D0311896

THE UNIVERSAL

BOOK OF HOBBIES

AND HANDICRAFTS

EVERY MEMBER OF THE FAMILY SHOULD HAVE A HOBBY

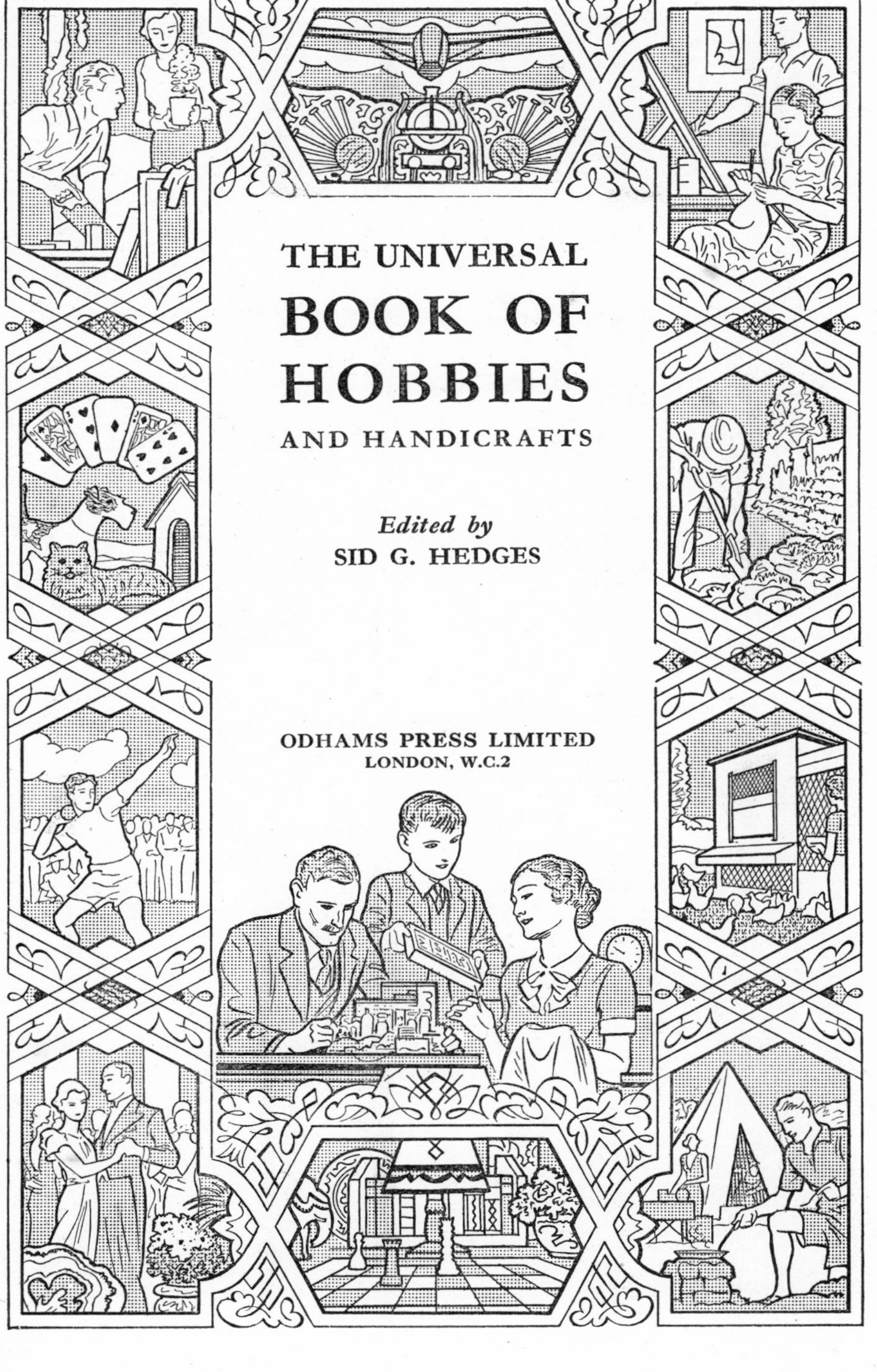

THE UNIVERSAL BOOK OF HOBBIES AND HANDICRAFTS

Edited by
SID G. HEDGES

ODHAMS PRESS LIMITED
LONDON, W.C.2

Printed in Great Britain

INTRODUCTION

A HOBBY is "a favourite subject or occupation that is not one's main business." Hobbies have always been important. They have been the salvation of many a man who has retired from business or ceased work with energies and faculties still vigorous; and for lack of them many such men have died before their time. But nowadays hobbies are coming to have much greater value, for three main reasons: there is more leisure; there is the tyranny of machines; there is the economic malaise which makes it difficult for young people to choose congenial careers.

Those of us with daily occupations have, on the whole, far more free hours than had previous generations. What is to be done with leisure? No real satisfaction comes from a mere pastime which can do no more than fritter away the hours. The value of the worth-while hobby is that it gives benefit to mind, or hand, or muscle. It constitutes a relaxation and change from ordinary occupation. It may effect economies in expenditure, or even be a means of earning. It makes leisure a time of delight instead of dullness; of opportunity instead of oppressive boredom; of achievement instead of inactivity.

In these days so many of us do routine work in which there is no spice of novelty or variety and no need for initiative. Life then can be very drab; mind and spirit can be almost quenched. But hobbies can save them. The soul-destroying machine may give no opportunity to the man who yearns to be craftsman or artist, but in his leisure his ambitions may be realized. There he may find the joy of designing, of constructing, of beautifying.

Similarly, the sedentary worker, sentenced to unnatural inertia during his working hours, may in his spare time revel in hobbies—swimming, to give but one example—which will call up all the abounding energy he desires to have and to use.

It is not easy, these days, to find congenial careers. When openings are few the boy or girl is thankful to get in anywhere. Work may be quite uncongenial, but it is better than unemployment. The pity is that often young folk with fine ambitions and abilities get so discouraged and settled that they resign themselves to a lifetime of drudgery. For these hard-used youngsters, too, hobbies may mean salvation. Spare-time work, after their own heart, may be indulged in and abilities gained so that later on it may be possible to plunge afresh and begin a happy career on new lines. A boy may, for instance, be compelled to do office work, though he longs to be a musician. If his leisure be spent in following the occupation of his choice he may one day become so competent a musician that he can step across into the world of music and make good there.

For those three reasons hobbies are playing an increasingly important part in the modern world. They will become more important still, for as mankind shakes itself clear of the old jungle habits of hating and arming and fighting so there will be more scope for living—"new arts shall bloom of loftier mould, and mightier music thrill the skies." Is it too much to hope that the various Whitehall Ministries of War may one sane day be replaced by constructive Ministries of the People's Leisure? This "Book of Hobbies" is towards that sort of future.

Equally this book is for the present. If you have no hobbies now, this book is to help you to become interested in the many things that you can do. One hobby may suffice, but it is better to have more. The sectional titles will show how every taste can be suited. Should you favour several, have them as different as possible. For example—*cardboard work*, for indoors; *nature study*, for outdoors; and *swimming*, for something strenuous.

Many subjects dealt with are as suitable for group or club activities as for individual enjoyment.

Notice the varied types of hobbies. If you like making things, then try a *Handicraft*; if you have a tidy mind and enjoy classifying, then some sort of *Collecting* will please you; certainly you should have at least one *Recreational* hobby and something on the *Outdoor* and *Cultural* side. The *Mechanic* and *Garden* topics clearly cater for very specialized interests.

May this book do something to increase the amenities of leisure—that has been my hope in preparing it.

SID G. HEDGES.

CONTENTS

APPLIQUÉ WORK

APPLIQUÉ work is the building of a design by applying cut-out shapes of one material upon another. In its simplest form it can be done by a child, but in the hands of an advanced worker it is an art form with infinite possibilities.

There are several forms of appliqué work, all having one great advantage over other forms of embroidery or tapestry work—large surfaces can be decorated in a short time without the use of innumerable small filling-in stitches.

The simplest way of doing appliqué work is to cut flowers from odd pieces of chintz or cretonne, and attach them to the article to be decorated. The designs, or flowers,

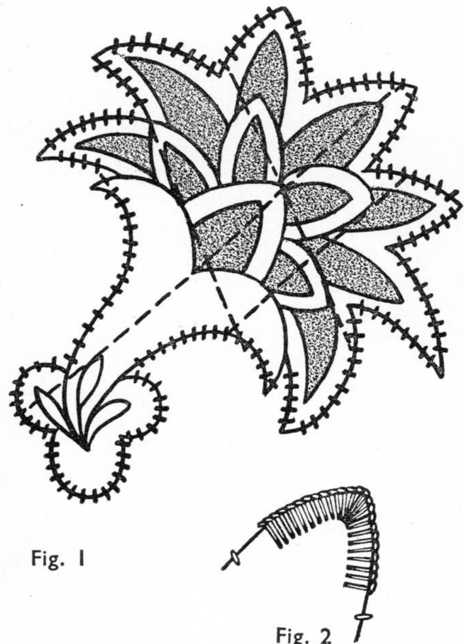

Fig. 1

Fig. 2

are carefully cut out with embroidery scissors, then tacked into position with two rows of tacking stitches lengthways, and two rows crossways, and one line of small tacking stitches round the edges. (*See* Fig. 1.)

Fig. 3.—Appliqué Design

The weave or thread of the material to be applied should run in the same direction as on the background. The number of rows of cross tackings would depend upon the size of the shape to be applied.

Edging Stitches.—The stitch generally used round the edge of the design is buttonhole - stitch (and sometimes satin - stitch), with other simple embroidery stitches to indicate the details. The buttonhole stitches should point inwards so that the ridge runs along the edge of the design. (*See* Fig. 2.)

Edging stitches vary. Besides buttonholing, chain-stitch, fine herring-boning, and flat-stitch may be used; or the edges outlined with tinsel thread or fine, coloured cord kept in place with overcast stitching in matching or contrasting colours.

In applying the shapes to the background there is always a danger of the edges

Fig. 4.—A Tray Cloth in coloured linen Appliqué

fraying as the work proceeds. To prevent this it is advisable to cut the design a fraction of an inch larger than is necessary. Then after it has been tacked in position the surplus material can be cut away a little at a time as the buttonhole stitching proceeds. The work should proceed patchwork fashion, one part being finished before the next is tacked on. When the shape has been applied, the details of the flowers should be stitched over to emphasize them, using stem-stitch or small running stitches. This should be done in suitably coloured silk or stranded cotton, following the colourings of the design. The applied material can also take the form of geometrical shapes cut out in plain coloured material and arranged to produce a formal design. As a rule it is advisable to begin the work from the top. When finished it should be pressed on the wrong side with a warm iron and damp cloth.

Appliqué Picture Designs.—Because of the vogue for appliqué decorations it is possible to buy cut-out chickens, rabbits, birds, cats, dogs, etc., in a variety of materials ready for attachment to children's cot or pram covers, pinafores, cushions, etc. If these are not obtainable in the size and material required it is quite

Fig. 5.—Detail of the above

Fig. 6.—Appliqué Picture

easy to cut them out oneself. Effective pictures can be built round these cut-outs with a minimum amount of embroidery stitching. For instance, for a child's bedspread, lightly pencil the outline of part of a little cottage, and a pathway leading to the door. Work over the marks in chain-stitch, using embroidery wool or thick mercerized cotton. Three varying-sized Teddy bears could be sewn invisibly in place along the path, illustrating the story of the three bears. (*See* Fig. 3.) If ready-made cut-outs have been purchased there would be no need to buttonhole-stitch the edges as these are well finished. The aim should be to make the stitches as invisible as possible. A little ingenuity could be used in adding details to the picture by means of embroidery work—a few flowers of the hollyhock type along the path, etc.

Or the cottage could be built up by means of shapes of material—roof, walls, door, etc.

To produce a picture successfully some skill in conveying an idea with the minimum number of stitches is necessary—just as with half a dozen strokes of his pencil or brush a "lightning artist" can convey his meaning. For instance, if a green field is to be applied, something more than the plain shape of green is necessary. The grass edges can be indicated by buttonhole stitches in irregular lengths. In this case the stitches should point in the same direction as the grass grows. This means that at the top edges of the grass shape the stitches will impinge irregularly upon the background. A few short, straight stitches here and there in groups should be added to give a suggestion of grass blades.

The same use of irregular stitches can indicate the thatch on a cottage roof, though in this case the stitches will always point inwards with the ridge on the outside. A few stroke stitches would provide the markings on a tree trunk.

Fig. 7.—An Effective Cushion Design

Attractive river- or sea-scapes can be built up very quickly on light blue linen. Draw a rough outline of the picture first. A few irregular-shaped hills in pale mauve, grey, or grey-green for the background, with a space between for a boat to sail through, a blue sea or river in the middle foreground, and in the lower foreground a strip of green on which grass and a few buttercups and daisies could be worked. An orange sun would have a few pink running stitches as rays, and a few similar stitches in pink or yellow would indicate the reflection on the water. Running stitches would also indicate the waves. A boat could be made of brown linen with orange or red sails. The mountains should be tacked in place first, then buttonhole stitched in self colour except at the lower edge, which should be of yellow irregular stitches to indicate sand, or green for grass. A tree shape or two could be added on the sides of the mountains, and in the foreground a few circles of running stitches in groups would mark the foliage. The boat should be added next, first the sails, then the brown boat, on which a few long stitches should be worked.

Another simple design for the beginner is the Dutch scene with the windmill and the two Dutch children. It is suitable for a tea cosy, or to be worked in the corners of a tablecloth, on a cushion, or indeed in a variety of ways with a little adaptation. (*See* Fig. 6.)

The suggested background is light blue or pale yellow linen. The roof of the windmill should be bright red. The sails should be of brown with darker stitches to indicate the markings on them. The body of the windmill could be cream with the doors and windows filled in with black satin-stitch. The path could be of light brick or stone colour and the field of light green, stitched in position with buttonhole stitches of irregular length in grass green. The little Dutch girl could have a white apron and cap and a mauve dress. The colour of the boy's garments could be made to fit in with the general colour scheme. Appliqué work is very much a matter of making use of odd pieces of material available, and the suggested colour scheme should be modified according to the stock of material on hand. The faces and arms of the children should be flesh colour with features slightly indicated by a few stitches.

An effective frieze for a

Fig. 9

Fig. 10

Fig. 8.—A Charming Decorative Panel in Appliqué

nursery curtain can be made by applying cut-outs of animals along the bottom of the curtain. The animals should be cut out in suitable material, and their features—eyes, nose, ears, hair, etc.—outlined with stitches. The patterns for this kind of work may have to be drawn and cut out by hand. This will not be difficult for the person who is handy at freehand drawing, but for those who are not skilled in this direction selected pictures from magazines, etc., can be fairly easily copied, enlarged or reduced as required, by ruling a number of small squares on the original. If the finished picture is to be twice as large as the original, an equal number of squares, but each twice as large, should be drawn on the paper to be used as a pattern. These squares will prove useful guides for the pencil, and the drawing will be automatically increased in proportion as the size of the squares is enlarged. (Fig. 9.)

Fig. 11.—Two more Animal designs for a Nursery Curtain

This idea of appliquéing pictures of animals can be extended to other articles in the nursery, notably cot covers. In this case the cot cover could be divided into squares of alternating contrasting colours —after the fashion of a chess board— and one animal appliquéd into the centre of each square. Simple pictures of other types could take the place of the animals.

It is possible to buy paper shapes of animals, birds, floral designs, etc., which can be used as patterns. Even if they cannot be purchased in the correct size they provide excellent designs for enlarging. Some of these paper cut-outs illustrate such well-known fairy tales as Cinderella, Hansel and Gretel, Snow-white and the Seven Dwarfs, and could be used in a score of ways in the nursery on cushions, hangings, bedcovers, rompers, toilet runners, etc.

Silhouettes.—More advanced work is to cut silhouettes in a plain material, such as felt, of human figures with distinctive outlines, such as a highwayman, a girl in a poke bonnet, a Victorian lady in a crinoline, or a Gallant of the Regency period. A more personal touch could be secured by cutting silhouettes of members of the family. It would require some considerable skill to draw the outlines, but a silhouette artist would provide this quite cheaply—they are often to be found at seaside places. In order to retain the clean-cut appearance of a good silhouette, the shapes can be carefully glued on to the background, special care being taken to see that the edges adhere firmly, and that the minimum amount of glue is used in the process. If the shapes are stitched on the stitches should be so small as to be invisible.

Appliqué Craft.—Another form of appliqué work which does not necessarily require stitchery is to use the coloured picture on an attractive magazine cover as a basis. The picture, for instance, of a child in a gingham dress could be cut out and mounted on a matt black board. The pictured dress should then be covered with a piece of suitably coloured gingham cut to shape. The outline might first be traced on tracing paper from the picture, and this used as the pattern. If, on the other hand, the child were wearing a fur-trimmed coat, the fur could be represented by plush, and the same material would do service for a muff. Ravellings from very fine silk, or doll's hair, could be used to cover the hair in the picture, but in many cases it would be better to allow the original picture to remain uncovered for flesh and hair. A picture of this kind looks quite effective when framed and glazed.

Appliqué is also used for the trimming of lingerie. The design is stamped on the material, and behind it are placed two layers of net. The outline of the flower or leaves is then stitched round finely, and then the material inside cut away carefully. The edges are then worked with buttonhole-stitch or satin-stitch. In the finished result the shape is seen outlined with buttonhole-stitch and filled in with the net. The surplus net at the back can be cut away.

AQUARIA

It is pleasant to reflect that the splendid tanks of fish from foreign seas in our large municipal aquaria are but developments of the urchin's jampotful of "tiddlers"! For young and old, aquatic life, particularly aquatic animal life, has always held a strong interest which is greatest when the water organisms have been personally collected and maintained alive.

Fig. 1.—A well-planted Aquarium with cover supported on corks to allow plenty of fresh air to enter

The hobby of keeping aquaria may be expensive or inexpensive at will. The person of very limited means can yet maintain a large variety of animals and plants, while the wealthy aquarist can obtain strange fish from foreign waters that add to the interest of the aquarium and live healthily in their new home.

To the serious student of biology a number of small aquaria is essential. The complete history of many small animals may successfully be worked out from observation on a jam-pot aquarium.

The ideal is to reproduce natural conditions as nearly as possible. This is, of course, impossible in some cases, but the following may be successfully imitated in aquaria: ponds, moderately fast streams, brackish water, seaside rock-pools, tidal zones.

Do not abandon hope if your first

Fig. 2.—Goldfish
Top.—Comet Goldfish
Middle.—Shubunkin Goldfish. Bred for colour variety
Bottom.—Young Fringe-tail Goldfish

aquarium is a failure. Making one is to some extent a matter of luck.

The Container.—First, the container. The beginner has many choices. A large special tank may be purchased, capable of holding a considerable collection; or a jam-pot can be used to house a single small organism. Other suitable vessels are earthenware sinks, enamel bowls, and zinc bowls. Perhaps the most useful is an old accumulator jar, such as is discarded when private electrical installations are dismantled. They allow observation without distortion and are easily cleaned.

An important problem is the provision of air for the animals. This is more easily solved in a tank that has a large surface in proportion to the bulk of water it contains. "Wide and shallow" should be the guiding principle. Therefore, avoid "goldfish bowls" and narrow-necked or very deep jars.

A wooden tub in a shady place out of doors makes an excellent aquarium, because lighting and aeration are nearly natural. It has not the drawback, that all glass vessels suffer from, of admitting light at the sides. It is also successful as a stock aquarium from which animals may be transferred to glass tanks for better observation.

Types of Aquaria.—Before proceeding to describe the preparation of an aquarium, it must be emphasized that different types of inmates call for different treatment. For instance, a mud-burrowing animal requires mud collected from its natural home spread over the bottom of the jar; an animal from the swift stream requires a continuous current of water. Again, marine and freshwater aquaria for general purposes need quite different treatment.

Fig. 3.—Common Aquarium Fish
Top.—Three-Spined Stickleback (Male)
Bottom.—Golden Orfe

Preparation of Freshwater Aquarium.—The vessel must be thoroughly cleaned. Old accumulator jars should be washed free of acid.

Sand to the depth of two or three inches can be introduced after it has been well washed. Avoid using sea-sand if possible, as the salt is difficult to remove.

Any rooting water-plants must next be planted.

Large stones should be arranged to provide hiding-places for the more retiring animals, while gravel may be spread over the sand, though this may render cleaning difficult.

The tank may then be filled with water. In the absence of rain or clean pond-water, tap-water is suitable provided it is not very hard.

Introduce the water gently. Siphoning from a pail which stands above the container is a good method.

Allow the water to reach the temperature of the room before admitting any animals. This may require several days.

A running-water aquarium can be prepared similarly. The water can run in from a tap and out through an opening in the side of the container. Cover the outlet hole with metal gauze to keep the small inmates from escaping.

Fig. 4.—Common Bullhead

Collection of Stock.—The collecting apparatus required depends upon the situation to be searched. Many small animals are to be found on the under side of stones in shallow streams, others cling to water-weeds which can be removed bodily by dragging a meat-hook on the end of a piece of string across the bottom of the pond. A muslin net is very useful, but for dredging the bottom or scraping the banks of a pond, a net made of stouter material, and having a metal rim, is necessary.

Small and large jam jars are useful collecting vessels. The "catch" must not be kept in such vessels very long, nor left standing in the sun. Should it be necessary to keep the catch overnight, empty the collecting jars into shallow dishes—pie dishes serve admirably—otherwise the oxygen dissolved in the water will become exhausted during the night and a sorry scene of death greet you in the morning.

Choice of Stock.—Bear this consideration in mind when you choose the creatures to inhabit your aquarium: animals which live in rapidly moving streams and rivers have, in general, a high oxygen requirement, supplied in nature by air thoroughly mixed with the water as it foams over waterfalls and rushes over rocks. For such animals to exist a considerable length of time, the problem of efficient aeration has to be solved. This problem is less acute if animals from ponds and slow-moving streams are selected, since their oxygen needs are less.

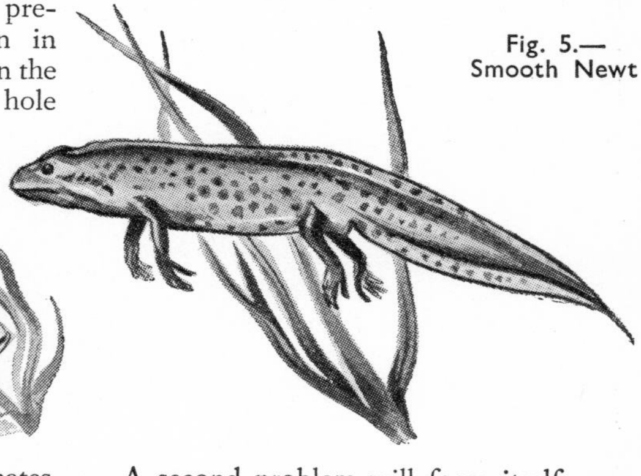

Fig. 5.—Smooth Newt

A second problem will force itself upon the notice very soon, particularly where only one aquarium is being kept. Some fierce animals will reduce the stock of vegetable-eaters to nothing; for instance, the voracious larva of the great water beetle will attack a defenceless tadpole or a fully grown newt. Those animals which may safely be kept together will soon become known after a little experience. Others, such as sticklebacks, are very pugnacious, and must be kept alone or given plenty of space, to reduce the chances of their meeting.

Overstocking will sometimes induce cannibalistic tendencies in the animals.

Aeration.—First, why is it so important to aerate the water in an aquarium?

Air consists chiefly of two gases, oxygen and nitrogen. Without oxygen neither animal nor plant can live. Aquatic animals gain the necessary oxygen from the water in which they live. The dashing of sea-waves against the shore and the bubbling of streams over a pebbly bed are but two examples of the ways in which air is mixed and dissolved in water. Some animals "breathe" the oxygen with their gills, others absorb it through their body-wall. The difficulty is to provide sufficient air for the aquatic creatures.

Several methods of aeration are available. Large public aquaria are aerated by methods which are too elaborate for the average person to construct. A simple apparatus may be arranged as follows—water from a large container standing above the level of the aquarium is made to run down a pipe through a glass nozzle into the aquarium itself. The stream of water is strong enough to carry air bubbles down with it. This method necessitates a periodical transference of water from the aquarium to the jar standing above it. Another simple variant of this method is to remove jugfuls of water from the aquarium and pour them back from a height. Air-bubbles will be carried down by the falling water.

It is obvious that these methods involve a good deal of trouble and frequent attention. Fortunately there is an equally satisfactory and far more interesting way of supplying oxygen to the water.

This depends upon the fact that one of the life-processes of plants involves the giving-out of oxygen. Water plants give this oxygen out into the water. Consequently, water plants are not merely an ornament in aquaria but, providing they are healthy, are an excellent means of oxygenating the water. The plants must appear fresh and green and no decaying pieces must be allowed to remain in the water. In strong sunlight streams of oxygen bubbles may often be seen rising from the plants.

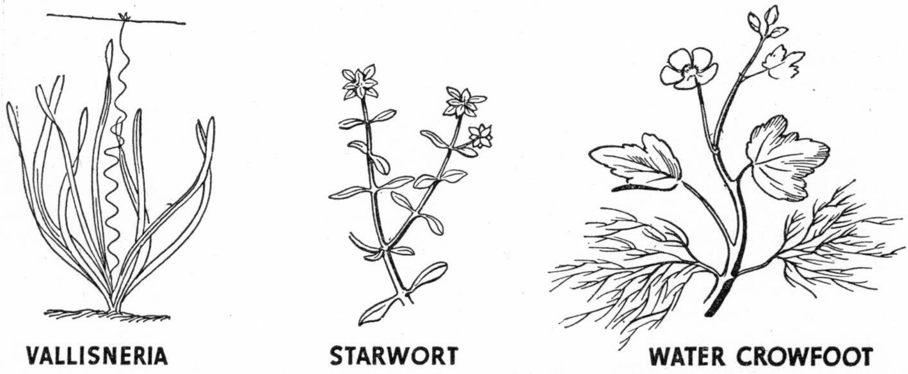

Fig. 6.—Oxygenating Plants for the Freshwater Aquarium

PLANT OXYGENATORS

The following freshwater plants are suitable for use in aquaria. The rooting plants must be planted before the water is put in the aquarium. Others will float on the surface or can be tied to stones to anchor them in the water.

Canadian Water Weed.—An efficient oxygenator that can be thrown on the water and left to do service throughout the year.

Duckweed.—An ornamental floating plant which is useful in providing shade. Excess due to rapid growth is easily skimmed off.

Water Milfoil.—A pretty plant with

fine thread-like leaves. Useful for winter aeration and a haunt for small insects.

Hornwort.—A hardy and excellent oxygenator, that will grow without rooting, though not so well.

Pondweeds.—A number of the Pondweeds are suitable for aquaria. Every aquarium should have one species at least.

Water Crowfoot.—This plant produces many beautiful white flowers in spring and the two kinds of leaves, submerged and floating, are attractive. A good winter plant.

Vallisneria.—A popular aquarium plant readily obtained from dealers. An excellent oxygenator.

Bladderwort.—This should be introduced for its interesting carnivorous habits. Water fleas, etc., are captured in the bladder-like traps.

This list is far from exhaustive but includes common, readily obtained, and useful plants.

Finally, air dissolves in the water at its surface. The use of a fairly shallow container has been advised above because this surface aeration can then play a considerable part.

ANIMALS FOR THE AQUARIUM

Fish.—Of the many fish, native and foreign, that live healthily under artificial conditions, the following are easily procured:

Goldfish.—A foreign fish easily kept and which adds to the attractiveness of the aquarium. Many varieties are obtainable.

Bullhead or Miller's Thumb.—A very unobtrusive fish for which hiding-places should be provided. Easily recognized by its large blunt head. Thrives best in shallow running water.

Eel.—A small eel is an interesting and hardy addition to the aquarium.

Three-spined Stickleback.—A common fish easily recognized by the three spines on its back. Will breed in captivity.

Molluscs.—Several kinds of molluscs are desirable in the aquarium. They are useful and attractive if their shells are cleaned. The following varieties are but a few of those available:

Ramshorn Snail.—Sometimes attaining a large size;

Swan Mussel.—Sufficient sand must be present to allow the Swan Mussels to bury themselves. Their mode of locomotion prevents them from passing rocks on the bottom, so their movements may easily be restricted;

Freshwater Limpets.—These small molluscs may be introduced in large numbers, say, about a score.

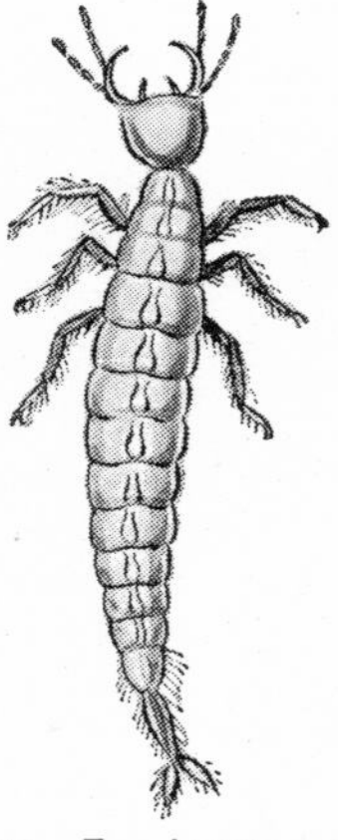

Fig. 7.—Larva of Great Water Beetle

Crustacea.—This class contains several species of use to the aquariist:

Crayfish.—This remarkable freshwater lobster, found lurking in shady places in streams, is not difficult to keep in shallow troughs about six inches deep, with stones on the bottom. An ideal inmate of the running-water aquarium;

Water Shrimp.—Like the Water Louse, the Water Shrimp is a useful scavenger.

Aquatic Beetles.—The aquatic beetles are suitable material for the study of life-histories. To keep them in separate large jam jars is a good plan.

Great Water Beetle.—An interesting beetle—but no small animal life, such as tadpoles, fish, etc., should be allowed in the same jar unless they are intended as food. The larva is amazingly fierce.

Water Boatman.—Easily known by its habit of propelling itself on its back by means of an oar-like pair of legs. Its relative *Corixa* does not swim on its back.

Whirligig Beetle.—This beetle swims about rapidly in a constantly curving path.

Amphibians.—Of this class the Frog is a common inmate of aquaria.

Newts.—The life-history of the newt is fascinating to observe, especially in the early stages—the laying of the eggs and the tadpole stage. Both newts and frogs must be given facilities (such as an island or raft) for emerging at times from the water.

Other interesting animals are the Leech, Hydra, Water-mites, and Pond-skaters.

Other insects worth keeping are Caddis-flies, Stone-flies, Alder-flies, and Dragon-flies.

FOOD

The following food suggestions will assist the beginner—but first a word of warning. Never put bread in an aquarium. It readily putrefies and has terminated the success of many aquaria.

Living Water Fleas.—Suitable for almost all animals.

Mealworms for amphibians and aquatic larvæ.

Biscuit Meal for Fish, Crayfish, Newts, Tadpoles, Snails.

Small Pieces of Meat, including Chopped Worm.

Microscopical Life.—Newly hatched fry of fish and small aquatic larvæ.

Ants' Eggs for Fish. Should be given only occasionally.

Fish.—Crayfish, Great Water Beetle.

Water Shrimps, Water Lice.—Large fish.

Dead Animal and Vegetable Matter.—Caddis-fly larvæ, Water Louse, Water Shrimp.

Water Plants.—Fish, Tadpoles, etc.

Feeding.—Never overfeed. The surplus food will decay and poison the water unless removed after the meal. It will be noticed that animals are often preyed on by others. Hence the necessity of several aquaria to obtain variety and to maintain stocks of living food.

Care of Aquarium.—All pieces of dead water plants and dead animals must be removed immediately they are noticed. The inclusion of scavengers, such as snails, caddis-fly larvæ, water shrimps, water lice, water beetles, and the Swan mussel will assist in the task of keeping the water free of refuse and check the growth of algæ, or "green shine." Strong sunlight also encourages the growth of this algæ, so that the aquarium should always be placed in a shady spot away from the direct rays. A north or north-eastern window is best. The side nearest the window should be covered by paper.

Fungus Disease in Fish.—A white "mould" is sometimes seen upon the fins of the fish. This is a fungus which spreads to the gills, often causing death. Other symptoms are dullness of colouring, back fin above the water, or fins closed. To cure, prepare solution of two heaped teaspoonfuls of salt in a gallon of water. Place the diseased fish in the solution, changing it daily for several days. The temperature of the solution must not be altered.

The disease is contagious and the other fish should be treated similarly. The tank itself must be thoroughly cleaned.

The Marine Aquarium.—If you have become expert in managing freshwater aquaria, experiment with a marine tank.

Sea-water may be obtained from Marine Biology stations or an artificial substitute may be prepared, according to Lulham's formula:

Sodium chloride (common salt) .	$46\frac{1}{2}$ oz.
Magnesium sulphate . .	$3\frac{1}{2}$,,
Magnesium chloride . .	$5\frac{1}{4}$,,
Potassium sulphate . . .	2 ,,
Tapwater	$13\frac{1}{4}$ gal.

Dissolve each constituent separately in water and then mix them. Leave a few days and then add seaweed. During the next few weeks stand in strong sunlight and from time to time add a small sea animal. The water is not fit unless these live.

Preparation of the Tank.—The tank must be thoroughly clean. Find pebbles or rocks bearing green seaweeds and place them in the bottom. It is best to keep down the number of sea weeds and achieve aeration by air-bubbling methods. In any case, avoid using red and brown seaweeds and also those which secrete much mucus, or the water will become foul.

Provision ought to be made for those animals, e.g. the short-crab, which prefer to leave the water. A rock projecting above the surface and forming a little island is a good plan. If the water does not fill the tank completely limpets are able to imitate tide-action by crawling above the surface.

The original level of the water should be

marked and, as water is lost by evaporation, river water must be added to maintain a constant solution.

Collection of Stock.—The best places to search are the rock-pools. Open-sea and fast-swimming forms should not be collected owing to their high oxygen requirements.

For transport, large containers of water are necessary and a change of water at the end of the journey is imperative. Molluscs, seaweeds, sea-anemones, echinoderms and some crustaceans may be more easily transported in wet seaweed in a closed case.

Seaweeds for the Marine Aquarium.—The aquarist should experiment with several kinds; those mentioned here are merely suggestions.

The Green Laver or Sea-lettuce is very useful and forms a thin wavy membrane up to about a foot in length. The Sea-grass or Mermaid's Hair, grass-like in appearance, is another useful form. Species of Cladophora are often attractive. The pretty *Bryopsis plumosa* is an excellent addition to the aquarium.

Animals for the Aquarium.—The greater attraction of the sea-water aquarium lies in the diversity of the animals that can be kept.

Bearing in mind the limitations of the still-water tank, various species can be experimented with. Many interesting creatures will not live very long, but the attempt to keep them in captivity is well worth while.

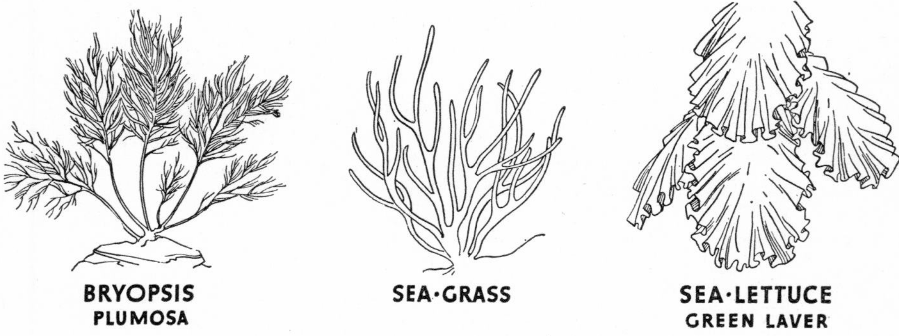

Fig. 8.—Seaweeds for the Marine Aquarium

Include snails and periwinkles for their scavenging habits. The beautiful smooth anemone, the edible mussel, the common shore crab and the porcelain crab, the carpet shell, the 15-spined stickleback—all these are worth attempting to keep.

Food.—Minute diatoms in natural sea-water are a universal food, while a little chopped lingworm or other meat can be added from time to time. (*See also* article on GARDEN PONDS.)

ARTIFICIAL FLOWER MAKING

ALMOST any kind of flower can be made with crêpe paper, and made to look real even to the minutest detail. To get good results use a good paper—it is cheap enough, and there is ample variety of colours from which to select.

Equipment.—This includes a pair of blunt-pointed, sharp scissors; a paper-knife (the bone variety is best) for curling your petals; wire (thick for stalks and fine for binding); a pot of good paste; and coloured crêpe paper. This is sold in sixpenny sheets about 20 in. wide by 10 ft. long. It is folded in a cardboard wrapper from which it can be withdrawn as required.

Make your flowers as far as you can by

copying real ones, or cut paper patterns of petals and leaves. (*See* Figs. 1–5.)

It is possible to have flowers for every season of the year, even when they are expensive in the shops, if you learn the art of making your own. Daffodil, narcissus, crocus, snowdrop, jonquil, violet, primrose,

desired width, and cut it off—it is a bad plan to remove the wrapper altogether.

The *grain* of the paper should be from the point to the base of the leaf or petal for almost all flowers. Only one or two kinds of leaves are cut the opposite way—pond lily pads and geranium.

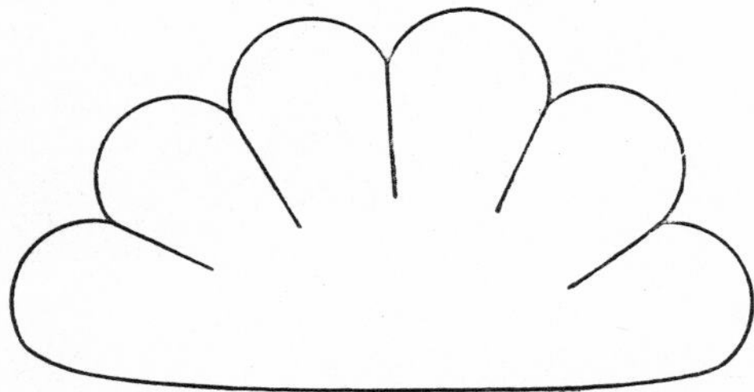

Fig. 1.—Wistaria Petal

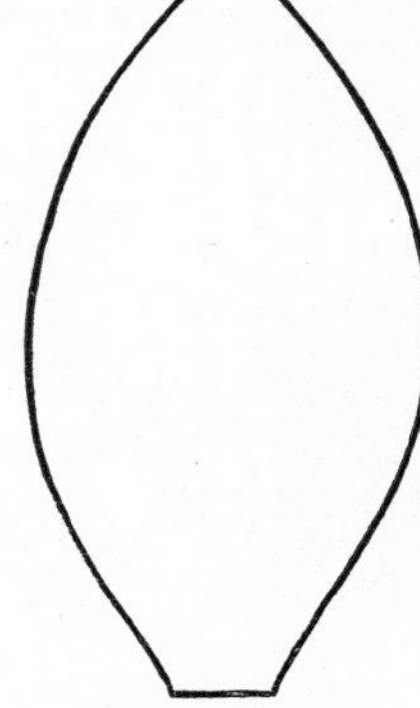

Fig. 2.—Wistaria Leaf

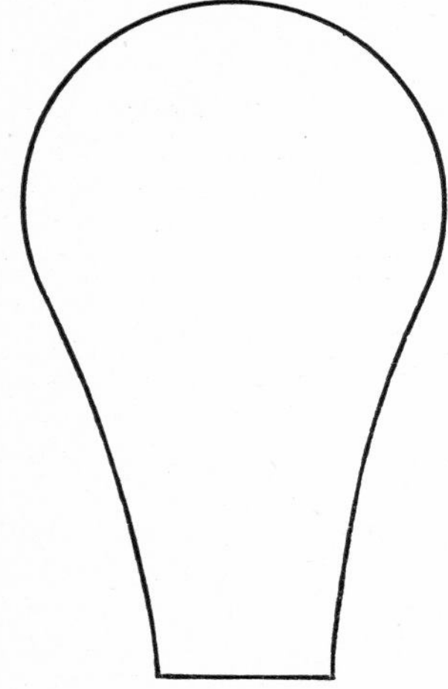

Fig. 3.—Rose Petal

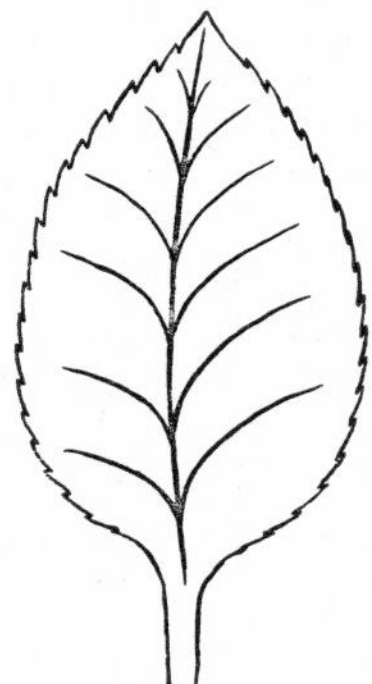

Fig. 4.—Rose Leaf

Fig. 5.—Rose Calyx

tulip, apple blossom, almond blossom, wistaria, laburnum, lily, hyacinth, carnation, roses (standard and rambler), sweet pea, poppy, sunflower, hollyhock, orchid, pansy, orange blossom, nasturtium, water lily, anemone, chrysanthemum, aster, dahlia, buttercup, field daisy, gladiolus, peony, geranium, fuchsia, can all be made at home in crêpe paper.

General Hints.—When using crêpe paper only draw from the folded packet the

When cutting out a number of petals draw out the paper to the width required—the wrapper will be a guide to cutting it perfectly straight. Shake out the fold and stretch slightly.

The Petals of roses are curled, with a paper knife or knitting needle. Hold the petal between the thumb and first finger of the left hand, and holding the knife in your right hand draw it up the back of the petal gently, but firmly, so that a nice curled effect

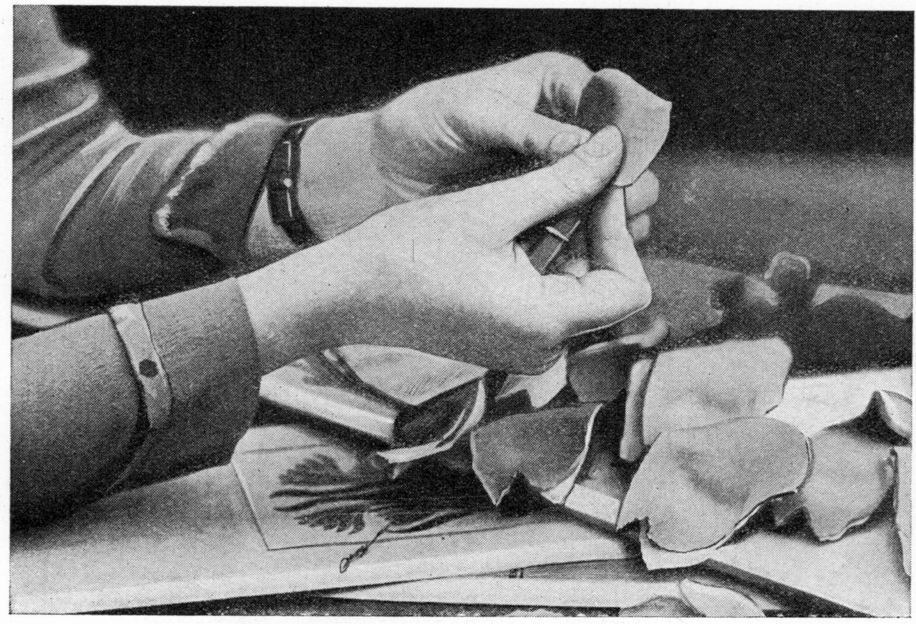

Fig. 6.—Curling the Petals with a Paper Knife

is gained. (*See* Fig. 6.) If a knitting needle is being used, lay the petal on the table and roll the paper over the needle. This method is used for rambler roses.

Some petals need to be cupped. Take the petal between the two thumbs and first fingers, and with the thumbs gently push out into the shape required—a sort of bowl effect. (*See* Fig. 7.)

Petals that have to be twisted, as for wistaria, are held in the left hand while the right gives them one or two complete twists.

It is essential, when wrapping stems with a strip of paper, to keep the paper well stretched as you go down the stalk and also with a distinct slanting movement. This makes them smooth. Hold the strip of paper between the thumb and finger of the left hand, twisting the wire with the right. In this way you can guide it more easily. Always put a little paste at the beginning and at the base to make a tidy finish.

If it is necessary to add wire to the stem already being wrapped in order to lengthen it, lay the two pieces together and stem as one.

When Wiring Leaves or Petals.—For orchids, water lily pads, lilies and so on, use straight wire not spool wire. Cut the wires a little longer than the petals to which they are to be pasted. Stem them and paste on the backs of leaves and leave till dry.

It is sometimes advisable to cut two leaves and paste together with a stem wire in between them: this needs careful handling.

Stamens for the centre of the flower can be bought ready-made, or can be made from pale yellow paper. Cut the paper into a fringe, and then twist between the thumb and finger. Use a piece about 1 in. long for most flowers. The poppy needs a thick black fringe cut very fine.

Use a good paper, it will not fade. Dust can be removed with a very soft paint brush.

Roses.—Many shades of colour can be used in the making of the standard variety of rose. Sometimes two colours can be curled together.

Single petals make the nicest roses. You may cut them in strips if you prefer, but you do not get such a tidy base, and you

Fig. 7.—Cupping the Petals

will want from twelve to fifteen for each flower. A piece of stem wire about 18 in. long, a calyx of leaf-green (*see* Fig. 5; where its lines are marked down you should cut with scissors) and some leaves. These can be bought or made. If bought, linen ones wear best.

Cut your petals, and cup them in the middle as already described, curling the top edges with your knife—it is best to have the silky finish of the paper nearest to you, for then you will get the "bloom" on the edges. Twist one straight petal into a cone-shape and work your others round it. (*See* Fig. 8.) Let the bottom of each petal wrap the previous one till all are used; bind together with your stem-wire leaving a long length protruding below the petals. Now paste your calyx round the bowl of the flower, and with a strip of green paper about 1 in. wide begin to stem the wire in a slanting direction. Add another length of wire if necessary. Put one or two sprays of leaves down the stalk as you stem. Now all that remains is to shape your flower to look as real as possible—hold the stalk between the knees very firmly, and gently cup the petals round.

Make your roses of red, coral pink, cerise, yellow, yellow and light orange—always use the darker shade in the centre when making two-colour flowers. Salmon pink and apricot curled together, with apricot outside, form one of the most popular roses.

Carnations.—These can be made in a number of shades—red, dark red, pink, apricot, yellow, striped red, salmon-pink, white, cerise, and so on.

To make the large variety eighteen to twenty-four petals should be used. Get your stem-wire and cover it with a small piece of the paper you are using for the flower, having turned it over at the top to prevent the sharp end protruding. Work your petals round and round this and bind with fine wire. Paste your calyx neatly; it is similar to the one used for the rose, except that this time it will not be cut down more than half an inch. With your stemming paper begin just below the bowl of the flower and work up towards the petals, then turn back and continue in the usual way, adding leaves as you go. To make the leaves for carnations, cut a piece of green paper about 5 in. wide, grain going lengthways; cut it into strips $\frac{3}{4}$ in. wide. Then cut again through the centre, pointing each at the top. Do not separate them at the bottom.

Wistaria.—Three shades of mauve are needed for this—purple, heliotrope, violet.

Cut a number of petals together—the diagram shows half of the pattern only. The best plan is to cut out of fine cardboard a whole pattern, then fold your paper into the desired widths for cutting out. There are three sizes of petals—the small ones are of purple and are 2 in. wide; the violet $2\frac{1}{2}$ in.; the heliotrope $2\frac{3}{4}$ in. Twist each petal as previously described. Then get a length of stem-wire and bend it over at the bottom. Pass the three or four small petals down the wire to the bottom and paste or use fine wire to bind them. If using wire, take a good length and work it up the stem as you go. Then four violet petals, keeping them fairly close together so that no part of the stem is seen; and next the heliotrope petals—how many will depend on the size of the bloom you wish to make. Stem up to the end of the stalk, having first pasted the stemming paper over the edge of the last petal.

Fig. 8.—Assembling the Flower. Two colours are being used

Cut a good number of leaves and, starting from the point of your new stem, wrap round the green paper, adding one leaf either side as you go down. Join to the stem of wistaria.

For decorative purposes wistaria may be made in shades of yellow as well as mauve.

Rambler Roses.—Cut your petals in circles and shape them, getting them narrower down towards the centre of the circle. Curl each separate petal with a knitting-needle. Make a small hole in the centre, and put one or two circles together for a rose, using fine wire for the stalk. Stem with a narrow green paper. When a good many roses are made, mount them up into a spray; two or three roses should be put together in stemming. You will need to have some sprays of leaves ready.

There are usually five leaves on rambler rose sprays, and these are cut smaller than the ordinary leaves. Use fine wire for the stems and a narrow strip of stemming paper. Put one leaf at the extreme end, and then insert the others as you go down. Have plenty of leaves among your roses. Real ramblers always have a good many.

Tulips.—Make a small ball of paper, and cover with leaf-green paper. Pinch it tightly. Now cut a piece of black paper into a fine fringe, rolling between the thumb and finger, and wrap a piece, about $3\frac{1}{2}$ in. long, round the ball.

Next the petals. Use the pattern illustrated for the rose, but cut it a little straight up the sides. Leave it rounded at the top for ordinary tulips; if "parrot tulips" are desired cut them a little pointed at the top.

Six petals are required, and each must be cupped. Place three petals round the fringed ball at equal distances and bind with stem wire. Now add the other three--these should be so placed as to come between the previous ones.

Two leaves should be used for each tulip, but they will not be needed till almost the bottom of the stem is reached. Have one or two in a bunch with their leaves curled outwards.

Water Lily.—These make a delightful centre-piece for a dinner table. They can be floated in a flower bowl if they are dipped in melted wax to waterproof them.

Make a ball of yellow paper and put a thick fringe of yellow paper round. Cut a 36-in. strip of white paper, or pink or lemon, 3 in. wide. Point the petals and cup them. Arrange round the ball. Now cut a strip of pink and leaf-green together to make six petals, pointing and cupping them. Place these petals round the outside of the previous ones, and bind with strong wire, leaving a length for the stalk.

Each lily should have two leaves—or pads. These pads are cut *across* the grain of the paper. They are 3 in. wide at the centre and rounded. Place a stem of strong wire through the centre, and stem in with the flower.

OTHER METHODS.—Flowers may be made of silk, organdie, rubber, or shells.

These materials are much more difficult to use than is paper, because you cannot cup the petals nor can you curl the edges so readily. Stamens must be bought, although some people use strands of embroidery silk for them.

Very effective posies of flowers, for use on dresses, can be made with lace. Ribbon also serves for delicate sprays. Lilies of the valley can be made with pearl beads and wire, and these look very attractive, and have the advantage that they can be washed.

When making artificial flowers always consider the general effect in preference to any imitation of minute detail. A charming "impression" of flowers is better than careful facsimiles that are rarely convincing.

ASTRONOMY

To begin this great and thrilling study needs no apparatus beyond that which Nature has provided, for many of the wonders of the sky are visible to the naked eye. As interest grows, and who can doubt that it will as knowledge increases, the need for equipment will arise, but there is much to see before that stage is reached.

Astronomy is one of the oldest of sciences and can be traced back to the Babylonian period of 3000 B.C. The early Egyptians made a study of astronomy and that their knowledge was fairly extensive considering the apparatus at their command, is shown by some of their buildings, which were constructed on definite astronomical principles. The Temple of Amen-Ra and the Great Pyramids are typical examples. It is possible, too, that the builders of Stonehenge had some knowledge of astronomy, judging by the way in which the circle of stones is laid out.

Under the Greeks, astronomy developed apace, assisted by Thales of Miletus and Pythagoras.

One of the great names in astronomy is that of Copernicus, who lived some 400 years ago. He postulated the theory that (*a*) the earth revolves and not the heavens round the earth, and (*b*) the earth is not the centre of the universe but only one of many planets revolving round the Sun, the true centre. It is upon his findings that all modern astronomy is based.

Another well-known name is that of Galileo, sometimes called "The Father of Astronomy," who, if he did not actually invent, improved the telescope and was the first to use it in astronomical observations. Among later astronomers of note mention

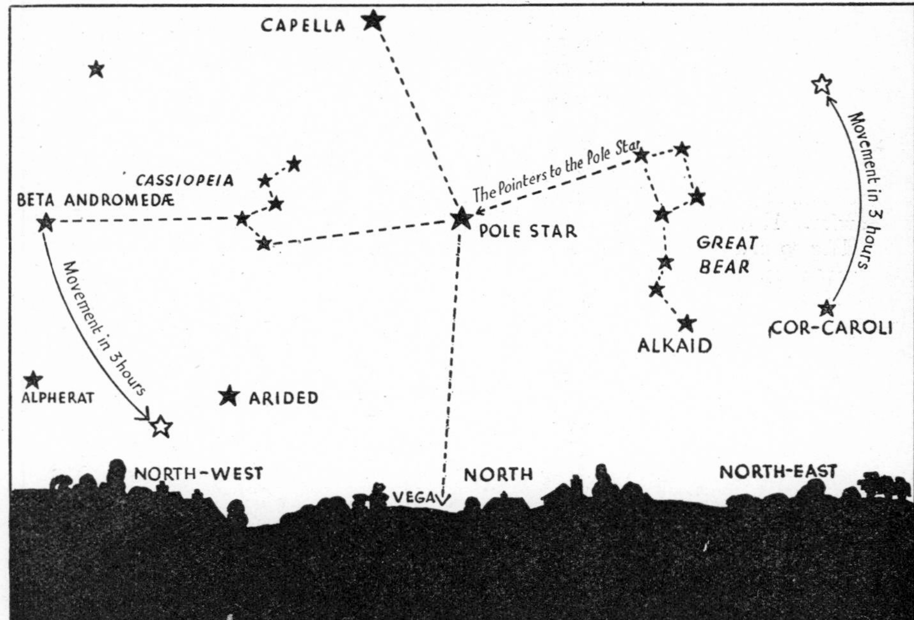

Fig. I.—The Northern Sky. October—March (Mid-month)

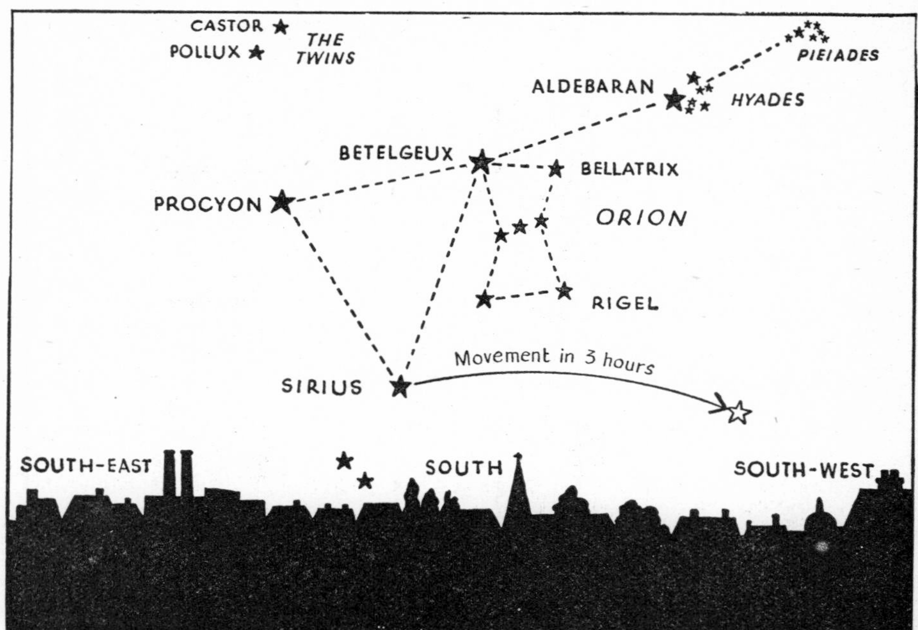

Fig. 2.—The Southern Sky. October—March (Mid-month)

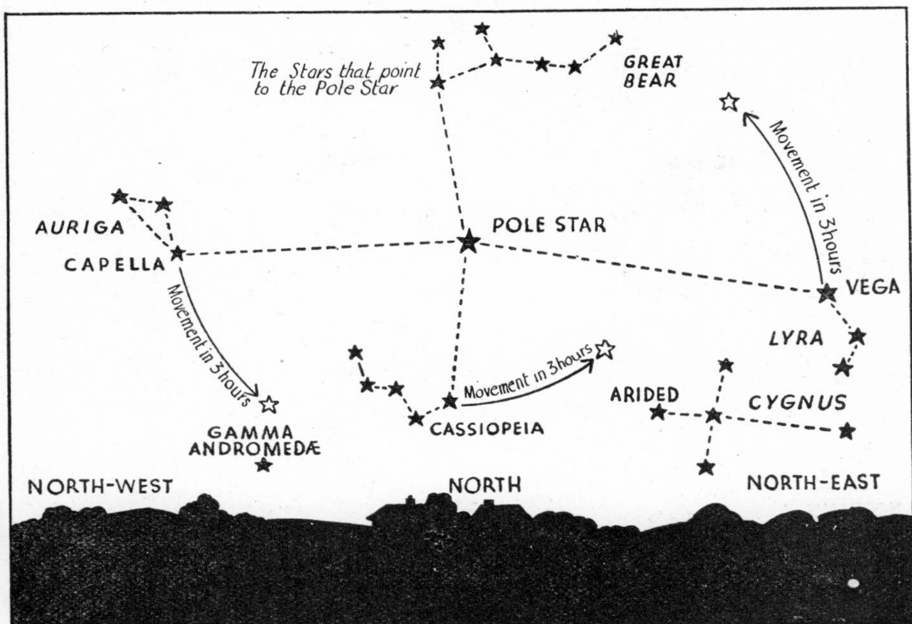

Fig. 3.—The Northern Sky. December—April (Mid-month)

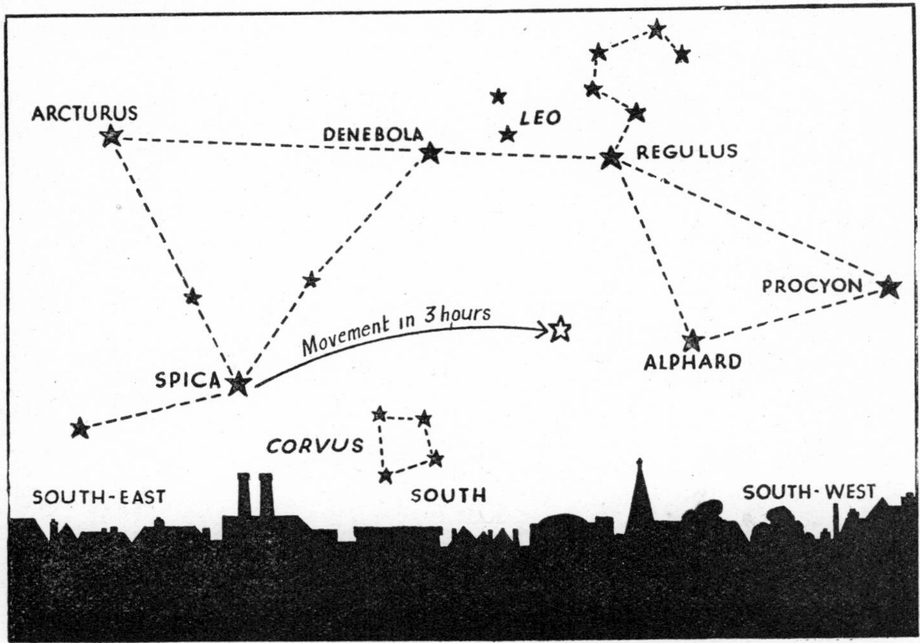

Fig. 4.—The Southern Sky. December—April (Mid-month)

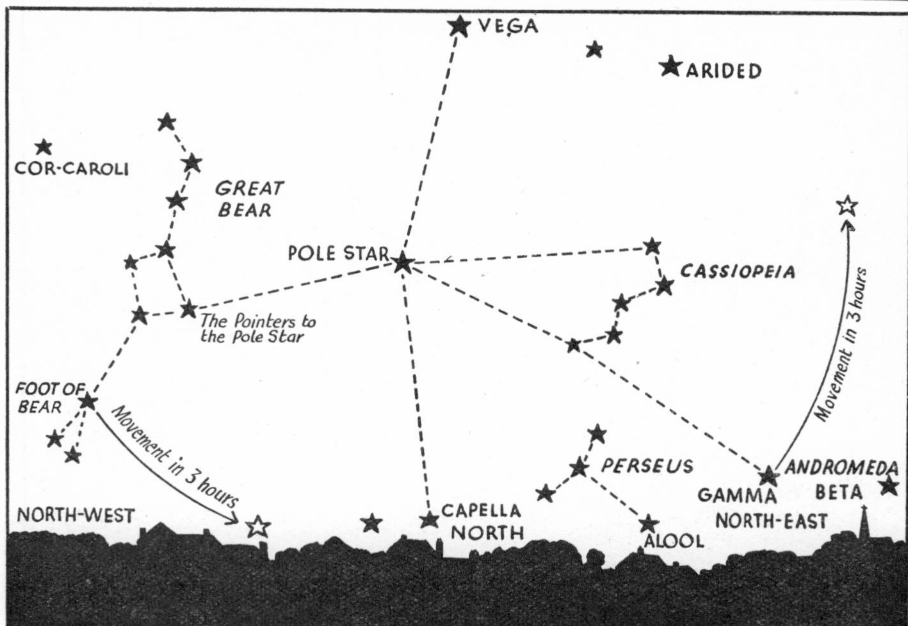

Fig. 5.—The Northern Sky. April—July (Mid-month)

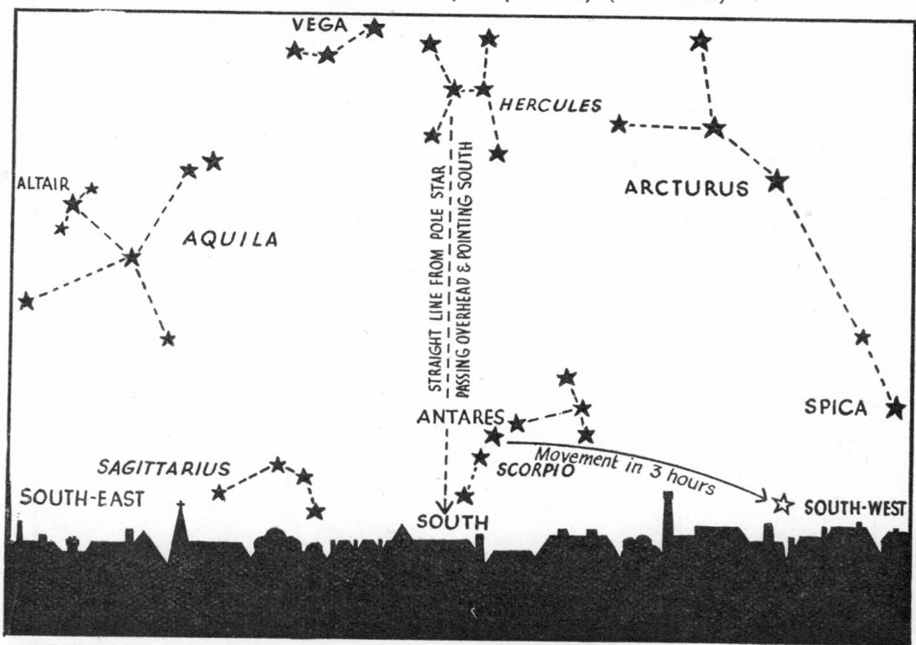

Fig. 6.—The Southern Sky. April—July (Mid-month)

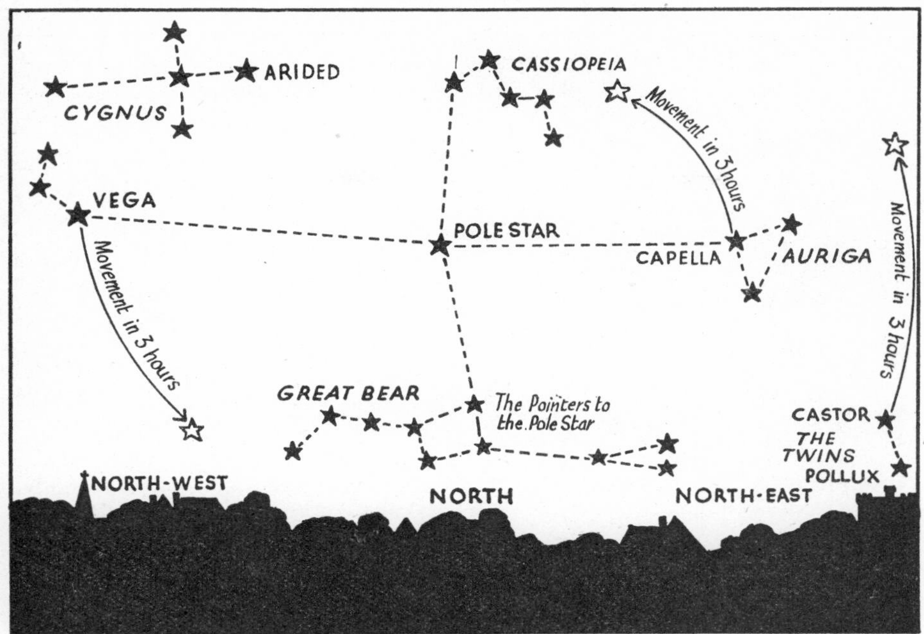

Fig. 7.—The Northern Sky. July—November (Mid-month)

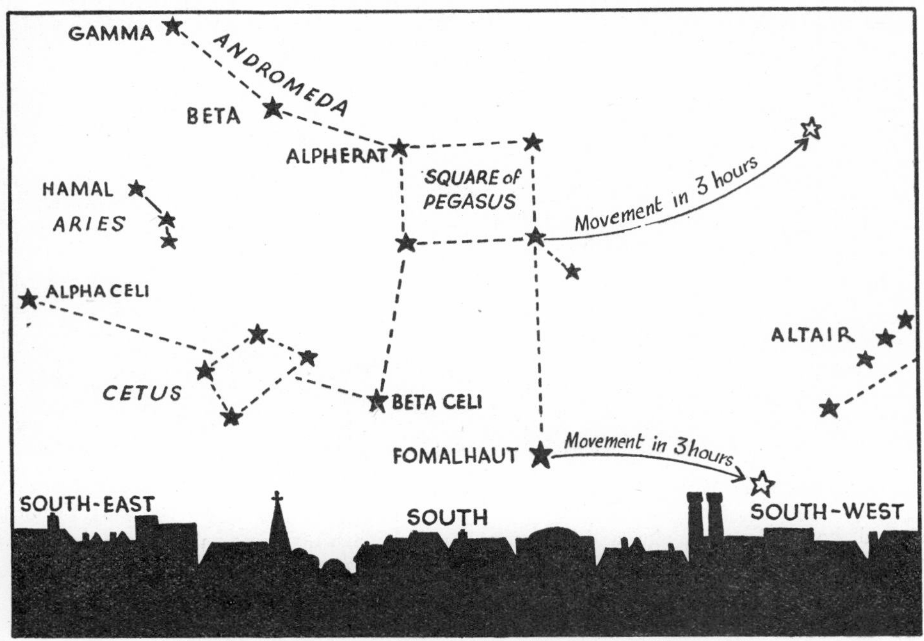

Fig. 8.—The Southern Sky. July—November (Mid-month)

Spencer Arnold

Fig. 9.—The northern portion of the Moon seen from the Mt. Wilson Observatory

should be made of Kepler and Newton, whose researches were of immense value.

Astronomy is the science which deals with the Sun, Moon, Planets, Stars, Comets and the Earth. It deals with their size, movements, distances and all other interesting facts concerning them. As a guide to the traveller, particularly sailors, and for many other purposes, astronomical knowledge is essential.

The most important instrument used by astronomers is the telescope. Until its invention man could only rely upon his own eyes for his observation of the stars and the number visible was thus extremely limited. When Galileo used his first telescope, which, crude though it was, admitted about 100 times as much light as the human eye, the number of stars visible was enormously increased. The giant telescopes of to-day are enabling us to penetrate still farther into the mysteries of the heavens and as still larger telescopes are constructed, so will our investigations extend.

Telescopes.— In its most complete form as used by astronomers, the telescope is a somewhat complex instrument, but essentially it is a most simple device. The function of the telescope is to make distant objects look nearer and it does this by using lenses which collect the light coming from an object to form an image of it. There are two ways in which the light may be collected, one by passing the light through a set of lenses and one by reflecting it from a concave mirror. Thus we have two types of telescopes called respectively, refracting and reflecting. The former is most frequently employed by amateurs. It consists of an object glass which forms the image of a distant object and the eye-piece through which the image is viewed. The power of the telescope depends upon the diameter of the object lens, which vary in size from 3 or 4 in. in the small telescopes up to 40 in. in a huge astronomical telescope. The power of a telescope is expressed as 25×, 50×, etc., which means that the glass has a magnification of 25 or 50 times as compared with unaided vision. The power of a telescope compared with the naked eye is not proportional, but increases with the square of the diameter.

A Simple Telescope may be constructed at home that gives surprising results. Procure a cardboard tube about 30 in. long and 2 in. in diameter or construct one by winding stiff brown paper, damped and glued, round a curtain pole of the desired diameter.

Now cut two strips of cardboard 1 in. wide and a little more than 6¼ in. long. Glue one inside the tube about 3 in. from the end. At the other insert a piece of wood 2 in. diameter and about 1½ in. long (a section of the curtain pole will do admirably), having previously drilled a hole 1¼ in. in diameter at its centre. This is glued in position to take the eye-piece which is similarly constructed to form a tube about 8 in. long and 1 in. in diameter. Two lenses, one 1 in. in diameter and the other with a focus of 30 in., must now be obtained from an optician. The latter is held in position by this second strip of cardboard mentioned above. Do not glue this as it

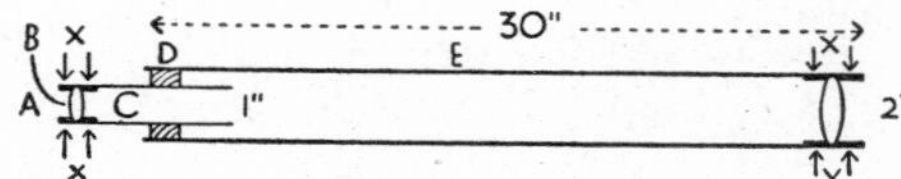

Fig. 10.—A Simple Telescope

must be removable for cleaning. The smaller lens is similarly secured by cardboard strips in the eye-piece. (*See* Fig. 10.)

Focusing is done by sliding the eye-piece in or out of its wooden socket. A camera stand makes an excellent tripod to mount the whole.

It must not be supposed that a telescope is essential to the study of astronomy, since it can be followed with no other apparatus than the naked eye. Much interesting work can also be done with an opera-glass or pair of field-glasses. (An interesting book dealing with this is "Astronomy With an Opera Glass," by Garrett P. Serviss.)

The Moon.—Perhaps the first object to which the amateur astronomer will turn his attention is the Moon which, relatively, is so close and yet so ever-changing. The various phases of the moon are a fascinating sight which never palls. There is no life on the moon. It is a dead, mountainous world without any signs of vegetation, without air and without water. The best time to begin observing the moon is when it is crescent shaped. One can then watch the advancing line of sunrise lighting up its peaks. The points of light which may then be seen are the sunlit mountain peaks, the valleys still being in dark shadow. There is no twilight on the moon and a step from the sunlit portion into shadow means

Spencer Arnold

Fig. 11.—The Great Nebula in Andromeda, from the Yerkes Observatory

complete disappearance. Both the sun and the moon attract the water and cause tides, but the moon has the greater power. At the time of the new and full moons the sun and moon unite their attractive power, which results in extremely high tides called spring tides. At other quarters of the year the sun and moon are pulling against each other with the result that the tides are not so high. These are called neap tides.

The moon is about one-fiftieth the size of the earth and is about 240,000 miles away. Sometimes it is 10,000–15,000 miles farther away and sometimes the same distance nearer. The moon revolves round the earth, taking about 28 days or a lunar month, and also accompanies the earth on its revolutions round the sun.

The amateur astronomer need not confine his activities to the night for there is always the sun to watch and in the right conditions the moon and stars as well. It is well known that the stars can be seen quite clearly from the bottom of a well in daylight, so if these conditions are reproduced—it is not suggested that the reader dig a well at the bottom of the garden—one may study the heavens at any time.

The Sun.—Care must be taken when viewing the sun directly. A sun diagonal should be used which causes the image only to be reflected to the eye, the heat rays passing out through a reflector. A star diagonal is a similar instrument which will avoid neck strain when looking at objects high in the heavens. By means of a prism the rays are directed out at right-angles to the tube.

The sun is a star and seems so much larger and brighter than the rest of the stars because it is so much closer. It is 93 million miles from the earth, and its diameter is over 100 times that of our own globe. It is not possible to see the inside of the sun but there is a great deal to watch on the outside.

An examination will show, for example, the sun spots which are now believed to be stupendous openings in the atmospheric envelope surrounding the sun. Daily observation of the sun spots can be made by arranging the telescope so that the light of the sun shining down the tube to the eye-piece falls on a sheet of white paper. The sun spots will be seen and drawings can be made of them from time to time. It is never advisable to look at the sun in broad daylight without the use of smoked or dark glasses. It is said that Galileo lost his sight through failing to take such precautions.

One of the most awe-inspiring spectacles is a total or partial eclipse of the sun which occurs far too infrequently for most amateurs.

The Planets, of which the Earth is one, are bodies similar to the Earth, the nearest to us being Venus, Mars and Mercury. The planets have no light of their own, shining only with light reflected from the sun. The planet Mercury is nearest to the sun and its temperature on the sunlit side is consequently very high. It is the smallest of the planets, its diameter being about 3,000 miles. Next to Mercury is Venus, which is the most brilliant planet. It is called the Evening Star. It is about the same size as the Earth but is much nearer the sun, and can be seen clearly with a small telescope or opera glasses.

Mars is another interesting planet which can be seen quite easily. There are many conjectures as to whether it is inhabited or not. Undoubtedly there is a possibility of life on its surface. Both air and water are present, though lesser in extent than on the earth. The largest of the planets is Jupiter, its diameter being nearly eleven times that of the Earth. Saturn is a very remote planet but is conspicuous because of its brilliance. It has a number of satellites and is surrounded by a marvellous system of rings, a fascinating sight. Other planets are Uranus, Neptune and Pluto.

The planets, with the exception of Mercury, shine with a steady light. The stars appear to twinkle. They are actually suns and many of them far greater than our own sun. There are twenty stars of the first magnitude.

Nebulæ are those misty spots which resolve themselves through the telescope into swirls of luminous matter. These consist of myriads of stars. The largest known nebula, in the constellation, Andromeda, is visible to the naked eye.

Comets when perfect consist of a nucleus, surrounded by a luminous envelope or *coma*, and a tail. This last points away from the sun. Their orbits appear to be parabolic or elliptic since they "approach from afar, go round the sun and then shoot back whence they came."

Meteors and Meteorites are bodies flying through space that become visible

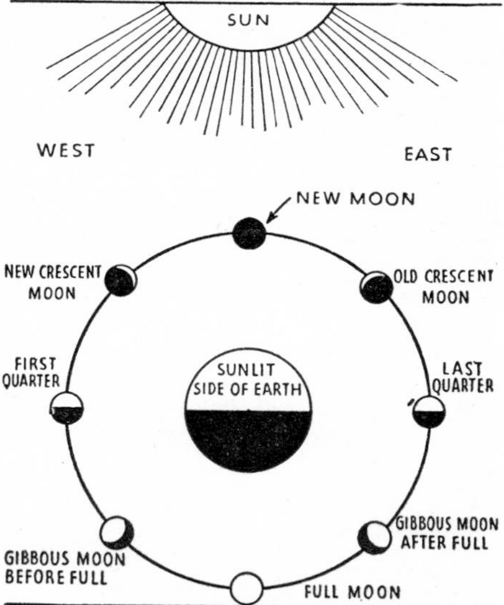

Fig. 12.—Diagram showing the Phases of the Moon

when they enter an atmosphere owing to the frictional heat developed. Meteorites are composed chiefly of stone or metallic iron. Meteors are small meteorites that are best observed during August and November when they occur in showers. It is possible that comets are composed of swarms of meteorites.

Every period of the year has its own particular celestial splendour and so frequent are the changes that there can never be any monotony in "star gazing."

ATHLETICS

THE following pages record some practical advice on some of the more usual forms of Amateur Athletics. Further information on other aspects of physical culture—surely one of the very finest hobbies—will be found under separate articles, such as Gymnastics, Keeping Fit, Self-defence, etc.

Running and Jumping are two of the most popular branches of athletics. The equipment is cheap, and the cost of being a member of an athletic club is very reasonable. For the beginner who wishes to take either running or jumping at all seriously, club membership is imperative. Nearly every town has its own clubs, and novices are generally made welcome.

Training for running or jumping can be recommended as one which will keep the ordinary person bodily fit. "Athlete's heart" (an enlarged heart, caused through over-strain of that organ) is not likely to trouble the person who combines tact with training. It is, however, advisable that the beginner first should be examined by a doctor. Even though you may be sure of your perfect physical health, the assurance of the medical man is extremely valuable.

Strict training should in no case be undergone by anyone under the age of 19; it is hindering and not helpful to the still-growing muscles. The best years are between the ages of 20 and 28, although many famous men have begun their athletics much later in life; and it is often found that the long-distance man enjoys a longer period in competitive athletics than does the sprinter.

To the runner and jumper reward is the result of perseverance. Athletes are not born ready-made—it is the man who trains the hardest who gains the most success. However, the beginner must not get disheartened if, after the first week or so of training, the result is a worse showing instead of better; this is the natural course, so it must be understood that it is impossible to find real success in a short time. The approach to strict training should be undergone slowly and as naturally as possible. A sudden change of régime is likely to have injurious results.

Fig. 1.—The Start of an 880 yards Race at White City

Fig. 2.—Hurdling at White City

Two months is the shortest time any athlete should devote to training before thinking about competition. The novice should prepare for the first half of the season.

The following gives a brief outline as to all-round athletic training, being suitable for all branches of the sport:

For the legs, walking is a good natural exercise, and is not beneficial to them alone; a couple of miles before breakfast is a fine tonic and appetizer. *Mix training with your everyday life.* If you do not have too far to go to work, walk instead of indulging in a bus, though the top of a bus is far better than a crowded train carriage. A walk home in the early evening is particularly health-giving. Do not use a cycle to excess, because for the athlete it develops the wrong muscles.

Exercise.—One of the finest forms of all-round exercise is skipping; it improves not only the legs, wrists and shoulders, but also benefits the liver and stomach, and, most important, the lungs and heart, thus improving the wind and stamina. The proper training skip is to jump off one foot to the other, just as though you were running; bringing the knees well up.

Another good exercise is running up and down stairs. The stairs should be taken one at a time, and two or three short bursts daily are excellent for the sprinter.

Immersion in water, in moderation, is good for the muscles. A cold plunge or sponge down first thing in the morning, followed by a brisk rub down, creates good blood circulation. Fairly warm baths (100°–105° F.) after training are excellent especially if the muscles are stiff; add a couple of tablespoonfuls of soda. Brine or sea-water baths are most beneficial, especially for hardening the feet against blisters. After a bath a massage is good for both circulation and toning up the muscles. The idea is to loosen the muscles away from the bone. The motion should always be towards the heart. Avoid very hot baths; they have a weakening effect and cause palpitation of the heart.

Sun-bathing is to be highly recommended; get as much of the body as you can exposed, but remember that the penalty of over-exposure is soreness and skin-peeling, and sometimes an unpleasant illness.

The feet are important. Great care should be taken of ingrowing toe-nails, blisters and corns. The toe-nails should be kept fairly short.

Bad teeth are frequently the cause of ill-health. It is advisable to have all decayed teeth extracted. The teeth should be cleaned regularly morning and night.

Diet.—It is impossible to be definite on this subject. That which suits one man's stomach does not agree with another's. We all know what food is most agreeable with our systems, and that food should constitute our diet. It is important that meals should be taken regularly, and it is bad to eat between meals. Constipation is often caused by eating the wrong food, and the effects of constipation are many.

With drink, alcohol, of course, must be avoided, and excessive tea or coffee drinking is not good, that is, more than half a dozen cups of either a day. Many people would not suffer from indigestion if they abstained from drinking with their meals. Liquid should be taken at least an hour after a big meal.

Smoking is definitely a bad habit for any athlete; and for those seeking the highest honours it should be taboo.

Nothing can be said against evening entertainments, such as pictures, dances, etc., unless it is that they are usually held in a stuffy atmosphere, and generally mean staying out late at night.

Sleep is an all-important point to the athlete. Eight and a half hours is sufficient, but less than eight hours is not enough. The nerves of some athletes mar their sleep on the night before a race. This cannot be helped, and the only thing to do is to relax the muscles and rest. This is really beneficial, and induces sleep.

Equipment.—The most important item of a track athlete's equipment is the shoes. These should be skin tight, with the uppers of soft, pliable leather, and the soles of stouter but still pliable leather; a steel plate for holding the spikes in position is not recommended. It is advisable to have the shoes made to measure at a little extra cost. The length of spikes varies with the distance of the race. It is generally agreed that sprinters should wear $\frac{3}{4}$- to $\frac{7}{8}$-in. spikes, and middle and long-distance men about $\frac{1}{2}$-in. The cross-country runner has special shoes, sometimes with rubber, and sometimes very short steel spikes. In addition to the six usual spikes the jumper and hurdler has two in each heel to enable a better grip on taking-off. Do not use your best shoes for

Fig. 3.—The High Jump : a fine action picture

Fig. 4.—Competing in the Long Jump

ordinary training, and do not walk about in them; carry a pair of plimsoles with you.

Shorts should be made to measure, and those kept up with buttons or a buckle, rather than elastic, are the best. The vest should be loose-fitting and sleeveless. Other necessary items are: a sweater, a tape measure (if you are a jumper), running corks (to grip during the final sprint), a pair of training trousers, and, for the sprinter, a trowel for digging starting holes.

Technique.—Something should be done towards physical improvement every day and hard training should be undergone at least three times a week. It is a good idea to plan out beforehand exactly what training is to be done.

Track athletes are advised not to let their training drop during the winter season. A trot a week with the cross-country section of the club, with indoor exercises on the remaining days, is beneficial.

A rest from training one day before competition is advisable for all athletes.

For the Runner.—In distances up to 440 yards the runner must become almost like a machine, owing to the fact that he runs at top speed throughout the race. His movements must be smooth and automatic; and the only way to achieve this is by constant practice, thus gaining a perfectly natural style.

The correct position of the trunk is slightly bent forward, but not overdone. The arms are used vigorously in a piston-rod movement; shooting out so that if they were both pushed forward at the same time the clenched fists would meet about 18 ins. from the centre of the chest. The swing should carry the fists to the point level with the collar-bone, and not lower than the hip-bone. The knees come fairly high at the front, but when bringing the feet up at the back they should not be taken off the ground any more than can be helped. The fact that the knees are brought up high means that the feet can stride a little farther, whereas when the heels are kicked up at the back no progress is being made forward—it is just a waste of time.

An excellent way of gaining a good style is to run on the spot in front of a full-length mirror. Wear as little clothing as possible, and by this means the little errors in style, otherwise unnoticeable, can be picked out. Draw a chalk line round the feet, and keep within its limits as far as possible.

One of the most important points that the sprinter must watch is the start. The "crouch" position should always be used. First get a trowel for digging the starting holes. They will be dug a little behind the starting line, because by leaning forward on to the hands the crouch position is taken. Kneel down on the right knee, or the left if it is preferred, so that the knee is on a line with the ball of the left foot, and this determines the position of the holes. Each hole should be dug big enough to contain the ball of the foot, but not too wide. The thumb and index finger of each hand should be placed on the starting line, with the other fingers spread out behind. That is the "Get ready" position, and on the command "Get set," the knee on the ground should be raised about a foot, throwing the weight of the body on to the arms and the forward foot. The eyes should concentrate on the spot where the first stride will come. The start should be practised until it is perfect, for to the sprinter a bad start is fatal.

Fig. 5.—The Pole Jump

A long stride is an advantage, but it is better to be able to take five strides of seven feet in a second than four strides of eight. During the stride the feet should glide as close to the ground as possible, and should be "flicked" forward at the end; this adds inches. Be careful not to bound off the ground like a kangaroo; this wastes a lot of time. When running, the feet should travel along an imaginary straight line. It is good to practise running along a chalked line. On reaching the finishing tape during a race, the arms should be thrust down and the trunk thrust forward; this is known as the "drop finish."

Middle Distance.—The half-mile and mile are usually termed the middle distances. The style of this distance runner is easier and not so keyed-up as that of the sprinter, as the speed is varied during the race. The stride is the same as that of the shorter distance man, but the arms should be carried more comfortably, except during the fast start and the final spurt.

Unlike the sprinter, the middle-distance man must have a knowledge of track tactics, and the premier rules are: (*a*) Do not pass on the bend; (*b*) Keep on the inside of the track. The ideal position during competition is to lie second or third until the race is three parts over—the miler a little farther than this—although on some occasions it is wise to lead throughout. However, do not be misled into following-up the person who goes tearing off for the first lap at a hundred yards pace—he will more than likely drop out, and so will anyone who follows him.

When once the final spurt has been started it should be carried on until past the finishing tape, for it is nearly impossible for a tired runner to speed up again after he has relaxed.

When training for one of the middle distances it is advisable to go a little farther than the actual distance to be raced; this gives extra stamina. Sprints, however, should also be practised to enable a good starting and finishing speed.

Longer Distances.—The tactics and technique of the long-distance runner are very similar to those of the middle-distance man. More stamina is naturally required, and this enforces a still easier style on the track. A thorough knowledge of pace must also be gained. For example, the three-miler, in running his race in 15½ minutes, should cover the first mile in just over five minutes, the second mile in five minutes twenty seconds, and alter his speed to cover the third in the scheduled time. Jog trotting over one and a half to twice the distance to be raced is useful in training for the longer races.

Cross-country running really demands a style of its own, because this has to be altered as the runner goes up and down the hills. Over the flat the style of the distance man should be adopted, but when ascending a hill a short stride with a more exaggerated arm-action must be employed, and the opposite to this when descending. Ploughed fields, soft and rough country should be taken with a short stride.

In a competition the athlete should get away fast over the first 200 yards, use a good stiff pace for the next 600 yards, and then settle down to normal racing speed until the final spurt.

The High Jump.—There are many different styles of high jumping, but all of them are controlled by the basic principle of combining the swing of the legs with a spring from the ground. When preparing to jump, it is a mistake to approach the bar at a fast pace. A slow, springy trot for about seven yards, quickening on the last two yards, should be used. When as near to the bar as possible the actual spring is taken. The "take-off" foot should be flat on the ground for a fraction of a second, in the act of making a tremendous stamp, the body being thrown forward. It depends on the athlete's build as to whether the spring or the leg swing is his greatest asset, but whatever the style adopted the swing of the legs over the bar comes straight from the hip, as in the act of kicking a football, the knees being perfectly straight. The next part of the jump—the lie out—depends on the style adopted, but the American "flat" style is usually recognized as the best. The jumper springs and swings his legs up. The leading leg is lifted over, the body follows, and is in turn followed by the other leg. Actually, while passing over the bar, the jumper is in a horizontal position. The landing should be made on the same foot from which the jump is made.

It is important that the high jumper should know the exact distance of his run-up. When training it is advisable to tackle jumps which can be cleared and work for the improvement of style. Once a week, see what height can be reached. High kicking is good for the balance and loosens the hips.

S. & G.

Fig. 6.—Putting the Weight

Long Jumping.—Unlike the high jumper the long jumper has to use speed in the run-up and the faster he can approach and hit the take-off board the better. In order that the take-off mark is hit, it is important that the run-up should be measured accordingly and accurately—the distance usually being between 25 and 35 yards.

The take-off is a powerful foot-stamp with the accustomed foot together with a downward pull of the opposite arm. This sends the jumper into the flight, and the knees are tucked-up as near to the chin as possible, or the running action is continued until the landing—these being the two recognized styles. The latter is known as being the better for landing, and as the distance of the jump is measured from the mark made nearest the take-off it is fatal to fall back on to the hands.

The long-jumper should aim at height, and the speed of his run will give him the distance. Sprinting practice is therefore essential.

Pole Jumping.—The uprights for pole jumping must be at least 12 ft. apart. A hole or slide-way or box is allowed in which the point of the pole can be planted so that it does not slip when the leap is made. The pole is made of strong but light bamboo.

A run of between 30 yards and 35 yards is made, speed being increased gradually so that maximum pace is reached by the time the runner is at the take-off. The pole is gripped with both hands, but it is not permitted that in the moment that the jump is made or after the jumper has left the ground his lower hand be placed above the upper one or that the upper hand move higher up the pole.

It is usual to have someone on the ground to catch your pole as it is falling, after you have released it and flung yourself over the bar, otherwise the pole might be broken when striking the ground. No hand support other than a binding is allowed on the pole.

Considerable nerve and acrobatic ability are required for the pole jump; there is a long way to go up and a long way to come down—world beaters have cleared more than 14 feet.

Before beginning a jump stand your pole in the hole; you will then be able to see where it touches the bar you propose to leap. Slightly above that is the point on your pole where your right hand will grip. About 30 inches lower your left hand will take hold. Now make your run, and finally plant your point in the hole and throw your legs forward and upward. Your knees will be drawn up as you rise and your left hand will have slid up close to the right, both will be pressing firmly on the pole. Then you will straighten your legs out above the bar, the body having begun to turn to the left. The feet must go as high as possible as they shoot over the bar and the body will continue its turn until it is face downwards. A last vigorous thrust on the pole forces head and arms clear over the bar—at this moment the body will be pointing upward. Then the hands release their grip, the pole dropping back, while you fall down towards the sand on the far side, landing with as little jar as possible.

Hurdling.—Remember first of all that every hurdle must be taken in your stride. You should never come to a standstill and then make a jump. Hurdling has really little to do with jumping at all. A hurdle course is simply a plain sprint, with every fourth stride rather bigger than the rest.

The length of a full hurdle course is 120 yards. It includes ten flights of hurdles, with ten yards between each pair. Before the first flight and after the last is a stretch of 15 yards. The regulation height of a hurdle is 3 ft. 6 in.

First master the method of going over the hurdle. The necessary movements can be rehearsed quite slowly. Stand against the hurdle and lift your right foot upward and forward, until it is over the top bar—if necessary, assist yourself by gripping the hurdle with your hands. When your right foot is clear of the top, give a forward spring from the left. At the moment when your body is midway over, thrust your right foot downwards to the ground and draw your left foot up behind you by bending your knee outwards, so that it comes cleanly over the bar. It is of special importance that you acquire the habit of darting your forward foot to the ground as quickly as possible. In actual hurdling, of course, your arms will be spread well out to the sides in order to preserve your balance.

Practice should consist in improving your style, until you can cover your ten flights with machine-like accuracy.

Taking off from the left foot, your first spring will be made two yards before the first hurdle. Your right foot will touch ground two yards beyond. Then will follow three strides, each of two yards, which will bring you on to the left foot once more and the correct two yards distance before the second hurdle. Repeat the performance for each flight.

Accustom yourself to the exact stride required so that you can go down the whole course without faltering. Always you will make your leap from the same foot. And, as your chief aim is to get to the other end of the course as quickly as possible, any unnecessary leaping in an upward direction means wasted time. Aim at getting over your hurdle with as little lift as possible. So long as you clear it, nothing else is needed.

S. & G.

Fig. 7.—Throwing the Hammer

Hop, Step and Jump.—In many respects this resembles the long jump, and the same general rules apply, but following the take-off you must first land upon the same foot with which you have taken off; the reverse foot must be used for the second landing, and both feet for the third landing.

The preliminary run is of great importance, for it has to give you impetus and speed. See that your steps fit in exactly; it is a bad fault to shorten or lengthen your strides in order to arrive at the take-off properly. If, in practice, your steps will not fit in, go back and start again, adjusting the length of your run as may be necessary.

Do not spring too high in the hop, or there will be too much strain on the single leg when you come down. And do not make the middle stride too long, for that will lessen the available power for the final jump.

In the jump you will get as high as you can, and use every bit of available vigour.

The judging of the height for the hop and the length for the step will have a good deal to do with the success of the whole hop, step and jump.

Let there be no check or pause at each landing. Simply come down on the heel, go forward on to the toes, then spring lightly and strongly. As far as possible let your original impetus carry you clean through, augmented, of course, by the full power of the leg at each landing.

Putting the Weight.—The weight

S. & G.

Fig. 8.—Throwing the Discus

forward off your balance give a thrusting hop from your right foot and swing the left leg forward once more. You will thus travel forward and your right foot will come to the ground almost at the centre of the circle. Your left foot will drop close to the front edge of the circle, and at the same time your body will twist, in counter-clockwise direction, bringing the right foot against the board. The left arm, and the whole body, assist the final movement, in which the right arm is thrust forward with utmost vigour, in a sort of punch, hurling the shot in the desired direction. And to save you falling forward out of the circle the left leg swings back and comes to the ground behind its fellow.

or *shot* is spherical and is made of brass, iron, or lead, the latter being least satisfactory. The 16 lb. shot is too heavy for a novice; lesser weights should be used at first. It may seem a fairly straightforward thing to hurl a weight, but it will not go very far—certainly nowhere near 50 ft. unless a great deal of skill as well as strength is used. Incidentally 50 ft. is close to world record figures.

The shot has to be *put*, or hurled, from a circle with an interior diameter of 7 ft. In the middle of the circumference at the front half a *stop-board*, 4 ft. long and 4 in. high, is firmly fastened to the ground. In making your *puts* the feet may rest against but not on top of this board. A fair put is one in which no part of you touches the stop-board, the circle, or the ground outside the circle until a shot has touched the ground.

To begin, stand with your right foot within the rear part of the circle, the shot balanced in your right hand against the right shoulder. Let your weight go on to your right foot for a moment while you swing your left leg forward, to gain impetus. Then bring the left foot back, still without touching the ground. As you begin to go

The first part of the journey across the circle is called the *glide*; the second part is the *reverse*—it is in this latter that the outside edge of the right foot hits the stop-board. The whole must be combined smoothly, with a crescendo of speed and energy.

See that you get an effective "follow through" of shoulder, arm, fingers.

Throwing the Hammer.—As in shot putting so in throwing the hammer, you must stand in a 7 ft. circle to make your throw, and no part of you must touch the ground outside the circle until the hammer has grounded. The hammer itself must weigh not less than 16 lb. and be not more than 4 ft. in length.

To begin, stand in the rear part of the circle, feet comfortably spread and with your back towards the direction in which you intend to throw. Your hands will be down towards your right knee as you grip the handle, and the hammer head will be on the ground to the right and slightly to the rear of you.

You begin by swinging the hammer round the head, three times, with arms fully extended. The circling of the hammer head should not be on a horizontal plane, but high over your left shoulder and nearer the ground on your right side. Following these three swings, which gain impetus, three more circling swings of the whole body, balanced on the left foot, are made. These add still more impetus. Finally the right foot comes to the ground towards the front of the circle, and the hammer is thrown.

In learning to throw, concentrate first on the preliminary head swings. When you can get those smoothly, continue to a single spin on the left foot, your right leg circling round the left, and make your throw. When all this is smooth, go on to make two spins. Finally do the three preliminary swings followed by the three spins. See that you make all swings as big as possible. But never let the hammer get in front of the body; there should always be resistance between body and hammer, and the body should be pulling—it is wrong to let the hammer pull you. In the final throw the hammer will go high above the left shoulder and every bit of power will go into the pulling throw.

Do not overdo practice; hammer throwing is exceedingly hard work.

Throwing the Javelin.—The javelin is made of wood with an iron point and is 8 ft. 1 in. long, weighing 1·6 lb. A grip of whipcord is wound round the shaft at about the centre of gravity. The javelin is thrown from behind the scratch line, and it is a foul throw if the point of the javelin does not touch the ground before any part of the shaft.

Hold your javelin at the grip, with thumb and forefinger at the back edge of the binding. During the run the hand is rather higher than the shoulder, and the palm is turned upward, with the shaft lying along it. Do not grip tightly until the actual throw begins.

In the concluding part of the run the right shoulder and arm are drawn back smoothly to full stretch, and the arm hurled forward, the fingers giving the final flick and follow-through as the shaft is released.

S. & G.

Fig. 9.—Throwing the Javelin. A Classical Pose

Do plenty of light practice, flinging the javelin easy distances so that you get thoroughly accustomed to handling and tossing. Get to know your javelin. Only occasionally, until you have cultivated good style, should you be concerned about longer throws.

Throwing the Discus.—This sport of ancient Greece is a splendid exercise, and deserves wider popularity. In many ways it resembles throwing the hammer, and the rules are the same, except that for the discus the circle from which the throw is made has an inside diameter of 7 ft.

The discus is made of wood with an iron rim and a smooth plate on each face. It weighs $4\frac{1}{4}$ lb. The discus is held flat against the palm and wrist, in the right hand, the ends of the fingers going over the rim. You will stand at the rear of the circle, with the left foot slightly forward, but with your back towards the direction in which you intend to throw, the discus being held above the head, partly supported by the left hand. At this moment the left side of the body is nearest the front of the circle.

A single full-arm swing is made to get impetus, and then the body turns and the right foot goes forward to the middle of the circle, followed by a step towards the front edge with the left foot as the throw is made. See that the fingers give a final flick to the discus as it leaves the hand; spin will be imparted to it by the forefinger.

In practising develop easy, correct movements by plenty of light throwing.

BADMINTON

Although it is possible to play garden badminton, the real game must be played indoors, because the standard shuttle is very light and easily deflected by wind. And as, of course, it is too warm to play indoors in the summer, badminton is thus restricted to the six months beginning with October.

Even if no club exists in your locality it is a fairly simple business to form one. Providing some sort of hall or other building is available with a floor space of 26 ft. by 50 ft. and a central ceiling height of 25 ft., then, with a few keen people, you may go ahead. Lighting, accommodation for club members, equipment, will have to be planned, but that will not be much trouble.

The Court.—Figs. 1 and 2 show plans of singles and doubles courts. The lines, which are marked in either black or white, are $1\frac{1}{2}$ in. wide. There is no ruling as to the material for the floor. Wood is generally used. The net must be of fine tanned cord of $\frac{3}{4}$ in. square mesh and may be 17 to 24 ft. in length, according to position of posts (*see* diagrams), and 2 ft. 6 in. in depth. The top of the net is 5 ft. in height at the centre and 5 ft. 1 in. at the posts, and must be edged with a 3-in. white tape doubled and supported by a cord run through tape, strained over and flush with the top of the posts, which must be 5 ft. 1 in. high.

One point of great importance in the badminton hall is its lighting. It is unwise to have lights spread equally over the full length of the court. A better plan is to concentrate them on either side near to the centre.

Badminton rackets are standardized in size and weight, so that in choosing one you should be guided chiefly by the thickness of the handle and the quality. The best plan is to pay as much as you can afford, good workmanship generally being cheaper in the end. But even a good racket can be spoiled if used carelessly. Look after it, therefore, from the outset. A press is essential, and always slip it on to the racket when you have finished play. Do not hang a racket up by the press, for nail or hook can easily damage the gut. Stand it upright, or lay it flat on a shelf. When the press is on, it is best to hold it in order to carry the racket; to carry by the handle may strain the thin shaft. Keep your

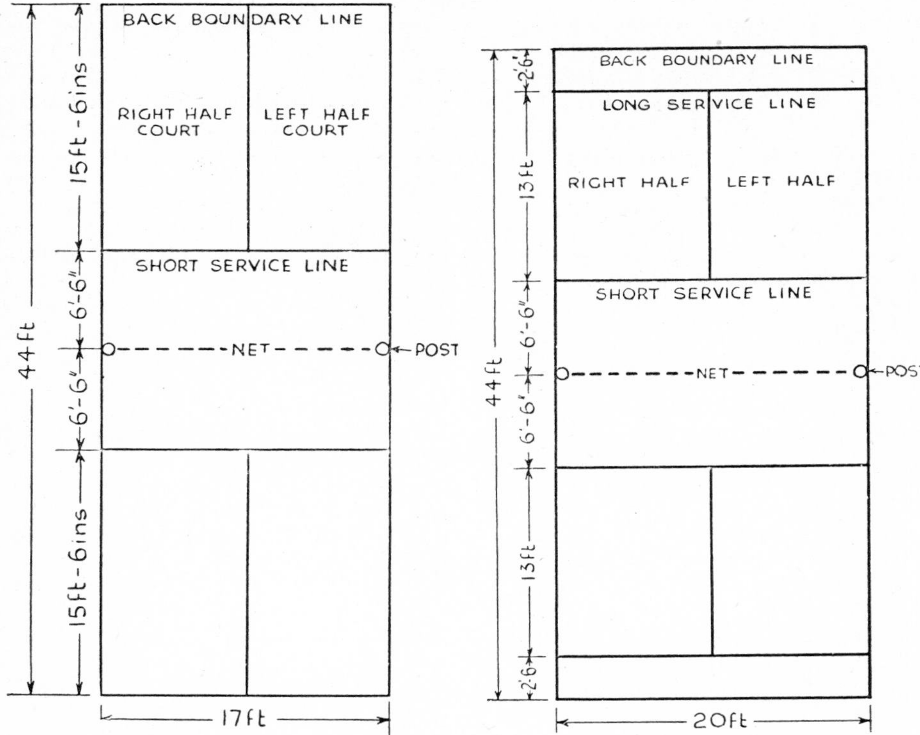

Fig. 1.—The Singles Court

Fig. 2.—The Doubles Court

racket in a dry place—like the rest of your badminton equipment. But remember never to put it away without its press.

The Shuttle.—The most expensive item of badminton is, curiously enough, the shuttle, not because its original cost is much, but rather that it is so short-lived. The usual thing is for a club to supply its members with shuttles, but, of course, the cost comes back on to the members just the same in their subscriptions or in some other way. Shuttles must not be treated roughly, for they are very fragile, and a single broken feather may mean a useless shuttle. Beginners often do unnecessary damage by knocking a shuttle along the floor. Train yourself to be careful of shuttles and you will have much reason to be thankful later on when you become so proficient that the sheer vigour of your play soon beats out the life of "the bird."

Dress for Badminton is about the same as for tennis. For men, shorts or white flannels with short-sleeve vest or white shirt. For women, white washable frocks, sleeveless and short, with enough material in the skirt to allow free movement. Some women favour shorts, as in tennis. Light tennis shoes are very suitable.

You should have something warm to slip on when you are not actually playing—a coat or pull-over. A badminton hall is often cold and draughty, and a chill is all the more likely when you have got thoroughly warm during a strenuous game.

Holding the Racket.—First you must get the right grip of your racket. The proper way is to have the V formed by thumb and first finger in line with the frame, on the side of the handle, not the flat of it. If you let the racket hang by your side it should rest flat against your leg, with this V to the front. Take care that you hold the end of the handle, so that the leather binding is within the palm. It is thoroughly bad to grip some way up the handle, for not only does the stump act as a sort of splint to the wrist, but the reach is considerably shortened. (*See* Fig. 3.)

Do not go on to the court with any preliminary ideas derived from tennis. The shuttle does not bounce, and points are scored when it falls to the floor.

As the game is very fast you must be thoroughly alert in mind and body, ready to move quickly in any direction. Should you have a moment's pause it is customary to rest the head of the racket on the palm of the left hand. Always stand leaning alertly forward, with left foot advanced. The usual position, in an ordinary doubles game, is the centre of the half court, unless of course you are receiving service or playing in a "back and front" partnership. Although you will necessarily have to move frequently from your position, form the habit of returning promptly to this centre of your half court, for this is very definitely the most convenient point from which to reach any other part.

SCORING

Fifteen aces, or points, usually make a game, and these can only be scored by the serving side. The four-handed or doubles game consists of 15 or 21 aces as arranged. The method of scoring, though straightforward enough, seems complicated at first.

In singles the server serves from each court alternately and counts each point he scores, until his opponent wins the shuttle. In doubles each pair of players has two *hands* consecutively. For example, supposing A and B are playing X and Y. A serves until he and his partner lose a point, then B goes on until they lose another point. Next the service goes over to X and Y, who continue in the same fashion. Each server, of course, serves alternately from each service court, his partner every time moving into the other half court.

The side which begins to serve takes only a single *hand* at their first time of service. The toss of a coin or the spin of a racket settles the original service. On spinning a racket it is usual to call "rough" or "smooth"—this applies to the fine gut at the top and bottom of the racket; on one face it has a smooth surface, on the other a rough. The side which wins the toss can either take the first service or choose from which end of the court they will play.

You should call the score always before serving, first giving the number of points belonging to your side, then the points of your opponents, and lastly the number of hands left to you and your partner. Thus you might call 6—7—2 or 12—9—1.

In the game of fifteen aces, if the score reaches 13 all, the side which first reached 13 may "set" the game to 5—so that 5 more points have to be played for. When the game is 14 all, the game may similarly be set to 3 more points.

A four-handed or doubles game consists of 15 or 21 aces, as arranged. In a game of 15 aces, when the score is 13 all, the side which first reaches 13 has the option of "setting" the game to 5, and when the score is 14 all the side which first reaches 14 has the option of "setting" the game to 3. After a game has been "set" the score is called "love all" and the side which first scores five or three aces, according to how the game has been "set" at 13 or 14 all, wins the game. In either case the claim to "set" the game must be made before the next service is delivered after the score has reached 13 all or 14 all. In a game of 21 aces scoring is by the same method, except that 19 and 20 are substituted for 13 and 14. Scoring is similar in men's singles but in ladies' singles the game consists of 11 aces. There is the option of "setting" the game to 5 at 9 all and to 3 at 10 all.

Both the receiver and the server must stand within the bounds of their half court. A service must not be overhand, and therefore the shuttlecock must be no higher than the waist of the server at the moment of striking, and the head of the racket must not be higher than the hand of the server. If a shuttle touches the net in a service it is a *let*, and a replay may be claimed.

Strokes.—Always hit the shuttle with the middle of the gut, and make full use of the body. The arm and wrist naturally participate in any stroke, but if you would hit with any force it is necessary to use the weight of the body, too. This generally means transferring the weight from one foot to the other.

Do not make a stroke with the elbow bent, for that not only reduces length of reach but lessens power. It is well to take the shuttle before it gets too close to the body so that a clean hit is possible.

Although in the preliminary swing some looseness and bending are allowable, the arm should be almost fully extended and stiffened at the moment of impact.

See that your racket "follows through" after its stroke. One of the most serious faults which can be acquired by the learner is that of checking his swing at the instant of striking. By having a smooth follow-through, not only do you gain much in power, but you greatly reduce muscular strain.

An equally important general rule is that of always keeping your eye on the shuttle. This necessitates much deliberate practice, for the shuttle moves very quickly.

Fig. 3.—Forehand Grip at beginning of stroke

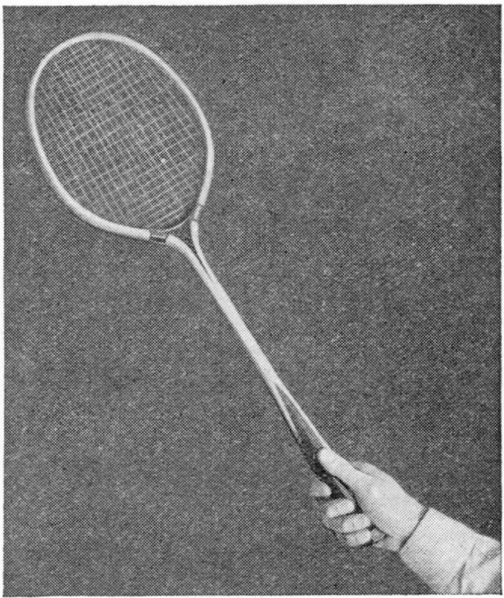

Fig. 4.—Backhand Grip at end of stroke

Serving.—Stand near your front service line with the right foot advanced a little and the weight of your body on it.

There are two chief services—the high lob to the back of the service court, and the low, short stroke which barely clears the net and drops close to the front service line. Play both of them smoothly in the ordinary forehand fashion. With practice you may make your actions so resemble each other that the opponent has no means of judging which he may expect. This disguise is helped still further if you always take up the same position whether giving a high or a low service.

Hold the shuttle lightly by the feathers, in the left hand. Do not throw it upwards, but simply drop it vertically on to your racket. Be careful, remembering that only one service is allowed to a *hand* at the beginning of each rally.

When receiving a service your best place is near the front service line, standing with left foot advanced. Thus you will be ready to spring back for a high service or jump at a low one. It is good to take a crouching position, racket and arms outstretched and body leaning forward. The more alert and dangerous your pose looks the more likely it is to upset the confidence of the server. Visual impression of this sort can play a great part, but remember that you must not let your feet come over the front line, however your body may be bent. It is a rule frequently broken that "the receiver must stand within the limits of his half court, and some part of both feet must remain in contact with the ground until the service is delivered." So avoid rushing forward before the shuttle has been hit.

There are a great many badminton strokes, but in the early stages of your play it is advisable that you should concentrate on a few. By serving well, and hitting hard, so that you can get the shuttle across safely and strongly to the back of the opponents' court, you will be laying a good foundation for future proficiency. The one or two strokes on which you concentrate should be offensive rather than defensive ones—for the best rule of all badminton play is "always attack."

Here are the principal strokes briefly defined:

Lob or **clearing stroke.**—In this the shuttle is driven high and sent to the back of the court.

Drive and **half-court shots.**—These are fast, direct strokes.

Drop shot.—A smooth little stroke which just lifts the shuttle over the net.

Smash.—A smashing, downward stroke.

The *lob* can be played forehand, backhand, or overhead. It should have good length and height. Aim at making your shuttle travel to within a few inches of your opponents' base line. It is a mistake, and a very common and serious one, to make it drop several feet short. In practising this stroke remember that it is better to drive too far than too short. The clearing shot, of course, is a lob which clears the heads of the opponents.

A deep and high lob can often get you out of difficulties, because it allows you maximum time to recover yourself. But when you are using the lob for attack your concern must be not to take maximum time in this way, but to get the shuttle clear over your opponents on to their back line as quickly as possible.

The *drive* allows you to send the shuttle to any desired spot in the quickest time. Do not just jab at the shuttle, but get a clean swing of your arm with a good follow-through. The racket should swing round the body, keeping at about the same level throughout, and at the moment of impact you should let your weight go forward from the right foot to the left foot.

The *drop shot* is very fascinating, it gives one such a sense of mastery to make the shuttle just trickle over the net so that it is quite unplayable. Naturally a good deal of practice is needed, for if the shuttle goes too high it offers an easy smash to an opponent. Play smoothly yet firmly, and let the wrist take its part—often the stroke may be made by the merest wrist flick.

Instead of making the shuttle drop very close to the net when you make a drop shot, there is a second variety of the stroke in which the shuttle falls farther into the court—the aim being to compel your opponent to hit upwards. An advantage of this type of drop shot is that it can be played faster.

A drop shot played overhead is very deceptive, for an opponent may even expect a smash, and only the slowing up of your stroke at the last instant takes out the sting and changes it to a shot which just creeps over the net. The underhand drop shot is more common.

Incidentally it is a sound plan to make all of your strokes look as much alike as possible so that those on the other side of the net can never determine what you are about to do.

The *smash* should generally win a point, if it is correctly made. In addition to the weight of the body the wrist must give the final sting to the stroke. Let your body come forward, the weight swinging vigorously from the right to the advanced left foot. And take the shuttle high in the air.

In the smash, particularly, a good follow-through is essential, and the racket should be pointing to the ground at its conclusion. Do not let your racket touch the net in this follow-through, if you happen to be near; check it in time.

The steeper the angle of your smash the better. But do not hit wildly: good placing is as important as proper force.

Many players neglect the varieties of strokes—forehand, underhand, overhead, backhand, particularly the last.

In a backhand stroke the body should be turned from the net so that the striking arm has complete freedom. Advance your right foot, pointing it to the side of the court, and letting your weight go on to it at the moment of striking. You should begin backhand work right from the outset so that it becomes thoroughly strong—so many poor players avoid the backhand and run across to play on the forehand. This wastes time and gives dangerous openings to opponents. Obviously if your backhand is weak that is all the more reason why you should give it plenty of work.

Singles and Doubles.—A singles player must get great variety in his strokes, and be careful to return to the centre of the court every time—for this is the ideal position. Although it pays always to attack it is worth while remembering that there is no one to rescue you if you err through over-eagerness.

It is not easy to get singles practice, especially in a popular club, so that you should seize every opportunity you can for it.

Doubles can be a *sides* combination or a *back and front*—this latter is generally adopted for mixed games, the lady playing at the net.

Study your partner, remember to guard her weakness and assist her strength. Have a thorough understanding. In a back and front game it is a common fault for the lady to retreat too far. She should keep between the net and the front service line.

Sometimes, when a game is not going well, a back and front pair may improve things by adopting a side-by-side combination—providing the lady can take her proper share of work at the back of the court.

Obviously a tall player is at a disadvantage playing at the net, though height is all to the good at the back of the court. If you are at the net allow yourself plenty of room, and don't hold your stroke till the shuttle is almost on you.

General Hints.—Do plenty of practice. You will soon learn your weak points, and they are the ones which you should cultivate, though it may be much easier to shirk them. If you have a particularly kind friend he may put up the shuttle for you in exactly the manner you desire so that you can repeat certain bits of technique over and over again.

Watch good players, and get them to criticize your own play if they will.

Study to acquire good footwork—quickness, nimbleness, balance, easy transference of weight. And be sure to develop the ability to run backwards, so that you can retreat with your eye on the shuttle and in position for your stroke.

Be considerate on the court. Acknowledge good shots by an opponent, but don't call any shot good merely because you failed to return it. Apologize if you let a partner down, but never get irritated when a partner makes mistakes.

Never question a judge's decision. Never give up hope until a game is actually lost. Get going at the first stroke, and keep going all through.

Become familiar with the official rules.

BASKET WORK

THERE is a great variety of work in cane and willow which may be so graded in difficulty that anyone beginning to learn how to work the material can produce something useful from the beginning.

The Materials.—The beginner is advised to avoid willow and concentrate on what is known as centre cane. This is about 1 in. thick. It is cut to various diameters from about $\frac{1}{16}$ in. to $\frac{3}{8}$ in. thick, into a flat segmental shape about $\frac{1}{4}$ in. wide known as lapping cane, and into a rough rectangular section known as flat cane.

The shiny skin that is cut off the outside of the cane is used for caning chair seats.

Centre cane is bought by the pound. Useful sizes for the beginner are Nos. 2 (thin), 4 (thicker), 6 (about $\frac{1}{8}$ in. diam.),

8 and 10 (the latter about $\frac{3}{16}$ in. diam.). A little handle cane, No. 18, about $\frac{3}{8}$ in. diam., will be necessary for the handles of strong shopping baskets.

Wood Bases.—If you have not done any of this work before you are advised to begin making baskets on wood bases. The latter may be of solid wood or of ply-wood. Ply-wood is cheaper and generally more easily obtained. If such bases are to be painted with enamel, quite cheap wood, such as may be obtained from tea boxes, might be used. Where a polished base is desired, the wood should be of fairly good quality and the edges and surface be well finished with tools and glass-paper.

Ply-wood bases may be purchased from the factory or the local carpenter, but they can be quite easily made with a fine-toothed bow or fret saw, a spoke-shave, a plane and glass-paper. On wood bases you can make teapot stands, cheese-box holders, bread trays, work baskets, tumbler holders, waste-paper baskets, knife baskets, linen baskets, and many others.

Cane Bases.—Instead of using wood for the base the latter may be woven in cane. The variety is much increased. Shopping baskets of all kinds, flower baskets, bread trays, etc., are all possible.

The Strokes.—As "stitches" in needlework, so "strokes" are the foundation of basket-making.

Sketches of some of the strokes are shown in connection with the making of a small tray, either circular, square or oblong, which can be used as a teapot stand, cheese-box holder, plant stand, etc. This is one of the easiest jobs to begin on and you will learn quite a lot from the making.

Bore holes in the ply-wood base as shown in Fig. 1, about $\frac{1}{4}$ in. from the edge of the wood, $\frac{5}{8}$ in. apart and a little less than $\frac{1}{8}$ in. diameter. Use a bradawl to bore the holes, or a small hand-drill, such as can be bought for two or three shillings. When using the former see that it is sharp or it may split the wood as it emerges on the other side.

Cut pieces of No. 4 cane, about 12 in. long, and put one piece in each hole as shown in Fig. 2, with about 3 in. on one side of the base and the remainder on the other side, which will be the top surface.

The Foot Border must be worked first. This is usually a "trac" border, which may be made as in Fig. 3, which is the simplest form, viz. in front of one, behind one, for each cane. This gives an insignificant and uninteresting border on which the one shown in Fig. 4 is an improvement.

This is made by weaving the canes "behind one, in front of one, behind one." Other variations which give a deeper border are, "behind one, in front of two, behind one." Again, "in front of two, behind one"; or, "behind one, in front of two, behind two, in front of one, behind one." Do not waste cane by leaving the ends of the weaving longer than is necessary for the ends to be prevented from slipping out behind the last cane on which they bind. Trim the ends off to equal lengths all round the base.

The Sides.—The usual stroke for setting up the rods is the "waling" or "upsetting" stroke. This is shown in three stages in Figs. 5, 6 and 7. Take three lengths of No. 4 cane each long enough to go easily twice round the base. Insert one in each of three adjacent spaces between the uprights. Begin to weave by picking up the one on the left, pass it over the other two, behind the next upright (*see* Fig. 6) and bring it outside again before the fourth upright from the starting-point. Repeat this operation with each cane in turn, working from the left to the right until two rounds are done.

Wooden beads of suitable colour may now be placed on the uprights, and the two rows of waling repeated, when the tray is ready for its border to be worked.

A more usual method is to weave a panel of thin cane. This is woven in one of two or three strokes which form the basis for most of the body work in baskets, etc. These are the "pairing," "randing" and "slewing" strokes. (*See* Figs. 8, 9 and 10.)

To weave by pairing, take two lengths of No. 2 cane, place one end of each piece in adjacent spaces between the uprights, pick up the left-hand cane, pass it over the other weaver and take it in front of one upright and

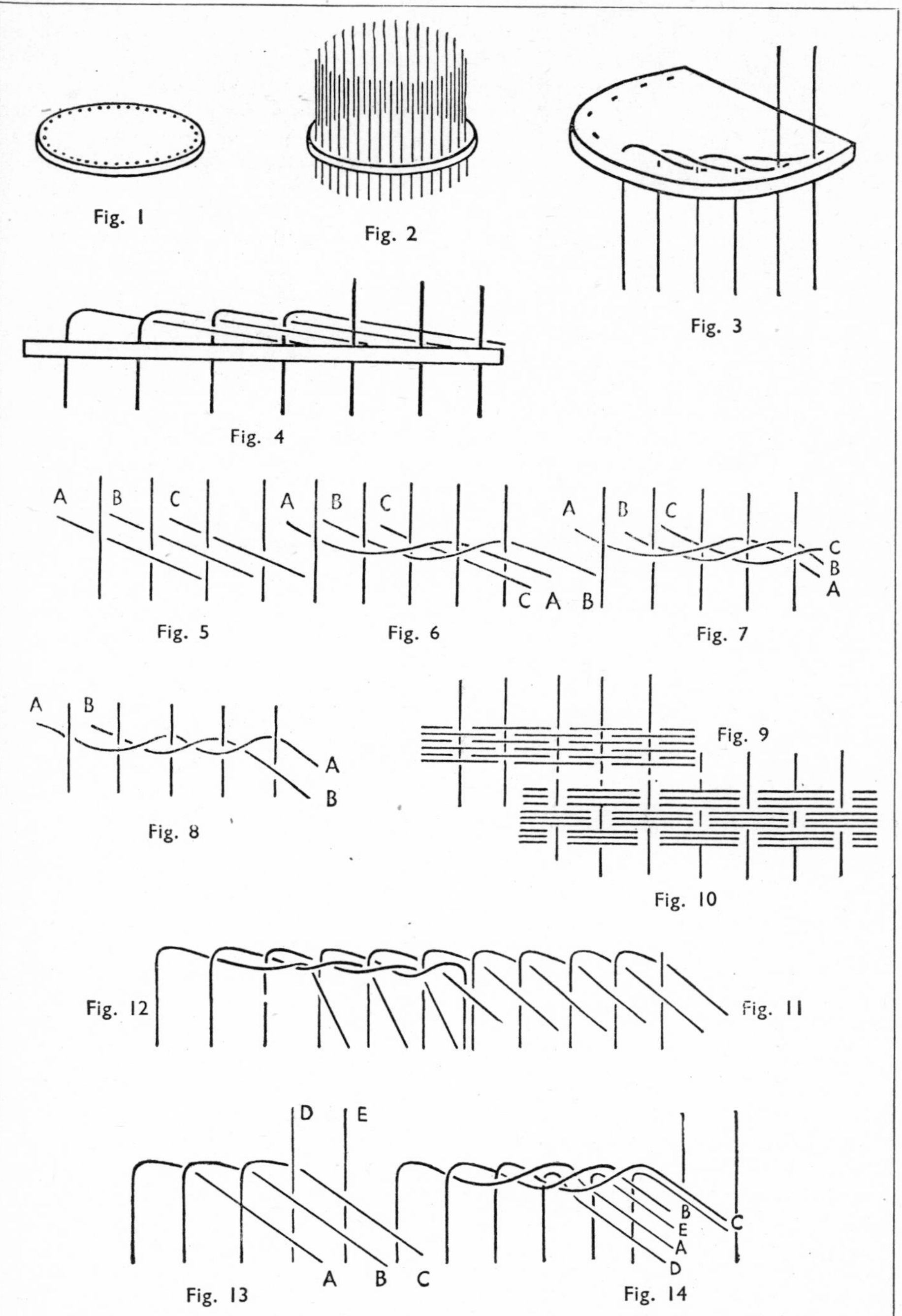

Fig. 1
Fig. 2
Fig. 3
Fig. 4
Fig. 5
Fig. 6
Fig. 7
Fig. 8
Fig. 9
Fig. 10
Fig. 12
Fig. 11
Fig. 13
Fig. 14

behind the next, bringing it out on the right of the other weaver. (*See* Fig. 8.) Repeat this process with each cane alternately and weave four or five rows. Repeat the two rows of waling and you are ready for the border.

Instead of "pairing," the "randing" stroke may be used for weaving this panel. This is woven with one cane only, in and out, to the required height. There must be an odd number of rods or uprights for this stroke so that the successive rows of weaving may be alternately inside and outside on the uprights. This stroke does not increase the strength of a basket, and the "slewing" stroke, which is done with two or three canes as shown in Fig. 10, is even weaker in this respect.

The Border.—A very simple and effective border is made as shown in Figs. 11 and 12. Take any upright and bend it down behind the next upright, bringing it out between the next pair. Repeat this operation until the last upright is reached. This is brought down and the end threaded in behind the loop of the first upright to complete the round of rods fixed behind each other. Now weave a second round by taking up one rod and passing it over the next and down in front of it as in Fig. 12. Fasten off the last rod in the loop of the first as before and go on to weave about five or six rows of border. The strokes should fit snugly behind each other, with no gaps between them, to make a tight roll-border which adds both strength and a good finish to any tray or basket.

Damping Cane.—At all times when working borders the rods must be kept in a damp condition. Before beginning to work them they should be dipped in water and allowed to stand for a few minutes, when they will be in a nice pliable condition. If this is not done there is a risk of the cane cracking or breaking. When a rod does break off, cut it level with the top of the weaving and insert another by pushing it down into the latter, leaving it standing at the same height as the other rods.

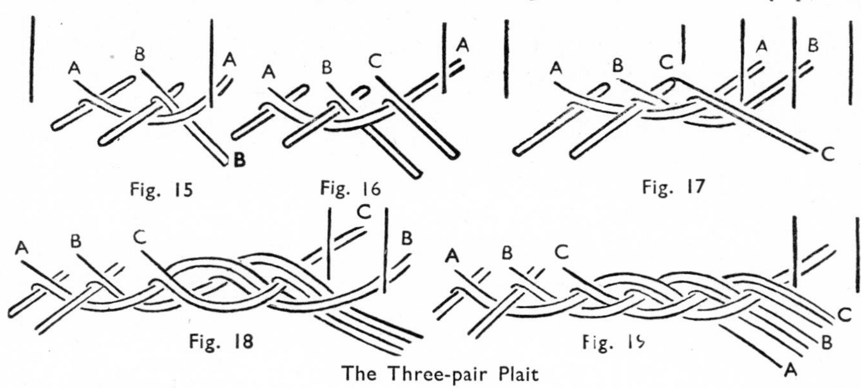

Fig. 15 Fig. 16 Fig. 17
Fig. 18 Fig. 19
The Three-pair Plait

Weaving cane should also be damped to make it pliable. If cane is over-soaked in water it will develop an objectionable hairiness. It will also be discoloured and the work will not look so smart. Rods which are to be bent at right-angles should first of all be squeezed with a pair of round-nosed pliers at the point of bending. This makes for regularity in the height and prevents breakage.

Singeing.—The hairiness mentioned above can be remedied by singeing the finished work with a clean flame, e.g. gas or methylated spirit, moving the work and the flame quickly across each other to prevent scorching.

If a piece of work has, through over-soaking in water, become badly discoloured, the whole job may be dipped in a dye to hide the bad colour.

Other Borders.—There are other borders which are suitable for trays of the kind just described, e.g. the three, four or five pair and the plait borders. The

Three-pair Border is shown in Figs. 13 and 14. Three rods are turned down as in Fig. 13. Pick up the rod on the left, pass it over the other two, behind the next upright and bring down both together (Fig. 14). Do the same with the next two rods and then with the fourth and subsequent rods pick up the rod which has only just been turned down and leave the other which has done its work. When the end is reached thread the last three rods to keep the sequence in the border.

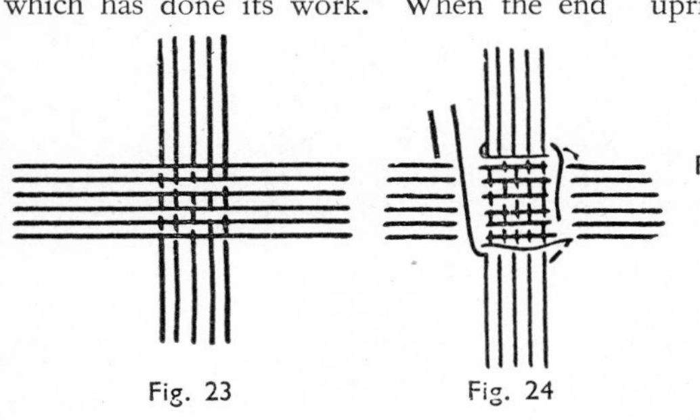

Fig. 23 Fig. 24

The Three-pair Plait.—The three-pair plait border is shown in Figs. 15 to 19. This is an attractive border which adds both to the appearance and strength of any tray or basket on which it is worked. Begin to make the plait at any point on the border. About 10-in. length of rod should be available above the weaving. Cut three pieces of cane about 9 in. long of the same thickness as the rods and two pieces of thick cane about 4 in. long. Damp the rods, bend down one over one short piece of thick cane and lay along side it one of the 9-in. pieces as in Fig. 15. Lay the other short piece across the top of these and in front of the next upright; bend down the latter and lay alongside it, on the right-hand side, another of the 9-in. pieces (Fig. 15). Now pick up the left-hand pair of canes, pass them over the next pair and in front of the next upright to the inside of the border and leave them for a moment (Fig. 16). Bring down the left-hand upright and lay alongside it the remaining 9-in. cane (Fig. 16). Pick up the left-hand pair of canes, pass them over the adjacent pair in between the next pair of uprights. There are now two pairs on the inside and one pair on the outside of the border (Fig. 17). Take the left-hand pair from the inside and bring it out to the right of the next upright, taking the latter down with it to the outside (Fig. 18). Pick up the left-hand pair on the outside and pass it inside again, making two pairs inside, with a group of three outside (Fig. 18). Bring out the left-hand pair from inside to the outside, bringing down the upright as before. There are now two sets

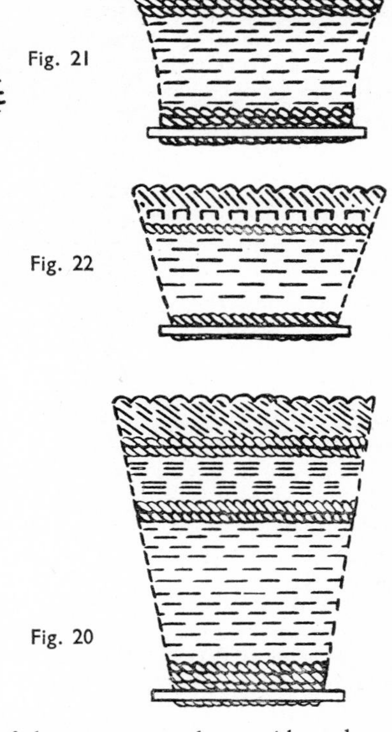

Fig. 21

Fig. 22

Fig. 20

of three canes on the outside and one pair inside (Fig. 19). This border shows three canes on the inside and two on the outside and this arrangement is formed in the next stroke. Take the left-hand pair of the left-hand set of three, leaving the right-hand cane, and pass the pair to the inside as before. The full weave of the border is now complete and the cane which has been left will be the one to leave each time, it being the one which has travelled the farthest of the three canes. If it is found during the working of the plait that the canes are running short, refer back along the plait and you will find that the wrong cane has been dropped and this third cane has been called upon to do more work than its length will allow.

Trays.—Quite a lot of variety can be put into the making of trays on wood bases, not only in shape and size, but in the sides and borders. Trays may be small and square for teapot stands, small and round for cheese boxes or teapot stands, egg stands and cruet stands; these are generally about 6 in. square or diameter. Made on square or round bases from about 12 in. side or diameter, they can be used for small tea-trays and lemonade sets. Larger trays, about 12 in. by 18 in., either oval or rectangular, serve well for use as tea-trays. The sides of any or all of these trays may be decorated by using beads instead of weaving between the bottom and top waling, or beads may be placed at the bottom of the rods instead of waling, so allowing crumbs, etc., to be more easily swept off the tray.

Interesting curves in the line of the plait border may be formed by the insertion of a few beads at the point where the curve is desired, passing the weaving over them and so raising the level of the border for a short distance. If this is done at the ends of an oval or oblong tray the raised curves act as handles. It may also be effectively done at the corners of a square tray.

The borders may be coloured by using dyed cane for the rods. The weaving cane may be natural or coloured, or both may be used together with good effect.

Work Baskets.—Very good work baskets can be made by using wood bases of about 9 in. diameter. A good design may be built up from ½-in. waling, 1½-in. pairing, two rows waling in coloured cane, about four rows of pairing in colour which harmonizes with the previous colour, then repeat the waling about four rows before the border.

Plenty of variety can be introduced by using coloured cane and varying the strokes, but the proportions of the parts and the harmony of the colours should be carefully controlled.

Waste-paper Baskets.—Waste-paper baskets are a development of the work basket. They should be made with rods of No. 8 or No. 10 cane and woven with No. 4 or No. 6.

It is generally advisable to use double rods for work of this kind so that the form and line of the basket may be kept under control. The extra rods are inserted when the first waling has been woven, being pushed into it alongside the first set of rods. The effect is to add such extra resistance to the weaving cane as will prevent the latter pushing the rods out of shape. The extra rods may be left in and used in the border or they may be cut off and the single rods only used. This depends upon whether the spacing of the rods and the type of border will allow the extra thickness of cane to be worked in conveniently.

Borders.—For all these deep baskets, whether on wood bases or woven bases, described later, the "trac" type of border is very useful. This border can be made in great variety—it is not difficult to arrange a sequence for yourself which will give you a desired effect in pattern.

A few of the forms are shown in Figs. 20, 21 and 22.

Woven Bases to Baskets.—Shopping baskets are generally made with a base woven from cane. The method of beginning a base is shown in Fig. 23, where the pieces of cane at right-angles to each other are of at least No. 6 thickness and about 8 in. long. Four of these are slit in the middle and the other four threaded through them. Holding these canes in the left hand, the thumb on the centre, pass the looped end of a thin cane, No. 2 or No. 4, over one group of four as in Fig. 24. Now begin the pairing stroke, i.e. first one "over and under" and then the other "over and under," no more than that with each weaver at a time, working over the groups of four. Carry this on for four times round the centre.

Now divide the groups of four into twos and weave four more rows, after which separate all the spokes into single canes and weave until the base is the required diameter. Cut off the weavers.

The reason for weaving on the groups of four and two spokes is that in this way it is

Fig. 21.—Examples of Cane Baskets with Handles

much easier to obtain a tight and regular centre to the base, a most important feature.

Rodding Up.—The next process is the insertion of the rods which are to be the framework of the body of the basket. Decide on the height of the basket, add 3 in. to be inserted in the base and 8 in. for the border and cut off a number of pieces of No. 4 or 6 or 8 cane to this length. In the base illustrated you will require 32 pieces. Sharpen one end of each of these rods and push them into the weaving, one on each side of each rod, as far as they will go towards the centre. Each rod should be fixed tightly when in position.

Wet the rods where they emerge from the weaving—do not wet the woven work; pinch them with the pliers close up to the weaving and bend them upwards at right-angles to the base. Now weave a few rows of waling and work the design as before.

Handles.—This is one of the most important operations in basketry. A variety of methods may be adopted for fixing or finishing a handle; the main principle is that either the thick core or the lapping cane or both must be fixed to the border and it must be impossible to separate them, even by very hard pulling. A very severe pulling test should be applied to every handle before it is allowed to be put into use.

The thickness of the core to a handle will depend upon the size of the basket. For an ordinary shopping basket No. 18 cane about $\frac{3}{8}$ in. thick should be used, and perhaps two pieces of it used together to give a wider and more comfortable handle. For a small cheese-box holder two pieces of No. 6 side by side would probably be best. This core is made of a length that will allow the ends to be pushed down through the weaving into the body of the basket, in the case of a shopping basket for three or four inches, and in the shallow type to the bottom of the weaving. The ends are sharpened to a point to enable the thick cane to be pushed in more easily. The height and shape of the handle will depend on use and ideas of good shape. The core is attached to the border by means of lapping cane. To enable this to be done quite satisfactorily a hole is bored with a bradawl through the core cane just underneath the border. The end of the lapping cane, whether of seg-

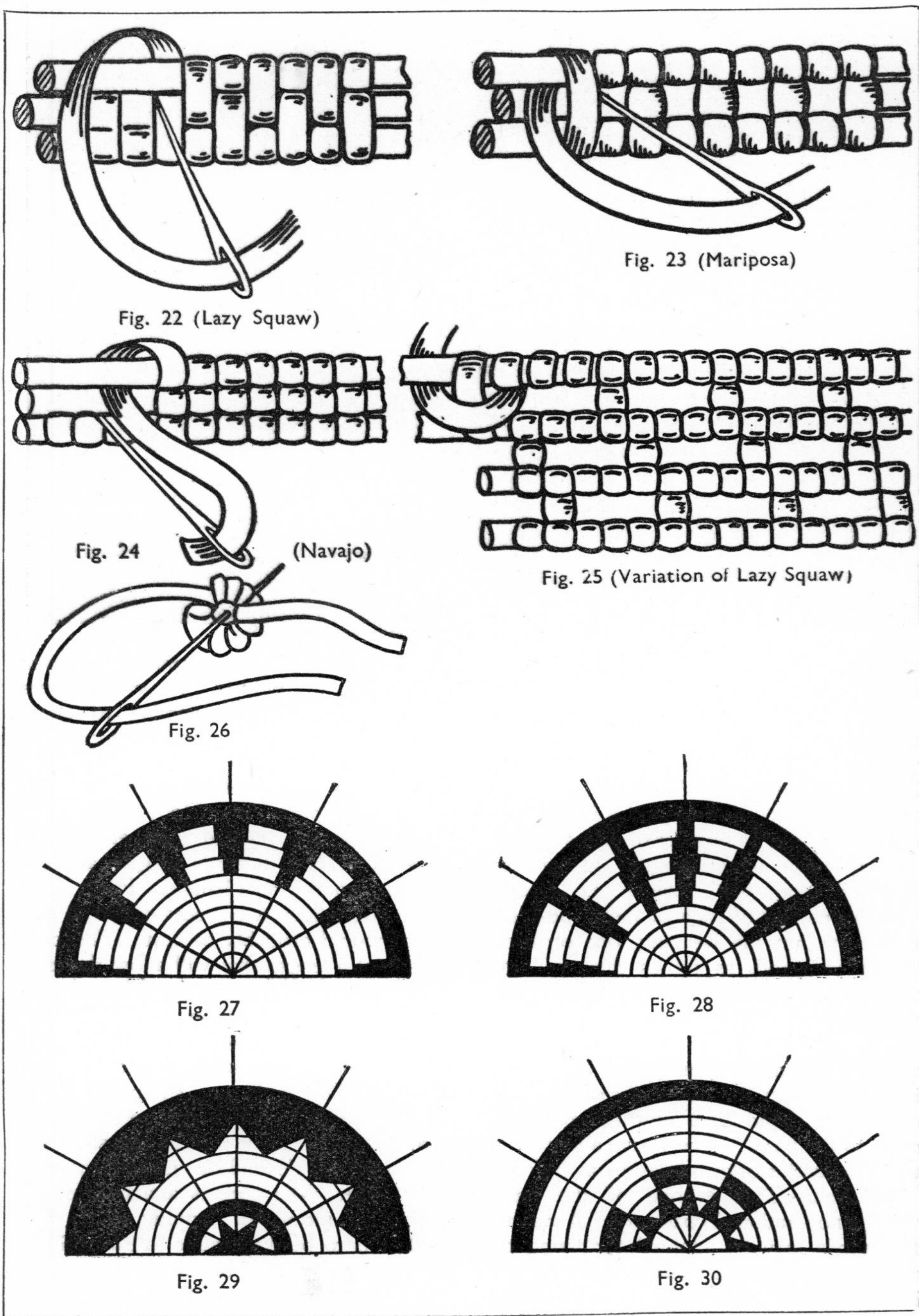
Fig. 22 (Lazy Squaw)

Fig. 23 (Mariposa)

Fig. 24 (Navajo)

Fig. 25 (Variation of Lazy Squaw)

Fig. 26

Fig. 27

Fig. 28

Fig. 29

Fig. 30

COILED BASKETRY STITCHES

mental shape or No. 2 round, is passed through this hole and a few inches of this cane wrapped round and through the border to form a pattern on the outside and at the bottom of the handle. When this is properly done it will at once be impossible to pull the lapping cane away from the basket. The lapping is carried on round and round the handle to the other side, where it is fixed in the same manner as at the beginning, finishing off the end underneath the border. Pattern can be worked on the handle itself by the insertion of coloured cane, which is exposed and covered at intervals by the lapping cane.

Coiled Baskets are made from raffia wrapped on a core of cane, string or raffia, held together by various stitches made with a blunt-pointed needle between the lengths of wrapping.

Raffia is obtained from the Raffia palm which grows in the island of Madagascar. In its natural state it is a pleasant creamy colour; it can easily be dyed or purchased ready coloured from florists or educational contractors. A good deal of coloured raffia is dipped in glycerine, which makes it soft and pliable to use. Unfortunately, as glycerine attracts moisture and holds it, any articles made from this kind are in a perpetual state of dampness, and may even develop a mould. The articles are also sticky and unpleasant to handle. You are therefore advised to use what is known as "dry dyed" raffia. If you dye your own raffia you will find a good deal of interest in obtaining your own colours. The mixing of dyes will give you the opportunity of producing something distinctive in the way of colour schemes.

Selecting Raffia.—Great care should be taken in the selection of raffia. Avoid that which is stiff, dirty in natural colour, badly torn or with many hard blunt ends. Choose the long fibre, soft and light-coloured material. Before using, the raffia should be soaked for a few hours in clear water. Lay it out to dry; do not hang it.

Variety, in colour, pattern and form, is the feature which gives interest and distinction to this work, that is, if it is combined with simplicity. Over-elaboration of either pattern or form will spoil the work. Before using a strand of raffia remove the hard edges and so make it more pliable and smooth.

If the raffia is inclined to be stiff and dry before brought into use each strand should be drawn through a damp cloth. It must not be too damp as this will cause the raffia to shrink when dry, making the sewing loose and the basket less firm.

The width of a strand of raffia should be in proportion to the size of the cane or string core it is proposed to use.

The Stitches. — There are several stitches in this work, some of which are derived from the Indians of North America, who do a great amount of beautiful work. Among these stitches are the Lazy Squaw, Mariposa, Pima Coil, Navajo, and so on. Illustrations of the method of making the stitches are given in Figs. 22 to 25. Simpler names for the Lazy Squaw, Mariposa and Navajo are "long and short," "lace stitch" and "figure 8" respectively.

Beginning the Base of a Basket.—Thread the needle at the small end of the raffia and tie a loose knot about four or five inches from the end. Sew over and over through this ring, working towards the left carrying the end along, until once round. (*See* Fig. 26.) Do not make the hole too large. Take a length of No. 6 cane, cut one end to a taper, moisten it and hold it in the left hand and lay it on the raffia centre. Continue sewing over and over until the core is fixed firmly in position, say, two or three rounds. The Lazy Squaw, or long and short stitch, may now be introduced. Hold the work in the left hand, with the thumb on top, and with the right hand wind the raffia once and a half round the core, holding the raffia near the ring. Pass the needle through the hole from the under side and complete the stitch. Repeat this operation till the required diameter is reached. Keep the raffia untwisted from the needle so that it retains its flatness and does not fray.

In making the stitches, do not split them —make them all perpendicular to the centre and close together, fasten off all ends so that no loose ends are visible, keep the core well covered, use raffia of uniform width and make the spaces between the stitches even.

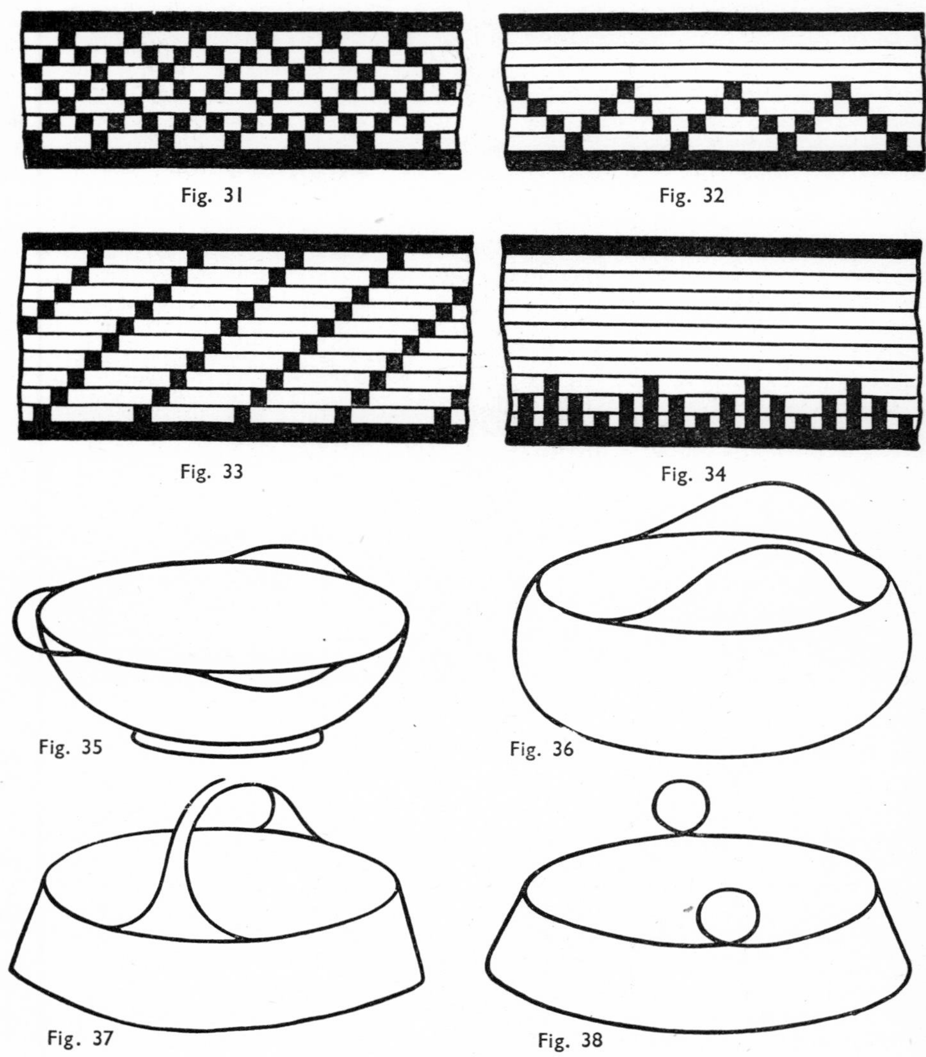

Fig. 31

Fig. 32

Fig. 33

Fig. 34

Fig. 35

Fig. 36

Fig. 37

Fig. 38

Side Patterns and Handles

Join in a new length of raffia by laying the end along the core, pointing to the right, make the stitches as usual and cover this end until it is well fixed; then drop the old strand, cut it off, thread the new strand into the needle and carry on with the stitching, covering in the end of the old one.

A Variation of the Lazy Squaw.—The Lazy Squaw stitch is rather slow to build up the work. Speedier growth can be obtained by extending the amount of winding between the long stitches which catch together the two coils. It must, however, be remembered that the fewer the stitches which connect the coils the weaker and looser the work will be. (*See* Fig. 25.)

A New Length of Core.—To introduce a new length of core pare the end of the old piece to a taper, put a similar taper on the end of the new piece, lay it alongside the former to make up a single thickness and carry on with the stitching to bind the two ends firmly together.

Turning up the Basket.—The sides of the basket may be turned up either gradually with a curve or abruptly and square. The former requires more skill as it is commenced very gradually and the turning up is spread over several rows, being scarcely perceptible at the beginning. It is done by slightly raising the core above the preceding row, the left forefinger applying the pressure necessary to give the shape and keep it while the stitches are being made.

The square turn-up is made by mounting the core on to the top of the outer coil of the base and continuing the stitching.

The Mariposa, Lace or Knot Stitch.—This stitch is used to give a more open appearance to the work. It also makes the work grow more rapidly. The details are shown in Fig. 23, where it will be seen that the open effect is obtained by passing the strand round the long stitch of the pattern already worked. It will be necessary to allow a little space between the coils in which to make this knot effect. Two or three rows at the top of a basket make a very pretty finish.

Navajo or "Figure 8" Stitch.—The "figure 8" stitch (Fig. 24) is probably the tightest and strongest of all the stitches in coiled basketry. Special care must be taken to keep all the strands of raffia of the same thickness and width or lumpiness will be apparent in the work.

Working out Patterns.—Patterns in this work must be planned full size on squared paper before any stitching is begun. It may perhaps be possible, when you are highly skilled, to carry out a design without previous planning, but it is inadvisable to attempt it at the beginning of your work in this craft. Figs. 27 to 30 show the method of planning patterns for a base. Figs. 31 to 34 show the planning of the side of a basket. Most patterns are carried out in coloured raffia and the planning of such is a very interesting part of the work; it is done on squared paper for the sides and on a basis of concentric circles for bases.

Fig. 39.—Raffia Baskets

It will be observed that all the patterns are geometrical in form and not free in movement. This is necessarily so on account of the size and squareness of the stitches. Also, there is always a step upwards in the pattern when one coil has been worked as you are working on a continuous spiral. This must be allowed for in arranging the pattern.

Handles.—Interest may be added to a basket if the handles are worked on to the top edge. Figs. 35 to 38 give suggestions for different types of handle.

The articles that can be made in this way include table mats, work-baskets, waste-paper baskets, fruit baskets, and (with very large core) log baskets.

BATHING AND SWIMMING

BATHING and swimming have been almost universally popular throughout the ages, but within this century their vogue has grown enormously.

One reason for this is the adaptability of this sport to individual requirements: it can be leisurely or strenuous, athletic or æsthetic. Age is no deterrent—the youngster of four may begin, and even his grandparent of four-score years is not necessarily too old to start.

Confidence is at the root of good swimming. To be confident you must really enjoy the water, and much depends on how you go in. The novice so often is afraid it is going to be cold and creeps in cautiously inch by inch. There is no worse way than that, for you will be chilled before you are in. Always enter with a rush, and duck straight under.

Standing.—Many learners, especially girls, find at the outset a good deal of difficulty in standing up whenever they want to. They make an attempt to swim, for instance, and swallowing some water get upset and want to jump to their feet—only to find it a very troublesome business. Yet the ability to stand up in water three or four feet deep can be easily acquired.

Begin by leaning forward in waist-deep water and pushing off gently from your feet, with arms stretched beyond the head, so that you float along the surface horizontally and face downwards. All you have to do in order to stand at any moment is to draw your knees underneath you, then to strike downwards with both arms and raise the head, at the same time placing the feet down on the bottom! Or you may put just one foot down by taking a step forward as you make the arm stroke. The same method applies whatever your position in the water, whether lying on breast, back or side.

The next stage will be to gain some knowledge of the buoyancy of your own body. Once you are convinced that you float easily you will be much more confident. An interesting way of experimenting is to stoop forward in breast-deep water, keeping your knees stiff, and trying to touch your toes. To your pleasant surprise you will find that the water tries hard to prevent your getting down. In the same way it will push you upwards if you take a good breath and try to sit down on the bottom.

Exercises such as these will help you to realize the buoyancy of the body, especially how buoyant it is when it is not held stiffly. This last matter should be especially remembered, for it will have a great deal to do with your early swimming.

Dog - paddle. — The best beginner's stroke is the dog-paddle. It is true that this stroke has the smallest practical value, yet it is of greatest importance to the novice, for its movements are so simple that it can be mastered after just a few attempts, and so can give that exhilarating feeling that comes when for the first time the feet get clear of the bottom.

Stand in water about waist deep, and lean forward until your shoulders are immersed. Then push off gently so that you glide along flatly on your chest—it is important that head and shoulders should not be kept too high. As soon as you are launched forward the arms will take up their pawing action, working alternately. Each in turn glides forward to full stretch in front of the body, and just under the surface. Then it drives downward and backward, supporting and propelling you head-first. Put the fingers together and the hands flat. Following the push-off the legs are left trailing straight behind, but then they begin their own independent movements—which are much the same as if you were crawling along the floor. Each knee in turn draws under the body, with limp, trailing foot, then drives vigorously back, foot held squarely so that the sole strikes hard against the water.

Do not attempt any particular combination of limbs; work all at a comfortable rate, putting chief vigour into the movements which support and propel. Do not shorten or quicken your strokes; do not stiffen the body; do not get flurried.

Breast-crawl Stroke.—The most popular of all the many ways of swimming known to-day is crawl, particularly breast-crawl. It is an easy, natural stroke, and very speedy, and is suitable either for long-distance swimming or for short sprints. It is an ideal first stroke, because it follows the dog-paddle so naturally.

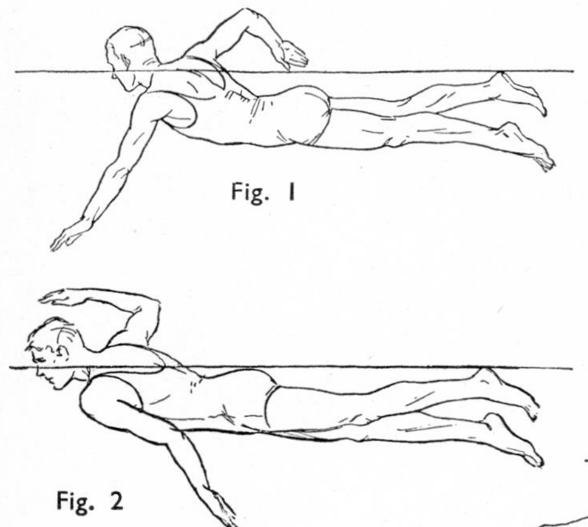

Fig. 1

Fig. 2

Crawl, like any other important stroke, needs to be learned with great care, or there will be danger of bad habits being acquired which may permanently prevent good style. There are various distinct parts of this stroke and the separate study of each is advisable—only when reasonable proficiency with these parts is gained should the full stroke be attempted.

Take breathing first, for there is no part of crawl more difficult and requiring such long practice. You may practise the method of breathing in a bowl of water at home. What you have to do is to breathe out through the nose, when the face is submerged, and breathe in through the mouth at one big gulp. *Aquatic respiration* is necessary to much modern swimming—notably to modern breast-stroke.

Whether in the basin at home or at the side of the swimming-pool, your mode of practice will be the same. Dip your face to the eye level, and blow out the air through the nose in a steady stream of bubbles. As you exhale turn the face slowly sideways so that by the time the last bit of air is expelled the mouth is above the surface. Immediately gulp in a big new breath, opening the mouth very wide, and then turn the face down again and begin the slow exhalation. There should be no strain about this breathing, you must continue with it until it can be performed easily and at a natural rate.

The leg actions come next. Cling to rail, rock, step or piece of bank, so that the body can be held horizontally along the surface, face downwards. The leg action consists of a continual, strong, up and down thrash, the legs passing and repassing each other. Each foot in turn drives down twelve to fifteen inches, and no more than the heels must break out of the surface as the feet rise. Each foot must be turned inward and pointed; so that the flat instep drives squarely against the water. In early practice it is advisable to keep knees and ankles stiff, in order that the thrash may be made entirely from the hips.

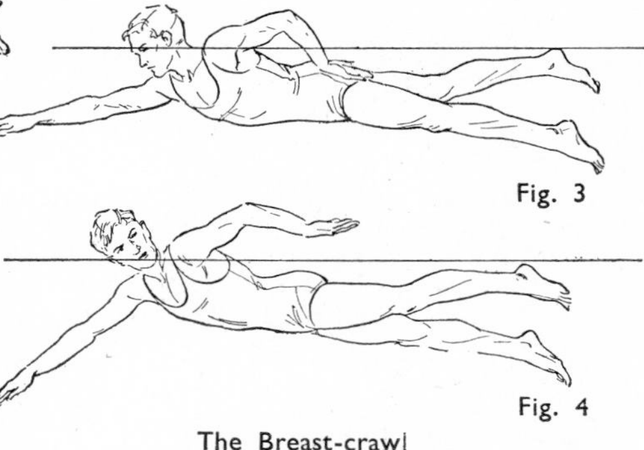

Fig. 3

Fig. 4

The Breast-crawl

Body poise must come next. This consists in a "push and glide" exercise for teaching relaxation and balance.

Begin from the side of the bath, standing with your back to the wall or bank. Bend forward with arms stretched beyond the head, just as a diver holds them, and have one foot raised behind you, doubled up. Suddenly raise the other alongside the first, and give a strong push-off, by straightening the legs. This will set you gliding face downwards along the surface, with arms, body and legs in a straight line. Remain relaxed throughout this glide, and concentrate your attention on obtaining perfect balance. Gradually you will be able to cover a longer distance. These smooth glides will teach you the ideal position for breast-crawl swimming and will help you to hold the body at full stretch yet comfortably limp.

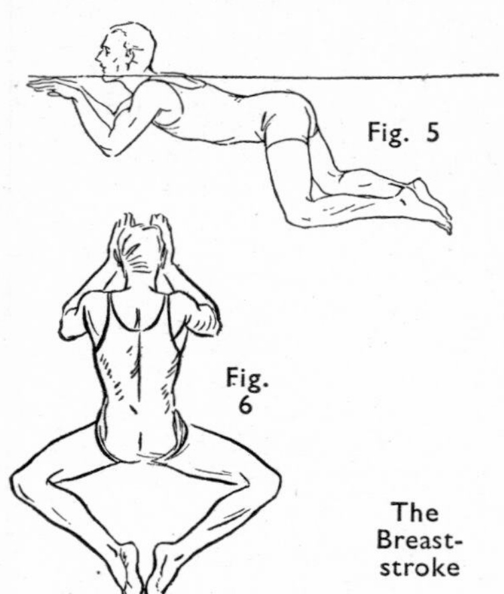

The Breast-stroke

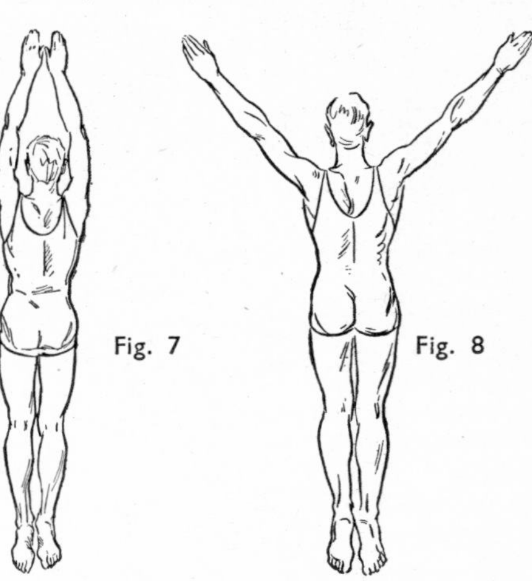

Your last bit of separate practice will be with the arm action. Roughly, in the crawl the arms work in a sort of windmill manner, alternately recovering forward through the air and driving backward through the water. As one arm drives its fellow recovers.

You should stand breast-deep, bending forward so that your shoulders are just submerged. Try one arm first, starting its recovery from down by the side of the body.

When the hand lifts from the water it twists at once so that the palm comes face downward. Next the forearm swings round just clear of the surface, until it is pointing forward, and to complete the recovery the whole arm glides forward to full extension in front of the head. The dip follows immediately. The flat hand descends into the water, increasing its pressure as it goes down, and travelling along an imaginary line running under the breast-bone. Keep the arm straight and rigid until it is at right-angles to the surface, then begin to bend the elbow, though without losing rigidity, so that the forearm remains more or less vertical and the hand, swerving outward, is able to continue its backward thrust until the moment when it reaches the thigh and so is ready to begin another recovery.

All that may seem rather complex, but when you have worked through it slowly it will soon become a smooth, harmonious whole.

And now the full stroke.

Make a push from the bath side so that you glide horizontally in the familiar way, and at once set the legs to work. As soon as they are thrashing strongly begin the arm action, and the breathing—and crawl forward along the surface. Be particularly careful to get full, regular breaths—inhaling always with the recovery of the same arm; which arm does not matter.

Go slowly. Do not let the body roll. Do not lift one arm from the water until the other at the front has begun its supporting pressure.

By degrees you will find a natural rhythm asserting itself in your stroke. When it does, encourage it. The most popular crawl mode is the six-beat, in which three leg strokes combine with each arm pull.

Fig. 9.—Practising the Crawl-stroke Leg Thrash

Breast-stroke.—The most useful of all swimming styles is breast-stroke. Nowadays there are two distinct modes of it. The old-fashioned stroke will never lose its value, although it is rather angular and ugly, because it has the unique recommendation of being the only method of swimming in which the head can remain comfortably above the water all the time. In this stroke the arms sweep round almost to the shoulder line, remaining practically at the same level, and all breathing is above the surface.

From this main style the *short-arm* or *racing breast-stroke* has developed, which is speedy, restful and exceedingly graceful. The main alteration in this newer style is that the arm stroke is very short and downward slanting and breath is blown out while the nose and mouth are submerged.

This short-arm breast-stroke is more difficult than crawl for a beginner, but once you have mastered it the ordinary breast-stroke can be derived from it quite easily.

It is best to begin with a land drill, for thus the parts can be acquired separately—arm action, leg action, breathing, and in fact much helpful practice can be done at odd moments by the beginner on land. Stand upright, with arms stretched to the front, parallel with each other and the ground, palms facing outward and downward. Count slowly:

One—make no movement.

Two—sweep the straight arms outward and downward so that each covers about eighteen inches and they finish at right-angles to each other.

Three—let the elbow sag to the chest and draw the hands together under the chin, thumbs touching.

Four—slide the arms forward into the preliminary position.

The body glides forward smoothly, in actual swimming, while the arms are at full stretch in *one*.

To practise both legs, lie across a stool, beginning by stretching the legs out, straight and together, feet pointed.

One—make no movement.

Two—make no movement.

Three—draw up the knees, spreading them apart, but keeping the heels together.

Four—kick the feet out until the legs are again straight, but spread as widely apart as possible. Then, without pause, sweep the legs together until the ankles meet.

The breathing should be fitted in with the arm pull.

One—breathe out through the nose.

Two—open the mouth and fill the lungs at one big gulp.

Three—let the air begin to trickle out through the nose.

Four—continue to breathe out through the nose.

Notice that, although the inhalation is by the mouth, this method of respiration conforms to that of ordinary breathing, with its quick intake of air and immediate but slow exhalation.

Now combine the full stroke, lying across a stool or chair, or get in just one leg whilst standing. Thus:

One—arms still; legs still; breathe out.

Two—arms sweep; legs remain still; breathe in.

Three—arms recover; legs recover; breathe out.

Four—arms glide forward; legs kick; breathe out.

As soon as the full action is fairly familiar go into the water and try the stroke. It is advisable to work with the separate parts first. Bend forward shoulder deep for arm action and breathing; grip the side of the bath for leg practice. In the breathing let the face submerge to the eye level for exhalation, and expel the last bit of air just as you rise again—this helps to blow the remnants of water away from the mouth at the moment when you take a new breath.

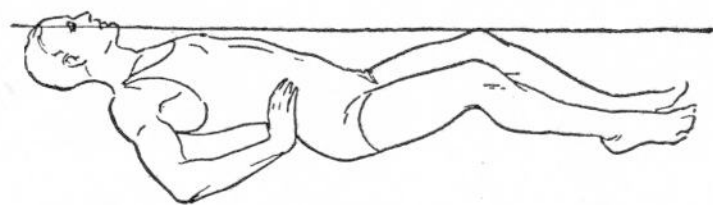

Fig. 10.—Life-saving Back-stroke

Do not stay too long with the practice of separate parts; go on to the full stroke.

To begin, lean forward with arms stretched to the front, and push off from bank or bottom so that you glide flatly along the surface with shoulders well submerged. As soon as your legs are properly trailing complete the exhalation—many beginners try to breathe in before they have breathed out—and make the sharp outward and downward arm stroke which lifts the head clear and so makes it possible for you to gulp a new breath. Follow this promptly by a quick, smooth recovery of arms and legs, and finally, as the arms glide forward, kick the legs outward and close them together. The impetus from this kick consequently finds you gliding smoothly forward with arms, body, legs, in a straight line, and face submerged. You have completed a single stroke and are back in the position in which you started—gliding.

On the power and length of this glide depend the effectiveness and beauty of the stroke. Always glide until impetus is almost exhausted. Each complete cycle of movements, when you become proficient, should carry you three to five yards, and the whole stroke should appear almost effortless, and beautifully regulated.

See that none of your movements are incomplete or hurried. Take care especially that the legs are kicked out straight before they begin to sweep together, and that they do not start to draw up for the recovery before they have closed together. Practise thoughtfully, giving attention to details, and aiming at smooth combination and constantly longer glides.

It is an excellent plan in this, as in other stroke practice, to strive regularly to cover a given distance with a fewer number of strokes.

Simple Back-stroke and Life-saving.—*Life-saving back-stroke* is, after breast-stroke, by far the most important method of swimming-crawl. This back-stroke is not particularly graceful, certainly it is not speedy, but it is powerful and dependable—and by means of it any swimmer in difficulty or any drowning person can be towed along with ease. This particular stroke is one of the easiest to learn, largely because it has no arm action. As soon, therefore, as you can travel about fifty yards by crawl or breast-stroke you should begin to acquire it.

A little land work is useful; you will be able to master the movements in just a few minutes. Stand "at attention," and try one leg at a time, counting to keep the parts of the stroke even:

One—make no movement.

Two—raise the foot backwards until the shin is horizontal; the knee will spread out sideways, three to four inches from its fellow.

Three—kick the foot out until the leg is again straight and stretched as far to the side as possible. Then, without pause, sweep the straight leg down until it crashes against the other, and so reaches the preliminary position once more.

To practise both legs together lie on your back across a table or bed, with legs overhanging the edge. Drop both legs down, from the knees—until the straight legs form with the body a huge letter Y; close the legs vigorously.

And now for the water:

If you have done some preliminary practice with floating, that will make things still easier. It is helpful also to have a friend standing by who can support you with a hand under your back. Should you, however, be unassisted there is no need to hesitate. Push off from bank or step and so set yourself gliding head-first, increasing your impetus immediately afterwards with your first kick. Keep your hands on your hips, and be careful that you lie flat along the water—ears immersed, chest bulging from the surface, stomach high as possible. On no account must you "sit" in the water.

You will have noted that *one* of the land drill allows for a glide at the conclusion of the kick. This is an important feature. But in actual life-saving it is generally impracticable to get this glide, for, in order to maintain the necessary momentum and support when hampered by the drowning person, it is necessary that the kicks follow each other continuously without any pause.

There are many alternative positions of the arms, and you may try these as you become proficient. The neatest style is with arms folded across the chest. But they may be clasped under the back or just trailed at the sides. A more difficult fashion is to stretch them beyond the head. By holding them upright in the air you may test the power of your kick.

To practise life-saving methods you must get the help of a friend who will act the part of drowning person, so that you may tow him.

Rescue Work.—The most useful rescue method—which is used when a drowning person struggles and so needs to be held firmly—is that in which his arms are gripped just above the elbows. Lie on your back. He is also stretched face upwards above you, the back of his head just above your chest. Seize his arms and drag them up in line with his shoulders—his forearms can trail anyhow. See that your own elbows are sharply bent and pressed against your sides. Your grip will be such that the backs of your hands are on the sides of his arms away from your face. In this position you will have firm control and will be able to swim along quite easily.

The rescuer's chief business is to keep the other person's head constantly above the surface. If his legs sink and interfere with your own you may force them up by pushing your knee into his back. When you become more skilled let your partner struggle like a frantic drowning person, so that your rescue becomes more realistic. If your grip is firm and your kick strong and fairly quick you will find yourself able to carry on no matter how much he struggles.

Another Type of Rescue.—Sometimes a person who is unconscious has to be brought ashore. Obviously he does not require the tight grip already described. Instead, therefore, of seizing his arms you will support him by the head, one hand on either side of his face, palms covering his ears. Although your elbows will be bent as before, the head grip will ensure that he is not quite so much on top of you, so that you have rather more freedom and can use your legs more effectively. His arms, of course, will trail limply in the water, but you will have no difficulty in keeping his mouth clear.

Life-saving work will soon strengthen this simple back-stroke. Later you will find it interesting, and not very difficult, to form other strokes, by adding various arm actions. A short, paddling sweep down by the sides of the body, and you have *short-arm back-stroke*; a long semicircular, underwater action gives *underarm back-stroke; overarm back-stroke* is simply this latter together with an air instead of a water recovery.

Back-crawl is something quite different. It is a breast-crawl inverted, so that the legs thrash instead of kick.

Watermanship.—The ability to perform one or two strokes does not make one a swimmer. Even the addition of diving is not sufficient. To be thoroughly competent in the water you must develop all-round *watermanship*—the ability to be always at home in the water; to move and turn as easily as a fish, without the violent scrambling that marks the novice; to be able to rest without clambering to the bank; to swim always in a graceful attractive manner.

Such ability does not come by chance. It is gained by developing certain technical aspects of swimming; and the earliest which will concern you are—treading water, sculling, floating.

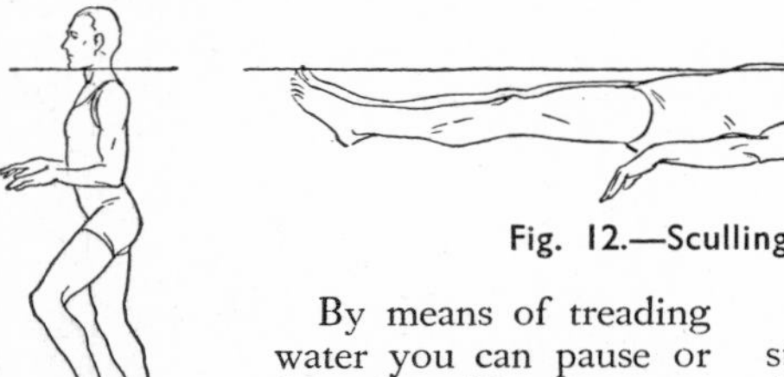

Fig. 11.—Treading Water

Fig. 12.—Sculling

By means of treading water you can pause or "stand still" when out of your depth. Sculling teaches one the value of apparently trifling flicks of the hand, which with the expert take on much of the characteristic usefulness of a fish's fins. Floating ability helps indirectly in every phase of swimming, and allows the floater to rest whenever he feels like it.

Treading Water.—There is nothing difficult about this, especially if you are a breast-stroke swimmer, for one common form of treading water necessitates a quick, short, breast-stroke leg action. Hang suspended vertically from the surface, and work your legs vertically—drawing them up, knees spread and heels touching; kicking them downward and outward, widely apart; sweeping them vigorously together. The kick is continuous and fairly rapid. While the legs work the arms paddle forward in front of the chest, palms facing downward and elbows being sharply bent.

In the second mode of treading water the same arm action is used, but the legs work alternately, with exactly the movement made as when running upstairs. Each foot trails limply as the leg is drawn up, so that resistance is minimized, but it becomes square and firm as it drives down and strong supporting pressure is thus obtained by the sole.

In both modes the head can be kept above the surface quite easily.

When proficiency is gained you will find it interesting to prove the power of your leg action by raising your arms right out of the water, above your head—your kick is pretty good if you can retain this position steadily.

Sculling.—You must lie horizontally on the surface for this, face upwards, with the arms straight down by the sides. The hands alone move, though later, when you desire to put fullest power into your action, a slight forearm disturbance will be almost inevitable.

Cup the hands just a little, and perform strong circular movements, swinging from the wrists—out, down, in, up—and so thrusting or scooping the water down the sides of the body towards the feet. Naturally this forcing of the water towards the feet results in the body being driven along head first. Providing you are straight and flat you may get quite a fair speed.

To propel yourself feet first simply reverse the action, scooping the water towards your armpits. This is a little more difficult.

It is a good plan to experiment with this sculling action, when you can perform it powerfully. Work one hand, and both hands, in all sorts of directions, until you become able to twist or turn the body wherever you will by the least flick of the hand—just as a fish turns by quick movement of tail or fin.

Floating.—There are two varieties of floating—perpendicular and horizontal—the former being much easier though less useful.

For perpendicular floating, tread water while you prepare your lungs. When they are well inflated spread the arms out to the sides in line with the shoulders, and lean the head right back until the ears are submerged. The legs hang down limp in the water.

Providing everything has been done smoothly enough, and that the lungs are properly full of air, then you will find yourself floating quietly, nose and mouth just clear of the surface. Take care not to breathe out heavily, but be satisfied with quick little breaths which keep the lungs well inflated and do not make violent variations in your buoyancy.

Horizontal floating will require more practice. It is largely a matter of balance.

If you swim on your back you may do it immediately following a kick. An alternative way is to stand shoulder deep, and begin from there. In this latter method take a really deep breath; spread your arms to the side, gradually carrying them back farther and farther, and lean the head backwards until the ears are submerged. Let the legs hang motionless and continue the slow arm sweep until arms are at full stretch beyond the head. Keep the lungs inflated and be careful to depress the diaphragm at the beginning of your preliminary inhalation, so that the supporting air is carried well down the thorax. This will result, on condition that the body is completely relaxed, in the legs rising very slowly towards the surface. Remain motionless, keeping the head right back so that the forehead is almost under, and remember to keep the arms at full stretch, for it is important that their weight beyond the head shall counteract the tendency of the legs to sink.

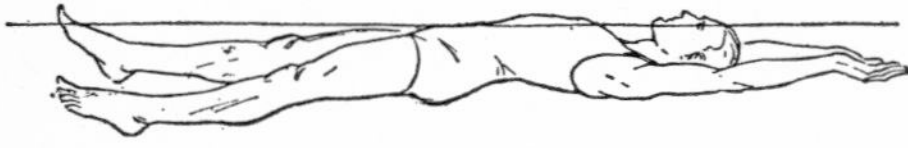

Fig. 13.—Floating

Horizontal floating is almost entirely a matter of balancing the legs by the head and arms. Press the biceps against the ears, and hook the thumbs together—more weight may be given to the head end of the body by bending the fingers up so that they protrude from the water. The feet must be held square, not pointed in line with the shins as in swimming, and thus the toes may protrude from the surface. Relaxation, which is such an essential thing if you are to succeed in staying horizontally at the surface, will be helped if you let the middle of the body sag a few inches, instead of keeping taut and straight in the normal back-stroke position.

Be patient, you will not master this floating at the first attempt; it may indeed take you a long time to get the knack of bringing up your legs and making them stay up. But persevere; once you gain the ability you are not likely to lose it.

Floating is naturally much more easy in salt water than in fresh, so that it is an advantage to begin the study of it in the sea—providing you choose a quiet day.

Just a few people of high specific gravity find it quite impossible ever to float. They are generally heavy, muscular folk, with large bones. But they are very few indeed—and you need not assume that you are one of the unfortunates simply because you take some time to master horizontal floating.

Fancy Swimming.—The highest branch of natation is generally called *fancy swimming*. It is in this realm that the finest mastery of the water is shown.

There are almost limitless numbers of feats available. You can, in fact, devise your own, for you will soon discover that it is possible to swim by the use of either pair of limbs, or even of single limbs, in face upwards, face downwards, or vertical positions.

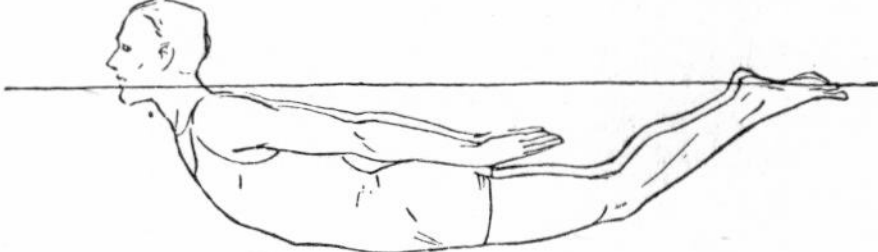

Fig. 14.—The Canoe

Also, you may revolve on the surface, travel sideways, feet first, head first, or by somersaults.

One of the most pleasing and popular feats of fancy swimming is the *canoe*. For this you lie flat on your breast, with body deeply curved, and arms down by the sides. Then, by a strong sculling action, you send yourself gliding smoothly forward, head and feet protruding from the surface like the ends of a canoe.

BEE KEEPING

Bee keeping, or as it is called apiculture, is a most interesting hobby, and one calling for much observation and thought. It is not so very many years ago that sugar first came into our households, and before this time honey provided the only means of sweetening. But bee keeping in those days was very different from what it is now.

In this article we are concerned with the subject as a hobby. No other country is able to produce better honey than is Great Britain.

Fig. 1.—*Left to Right:* The Queen, a Worker Bee, and a Drone (the Male Bee)

The Colony.—This consists of a queen, workers and drones, there being one queen to thousands of workers and perhaps two or three hundred drones. The queen is, of course, the centre of the colony. She is, in fact, the mother of them all. The queen is the only perfectly developed female in the hive. She is about $\frac{7}{8}$ in. long and is larger than either the workers or the drones. The average length of a worker is $\frac{1}{2}$ in.

The queen, as mother bee, is responsible for the colony. It is she alone who lays the eggs, and in the height of the prolific season she will lay between two and three thousand eggs a day. Next in importance to the queen is the worker, which is a female bee that is highly developed for work but under-developed for reproduction. It is this worker bee that we see going from flower to flower. The life of the worker during the summer months is only about seven or eight weeks, and it is a literal fact that she works herself to death in this period. The last inhabitants of the colony are the drones, or male bees, and these exist only to fertilize the queen. Drones do no work and are only kept in the hive until they have done their task of mating with the queen. Only one drone from the colony is required for this and the remainder of the drones are usually expelled by the workers at the end of the season.

The Labour of the Bees.—When the worker bees go from flower to flower they collect nectar, water, pollen and propolis. It is the nectar from which honey is formed. It is partially digested by the bee and stored in cells in the hive. Pollen is required for feeding purposes. It is carried in the pollen basket or "corbicula" on the hind legs of the bee. A bee never mixes the pollen. It will go to one kind of flower only until it returns to the hive. Later on it will perhaps go to another kind of flower and so on. This fact makes bees so valuable for the pollination of flowers. Propolis is also collected in the pollen basket. It is a sticky substance sometimes called bee-glue and is obtained from horse chestnut trees and so on. This is collected to seal crevices in the hive.

Swarming.—Should the hive become overcrowded with bees they form a number of queen cells and a part of the colony departs in search of a new home. This split in the colony is known as swarming, and takes place as soon as the queen cells are sealed.

Great numbers of them fly around the hive, gradually rising higher and wider. With them is the queen.

If they are not in the mood to fly far they will cluster on the branch of a nearby tree. Should the bees leave the bee-keeper's own ground he must follow them to establish his ownership and right to take them.

As soon as they have clustered, the bee-keeper, wearing his veil, etc., should place a box, with an easy-fitting lid or a piece of cloth to cover the top, under the cluster of bees and gently shake them into it. If the majority of the bees are not shaken into the box at first, replace the lid or cloth, and wait until the remainder have clustered again, and then repeat the operation.

Of course, a number of bees will still be flying around, but if the queen is in the box they will gradually settle on it. If it is certain that the queen is within, the box may be turned upside down with the usual ½-in. space for the remaining bees to enter.

The box should then be placed in the shade, if possible, or covered with a white cloth.

Should the bees swarm on the trunk of a tree or post, place the box underneath the bees and proceed to brush them into it with a stiff feather.

Position of Hives.—Not many people realize that locality plays a large part in the success or failure of bee keeping. Hives should be fairly close to suitable flowers, say, within a mile and a half or so. The quality and kinds of flowers grown vary with the district and it is worth knowing that white clover and heather are much favoured by bees. The reader is advised not only to read some of the many excellent textbooks on the subject but also to join a bee-keeping society or at any rate to discuss the subject with a keen apiarist. Whilst no amount of book-learning will ever be a complete substitute for practical experience it is as well for the amateur to read as much as he can about his new hobby.

Starting the Colony.—The best time to start keeping bees is in the spring, and the best way of obtaining a colony is to purchase one complete. You may either purchase a whole stock on its ten frames, a swarm, or a nucleus. The latter is simply a miniature colony and usually comprises three or four combs of stores and brood with a young queen and workers adhering to them. Buy your nucleus only from a reliable dealer. Before actually purchasing, however, you should prepare for your colony. You will require hives and sundry appliances which will be described later. Avoid the old-fashioned straw skep. Although the skep is picturesque it is unsuitable and inconvenient to use.

The Hive.—There are many kinds of hives on the market, but the beginner is strongly recommended to purchase those of a good quality only. Another point to be noted is that not only should the one type of hive be purchased, but one size and one pattern, in order that parts may be interchangeable.

A modern hive is shown in Fig. 2. It is made up of sections. First there is the floorboard which is mounted on legs, then there are the outer case, two lifts and a roof, all of which are detachable. The hive is, of course, made of wood, and it should be given a few coats of paint before the tenants are allowed to move in. White paint of a good quality is best, for white reflects the sunlight and helps to keep the hive cool.

Fig. 2.—A Cottage Hive

Types of Bee.—There are many kinds of bees, including the Black bee, the Carniolan, the Cyprian, the Syrian and Dutch bees. For gentleness, however, the best of all is perhaps the Italian bee, of which the five-banded species is the most popular.

Handling Bees.—Everything should be done slowly, and with sureness in oneself. The bees will detect at once any bee-keeper who gets flurried and lacks confidence.

A veil to protect the face should always be worn. The coat arms should be tied at the wrist to prevent bees from climbing up the sleeves and, if preferred, thin gloves may be worn. Never approach the hive from the front; always work from the back. First lift the roof from the hive, taking care not to jar it, then raise a corner of the quilt and blow a few puffs of smoke from the smoker. The bees will start to gorge the honey and become easy to handle.

Housing a Swarm.—The reader who has purchased a nucleus or a swarm must know how to get them satisfactorily into their new home. No attempt should be made to induce a swarm to take up their lodging until the evening. When the hive has been placed in the most suitable position —that is with the front facing south or east —the top of the hive and the outer casing should be removed, so that only the lower or brood chamber is standing on the floor-board. A wide board should then be placed with one end against the ground and the other end against the step or alighting board of the hive and over this should be spread a piece of light cloth. The bees are then shaken on to the sheet from their temporary home and as a rule they will proceed to walk up hill and take possession of their new home without much delay. As soon as they are all in, the remainder of the hive is built up, and some additional protection from the cold, such as a piece of old carpet or felt, should be put on before the roof is fixed.

To House the Nucleus a different procedure is necessary, for the bees are invariably quite lively. First give the bees their liberty by opening the entrance of the travelling-box to enable them to learn the position of their new home. Shortly after, the bees and frames can be transferred. It is here that the bee-keeper will use his subjugator, which is a long name given to a simple instrument for puffing smoke. A few whiffs of smoke will render the bees sufficiently quiet to enable them to be handled, and the combs should then be lifted from the travelling-box and placed in the brood chamber of the hive. The best time of the day to handle bee colonies once they are established is in the heat of a fine, bright day. The reason for this is that the majority of the bees are then away in the fields and gardens.

The Combs.—Combs are used for four purposes—for breeding workers, for breeding drones, for storing honey and pollen and for breeding queens.

Worker combs are built entirely of wax by the worker bees. The cells are originally made quite round in section, but owing to the vast number of them they very quickly become hexagonal in shape. The diameter is approximately $\frac{1}{5}$ in. When a brood is occupying these combs, the cells are capped over with a mixture of pollen and wax as soon as the feeding stage of the larvæ is finished. The capping on the worker-brood comb is slightly convex and is rather dull in appearance. Sometimes honey is stored in these worker cells, in which case the cappings are shiny and not quite so evenly convex. The cappings for honey cells are made of wax. The drone comb is exactly the same as the worker comb except that the cells are much larger, usually being about $\frac{1}{4}$ in. in diameter, and slightly longer than those designed for the workers, although additional length is gained by a higher dome.

The Queen is produced in a much larger cell than those used for workers, drones or for honey. Certain of the worker larvæ are set aside by the inmates of the hive to become queens. These, as we have said, are placed in a cell about the size and shape of an acorn. Directly an egg is hatched, which is usually about three days after it is laid, the larva is fed with a special food called royal jelly. It is this food which is largely responsible for turning the worker-bee larva into a queen. The larva and the food occupy the cell together, and during the actual feeding the cell is gradually made longer by the bees and eventually it is capped over. Fifteen days after being sealed up a perfect queen emerges, and usually after a few days and one or two trial flights, the young queen flies high into the air, pursued by the drones. Maeterlinck, in his book "The Life of a Bee," gives a wonderful description of this flight. The queen and the drones fly higher and higher until, when only one drone is left, the queen is mated. Immediately this has been done, the drone falls lifeless to earth and the queen returns to her hive, where, in about 48 hours or so, she begins to lay her eggs.

The larvæ are fed by the other bees, and in about three weeks' time the new workers emerge and set about their task of cleaning the hive, feeding larvæ and so on. Later, they go to the fields to collect nectar for the honey.

The Honey Cell.—The last type of cell is that in which the honey is stored. It is exactly the same as the drone and worker cells, and both of these are used indiscriminately for the storage of honey. It should be remembered that when honey is stored in a cell, pure wax is always used for the capping.

Feeding the Bees.—The bees require feeding at certain times of the year. When starting a new hive, the store of food purchased with the nucleus may not last until the worker bees can go out and collect their food. In any case it is necessary to feed the bees in the spring. Usually this food takes the form of syrup, although some bee-keepers prefer to use candy. The syrup is quite easily made. To 1 lb. of sugar (either loaf or granulated) add ¾ pint of water. Put the pan on the gas or fire, and stir. As soon as the sugar is quite dissolved, the syrup is ready. It must on no account be brought to the boil, or it will crystallize on getting cold. Some bee-keepers add a pinch of salt and a teaspoonful of vinegar to every twelve pounds weight of sugar.

Candy should be quite soft, and a good recipe is the following: To every 10 lb. of sugar add 1¾ pints of cold water and a teaspoonful of cream of tartar. Put the pan on the fire and stir to prevent burning. Boil until the sugar commences to froth, but do not let it go over the side of the pan. In a few minutes it will boil with a cracking sound and will not froth. After this happens, keep boiling for three minutes, and then remove to cool. Not long afterwards the mixture should be stirred, when it will become creamy and thick. Stirring should be kept up until it is almost too stiff to continue, then the candy should be poured into plates or shallow tins to set. In the early part of the year a certain amount of pea flour is required by the bees. This is about the best substitute for pollen which is, of course, very scarce at this time of the year. To provide this pollen substitute, then, candy may be made up as above, but a packet of pea flour (costing approximately 1d.) should be added for every 10 lb. of sugar.

Some manufacturers of bee-keepers' supplies market a special thermometer which is used for candy making. This saves a lot of guesswork and its purchase is advised. The thermometer is hung so that the bulb is in the liquid, and immediately the top mark, which is clearly indicated, is reached, the pan is taken off the fire and allowed to cool until the mercury falls to the low mark.

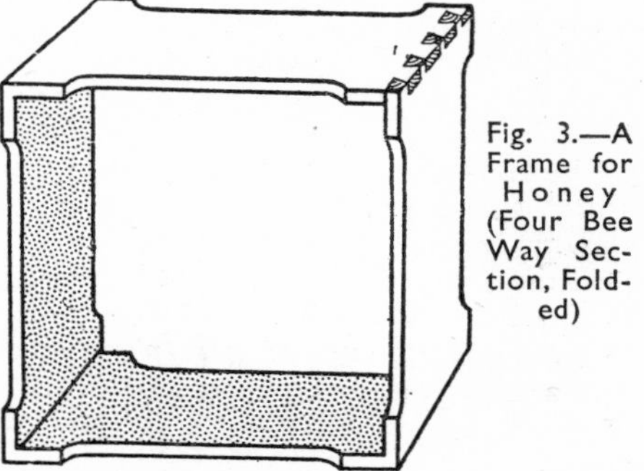

Fig. 3.—A Frame for Honey (Four Bee Way Section, Folded)

The Honey.—We have seen that the lowest "room" in the hive is used as a brood chamber. It is here that the queen lays her eggs and the workers and drones are hatched out. It is here also that the bees make their store of honey, but there comes a time when this chamber is not large enough. Above the brood chamber, then, is set a compartment or "super" in which the surplus honey is stored. In the super, or rack, above the brood chamber are placed a number of section boxes (21 in a standard-sized super). Several supers may be required.

Bees will put their honey in any sort of box, but in order to have orderly sections, the bee-keeper inserts sheets of bees' wax called "foundations." Each row of sections is separated from the next by "separators" so that the bees will not join them all together. Shallow frame "supers" are used for the production of extracted honey. (The honey from a hive may either be sold complete in its section box, or the bee-keeper may extract it from the combs and put it into bottles or jars.) The combs used for the extracted honey are usually of a smaller size.

The Foundation.—This consists of sheets of beeswax impressed so as to form indentations similar to the base of the natural cells. It is upon these foundation sheets that the bees make the rest of the cells and fill them with honey.

Foundations are made in various patterns and grades, namely, for workers, drones and so on. The beginner is advised to experiment with several different makes if he is unable to get advice from an experienced apiarist. It should be noted that not every colony should be given supers in which to store the honey. Much depends upon the strain of bee in the hive. When working for extracted honey, sections are not used, but instead, small frames are given in an extracting super. Sometimes the foundations for these are of the drone variety, as when these are used the cells are larger, so that more honey is stored.

Extracted Honey does not fetch such a big price as section honey, but usually there is more of it. Honey is extracted by cutting off the cell cappings with a warm knife, and removing the honey in an extracting machine that rotates the decapped cells so that the honey is ejected by centrifugal force. When extracting honey, make sure you do so in a bee-proof room, otherwise, hundreds of bees, smelling the honey, will come in and try to get it back. The combs can be used again, which saves the bees the trouble of building new ones. Bees will fill a rack of sections or a super for extraction in a week to ten days in the height of the season.

Heather Honey is much denser than ordinary honey, and it will be found that the centrifugal extractor is insufficient. The usual method is to put the combs in a press, the honey escaping through a perforated metal plate and the comb being left above it in the form of a cake. It is impossible to avoid getting small particles of the comb wax in pressed honey, and for this reason heather honey is more frequently sold in sections.

There are two kinds of heather—Bell and Ling. The Ling or *Calluna vulgaris* is the real heather which is, of course, usually found on hills. Ling honey has a better flavour than ordinary heather honey (Bell heather, or *Erica cinerea*). Heather and Ling honey is chiefly produced between the end of July and the beginning of September, and it is of a darker colour than clover honey.

Owing to the nature of our climate no definite dates can be given as to when the honey flow starts. The clover honey is usually the main flow, although it is by no means the first produced by the bees. Fruit trees enable the bees to start their store, and the bee-keeper is wise if he allows them to retain this for their own use.

Once the white clover starts to bloom, however, the apiarist can begin to look for honey. As a rule the early honey flow starts in May, but, as we have said, it varies from year to year according to the weather. Where there is no heather, the final flow will stop about August, although if there be any buckwheat about, it will go on for a longer time.

"Robbing."—There is not sufficient space to enable us to deal fully with every phase of bee keeping, and we must leave out of this article all reference to the ills to which bees are subject. If care be observed at all times, however, there is little likelihood of illness. Some things, nevertheless, must be carefully guarded against, even though the colony be in a healthy condition, and one of these is robbing.

Bees will not rob if honey is coming in plentifully, but when the supply fails they will not hesitate to try and get some from other hives. It is then that the keeper is advised to get out of the way, for thousands of angry bees will be fighting and struggling in an endeavour to steal honey. The bee-keeper should, therefore, watch his charges very carefully towards the end of the honey flow, and it is a good plan to restrict the opening to a weak hive in order that intruders may be dealt with one at a time! When a robbing bout is on, the apiarist may lose hundreds of his bees, so he should always be prepared. Robbing is easily prevented but not so easily cured.

Another thing that should always be

looked to is the safety of the queen. If she is absent just before the honey flow is due to start, it is a serious matter. Sometimes birds will kill the queen when she is on the wing, and sometimes, when returning from her nuptial flight, she will go to the wrong hive. At other times, when the bees wish to get rid of a queen, the workers will mass themselves round her so much that she is suffocated. This latter is called "balling," and the way to release the queen is to drop some honey on the mass of bees or to immerse the ball of bees in water.

A queenless colony will be detected by the conduct of the bees. They become very restless, and run about in all directions, apparently looking for her. A new queen should be introduced without delay. This is a matter requiring care, otherwise the bees may kill her. There are many textbooks which deal with this subject.

It is obvious that there comes a time when the queen will no longer be prolific, and when this happens she must be replaced. The bees, will, of course, feed one of the larvæ and make their own queen, but it is sometimes advisable to introduce a queen right away, in order that the colony does not suffer through a lack of egg production.

Showing Honey.—Just a word about honey for show purposes. This is undoubtedly one of the best methods of getting customers if one is taking up the hobby in order to make it pay dividends. First, then, the bees selected for the colony must be of a good strain, then everything must be carried out with scrupulous care so that they are maintained in a healthy and happy condition. When the honey flow comes, and the sections are ready for exhibition, they should be cleaned well by scraping them with a piece of glass, and only the best-looking sections entered. Sections with the most even cappings only should be chosen. A special show-case—this being a double-sided box with glass windows in it—should be used.

For extracted honey, use glass jars of ½-lb. or 1-lb. capacity, preferably with screw tops. There are three grades of honey: light, medium and dark, and there is a special colour-grading glass obtainable.

BILLIARDS

BILLIARDS is a non-strenuous indoor game which can be enjoyed for hours at a stretch, and one of its chief advantages is its adaptability. Whether you have a huge table weighing round about a ton or a miniature board laid on your dining-room table, the game in essence will be the same. The ideal game is naturally on a full-sized table, and in buying a table for your home it will be well to get one as large as will be convenient.

Care of a Billiard Table.—To keep the cloth in good condition brush it regularly and occasionally iron it. The nap runs towards the top of the table from baulk, so see that brush and iron are worked only in that direction. An iron should not be too hot; it should be pushed along from one end of the table to the other in a straight line, covering strip by strip until the whole width is traversed. A table that is regularly used should be ironed every few days, especially in damp weather.

The Cues.—Choose your cue with care. If you are inexperienced it will be a little difficult to judge the most suitable weight, and you will do well to experiment with a few until you are able to form an opinion—a few half-hours on some public table, or at a friend's house, will give you the opportunity. Medium weight may suit you, but a fairly heavy cue is most generally preferred. Try a weight of 16 oz. The well-balanced, heavy cue obviously eliminates much arm and shoulder work. Length, thickness, degree of tapering, balance, type of handle, size of tip, all these things have to be taken into account as well as weight.

When you have a good cue look after it. There is no more common fault amongst inexperienced players than that of leaning a cue against a wall when it is not in use.

This is a most harmful thing, and will very soon ruin the straightness of the best cue.

Chalk.—Get good chalk. Even the best quality is so cheap that it is not worth while economizing. Chalk your cue tip frequently and sufficiently during play—the chalk of course helps the tip to grip the ball. Before actual play you must learn something of the rules of the game.

Terms Used.—The billiard table has *six pockets*. The cloth-covered strips of rubber round the edges of the board, which keep the balls in play are *cushions*. Across the lower end of the table is a straight mark, the *baulk line*; the small section of table behind this line is *baulk*. On the baulk line, and in baulk, is marked a small semi-circle, from which play begins, this is the *D*. At the centre of the table is a spot, called the *centre spot*; near the top end is the *billiard spot*, and between this and the centre spot is the *pyramid spot*.

Three balls are used—the *red*, the *white*, the *spot white*—this latter is distinguished by a small black spot. When you are playing, the ball which you have hit or are about to hit is the *cue ball*, and the *object ball* is that at which you aim the cue ball.

The red ball is placed on billiard spot and the white inside the D to start a game.

Scores are made by losing hazards, winning hazards and cannons. It is a losing hazard when the cue ball goes into a pocket after striking another ball—three points are counted if the red is first struck, and two if a white ball is first struck. The losing hazard is also referred to as *in off*. A winning hazard is when a ball other than the cue ball is driven into a pocket. This pocketing is also referred to as *potting*—three points are scored when the red ball goes down and two when a white is pocketed. It is a cannon when the cue ball strikes both the other balls—and two points are scored. If a winning and a losing hazard are made in the same stroke the score of each is counted, and should there be a cannon as well that will also be added. When the cue ball runs into a pocket following a cannon two points are counted for the losing hazard if the white ball was struck first and three if the red was struck first; two are scored if the cue ball struck both the others simultaneously.

After the red has been pocketed or put out of play it is started off again on the billiard spot. When a white is similarly brought back into play it is replaced in the D, and must play out of baulk; it is not allowed to play on to any ball in baulk by a *direct* shot.

Should a cue ball miss both other balls the player gives one point to his opponent; and, in such a miss, if the cue ball goes into a pocket or is driven off the table the opponent gets three points. If, without there being a miss, any ball is forced from the table, the player responsible forfeits two points.

Although there is not a rule against it, it is generally considered bad form among amateurs for a player to pot his opponent's ball, and the conventional thing for any person doing this unintentionally is to declare that he is sorry. The potted white ball scores two points, but it is left "down" and so is lost to the player who has potted it.

Fouls.—It is a *foul* to touch the cue ball twice in one stroke—as when a player accidentally touches it in taking aim and then makes his real stroke. It is a foul if the ball in play is touched by any part of the cue other than the tip, and if the ball is pushed rather than struck. Other fouls are: playing with the wrong ball; failing to play out of baulk when one's ball has been replaced in the D; playing out of one's turn; failing to have one foot on the floor when making a stroke; striking any ball which has not come to rest. For a foul the striker forfeits his turn; and any points which were made by the foul stroke. The opponent can continue with the balls as they are or may have them *spotted*—the red on billiard spot, his own in D, his opponent's white on the centre spot.

If at any time it is impossible to replace the red ball, as desired, on the billiard spot, it should be put on the pyramid spot, if that also is occupied by another ball the red will go on the centre spot.

With this preliminary knowledge you will be ready to begin playing.

Stance.—Assuming that you are a right-handed player you will stand with your left foot nearest the table, the foot pointed in line with the cue and the knee bent. Your right foot will be back at a comfortable distance, turning outwards, so that your whole body is half turned to the right and your cue arm has ample freedom. The position to be avoided is with both feet at an equal distance from the table, with the body square.

The Bridge, on which the cue runs, is formed by the left hand. Rest this left hand easily on the table, bending forward, so that the finger tips and the lower part of the palm are firm on the cloth. The thumb is stretched along with the first finger, and it is in the groove formed by this finger and the thumb end that the cue slides. Keep the left arm at full stretch, and bend forward from the hips. The head should be low, for this will enable you to get better aim when sighting along the cue.

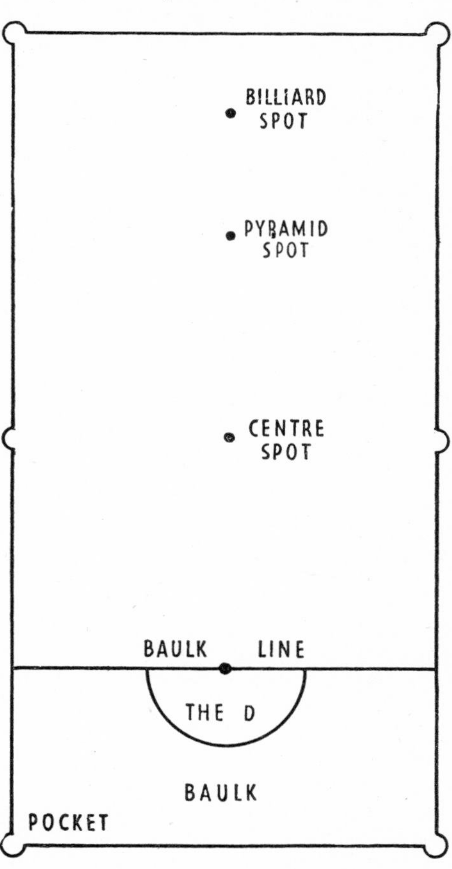

Fig. 1.—The Table

Holding the Cue.—You must not clutch the thick end of the cue with your full hand, for this would hamper both arm and wrist play. Hold it firmly but lightly between the thumb and first finger, or the first and second finger and the thumb. Make all cue movements smooth and as horizontal as possible. Your hold on the cue should not be at the extreme end of the butt or, unless you are a person of remarkable arm length, your left hand will be compelled to make its bridge too far from the cue ball. The best grip is about 3 in. from the thick end, for this enables the left arm to reach near to the tip without strain. Do not have too short a grip, however, by holding the cue too far from the butt end, or you will upset balance and fail to get proper power in your stroke. For special power or cue control the remaining third and fourth fingers may wrap round the cue.

Striking the Ball.—When you begin to make strokes you will discover the importance of gauging the right position for your left hand. If your bridge is too far from the cue ball you will have insufficient control of the cue tip when striking; if the bridge is too near you will lose that smooth power which characterizes a good stroke. About 8 in. is the best distance between bridge and cue ball.

In all strokes keep the cue as close to the side of your body as you can so that your arm swing is free and you are able to aim comfortably.

By this time you probably want to go straight ahead to play a game. But do not fall into the mistake which so many make of thinking that providing you play sufficient games you will automatically become a good player. That certainly is not true, however much it may apply to other forms of recreation. There is only one way of becoming proficient on the billiard table, that is by systematic practice. If your table is in your own home and so available at all times this is ideal, for you will then be able to practise by yourself whenever you wish.

Exercises.—Place your ball in the centre of D, on the line, and take sight straight up the table. With a firm, clean stroke drive the ball up to the top cushion and back, so that it passes over the three spots, and returns above them when it has struck the cushion. At the conclusion of your stroke you should have allowed the cue to remain motionless, and thus the ball, providing it runs as you intended, will come down the table again and collide squarely with the cue tip. You may vary this practice by lifting your cue after its stroke and seeing that the ball returns exactly over the centre of the D, from where it started. Another alternative is to put the other white and red ball side by side against the bottom cushion, in line with the spots down the middle of the table—your own ball will then arrive back just between them, hitting them both. Your early failures in all this practice will be due to the faulty aim, or because you have not hit your ball squarely in the middle.

Next put your ball on the centre spot and try driving it into each pocket in turn. It should not be long before you can manage this cleanly enough. And then you may begin to drive at an object ball.

Put the red on the billiard spot, and drive up the table as before from D, striking the red full and squarely and so sending it on to the top cushion.

The Half-ball Stroke.—You will need to practise this untiringly, for it is the basis of almost all billiard play. In your last bit of work the cue ball met the object ball squarely, both being exactly in line. In the half-ball stroke the cue ball is moved to one side just half of its width, so that at the moment of impact its centre is in line with the outer edge of the object ball. As a result, the object ball is driven off at an angle, perhaps to the left and the cue ball will therefore slant off to the right. This half-ball stroke gives the widest angle in billiard playing. An excellent way of practising is to put the red on the pyramid spot and your own ball on the left corner of the D. If you now make a half-ball shot, striking the red on its right side, then your ball will go into the right-hand top pocket of the table. This is a most useful practice stroke, since you have definite spots for placing your balls, and the white runs squarely into the pocket, securing the widest possible entry.

With reasonable mastery of the half-ball shot you may go on to explore the intermediate angles between the half-ball and full-ball impacts, for it is necessary that you should be able to judge angles—the angle of the half-ball stroke will become a sort of measurement standard.

By switching your attention over to the effect of your shots on the object ball you may begin to concentrate on potting the red. Strive to get it in the various pockets from all sorts of positions. Only when you are getting fair confidence with plain winning and losing hazards should you begin to consider the new matter of what happens to the secondary ball—your own white after you have potted the red, or the red when your white has gone in off it. For since your aim is to score continuously by a number of strokes—for only when no score is made does the opponent follow on —then how you leave your balls is of the greatest importance.

In making a cannon it is often advantageous not to hit the second ball direct for this will probably drive it farther from the first; but if you approach behind it from the cushion you may even bring it nearer to the first ball and so make a succeeding cannon practicable. Similarly, if it is impossible for you to score then you will want to leave the balls as badly placed as possible for your opponent—in baulk, perhaps, if his own has to make a restart from the D.

It is at this stage where billiards begins to get really interesting, for the absolute novice thinks of nothing but the possibility of scoring from the immediate stroke, and all his "leaves" are entirely unpremeditated.

"Top," "Bottom" and "Side."—A new complication, and a very important one, also arises when you have advanced thus far. You must now study how to put *top*, *bottom*, *side*, on the cue ball.

Chalk your cue well and drive your ball straight at a cushion, hitting the ball, however, on the right side instead of squarely in the middle. You will find that instead of the rebound being square the ball will glance off to the right—because of the right-side spin imparted to it.

If you put the red ball on the centre spot, and your white between it and the right-hand middle pocket you should be able to pot the red easily. If, however, you strike your ball at the top, so giving it a strong forward spin, you will, providing you have hit straight and square, not only pot the red, but follow on with your own white ball, and so score six—that illustrates *top*. Conversely, if from the same position in the middle of the table, you hit your own ball low you will pot the red as before, but the white, after the impact, because of the backward spin acquired, will tend to come back towards you and so drop into the right-hand middle pocket. This same principle of *bottom* is familiarly illustrated in the common trick of throwing a child's hoop forward in such a manner that when the forward impetus is exhausted the backward spin causes the hoop to return to the sender.

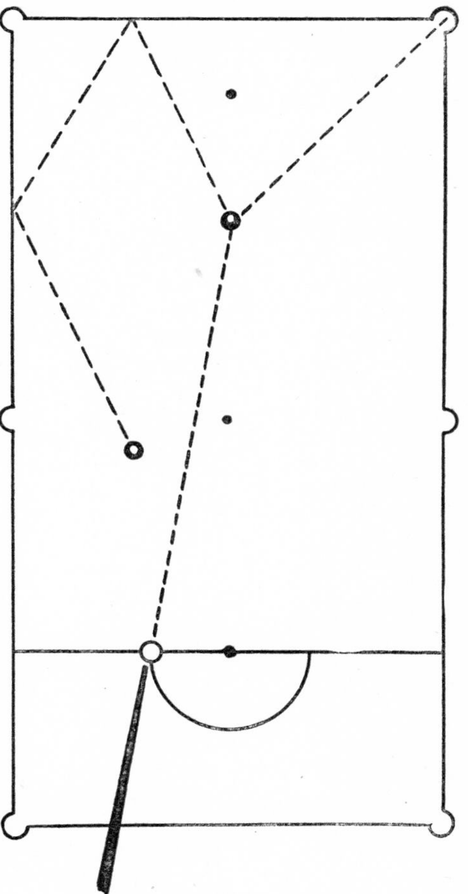

Fig. 2.—The Half-ball Shot

You will therefore practise all these features, of side, top, bottom. Putting top on a ball will be the thing which will give you most satisfaction first, for it will frequently enable you to make useful scoring strokes by compelling the cue ball to "follow on" after it has impelled the object ball forward.

But remember that the first great aim of the billiard player must be to hit his ball squarely—until you can do that you can obviously do nothing else dependably.

Sometimes it happens that a stroke must be played with a cue ball against the cushion. In such circumstances the ordinary bridge obviously cannot be made. Instead you must rest your cue on the edge of the table itself, fastening the fingers over it to keep it steady; the first finger should be on one side and the second finger and thumb on the other. Do not dig your cue downwards, keep it as horizontal as you can, but be careful not to miscue.

Using the Rest.—When it is not possible to reach the ball with the left-hand bridge the *rest* must be used. Do not keep the handle of the rest raised in the left hand, but let it lie on the table, merely holding it in position with the hand. The cue should be just over the rest, held with the back of the right hand towards the body, thus during the stroke the shafts of cue and rest are just in line, both of them running to the middle of the player's body.

Do plenty of experimenting with a ball driven on to one or more cushions, in order that you may know what to do when you are left a double baulk. In all sorts of strokes cushion play is important.

In making any stroke, first see that your cue and cue ball are in line as you desire, then move your gaze to the object ball, and work out the desired angles. For the actual stroke your sight must remain safely on the object ball, if you glance away the shot will be spoiled.

Do not give a lot of nervous little swings before making a stroke; just three or four quiet movements are enough to ensure that the stroke can be made loosely and freely.

Always stand still while an opponent is making a stroke, to speak or move will distract and spoil his stroke.

Do not suggest, when you are beaten, that your opponent had some extraordinarily good "leaves," while the balls simply "wouldn't run right" for you.

Snooker, Pool.—Snooker is a sociable sort of game for four or any reasonable number of players. For those who have not much skill, snooker is very attractive since they often have quite a reasonable chance of winning against opponents of much more ability. In addition, snooker is very interesting for onlookers.

The game consists of winning hazards or "potting." The same technique of strokes is employed as in billiards, so that you have merely to acquaint yourself with its rules in order to begin playing.

At the beginning of snooker fifteen red balls are placed in pyramid formation at the top end of the table, with the inverted apex on the pyramid spot. On the billiard spot is a black ball, and a pink ball touches the red which is on the pyramid spot. On the centre spot is a blue ball; a brown on the middle of the baulk line; a green on the left-hand corner of the D, and a yellow on the right-hand corner. The scoring values of the balls are: red, 1; yellow, 2; green, 3; brown, 4; blue, 5; pink, 6; black, 7.

Of the 22 balls 15 are red, and the other colours have one ball each. The white is the ball to be played with the cue, by all players alike. The game consists in potting first a red, then a ball of another colour, then another red, and so on. The single balls of the six other colours are always replaced on the table; the reds stay down until all the reds are pocketed. Then one after another the other coloured balls are pocketed and put out of play, until all are finished. Those other than red and white are called "pool balls."

A player continues at the table until he fails to score, or commits a fault. It is a fault to strike or pocket the wrong ball, or to miss the object ball. For any fault or foul stroke the player is penalized according to the score value of the ball in question—except that the minimum penalty is 4. If, for instance, he hits a pink instead of a red ball then he forfeits 6; but if he fouls with a yellow then he forfeits 4. The general fouls of billiards—like playing with both feet off the ground—apply also in snooker.

After all the reds have been pocketed the pool balls must be put down in proper order, beginning with yellow and finishing with black.

It is not necessary that a player shall always try to score directly. Often it is better tactics to "snooker" an opponent, by interposing a ball so that his next stroke is obstructed and he is forced to commit a fault—and so lose at least 4 points. One's score is often benefited by such snookering, and it is in this that much of the finesse of the game lies. For example, supposing all the reds are "down" and only the pool balls remain. They have to be played in proper order. The player who intends to snooker may therefore play on to the yellow, but without the intention of pocketing it. If he did pocket it he would score only 2, whereas if he can so leave it covered that his opponent, following, is unable to hit it, either by a direct or any indirect stroke, then the opponent yields 4 points.

A pool ball is always replaced on its spot after being pocketed or forced off the table; so is the white cue ball. If a player misses the black ball twice, when the black is "on" or due to be played, he loses the game.

BIRDS AND BIRD WATCHING

Bird watching can begin in your garden and progress to a hide built in a cleft on a Scottish mountain; but you are just as likely to find out valuable facts about birds when in the former as in the latter. It is not an expensive hobby, a note-book for entering dates, sketches, etc., and a pair of field glasses being the main requisites.

It is advisable at the outset to determine from what point of view birds can be studied, as aimless gazing at them is a waste of time. The beaks, feet, and plumage of birds, and the influence of such on their habits, may form separate studies. The flight of birds, the song, call, and alarm notes of birds; birds as agricultural pests, offer other aspects for study. Birds may be studied as winter and summer migrants; as parents; or watched as subjects for photography.

The Best Time for Observation.—Perhaps the most fruitful period for general bird watching is the mating and nesting season, which begins about the middle of February and continues until the end of July—later in the case of birds like the swallows, who often nest in September. August on the whole is not a good month, for most wild birds are moulting and living lives of retirement; though new facts about partridges and other game birds can often be gathered then. In autumn, though, there is a good deal to see, for birds begin flocking, or separating for the winter. Spring and autumn are definitely the seasons, too, for studying migration.

Attracting Birds.—Bird tables and nesting boxes are a great aid to bird watching in your home, though, if you have only a small town garden, the latter will offer too great a temptation to the neighbouring cats. Two or three stout stakes with a flat board nailed on top, set away from the walls so that no cat can reach them, will make excellent bird tables. Place a bowl of water on each, but vary the food; putting seeds on one table, chopped crusts and fat on another, and nuts on a third. Then you will begin to see how beaks and choice of food are allied.

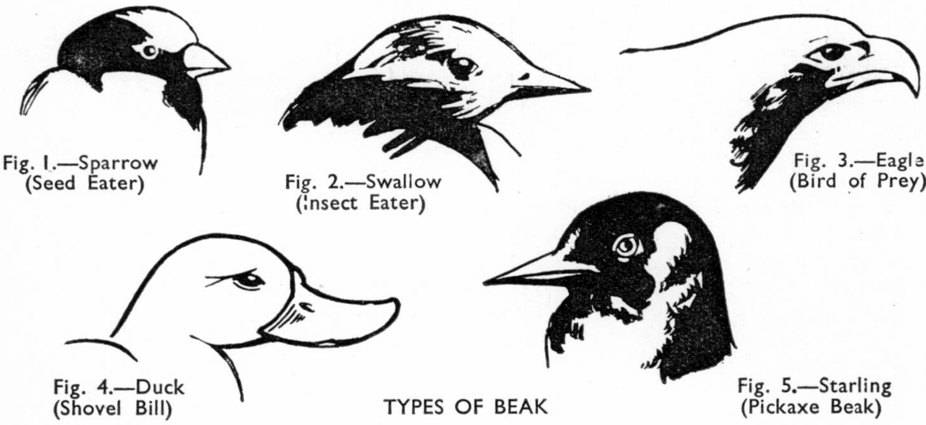

Fig. 1.—Sparrow (Seed Eater)

Fig. 2.—Swallow (Insect Eater)

Fig. 3.—Eagle (Bird of Prey)

Fig. 4.—Duck (Shovel Bill)

Fig. 5.—Starling (Pickaxe Beak)

TYPES OF BEAK

Types of Beak.—Birds that eat seeds with hard husks, needing cracking, have strong, short beaks like those of the sparrow and the chaffinch. Birds that like worms have long strong beaks with which they can pull their meal out of its hole in the lawn; look at the blackbirds and thrushes. Birds which catch insects on the wing have small, rather weak beaks, but mouths which open widely and in which they can store several insects before eating them *en masse;* swallows and flycatchers have such beaks. Insect eaters who search for food under leaves and along hedge bottoms, as the wren does, have similar, but slightly longer beaks.

On the other hand, birds of prey—eagles, hawks, and owls—have very strong beaks, with a pointed, down-curving upper part with which it is easy to tear the flesh of their catch. Birds like the moorhens and wild ducks have spoon-shaped bills with fringed plates at the edges, which act as a mud-scoop and strainer. Rooks and starlings have pickaxe-like beaks with which they can dig out grubs from the soil and peck into vegetable and fruit crops.

Feet.—When you are studying birds with regard to their feet you may divide them into perchers, darters, swimmers, waders, scratchers, and birds of prey.

Perching birds have three long toes in front and one short one behind; the front ones automatically close on the perch directly the bird bends its leg. Sparrows, thrushes, robins, and linnets belong to this class.

Swallows, flycatchers, etc., who are always on the wing, belong to the darters. They come to the ground so little that their feet are weak and short, with all four toes pointing forward.

Swimming birds often have webbed feet as have ducks, while the waders have long legs with flat, three-toed feet. Scratching birds, like the pheasant and partridge, have short strong legs, with blunt claws; three toes in front and one shorter one behind.

Birds of prey have strong, curved talons with which they grip their prey on pouncing.

The plumage of birds, the changes of feather according to season, and the differences in colour between the cock and the hen birds, form a study which will appeal to the artistic mind.

The Flight of Birds is indicative of their mode of life. Migratory birds have longish wings with strong flight feathers and their movements in the air seem effortless. Partridges, who fly very little, have short stumpy wings and a whirring, bothered start to their flight. The wren, who flits mostly from bush to bush, has short, quickly flapping wings. Observation will help you to build up your own table of flight.

Notice, too, how certain types of birds fly always with outspread wings, others close them at intervals when undulating; also, how some hover, then fold their wings and drop like stones. The flight of birds offers limitless opportunities to the bird watcher, and it is a little-explored field, too.

Bird Song.—Interest in the songs of birds has grown so of late that bodies of bird watchers have spent many nights awaiting the dawn chorus, so that they can find the actual time at which each type of bird begins to sing. Interesting experiments of this nature can be made each year by anyone, and much valuable data can be so collected. It is the spring dawns which are spent thus, but it is the summer nights which must be devoted to the song of the nightingale. Sunny November afternoons are going to tell you about the robin's thin song; and storm-tossed February days give you the blithest song of the missel thrush.

Any new call notes should be located and followed up on the chance that it will lead you to the bird or its nest.

Winter flocks and nesting birds offer the best opportunity of watching the food of birds from the point of view of the farmer. Rooks, for instance, can be seen pulling up the growing corn, but it is merely to get at the grub at the roots, which would otherwise breed and do extensive damage. The regular analysis of crop contents of the birds shot by the farmer offers statistics for checking up such birds as agricultural pests.

Bird Photography.—With bird photography we come to the niceties of bird watching. Though walks through woods and fields, over moors, and along river banks, with a reasonable amount of field-glass observation, will yield an enormous amount of knowledge under the aforementioned headings, really intimate bird study is best done from a hide; except perhaps in bird sanctuaries and island colonies, where exceptional conditions prevail.

Ground nesters, bush nesters, and tree nesters; flocks too, if you will, can be studied and photographed from a "hide." When you have found a nest you want to watch, set up your hide before the eggs are hatched so that you can study the feeding and brooding habits of the cock and hen. Eggs take about twenty-one days to hatch, and then an even more delightful time begins. The feeding of the fledgelings, their first appearances abroad and their lessons in flight, offer priceless opportunities to the bird lover.

Hides in trees for watching and photographing rooks, herons, etc., need only be constructed of weathered sacking. The chief thing here is that the birds should be allowed to get used to the hide before you occupy it; and when you do, their attention must be distracted by one or two friends approaching it with you and then going audibly away. That, in fact, applies to taking up occupation in all hides.

For bush nesters, hides made of surrounding bushes tied on to a one-man canvas tent, or "property" tree trunk on a wire frame, are satisfactory. Judicious pruning of the actual nesting site is often necessary in order to obtain a clear picture. For ground nesters, often covering the photographer with grass, straw, bracken, or heather, and then going obviously away yourself, is enough to get the bird back on to the nest.

It is more satisfactory to consider the commoner birds under the following headings: In your garden; in fields and hedges; in spinneys and woods; on commons and moors; by river banks. Of the whereabouts of rarer birds, knowledge must be obtained from keepers and bird societies.

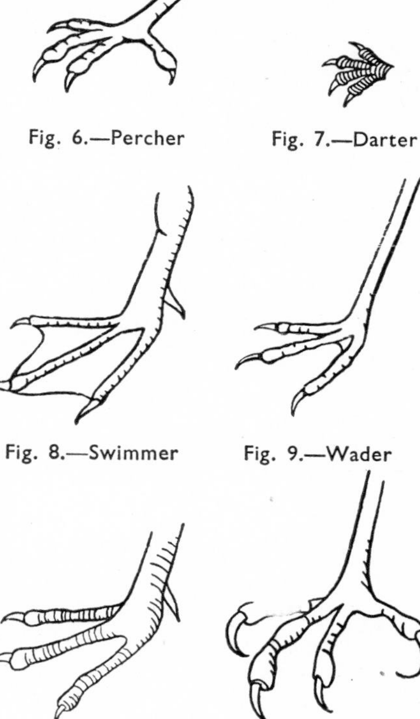

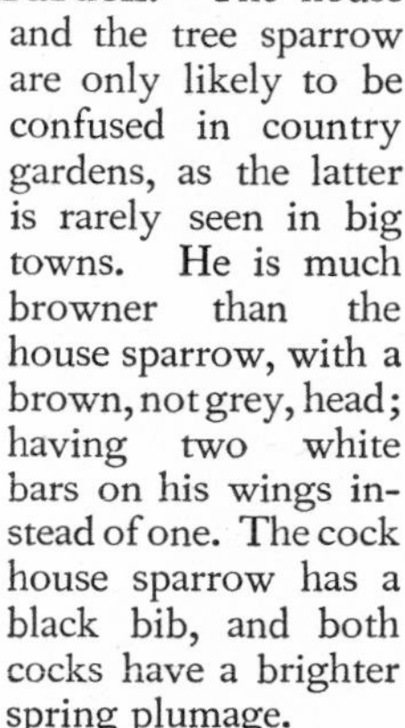

Fig. 6.—Percher Fig. 7.—Darter

Fig. 8.—Swimmer Fig. 9.—Wader

Fig. 10.—Scratcher Fig. 11.—Bird of Prey

TYPES OF FEET

Birds in Your Garden.—The house and the tree sparrow are only likely to be confused in country gardens, as the latter is rarely seen in big towns. He is much browner than the house sparrow, with a brown, not grey, head; having two white bars on his wings instead of one. The cock house sparrow has a black bib, and both cocks have a brighter spring plumage.

Robins and chaffinches are sometimes confused; but, though they are similar in size, the robin has a brown back and orange-red breast, and the chaffinch has a pink breast and slate-grey head, and also white wing bars; his wife's plumage is grey. The robin's song has a definite melody, its call note is like the noise made by a zip fastener, while the chaffinch calls "Spink! Spink!" Robins lead solitary lives in winter, but male and female chaffinches spend that time in separate flocks.

Blackbirds and starlings also are confused at a distance. Cock blackbirds have jet black, streamline bodies, and orange bills; the hens are sooty black with brown bills. Starlings, which appear black in the distance, have greenish-purple speckled plumage and brownish beaks. Their neck feathers are untidy, and they walk awkwardly when on the ground. Starlings are seen on refuse dumps, for they are dirty feeders.

The missel thrush is a bigger bird than the song thrush, its breast is lighter, and though it is speckled, the spots are triangular and not round. Both thrushes move in a hopping run on the ground, and both will stop suddenly with head on one side as if listening. A large stone surrounded by broken snail shells is the thrushes' dining table; to it they have carried snails in their beaks, and dashed them against the stone to break the shells. Their song is a repetition of several phrases but the blackbird's is a continuous melody.

Two of the tits are common garden visitors. The great tit, the size of a sparrow, has a black bib and head, yellow breast, green back, white cheeks and a grey tail. The blue tit, a small bird, with a bright blue head, has a greenish back and wings, and a yellow breast. Both love coconut, but they also hunt the bark of trees for insects. The great tit calls "Pi—ter, pi—ter, pi—ter pee!" and the call note of the blue tit is "Tzee—tzee tzee!"

The pied wagtails may be seen as often in the gardens as by the stream side. Their distinctive black and white plumage, quick nimble run, and jerking head and tail mark them out from other birds.

Swallows and house martins, too, haunt house and river alike. The swallow is blue-black with yellowish underparts, long wings, and forked tail; the house martin is a stumpier bird with a white rump and throat, pickaxe-shaped wings, and shorter tail.

Field and Hedgerow Birds.—Yellow-hammers, greenfinches, bullfinches, goldfinches, wrens and hedge-sparrows, are all likely to appear out of the hedges as you pass. It is the yellow-hammer who says: "A little bit of bread and no cheeeeeese!" from a gate post; he is a bright yellow bird streaked with brown. In winter he joins the finch and lark flocks.

The green-plumaged greenfinch, with yellow wing edges, has a wife with duller plumage; his cousin the bullfinch is more brightly coloured; he has a salmon-pink breast, and black throat, head and tail. He is destructive in orchards, nipping off fruit buds with great rapidity. The goldfinch is smaller; you will see him flying to thistle heads in summer, where, with his black, white, and red head, and black, yellow-banded wings, he looks like a gorgeous butterfly. Like the other finches, he is a seed eater, but his beak is not so parrot-like as that of the bullfinch.

The slim, dark brown bird which slips so quietly out of the hedge is the hedge-sparrow; he belongs to the finch family. He sings all the year round, and searches for insects in the hedge bottom, as does the stumpy, stiff-tailed wren, whose whirring flight from bush to bush is impossible to mistake.

From the grass in the field itself you may put up the skylark, and though you will often hear the landrail "Crek—Crek—ing" from the hay field, you will not often see this large migratory bird with its buff-coloured, spotted plumage. The skylark is brown, streaked with darker brown, and with white wing edges; on its head is a crest. The titlark is smaller, flies more jerkily, and has dark spots on its breast. Its song is not so sweet as that of the skylark, with whom those who do not migrate in autumn, flock.

The large brown-back bird, with grey tail and dark streaked underparts, which you see hovering with outstretched wings and head to wind, is the kestrel. He is waiting to pounce on mice and voles in the grass. The grey-plumaged sparrow-hawk, a much rarer bird, preys on other birds and is therefore to be seen darting along the hedge seeking the small birds which perch there, or haunting woods and heaths where game birds abound.

Do not confuse the cuckoo and the kestrel when perching, for though their greyish dark-streaked plumage is somewhat similar, their call notes and the swift, flapping flight of the cuckoo mark them out from one another,

Rooks and jackdaws are sometimes mistaken one for the other, but though both are black as to plumage, the bare face of the former and the grey nape of the latter distinguish them at closer view. They live together in flocks during the winter, but in February the rooks may be seen walking in pairs in the fields. Rookeries and jackdaw colonies in towers or ruins offer some of the most entertaining and fruitful hours of watching to the bird lover.

Another bird which takes insects on the wing is the spotted flycatcher. A summer migrant, this grey-brown bird sits on a post watching for flies, which he pursues relentlessly, returning to his post after each sally.

Birds in the Woods might be separated into those you see and seldom hear, and those you hear and seldom see. To the former class belong the nuthatch and the tree creeper. The tree creeper has a brown back, white underparts, a stiff tail, and long, curved beak. He creeps up trees in search of insects living under the bark. The larger nuthatch has a gay chestnut breast, white cheeks and grey back; he runs up and down trees after insects, but also seeks nuts which he wedges in the bark and cracks with his sharp bill.

Fig. 12.—Great Spotted Woodpecker

Fig. 13.—Green Woodpecker

Fig. 14.—Lesser Spotted Woodpecker

The wood-pigeon falls between these two divisions, his "Tak too coos Davy!" being as well known as his grey plumage.

The jay, the woodpeckers, the owls, the magpie, and the chiffchaff are birds whose call notes are familiar. The harsh screams of the crested, rosy, blue-tipped jay, and of the black and white magpie are the danger signals best known to the woodland inhabitants. The tapping of the woodpeckers, either the common green, or the rarer spotted types, as they hunt rotten trees for grubs should be followed up for a sight of the bird.

The barn owl, the long-eared, the tawny, and the little owls may be heard calling at night. The barn owl calls mostly "To-whit to-whoo!" the tawny owl calls "Whoo-whoo-whoo-wit!" the long-eared owl calls "Whoo-o!" and the little owl "Hoo-hoo!"

The song of the olive-brown nightingale is too famous to need description.

Birds on Moors and Commons.—The chestnut-backed, crimson-headed linnet, crying "Twit! Twit!" as he flits among the gorse bushes, is more common than the black-headed, chestnut-breasted stonechat, who loves to sing a bit of his queer clinking song as he fusses from bush to bush. The wheatear, a summer visitor, will flit before you on bare hillsides, flirting his white-topped tail over his grey back, and showing his white breast and black wings as he twists in the air after flies. The jerky flight of the lapwing as he flaps over waste places is well known. When on the ground his greenish black crest can be clearly seen.

In the spring the cry of the curlew is often heard over moors and sands. This big brown bird is dark streaked and has a very long, thin, down-curved beak.

River Birds.—The blue and emerald kingfisher darting to the stream centre and returning, fish in beak, to an overhanging branch, is a sight to look for on a riverside walk. Black moorhens, and grey-backed coots sallying forth from their homes in the reed beds offer an opportunity for "family life" studies to the watcher. Look for the small red-legged dipper bobbing on a stone set mid-stream near a lasher where scythe-winged swifts scream overhead. Herons frequent certain localities, and in such are easy to see standing motionless in shallow water as they watch for fish.

BOATING

Apart from engines, there are four general ways in which you can propel a boat—by pole, paddle, oar and sail. Naturally, when you begin to spend your leisure on the water you will come to have a preference, but it is a good plan to develop all-round watermanship by gaining at least some mastery of punt, canoe, sailing boat and rowing boat. Incidentally, you should have nothing to do with any of them before you can swim—but as soon as you can, boating offers a most fascinating recreation.

Punting.—The punt is the commonest type of boat on most rivers. There are many advantages possessed by this square flat-bottomed craft—it does not require much depth of water, it is roomy, it is not easily overturned, it is easily manageable.

In your early experiments at punting you may feel safer in the middle of the boat, and it is all right to stand there, providing you have no companions whom you are likely to wet. But as soon as possible take your place properly in the sloping end of the boat. The gratings will prevent you from slipping, but it is advisable to have suitable shoes, too. It does not matter whether you stand on the right or left side of the boat; many prefer the right, but a few experiments will soon settle where you are likely to be comfortable. If you are on the right hand your left foot should be spread a moderate pace in front of the right. You must be able to look towards the front although you are standing sideways.

You should choose a pole of moderate weight, and one that is not splintered or rough anywhere in the upper part where you will need to handle it. Poles vary in length and weight, though usually they are approximately the same on the same stretch of river.

Before beginning, take off your wrist-watch, if you object to water running on it, and roll up your sleeves.

Some novices think that punting is perfectly easy, nothing else being required than to drop the pole into the water and push the boat along. A few trials soon show that it is not so simple. Everything depends on details that are not at all obvious at first. For instance, the problem of steering arises immediately. A rowing boat can be made to go straight forward fairly easily, because it has an oar on either side; but the person who is punting does all his work on one side, so that at every thrust the front of his craft is liable to swerve sharply. The major problem of punting is to overcome that tendency to swerve.

Three main things have to be learned—putting the pole in, taking it out, steering.

The iron point should be dropped into the water close to the side of the boat, and about a yard farther forward than your head. Thus, by the time the point is on the bottom of the river, the boat will have glided forward sufficiently to bring the pole to the requisite angle at which you can apply a backward, propelling push. Clearly, if you drop the pole vertically the forward momentum of your boat will carry you on so that only a trifling push will be possible before the pole must be lifted from the water. It is even necessary to point the tip of the pole slightly forward as you drop it, so as to overcome the drift tendency. When your pole is on the bottom, push back steadily, hand over hand, until you reach the top. The depth of the water will determine the amount of push practicable just as it will settle the allowance which must be made for drift as you drop the pole in.

Do not change your stance—a punter does not walk down his boat in the manner of a ferryman or man poling a barge.

Recover the pole upwards hand over hand, until the iron tip comes above the surface, and the pole is vertical, ready for a new dip. Do not trail the tip in the water as you carry it forward.

Now for the most difficult part—steering, or overcoming swerve.

During the thrust the left hand should be two or three feet higher up the pole than the right. To check the boat swerve you must pull or push against the pole, during the thrust, with the lower hand. If you imagine the pole to be a fixed point detached from the boat when resting on the bottom and supported by the top hand, it is easy to see how, by pulling the stern of your punt across to this point, or pushing away from it, you can make your craft travel to right or left as it goes forward. Of course you can push away when the pole is close against the boat, but the pole must be some distance out if you want to pull your boat towards it. Anticipation is necessary, so that you may know just how far to the side the pole must be dropped. The experienced punter keeps a straight course by anticipating and preventing tendencies to stray, as does a motorist, rather than by getting widely off his intended track and then steering back.

Ordinarily, providing you are on the right side of the boat, you will need to push outwards with the right hand, with every thrust. This outward pressure must be combined with the backward push which propels the boat.

There is one other means of steering. When you are lifting the pole it is naturally trailing behind the boat, at the end of its thrust, and so you may swing it slightly in either direction—even over the stern—in order that it can act momentarily as a rudder.

One last point. There is no need to ship a lot of water. If you are careful not to grip the pole too closely as you lift and drop it in again, you will be able to keep your arms fairly dry, and the boat, too.

Paddling.—A canoe is a comparatively fragile craft. It can be overturned fairly easily. One's position in it is therefore of much importance.

When using a single paddle, alone, you should kneel or sit in the stern, for this gives best control. There is no need to get so far back that the prow is tilted high in the air, though it is an advantage to have it raised when traversing rough water. Your chief concern is stability, and this will necessitate that you get as low as possible in the canoe. Do not sit on back-rest stays or even seats; keep your weight well down towards the bottom. If you have a companion you should be well spaced along the craft so that the canoe remains level and steady; should one of you be heavier than the other he should sit behind.

Fig. 1.—Using a Single Paddle

There are two sorts of paddles—single blade and double blade. The single blade is more difficult to handle because it is used on one side of the canoe only, and therefore is liable to swerve the craft from a straight course just as is a punt pole.

To use a single-blade paddle on the right-hand side of your canoe, you must grasp the knob of the handle with your left hand, and hold the shaft low down with the right;

the greater the distance between your hands, the greater leverage you will obtain, providing that your position is not strained or uncomfortable. The left hand acts as a socket, mainly, and the right does the pulling. Have the left elbow bent as you recover the paddle above the water, pushing the blade forward until the right arm is at full stretch. The body should also lean forward from the waist with this movement, so that when the blade is ready to dip it is almost horizontal. This reaching forward should not be exaggerated, or you will get little power from the first part of your stroke.

Dip your blade cleanly, and close in to the side of the canoe. Do not put maximum pressure on it immediately, but increase pressure as the blade gets lower, sweeping it back, until it drives right past your body—in the latter part of the movement fullest strength will have been put into the stroke. The right hand pulls the paddle shaft back, and the left assists the movement by pushing forward, though the left hand should not travel nearly as far as the right.

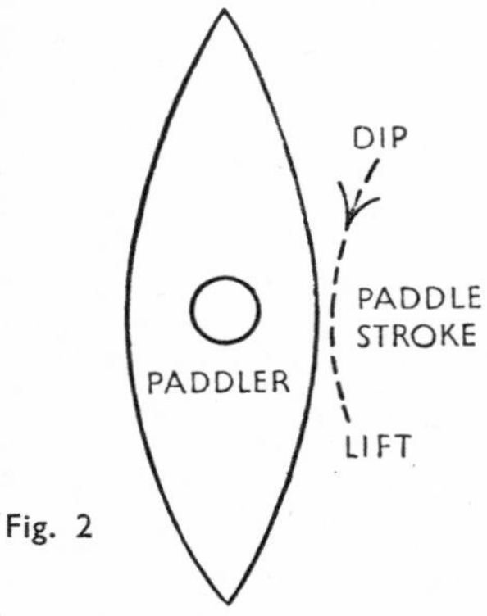

Fig. 2

Throughout the stroke keep the paddle vertical, and close in. If you make an outward, flattened sweep, in the manner of an oar, you lose a great deal of power and make the task of steering still more difficult.

Steering.—As all the strokes of a single-blade paddle are on one side the canoe tends to turn away from the paddler. To keep a straight course you must turn your blade slightly outwards as you finish each stroke, forcing out the inner edge, so that the blade becomes flattened away from the side of the canoe as you lift it from the water.

Do not waste power on this steering movement, for it has no propulsive value; in fact it hinders progress. Give it no more force nor time than is needed to keep the canoe straight.

Should you prefer to sit in the middle of your craft paddling is slightly more difficult. Your blade will now dip well to the front, so that as before your whole body can swing forward and backward to aid the stroke, but now the blade must immerse out from the side of your canoe. Thus the first part of the backward drive slants inwards, and the latter half is an outward slant as already described.

All paddling movements should be even, fairly long, and rhythmic. One long stroke is better than two short ones. As you gain experience you will find that a certain added vigour can be imparted to the close of a stroke, just as it reaches the point by the body where it has greatest propelling power; but do not let this deteriorate into a mere jerk.

When two people are using single-blade paddles it is better that they work on opposite sides. Their strokes should be timed together, the rear paddler taking the pace from his companion. Steering is effected by the person behind, who can cease his own strokes or ask his companion to hold up momentarily; also, of course, he can use his blade as a rudder. The bow paddler keeps up a straight, regular stroke; normally he does not steer, though in an emergency he can pull the prow across to either side. In rough water it is an advantage to have the two blades dipping alternately, so that there is always one in the water to steady the canoe.

The Double-bladed Paddle.—Spread your hands well in gripping the paddle shaft, and dip each end in turn with regular speed and force. Naturally your craft will be swerved first to one side then the other, but the movements will negative each other and the general result will be a straight course. To minimize the swerves, dip deeply, and get what you can of steering pressure when lifting your blades. When two paddlers are working together they should keep in unison. Two strokes on the same side will swing you round, or you may drag one blade in the water.

Although the length and form of the double-end paddle makes it impossible for blades to dip close to the canoe side, this wider spread is an advantage in a strong wind or a tide, and it helps to steady the craft in rough water. You should remember when making your stroke that one hand must push equally as the other hand pulls, so that the positions of the blades are exactly reversed at the conclusion of each stroke.

Be careful in handling a canoe. You must never attempt to change places with a companion, except when at land. To get into a canoe step into the middle, carefully, and grip the two sides with your hands opposite each other. Never stand up—the lower your weight is the better.

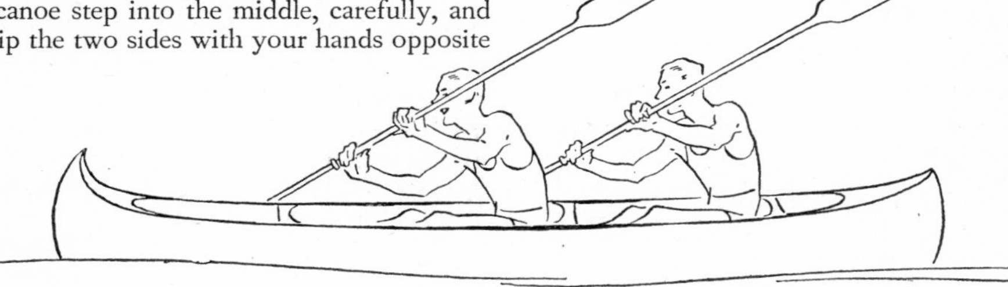

Fig. 3.—Two Paddles should keep in unison

Rowing.—Handling a pair of oars is generally termed *sculling*. You *scull* in the usual light pleasure skiff on river or lake. If you use only one oar, in a pair or four or eight, it is *rowing*—boat-race teams *row*. But apart from technicalities it is convenient to use the term *rowing* whenever oars are used in a *row-boat*.

Roughly, the same principles apply whether you are dealing with a river skiff or a sturdily-built sea boat. The forepart of a boat is called the *bows*, and the *stem* is that part of the keel which runs up the bows. The *stern* is the *rear* or *after* part, and that section of the keel rising in the stern, and corresponding to the stem is termed the *sternpost*. When the top of the rudder has a cross-piece, attached to which are fastened the rudder cords, this cross-piece is the *yoke*, and the cords are the *yoke lines*. In heavier boats a protruding spar takes the place of the lines and it is called the *tiller*. The foot-rests across the

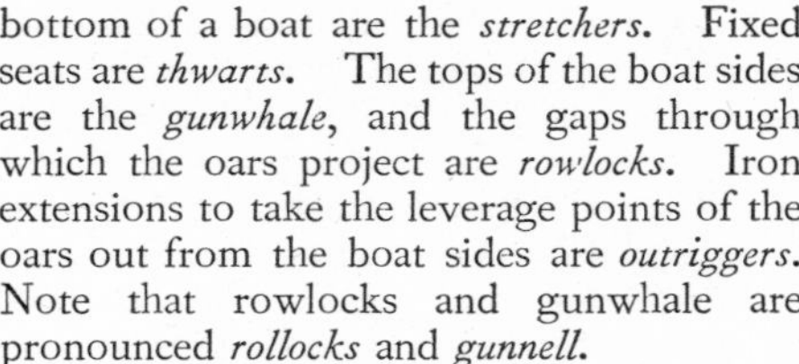

bottom of a boat are the *stretchers*. Fixed seats are *thwarts*. The tops of the boat sides are the *gunwhale*, and the gaps through which the oars project are *rowlocks*. Iron extensions to take the leverage points of the oars out from the boat sides are *outriggers*. Note that rowlocks and gunwhale are pronounced *rollocks* and *gunnell*.

Mooring ropes attached to front and stern are *painters*. Most large boats have *bottom boards*, which give a level footing, and prevent treading on the actual framework of the craft.

One end of an oar is the *blade*, the other the *loom*—this latter is generally tapered down to a more convenient size for the hand.

When you take your seat in a boat be sure that you are in the middle of the thwart in order that your oars may be equally immersed and balanced. Put your outer oar through its rowlock and push off from the bank. When you are clear, slide the other oar into position.

Your feet should be braced against the stretchers, which will have been adjusted to the requisite distance.

Your first impression when you grip the oars and have them in position will probably be that they are too long, for the ends or looms will slightly overlap. But this length is necessary to obtain requisite leverage for efficient rowing, and you must consequently arrange that one hand comes above the other when you pull. Decide which hand shall come on top, and stick to the habit.

You must sit easily, and be prepared to let the swing of your body help the arms, so that you get long, clean pulls.

Grip the handles at their ends, with thumbs underneath. The arms will be at full stretch, with the body leaning forward, hands slightly lower than the knees, and feet firm. Lower the blades cleanly into the water, behind you. Then, pull smoothly.

Your body swings back, moving from the hips and not the waist, until it is just past the vertical. The legs themselves will be thrusting vigorously against the stretcher and, providing you swing from the hips, this vigour will be imparted to the whole of the body. Finally, the arms draw up strongly until the thumbs touch the chest.

Take especial care to keep the elbows well in to the sides during this latter part of the pull; it is a common and serious fault for elbows to spread sideways in ungainly fashion.

Throughout the stroke each blade should be upright, and with its top edge only about an inch under the water. Until you have some facility lift the blades clear of the surface after each pull, and swing them back well in the air, concentrating on even, long strokes. But then you may proceed to *feather* the oars—which reduces the air resistance of the recovery by turning the blades flat, and also allows more relaxation of the arms by reducing the amount of support they are compelled to give.

Feathering.—Drop the wrists as the blades lift from the water, thus turning the blades almost on to their backs so that they skim the surface flatly as you recover them backwards for the new stroke. Keep the back edge of the blade higher than the front in this feathering, so that the wood rides lightly on the water, merely skimming a flicker of foam from it. If the back edge is turned right over the oar may bury itself. Also, be sure that the blade is lifted clear before it begins to recover; should you turn the oar too soon the blade may flatten under the surface, and disconcert you by refusing to come out of the water.

Do not jerk in any of your movements, though the latter part of a pull should be very strong.

It is preferable, when starting for a few hours of sculling, that you should go against the current first. You will find the return easier, with the assistance of the stream when you are tired. If other boats are about, observe the rules of the water. A boat going against the current or tide keeps by the bank or shore when passing another craft: a boat going with tide or current keeps in midstream, and so inside all boats which it meets. Row boats give way to sailing boats, and an overtaking row boat must give way in order to pass another row boat which is going in the same direction. In crossing a stream try not to intercept boats travelling up or down. Remember that punts need shallow water, and be prepared to give way in order that they may not be forced into the deep.

Sailing.—In beginning your sailing experience choose a short, broad boat, of a size and build that you can row easily if wind should drop.

First you should be familiar with a few terms.

Boom, the lower spar on a sail.

Tack, the rope which ties the sail to the bottom of the mast. The word has other meanings too.

Sheet, a rope fastened to the free end of the boom. The sheet must be held in the hand in the small boat; to tie it to anything is exceedingly dangerous, for this would prevent the sail being moved with perfect freedom.

Halyard, a rope running over a pulley or block near the top of the mast, by which the sail can be raised or lowered.

Lugsail, the simplest sort of sail—the best with which to learn how to sail a boat.

Yard, the top spar of a lugsail.

Starboard, the side of the boat on your right hand as you sit in the stern and look forward.

Port, the side on your left hand.

Weather and *lee* are more often used in connexion with small boats than port and starboard.

On a calm day, when you have cleared the shore, you may put up your lugsail by standing in the boat and lifting the yard up with sail attached. But, when windy, it will not be safe to do this and you should hook the top of the sail to the yard and then haul it up into position by the halyard, securing the rope by a twist round the hook at the bottom of the mast. When the sail is right up, the end of the boom must be hooked into the metal eye which is also at the bottom of the mast. You will see that the tack hangs from the lower corner of the sail. This must finally be laced through each loop and secured to the mast.

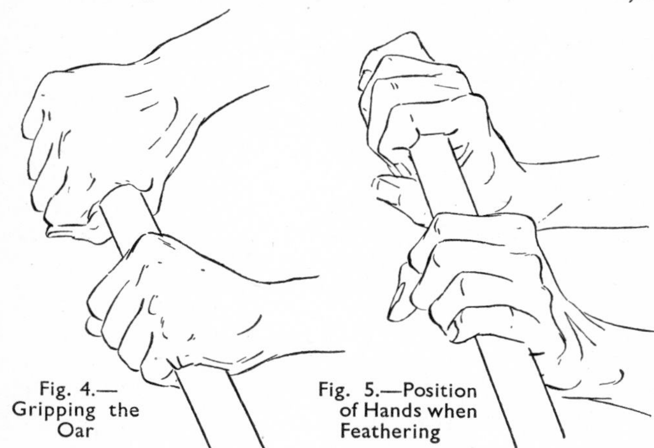

Fig. 4.—Gripping the Oar

Fig. 5.—Position of Hands when Feathering

Tacking.—With a wind behind a boat can travel forward with the sail out so that full advantage is taken of the breeze. But the wind is not always behind, and when it is necessary to sail into the wind the boat must *tack*, or take a zigzag course.

When being carried along before the breeze do not be lulled into carelessness. A sudden gust may swing the sail back, and you must be alert to catch the boom as it comes above your head. The sheet must be constantly in your hand. To run to land with the wind you may lower your sail at a suitable distance, and so run in on to the shelving beach; but in landing at a jetty or similar place you should run on a short way to right or left, then turn your boat so that the sail flaps and the bows are pointed into the wind. This will check you.

In sailing against the wind the position of the ballast, which keeps the boat well down in the water, is important; it may be necessary to move it. Also you yourself must be prepared to move to adjust balance, for the boat will not remain on an even keel.

To start into the wind seat yourself on the windward side of the stern—that is in the direction from which the wind blows, and pull in the sheet. As the sail comes towards you the boat will begin to move. Providing the boat glides on smoothly all will be well, but if she swings round and the sail flaps you must put her across the wind again by the rudder. Probably the ballast will need moving too, for you must aim to have the boat so balanced that it keeps on the desired course with scarcely any use of the rudder—the rudder obviously acts as a drag. See that the wind takes the sail well in the middle; if the bulge is close to the mast you should use the rudder to put the boat a little more "off the wind."

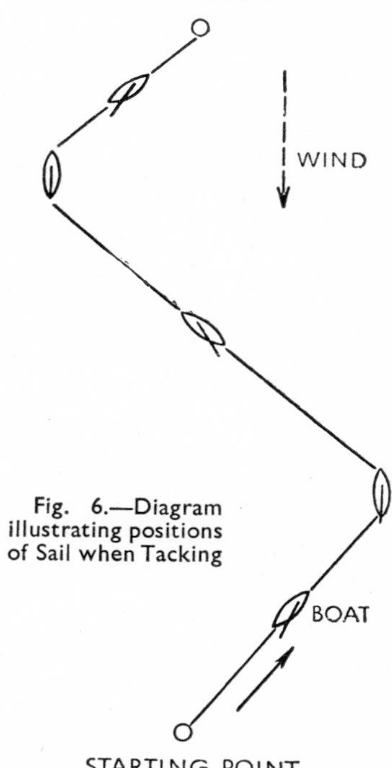

Fig. 6.—Diagram illustrating positions of Sail when Tacking

Having in your mind to go to a certain spot, against the wind, you will naturally plan your zigzag course so that you sail from side to side a convenient distance. When you have reached the end of one tack your position and that of the sail are reversed, and the boat thus slants across in the opposite direction.

In any trouble head your boat into the wind, and remember particularly to be ready to loosen your sheet.

An hour in a sailing boat, with an experienced sailor, will teach you more than any amount of reading. Start with a simple lugsail so that you are not overwhelmed with technicalities and complicating factors.

Experiment yourself cautiously, under the eye of a companion who can point out faults, and prevent serious consequences from them.

And be sure that you can swim. This should be understood before you do any sort of boating, but especially for sailing.

BOOKBINDING

This section is intended to show you how you can put your paper-backed books into better and more substantial covers, and how to bind together the serial parts of volumes issued periodically.

Materials.—The materials are fairly easily obtained. They consist of strawboard or cardboard or millboard, cartridge or other plain white paper, paste, glue, thin paper for repairing, bookbinders' cloth, coloured papers for covering the boards, tape and bookbinding cord, mull or bookbinders' muslin. Millboard is a dark brownish-grey board used for boards on good books. It is very hard and tough and is more expensive than strawboard. Cardboard boxes can be cut up for this work and used instead of sheet strawboard. If a board is not thick enough, glue or paste together two or more thicknesses, but be careful that they do not wrinkle or warp.

Ordinary cheap cartridge paper is necessary for end-papers for making small books, and for decorating.

Any home-made paste can be used for this work, but it must be thick and not too wet so as to avoid soaking the cloth or leather and spoiling it. Carpenters' glue, or almost any prepared glue will serve the purpose for stronger work.

Bookbinders' cloth can be obtained in a great variety of colours, textures and qualities. There are good cloths to be obtained at 9d. per yard, while very good material can be bought at prices up to about 2s. 6d. per square yard. Avoid papers which masquerade as cloths and cloths which pretend to be leathers. All this patterning on the surface of cloth makes it more difficult to handle with paste. Goatskin is by far the best leather for bookbinding. Avoid patterned leathers. Any reputable firm will send you the real morocco on request.

Brown papers of various shades, blue, buff, orange, dark red, green and grey papers are most useful. They can be used in the production of coloured cover papers, decorated by marbling or paste-coloured papers or hand painted in pattern. Many other odd materials will be found useful at times; such stuff as hessian, calico, linen, cretonne, crash, Doric cloth and so on might be found just right for the character of a special book.

Tools and Apparatus.—Essential tools are a cutting or lying press for pressing books while the backs are being rounded and for holding them while being cut (*see* Fig. 1); backing and cutting boards for use in the press (*see* Figs. 2 and 3); sewing frames or presses in which the sections of the books are sewn on to the cords or tapes (*see* Figs. 4 and 6); scissors, knife, non-slip metal ruler (*see* Fig. 5). Glue pot, brushes, set-square, backing hammer, a small tenon saw and large darning needles are also required.

The Operations.—Beginning with what is known as a single-section book, i.e. a book similar to that shown in Fig. 7. This may have a paper cover which you may wish to renew. The operations are as follows:

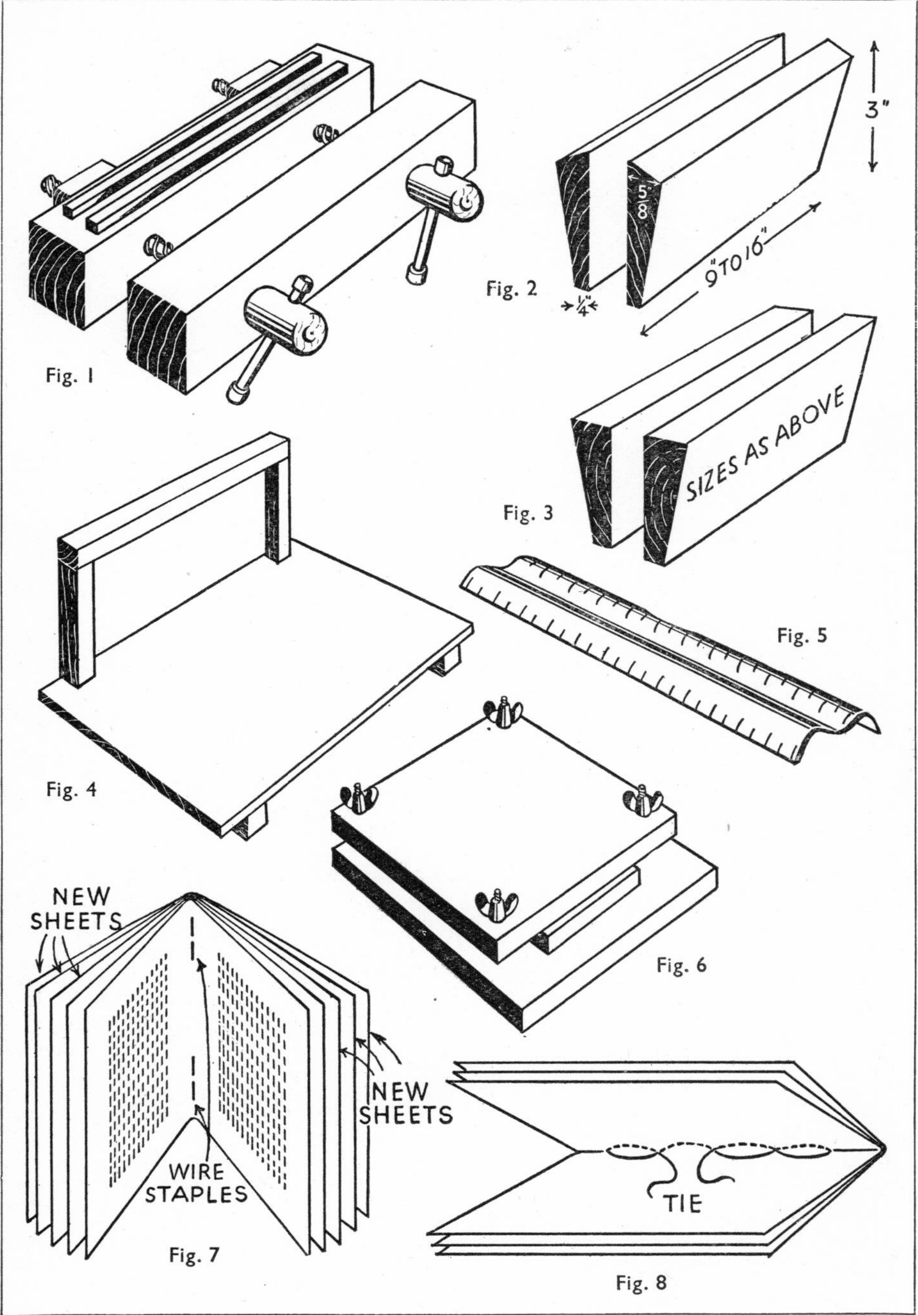

BOOKBINDING TOOLS

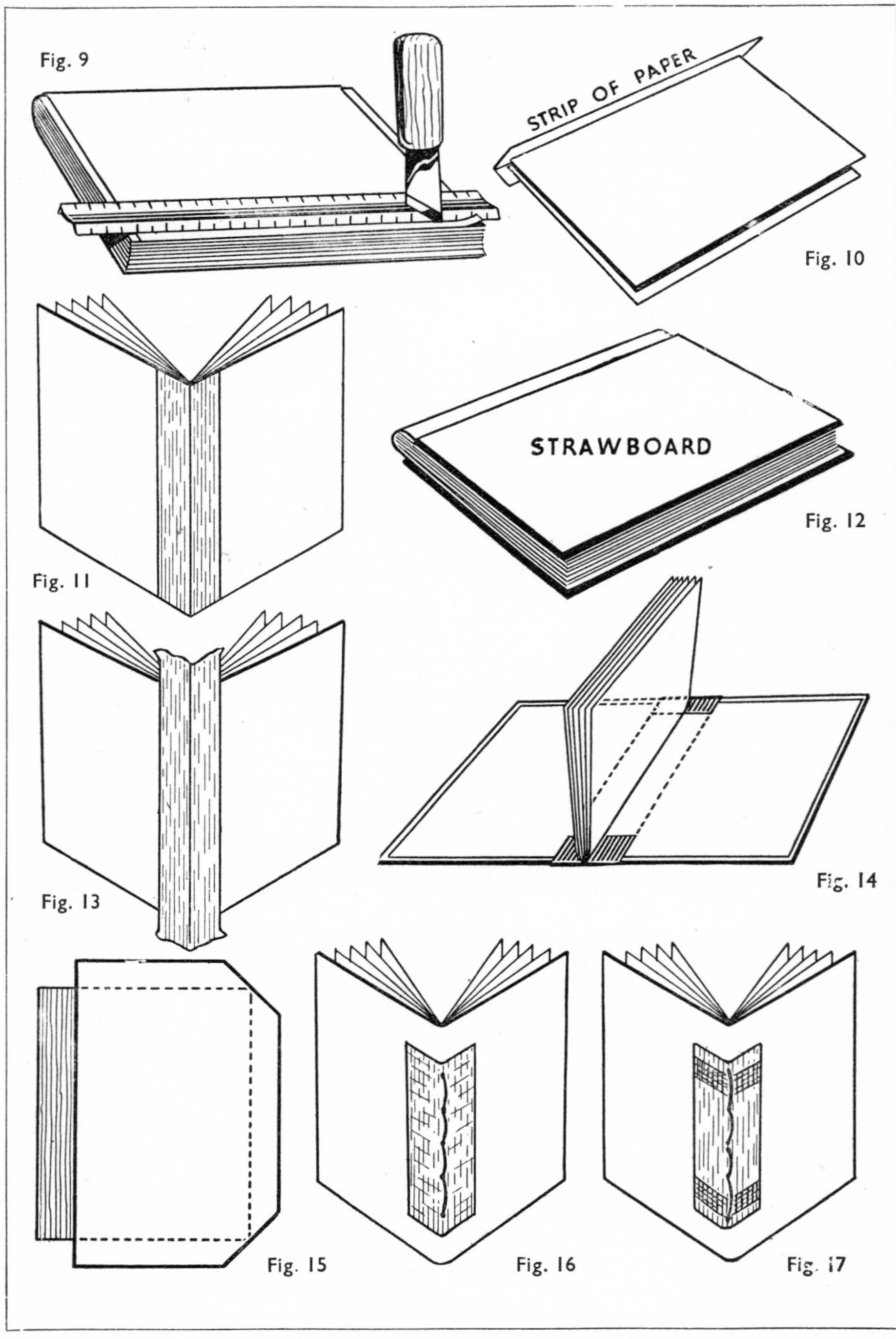
Fig. 9
STRIP OF PAPER
Fig. 10
Fig. 11
STRAWBOARD
Fig. 12
Fig. 13
Fig. 14
Fig. 15
Fig. 16
Fig. 17

Remove the old cover, do *not* cut the stitches or take out the staples at this stage. Cut three sheets of white paper the same dimension as the height of the book and about $\frac{1}{4}$ in. longer when it is opened out. Fold the sheets in the middle and place them on the back of the book as in Fig. 7. Sew the book and sheets together with four stitches of white thread as in Fig. 8. Now remove the wire staples by lifting the ends and drawing them out with the point of the scissors through the back underneath the end papers, or cut the old stitches and remove them. Open the book out flat, back upwards, paste on a piece of plain coloured or decorated paper, fold the book, turn out old folded corners of leaves and leave to set. Clean the edges by cutting them with the knife and ruler as shown in Fig. 9 to give clean, square edges.

Repairing Damaged Leaves.—Perhaps some of the leaves are torn apart for some distance up or down the back so that they cannot hold the stitches and must be repaired. Take out the damaged leaves. Use thin typewriting paper for repairing. Cut narrow strips $\frac{1}{2}$ in. wide, a little longer than the book. Fold the strips down the middle and unfold again. Lay them out and paste one side. Put on to the back of the book as in Fig. 10. Repair all damaged leaves in this way, replace in position in the book and then proceed as previously described.

Other Methods of Covering the Book.—The following method gives a stronger back to the book. When the book is stitched and the old stitches or wire staples have been removed, take a piece of book cloth about 2 in. wide and the same height as the book. Paste it on the inside and stick it on the back of the book as in Fig. 11. Then take a piece of coloured paper and cover the remainder of each cover, overlapping on to the cloth no more than $\frac{1}{16}$ in. Then cut the edges as before.

Another method is to put on a whole binding in cloth instead of in paper.

Stiff Covers.—To put the book into stiff covers. Stitch up the book and end-papers as before and cut the edges. Prepare two pieces of strawboard $\frac{1}{4}$ in. longer than the book and $\frac{1}{8}$ in. narrower. Paste these in position as shown in Fig. 12, allowing $\frac{1}{8}$-in. margin at the top, bottom and front edges, thus leaving a margin at the hinge on the back of $\frac{1}{4}$ in.

Now take a piece of book cloth or leather, 1 in. or $1\frac{1}{2}$ in. longer than the book and about 2 in. or $2\frac{1}{2}$ in. wide, paste it and place it on the back of the book as in Fig. 13. Rub it well down on the latter with a bone folder and then turn in the top and bottom as shown in Fig. 14. The folder is flat, about 9 in. long by 1 in. with a rounded end. The cover paper is cut and laid in position as shown in Fig. 15 and the edges are turned in on to the inside of the cover. Paste the end-paper and lay the cover down on to it, so as to finish neatly the inside of the book.

The backs of these single-section books can be further strengthened by the addition of a strip of book muslin about $1\frac{1}{2}$ in. wide and a little shorter than the book. This is sewn in with the leaves and end-papers as shown in Fig. 16 and is then stuck down to the outside paper before the covering cloth or boards are put on. Further strength can be added by the insertion of two pieces of $\frac{1}{2}$-in. tape, about 2 in. long. Pass the tapes underneath the stitches as shown in Fig. 17.

Half-bound Books.—The methods of covering the backs which have just been described are known as quarter-binding. Half-binding consists of the addition of corners of cloth or of leather after the back has been covered. Fig. 18 shows the shape of the piece of cloth or leather which is cut to fit on each of the four corners. Fig. 19 shows it in position. Fig. 19 also shows the method of obtaining the exact shape and size of the cover paper. The end-papers are then pasted back as described above.

Split Boards.—Another method of fixing the boards so that the tapes and muslin are hidden is shown in Fig. 20. The boards are made of two thicknesses of strawboard.

Finishing the Cover.—When rebinding books do not discard the old paper covers until it has been decided whether the title can be cut out and stuck on to

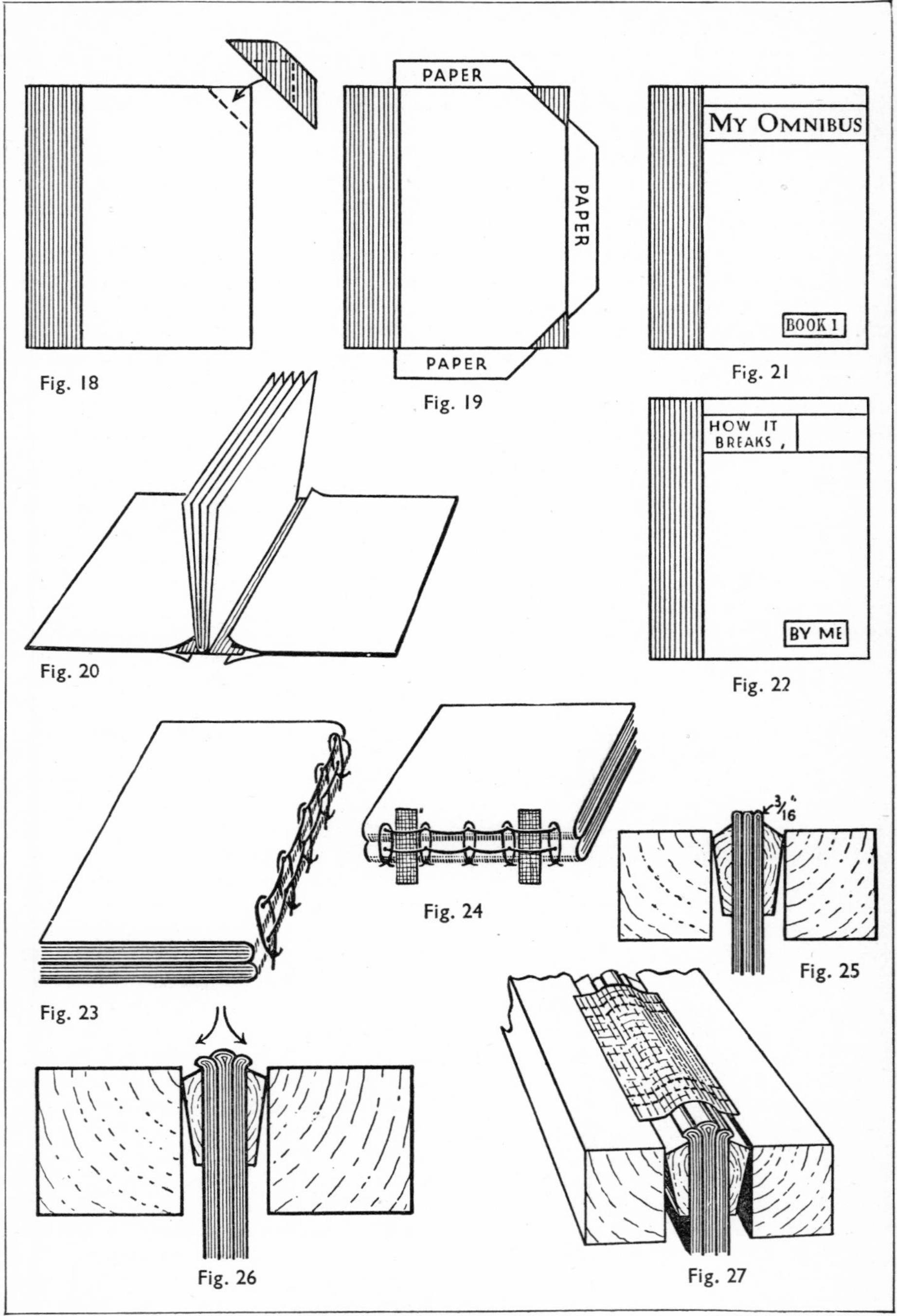

Fig. 18

Fig. 19

Fig. 20

Fig. 21

Fig. 22

Fig. 23

Fig. 24

Fig. 25

Fig. 26

Fig. 27

the cover as a useful panel of decoration. It may be possible to use it in several ways as shown in Figs. 21 and 22.

Two- and Three-section Books.—Small books containing two or three sections can be sewn together without the aid of a sewing frame and they can be cut with a knife and ruler as described for the single-section book. A press is necessary when gluing the back. Fig. 23 shows two sections or two single-section books, each sewn as previously described, being fixed together by tying the stitches with a separate thread at five points in the sewing. A stronger method is shown in Fig. 24 where pieces of tape are enclosed in the stitches, or inserted afterwards. Allow about 1½ in. of tape to project on each side of the book.

Ready for the Press.—The book is now ready for the press where the back is held tightly in position while it is shaped, glued, muslin put on and allowed to set. Pairs of backing boards are necessary for this operation. These backing boards should be made of fine-grained wood such as birch or beech. The boards are placed one on each side of the book about $\frac{3}{16}$ in. from the fold as shown in Fig. 25. Screw up the press fairly tightly, paint the back with hot glue, which is rubbed well into the spaces between the sections. Screw up the press as tightly as possible. Use the fingers for rubbing. Leave the glue for about twenty minutes until it is just *not* sticky to the fingers.

Shape the back by hammering it in the direction shown in Fig. 26. A cheap cobbler's hammer is useful for this work. The aim of hammering is to form a good flattish convex curve on the back. After hammering, brush on another layer of thin hot glue and lay on it a piece of book muslin, or mull, projecting about 1 in. on each side of the book and a little shorter than the latter as shown in Fig. 27. Rub the glue up through the muslin and enmesh it thoroughly and leave to set for at least twelve hours. Then take the book out of the press and get it ready for cutting.

Cutting.—This may be done as described with the aid of a knife and ruler. Or it may be better to use a press. Fig. 6 shows a simple press which can be used with a knife. It is made from pieces of thick plywood and four ¼-in. or ⅜-in. bolts with wing nuts. Another press is shown in Fig. 1. This is made from a pair of wood bench screws and two pieces of beech about 2 ft. 6 in. long by 4 in. by 3 in. A chisel will do for cutting. Fix the book in the press as shown in Fig. 28 with a wooden board or a piece of stiff cardboard behind it. Cutting boards shown in Fig. 3 may be used instead and they do help in concentrating pressure at the edge of the book should they be where the cutter is to be applied. The amount cut off the book should be as little as possible but the edge must be set so high that every leaf is cut to produce a perfectly clean edge. Fig. 28 shows how the chisel is applied. It is moved forward to cut on one corner only. The chisel must be perfectly sharp and kept quite flat on the top of the press when cutting. If the angle of inclination of the cutting edge is more than 80° the edge of the book will be torn and spoiled. Fig. 28 shows the fore edge being cut. When this has been done take the book out of the press and fix it up again with one of the other two edges upwards. More books are spoiled at this stage than at any other. Remember that there is a projecting ridge on each side of the back of the book. This must be retained and the danger is that it will now be crushed down in the press. To avoid this pack up the sides of the book with cardboard so that the depression is filled and the ridge is clear of the sides of the press. Set the top edge of this packing cardboard to the line to which the book is to be cut. That which is put in on the far side of the book should project above the edge. The appearance will be as in Fig. 29. Now cut the top edge, take out, re-set the cardboards, fix in the press and cut the bottom edge.

Fixing the Boards.—The covering boards may be fixed as described for the single section book or split boards may be used. For very small books two pieces of thin cardboard may be strong enough, for larger books one piece of strawboard $\frac{1}{16}$ in. thick and one piece of manilla or thin card,

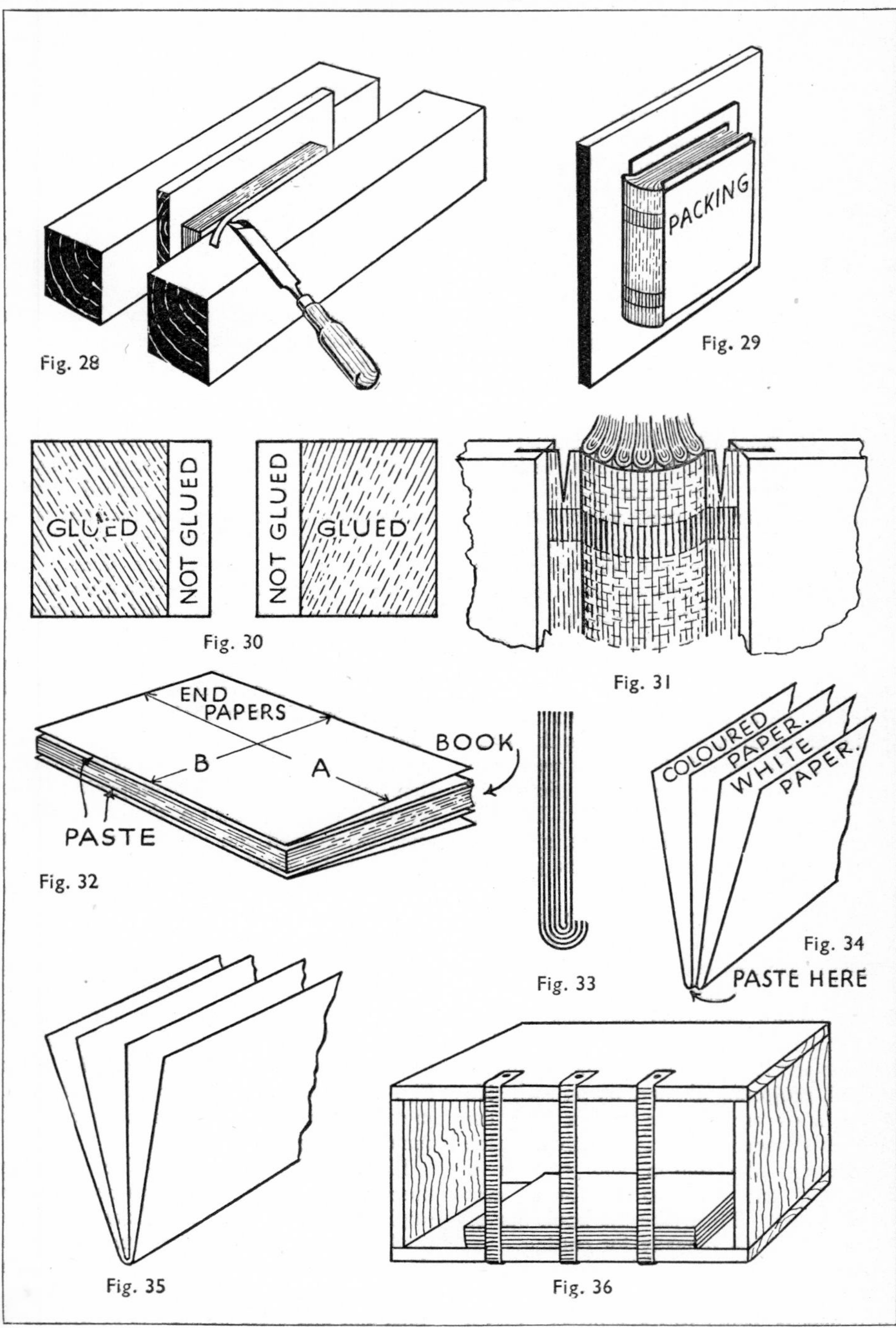

Fig. 28

Fig. 29

Fig. 30

Fig. 31

Fig. 32

Fig. 33

Fig. 34

Fig. 35

Fig. 36

and for large books two pieces of board $\frac{1}{16}$ in. thick may be all right. Cut to size, paste or glue them as shown in Fig. 30, leaving 1 in. unpasted. Make a pair of these. The muslin and tapes on the sides of the books have been stuck down to the end papers and trimmed off with the latter to about 1 in. wide. Now open the edges of the boards and paste inside. Open this edge a little more and insert the muslin, etc., as in Fig. 20, on both sides. Leave to set under flat pressure.

Covering the Back with Cloth or Leather.—Prepare the cloth or leather to

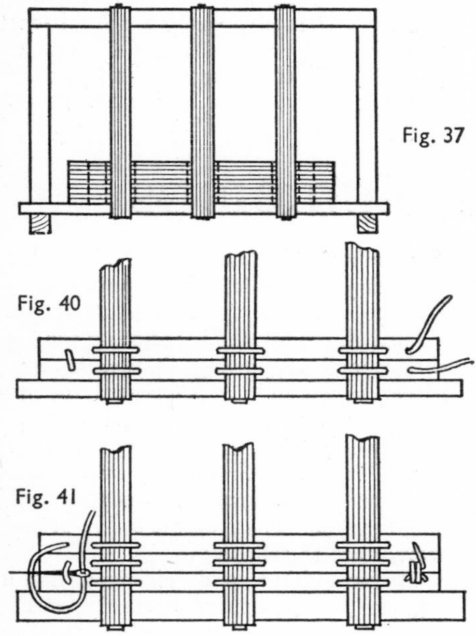

Fig. 37

Fig. 40

Fig. 41

be used for covering the back and corners for a half-bound book as previously described. In fixing the cloth on the boards and back of this book it is not possible to turn it in at the head and tail unless the muslin is about $\frac{3}{4}$ in. shorter than the boards at each end or unless the joint in the muslin is cut on both sides at the top and bottom of the book as in Fig. 31. When this is done the cloth is turned in by passing it through the slits and on to the back of the book and out on the inside of the boards as in Fig. 14.

The next stages follow as previously described for half-binding: put on the cloth or leather corners, cut and fit the covering papers, and then paste the end papers to fix them on to the boards, finishing all off neatly inside. When doing the latter operation the cover should be laid down on to the pasted surface; the end papers should not be lifted up to the cover. If the latter is done an ugly fold will be formed in the paper near the hinge.

End Papers.—You will need end papers for the beginning and end of the book. These may be made in several ways. Fig.

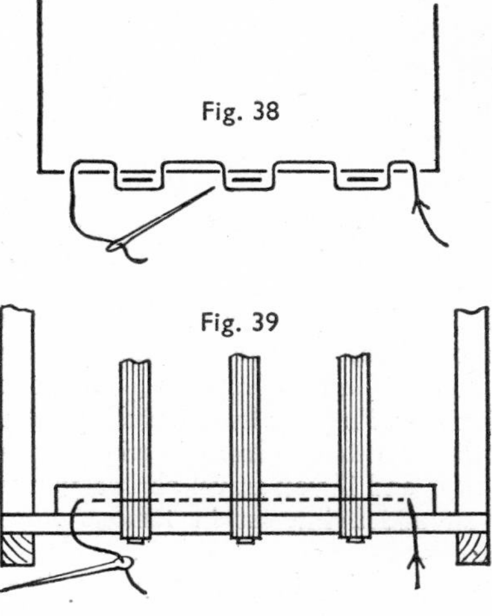

Fig. 38

Fig. 39

33 shows three sheets of white paper in size equal to the height of the book and about $\frac{1}{2}$ in. wider to allow for the fold over the back of the first and the last sections. These sheets are sewn in with the sections. Other simple methods are shown in Figs. 34 and 35.

Sewing Frames.—Figs. 4 and 36 show simple forms of sewing frame which are easily made.

Arranging the Tapes.—The position of the outside tapes is fixed by measuring about $1\frac{1}{4}$ in. from the head and about $1\frac{1}{2}$ in. from the tail of the book. Then space the other tapes equally between these two as shown in Fig. 37. Fix the tapes with drawing pins. The position of the kettle or catching stitch is fixed midway between the end of the book and the edge of the tape at each end.

Place the sections on the sewing frame as in Fig. 37 and mark off the position of the tapes in pencil on the back.

Now put back the first end-paper and begin to sew. Keep all the sections in order. Take a No. 4 darning needle and a yard of linen thread. The plan of the line of sewing is shown in Figs. 38 and 39. When sewing in this direction half the leaves of the section are lifted and held up by the left hand which also receives the needle as it is pushed through the fold of the section and pushes it back again on the right-hand side of each tape. The sewing of the first section being completed, add the second one, i.e. the first section of the text, place it title page down and head to the right hand and sew it in, working from left to right, as in Fig. 40. Tie the ends of the thread together again, retain the length in the needle and add the third section, to be sewn in as the first.

Kettle Stitch.—When the left-hand end of this section is reached the "kettle" or "catch" stitch is necessary to fix it firmly to the previous sections. This stitch is made in exactly the same way as the button-hole stitch as shown in Fig. 41. Pull the stitch taut and repeat it so as to fix it securely. Carry on in this way until all the sections and the second paper are fixed. Cut the tapes about 2 in. above the book.

The book is now ready for the back to be glued and rounded and the edges cut. Then follows the fixing of the boards and covering with cloth or leather and paper.

LOOKING AT BUILDINGS

THE world becomes immediately a much more interesting place when you take the study of architecture as your hobby. Beginning with your local church your eye will discover fresh charm in village, town and city; and if you travel abroad you will find an added interest in famous foreign buildings.

In this restricted space it is impossible to do more than outline the principal styles—in the hope that appetite may be whetted for fuller studies.

Greek Architecture.—Architecture as we know it began with the Egyptians and the Greeks. The latter were a race with a highly developed sense of beauty, logical, appreciative of form and balance, and of great skill and craftsmanship.

For sheer beauty their buildings have never been excelled. Many to-day consider that the Parthenon, the temple of Athena standing on the Acropolis of Athens, is the most lovely building the world has seen. Most museums have a model of it, and at the British Museum the Elgin Marbles—fragments rescued after war had devastated the Parthenon—can be seen.

The Greek temple was usually in the shape of a simple rectangle, but of wonderful symmetry. Simplicity and dignity were the keynotes. Regularly spaced stone columns formed the outer sides, enclosing the inner shrines and supporting the *entablature* or block, which in turn supported the roof. The entablature had three parts: *architrave*, the lowest; *frieze*, the middle; *cornice*, the top. From the Greeks we have derived the types of columns with the corresponding entablatures. These classic *orders* of architecture are as follows:

Doric—oldest and plainest; has no separate base; broad and sturdy; shallow flutings; plain, outward sloping top surmounted by square slab. The Doric entablature consists of *triglyphs*, or three-grooved tablets, at intervals along a plain or carved frieze.

Ionic—more slender, with narrower, deeper flutings; ram's horn "curls" at the top, so that the side view differs from the front. The entablature has continuous carving for its frieze, instead of the squared sections of the Doric.

Corinthian base and flutings like Ionic; capital consists of flat slab resting on clustered foliage of the acanthus or

Greek thistle. Entablature, like the Ionic, has no squared sections breaking up the frieze.

Roman Architecture.—The Romans made use of many new constructional devices—the arch, the dome, and rubble bound together into a kind of concrete instead of merely solid blocks of stone or marble. The Greek orders were used principally for decorative purposes. Whereas a Greek column had always been made to support something, the Romans used it merely to give an air of dignity even though it was structurally superfluous. The Romans favoured circular buildings, and built many triumphal arches and commemorative columns; they were less concerned about pure style than the Greeks, and the famous Colosseum contains Doric, Ionic and Corinthian columns more or less indiscriminately. They were master builders, making colossal aqueducts running over huge round-topped arches, great bridges, massive open-air theatres, roads of masonry, and so on.

Famous examples of Roman architecture abound in Rome—Pantheon, Temple of Vesta, Arches of Severus and Constantine, Trajan Column, and Forum. Italy and southern France have many notable examples, and the enduring strength of the Roman work may be seen in our own country, where Hadrian's Wall still runs for miles over the northern moorland.

Byzantine Architecture. — When Constantinople became the capital of the Roman Empire, the name of the city was Byzantium. From here developed a new style of building called Byzantine, best exemplified by the wonderful church of Santa Sophia—a combination of many domes, with complete absence of the familiar columns. The domes were supported by arches and piers, or built-up masses of masonry which allowed the domes to cover square buildings instead of only circular, as in the earlier Pantheon. Colour, too, came into the buildings—the great dome of Santa Sophia was gilded. Saint Mark's of Venice is another wonderful example—a wealth of coloured stones and mosaics covering every visible part of it. Westminster Cathedral is a more modern example of Byzantine influence.

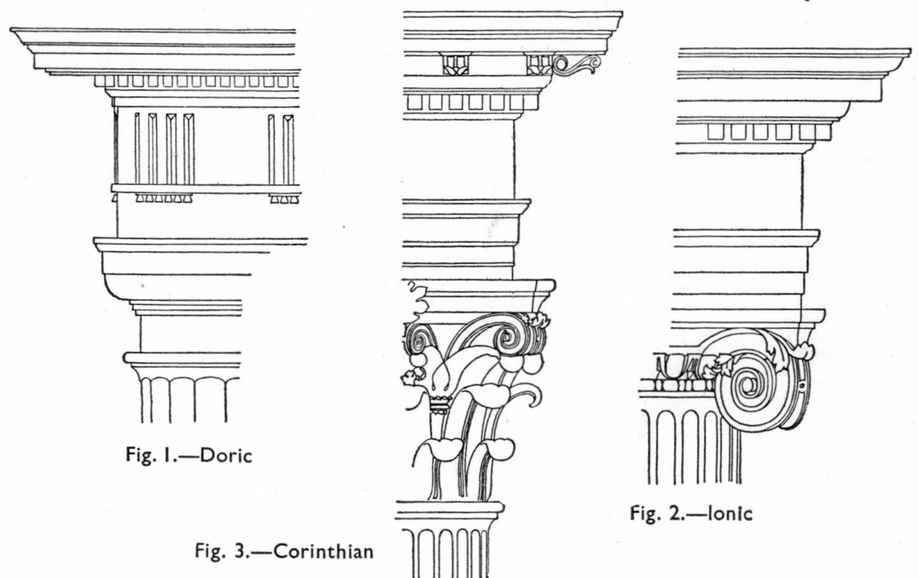

Fig. 1.—Doric

Fig. 2.—Ionic

Fig. 3.—Corinthian

THE CLASSIC ORDERS OF ARCHITECTURE

Romanesque Architecture.—With the Roman domination extending across Europe, Roman ideas of architecture naturally spread too. But these ideas did not remain in their original form; they were assimilated, modified, adapted by the various peoples, and so there at last emerged widely different types based on the same foundations. These adaptations are termed Romanesque.

Some of their difference is due to the influence of northern or Teutonic ideas which became merged with the original Roman and so gave birth to something new.

The Romanesque retains the round column and the round arch of the Romans,

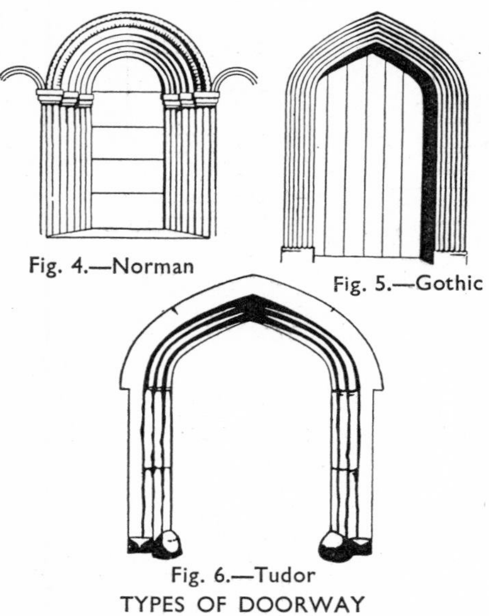

Fig. 4.—Norman

Fig. 5.—Gothic

Fig. 6.—Tudor

TYPES OF DOORWAY

but it introduced the Christian cross-shaped church by adding the transept to the plain basilica of the Romans. Then the chancel was added, and the original simple rectangle began to offer increasing scope for elaboration of interior ornament.

Later Romanesque, increasingly influenced by rude forces of the north, shows evidence of the Teutons in quaint decorations, grotesque pieces of ornamental sculpture, and conspicuously by towers. Towers were of two main kinds—those for military purposes, and bell towers for churches. These latter were especially developed in Italy, where they grew up as structures standing by but separate from the churches. Two of the most beautiful specimens are Giotto's Tower of Florence and the Venetian Campanile.

Norman Architecture.—The English form of Romanesque is the familiar Norman, and one of the best-known examples is the Chapel in the Tower of London. Durham and Carlisle Cathedrals are notable too. In these are the characteristic Norman features—round arches; massive pillars, piers, walls; small windows; deep door recesses and considerable decoration.

The early Norman had plain exteriors. Gradually decoration inside and outside grew more elaborate; massiveness gave way to lightness; and the beginnings of a new style appeared—the Gothic.

Gothic Architecture.—The Goths who swept down Europe had in their architecture memories of their wild forests, and so their buildings soared like forest trees. Instead of the plain single column of Rome, the Gothic builders substituted clustered columns—like a group of tree stems standing together. The clustered column is typical of Gothic; still more so is the pointed arch. The pointed arch came into use as the solution of the vaulting problem, to get arches of equal height over varying spans, which had been impossible with round arches. It was not just an idea for a new shape, but the underlying structural motive of Gothic architecture.

Not merely was the rounded arch of Rome pushed upwards to a point, but a gable was frequently added above it to give additional emphasis. Often, in churches, these gables were ornamented with little crooks or crockets.

Stonework became finer and more fretted. Leaf-shaped and traceried windows began to appear, of increasingly intricate design, and soon coloured glass began to fill them.

Interior roofs became vaulted and complex, with more and more elaborate ribs and spokes—like the many-branched natural vault of forest trees. And, because of height and lightness, buttresses and flying buttresses came to be built, and from being merely utilitarian grew into things of beauty in themselves, with their accompaniments of gargoyles and decorations.

The soaring tendency of the pointed arch found another mode of expression in the spire, and great spires began to crown our Gothic churches and cathedrals.

Of Gothic cathedrals Europe has, fortunately, many lovely examples—Milan, Cologne, Rouen, Amiens and Salisbury. The more one explores such wonders in stone the more one appreciates their beauty and mystery. The Grecian temple had a symmetry of beauty that enthralled, because it was so obvious, so inescapable; Gothic beauty is romantic, wrapped in mystery. It makes one wonder.

Renaissance Architecture.—When Europe rediscovered classic learning and art she rediscovered Greek and Roman architecture too, and so came a rebirth of the old styles—but interpreted now in the light of experience gained in the intervening centuries.

The horizontal rather than the vertical are again emphasized; Doric, Ionic and Corinthian orders appear, with the rounded arch; domes replace towers, and severity and proportion are to the front instead of the luxuriance of Gothic. Often Renaissance buildings became merely dull and uninspired in their imitative accuracy. Some, on the contrary, were confused medleys of Classic and Gothic.

A few of the characteristics recognizable in many Renaissance buildings are: high and large column; rusticated masonry—sunk joints which mark out regularly sized slabs, with roughened surface; rounded window tops; heavy cornices, with statuary on the projecting ledges; balustrades; such ornaments as festoons of flowers and fruit, musical instruments, shields, scrolls, heads of cupids and lions.

The two best-known examples of Renaissance work, showing this period at its best, are St. Peter's of Rome and St. Paul's of London. Paris also has its Pantheon.

English Architecture. — The main trends of architecture so far touched on have been reflected in most European countries, but in each there have been individual developments. It will be helpful to consider very briefly the main course of change in this country.

Study of Churches.—By far the best idea of the development of architecture can be obtained from a study of your own parish church, if this is at all an ancient one. Most

Fig. 7.—Architectural Styles

of the individual trends of English building have had their origin in church architecture.

Considered in its simplest form, the basis of all church construction is the rectangular nave, built out at the east end to form the chancel. When they wanted to increase the accommodation the builders cut arches through the sides of the nave, forming aisles to the north and south. Later, as the design became more and more fully developed, the chancel end of the nave was widened so that the building was shaped

Fig. 8.—The West Front of Salisbury Cathedral

like a cross, the short arms between nave and chancel being called the north and south transepts. To this were added from time to time the tower, at the west end; often a smaller chapel to the south of the chancel; perhaps a porch opening from the south aisle; and in modern times the vestry, leading from the chancel. (*See* Fig. 9.)

The Four Earlier Types of Architecture are usually to be found in the older country churches. You can recognize the *Norman* style—approximately 1050–1200—by its massive, solid workmanship; square towers; rounded arches and pillars; and narrow, round-headed windows. The ornament was often of the simple zigzag type. The *Early English* style which followed this period—1150–1300—was gradually developed from the Norman. Buttresses began to appear, and lancet windows, often grouped. Buildings, windows, vaultings, arches became lighter and higher, more acute than the Norman; spires were added; and the zigzag ornament was replaced by the more elaborate "dog-tooth" design.

Gradually, as the centuries advanced, the craftsmanship of the builders became more ambitious. During the *Decorated* period — 1250 – 1400, ornament, instead of being something merely added for decorative effect, became an integral part of the structure itself. You can see this striving after architectural pattern in the high, graceful arches of many churches of this period; in the larger, mullioned and traceried windows, the triple doorways grouped under one arch, and the more intricate vaulting. Crockets, carved and traceried roofs, and tiered buttresses with niches for statues, began to appear; and ornament became richer and more complicated.

The *Perpendicular* style—1350–1500 — was a further development of these Gothic tendencies

A NAVE CHANCEL

N W E S

B NORTH AISLE NAVE CHANCEL SOUTH AISLE

C NORTH TRANSEPT VESTRY NORTH AISLE PULPIT TOWER NAVE CHANCEL SOUTH AISLE SOUTH CHAPEL SOUTH PORCH SOUTH TRANSEPT

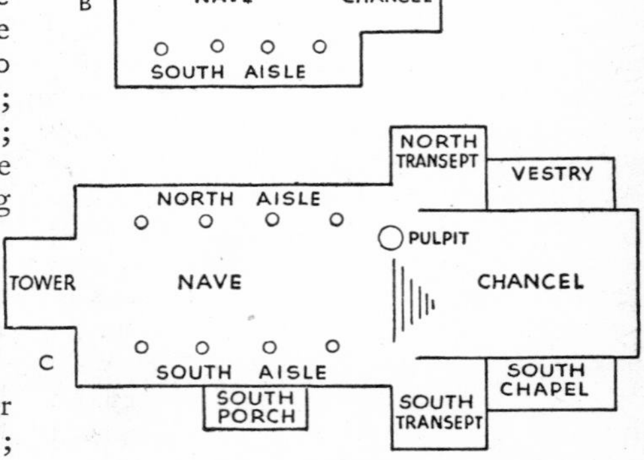

Fig. 9.—The Development of the Church

to lightness and delicacy. Perpendicular lines became very conspicuous in the square doorways and mullioned windows; piers were moulded in clustered shafts; walls were panelled in straight lines; and the lovely fanlike tracery of vaultings was more fully evolved. Thinning, tapering, panelling became more and more common in order to remove all appearance of heaviness. Ornament of this period is profuse; there is much carving of natural foliage, and of imaginative grotesques such as adorn many of the flying buttresses.

Church Window Development.—An interesting feature to trace when looking at churches is the development of the window; and this will, incidentally, give you many enlightening glimpses into the life and history of the times. The earliest type of window found in our English churches is the small, deep-set Saxon one, which was purposely made narrow for defensive reasons in an age when war was ever at hand. You will find the sides of "jambs" of these windows splayed—that is, narrowed as they approach the aperture—both inwards and outwards; and they are always round-headed.

In Norman times windows, though still round-headed, were splayed only on the inner side, and the opening was set very much nearer to the outside of the wall. As the transition to Gothic appeared, windows became more pointed and sometimes twin or triple windows were set close together and the dividing stonework replaced by a small column. But it is in the Early English period that the beginnings of what is called "fenestration" are seen—decorative grouping of windows beneath a central arch or hood. Narrow, pointed "lancet" windows now appeared, clustered under one main arch whose stonework was delicately patterned or "traced." "Plate" tracery—where a flat plate of stone was set between the two main windows and the third circular light—developed into "bar" tracery in which the stonework was cut out into narrow, bar-like shapes. Projecting ornamental points of stone, or "cusps," added to the decorative effect.

Stained Glass.—About this time the craft of painting glass was developing in England, and the masons were consequently adapting their work to the new fashion. Tracery became popular because it gave accommodation for the display of the glass. As stained-glass work became more ambitious, windows became larger and broader, the bars being fashioned in geometrical or flowing patterns, so that the effect of the windows of this period is one of great

Fig. 10.—A Tenth-century Church

Universal Pictorial Press

Fig. 11.—Hampton Court: A Renaissance Country House

richness and delicacy. In the later Decorated and Perpendicular periods they assumed still larger proportions; so extensive were they that the masons found it necessary to strengthen them both by upright bars (mullions) and by horizontal ones (transoms). This effect of squareness was still further enhanced by the flat hood of stonework which was fitted to the head of the window.

Vaulting. — One of the difficulties which the early builders had to contend with was that of roofing a large space such as the top of a church. Usually the roof was made of timber, but a stone ceiling was frequently desirable to protect the wood, and it was the problem of how to build this ceiling which gave to the world the beautiful forms of vaulting seen at their best in our English cathedrals—the builder's answer to the difficulty.

The first method experimented with was the simple "barrel" vault of the Normans—rather like a miniature railway tunnel. Later the discovery was made that by causing one vault to cut across another some very graceful effects could be obtained. In Early English times the ribs were built out to meet from side to side and diagonally, and also at the top or apex; and the possibilities for varied and beautiful patterns were still further increased by the addition of a number of short intermediary ribs between the main ones. Later, fan vaulting began to be elaborated, spreading out and supporting a flat ceiling composed of horizontal ribs; the upright ribs sprang from the wall in a circular manner, like the spokes of a wheel, giving the delicate effect best seen in Henry VII's Chapel at Westminster Abbey—the perfect example of fan vaulting. Pendants of stone suspended from a hidden arch, and supporting the fan vault, gave still another touch of beauty to this intricate stonework.

With the coming of the Tudors, experiments in stone roofing were largely replaced by experiments in timbering. This is the period of carved woodwork and of the hammer-beam roof sometimes seen in Tudor halls and country houses; and this brings us to another subject—the effect of the Renaissance upon English architecture.

Renaissance Architecture in England, from 1500.—Gothic architecture came to an end with the Tudors and the Renaissance properly began in the Elizabethan age. The influence of the Church and of the religious guilds, which had hitherto brought unity into architecture, gave way now to the demands of society and common life, and domestic architecture came to the fore, the corporate element in building being replaced by the personal, individual touch. The first great architects, Inigo Jones and Christopher Wren, were products of this era of individual building.

Country houses now made their appearance, built (like Hampton Court) of brick and timber, and decorated with external embellishments rather than structural features. Clustered chimneys are seen, elaborate plasterwork, carved timbers and curved, pointed or pinnacled gables.

In the seventeenth century appeared Inigo Jones, leading the way to a purer classicism. With his intimate knowledge of the best Italian architecture, he set before Renaissance builders the ideal of the building as a unit—perfect in itself, simple and unspoilt by alien tendencies. Christopher Wren (1632–1723) carried on the classical design; the severity and refinement of his work is best seen in his masterpiece, St. Paul's Cathedral.

Meanwhile houses, in keeping with the classic tradition, were becoming higher and flatter, with plain façades and balanced windows. To preserve this simplicity and yet to allow liberties of decoration was the task of the famous brothers Adam, who in the Georgian period built many of the stately houses to be seen in the neighbourhood of the Adelphi, London. Curves, alcoves and embowed windows were emphasized, giving the effect of lightness without departing from the old simple forms.

Some of the most beautifully proportioned rooms were constructed at this period, whose elegance seems to reflect the temperament of the age as distinctly as do the pages of a novel by Jane Austen or a Morland print.

Modern Trends in Architecture.—Following the Gothic revival of the later nineteenth century—of which the Houses of Parliament at Westminster are an out-

Fig. 12.—St. Paul's Cathedral

standing example—modern architecture is being shaped by new demands necessitating new methods of thinking. More attention now is given to service: buildings are planned for hygiene and utility; for labour-saving and economy of space; and to suit an age of machine production. Steel and concrete as building materials are encouraging simpler shapes; vertical planning is replacing horizontal where ground space is precious.

Architecture is again on the move. The student is likely to find his hobby of still more absorbing interest as new achievements come to light in the modern world.

CAMPING

NOWADAYS there are so many ways in which one may camp—hiking, cycling, motor-cycling, motoring, caravanning, boating. Not only may you choose from one of these types of "mobile" camps, but if you prefer to have things done for you, you may take a very inexpensive holiday in a "stationary" camp—there are many such, large and small, at the seaside and elsewhere, the holiday pages of papers and magazines advertise them. But healthy and pleasant as the life in these organized centres can be, to get the real thrill of camping you must do things for yourself.

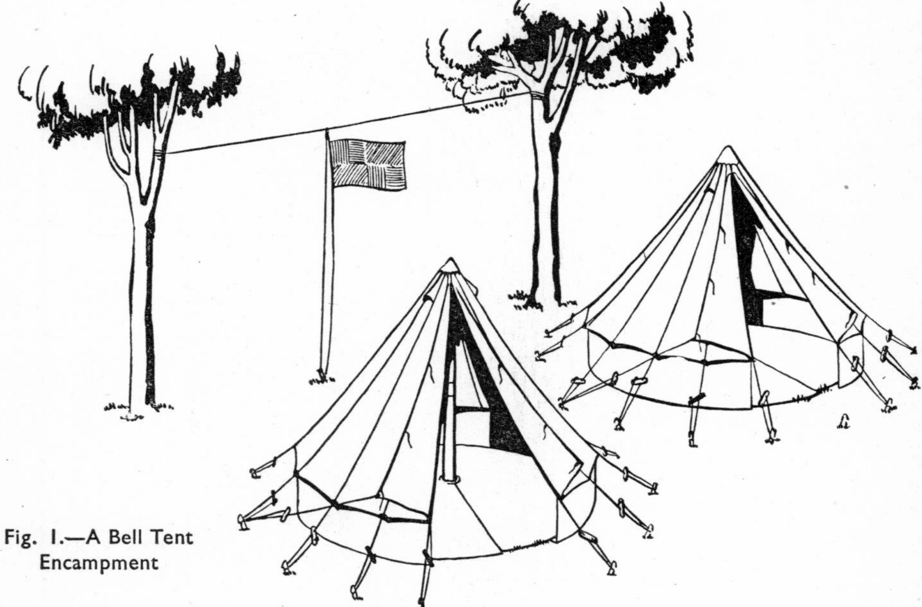

Fig. I.—A Bell Tent Encampment

The arrangements to be made can vary considerably. There is a vast difference in planning a "one night one site" cycling trip for yourself, and taking half a hundred boys into camp for a fortnight; but it is pretty certain that you cannot hope to do this latter successfully unless you have had some experience by yourself, or at any rate with just one or two companions. It is in the small camp where one acquires vital, first-hand knowledge. The general principles underlying any form of camping are, of course, pretty much the same.

Incidentally, if you do camp with a companion, choose the right person. Living closely together, day and night, sharing difficulties as well as pleasures, is a stern test of friendship.

It is important that you take all the things you are likely to need, but do not lumber yourself with non-essentials. Circumstances will determine the inclusion or exclusion of any extras, but the following should certainly not be missed.

The Tent.—The choice nowadays is almost illimitable, and you may buy one particularly adapted for your type of camping. (*See* Figs. 1–5.) Get good quality, then it may last almost a lifetime. Do not have it too small—it is better to carry a few extra ounces than to be cramped.

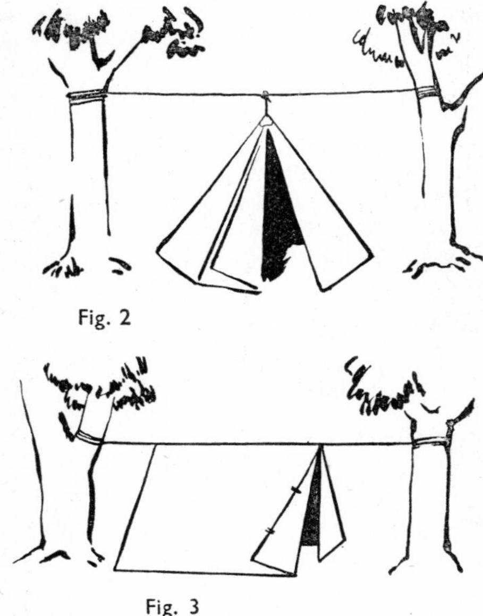

Fig. 2

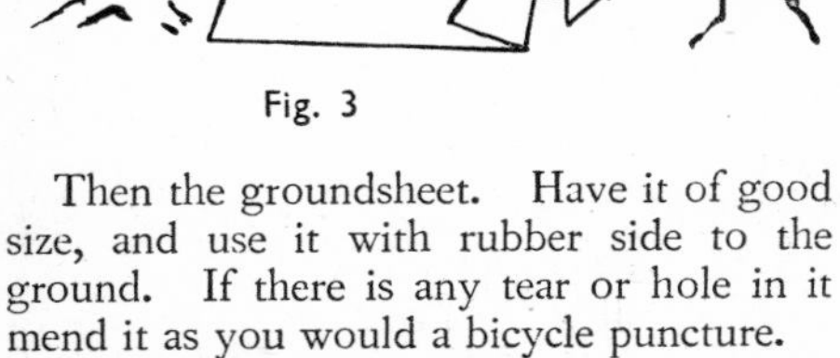

Fig. 3

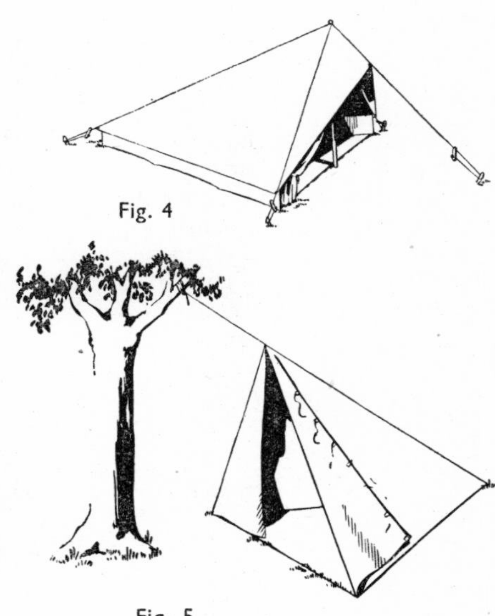

Fig. 4

Fig. 5

Then the groundsheet. Have it of good size, and use it with rubber side to the ground. If there is any tear or hole in it mend it as you would a bicycle puncture.

A Sleeping Bag is the cosiest way of sleeping. You may procure one warmly lined and waterproof at comparatively low price. See that it is big enough. It is a fairly simple matter to make such a bag. If you do not care to have one, then take two or even three blankets—do not think that one will be warm enough. And do not choose the hard, heavy kind; they may look and feel impressive but there is generally more warmth in the light, fluffy blanket. Whether you take a camp bed will depend on many things; certainly you will not want one if you are hiking or cycling. The bed is very comfortable, especially in a long-standing camp. Otherwise you may much reduce the hardness under your groundsheet by a layer of dry straw, leaves, bracken or heather.

A Billycan for food and cooking is necessary; and fork and spoon which may fit into it. Every camping shop has multitudes of gadgets, and it will pay you to make careful choice. Your knife should be of the strong folding variety. If it contains a few tools so much the better; certainly it should have a sturdy tin opener.

A Small Axe for wood chopping is most useful, for firewood and knocking in pegs. Of course there are many kinds of stoves and lamps available for cooking purposes, but they do not give the same enjoyment as an open fire.

Enamelled mug and plate; candles and matches, or a small, safe lantern; a canvas bucket, which collapses into little space, a trowel—all these should be included.

Clothes.—Your personal things may go into rucsac or kit-bag. Change of clothes, and an extra pair of strong shoes, perhaps with slippers or plimsols for actual camp use. Also pyjamas. Remember to allow for chilly nights. In an emergency you may slip on spare clothes over pyjamas. Warmth, however, depends a good deal on how a bed is made—there should be as much blanket underneath as on top, and feet should not escape from the blanket ends.

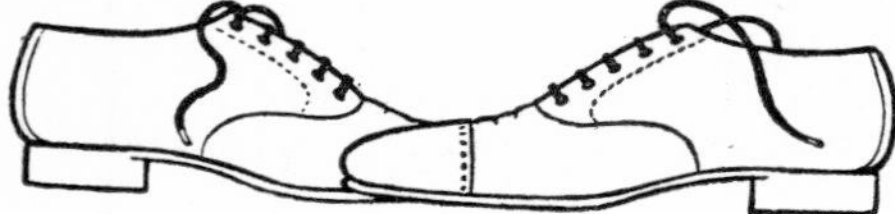

Fig. 6.—Arrange Shoes like this and cover with folded garment to form pillow

Providing they are dry, shoes can be used as a pillow, with a folded garment on top (*see* Fig. 6), or you may have rucsac or kit-bag. Do not use a damp towel for a pillow—some novices, tempted by the softness, develop neuralgia in this way.

Old clothes should be the rule if you would be comfortable—there is nothing to equal shoes, shorts, vest, when the weather is right. Have a mackintosh, too—a wet day loses half its terrors if you are prepared.

Toilet things need not be bulky—a towel, which will serve for bathing, too; soap; toothbrush; shaving kit; comb and brush; mirror made of metal. The Camping Club Handbook is useful as it gives details of lightweight kit for walker and cyclist with weight of full equipment.

A First-aid Outfit is essential. Details of this are given later. You may buy a well-packed tin from the chemist, or make up the outfit yourself.

Food.—Give a good deal of thought to your food. Camping helps appetite, so when catering allow for more than you would eat at home.

Other Equipment.—The remaining things will depend largely on the style of your camp. You may find that equipment like clothes-pegs, to attach to the pole, hanging shelves, wall pockets are worth while. You will need a few books. A football may be included, and some stationery. The following odds and ends will almost certainly be worth packing: a swim suit; shoe-cleaning materials; tea infuser or piece of muslin; some string; tenikoit ring for ring tennis; spare shoe laces; a few safety-pins; diary; pencil; housewife — containing buttons, needles, cotton and so on; a musical instrument—flute, mouth organ, violin, mandolin. But remember that campers must not make a nuisance of themselves to the district they are in! Should you happen to be in charge of a group of campers, especially young ones, one important extra is a wooden chest with a lock to it in which you can store stationery, stamps, medicines, and deposit, when necessary, money or valuables belonging to the others.

It is a good plan to read through a complete list like the foregoing, or one which you yourself have compiled, so that before setting out for camping you may check your things and ensure that nothing is missed.

The Site.—It is possible to obtain a list of camping grounds from railway companies, camping and other associations, and sometimes from local authorities. Recognized camping sites, particularly those available for motorists, usually involve some small fee. It is much more fun to find your own ground—the experienced camper learns to choose an ideal position merely by examination of a good map.

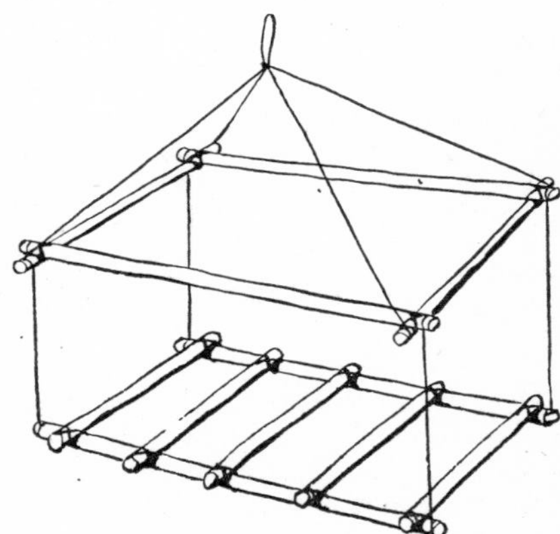

Fig. 7.—A Useful Hanging Shelf

When you have arrived at what seems a

suitable piece of ground, get permission to use it, and make careful enquiries about drinking water. It is important, too, that you shall get information about such things as firewood, fresh milk—perhaps fruit and vegetables, sanitary conveniences, bathing conditions.

Remember that if you are a good camper a farmer may be glad to see you; but the other sort of camper—who leaves gates undone, breaks hedges, pollutes water, spreads litter, disturbs cattle—is anathema.

Look round well before choosing the place for your tent. There are some spots which you should not choose—the foot of a slope, where water can drain in on you; the high, exposed place; the hollow, where water will collect during heavy rain; among thick, damp undergrowth; in a wood with sodden ground; or under a tree where lightning may be dangerous and where rain can drip unpleasantly. The best place is the crest of a gentle slope, covered with short grass, especially if it is sheltered by a wood or high hedge. The wood will be convenient for your fire. Water should be near, but not too near—you do not want flooding or moist ground, nor mosquitoes, which are generally attracted by water.

Notice the bend of the grass and bushes; this will help you in placing your tent, the mouth of which should be away from the prevailing wind. It is best to face south-east, but do not cut off light and air by being head-on to a near hedge. Remember that one of the pleasantest ways of spending leisure is to lie in your tent so that you have a clear view outside.

Pitching the Tent.—When you start to pitch your tent first lace it up, if it has lacings. Should there be one or more poles, get these upright and fix the main ropes, tent pegs slanting outwards, their notches towards the ground. Pegs should not be driven in too far at first, they may need altering. When a tent is fully stretched move pegs as needed, and tighten all down, so that the ropes pull squarely and are properly spaced. Now you may unlace the door—if you had put the tent up without fastening it, the door flaps would never have come together. Possibly you will need another couple of pegs for holding back the door flaps when you wish the tent to be fully opened.

Always make preparations against rain—you do not want to have to turn out for emergency measures when a heavy shower is on. It is a good plan to have a hole dug just beside a tent pole, so that if it rains you may drop the pole down several inches into the hole, thus slackening all the ropes together without need to go outside. Wet, of course, causes ropes to tighten, and if they are already taut pegs may pull out of the ground, especially as the ground itself becomes softened with the water.

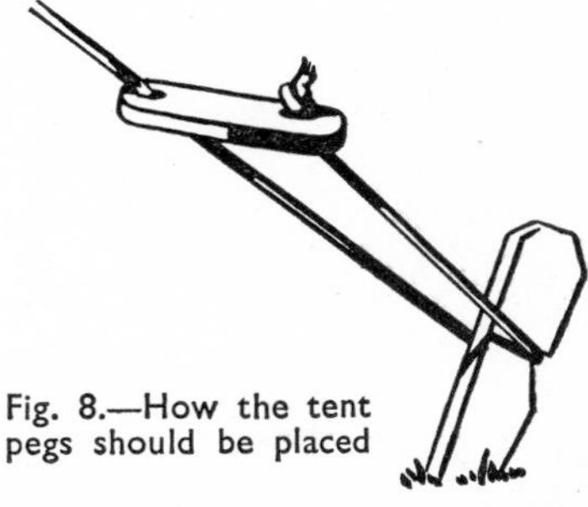

Fig. 8.—How the tent pegs should be placed

No bedding or kit should touch the side of the tent when it is raining, or water will drip through the canvas at that point. If you have such a drip, run your finger down from the spot to the bottom edge; this will take the drip down where it will be harmless. If you must turn out in rain wear no more than shoes and waterproof. You can then towel yourself dry—wet clothes in camp are a nuisance.

A trench around the tent is another valuable safeguard against wet. It should be about six inches out from the canvas. Make it at least three inches deep, and slope it so that the water drains away from the tent. Should your site lie on the side of a slope a horseshoe gully will serve, the deepest part being, of course, on the top side, and the two arms carrying the water down clear of the enclosed tent.

There should be a lantern or candle fixed to your tent pole. Plan where everything is to go before darkness comes.

Dig a latrine trench or hole at some distance from the tent, beginning the task, if possible, by removing a piece of turf which can later be replaced. Leave the loose earth close by so that it can be tipped back as required.

Camp Fires.—The choice of site for a fire and the ability to get it going efficiently is a sure test of the practised camper.

A sheltered spot is best, on the leeward side of the tent. Remove a square of turf, or find a bare piece of ground. Do not burn a patch in the grass. Keep clear of brushwood, dry gorse, or anything likely to catch alight.

A scrap of paper, or a few dead leaves, and some dried twigs no thicker than a match should start your blaze. Build them pyramid fashion. Gradually add bigger twigs until quite large bits of wood are being used. Do not overload; do not attempt to hurry. The lighting of a fire depends on starting well, and getting the tiny centre properly ablaze. It is worth while keeping a good supply of small stuff to light or rekindle the fire. But when the blaze is going you need plenty of bigger wood, which must be dry. It is a good plan to have three or four logs, placed wheel-spoke fashion, with the fire as hub—as they burn, their ends can thus be pushed inwards to the fire (Fig. 9). For cooking and warmth glowing embers are needed; flames are cheerful when you are sitting round in the dusk.

Fig. 9.—A Star Fire

Wind is a great nuisance, it may make a fire roar away, squandering all its energy in scorching legs and blacking faces. To cook in a wind you may have your fire in a trench, so that the heat can get at your pots. It is often easier to keep a fire together if you have some stones round it; the stones themselves retain heat.

It is a mistake to think the biggest blaze is the best one. The wise camper has a fire no bigger than he needs, thus economizing his fuel. The procuring of dried wood can be a very big business if there are few trees in the neighbourhood.

But certainly do not break down branches or pilfer from hedges or fences. Dead, dried stuff can generally be found with a little perseverance. When you get it to your camp store in a sheltered place that which is not being used.

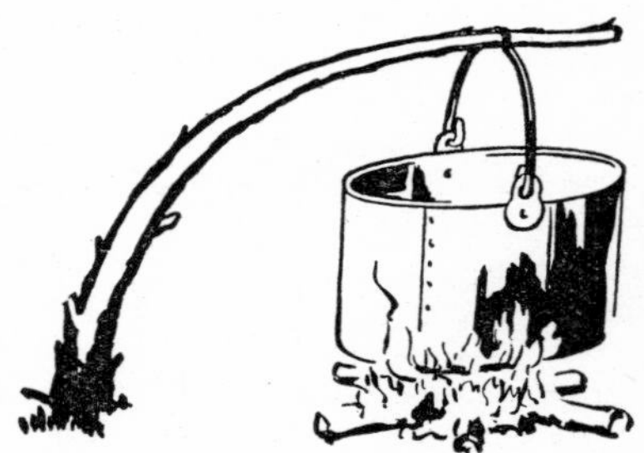

Fig. 10.—Green Stick Cooking Bracket

Your billy, for cooking, may rest on one or two stones over the fire, or right in the hot ashes. Alternatively you may have some sort of tripod spread so as to support your cooking pot. A simpler method is to have a single green stick driven slantingly into the ground by the side of the fire. Notch this stick at the top end and on it hang your billy—the stick will then bend with the weight so that the billy comes just over the desired mass of embers. By having a green stick you will not only get pliancy but ensure that it will not burn (Fig. 10).

Meals.—Do not yield to the temptation, when in camp, of having too much tinned stuff. Plenty of fresh food is essential. Tinned milk may be handy—remember two holes are needed when you wish to pour from such a tin, one to let the milk out, one to let the air in.

Be especially careful about water; if your supply is not regularly used for drinking, always boil it.

Cooking can be part of the fun of camping. No doubt you can make tea or cocoa, boil an egg and even a potato, fry bacon or sausage. Bloaters are quite easy to prepare, and so are the forms of porridge which can be made quickly with boiling milk. "Greens" are not much trouble—clean them thoroughly, and boil, not forgetting to put in a pinch of salt.

If you wish to do much cooking, and are inexperienced, it is best to practise at home, where mistakes will matter less than in camp. But try at any rate a few experiments outside your tent. Potatoes can be baked in hot embers, in their skins; so can bananas and apples. You may do a sausage similarly wrapped in a banana skin. To roast an apple smear it with butter and hold it over the fire—not in a flame—on the end of a peeled stick. A fresh-peeled stick, especially a forked one, can be very useful. You can toast a chunk of bread with some cheese inside by the aid of it, or grill a sausage or chop.

Clear up properly after each meal. Wood ashes are good for scouring greasy utensils. All refuse which cannot be burned should be buried. Should you have no spade to make a hole for tins, glass and suchlike, then you may dig with a pointed stick.

The sooner things are washed up the easier the task will be. A greasy pan should first have water boiled in it, and afterwards be cleaned with wood ash, mud, or grass, finally being rinsed with cold water. Wood ashes are useful for cleaning almost anything, so is grass. To clean a pot which has burned when cooking put in salt and cold water and leave it to stand for a few hours.

Do not throw greasy water about carelessly; pour it under a hedge, or somewhere where a grease film will not matter.

Keep your diet varied. Eat plenty of fresh fruit.

Health and Hygiene.—Camp life is healthy, or ought to be, but its benefits may be missed through carelessness. The first rule should be cleanliness. Have no litter—from courtesy to the land owner, and to keep away flies. Watch that your latrine and rubbish trenches are deep enough, and are kept adequately covered with loose earth.

Cleanliness is the best safeguard against insect pests, but be prepared if some do come. Oil of pennyroyal, smeared round the bottom of your tent, will keep out earwigs. Even snakes can be warded off by a ring of salt! For gnat and other small insect bites dab the affected place with dilute ammonia—your chemist will supply a small bottle. You may prevent such bites by dabbing oil of cloves on neck, arms, or legs.

The Medicine Pack is important. It should contain gauze, bandage, scissors, adhesive plaster, clinical thermometer, fingerstalls, cascara sagrada tablets (for constipation), bismuth tablets (for stomach disturbance), vaseline, iodine, and a few other first-aid odds and ends.

Take some quinine, or a few spots of camphor on a lump of sugar, if you fear a cold. For a headache, a cup of strong tea, two aspirins and a rest are usually efficacious. For blisters, put on iodine, and then prick, having sterilized the point of the needle in a flame.

You need not expect all sorts of trouble in camp—but the practised camper can look after himself, and others too. Obviously it is a notable advantage to understand something about first-aid. And, when you have a chance, find out where the nearest doctor and chemist live—just in case! "Safety first" should be the rule in all matters of health. You should not, for instance, cut towards the body when using axe or knife; nor should you over-expose when taking your first spells of sun bathing.

The Daily Routine.—Early to bed and early to rise apply very definitely to camp life. But there is no need to rise with the sun. Take at least nine hours sleep, with plenty of it on the right side of midnight.

Do not sleep in the clothes you have worn all day, they will need to be aired during the night—though not outside the tent; a peg high up your pole will serve, or the foot of your bed. For sleeping put on pyjamas, adding spare shirt or jersey if you should get chilly.

It is good to begin the day with a large cup of cold water. There is no better safeguard against constipation, which is one of your worst enemies. Do not fly too readily to the remedy of medicine; it is infinitely better to drink more water and eat more vegetables and fruit.

Have meals regularly, but do not take supper later than an hour before bedtime. Snacks between meals are bad.

Do not sit about in damp clothes. Change quickly. Should your feet get wet dry them with a towel and put on fresh shoes. Shoes that have been wet will be liable to get hard unless you put plenty of polish on. Wear woollen socks or stockings.

The tent should be ventilated each morning, by raising the flaps or opening out as much as possible. Bedding should be hung out to air, first one side up then the other. After the airing replace everything and make the tent tidy—slovenliness never goes with good camping.

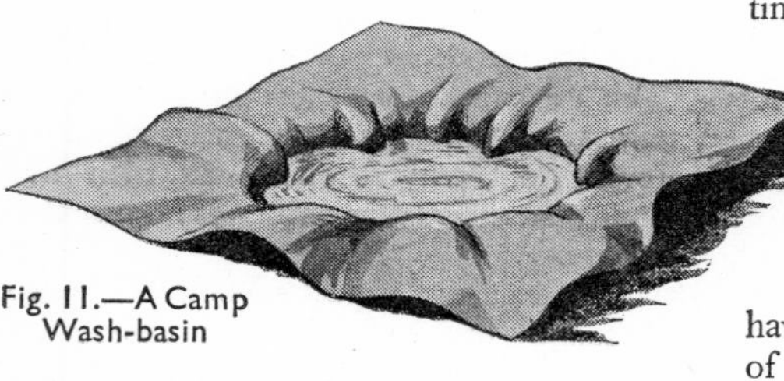

Fig. 11.—A Camp Wash-basin

To get a makeshift bath, or wash-basin, put a groundsheet, rubber upwards, over a hole in the ground, and pour in the water. (*See* Fig. 11.) Alternatively raise the edges of the sheet on stones or logs, and pour into the hollow between. But do not put back the sheet under your bed until it is dry.

If possible food should never be left inside your tent, especially at night. A sound plan is to suspend it from a tree, under a waterproof cover; this will keep it safe and cool. Or you may partly bury a biscuit tin. But do not use the ordinary tin lid for this type of cold storage; a flat wood cover is much better, for it allows the air to circulate. A heavy stone will keep the wood lid in place.

Providing, however, that you can get fresh supplies easily there will be no need to keep too much food in camp.

In order to get meals at regular times you will need to take the fire into consideration. Always have firewood ready at hand. On a windy day it is advisable to allow an extra quarter of an hour because of the difficulty of concentrating the heat where you want it.

General Hints.—When camp routine is well planned there is ample leisure and, if you are staying in one place, the problem arises, what shall you do with it?

One of the best things is to live near to Nature—to do rambles; to study birds, trees, flowers; to collect insects, footprints, Nature photographs; to explore with an eye to old history. This book itself is an answer to the question of what to do with one's leisure. Painting or sketching; wood-carving with your pocket knife; clay modelling with lumps of clay fetched from the stream—all such things help to pass the time happily. Particularly there is the making of gadgets of camp equipment—pegs, chairs, table, plate racks, shelves, and so on, both useful and ornamental things can be improvised, and your camp will be all the more cosy because of them. Incidentally, you will find it a great advantage if you have some knowledge of the various kinds of knots—and the study of knot-tying itself can be a very profitable occupation.

Naturally you will bathe if there is any chance. But always wait two hours after a meal; and know the water. There is no time to compare with the early morning for a dip, providing breakfast is not long delayed afterwards. Never stay in the water too long, nor sit about afterwards in a wet costume.

Rest awhile after your midday meal. Perhaps take half an hour's nap, then lie around for another half-hour. Reading is delightful for this part of the day. There should always be a few books in your tent. But do not strain your eyes over them when it is nearly dark, or by candle-light.

With one or more companions you will want a few games. Plenty of suitable ones are described in other sections of this volume. *Net* games, like *ring tennis* and *toss ball*, are very suitable; they can even be played over a fence or low hedge. For a rough and tumble bout try *hog tie*—the two taking part each having a short length of cord and trying simultaneously to tie each other's ankles together. When your camp is still larger novel ways of running races can be appreciated—on all fours, blindfolded, leapfrog, back to back, heel and toe, somersaulting, with legs and arms stiff, hopping, with sticks balanced on hands, rolling, touching ankles.

Packing Up.—When finishing camp be just as careful still to do everything properly. Pack your tent, taking care that it is dry, or you may be troubled afterwards by mildew. See that no broken cords or pegs are left about. Go over the camping ground with a wooden rake—you may have made this as a "gadget" and have used it every morning to tidy up. Collect and burn all paper and rubbish. Fill in holes and replace turf over latrine and fire. Clean up, in fact, so thoroughly that any person afterwards would find it difficult or impossible to say where your camp had been. If you can achieve that you are no longer a novice.

CANVAS WORK

STITCHERY in canvas can be carried out with a variety of threads and canvases. The scope for pattern work and colour is very wide. As a hobby this work is particularly suitable for those who are perhaps unable to move about freely or have little room in which to work. It is also useful where it is desired to have something in hand for odd moments.

The articles which can be made include mats of all kinds, cushions, pochettes, bags, tea cosies, book covers, blotters, work boxes, slippers, table runners, chair and stool seats, etc.

The Material.—Canvas can be obtained in various grades of mesh, but the three most commonly used are, first, "coarse" which is mainly used for rugs and does not give sufficient scope for design on a small scale. If rug wool is used with this canvas and large articles made, such as rugs and floor mats, quite a large amount of saleable work can be done. In fact many rug-makers are using these two materials together with such stitches as cross stitch, herring bone, etc., and obtain excellent rugs.

The next canvas is called "medium." This has a mesh of about $\frac{1}{10}$-in. It is used with a three- or four-ply wool.

Both these canvases are now largely made from a twisted paper cord. They are quite satisfactory in use.

"Fine" canvas is white, made from a finer thread and woven to a smaller mesh with double threads as in the coarse canvas. The double threads are used as single ones in the stitchery.

Coloured canvas can also be obtained and this is sometimes useful in giving a certain quality of colour to the background of the design or where it is not desired to cover the canvas with stitchery. The price of canvas depends upon the size of the mesh, width and whether plain or coloured. It varies from 7d. per yard 12 in. wide for rug canvas to about 2s. per yard 36 in. wide for fine white canvas.

The Stitches.—The principal stitches used in this work are block or satin stitch, running or darning stitch, herring bone, cross stitch and buttonhole stitch. These are illustrated in Figs. 1 to 18. Stitchery can be carried out in raffia, wool, cotton, silk, etc. The former is not so much used now as formerly. It can, however, be used with great effect and it does withstand a good deal of hard wear. It can be obtained in all colours or natural raffia can be purchased and dyed to any colour in one of the many dyes on the market.

Of the wools which can be used, that generally used for weaving is best. It is spun to a harder twist than embroidery wool and therefore does not rub up so easily as the latter. Either two-, three-, four- or five-ply can be used according to the size of the mesh in the canvas. The wool should generally fill the latter so that none of it is visible when the stitchery is finished.

Silk or its mixtures can be well used on the fine mesh canvas, and very fine designs can be worked in it.

The question of design and colour is a most important one. It is easy to purchase canvas with the design stamped on it in

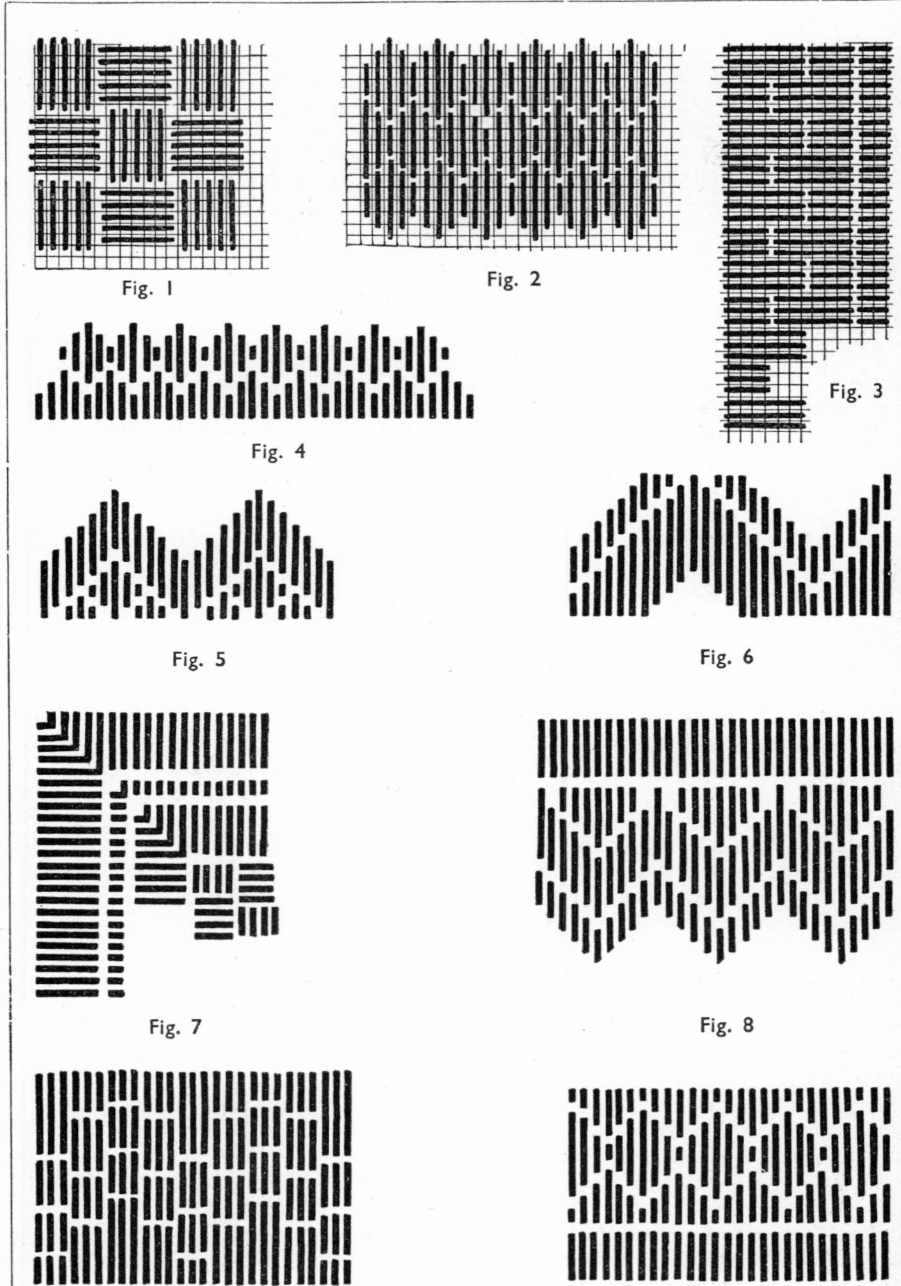
Fig. 1
Fig. 2
Fig. 3
Fig. 4
Fig. 5
Fig. 6
Fig. 7
Fig. 8
Fig. 9
Fig. 10

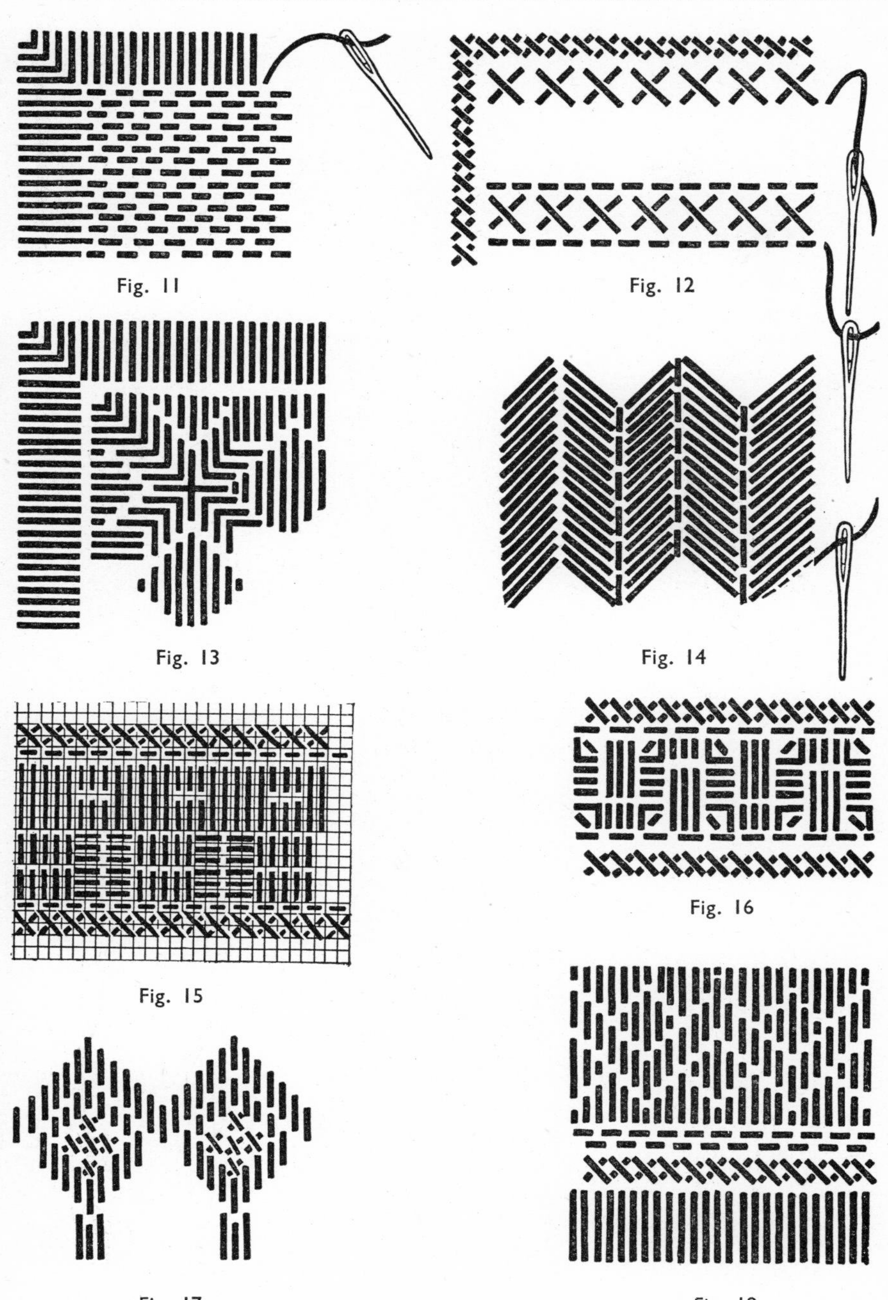

Fig. 11

Fig. 12

Fig. 13

Fig. 14

Fig. 15

Fig. 16

Fig. 17

Fig. 18

Fig. 19.—Tapestry Motifs and Stitches on Canvas

colour. All you have to do is to buy the appropriate colours in wool, etc., and work over the design exactly as printed. A better way, with much more pleasure in it, is to make your own designs either by adapting something you have seen and like, or by taking a number of simple geometric figures and using them to make a design.

An important point is, that as the mesh of the canvas is at right angles to the sides it will be easiest and best to use this as the foundation of any design. This will confine you to geometrical form somewhat, but that is quite the safest and best type of design for this class of work. Do not be tempted to copy the shapes of flowers, sprays of foliage, cottages by the sea, complete with chimney and smoke emerging from it. It will be observed that, excepting the fine cross stitch, none of the suggested stitches are worked diagonally on the canvas. If it is so stitched it will be found that the canvas is pulled out of shape and cannot be corrected. The fine cross stitch corrects itself, a large one might be difficult. Do not use long stitches which catch on the clothing. The length of the stitch should not exceed $\frac{3}{4}$ of an inch, covering about six holes in the canvas. When the designs have been stitched in while the canvas is on the flat, the latter is folded to the shape and proportions designed, whether it be a bag, pochette, purse, etc., and the sides stitched together by oversewing. Take care to cover the join adequately.

The Illustrations.—Fig. 1 shows the block or satin stitch worked in squares at right angles to each other. This is useful for a large plain background. Fig. 2 shows a diaper pattern in the same stitch also used as Fig. 1. The long and short stitches in Figs. 3 and 4 are very useful for borders, or all-over patterns. Figs. 5, 6 and 8 show a zigzag which is very useful. It can be worked in parallel as in Figs. 6 and 8 or in conjunction with squares as in Figs. 5 and 18. Fig. 7 shows the planning of a corner and Fig. 9 shows the effect obtained by zig-zag groups of long and short stitches. Fig. 10 shows the effect obtained from squares and half squares inside a border. Fig. 11 shows a corner and a running stitch. This stitch is useful where you wish to show up the colour of the canvas a little. Figs. 12, 15, 16 and 18 show this stitch in conjunction with the cross stitch. The latter can be made more interesting by running a line of wool of contrasting colour along the line of the cross stitches, fastening it down with the latter, at the same time exposing some of it between the stitches. The herring-bone stitch in Fig. 14 can be used very effectively, but care must be taken not to pull it too tightly and to make short stitches.

Suggestions for Colour.—Just a few hints on colour in this work. The following combinations will be found very safe and good until you have experience and knowledge from which to experiment.

Three shades of brown and fawn; light brown with fawn and a small amount of pale or dark orange, three shades of blue with a small amount of orange or grey; dark red, brown and fawn are useful, two blues and a grey; dark green, light brown and orange; three shades of purple with small amount of yellow-green; fawn, light brown and soft green; rust, pale rust, fawn and a little green. Generally avoid putting together blue and yellow, or red and blue, or yellow and red, unless you require strong sharp colour values. They can be safely used together if one or both have been darkened. Keep your eye on the colour schemes in well designed clothing and you will find plenty of ideas.

CARD GAMES

TWO PLAYERS

Bezique.—Played with two picquet packs (2–6 withdrawn from both), this is one of the best of all games for two players.

Shuffle and cut, dealing three cards to each, then two, then three. The top card is then placed face upwards beside the remainder of the pack which is placed between the players; it shows the trump suit.

Each player examines his hand. The scoring is as follows:

Four Jacks—40 points.
Four Queens—60 points.
Four Kings—80 points.
Four Aces—100 points.
Sequence (A, K, Q, J, and 10 of trumps)—250 points.
Bezique (Queen of Spades and Jack of Diamonds)—40 points.
Double Bezique (*both* as above)—250 points.
Royal Marriage (King and Queen of trumps)—40 points.

Common Marriage (any King and Queen of same suit)—20 points.

The object is, by leading a card and winning a trick, to declare a scoring combination. The winner of a trick takes the top card of the pack and the loser the next. Both players must always have eight cards each, until the pack is exhausted.

At any time immediately after winning a trick and before taking the top card, a scoring combination may be exposed on the table and claimed. The exposed cards still continue to form part of the player's hand and may be led or played to a trick.

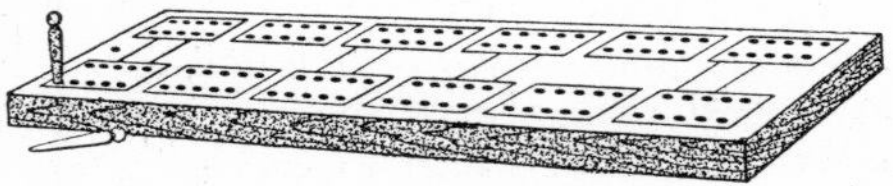

Fig. I.—Cribbage Board

The seven of trumps may be exchanged for the trump card exposed. Scoring 10 points for the exchange. The ten ranks as the highest card after the Ace (as in Eucre). During play there is no need to follow suit. Aces and ten score 10 points at the conclusion, to the player who has won them among his tricks.

Fuller details of rules and play are given with full Bezique packs and scorers.

Cribbage.—This is one of the best games for two persons. In addition to an ordinary pack of cards, a cribbage board is required. This consists of a wooden rectangle drilled with holes. (*See* Fig. 1.) There are 60 holes for each player, an additional hole—called the "home hole"—being placed in the centre of each end as shown.

The pack is cut by each player, the one turning up the lowest card dealing and taking the crib. Ace counts low when cutting for deal. During the game itself all court cards count equal (ten). The non-dealer scores 3 points by way of consolation. After the cards have been cut and shuffled, they are dealt one at a time until each player has five.

Each player then takes up his hand and sets aside two of the cards he does not want; they are placed face down and to one side of the dealer and form the crib. The balance of the pack is then cut by the non-dealer, the dealer taking the top card of the under pack and placing it face upwards on the top of the pack.

The game is won by the first player to move his pegs the entire 60 holes. Scores are as follows:

"*Pair*," i.e. two cards of the same value, such as two fours, two tens, etc.—2 points.

"*Pair Royal*," i.e. three cards of the same value, such as three tens, three fours, etc. —6 points.

"*Double Pair Royal*," i.e. four cards of equal value—12 points.

"*Fifteen-two, fifteen-four*," etc. When the hand has been played out (described later) each player in turn takes his cards and tries to make up fifteens, thus a seven and an eight would count as 2 points, two sevens and an eight would be 4, and so on.

"*One for his Nob*." The player who, in hand or crib, holds the jack of the suit turned up scores "one for his nob."

"*Two for his Heels*." The holder of the crib, if he turns up a jack on the "cut" is entitled to 2 points.

"*Flush*." If all the cards held in the hand are of one suit, this is called a flush and 1 point is scored for every card. If the turned-up card is also of the same suit it may be counted in, thus giving an additional point.

"*Sequence*." A sequence, or, as it is sometimes called, a run, can occur either in the hand, in play, or in the crib. It consists of a minimum of three cards, of which the turned-up card may be counted as one, when scoring at the end of the game. As an example, the first player may put down a three, the second follow with a four, and the first again with a five, thus scoring 3 points. If the fourth card played were a six, the player of it would score 4 points.

Method of Play.—Suppose A deals the following hands with the ace of clubs as the turn-up card: B's hand: king, six and three of hearts, eight and ten of clubs. As there is an ace for the turn-up-card, B will probably decide to put the king and three into crib. A's hand: eight and six of diamonds, four of hearts, five of clubs, seven of spades. He discards the four of hearts and five of clubs for his crib. B leads with an eight, calling as he does so "eight." A plays the eight of diamonds, calling "sixteen" and taking 2 for a pair. B plays a ten, calling "twenty-six" and as the highest they may go is thirty-one, A cannot go, so B scores 1 point. The cards played are then turned over so that they are face down on the table, each player keeping his own hand in front of him. A leads with his six of diamonds, B follows with six of hearts and takes 2 more points. A puts his last card down and scores another point. B as the non-dealer counts up his hand first. The six and eight used with the ace turned up, total fifteen. B's score is therefore 2. A takes up his hand. He has a six and an eight which with the turned-up ace make fifteen for 2. The eight and seven make fifteen for another 2, and a sequence of six, seven and eight gives him a further 3. He then takes the crib which comprises king, four and three of hearts, five of clubs and of course the turned-up ace. The king, four and ace make fifteen and score 2; the king and five make another fifteen for 2; the three, four and five form a sequence for 3, totalling 14 for the two hands.

In the next hand B is the dealer and takes the crib.

WHIST AND ITS DERIVATIVES

Whist.—The full pack of 52 cards is dealt to the four players, each receiving 13. The final card may be turned up to denote trumps or the other pack cut. The player on the dealer's left leads, and each other player must follow in turn, playing a card of the same suit if he can, otherwise playing a trump or a card of another suit. The winner of one trick leads for the next and so on until the 13 tricks have been played. Players sitting opposite one another are partners, their object being to win as many tricks as they can.

Although players must not communicate with or signal to each other, much information is conveyed by the way in which cards are played. It is necessary of course for the two partners to understand the various signs in order that they be of benefit. There are a number of conventional leads ; for instance, if a player leads with a king, it is generally understood that he possesses either the ace or the queen. Should he play the ace it indicates that he has not the king in his hand. If the queen is led it indicates that the player who leads it holds neither the ace nor the king. As a general rule it is the duty of the third player to play his highest card on his partner's small card, and if after the round has been played he still has two more of the same suit, he should generally lead the higher of the two, but if he has more than two he should play the lowest. A knowledge of these conventions is advisable, but not essential.

It is wise to lead trumps when five or more are held. The player who does not do this will lessen his chance of winning. There are occasions, of course, in which the player who wishes to lead trumps is unable to obtain the lead, and there are methods of signalling to his partner when he desires trumps to be played. The "trump call" is made by playing a high and then a lower card on two consecutive tricks of the same suit, but of course this cannot always be done. Once trumps have been started discretion should be used, for it is quite easy to over-run and lose what would otherwise be a winning hand.

Solo Whist.—Solo whist is an interesting game which gives much more scope for individuality than does ordinary whist. The full pack of cards is used, these being dealt out to the four players, three cards at a time, the last four being dealt singly. The final card, which, of course, always belongs to the dealer, is turned up to denote trumps. The player on the left of the dealer then inspects his hand and declares the number of tricks he thinks he can make, either by himself against the other three or with a partner. Unless four practically certain tricks are held it is wise for him to pass.

The calls for solo whist are as follows:

1. *Proposal.*—This is commonly called "prop," and is given by the player who has four tricks in his hand, and who feels that if another player can provide suitable backing they will between them secure eight tricks. Any one of the three remaining players may complete the partnership (cop), but the calls proceed from right to left.

2. *Solo.*—Five tricks must be obtained, the caller opposing the other three players.

3. *Misère.*—All thirteen tricks must be lost.

4. *Abundance.*—The caller must take nine tricks, but has the privilege of choosing his own trumps. (If one player has called Abundance, another may call Abundance in Trumps, which is superior.)

5. *Misère Ouverte.*—The caller undertakes to lose all the thirteen tricks, but after the first round has been played, he places the remainder of his hand face upwards on the table. (There are no trumps in Misère or Misère Ouverte.)

6. *Abundance Declared.*—The caller undertakes to win all thirteen tricks. He can choose his own trumps and must make the initial lead.

Players can over-call one another in turn, so that although a prop, solo, misère, abundance may have already been called, the caller of the misère may, if he desires, over-call the abundance by calling misère ouverte, whilst of course the abundance caller may, if he wishes, over-call misère ouverte by abundance declared.

Bridge.—There are several variations on bridge, and it is only possible here to give a brief outline. Bridge is more difficult to master than the majority of card games, but once the scoring, etc., is understood, the game is full of absorbing interest.

With ordinary bridge the cards are dealt and the leads are practically the same as with whist, but bridge differs from whist in the following main features: (1) The dealer's partner's hand is exposed, and the dealer plays both hands himself. (2) Trumps are declared either by the dealer or by his partner. The dealer upon examining his hand will call as trumps the suit in which he expects to be able to take the greatest number of tricks. If he is unable to decide from his own hand, he may leave it to his partner to declare trumps. After the trump suit has been settled the eldest hand, that is the player on the left of the dealer, or his partner may call double, which means that the value of each trick is doubled. The dealer or his partner may redouble if they desire, which means the value of each trick is multiplied by 4. Re-doubling may be continued until the maximum of 100 points a trick is reached, although, of course, this may be dispensed with if desired. The eldest hand leads a card and the dealer's partner then lays down his cards face upwards so that all may see them. Play then proceeds as in whist.

Scoring is as follows: If spades are trumps, count 2 points for every trick above six; if clubs, 4 points; if diamonds, 6 points; if hearts, 8 points; and if no trumps, 12 points. Scoring is recorded on paper ruled with two vertical columns crossed by a horizontal line about half-way. The value of the tricks above six is scored below the line, to either side, according, of course, to which is the winner, whilst the space above the horizontal line is for recording the scores for honours, chicane, and points for grand and little slam. Honours consist of ace, king, queen, knave and ten of the trump suit, the points scored for the whole five if held between the partners, being five times the value of a trick in the trump suit, if held by one partner, ten times the value; for any four honours between the two partners, four times, but if held by one player, eight times; three honours, three times, but if one player, six times. If the hand played is a no-trump one, the honours are the aces, and if two partners hold all four between them they add 40 points to their score, 30 if they hold three. If one player holds the four aces 100 points are added to his total.

If either side succeeds in taking the whole thirteen tricks this is called the grand slam and 40 points are added to the honours score. If they succeed in taking twelve, this is called the little slam, and 20 points are added. Chicane means that one or more players does not hold a single trump in his hand, and in this case, twice the value of a trick is added to the honours score.

The game is completed when one side makes 30 points below the line. The first side to win two games is awarded the rubber for which 100 points are secured in the honours column. The total score is arrived at by adding all the points both above and below the line together.

Auction Bridge.—This is a variation of ordinary bridge, but it is more popular.

It differs from the former game in several ways, for the declaration of trumps is put up to auction. The dealer makes the first bid which consists of the trump and the number of tricks he undertakes to make above six. The leading hand may pass, double, or increase the call if he wishes. Bidding goes on until one player calls the highest, and this player then plays his own and his partner's hand, the partner laying down the hand and becoming the dummy. The player on the left of the highest bidder always makes the initial lead. If clubs are trumps the score for each trick is 6 points; if diamonds, 7 points; if hearts, 8 points; if spades, 9 points; no trumps, 10 points. Should the highest bidder and his partner fail to make the number of tricks stated, the opponents count 50 points in honours, for every trick short of the number declared. If the call was doubled 100 points would be scored for each trick short.

Declarations can be doubled and re-doubled, but not more. Doubling does not alter the value of the bid, but it increases the scoring value. Thus, though the call may be for two hearts and this is doubled and re-doubled, only two hearts are required to win, though 32 points are scored per trick.

The double is, of course, made by the opponents of the declarers, and is called for a penalty scored according to the number of tricks which the declarer fails to make. The re-double is made by the confident declarer (or his partner) when he is sure of making his contract. Tricks under contract count 100 points above the line to the opponents when doubled, 200 when re-doubled. Bids are made in ascending scale, one diamond (six tricks and one) taking precedence over one club, and so on, seven no trumps (six tricks and seven) being the highest. The point valuation has precedence over the number of tricks called.

Contract Bridge.—This immensely popular game for four players has become very much governed by conventions and "Systems." It is essential for a would-be player to take lessons or study one of the many books on the various systems in general use.

Played in the same manner as Auction Bridge, the main difference lies in the fact that only the number of tricks called during the auction can be scored towards the rubber. Penalties for failing to make the contract are heavy, but the points for achieving it are proportionately great. The penalties are also increased when one side has scored a game (vulnerable).

The principal systems in play in England at present are: the Strong (forcing) Two, (Culbertson); The Two Club (Lederer and others); The One Club (Barton and, seldom used, Vanderbilt); The One Over One, The Four Aces, and with most of these are combined the Four Five No-trump. A decision (on advice from a player or teacher) as to which system to learn should be made and books purchased or lessons arranged. A player should, however, have a knowledge of all the general systems. Culbertson and Lederer—with or without variations—are probably the most generally played.

ROUND GAMES

Hearts.—This is a very popular game which originated in America. It can be played by four, five or six people. The dealer uses the full pack and gives out one card at a time to each player. The eldest hand then leads a card, and the rest of the players in turn follow suit, if possible. The object of the game is to conclude with as few hearts as possible among one's tricks. The winner of each trick takes the cards played and places them face down in front of him, then leads for the next trick. It does not matter how many tricks are gained so long as there are no hearts among them. Players naturally try to get rid of their hearts, particularly the high ones, for if they are forced to lead or follow with a high heart, they will probably have a handful of the same suit added, and this will of course count against them. The best hands are those which contain practically no high cards at all, and it is wise for leaders at the beginning of the game to lead a high card of a suit that has not been played, for in the majority of cases the other players will have to follow suit; it is very unlikely that a heart will be thrown away the first time round. It is sometimes advantageous to lead a heart, but it must be a small one, so that someone else will have the doubtful pleasure of raking in the trick! The game is perfectly simple, and after one or two rounds players will discover the best leads and mode of play. Scoring is usually kept by counting up the number of pips on the heart cards held at the end of the game, and one may, of course, play for 500 points or so. The player who has the least number of points wins the game.

The queen of spades is sometimes included in the penalty cards. She scores 20 points in the tricks at the end. A variation sometimes played is to allow as a winning hand any player who secures *all* the hearts and the queen of spades. 100 points are scored against all the other players for this unusual hand.

Nap.—For this game five is the best number of players, and the limit should be seven. Five cards are dealt to each player, one at a time, and it is usual for counters to be used for stakes. Each player looks at his hand, the eldest hand making the first call. He has the right of choosing his own trump suit should he be left with the call and volunteers to make 3, 4, or 5 (nap) tricks against all the other players. Alternatively he may call misère (no trick at all, in which case there is no trump), and it should be decided beforehand whether or not misère takes precedence over a call of 4. When all have called, the highest call has to try to make his bid. The first card led by the bidder indicates the trump suit. The winner of a trick leads for the next. An agreed stake per call is paid by each player to the declarer should he make his call. Should he fail, he pays the same amount to each of the others. The exact proportions of the stakes vary considerably. An average might be, say, 2 for three tricks, 3 for four tricks or misère, 6 for nap and 10 for double nap. (Double nap is called over nap. The declarer plays his hand on the table after the first trick is taken. It cannot be called if nap is not called first by someone else.) A variation of the ordinary game of nap is called purchase nap, and is played as follows: after the original five cards have been dealt and the players have examined their hands, each in turn may purchase fresh cards from the pack, throwing away a similar number, face down, which are not used until the next deal. Purchase money is put in the pool, and this may either be taken by the next to win a call, or may be left for the first to pull off a "nap" call. Scoring for either game is quite simple, being usually one counter per trick; thus, if a player wins his "three" call, he receives three counters from each of his opponents, if a "four" call, four counters; the nap call is usually at double rate. Should the player fail to get the number of tricks declared, he pays away at the same rate except that in the case of a nap hand he only pays away five counters.

Pelmanism.—This is a good lively game for the start of an evening. It is for any number of players. The full pack is spread face downwards over the table, and shuffled in this position, no two cards touching one another. One player takes up two cards and exposes them. Should they be a pair he will remove them, and they count as a trick in his favour. If they are not a pair he replaces them face down, and the next player picks up two more, one at a time. If his first card happens to be similar numerically to one previously turned over, he naturally tries to remember the position of this former card in order that he may pick it for his second choice, and thus gain a trick. The player who in the end has the largest number of pairs, wins the game.

Pontoon (or Vingt-et-un).—This is quite an exciting game for a party. One player is chosen to be the banker, and after shuffling the cards, the maximum stakes having been agreed upon, he deals one card at a time, face downwards to every player in turn, giving one, also, to himself. Each player except the dealer looks at his card and places his stake in front of him, basing the amount on the chances of obtaining cards to the value of 21. Picture cards count as ten, and ace as either one or eleven. After the stakes have been laid, a second card is dealt, also face down, to each player. If the two cards together make 21, for example a queen and an ace, or a king and an ace, this is called a "natural" and they are turned up for everyone to see. Should the two cards total, say, seven, the player will ask for another. If this is a four he will ask for yet another in the hope of getting a nine or a ten, to bring his total as near 21 as possible. If the cards thus dealt total over 21 the stake is lost and the cards are placed underneath the pack. The player who reaches 18 or so generally decides to stop, but of course does not say what his score is, and the dealer passes on to the next man. Should a player's first two cards both be aces, he is at liberty to split them into two separate lots and place a stake on each one. He is then dealt one more card on each, and play proceeds in the ordinary way. When all have been served the dealer looks at his own cards, turning them up for all to see, and dealing himself additional cards as he thinks fit, finally declaring his score. If he has a "natural" he receives from each player double the stakes laid, except in the case of a player who has also turned up a "natural," for in this case the player merely takes back his stake. If the dealer has not a "natural," and has under 21, he collects the stakes of all those who have the same number or less than himself, and pays those who have more. If one of the players has a "natural" the dealer pays him double his stake and hands over the pack of cards. Should two players turn up "naturals," the first one becomes banker, but both are paid double their stakes. If any player has five cards and still totals less than 21 the dealer pays him double his stake. If the dealer has more than 21, he pays all those who have not already handed in their stakes.

Fan Tan.—This is another good game for six, seven or eight players. The whole pack is dealt, one card at a time. The eldest hand then, if he can, lays down a seven of any suit; if unable to do so he places one chip into the pool. The second player must then lay a seven or forfeit a chip and so on until any seven is actually put down. When the seven has been laid down the next player may put a card of the same suit either side of the seven, but it must be one that is numerically one point lower or higher; thus if a seven of clubs is laid, the player can put the six or the eight. Each player when his turn comes tries to add to the cards on the table. If unable to put any of the same suit, he must either play a seven if he has one or pay a forfeit. The game is, of course, to hold back the sevens as long as possible in order to get rid of the rest of the cards in the hand. The player who puts down all his cards first wins. He takes the contents of the pool and one chip from every player for every card that player holds.

PATIENCES

Tower of Hanoy.—Out of a pack of cards select nine of one suit, from the deuce to the ten. Shuffle them and then lay out on the table in three columns of three. (*See* Fig. 2.) The game is to get them into one single column, moving only the bottom card of any column, one at a time.

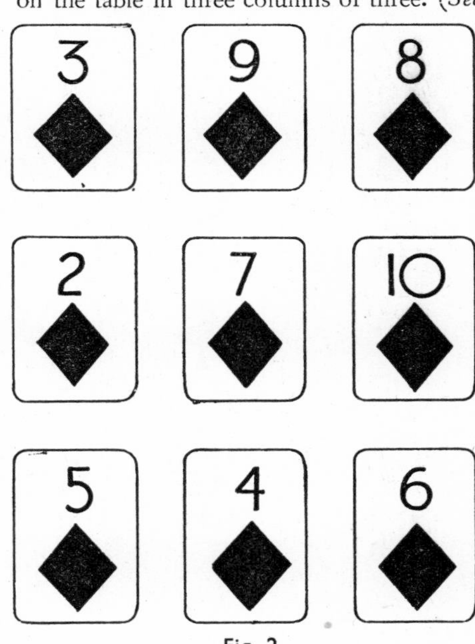

Fig. 2

No card may be set under a card of lower denomination; thus, if the three bottom cards are five, four and six, either the five or the four may be placed under the six, but only the four can be put under the five.

When all the cards in one column have been moved, the bottom card of either of the remaining columns may be placed in the vacant space in the top row.

Demon Patience.—Take a full pack of cards, shuffle them and count off thirteen.

These are to be put on the table, face upwards and to the left of the player. Then count off four more cards and put these also face upwards, and to the right of the pack of thirteen in a single row. One more card is then dealt and placed face upwards above the first of the last four cards The thirteen cards are called the stock, the four next to it are the column heads, whilst the one above is called the foundation.

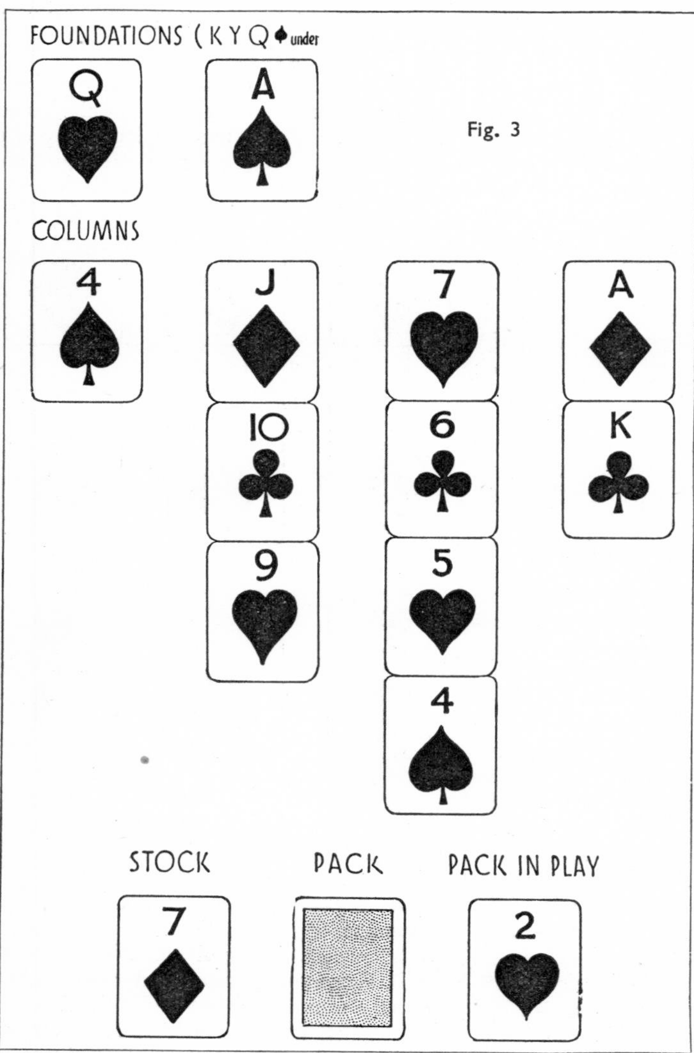

Should any of the column head cards be of the same denomination as the foundation card, move upwards to make further foundations, similarly, with the top card of the stock. If any column head card is taken away, either to build up another column or to take its place in the foundation, the place should be filled with a card taken from the stock. If the foundation card is, say, a queen, and one of the column cards is a king of the same suit, it is placed on top of the queen; the ace, two, etc., being played as they are available. The aim of the game is to build up these foundation columns until each suit is completed. No matter what the foundation card may be, that placed immediately on it must be one number higher, and of course of the same suit. On to the columns, cards are played in contrasting colours and descending order, i.e. the jack of diamonds may have the ten of clubs or spades played on to it and then the nine of hearts or diamonds—and so on.

With the rest of the cards in the hand and held face downwards, remove three at a time without changing the order, placing them face up on the table. If the exposed card of the three is a foundation card, place it with the others. If it is not, see if it will

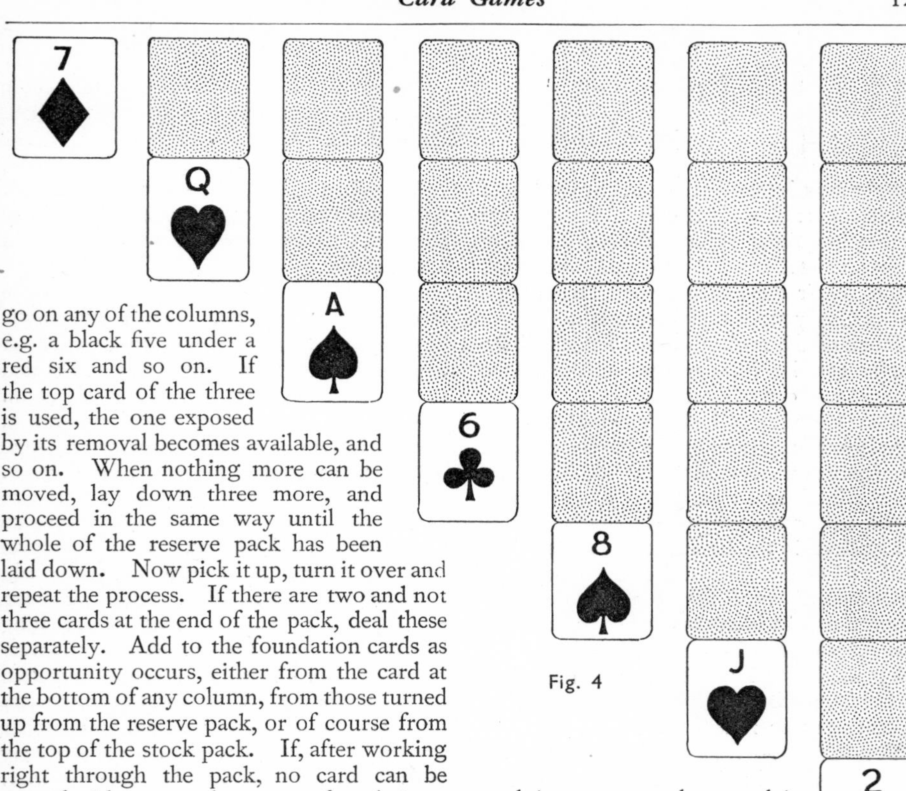

Fig. 4

go on any of the columns, e.g. a black five under a red six and so on. If the top card of the three is used, the one exposed by its removal becomes available, and so on. When nothing more can be moved, lay down three more, and proceed in the same way until the whole of the reserve pack has been laid down. Now pick it up, turn it over and repeat the process. If there are two and not three cards at the end of the pack, deal these separately. Add to the foundation cards as opportunity occurs, either from the card at the bottom of any column, from those turned up from the reserve pack, or of course from the top of the stock pack. If, after working right through the pack, no card can be moved either to columns or foundations, the game must be abandoned. Fig. 3 shows a game in progress.

Monte Carlo.—Shuffle the pack, cut, and lay the top card face upwards on the table. From this lay six cards singly face downwards, making a row to the right of the first card. Turn up the next card (the seventh) and lay it face upwards, overlapping the first downward card. From it lay a row again facing downwards and overlapping the row of downward cards. Continue until there is one card laid face upwards on the right-hand column, which should now contain six cards face downwards and one up. (*See* Fig. 4.)

Above this wedge are laid the aces, followed by their twos, threes, etc., up to the kings, as they come into play. The object is to have all the cards out in order on top of their own aces, the kings on top.

Referring to the diagram, the first move would be to place the ace of spades above the wedge as a foundation. The downward card is now turned up and is in play.

On the seven upward cards may be placed any card one pip less than itself, in a contrasting colour. For example, the six of clubs may be placed on the seven of diamonds, and both be placed on the eight of spades. Into a space only a king may be played. The downward card in each case is turned up as soon as it is released.

When there is no further move from the wedge, either to the foundations or to the upward cards, the pack is played out, one card at a time. When the pack is exhausted by being turned through once only, the game is over. The number of cards on the foundations may be counted and constitute the score. Two players may compete, each with a pack, the highest score (or number of cards on foundations) winning. Ten cards on the foundations is good and it is rare to get this patience out.

CHAIR SEATING

SEATS may be worked on to the frames of stools and chairs, either new or as repairs, in quite a variety of ways, including leather, twisted sea grass, twisted paper cord, rushes, chair cane, string, macramé thread and ordinary upholstery materials.

None of the methods are difficult and the results can be just as serviceable as the professional can make them.

The Wooden Chair-frames may be already made quite cheaply by yourself, or purchased from a woodworker's. They can be obtained at prices from 2s., in birch, beech, oak, mahogany or walnut.

Leather is the best material for seating, if of calf or cowhide, either cut into strips for stools, or used in the whole piece to cover a seat which has been stuffed and covered with hessian and calico, the leather being used as a final cover. The seat and its frame may be entirely covered or a drop-in seat may be necessary.

Sea Grass.—Quality, size and colour vary a good deal as it is a native production. It can be purchased at from 8d. to 1s. per lb.

Paper Cord in two- or three-ply is often preferred to sea grass as it is stronger and can be worked in longer lengths. It is obtainable in several colours and a brownish-grey, which is its natural colour. It costs about 1s. per lb.

Rushes.—River rushes are from 6 to 8 ft. in length and vary a little in thickness from the root end to the top. They must be hardened by twisting when being worked.

Chair Cane.—This is a thin, narrow cane, flat on one side and curved on the glossy side, which is used for the seats and backs of good-class work. It is fairly expensive—from 3s. to 7s. a pound according to width, size 1 being the narrowest and most expensive and size 6 the widest and cheapest. Not much material, however, is required to work a chair seat.

String and Macramé Thread are substitutes for sea grass and paper cord and are used in the same way.

Weaving Rushes.—The lengths of rush must first be soaked in water for a few minutes. Take them out and place them under a damp cloth for about 24 hours, when they will be found pliable and not liable to crack when twisted. Fig. 1 shows the beginning of the weaving on a seat. A length of rush is taken, its thick end is tied to a leg of the stool or chair as at A. The rush is then passed under the rail B, at number one across and over the top edge of rail D as shown by the arrow mark. Here take the rush in the hands a few inches away from the rail and twist it, say, three or four times to the right. This operation hardens the rush at the point where it will be subject to wear. Now pass it under the rail D up and to the right of the long strand and over the rail C as shown at number two. Here it is again twisted, passed *under* the rail, across the frame and over the rail E. Twist again, pass under the rail at number three, across the long strand and over the rail D at number four. Twist a little more and pass under the rail to the opposite rail B where it will go over at number four. More twist, under the rail, up and to the left across the long strand and over the rail E at number five where it is again twisted. Pass under the rail E, take across and over rail C, twist again, and so on, round and round each side until the hole is closed. If the seat is rectangular there will be a rectangular hole in the middle after the corners are filled. The weaving will then be from side to side as in Fig. 2 until the hole is filled up.

It will be observed that there is no twist put into that part of the rush which is out of sight underneath the seat. The knots to be tied in the rush must all be placed underneath the seat and tucked away as neatly as possible. A well-pulled reef knot is the best to use. The end tied to the leg at the beginning is now tied in with the strands underneath to finish off.

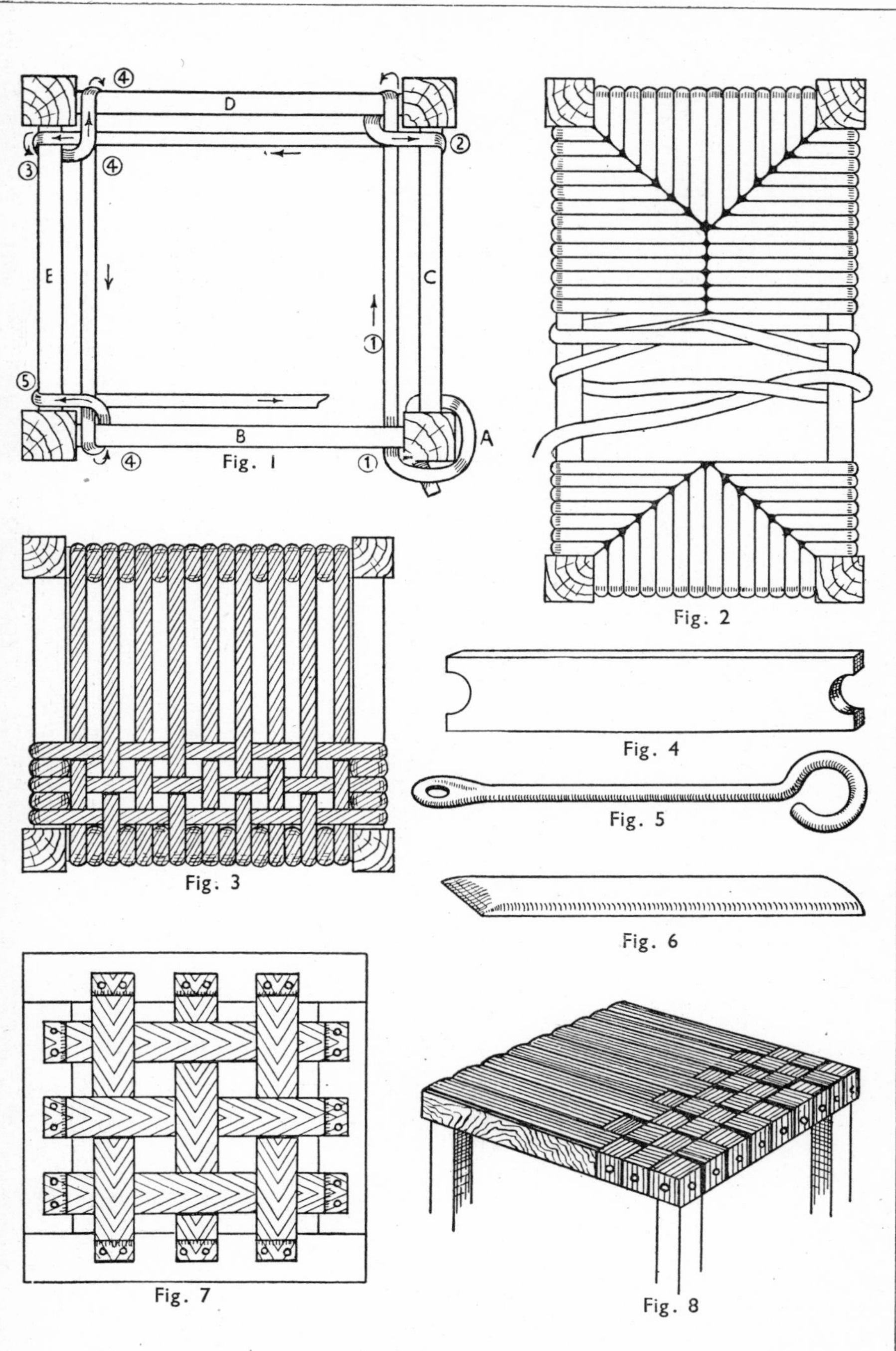

Fig. 1

Fig. 2

Fig. 3

Fig. 4

Fig. 5

Fig. 6

Fig. 7

Fig. 8

Some chair seats are wider in front than at the back rail, this giving more space to be filled with the rush on the front rail. This difference is made up by wrapping the rush twice round the front rail instead of once before passing it underneath to be carried over the side rail adjacent to it, at the right- and left-hand front corners. This is done until the space to be filled with rush has assumed a rectangular form, when the above method is resumed.

Sea Grass, String and Paper Cord.—The method just described is equally suitable for seats in twisted sea grass, paper cord, macramé thread and string of all kinds. Quite good work can also be done with the cheapest binder twine. Chair cane and ordinary flat cane can be used with equal success.

A greater variety of pattern can, however, be obtained by a system of weaving on stool or chair frames. A simple check pattern is shown in Fig. 3. For the sake of clearness the strands are shown very much thicker than the right proportion. A few yards of sea grass or any other material that is to be used is wrapped on to the wooden shuttle shown in Fig. 4. The latter is made from a piece of wood about 12 in. long and $1\frac{1}{2}$ in. wide by $\frac{1}{4}$ in. thick. Tie the end of the sea grass now on the shuttle to one leg of the stool and proceed to pass the grass over the rail, beginning at a corner, across to the opposite side, over it and then round it completely before going back again to the first rail to repeat this. Carry on until the whole of the top is filled with a warp of long threads with a short thread between each pair of long ones. The reason for wrapping this short thread is that space must be allowed between the warp threads for the weft threads to be passed through fairly easily. Pull the warp threads fairly taut when wrapping them, not too tight or it will be very difficult to weave the weft, nor too slack because the seat must not sag when sat upon.

Fix the end of the warp temporarily to a leg of the stool or chair. Join new lengths of grass with a reef knot underneath the seat.

To complete the seat, thread a long length of grass through the eye of a large needle made from $\frac{1}{4}$-in. iron as in Fig. 5. Push the point of the needle carrying the grass in and out of the warp threads from one side to the other. Wrap the grass once round the rail as in wrapping on the warp, then weave another strand back over and under warp threads alternate to the previous row. When the other side is reached wrap the grass once round this rail and proceed in this way until finished. It will be found that as the weaving proceeds the warp threads offer more resistance to the lifting by the needle. This can be overcome by using the shed stick shown in Fig. 6. This is of wood, shaped to an oval section, sharpened as shown at one end and rubbed perfectly smooth with glass-paper. Thread this stick in and out of the warp to open the way for the needle which now easily passes through. If the shed is not quite deep enough to admit the easy passage of the needle raise the stick on its edge and so increase the depth of the shed.

When the weaving is finished untie the loose ends on the legs and fasten them in underneath the seat.

Patterns.—A very great variety of patterns can be woven in these materials, all planned on the same principle as that just explained. Instead of one warp thread and one wrapping thread, you might take two warp and two wrapping threads or three and three. You would then have spaces two or three threads wide between groups of two or three warp threads. The weaving of the weft could be done to the same plan and a broad check of squares would be the result. A closer pattern, still fairly large in detail, could be obtained by wrapping only one thread between the groups of the warp threads. Colour can be introduced to add interest to the pattern, the warp in one colour, the weft in another, or a warp with a group of coloured strands to give a striped effect, and, when combined with stripes in the weft, a large check pattern. There is plenty of scope for individuality.

Leather Seats.—As previously mentioned, cowhide, technically known as "hide," is the best material for cutting into strips to be woven into a seat. Calf and goat may also be used with success and, indeed, sheep may also be satisfactory if the precautions to be described are taken.

As leather strips will stretch when sat upon and almost any seat of the kind will develop a sag unless some preventive means are adopted, the seat is first made by stretching chair webbing across the frame as in Fig. 7. There are two sets of strips of 2-in. webbing, the ends of which are nailed to the frame with strong tacks. The webbing must be pulled very tight before the second end is nailed down.

If this method is not desired very good results can be obtained by nailing the first ends of the webbing to the underside of the seat, bringing it up over the side, across the top, down the other edge of the latter and on to the underside to be pulled very tight and nailed down.

Before the webbing is nailed down a piece of hessian may be nailed down to cover the frame. The webbing is then nailed down as shown. This gives a neat finish to the underside of the seat. Another layer of hessian may be put on if required after the webbing has been fixed. This gives a smooth finish to the top surface before the strips of leather are tacked down.

Further, if a little padding is required to give a slight roundness to the top of the seat, a layer or two of felt or any thick cloth may be put on the top of the webbing to be covered by the leather.

Fixing the Leather Strips.—Cut the strips of leather, if not purchased ready cut, to widths of 1 in. to 2 in. and lengths equal to the distance from the bottom edge of one rail, across the seat and down to the bottom of the rail on the opposite side. It is advisable to allow about an inch extra on this length on account of the taking up of the leather when the strips are woven to form the seat. Cut twice as many strips as are necessary to cover one width. Tack the ends of half of these strips on the edge of one side, pass them across and tack down the other ends on the edge of the opposite rail as shown in Fig. 8. Now fix the ends of the remaining strips on the edge of another rail at right angles to the first two and weave the strips in and out among the first set alternating the in and out of each strip with its neighbours. Tack down the ends of these and cut off any superfluous length on the ends. One or two brass- or copper-headed nails for each end of each strip and knock them into the ends of the strips, in addition to the tacks; add an ornamental line of spots on the rails.

Variety of pattern can be obtained by using different widths of strips in combination and by using leather of different colours.

Solid Leather Covering.—A one-piece covering of leather can be put on if the seat is prepared with hessian, webbing, hessian, a layer or two of thick felt or several layers of cotton-wool trimmed off neatly to a little less than the square or rectangle of leather. The latter may be decorated by tooling, as described in the section on Leather Work, stained or left natural colour, or a piece of plain-coloured leather may be preferred. When the seat has been prepared and the leather top cut to about ½ in. larger than the felt, etc., on each side, it is tacked down into position by nailing into the top surface of the rail, first on one side, then on the *opposite* side. Then the other two sides are fixed, care being taken to obtain a smooth surface to the leather. After the tacks have done this work, a row of brass-headed nails are driven in to give a line of bright spots all round the edge of the leather.

If desired, this leather covering may be extended down the sides of the seat and fixed either on the sides of the rails or underneath them. In this case the slight padding should be brought out to the edges of the rails. The corners must be worked very carefully and neatly so as to give a fine neat finish.

CHESS

Many more people would play Chess if they realized that it is by no means difficult to learn and can be played at odd moments, if desired, or even by post with friends who are far distant.

Fig. 1.—The Pieces

The game is played on a board that is marked out exactly the same as a draught board—that means it has 64 squares alternately light and dark. Upon this board are placed a number of men: eight pieces and eight pawns for each player. These are King, Queen, Bishop, Knight, Rook, Pawn—there being two Bishops, two Knights, two Rooks and eight Pawns, with one King and one Queen for each player. One set of men is white and the other red or black. The board is placed so that each player has a white square at the corner of the board nearest his right hand. It is usual for the players to draw for colour. The pieces are then placed on the board as indicated.

The Moves.—First the King. This piece can only move one square at a time, but in any direction provided the square to which it is moved is not occupied by a piece of the same colour as the King itself, nor commanded by an enemy piece. The Queen may move in any direction and any number of squares but must not jump over any piece. The Bishops can only move diagonally, that is, the Bishops which are on white squares can only move on white squares, whilst the Bishops on black squares can only move on black squares. Bishops can move any number of squares at one time but must not jump over any piece. Knights have a move which to many people is confusing, but it is best described as one square in a lateral direction followed by a diagonal move of one square in the same direction. It should be noted that the Knight, unlike the others, can jump over pieces situated on neighbouring squares. Fig. 2 shows eight possible moves of the Knight from the square on which it stands. It may be moved to any one of the numbered squares. The Rook moves upon straight lines, only, and may occupy a square of either colour. Its movement is, of course, checked by the presence of other pieces. The eight Pawns can only move forward unless they are taking another piece, in

Fig. 2.—The Knight's Moves

which case they take a diagonal square in a forward direction, only replacing the piece taken. It is permissible, however, for a Pawn to move two squares on its first move, but at no other time. The Pawn cannot take any piece without moving diagonally, except under a certain circumstance called "taking *en passant*." This occurs when, say, a white Pawn has moved to the sixth square and a black Pawn makes its initial move of two squares and occupies the square beside its enemy. (*See* Fig. 3.) The white Pawn can then take the black Pawn *en passant* and moves to the position that would have been occupied by the black Pawn if it had only moved one square forward. White can only do this immediately after black has moved.

If a Pawn succeeds in reaching the far side of the board, it may be exchanged for any piece the player thinks fit. He may thus have two Queens if he so wishes.

Capturing.—A piece is captured by occupying its square and removing it from the board.

The Board.—In order to understand Chess properly it is necessary to learn the names of each square; thus assuming that we are playing white, the squares on the

Fig. 3.—The "En Passant" Move

QR1 QR8	QKt1 QKt8	QB1 QB8	Q1 Q8	K1 K8	KB1 KB8	KKt1 KKt8	KR1 KR8
QR2 QR7	QKt2 QKt7	QB2 QB7	Q2 Q7	K2 K7	KB2 KB7	KKt2 KKt7	KR2 KR7
QR3 QR6	QKt3 QKt6	QB3 QB6	Q3 Q6	K3 K6	KB3 KB6	KKt3 KKt6	KR3 KR6
QR4 QR5	QKt4 QKt5	QB4 QB5	Q4 Q5	K4 K5	KB4 KB5	KKt4 KKt5	KR4 KR5
QR5 QR4	QKt5 QKt4	QB5 QB4	Q5 Q4	K5 K4	KB5 KB4	KKt5 KKt4	KR5 KR4
QR6 QR3	QKt6 QKt3	QB6 QB3	Q6 Q3	K6 K3	KB6 KB3	KKt6 KKt3	KR6 KR3
QR7 QR2	QKt7 QK2	QB7 QB2	Q7 Q2	K7 K2	KB7 KB2	KKt7 KKt2	KR7 KR2
QR8 QR1	QKt8 QKt1	QB8 QB1	Q8 Q1	K8 K1	KB8 KB1	KKt8 KKt1	KR8 KR1

Fig. 4.—The Names of the Squares

row nearest to us reading from left to right are named as follows: Queen's Rook's square, Queen's Knight's square, Queen's Bishop's square, Queen's square, King's square, King's Bishop's square, King's Knight's square, King's Rook's square. The Pawn in front of the King, then, would be on King's second square and so on right across the board. As, however, each player reads the board from his own side it is necessary to give a diagram showing the square names. (*See* Fig. 4.) A study of this will make the matter quite clear. The advantages of learning the names of the squares are (1) that it enables Chess problems to be given without illustrating the board and (2) it enables persons at a distance to play by post, as each player by receiving his opponent's move may make the necessary alteration to his own board.

Having set the board in the manner indicated, we must next learn what the object of the game is. Briefly it is to force the King of the opposite player into such a situation that he can neither move nor remain in position without the danger of being taken by some other piece. He cannot actually be taken, but if he be placed in the position described (called checkmate), the game is at an end.

The Rules.—We are now ready to

learn the main rules. A player must not move any piece if by doing so his King becomes what is known as "in check," which means that the square on which the King stands is threatened by an opposing piece; nor can he move his King into check. But should a player be in such a position that he cannot move any of his pieces without putting the King in check, the game is drawn and the result is called "stalemate." A draw may occur if neither player has enough force left to checkmate the other.

Castling.—One important move that may be carried out by the King and either of the Rooks remains to be stated. If the King's Bishop and King's Knight no longer occupy their squares, these being left blank, and neither the King nor his Rook have been moved since the commencement of the game, it is possible to alter the positions of these two pieces in one move, and this is called "castling." The Rook is moved up to the King, and the King to the square on the other side of the Rook. Castling may not be carried out if an opponent's piece commands any of the vacant squares which the King has to cross. The King may also castle with the Queen's Rook, and in this case the King is placed on the Queen's Bishop's square and the Rook on the Queen's square. Castling cannot be carried out if the King is in check.

The next step is to learn how the moves are recorded and we will begin by playing a common opening. White moves first. The Pawn in front of the King is moved forward two squares and this move is recorded as P–K4. Black does the same, so the same record is set down. Going back to the white side it is found that in addition to the seven remaining Pawns, the Queen, the King's Bishop and both Knights may move. We will continue the game to its conclusion in order not only to show how the moves are recorded for each player, but to show a Giuoco Piano game in which white wins in ten moves.

Move 2.—(White) Kt–KB3. Black moves Kt–QB3. At this point it will be seen that the white Knight threatens the black Pawn, but the black Knight covers this piece, so that should the white Knight take the black Pawn the black Knight will take the white Knight.

Move 3.—(White) B–B4. Black moves B–B4. The rest of the game is as under:

	White.	*Black.*
4.	P–Q3.	KKt—K2.
5.	Kt–Kt5.	O–O (castles).
6.	Q–R5.	P–KR3.
7.	Kt takes P.	R takes Kt.
8.	B takes R (check).	K–R1.
9.	B takes P.	P takes B.
10.	Q takes RP (mate).	

If the reader sets out the board as directed and makes all the moves given in the above game, he will very quickly learn how fascinating Chess is. There are, of course, dozens of different openings and millions of different games, and it is for that reason that Chess will never be entirely mastered. At the same time the earnest player is able to recognize certain typical positions and can at any rate attempt to bring about mate as early as possible. Perhaps the quickest mate of all is that known as "Fool's Mate," the moves of which are as follows:

White.	*Black.*
P–KKt4.	P–K4.
P–KB3.	Q–KR5 (mate).

This is not regarded as serious Chess!

Another very quick game called "Scholar's Mate" is completed in four moves, as follows:

White.	*Black.*
P–K4.	P–K4.
B–B4.	B–B4.
Q–KR5.	P–Q3.
Q takes KBP and mates.	

Too great a stress cannot be laid on the importance of the opening moves, for a bad start means a perpetual fight against long odds. There is a great variety of openings, each being the result of much study and thought, and the player who takes the trouble to learn as many as possible will find that not only is his interest in the game increased but his play will benefit considerably.

The student should make a particular

study of those openings which will lead to rapid development, but it is necessary to know *why* certain openings are used.

Other Openings.—Consider the Giuoco Piano opening given above. The first three moves of each side are used by the greatest of Chess players simply because they provide a fine opening. The Scotch Gambit and the Ruy Lopez are other good openings. In the former the moves are:

1. P–K4.	P–K4.
2. Kt–KB3.	Kt–QB3.
3. P–Q4.	

The difference between the Scotch and the Giuoco Piano opening is in the third move of the white player who, by moving his Pawn to Q4, opens the way for the Queen to come out. The Ruy Lopez opening, however, in which white's third move is B–Kt5, provides a formidable attack.

As will be expected, there are many schools of thought regarding the opening moves of Chess. One of these holds that the best opening is that in which no piece is moved twice before all the other pieces have been developed. A moment's thought will, however, show that this plan is practically impossible, for it does not take into account the opposing side. Another school makes a practice of clearing a few pieces—and Pawns—from the board in the early moves, so as to allow greater concentration upon the remainder of the game. Such a procedure is, to many, an evasion, for they consider that it lessens interest. At all events, there is much soundness in the claim of Philidor that "Pawns are the very life of the game, and on their good or bad situation depends the gain or loss of the party." Philidor believed in advancing his Pawns until they reached the far side of the board, each Pawn being well protected at every step of its progress. Beginners are advised to study the methods advocated by such players as Lasker, Pillsbury, Dr. Tarrasch and the host of other eminent Chess players who have done so much to make the game interesting to their followers. It is, in fact, an excellent plan to follow a good game, step by step, and try to see the reasoning of each player's mind as the pieces on the board are moved. The advantage of playing with better players than oneself cannot be over-estimated, but opening moves should be studied first in order to avoid early defeat. Always be wary of traps, for an opponent will frequently sacrifice one or two pieces in order to gain a position of ascendency by drawing attention away from the actual point of attack. White always moves first, and may thus be considered the attacker, at least in the beginning of the game.

Openings for the Queen's Side.—So far we have only dealt with a few openings which have opened up the King's side of the board. Below are some well-known gambits for the Queen's side. A gambit is a particular kind of opening in which a piece or pawn is given up for a good position.

1. P–Q4.	P–Q4.
2. P–QB4.	P–K3.
3. Kt–QB3.	Kt–KB3.

Note how the game starts. The two first Pawns oppose further movement. White's second move threatens black's QP, so the KP is brought forward one square in support. White again threatens the QP with his QKt and the black Pawn is again covered with the Kt–KB3. Here are a further three moves, to show how the game progresses:

(4) B–Kt5. The Bishop threatens the black Knight, so black covers by moving his other Knight to Q2. White moves again: (5) Kt–B3, covering the Bishop should black move his Knight and expose white's Bishop to the Queen at a later stage of the game. Black moves B–K2. White's sixth move is R–B1, that is he puts it by the side of the Queen. Black castles, and so the game goes on.

Another good opening on the Queen's side is:

1. P–Q4.	P–Q4.
2. P–QB4.	P–K4.
3. P X KP. (X = takes).	P–Q5.
4. Kt–KB3.	Kt–QB3.

Note how the white Knight threatens the black Pawn which is covered by black's next move.

Occasionally a player will bring out the Queen's Bishop's Pawn as his first move, but all attempts to depart from the usual practice should be postponed until a fair measure of skill in the game has been attained.

A gambit that every player should know is one called the Evans gambit. This is a King's side opening, the first four moves being as follows: (1) P–K4, P–K4; (2) Kt–KB3, Kt–QB3; (3) B–B4, B–B4; (4) P–QKt4. The black player who finds that this opening is made by his opponent may meet the attack by moving Bishop to Knight's third. This is considered safe play.

A Blindfolded Chess Player.—A study should be made of methods of defence, and below are given the moves of an actual game that was played simultaneously with nine others, by one man (Mr. Blackburne), who was blindfolded throughout the whole series.

	White.	*Black.*
1.	P–K4.	P–K3.
2.	P–Q4.	P–Q4.
3.	Kt–QB3.	B–Kt5.
4.	P X P.	P X P.
5.	B–Q3.	Kt–QB3.
6.	Kt–B3.	Kt–B3.
7.	Castles.	P–KR3.
8.	R–K1.	Kt–K2.
9.	Kt–K5.	Castles.
10.	Q–B3.	P–B3.
11.	B X P.	Kt–Kt3.
12.	B–KKt5.	B–K2.
13.	B X QKt.	P X B.
14.	Kt X KtP.	R–B2.
15.	B X Kt.	B X B.
16.	Q–R5.	R–Q2.
17.	R–K3.	R–Q3.
18.	QR–K1.	B–Q2.
19.	R–K7.	B X R.
20.	Q–R8 Check.	K–B2.
21.	Kt–K5.	K–K3.
22.	Q–R3 Check.	K–B3.
23.	Q–K4 Check.	P–Kt4.
24.	Q–R6 Check.	K–B4.
25.	P–Kt4 Check.	K–B5.
26.	R–K4 Check.	P takes R.
27.	Kt–K2 Mate.	

This game is particularly intriguing, for it shows how quickly white started to harass the black King and ultimately drove him away from his base and from his supporters. It is interesting to note that Mr. Blackburne announced, at the end of his nineteenth move, that he would mate in another eight moves!

Traps and Stratagems.—It would be as well at this point to mention a few of the traps and stratagems the player will encounter, especially if his opponent is a more experienced player. Some of the standard openings given are full of traps, particularly the Ruy Lopez and the Giuoco Piano. Many players set a trap by moving quite carelessly the guard of an important position, but such moves should always be treated with suspicion. It is a good plan always to assume that your opponent does not make mistakes, and that every move has a real significance.

An excellent example of a trap is shown in the following game.

1.	P–K4.	P–K4.
2.	P–KB4.	P–Q3.
3.	Kt–KB3.	Q–K2.
4.	B–B4.	P X P.
5.	Castles (trap).	Q X P.
6.	R–K1.	

Here we see that the Queen is lost, for to move the piece to either side is to put the King in check, and this cannot, of course, be done. It will thus be gathered that to bring the Queen out early with the idea of taking a few Pawns is not always a wise plan.

Another common trap is shown in Fig. 5. White plays Kt–R4, and black, seeing that there is a chance of mating by moving his Queen to B7, takes the Knight that is offered him. White then removes his opponent's King's Pawn with his Bishop, thus putting black in check. Now a player can do one of three things when his King is in check—he can take the offending piece, he can move the King out of check, or he can place a piece or Pawn in between the King and the piece threatening him. In the example given above, he has the choice of moving the King to Rook's square or to the KB square, or of removing the white Bishop with the Rook. He does the latter, but loses his Queen.

Players should never overlook the fact that an opponent will sometimes try to lead a piece away from safety by dangling a prize. An instance of this is shown in the following. (Fig. 6.)

Black has just moved, playing his Queen to B3. Now note how white leads black on:

White.	*Black.*
Kt–Q2.	B–Kt5.
Q–B2.	P–R4.
P–Kt4.	Q X R.
P–Q4.	Kt–Q6 Check.
B X Kt.	P–QB4.

Kt–Kt3, and the black Queen is lost.

Fig. 5.—A Common Trap

To terminate a game satisfactorily, even if one has the advantage of pieces, is not such a simple matter as it at first looks. There is a tendency for the player—unless he is an old hand—to speed up his moves and at the same time to relax his vigilance; but careless play has many a time lost the game to the player who actually held the whip hand. For instance, how many people would back white to mate in two moves in the following:

White.	*Black.*
Kt on QKt1.	R on Q4.
B on QB1.	K on Q5.
R on QKt3.	P on KR6.
P on KB3.	P on KKt6.
B on QB4.	R on KR7.
K on KKt4.	Kt on QB7.
R on KR4.	B on KB8.
P on QKt5.	B on K8.
Kt on KKt6.	
Q on QB7.	

White moves his Knight to QR3. Black moves his Rook across the board to KR4, whereon the white King takes the black Rook and mates. Of course, the black Rook could have been moved to KKt4, giving check, but this would be a foolish move as the Rook is not covered. Again, black could have gone to KB4, but the result would be the same. Black would do no better to move the other Rook.

Tournaments.—The fascination of Chess eventually leads most players to partake in a tournament. It may be quite a private affair, or it may be a club event, but in any case, it is as well to know something about general conduct. First of all, the umpire's word must be taken as final in the event of dispute. The umpire does not comment upon any game unless he is appealed to, but the following rules should be observed by all players. The rules are now standard in the British Empire and also in the United States of America.

Fig. 6.—A Problem of Strategy

1. The player should never allow his hand to hover over the board. It is distracting to his opponent.
2. A player should make up his mind what piece he is going to move, and where he is going to move it, before actually touching the piece. Occasionally it may be necessary to adjust a piece, and in this place the player is required to say "*I adjust*" or words to that effect, before actually handling the piece. Failure to do this may result in the opponent's insisting that the piece be moved.
3. Should a player move out of his turn, he must retract the move. After the opponent has moved, the piece touched must be moved provided it can legally be played.
4. If the wrong player opens the game, a fresh start must be made if four moves have not been made when the error is discovered. After the fourth move the game must proceed as if the correct player had led.
5. Choice of colour is decided by lot.
6. If a player plays a piece on to a square to which it cannot legally be played, he must, according to the choice of his opponent, either move the piece legally, or move another piece legally movable.
7. If, in the course of a game, it is discovered that one of the Kings has been in check for one or more moves, all moves made after the check must be retracted, but if no recored has been kept or they are not remembered, the game is declared null and void.

As far as general rules for play are concerned, it is usually better for beginners to open a game on the King's side in preference to that of the Queen.

Speaking generally, the beginner is advised to castle early in the game, but it should not be done merely for the sake of doing something. As has already been pointed out, every move should be the result of much thought, and in accordance with a plan. Try to play with better players and to learn from every defeat.

HOME CINEMATOGRAPHY

Few pastimes have aroused so much attention in so short a time as the twin hobbies of Home Cinema and Cinematography. Although they are called twin hobbies, the projection of films has the wider appeal, and as the projector is the logical introduction to this new and fascinating hobby, the Home Cinema will be dealt with first.

These small projectors are very easy to operate, and a few minutes' instruction from the dealer from whom it is purchased will enable the novice to obtain good results.

When considering the purchase of a projector a number of points should be taken into account. One of these is the possibility of taking up Cinematography at a later date so that the projector and camera should be considered together, even if the purchase of the latter is not being thought of at the moment.

First cost and running costs will also have their bearing upon the ultimate decision, but the range is sufficiently wide to suit all pockets.

Projectors can be obtained which operate either by hand or by an electric motor.

Many of the former are so designed that an electric motor can be added afterwards if desired. When a motor is fitted, the operator is left free to prepare new spools, re-wind those just used or enjoy the programme. Both lamp and motor operate from the normal lighting circuit, though generally a resistance unit is used to reduce the voltage to that of the lamp and motor.

The lowest priced model—9·5 mm. projector—is hand-operated. A super reel attachment can also be obtained for larger models enabling super reels 300 ft. in length, equivalent to a twenty minutes' showing, to be used, thus bringing all the subjects in

Fig. 1.—The Pathéscope 200B Projector

the 9·5 mm. library within the owner's reach.

The 16 mm. is the de-luxe of the Home Cinema range, and prices are even more varied, being from a few guineas up to £100 or more; the latter compares in everything but size to the standard commercial projectors. These are rather beyond the scope of the individual, but are used by many Cine Societies.

The Films used range in size from 8 mm. ($\frac{1}{3}$ in.) to 17·5 mm. The standard commercial film is 35 mm. Naturally the larger the film the better the results and, generally, the larger the projection. In this, as in other things, it is well to get the best possible, but so great have been the technical advances during the last few years that even the lowest priced and smallest piece of apparatus will give a clear bright picture free from flicker.

The 9·5 mm. film was introduced from France in 1921. It differs from the 16 mm. in that the whole width of the film is used for the picture, the winding perforations being central on the film between each picture or "frame" as it is called instead of at the side as in the 16 mm. Because of this the 9·5 mm. film picture is not a great deal smaller than the 16 mm. This size is very popular with amateurs.

All sub-standard (by which is meant under normal size) films, such as are used in Home Cinema projectors, are non-inflammable and can be projected without any special precautions against fire.

The Screen.—One important aid to perfect projection is the screen. The usual is what is known as a "silver" screen, which not only gives good definition but makes the most of the light by its own reflecting properties. One unusual screen has a gold surface on one side which gives a soft pleasing appearance to the picture. The latest type of screen is the "beaded," which gives most amazing definition and brilliance, but which at the same time is very "directional." This means that when viewed from the side, the illumination falls away very rapidly. This is true also of the silver screen, but in a much smaller degree. A white screen gives the same illumination at whatever angle it is viewed, but the projected image is apt to appear "flat" and to lack the "sparkle" so essential with motion pictures.

Programmes.—Once the projector has been chosen the next thing is to obtain films and build up a programme. The first problem presents little difficulty as there are numerous film libraries which enable the user to offer a most ambitious programme. These films are just as easily obtained by the country dweller, who perhaps needs them most, as by those living in towns, for there is an efficient postal service. Films ordered by letter will be forwarded by return. In the 8 mm. film, libraries have a large selection of subjects which is being rapidly added to. Reels may be hired at a nominal charge per night or week-end, but if films are required regularly it is better to have a library subscription ticket, which enables the user to obtain any film in the library for one week. Rates vary from two guineas upwards.

The range of subjects in the film libraries is very large and increasing every day. There are sections relating to Educational and Instructional films, Travel, Sports, Manners and Customs, Industries and Agriculture, Popular Science, Useful Arts and Natural History, Reconstructed and Modern History, Comedies and Juveniles (which include many Charlie Chaplin films) and such favourites as "Mickey Mouse," "Felix the Cat," "Oswald the Rabbit," and "Æsop's Fables." Lastly there are Dramas and Light Dramas which include works by many well-known writers, and feature many well-known stars. These include such famous films as "Metropolis," "White Hell of Pitz Palu," "Q-Ships," "The Spy," "The Blue Light," etc. etc. Some of the latest talking pictures are now being re-edited as silent films and are proving very popular. Nor does the list end here, for news reels have now been placed on the market, each issue showing selected news events of the month. It will thus be seen that the owner of a projector has at his disposal an almost infinite variety of films, which will enable him to build up a really effective programme.

To get the best out of the hobby the programme should be chosen carefully and this is where the Home Cinema undoubtedly scores over the commercial cinema. The whole programme can be built up with the idea of creating the maximum interest together with an artistic presentation. If Home Movies are to mean anything at all, it is better not to "have a few films" but rather to undertake the task of building a balanced, harmonious, and pleasing programme, such as the commercial cinema is frequently unable to provide. Variety is the essence of real entertainment, therefore see that the films are varied. Children generally form part of the audience, and their interests should be studied, though adults are generally just as interested in the so-called children's features.

A Six-reel Programme will take about two hours to run, allowing for changes of films and a short break in the middle for refreshments. The programme could consist of a single-reel comedy followed by a long "feature film." A general interest film could follow, and the programme could be continued by another comedy or perhaps a news-reel, and concluded in real professional fashion by a trailer of "The King."

Seating, Lighting and Music.—When planning your programme plan your arrangements also. Have the seating accommodation prepared beforehand, the projector ready and in its place, and the light switch close at hand. If you can "dim out" your lights by means of a resistance so much the better, and if you can have a musical accompaniment to your films as well you will add considerably to the enjoyment of the entertainment.

A suitable musical background or accompaniment makes a vast difference to your programme and the gramophone pick-up is here a valuable ally. A good amplifier of adequate power and quality should be used, and the loud-speaker placed behind or below the screen. Unfortunately a record does not last as long as a film and it is not easy or convenient to change a disc in the dark. There is, however, a device called a "fader," which is a combination of two volume controls in one, which can be used with two pick-ups. With this device the two gramophones can be running at the same time with both pick-ups on the records. As the fader is turned in one direction one record will be heard, while turned in the other direction the music fades out to be replaced by the other record which is "faded in." This method can be operated through the amplification stages of a wireless receiver also.

Fig. 2.—Pathéscope Vioto camera "B"

Various gramophone manufacturers are catering for the home cine enthusiast by issuing records suitable for film accompaniment. There are also "effects" records which can be faded in or out as required.

It will be understood that we are referring to the use of silent films. Quite recently home talkies of a really practical kind have appeared, and will be dealt with at the end of this section.

Cinematography.—There is little doubt that once the novice has taken kindly to his new pastime, and has learnt to prepare his programme with skill and showmanship, he will desire to take the next step and make his own films. With modern apparatus the film produced by the amateur can, if intelligence has been used in its making, possess an appeal and a charm entirely its own.

It is a mistake to think that cinematography is far more expensive than ordinary snapshotting, and an examination of costs and prices will easily prove this. The home movie enthusiast must, of course, supply himself with a camera, but it is possible to get a really efficient 9·5 mm. camera for as low as 75/– which is quite a practical affair. He must also have a projector, which again can be obtained for a very low figure, as mentioned previously. With this equipment to start with the only extra cost is for films and developing. This naturally varies with the size, but a 30-ft. spool of orthochromatic 9·5 mm. film costs 4/6 including development. The film is returned mounted on a small reel all ready for use. A short length of film such as this can contain half a dozen cameos of action—baby playing with the puppy, Tommy diving at the baths, Tommy lighting the camp fire, Dad playing cricket, etc. There are no mounts to buy, no prints to pay for, no enlargements to be made. The first cost is the last.

Another point in favour of cinematography is its simplicity. With an ordinary camera you have to wind the film to the correct exposure and try to persuade your subject to remain still—and only those who have tried to photograph children and animals can realize how difficult this is, and how, when achieved, it results more often than not in a tenseness of expression which makes the subject quite unlike his real self. With the cine, on the other hand, after the camera has been loaded it is wound up, for it has a clockwork mechanism inside to turn the film, and when the release button is pressed the film moves continuously across the lens. The more the subject moves the better. Focusing is equally simple. The camera is held at eye-level, the subject is seen through the view-finder and the pictures are taken with ease. You cannot forget to turn the film on, for that is done automatically if wound up. If you have forgotten to wind it up then nothing happens. With a good camera and a reasonable amount of care, you will find that all your films will be good ones. Even mistakes will not ruin your film, for a few bad frames can be cut out of the film after developing, and generally such cutting will not be noticeable.

Films.—One of the most pleasing aspects of this hobby is the simultaneous improvement in and the lowering of cost of first class apparatus, and even the lowest priced camera, if correctly used, will give unvarying results. Correct usage, apart from focusing, generally means choosing the proper kind of film and right aperture for the light available. There are so many different films from which to make a choice that the novice is likely to be bewildered, but the dealer will always give good advice in this matter. Films may be classified as orthochromatic, panchromatic, and super-sensitive film, but great care should be taken when handling all these films before exposure, in order to prevent fogging. Films are loaded into the camera in several ways, but in the majority of cases may be loaded in daylight.

Choice of Subject.—The most beautiful of Nature's pictures are poor material for a film unless there is movement. It is movement that makes the film, so always photograph movement, if only trees waving in the breeze or a cascade of water over the rocks. Children, holidays, members of the family at sport and games, home pets such as cats, dogs, and birds, horses in the field all make good subjects. Incidentally, a film of yourself playing golf, cricket or tennis might well show you some of those faults which you suspected but were unable to cure. The movie camera is a candid but not always an unkind critic.

Whatever you take, avoid the commonplace. Do not take just some odd shots of the family doing nothing in particular, but try to arrange some continuity in the shots so that they will link up together. Keep each shot short—about six feet of film is plenty for one of those humorous holiday interludes—and have them as nearly as possible the same length. A six-foot length of film will take eight or ten seconds to shoot. After a little practice no difficulty will be experienced in this direction. One camera has an audible "footage" indicator, which clicks as each foot of film is passed through the camera. The nearer the subject is to the camera, the better the result. The exposure must be varied according to light conditions, aperture of camera, etc., otherwise the film will be spoiled. Instructions are always sent out with cameras, and an exposure meter will be of great assistance.

It must not be supposed that the camera is still limited to outdoor use as it was not so long ago, for in these days, with super-sensitive film and fast lenses, not only is the daylight range extended, but with the lamps that are now available scenes may be shot in the home, so that children romping in front of the fire, or the family Christmas gathering can both be permanently recorded.

Most sub-standard films are sold at a

price which includes developing or "processing" as it is called, and it is generally best for the amateur to have his films done in this way. Many experienced enthusiasts, however, prefer to develop their own films, this resulting in a certain saving in costs as some makers quote for films and processing as two separate items. Home developing outfits are also marketed, and these will take up to thirty feet of film.

Developing must, of course, be done in a dark room, and a good dark-room lamp is essential. Home developing is advised only for orthochromatic film, as panchromatic film, unless de-sensitized, is so highly sensitive as to require development in total darkness or in a weak green light.

It is not possible to give details here of the various processes, but information may be easily obtained from the manufacturers of equipment for this purpose.

Editing.—When the film has been shot and processed, there comes the difficult yet perhaps the most interesting operation of all, that of editing the film. This is for the purpose of making the action continuous or maintaining the sequence, and is just as necessary with a series of holiday shots as with a professional film.

The film should be run through first and a note made of any badly exposed portions, or anything else regarded as unnecessary. It should then be cut and spliced again. Shots can in this way be arranged in better sequence so as to give greater continuity, and portions of previous films can be included to assist the construction. Careful editing will make a tremendous difference to the effect produced, and it must not be forgotten that the introduction of an occasional "close up" will give the film something of the professional touch which is so greatly desired.

Splicing.—When editing, bear in mind that good splicing is essential for trouble-free projection. The reader is advised to purchase a splicer specially made for the size of film with which he is working. When films are joined, the two pieces of celluloid are actually welded together, the film cement dissolving the base of both strips. Each strip of film to be joined should be cut to about $\frac{1}{16}$ in. beyond the sprocket hole. Insert one of the strips in the splicer, shiny side up. Film cement will not dissolve the photographic emulsion of the image, and it is therefore necessary to scrape off $\frac{1}{8}$ in. of this emulsion from the remaining strip. Place this strip in position in the splicer, apply film cement to the scraped end (not too liberally), and clamp down for ten seconds. At the end of that time remove the film, and the result is a perfect splice.

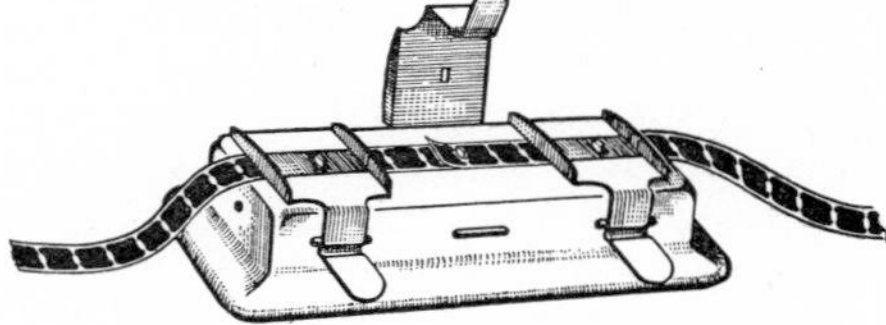

Fig. 3.—9·5 mm. Splicer

Part of the film editor's duties consist of inserting titles—such titles introducing the film, naming the actors, and explaining the action. There are many methods of making these titles, and the amateur may exercise

Fig. 4.—Home Titling Studio

his ingenuity in a variety of ways. Printed or written titles and drawings may be used, while even animated titles present little difficulty. The titles must be carefully photographed and inserted in the film at the correct places, the photography being done either by natural or by artificial light. There are some excellent titling benches, with which the amateur can produce titles of professional standard, now available at low prices.

One outcome of the interest in cinematography is the number of Cine Societies which have been formed to foster interest in the hobby and to widen the scope of the individual.

Membership in a Cine Society is often a valuable training ground for commercial cinematography as well as being a source of tremendous enjoyment.

Home Talkies.—No section on cinematography would be complete without a reference to home talkies. It is only recently that they have become a practical proposition, but already they are receiving much attention and are developing rapidly.

Two systems have been developed for home talkie work. One is the sound-on-film method, such as is used in professional studios. On the edge of the film is the "sound track." In the projection, as the light passes through, this track falls on a sensitive electric cell which sets up a varying electric current which is fed to amplifiers and loud-speakers. Thus the sound which was "photographed" on to the edge of the film is re-created and transmitted.

At present sound-on-film apparatus is rather expensive for home use, though many societies are now making and projecting their own talkies. The cheapest S.O.F. projector is £60, which includes amplifier and loud-speaker. Rapid progress is being made in this particular sphere, and there is little doubt that soon the size, weight, complication and cost of these outfits will be reduced. Already many professional productions are available in 17.5 mm. and 16 mm. sound-on-film versions.

In the second method—sound-on-disc—the sound is recorded on large-sized gramophone discs. Arrangements have to be made to synchronize the disc with the film and also to carry on from one disc to another without a break. One manufacturer has a library of sound film with discs available for hire. Apparatus can also be purchased enabling the amateur to make his own discs, which can be used to give running commentaries on his films, or may even be used for actual dialogue.

A complete home recording and reproducing outfit, comprising synchronizing, turntable, amplifier, batteries, microphone and recording attachment and discs, can be obtained for about £35.

COINS AND TOKENS

Many interesting collections of coins and tokens have resulted from a few old coins in mint condition (i.e. unused) having been preserved as mementoes of new currencies. The possession of such pieces has given an impetus to the hobby, and collectors, young and old, have frequently been thus influenced in their selection of a specialized group upon which they have centred their attention.

The coinage of the world presents a varied selection of currency, both in metals and values. To some the moneys of ancient times chiefly appeal; to others foreign currencies have a special fascination. To most people in this country, however, the coinage of the British Empire, especially that of early English coins, seems to be the most important branch of numismatics to pursue.

Briefly then, some of the more salient features in these varied currencies may be enumerated as a guide to collectors just beginning to assemble a nucleus of a cabinet of coins and tokens. It may be pointed out in the first instances that regal and authorized coinage has in many instances during the centuries been supplemented by irregular issues and by token currencies, sometimes issued by local authorities, at others by private persons in that at many periods the governments of this and other countries have failed to supply the needs of increasing commerce, or to give sufficient small change required for the payment of wages and for small purchases from retail shops.

Pre-Roman Coins.—When the Romans invaded England and settled in the land, they brought with them a plentiful supply of coins issued by the early Emperors, supplementing them later by coins struck in Britain, sometimes bearing the effigy of the Emperor, at others portraits of the generals who from time to time assumed almost regal power in this country. Many examples of Roman coins have been found on the sites of camps and villas, those bearing letters in the exergue, indicating British mints, having the greater interest. One example must suffice — "PLON" meaning Pecunia Londinensis, or money of London. There are extant gold coins imitating the gold staters of Philip of Macedon, then circulating in many countries in Europe, other early British coins bearing the ancient emblem of the triple-tailed horse. There are several types of Roman coins obtainable both in gold, silver and bronze, chiefly minted in Britain during the Constantine period.

Fig. 1—Coin Portraiture. Top L. Vespasian; Top R. Domitian; Mid. L. Septimus Severus; Mid R. Julia Augusta, his wife; Bottom L. Antoninus Pius; Bottom R. Geta, son of Severus.

Saxon Coins are rare. These bear the names of Alfred the Great, Canute, Edward the Confessor, and others of lesser fame. After the settlement of the country under Norman rule the number of mints increased. The silver penny, however, remained the chief coin of currency, supplemented in a few instances by halfpennies. The long cross, deeply engraved on the reverse, facilitated the breaking of pennies into halves, and also into fourthlings or farthings. As the centuries passed higher values were required, and gradually silver groats became popular coins. In size they were larger than the shillings of to-day, and their buying power much greater. In time they too were supplemented by shillings and eventually by crowns and half-crowns.

Silver Currencies.—Collectors desirous of building up an imposing cabinet may acquire large coins representing the more important silver currencies of the last few reigns. The current issue of crowns from Charles II onward are easily obtainable at moderate prices, although scarce issues and pattern pieces, representing the currencies of most of the reigns are more expensive.

Among these may be mentioned the beautiful Gothic crowns of Queen Victoria, and the florins of that monarch, following the earlier so-called "graceless" florin because of the omission of the "D.G." (Dei Gratia).

As the scarcity of silver was experienced from time to time the kings of England resorted to the expedient of reducing the size of the coins, and also their quality, notably during the reign of Henry VIII

Fig. 2. L. Silver Crown, William and Mary; Mid. Gold Noble, Edward III; R. Commonwealth Shilling

when the groat became merely copper washed with silver. Soon the more prominent features of the coins showed the copper base, thus giving rise to the nickname "old copper nose" given to Henry by many of his loyal subjects. It is interesting to note that in the reign of Elizabeth the introduction of the mill and screw made a marked change in the method of coinage, the milled coins contrasting favourably with the older hammered money. During the Civil War in England in order to find money with which to pay the Royalist troops in some of the besieged strongholds "Money of Necessity" was issued. These scarce pieces were struck at Beeston, Carlisle, Colchester, Pontefract, Newark and Scarborough, out of small pieces of silver plate, and are among the more envied treasures in English silver collections. The coins of Charles I, struck at the Oxford mint, represent the King on horseback carrying in his hand a drawn sword. There are several varieties.

Georgian Dollars.—In the early days of the 19th century the introduction of machinery in factories gave an impetus to production, and mill owners and others, owing to the shortage of current coins, issued token sixpences, and in some instances change in silver. Many of these minted in Birmingham were from well sunk dies, and are interesting souvenirs of the commercial history of this country at that time. The Bank of England also supplemented regal coinage, issuing Bank of England dollars and their lower divisional values. They were of equal weight and size to the current coins of that day, the so-called dollars passing as crown pieces. The Bank of Ireland also issued token money. Much treasure had been secured during the wars with Spain, and many Spanish dollars instead of being melted up and re-minted were put into circulation by the Government after over-stamping them with a portrait of George III or some emblem by which their currency could be recognized.

King John and Cromwell.—All periods of English history are full of reminders of insurrections, and in some instances coins bear portraits of rulers holding lesser positions in certain portions of the country or of British possessions like those of King John, which were struck in Dublin and bear the title of "Lord of Ireland." Another example are the coins of the Commonwealth with the legend "Commonwealth of England," and the motto "God With Vs"; and afterwards the issue of silver coins and lesser denominations bearing the bust of Oliver Cromwell as Lord Protector, and the somewhat unusual and interesting legend round the crown and shield of arms of England "Pax Qvaeritvr Bello" (Peace is sought by war). Incidentally it is interesting to note that the pattern coins of Cromwell, few of which passed into circulation, were the first to bear an inscription on the edge, in Latin, meaning, "A protection to the letters; a garland and a safeguard to the coinage."

Ecclesiastical Mints were at one time active, and the initials of Archbishops and Bishops are found on small coins issued in the Middle Ages from the Canterbury, Durham and York mints. Fortunately many English coins, although hundreds of years old, are in a fine state of preservation owing to their retention as souvenirs in many old families, and in some instances because they were buried or concealed for safety, forgotten by the owners to be discovered perhaps in an earthenware jar many feet beneath the ground or in the thatch of some old house in these later years.

Copper Coins have been popular both with amateur and professional collectors. English regal coins in copper may be said to begin (excepting for a few trial pieces) with halfpennies and farthings issued for general circulation in the reign of Charles II. From that time onward copper currencies have been issued in practically every reign. Pennies were introduced when higher values were needed, these larger pieces culminating with the cartwheel twopenny pieces of 1797. There are also collectable pattern halfpennies and farthings. The half-farthings and one-third farthings struck in the reign of Queen Victoria, mainly for use in Malta, are also interesting.

Tokens.—Cabinets of copper currencies should contain tokens which circulated in thousands of varieties in the later years of the 17th century. They were issued by traders, in some instances retail shopkeepers, and also by local authorities, who recognized the need of small change. They were redeemable by the issuers but gradually assumed a very general circulation. Thus numbers never found their way back to the tills of the issuers. These small copper tokens circulated until the year 1671 when they were suppressed by the Act of Parliament on the issue of regal currency considered to be sufficient for the public's need. Many of them bore the monograms and emblems of the traders by whom they were issued, mostly reading after the name of, say, John Smith, "His Halfe-penny"; there were farthings too and in some rare instances, pennies. These tokens included issues by tavern keepers, overseers of the poor and town authorities. Traders' tokens of the more recent periods have generally been of larger size, closely following the type and denomination of concurrent regal coins which they supplemented. They were issued in considerable numbers during the closing years of the 19th century, and in a few instances by traders in the reign of Queen Victoria in villages where works began to be established, and where there appears to have been no means of securing regal currency in sufficient numbers.

Scottish and Irish Currencies.—An interesting collection may be made of the currency minted by Scottish kings before the union of Scotland with England. They were of different sizes and somewhat irregular values, but it may be assumed that their buying power was regulated somewhat

Fig. 3. L. Sieze piece, Pontefract; Mid. Pattern Crown of Oliver Cromwell; R. Sieze or obsidial currency struck at Carlisle

by the size of the coin corresponding with similar issues across the border. Early Irish kings issued silver coins, but they are rare and difficult to discover. At a later period during the closer intimacy between Great Britain and the Sister Isle copper coins similar to English money were minted, the only difference being the reverse on which was the Irish harp and the legend "Hibernia" instead of Britannia. There are also a few interesting currencies collectable once circulating in the British Isles, such as the separate coinage of the Isle of Man, the earlier pieces bearing the crest of the Earls of Derby when they owned the island, the "Legs of Man" on the reverse denoting their origin. Later Manx halfpennies were superseded by regal coins bearing the busts of George III and his successors, and the usual legend on the obverse and the type of the Triune on the reverse. The coinage of the Channel Islands is also interesting, including the coins issued for use in Guernsey and Jersey on which are the respective arms of the islands.

Empire Currencies. — The British Empire has always been served with special currencies, both in values and in metals, the variety increasing as the Empire expanded. In the early days of the Plantations special currencies circulated in Virginia and other North American settlements—but these are all rare and difficult to secure. The Canadian Government issues its own currency now; in the time of Queen Victoria tokens as well as coins circulated, some of the former being issued by the Bank of Canada, the Bank of Montreal and by a few traders. Then there was a separate coinage for each of the provinces of Nova Scotia, Newfoundland and for Prince Edward Island. The needs of the growing commercial interests of Australia, insufficiently recognized by the government of this country, necessitated the issue of tokens by local business firms early in the 19th century. In later years British coins have mainly been used. Collectors will note that the Australian sovereigns bear the mint mark of Perth from which mint Australian gold is still issued. An Empire collection should include pieces of the Transvaal Republic with Kruger's head on the obverse to remind us of the days before the consolidation of South Africa.

Fig. 4.—Mid. Charles I crown minted at Oxford. L. & R. Obverse and Reverse of Charles I shilling

Foreign Currencies.—Only the briefest reference can be made to the coins of foreign countries. Almost every civilized country has issued separate coinages from early times. Many of the older nations possess coins carrying us back to earlier days, especially so Eastern currencies, among which may be mentioned ancient Chinese and Japanese currencies of gold and brass. The Chinese coins were at first in curious forms like knives and spades, and later the round or oblong coins had square holes in the middle by which they could be strung and thus carried conveniently. There are curious pieces, too, from

Persia and the Near East. To some the collection of early Jewish coins is of interest, especially those issued before the Roman Conquest showing types like the Rod of Aaron which blossomed and the Pot of Manna.

European Currencies.—Of these it is not possible to say much more than to point out that these go back to early times, like the Roman coins indicating the victory of the conquerors over the German hordes, inscribed "VICTORIA GERMANICAS." French coins include also Roman issues in Gaul and historically record the rule of kings, emperors and republicans; they bear legends of local value. There are eagles of many types noticeable on European coinages, thus the two-headed eagles of Austria are distinguishable from the eagles of Russia and some other provinces. More easily

Fig. 5.—Top. John Wilkinson halfpenny, 1788; Mid. Townpiece of Aylsham, 1795; Bottom, Cronebane halfpenny payable in Dublin, Newry or Belfast

Fig. 6.—Examples of 17th Century Trader Tokens

distinguishable are the separate coinages of Norway, Sweden, Denmark, Belgium and Spain. Italian currencies begin, of course, with the Roman consular coins, followed by the Imperial series of gold, silver and bronze from early days to the break up of the Empire and the separation of the Eastern and Western Empires of Rome. The Italian coins of later days have little connection in appearance with the Byzantine coins of the East—and so the story of coinage goes on and new issues are added as the result of changes in Governments and the creation of fresh states, and the growth and development of international commerce.

CONJURING AND CARD TRICKS

Most people wish at one time or another that they could do a little conjuring, but the belief that costly apparatus is necessary frequently deters them. There are many tricks, however, that can be carried out without the aid of expensive equipment, and there is no doubt that both conjurer and audience may spend a pleasant hour with a few simply learned tricks that require very little practice.

Need for Patter.—Quite half of the amateur conjurer's success is due to the ability to keep up a running fire of chatter which not only in itself causes much fun, but cloaks many a move on the part of the performer. For instance, if, when standing in front of several people one suddenly points upwards, it is safe to say that everyone watching will look to where the hand points. The action of pointing may be a perfectly natural one—merely emphasizing a remark or illustrating a happening—but all the same, the conjurer is able to do many little things whilst the attention of the audience is engaged elsewhere.

Capturing the Audience.—Speaking generally the performer should attempt to put his audience into a good humour in the first few minutes either by the performance of a trick that is so simple that everyone sees how it is done, or perhaps by pretending to make a deliberate blunder and apparently giving the secret away. It is a wise plan to grade the tricks so that the most impressive is performed last of all.

Although there are a large number of tricks which can be carried out without the aid of special apparatus, it must be admitted that the conjurer will gain much in prestige if he will expend a few shillings in the purchase of some simple apparatus.

False Fingers.—There are for example several excellent tricks which may be performed with the aid of a false finger or a false thumb. These are made of tin and painted a flesh colour.

A very puzzling trick may be performed with the aid of a false thumb. The performer borrows a handkerchief from a member of the audience, insisting that it be a good one. The more expensive, the better will be the trick. He then takes the handkerchief and drapes it over his right fist and cups his left hand to take the extended thumb of the right. To all intents and purposes he merely makes a depression in the centre of the handkerchief, which is then, of course, held in the left hand. After a few remarks in which he points out that he cannot of course guarantee the success of the experiment, and that handkerchiefs do sometimes become damaged, he withdraws a cigarette from his mouth, and, in full view of the audience, drops it, lighted end downwards, into the cavity. He presses the cigarette well home with his right thumb to make sure, as he informs the audience, that it has gone right through, and then takes the handkerchief by two corners and shakes it out, showing an unharmed square of silk. The cigarette has apparently disappeared. At the beginning of the trick the false thumb is placed over the thumb of the right hand, but whilst making the cavity—that is forcing the handkerchief into the half-doubled left hand—he leaves the false thumb behind. The cigarette is, of course, pushed into the tin cap, the pressure on the end being sufficient to exterminate the glowing tobacco. When shaking out the handkerchief, of course the false thumb is once more in position on the hand. It should be noted here that the cigarette should be as short as possible, for the tin thumb is not large enough to take more than half a cigarette.

The Divided Nut.—Another trick is performed with two brass nuts (engineering type) and a piece of string. One of the nuts is so constructed that it is in two parts, the halves fitting together so closely that they are looked upon as one. These may be purchased for a shilling or so. The magician hands round the whole nut for inspection, then he takes this and hands round the piece of string, and whilst this is being examined he quietly palms the good nut, or slips it into his pocket, and takes out the prepared one. The performer then asks a member of the audience to hold one end of the string and to make sure that the nut is definitely threaded on to the other.

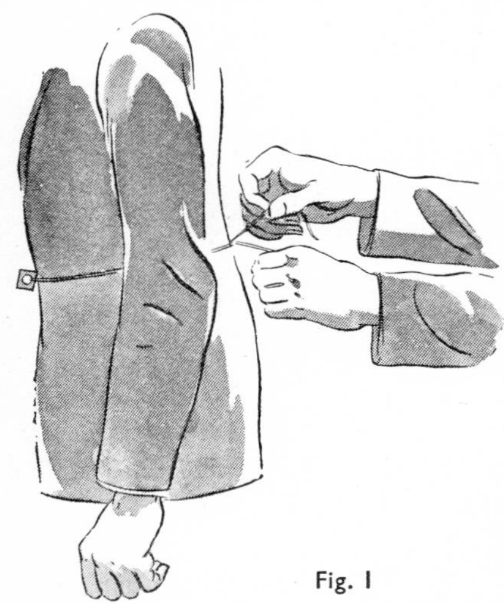

Fig. 1

When this is done he gives the other end to the assistant (who is not, of course, in the trick) and asks him to tie the string securely round the performer's waist. (Fig. 1.) The best position is for the performer to turn his back on the audience so that all can see that the string is securely tied. Even while the tying is going on the performer pulls apart the nut (Fig. 2), slips it into his pocket and takes out the original and untouched counterpart. This is a most mystifying trick and well worth its cost.

The Pocket-book Trick.—At most fancy goods stores one may purchase for sixpence or so a three-fold imitation leather pocket-book. The kind of thing designed for stamps, season ticket and a few visiting cards, etc., will suit admirably. The performer purchases two of these and makes quite sure that they are absolutely identical. If they are fastened by means of a press stud, so much the better. The design of the book should be such that on one side there is a pocket with a transparent ticket window. Into one of the season ticket pockets insert a piece of tin and then turn the book over and with a sharp knife, cut a rectangular hole through the leather. The hole should be about 3 in. long by $1\frac{1}{4}$ in. or so deep, but this will depend, of course, upon the size of the pocket-book. At all events, see that the larger part of the fold is cut away. Now remove the tin, and in place of it substitute a piece of white card. On this may be written the name and address of the performer. This prepared pocket-book is then secreted in one pocket. The other book is fitted with a piece of card the same as that in the prepared book. The performer then tells the audience that he is possessed of second sight. He asks one of them to write down on a

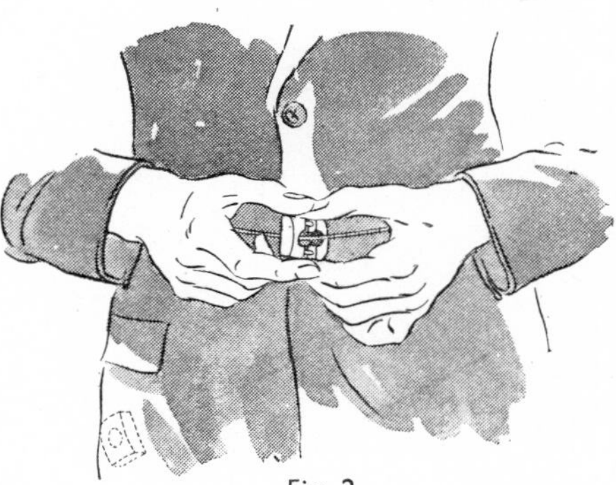

Fig. 2

piece of paper, which he of course supplies, as it must be of the correct size, a question which he would like answered. Whilst this is being done the pocket-book is passed round for inspection, but on being returned to him he substitutes the prepared book. In full view of the audience he then slips the paper on which the question has been written face downwards into the pocket behind the address card. The effect of this is, of course, that when closing the pocket-book the performer is able to read the question through the hole cut in the book. The flap is then fastened down, and with many weird gestures the magician holds the book to his forehead and pretends to transfer what is written into his mind.

During this transference he is able to think out a suitable answer to the question. This he gives. He then opens the pocket-book and withdraws the paper, reading aloud the actual query. This not only enables the rest of the audience to understand the answer, or at least to check the fact that the question answered was the one asked; but it also enables the performer to slip the prepared pocket-book away and produce for inspection the original and untouched one.

The Coin in a Box Trick.—The performer picks up from his table an ordinary polished wooden box about 3½ in. long by 2 in. wide and about ½ in. deep. The box has a sliding lid, similar to those made for pencils, etc. After showing that the box is empty, the performer asks a member of the audience to drop a penny or a shilling into the box. This done he closes the lid and rattles the box to show that the coin is still inside. He then drops the box into an envelope and seals it down, after which he takes the envelope in his hand and gives it a shake so that all can hear the rattle. The

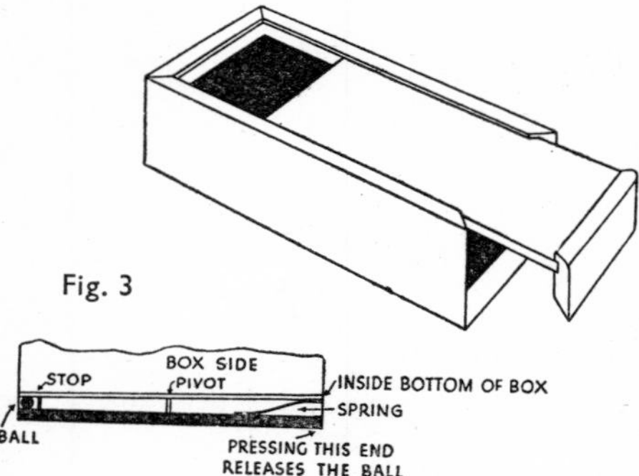

Fig. 3

sealed envelope is then placed on the corner of the table. It is as well to mention here that this moment is opportune for carrying out another trick, say the first one described, and on completion of this the performer will go back to the envelope, and drawing the attention of the audience to the fact that he has not been near the envelope and that it still remains sealed, he picks it up and shakes it. There is no sound. In apparent consternation he rips open the envelope, takes out the box, pulls off the lid and discovers the box empty. After pretended search he picks up a ball of wool and asks a member of the audience to unwind it, and inside is found the missing coin. This trick is delightfully simple to carry out. The box has a false bottom and works on a pivot. (Fig. 3.) When one end is pressed a ball-bearing is released and is allowed to rattle. It is this that gives the illusion that the coin is still in the box. Actually, however, the end of the box and the lid are joined together so that when the lid is pulled open the coin slides along the bottom of the box and into the hand. The lid is pushed back, the bottom pressed and the box gives out a rattle As of course the ball gives the only rattle, it does not make any difference whether the coin placed inside be a penny or a shilling, etc. To get the coin inside the ball of wool is quite easy. A small flat tube of tin can be constructed from an old cocoa tin. It should be sufficiently large to take a half-crown and should be about an inch long. (Fig. 4.) Around this tin tube is wound the wool to form a ball. Any odd moment is secured to drop the coin through the flattened tube and when the ball itself is picked up and handed to a member of the audience the tube is withdrawn and the ball pressed into shape. The trick is all the more exciting if the coin is marked in some way unknown to the performer. The ball of wool trick can of course be performed independently of the box and coin.

Fig. 4

The Wine and Water Trick.—Most conjurers at some time or other like to manufacture wines, and here is a trick that is particularly effective. The conjurer asks for, or has previously obtained, a jug of water and a couple of glasses. At the end of his wand are fixed a few grains of permanganate of potash. After pouring out half a glass of water the conjurer produces a piece of cardboard tube sufficiently large to cover the glass. He shows this to the audience and then carefully places it over the glass, hiding it from view. The wand is next brought into service, and to prove that the glass of water is still inside the cardboard tube the magician rattles the wand in the glass, lifts it out occasionally to show that the water is still there. After a moment or two's patter, he withdraws the wand and lifts up the cardboard tube, exposing a glass of "burgundy." He then goes on to say that perhaps some of the audience are teetotallers, and possibly the trick has rather upset them, so he picks up the other glass and pours some of the burgundy into it. To the amazement of all the liquid turns perfectly colourless. The magician may then say that he has gone from the sublime to the ridiculous and perhaps a compromise in the shape of a glass of cider would meet requirements. He thereupon pours the remainder of the burgundy into the glass, and to everyone's surprise the whole turns the golden colour of cider. The explanation of this trick is simple. Stirring the prepared rod in the glass of water quickly changes the colour to that of burgundy, but in order to change this into a clear liquid once more it is necessary to have some peroxide of hydrogen in the other glass. About a quarter of a glass is ample. If half the burgundy be poured into this peroxide all the colour is bleached and the liquid is to all intents and purposes clear water. But if more of the permanganate fluid is added, the resultant colour will be amber. It is necessary to point out that neither of the liquids is drinkable, and they should be thrown away immediately the trick has been performed.

The Magician Drinks.—Whilst conjuring with liquids the performer says that he would like someone to pour a certain amount of water into a tumbler, and then in full view of the audience to seal the tumbler with a few strips of gummed paper across the top, say two strips running each way. He then calls for someone to tie his hands behind him, and informs the audience that although his hands are tied behind him and the glass is sealed, he will nevertheless drink the water without either breaking the seal or freeing his hands. In order to perform this delicate trick, however, it is necessary for the room to be in complete darkness, so he calls upon someone to switch out the light. In a few seconds' time he asks for the light to be put on, and the glass is found to be empty, there is no trace of water on the edges and the performer's hands are still bound tightly behind him. This is an easy trick to perform. All the magician needs is a couple of straws, such as are used for lemonade, in the top pocket of his waistcoat. Immediately the lights are put out, he bends down and takes the straws in his mouth, pushes them through the open seal of the glass and draws the water up. The straws are then put back into the waistcoat pocket and a request made for the lights to be switched on.

The Coin and the Handkerchief—A very puzzling trick can be performed with no more apparatus than a handkerchief and a coin. After folding the handkerchief

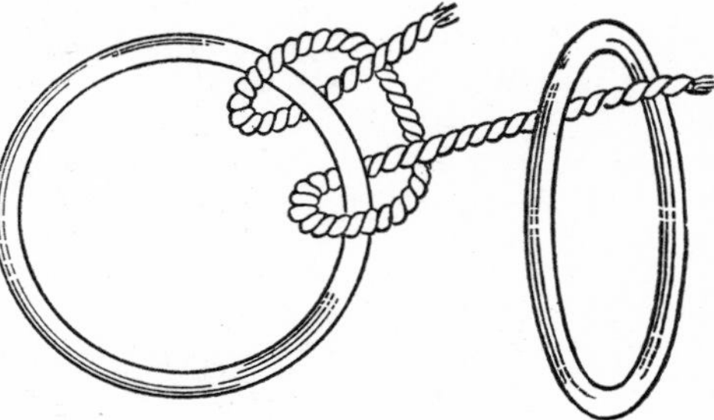

Fig. 5

once over so as to form a triangle, the two corners farthest apart are held, one in each hand. The handkerchief is then twisted, one end one way and the other end the other, after which the centre is tied in a knot and the handkerchief handed to a member of the audience.

The performer next takes a coin and causes it to disappear, either by palming or by other means. The handkerchief is then untied by the person holding it, and the coin found inside.

Two coins are needed for this trick. One is held in the fingers of the right hand, and after two turns have been loosely made in the handkerchief, the coin is introduced into the tube thus formed; it slides to the centre where it is tied.

Another mystifying trick, and one requiring only a dozen curtain pole rings and a piece of string or cord, is the following.

The cord should be about six feet long. Double the cord and pass the loop through one of the rings, then passing the ends of the cord through the loop as shown in Fig. 5. Two members of the audience are now asked to come forward and to drop the remaining rings on to the doubled cord, until the whole twelve are hanging together in the middle of the cord. The magician can then make the trick all the more intriguing by appearing to make it more difficult. He obtains an ordinary coat and passes one end of the cord through each sleeve so that the coat hangs down over the rings. He then gives one end to each of the assistants. A great deal of patter is going on all the time, the performer not, of course, saying what he is going to do, but stopping every now and again to show the audience that the rings are still firmly on the cord. He then announces that he is going to perform what is to all intents an impossible feat. Everyone saw him put the rings on to the cord. All know that the rings are still there—he shows them again to make quite sure. He will, he says, without cutting the cord, or interfering with it in any way, remove the rings, *whilst the two ends are held* by members of the audience. A quick movement beneath the coat, and the whole twelve rings drop on to the floor! It is perfectly simple to remove them, for by taking hold of the cord where it loops round the centre ring, and drawing it down the sides of the ring, all of them are released. Make sure that there is enough slack in the cord before releasing the rings.

CARD TRICKS

The ability to do a few card tricks is an asset to all, and here are a few of the lesser-known tricks which are well worth learning. None of them requires any apparatus, but the performer is strongly advised to learn a little patter as an introduction. Any performance will lose half its value unless the tricks are carried out with the maximum of flourish. It is not always wise to inform the audience of your intentions, although with some card tricks it is necessary to do so. This happens to be the case with the trick which may be termed the Divination Trick.

The Divination Trick.—The performer begins by talking about water divining, and may perhaps refer to some of the instruments necessary for discovering metals and so on. Whilst doing so he should take an ordinary pack of cards and thoroughly shuffle them. He can then ask someone to select ten pairs of cards which he places in pairs face downwards on the table. He then invites two persons in the audience to come forward and to pick up any pair of the cards, each person to make a note of the pair he has chosen. The cards are then gathered up a pair at a time in any order the member of the audience may like. The performer then drops the cards down on the table, one at a time, in a seemingly irregular manner, so that when finished he has four rows each consisting of five cards. He then turns his back whilst the two people who had chosen the pairs turn each card over to find out exactly where the pairs chosen are placed. He then calls upon each of them in turn to point to the row or rows in which the two cards are (they are, of course, now face upwards). The performer thereupon brings his powers of divination into play, and is successful in turning up the correct cards.

To carry out this trick successfully the performer must use a code, so that each card has a letter. For instance, the following code words can be used:

M U T U S
N O M E N
D E D I T
C O C I S

It will be noticed that every letter in the above code is duplicated, and as there are ten pairs of letters, one pair will represent the corresponding pair of cards. Now it does not matter in what order the cards are picked up, provided, of course, they are kept in pairs, but when throwing the cards down on the table in the form of four rows of five, they are dropped in a deliberate order. Looking at the code words it will be seen that the letter M is number 1 in the first row, whilst the corresponding M is number 3 in the second row. T is the third letter in the first row, the other T being the last letter in the third row, and so on. Thus when the cards are thrown down they should be dropped in the following order:

1	3	5	4	7
9	11	2	13	10
15	14	16	17	6
19	12	20	18	8

Each card should be dropped in turn according to the above figures, running, of course, from 1 to 20. Thus the first card down will occupy the top left-hand corner. The second card will be two spaces to the right and one down. The third card will be next to the first; the fourth card will miss one space, and go to the right of the third. The fifth card will fall in between. All the performer has to do then is to memorise thoroughly the code, and to practise dropping the cards in a careless manner, to see that they fall in the order given. Recognition is then rendered perfectly simple. If, for instance, one of the persons who chose a pair of cards says that the two he chose are in the first and fourth rows, it is obvious that these can only be the seventh and eighth cards thrown down, or, in other words, the two cards representing the letter S, therefore the two end cards in each row are the pair concerned. Should the other person point to rows 2 and 4, his cards will be found in the second place in each row, corresponding, of course, with the two O's in the words NOMEN and COCIS.

With the appropriate patter this trick is most effective.

Kings and Queens.—This is a very simple little trick, but nevertheless one that few people can do the first time.

Take all the kings and all the queens out of the pack, hand them to a friend and ask him to put them into such an order that when played in the manner described they will read, queen, king, queen, king, queen, king, queen, king. The method of play is as follows: Take the top card from the pack and turn it face upwards on the table. Place the next card underneath the pack. Put the third card on the table, the fourth underneath the pack, the fifth on the table and so continue until the whole of the eight cards have thus been played.

The cards must be arranged as follows: Q, Q, K, Q, Q, K, K, K. (*See* Fig. 6.)

The Infallible Choice. — The following trick will cause a good deal of amusement, particularly if the performer is able to add a certain amount of lively patter, and also to have a confederate (although the latter is not always absolutely necessary).

Take a pack of cards and ask someone to shuffle them, then spread them out roughly on to the table. Call upon different members of the audience to point to a card which you name. Finally you turn up the cards thus selected, showing them to be those named.

The method is this: After the pack has been shuffled, take a glance at the last card or last but one—suppose, for instance, this is a two of diamonds. You then call upon someone to pick out the two of diamonds. They will choose any card in the pack—perhaps the seven of clubs. (Of course, all the cards are face down on the table.) You take the card indicated, glance at it, and without showing it to anybody, ask another person to pick the seven of clubs. We will suppose that he points to the king of hearts. You thereupon take up this card, and after looking at it, ask

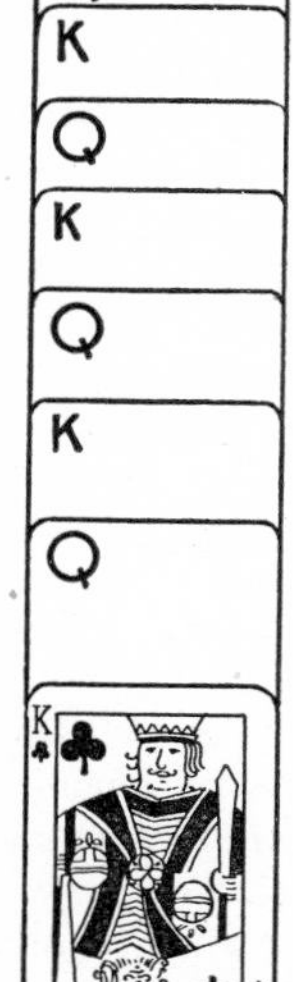

Fig. 6

someone else to pick out the king of hearts. This can be carried on indefinitely, although half a dozen cards is usually the best number. The confederate is requested to choose the last card, and he will, of course, point to the real two of diamonds. The performer takes this card, and then displays all the chosen cards, thus proving that each member of the audience has taken the card he was told.

Clairvoyant Whist.—There are numerous tricks which depend entirely upon mathematical calculation, although of course the performer has no actual calculating to do. An interesting prelude to a game of whist is the following: The performer takes a full pack of cards, hands them to a member of the audience and asks him to shuffle them, and then to take out any four cards. He does this with three other people, so that each one has four cards. He then tells them to imagine that they are in the middle of a game of whist, and asks each one to look at his hand and mentally to choose the card he would play if it were his lead. Each player may choose his own trumps, and, of course, play any one of the four cards. The performer collects the cards and shuffles the pack in full view of the audience. He then deals them out into four hands and takes up each hand in turn, spreads them out so that all can see them and asks each one of the players if the particular card selected happens to be in the hand displayed. If one of the players says that his card is among the four, the performer will immediately tell him which one it is. He then proceeds in the same way with the remainder of the hands, telling each player which card was chosen.

The secret of this lies in the fact that as each four are collected, they are slipped to the bottom of the remainder of the pack, and that whilst shuffling care is taken that the last sixteen cards remain undisturbed. It is quite easy to shuffle cards without altering the position of a number of them. It is here that the mathematics of the trick comes into operation, for when the cards are dealt round in four hands, the first nine of each pile are merely ordinary cards, but the last four of each pile together make up the sixteen chosen by the players. Now as the first player's cards were together, upon the second deal, one of his original choice will be found in each hand, and the same of course with the other three players. We see then that the first player's cards take the tenth position, the second player's the eleventh, the third player's the twelfth, and the fourth player's the last card dealt on each hand. When the performer exhibits the hand and one of the players claims that the card he mentally selected is in that hand it is easy enough to pick it out. Thus if the last player states that his card is there, it is quite obvious it will be the end card. This is a very mystifying trick, and one which causes a great deal of fun.

The Spelling Trick.—The performer takes a full pack of cards, shuffles them and asks a member of the audience to select any one. The pack is then cut several times, and the person who chose the card is asked to replace it. The performer then asks the name of the card, after which he proceeds to count off the cards one by one, spelling out the name of the card chosen as he does so. He turns up the last card and shows it to be the one selected. For example, suppose the two of spades were chosen, the performer would spell t-w-o o-f s-p-a-d-e-s, and the next card he turns up and exhibits is the two of spades.

This is quite a simple trick, for whilst the selected card is being passed round, the performer counts off 11 cards into his right hand, the chosen card then being placed on the top of the rest of the pack. This may be cut if desired, but care should be taken to see that the original top cards are also the top cards of the newly arranged pack. When counting out the performer must make a note of the number of letters in the name of the card chosen, for instance, if the seven of clubs were selected, the card representing the s in clubs should be turned over to exhibit the seven of clubs. It is a simple matter to calculate the number of letters and a little practice will enable the performer to carry out this trick without any hesitation.

A good many mystifying tricks can be played if the performer obtains two packs of cards that have the same design on the backs. Any cheap cards will do and they may be purchased at almost any stationers. Open one of the packs and arrange the cards in a certain definite order. It is best to see that the suits come in turn, and this may be alphabetical, such as clubs, diamonds, hearts and spades. The thirteen cards of each suit are then set out according to some particular plan, the following being one of the simplest, each word of the couplet suggesting, as shown, one or more of the cards of a suit:

"Eight Kings threatened to save
8 King 3 10 2 7
Ninety-five Ladies for one sick knave"
9 5 Queen 4 ace six Jack."

The cards are then placed so that the eight of clubs is on the top of the pack, the king of diamonds follows, the three of hearts is the third and the ten of spades is the fourth card. The same order is carried out until the pack is completed. This prepared pack is placed in a waistcoat pocket beforehand. When the trick is to be performed the other pack is unfastened and handed to a member of the audience with a request that they be well shuffled. The performer then takes them and, turning his back upon the audience, walks towards the end of the room or to his table. Whilst doing this, he slips the shuffled pack into the pocket and extracts the prepared set. After picking up a wand, he turns to one of the audience, places the pack in his hands and announces his intention of naming every card in the pack in the order in which they happen to be. With a great show of divination he calls out the first card—the ace of clubs—and this card is then turned up. The performer goes thus through the entire pack, calling each card in turn.

Another Spelling Trick, but one which requires the use of a second pack, is this: Count out thirteen cards on to the table and hand them to a member of the audience to shuffle. Then, returning to the table, the performer spells out each letter of 13 cards, ranging from the ace to the king. As each letter is called out, the top card is placed underneath the pack, but *on the last letter of each word* the card is thrown face down on the table. T-W-O and the deuce is dropped. T-H-R-E-E and the three follows. This is continued until every card has been dropped in the right order.

A little preparation is necessary for the trick, for the performer selects beforehand 13 cards, from the ace to the king, and arranges them in the following order: Q, 4, 1, 8, K, 2, 7, 5, 10, J, 3, 6, 9. The word "Jack" and not "knave" must be spelt. After the member of the audience has shuffled the 13 cards, the performer when returning to his table, changes this pack for the prepared one. The prepared pack is arranged, of course, so that the queen is the top card.

The trick can be made even more mysterious if a second prepared pack is concealed, this one being in a slightly different order so that when each card has been spelled out the NEXT one is turned up to reveal the card spelled. The order in which the cards should be arranged for this trick is 3, 8, 7, 1, Q, 6, 4, 2, J, K, 10, 9, 5.

The pack that has been used once is passed to a member of the audience, and substitution made as before.

The Travelling Cards.—The performer who does not mind going to a little trouble, can prepare, at very small cost, some interesting tricks for his repertoire. One such trick is performed as follows: During some entertaining patter the magician places two chairs, one on each side of the room, and upon each stands a bowler hat, brim upwards. He then takes a pack of cards, shuffles them, and selects two, these being, let us say, the two of hearts and the six of spades. He holds these cards up so that the audience may see them. It is his intention, he says, to place the two of hearts in the hat on his left and the six of spades in the hat on his right, then, standing between them, he will wave his wand and the two cards will change places. He then turns to the audience and says that a miracle has been performed, but states that his powers do not end there, for by waving his wand once more, and uttering some different magical words, the two cards will be changed again, and thus be as they were at the beginning of the trick. Having done this he walks to the hat on the left and exhibits the two of hearts, and from the hat on his right draws the six of spades. (Fig. 7.)

Fig. 7.—The Travelling Cards

The audience will, of course, say that the cards have never been changed, and in order to prove that they are wrong he proceeds to do the trick once more, but when he has changed the cards once, someone will want to see them. The magician will pretend to be embarrassed, and walk over to the hat on his left and draw from it, to everyone's amazement, the six of spades, whilst from that on the right he will take the two of hearts. The explanation of this trick is quite simple. From two similar packs of cards withdraw the two of hearts and the six of spades (or, of course, any other two cards desired). It will be found on examination that the cards are composed of two pieces of paper. On one is printed the card's denomination, whilst on the other is printed the back design. It is quite easy to separate these two cards. Having separated all the four cards, that is the two twos and the two sixes, paste them to form double cards. This means that there will be two cards, each showing a two of hearts on one side and a six of spades on the other. In performing the trick the magician naturally inserts the two prepared cards in the ordinary pack (if a third pack is used the corresponding untouched cards should be withdrawn, to avoid mistakes). He selects the prepared cards and shows them to the audience, taking care, of course, that only one side of each is exhibited. When it is required to show that a change of position has taken place, the card, as it is lifted out of the hat, is merely turned over.

CROCHET

CROCHET is an ideal type of work for the woman who dislikes her fingers to be idle, but who does not want to choose a hobby that will make demands on her mental energy and that requires little "fuss." It has one disadvantage when compared with knitting: it takes considerably more thread, with the result that it easily becomes rather expensive. Also, it is not so elastic. On the other hand these apparent disadvantages can be turned to good account. The extra thread and consequent thickness and warmth, if in wool, make it practical for children's clothes, while its firmness is a great advantage when knitting garments that are not intended to stretch much.

Materials and Tools.—Crochet is done with a crochet hook and this tool is obtainable in steel, wood, bone and celluloid. The last for wool work is much to be preferred as it is lighter and free from any roughness which can easily spoil the evenness of the work. The steel hooks for very dainty lace are extremely fine, while for coarse work the hooks are very large. One word of warning; the fine crochet hook is a really dangerous tool with its hooked end, and when not being used it should always be protected.

The threads used for crochet work are very varied. Almost all kinds of wools are used, although the finer, light-weight wools are most popular. Recently the wool firms, catering for the rising popularity of crochet during the last few years, have produced a firmly twisted thin wool that is excellent for jumpers, berets, etc., as it is not easily split by the hook. In addition to wool, there are numerous crochet cottons, linen and silk threads. For modern dress accessories, such as bags, belts, etc., a fine macramé string is sold.

The Stitches and First Exercise.—The beginner should first master several of the elementary stitches and try to acquire a quick and even rhythm of working. A No. 8 hook and fairly coarse wool should be used for practice work.

To Hold the Work.—With the left-hand thumb and first finger, hold the first stitch or the fabric. The wool as it comes from the stitch passes over the first finger, which is held well up, and then under the third and round the fourth finger.

To Commence Chain Stitch.—Make a loop on the hook, which is held in the right hand, and hold the thread as described above and hold on to the bottom of the stitch on the needle. Fig. 4 shows how the hook is directed under and over the thread to pull it through the loop. Continue making chain in this way, trying to keep all the chain the same size and very even.

This makes a good cord for vests and jumpers and is the beginning of most patterns.

Single Crochet makes a very narrow row of stitches and is the shortest in height

Fig. 1.—Single Crochet

of all the stitches. It is used for joining at the ends of rounds and "slip stitching," as it is often called, along a piece of fabric to continue the pattern elsewhere.

To crochet, make a length of chain and then insert the needle through one of the foundation chain loops and proceed as in Fig. 5. Pull the thread through both loops on the needle.

Double Crochet (*see* Fig. 6) is an excellent stitch for a firm and flat surface.

Make a length of chain and on this work as follows:

1st Row.—Miss 2 chain, * draw a loop through the next chain and then draw a loop through both stitches on the hook. Repeat from * to end of row.

2nd Row.—Make 2 chain, * draw a loop through the next chain and then draw a loop through both stitches on the hook. Repeat from * to end.

Repeat this row all the time.

If a Flat Surface is Desired insert the hook through both threads forming a chain along the top edge of the previous row.

For a Ridged Surface insert the hook through the back one of the two stitches forming the chained edge.

Half Treble (Fig. 7).—Make chain the required length. Miss 3 chain, * wool round the hook, draw a loop through next stitch and then draw a loop through all three stitches. Repeat from * to end. 3 chain, turn.

Fig. 2.—Treble

2nd Row.—Crochet as from * in first row.

Treble (*see* Figs. 2 and 8).—Crochet a length of chain.

1st Row.—Miss 3 chain, * wool round hook. Draw a loop through the next stitch to the height the stitch is required to be when finished. Draw a loop through the first 2 loops on the hook, then draw a loop through the two remaining loops. Repeat from * to end. 3 chain, turn.

2nd Row.—Count the 3 chain as 1 stitch, then work 1 treble into the next stitch and then into every following stitch. Work 3 chain at the end and turn.

Repeat the 2nd row.

Long Treble (*see* Figs. 3 and 9).—Make a length of chain.

1st Row.—Miss 4 chain, * wool twice round needle, draw a loop through the next chain stitch, draw a loop through the first two loops on the needle, draw a loop through the next two loops and another through the last two loops. Repeat from * to end. Make 4 chain.

2nd Row.—Repeat from * in previous row.

Abbreviations for Above.—ch.=chain stitch; s.c.=single crochet; d.c.=double crochet; half tr.=half treble; tr.=treble; long tr.=long treble.

To Increase.—Work two stitches in one stitch, or in the case of a pattern, 2 groups of stitches into a stitch.

To Decrease.—In plain fabric, miss a stitch. In fancy patterns, directions are usually given.

A Ball for Baby.—Fig. 6. It is always important for the beginner in a craft to make one or two simple things first and the little ball described here is an exercise of this kind; simple and quick to do, it makes a delightful little gift for a baby.

To Crochet.—Make 16 chain, into this work 4 d.c., 8 tr. 4 d.c. and then 1 ch. to turn. 2nd and all other rows, 3 d.c. 8 tr. 4 d.c. When 18 rows have been worked, gather each end up tightly and fill the ball with crumpled tissue paper. Sew up the side. If a string is to be attached to the ball, crochet a chain the required length. The ball can be made any size desired and can be worked in stripes of various colours.

A Round of Crochet (*see* Fig. 6).—This is another easy exercise that can be quickly worked. In the illustration it is worked in wool with a fairly large hook and as such is ideal for the top of a beret or tam-o'-shanter. Worked in knitting cotton it would be suitable for a mat for a washstand. In crochet cotton it could be developed for a d'oyley or table centre and with still finer crochet cotton it would make an attractive inset for lingerie.

Fig. 3.—Long Treble

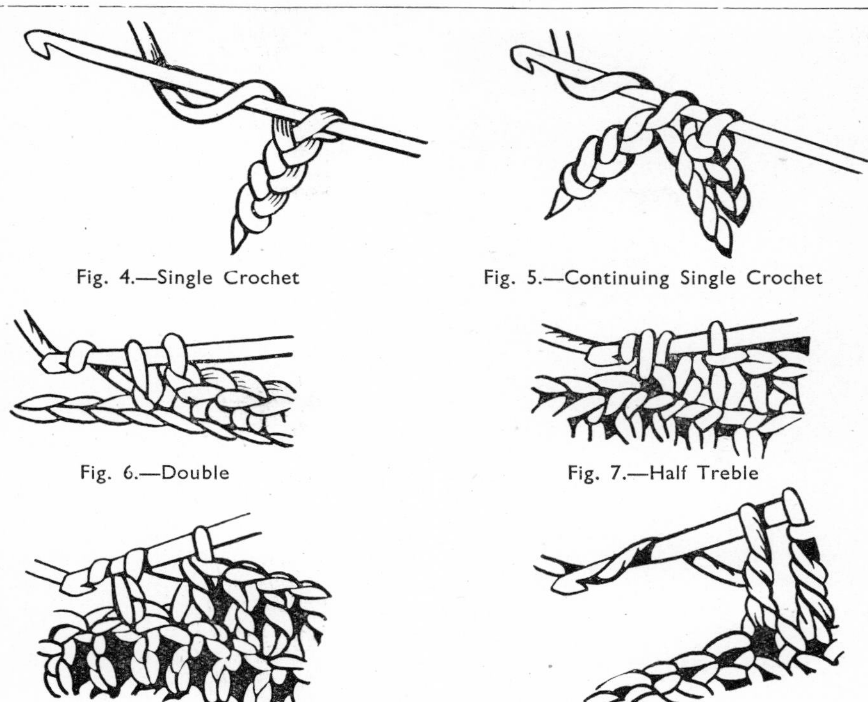

Fig. 4.—Single Crochet

Fig. 5.—Continuing Single Crochet

Fig. 6.—Double

Fig. 7.—Half Treble

Fig. 8.—Treble

Fig. 9.—Long Treble

How the Stitches are made

To Crochet.—Make 6 ch. and form into a ring.

1st Round.—* 6 ch. 1 d.c. taken into the ring. Repeat from * 5 times, i.e. 6 loops in all.

2nd Round.—Slip stitch (2 single crochet) 2 stitches, then make 4 ch. for the first long tr. Then make 5 long tr. * 2 ch. 6 long tr. Repeat from * to end of round, i.e. 6 groups altogether.

3rd Round.—1 d.c. into every stitch.

4th Round.—1 d.c. into every stitch.

5th Round.—6 ch. * 1 tr. into 3rd stitch, 3 ch. Repeat from * to end of round and then join.

6th Round.—5 ch. (for first long tr.), 5 long tr. into first space, * 2 ch., miss space, 6 long tr. into next space. Repeat from * to end of round and join.

7th Round.—1 d.c. into each stitch.

8th and 9th rounds, as the 7th round.

If it is desired to develop the circle into a wider one the pattern can be continued as from the 5th round. If, however, it is desired to make this into a beret, the 10th round (for increasing) would be * 2 d.c., 2 d.c. into one stitch. Repeat from * to end. Do two plain rows of d.c. and then an increasing round and so on until the crown is large enough.

When no increasing is done the shape will curve in and when the edge near the forehead is approached rounds of decreasing should be worked, e.g. * 2 d.c., miss a stitch. Repeat from *.

A Very Attractive Beret.—The beret described below is not only very effective and becoming to the wearer, but is an excellent exercise for the amateur as it introduces a variety of stitches and patterns. (*See* Fig. 6.)

To Crochet.—Make a ring of 4 chain.

1st Round.—8 d.c. into ring and join with a slip stitch.

Fig. 6.—A Round of Crochet, a Ball and a Beret

2nd Round.—3 ch. 1 tr. into 1st stitch, 2 tr. into each stitch of ring (16 altogether). Join with a slip stitch.

3rd Round.—3 ch. and then 2 tr. into each stitch and join with a slip stitch.

4th Round.—3 ch. * 2 tr. into 1st stitch, 1 tr. into next stitch. Repeat from * to end of round (48 stitches) and join.

5th Round.—3 ch. and then 1 tr. into each stitch and then join.

6th Round.—3 ch. * 2 tr. into 1st stitch. 1 tr. each into next 4 stitches. Repeat from * to end and join.

7th Round (commencement of open-work).—* 7 ch. 1 d.c. into 4th stitch. Repeat from * all round.

8th Round.—Work slip stitches to top of loop and then * 7 ch. 1 d.c. into 4th chain (top of loop). Repeat from * to end.

9th and 10th Rounds as 8th Round.

11th Round.—Slip up 4 stitches. Then 4 ch. (for 1st long tr.) 3 long tr. into loop made by the chain in previous round, * 1 ch. 4 long tr. into next loop. Repeat from * to end.

12th Round.—3 ch. for 1st tr. and then 1 tr. into each stitch.

13th Round.—1 ch. stitch for first d.c. then 1 d.c. into each stitch.

14th Round as 13th Round.

15th, 16th and 17th Rounds.—1 s.c. into each stitch.

18th Round.—4 ch. 1 tr. into 4th stitch, 3 ch. 1 tr. into same 4th stitch, * 1 tr. into the 3rd stitch further on, 3 ch. 1 tr. into the same stitch as last tr. Repeat from * to end.

19th, 20th and 21st Rounds.—1 s.c. into every stitch.

22nd (last) Round.—5 s.c. * 5 ch. twist this chain to make a picot, 5 singles, repeat from * to end.

THREE SIMPLE FABRIC PATTERNS

Shell Pattern.—(Fig. 7.)

This is ideal for shawls, scarves, berets, bed-jackets, babies' coats, jumpers, etc.

Fig. 7.—Shell Pattern

Make a chain the desired width of fabric.

1st Row.—4 ch. more, 6 long tr. into 5th ch. from hook. * 1 ch. 7 long tr. into 7th ch. stitch further on. Repeat from * to end. Turn with 4 ch.

2nd Row.—* make 1 d. into 4th long treble. 7 long tr. into the 1 ch. between the groups of 7 long trebles in previous row. Repeat from * to end. Turn with 4 ch.

3rd and successive Rows.—* 1 d. into 4th, 1 tr. then 7 long tr. into the 1 double in previous row. Repeat from * to end.

Crossed Treble Pattern.—(Fig. 9.)

This is not such a close pattern as the Shell one, but forms quite a firm enough pattern for babies' garments and jumpers, scarves, etc.

Make a length of chain.

1st Row.—Miss 3 ch. * 1 d.c. into the 4th ch. 3 ch. 1 tr. into the same 4th ch. 1 tr. into each of the next 3 ch. Miss 1 and repeat from * to end of row. 3 ch. to turn.

2nd Row.—* 1 d.c. into loop formed by 3 ch. in previous row and then 3 ch. and 4 tr., all under the same 3 ch. of previous row. Repeat from * to end.

All rows as 2nd row.

Open Lace Pattern.—(*See* Fig. 8.)

Because of its open nature this pattern is suitable for summer jumpers, scarves, summer caps and simple lace edgings.

Commence with length of chain.

1st Row.—Miss 4 ch. 1 d.c. into next chain * 1 ch., miss 2 ch. 1 tr. 2 ch. and 1 tr. all into the next chain, 1 ch., miss 2 ch. 1 d.c. into next ch. Repeat from * to end.

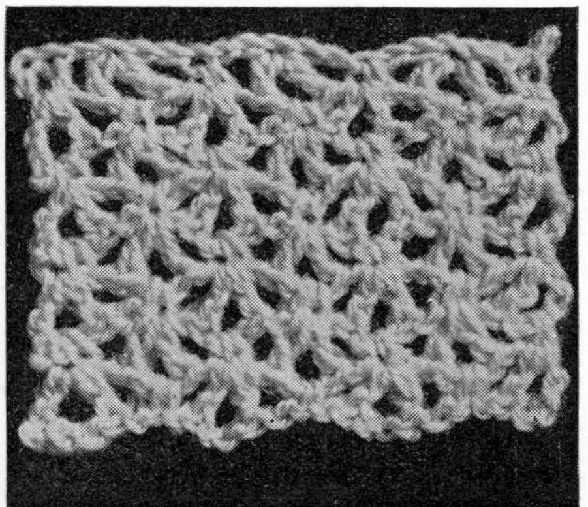

Fig. 8.—Open Lace Pattern

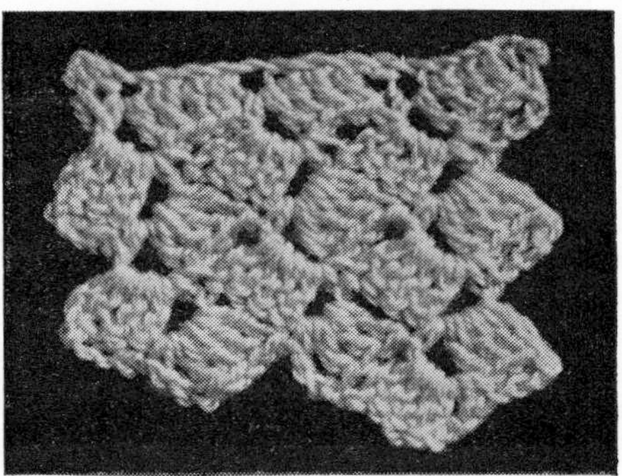

Fig. 9.—Crossed Treble Pattern

2nd Row.—4 ch. 1 tr. into the first d.c. below * 1 d.c. into next 2 chain space, 1 ch. 1 tr. 2 ch. 1 tr. all into next d.c. Repeat from * to end. 1 ch. turn.

3rd Row.—1 d.c. into first space * 1 ch. 1 tr. 2 ch. 1 tr. all into next d.c. 1 ch. 1 d.c. into next 2 ch. space. Repeat from * to end. Repeat these last 2 rows.

Fig. 10.—Lace Edging

Two Charming Lace Edgings.—(*See* Figs. 10 and 11.)

Many readers will be anxious to try their skill at finer work, such as lace edgings for little cloths and children's things. Directions therefore are given below for two easy edgings which can of course be worked just as well in wool for the edgings of shawls, quilts, etc.

No. 1 Pattern.—(Fig. 10.)

Commence with a ring of 10 chain.

1st Row.—10 d.c. into this ring, turn.

2nd Row.—* 4 ch. 1 d.c. in 2nd d.c. Repeat from * 4 times (5 loops in all), turn.

3rd Row.—* 4 ch. 1 d.c. into 1st loop,

4 ch. and 1 d.c. into the same loop. Repeat from * into the next 2 loops. Then 4 ch. 1 d.c. into next loop, 8 ch. 1 d.c. into next loop, turn.

4th Row.—As the 1st, putting the 10 d.c. into the loop of 8 ch.

5th, 6th, 7th and 8th Rows as the 2nd, 3rd, 4th and 2nd Rows respectively.

9th Row as the 6th Row, except that the first loop of chain which after 2 ch. are worked is caught back with a d.c. into the

Fig. 11.—Lace Edging

2nd loop of previous fan on the same side. Then work 2 ch. and proceed as in the 6th row.

Repeat from 7th Row.

Top of Edging

1st Row.—Join thread on to the first loop of a fan and work 3 ch. (for 1 tr.) * 5 ch., miss a loop, 1 tr. in next, 6 ch., miss a loop, 1 tr. into next (or next fan) and repeat from * along the length.

2nd Row.—* 5 d.c. in loop of 5 ch. 1 d.c. in tr. 7 d.c. in loop of 6 ch. 1 d.c. in tr. and repeat from *.

If the above two rows are worked on the other side as well an insertion is formed.

No. 2 Pattern.—(Fig. 11.)

Commence with a ring of 10 chain.

1st Row.—10 d.c. into this ring. Turn.

2nd Row.—* 4 ch. 1 d.c. into 2nd d.c. Repeat from * 4 times. Turn.

3rd Row.—4 ch. 1 d.c. into first loop, 8 tr. into next loop, 1 d.c. into 3rd loop, 8 tr. into 4th loop, 1 d.c. into 5th (last) loop, 8 ch. and 1 d.c. into same loop. Turn.

4th Row.—As 1st Row, putting 10 d.c. into loop of 8 ch.

5th Row.—As 2nd Row.

6th Row.—As 3rd Row.

7th Row.—As 4th Row.

8th Row.—As 2nd Row.

9th Row.—As 3rd Row, except the first loop of chain, after two chain are worked, is caught back with a d.c. into the 4th tr. of fan below on the same side. Then work 2 ch. and proceed as 3rd Row.

Repeat from 7th Row.

Along one edge work as follows:

1st Row.—1 d.c. into first fan, * 6 ch. 1 tr. into 2nd fan, 6 ch. 1 d.c. into next fan. Repeat from *.

2nd Row.—1 tr. * 2 ch. 1 tr. into 4th stitch. Repeat from *.

CURIOS AND ANTIQUES

Buying curios for home use and decoration is naturally governed by the opportunities for their display and by the character of the building in which they are to be housed. Modern architecture is especially helpful to the householder, in that many of the new buildings are adaptable to furniture representing well-known periods when certain types of furnishing were strictly observed. Others, although quite different in the arrangement of the rooms and their appointments, are suitable for the display of ornamental curios. Foremost among such are fireside appointments and ornaments. Some modern grates and fireplaces suggest the use of the beautifully perforated brass fenders, hand made a century or more ago, many of which are to be obtained in excellent condition, and which are exceedingly decorative when used in conjunction with little brass trivets and perforated circular and oblong stools. Then there are chimney-piece ornaments, many of brass, some representing miniature tables, others little coal boxes, the brassworkers evidently drawing their inspiration from the larger pieces they fashioned for regular use. Dogs and other animals cast in iron as well as in brass, occasionally painted realistically, are interesting examples of the ornaments

Fig. 1.—Fumigator

Fig. 2.—Candlestick

Fig. 3.—Early Jug

Tudor Pottery

on the hob grates of old-time fireplaces. Where there is wall space, and especially if you have an inglenook, copper warming-pans, many of which were beautifully engraved, can be hung side by side with carved wooden bellows for use or ornament. Old kitchen utensils, such as brass fish slices, long ladles and brass and latten spoons, are also appropriate ornaments upon the chimney jamb.

Trays.—Birmingham metal ware, especially tea trays, look charming. Some of these are painted with representations of old English scenes, others with birds of Paradise, and other fanciful creations. Some are inlaid with mother-of-pearl and even tortoiseshell with curious effect. In earlier times tin-ware of a specially ornamental type was decorated and enamelled and japanned at Pontypool in South Wales. This includes canisters, waiters and snuffer trays, as well as beautifully modelled tea urns and decorated caddies. Old tea caddies of wood and metal have always been favourite household curios and can still be put to a practical use, especially caddies with the central compartment holding a glass sugar bowl and fitted with a silver caddy spoon. Then there are the string boxes and curious receptacles for needlework which our grandmothers used, and the workbox, too, with its delightful little fittings in ivory, pearl and, in a few instances, tortoiseshell, often still retaining traces of the silks and cottons used, and of the beeswax reel. Small inlaid woodware is among the scarcer objects on which the cabinet-maker showed much skill and originality of design, notably the famous Tonbridge ware, representing in mosaics floral sprays and rural scenes. Among the scarcer examples are boxes having on their lids pictures of old castles, churches and family mansions and ruined abbeys. These charming souvenirs, purchased by visitors to the famous Tunbridge Wells, were inlaid with thousands of tiny fragments of wood.

Old Silver for the sideboard and for use upon the table has always been regarded as among the choicer collectable objects for the home. There are cups and porringers as well as dainty cruets, salts, peppers and casters. Silver candelabra and pillar and dished chamber candlesticks are attractive pieces and still useful. There are taper-holders and many curiosities associated with letter writing in olden times, when the quill pen was used, necessitating a special sharpener as well as the pen-knife, together with many oddments, such as seals of ivory and silver with ornamental handles.

Pewter is a favourite subject for the collector, and even when its collection is not taken seriously odd pieces of old pewter, which polishes almost like silver, adds to the lustre of the sideboard or of an old Welsh dresser on which it can be appropriately shown. Pewter platters and dishes, especially those engraved with armorial bearings, may be hung on the walls or arranged on the sideboard or overmantel. There are also many little objects of pewter still suitable for table use, such as salt cellars and pepper boxes.

Fig. 5.—Silver Cream Jug, 1797

Fig. 4.—A Silver-mounted Coconut—George III, about 1800

Kitchen Utensils and cooking vessels of wood turned from locally grown apple, cherry, box and yew still retain an excellent polish. Then there are the smaller inlaid wooden articles following the designs of contemporary furniture, such as clock cases, barometers, tea caddies and knife boxes, and also salt boxes, all of which make interesting decorations.

Pictures no longer crowd the walls; fashion decrees that they shall be few in number, and when used should correspond in style and character. Obsolete styles, such as paintings on glass, are curious and contrast well with distempered walls or modern styles of decoration and panelling. Pictures in needlework have been popular at all periods of English history. Especially noticeable are the delicate floral petit-point pictures and later cross-stitch, wool work and the scarcer types known as print work, imitating the lines of the engraver, who worked mainly during the last few years of the eighteenth century and during the first decade of the nineteenth century. For small rooms miniature portraits on ivory or copper, portraits in water colours on card, daguerreotypes and even early photographs on glass are better than larger pieces.

Enamel. — The rarer enamels of Limoges are especially fascinating, and also the old enamels of Canton and the cloisonné enamels of China and Japan.

English enamelled trinkets of Battersea and Bilston in rose and blue are especially charming and include oddments such as patch-boxes, knife-handles, etui-cases, and scent-bottles. Many of these are doubly interesting because of sentimental mottoes on them, such as "Think of me" and "This Trifle in your Mind I hope will Favour Find."

Fig. 6.—Needlework Picture

Those who have a cabinet suitable for the display of mosaics and inlays have an endless variety of choice.

A Glass-topped Display Table can appropriately be included in any modern room. Wall cases, too, are useful and economize in space.

Derbyshire spas were at one time made up into ornaments for the drawing-room table, including little vases, bowls and curiously shaped dishes for trinkets. Among the different spas is the rare variety from the Blue John mine, rich in colour effects, and sparkling when the sun shines on it.

Antique "souvenirs" are a study in themselves. Perhaps the most interesting are those from Buxton, Cheltenham, Bath and Tunbridge Wells, and others mostly ornamented with views. In some places fossils found locally have been mounted as brooches and for paper weights.

Leather Work was once put to odd uses, including vases for flowers, ornaments for the wall or for the table, and sometimes as substantial brackets for china figures. There are also leather baskets of flowers, many framed for hanging on the walls in deep recessed frames.

Tobacco Boxes make an interesting collection, both the larger types, formerly kept near the chimney corner, made of wood, copper, lead or pewter, and the small pocket boxes of brass, principally engraved by Dutch artists and introduced into this country at an early period. They were followed by boxes in iron and steel in later days and have now been supplanted by rubber pouches. Then pipes of all periods, from the introduction of tobacco into this country in the days of Sir Walter Raleigh, are curious, including the simple pipes of clay and the decorative Meerschaum pipes, many of French and German manufacture. Many quaint old pipes have been found in ancient rubbish heaps and have upon the heel makers' initials; of later varieties are the Broseley clay "churchwarden" pipes.

Fig. 7.—A Collection ranging from Ancient Greece to Nineteenth Century France

There are also metal racks which were at one time used in all houses for the renewal of the pipes by burning them in the oven. There are pipe stoppers and knives with stopper ends, and there are, of course, snuff-boxes of wood, *papier mâché* and in all metals, including presentation snuff-boxes of gold, frequently encrusted with jewels.

Sportsmen will find many things suitable for the decoration of their halls, smoke-rooms and lounges, including guns and relics of ancient amusements and sports. Others take a delight in curios brought back by early explorers, such as savage weapons and relics of primitive man. Daggers and knives are worth collecting, especially the daggers from the South Seas in which were cunningly concealed rows of sharks' teeth —terrible weapons when deftly handled. Native dress and ornaments of beads curiously wrought are interesting but apt to collect dust.

Glass Curios.—Old English and Irish glasses have always been favourites because of their variety. Modern reproductions of Georgian tumblers and jugs indicate that the designs are still popular. Glass chandeliers and candelabra are expensive and suitable only for the larger house, but old lustres with their cut-glass droppers make beautiful ornaments. So also are Bristol glass and Nailsea vases with their quaint markings and colours.

Sheffield Plate is, of course, quite a different thing to modern electroplate. Genuine Sheffield plate was an art discovered and practised by Thomas Bolsover in 1740, providing household plate at a less cost than sterling silver. It was produced by welding together two thin sheets of silver under and over a plate of copper. From this material table plate similar to that which had previously been made in solid silver was fashioned. To cover the copper edge of the vessels showing between the two plates of silver a gadroon border was welded on, preserving the plate and giving it a better appearance. Much old Sheffield plate has been preserved in good condition and it will often be found that an extra shield of solid silver has been fastened in a prominent place, its thickness being sufficient to admit a monogram or the arms of the owner being engraved thereon.

There are many more objects that may be studied by the amateur collector, but space forbids their mention. It is hoped, however, that enough has been written to indicate the wide and fascinating field of action and to inspire the amateur to search for specialized information on the type of antique ornament that takes his fancy.

ANTIQUES

Genuine antiques should be distinguished from old things which, although out of date, are by no means necessarily types of ancient craftsmanship or arts which have no modern replica. Antique furniture has always had a special fascination for the collector and for those who are fortunate enough to possess homes in which they may be appropriately displayed and used. Period furnishing is a favourite hobby, and in order to give the right atmosphere and environment to the furniture there must be a well-arranged scheme of decoration and an appropriate setting for antiques and appointments used in conjunction with them.

Fig. 8.—Dark Blue and Gold Worcester Mug. Crescent Mark

Period Furniture.—Old oak furniture is seldom quite suitable for the requirements of the present-day householder, although some pieces are useful and attractive, as for instance the old oak chests once general in houses of timber and plaster and blackened beams. The oaken settles which occupied an important position in the inglenook of some old farmhouse may be appropriately displayed in the entrance hall or even in the modern lounge. Again, there are the massive oaken chairs of the Cromwellian period, the richly carved tall-backed chairs of Jacobean taste and those rich in the scroll work of Carollian times. The furniture of William and Mary showing indications of Dutch influence is also attractive; and the later developments of Queen Anne's reign provide useful examples for home use.

It was then that needlework was a popular amusement, and ladies of the household embroidered curiously designed coverings for their furniture and bed hangings, as well as fashioning rich Genoa velvets for their settees. These beautiful fabrics and the finer petit-point work were used by old-time upholsterers, and the screens they made and the stools they covered are choice objects to acquire. Smaller pieces of old furniture and household appointments are also collectable, such as the carved Bible boxes which

Fig. 9.—Crown Derby Cup in Blue, Red and Gold

Fig. 9.—Worcester Cup with Square Mark

Fig. 10.—An Oak Chest Studded with Iron Nails from the Door of an Ancient Castle

now serve as ornaments in the modern home.

Throughout the whole of the periods of furniture-making, craftsmen have introduced special features which give the collector to-day an ample choice in design and ornament, if not in purpose. Dutch marquetry has a special fascination for some; others prefer the more delicate tracery of Sheraton's designs or the elaborate carvings of Chippendale. These great artists left designs which are still followed, altered in some instances to suit modern conditions. Bedroom furniture is mainly assembled in representative rooms in leading museums where the old four-post bed and its hangings accord well with carved overdoors and mantelpieces.

Metal Work is especially interesting and among favourite antiques are the works of the smiths of old. They fashioned fireplace ornaments and dog grates, and in the Sussex foundries were moulded quaint grate backs on which were heraldic ornaments; often the monograms of reigning sovereigns, especially of Charles II and William and Mary, together with royal arms were added. Antiques associated with the home are naturally among the more appropriate collectable curios, other than objects sought by connoisseurs who have galleries at their disposal for the display of their hobbies and the things they discover and collect.

The term "antiques" seems to embrace the products of every workshop and village smithy, and of old-time crafts which have fallen into disuse as well as relics of the ancient practice of the several crafts. Thus we have the beautiful spinning wheels which may well be sought by the collector of old things and given a prominent place in a home furnished according to the style of almost any given period. Even the tools that once served the village blacksmith, who has left so much hand-wrought metal work for us to admire, are objects of interest.

Clocks.—Among the more valuable antiques acceptable in the modern home are the grandfather clocks, many of them, perhaps after some two hundred years' service, still working accurately. Then there are the so-called Cromwellian bracket

Fig. 11.—A Fine Elizabethan Settle

clocks and cruder clocks working with chains and weights, such as may be secured in country sales for a trifle and easily restored, ready to adorn the walls of modern dwellings, especially those representing old styles. Again among antiques are the things associated with architectural work, whether attached to the buildings or merely used as adjuncts in accordance with the architectural style adopted. In olden times the City Companies and Guilds, like the Worshipful Company of Braziers, had a supervising influence over the work of their members and directed the training of apprentices, hence it is that in metal work of those times there is a distinct evidence of quality, many pieces made by country smiths having indications of local origin and use.

Arms and Armour.—There has always been a special fascination about arms and armour. It is true that most of these relics find their place in museum collections, or are retained in one of the few baronial halls where ancient style is kept up and the relics of traditional use are treasured as mementoes of the past. There are, however, odd pieces of armour which may possibly have been used during the Civil War in England, met with from time to time in the sale-rooms. There are also interesting examples of old guns, such as were in use in this country by sportsmen a century or more ago, including the earlier wheel-locks and flint-locks, and later the percussion guns, which sportsmen used before the days of breech-loaders. There are swords and pistols reminiscent of duels fought often, and blunderbusses carried by the "Stand and deliver" type of "gentlemen of the road" in former times.

Fig. 12.—Jacobean Oak Dresser

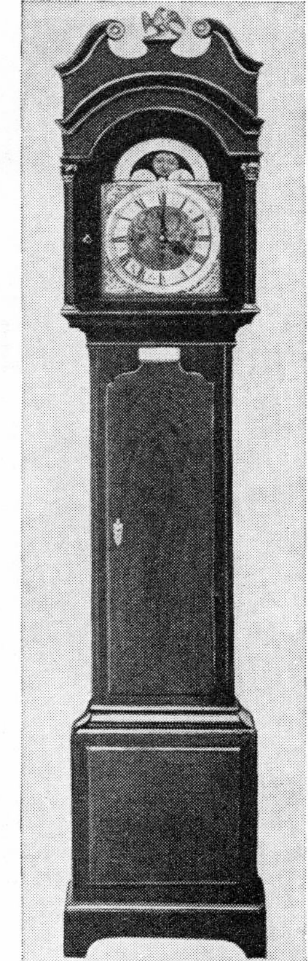

Fig. 13—Grandfather Clock of Chippendale Period

Another interesting hobby is found in the collection of fire-making appliances, and tracing the way in which civilized peoples gradually acquired the art of kindling a fire by striking flint and steel and igniting tinder by the spark. Old tinder-boxes and many curious relics of early fire-making are to be found stowed away in the attics of old houses. There is a special interest, too, in ancient lanterns of horn and of candlesticks and candle boxes. Many people are fond of relics of the days when horses and wagons carried the traffic of the road.

Horse Brasses are of many different types, emblematic of ancient beliefs and

Fig. 14.—Windsor Armchair on Rockers, Period 1810, made of Yew, the seat of Ash

superstitions at one time inseparable from those who used the road. They are still to be seen in use. The more favourite emblems were the crescent moon, the lotus of Egypt, the Kentish horse, card diamonds and hearts and the sun's radiating rays. A horse laden with these talismans against the influence of witches and evil spirits was thought to be also immune against accidents.

The mention of brasses suggests the collection of rubbings of the brasses on ancient tombs, among them the effigies of medieval knights which, when mounted in an album, make an interesting souvenir of visits to old cathedrals and churches. It has been said that many who fought in the Great War brought back with them curios acquired in the villages of France where they were located. War relics and medals have always been a favourite study, and not infrequently curious objects are met with in the sale-rooms connected with earlier wars, and in many old houses there are still treasured relics associated with Waterloo and Trafalgar and of the more recent Crimean War and the Indian Mutiny.

Weights and Measures.—A very interesting collection may be made of these, including measures used for grain and other products of the land as well as in ordinary business. There are collectable measures of bronze, moulded when Elizabeth was Queen, bearing the royal monogram and sometimes dated. Although steelyards dating from Roman days have been found, weighing machines are not exactly collectable objects, other than the scales and weights which were formerly used by business men everywhere for the weighing of gold coins in the days when much worn gold circulated. Some of these are in the form of balances; others like ordinary scales in miniature with loose weights, such scales and weights usually fold up and can readily be carried in the pocket.

Old Keys make an interesting hobby which may be pursued at small cost. Some are weighty, others delicate in their intricate cutting, and are suitable ornaments for a lady's chatelaine. Many interesting examples have been found on the sites of old buildings. Curious padlocks have also been turned up when ploughing fields, relics of the times when farmers carefully padlocked their gates to prevent their cattle from being stolen.

Fig. 15.—A Beautiful Example of a Chippendale Chair

A Curious Hobby.—The necessity for insuring premises against fire has long been recognized. The earlier insurance companies issued to their insurers labels or shields indicating that the premises were insured by a given company. These, many of them of considerable size, in lead or tin, and in some instances copper, were painted or gilded emblematically, generally with the arms of the Association, thus forming a useful advertisement for the company, perhaps giving the semblance of security to the insured. These labels have in many instances been preserved when pulling down old buildings, and now and then quite large collections come into the market in the sale-rooms. In lesser numbers, many of them in excellent condition, these fire labels may be secured from dealers' shops and from builders when demolishing old houses.

Rural Collections.—Country folk are sometimes at a loss to know what hobby to take up at small cost. They feel a special interest in things relating to their own craft or occupation or to their country surroundings. Quite recently interest has been shown by advanced agriculturists in the quaint tools and implements which served in the days before agricultural machinery was commonly used.

Prehistoric Remains.—The collector might go back further and add to his hobby the prehistoric implements which served both the tiller of the soil and the primitive worker in wood, so many of which have been found in all parts of England. These flints were fashioned in the form of simple axe-heads, hammers, scrapers, borers and in a few instances implements which have been designated "saws," which were simply knife-shaped flints, chipped so as to give them some resemblance to the teeth of a saw. With these tools they wrought some of the curious relics of ancient Britain which have been found in the barrows and mounds and during excavations far below the foundations of modern dwellings. Curious objects too have been dredged from the Thames and other rivers, including weapons of war and the chase, as well as domestic implements and primitive pottery which had been made on the spot from local clay.

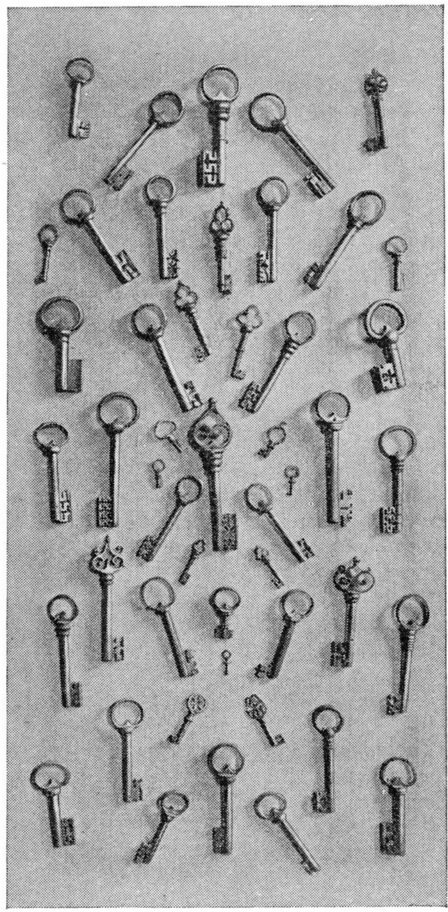

Fig. 16.—A Rare Collection of Old Keys

Reminiscent of the old-time woods of England may be mentioned the box and the yew and also the beautiful bog oak found mainly in Ireland from which so many curios were fashioned a century or more ago; these in their turn have become antiques linking up the more remote periods of Britain with present-day hobbies and museum exhibits.

Finally a word of warning. In these days of organized faking it is often very difficult to distinguish a clever modern copy from a real antique. Curators of local museums are usually helpful and it is always wise to get the opinion of a qualified expert.

CYCLING

CYCLING is a very delightful pastime. To the young and the old, to those who wish to attain fitness, those who wish to keep fit and those whose vitality demands a strenuous athletic outlet, cycling, in its many varieties, makes an immense appeal. In itself, purely from a health point of view, it plays a great part in the creation and upholding of physical well-being. To the not-so-strong it offers a means of gentle open-air exercise. To those of normal health it offers more strenuous exercise. To the athlete it gives the opportunity for the fierce struggle against time or his fellow-man, on road or track.

Choice of Machine.—Do not be in too much of a hurry when getting your first machine. It may not be an advantage to get an inferior quality or a machine that does not meet your requirements, merely for the sake of having it new or of making full payment straight away. If you can make your choice without troubling about cost, then this way of buying a bicycle is ideal.

To buy second-hand you need either to be experienced or to deal with someone on whom you can entirely depend. The instalments plan is particularly attractive to those who, by cycling, can save bus or tram fares to work each day, and so have this economy to put against the instalments.

Types of Bicycle.—The two extremes, or basic types, are the full roadster and the racer. The full roadster is strong, inclined to be large, built for security and comfort, probably an all-weather machine, fitted with all manner of accessories. It is consequently heavy, and is useful only for big and heavy riders in rough country—the racer cares nothing for comfort. It is slim, very light, may look fragile, though it is not, is sparsely equipped and has weight saved at every point.

It is possible to get machines of all grades between these two extremes, and so it is necessary before buying that you shall know exactly the purpose for which your machine is required. Remember that you will have to supply the motive power, and that the lighter your machine the easier it will be to propel. Do not confuse lightness with flimsiness—modern methods of construction have made even the lightest of bicycles strong enough to stand heavy wear.

If you intend to use your machine solely for business purposes, in all weathers, then you will need one with ample protection. Many firms now manufacture a light type of machine, fitted with gear-case and full mudguards. These machines, being low-built, are particularly handy in traffic.

The club cyclist, whose chief interest will be in fairly long runs with his fellow-members, will need a machine more akin to the racing type. He will forego the gear-case, the large saddle, the heavy tyres and the upturned handlebars of the business man's mount. The ideal clubman's mount has a light frame, a smallish but comfortable saddle, lively but strong tyres and handlebars with a moderate drop.

For general purposes, the light roadster, which comes between the gear-cased model and the clubman's machine, will suit the average person who is not interested in club riding, and wishes to use his bicycle for occasional town work and for modest country rides. It is low-built and has reasonable weather protection.

Frame Size.—This is most important. If you get a machine which is too big for you, you will not only lose efficiency and comfort, but may also harm yourself physically. It is better to err on the small side and to show 2 or 3 in. of seat-pillar than to be compelled to stretch and strain to reach the pedals. As a rough guide to the size of frame required, subtract 10 in. from your inside leg measurement. If the result is, say 23 in., then the frame size of your machine should not exceed that figure. It may even with advantage be less, for a smaller frame will be lighter and easier to propel. If you are buying a second-hand

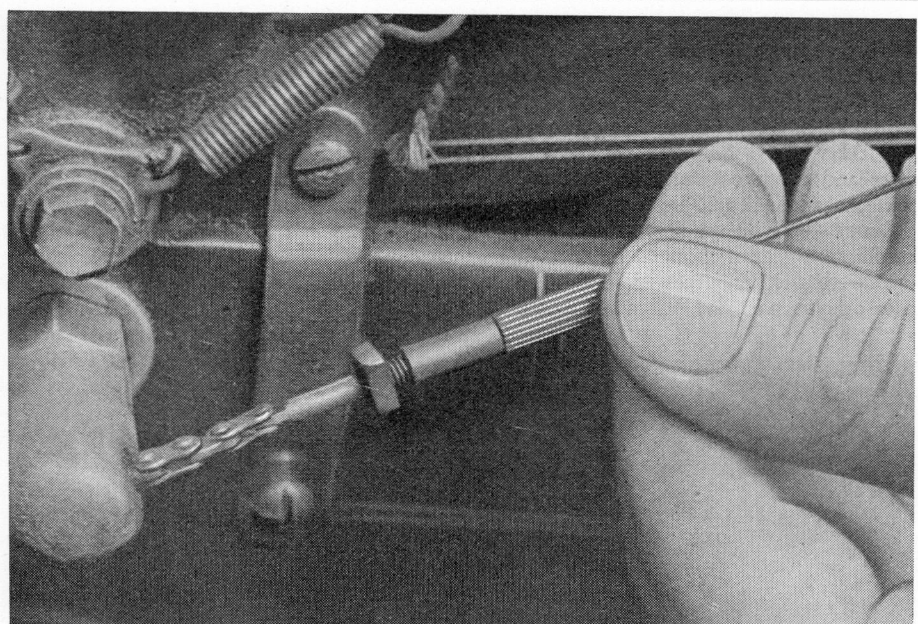

Fig. 1.—Adjusting the Three-speed Gear

machine or one from stock, get astride it. You should be able to reach the pedals at their farthest point without stretching the legs to their fullest extent. The knee should never be fully straightened when riding. It is also a great advantage to be able to touch the ground with both feet, particularly in the case of town cyclists. You can then stop and start in the minimum room, and with no waverings which may be dangerous to other road-users.

Handlebars.—There are many different types. The North Road upturned bar is very popular on light roadster machines, and the same bar in its reversed or dropped form is used by many riders who like a moderately low position. Flat bars, too, have attained some popularity in recent years. The club cyclist has an almost bewildering choice of bends amongst those with a more pronounced drop, and must be left to follow his fancy or that of his favourite racing man.

Avoid narrow handlebars, which cramp the chest. The comfortable cyclist leans forward, without stiffness, and his handle-grips slope downwards a little so that the hands fall into a natural position. It is a mistake to have the bars too close to the saddle in order to gain a bolt-upright position. At the other extreme, the back should not be arched in order to get a low position. If you use dropped handlebars, keep your back straight. If you lean forward from the hips you will avoid the curved spine, your breathing will have full play and the amount of your forward leaning will not matter.

Saddle.—Comfort must be your main object, and here again your choice will depend on the use to which you are going to put the machine. The size, springiness and softness of your saddle should vary inversely with the speed and distance of your intended riding. If you intend to ride solely for business purposes, mainly in a town, where stone setts abound, then you need a fairly large springy saddle. If you are going to ride moderate distances for pleasure, then one of the lightweight "mattress-spring" type will be a good choice. Long rides at a fairly good speed call for a rather harder, less-sprung saddle, and so down to the microscopic, almost springless saddle of the racing man. You can get some idea of the "feel" of a saddle by getting astride it, but remember that although it may feel a trifle hard when new it will get softer and more comfortable. Except for racing, a saddle should be 8½ in. wide.

Gears.—If you are new to cycling you should use a gear of about 65 in. with 6½ in. cranks—that is, ten times the crank-length. Later on you will find out whether it suits

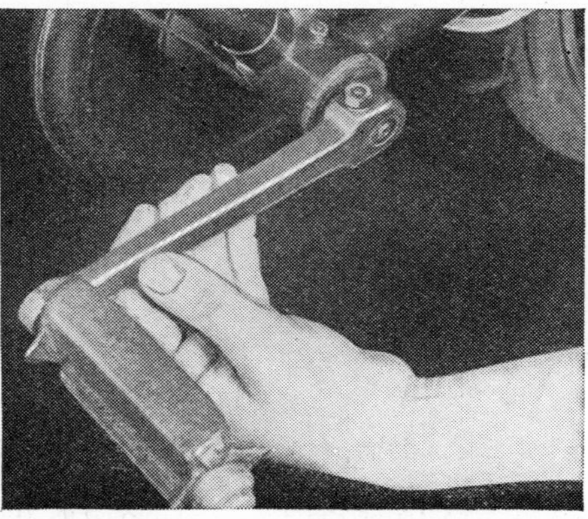

Fig.2.—Test for Play in the Bottom Bracket by Pushing Crank to and fro

you better to push a fairly high gear or to pedal nimbly on a lower one and you can then alter your gear accordingly. The average man will find 65 quite suitable for normal purposes, while a woman will require a gear slightly less.

For the tourist, or the cyclist who lives in a hilly district, the three-speed gear is of great help. The hub type has the advantage of being entirely enclosed, but the ratios of high and low gears to normal are fixed, and you cannot vary them.

On the other hand, with gears of the derailleur type (in which there is usually a triple sprocket, the chain being "derailed" from one to another), one can choose any ratio which appeals. It is merely a matter of varying the size of the sprockets. The mechanism of the derailleur gear is simple, but it has the disadvantage of being exposed to dirt and weather. Hub gears can be obtained with two or three speeds, wide-ratio or close-ratio alternatives being available with the latter, while gears of the derailleur type offer in addition, by the use of a double chain-wheel, four or six gears. You will find either type of gear perfectly satisfactory.

Brakes.—The roller-lever brake, actuating through the medium of rods, is now rapidly disappearing before the sweeping advance of cable-operated brakes. Cable-operated brakes are of two forms—the calliper, in which the tightening of the cable draws brake-blocks on to the side of the wheel-rim by a scissors-like action, and the internal-expanding, in which a band is expanded against the inside of a drum which forms part of the hub shell. Both are simple and give little trouble, but the efficiency of the rim brake is liable to be affected by any inequalities on the rim and also by rain on the rim.

Tyres.—The roadster has a broad heavy tread, non-skidding and strong, ideal for town and business riding. The lighter machines have correspondingly lighter tyres, from the light but fully-rubbered ones, through the lively open-sided (skin-sided) tyres of the speedy clubman's mount to the relatively flimsy stuck-on "tubulars" of the racing machine. In the case of a new machine the maker can usually be relied upon to fit the most suitable tyres for its purpose.

Mudguards are usually made of steel or celluloid, the former being cheaper but heavier. The latter are more susceptible to hard knocks, but are easier to keep clean.

Bells.—The cyclist is required by law to give audible warning of approach, and though no particular means of giving the warning is specified, a bell is the most usual and the best method. Get a good one. Syrens, bulb horns and electric horns are also available. It is as well to get something which makes a loud but pleasing sound, instead of merely a noise. There is too much harsh clamour to-day.

Lamps.—Oil lamps are the cheapest, as they are the oldest, but they are not of much use for long rides in the country. Acetylene lamps give a brilliant light, but need a good deal of attention. Electric lamps have now achieved great popularity. They are of two kinds—those running from a battery, and those supplied by power generated by a dynamo run from the bicycle. In town, one rides by the street lighting more than by the light of one's cycle lamp; for country riding a much stronger beam is required. The electric lamp may conveniently have dimming or dipping arrangements. Rear reflectors are compulsory, and you should buy a good one and see that it is kept clean. A white patch on the rear mudguard is also required by law.

Clothes.—It is purely a personal question of whether you favour shorts or knickers, tweed sports coat or suède zipp-jacket. A black or grey alpaca jacket is ideal for hot-weather wear. Whatever you wear, let it be light and free. There is very little need for extra muffling-up in winter, for the cyclist generates his own warmth by exercise. Your bad-weather equipment should include a cape which will hang down over the saddle and handlebars, a sou'wester, and leggings which come well above the knees. These can be obtained in light, waterproof material.

Tandems.—The tandem has become extremely popular during the last few years and is made on the same low light pattern as the solo machine. It has the advantage that two people can travel together, without taking double road space and so incurring greater risk from traffic. It is relatively faster than a bicycle and gives a delightful sense of companionship. It is not necessary for the rear rider to have had any previous cycling experience—all that is needed is confidence in the "pilot."

How to Achieve Cycling Fitness.—Start off with short distances at first. A ten- or fifteen-mile ride on two evenings in the week will put you in trim for a ride of twenty-five miles on the Saturday afternoon, and possibly thirty or thirty-five on the Sunday. Take things easy at first. Don't hurry. Learn to "ankle"—the hall-mark of the good cyclist. Drop the heel as the pedal nears the top of its stroke, so as to push it over dead-centre, and drop the toe as the pedal nears the bottom of its stroke, so as to "claw" it over bottom dead-centre.

Fig. 3.—This Nut Tightens or Loosens the Chain

Practise this a little and it will soon become quite automatic.

Keep your body still. All the movement should come from the hips downwards. To sway from side to side as you put pressure on each pedal in turn is unsightly and a waste of effort, and, if you have your position on the machine correctly adjusted, quite unnecessary. For ordinary riding the peak of the saddle should be 2 or 3 in. behind the centre of the bottom bracket, and should be only very slightly tilted upwards. The grips of the handlebars should be level with or slightly below the peak of the saddle.

If your position is correct—and a slight alteration will sometimes work wonders—and you continue your cycling regularly, you should have little difficulty after a short time in achieving fifty or sixty miles in a day without undue fatigue. You will find, too, that your speed will increase, though unless you are young and fairly strong it is not advisable to push yourself hard. Better a modest but enjoyable eight or ten miles an hour than a frenzied effort to reach a higher speed which leaves a feeling of over-fatigue.

After some months of regular and improving riding you may feel inclined to tackle a hundred miles in a day. This is not at all difficult if you have gradually

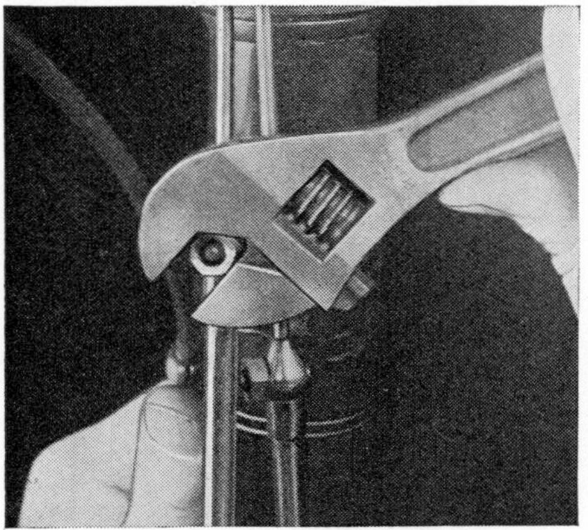

Fig. 4.—Adjusting the Front Brake

accustomed yourself to fairly long rides, and have felt no ill-effects. Plan your route beforehand, on good and not too hilly roads, if possible. Make an early start and ride steadily and at your normal speed for about forty miles before pulling in for lunch. Don't try to rush the hills or to gain on your schedule. The whole secret is to take things easily and calmly. Allow yourself an hour for lunch if you like, and then put in another thirty miles before tea. An hour for tea, if you wish, and then a nice, comfortable thirty miles to reach home and the coveted century.

Don't be afraid to dismount and walk up some of the less steep hills. The change of exercise is frequently very beneficial. Even in a flat district it may be a distinct gain to walk for a minute or two when one is on a long journey. This exercises fresh muscles, and gives the "cycling muscles" a rest. It may also prevent one from getting the "knock."

Nearly all cyclists (even the super-fit racing men) get the "knock" at some time during their career. It is characterized by a feeling of lassitude—the hills seem twice as long and steep as they really are, the wind seems to blow twice as hard in the wrong direction and the pedals simply will not go round. The remedy is to reduce speed. Take it easy for a little while, walk that next hill, and a little later you will be sailing along normally again.

If you are on a long journey, provide against the "hunger knock" by carrying an emergency ration of chocolate or nuts and raisins.

A Cycling Tour is one of the finest holidays imaginable. It may be made alone, with one companion, or with several. If you are used to solitary riding, then go alone—you will meet with and chat with many people on your way. If you like companionship, then go with a friend or friends, but be careful to choose for your tour-mate someone with whom you have kindred tastes, so that neither of you is bored by the other's enthusiasms.

There are two kinds of tours. One in which you move on from place to place, sleeping in a different town or village each night; the other, touring from a centre, in which you choose a certain place as your headquarters, riding out from it each day and returning to it at night. For the latter, it is essential that you should choose a place which is a good centre, so that whichever way you go you are sure of finding much to interest you. Its chief advantages are that you can send your luggage in advance (and, if you like, more luggage than you would take on the other kind of tour), you have a definite address for letters, etc., your nights' lodgings are all arranged beforehand, and you can take your rides with no more baggage than you would carry on a normal day's ride from home.

You will probably find, however, that a straightforward tour will give you more pleasure. The ideal holiday is one which provides as wide a contrast to your normal habits as possible, and there is a subtle thrill about waking up to the life of a different (and strange) place every morning.

If you wish to keep in touch with home, you can arrange to pick up your letters at a certain post office *en route*.

Planning a Tour.—Having decided where you are going, the next thing is to plan your route. Much depends on the time you have available, your fitness and the length of your usual day's ride. Don't make the mistake of planning on too big a scale. The fact that you ride sixty miles every Sunday does not mean that you can keep up sixty miles a day for a fortnight. Cut down your mileage. You will be in a strange district and there will be much to see. Fifty miles a day is ample for touring, and if you are observing and learning all the time there is no need for you to feel disgraced if you do only thirty or even twenty miles in the day. Measure your tour by enjoyment, not miles.

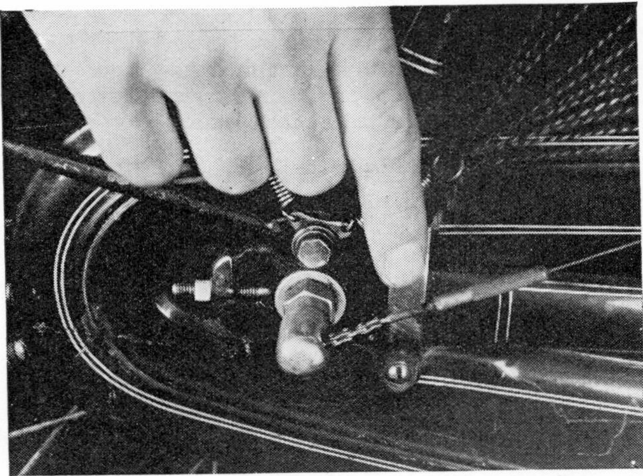

Fig. 5.—The Locknut must be unscrewed before adjusting the Three-speed

Equipment.—See that your machine is in perfect order—brakes adjusted, bearings oiled and adjusted, tyres in good condition. You will need a fairly big touring bag. In this you will carry your maps, guide books (if necessary), tools and puncture repair outfit. The ideal clothing for touring consists of alpaca jacket, open-necked shirt, shorts, stockings and shoes, so for spares you will need another pair of stockings and a shirt, in case you get wet. You will also need a supply of handkerchiefs, your shaving tackle, and possibly soap, towel and bathing costume. Include a pullover—even in the summer there are occasional cold spells. The items mentioned are the absolute minimum, and it depends on your own inclination as to what you add to them. The golden rule is—travel light.

Get your machine ready for the road the night before you are due to start. It is an excellent plan to draw up a list of things which need attention on the bicycle, things which are to be packed on the bicycle and things which you intend to carry on your person. Make this list a few days beforehand, and as you think of anything else add it on. Then, as you attend to each item in making your preparations, cross it off your list. In this way, you guard against forgetting some important thing.

If the district selected for the tour is a long way from your home, it is often advantageous to take your bicycle by train to some convenient jumping-off point. This cuts out a certain amount of riding in country with which you are familiar, saves perhaps a day which can be utilized in the touring ground proper, and so gives you a flying start. If you return by train from the same place at the end of the tour you can probably save another day.

Meals.—Some people like a four-course luncheon, a light tea and a late dinner. Others prefer a snack lunch, a right-royal tea and a good supper. Please yourself—but do not ride immediately after a heavy meal. And do not drink too much in hot weather, especially gassy mineral waters.

Finish your riding fairly early in the evening, say about seven o'clock. This will give you plenty of time to find accommodation for the night, and if your search should prove fruitless in that particular town or village it will give you the chance to ride a little farther on.

Cycle touring is not expensive. Staying at country inns or at commercial hotels you should manage comfortably on ten shillings a day, or, if you care to stay at farmhouses or youth hostels you can make a considerable cut in expenses.

Clubs.—Every cyclist should join one of the great national organizations which look after his interests. The National Cyclists' Union caters principally for racing men, though it offers touring facilities also. The Cyclists' Touring Club, as its name implies, caters principally for the tourist. It has numerous District Associations, which provide the advantages of a club within a club, and issues to members a very useful handbook and hotel list. The National Clarion C.C. and the N.C.U. also have their local centres. Membership of either of these associations costs but a moderate annual fee. In addition, there are many hundreds of local clubs, offering runs, racing fixtures and social activities to suit all tastes.

Cycle Camping.—Cycle camping is very delightful, especially if you go with one or two friends.

Your bicycle must be in sound condition for it will be carrying more weight than usual. Overhaul it, looking to the adjustment of brakes and so on. See that your tyres will stand up to the hard wear. Replenish your repair outfit and look over your tools.

Clothes need some thought, for you do not want to carry extras if you can help it. The successful camper has not a thing more than he needs, and yet has everything that is necessary.

If you do carry a lamp a small electric one is the best. Take a spare battery with you.

If there are three of you there should be no difficulty in apportioning things. One will have the tent, and the remaining equipment will be divided among the others. Jointed tent poles can generally be secured down the back stay of a bicycle between the saddle and the rear hub. The best arrangement for bulky luggage is in two large pannier bags hung on either side of the back wheel, across a broad carrier. These bags balance each other, and they should so fit that they can be readily lifted off or on. The back carrier itself will also be utilized, and so will the front carrier and the handlebars. For the latter you may have a single large bag or basket, and small balanced panniers on the top tube.

Do not overload the front of the machine; it has not the advantage of keeping the weight low and so giving maximum security, like back panniers.

Tents are of multitudinous variety, the choice being an entirely personal matter.

Besides such things you will also be guided by your general plans—if you intend to seek shelter in a nearby house in the event of bad weather, then a very light tent will serve for the fine nights; but to withstand heavy rain and wind you will need something sturdy.

More complete advice on the normal routine of camping will be found in the other Sections of this book on CAMPING and HIKING.

Have a fair idea of the route you intend to take before starting your cycle-camp tour, and do not try to travel too far each day. You do not want to be tired when you arrive at your camping site, neither do you want to be pitching camp when it is dark.

The Upkeep of the Bicycle.—If your bicycle is to give best service it should be kept in good condition. You should overhaul it periodically, and keep it always clean and properly lubricated. Do not assume that because it is new it needs neither oiling nor attention; look over it, or have it looked over thoroughly before you begin to ride. After your machine has stood for any time—as, for instance, through a winter—then go over it thoroughly before bringing it out afresh.

If the machine is cared for, upkeep expenses are very low indeed. They naturally vary with the amount of riding you do. Tyres may require replacing after 5,000 or 6,000 miles; a chain may last for 10,000 miles, with care; infrequent replacements of bearing and brake or gear cables; lamp expenses and puncture repair stuff—all these involve no more than a few shillings, and when you have added oil for lubrication, and cleaning materials, you have included practically all normal costs.

Cleaning.—Do not let your machine deteriorate, for that will involve depreciation in comfort as well as in value. Keep it thoroughly clean. The old-type enamelled parts needed to be treated with any ordinary furniture polish, for that gave a gloss without scratching. Turpentine would clean the parts that were plated, and then these could be wiped over by a rag smeared with vaseline—a very thin coat of this gave ideal protection and yet was almost invisible. The best way to preserve the more modern chromium plating is to rub the parts with a well-oiled rag, polishing with a soft cloth.

Modern saddles need no attention. For a saddle with the old-type leather top you can use ordinary leather or boot polish, which contains no colouring matter or stain, for the top. The underside should be rubbed with dubbin, which will preserve the leather.

Your chain must be cleaned occasionally. Having taken it off, lay it in a flat dish containing paraffin and give it a thorough shaking and brushing, with a small stiff brush, until every bit of dirt has been brushed away. Hang the chain up to dry after this, and wipe it. Next get the same dish containing some fairly thick lubricating oil which you have warmed so that it becomes thinned, and put your chain into it, coiled up as before. See that the oil can penetrate everywhere. Better still, heat the oil for ten minutes, with the chain in it, but do not boil. Leave until the oil is cold, then hang up the chain to drain, and finally wipe it clean. The oil is needed inside the tiny rollers of each link, not on the outside. Many novices imagine that they are oiling the chain when they simply drip the oilcan along the outside of the links, but actually this does very little good, and helps the chain to collect dirt which otherwise would not adhere to it.

Oiling.—When oiling your machine, look after the five main points—two on the hubs, two on the pedals and one on the bottom crank bracket. After attention to these, go on to the steering head, freewheel and brake joints. If your saddle top should squeak, you may put a spot of oil at the places where it is fastened to the frame. Take care that no oil runs on to your tyres, for it can rot them. Too much oil is bad.

In looking after your machine after it has stood by, you will need also to examine the tyres. See that there are no old patches which have come loose. If necessary, fit a new piece of valve rubber. Possibly the suction washer of your pump will need softening in oil; the pump will not work if the washer is dry and hard.

Fig. 6.—Oiling is done through small valves such as this

Then you will need to see about adjustments. Perhaps your chain may need tightening, or there may be too much play in the wheel bearings, or the saddle nut may need a turn to bring the leather more taut.

Since the bicycle needs comparatively little lubrication, it is worth while to get good quality oil. The same oil is not advisable for the whole machine; it is best to have a heavy and a light weight. The heavy oil can be used for the chain, bottom bracket, hubs, pedals and steering head, and the light oil for the brake joints, etc.

Tyres.—Do not let your machine stand for a long period when not in use, or the tyre will suffer at the point where it is carrying the weight of the machine. Put the machine on a stand, or hang it up. About half-pressure is sufficient for such a time. Normally a tyre should be fully inflated, so that there is only the slightest bulge when riding. To ride with a tyre insufficiently filled with air imposes a severe and unfair strain on the sides of the cover, and will most likely result in splits or cracks.

Never ride with a flat tyre; you will probably ruin both tube and cover, and may dent and deform your rims. In hot weather your tyres should be a little less hard than usual, so as to allow for air expansion due to the heat. Bright sunshine is injurious to rubber, and during the summer months you should keep your bicycle in the shade as much as possible.

Oil and grease are also harmful to a tyre, so see that no oil runs from your hubs down the spokes and through the nipple holes. In mending a puncture on the rear wheel take the tyre off on the opposite side to the chain so that there will be less risk of rubbing on oily metal. It sometimes happens that you go over a patch of oil left by a motor on a garage or a road. When this has happened run your machine through some sand or dirt so as to clean the tyres; grass will do, though it is less effective.

It is a good thing to examine tyres occasionally for flints, thorns or nails. Nails will generally go through, of course. Incidentally, if one should cause you a puncture, pull it out at once—if it is still embedded as you push the machine along it will probably punch a few more holes.

For small cuts or injuries to a tyre there are plenty of satisfactory "fillings." These cannot be applied at the roadside, as the tyre requires a thorough cleansing, and the filling needs a considerable time to set. A really severe gash means a new cover.

Punctures.—When you get a puncture stop and look for the cause of it at once. If you find nail, flint or piece of glass in the tyre, take it out and put a pencil mark to show the spot. The cause may not be visible from the outside and you may need to run your fingers round the inner side of the cover until you find the cause. Provided that such a puncture is at some distance from the valve you may be able to pull out the few necessary inches of the tube without disturbing the valve itself. Otherwise the valve must be withdrawn, as it must if your preliminary search has not revealed the puncture. Having drawn the tube out you must put some air into it to make a further search. Hold the inflated tube between your two hands, stretching it slightly, and pass it round section by section until you hear the air escaping; failing that you may hold it close to your lips and you will probably feel the tiny rush of air. Should that method fail, you must insert the tube in water, a length at a time, and watch for the small air bubbles which will show the leakage point.

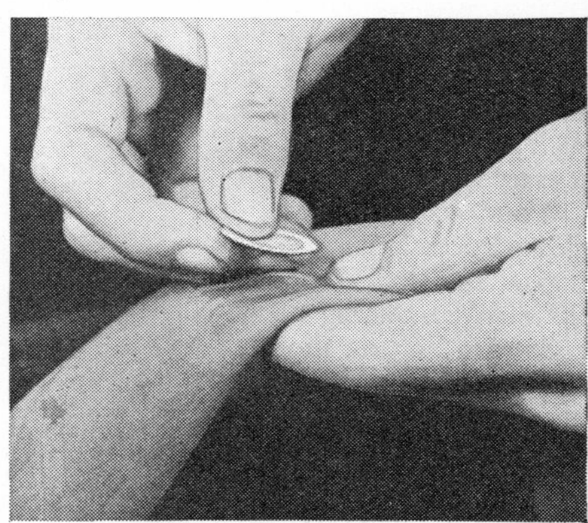

Fig. 7.—Allow the Solution to become tacky before applying the Patch

To mend the puncture, thoroughly clean the spot with glass-paper or petrol. The air will first have been let out of the tube, and it may be thought advisable to put a pencil-mark round the puncture-hole. Apply the solution thinly to the tube and patch, and let it get almost dry before you apply the patch. It is a common mistake to put the patch on too soon. (There are on the market some specially prepared patches, which do not need the use of solution. If you are using these, simply peel off the protective cover and apply the patch at once.) Press the patch down firmly, seeing that the edges are properly down, and finally dust over with french chalk, so that the solution will not stick to the outer cover.

If your tube has a slit instead of a mere puncture, you must use a patch that is big enough, and cut a tiny circular hole at each end of the slit so that it will not spread. A patch may also be required inside the tube. You may get the solution in with the tip of your finger. Draw the edges of the slit together as you press them down on to the inner patch, and put a second patch on the outer side in the usual way.

Lamps.—With an oil lamp you must see that the flame does not smoke. When it gets warm it has a tendency to burn more brightly, so that the wick needs to be turned down a little soon after lighting. See also that the lamp is upright—the bracket will determine this—so that neither the reflector nor the front glass gets smoked.

The water container of an acetylene lamp should be filled, but the carbide container should be no more than half full. The inexperienced cyclist is apt to run too much water on to his carbide. To light an acetylene lamp you must turn on the water and wait until the gas comes up. When the lamp is finished with, turn off the water and blow out the flame before it goes right out. The smell of acetylene gas is most unpleasant and an extinguished lamp should not be taken into a house. The smell, of course, is made by the gas which is emitted when there is no longer a flame to burn it. Do not allow the flame to burn itself right out, as this will cause the burner to get choked up with carbon.

If you have an electric light, choose one if possible which has a dimming arrangement. Not only does this allow you to be courteous to other cyclists and motorists, who will thus be prompted to show the same helpful consideration to you, but you will also be able to economize your resources by riding with a dim light when street or other lighting makes a stronger beam unnecessary.

Bearings.—At least once a year all the bearings of a bicycle should be overhauled. Ball bearings may need replacement; wheels may have developed some side play which needs to be taken in, and so on. A properly poised and lubricated wheel should, when raised from the ground, turn easily by the weight of the valve until the valve comes to rest at the lowest point.

General Cycling Hints.—Study the Highway Code, and follow its recommendations. Learn the recognized road signals and use them. Your right arm outstretched indicates that you intend to turn to the right—keep it straight out at shoulder level. The same arm outstretched and moved slowly up and down signifies that you intend to slow down or stop. To indicate to overtaking traffic that it may pass you on the right, hold the right arm out below the shoulder level and sweep it backwards and forwards. Warn overtaking traffic that you are about to turn left by holding out the right arm below shoulder level and rotating the hand and forearm in an anti-clockwise direction (in certain circumstances it may be wiser to give the older signal—raising the left arm and holding it out at shoulder level—particularly if any pedestrians are crossing the road into which you are about to turn). Learn also the traffic signals given by a policeman. An arm held straight up above his head is to stop on-coming traffic. An arm out at shoulder level stops traffic coming up behind him. One arm raised and one arm outstretched signifies "halt" to traffic in front and behind. Beckoning hands instruct traffic to proceed.

Become familiar with the road signs, and remember that you *must* STOP at a "Halt—Major Road Ahead" sign.

Do not use a chain that is worn out or slack. Slackness can be adjusted by the nuts at the end of the chain-stays. A little slackness is proper, but when you take the unsupported parts between the finger and thumb you should not be able to press them inwards more than an inch.

Always remember to free-wheel when changing gear on a hub three-speed gear, or you may damage the mechanism. On the other hand, if you use a gear of the derailleur type, you must keep on pedalling gently while you change gear, so that the chain will jump on to the correct sprocket.

When going uphill, and having changed gear, do not increase the speed of your pedalling, otherwise you will lose the benefit of your low gear. By working on at the same speed your machine will move on smoothly at a reduced pace.

Should you be stranded with a puncture and no solution in your repair outfit, hold the front of the patch in a match flame. When the rubber melts apply some of it quickly to the tube with your fingers and promptly put the patch on.

A child may begin on a miniature cycle at about four years of age, but nine is quite early enough for proper cycling, and even then the youngster should be supervised, for he will not develop road sense for some time. Do not buy a bicycle that is much too large for a child, with the idea that he will grow into it; he may seriously injure himself in straining to reach the pedals and hand-grips. If a child's bicycle has a back-step it is best to take this off, for he will not then be tempted to take the risk of giving another youngster a ride.

The front rider of a tandem does the balancing and steering; he should be able to ride comfortably without his partner. The rear rider may be a complete novice at the outset—a little practice in adjusting balance to his partner and he should be all right.

Beware of tramlines. Cross them smoothly and as squarely as possible.

When riding out with the wind remember that you have to return. It is better, when out for a pleasure trip, to start out against the wind, so that when you are rather more tired on the return you will have the helpful breeze behind.

Remember that a saddle can be adjusted in three ways—higher or lower, nearer to the handlebars or farther away, tilted forwards or backwards. Get comfortable.

A celluloid mudguard can be softened by immersion in hot water, thus allowing any part of it to be straightened or shaped.

Bicycles can be insured in the same way as cars; it costs very little to protect oneself against fire and theft.

The tightening of spokes and the setting-true of a wheel are delicate matters which should only be tackled by a skilled repairer.

Never ride all out when you are cycling for pleasure; if your machine is adjusted properly it will run smoothly enough with the expenditure of comparatively little energy.

Learn all you can about your machine, so that you are competent at emergency repairs.

DANCING

Many people protest that it is useless to learn to dance nowadays as steps are always changing, and there is not a set sequence as there was in pre-war days. This is not true; there are basic steps for the main dances: the Quickstep, the Foxtrot and the Slow Foxtrot, the Waltz, and now the Tango; and these rarely change. On to them are fitted different variations, many of which form a sequence of steps in universal use.

In the autumn there are often notes in the papers of a new dance, but few of these ever seriously rival the popularity of the main dances. Of such, the Charleston and the Black Bottom have had their day, and all that remains of them are odd steps introduced here and there as variations in the Foxtrot. The Rumba, introduced in 1934, is danced a good deal in some parts of the country, and not at all in others. What you must know then, are the basic steps of the Quickstep, the Foxtrots, the Waltz, and the Tango. As the Rumba may be popular in your district, the basic steps will also be given later in this article.

People who danced before the war have not all realized the main difference between pre-war and post-war dancing, and this is often the stumbling block to older people when doing modern steps. The thing to remember is that then one danced on the toes with feet well lifted from step to step. Now one dances chiefly on the ball of the foot, using the heels for turns, etc., and gliding from one step to another.

The first thing that you and your partner must realize is that you must RELAX when dancing. Don't tense your muscles in an effort to do a step correctly, you will become stiff and unwieldy to one another at once. Each step must be a natural movement, smooth and effortless. This you will never achieve unless you learn the correct hold, the correct poise, and the correct balance.

Tunbridge

Fig. 1.—Position for most modern dances. Notice that the man leans slightly forward and the girl slightly back

The Hold.—The girl should place her left hand lightly, on the man's right shoulder, leaning no weight on it, and keeping her elbow up. The man puts his right arm round her, laying his hand with fingers closed beneath her left shoulder-blade; with his left hand he takes her right hand, she folds her fingers over the space between his first finger and thumb; elbows must be kept up. The hold should be close so that the two dance as one, and toe to toe. At the moment there is an attempt at introducing a "no hold" type of dancing, in which the two do not touch one another at all.

With the hold previously described, the man should lean very slightly forward from the waist, and the girl very slightly backwards, but not with a noticeable slant in either case. Any tendency for the girl to droop over her partner is ugly, uncomfortable for him, and spoils the line of her dress, besides making good dancing impossible.

Here is another golden rule for the girl: Let the man do the steering and the indicating—don't interfere. He will steer with his right arm, and indicate with the body.

Movement in dancing must be made from the hips, and the knees must be kept straight when stepping backwards and forwards, except in the Tango and occasionally in more complicated turns in the Waltz. Weight should go from heel to toe when taking a forward step; don't step forward and then transfer your weight on to the forward foot, or you will step on your partner's toes. When stepping backwards, however, move from the toe first on to the ball, with weight going on to that leg as the heel touches the ground. This weight transference is of the utmost importance. Weight must always be forward, and therefore when stepping forward, girls especially must be careful not to bend at the knee. In a step backwards, by keeping the weight on the forward foot and stepping back on to the toe, then to the ball of the foot, and then transferring the weight as the forward foot passes backwards in its turn, you *are* keeping the weight forward all the time.

Feet must move backwards and forwards one behind the other. Nothing looks so bad as a person dancing with feet wide apart. Don't turn your toes out, either.

Keep your head up, and don't hold your head on one side. Many people do it, but it is ugly, and it makes your neck ache after a time. Another thing many people do if they are not sure of themselves on the dance floor is to hold their breath. Watch the effect of this next time you are sitting out, and don't do it yourself!

Yvonne

Fig. 2.—The Quick Step. A Twist after Chassé into Promenade Position

In spite of all this, you will step on somebody's toes sometimes! Don't get upset about it, just say "Sorry," and smile; worrying about it will make you do it again. If a girl is not sure where her partner's foot is going next, she should not put her foot down first. If she uses one as a pivot she will not be so likely to step in the wrong direction with the other.

All good dancers take long steps, and although a girl has to adapt herself to her partner's steps and variations, most men get on better with a partner who takes long steps. A man who dances well indicates well, i.e. by movement of hip or by raising his partner on her toes, to indicate that he is about to do such and such a variation. If his partner has learned the same steps at the same class she will at once follow any out of the ordinary variation; but to follow the variations of a partner she has not met before is not difficult if she will remember not to tense up but allow herself to be swung into the required movements.

Rhythm.—As it is the man who "sets the pace," as it were, in modern dancing, he must have a good sense of rhythm. There is nothing so frightful as a man who trots round entirely oblivious of being "off the beat," and then wonders why he treads on his partner's toes. The Quick Step and the Slow Foxtrot are four-beat tunes, the former having about 50 bars to the minute and the latter about 33. The Waltz, with its 36 three-beat bars to the minute; and the Tango, with two beats to the bar, and played at a speed of about 30 bars to the minute—are unmistakable in their rhythms.

In many basic steps the first half of the man's steps for the movement are the same as the second half of the lady's, and vice versa. This is because at the beginning the man starts with a forward movement and the lady with a backward one, and as they turn, the man takes the backward position and the lady the forward moving one. In some variations, however, the man's step is different, for he often does one long step, a pivot, or heel turn, while his partner is doing two short steps.

THE QUICK STEP

Because of the speed at which it is danced, this is a much easier dance than the Slow Foxtrot. There are eight well-known variations, together with the primary steps, the Promenade and the Chassé.

The Promenade or Walk is a sequence of fairly slow walks, each step taking two beats of the tune. The man usually is moving forward, and the lady backwards. Each forward step should be a gliding movement, heel down first, and weight going forwards with the foot. Each step backwards is a straight swing from the hip, the ball of the foot down immediately the toe touches the floor, with the weight still all on the front foot; this passes to your front heel as your front toes come up. Then, as your forward foot passes the other in its backward swing, the weight goes on to that back heel as it comes to the ground.

It is this transference of weight from the ball to the heel which is important, and, until practice has made it automatic, you cannot hope to dance really well.

The Chassé, taken in various positions, is: Step (forward or backward), close feet together, step; i.e. L.R.L.; the first two steps being short and quick, one to each beat; the third a long one, counting to two beats.

It is easier always in dancing to think of steps in terms of QUICK and SLOW; so the Chassé rhythm is QUICK, QUICK, SLOW.

The eight best-known variations are: The *Quarter Turns, Right and Left* (known as the Quarter Right and Left), *The Ordinary*

Yvonne

Fig. 3.—Quick Step. Reverse and Cross Chassé

Yvonne

Fig. 4.—Quick Step. The Zig-zag

and the *Reverse Turn*, the *Cross Chassé*, the *Zig-zag*, the *Drag* and the *Pivot Turn.* The ordinary *Chassé* is incorporated in the *Quarter Right*, the *Forward Turn*, and in the lady's steps in the *Reverse Turn*, the *Quarter Right and Left.*

These two turns may be used separately, or in sequence.

Man : (*a*) Forward on R. turning R. S
(*b*) L. sideways, continuing turn . . . . Q
(*c*) Close R. to L. . . Q
(*d*) Diagonally back on L. turning L. . . S
(*e*) Back on R. still turning . S
(*f & g*) Close L. to R. with right heel turn . . Q Q
(*h*) Forward on L. . . S

Lady : (*a*) Back on L. turning R. . S
(*b*) Sideways on R. continuing turn . . . . Q

(*c*) Close L. to R. . . . Q
(*d*) Forward diagonally on R. S
(*e*) Forward L. turning L. . S
(*f*) Step sideways with R. . Q
(*g*) Close L. to R. . . . Q
(*h*) Back on R. . . . . S

The Ordinary or Forward Turn.—This is the turn used on corners; it contains six movements and the rhythm of it is SLOW, QUICK, QUICK, SLOW, SLOW, SLOW, and there is a small amount of lilt obtained by rising for the two QUICKS.

Man : (*a*) Forward on R. turning R. S
(*b*) Sideways with L. continuing turn . . . Q
(*c*) Close R. to L. . . . Q
(*d*) Back on L. turning R. . S
(*e*) R. beside L. in heel turn . S
(*f*) Forward with L. . . . S

Lady : (*a*) Back on L. turning R. . S
(*b*) Sideways with R. continuing turn . . . Q
(*c*) L. beside R. close . . Q
(*d*) Forward on R. turning R. S
(*e*) Step sideways with L. . S
(*f*) Brush through with R. and back on it . . . S

The Reverse Turn.—This is often taught in two parts because the first half is used to make variations such as The Drag, and the second half is the same as the Quarter Left.

Man : (*a*) Forward on L. turning L. on heel . . . S
(*b*) R. to side continuing turn. S
(*c*) Back on L. . . . . S
(*d*) Back on R. turn on heel . S
(*e*) Close L. to R. in heel turn. Q
(*f*) Heel turn L. on R. . . Q
(*g*) Forward on L. . . . S

Lady : (*a*) Back on R. turning L. . S
(*b*) Close L. to R. in heel turn. S
(*c*) Forward with R. . . . S
(*d*) Forward with L. turning L. S
(*e*) R. to side in short step . Q
(*f*) Close with L. . . . Q
(*g*) Back on R. . . . . S

The Zig-zag

Man : (*a*) Forward on L. turning L. S
(*b*) Sideways with R. continuing turn . . . S
(*c*) Back on L. behind R., turning partner outside. S
(*d*) Close R. to L. in heel turn S
(*e*) Forward on L. . . . S

Lady : (*a*) Back on R. turning L. . S
(*b*) Close L. to R. with heel turn S
(*c*) Forward with R. outside man . . . . . S
(*d*) L. to side . . . . S
(*e*) Brush through and back on R. . . . . . S

The Drag.—Both the man and the lady begin with the first four steps of the Reverse Turn, then

Man : (*e*) Forward on L. . . . Q
(*f*) Diagonally back on R. . Q
(*g*) Close with L. . . . S
(*h*) Back on R. outside partner S

Lady : (*e*) Back on R. . . . . Q
(*f*) Diagonally forward on L. Q
(*g*) Close with R. . . . S
(*h*) Back on L. . . . . S

A good sequence of steps in the Quick Step is: Promenade Quarter R. and L. into the Drag; Promenade, Natural Turn.

THE SLOW FOXTROT

The two main differences between the QUICK STEP and the SLOW FOXTROT lie in the speed at which they are danced, and in the turns. In the Chassé in the QUICK STEP turns the movements are: Step—Close—Step; but in the SLOW FOXTROT the turns are open turns, and the movements are: Step—Brush through with the other foot—Step.

The two primary steps are the Promenade, with its movements as for the QUICK STEP, only taken more slowly; and the Three Step. The latter consists of three ordinary length steps forwards or backwards, counted QUICK, QUICK, SLOW. The main thing to remember is the first step, when moving forward, begins on the heel, and when moving backwards, the heel comes to the ground at the end of the second QUICK.

The most necessary steps to know are: the Ordinary and Reverse Turns, the Feather Step, and the Change Step.

The Ordinary Turn

Man : (*a*) Forward on R. turning R. S
(*b*) L. to side continuing turn. Q

Fig. 5.—Foxtrot. A typical error. The lady has "overturned" in placing the R.F. to the side and will therefore be too much on her partner's right side in the following "feather"

Yvonne

Fig. 6.—The lady's R.F. should be slightly turned out at the **beginning** of the 5th step to prevent "overturning"

(*c*) Back on R. . . . . Q
(*d*) Back on L. turning to R. . S
(*e*) R. by L. in heel turn . S
(*f*) Forward on L. . . . S
Lady : (*a*) Back on L. turning R. . S
(*b*) Close R. to L. in heel turn. Q
(*c*) Forward with L. . . . Q
(*d*) Forward on R. turning R. S
(*e*) L. to side . . . . S
(*f*) Brush through and back on R. . . . . S

The Feather Step

Man : (*a*) Long step on R. forward . S
(*b*) Forward with L. . . . Q
(*c*) Forward with R. outside partner . . . . Q
(*d*) Forward with L. in front . S
Lady : (*a*) Long step back on L. . S
(*b*) Back on R. . . . Q
(*c*) Back with L. . . . Q
(*d*) Back on R. . . . S

To make this step satisfactorily, rise at the end of (*a*) and dance the two Q's high on the ball of the foot, dropping on to your heel on the last backward SLOW.

Reverse Turn

Man : (*a*) Forward on L. turning L. S
(*b*) R. to side continuing turn. Q
(*c*) Back on L. . . . Q
(*d*) Back on R. turning to L. . S
(*e*) L. to side . . . . Q
(*f*) Forward on R. outside partner . . . Q
(*g*) Forward on L. into line of dance . . . S
Lady : (*a*) Back on R. turning L. . S
(*b*) Close L. to R. in heel turn. Q

Yvonne

Fig. 7.—The Waltz. The Balance. Notice relative position of dancers and length of step

(*c*) Forward on R. . . . Q
(*d*) Forward on L. turning L. . . S
(*e*) R. to side . . . . Q
(*f*) Back on L. . . . . Q
(*g*) Back on R. . . . . S

The Change Step.—This step is used as its name suggests, when you wish to change your direction. It follows the Feather or the Reverse Turn as a rule; and consists of two SLOW movements. The man steps forward and sideways with his R., turning to L., then brushes through and forward with L. The lady steps backwards and with the Right Foot.

THE WALTZ

The secret of waltzing well is to remember that the first beat of the three in each bar is accentuated and is therefore a long step, and that you must rise for the second and third steps, then drop for the first step. In the turns you must close your feet together on the third beat.

There are three basic steps, the Ordinary and Reverse Turns, and the Change Steps.

The Ordinary Turn

Man : (*a*) Forward on R. turning R.
(*b*) L. to side continuing to turn.
(*c*) Close R. to L.
(*d*) Back on L. turning R.
(*e*) R. to side continuing to turn.
(*f*) Close L. to R.

The lady's step is exactly the reverse, she does:

Lady : (*a*) Back on L. turning R.
(*b*) R. to side continuing to turn.
(*c*) Close L. to R.
(*d*) Forward on R. turning R.
(*e*) L. to side continuing to turn.
(*f*) Close R. to L.

The Reverse Turn

Man : (*a*) Forward on L. turning L.
(*b*) R. to side continuing to turn.
(*c*) Close L. to R.
(*d*) Back on R. turning L.
(*e*) L. to side continuing turn.
(*f*) Close R. to L.

Again the lady's step is exactly the reverse, i.e. d, e, f, a, b, c.

There are two Forward Change steps, one used after an Ordinary Turn and the other after a Reverse Turn. As the usual sequence of steps here is Ordinary Turn, Forward Change 1, Reverse Turn, Forward Change 2, then you can either go into the Promenade or continue with an Ordinary Turn again.

Forward Change 1 (Following Ordinary Turn).

Man : (*a*) Forward with R.
(*b*) L. to side.
(*c*) Close R. to L.

Lady : (*a*) Back on L.
(*b*) R. to side.
(*c*) Close L. to R.

Forward Change 2 (Following Reverse Turn).

Man : (*a*) Forward on L.
(*b*) R. to side.
(*c*) Close L. to R.

Lady : (*a*) Back on R.
(*b*) L. to side.
(*c*) Close R. to L.

THE TANGO

Yvonne

Fig. 8.—Completion of step illustrated in Fig. 9

Here we have a dance which is growing in popularity although many people are still afraid to tackle it, and Tango tunes are often played to a half-empty floor. But since the basic steps have been standardized there is no chance of that humiliating experience of taking the floor with an unknown partner and finding that his Tango is another of the 57 varieties. Knowledge of a few of the basic steps is enough for you to be able to take the floor and acquit yourselves worthily.

The Tango rhythm, with its staccato half-beats, is easy to recognize. There are only two rhythm patterns: SLOW, SLOW, and QUICK, QUICK, SLOW. Remember that the Tango is the nearest you can get to the movements used in ordinary walking. Instead of dancing with straight knees, on the ball of the foot, your knees should be slightly relaxed as you walk each step. Quite a good way of achieving this is to "think" yourself heavier than your knees can bear, so they have to "give" a little to carry your body weight.

The whole of this dance is flat; you do not rise on your toes for any step, as you do in the Waltz.

There is very little difference between the Tango and the Foxtrot holds: the man holds his partner somewhat more to the side with his left hand well under her right shoulder-blade, that is all.

The Forward and Backward Walks, i.e. Promenades, are most important; and it is a very good idea to put a Tango record on the gramophone and practise walking only to the rhythm. To Walk Forward, take ordinary-sized steps, putting the weight first on the heel, then on to. the flat of the foot, but taking care not to take the back foot from the ground until you absolutely must. Keep your weight forward. For the Backward Walk, swing the leg back from the hip, placing the ball of the foot straight on the ground. Keep your weight forward, transferring it to your front heel then to the back foot. Each of these steps is a SLOW.

The Progressive Side Step

Man: (*a*) L. forward and slightly to right . . Q
(*b*) R. to side with small step . . Q
(*c*) L. forward and again slightly towards right . . S

Lady: (*a*) Back on R., stepping slightly to left . . Q
(*b*) L. to side with small step . . Q
(*c*) Back on R. again slightly to left . . S

The last step here is brushed through.

The Reverse Turn

This consists of six steps, the first three making a half-turn, and the last three a quarter-turn. Here the man in steps (*a*) and (*b*) achieves the half-turn by two quarter-turns on the ball of the foot. The lady in step (*a*) achieves a half-turn on the heel.

Man: (*a*) Forward on L. turning on ball of foot to L. . . Q
(*b*) R. to side completing half turn L. on ball of foot . Q
(*c*) Cross L. over in front of R. S
(*d*) Back on R. turning towards L. . . . Q
(*e*) L. to side with small step . Q
(*f*) Close R. to L. . . S

Lady: (*a*) Back on R., heel turn to L. Q

Yvonne

Fig. 9.—Waltz. Changing direction

(*b*) Complete turn with small step with L. . . Q
(*c*) Close R. to L. . . S
(*d*) Forward with L. turning L. Q
(*e*) R. to side with small step . Q
(*f*) Close L. to R. . . S

The Side Promenade.—In this step instead of the man facing the way he is going and his partner having her back to it, both stand sideways, as for the old Valeta, for instance.

Man : (*a*) Long step to side with L. S
(*b*) Cross R. in front of L. . Q
(*c*) Small step to side on L. . Q
(*d*) Close R. to L. . . S

The lady's step is exactly the same only she starts on the other foot.

Lady : (*a*) Long step to side on R. . S
(*b*) Cross L. right over R. . Q
(*c*) Step to side on R. . . Q
(*d*) Close L. to R. . . S

The Back Corté

The "back" in this case refers to the man's step, for in this movement the lady is travelling forward all the time.

Man : (*a*) Back on L. . . . S
(*b*) Back on R. with slight turn to L. . . . . Q
(*c*) L. to side . . . Q
(*d*) Close R. to L. . . S

Here again the lady's step is just the reverse of the man's.

(*e*) Forward on R. turning R. S

Lady : (*a*) Forward on R. . . S
(*b*) Forward on L. turning a little to L. . . . Q

Yvonne

Fig. 10.—Waltz. Follow on from position in Fig. 9

(*c*) R. to side with small step Q
(*d*) Close L. to R. . . S

When you are dancing the Tango it is a good idea to start off with several walks to get the tempo of the dance really in your mind; after that try to construct a sequence for yourselves. A good sequence consists of a few walks, then the Progressive Side Step, because you are facing the right way to begin it; then after the last step of that, i.e. the third, the man can take one step forward and the lady one back, closing the feet ready to start immediately with the Reverse Turn. As you will have taken altogether a three-quarter turn you will be facing sideways and so ready to do the Side Promenade. You can follow this with the Progressive Side Step to get you back on to the line of dance, and so continue as you will.

Tunbridge

Fig. 12.—The Tango, showing the hold and position

Yvonne

Fig. 11.—Completion of movement illustrated in Figs. 9 and 10

THE RUMBA

The great thing to remember when you set out to dance the Rumba is that although it is a four beats in the bar dance it has nothing to do with the Foxtrot. When you first try to think of these in SLOWS and QUICKS, you will get on best if you call it a Slow, Quick, Quick rhythm, although the true Cuban rhythm is not quite like this. They make it almost a three-beat rhythm,

i.e. $1\frac{1}{2}$, $1\frac{1}{2}$, 1 (♩. ♩. ♩. $= \frac{4}{4}$)

But when you have mastered the basic steps of the straight Rumba, as the Slow, Quick, Quick rhythm is often called, you will find that dancing it to a good band playing the correct rhythm, you will

Yvonne

Fig. 13.—The second and third basic steps of the Rumba. Note relaxed knees in last position

probably fall into the true Cuban rhythm automatically.

The hold for this dance is quite different from that of the other dances, for instead of the partners touching one another at the hips, they stand well apart. The man should put his right hand on the left side of the lady's waist, and takes her right hand loosely in his, while she places her left hand on his right arm. Both should have their knees relaxed, as for the Tango, but with weight rather on the heels. Hips should be forward and both should be leaning slightly back from the waist. This is known as the non-clasp hold.

Don't forget to keep your knees somewhat relaxed all the time, for the definite "relax" movement on the second and fourth beat in most of the steps is the outstanding characteristic of this dance.

First Figure

Man : (*a*) Forward on L., turning a little to L.; relax knees, and . . . . . S

(*b*) R. forward level with L. about 4 in. away . Q

(*c*) Close L. to R.; then relax knees, and . . . Q

(*d*) Back on R. turning a little to L.; relax knees, and . S

(*e*) Step back on L. to level of R. . . . . . Q

(*f*) Close R. to L.; relax knees, and repeat a, b, c, d, e, f. Q

Then you will find that you have made a half-turn.

Lady: (*a*) Back on R. turning a little to R.; relax knees, and . S
(*b*) Bring L. level with R., about 4 in. away . Q
(*c*) Close R. to L.; relax knees, and . . . . Q
(*d*) Forward on L., slightly turning to R.; relax knees, and . . . S
(*e*) Forward on R. level with L. . . . . . Q
(*f*) Close L. to R.; relax knees, and . . . . Q

Repeat a, b, c, d, e, f.

Now you are standing ready for the second figure.

Second Figure

Man: (*a*) Brush forward with L. then step back with it. . S
(*b*) Small step back on R. . Q
(*c*) Small step back on L. . Q
(*d*) Brush forward with R., then step back on it . S
(*e*) Small step back on L. . Q
(*f*) Small step back on R. . Q

Repeat a, b, c.

The lady's step is exactly the same, except that she starts off on the right foot, and steps forwards.

Another good "step" which will fit on to the second sequence is as follows:

Man: (*a*) Bend left knee towards right knee, then forward on L. . . . S
(*b*) Forward on R. . . Q
(*c*) Forward on L. . . Q

Repeat, starting alternately on R. and L. to achieve a quarter circle to L.

The lady's step is again the reverse, beginning by bending right knee towards left knee, then stepping backwards on R., etc.

This sequence is often followed by the steps given below, though when you have learned these few movements you will be able to vary the order.

Man: (*a*) Back on L. to side, also turning somewhat to left on R. . . . S
(*b*) Relax knees and bring instep of L. to heel of R. S
(*c*) R. to side and backwards . S
(*d*) Relax knees and bring instep R. to heel of L. . S

Repeat to achieve quarter circle to left.

Lady's step begins "Forward on R.," etc., doing the same as the man but with the other foot and moving forwards.

DEBATING

"In the case of any person whose judgment is deserving of confidence," wrote John Stuart Mill, "how has it become so? . . . Because it has been his practice to listen to all that could be said against him; to profit by as much of it as was just, and expound to himself, and upon occasion to others, the fallacy of what was fallacious. Because he has felt that the only way in which a human being can make some approach to knowing the whole of a subject is by hearing what can be said about it by persons of every variety of opinion, and studying all modes in which it can be looked at by every character of mind."

In these words, one of the greatest of English thinkers has pointed to the real value of debating. A debate is an organized public argument. It provides you with an opportunity for exchanging your opinion with others, of adding to your knowledge and of developing your critical faculties. Above all, debating helps you to understand more fully and express more clearly the *reasons* for holding any particular opinion.

The accomplished debater is sometimes regarded with awe. Yet there is nothing to prevent any person of average intelligence from achieving skill in the art of public discussion. Once the initial nervousness has been conquered, the beginner will gradually learn how to express his thoughts in clear and forceful language. Constant practice is the only key to success.

There are several ways in which the beginner can get practice in debating. If you belong to a political or religious body, to a trade union or a professional association, the best plan is perhaps to attend meetings of your organization and contribute your views on the questions discussed. On the other hand, you may prefer to join your local debating society. If no society of this kind already exists in your locality, it should be possible, in co-operation with your friends and acquaintances, to form one yourself. In such a case it would be advisable to invite an experienced public speaker to preside over the first few meetings.

Procedure.—The majority of debating societies meet regularly to discuss a wide range of subjects. Procedure is governed by rules or standing orders, and the new member should master these thoroughly before attempting to participate in debates. At the beginning of each meeting, the chairman announces the terms of the resolution to be discussed, e.g. "That the House of Lords should be abolished." The proposer of the resolution then makes his speech. He is usually followed by the first speaker for the opposition. The seconder of the resolution then speaks, and is followed by the second speaker for the opposition. When the four principal speakers have concluded, the chairman throws the meeting open to discussion. At the close of the general discussion, the principal speaker for the opposition and the proposer of the motion are called upon in turn to sum up. The chairman finally puts the resolution to the meeting.

The above is a summary of the most usual form of debate. Procedure varies, however, according to the standing orders of the society concerned. It is customary to impose a time limit on speeches. The proposer of the resolution and his principal opponent may, for example, be required to limit their remarks to fifteen minutes each. These two speakers are generally given an additional five or six minutes in which to reply at the conclusion of the debate. The seconder of the resolution and the second opposition speaker may be allowed seven minutes each, whilst the remaining speeches may be limited to three minutes.

Amendments.—In some societies, the resolution must stand or fall in its original form, i.e. it cannot be amended. In others, amendments are allowed. The most important thing to remember about an amendment is that it must not be a "direct negative." In the case of the resolution mentioned above, for example, it would *not* be in order to move as an amendment: "That the maintenance of the present House of Lords is essential in the interests of stability." It would be perfectly in order, however, to move the following amendment: "That an elected Second Chamber should be substituted for the present House of Lords." Such an amendment is permissible, for it represents a *modification* of the original resolution and not a *direct negation* of it. When an amendment of this kind has been carried it becomes the *substantive motion*, and, in the absence of any further successful amendment, is finally put to the meeting in place of the original resolution.

"Parliaments."—Some debating societies take the form of Local Parliaments in which the proceedings are modelled on those of the House of Commons. A "Speaker" presides, and the majority of members are organized in political parties. The standing orders of the Local Parliament concerned provide either that each party takes office in turn, or that one party holds office continuously until defeated. The leader of one of the parties becomes Prime Minister and chooses his Cabinet. Each sitting usually begins with questions to Ministers. At the end of question time a debate takes place either on a Government Bill or on a private member's motion. Procedure and forms of address at Local Parliaments differ in many details from those adopted at ordinary debating societies. (For example, you are allowed to applaud by saying "Hear, hear," but *not* by clapping your hands. Again, you must refer to another speaker not as "Mr. So-and-So," but as "the Honourable Member" or, in the case of a Cabinet Minister or a member on the Front Opposition Bench, as "the Right Honourable Gentleman.") New Members of Local Parliaments should buy a copy of Hansard in order to acquaint themselves with the procedure and forms of address actually adopted at Westminster.

Your Maiden Speech.—Let us suppose

that you have joined either an ordinary debating society or a Local Parliament. Before attempting to take part in the proceedings, you will be well advised to attend a few meetings for the purpose of listening to other speakers and of learning how debates are conducted in practice. As soon as the society discusses a subject in which you are particularly interested, or of which you have some specialized knowledge, you should take the opportunity of making your "maiden" speech. Your best plan will be to limit yourself to a few brief remarks for or against the resolution. Do not attempt to cover the entire subject. A short speech is always more effective if confined to *one point*, and one point only.

Every beginner should profit by the advice of the late Lord Balfour: study the subject, not the phrase. In other words, clarity of expression naturally follows clarity of thought. Even if you feel nervous before your turn comes—and it is well to remember that many experienced debaters suffer in this respect—a sure knowledge of your subject will give you a large measure of self-confidence once you have risen to speak.

Preparing Your Speech.—Your first speech, however short, should be carefully prepared. Make a note of the resolution beforehand, study the views of writers on either side, ponder over the pros and cons, and finally decide what your own attitude is to be. Set out clearly in writing the various stages of your argument, and make absolutely certain that all your facts are correct. Provided that you have mastered the subject, it should be unnecessary to refer to notes during the course of your speech. You may find it useful, however, to write down the principal headings (preferably on a postcard) in order to refresh your memory on any specific point. Do *not* attempt to write out your speech in full, or even to prepare elaborate notes. Memorize arguments and facts, not words and phrases. The most effective speaker is he who has grasped the essentials of his case and arranged his ideas in logical sequence. If you intend, however, to support your case with quotations from books, newspapers or speeches, the relevant passages should be written out fully on separate cards. You will then be in a position to make an effective rejoinder to anybody who challenges your accuracy.

Impromptu Speaking.—Your first few contributions to debates will necessarily take the form of set speeches prepared in advance. The real art of debating, however, lies in the interchange of ideas, the refutation of arguments put forward by other speakers, the examination of evidence quoted during the course of the discussion. As soon as you have gained sufficient confidence in your ability to speak in public, you should attempt to make an impromptu contribution to a debate. Listen carefully to what other speakers have to say, make a note of any statement of fact or opinion which appears to be open to challenge, and turn the question over in your mind as the debate continues. Take the earliest opportunity of putting your point of view to the meeting. Begin by quoting the statement with which you disagree, then give briefly and succinctly your reasons for challenging it. Point out any logical flaw or error of fact. Your case against the preceding speaker will be the more effective if you can support it by citing personal experiences or published facts and figures.

Opening a Debate.—Sooner or later you will probably be invited to open a debate. As proposer of the resolution, your task will be more difficult than that of any other speaker at the meeting. Your statements will be challenged by your principal opponent and probably by many of the succeeding speakers. Here again, a thorough knowledge of your subject will help to give you self-confidence. Prepare your own case carefully and try to anticipate any criticisms which may be made during the debate. Do not forget that your principal opponent will also come to the meeting well prepared. "He who knows only his own side of the case," wrote John Stuart Mill, "knows little of that." Cicero, the greatest orator of ancient Rome, always studied his opponent's case even more thoroughly than his own. Your chances of success in the debate will be vastly increased by understanding clearly the main arguments against your proposition.

Your opening speech should consist mainly of a straightforward statement of the facts and arguments in support of the resolution. It is advisable, however, to reserve one or two strong points for your reply at the end of the debate. In your opening speech you should also try to disconcert your principal opponent by anticipating a few of his criticisms. Listen very carefully to his speech and make a note of his chief objections to your case. Note briefly the criticisms made by succeeding speakers. As the debate proceeds, try to link up the various points made by the opposition and decide upon your replies. Your closing speech should combine a final summary of your case with answers to all important criticisms. If you have planned this speech carefully, you will probably find that many of your answers to opponents will fit conveniently and effectively into the existing framework.

In conclusion, here are a few general hints for beginners:

Do Not Speak Too Quickly.—Remember that the members of your audience may not be well informed on the subject under debate. Give them a fair chance of grasping your arguments.

Speak Clearly.—A debater should articulate every syllable distinctly. Do not shout, but speak loudly enough to be heard by everybody in the audience.

Do not use any gesture unless it helps to increase the effectiveness of your speech.—Try to emphasize the key phrases and words by gesture and inflexion.

Keep Your Temper.—You will strengthen your own case by treating your opponents with courtesy and good humour.

Above all, **never forget your audience.** Remember that you are taking part in a debate, not delivering a lecture. Try to understand the "sense of the meeting," and present your arguments in the manner most likely to appeal to the majority of those present.

DIVING

EVERY swimmer should dive. It is the mark of the beginner to creep down steps or wade in shiveringly through shallows. And on a cold day the water will seem very much colder if you enter inch by inch, whereas if you plunge in boldly the shock is over so quickly that you scarcely notice it.

Quite apart from these preliminary advantages, however, diving is tremendously worth while for its own sake. It is an art to which a lifetime of study can be devoted, and in which every quality of the artist, athlete, and acrobat can have fullest scope. When you have learned to take simple headers you have only made the first step on the fascinating path which may finally lead you to the fifteen-metre board and to all sorts of delightful evolutions calling for great courage and muscular control.

If you are wise you will develop swimming and diving together, though naturally you will need to swim a little before you begin plunging into deep water. Many bathers neglect diving too long, until they have become fairly proficient swimmers, and then shrink from becoming novices again on the diving board. Do not let that hamper you, for only ten minutes' real work will make you able to plunge in boldly from the side of the bathing pool or from a low board. The one big difficulty is the first header, and the rest of diving will follow with less trouble once that is achieved.

The First Lesson.—As it is a most novel experience your first header is bound to be a bit of an ordeal. It can be much simplified if you start properly. There is no need to stand on the diving board at all. You may kneel on the edge of the bath, and then fall with outstretched arms until your fingers are almost, or quite, touching the water. Then, all you have to do is to topple forward, keeping your head low. It is so easy, and yet it will be a very important stage passed.

As soon as you are on your feet—the water should be at least breast-deep—you may come out and repeat your performance. After a few trials you should stand on the edge, and tackle the next stage. Bend forward, just as when you are kneeling, with head dropped between the arms, thumbs touching, palms flat and facing downward. Be careful not to jump at the last moment, but leave your feet on the bank as long as possible. In subsequent tumbles you may get some sort of push-off from the bank by straightening your legs as you fall.

For this preliminary practice see that the water is no less than five feet deep; even that is scarcely enough, and certainly is not sufficient to give proper safety for future diving. One fundamental rule for the learner is that he must always endeavour to go deep. It will help you now if you try to touch the bottom with your finger-tips at each tumble, for this will ensure that you go in more steeply—you have doubtless noticed that going flat is the commonest fault with beginners.

The First Real Dive.—Stand a foot or two above the water, with your toes curled over the edge of the bank or board. As you remain upright take one or two deep breaths. To steady your poise you may raise the arms forward once to the shoulder level and drop them again—do not swing them backwards and forwards several times. (Fig. 1.) As they drop to your sides let your balance go slightly forward so that your weight is on the balls of your feet, and the knees are giving a little. Immediately, the arms must be flung forward once more and the leap made, in an upward and outward direction. The arms are carried beyond the head till the thumbs meet; the feet are flicked backwards and upward; the head is dropped forward so that the chin approaches the chest—this will result in your turning over in the air and dropping down into the water at a proper steep angle. During the flight your arms, body, legs, and feet, should be in one straight line. (Fig. 2.)

After the arms and head have broken the surface the rest of the body should follow on cleanly, making very little splash. Do not tilt the flat hands forward so as to bring you gliding back to the surface, until the whole body is submerged.

Take care that the feet flick upwards at the outset and that the limbs do not sag.

The Second Stage.—Before long your plain header will be fairly good, and you will be ready to proceed to the running header. You have merely to take a short run and leap into the air—from one foot if the edge is firm, from both feet if you are on a springboard. The dive is the same in other respects.

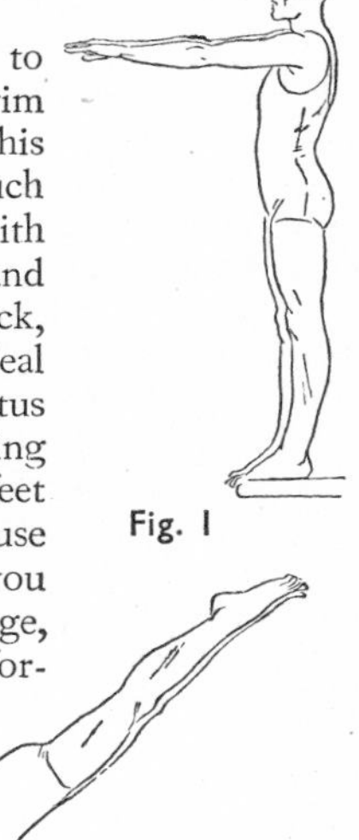

Fig. 1

Fig. 2

It is a good plan to begin any plain swim with a plunge. For this you need to go much more flatly. Start with the body crouching and the arms stretched back, then get a good deal more outward impetus into the spring, entering the water about ten feet from the bank. Because of the shallow entry you will scarcely submerge, and so will travel forward much farther. As impetus slackens you will take up your stroke. You may also plunge for distance—holding your position and gliding as far as you can.

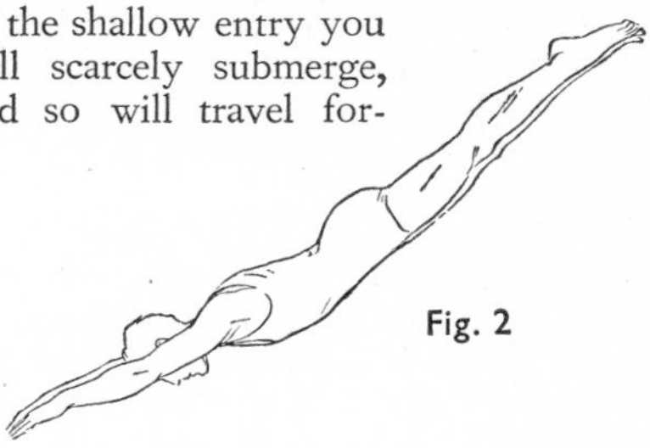

The Springboard and High Dives.—A reasonable mastery of plain and running headers will naturally lead you to think about fancy dives.

Do not be in too great a hurry. Two preliminary things which have to be considered before you enter this new realm of enjoyment—the use of the springboard, and high diving. In all fancy diving it is necessary for the body to get high into the air, in order that the flight to the water is prolonged as much as possible, and thus the "fancy position" is retained for the maximum length of time.

The purpose of a springboard is to throw the diver upwards, so that the effect is as if he were taking-off from a fixed board of considerable height.

Your first stage of preparation should therefore be the performing of plain headers from a fixed platform up to eight or ten feet above the surface. This is straightforward enough, providing you remember that fundamental rule of diving—always spring *upwards* as well as outwards. The higher you get, so you will find, the less need there will be to throw up your legs behind, for the body will be brought over sufficiently to the necessary steep angle entry by the weight of the head.

Preliminary Springboard Exercises consist merely of jumping up and down on the end of the board, timing yourself so that you synchronize exactly with the up and down movement of the board. Do plenty of work with this, for this precise timing is almost the entire secret of good work on the springboard. Bounce and bounce, from the balls of your feet, until you can so judge height and speed that the board is always yielding downwards as you drop and pressing upwards as you rise.

After this, practise taking a few short, quick steps along the board and finishing with a single jump on the end. Jump high and come down with feet together; knees bending, and arms and every bit of your body sagging. Then, as the board reaches its lowest point spring upwards with it, flinging your arms up too and stiffening the body so that you rise almost vertically from the strong push under the feet. It is important at this point that the body shall be upright; your legs will get thrown up without your body if you are leaning forward.

Jumps.—The novice, beginning fancy diving, has to give much of his attention to the high board or springboard itself, and when—besides the special position that is to be held for the flight—the dive has to finish with a readjustment of limbs for the steep head-first entry, then there is likely to be too much for the learner to think about. For this reason fancy jumps are very useful. It is much simpler to enter the water feet-first than head-first, so that by jumping instead of diving off all the trouble of turning the body over in the air is avoided. Also, it does not much matter if a feet-first entry is faulty—but it is not pleasant to experience a bad header from any height.

The take-off and entry of most fancy dives are performed in straightforward fashion. The complicating factor is that the body and limbs are adjusted into the "fancy position" immediately the board is left, and readjusted for the plain entry just before the water is reached. These requirements may be met quite well in the fancy jump. You may proceed to the real dive when limb adjustment and readjustment have been mastered.

Start with plain jumps, leaping into the air and holding the body quite vertical, with arms at the sides, until you have dropped beneath the water surface. Your attention should be concentrated on a correct attitude—muscles tense, feet pointed, head up, and so on. To prevent yourself going too deeply you may spread arms and legs as soon as they are submerged. But do not spread them too soon!

The Swallow Jump can be taken next. As soon as you are in the air swing the arms forward, then outward, so that they come to rest stretched out in line with the shoulders. Just before your feet reach the water swing the arms up above the head, and so submerge. Those movements will have imitated exactly the movements of a *swallow dive*—and when you come to try this dive later it will be naturally easier.

The Balled-up Jump.—Take the same high leap, but draw your knees tight up against your chest when you are at the highest point in the air, clutching the fronts of the legs with your hands, keeping your elbows close down by the sides. Fall towards the water in this sitting position—sometimes it is called a *tuck* position—and at the last moment straighten so that you are vertical for the water entry.

The Jack-knife Jump will help towards future *jack-knife dives*. Jump high, as before, keeping the trunk upright, but raise the legs to the front until they are horizontal, and at the same time reach the arms forward and touch your ankles. The position during the fall is just as if you were sitting on the floor with legs straight in front and hands reaching towards the feet. At the last moment drop the legs, and make a vertical entry.

Fancy Dives.—And now you will be ready to go on to fancy dives, which must all be taken either from a springboard or a fixed high board. Begin with the most popular dive in the world, and the most graceful:

Swallow Dive.—This happens to be about the easiest of fancy dives. It is simply a plain header in which the arms, during the flight, are spread out in line with the shoulders, as in the *swallow jump*.

Take-off as for a plain dive, with an upward and outward spring, but do not let the hands go beyond the head. Instead, they rise only halfway to the front, and then swing outwards, and finish up fully stretched to the sides. You will thus fall with the arms spread and the head kept up so that the body is almost horizontal. (Fig. 3.) As you near the water the head is dropped, the arms swing down and you thus submerge in ordinary header fashion.

A good deal of practice is needed to acquire perfect timing. The adjustment and readjustment of the body must be made at the right instant if the dive is to be neat and graceful. Remember to keep the head up throughout the flight, and the legs too, and be specially careful to keep knees and feet under control—the dive will be marred if they drop apart.

In this and all such dives there is much less time available than is taken in reading this account, so that the right thing has to be done very quickly, and thorough limb control is essential. Remember to assume the flight position promptly after your upward leap, then hold the position as long as possible. There are two extremes against which you must guard: you must not adjust for the entry too soon, or the flight position will scarcely have time to show; on the other hand, you must not leave the adjustment too late, or you will not be straight in time for a clean entry. Even when you have mastered the precise instant for the body straightening you must still aim at making the adjustment smooth, and free from any suggestion of jerkiness or haste.

Incidentally, be sure that the water is deep. This is really an essential for all diving, and particularly for fancy dives—it is not advisable to try any of the dives here described in water shallower than $8\frac{1}{2}$ ft. A rough standard of measurement for high boards is that the water should not be less than half the height of the board—with a minimum of $8\frac{1}{2}$ ft.

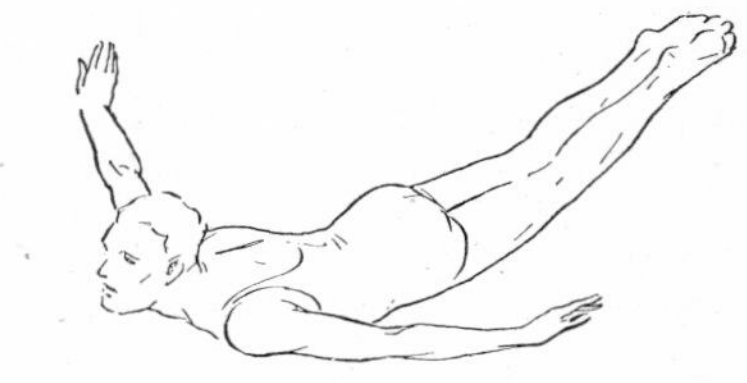

Fig. 3—Swallow Dive

Backwards Header.—This is not so difficult as it may look. The great essential is nerve; unless tackled boldly it cannot succeed.

Take up your position on the edge of the board facing the bank. Your arms should be stretched in front of you, palms down. Make an upward and backward spring, at the same time swinging your arms above your head. As you rise your head also will travel back between the arms, and these two factors combined will cause you to turn over in mid-air and fall steeply towards the water with your back to the bank. You will make the entry vertically—it is a matter of choice whether you rise to the surface in the direction of the bank or away from it.

Success in a back dive depends on the accuracy of the backward swing of arms and head, and of course the boldness with which it is made.

Jack-knife Dive.—Let the body leave the board in an ordinary upward and outward spring, and finally enter the water stretched out straight, exactly as in a plain header. But during the flight the "jack-knife" position is held. You may try it over on land. Stand with stiff knees and bend forward so that the hands are able to reach down and touch the outside of your ankles, the head meanwhile keeping up. For the actual dive the head and feet are about on the same level, the body tilting forward slightly from the leap.

Take up the jack position when you are at the highest point of your spring. Aim at bringing the legs forward, rather than reaching down with the arms, for unless you do there is the chance that you may roll over too far in the air and perhaps even perform a somersault. To help to preserve the right position during the flight keep your head up.

The straightening out must be done when you are something like six feet from the water. Drop the arms down; allow the head to fall between them; whip the legs backward and upward, until once more the body is completely straight. The water is thus entered in clean header fashion, almost vertically.

Somersaults.—Of the many types of somersault the easiest is with the body in a *balled-up* or *tuck* position—that is with knees drawn up against the chest and hands clasped around the fronts of the legs. You will have practised this position for the *balled-up jump*.

Start from a very low board, providing it juts out well from the bank. Squat on the end with the knees tight against the chest, hands clasped firmly on the fronts of the legs, and elbows tightly into sides. Then topple forward, letting the head go over vigorously so that the chin approaches the knees. This will cause you to turn a quick somersault and, providing that the water is only a few feet below, you will drop into it in an upright sitting position. Proceed to the high board or springboard when you have tried this a fair number of times.

Make your leap well into the air, and immediately assume the *tuck* position. Swing the head forward simultaneously and this will result in the somersault. You may hold the sitting position, or straighten out at the last moment, dropping in vertically with limbs straight and rigid. By putting more vigour into the somersault one and a half turns can be made, and then the straightening will bring you to a head-first entry—but do not be impatient to try this; master the single turn first.

Handstand Dive.—For this, grip the end of the board firmly with both hands and throw the legs upwards. You must reach and hold a hand balance for a moment with the body vertical, legs together, feet pointed, the whole weight resting on the palms of the hands. Then give an outward and upward push, which will carry you well clear of the board, and release your grip. Drop towards the water with body vertical, and so enter in a steep header, arms adjusted below the head in the customary manner.

Take care to get the head down between the arms, so that you take the water almost with the crown of the head. It is a very common fault for a diver to strike the surface with his forehead or the front part of the head, through failure to carry the chin sufficiently forward towards the chest. This applies equally to all head-first entries.

Be very careful in the handstand dive to push out clear of the board at the beginning. Unless you do there is danger that during the first part of the fall the legs or feet may be grazed.

Dead-drop.—The safest way to perform this is with arms stretched above the head all the time, but you may begin with the arms at the sides, and then drop them below the head just before you enter the water.

Stand on the end of the board in ordinary fashion, though with the arms above the head. Instead, however, of holding the body limp and prepared for a spring you must have every muscle taut. Rigidity is the secret of the dive. Allow yourself to topple forward, keeping your feet on the board end. Thus you will drop until your feet eventually come away from the board, without making any push. Keeping the same stiffness you will enter the water at an angle whose steepness will depend on the height from which you have taken off.

KEEPING A DOG

To get the full pleasure out of keeping a dog you should make quite certain not only that he is the kind of dog you fancy, but also that he is the kind best suited to the circumstances in which he will have to live.

If your spare time is limited do not buy a sporting dog like a Greyhound or a Borzoi, for these need a lot of accompanied exercise in fields or parks to keep them fit; neither should you have a long-coated dog which will need much daily attention with the brush and comb.

The Terrier breeds offer wide variety, ranging as they do from the Airedale to the tiny West Highland; practically all of them adapt themselves well to town or country conditions; and all make good watchdogs because they are ever ready to bark impressively at strangers. Bulldogs are excellent where there are children as they are very docile despite their expression. Any of the toy breeds require little room, and are inexpensive to feed. They are ideal companions for flat-dwellers. Alsatians and Chows are one-man dogs and not ideal for household pets.

Whatever breed you choose it is best to buy a puppy about four months old. Whether it is a bitch or a dog is for you to decide. Bitches are cheaper than dogs, but every six months they come on heat and then great vigilance has to be kept over them.

Where to Buy.—Mongrels are on sale for a few shillings at a dogs' home; or, if you are prepared to spend a guinea or two, you may buy a dog through the classified advertisements of one of the canine papers—getting him sent on approval if you are unable to go to the kennels personally.

Fig. 1.—Training a Dog. When called, the dog is prevented from running across the flower-bed and compelled to go round it

The least troublesome way is to buy from one of the big London shops where dogs are sold "across the counter" but it is always best to go direct to the breeder.

Having got the puppy home, make friends with him but do not be too fussy or introduce him to a lot of strangers.

Meals.—At the start, give him three meals a day: breakfast, consisting of stale brown bread and milk; midday dinner of green vegetables, gravy, and raw or underdone meat; supper, just before he goes to bed, of dry puppy biscuits. This diet can be varied now and then with sheeps' lights and puppy biscuits minced together, cooked paunch, and even with plate scrapings, providing they contain no brittle bones or fat.

Letting him gnaw big bones will aid your dog's digestion and keep his teeth healthy—bones like those from rabbits or chickens which splinter easily, and do internal injury, must *never* be given.

When the dog is eight months old you may omit the midday meal, making up with extra at morning and evening. The late meal will help him to sleep soundly and prevent any whining at night.

Sleeping Quarters.—During his early puppyhood, at any rate, let him sleep in the house. His bed may be simply a wooden box in the bottom of which is a layer of pine shavings or wheaten straw covered with a few old newspapers. A dog-basket containing a cushion or an old blanket is even more luxurious.

If it is essential for him to sleep in an outhouse, see that his bed is clear of draughts and damp—and never send him straight from the warm fireside to his chilly sleeping quarters.

An outdoor kennel is easily made; it should contain a low platform at one end on which the dog can lie. The door should be as far from the sleeping shelf as possible, and in one of the sides, not at the end. The kennel may be insulated from damp by raising it on bricks. A shaded veranda and a wired-in run are two refinements well worth adding.

Exercise.—While his bones are still in the soft, puppy stage a short walk each day will be sufficient and if he shows signs of tiring you should carry him. But, as his strength increases, he will need anything up to two hours' exercise a day, according to his breed.

Naturally, short-legged or heavy dogs cannot travel so far as the lighter, more athletic breeds. You can best tell the right distances for your dog by watching him when he comes back from his run; he should be ready for a feed and a drink, but not so tired that he goes at once to his corner and drops asleep. It will be best if you can give him one outing in the morning and another at night. If necessary, encourage him to make the most of his liberty by throwing a rubber ball (stones will damage his teeth) for him to fetch.

A thing that is to be avoided is giving him only a short run each week-day and then at the week-end, taking him into the country on a twenty-mile hike. Exercise must be regular as well as adequate.

Grooming.—Your dog needs *daily* grooming to keep his coat in condition. Comb out the hair, patiently working loose any tangles, and then finish off by rubbing briskly with a hound-glove if the coat is short, or with a brush if it is long.

Occasionally you may give him a dry shampoo, either with a proper shampoo powder or by simply rubbing warm bran into his coat and then brushing it out again. By doing this you will make it unnecessary to bathe him except when he picks up an unpleasant smell or when he is infested with fleas or lice (mild attacks by these pests can be warded off by dusting the coat with ordinary insect powder). Bathing tends to soften and take the vitality from his coat. When it becomes absolutely essential stand your dog in a bath of luke-warm water (no hotter) and lather him all over with special dog soap. Be careful that it does not get into his eyes, but at the same time make sure that he is soaped from the tip of his nose to the tip of his tail.

Having done this, sluice off as much of the lather as possible with the washing water. The remainder can be rinsed off with clean, luke-warm water, and finally the dog must be thoroughly dried with hot towels. In cold weather keep him by the fire some time after the bath, but in

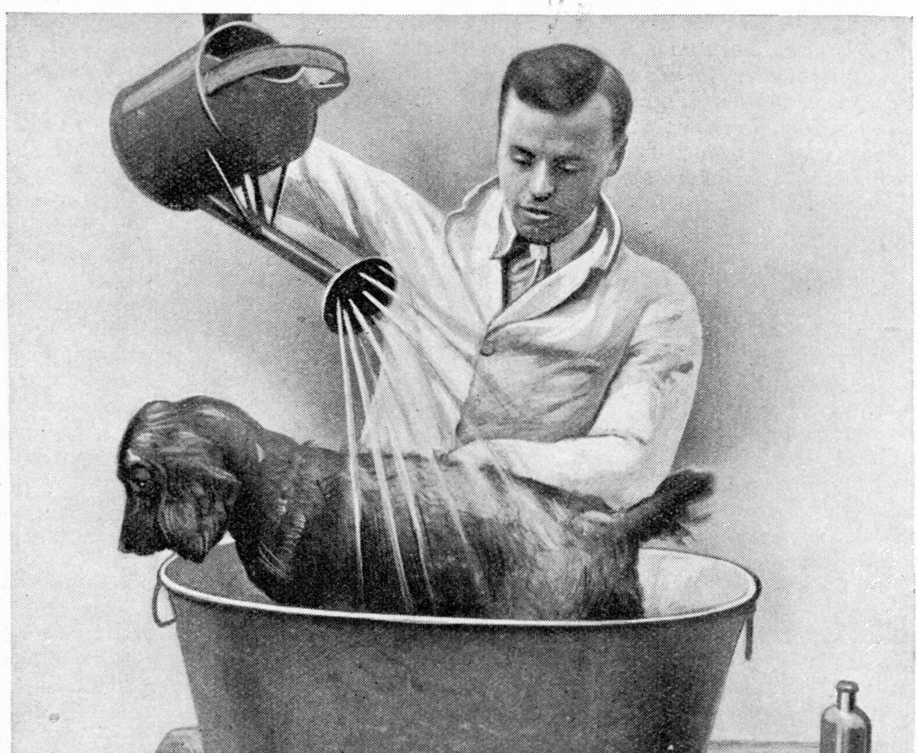

Fig. 2.—Bathing a Dog. A shower-bath like this greatly facilitates the operation. It should never be more than lukewarm

summer time you may let him out in the sun.

The Toilet.—Points that may need attention are nails and teeth. House dogs often fail to get enough exercise on hard roads to wear their nails down and so keep them short; therefore they must be clipped occasionally. If this is neglected the nails will curve round till they actually puncture the pads. Use strong, sharp scissors, and be careful not to injure the quick or you will fetch blood. If the nails are pale you may be able to see the pink quick, but if they are dark you will have to cut back till the dog shows that you are beginning to hurt him.

Keep a sharp watch on the teeth. One of the first signs of distemper is brown stains on the teeth and these should be cleaned daily with a solution of Milton and a little good toothpaste. In no circumstances must the teeth be neglected as these brown stains eat into the tooth and cause decay. With constant effort it is possible to prevent these stains becoming permanent, but the teeth should be cleaned at least twice a day.

Indoor Training.—First you will have to teach him to be clean in the house. Remember that, on the day of his arrival, he will probably be suffering from diarrhœa due to the shock of changing his home. Make allowances for this. When, having recovered from the attack, he misbehaves take him to the scene of his crime and scold him, trying to indicate by gesture what he has done wrong. Then turn him out of the house for a few minutes. Let him out after he has a meal or a drink and first thing in the morning. Also encourage him to whine or bark when he wants to go into the garden, and never refuse him when he asks in this way. Thus you will make it easier for him to be clean, and soon he will understand what is required of him and act accordingly.

You must also teach him not to trespass on arm-chairs, in bedrooms, and so on. This is mainly a matter of turning him off the forbidden spots with a scolding. But it will help if he is given some snug corner of the house which is his own and to which he can be taught to retire on command.

Outdoor Training should start with that indispensable accomplishment—walking at heel. Take your dog along a quiet footpath and tie a long piece of cord to his collar, letting him run to the full length of it. Then say sharply, "To heel!" at the same time pulling him to you with the cord. Make him take up his station on your left-hand side with his shoulder level with your body. Next slacken the cord, but immediately the dog darts forward, as he is practically certain to do, force him back, saying once more, "To heel!"

Keep on in this way till you think he has had enough instruction for one spell, and then let him go, saying as you release him "Away!" When this has been repeated on several excursions he will get to know what "To heel!" means; also he will recognize "Away!" as the word which releases him from his station.

The next step is to loop the cord through his collar instead of tying it. Holding both ends in your hand, bring him to you in the usual way. When he is at heel, let go of one end of the cord, thus freeing him. On discovering his liberty he will probably bound forward, but you must make him return, re-tying the cord if necessary.

Persevering with this process, you should in a short time be able to dispense with the restraining cord altogether. But do not think that you are justified in letting your dog run loose through the streets because he will walk to heel. However well trained he may be, there will come a day when the temptation is too great—perhaps a very attractive-looking dog on the other side of the road; perhaps an enticing smell just off the pavement—and in an instant he will dart blindly into the street. If he is lucky the road will be clear; if not—— Is it worth running the risk just to save yourself the trouble of putting him on the lead?

The next lesson to teach your dog is the "Sit" position. Walk along with your dog at heel, then stop and say sharply, "Sit!" Press him down into a squatting position, and pat him or say, "Good dog," to let him know that he has done as you wished. Repeat this a few times and he will squat when you command if you just tap his back gently with the lead. And, finally, this tapping may be dispensed with and the command will be sufficient.

It is also useful to get your dog to obey the order "Stay there!" Tether him to a low post with about five feet of cord. Make him sit by the post, then walk away from him, saying "Stay there!" He will probably advance to the length of the cord in an effort to follow you, and you must turn back and make him sit by the post again. Repeat the command "Stay there!" and walk away once more. Every time he tries to follow you go through this procedure until he will remain by the post obediently. The next step will be to omit to fasten him with the cord and this will follow quite easily after the preliminary training.

It is a good idea, by the way, whenever you leave him alone, to leave with him a handkerchief or cap or some other article in which he can detect strongly your own friendly scent. With this to keep him company he will not feel half so lonely, and consequently will not be so inclined to bark.

Tricks.—Most people like to finish off their dog's education with a few parlour tricks. The real dog-lover, however, avoids such things as "dressing up," "smoking a pipe," or "dancing." These merely make a clown of a dog, instead of exhibiting his intelligence.

Fetching slippers, or shutting doors, on the other hand, are two tricks you might well teach him. The first is quite a simple one. Sit down as if to take off your shoes, and say "Slippers!" Another member of the family should lead the dog to the shoe box or cupboard and encourage him to seize the slippers, then leading him back to you with them. It will not need much practice before your dog will do the trick

Fig. 3.—Training a Dog. He should always be taught to keep "to heel"

without any prompting, and then you can go on teaching him to put your shoes away by a similar method.

The "shutting doors" trick is a little more difficult. Place a tit-bit on the handle of a half-open door, saying "Shut!" Your dog will rear up with his fore-feet against the door in order to reach the tit-bit, and his weight will slam the door. When this has been done successfully a number of times, try him without the tit-bit, merely touching the door-handle and saying "Shut!" If he refuses, stand him up gently with his fore-feet against the door, and, as soon as the door slams, reward him. Soon he will slam the door on the word of command alone.

Here are one or two things you should remember, whatever training you give your dog—never continue your instruction when he is tired or sulky; never lose your temper with him; let the command words be short and distinctive, and speak them clearly; never enter into conversation with him like this, "That's not right! Get back, you little brute! Yes, that's better. . . ." This will only bewilder him, and you would make your meaning much clearer to him with gestures and grimaces.

Your Dog in Sickness.—So far all the points dealt with have concerned your dog in health. But few dogs go through life without some off-colour periods, and, unless these mild attacks are taken in hand, they often end in something more serious. With many dogs the first serious illness is the last; they die, simply because their owners treat them wrongly—or do not treat them at all.

The following alphabetical veterinary guide will enable you to deal intelligently with most of the ailments that may come your dog's way. For many of these ailments there are proprietary "cures" on the market; and, generally speaking, those made by the first-class firms may be used with confidence. However, there are people who will prefer to get their own remedies made up by a chemist, and, for them, I have suggested a number of well-proved and inexpensive prescriptions.

A word of warning: never fail to call in the vet. if your dog's condition shows signs of becoming serious. With his experience he can notice developments which you would miss and vary treatment accordingly.

Anal Glands.—These sometimes become swollen and inflamed, exuding a foul-smelling discharge. As the dog often draws himself, sitting, along the ground, this complaint is quite frequently mistaken for worms. Apply warm fomentations and later smear the anus with boracic ointment.

Sometimes the rectum will protrude alarmingly during a bad attack of diarrhœa. Wash the protrusion in warm water, smear it with vaseline, and gently restore it.

Bronchitis.—The dog pants and wheezes, also there is a dry cough which becomes looser as the illness progresses. Keep the dog warm, wrapping him in flannel. Give him 5–20 drops of ipecacuanha wine and continue by giving him this pill three times a day: Rhubarb powder 2 grains, ipecacuanha powder ½ grain, extract of opium ½ grain, compound tincture of benzoin 2 drops. Inhaling the steam from hot water containing friar's balsam is excellent.

Burns.—Apply boracic ointment, or, if this is lacking, starch. Bandage carefully. If the burn discharges, bathe it with warm salt water.

Colds.—If your dog wheezes and coughs, and there is a discharge from his nose but no rise in temperature as in distemper, he probably has a cold in the head. Give him a dose of 2 drachms of Mindererus spirit at night, followed by Epsom salts with a taint of spirits of nitre and from 1 to 6 grains of quinine next morning. A different kind of cold is that known as Husk. The dog coughs frequently, sometimes almost choking. Let him inhale the steam from a mixture of 1 tablespoonful of iodine to 1 pint of water. Give him daily doses of cod liver oil, and rub his throat and chest with liniment, afterwards applying warm flannel.

Constipation.—This is usually caused by irregular and unsuitable feeding, and lack of exercise. Your dog will have difficulty in relieving himself, and the motions will be large and dry. Do not give him a strong purgative; only a dose of medicinal paraffin is permissible. The diet should be regular and should consist of coarse wholemeal bread; meat (a little raw liver is most effective), and green vegetables. A mild daily dose of magnesia will complete the cure.

Deafness.—Some dogs, especially white ones, suffer from a form of deafness which is quite incurable. But many cases of canine deafness are due to wax in the ear. First soften the wax by dropping a little warm almond oil or olive oil into the ear. which should later be syringed with warm water. Sometimes deafness is caused by the growth of a polypus, and for this the only cure is an operation.

Diagnosis.—The first thing to do when your dog goes off-colour is to examine him carefully to find the nature of his ailment. If he shows signs of local pain this will lead you to the seat of the trouble. He may lick the part that hurts, or you may have to feel him all over till he shows where the pain is.

Take his temperature and feel his pulse as directed under separate headings. Does he cough? Is there any discharge from the eyes or nose? Does he breathe with difficulty? Is he suffering from constipation or diarrhœa? Does he vomit? Is he emaciated or do any parts appear swollen?

Compare your observations with the symptoms of diseases in the list, and you should be able to name the trouble.

Diarrhœa.—This is brought on by lack of cleanliness in feeding-dishes, etc., change of home or food, unsuitable food, or cold. Decide what is the cause in your particular case and proceed to set it right. Whatever it is you will open the path to recovery by giving your dog ½ teaspoonful to 2 tablespoonfuls of castor oil. If he seems in pain, add to this 5–20 drops of laudanum or the same quantity of brandy. In all probability no further dosing will be necessary, but if the attack continues give the following: aromatic chalk 3 drachms, tincture of opium 5 to 8 drachms, rice water 7 oz., the dose being from 1 teaspoonful to 2 tablespoonfuls given after every loose motion. For a time the diet should consist of binding foods like sago, arrowroot, rice.

Distemper.—Careful nursing counts even more than careful dosing in the treatment of this, your dog's worst enemy.

The disease has two phases, the first just a feverish cold and cough with wasting, and the second much more severe stage when complications often set in. As soon as you recognize the first symptoms—dullness, loss of appetite, slight cough, rise in temperature, perhaps sickness or diarrhœa—keep the patient in a warm, well-ventilated room. Wrap him in flannel and, if possible, get him used to relieving himself in a tray littered with cork-dust so that he need not go out of doors. Give 2 aspirins crushed in a spoonful of milk as a dose. This will help to bring the temperature down. Put him on a light, tempting diet—oatmeal gruel made with milk, beef tea, arrowroot, fish, and very small quantities of shredded lean meat. If wasting is acute you will have to feed him forcibly. The gruel and beef tea should be given by holding the cheek away from the teeth in the same way as if you were giving him a dose of medicine and pouring the liquid spoonful by spoonful down his throat. Another excellent strengthener is white of egg. Break an egg into a cup and separate the yolk from the white. With a teaspoon take up a little of the white and pour it into the dog's mouth through the cheek. He will swallow it easily and it will do an enormous amount of good. Little pimples may form on the dog's stomach and on the inside of his thighs. Squeeze the matter out of these to rid your dog of poison, and bathe the eruptions with permanganate of potash solution, afterwards drying them carefully.

There will be a discharge from the dog's eyes and nose, and this should be frequently wiped away with a dilute solution of disinfectant. As regards dosing, there are several good distemper cures on the market graded to be given at different stages of the illness, or you may give this mixture three times a day: solution of acetate of ammonia 30 to 60 drops, sweet spirits of nitre 15 to 60 drops, salicylate of soda 2–10 grains, in camphor water. Any tendency to sickness may be checked by adding 1–4 drops of dilute prussic acid to his drinking water. Diarrhœa to a mild extent is not harmful, but if it becomes very bad feed the dog chiefly on arrowroot.

Watch carefully for any complications. If the brain is affected, symptoms of which

Fig. 4.—Training a Dog. Teaching him to come to heel when called

are bloodshot eyes, convulsive movement of the jaws, frothing at the mouth, or a vacant expression, apply to the patient's head lint saturated with a solution of methylated spirit and milk in equal quantities. If this is without effect, a blister may be applied to the base of the skull, which is an operation the vet. should superintend. These precautions may prevent fits which are usually incurable once they get firm hold.

Blood in the nasal discharge, and quick, difficult breathing show that the lungs are disordered. Redouble your efforts to keep the dog warm. Under his woollen or flannel jacket put pieces of flannel which have been sprinkled with liniment and then wrung out in hot water.

Perhaps the most important instruction is: do not let your dog out and about till his temperature has been normal for over a week. During this convalescence he should be given tonic foods like raw meat and beef tea, to help him regain strength. Furthermore, during this time watch carefully for any "off colour" signs, since it will be at least a month from the time the temperature is normal before your dog is fit again.

Dosing.—To give your dog liquid medicine, tip his head gently back, and, holding the cheek away from his teeth so that it forms a funnel, pour the medicine into this. (*See* Fig. 5.) A pill or powder is best given by pressing the dog's lips between his teeth so that his jaws are forced apart. The pill can then be dropped down his throat and his head held with mouth closed till he has swallowed.

The lower quantity of the doses prescribed in this list mentioned is always for a toy dog weighing about five or six pounds, and the larger for big dogs weighing over a hundred pounds. If you know how much your dog weighs a little calculation will soon show you the correct dose for him.

Ear Troubles.—Most common of these is canker. It is most frequent in the long-eared breeds, and sometimes accompanies worms, though not drying the ear after a wetting is the usual cause. The dog scratches his ear and shakes his head. There is a foul-smelling discharge, at first dark brown but later pale. Give a dose of 20–60 grains of Epsom salts sweetened with castor sugar, and syringe the ear with lukewarm solution of permanganate of potash or a solution 3 grains of dried alum to 1 oz. of water. Dry thoroughly and dust with boracic powder.

The ear flap itself is sometimes attacked by "external canker." Sores appear on the inside of the flap and discharge. First cut away any matted hair near the affected spots, bathe with warm water, dry, and finally smear with benzoated oxide of zinc. In all cases of canker you should give your dog a canker-cap to prevent him scratching his ear. The cap is a wide band of linen to go over the top of his head and be tied under his chin.

Eczema.—The dog will scratch and bite itself. Sores will appear along its back and perhaps on its face and ears. This condition may be a result of worms, so dose the dog for these first. If this has no effect, unsuitable diet, lack of cleanliness, insufficient grooming or exercise are probable causes. Should you suspect any of these, set it right and so remove the seat of the trouble. The sores should be bathed with weak permanganate of potash and then dressed with benzoated zinc ointment. Giving alternate doses of orange juice and cod liver oil will help. Generally speaking, the best food for dogs suffering from eczema is meat but there are exceptions. Sprinkle a pinch of flowers of sulphur on the food.

Eye Troubles.—If your dog's eyes are sore and watery examine them to see if grit, a fly, or hair has found its way into them. If so, remove the foreign body and bathe them with 2 grains of powdered alum in 1 ounce of water. The inflammation may be caused by sleeping in a draught. In this case, move your dog's bed and bathe his eyes with the alum eye-wash.

To treat wounded or ulcerated eyeballs crush up three poppyheads and boil them for ten minutes in three pints of water, then strain the liquid carefully. While it is still warm dip a pad of lint into it and apply this to the eye. Do this three times a day, afterwards bathing with alum lotion.

Always keep your dog's eyes clean by

wiping away any discharge with cotton-wool soaked in a weak solution of boracic crystals.

Foot Sores.—Painful swellings may occur between your dog's toes. If you detect them at the outset just painting them with iodine may effect a cure; but at a later stage they will have to be poulticed (do not have the poultice hotter than you can bear on your elbow) and then opened with a sharp penknife or a razor-blade sterilized in boiling water. Keep the foot bandaged till the wound has healed cleanly. However, prevention is always better than cure and one of the chief causes of sores between the toes is that tar and grit are picked up when your dog is out walking and these become matted in the hair. His feet should be inspected regularly and particularly after a walk on tarred roads. If the swellings continue to come, the only permanent cure is an injection by the vet.

Gastritis.—This is symptomized by sickness and great thirst. It is caused by irritation of the stomach usually due to bad food. First dose for worms if their presence is suspected; if not, give a mild dose of castor oil. Instead of water give soda and milk, or let the dog lick ice. Diet should consist of milk foods and meat essence. If sickness is acute you will have to give nourishment by means of a meat suppository obtained from the chemist.

Harvest Bugs.—These tiny red insects often attack dogs on the nose, legs and stomach during harvest time. You can get rid of them by washing them off with vinegar or by bathing the dog as you would if he had fleas.

Mange.—There are two forms of mange, the more common being known as sarcoptic mange; I will deal with this first. The only way to distinguish sarcoptic mange from eczema is by actually seeing the tiny mange parasites with the aid of a powerful magnifying glass. They are oval, have eight legs and will be found on the sore patches; the best way to make certain of their presence is to take a scraping from the dog's skin to be examined under the microscope. This disease is very contagious to human beings as well as to other dogs so you should take every precaution to prevent it spreading.

Treatment should be begun at once by bathing the dog in water to which iodine tincture has been added. Having dried him, paint the affected spots with iodine, too. This will check the parasites and give you time to prepare more extensive remedies. You can make up this dressing: 2 ounces of flowers of sulphur, ½ ounce of rectified spirits of tar, and ½ pint of olive oil; though you may find it as cheap and less trouble to buy a ready-made cure from the shop.

As soon after the bath as possible apply whatever dressing you have decided upon.

Fig. 5.—When administering medicine, pour it down the side of the mouth

Renew the dressing every day and bath the dog twice a week till a cure is effected.

With follicular mange little bald patches appear just as in sarcoptic mange, but the irritation is not so intense, and the dog will probably shake himself instead of scratching. The bare patches turn blackish and a few pimples usually appear. The disease may stop at this stage, the skin merely becoming encrusted and thickened; this is the dry form of follicular mange. To treat it, first clip the hair round the affected spots, this not only makes it easier to bathe and anoint them, but also seems to check the parasites. Paint the patches with iodine tincture and then smear them with a mixture of one part of benzine to four parts of lard. Continue this treatment for several months, until all signs of the disease have disappeared, for the parasites are very tenacious and sometimes break out again.

In the case of acute follicular mange the skin passes from the dry stage and becomes raw. Also the legs and head swell.

There are only two courses recommended—either have the dog destroyed or else call in a vet., for actual observation of the case is really essential to effective treatment.

Nettlerash.—The skin puffs up in patches as the result of a chill. Wrap the dog up well in his bed and give a mild dose of castor oil. Feed him on light tempting food and the skin should soon return to normal.

Pulse.—Place your finger-tips on the inside of your dog's thigh, about the middle and close to where the leg joins the body. When you have found the precise spot where the femoral artery crosses the thigh-bone you will be able to feel the throbbing of the pulse. Using the second hand of a watch, count the number of throbs in a minute. If your dog is in health the number should be between 80 and 100, according to his size—the smaller the dog, the faster being his pulse rate.

The *feel* of the pulse can tell you more about your dog's condition than the number of beats, so you should get accustomed to the character of the pulse while the dog is in health. It will most likely be irregular, but this is quite usual. If the irregularity is more marked and the pulse weak and slow, some form of heart trouble is indicated. When the pulse is faster there is a probability of some kind of fever.

Skin Irritation.—If your dog scratches and his skin appears scurfy, give him several baths at intervals of three or four days and rub a little olive oil into his coat. Give him a dose or two of flowers of sulphur, followed by a course of good condition powders.

Irritation will be set up, too, when your dog is changing his coat in the spring. All he needs is extra grooming to help get rid of the dead hair, though, with most of the terrier breeds it is as well to pluck out the old hair with a stripping knife.

Worms sometimes cause skin irritation. Though nothing is visibly wrong with the skin, the dog will scratch and bite itself. When he has been ridded of the worms the trouble will soon disappear.

Specific Hysteria.—The dog starts suddenly to career about, howling and barking. He will crash blindly into walls and chairs. The attack will soon pass, but will probably be followed by another in anything up to three days. Catch the dog (taking care not to get bitten) and take him somewhere quiet and dark. As soon as possible give him a dose of castor oil mixed with from 15 to 30 drops of brandy. Five to 22 grains of sodium bromide or ammonium bromide will calm the dog's nerves. After the attack, feed him on light, easily-digested food, and keep him quiet. Dose him for worms if you suspect their presence.

Apoplexy and epilepsy are sometimes mistaken for hysteria, though there are features by which apoplexy, at any rate, can be distinguished. It takes the form of complete or partial loss of consciousness, the dog either falling down or staggering about. Heavy breathing and bloodshot eyes are other symptoms; frothing, champing jaws are absent. Epilepsy usually begins with the dog walking unsteadily, and then falling down in convulsions. Later he will rise and dart off dementedly. The treatment in both these complaints is practically the same: see that the collar is loose, apply cloth dipped in cold water, or ice to the head. Take the dog into a quiet, dark corner, and, if his pulse is weak, give him a few drops of brandy in water when he can swallow. A dose of castor oil should also be given in the case of epilepsy. A light and tempting diet should follow fits of any kind.

Temperature.—To take your dog's temperature use an ordinary clinical thermometer. There are three places where this can be inserted—the rectum, under the armpit, and in the mouth. The most accurate reading can be obtained in the rectum. Vaseline the thermometer and pass it gently into your dog's rectum, taking care to prevent him struggling and perhaps breaking the delicate instrument. Leave it there a little longer than you would if you were taking your own temperature. If you put the thermometer under the armpit, see that its point is well buried in a fold of the skin; here it must be left for longer than in the rectum to get a true reading. The other alternative is inserting the thermometer along the inside of the dog's cheek, but there is always the danger that he will bite it; the armpit is the safest place.

Your dog's normal temperature is about 101° F. If you take it once or twice when he is in good health you will get to know exactly its healthy reading.

Whenever your dog is taken ill, keep a record of his temperature day by day in the form of a neat chart; you will thus be able to see at a glance exactly how the patient is progressing. Such a chart will also greatly assist the vet. should his services become necessary.

Whelping.—The usual period for carrying puppies is nine weeks. During this time the bitch should be exercised frequently but not violently, and her food should be as concentrated as possible. About six weeks before the puppies are due, dose her for worms, and then give her a dose of cooling health salts twice a week. One of the chief causes of puppies dying is that the bitch's milk is acid. Doses of milk of magnesia should be given during the last month to prevent this or, if the bitch has had puppies before and is known to have acid milk, dose during the whole period. When the puppies are shortly due she will seem restless and will probably seek some quiet corner by herself, also the parts will be a little distended and a discharge will be seen. Absolute cleanliness is now essential, the place where she lies must be as clean as possible, and the dog's underparts should be cleansed with weak tepid Condy's Fluid.

As far as possible she should then be left to herself. Most probably the puppies will appear without any trouble, but if an hour or two of straining passes without a puppy being born, consult the veterinary surgeon, who will come and put things right.

The puppies will probably be born at regular intervals of about half an hour or perhaps more. As they appear the mother should sever the navel cord herself; if she fails to do this, tie a piece of thread around it about half an inch from the pup's body, and cut it with scissors.

By feeling the bitch carefully, you will be able to detect any puppy which remains unborn, and which must be removed by an expert.

After the birth of the puppies, feed the bitch on light food for a day or two, then she may go back to her ordinary diet except for a more generous allowance of meat and milk.

The bitch herself will naturally keep her puppies clean but you should also bathe her underparts occasionally with warm boracic lotion. At five weeks you can begin weaning the puppies. Get them lapping from a dish of one of the milk foods before referred to, and take their mother away from them for gradually lengthening periods every day, leaving her with them all night at first till in about a fortnight they are quite weaned.

They must be fed half a dozen times a day as their little stomachs cannot take on a large meal at a time. After a couple of weeks the milk food can be diminished and shredded raw lean meat, gravy, and puppy meal included in the diet.

Worms.—Worms generally affect dogs during puppyhood, and are responsible for thinness, poor coat, loss of condition, and sometimes they even bring on other illnesses by weakening the dog's power of resistance. The most common are tape worms, which can usually be detected by the little white sections, about half an inch long, seen moving either in the evacuated matter or clinging to the dog's coat round his back parts.

Home-made vermifuges are not to be recommended, especially as there are so many good, ready-made cures on the market. When buying the physic always mention whether your dog is a puppy or not, as most firms make a specially mild form for puppies.

The best plan is to dose your dog for worms twice a year, as it is quite possible for him to be infested with them without showing any noticeable signs.

DOMINOES

Although there is a certain element of luck in the game of dominoes, it is a mistake to class it among mere games of chance, for skill does, to a large extent, enter into it. The game is played with black oblong "pieces," usually of wood, ivory or bone, between $\frac{1}{4}$ in. and $\frac{1}{2}$ in. thick, being thus capable of standing on edge. The faces are either white with black spots, or black with white spots, and each is divided by a line down the centre into two sections. Into the centre of the face of each piece a brass rivet is often fitted so as to make the pieces spin easily on their faces when shuffling. Except in the case of the double-blank, each face has on either or both ends a certain number of spots or pips, from one to six, and as there is also the "blank," there are twenty-eight different combinations of numbers and therefore twenty-eight pieces in the game. We thus have, taking them at random, the double-three, which is a piece having three pips on each section; the six-two, which has six one end and two the other; the five-blank, which has five pips one end but nothing the other; the double-blank, etc. Some domino sets number up to double-nine and even double-twelve, these having, of course, fifty-five and ninety-one pieces respectively. The double-six sets, however, are the most usual.

There are a great many different games that can be played with dominoes, two players usually being the best number, although in some of the games it will be found that three or even four may join. One of the most popular games for two players is Matador.

Matador.—The players sit on opposite sides of the table, shuffle the pieces in the centre and draw for lead. The one who draws the highest piece takes the lead. Each then draws seven pieces, the remainder being put, still face down, on one side to form the stock. Each player stands his pieces on edge with the faces towards him. The leader then lays down face upwards (or "poses" as it is called) any piece he so wishes, and his opponent must then pose either a Matador (this is explained later) or a piece the number on either end of which will make either end of that already played up to seven. It is understood, of course, that the pieces are placed end to end. Thus if the first piece were a double-four, the second, if it is not a Matador, must have a three at one end, and we will say for the sake of argument that the three-six is played. We now have four at one end of the game and six at the other, which means that the first player must produce either a three or a one. If he cannot do so and has no Matador, he must draw from the stock, and if he still cannot play, he must continue to draw until he can. The last two pieces in the stock must, however, never be drawn.

A Matador is the double-blank or any of the pieces on which the numbers of the two ends together make up seven—i.e. four-three five-two, or six-one. Such pieces may be played at any time, no matter what the pieces already played, and may be laid down in the position which best suits the player. It is usually wise, however, to save them for use when one would otherwise have to draw from the stock. (If double-nine dominoes are being used, the number to be made up is ten, instead of seven, and in the case of double-twelves, the number is thirteen.)

The game is won by the first player to get rid of all his pieces. If neither player can move and the whole of the stock has been exhausted, except, of course, the last two pieces, the game is won by the player with the smaller number of pips. It will thus be seen that it is generally good policy to rid oneself of high numbers as early in the game as possible. The winner scores the total number of pips left in the hand of the loser, although in the case of a block (that is, when neither player is able to move) this rule is sometimes modified, and the winner only scores the number of pips his opponent holds over and above the total of his own. The game may, of course, be played for any total, but the usual is 100.

The Draw Game.—As before, the pieces are shuffled, the players draw for lead and each takes seven pieces. Again, as before, the leader poses any domino, but in this game the object of the players is to match the numbers. Thus, if the first player leads the double-six, the second player must lay against it another six, say, for example, the six-four. Now the first player must pose either a further six for the one end or a four for the other, and so on. The game is continued in this way, each player, when unable to match either number, drawing, as in the previous game, from the stock. He can, if for any reason he so wishes, draw from the stock at any time, even if he can already follow from his own hand, but he must always leave the last two pieces in the stock. The game is won, as before, by the player who lays down all his pieces first and calls "Domino," or who has the lower number of pips in his hand. This game can be adapted for four players, but in such a case there will, of course, be no stock.

A good variation of the game is as follows: each player takes an equal number of pieces, leaving at least four in the stock. The lead is not drawn for in this game, as the holder of the double-six must lead with this piece. If none of the players has this, the double-five must be played as lead instead. The pieces are matched as before, but the player of a double at any time during the game is allowed a second move.

Threes.—As many as four people may join in this game. Each player draws six or seven pieces, the number depending upon the number of players taking part. In any case, not more than seven pieces may be drawn and there must be at least two left in the stock. The object of the players is to make up multiples of three. Thus number 1 player, let us imagine, poses the double-six, and scoring 4. (In this game double pieces or "doublets" are always laid cross-wise or "à cheval" and count the full number of pips of both ends.) Number 2 player then lays down the six-three, so that at one end of the game there is the twelve and at the other the three, and he therefore calls fifteen or 5 points. Number 3 player poses three-blank, and scores 4 (i.e. 4 × 3, the equivalent of the original double-six),

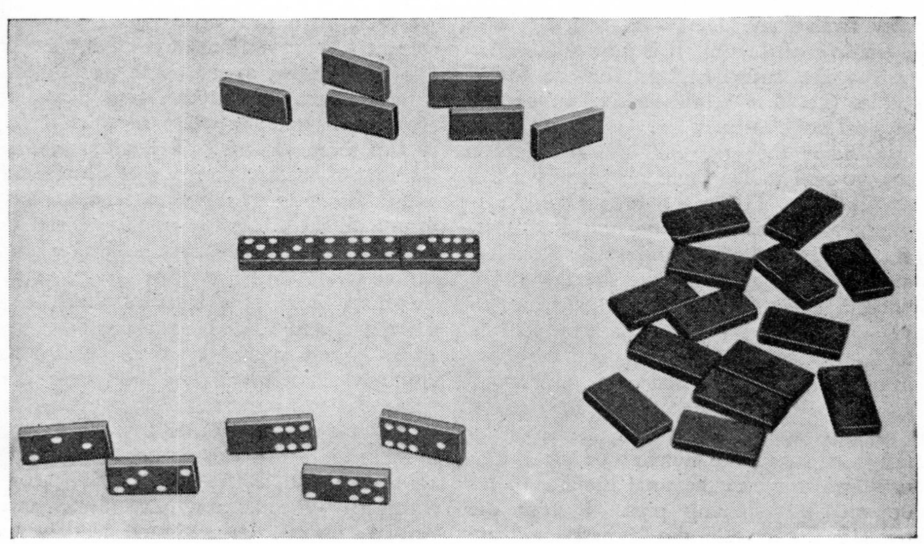

Fig. 1.—The Game of Matador

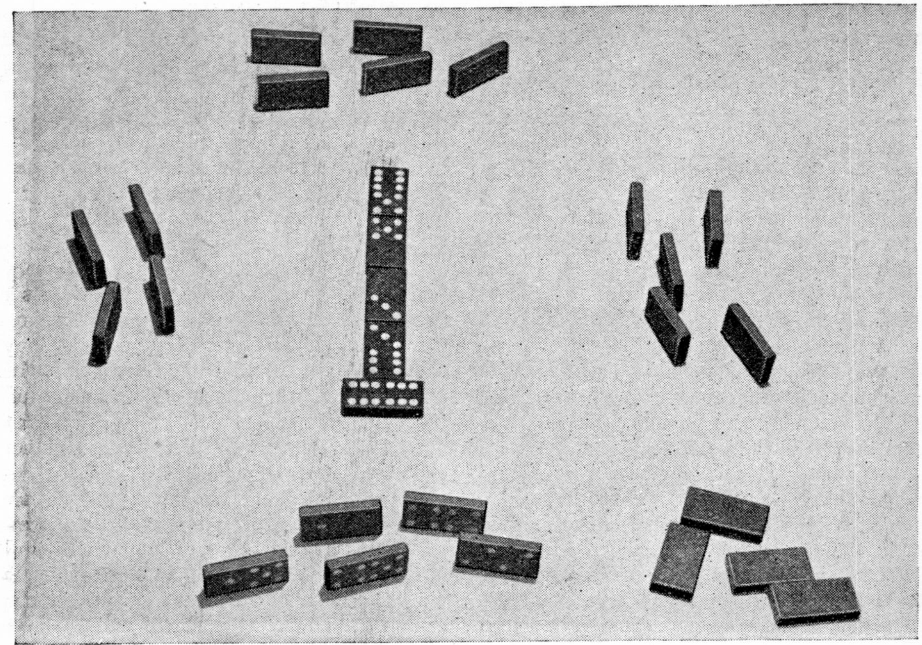

Fig. 2.—The Game of Threes Showing a *Doublet* laid *à Cheval*

number 4 following with blank-five and scoring nothing (because the two ends are now twelve and five = 17, which is not a multiple of three). It is now number 1's turn again, and he plays five-six for 6 points (i.e. 6 × 3, the equivalent of the original double-six, at one end plus the six just laid at the other). Number 2 is not able to add to his score but merely plays the six-two. Thus the game proceeds. It is not always wise to play the double-six at the beginning of the game, for although it may bring in a good score for the player himself, it also gives a splendid chance to his opponents. The art of dominoes is to note what pieces are out, and with this in mind, to try and block one's opponents' game, while leaving an opening for oneself.

When one player is out, he scores a figure equal to the number of times that three will go into the total number of his opponent's remaining pips. If four are playing the pips in the highest hand are divided in this way. If, however, there is a block, scoring is made as in the game previously described.

Fives and Threes.—This is a rather more exciting version of Threes, and in this it is necessary to concentrate one's whole attention upon the game. It is played in the same manner as above except that multiples of three or five *or both* are made up. For example, let us suppose that A leads with the six-five, B adds the six-one, and, the ends thus totalling six, he scores 2. C can do nothing but the one-blank, making a total of five for which he scores 1. D plays the five-three, making a total of three, thus scoring 1, and A, playing again, poses the three-six and scores 2 more. The game continues in this manner, the player who succeeds at any move in making the numbers at the two ends add up to fifteen scoring a double figure, for this counts as not only three fives, but five threes, and thus scores 8 points. Of course each player endeavours to make up this figure himself, at the same time doing his best to prevent his opponents from producing it. This game is one of the best-known forms of dominoes.

Domino Pool.—Each player pays five counters into the pool, then draws pieces according to the number of players—five pieces if four are playing, seven pieces if three are taking part, and so on. The play is as in the Draw Game, that is to say, the pieces must be matched, but if a player cannot follow he must pass, and cannot draw from the stock. At the end of each game the total number of pips left in the hand of each player is scored against him, and when he reaches 100 he is out of the game unless he likes to put another five counters into the pool, in which case he again enters the game, but with a score against him equal to the highest of those still left in. He may only buy his return once. The game is continued in this way until there is only one player left, who, of course, takes the pool.

Bergen.—This game can be played by two, three or four people, although in the case of four, there is not sufficient stock upon which to draw during the game. The pieces are shuffled and each player takes six, after having drawn, of course, for lead. The object is to make the numbers at each end of the game match. At the same time the players must follow suit, that is, match up the numbers upon which they follow. For example, if the leader is able to do so he plays a double, thus scoring 20 points for matching the ends, and in this case we will suppose he leads a double-four. The second player cannot, of course, match the ends, as this would need another double-four; he therefore plays the four-three, and cannot score. The first player continues with the four-five and his opponent then produces the three-five for the other end, thus scoring 20 points for a match. If a player is not able to move he draws from the stock, but if he still cannot move he may draw no more, and his turn passes to his opponent. The game goes on in this way, the players scoring 20 points for every time they are able to make the ends match. If the ends are already the same and the next player is able to pose the corresponding double, 30 points are gained.

The player who gets rid of all his pieces first scores a further 10 points, but in the case of a block, where neither is able to move and the stock has only its two pieces remaining, the player who is left with the smaller number of doubles takes the 10 points. If both hold the same number of doubles, the player who holds the lowest double scores. Should neither player hold a double, the one with the lower total of pips in his hand scores the 10 points.

DRAUGHTS

Draughts is a very fascinating game of absorbing interest and of great value as a mind trainer. The player who takes his game seriously is taught to refrain from making hasty judgments or moves, and there is no doubt that the game is an aid to concentration.

The Board.—A complete draughts outfit can be purchased for under a shilling. The board is square and is made up of sixty-four small squares, alternating black and white. There are twelve black men and twelve white. The board should be set so that there is a double square to the right hand of each player. The players, of course, sit opposite one another with the board between them. It is usual to have the double black corner at the right hand and for the men to be placed on the black squares. Fig. 1, however, illustrates a board with all the white squares numbered. This is done for ease of illustration. Black places his men on squares 1–12 and white places his men on squares 21–32. It is worth noting in passing that draughts can be played by post as can chess.

The players cast lots as to which plays first, the winner to have the choice of either black or white men. It is a law that the person playing the black men makes the first move. Pieces are moved in a forward direction only, one square at a time, and they must keep to the squares of the same colour.

The Object of the Game is to remove all the pieces belonging to one's opponent. A piece may take an opposing piece by jumping over it and occupying the vacant square on the other side, still, of course, keeping to the one colour. For example, if there are black and white pieces respectively on squares 16 and 20 white may take black by jumping over this to square 11. A piece may take any number of opposing pieces, provided there is a vacant square of the correct colour in between them. After the player has moved his piece over one or more of his opponent's, the pieces passed

Fig. 1.—The Board

over are taken from the board as being captured. Should any piece reach the back row (that is the row nearest to the opponent) it is crowned with another piece of its own colour and becomes a king. It is then free to move both forwards and backwards and to take pieces in its way. If a person whose turn it is to play touches one of his own pieces, he must either play it or forfeit the game. Many people, however, have altered this rule, so that instead of the game's being forfeited, the piece itself is removed from the board. A move is concluded immediately the hand is withdrawn from the piece played, so that if a player takes one of his opponent's pieces, and could have have taken another one, if he has removed his hand from the piece after taking the first, the second move is lost. If neither player can force a win the game is drawn.

Draughts is a much more difficult game than most people imagine. It is full of tricks and stratagems, and although a player may be in a very strong position at one moment, it by no means follows that he will win, and he should therefore not relax his vigilance for an instant.

Openings.—There are many different openings in draughts, and the reader who wishes to be able to play well is advised to study the following openings. By practising each one a dozen or more times, and by studying the intention of each player, the reader will pick up far more about the game than it is possible to give in a short article. There are many people who believe that centre board play is much better than side board play, but whilst it is true that the moves of a piece which is at the side of the board are limited, this is frequently more than compensated for by the side of the board itself, for in many cases the side of the board acts as additional piece. Each player must, however, choose for himself. Every move should be made according to a definite plan, and a study of the following regular openings will show what was behind the mind of the inventor.

Ayrshire Lassie.—This is a very popular opening and one which quite early forms a trap. Refer to Fig. 1 for an interpretation of the numbers.

	Black.	White.
1.	11–15	24–20
2.	8–11	28–24
3.	9–13	23–19
4.	4–8	20–16
5.	11–20	22–17

Black in his fifth move takes one of white's men as he moves from 11–20. This particular game which was played out by a former chess champion, resulted in a win for white.

Single Corner.—After the first four moves of any game the play resolves itself into one dependent upon the personality of the players. Here are two methods of playing a game called Single Corner. Black, who of course leads, can often lay a very neat trap for his opponent, and the following are the moves which lead up to this:

	Black.	White.
1.	11–15	22–18
2.	15–22 (takes white)	25–18 (takes black)
3.	8–11	29–25
4.	4–8	25–22
5.	12–16	24–20
6.	10–15	27–24
7.	15–19	24–15 (takes black)
8.	16–19	23–16 (takes black)
9.	9–14	18–9 (takes black)
10.	11–25 (takes 2 white)	28–24

etc. Black should win.

Here is another game utilizing the Single Corner opening. It was played some years ago by correspondence. The first two moves on each side were as those given above. The game then proceeded as follows:

	Black.	White.
3.	9–13	29–25
4.	12–16	24–19
5.	16–20	26–22
6.	5–9	21–17
7.	10–15	18–11 (takes black)
8.	8–24 (takes 2 white)	28–19 (takes black)
9.	6–10	25–21
10.	9–14	19–16
11.	4–8	23–19
12.	8–11	30–26
13.	2–6	27–24
14.	20–27 (takes white)	32–23 (takes black)
15.	11–20 (takes white)	22–18
16.	13–22 (takes white)	18–2 (takes 2 black)

Black resigns.

It will be seen from the above game that it is not always essential to work the game out to its conclusion, although the amateur is well advised to do so.

Old Fourteenth.—The opening to the Old Fourteenth is a very familiar one to advanced players, and it will usually be encountered in a club match.

	Black.	White.
1.	11–15	23–19
2.	8–11	22–17
3.	4–8	17–13
4.	15–18	24–20
5.	11–15	28–24
6.	8–11	26–23
7.	9–14	31–26
8.	6–9	13–6 (takes black)
9.	2–9 (takes white)	26–22
10.	1–6	22–17
11.	18–22	25–18 (takes black)
12.	15–22 (takes white)	23–18
13.	14–23 (takes white)	27–18 (takes black)
14.	9–13	17–14
15.	10–17 (takes white)	21–14 (takes black)
16.	6–10	30–25
17.	10–17 (takes white)	25–21
18.	22–26	21–14 (takes black)
19.	26–30 (crowned)	19–15
20.	30–26	15–8 (takes black)
21.	26–22	32–28
22.	22–15 (takes white)	24–19
23.	15–24 (takes white)	28–19 (takes king)
24.	13–17	8–4 (crowned)
25.	17–22	4–8
26.	22–26	19–15
27.	26–30 (crowned)	

Of course, only the first few moves on each side are counted the opening, but the game is run on to show developments. In

Fig. 2.—How two Black Kings get White King out of Double Corner, and Win. Blacks are on 19 and 23 ; White on 28. Black Moves and Wins, as follows : 23–27 ; 28, 32 ; 19–23 ; 32, 28 ; 27–32 ; 28, 24 ; 32–28 ; 24, 20 ; 23–18 ; 20, 16 ; 18–15 ; 16, 20 ; 15–11. Black Must Avoid 23–19 in his Fifth Move, and 15–19 at The End

the particular instance given it ended in a draw.

Below are some other popular openings,

and the reader is advised to make himself familiar with them:

Whilter.	Souter.	Fife.	Laird & Lady.
11–15	11–15	11–15	11–15
23–19	23–19	23–19	23–19
9–14	9–14	9–14	8–11
22–17	22–17	22–17	22–17
7–11	6–9	5–9	9–13

We will now play the game called the White Dyke, in order to introduce what is known in draughts as "the move." It is

Fig. 3.—"The Move"

noticeable in books on draughts that after a number of moves have been given, one of the players resigns or the winner is stated, without the concluding moves of the game having been given. It is quite obvious that one player is to have the last move, and although at the beginning of the game it is obviously white who must enjoy this privilege, later on it is possible that black may finish off the game. When the board is comparatively clear it is quite easy to calculate which of the players is to have "the move." Before explaining how it is calculated, however, take your board and play the following game:

	Black.	White.
1.	11–15	22–17
2.	8–11	17–14
3.	9–18	23–14
4.	10–17	21–14
5.	4–8	26–23
6.	15–18	24–19
7.	11–16	25–21
8.	16–20	29–25
9.	6–9	28–24
10.	1–6	32–28
11.	9–13	30–26
12.	6–9	26–22
13.	7–11	22–15
14.	11–18	14–10
15.	9–14	19–16
16.	12–26	31–15
17.	14–18	24–19
18.	5–9	10–6
19.	9–14	6–1 (crowned)
20.	2–6	1–17
21.	13–29 (crowned)	15–10
22.	29–25	10–6
23.	25–22	19–15
24.	22–26	6–2 (crowned)
25.	26–23	2–6
26.	23–32	6–10
27.	8–11	15–8
28.	3–12	

Black wins.

After the move 3–12 at the end, it will be found that the pieces occupy the squares as shown in Fig. 3. (Note here that play usually takes place on the black squares, but for the sake of illustration they are here depicted on white.) The method of ascertaining who has the last move is as follows: On the row nearest to you are the four white squares (which, of course, will be black if you are playing on the black squares), and it is with the columns running away from you that you are concerned. For instance, the square on the left hand corner of the board is white, and running back to the opposite side there is one white piece on that column. In the next white square and column there are no pieces, nor are there in the third. In the last, however, we find the king. So far, then, we see that on the four columns there are two pieces, and the rule to be followed is this: If the number be an odd one, with your turn to play, you have "the move," but if it be even, "the move" is with your opponent. Assuming, then, that you have been playing white, and it is of course white's turn to play, your opponent will have "the move." It is frequently very important to know who will play last because the finishing moves of the game very largely depend on this. It is not always, however, that the player who has the move possesses the advantage, for instance, if the men are placed out as follows: Black 1, king 18. White 9, king 29, and white has to play, black will be almost sure to win, because he forces the white man on square 9 on to square 5 after white has moved from 29–25. This is an exception to the rule that if a player has "the move" and it is his turn to play he wins.

DRESSMAKING

SOONER or later and whether she likes it or not, almost every woman finds herself dressmaking. Sometimes she is driven to it by necessity, but often she does it as a hobby and derives from it pleasure, satisfaction and a real sense of economy.

There is not the slightest doubt that if one enjoys using a needle—as a large number of women do—it is really economical to make one's own garments. Better material can be purchased than one could hope to find in a ready-made within the range of one's purse; a style can be selected that will be suitable; the pattern and colour of the material can be her own choice; "cheap" looking methods of finishing can be avoided and finally there will be the pleasure of making the dress, occupying hands which might otherwise be idle and having the great satisfaction of doing a "real job of work."

Dressmaking is one of the oldest and largest crafts and the space allotted to it here is much too small to deal with it in great detail or with the really advanced side of it. So the following hints are intended mainly for the amateur who for the above reasons is anxious to make some, if not all, of her own clothes or those of her family.

Tools.—The following are important items—these should be steel: thimble, dressmaker's pins, a good assortment of needles, a fairly large pair of really sharp scissors and a small sharp pair; soft tacking cotton, tape measure, tailor's chalk, a good-sized table for cutting-out, pressing equipment (dealt with further on) and a machine. The last is not essential for children's clothes, summer dresses, etc., but it becomes so as soon as the worker is dealing with heavier materials.

A long mirror is a great asset as the tilted swing mirror often fails to give the right effect for the hem.

A 36-in. ruler is a great help in all sorts of ways.

Materials, Styles, Patterns and the Wearer.—There are a large number of pattern books on the market to-day full of current styles and a great deal of advice. The amateur may well be bewildered! The great danger, when the worker is inexperienced, is that she is carried away by a current style or a new material, and desiring above all things to be fashionable, finds herself the possessor of a very unbecoming garment.

The average person, presumably, decides that she needs, for example, a simple business dress. Next she has a good look in the shop windows and in current fashion books to get a clear idea what the current designs for such dresses are like and of what material they are made. All the time she should be thinking "Can I wear that?" or for example: "I could wear that if I altered the line of the neck." The great advantage of being one's own dressmaker is that one need not be dictated to by other people. We learn to know ourselves and what suits us best, and while keeping the general characteristics of the current styles we can ignore some style point that is not flattering to us and add some feature to the dress that not only makes it suit us but gives it individuality.

A few Hints about Materials.—It is in the choice of materials that many people go astray, and the following hints may be useful.

Woollens.—Choose closely woven, smooth-surfaced cloths. The more openly woven ones tend to stretch at the knees and seat and fray at the seams. Some woollen materials, especially if plain in colour and rough in texture, pick up threads and hairs and are very difficult to keep clean in appearance.

Wool Crêpes are very flattering, as they hang gracefully and do not easily crease. The chief disadvantage is that they shrink, so that they should be well shrunk *before* the garment is cut out. Therefore it is better to buy more than one requires, as a dress length may lose many inches when shrunk.

Tweeds, both heavy and light in weight, are very serviceable as the patterned surface prevents any spot of ink, etc., being obvious. Also the pattern breaks up the surface of the figure and gives a slimmer effect.

Silks.—These are so various in make that it is difficult to give any definite advice. Many of the artificial silks are just as lovely and often better wearing than the pure silks, but some of the cheaper ones have a very bright sheen and this accentuates the figure, often to the disadvantage of the wearer. Moreover these artificial silks tend to fray badly.

Silk georgettes and ninons are delightful, but the inexperienced worker should avoid them as they are extremely difficult to make up.

Mercerized Cottons often have the appearance of silk and they give excellent wear for little outlay.

Cotton Prints and Plain Cottons are very inexpensive and are easily washed and ironed. The chief disadvantage is that they crease badly, but as children's dresses have to be washed very often this is not a serious drawback. Moreover it is now possible to get crease-resisting cotton fabrics.

Linens make delightful summer wear but be sure to demand the crease-resisting kind since otherwise a dress needs thorough pressing after every time it has been worn.

There is an increasing demand for materials that do not crush; cruises, holiday week-ends and the general tendency for everyone to pay more attention to clothes have given impetus to research in the manufacturing of such fabrics. The following fabrics keep their freshness for a long time: Voiles and linens sold as "crease resisting," crêpes, georgettes, ninons, most pure woollen fabrics and real silks, wool voiles, dress lace.

Hints for those who want to appear slim and tall.

1. Select materials with a dull surface.
2. Choose a fabric with an all-over design in preference to a plain one, but avoid a large detached design which would attract undue attention.
3. A striped material with the lines running down the figure adds height. If the dress is cut so that the lines run diagonally to meet in the centre, back and front, this gives a slim effect.
4. Choose styles with style lines running down, e.g. pleats, decorative seams, a hanging sash, rows of buttons, etc.
5. Avoid cutting the figure across with a contrasting or wide belt.
6. If the waist line must be defined cut it slightly lower than the natural line and let the belt drop a little in front.
7. Emphasis on the shoulder in the form of cape or puff may be worn by the taller woman and this will suggest narrowness at waist and hips.
8. A long neck line tapering to a V in front is flattering.
9. A straight plain sleeve is usually better than a very full one.

The Paper Pattern should be bought with care.

If your figure is stock size (that means a bust measurement of 32, 34, 36, 38 or 40 in.), you will find a variety of patterns on the market from 9d. or 1/– upwards. Special designs are often available for the small woman with a 30-in. bust measurement or for the "outsize" one with a bust of 40, 42, 44, 48 or sometimes 50 in.

If you are inexperienced choose a pattern where ample making directions and diagrams are provided. With free patterns explicit dressmaking lessons are generally printed in the book presenting them, but there is an absence of trace lines and stamped directions on the actual pattern which is confusing to the novice. Some cheap patterns are provided with step-by-step

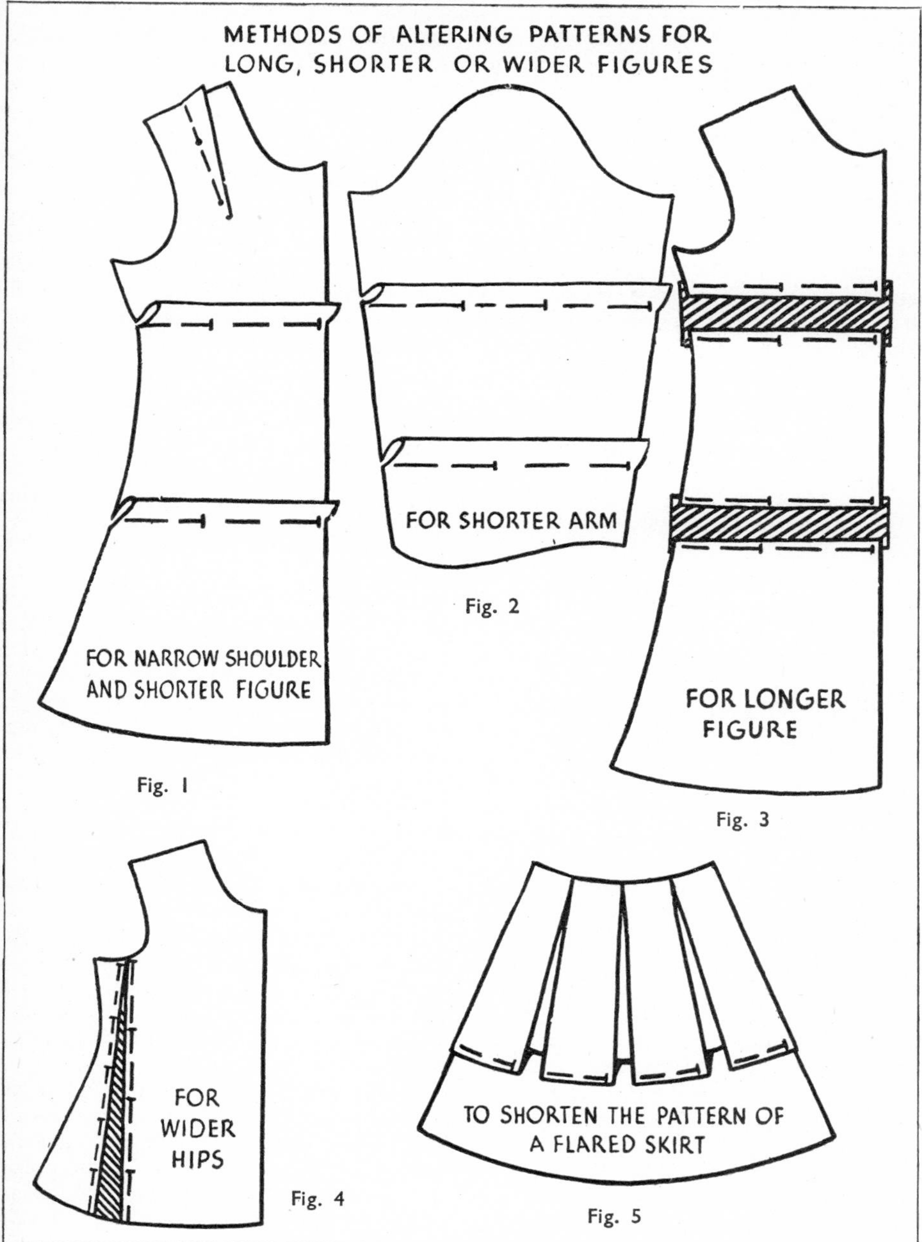

picture lessons which are simple to follow. Diagrams showing the paper laid out on different widths of material are also very helpful.

Altering the Pattern.—Most women have to make slight alterations as very few of us are in true proportion. We may have a bust measurement that is 34 in. but our shoulders may be too narrow, our hips too big or our waist too high. No pattern-maker can cater for all our little idiosyncrasies. Always buy the pattern that is nearest to your bust or hip measurement (whichever is more normal in comparison with the rest of you).

If on the other hand your figure is badly out of proportion (meaning that individual measurements are far from stock size in relation to the others), your best plan is to invest in a cut-to-measure pattern in linen or leno which fits exactly. This foundation garment is really worth while as it can be incorporated from year to year either with a style pattern of incorrect size or with an actual garment.

Figs. 1 and 2 show how the pattern can be pleated for small chest measurements and narrow shoulders. Fig. 5 shows how a skirt pattern can be pleated for a short figure. Never cut a piece off the bottom of a sleeve or skirt, but pleat the paper above and below the waist or elbow.

Fig. 3 shows how to lengthen a pattern without altering the width at the hem. It is quite usual to have a hip measurement out of proportion to the bust and the pattern can be widened in exactly the same way as the diagram shows it being lengthened.

Figs. 1–5 show some of the best methods of adapting patterns, illustrating the simple principles underlying all pattern alterations for different sizes.

Cutting Out.—If the intending dressmaker is nervous of cutting out, most of the large shops will do it for her providing that the pattern and the material have been purchased there. For the inexperienced worker it is a good way to begin and she is helped over the first and rather frightening stage, but the serious and more experienced worker will realize that the best way to success is to follow the work right from the beginning. The following are several very important points concerning cutting out:

1. The crease down the centre of the fabric should be pressed out before cutting out is done.

2. Woollen material should be tested for shrinking when pressed under a damp cloth. If it shows signs of shrinking then it should either be pressed all over with a damp cloth and warm iron or rolled up in a damp cloth for a night and pressed the next day.

3. All notches, darts, holes, etc., in the pattern should be marked on the material, on both sides, left side and right side of the dress. Tailor's tacking is the best method of marking up if a tracing wheel cannot be used, as this will stay in, no matter how long the construction of the dress will take. This is done with double cotton and long, very loose stitches, which can be taken through both pieces of the material. You cut the threads in between the pattern pieces when you come to separate them. Loose back stitches in tacking cotton are made to mark notches. If the making up will be done quickly, tailor's chalk can be used. A pin should be inserted through both thicknesses of material at the notch or hole and then the spot marked on both sides with chalk. Pencil can also be used on the wrong side of the fabric.

4. When using a new pattern it is by far the wisest plan to make a little extra allowance on all side seams just in case, after fitting, it is necessary to let the seam out at some particular point. It is, however, important to mark the position of the edge of the pattern with chalk so that it is easy to see where the stitching line should be.

First Fitting.—After the material has been cut out, tack up the dress as indicated in the directions and try it on and adjust where necessary. The shoulder should be carefully noted. It is most important that it should be narrow enough. Of course, the *pattern* ought to have been narrowed if necessary by making a pleat in the shoulder but otherwise a dart can be made in the centre of the front shoulder and the back adjusted to fit it.

Making Up.—If a bought pattern is used and directions for the construction of the garment are given, these should be carefully followed. Usually the wisest plan is to seam up the shoulders and then complete the neck which would easily stretch if not soon finished. Experienced dressmakers often trace the neck line and do not cut it out until it is fitted ready for finishing.

Next, if possible, stitch the front skirt to the front bodice and similarly the back.

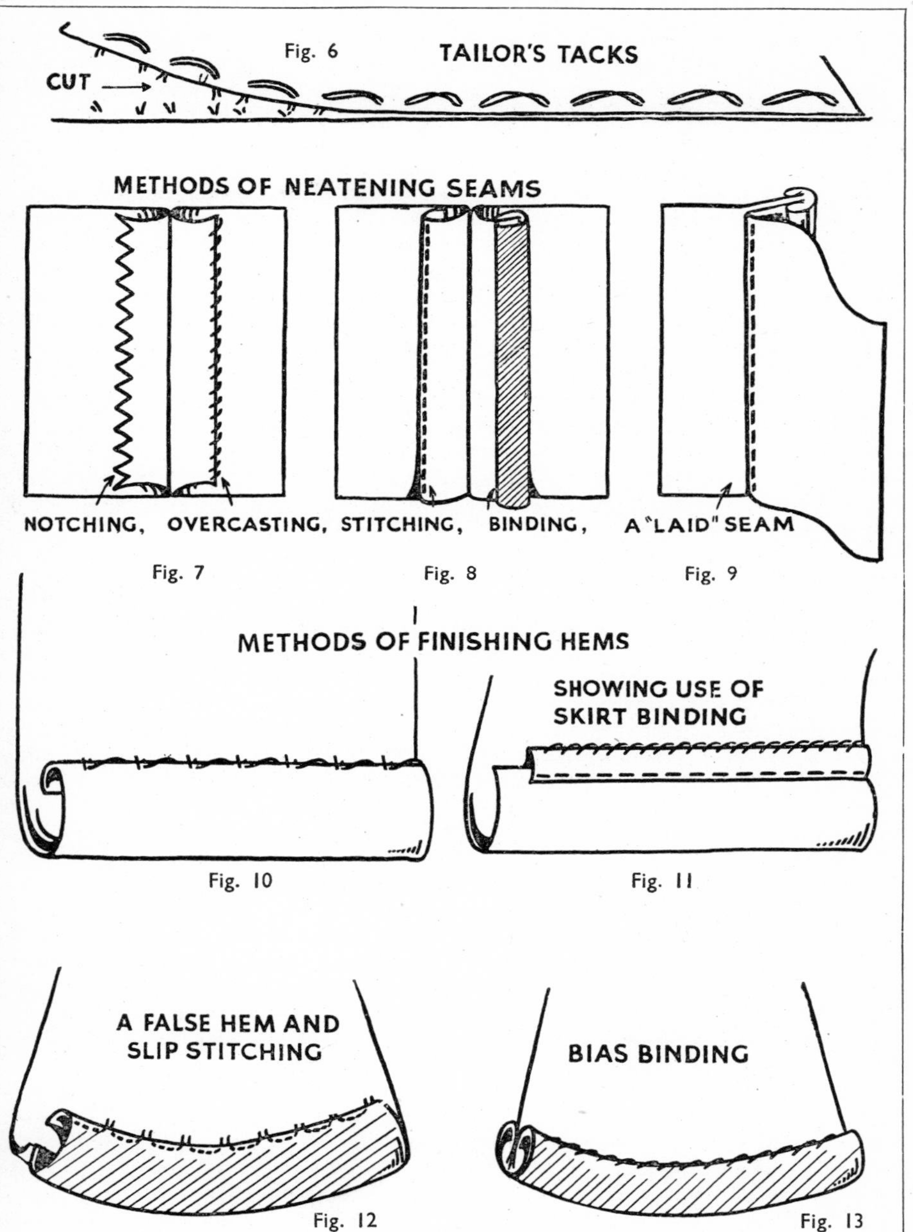

Fig. 6

Fig. 7

Fig. 8

Fig. 9

Fig. 10

Fig. 11

Fig. 12

Fig. 13

Then make the long side seams, altering them if necessary to fit the figure.

Then set in the sleeves. (*See* further on.)

Seams.—For very thin and cotton fabrics a french seam is used, but the most usual seam is the single seam, i.e. one line of stitching and the two edges pressed open. (*See* Figs. 7 and 8.) The edges are neatened by notching or are overcast (*see* Fig. 7), or by binding or stitching back the raw edge. A laid seam (*see* Fig. 9) is very common at present on all silk materials and light tweeds. One edge is turned back to the stitching line and carefully tacked. It is then laid in position on the corresponding section of the garment, with the edge placed exactly to the stitching line. It must then be carefully tacked into place and stitched very close to the edge. The raw edges are neatened together in any one of the usual ways.

Setting in Sleeves.—It is essential that the pattern be darted narrow enough on the shoulder before the garment is cut out. An armhole that overhangs the arm will ruin a sleeve and it is no good cutting away any material to make it right as that will simply make the armhole too large for the sleeve.

Be absolutely accurate in taking turnings. There are usually three seams running into an armhole and the seam which sets in the sleeve. If these have been stitched in a haphazard way there is no need to be surprised and no excuse for blaming the pattern if the sleeve does not set in properly.

First tack up the two sleeves, making sure that there is a left and right one. The wrist often indicates more clearly than the top nowadays for which arm the sleeve is intended. The notches in the pattern are the best guide.

Next with tacking cotton or tailor's chalk mark the highest part of the sleeve and the armhole. The latter usually comes 1 in. to the front of the shoulder seam. (*See* Figs. 15 and 16.) Then run a gathering thread very finely round the top half of the sleeve (Fig. 16).

To Set in the Sleeve.—Have both garment and sleeve right side out. Put one hand inside the garment with the fingers holding on to the highest part of the armhole. Hold the highest part of the sleeve in the other hand and then place the two highest points together (Figs. 16 and 17). The hand inside the garment should take hold of the two raw edges. Then turn the garment over the sleeve so that it is wrong side out. Pin the two highest points together and also make representing notches on the front and back armholes.

The sleeve head is gathered and now working down the back first, pin the sleeve in. Put the pins in parallel to the raw edges, but only take up a very little material. There should be very little fullness at the back of the shoulder seam and none down the back. The sleeve seam will probably come a little to the front of the underarm seam even if it is a "seam to seam" sleeve.

Some sleeves fit the armhole exactly. If they do, fit the centre top in position first and tack the sleeve in place. If there is fullness run a gathering thread round the sleeve and case it to the top or the front top, according to the style of sleeve you are making.

Continue pinning up the front until about 4 in. from the shoulder seam. Then distribute the gathers very evenly. Turn the garment right side out and put the sleeve over the hand and see how it appears. Note that if the pins were at right angles to the edges this could not be done.

If the distribution appears satisfactory, tack the sleeve in with very small stitches and try on. One set of threads in the material should be travelling parallel to the floor and the other threads should be vertical (Fig. 20). Adjust the sleeve if necessary by taking it in or letting it out at the armhole seam. Then stitch, but be most particular that there is not a single little gather visible on the sleeve head. Neaten the raw edges by binding or overcasting.

To press the sleeve head, make a thick round pad of a clean duster and place it inside the top of the armhole seam holding the pad in the left hand. See that the raw edges face down *into the sleeve.* Place a damp cloth over the seam and with a warm iron press the seam, a small piece at a time.

Hems are much more important than many people realize. Styles, fashions, materials, all influence the choice of methods, especially in the more light-weight fabrics, such as silks and georgettes.

The following methods are used:

(*a*) A wide hem turned up and lightly sewn into place as shown in Fig. 10.

(*b*) A very narrow hem, e.g. $\frac{1}{10}$ in. turned in and machined. Be careful not to stretch the edge.

(*c*) Turned up $\frac{3}{8}$ in. or $\frac{1}{2}$ in. once only

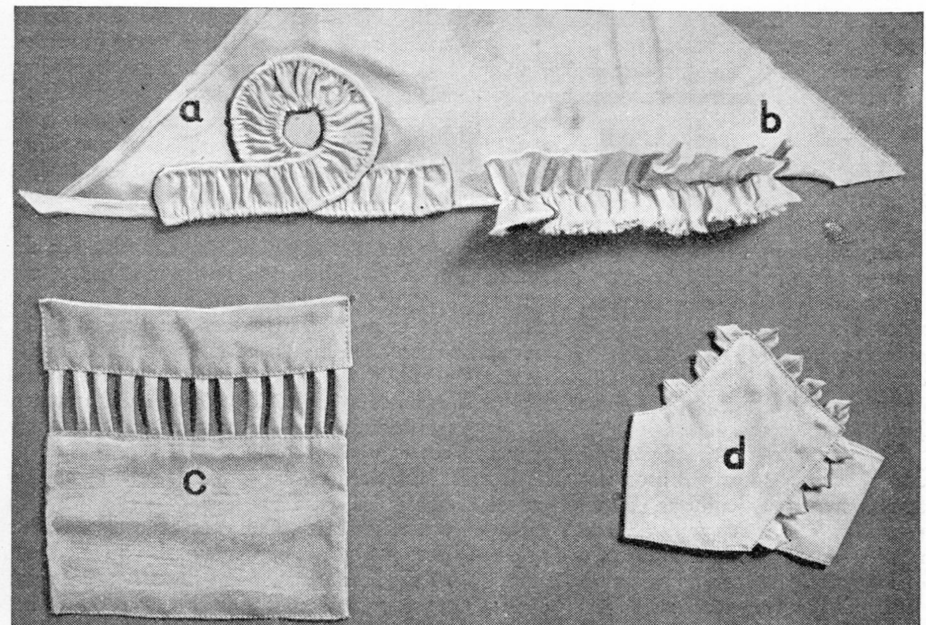

Fig. 14.—Trimmings from material cut on the cross. (**a**) Appliqué ruching. (**b**) Ruched frill. (**c** and **d**) Two decorative trimmings with rouleaux

and machined twice on the right side. The raw edge can be overcast or cut close to the stitching.

(*d*) A hem about $\frac{3}{8}$ in. turned up and machined.

(*e*) When a very supple edge is required on a very thin dress turn it up once, machine it and overcast the raw edge which should be only very narrow above the stitching.

(*f*) Binding with bias strips. This always looks smart and is very good for flared skirts.

(*g*) Picot edging is good for georgettes and silks, but it has to be done at a shop.

When firmer fabrics are being used, the methods shown in Figs. 11–13 are satisfactory.

On a straight or nearly straight hem it is often possible to turn it up as in Fig. 10 and fell it, only catching up the tiniest possible amount of the skirt. This shows a very good way of hemming which avoids too many stitches and yet keeps the hem in place. Take one almost vertical hemming stitch and bring the needle straight back to the hem. Then take one false and long hemming stitch which does not take up the underneath part. Then make a vertical stitch and so on. Slip stitching as shown in Fig. 12 would do just as well, but it does not keep the hem so flat. In this stitch the needle is slipped along inside the fold. It is brought out at the required spot, a tiny thread of the skirt is taken up and the needle inserted in the hem just where it came out.

In Fig. 11 is shown binding rubber, sometimes called prussian binding and used as a successful finish for any turned-up hem, especially one with a fraying edge. If the latter is curved, a gathering thread must first be run in to pull up the raw edge to the required length. The binding is then run or machined to the edge and then felled to the garment. This is a "tailored" method and is very satisfactory. Very curved edges should not be turned up. A crossway facing of some thin fabric is an excellent way of finishing them. (*See* Fig. 13.)

Pressing.—A famous dressmaker who once took pupils always impressed upon her students "*Work with the iron always beside you.*" Expert pressing at every stage of the work makes all the difference to the finished look of a garment—it must not be shirked.

Any garment—from lingerie to a top coat—must be pressed at every stage of its making. On heavy materials, serges, velours or suitings, when pressing open seams or pressing hems, always work with a damp cloth—preferably a piece of the actual material you are making up—between your iron and the seam.

Keep your iron moving gently backwards and forwards to avoid iron marks. On fragile materials, chiffons, crinkly crêpes, thin silks, etc., press with a circular movement and a warm, not a hot, iron, taking part of the weight off the fabric as you press.

Velvet or velveteen needs very careful handling. Until a year or two ago the recognized way was for a willing helper to hold a warm iron face upwards while the pile was passed gently *wrong side* next to the iron—backwards and forwards. Nowadays the modern fabrics are often treated like any fragile material and ironed with a circular motion. This needs careful doing. Always remember that the iron must be only warm and that most of the weight must be kept off the fabric.

The use of material cut on the true cross of material.—There are many ways of using material that is cut on the cross, and anyone who is anxious to do really good dressmaking should accustom herself to cutting and handling such material.

To cut material on the true cross, first take the fabric to be cut and trim two adjacent edges straight with the threads of the fabric. One edge can be the selvedge and the other along the threads going straight across the width. Turn down the right-angled corner so made so that the sides are turned exactly at right angles to themselves. Crease the fold and cut along it. The result is an edge absolutely on the cross. Notice how it stretches easily and is very pliable. It is this quality which makes it useful for many purposes.

Binding with crossway or bias binding is very common. Strips of material must be cut 1 in. wide or less. Stretch well under a warm iron before putting on. Then bind an edge, place the two right sides together and the edge of the garment and binding quite level. Run or machine a quarter of the way down the width of the binding. Use a hot iron and press the binding up over the stitching. Fold it over the edge of the garment and press again. Then fold in the edge of the binding to touch the other edge and hem the fold so made to the back of the running stitches.

Binding must be narrow and accurately cut to look correct.

On very flimsy materials such as chiffon or triple ninon it is often easier to work with a double bind. Cut your strips 1½ in. wide (less if you are expert, unless you are afraid of them fraying), press them double, right side out, and run the double raw edge to the right side of the garment as before.

Then all you have to do is to press your binding up over your stitching and fell its fold lightly in place on the wrong side over the first line of stitches; that is much easier than attempting to turn in a second turning on a springy, stretchy material.

Rouleaux.—This term is given to bias strips stitched into tubes and used for trimming.

The rouleaux can be faggoted to the edge of collars, cuffs, necks, jabots, etc., and makes a very attractive finish.

Ruchings.—This is another way of using bias strips as a trimming and it is used a great deal in taffeta evening dresses. (*See* Fig. 14.)

Another form of this trimming is to have the edges frayed first by straining them over the edge of the scissors or a paper knife. Then a line of running is put down the centre and the fabric is pushed along it to give the required fullness. This is regulated by back stitches. Sometimes instead of gathers boxpleats are used instead. When ready for use the ruching is run into position.

False Hems on Dresses.—A bias strip about 2 in. wide of jap silk or sateen is

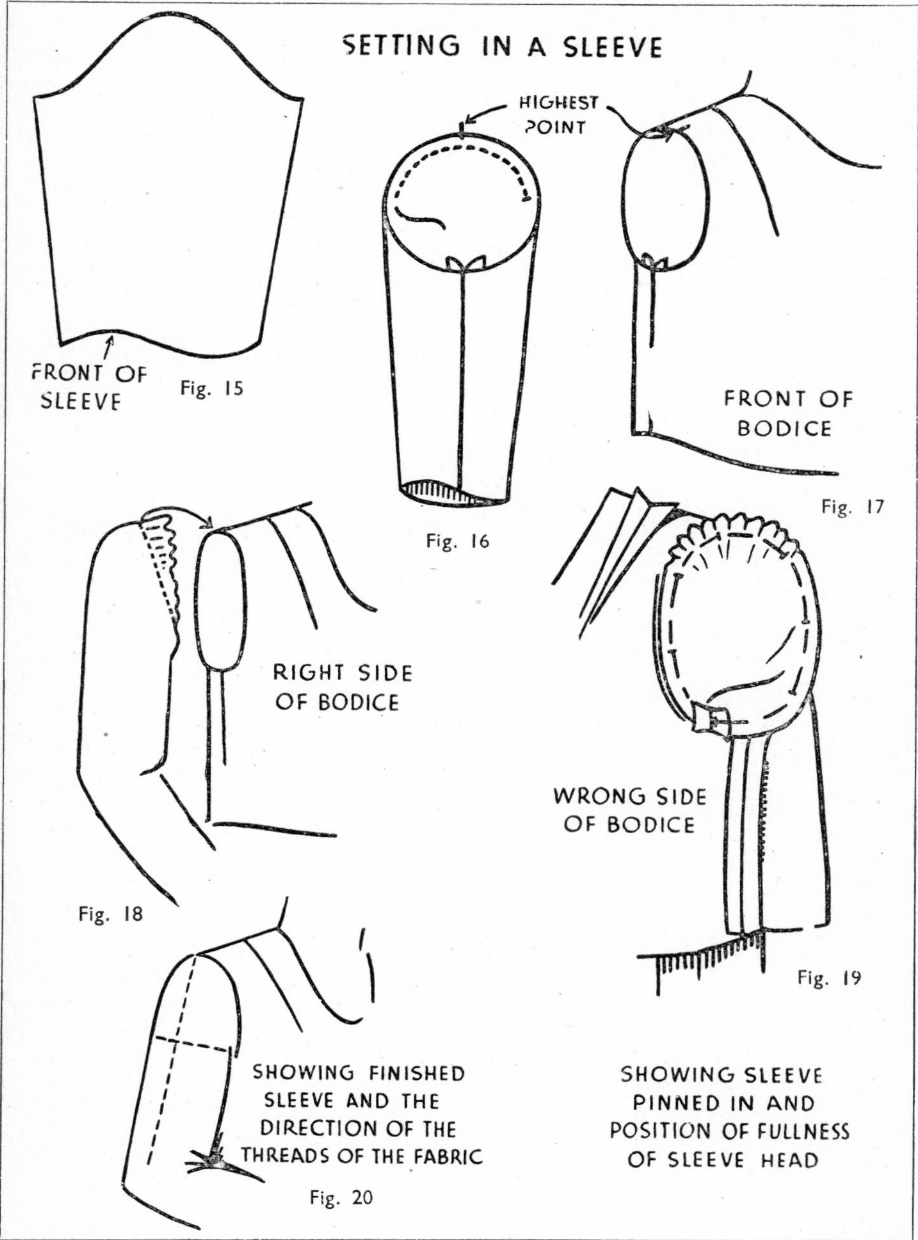

often used to face the hem of a dress. This may be done because there is insufficient material or the edge is very curved or because the fabric will not lie flat when turned up. The facing is run to the right side of the dress first and then turned to the wrong side and very lightly hemmed into position.

Skirts.—Many readers may be anxious

to make themselves a simple skirt. Figs. 21–23 show how to deal with the opening and set it on the petersham. First make the opening by facing the upper side or neatening it with skirt binding and arranging for a wrapunder of the other side. Then take the petersham and cut it the exact length the extreme edge of the under wrap, and arrange for the other end to be the width of wrap in from the edge of the upper part of the skirt opening. Bring the top edge of the skirt over the petersham on the side nearer the body. Tack it into place and lay a piece of binding over the raw edges and

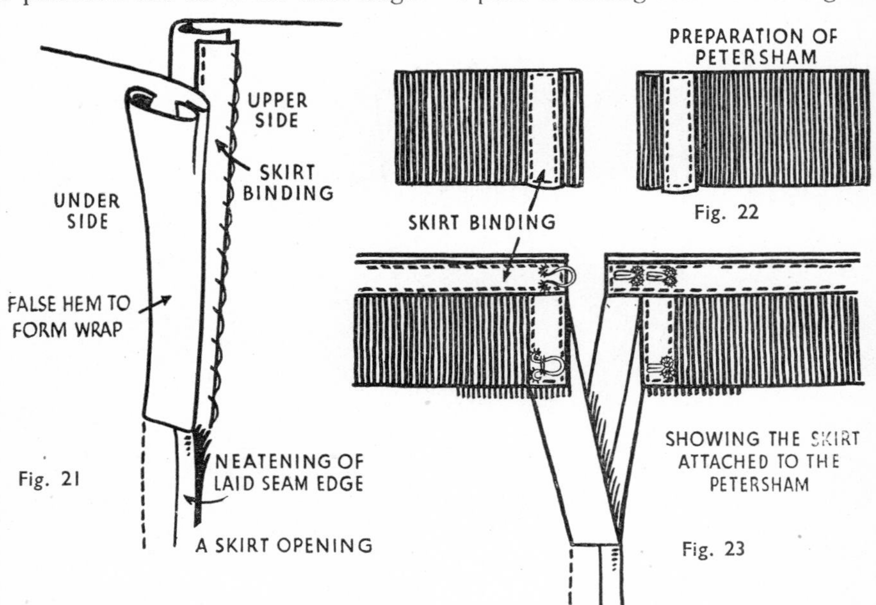

Fig. 21

Fig. 22

Fig. 23

required, i.e. waist measurement, plus ½ in. at each end. Turn these half inches back at each end on to the side that will be near the body. Stitch over them a piece of material or skirt binding.

Next place one end of the petersham to machine along top and bottom but not through the skirt on the right side.

Attach hooks and eyes to the petersham and sew these on with buttonhole stitch as in Fig. 23. Sew clips on to the skirt opening, also using buttonhole stitch.

EMBROIDERY

MODERN embroidery is a hobby as profitable as it is pleasant. It is quick, easy and effective work. More than that, it adds definite distinction both to your household linens and furnishings and to your own clothes and those of the family.

"Embroidery" includes such a wide range of needlecraft that it is not possible to deal with it comprehensively in this section. But certain stitchings are more popular and useful than others; appliqué, for instance, cutwork, drawn-thread work, English embroidery (or *broderie Anglaise*), smocking, tapestry and quilting. These are briefly described here.

A knowledge of the most used stitches is necessary. Once you have mastered these you will be able to tackle far more complicated embroideries than those mentioned and will have no difficulty in carrying them out for yourself. The Dictionary of Stitches tells you how these are worked.

Your equipment is quite simple. You will need crewel needles, which have long, narrow eyes that pass through your fabric without making big holes. (It is essential, on the other hand, that the needle should make holes sufficiently large for the wool, silk or thread you are using to follow through without dragging and becoming rubbed). Get wool or tapestry needles with blunt ends for working in wools or on canvas. Add embroidery scissors; these have fine points and are small.

Choose good materials, both to work on and to work with. Start with something simple that you will be able to finish before you get tired of it. For almost every type of embroidery you can obtain transfers of appropriate designs, which have only to be transferred to your material by pressing under a warm iron.

Take pains over your starting and finishing. Be sure, for instance, that you have the right needles and appropriate thread for your material. See that the latter is clean and smooth and if you use a transfer place it carefully before you iron it off.

Finish your embroidery by pressing it. Spread it face downwards on a blanket covered with a white cloth. Raised embroidery, such as satin stitch, needs a thicker blanket than flat embroidery like hem stitch. Press from the wrong side with a warm iron. For white and colour-fast embroidery the cloth should be very slightly damp, but not for silks and pastel colours. Embroideries on linen and cotton need a hotter iron than silks or delicate fabrics like organdie.

If the embroidery has puckered, as cut work or eyelet embroidery are apt to do, it will need stretching. Pin down your blanket and cover-cloth, then pin the upper edge of the work in place through these to the table or board beneath. Smooth the embroidery downwards to its full extent and pin the lower edge. Smooth out to the sides and pin these in place. Damp the back of the work with cloth or sponge squeezed out of cold water, cover with a clean press-cloth and pass a hot iron lightly over the back. Do not let the iron actually press the work; its business is to steam it. Leave the work pinned out until quite dry. If necessary repeat the steaming.

Appliqué.—*See* separate article.

Cut Work.—This is done in buttonhole stitch, with part or all of the design cut away, or the background. The two principal types of cut work embroidery are Richelieu and Venetian Ladder; in the first the background is cut away and in the second the design. Buttonholed bars connect the cut edges. It is a hard-wearing embroidery and is used a great deal for household linens. Transfers are specially designed for this work; you can carry out any design if you follow these simple rules.

Richelieu Embroidery.—Iron the transfer on to the right side of your work. Choose a firm fabric, linen for preference. Go along every line in the design with running stitch, but when you come to a bar (more correctly called a "bride") take your thread across this to the other side, then back again, back once more and then return, buttonholing the "thrown" threads together firmly until you reach the starting point of the bar. Be sure that no buttonhole stitch catches in the material under the bar. Carry on with the running stitch until you come to the next bar, and so on. When the outlining is done and all the bars buttonholed you begin again, this time buttonhole stitching over all your running stitch, the head or "purl" of the stitch towards the openwork.

This finished, take small, sharp scissors and very carefully cut away the material from the back of the bars, close to the buttonholing. If you are inexperienced make a faint pencil mark on the portions to be cut away; it will prevent your cutting out the wrong piece and spoiling your work! Be very careful not to snip the bars.

Sometimes the bars are bound together by twisting the thread round and round them, but this is not so strong as buttonholing.

Venetian Ladder Work.—Run-stitch the outline as for Richelieu, but when you come to a bar take a single thread over it and in returning twist your needle several times round the thread. When outlining and bars are finished cut away your material, but this time leave fairy-like turnings just round the run edge. Now instead of buttonholing the edges work along them with oversewing stitch, as for eyelet embroidery, taking in the turnings and the running stitch. Keep your stitches even and close together and pull them tightly.

Drawn-thread Work.—This term is applied most frequently to those white embroideries in which horizontal threads are drawn and the vertical threads grouped with any of the simple or complicated varieties of hem stitch. These decorative forms of hem stitch are used a great deal on table linen, either in lines or squares, and also for trimming frocks and lingerie. When a wide band is drawn the vertical threads are bound together in fancy patternings, or darned in groups.

But there are other varieties of drawn-thread work, some of them too complicated to deal with here, and some very simple to master, such as needle-weaving. The threads are drawn from the material, as for hem stitching, and replaced with coloured threads, which may be woven in and out just as the original threads were woven, or darned in in patterns.

For drawn-thread work of any kind choose a good quality material; linen is the favourite. It is possible, however, with a little practice and patience, to draw threads in a fine material like *crêpe de Chine*, and hem stitch on such a background has a dainty and delicate effect that repays the trouble taken. If you choose linen be sure that it is free from dressing.

English Embroidery or *Broderie Anglaise*.—Eyelet work is the main feature of this very favourite embroidery; round, oval and leaf-shaped holes are combined into decorative openwork designs, but in most cases certain of the rounds and ovals and leaves are worked in well-padded satin stitch, making an effective contrast. Where stems or lines are added these should be worked in cordonnet, or whipped running stitch . . . all the stitches required are described in the Dictionary of Stitches. Scalloping is very frequently used as an edging for this embroidery, or a line of shaded eyelets may be worked.

You will have no difficulty in finding transfers with suitable designs, whether you want just simple sprays for a baby's frock or coat or something much more elaborate for an afternoon cloth. But whichever you work, do use a firm material of really good quality. This embroidery will wear and wash splendidly and it is a waste of time to put it into poor fabrics. Choose good embroidery threads, too.

It is most usual to work in white on white, especially for household linens, but collars and cuffs, baby garments, luncheon mats and so on can be delightfully embroidered in white on colour or the other way about. Fine materials such as *crêpe de Chine* may be trimmed with *broderie Anglaise* and in this case a fine silk should be used for the working.

Press your work thoroughly from the wrong side to finish.

Quilting.—The actual stitchery used in quilting is exceedingly simple, being a form of running stitch. It *is* running stitch, actually, but instead of picking up two or three stitches at once on your needle, or even one, you must put your needle right through every time . . . from front to back, then from back to front, drawing your thread through each time. Occasionally back stitch is used instead of running, but this is not general.

You will need cotton wadding, flannel or domette for padding your work, and a lining. Choose a pretty material for the outer layer; satin, taffetas, a good artificial silk or a cotton can be used.

Transfer the design for your quilting to the right side of this outer layer. Lay the padding over the wrong side of the lining and the outer layer over the padding, right side uppermost. Tack the three layers together, so that the padding won't move out of place as you quilt, and run a line of machining round the edges.

Begin your work in the centre and work out towards the edges. If you are quilting in plain diagonals stitch the longest lines first. Use cotton or silk, according to your material, exactly matching the ground colour.

Smocking.—The initial stage in smocking is to gather your material into even pleats, so that their edges can be caught together with various fancy stitches and in various patterns. On the regularity of your gathers depends the success of your smocking, so it is a wise plan to use a smocking transfer, stamped with rows of accurately-spaced dots. Allow a row of dots for every row of gathers in the design you are going to work, with one row extra, and use a strip three times as long as the finished smocking will be.

Transfer the dots to the wrong side of the material and gather from the wrong side, too. Your thread must be long enough to go right across the material and a bit over. Begin at the right end of a row; give your thread a knot much too big to be pulled through, however great the strain. At every dot pick up a small stitch, not more than an eighth-inch. Your gathers finished, pull the threads up as tightly as they will go; this pleats the material. Before you begin your smocking let out the gathers until you have the required width. Place a pin, point downwards, at the end of every two rows, so that you can twist the threads of these rows round the pin in figure-of-eight. Adjust the pleats evenly and then you can begin.

Honeycombing is the simplest form of smocking, and the basis of all more elaborate varieties, so it is good to start with.

Beginning at the left end of the second row of gathers, the right side of the work towards you, bring your needle through from the edge of a pleat at the wrong side. This gives a firm start. Now pass your needle through the edges of the first two pleats, *from right to left*, catching them together. Then put your needle once more in at the right side of the second pleat, but this time pass it downwards, inside the pleat, to the next row of gathers, and bring it out again at the left side of this pleat. Link this pleat with the one to the right of it, as before, the needle going through them from right to left.

Pass your needle up inside the right hand pleat to the gathered line above; bring it out at the left side of the pleat. Repeat across your strip. Work two rows at a time in this way until your band of smocking is complete.

In more elaborate smocking the thread is often passed up and down outside the pleats instead of inside.

The gathering threads are drawn out after the smocking is done; untwist them from their pins and draw them out gently by their knots. When pressing smocking pin it out face downwards so that it is stretched to the right width. Have a thick blanket under it and put a damp press cloth over it. Press it very lightly, you do not want to flatten the pleats. The iron should be only moderately hot.

Tapestry.—This is very definite and straightforward work, using the simplest of stitches; it demands patience and accuracy, but as it will wear almost indefinitely when it *is* done it is worth the time spent. It is worked on canvas, and as the entire surface is to be covered the finished work is very hard-wearing and especially suitable for such things as chair-seat covers, stool covers, cushions, screens, hand-bags and so on.

There are two kinds of canvas, one with single threads and the other with double threads, generally known as Penelope. For working you can use wool, silk, mercerized cotton or raffia. You will want a blunt-ended needle to prevent splitting the threads; you can buy these wool or tapestry needles in any size you need.

For embroidering a large piece of canvas an embroidery frame is useful, because it keeps the work stretched properly and also leaves both the worker's hands free. Great speed can be achieved if you can use your right hand on top of the work and your left hand under it.

You may want to copy a piece of tapestry you admire. That is a case of counting stitches carefully and reproducing them on your canvas, taking your stitches over its threads. If you want to plan out your own design draw it on paper ruled in one-tenth inch squares. The design does not necessarily cover the whole canvas; the background may be filled in with the same kind of stitch in a neutral shade. An easier method is to buy one of the tapestry charts you can get through any needlework shop; you can work this stitch by stitch without any difficulty, and will be advised what colours to use for them. Still another method is to buy a canvas stamped in colour with your selected tapestry design and to fill in the different coloured surfaces with appropriate threads. Sometimes when it is wished to cover a surface quickly the stitches are worked over a strand of the wool or silk being used, and it is possible to buy your canvas with these threads in position. The work is said to be "trammed" when this is done.

The stitch most used in modern tapestry is *petit-point* or tent stitch, which is actually

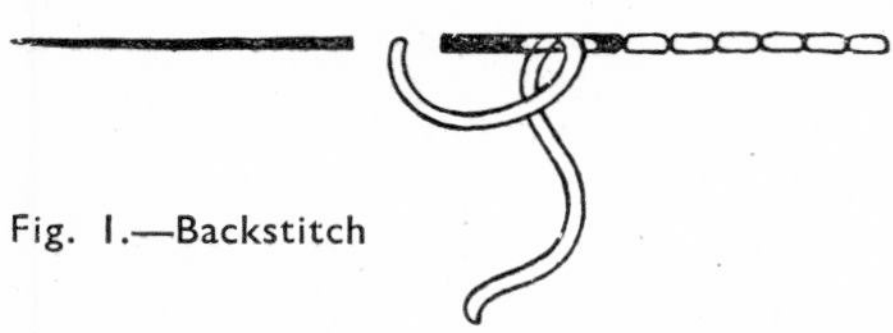

Fig. 1.—Backstitch

half a cross-stitch. But for a first attempt at this work cross-stitch is better; tent stitches all slant in one direction and this is apt to stretch the canvas out of shape in inexperienced hands. Cross-stitches slant both ways and so do not drag at the canvas. The stitches are taken across one or two threads of the canvas, according to the size of stitch required.

Other important tapestry stitches are *gros-point* and Gobelin stitch. You will find them described in the Dictionary of Stitches.

It is very important to keep the back of the work as tidy as possible, and especially to avoid long threads crossing the canvas. When your work is finished it should be stretched.

Remember that owing to the thickness of the work and the slantwise strain of many stitches several stretchings may be necessary. Don't scamp this part of the finishing.

Mounting is also very important, and if you are inexperienced it is better to let an expert do it for you; it is a pity to spoil the effect of your painstaking stitchery by clumsy or careless making-up.

Backstitch.—(*See* Fig. 1.)

This is used when you want a continuous line of stitching, resembling machine-stitching; it is very useful for outlining, for working straight lines and in quilting. Decide on the length of stitch most effective for your purpose (a few sample stitches will soon show you this). Bring your needle through from the wrong side of the material a stitch-distance from the right end of your line then put it back again at the very beginning. Bring it through again a stitch-space to the left of your starting point. You have now made one back-stitch and are ready to make the second by putting the needle through where you started, this time from right side to wrong. Bring the needle through a stitch-space to the left of your second backstitch and repeat.

Variations.—**Spaced Backstitch** makes an effective broken line or a filling for a surface that needs breaking up. Make small back-stitches and instead of putting your needle back to the previous stitch pass it through the material a space to the left of this, producing a line of alternate stitches and spaces. As a filling work in rows, making the stitches in the alternate rows come under the spaces in the other ones. This is also known as Seed stitch.

Threaded Backstitch gives a thicker, more decorative outline. Work the back-stitch in the usual way then, using thread of

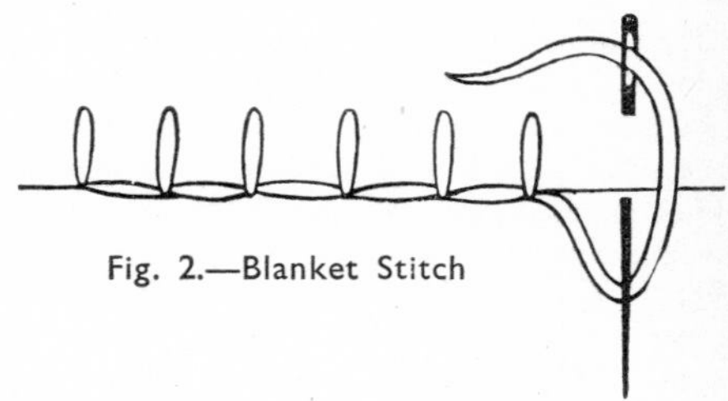

Fig. 2.—Blanket Stitch

a different tone or colour, bring it through at the right end of the line. Pass it under the first stitch from bottom to top without catching in the material then down under the second stitch from top to bottom. Repeat. A bolder effect is gained by adding a second thread worked the opposite way: pass it under the first stitch, from top to bottom and under the next from bottom to top. Repeat. The threads may be in matching or contrasting shades. Threaded backstitch is most effective for working simple monograms.

Blanket Stitch

An edging worked in Buttonhole stitch (*see below*).

Bullion Stitch.—(Fig. 3.)

This is actually an elongated French knot, and when made looks somewhat like a little caterpillar lying on your material. It is used particularly in raised embroideries and when grouped, forms attractive little "roses."

Bring your needle through from the wrong side and put it back again as close as possible behind first stitch-hole. Pick up on your needle a bit of material the length you want your stitch to be, bringing the needle partly through towards you where the other end of the stitch comes. When the needle is half through wrap your embroidery silk round the point of the needle *from right to left*, and close to the material. (If wound the other way it will untwist.) The number of twists required depends on the length of the stitch; usually six to nine twists are needed, but it is a matter of practice to find out. Place your left thumb on the twists and pull the needle and thread gently through; give these a pull in the opposite direction. Let the "caterpillar" lie along the material where your stitch is to be and put back your needle at the starting point, drawing it through to the wrong side.

It is a good plan to practise with a coarse thread first of all.

Fig. 3.—Bullion Stitch

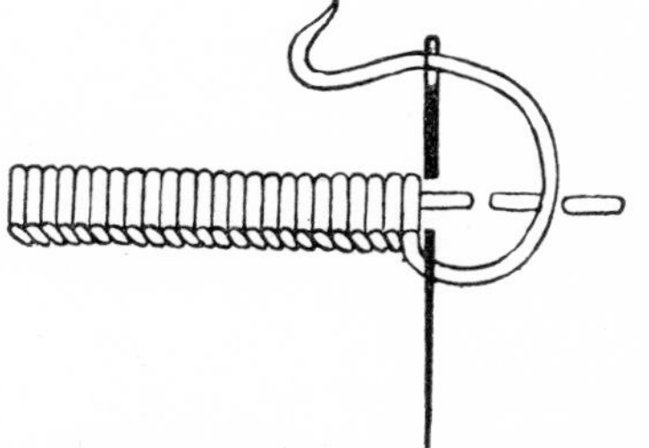

Fig. 4.—Buttonhole Stitch

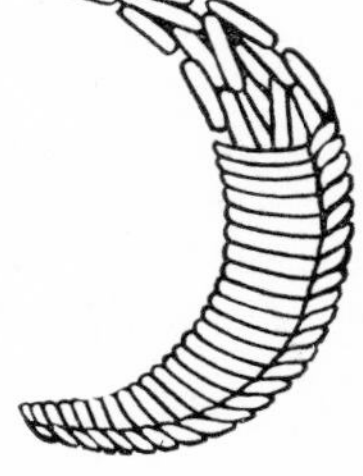

Fig. 5.—Scallop

Buttonhole Stitch.—(Fig. 4.)

One of the most useful and most used of embroidery stitches. It is worked from right to left: to begin bring your threaded needle through from the wrong side at the lower left-hand edge. Put the needle back again just to the right, the height of a stitch above your starting point. Hold the working thread down with your left thumb. Bring out your needle again on the lower line, immediately below where it went in, *over the working thread*, pulling this down loop-wise. Repeat, the stitches just touching one another.

Scalloping is worked in buttonhole stitch (Fig. 5), the loop or "purl" of the stitch at the outer edge. The design is usually stamped on the material a little distance from the raw edge and worked before this raw edge is trimmed away. You can cut close to the "purl" edge without danger of fraying.

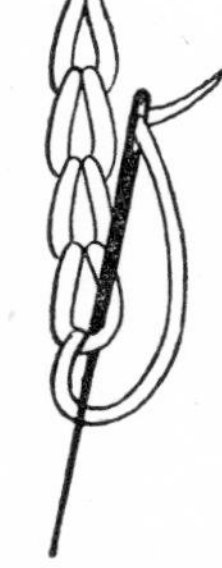

Fig. 6.—Chain Stitch

Flowers and formal circular designs are often worked in spaced buttonhole stitch, the purl edge forming the outline and the stitches radiating from the centre.

Blanket-stitch is really spaced buttonhole stitch worked along an edge (as on blankets). The raw edge is blanket-stitched when the material is non-fraying, but the stitches are worked over a single turning when the material may fray. True blanket-stitch is buttonholing with the stitches grouped, three stitches spreading fan-wise from one point, but the term is applied generally to any edge finished with spaced buttonholing (Fig. 2).

Chain Stitch.—(Fig. 6.)

A popular outline stitch, very quickly worked. It is also useful as a padding for satin-stitch, monograms, scalloping and embroideries with a raised effect. It is worked downwards. Bring your needle through at the top of your line and put it back again as close as possible to the same spot, holding down the working thread with your left thumb as you do so. Bring out the needle again the depth of a stitch along your line, drawing it through the loop of thread you are holding. Pull down the thread to form a "link."

To make the next stitch hold the working thread down with your thumb as before, and put the needle back again just inside the link, close beside the place where it came out last time. Repeat. *Always keep your working thread to the left* and always begin a stitch just inside the previous link. Keep your stitches of even length, not too long, and do not pull them too tight.

There are many variations of chain stitch used in embroidery, but this is the foundation of them all.

Coral Stitch.—(Fig. 7.)

A knotted outline stitch, useful when something rather bolder than the usual outline stitch is needed. It is worked from right to left. Bring your needle through at right end of your outline and with your left thumb hold down the working thread along the outline. Where your first knot is to be, pick up a slanting stitch, passing the needle under the outline of an angle; it passes under the thread, too. In drawing it out pass it *over* the working thread at the other side of the thumb, so that as you pull it fairly tight you form a knot. Carry your thread along to where the next knot is to be and repeat.

The spacing of the knots depends on the effect you want to get; practise a few before you decide.

This coral knot is used in various kinds of embroidery and is important to know.

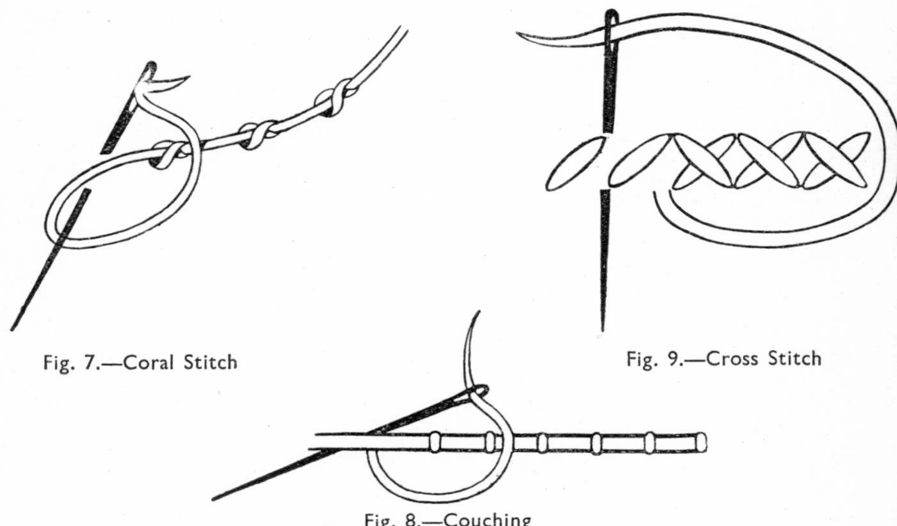

Fig. 7.—Coral Stitch

Fig. 9.—Cross Stitch

Fig. 8.—Couching

Couching.—(Fig. 8.) A quick and

effective method of outlining often used to finish an edge in appliqué or satin-stitch embroidery. You will want a fairly thick strand of wool or silk and a thinner one; they may be in the same colour or form a contrast. Hold the thicker thread down along the line to be couched and catch it down at intervals with the finer thread, using an oversewing stitch. If more convenient, use three or four strands of silk for your outline and couch them with a single strand.

For more decorative effect the thick strand may be couched with cross stitches instead of single stitches, or with groups of stitches.

Cross Stitch.—(Fig. 9.)

Diagonally crossed stitches of even size. It is most easily worked on canvas, as in the old samplers, when the threads can be counted and a definite number crossed each time, but it can quite well be worked on finer material by using special canvas, sold at any embroidery shop, or by using a transfer.

The canvas is mostly used for bold embroideries and is tacked to the ground material. The design is then worked over the threads (pull your working thread rather tightly), and these threads are gently pulled away afterwards. Transfers are stamped with a cross for every stitch in the design and all you have to do is to cover each of these.

All the first stitches in your crosses should slant in the same direction. For instance, if the first half of your first stitch crosses from left to right the first half of every other stitch should cross in the same direction. Pull the second stitch a little more tightly than the first. In working a line of cross stitch, go from one end to the other making the first halves, then come back making the second halves.

Cross stitch is one of the most popular tapestry stitches. It is also particularly useful in general embroidery for working formal or quaint peasant designs, borders for towels, runners and cloths, and for trimming children's clothes. In Assisi embroidery cross stitch is used to form the background, the design being left plain.

Daisy Stitch.—(Fig. 10.)

This is very often called Lazy-daisy stitch, because it is so easy to work. It is used a good deal in simple flower embroidery, since each stitch looks like a daisy petal, and when a number are arranged round a centre of satin-stitch or French knots a flower is formed.

It is very like chain stitch. Bring your thread through at the base of the "petal," and hold down the working thread with your thumb, just to the left. Put your needle back quite close to the starting point and bring it out again at the other end of your petal. Pass it over the working thread to form a loop. Draw the thread through, then put back the needle just outside the tip of the loop, and draw the thread to the wrong side so that the loop is caught down with a tiny couching stitch. Bring your needle out again where the next stitch is to begin.

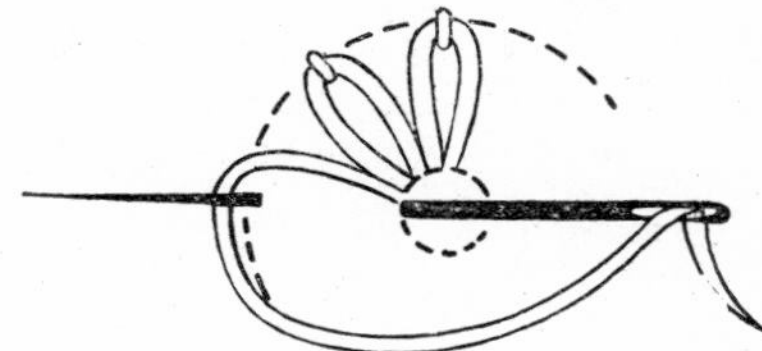

Fig. 10.—Daisy Stitch

Worked on either side of a flower stem these stitches make realistic leaves and may be varied in size. The caught-down end is the tip of petal or leaf.

Darning Stitch

In embroidery darning stitch is usually worked with a long stitch on top and a short one under, over an accurately counted number of threads . . . say over five threads and under one alternately. It is useful as a filling stitch, when the stitches are worked in rows across the surface in brick fashion; that is, the spaces in the alternate rows coming under the centre of the stitches in the row above. For borders it can be worked in formal patterns and is very effective for guest towels, runners, curtains and similar household furnishings. On huckaback and linen it is easier to count the threads than on a fine material. In carrying out patterns these are formed by the stitches on the right side of the material and in such work the thread is carried across the back in long stitches when long spaces are required. For towels, and when the wrong side must look as tidy as the right, avoid patterns where wide spacing is necessary.

Eyelet Embroidery

A feature of English embroidery (or *broderie Anglaise*), in which round and leaf- or petal-shaped holes are combined with raised embroidery. Eyelets are also useful for ribbon slots.

Trace the design on your material. If you are drawing your own eyelets and not using a transfer use something round as a guide, for if the outline is not a perfect circle your hole will not be a good shape. Work over the outline with small and even running-stitch in your embroidery cotton; this serves as padding. For a large hole snip the

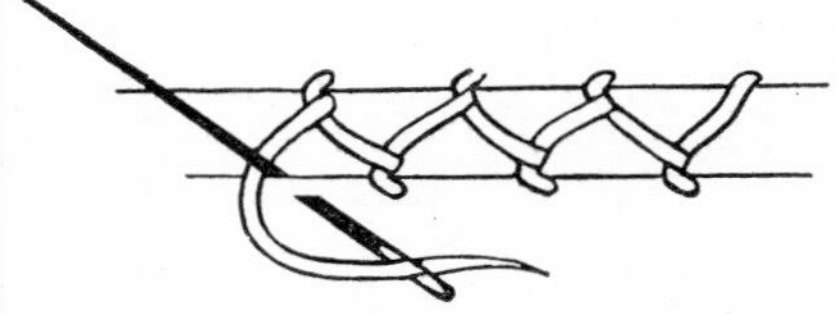

Fig. 11.—Faggot Stitch

material in the centre cross-wise; *never cut out the hole.* For a small hole simply push a stiletto through. Do not go right to the outline either with stiletto or cross-cuts.

Now work round the outline with close oversewing stitch, taking up the same amount of material every time and also taking in the snipped edges. Pull your stitches firmly each time. The result should be a firm, cord-like edge. Large holes are sometimes buttonholed.

Leaf-shaped or oval "holes" are worked in the same way. Long slots, for passing belt, tie or ribbon through, should be worked down either side of a pencilled line and the slot cut along this line afterwards.

Always work from right to left in eyelet embroidery, to avoid twisting your cotton.

Large eyelets are sometimes "shaded," the upper half worked in overcast stitch and the lower in buttonholing (Fig. 4). In this case the lower half should be well padded first with running stitch. These eyelets may be used along the edge of a collar or round a mat. When worked in a row like this they should all be outlined and padded before any of them are embroidered. When used along an edge the raw material should

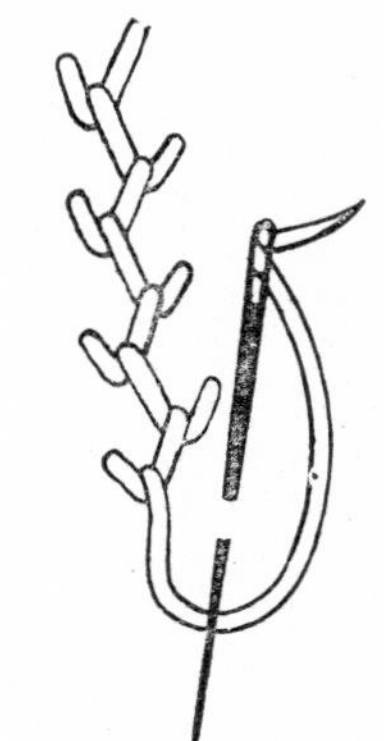

Fig. 12.—Feather Stitch

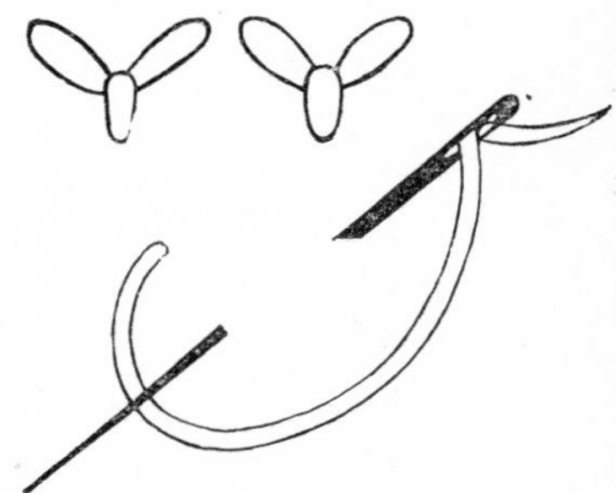

Fig. 13.—Fly Stitch

be trimmed away after the working and pressing are finished.

Faggot Stitch.—(Fig. 11.)

A decorative stitch for an openwork join; it can be used for seams, for putting on a hem or as a trimming strip between bands.

When joining single material, as for seams, make the narrowest possible hem along each edge and tack them both in position on a strip of stiff paper, leaving between them just the width your faggoting is to be. When putting on a border use a bias strip, doubled, and turn in its raw edges narrowly to face. Tack them together, then tack this double edge to the paper, opposite the other prepared edge of material. (The space should not be much more than quarter-inch.)

Holding the work horizontally, bring your needle through from the wrong side of the upper edge, at the right end. Holding your thread down with the left thumb, pick up a stitch in the lower edge just below your starting point. Now pick up a stitch in the upper edge, to the left, then another in the lower edge, again to the left, *always keeping your working thread to the left of your needle.* Repeat.

There are many variations of faggot-stitch; this is the simplest.

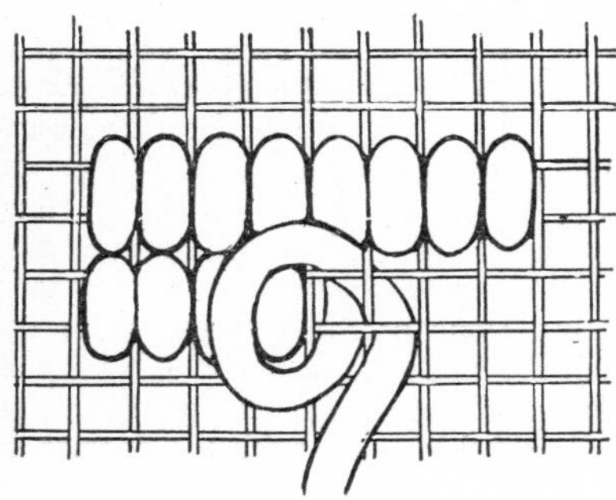

Fig. 14.—Gobelin Stitch

Feather Stitch.—(Fig. 12.)

A trimming stitch used in embroidering babies' clothes, in smocking and for hems and borders.

It is worked like buttonhole stitch, except that you go downwards instead of from left to right. Begin at the top, bringing your thread through from the wrong side. Hold the thread down with the left thumb and pick up a small vertical or very slightly slanting stitch to the right, just below the starting point. (Sometimes you will find the stitches quite vertical, at others just a little slanted, in feather stitch.) Draw the needle over your working thread, pulling this down loop-wise, as in buttonhole stitch. Now pick up a similar stitch at the left, its top level with the lower end of the previous stitch; repeat down the line. It is important to keep the stitches at either side exactly under one another, and of the same size.

Fly Stitch.—(Fig. 13.)—A variety of Chain Stitch—it is also called Y-stitch, because it looks like a Y when finished. Bring your needle through from the wrong side at the top of the left arm of the Y and put it back at the top of the right arm, meantime holding down the thread with your thumb. Bring the needle out again at the top of the stem, over your thread. Pull down the stitch into a V, then form the stem by making a little straight stitch which keeps the V in shape and incidentally forms a Y. Sometimes the stem is kept very short and sometimes it is as deep as the upper half of the letter; it

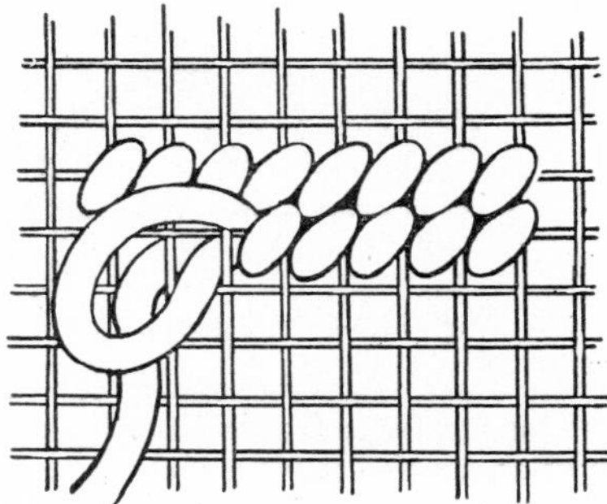

Fig. 15.—Petit Point

depends on the effect you want to get. You can work this stitch in lines as a hem or border trimming, or scatter detached stitches over a surface you want to fill.

French Knots.—These are used a great deal in embroidering baby wear, and in flower embroidery, when they make realistic

Fig. 16.—Hem Stitch

stamens. They are also used for trimming hems, in lines between tucks and so on.

Bring your needle through from the wrong side of the material where the knot is to be, drawing the thread right through.

Hold it down with your left thumb quite near the starting point. Slip your needle under the thread and twist it round the thread two or three times. Still keeping the thread taut with your left thumb, turn the needle round and put it back through the starting point. Pull needle and thread through the spiral and fasten off firmly at the back. If you are making a number of knots bring your needle out again where the next knot is to be, instead of finishing off the first knot. Do not draw the knot too tight.

Gobelin Stitch.—(Fig. *14.)

A tapestry stitch, worked on canvas.

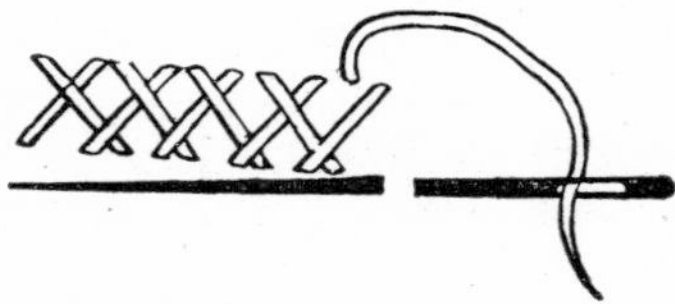

Fig. 17.—Herringbone Stitch

There are several varieties of it. Straight or Upright Gobelin is worked in horizontal rows across the canvas; each stitch is taken over two horizontal threads of plain canvas. Oblique Gobelin stitch, as the name suggests, slants slightly, being taken over two horizontal threads and one vertical; that is, it is taken into the adjoining vertical row of holes, crossing two horizontal threads. Encroaching Gobelin stitch is used for covering large surfaces; these are much bigger stitches, taken slantwise over five horizontal threads and one vertical. After the first row the succeeding rows begin four threads below the previous one, so that in making each stitch it takes in the lowest thread of the row before, so "encroaching" on it.

Gros Point.—This is a larger version of Petit point (Fig. 15), worked over two or sometimes more threads instead of one. Gobelin stitch is sometimes called Gros point.

Hem Stitch.—(Fig. 16.)

An important stitch in drawn-thread work; it is most often used as an openwork finish to hems on household linens of all kinds. It can only be worked along a straight line, as it depends upon drawn threads. Choose for your first attempt a material from which threads can be drawn easily, such as linen or canvas-weave.

Draw a thread to mark the fold of your hem turning; from this measure twice the depth your hem is to be and draw another thread. Below this draw as many threads as required for your openwork line; the number varies according to the weave of your material. Draw the threads one at a time, easing them through gently.

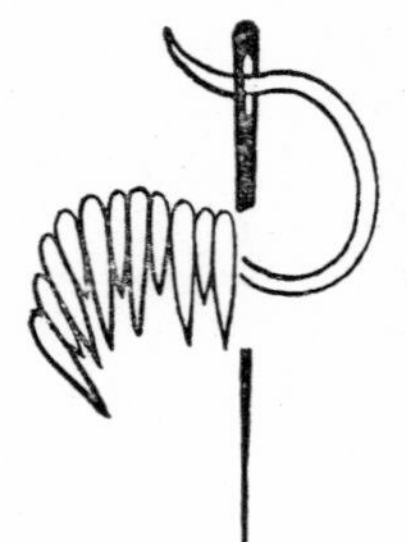

Fig. 18.—Long and Short Stitch

Tack your hem with the turning (just along the first drawn line), touching the second drawn line. Turn the material with wrong side towards you, hem downwards, and bring your needle through from the inside of the hem at the left end. Now pick up a group of threads (four is a good average number, but this varies with the coarseness of the threads), passing your needle behind them from right to left. Bring the needle through to the right side without catching in the material, and across the front of the group. Put it in again at the right of your picked-up group so that you can bring it

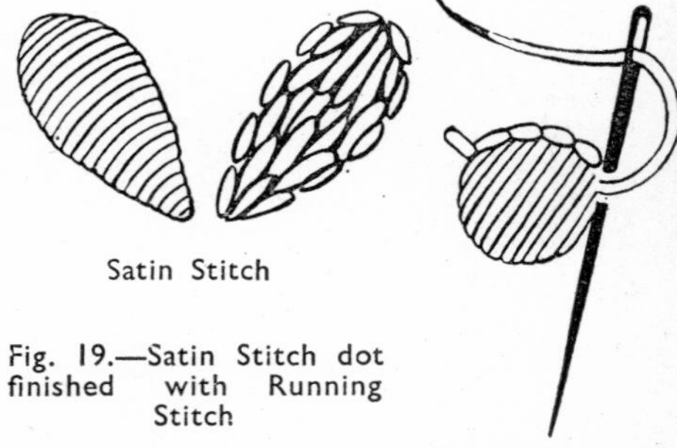

Satin Stitch

Fig. 19.—Satin Stitch dot finished with Running Stitch

through the edge of the hem. (*See* Fig. 16.) Repeat.

This is single hem stitch. For double hem stitch repeat along the other edge of the drawn line.

Herringbone.—(Fig. 17.)

A quickly-worked stitch for borders,

hems and straight lines of trimming. The stitches should be as regular as in cross-stitch, which it resembles, so it is best to choose a material which shows its threads clearly, for example, either a huckaback or a canvas-like weave. Otherwise you must carry a double straight line in your eye. Begin at the left end of the upper line and bring your needle down to the lower line, to the right of the starting point. Pick up a horizontal stitch, passing the needle from right to left, and take the needle up to the upper line. Pick up a similar stitch here and repeat along the line. Keep the thread to the right of your needle.

Long-and-short Stitch.—(Fig. 18.)

This is used a great deal in flower embroideries when petals are too large to be covered with single stitches, or when you want to shade the colours. It is simply a series of alternate long-and-short, straight stitches. Begin at the top of your petal or of the surface to be embroidered and take a series of long-and-short stitches along the upper outline, the upper ends all touching the outline, but the lower ends long and short alternately. In the succeeding rows keep your stitches of even length, each touching the lower end of the stitch above it. Fill the surface in this way. The irregular effect of the stitches will blend colours well if you want to shade the petal from light to dark or the other way about. The actual separate stitch is really a satin stitch.

Outline Stitch.—*See* STEM-STITCH, of which it is a variation.

Running Stitch.—The very simplest stitch and one of the most important. It is used for outlining, especially where the outline stitch serves as a padding, as in eyelet embroidery. It is worked by running the needle in and out of the material, making short, even stitches on the right side and picking up a tiny stitch between, of one or two threads. It can be worked in bands of several rows as a trimming, stitches in alternate lines coming below the spaces in the lines above them, or worked backwards and forwards in rows as a filling. The length of the stitches depends on the effect required, but all the surface stitches should be quite regular in length.

Whipped running stitch, or cordonnet stitch, makes a neat outline and can be worked in two colours. After working the outline in running stitch pass a whipping stitch over each running stitch, working from right to left and passing the needle under each running stitch from top to bottom. Be careful not to catch up the material.

Satin Stitch.—(Fig. 19.)

A very simple stitch, which must be worked neatly and accurately. It is used in many types of embroidery, and particularly in English embroidery, monograms and white embroideries. The stitch is taken across from one edge to the other of a surface to be covered, and may be worked in any direction. It is important that the needle should come out and be put in again

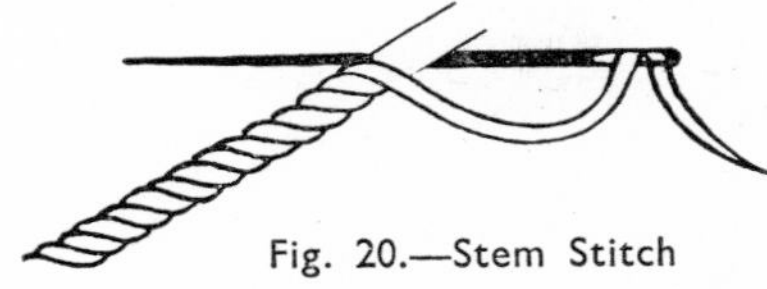

Fig. 20.—Stem Stitch

every time exactly on the outline, so that the outer edge is clean and neat, and that the stitches should lie evenly side by side with no gaps and no overlapping. It is also essential to keep the tension even.

As a rule the surface is padded with running stitch or chain stitch, to give a firm, cushioned effect to the finished work. Unpadded satin stitch is apt to look very flat and thin. To begin, work round the outline with running stitch, putting in your needle and bringing it out again just outside this when working the satin stitch. When covering narrow surfaces, as in a monogram, the surface is passed with a line or two of running stitch.

Satin stitch "dots" are used a lot in English embroidery. Outline these as before. Make a satin stitch across the centre, from top to bottom, then work first one half, then the other, with satin stitch. Keep all these stitches just within the outline, because they serve as padding.

Now cover them all with satin stitches taken the other way across. When you finish off pass your needle under the satin stitches to the opposite side of the dot, then through to the wrong side of the material, drawing the thread firmly. This prevents making a little point where the last stitch ends.

These dots are sometimes edged with backstitch to finish, as in Fig. 19, or they may be surrounded with French knots or edged with stem or outline stitch.

Seed Stitch.—*See* BACKSTITCH, of which it is a variation used as a filling stitch.

Stem Stitch.—(Fig. 20.)

This is used for outlining, for stems and for fine lines. Sometimes it is worked from left to right, but usually from the bottom of the line upwards. Bring the needle through from the wrong side at the bottom of the line and put it back a stitch-space above, bringing it out at the starting point. Put it back again a stitch-space above the first stitch, bringing it through at the top of the first stitch. *Keep your thread always to the right.* The lower end of each stitch should just touch the top of the preceding stitch.

Outline stitch is worked in the same way except that in this case *the thread must always be to the left.*

Stroke or Straight Stitch.—This is fully described by its name. It is a single satin stitch, and may be taken in any direction. Stroke stitches radiating from a centre are used to form flowers, and stroke stitches often represent grass, leaves or stems in flower embroideries. The stitches must not be too long, or they will loop; when a long straight line is to be covered it is better to use stem or outline stitch.

Tent Stitch or Petit Point.—(Fig. 15.)

Probably the most-used stitch in tapestry work. It is actually just the first half of a cross-stitch, passed over a single thread of plain canvas and is used mostly for fine work. Sometimes it is worked over a horizontal strand of the embroidery wool or thread, laid along the line of canvas being worked over: this helps to cover the surface more quickly.

ETCHING

ETCHING is a process by which drawings are reproduced from copper plates on which the design has been "eaten into" by acid. Actually a variety of metals can be used for etching. The most commonly used are copper and zinc, but copper has so many advantages that the amateur should learn his art on copper plates.

The pencil or pen-and-ink artist is most likely to make a success as an etcher, for although it is possible to trace designs and drawings it is obvious that the greatest pleasure comes from producing original work. It is a hobby which can call for the use of very expensive and elaborate outfits, but although it is never likely to prove a very cheap hobby, it is possible to branch out on a modest scale by the expenditure of a pound or two. The cheapest way of taking up this fascinating hobby is to join a class at an art school.

As the etcher becomes more experienced he will probably prefer to do much of the preparatory work for himself. Here we will assume that he would rather purchase his material ready-prepared as far as possible.

The Plate.—A copper plate, which can be purchased ready for use and cut to size, is first thoroughly cleaned with a mixture of ammonia and whitening. The plate must now be heated until it is hot enough to melt the "ground" which is to cover the plate with a thin film that will protect it from the action of the acid. A ball of "ground," which consists of bitumen, Syrian asphaltum, Burgundy pitch and bees-wax, is obtainable at etchers' supply houses.

Heat the copper gently on an iron plate over a gas-ring until the ball of ground melts on being rubbed thinly and evenly over the surface. The melted ground is equalized by rolling out with a special roller, or dabbing with a dabber. A "dabber" consists of a disc of cardboard 2–3 in. diameter on which is placed a pad of horse-hair covered by a layer of cotton-wool. Next, a piece of soft kid (a kid-glove) or smooth silk is placed over the cotton-wool and drawn tightly over the pad, leaving no folds on the front surface. The ends are bunched together on the other side and

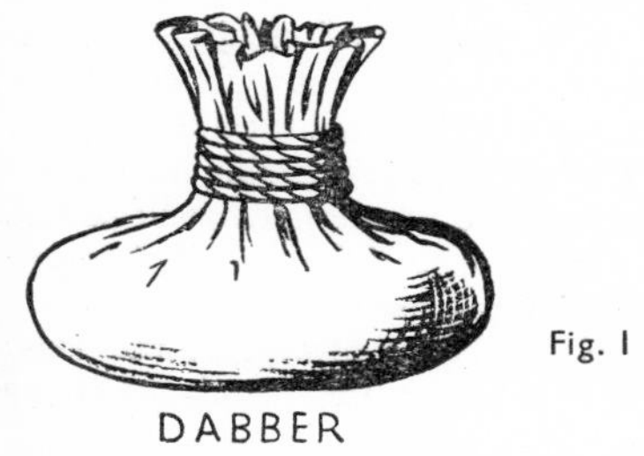

Fig. 1

DABBER

wound and tied with string. This keeps the kid in position and forms a handle (Fig. 1). The ground-covered plate is next smoked by passing a bunch of five or six burning wax tapers under the up-turned plate backwards and forwards until the ground is blackened. To avoid scorching the ground the flame should just touch the plate which must be kept moving. This is generally considered necessary in order that the needle lines should be clearly visible. Some artists do not consider this blackening necessary or advisable, but the beginner will certainly find it a help.

Engraving the Plate.—The plate is now ready for the etching needle. It is possible to work direct on to the plate, but the beginner had better trace his design on to the grounded plate first. A piece of tracing paper, somewhat larger than the plate, should be chalked and folded over the plate, chalked side to the ground. Another piece of tracing paper, this one bearing the design, should then be folded over the first piece, and the design worked over with a sharp, hard pencil. When the tracing sheets are removed, and the surplus chalk dusted off, the design will be clearly visible on the ground.

The etching needle is usually a fine-pointed needle mounted in a wooden handle. Some great etchers have used very primitive needles—J. M. W. Turner used a prong of an old steel fork—but the beginner will do well to purchase one of the instruments sold for the purpose. It is not everyone who favours the fine-pointed needle, some artists grinding their needles to present a cutting edge, which enables them to get a broad line. These experiments, however, are more for the advanced worker.

The needle should be held practically vertical, the drawing being made in fine lines of uniform thickness. The degree of pressure is very important. It should be just sufficient to penetrate the ground. It should be noted that the thickness of the lines in the finished print depends not upon the pressure exerted in using the etching

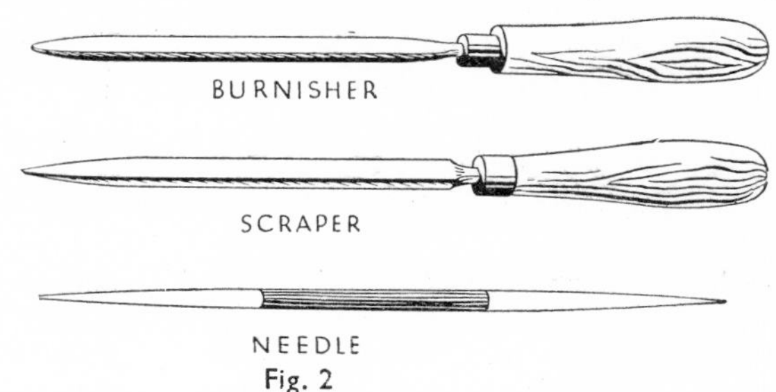

Fig. 2

needle, but upon the length of time the lines are subjected to the action of the acid.

"Biting" the Plate is the next process. For this purpose the following mordants are used.

1. For Copper

Nitric Acid and water in equal volume (for a weaker and slower bath 40% acid to 60% water). In mixing the parts the water should not be poured into the acid or the heat generated might cause the bottle to crack. The water should be measured and poured into the bottle first, the acid being then added. It should be allowed to cool before being stoppered.

Hydrochloric Acid (known as the

"Dutch bath").—20% acid, 77% water, 3% chlorate of potash. Dissolve the chlorate in hot water, allow to get cold and pour into the bottle, then add the acid.

2. For Zinc

Nitric Acid.—25% + 75% water.

Hydrochloric Acid.—10% + 2% chlorate of potash + 88% water.

The back and edges and any mistakes in drawing are now painted with "stopping-out" varnish and allowed to dry. The plate is next placed in a porcelain, enamel, or

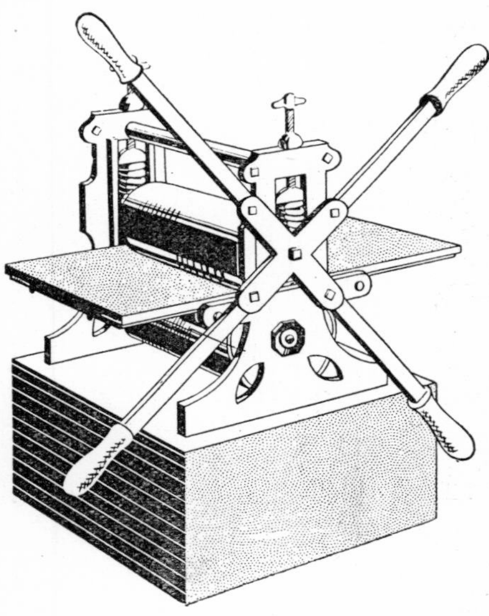

Fig. 3.—The Etching Press

glass bath containing the solution. After a few minutes bubbles will appear over the lines of the drawing, produced by the action of the acid upon the metal. They should be cleared away with a feather. The plate is left in the acid until the etcher considers that the lines which are to appear lightest have been sufficiently "bitten." The plate is then removed to a dish of water and afterwards dried gently between blotting paper. During this operation care should be taken to prevent acid remaining on the fingers. The acid has such disastrous effects if spilt that it is well to have a bottle of ammonia handy, as if applied quickly it neutralizes the effect of the acid.

If the etcher's judgment is correct the lines which are to appear lightest have been sufficiently etched. They are therefore painted over with stopping-out varnish, leaving the lines which require further etching still exposed. The plate is now returned to the acid and the lines which are to appear slightly darker bitten a little deeper. This process of etching, drying, stopping-out and re-etching is continued until the contrast desired in the finished print is achieved. Considerable experience is necessary before the desired result can be secured straight off. The acid will work quicker in a warm room, so that it is advisable to etch the plate always at the same temperature in order that results may be uniform.

Printing.—The ground and stopping-out varnish is removed by warming the plate and cleaning with turpentine. The plate is ready for printing. For this a press is necessary. Only a few amateurs will be able to have the genuine article at first, but there are several ways of getting over this difficulty. The etcher can send his plate to be printed by a professional printer. This, however, in addition to being expensive, has the disadvantage that too much time elapses between making the plate and seeing a proof. The beginner especially will want to see proofs as his work proceeds. Another plan is to secure the use of a professional's press after normal working hours. Art schools also have presses. Another alternative is to use the domestic mangle with a smooth, hard plank between the rollers to act as a travelling bed.

The sketch gives an idea of how the press should work, and will also suggest how the mangle might be adapted. If a proper press is used, blankets consisting of about two of thick "swan-cloth" and two of fronting or coarse sheeting should be supplied with it. They are needed to give elasticity under pressure, so that the paper is driven down into the lines in the plate. They are therefore used between the printing paper and the roller (the upper roller, in the case of the mangle). They are best arranged to

Reproduced by permission of Denise Brown

Fig. 4.—Etching: "The Gipsies' Breakfast," First State

overlap each other slightly so that the full thickness is not taken under the roller at once. On the other hand, they should be of uniform thickness over the plate, which should be placed in the centre of the travelling bed.

Inking.—The plate, after having been cleaned, is heated. It is inked with special etching ink by means of a roller or dabber, the ink being worked well into the lines. When cool the ink should be wiped off, first with coarse mosquito netting and then with tarletan. The polished surface of the plate will then be bright and clean, but the lines will be full of ink.

Paper.—There are various kinds of printing paper especially prepared for printing etchings. The paper should be damped with a sponge and left for about 24 hours and pressed between plate paper and zinc until free from surplus water.

The plate should be warmed a little to thin the ink, and placed upon a sheet of tissue paper on the travelling bed of the press, inked side uppermost. The damped sheet of printing paper should be placed over this; covered first with tissue paper and then a piece of damped plate- or blotting-paper and then with the blankets, and run through the press.

The resulting print will show the etcher where he has gone wrong. Because the plate was wiped clean before proofing the result will show the lines rather barely and harshly, and without the richness and softness the etcher was possibly hoping for. The achieving of this is a stage farther on and will be returned to presently.

Burnishing.—The immediate question is: what is wrong with the etching? Some parts of the print will be too dark. This will be because these particular lines were exposed to the action of the acid too long. This fault can be corrected by burnishing, which is done by rubbing as far as possible in the direction of the lines affected with an instrument called a burnisher. If the lines need considerable reduction a scraper is used. This is a three-edged knife, and like the burnisher is used with a little oil. After working with the scraper the burnisher should be used to remove scratches. Slight reductions can be secured by the use of engraver's charcoal and oil. Lines can be effaced entirely by the use of the scraper and burnisher.

While some parts of the picture will come out too dark others will appear too light. The lines in these parts used to be darkened by re-biting with acid. The plate is covered with ground again, and the underbitten parts worked over as before. Instead of using the bath, acid can be applied with a feather to the lines which need further treatment.

Added Effects.—When the beginner is satisfied with his plate he should study the methods by which different effects are obtained in printing. We have already seen that a proof from a plate that has been wiped quite clean has lines that are very clear cut and cold in appearance. Rich effects can be obtained by arranging the ink over the plate. One method of doing this is known as *retroussage.* The heated plate is inked and wiped as before. The plate is then heated and gently brushed over with a pad of soft muslin. This draws a portion of the ink over the edges of the lines, and the result when proofed is softer.

When the tarletan has been used a number of times it holds a certain amount of ink, and in this condition, if applied lightly, leaves a small amount of ink hanging over the edges of the lines. This also gives a fuller effect. Tone is given to the print if the heavy, or "fat," tarletan is used without cleaning up the plate too brightly. The palm of the hand can also be used to clean the plate, either entirely or in selected parts.

Dry Pointing.—A process which is usually classed with etching. It is a simpler process, no acid being used. The copper (or zinc) plate is worked on with a steel drypoint needle in such a way that a "burr" or ragged edge of metal is thrown up. It is this burr which holds most of the ink. The steel needle has to be constantly sharpened, for if the point becomes blunt the resulting burr is weak and will not stand up to the pressure of printing. When the needle is held vertically two burrs are thrown up, but when it is held slanting a single burr is the result. According to the nature of the subject, the burr is removed in certain parts —on the "distant" parts, for instance— and this is done carefully with the scraper, and not with the burnisher. Drypoint can be used alone, but it is also useful in conjunction with ordinary etching. Plates on which the drypoint process has been used, however, do not yield a large number of prints unless they are steel-faced because of the weakness of the burr.

Etching is a very pleasant hobby, and one well worth the consideration of those of artistic tastes. But because dangerous acids and poisons are used, great care should be taken to keep the bottles properly labelled and out of the reach of children. The etcher himself should be careful also. The fumes from the acid working on the plate can be more than unpleasant—they can be dangerous—so that he should work in a well-ventilated room, and take care that his enthusiasm does not lead him to lean too much over the acid bath.

Reproduced by permission of Denise Brown

Fig. 5.—Drypoint: "Study"

FANCY DRESSMAKING

Fancy dress should be original if possible; if not it should be pretty. The principal delight in wearing fancy dress is for the dancer to feel that she has designed and made her own costume. It is not as difficult as it sounds. A great deal of pleasure can be gained from imagining and planning a suitable dress. Let the mind roam round the titles of books, plays or films that have recently made history and if possible let your costume represent a play upon the title.

Pictures and literature of past and present are teeming with suggestions of characters that can be impersonated. History can be drawn upon with very good results. Advertisements often lend themselves to novel and humorous impersonations. Many firms will be glad to help by providing posters, etc., and in some cases the costume, in order that their name may thus achieve still further publicity.

Use Imagination.—Fancy dress gives scope for imagination and ingenuity in a way in which it is impossible for any other form of dress to do. Fashions change, and though, at the fancy carnival, Pierrot and his Pierrette are there as they were 40 years ago, yet they too have moved with the times. We recently saw a black and white Pierrot with an almost square tunic ending in vandykes, with a pompon upon each for decoration. He had black tights, also black tight-fitting sleeves with white points over the hand, made of stiff material, so that they stood out smartly. Bootees, of bedroom-slipper-like appearance, were worn, and like the cap, which was finished with upstanding points in the form of a corolla, these were decorated with pompons.

His partner, Pierrette, had a simple black and white costume consisting of a black frock with white points of material falling from the neck, and white vandykes upon the skirt to complete the design.

There is no limit to the variety of effects that can be achieved in costumes for Pierrot, Harlequin, Pierrette or Columbine. An exaggeratedly long feather in Harlequin's cap will give an air to the whole costume. An unusual colour for her costume, with a deep ruffle contrasted by an otherwise *décolletée* effect, and Columbine will have a dress smart enough for musical comedy.

A young man on board ship carried off the prize for a costume made without expense. He was a Black Cat and his costume was collected chiefly from an elderly aunt who gave him two old vests, one with long sleeves, and a pair of black stockings. The vests he dyed in the ship's ink, and with his own black shorts he covered himself from head to heel. In the head-dress, made out of one of the vests, were slits for the eyes and nose and mouth. At each side were sewn black woollen ears, and whiskers and tail were made of a piece of ship's rope touched up with black ink.

Holly and Mistletoe.—It is always a good idea to partner your character. Holly and Mistletoe suggest themselves for a Christmas dance. Holly should have doublet and tights of dark green, edged with red swansdown and appliquéd with holly berries, and Mistletoe a pale green chiffon dress edged with white swansdown at neck, hem and sleeves. The head-dress in the form of a corolla, should consist of long and upstanding mistletoe leaves in pairs, each one finished with a berry between.

A Salad is another idea that is suggested by the colour scheme. The main part of the dress should be of dark cream sateen, the colour of salad dressing, lettuce leaves shaped out of green crinkled paper, two tones if possible for the heart and the outside leaves, should be sewn on the bottom of the skirt. Pieces of red material to represent beetroot, and of another red to show tomatoes, blobs of white with yellow centres, to register sliced egg, should all be sewn or pasted in a careful border above the lettuce leaves. The head-dress should suggest tomato, a touch of the red with the green corolla on top.

My Lady Nicotine can be suggested

by a sleeveless dress of gold and white with little bundles of artificial cigarettes on either shoulder. Sea Symphony might be the name given to a sea-green chiffon dress with strings of shells worn round the neck.

Autumn, Spring, Summer and Winter can be portrayed in any way that takes the fancy.

For Autumn, make a chiffon dress such as dancers wear consisting of long loose pieces of material in every colour of autumn tints, from dark brown to chestnut and flame. A chaplet of leaves would look well in the hair.

Spring can be suggested by a similar chiffon dress of pastel shades. Posies of spring flowers might be worn at the shoulders. A floral coronet would complete the effect. Spring would also look charming carried out in various shades of the anemone. The dancer would wear a chaplet of anemones of every shade in her hair.

Summer might be represented by a dress of deep corn colour with corn stalks sewn here and there to suggest harvest; a sheaf of corn should be carried.

To represent Winter is simple. A dress of white velvet outlined with swansdown, or white fur at neck, armholes and hem would be sufficient. This dress should be sleeveless and worn with a chaplet of pointed crystals.

Ideas from Past and Present

Man or boy might represent Rival Blues. The suit might be of the Pierrot variety, one half made of light and the other of dark blue. The oars should be embroidered or appliquéd on the bodice.

A girl in black and white velvet seen at a fancy dress ball recently represented Dominoes; her costume was completed by a mask. The Queen and Ace of Spades were equally effective.

A costume for the Queen of Diamonds could be carried out in red and white; the red diamond-shaped bodice would provide a splash of colour on the white dress. Red diamond-shaped pieces of material should trim the skirt.

The Fortune Teller can be impersonated in two different ways—first, by means of a gipsy costume, with a coloured handkerchief over the head; secondly, by means of a dress trimmed with horseshoes, swastikas and appliquéd black cats in velvet, while the wishing bone and lucky bean and other symbols that appeal to the superstitious might be attached as ornaments.

The Pirate, the Irish Colleen, the White Rabbit and Alice in Wonderland are other characters that can be very effective.

The Grotesque.—For originality, the Skeleton cannot be beaten, if its wearer does not mind suggesting the gruesome. Its very appearance will attract a good deal of notice, drawing peals of laughter from some and expressions of repulsion from others.

A black costume is worn to cover the entire figure, and the spinal column, ribs and arm and leg bones are worked in white. A papier mâché skull can be hired to cover the head.

The Jockey's Suit can be worn by either sex and carried out in any number of colours. The Fisher Girl can be impersonated in sombre hues and the Coster may be presented by man or woman.

Circus Folk.—The Clown, the Ballet-dancer, the Circus Proprietor (in top hat) and the Giant can all be achieved with a little thought. Elongated head and shoulders can be hired and worn over the real head and shoulders to give an effect of considerable height, or any person who is clever with her fingers might manage to make this elaborate mask and at the same time create an illusion.

History Book Suggestions.—Henry VIII and his six wives, all members of the same house party, would cause a good deal of amusement. Queen Elizabeth and Sir Walter Raleigh, Mary, Queen of Scots, Cardinal Wolsey and Guy Fawkes are characters that have been impersonated time and time again, but they never fail to interest and attract. The costumes in each case should be hired if they are to be really effective.

Bruce and his Spider are historical numbers suggested by a very successful play. George Washington with his little Hatchet or George Stephenson with Puffing Billy, would be amusing and interesting impersonations.

Characters of the French Revolution, such as Robespierre and Marie Antoinette, are a little difficult to portray, but the costumes of the women of that period especially lend themselves to good effect with inexpensive materials.

A costume was copied from a French engraving showing a dandy of the 1830 period (Second Empire), made at a cost of five shillings approximately and worn by a woman with huge success at an important fancy dress ball. The coat was part of an old tailor-made, fitted at the waist and coming well over the hips in length. The trousers were of grey sateen, made like children's leggings, to fit closely below the knees and to come over the top of the foot. She borrowed a white waistcoat, a top-hat and a monocle and purchased a butterfly collar and a very large black sateen bow. The whole effect was very dandy!

The curators of a museum will generally be willing to supply any details about the dress of a particular period, and those who wish their costume to be correct in every detail, should seek expert advice upon the subject.

Children's Costumes.—For children nursery-rhyme characters suggest themselves and when there are two or three members of one family they might all be associated with the same rhyme or fairy story. Boys or girls, for example, could represent the Three Little Bears, while Cinderella naturally needs her Prince and Dick Whittington his Cat.

With a small boy as Aladdin in a somewhat elaborate costume, his little sister in a wired outstanding skirt should represent his Lamp. Aladdin wears yellow sateen Chinese trousers turned up with blue and a blue tunic with wide sleeves lined with yellow. An effect of embroidery is obtained by sewing or pasting a gold doily on the back and front of the tunic.

The Farmer's Wife and the Three Blind Mice are other suggestions. The Farmer's Wife is easy to dress. She should wear any skirt and a spotless white apron and carry a carving knife. An imitation one must be used for safety. The masks of the mice can be hired, or made of papier mâché, and their costumes might consist of grey tights or overalls that will cover the entire body.

The Guardian Angel is a classic figure that is very striking. A simple white dress relieved with gold tissue, a gold cardboard halo and golden wings, upstanding and curved so that they meet over the head—what could be lovelier? It is so simple to contrive and the contrasting effect of gold and white is lovely. The wings rely largely on gold paint and patience as they are time-taking to make.

With green wings and a similar halo of green the River Fairy can be represented. The simplicity of such a costume is its chief point.

Illustrations from legends and fairy tales are worth studying and copying. The Moonbeam Fairies and the Toadstool Elves are to be seen in a hundred different guises. Tiny children may impersonate any of these fairy figures with excellent effect. A yard or two of chiffon and a little ingenuity will work wonders.

A three- or four-year-old in a little leopard skin with his face and limbs made up an attractive sunburnt shade if desired, would make a charming little Changeling Boy from "A Midsummer Night's Dream."

A child of either sex might wear a page boy's costume and give himself or herself the title Grand Hotel.

The Bride and Bridegroom are always popular figures. The bridal veil can be made from a lace or net curtain to spare expense. Again, if there are several children in the family or if a party of friends are going to the dance together, pages and bridesmaids can form a bridal retinue. They will look well in the grand parade, which is invariably a feature of a fancy dress dance, since it gives the judges an excellent opportunity of studying the costumes.

Flower frocks are pretty for dainty children. The Harebell would look particularly attractive. The skirt should be cut in the form of petals and each one lightly wired. The head-dress might also represent the flower. Little green dancing shoes and

Fig. 3.—Diagram of Flame's Head-dress

Fig. 1.—The Lady of the Bath

Fig. 2.—The Flame

Fig. 4.—The Siren

stockings could be worn, or bare legs and shoes to match the dress.

The Fuchsia might be represented in similar fashion, although the colourings would be less suitable for children.

The Wild Rose is pretty. It consists of a pink ballet dress and a wreath of wild roses in the hair. Round the waist an imitation green rose briar should be twined.

The Marguerite can be represented by sewing imitation flowers on any foundation. Put them so close together that the heads of the flowers touch. A wreath of marguerites should be worn in the hair. A large white marguerite might also be sewn to each dancing sandal.

The Bluebell, consisting of blue petal frock, green stockings and a little blue cap, is a pretty frock for a small girl, while the Daffodil can be effectively carried out in two shades of yellow crinkled paper with the bodice of the palest shade.

Materials to Use.—The illustrations show costumes that are highly original. The Siren and the Lady of the Bath should be adults, but child or grown-up could represent the Flame. Each costume, particularly that worn by the Lady of the Bath, shows how, with ingenuity, the most ordinary article can be used in creating a clever costume. Do remember to look round the house before going to buy articles that may be quite unnecessary. Anyone with sufficient money and taste can hire an effective fancy dress, but it is the clever woman who can make her own from the least expensive materials. She will have to show resource and ingenuity. She must exercise her imagination and use discretion and taste in designing and making the garment. In the first place a bright idea is needed; this is important but not enough in itself, for that idea must be cleverly carried out, never forgetting to bear in mind the character that is to be represented in silk, satin, velvet, cotton or, perhaps, merely crinkled paper.

Silk and satin are expensive materials and should be eliminated from the design whenever possible and replaced by sateen or mercerized cotton material, which can be bought at a cost of about one shilling per yard. Cotton-backed velveteen can be bought at about two shillings per yard and is indispensable in some costumes.

White *bleached* calico is a most useful material for making fancy dresses. It makes a strong, smooth foundation on to which can be sewn or pasted all kinds of appliqués and ornamentations, and its colour can be changed with the help of the paint-pot or a packet of dye to whatever is required.

Crinkled paper is used a great deal for effect, especially in the "made-in-five-minutes" dresses, but it is always advisable to have a foundation of some stronger material. Crinkled paper and smooth tissue paper can be bought in nearly every colour at any stationer's; as can gold and silver paper.

Chiffons and fine mercerized lawn can be procured in lovely colours for the more dainty dresses, sometimes quite cheaply, and inexpensive organdie or fine book-muslin should be used for ruffles, or to assist in getting any bouffant effect with sleeves or skirt. For stiff effects, use a heavier book-muslin to line your material. Tailor's canvas can be bought in black, white or buff colour, and is very helpful for head-dresses and more solid stiffening. Millinery buckram is sometimes needed, but it is very stiff and brittle indeed.

Millinery wire is helpful in obtaining outstanding effects and can be bought at the drapery stores in black and in white, in a variety of thicknesses.

Making the Fancy Dress.—If you have a new and original idea for a fancy dress, something which you hope has never been done before, it will, of course, be impossible for you to find a paper pattern which exactly fits your idea. But more often than not you can find something very near it, in the magazines or fashion journals, which you can adapt to suit your purpose.

It is not advisable to spend too much time on the actual sewing of the dress. It is very seldom that a fancy dress is worn more than once.

The Distinguished Dress.—Colour and design play a great part in the success of fancy dresses. It is not only essential to see that the colour of the dress in question suits the potential wearer and that the design completely suggests what it is intended to represent, or that its period is correct, but it is necessary to make sure that the colour of the dress will be seen at its best in artificial light.

Nor need the dress be too quiet, if it is to catch the eyes of the judges, whose task at selecting the pretty or original from several hundreds is not one to be envied. Originality will catch the eye; attractive colour will hold it and sound design and workmanship and a realization of purpose will satisfy discriminating taste.

In the ballroom, as on the stage, an effect must be gained quickly and the dancer, like the actress, must impress her personality, on to the image of her partner, the judges and spectators. She can do this by carrying herself well, moving gracefully, letting her face show radiance as she dances and by being sure that every detail of her appearance is as perfect as she can accomplish. Further, she must achieve her effect to a large extent by the clothes she wears.

FISHING

To the uninitiated, fishing merely means buying a rod, a line, some hooks and bait, attaching the bait to the hook, dropping it into some quiet stream and waiting for the fish to bite. It is a more complicated matter than that, however, and is a hobby which requires not a little skill, quite apart from some degree of wisdom in choosing one's apparatus.

There are several kinds of fishing, each requiring special equipment and knowledge. For instance, we have fishing for coarse fish, among which are perch, tench, gudgeon, bream, chub, dace, roach and carp. There is a special form of fishing for pike and for what are termed "game" fish, which include trout, salmon and grayling. Lastly, we have the ever-popular sea fishing.

Sea Fishing is a most delightful pastime. There is nothing more refreshing to mind and body than to go down to some quiet fishing village, taking with one the necessary line and tackle (to be described presently), to hire a boat—and to spend a few hours in this way, absorbing the fresh sea air.

Fishing may be expensive or otherwise—it all depends upon the fisher. For sea fishing the expenditure of five shillings will cover the cost of all that is needed for apparatus, that is about 30 fathoms (60 yards)

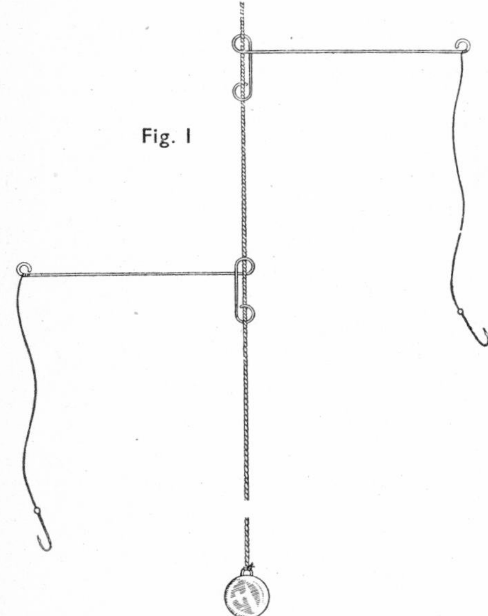

Fig. 1

of good brown line, a few hooks, some whipcord, one or two lead "sinkers" and a good strong pocket- or jack-knife. Bait varies considerably, and perhaps the wisest plan is to leave the selection of it to one's boatman. Later on, however, we will give some useful baits for the various kinds of fish.

The next step is to arrange the hooks ready for the catch. One of the best methods is to employ what is called a paternoster. (Fig. 1 shows a paternoster already made up by the tackle seller.) It is, however, a simple matter to make one's own to the same or to a similar design, using brass wire for the centre rod and extending arms. The arms should be about 8 in. long, and a sinker attached as in the picture. By joining several pieces of wire by loops, the whole apparatus can be made so that it folds up. If one does not wish to go to the trouble of making one of these paternosters, an excellent substitute may be made from the brown line itself in the following manner: cut off four 2 ft. lengths of the line and fasten a hook to the end of each piece. Some hooks have eyes at the ends, and, as a rule, these are better than those which have to be whipped to the line with gut. Tie a knot in the end of each piece of line so that the hook is held securely. Then tie each hooked piece to the main line at intervals of 2 ft. or so from the end. Take one of the sinkers, or lead weights, and fasten this to the extreme end of the line by means of a yard or so of whipcord, and the rig is quite ready for use. It is possible, of course, to fasten the sinker direct to the end of the line, but sometimes these sinkers get stuck, and a sharp pull may sever the line and so mean the loss of the hooks. The whipcord, being weaker than the line, snaps first, so only the sinker—which costs but a few pence—is lost.

Bait.—Many people think that fish—especially sea fish—will bite at anything, but this is a fallacy. Fish have their likes and dislikes, so in order to stand a fair chance of being successful, you must have an assortment of baits. Do not always believe that the local fisherman—the professional man—knows the best baits to use. Many a time an amateur has made a record catch with a bait that would be scorned by the local expert.

Crab, lugworm, a mussel, a piece of fresh herring or a lump of cheese will be found good for most localities, but do not ignore the bait recommended by your boatman. Having arrived at the fishing ground, if you are a novice, get the boatman to show you how to bait the hook. It must be "threaded" through the bait so that as little as possible shows, yet the barb must be exposed so that it penetrates as soon as it is snapped.

When the hooks are baited, pay out the line until the sinker touches bottom, and then hold the line between the first and second fingers, ready to feel for the first bite. No doubt you will lose bait, and will wonder how it is that fish get it off the hooks without your knowing, but after a time you will get accustomed to the "feel" of the line, and will know just exactly when to give it a little tug and so hook your fish.

The above is a brief sketch of the procedure, but there is more in fishing than just that. One must get to know the best fishing grounds, the type of fish that frequent them, the baits that these fish prefer, and so on. Only practical experience can teach you this.

Fig. 2.—Paternoster in Use

A Rod may be used instead of the hand line. In many ways it is preferable as it leaves one hand free. The selection of a rod is a matter demanding careful consideration. Do not always take the unsupported advice of the tackle merchant. If possible, ask a friend to accompany you who knows something about rods and their use. You will find his advice valuable.

The Line.—Remember to keep your rod well oiled when not in use. Olive oil is as good as any. There are many qualities and thicknesses of line. Lines are sold according to thickness, being numbered 1, 2, 3 and 4. No. 1 is the thickest, and should be used for such fish as conger. No. 3 is probably the best for sea fishing, although if the water is shallow, No. 2 will do. These lines weigh, approximately, 21 lb. for a 60 yard length of No. 1 line, 15 lb. for the same length of No. 2, and 9 lb. and 6 lb. respectively for the others.

Sinkers.—The weight used must vary according to conditions. The object of the sinker is to hold the line to one spot, but unless a heavy sinker is used, one may find the line drifting, especially if there is a strong current running. All lines that are operated by hand should be wound on to a frame. This can be purchased for a few pence, and saves much time and trouble. After fishing, however, the lines should be carefully dried before being wound on to the frame. This will add enormously to their life.

Waterproofing Lines.—Lines should not be used just as they are purchased, unless, of course, they are guaranteed waterproof. Even then it is wise to dress them oneself. A good dressing is made from 4 oz. of catechu and about a quart of water. Bring to the boil and drop the line in it, leaving it there for about 24 hours. At the end of that time take it out, rinse it in fresh water and hang it out to dry. Drying such a great length of line may present some difficulty to the town dweller, but a good frame drier (something like a wool-winder) may be purchased quite cheaply.

The Reel.—A good reel is the next essential. Cheap reels are unsatisfactory, and usually jamb at awkward moments.

Attention should also be given to the rod rings. Porcelain-lined rings are good for allowing the line to run freely, but they are apt to get broken. There are several kinds now on the market with protecting wire to prevent damage should the rod be dropped.

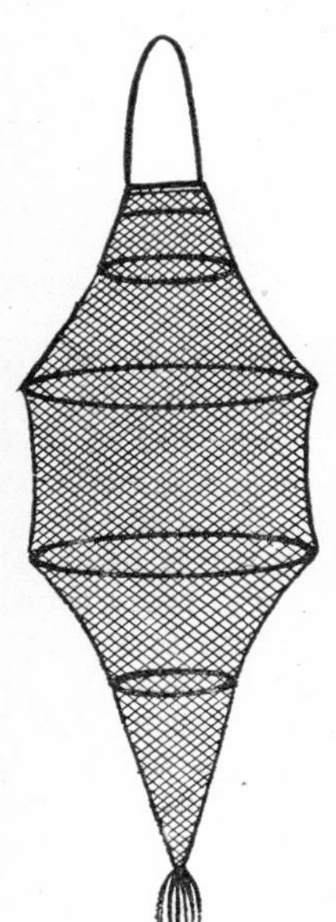

Fig. 3

Coarse Fish.—Different apparatus is required for this form of sport. A lighter but longer rod is needed, also a finer line and smaller hooks. Much depends upon whether one is going to fish from the river bank or from a boat or punt, but no hard and fast rule can be laid down about the choice of a rod. The best thing to do is to obtain the advice of an angler friend.

Bait. — As with salt-water fish, river fish have their own particular spots and their own particular foods, and the question of bait must of course be carefully studied. Roach, for instance, like wheat, bread and bran, or even rice or pearl barley. To prepare the wheat, rice or barley put a quantity, say, a tumblerful, into a stone jar, fill with water and then put into a slow oven for several hours. The slower the wheat cooks the better. Gentles (maggots) are also attractive to the fish, although perhaps not to the angler.

Many people do not use ground bait on the score that the fish usually eat this in preference to that on the hook. A little ground bait, however, certainly attracts the fish to the vicinity. Well-soaked bread mixed with meal and then squeezed into small balls makes excellent ground bait, and a supply should be made just before beginning the day's sport. Ordinary baits should consist of three or four kinds, because fish are sometimes more attracted by one kind than another. Paste made of the boiled wheat, gentles and worms are usually attractive to roach; and in some cases even earwigs will result in a good day's fishing. Make certain that the baited hook is as near to the ground bait as possible—to provide a good feed some distance from one's hook is to invite failure.

A good general rule is to fish just off the bottom, that is, as near as can be judged to 2 in. from the bed, the depth being gauged by a "plummet," obtainable from all tackle shops.

To Catch Perch we use the paternoster, only this time one of much finer construction. It should be borne in mind that rivers are usually much clearer than the sea, and that fish can see thick lines and tackle. The object of the angler should be to hide his traps as much as possible. Usually, gut is used for river fishing with the paternoster, and, of course, smaller and finer hooks. If ordinary float tackle is to be used, employ a gut line and a quill float.

The size and weight of the quill float depend largely on the state of the water. Unless a large and heavy one is used in running water, the current will knock it flat on the surface and bites, or "knocks"

Fig. 4.—Keep Net in Action

as they are called, will not be seen. In dead calm, the smallest and lightest obtainable is advisable.

A Keep Net should be used. (*See* Figs. 3 and 4.)

As a rule, perch prefer live bait, such as small gudgeon, minnows, etc., although sometimes an artificial bait will do. Minnows are, however, the best, and the angler is usually able to catch these in large quantities by making a round net, something like a basket, and lowering it into the river near weeds. Directly some minnows are over the net he lifts the pole sharply and the bait is his.

Another good fish for sport—but not for eating—is the chub. This sometimes reaches five or six pounds in weight, but the larger ones are rare. The usual weight is in the neighbourhood of from three to four pounds. Chub are most likely to be found near holes which are overhung with shady trees, or beneath quiet bridges. The bait for chub is a fly, and your dealer will provide a good selection. When angling in fresh water avoid casting a shadow on the water, for fish become wary of it. Take up a position on the bank facing the sun.

Fishing for Gudgeon is good fun, for these are fairly easily caught, especially in the summer months. The gudgeon is quite small, being only about four to six inches long, but he makes delicious eating. Begin fishing for gudgeon about June—at the end of the month preferably—and continue until September. Like the chub, gudgeon are more usually found near holes in the bank. A small hook, a fine line and a light float are necessary, and a tiny piece of worm makes good bait. Gudgeon-fishing may also take place from a boat or punt—on the Thames much of the gudgeon-fishing is done in this way. An advantage is that one may the more easily stir up the mud at the river bottom, when the gudgeon will come along in large numbers to see what food they can find.

Sporting Fish.—No angler is happy until he has tried to fish for what are known as "game" fish, which term includes salmon, trout and grayling. It is here that the angler must exercise every wile, for these lordlings are not easy to catch. Few people realize that salmon and trout are probably descendants of the same fish—indeed, not everyone can tell the difference between them even to-day. Both salmon and trout are known by a variety of names, these usually being given according to the age of the fish. Different localities, too, have their own special names, so it is wise to consult some authoritative book before believing that no trout are in the vicinity.

As these fish are caught chiefly with a dry-fly bait, and are very powerful, the angler will need a fairly stout rod of from 10 to 12 ft. long. The line must be of best quality, preferably of plaited, waterproofed silk. A landing net is necessary in most cases, while of course every fisherman will carry a creel, which is a wicker basket to hold the catch. The stronger the creel the better, for it will then form a comfortable seat. Space does not permit of a description of the various fly baits, and the reader is advised to get an angler friend to help in the purchase of them.

Night Fishing can provide good sport and it will be easy for those who live by the sea to enjoy angling for sea trout. These fish are frequently quite large—10 lb. or so—but the size varies according to the locality.

Those readers who live in Hampshire will find there many excellent spots for catching grayling. The method of fishing is very similar to that used when catching trout, fly bait being chiefly used. As a rule grayling prefer deeper water than trout, although they will sometimes rise to the surface for a moment to grab a tempting fly.

Another fish which is fond of deep water is the char. This is very much like trout, but has brighter colouring, being red underneath, especially in the spawning season. Char are seldom found in South England, but are more common in the North, in Scotland and in Ireland. Char are also caught with a fly bait, and a fine tackle must be used.

The Salmon—king of fish—is to be found in deep pools and swift-running streams, such as those in Devon. The

River Wye is famous for salmon fishing, but many of its best reaches are "privately owned." As the salmon is a fighter, the best quality tackle only must be used. A good-sized salmon will always fetch a fair price with a local fishmonger—a point to be borne in mind on occasion.

Everyone has heard of the herculean fights between angler and salmon, and, allowing for some exaggeration, much skill is nevertheless required in playing these fish. The main rule is never to allow the line to slacken.

In this short article it has only been possible to describe in a very brief form some of the methods and baits used for catching various fish, and obviously even to mention all the various kinds of fish that frequent our shores, lakes and rivers has been quite impossible. The angler should most certainly purchase one of the many excellent handbooks which cover every field of this famous sport.

The best month for fishing is September, and you will be saved some inconvenience if you remember that "when the east wind blows, go home"—since you are unlikely to get a bite. When coarse fishing, do so in comfort. Use a seat and do not rise every time it is necessary to cast, or when "striking." And avoid trees, or you will tangle your line and may even damage your rod.

With fishing, the wealth of the angler has little to do with his success, for frequently a poor lad with his crude equipment will make a finer catch than many another sportsman possessing the latest and most expensive appliances. Angling is a sport which must be learned thoroughly if success is desired. It is true, of course, that there is such a thing as beginner's luck, but the true angler never rests in his search for knowledge. He will quietly go about from place to place, picking up hints here and there, conversing with more experienced men than himself, and learning all he can about this king of sports. No one need be discouraged because he cannot go salmon fishing, or undertake a pike-fishing expedition. There are fish in plenty to be found in most of our rivers, and round our coasts.

FLOWER GROWING

A FLOWER garden should be a picture and like all good art it should begin in the mind of the creator.

But how uncertain some of us are in our gropings after this picture! We have had day-dreams but, alas! how disappointing are our attempts to make them come true! A garden may be filled with pretty flowers; there may be a riot of colour which passers stop to admire. Stately delphiniums vie with the roses and some fine beds of summer annuals make a dazzling display. But there is no harmony; it is not a picture.

Why? Because that garden has grown up in a higgledy-piggledy way; the owner has crammed his beds and borders with flowers and flowers and yet more flowers. But there is no rest. There is something lacking, some quality which only an artist can supply. Gardens need *planning*.

A few actual examples will show the kind of faults that often ruin an effect towards which much time and money may have been contributed.

In one case the design of a villa garden was faulty in spite of its lovely blooms because there were far too many paths, small, narrow, and meaningless paths. One wide path leading to the house door is all that is necessary for most small front gardens.

Given a dignified approach to the house where roses can clamber on the gable, the view from the house comes next in importance in a country where so much of our time is spent indoors. Where, as you sit, you look straight across into a neighbour's sitting-room, plant a screen of pillar roses, something beautiful for all to look at and yet providing the necessary privacy and shelter. Another quick-growing screen is polygonum baldschuanicum, which produces decorative masses of pinkish-white flowers in early autumn. Another garden had a magnificent perennial border overflowing with good things, but a tiny lawn flanked by narrow paths spoiled it and it lacked a background—especially in winter.

Every gardener should try to visualize his garden at every season of the year and make due provision for the colder months by planting evergreens where they can show to advantage and furnish the garden between autumn and spring flowering, as well as ornamental shrubs to serve as foil to more delicate plants.

Soil.—The best kind of soil is composed of lime, humus, which is decayed vegetable matter, clay and sand, but seldom will the ideal proportions be found. A good rich loam is usually prized for its nourishing qualities for all kinds of plants. But whatever the nature of the soil at first you will have to make the best of it till you learn by experience how to improve it. Any additions of organic manure or chemicals will be determined, as you go along, by the kind of crops you are growing. To worry, at the beginning, about the chemical constituents of soil is not worth while.

Evergreens are best planted just before growth commences for the summer. At the windy end of a border a short yew hedge may be planted or a group of hollies may be more attractive and just in front rhododendron ferrugineum, the alpine rose, would look well. A bushy laurel is not to be despised; it will make a fine foil for a pillar rose. Cupressus looks well associated with the pretty blue flowering shrub ceanothus, Gloire de Versailles, a deciduous shrub. It is good to mingle evergreens with the leaf-losing shrubs; it takes away bareness in winter. Shrubby spireas and good hybrid rhododendrons look well if planted in irregular masses in the herbaceous border so as to break straight lines. But remember that rhododendrons, to do really well, need lots of room and preferably a peaty soil. Arbor vitaes look distinguished and the low-growing mahonias look well with winter rime upon them.

Planting Trees and Shrubs.—Trees and evergreens must be put in at the right time only or the result will be disastrous. Deciduous, or leaf-losing trees, must be planted in the autumn or winter while the sap is not flowing. So if you are planning to have small trees such as laburnums, lilacs and any of the other flowering shrubs like mock orange and flowering currant, or any of the flowering cherries or crabs, remember to plant them in the autumn. Evergreens are best planted just before growth commences in the spring, usually April or May, or in the autumn about September when the second new growth of the season appears. This is very important for such shrubs as holly, yew, laurel, bay, cupressus and arbor vitae.

Hedges.—If you prefer to plant a hedge the same rules apply, according to whether it is a leaf-losing or evergreen subject you are using. Privet makes a cheap hedge, yew an everlasting one but slow growing and, like holly, apt to be dull. A small garden is better with the indefinite boundary of trees and shrubs. Low hedges are useful and beautiful within the garden for dividing kitchen garden from flower garden.

Annuals.—Beginners usually fill beds and borders too with annuals and biennials. It is a good idea, for the seeds are cheap and give a display the first year, but they are not the easiest to grow. Great care is necessary if these beautiful flowers are to be well grown. A light sandy soil is required and not too rich; a little well-decayed manure and some well-rotted leaf-mould should be worked into the beds which should then be neatly shaped with a rise in the centre.

Annuals are, of course, sown in the spring as soon as the weather permits of the soil being worked to a fine crumbly condition or tilth. Sow in moist genial weather when the danger of frost is over. The hardier ones should be sown in the open where they are to bloom; the half-hardy ones like stocks and asters, antirrhinums, lobelias, and pentstemons will need the protection of a frame till they are ready for transplanting.

When sowing, cover seeds to about their own depth with soil, and water if necessary with a fine-rose watering can.

Beds look best filled with one kind of

Fig. 1.—"The Garden should be a Picture"

flower. A bed filled with nigella (Miss Jekyll) looks well. Brilliant tomato red eschscholtzia (Mikado) would look well in another. Others suitable for beds are marigolds, annual chrysanthemums, cosmos, jacobea, lupins and godetias.

Some annuals are more suitable for borders, either entirely of one kind or grown as a mixed border in a colour scheme devised according to your own taste with some regard for heights and habits of the plants. Poppies, cornflowers, coreopsis, clarkia, delphiniums and helianthus are good for mixed borders with candytuft, mignonette, sweet alyssum or lobelias as edgings.

Sweet Peas, the loveliest of all annuals, show to best advantage at the back of the herbaceous border, trained on canes or dead branches, or in clumps round hollow "pillars" of wire netting.

The soil should be deeply dug and some decomposed farmyard manure worked in. The lighter the soil the more need for manure, but if it is clay or heavy loam the manure should be of a light strawy nature. Seeds should be sown 1 in. deep in March or April or young plants (previously raised under glass) planted after all fear of frost has passed.

All dead flowers should be snipped off regularly as this extends the period of flowering.

The hardy annuals should not be transplanted but they must be thinned in the beds where they are to bloom to ensure good plants and large blooms. Keep the weeds down by hoeing.

The half-hardy annuals raised in frames are, of course, easily transplanted when large enough to handle. The secret of success in transplanting them is to keep the ball of soil about the roots intact. This rule applies to transplanting of all plants. The boxes containing the plants should receive a good soaking with water before the plants are lifted. This helps to keep the soil together.

Biennials or flowers which are sown like annuals, but later in the season (about May, June or July), and bloom the following season, are wallflowers, canterbury bells, sweet williams, foxgloves, myosotis (forget-me-nots) and scabious. These should be transplanted to nursery beds when large enough to handle and in September transferred to beds where they are to bloom.

Perennial Flowers are usually grown in a herbaceous border. These are the flowers which, once planted, come up every year. To the true gardener they are a source of never-failing delight. In the border where they grow there is always something interesting in bloom practically all the year round.

In September and October when the glorious display of annuals has died down there will be a miserable blankness which will make you thankful for the greenness of grass. It is at this time that you should turn your attention to getting some of the permanent inhabitants into the herbaceous border which you have marked on the paper plan.

The herbaceous border looks best when you look along it, so have it as long as possible. It may be straight, curving or even go round three sides of a lawn. Eight or ten feet is the best width to allow for a background of shrubs and small trees. If this must be dispensed with, then cut it out of the lawn on two sides or have it shaped like a L so that there may be a foreground of grass to help the picture. A grass path looks effective if well kept.

The Soil is better to be a good heavy loam that has been well manured, for many of the plants to be put in will have to occupy their positions for years. The informality of this part of the garden is its chief charm, but it is achieved only after much effort and with much art. Even if your border is only 20 or 15 ft. long begin by planning it on paper. Mark off the paper into 3 or 4 ft. squares. On these squares write the names of the plants you would like to see blooming in your border. When you have decided that, the next thing is to plant the background. A good clump of rhododendron at one end is effective. Choose Pink Pearl or Alice. Hollies, brooms, a rose pillar or two, ceanothus shrubs and sweet briar will all be useful.

Edging Plants should be pinks, saxifrages, aubrietias, iberis, foam flower, arabis and any grey or green alpines which look well grown thus. A successful herbaceous border will have bloom after bloom, though its chief glory will come in June.

Plant delphiniums well to the back or in the centre of border. Nearer the front place blue and white and mauve lupins with some oriental poppies and white campanulas and you will be sure of a show in June. In a bay backed by evergreens plant crimson pæonies and on no account shift them or divide, even for your best friend who comes to beg for some of your surplus later on. Pæonies, lupins and oriental poppies have long tap roots and all such plants resent being transplanted.

Irises and montbretias have stylish lance-like leaves which look well planted in the foreground. Michaelmas daisies in large clumps will give masses of bloom in autumn and so will heleniums and Japanese anemones. Anchusa, being the truest blue flower in the garden, should be given a place not too far back. It has roots which work to the surface, so plant it deeply.

The scarlet geums (Mrs. Bradshaw) do well associated with a clump of mossy saxifrage at the edge, and heuchera, although not low growing, has a delicacy which should not be hidden among clumps farther back.

The bright yellow of the day lily (Hemerocallis), although short lived, has a vividness almost as delightful as the high lights which white marguerites give. Lychnis, the lightning flower, brings a dash of scarlet to the border which can be startling, but used with care it gives distinction. Perhaps it is best to surround it with pale yellow annuals as these are not so harsh as a mass of white would be. Lavender growing well out on to the path in a careless clump will impart an old-world look.

Phloxes are so effective that if there is room a special border should be set apart for them. Failing that, good clumps of white, pink and mauves should find a place in the border. Choose the best varieties you can afford.

Japanese chrysanthemums are the best autumn flowers to use; when other plants are over and cut down their beauty prolongs the show until, at last, regretfully we turn indoors till the promise of Christmas roses draws us forth to have another peep at the everlasting border.

Fig. 2.—Vivid Annuals for the Border. 1, Nemesia. 2, Phlox Drummondii. 3, Zinnias

Remember that flowers which bloom early in the season should be planted in the autumn; autumn bloomers can be put in in spring. But in the colder northern regions planting of all herbaceous flowers should be done in spring. Delphiniums must not be disturbed in the autumn. The spring is the only time to transplant them. They should be protected from dampness and slugs in winter by a covering of ashes.

Cultivation.—A large collection of herbaceous plants can gradually be acquired but only the best should find room. The management of such a border consists of forking over in spring, weeding and careful staking. Long single plants need only one stake, large clumps will require several stakes surrounding the clump and tied with tomato twine in as natural a position as possible. A top dressing of well-decayed manure is beneficial in spring. When plants become overgrown they should be divided. Use only the outer parts of plants and throw away the middle. Some need division frequently, others not at all, such as pæonies. Phloxes are better divided every three years. They have very woody roots so use a sharp knife; do not hack blindly at any root with a spade. Some will divide easily with the fingers, others need to be torn in pieces. These things are learned by handling the plants themselves.

Bedding Plants.—For brilliant displays there is nothing to beat bedding plants. There are two kinds of these, spring and summer. Every grower of herbaceous plants feels that the best of his garden is over when July has passed, unless he has provided for this by filling summer beds with antirrhinums, stocks, asters, calceolarias, violas and pentstemons.

Use a span-roofed frame placed on ashes and facing north and south. This kind of frame should never be out of use. In September, after the summer bedding plants are over, prepare it to receive cuttings of plants you wish to propagate. The best soil for striking cuttings is a compost of equal parts of leaf-mould and sieved loam with a good proportion of coarse sand. Spread this over a foundation of coarse rubble or stones and level off with a thick layer of sand.

Cuttings.—A cutting is a new shoot of a plant which is inserted in soil, either out of doors or under glass, and kept moist till roots have formed. It is a method of increasing which ensures that plants will come true to type and is sometimes quicker than raising from seed. Select healthy side shoots of antirrhinums, calceolarias, pentstemons and violas, taking them from low down on the plants. Cut them across clean and sharp just below a joint, leaving only one or two joints below the foliage. Remove lower leaves to prevent rot, leaving some leaves at top of shoot, for it is through the leaves that a plant breathes. Hollow-stemmed cuttings of violas should not be used; they are useless. The small young shoots from the centre of the plant are the ones to take. If soft cuttings of shrubs are required, prepare and insert in frame as for flowers. Hard-stemmed cuttings of flowering shrubs such as mock orange, lilac, flowering currant or heaths should be inserted to about two-thirds their depth in a cool shady place out of doors.

The soft-flower cuttings are inserted in the soil about a third of their length and about $1\frac{1}{2}$ in. apart. Some of the surface sand will fall into each hole as it is made and allow of faster root formation. Water should be given and the lights closed and kept closed for about six weeks or until roots have formed. Ventilation is important to prevent the fungus "damping-off" which spells ruin. Keep glass free from moisture by cleaning with a dry cloth and in frosty weather protect with straw mats. These must not be allowed to become sodden. When wet, remove them and dry thoroughly or replace by dry ones.

These cuttings will be the new plants ready to fill summer beds by June of the following season.

Spring Bedding.—September or October is the time to be thinking of spring bedding. When autumn leaves are flying and most people are thinking that nothing happens in October the gardener is beginning all over again. His fertile brain is busy with glowing tulip beds, drifts of daffodils in grass and long lines of scented wallflowers.

Clear out summer beds. Dig them and give a good supply of well-rotted manure. Six ounces of bone-meal to the square yard and some lime will be beneficial. Begin with wallflower plants. Vulcan wallflower with a sprinkling of Victoria daffodils among it and with an edging of myosotis (forget - me - not), although a common scheme, is hard to beat; or use a mixed border of all kinds of wallflower with an edging of Maggie Mott violas.

Spring Bulbs.—Tulips of the bedding variety such as Kaiser Kroon look well alone. Rose and pink ones are charming if a ground work of mauve aubrietia is used or double white arabis. The single white arabis blooms earlier and is only suitable for using with very early tulips, for it is important that all flowers massed together should bloom at the same time. Darwin tulips such as Pride of Haarlem and T. Gesneriana are good ones to incorporate in groups in the herbaceous border. If left alone they will come up year after year. Cheiranthus Allioni, the Siberian wallflower, is of a startling orange colour but delightful and lasts long in bloom. Bedding hyacinths of mixed colours will give a rainbow effect to your lawn in spring if you fill a bed there with them. You need not buy very expensive ones so long as you get pretty colours. Mixed polyanthuses make fine beds; they are also useful as edgings in spring. They should be lifted and reserved for another year after blooming. They need frequent division.

Nothing looks more charming in spring than a long straight line, fairly wide, of lilac crocuses. Clumps of yellow ones brighten the lawn after the snowdrops have passed. Daffodils should be generously planted in long informal drifts on grass or crowded under apple trees, in groups in the herbaceous border or even in beds all by themselves. Planted the last way they will, of course, have to be lifted after blooming and planted in a reserve part of the garden till the leaves die down. This is an important rule in the management of all bulbs; allow the foliage to die down naturally, never cut it and do not take them out of the soil till this process is over. After that they may be lifted and stored, though daffodils are better left in grass from year to year.

Roses need a volume to themselves and only the simplest advice can be given here. No garden should be without some, at least, and if you can only have one dozen rose bushes have a bed of Mrs. Henry Bowles, a good pink, or select a mixed dozen from a catalogue and plant in a long narrow bed or border. A heavy loam with some rotted turf and a plentiful supply of manure is necessary for roses. November is the month to plant the bushes but any time during the winter does, if there is no frost in the ground. Firm planting is essential.

Fig. 3.—The Queen of Flowers

Pruning should be done in April or May when you are sure that all danger of frost is over. Simple rules for pruning are given in most good rose catalogues. The thing to remember is that vigorous roses should be lightly pruned; less vigorous growers more heavily. Every rose, like every flower, has an individuality of its own. It is only by growing them, reading about them and studying them that you will learn how to manage them. The great thing is to plant some and find out for yourself.

FOLK DANCING

No book on the hobbies and pastimes of the English-speaking peoples would be complete without some reference to Folk Dancing for this is as English as our countryside and nearly as old.

The Origin of many of these dances is wrapped in mystery. Some, perhaps, such as the Padstow Hobby Horse Dance and the Helston "Furry Dance," which are held annually, have their beginnings in pagan rites now lost in the mists of obscurity. It is not within the scope of a book of this description, however, to give a detailed history of these dances, interesting as such a history is.

Suffice it to say that, owing to the energy of the late Mr. Cecil Sharp and a band of enthusiastic workers, many of the traditional English Folk Dances in danger of being lost even to the country people themselves were revived. Mr. Sharp spent many years touring, not only the British Isles but also parts of Europe and North America collecting Folk Dances and Folk Songs and, as a result, during recent years there has been a great revival of these pastimes.

The beauty of Folk Dancing lies in its simplicity. The dances may be performed either in the open air—excellent displays are held each summer in Hyde Park and in Greenwich Park—or in a hall with an unpolished floor.

The Music in the original dances, as discovered by Mr. Sharp, was usually provided by a single instrumentalist using a violin, a concertina or a pipe and tabor. While the violin is perhaps the best instrument for the interpretation of Folk Dance music, the piano is now the most generally used, especially for indoor performances. Since, however, many of the dances have been recorded for gramophone reproduction even a piano is not a necessity.

Clothes.—These should allow complete freedom of movement and action. White flannels for men and light summery dresses of cotton or silk for women together with rubber-soled shoes are to be recommended if the dancers are to feel comfortable.

Types of Folk Dances.—These may be divided into three sections—Country, Morris and Sword Dances. The Country Dance is less strenuous than the Morris and less exacting than the Sword. Originally the Country Dance was the only one of the three danced by both sexes, Morris and Sword Dances being confined to men performers. Nowadays it is quite usual for women to learn the Morris and Sword, but it is probable that the Country Dance which is meant for social occasions will always be the favourite. It has no real technical difficulties, as it depends for its effect on the weaving of patterns, so that the only essentials are balance and a sense of rhythm. Consequently the steps are few in number and simple to perform.

Steps.—Here are some simple directions which should help the intending Folk Dancer at the first class or party.

The normal Country Dance steps are:

An ordinary running step—executed neatly and lightly;

A walking step with a scarcely noticeable spring;

A skipping step—the usual step and hop on alternate feet;

A slip step—springing to the right or left for use in ring movements.

In all these steps the weight of the body should be supported wholly on one foot or the other and the transference of the weight from one foot to another should be effected by a spring high enough to raise the body off the ground. The body should be well poised and balanced in order that the dancer may be graceful in his or her movements, and the steps should fall on the ball of the foot with the heels slightly raised. The knees should be bent as little as possible and movements should be chiefly from the ankle joint. At the same time there should be no scraping on the ground with the free foot. The arms should be allowed to swing quietly and loosely by the side of the body unless the dancer has to make use of them to maintain balance, but all hand movements—as all other movements in the Country Dance—should be made simply and without exaggeration.

The Movements.—Each dance has its own particular figures which may be quickly learnt, especially if the performer has a good memory for tunes. This will enable him to fit the steps to the music. The following movements occur in most of the simple country dances and should be memorized as early as possible.

1. Forward a double means four running steps forwards.

Dancing "Speed the Plough"

2. Back a double means four running steps backwards.

3. Set and turn single. Partners face, spring to the right, spring to the left, turn on the spot completely round in four steps.

4. Siding. Two dancers—not necessarily partners—face one another, pass with four steps obliquely to the right, that is passing left shoulder, turn and retrace their steps along the same track.

5. Arming. Two dancers meet, link right or left arms, and swing round for four steps then fall back to places. Arms should be linked at the elbows, dancers leaning slightly away from one another.

All these movements must be performed in exact time with the music which is described in the music book by means of letters A, B and C. When an air is to be played more than once it is marked A1, A2, or A3. Similarly with B and C music.

The dances which may be attempted by beginners are many and varied. In the Progressive Dances the performers change places in every round by the top couple moving to the bottom of the set and all other couples moving up one place. Some of the best known and easiest to learn are: Haste to the Wedding, Sir Roger de Coverley and We Won't Go Home till Morning.

In the Longways Dance there may be six or eight dancers in couples. The dances are usually in three parts, the first part beginning with "Forward a Double and Back a Double" followed by a special figure, the second part "Siding" followed by a special figure and the third part "Arming" also followed by its own special figure. Examples of this type are The Old Mole (for six), The Bonnie, Bonnie Broom (for eight) and Upon a Summer's Day (for six).

There are also many dances for two couples only, perhaps the most popular of these being Rufty Tufty. Of the Round Dances, often for eight people, one of the simplest to learn, owing to the familiarity of its tune, is If All the World Were Paper. The music is that of the nursery song:

If all the world were paper,
If all the sea were ink,
If all the trees were bread and cheese,
What should we do for drink?

A "Hey" from the Morris Dance "Trunkles"

There are three parts to this dance and the music is repeated as often as is necessary for the completion of each figure. It includes the three movements. Forward a Double and Back a Double, Siding and Arming. There is also in the last figure a circular "Hey." This Hey is a figure like that of the Grand Chain in the Lancers in which the dancers take hands alternately right and left as they move round the circle to their places. The Hey may occur in many forms in country dances, sometimes in a straight line or as a figure of eight for three people or as in the above dance in a circle either handing or passing without hands.

It is very necessary that the dancers should note the rhythm of the music and that all steps should be fitted to each phrase of the tune.

At the same time each dancer must move in time with his companions in the dance. Not all dances are gay, some of the more intricate dances being quiet and subdued in style and requiring great restraint on the part of the performers. In consequence these dances are not, at their first introduction, as popular at an ordinary class as the more care-free dances, though eventually they are the dances that hold the interest of the intelligent folk dancer and provide an ideal of rhythm and beauty of movement. For the more advanced dancer there is the Running Set with the fascinating evolutions of The Back Door Key, Bird in the Cage and Going Down Town, only to be achieved after considerable practice. This dance was discovered when Mr. Cecil Sharp visited the Appalachian Mountains, and nowadays there are few Folk Dance Party programmes which do not include one or more figures of this famous dance.

"Honouring."—At the end of each dance partners "Honour" one another. This takes the form of a bow—polite but not elaborate—on the part of the man or the lady taking the part of the man for that particular dance, while his partner responds with a graceful "bob" or curtsey. This delightful old-fashioned custom is in keeping with the atmosphere of the dance, being gracefully formal. One cannot leave the actual dances without a reference to Sellingers

The Rapper Sword Dance

The Kentucky Running Set

Round which concludes most open-air programmes of country dancing. Sellingers Round is the country dancer's Auld Lang Syne. In this dance the dancers form several concentric circles and the alternate circles move in a clockwise and an anti-clockwise direction.

The Morris Dance.—Like the Sword Dance this is a team dance, a team in the Morris consisting of six men wearing pads of bells on their shins and carrying stick or handkerchiefs. The dancers begin in two columns but the formation is varied as they dance into rings, figures of eight and other patterns. Different villages had their own traditional dances and at Bampton in Devon and outside Balliol College, Oxford, two of these dances may be seen annually.

The Sword Dance is performed by a team of from five to eight men who form a circle. The dancers move with a simple running step and go through a series of evolutions, finishing with the swords, which have no sharp edges, interlocked in a pattern. At the end of the dance one of the performers usually holds the star of locked swords above his head.

The Morris and Sword Dances being more ceremonial are not so easy of description and no attempt is made here to give instructions for their performance. Suffice it to say that anyone who has mastered the rudiments of Country Dancing should have little difficulty in becoming proficient in the other branches of Folk Dancing.

Folk Songs.—Mention must be made here of Folk Songs which also received the attention of Mr. Sharp. It is an excellent thing that these songs with their fascinating airs and words should be sung by both adults and children of to-day. While resting from the activities of the actual dance it is pleasant to gather round a piano and sing such melodies as: *Green Grow the Rushes Ho!; The Keeper;* and *The Twelve Days of Christmas.*

There is now a permanent headquarters of the English Folk Dance Society at the corner of Regent's Park Road in London. This magnificent building with its library of folk lore and folk music, its rooms for dances and lectures, is a memorial to Cecil Sharp, to whom folk dancers owe so much. You can obtain here all information about the various dances, together with the music to use with them. H.M.V. and Columbia also have folk dance records. Folk Dance classes and parties are held in practically every suburb of London and in large towns, while the villages are showing ever increasing enthusiasm for their national dance. The annual Folk Dance Festival at the Albert Hall is probably known to most people in the British Isles through the medium of Broadcasting. To this festival come dancers from all parts of our islands and from many parts of Europe.

FRETWORK

There are few hobbies which have had so wide an appeal as fretwork. Almost every boy—and a large number of girls—at some time or another is keen on fretwork, whilst there are still thousands of grown-ups who spend many a happy hour working at this delightful and useful pastime.

Equipment Required.—One of the great advantages of fretwork is its cheapness, as really serviceable outfits can be purchased for from one shilling and sixpence upwards. It is true, of course, that these cheaper outfits limit both one's output and the range of articles that can be made, but nevertheless a little ingenuity goes a tremendously long way. The essential parts to a fret kit are the saw frame, which is a deep U bent metal frame with a handle; a number of fine saw-blades, a small clamp and a steel cutting-table. This latter is merely a guard, and it may be dispensed with if desired. It costs so little, however, that it is wise to use it if only to prevent damage to the table or bench upon which one works.

Better sets include such things as a rule, a drill with a few small "bits," a light tack hammer, a sand-paper block and a small plane. As the fretworker progresses with his hobby, he will want to add still more tools, but none of them cost more than a few pence. Of course, the day may come when a treadle-operated fret-sawing machine is desired, but even these can be bought for from 25/– or so. The great advantage of a treadle machine is that at all times it cuts absolutely vertically and, of course, at a great speed. Electrically operated saws are also marketed, but these are usually beyond the requirements of the amateur.

Let us assume that the reader has purchased the small outfit comprising the saw, saw-blades clamp and steel cutting-table—an outlay, as we have seen, of one shilling and sixpence. The only other thing necessary is the wood upon which to work.

There are many kinds of wood used in fretwork, and such woods as mahogany, sycamore, white chestnut, satin walnut, padouk, light oak, figured oak, Spanish chestnut, satinwood and beech are available from most dealers. It is as well to make a start by using the cheapest, for then one's mistakes will cost but little. A square foot of satin walnut, which is a soft, brown-coloured wood, evenly and yet richly grained, will cost about 5d. Three-ply wood is even cheaper and it has the added advantage of being stronger. For back panels it cannot be beaten.

Fitting the Fret-saw Blade.—Now for a little practice. Clamp the steel cutting-table to an ordinary kitchen table or bench about 3 ft. high so that the whole of the V opening projects over the edge of the wooden table. Now take one of the fine saw-blades and set it in the fret-work frame so that the teeth point downwards towards the handle. This is necessary so that the saw may be drawn downwards to make the cut. If the blade is put in the other way up, it will break. The old-fashioned frames required the blade-end to be heated and bent over to form a hook, but the modern frame is provided with two small clamps which tighten on the blade by means of thumbscrews. Blades should be quite taut or they will break directly one starts cutting.

A word is necessary here about the quality of blades. There are many qualities on the market, some of which are extremely brittle. All blades are delicate and must be handled with care, but the best quality will prove to be by far the cheapest in the long run. They cost very little more to buy, and are infinitely superior.

It will be found useful to have a small bottle of thin oil handy, and occasionally to apply a little to both sides of the blade from time to time. A camel-hair brush is the best means of applying it.

How to Use the Fret-saw.—The next thing is to practise a few simple cuts before starting on some more ambitious

Fig. 1.—Using a Treadle Machine

work, so take your piece of wood and first of all cut it in half, so that you have two pieces, each six inches wide. This cutting is, of course, done with an ordinary saw. Now take a pencil and draw a line on the wood as shown in Fig. 2.

Keep the line well to one end of the wood in order to avoid waste. Note that the line is first of all straight, then it curves gradually, then with sharper bends until we get a right-angled turn or two. This will be good practice, for after a few minutes of this, you will be ready to start making something useful or decorative. Place the wood on the cutting-table so that the line is between the points of the V opening. Hold the wood with one hand and with the other take up the saw. With a downward stroke start to cut along the line. At the end of each down stroke, draw the saw back just a little and raise the handle, then make another downward cut. Proceed thus, without haste, holding the saw-blade upright. Slide the wood about on the table as bends are encountered and try to keep the saw away from the edge of the steel table.

With most fretwork outfits, a few designs are supplied, but in any case these may be purchased quite cheaply at any fretwork shop. The next thing to do after you have

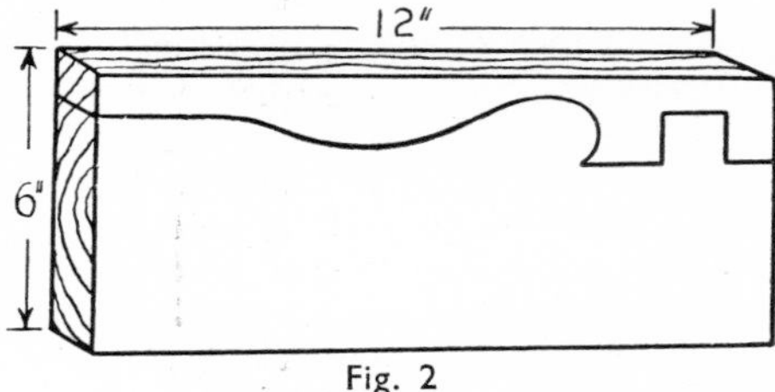

Fig. 2

gained proficiency in closely following the guide lines is to set about making something. Before doing this, however, the correct wood should be chosen. This will naturally depend upon the article to be made. Some descriptions of the various woods will be given later. The wood selected, the next job is to paste the design on to it. Any paste—such as that made from flour and water—will do, and it should be spread smoothly over the back of the design by means of a brush. Then take up the design and lay it on the wood, smoothing it with a piece of clean soft rag, working from the centre to the edges. If the design cockles, raise it from the wood and smooth it down again. When all is smooth, set aside to dry thoroughly. If an attempt is made to

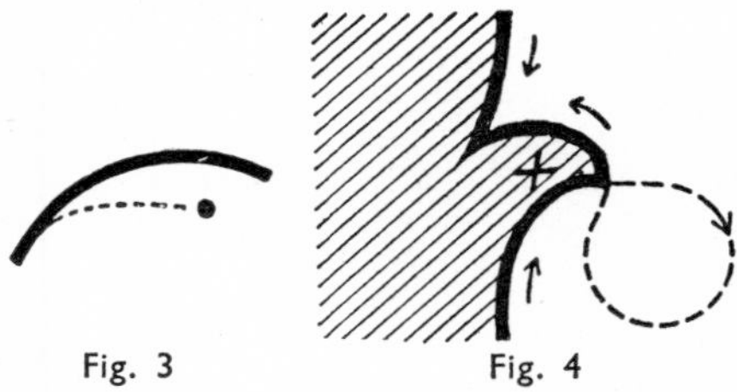

Fig. 3 Fig. 4

cut whilst the paste is still wet, the paper will tear and the work will stand a good chance of being spoiled. When pasting designs, always see that wastage of wood is avoided, and make sure that the design is pasted the right way of the grain. Most good designs have an arrow printed on them showing the way the grain should lie. The general rule is that the pattern runs lengthwise with the grain in order that the full strength of the grain be utilized. Were the grain to run across the piece, there would be a danger of breakage.

It will be found that there are many holes to be cut for each design, and so the small drill is used to enable the saw-blade to be inserted. One end of the blade is released from the frame for this purpose. The holes are made with the drill (called an Archimedean drill), which will most likely be provided with the kit. At all events, these drills only cost a few pence. Hold the drill perfectly upright, and do not drill the holes too closely to the guiding lines. Where possible, place them so that a gradual curve can be cut, enabling the design lines to be followed with ease. Figs. 4 and 5 will make this clear. One frequently comes to a sharp corner, and it is useless to try to turn this with the saw-blade, so the practice is to approach it from both sides as shown in Fig. 3.

Always, when cutting an acute angle, note the way of the grain so that breakage of the wood can be avoided. In Fig. 6, for instance, the shadowed lines denote the way of the grain, and it will be obvious that to cut from A to B and then round and back to A via C would mean that a great strain is placed on the wood near point A. It is more than likely that it would break. The better plan is to cut from A to B, and then to take the saw back again to A and cut to C, for the wood is stronger at its greatest width.

When the whole of the design has been cut, the wood is then sand-papered carefully, not only to remove the sharp edges left by the saw, but to take off the paper design and to impart a smooth surface to the finished job. Smoothing is best done with the aid of a sand-paper holder block, for it gives much better results than if the paper is held in the hand. Any piece of wood of a suitable size will do for a block—a piece of 1-in.-thick deal, 4 in. long, and cut wide enough to make a comfortable grip for the hand will do admirably. If desired, the block may be faced with cork. Proper blocks may be purchased so cheaply, however, that it is scarcely worth troubling to make one.

Two grades of sand-paper should be used, one to remove the remains of the paper design—this can be fairly coarse—but a fine glass-paper should always be used for imparting the actual finish. The more the

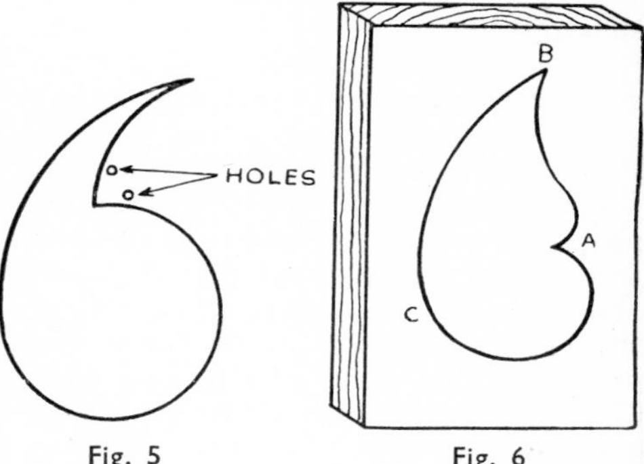

Fig. 5 Fig. 6

wood is polished with sand-paper, the better will it look when stained and finished. After every part of the article has been smoothed, it should be assembled. This may be done either with tacks or with glue. Cabinet pins should be used for tacking, but the more general method of assembling is to use one of the many kinds of glue. That purchased in twopenny tubes is quite satisfactory, but it should be used sparingly and allowed to become tacky before the parts are pressed together. It is, however, better to use hot glue.

String may sometimes be used to hold the newly glued parts together until the adhesive has set, but special clamps can be purchased if desired. Surplus glue may be scraped off with a knife, but it is not wise to do this until the glue is thoroughly dry.

Staining and Polishing.—The article is now ready for staining and polishing. Fretwork may be left in its natural colouring, but the appearance will be greatly improved if it is stained and polished. Never use varnish-stains on fretwork, for they not only make the work look cheap, but the varnish scratches easily. The best polishing medium is undoubtedly french polish. Use a good water stain and apply it with a brush, allowing it to dry thoroughly before attempting to polish.

There are many designs which are improved if a transfer is used, for they give the appearance of inlay work. Transfers can be obtained quite cheaply and in a great variety of designs and colours. They consist of a brightly-coloured design printed on stout paper in such a way that when affixed to the wood or to other surfaces, the paper can be removed, exposing the coloured design firmly adhering to the surface.

If you examine a transfer, you will find that one side is composed of the thick paper or backing, and the other of a dull satin-finished surface which hides to a great extent the coloured design. This dull side is first coated with varnish which is afterwards allowed to become tacky. It is then applied to the wood and gently pressed down with a piece of cloth or other pad, and allowed to harden. To remove the paper covering, water is applied by means of a brush, and when the paper is thoroughly soaked, it may be stripped off exposing the design in its proper colours. It is usual to affix transfers after the wood has received a certain amount of polish, the remainder being put on after the transfer is dry. This acts as a protective medium.

There is a great fascination in making mechanical models out of wood, and although this subject has been dealt with elsewhere in this book, a few words concerning it will not be out of place here. Designs of all descriptions can, of course, be purchased, but it is much more enjoyable to make your own. Suppose, for instance, it is desired to make a model aeroplane. This consists of the wings, fuselage or body, and tail. The reader should make a sketch of the type he wishes to make—biplane, monoplane, triplane, seaplane, flying boat, etc., and plan every step carefully, bearing in mind the fact that the parts must be securely fixed together when made. Such an exercise is in itself good training, and many a delightful hour may be thus spent.

Jig-saw Puzzles.—There is a great demand for jig-saw puzzles by people of all ages, and it is both a fascinating as well as a profitable hobby to make them. You may even find a local shopkeeper ready to buy as many as you can turn out. Any good picture, provided it is nicely graded in colour, will do, and this is pasted on to wood as previously described. Most children welcome jig-saw puzzles for birthday and Christmas presents, and excellent little ones can be made by pasting picture-postcards on to three-ply wood and cutting them out.

When the picture is dry, the next job is to mark it out lightly so as to make good shapes. A pencil will do for this, and with a jig-saw it does not matter if the lines are not kept to accurately. A straight line jig-saw puzzle is a good thing to start on. The pieces may be triangles of all shapes. Always be sure to hold the saw upright or it will be difficult to build up the picture afterwards.

Fretwork has progressed far beyond the picture-frame and corner-bracket stage, for some really beautiful pieces of furniture can be made quickly and cheaply. Wireless cabinets, for instance, provide an almost endless variety of designs, and they give much scope for the artistically-minded fretworker. Gramophone cabinets and radio gramophone cabinets can also be made, whilst such things as screens, clock cases and so on are common.

The keen fretworker will find that he is able to make many things of use to others, especially for selling at local bazaars and sales of work. At a scout's bazaar, for instance, the fleur-de-lis can be introduced into the design quite easily, whilst people's initials are equally simple and much appreciated. Many beautiful models of great engineering feats can be constructed—such things as bridges, motor-cars, motor-coaches, and so on, being very popular with children. A huge variety of toys can also be constructed with the aid of fretwork tools. A farm, complete with little thatched houses and barns, animals, and so on, can be made, or a model village complete with pond (made out of a piece of looking-glass), village pump and the village green.

Now that photographs can be printed directly on to wood, it is a simple matter to take a snap of a friend and then to present him with a cut-out photograph complete with a stand. It makes a delightful present and one that is much appreciated.

Woods to Use.—We have already mentioned, by name, some of the woods used in fretwork. The fretworker will, however, want to know more about them, so below is a list of the woods most commonly used, together with a short description of their characteristics.

Beech.—This is of a yellowish-white colour, very durable and close-grained. It takes stain and colours admirably.

Chestnut (*Spanish*).—Very similar in appearance to oak, but much softer. It is very popular.

Chestnut (*White*).—A soft, close-grained wood.

Mahogany.—A more expensive wood, possessing a rich red colour. It is easily polished.

Oak.—Obtainable in light and dark. Both varieties are popular. They are not difficult to cut, and they take polish well.

Padouk.—Another red-coloured wood that is beautifully figured.

Satinwood.—An orange-yellow wood, close-grained and hard. It is more expensive than the others and is used for first-class work.

Sycamore.—A cheap wood of close grain.

Walnut (*Satin*).—A soft brown-coloured wood, beautifully grained.

FRUIT GROWING

FRUIT in small gardens is not nearly so common as it might be. The apple orchards of Britain were at one time famous, but now that apples can be bought so cheaply the growing of trees in gardens has been discouraged. But apart from economic reasons the hobby can give much pleasure. The trees can be grown in such a way that they take up very little room; they give feature to a garden, the blossom is beautiful in spring and the fruit is equally beautiful in autumn.

Planting.—Fruit trees, like other deciduous trees, should be planted in the autumn. October or November, preferably the latter, are good months in which to commence planting, which may go on right up to March, provided it is not done when the soil is sodden. The position of fruit trees in a small garden is governed by æsthetics rather than utility. The beauty of the garden has to be considered as well as the well-being of the trees. Old-world orchards are very nearly a thing of the past; but if you have an old wall there is no reason why it should not be clothed with a fan-shaped pear tree. A double row of apples or plums can make an effective screen at the back of a garden and raspberry canes will take the place of an unproductive privet hedge, surrounding or shutting off the vegetable garden. Currants and gooseberries are, however, better grown in orthodox lines inside the kitchen garden.

The form of fruit trees is of great importance. Nurserymen supply standards, half-standards, pyramids, bush, cordons or espaliers, all trained ready for planting. Standards have stems or boles 5 or 6 ft. high and are most suitable for planting

Fig. I.—An Obelisque Condon Pear

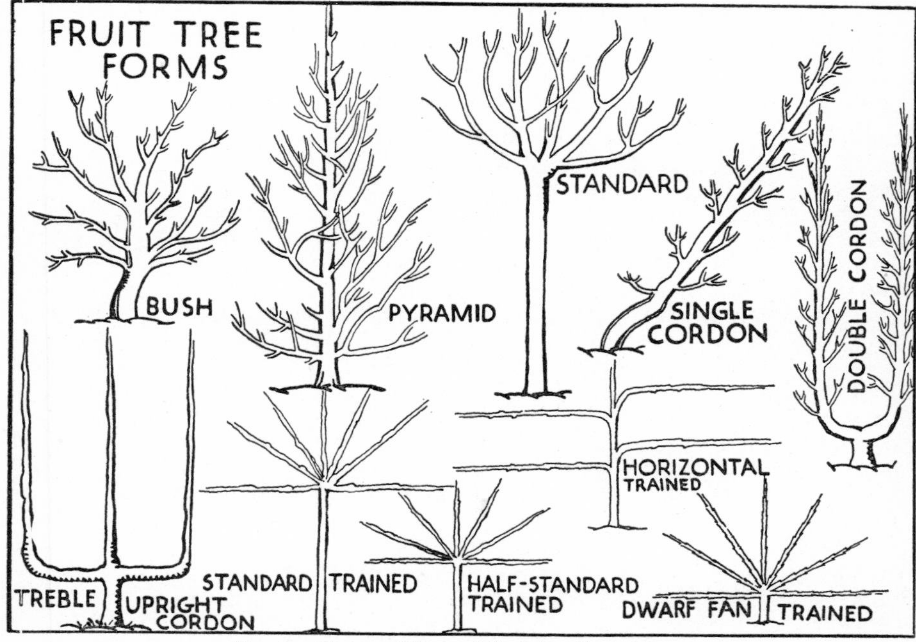

Fig. 2.—Various Ways of Training Fruit Trees

singly where there is plenty of room to develop, or as orchard trees. Half-standards with a height of 4 ft. are more suitable for the small garden, being more easily managed at pruning time. Bush and pyramid forms, bearing fruit right from the bottom, are ideal in a limited space, while cordons or espaliers take up least room of any and they give an air of distinction to a place, if well-cared for. Nothing looks better than an espalier apple arch over the paths of a kitchen garden. Cordons trained in single, double or treble lines against a wall, while perhaps looking too formal for some tastes, have points where economy of space and the maximum amount of fruit have to be considered. Cordons may also be trained horizontally, being single stems, to right and left of main stem or trained on each side ladderwise. It is important to state the type of tree required when ordering from a nurseryman, for trees for various purposes are grafted on suitable stocks and it is better to buy them with the first stage of training as standards, half-standards or cordons over, for nurserymen are experts and usually make a better job of this operation than amateurs. Besides, it takes too long to grow the trees from the beginning yourself, unless you have a complete knowledge of grafting and training.

When planting fruit remember that shelter is essential. See that there are good walls, fences, hedges or shelter trees, sufficiently well back to cause no shading in the fruit ground. Ground sloping south or south-west is ideal. Trenched soil that is well drained is imperative, for deep cultivation is necessary and fruit trees will not thrive if there is water about the roots. Humus or vegetable refuse should be dug into the soil but use no manure. A dressing of bone-meal is beneficial.

Remember that the roots that matter must be kept near the surface. The long tap root should be cut away. (*See below.*) Another method is to put brick chips, rubble or stones at the bottom of the hole to prevent the tap root penetrating too deeply into the subsoil. In both cases this is to avoid unfruitfulness when the tree begins to be established and to send its roots too deep. Keep the tree in the same position in the soil as it has occupied in the nursery, that is, plant only up to the soil mark on stem, not deeper or disease will set in. Keep the fibrous roots spread out and fill in gradually with soil, pressing very firmly with the foot as you go along and stake as you plant with stout wooden stakes but do not tie too tightly at first. After the tree has settled down in the soil go over the ties and re-adjust more firmly. Roots which have been damaged in transit from nursery should be removed with a very sharp knife.

All fruit trees—apple, pear, cherry, plum—and fruit bushes are planted according to these rules at the same season, autumn. The distance apart is usually decided by the space at one's disposal, but allow enough room for every tree or bush to develop properly. Gooseberries and currants need to be about 3 or 4 ft. apart, but a good deal depends upon the variety grown. The nurseryman who supplies them will advise. Raspberries should be about 3 ft. apart.

Apples should be grown out in the open where they can get plenty of sun; they are not suitable for growing against a wall, except in very inclement districts. Pears do well in the open but they are also suitable as fan-shaped trees against a wall. Plums are perhaps best planted in groups in the open garden though they do well on walls. Cherries do well on walls or out in the open garden. Apples and pears make good cordons though when well trained and managed almost any fruit can be so grown.

Cultivation.—The surface roots of trees do not bear disturbance well so the subsequent management does *not* entail digging with a spade about the trees every year; this treatment damages the roots and consequently the trees. While it is important that these roots should be free from annoyance it does not mean that grass and weeds should be allowed to grow close up to the trees as in some old orchards. This, while picturesque, is not good gardening. Cultivate the soil about the trees by hoeing and weeding and keep the soil around the roots—not close up to the boles—stirred so that nourishment may be obtained without injury to roots. A mulch of cut grass or well-rotted manure is good for old trees and particularly good for raspberries.

In selecting varieties to plant it is well to have regard to the kinds found most suitable to the district in which the garden is situated rather than to the names of exhibition prize winners.

Pruning.—The successful cultivation of fruit depends on a thorough understanding of the principles of pruning. While individual kinds of fruit tree have their particular needs, and even varieties of apple or pear need different treatment according to their kind, the general principles which apply to all are a very good foundation for managing any kind of fruit tree. The peculiarities of bush fruits, such as currants and raspberries, will be dealt with separately.

Newly planted trees are more rigorously pruned than older ones; the object being to promote a healthy growth of wood and to make a shapely tree. It depends on the kind of tree for the amount to be cut off. Apples and pears should have half the length of branches cut away. Cherries do not bear pruning so well, and should only be cut to two-thirds their length; plums may have more wood left, but in all of these trees weak wood should be sacrificed and all vigorous shoots cut back to an outward pointing bud. Clean cuts with a sharp knife should be made, the cut sloping upwards to the bud and projecting just beyond

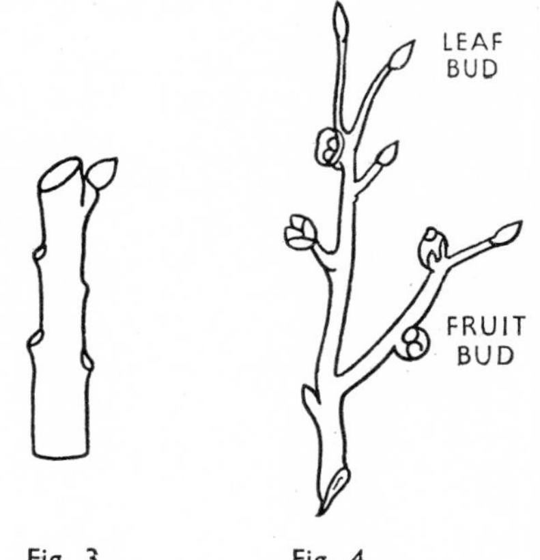

Fig. 3 Fig. 4

the end of bud. (Fig. 3.) This first pruning should be accomplished in February or March before the sap has begun to rise in the trees. Due care should be taken to preserve the shape of tree or to improve it according to the type that you are growing. It is important to be able to recognise a fruit bud and a leaf bud. Fruit buds are round and plump, leaf buds are long and slender and come at the end of shoots, while fruit buds usually appear at the end of old shoots. (Fig. 4.)

When trees are established, pruning need not be so drastic as for young newly planted ones, unless they have been neglected. After the first pruning, a routine of three kinds of pruning, summer, winter and root pruning, is usually adhered to by good fruit-growers and this must be borne in mind if good harvests are to be gathered.

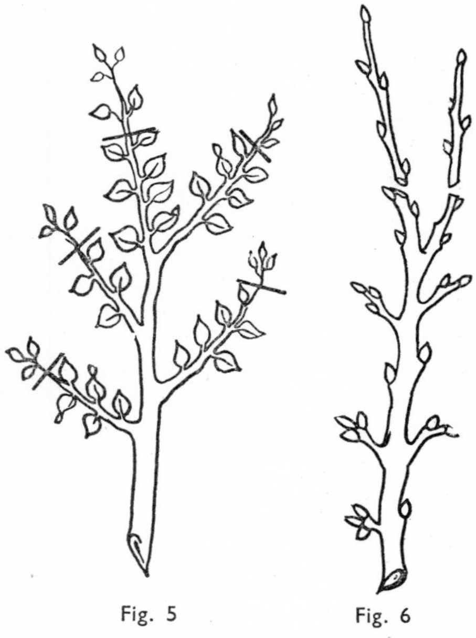

Fig. 5 Fig. 6

During the summer new shoots will be observed all over the trees, especially side shoots from main branches. It is usual to shorten these, leaving about five or six leaves. (Fig. 5.) This encourages the formation of fruit buds or spurs and is best done about July. Any other side shoots which grow as the result of this pruning back should likewise be shortened to a few leaves.

In winter these same shoots should be further cut back to a few buds; four is best. (Fig. 6.) The tips of these will develop into leaves while the other buds will become fruit buds. Apart from this, winter pruning should consist only of keeping the trees a good shape.

Trained Trees are usually allowed to grow sufficiently large to cover the space allotted to them before pruning is resorted to as they are usually trained to shape before leaving the nursery. With pyramids and bushes the pruner's task is easy, the only thing necessary is to preserve the shape and to keep trees open to admit sunlight. All crossing branches are cut out as these spoil appearance of trees and much damage is done by one branch rubbing against another.

Cordons, espaliers and fan shapes should, like other trees, have side shoots pruned in summer. Besides this they should, of course, be kept to their original shape, no shoots being allowed to grow out where they would spoil the effect. Newly planted ones will, of course, have to have main branches shortened till the trees gain strength after transplanting.

Root Pruning is an operation resorted to when fruit is not being borne although the trees are obviously healthy and making good length of wood. Young trees are bodily lifted and replanted. As this means that much of the old root dies and fibrous roots are, of necessity, formed after the replanting, actual cutting is not always necessary; but tap roots, which are the long, strong roots which are growing deep into the soil, should be cut away. Make the cut upwards as this helps to encourage the growth of the surface roots which are required for the production of fruit.

Old trees which are not bearing should have a trench dug round them at about the distance from the trunk that the branches are spreading. Make this trench a few feet wide and a few feet deep. Keep the fibrous roots intact by protecting with moist sacking and cut off all old thick roots. Roots striking straight down should be severed with a spade and the trench filled in with good soil. Sometimes only one half of the tree is thus pruned in one autumn, the other half being done the next season.

Very old trees or neglected ones need drastic pruning. Old and dead wood must be removed, crossing branches removed so that sunlight gets into the tree, but sometimes this is too severe treatment if the trees are dried and gnarled. Sometimes regrafting is performed, but unless done by an expert old trees are better left to be merely picturesque or they may be ruthlessly removed to make room for new plantations.

Fruit Pruning.—In addition to pruning for shape and fruit, pruning for large fruit is necessary. This consists of thinning fruit spurs in autumn or winter when these have become too numerous or too large. This is usually done in two operations, the tip of fruit spur being removed one year, the spur being cut well back to the base the next year. Fruit, after it is formed, needs to be thinned so that those allowed to remain on trees shall be of good size and shape. Remove all weak fruit, leaving just sufficient for the strength of the tree to ripen. Keep an eye on trees and pick off, as you notice it, the fruit you do not desire to ripen.

Further, it is important to remember that special varieties of fruit trees have often special ways of bearing, some bearing on the season's growths, others bearing on the previous season's growth. The nurseryman who supplies the trees should be consulted.

As pollination of fruit trees is very important some growers always keep bees to ensure that this is satisfactory. Some kinds of trees are self-fertile; others are self-sterile and require to be planted in association with other trees to ensure a crop at all. It is well to find out from the nurseryman any particulars about this matter when purchasing trees, for one wants trees which will be useful as well as ornamental.

Apples.—While the foregoing instructions are general for most fruit trees, each individual kind has to be considered in certain respects. Apples are better grown in the open in a sunny, well-drained position and should be summer pruned in July, August, September. Winter pruning should be done in December or January and consists of shortening main branches by about a third of their length and laterals or side shoots to about two buds. Standards and half-standards are best left to grow as freely as possible; the less pruning the better. When large branches are removed the wound should be treated with mastic varnish. Good apples to grow are: (dessert) Cox's Orange, James Grieve (a good one for growing in Scotland), Allington Pippin and Blenheim Orange; (cooking) Bramley's Seedling, Newton Wonder and Rev. W. Wilks.

Pears.—The best pears are grown on walls, the flavour being finer than that of those grown in the open garden and the fan-shaped tree is best. Prune as for apples in summer and winter. Basic slag used at the rate of $\frac{1}{4}$ lb. to the square yard is beneficial. Good dessert pears: Bon Chretien, Superfin, and Jargonelle; good cooking pears: Beurre Clairgeau and Verulam.

Plums delight in lime and owing to the early blossoming should not be planted in a low site as this means that they will be damaged by frosts. They are best grown in groups as pyramids. They need much water. Pruning should not be so severe as for apples and pears. If you have only room for a few, grow greengages and Victorias.

Cherries profit by lime rubble in the soil and while nothing looks so well as a standard tree in the garden, wall trees are usually best as they can be secured by netting from the ravages of birds. It is important to prune cherry trees into a desired shape when they are young, for they do not bear pruning well and should only be lightly pruned when established. Summer pruning should be omitted altogether. The reason for this is that all cherries bleed when cut too freely and this damages the tree as well as being a source of disease. The best cherries are: Morello (north wall), Black Tartarian, Early Rivers, May Duke and Governor Wood.

Figs.—If you want an ornamental tree for a wall, even if there should be no fruit, grow figs. The large leaves are most artistic when the tree is trained in a fan shape against a sunny wall and pruned carefully, though for fruit too much pruning is bad. Some growers build the roots in with brick or even cement to prevent too free root development at the expense of fruit. The Brown Turkey is the most satisfactory fig for growing out of doors.

Damsons while not so popular as plums are hardy and, after being pruned to a good shape when young, can safely be left alone and can be depended upon to bear well. Varieties: Bradley's King of the Damsons, Farleigh Prolific or Cluster and Aylesbury Prune.

Gathering Fruit is one of the most delightful garden tasks. It should always be done in dry weather. Cooking apples should be harvested as soon as ripe, desserts usually need to be removed a few days before quite ripe and allowed to sweat in a dry, cool place before being stored. Some pears are quite hard when gathered, but ripen later in the store. If fruit parts easily from the stem on the branch or if one fruit being cut through has dark pips it is ready for gathering; this rule applies to all fruits, except stone fruits which are, of course, soft when ready for use. No bruised or diseased apples or pears should be stored along with sound fruit, and fallen fruit is not suitable for storing, as it is usually diseased or damaged. A cold place is not suitable for storing fruit, a temperature of 45° being the best and, if possible, all fruits, thoroughly dry, should be placed on shelves rather than barrelled.

Canker is one of the worst disasters that can befall a fruit tree. It attacks the wood of the tree, causing deep, wide cracks, which means decay, and as these wounds usually get wider there is only one remedy—to cut off affected branches or destroy badly injured trees. When branches are removed the wound left from cut should be treated with Stockholm tar to prevent the ingress of other disease or decay of the tree at that place. Damp situations are usually to blame.

Greenfly or Aphides is also an enemy of fruit trees and Apple Aphides should be fought, in April, with a spray of 1 lb. quassia chips boiled in a little water. Dissolve ½ lb. soft soap in hot water and add more water till there are 10 gallons and add the quassia chips to this and use in spray.

Apple Maggot.—Fruit-growers are caused some anxiety by various troubles to which trees are prone and as these trees are expensive it is as well to have a knowledge of how to combat them when they come. The falling of fruit is caused by the ravages of the Codlin Moth or Apple Maggot. The eggs of this insect are laid on the eye of the fruit as the blossom falls and the larvæ, hatching out there, enter the fruit and eat a tunnel through it, causing it to fall. The larvæ emerge and lie dormant in the soil before pupating in the spring. The remedy is to spray the eye of the fruit, as the blossom falls, with arsenate of lead, 1 oz. to 2 gallons of water. This is poisonous. Grease banding is, surrounding the trees in the autumn, about September, with brown paper bands smeared with grease to prevent the adult female creeping up to lay eggs. Special bands for this purpose are sold. They should be placed about 2 ft. from the ground.

Falling Blossom is often caused by frost and in the open garden little can be done to prevent this. Canvas blinds or tiffany, a kind of transparent gauze, is sometimes used to protect wall trees. Another cause of dropping blossom is lack of moisture and this usually occurs when trees are grown on a gable or wall which has very dry soil about it. Copious watering is necessary at blossoming time to prevent the loss of bloom.

Old trees which are covered with moss or lichen can be cleaned by using a solution of 1 lb. caustic soda in water mixed with 1 lb. of soft soap and made up to 10 gallons with water. This should be sprayed on to the trees when they are leafless in December or January. It is poisonous.

Raspberries are easily grown on a trellis as a screen for the kitchen garden or in clumps. The root of this fruit is permanent but the stems, or canes as they are called, are biennial, bearing one year and dying the next, though some of the newer introductions have annual canes and this has to be borne in mind when pruning. The soil most suitable is that enriched with vegetable refuse or well-rotted manure. Shady positions are best and a rainy district suits them as they need much moisture. For this reason mulching with cut green grass is used to keep the roots, which are near the surface, cool in hot, dry weather. The canes can be planted early in autumn and should be cut hard back to within 6 or 7 inches of the ground to encourage new growth; this pruning is done when they are planted. Established canes are pruned as soon as the fruit is gathered, old canes which have borne fruit being cut out: this treatment is for the old biennial stem type. The newer annual type is best cut back almost to the ground in spring. The biennial type should have the ends of canes shortened in spring.

A wire trellis is best for rasps, but if you do not wish to have this trouble grow the canes in clumps of three roots and tie the canes together at top. This should be done in autumn and the canes left free in summer. Superlative is one of the best rasps; other summer fruiting varieties are Baumforth's Seedling and Hornet. Autumn fruiting kinds are: Hailsham and November Abundance. Lloyd George bears fruit in summer and in autumn.

Black Currants do best in a shady position. Prune hard back, if newly planted, to encourage new growth. After that, old wood should be cut down hard in autumn and at the same time examine bushes for any signs of the Black Currant Mite, an insect which gets into the inside of buds. The only remedy is to pick off affected buds and destroy them; if the trouble is widespread throughout the plantation the bushes must be uprooted and burned and, in some cases, it is not advisable to replant the site with black currants again. Laxton's Mite Free is practically immune to this blight. Boskoop Giant, Edina and Daniel's September are to be recommended.

Red and White Currants and Gooseberries.—It is becoming the fashion to grow them as cordons. They look well along the edge of paths on wire trellis work or they may be trained against walls, two or three branches being allowed to each. But they are more often grown in the open as bushes. Moderately manured ground suits them. Prune hard back the first year. After that summer and winter pruning is essential. Pinch back side shoots to five or

Fig. 7.—A Heavy Growth of Raspberries

six leaves but leading shoots should not be touched. This process should be begun in July and continued throughout the summer as the shoots develop and are observed to be ready for stopping. In winter, shorten these again back to two buds; main branches are cut half-way back. This treatment is suitable for both red and white currants. Good red ones are: Fay's Prolific, Raby Castle and Red Dutch. Good whites are: White Grape, White Dutch and White Transparent.

Gooseberries make a very profitable crop if well manured and the pruning not neglected. If intelligently managed, bumper crops will be the result. Too severe pruning means failure, unless when grown as cordons, when training makes more drastic pruning necessary. These should have side shoots stopped in July to 5 or 6 inches and in winter should be cut hard back. Much manure is required for this fruit.

Like other newly planted trees and bushes, hard pruning is necessary at the beginning. After that the ideal should be to have nice-open bushes with long branches heavily laden with berries. Old and weak wood should be removed in winter and only soft tips removed in summer. Crossing branches should be removed at the winter pruning. Red gooseberries include: Crown Bob, May Duke (the earliest), Whinham's Industry and Red Champagne. Green ones are: Greengage and Thumper. Yellows are: Yellow Sulphur and Champagne Yellow.

Gooseberries sometimes need to be protected in spring from birds. Wire netting or fish netting is suitable for the purpose. Caterpillars are often troublesome. Hand-picking is the most efficacious way of getting rid of them. Spraying with arsenate of lead is sometimes resorted to, but as this is poisonous it should not be used by amateurs. A spray of Paris green is also recommended.

Loganberries are hybrid berries newly introduced, being derived from red raspberries and blackberries. Their dark red, long-shaped berries are much prized by cooks for preserves, but some gardeners look askance at them, alleging that as the berries ripen only a few at a time, they cause a good deal of trouble in picking. Apart from this irregularity, they are prolific croppers and easily grown either on trellises or as bushes. Moist conditions suit them. Old fruiting shoots should be cut down nearly to the soil level in autumn, weak growths removed and the best of the shoots which are retained tied to the wires to prevent damage from winter storms.

New Berries.—For those who like novelties there are the wineberry of Japan, or filberts. The wineberry or *Rubus Phoenicolasius Argenteus* is ornamental as well as useful. It is perhaps best described as a very fine climbing bramble with decorative leaves which look very well on arches or pergolas. It has pink blossom and scarlet berries with a slightly acid flavour. These can be used as rasps and blackberries or brambles are. Like brambles, they need not too much manure and shelter from winds. Cut out old wood, leaving a sufficient number of canes to cover trellis or poles and shorten tips in spring. The veitch berry is also new.

Nuts are not common in gardens and yet there is no reason why filberts should not be tried. Plant in a sheltered spot and keep ground about them well dug and lightly manured. Prune in spring just after the falling of the pollen. Old wood should be cut out and the spring pruning consists of cutting back side shoots almost to the base of shoot. It is the fine growths of the previous year which bear the fruit. Do not gather nuts till quite ripe or wait till they fall. They will keep better than less mature ones. Cobnuts are related to filberts and need the same treatment.

Strawberries are easy to grow but they have an individuality of their own and need special culture. The best time to begin preparations for a new plantation is in the autumn when the land should be trenched or deeply dug. If the soil has been previously trenched for a crop, deep digging will be enough, in spring. The best soil is a deep sandy loam which must be well drained. If natural drainage is good, such as that on a sloping bank, the expense of draining can be lessened. A sunny position facing south is ideal. After the digging manure the beds with stable manure, in May. Allow a few months to elapse, not using the beds for any other crop and keep them free of weeds.

In September plant the strawberries. At first these will have to be bought, unless a friend gives you some of his surplus stock. Once a stock is obtained, the strawberry, being very prolific plants, can easily be propagated to keep up supplies. In cold districts in the North of England and in some parts of Scotland planting cannot be done in September but has to be done in the spring because the frost heaves the new plants out of the ground and damages or even kills them during the winter. September planting is, therefore, only suitable to mild districts.

To Plant.—The best plants are sold in pots, having been layered beside the mother plants. Keep the pots in a shady place till you are ready to plant them. In dry weather they should be watered every day before planting out begins, giving a good soaking just previous to planting. The bed prepared for them should be made firm and this also should be well watered before the transplanting begins. Knock each plant out of the pot as you plant it, keeping the ball of soil about it to prevent

Fig. 8.—Plum: "The Czar" trained on a wooden fence

damage to the fine roots, for a plant thus injured is either lost or seriously retarded in its development. Use a trowel for transplanting and plant in rows, allowing 10 in. between each plant and about 2 ft. to 2 ft. 6 in. between the rows.

In October give a liberal dressing of stable manure. This should be forked in about March. Weeds must be ruthlessly kept down by hand forking and hoeing between the lines. Feed with artificial manure in May, just before the flowers appear on plants. Nitrate of soda at the rate of 1 oz. to the square yard is a suitable artificial to use. A dusting of soot is given at this time. Next straw should be laid under plants. If late frosts come this straw should be pulled up about the plants to protect them during the severe spells.

You *must remove all tiny berries*, for strawberries should not be allowed to bear the first year; it weakens the plants. Layers, which are the long shoots that grow out from the central plants and are used for making new plantations, should be reduced in numbers, leaving only those which may be required for new beds. This gives the new plants a better start in life.

Propagation.—Strawberries bear best in their first season and deteriorate in the second and third. To keep up a supply it is therefore desirable to plant fresh beds every year, drawing each year on a third of the original bed for supplies of layers. Strawberries can be increased by division of the root, but the best and the usual way is by layering. This work is done in July. Select vigorous shoots or runners from plants with good centres and which have fruited heavily. Use only runners with good nodes or joints from which the roots of the new plant develop. These runners will be found growing out from all the healthy plants. They spread themselves over the soil and would naturally take root. It is the gardener's duty to assist Nature. The joint nearest the mother plant is the one to bring into contact with soil as it makes the strongest plant. These runners are pegged down into the soil beside the mother plant. They are not severed from the parent. Tiny pots of soil are prepared and laid along the rows directly under the runners, the joints being firmly pegged down either with pegs bought for the purpose or made from birch branches. The use of pots makes transplanting or transport easy when the time comes to remove them to new beds. If pots are not used, simply peg them down into the soil under joints. Some growers peg down on to small pieces of turf and these are removed with the roots at transplanting time.

In August or September separate these new runners from the parent plants and plant in beds prepared for them.

An Important Note.—The main time to feed the plant is after fruiting. There is a temptation to be careless after the harvest has been gathered. Do not allow the plantation to lie neglected. To lose interest at this time is fatal. The plants must have their constitutions built up for the following year. This is the most important point in the cultivation of the strawberry. Either artificials or natural manures should be given in July or August. Ordinary mixtures of ammonia sulphates, fish-meal and nitrate of soda are suitable. This treatment refreshes the plant. Except in the case of a new plantation, where no fruiting is allowed, this feeding will be found to be more effective than feeding applied just before fruiting. You will always find in spring that leaves, flowers and fruit come with a rush before any chemicals would have time to act. To apply them at this time would therefore only be to waste them.

In choosing the kind of strawberry remember that nearly every district has a popular variety and it is often wise to grow that berry. There is, of course, always room for experiments with kinds unknown to the district, but for main crop use a reliable one—one that has been recommended by a neighbour. A few new ones may be grown for experience. Good earlies are: The Duke, King George and Royal Sovereign. Mid-season: Veitch's Perfection and British Queen, the latter highly recommended for flavour. Late: Sir Joseph Paxton and Waterloo. Dr. Hogg is a late one, suitable for heavy soil. Ruskin is the best one for jam-making, being small and a good cropper, but it is very liable to the strawberry disease which destroys many a plantation and makes it hopeless to lay down new ones, so dangerous has it become. By planting earlies, mid-season and lates it is possible to prolong the feast.

FRUIT AND VEGETABLE BOTTLING

In fruit bottling sterilization is essential to arrest the growth of germs, which would otherwise destroy the fruit, while effective sealing of the bottle will prevent attack by germs from without. Since bacteria dislike acid products, fruit, owing to its acidity, is easily sterilized.

Bottles.—It is false economy to buy cheap bottles. Those of good quality will last a life-time, if sufficient care be taken.

The most popular are those with glass lids, flat rubber bands and metal screws, or spring clips. In most cases lids and rubber bands can be renewed.

Strict cleanliness is, of course, essential. The bottle should be well washed and sterilized by holding it over the spout of a boiling kettle. When filled with steam, place upside down on a wooden table until required.

Fruit for bottling should be freshly gathered and of good quality. It must on no account be over-ripe. Its final appearance must be considered when it is placed in the bottle; that is why the best demonstrators see that all the fruit is placed the same way. It should be packed as firmly as possible, then covered with syrup which has previously been allowed to cool.

The Syrup is made in the following way. Take 1 lb. of loaf or granulated sugar to 2 pints of cold water, boil for five minutes and stand aside to cool. It may be necessary

Fig. 1.—Fill the jar to overflowing with syrup

to strain through muslin. The syrup should fill the bottle to overflowing.

Water can also be used. The jars are packed with fruit and cold water instead of syrup poured over them. The successive procedure is the same in both cases.

The rubber band should be pressed in position with the thumb, and the glass lid and screw band put on loosely to allow the gases to escape. When the bottle becomes hot, the glass will expand, and if the metal band is screwed too tightly the bottle may burst.

Do not insert a knife to force open the lid. It can always be removed when the bottle is warm.

Sterilizing.—If a fish-kettle or the scullery copper is used for sterilizing the fruit, instead of one of the special articles that can be bought for the purpose, the glass should not be allowed to come into direct contact with the heat beneath. A false bottom, consisting of thick felt, cardboard, or slats of wood will prevent this.

The filled bottles should be placed on the false bottom and the cold water should be allowed to reach their necks. The heat must be gentle at first, and it must be remembered that sterilization should last from one hour to an hour and a half. Water which has come gradually to the necessary heat must be held at that temperature from five to ten minutes. The water round the bottles should register 155 degs. F. at least.

When the bottles are taken out, the screw band should be tightened; another turn of the screw must be given when the cooling glass has contracted. If the bottle is properly sealed, the contents will last for years.

Experts, who intend to exhibit their fruit, store it away from the light after it has been wrapped in dark blue paper in order to maintain its colour. Even on the dinner table the rich natural colouring of the fruit adds considerably to its attraction, so that the housewife might well follow their example.

The Choice of Fruit.—Plums and pears are among the most popular fruits for bottling and Victoria plums are best for the purpose. They should be carefully chosen and graded, and they must be washed before they are cooked with syrup. A temperature of 170 degs. F. is required, but they should be very slowly raised to this heat.

Pears on the other hand need to be sterilized at a temperature of 190 degs. F., and this again must be reached very slowly. It is impossible to over-emphasize this point.

The best dessert pears should be used. They must be peeled, cored, and when they are very large, halved. They should be dropped into cold water containing one

Fig. 2.—Cover loosely after filling jars

teaspoonful of salt to two pints of water. Experience will prove which species of pears will best retain their colour.

The pears should be put in syrup made of $\frac{3}{4}$ lb. of sugar to the pint of water.

Other Fruits.—When bottling apricots, the temperature should be brought to 130 degs. F. in the first hour and 165 degs. in the next half-hour. This temperature must be maintained for ten minutes.

The same temperature should be reached in the same time for sterilizing rhubarb.

A syrup containing 8 oz. of sugar per pint of water should be used for apricots and rhubarb.

Cherries are also suitable for bottling, but they must be nice plump cherries of good size and quality. White should not be used. Morello and May Duke blackheart are good. Avoid fruit with any blemish.

The fruit is stoned, and when covered in syrup, heated to 180 degs.

Gooseberries, which need heating to 165 degs., should be young and green. They must be topped and tailed, well washed and graded. The fruit should be packed and shaken down. It is unnecessary to worry about any bubbles which may rise. They will disappear later.

Soft fruits require careful handling, as they are apt to rise in the bottle. An asbestos mat under the pan will prevent the bottles heating too quickly. Always raise the bottles from the bottom of the pan on a wire rack or wooden slab.

Blackberries are easy to bottle and they keep in excellent condition. The beginner may well use them for her first attempt at bottling, either alone or with apples. The latter should be peeled, cored and cut thin. Blackberries must be brought to a temperature of 165 degs. F. in an hour and a half and the temperature must be maintained for fifteen minutes.

Use a syrup of 8 oz. to the pint.

For raspberries and loganberries raise the heat to 160 degs. F. and remove the bottles immediately, but remember that black-currants, owing to the toughness of their skins, require a little more heat and should be given a temperature of 170 degs.

In bottling loganberries, which should be firm and not ripe, care must be taken to rid the fruit of a pest by which it is frequently attacked—the white maggot.

The berries must be packed and covered with one teaspoonful of salt to a pint of water in the bottle, and the fruit should be allowed to stand in this solution for half an hour, so that the maggots will be drawn to the surface.

Fruit Salad.—A fruit salad consisting of raspberries, loganberries, red-currants and black cherries is easy and effective. The different fruits should be arranged in layers in the bottles, as tightly as possible, so that they will not rise during sterilization. A syrup consisting of 4 lb. sugar per gallon of water should be used to cover the fruit. The temperature of 180 degs. F. should be reached in $1\frac{1}{2}$ hours and maintained for 20 minutes.

Tomatoes are delicious when bottled, and they look attractive. Moreover, owing to their acidity, they are easy to sterilize.

Choose young tomatoes of the same colour, wash thoroughly and remove the stalks. When packing use packing-sticks to place them in position at the bottom of the bottle, and in order to ensure that they are placed the right way up. Add one teaspoonful of salt to each 2-lb. bottle, cover with cold water to overflowing, put on a rubber band lid clip, or screw loosely to allow for expansion of the glass and place them in a pan on a false bottom. Cover with cold water and heat slowly to 190 degs. F., taking one hour to do so. They should be kept at this temperature for half an hour. If they are heated too quickly the tomatoes will rise in the bottle.

Bottling in Open Glasses.—Although bottling is likely to be more successful when the proper utensils are used for the purpose, it is possible to preserve fruit in open glass jam jars. It is essential to keep the jars in a dry atmosphere. A shelf in a passage that has a continual current of air is the very best position.

The glass jars should be filled quite full with fruit and placed in a cool oven after newspaper has been stood on the oven-shelf to protect the glass. The fruit should be allowed to get hot right through, so that it will shrink to below the neck of the jar. The oven should not be too hot and the time taken should be half an hour to three-quarters. Take out each bottle separately and cover the fruit with bottling syrup. (Allow 1 lb. of sugar to 2 pints of water.)

The syrup should reach to within an inch and a half of the top of the jar. Take some rounds of white paper, paste the edge and cover the jar, while the steam is still rising. Press the pasted edges to the sides of the hot jar. Snip the edges of a second paper, paste it all over and press down over the first. Take a third paper, paste it all over and press down over the second, tie with fine string, and then paste all over the top and round the sides, pressing the paper flat to the sides of the jar.

Thick boiled starch will also make a useful paste if used cold. Bottles sealed in this way will remain in perfect condition for twelve months.

Many people still use liquid mutton fat instead of paper and substitute wide necked bottles for jam jars. The sealing must be done with great care. The inside of the bottle neck must be wiped to ensure the fat adhering to the glass. The fat must be carefully heated and on no account must it be allowed to smoke. The layer of fat, poured gently on top of the syrup (which should come well up the neck of the bottle), must be ½ in. to 1 in. deep. If the bottles should be jerked and the fat moved, the air will get into the bottles, so the utmost care must be taken.

If the syrup should come through any cracks in the fat, a second layer (lukewarm) should be put on. The bottles should be papered and tied before they are stored in a suitable place. Melted refined paraffin wax can be used instead of mutton or beef fat.

Vegetable Bottling has its own technique. The acidity of fruit makes it easily sterilized, but vegetables lack this acidity and sometimes the bacteria which they contain are not destroyed in a temperature of 212 degs. F. (boiling point).

Canning factories use a steam pressure for the sterilization of vegetables. A tin can is undoubtedly the simplest and most suitable container, but bottling is still prevalent among housewives. An American steam pressure cooker will enable the housewife to bottle vegetables under 10 lb. pressure, which corresponds to a temperature of 240 degs. F. This means that a 2-lb. bottle can be sterilized in just over half an hour at this pressure. Thorough sterilization is essential.

Bottling Without a Pressure Cooker.—When the bottles have been packed, they must be put into a pan with the necessary false bottom containing cold water, which must be brought to the boil. The vegetables must be boiled for 1½ hours at 212 degs. F., and care must be taken to see that the heat is maintained throughout.

Fig. 3.—Stand jar on false bottom in pan

A second sterilization is necessary in order to make sure that all the bacteria are destroyed. Twenty-four hours after the first sterilization the sealing should be tested by removing the clip or screw band. If satisfied that the lid is fast, replace loosely the clip or screw band, put the bottle into a pan containing cold water and sterilize a second time for an hour and a half at boiling point.

The Brine.—Young, freshly cut and carefully selected vegetables should be used.

The acid brine to serve as a covering liquid should be made from 1 gallon of water, 2½ oz. of salt and 5 oz. of lemon juice, which provides acidity and thereby helps to destroy bacteria.

As in fruit-bottling, utensils with glass lids will be found most suitable. The bottles must be held over steam to sterilize them and should be placed in cold water, or turned upside down until required. New rubber bands are necessary each time as they are considerably weakened by use.

Cauliflowers.—It is essential to see that a freshly cut vegetable of good colour is used. It should be broken into pieces and soaked for an hour in salted water. Later, to preserve its whiteness, it must be blanched for about five minutes in water that has been brought to the boil and which contains 1 oz. of citric acid to the gallon.

The vegetable must be rinsed in cold water, packed and covered with brine and sterilized for an hour at boiling point. It is then necessary to fill up with boiling brine and sterilize for another hour, repeating the process on the following day.

Carrots should be bottled in the later part of June, or early in July, when they are only about 3 in. long. They must be washed very carefully and the tops must be cut off. They should be placed in a saucepan of boiling water and boiled for ten minutes if very young. A few minutes' extra boiling will be required if they are older. Next they should be taken out of the hot and put into cold water. Remove the skins with a coarse cloth; cut away any dark parts and take care not to break the points of the carrots after they have been skinned.

The carrots should be laid in cold water so that they may be kept fresh and the brightness of their colour may be preserved. The carrots must be graded and packed into the bottles to within ¼ in. of the top. They must be covered with acidified brine and sterilized for 1½ hours at boiling point.

Beetroot for bottling should be of the deep red variety. The tops must be removed and the beets must be soaked in water till all the soil has been softened; then they must be washed thoroughly so that all the grit is eliminated. Place them in boiling water and boil for ten to twenty minutes, according to size. The skins must next be removed, and if the beets are too large, they should be cut into slices about ¼ in. thick.

Broad Beans. — Wash the pods thoroughly, shell and blanch for three minutes, then plunge them into cold water for a few minutes.

Broad beans should be packed loosely into the bottles to within ¼ in. of the top and completely covered with brine. The bottles containing the beans must be sterilized at boiling point for an hour. Then take out the bottles, one by one, remove the lids, hold back the beans with a spoon and pour off the covering liquid.

Fill the bottles with boiling water, then pour it off and repeat three or four times. Then the bottles must be refilled with boiling acidified brine and the fittings should be replaced with the screw bands left rather loose. The bottles must be replaced in hot water in the sterilizer and when all have been rinsed and filled up again, the water in the sterilizer must be brought again to boiling point and the bottles must be boiled for half an hour.

Asparagus.—The young fresh stalks with closed buds must be used and little time should be lost between cutting and bottling. Tips of the same maturity should be selected. The stalks, which must be scrutinized and any inferior ones rejected, should first be washed and cut to the same height as the bottle. The outer skin must be scraped off and the asparagus must be tied into bundles, each one containing more stalks than will fit into the bottle.

The bundles should be tied in muslin with the tips upright and lowered into a pan of boiling water, so that the heads are just above the surface. The lid should be put on and left for two or three minutes. By such means the heads may be prevented from becoming over-cooked.

The asparagus must be removed carefully from the hot water and dipped into cold for a few minutes.

The heads must then be immediately packed into spotlessly clean bottles to within $\frac{1}{4}$ in. of the top. The tips should be packed downwards, in order to facilitate turning out the asparagus.

The bottles must be filled with cold acidified brine. (Use a double quantity of salt.) Sterilize for an hour. Lift out each bottle, then fill with boiling brine and put back for half an hour.

When serving, asparagus should be warmed in the bottle in which it has been sterilized, as the heads may otherwise break off. The liquid should be drained away and the asparagus placed on toast to complete the draining. Serve with melted butter.

Peas.—Pea-pods, often very dirty from the soil, should be washed thoroughly before the peas are shelled, so that no infection is transferred from the pods to the peas. Washing in water is not really sufficient; it is better to use a diluted solution of potassium permanganate, taking sufficient crystals to make the water a deep magenta.

When the peas have been shelled they should be tied loosely in muslin or cheese cloth, then dipped for two or three minutes in a pan of boiling water, which contains a pinch of salt and a sprig or two of mint. By this means the peas will be shrunk and it will be possible to pack a larger number. They should then be taken out of the bag and placed into cold water for a few minutes.

When they have been cooled in this way, they should be packed into bottles, shaken down and covered with a cold acid brine solution made from 1 gallon of water, $2\frac{1}{2}$ oz. salt, 5 oz. lemon juice and 4 oz. sugar.

Put on the rubber band, lid, screw or clip, cover with cold water, bring to the boil gently and boil for an hour. Vegetables absorb much of the covering liquid, so it may be necessary to add more of the solution. In this case it should be boiling. Replace the bottles in the pan and boil for another half-hour, then take out, tighten the screw band and put aside for 24 hours. Then take off the screw band, and if the lids are firm, replace these bands lightly, place the bottles on a false bottom in the pan, cover with cold water again, bring to the boil and let them remain at boiling point for an hour and a half. Experts are agreed that a second sterilization is necessary for peas, broad beans and runner beans.

Peas are generally considered to be more difficult to bottle than any other vegetable. The housewife, then, should take care to see that she only uses for the purpose young and freshly gathered peas, that she washes the pods, drops the peas into cold water when shelling, that they are then plunged into boiling water for three minutes and allowed to cool, that they are covered with acid brine and that they are sterilized twice—for the last time on the next day. If she remembers each of these points and undertakes the sterilization carefully, she need have little fear about the success of the venture.

Fig. 4.—Be sure to tie securely, having pressed the cover well on

When the bottle is opened place the peas in a colander and heat over a saucepan of boiling water for 10 to 15 minutes.

Runner Beans.—Once again only very young vegetables should be used. Like the peas they may be washed in a solution of potassium permanganate, only in this instance it should be diluted to a pale pink solution. The beans should be strung and cut as if for cooking, then dipped first into boiling water and then into cold. The bottles should be packed to within $\frac{1}{4}$ in. from the top, and a solution made from $2\frac{1}{2}$ oz. salt, $\frac{1}{2}$ oz. lemon juice and 1 gallon of water should be used to cover the beans, which must be sterilized in the same way as the peas. If necessary the bottles should be filled up with boiling brine before they are sterilized for the second time for 20 minutes. The second sterilization should take place after 24 hours. Bottles should be filled up with acid brine at the end of the first hour to prevent the vegetables, otherwise left uncovered at the top of the bottle, from turning brown.

Macedoine of Vegetables.—Carrots, turnips, runner beans and celery may be used together to make a delicious macedoine of vegetables.

After washing them carefully the carrots and turnips should be cut into small squares and the runner beans should be sliced. Every kind of vegetable should be blanched separately and packed into bottles to give an effect of colour contrast. The bottles should be filled with acidified brine and sterilized at boiling point for 1½ hours.

Preserved vegetables should be tossed into butter over the fire when cooking. It will make all the difference to their taste.

If through faulty sterilization the preserved products smell bad when the bottles are opened, they must not be eaten, or given to poultry or animals. With care, however, this can become a fascinating and useful hobby.

GARDEN PLANNING

FEW hobbies are more fascinating. Given a new piece of ground, attached to a new house, there are so many possibilities. You may fill it with turf, flowers, trees, vegetables, or have a mixture to taste. And not only are there these main divisions to be settled, but there are in addition paths, pavings, rockeries, ponds, walls, hedges, summer houses, and so on. When you consider that a garden cannot be made in a month or a year, that it must develop slowly, then it is easy to realize how important the original planning is. It will be difficult, it may be impossible, to make radical changes when once things are done.

Consider first the general type of garden which you desire. What is to be its keynote—usefulness, beauty?

And having decided on your general requirements you may set about the actual planning or designing. One of the first things to be decided will be the paths. And do not hurry in making up your mind about these, for not only are they more or less permanent when once made, but they are usually such a prominent feature that there is need for them to be as suitable and attractive as possible.

Paths.—Any garden can be made to seem bigger than it is if its paths wind circuitously. A well-shaped path, of bold outline, can give pleasing symmetry to a garden in bare winter. The structure and colour can be such that it adds to and sets off the beauty of its surroundings.

When planning your paths take all such points into consideration. Work out various designs on paper and balance them against each other. Next decide on most suitable material, for there are many ways of making paths.

The Cinder Path.—This is cheap—that is its chief virtue. It also stays fairly dry, and weeds do not grow in it too easily. On the other hand the cinder path is undeniably ugly. It may be made in haphazard fashion, simply by throwing daily the cinders from your fires on to a stretch of ground which has previously been trampled down. Or you may do the thing thoroughly by getting a load of cinders from the gasworks. Excavate to about 6 in. and put in a firm foundation of big cinders or stones. Put the roller over these until they are well settled, then add layer after layer of smaller stuff. The top surface should be curved to run off wet, and packed tightly with finer ashes. You will do well to have borders of wood or brick or tiles, so that the edges of the paths are kept intact.

The Gravel Path.—This looks decidedly better, though it is made in the same fashion. The cost will naturally be higher. Begin with a foundation of stones to allow for drainage, and to discourage the growth of weeds.

The Chippings Path.—Stone chippings of the sort used for mending road surfaces, can often be procured in cheap loads. Such chippings make excellent paths, of the same type as gravel. They can be used with or without tar, but must in every case be thoroughly rolled.

In these three similar types of path—cinder, gravel, chippings—satisfactory drainage and a good camber are important. If your soil is wet and heavy it may be advisable to have foundations built over proper gullies so that the water can drain off into a soakaway or some other convenient place. A soakaway is a deep hole filled with stones and rubble and covered with soil.

The Asphalt Path.—Asphalt is very durable and waterproof, but not easy to lay. A similar foundation is required as for the paths already dealt with. Sometimes it is possible to buy your material from builders or local authorities when roads are being made in the vicinity, and it is certainly an advantage to get asphalt laid by a man experienced in the work.

The Cement Path.—This is splendidly tidy and strong. You may have the top smooth and grey, or sandy and rough—this latter effect will be obtained by brushing the surface with a hard broom before it has quite set, and so removing the grey scum which rises to the top.

You may have cement in any colour nowadays, and reds, yellows, black, white, especially when mixed in broken or geometrical designs, can add a great deal to the brightness and gaiety of a garden.

There must be a solid foundation of stones before you put down your cement.

Crazy Paving is very attractive, but should not be used where barrow or roller must often be taken. If a really strong path is required, which can readily be swept and will need no further attention, then set your slabs of stone in cement, on a solid foundation. By mixing lamp-black, or other colouring matter, with the cement, the shape of the stones will be shown up more distinctly.

But stones can be placed directly into the soil, so that rockery and alpine plants can be grown between them, or the interstices may be filled with ashes, through which weeds do not easily grow. One advantage of a crazy path set in soil is that it can be very easily moved or altered.

The Tiled Path.—This looks extremely clean and neat, but it is expensive. The tiles, being thin, need to be bedded in cement on a good foundation.

The Brick Path.—Old bricks are fairly easily obtained, and they make a good path, and one that is easily constructed. First level and roll your soil, but before bedding the bricks loosen the top earth slightly with a rake. If the path is to get much heavy work, and if you have plenty of material, put in your bricks edgeways.

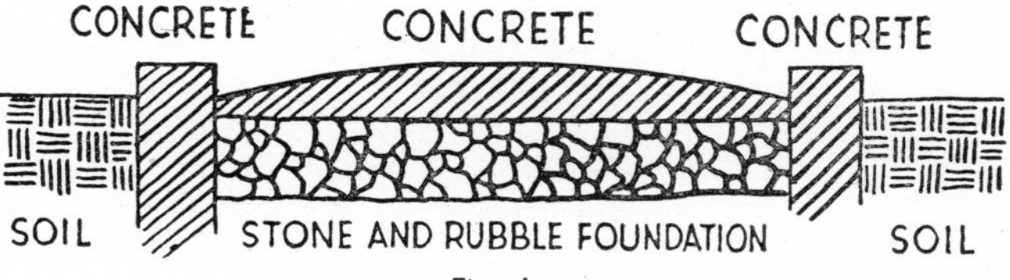

Fig. 1

Useful little tracks can be made 9 in. wide, of single bricks put flat-ways; these enable you to get to awkward parts of the garden without treading on the soil.

For a path which is to be serviceable in wet weather you should use grooved bricks set in cement.

The Grass Path.—This looks attractive, and is fairly easy to make and keep in good condition. But it is no use in bad weather, and it will not stand hard wear.

Edgings.—In most paths it is an advantage to have some sort of edging, to keep the sides of the path from becoming broken and to prevent the garden soil from encroaching. You may use tiles, bricks, concrete, metal-strips, boards or stones. Generally stones are cheapest and easiest to fix. Fair-sized flat stones, buried to about half their depth, serve best. Metal edging is neat and easy to fix, but expensive.

Boards, even when tarred, have but a limited life, and are becoming less popular than formerly. Bricks, stood edgeways or endways, are fairly good, but like tiles they are apt to get out of condition and break the regularity of your border. Concrete edging is easy to make and is very strong. Simply put down two boards, perhaps 3 in. apart; fill between with cement, and remove the boards when the mixture is hard.

Whatever edging you choose see that it harmonizes with your path.

Crazy Paving.—There are many uses to which you may put this paving—it

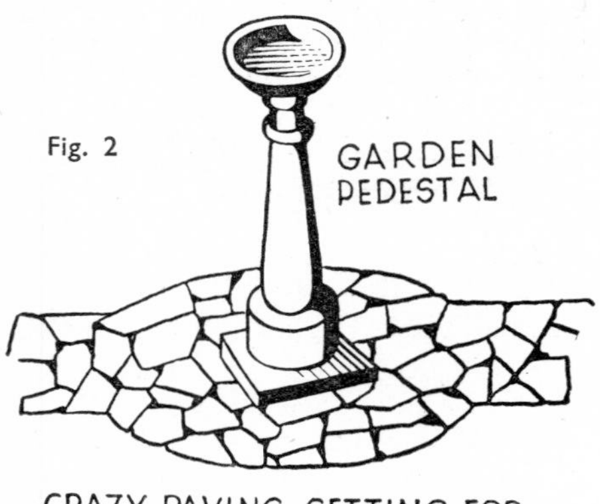

CRAZY PAVING SETTING FOR ORNAMENTAL PEDESTAL

can form paths; pave large courts; make ornamental centre-pieces on which to stand pedestals; form a rosary, by having holes left where standards and bushes may grow; surround ponds and flower beds.

You may be fortunate enough not to have to buy new stone at all. Often it is possible to obtain suitable slabs from local authorities, or from builders who have taken up old stone floors. Before embarking, therefore, on more expensive dealings for newer and less attractive stone, search your own district. Providing you do not need a great deal you may even find suitable stuff in odd pieces, all over the place. Form a habit of looking for flat slabs and it is surprising how many bits you will find.

But if you have to buy it you must have a good idea of how much you will need. Crazy paving is generally sold by the ton, and the average ton of $2\frac{1}{2}$ in. stone covers approximately 10 square yards (not 10 yards square). Thinner slabs of $1\frac{1}{2}$ in. may cover as much as 14 square yards. Thickness is an important consideration. Two inches should generally be considered as a minimum where the paving will get a good deal of use.

Crazy paving stone can be of two kinds: *sawn*, which leaves a flat, smooth face; or *split*, which has a rough surface.

If the stone is carted to your garden be quite sure that it is dumped at the most convenient spot ; it is unpleasant to have to handle the stone more than necessary, especially if you are laying it yourself. And do not let a lorry with a 5-ton load drive down by the side of your house on a private road which was never intended to carry more than a bicycle or light car.

Laying the Stone.—One way is to bed it in cement, on a foundation of small stones or gravel. This will make a solid and water-tight job, with no fear of weeds growing. But it will not give the best appearance, even if you vary it by using black cement.

Another way is to fill the gaps between the stones with fine ashes.

The third, and most attractive treatment, is to fill in soil between the stones so that plants can be put in. But there is the danger that weeds and grass will come up, too.

Having settled on your style you will begin to fit your stones together, rather in the fashion of a jigsaw puzzle. You will need patience, and a quick eye to grasp the sizes and shapes of the pieces of stone lying about you. There is no need to leave deliberate gaps between the slabs, the gaps will come unavoidably of themselves quite often enough. Aim at getting the stones as closely together as you can. A rock plant can grow quite well from a crevice just $\frac{1}{2}$ in. wide, providing soil is good—and most of the time you will not be able to fit your stones together as closely as that. Try not to have gaps wider than a couple of inches, however.

As you are sure to have definite boundaries or outlines for your crazy paving you must settle these at the outset, while you have your biggest choice of stone. For example, you may be planning to have a circular flower-bed left in the middle of your paving. Do not work towards the centre, hoping to make your circle with the final stones; make sure of the circle first, and then work away from it. Do not break any stones until you have tried every possible bit of juggling with the available pieces; large slabs are always preferable to small ones—they look better, are stronger, and keep their position more safely.

In order to get your paving flat and even you must be careful of the bedding of each stone. The cement method is easy enough—each slab is laid on cement in the same way as a mason lays a brick. But in the other types of paving the stones must be put down in soil.

Level your garden surface with great care, removing all stones on which your slabs will be liable to "ride." Then roll the ground until it is well settled. This rolling will very likely make the surface quite uneven again, so that you will need to go over it with a spade, levelling the hollows and bumps. Roll it again after this, and continue until you are satisfied that the ground is really firm and settled. Next go over with a fork, to the depth of 2 or 3 in. and finally rake over until the top is level once more. Thus you will have a stretch of fine, soft soil, and a good foundation, and you will find that your stones will settle in firmly, and yet have a level surface at the end.

Laying the Slabs.—Have all your slabs spread out close at hand, so that you can pick out the requisite pieces readily. Do not step on the soil ; keep on the stone which is already laid, or run a plank across so that it just clears the surface.

Use your largest slabs in those sections of your paving which are likely to be traversed most frequently; and fit your final pieces in some unimportant corner, for at the end the slabs are likely to be small and the gaps between less regular than you would wish. Having finished, the interstices will be filled in with fine soil, or ashes—shovel and broom will best do the work.

If rain comes early so much the better, for it will harden down your soil and settle the stone firmly. Perhaps some of your small slabs may need taking out and re-bedding, for naturally they are more likely to sink than the large pieces. And almost certainly you will need more and more soil for the crevices.

An alternative method of making crazy paving is to put down a flat cement surface, and then scratch imitation crevices in it, possibly filling them with black cement.

Rockeries.—No garden nowadays is complete without some form of rockery. This is easy enough to understand, for the rockery has that natural, quiet beauty which can so easily be missing in the formal layout of a new garden; when once a rockery is in good condition, it needs but little attention. Still another reason for popularity is that the rockery can look almost equally attractive in winter and summer, for severe weather conditions have little effect on many attractive alpine and other suitable plants.

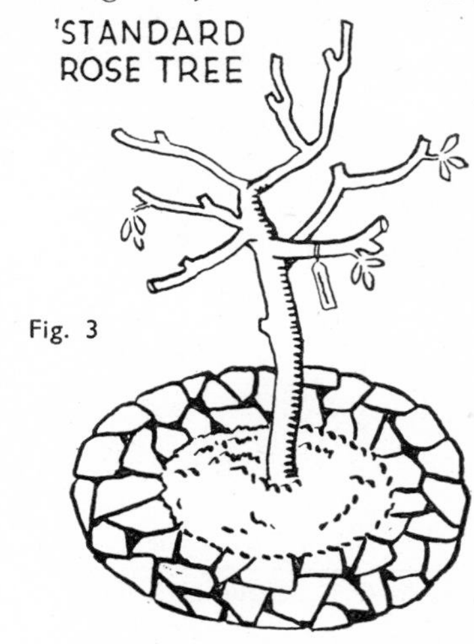

CRAZY PAVING EDGING

It is not enough to pile some earth and scatter a few stones on top ; that does not make a rockery. You should remember that you are trying to imitate nature, so that your plants may grow in ideal conditions, but in a seemingly natural state.

Rockeries are of several kinds, but all of them require rock, or stone—and a surprising lot of it, too. Your own locality will determine the way you procure your stone. The demolition of old walls or buildings often gives opportunity for loads merely at the cost of carting; a builder or road contractor may have stocks conveniently at hand; you may collect odd lumps until you have enough for your purpose; or there may be a quarry close at hand where you can actually pick and choose the shape, size and colour of your material.

Remember, in buying stones, that carting will cost as much or more than the material itself.

Avoid flat stones, of the kind frequently used in building walls. Large irregular lumps are what you want. As far as possible your rockery should give the appearance of natural masses of rock out-cropping from the ground, and obviously straight-cut stuff, broken paving, old bricks, and that sort of thing, are quite unsuitable. You must have good-sized pieces, too—little stones are covered too easily with soil or plants.

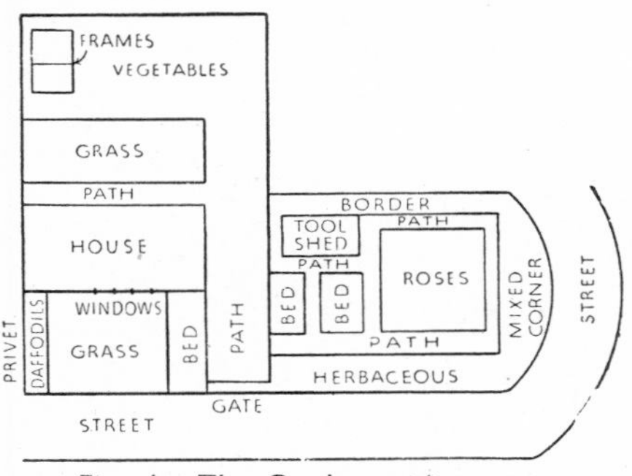

Fig. 4.—The Garden as it was

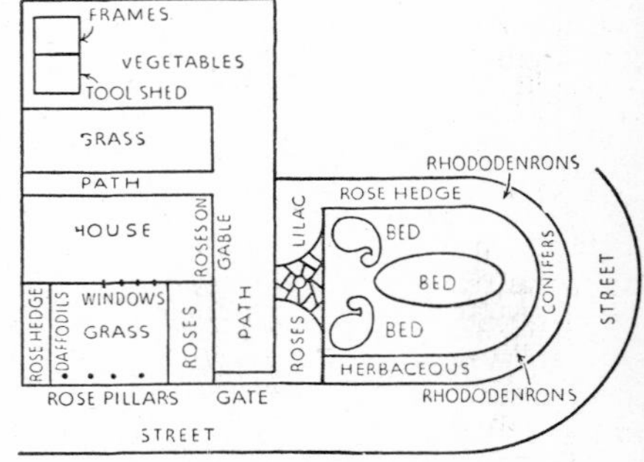

Fig. 5.—The same improved

Preferably your stone should be all of a sort: you do not want jarring colour contrasts. There is such a wide range of shades, even in common kinds of stone, that if you are planning a number of rockeries, suitably scattered, it is very interesting to use different material for each.

The following are the commonest kinds of rockeries: corner, border, mound, single-face wall, double-face wall, edging or flat. When planning, always try to visualize the rockery as it will eventually appear draped with foliage and flowers, not merely as the stone structure which you will see when you have done your preliminary work. And do not think, either, just of the ground space, but of the appearance from other parts of the garden and from the upper as well as the lower windows of your house.

The Corner.—A shady corner is a problem in a good many gardens. Few things seem to thrive in it, yet it is untidy. A corner rockery is often a happy solution.

Should your fences be of wood it will be advisable to begin by building up some protection to keep the soil clear—slates will serve, old bits of asbestos roofing, flat stones, galvanized iron. Then, having got this protection in position, fill the back corner to a depth of a foot or so with rubble, to enable the water to drain away. Above this put smaller stones to fill the crevices, and finally soil. Use good soil, free from weeds, and build the approximate shape of your rockery with it.

Lastly begin to insert your masses of stone over the face. You may have tier above tier, fairly symmetrical, but not too regular. Have plenty of soil between, and gradually slant backwards until you reach the apex of your pyramid. See that your stones have the air of protruding from the soil rather than just lying on it.

The Border.—This type of rockery looks very attractive when stretching along the edge of path or lawn, facing on to it. The rockery may be 3 ft. wide and 2 ft. high at the back, sloping down to the ground level at the front. Build your framework first, so that you have a sort of stone box into which you can fill your other material. The back wall may consist of piled lumps, or perhaps flat slabs standing edgeways. Should your rockery, however, be seen from both sides you will need just single stones all round, for your highest point will then be the middle instead of the back.

Spread some rubble in the bottom, for drainage, and then fill in with soil to the desired height, remembering to allow a good deal for the inevitable settling. As in the corner rockery, try to get the appearance of shelving ledges of rock, rather than a bed of soil over which a few stones are strewed. The stones, of course, should be more conspicuous than the soil.

The Mound can be of any size or height. It forms a pleasant change from the ordinary small flower-bed.

Having made your rubble foundation, build up with soil and add your stones to the surface, filling gaps also with soil. Let your stones incline inwards so that water runs to the centre and not to the outside.

The mound rockery looks especially attractive in the middle of a lawn, or similar places where it can be viewed from every side. It will look better still if you put a fountain or sculptured figure of suitable size in the middle of it.

A Single-face Wall.—It is often desired to cover up a brick boundary or an unsightly fence, and for this purpose the single-face wall rockery is ideal. Providing the bottom is sufficiently broad you may continue it up to any height. Of course, the front face of your rockery should slope backwards, thus allowing for more soil behind and adding to the stability of your stones, which have only the soil to hold them in place.

If you are building against a wood fence have some sort of protection behind, as described for the corner rockery, and try not to allow too much weight to press against the fence.

Put in your lowest tier of stones, placing them not too closely together. Fill between them, and on top, with good soil, then add your next lot of stones. Do not have your tiers too regular.

See that the top surface of every stone slopes backwards, as mentioned for the mound, so that water falling on the front edge drains into the wall and reaches the roots of your plants. Should your stones be flat, or sloping forward rain will drain out.

The Double-face Wall.—A flat garden becomes much more interesting and attractive if it is broken up into several sections, so that the whole of it cannot be seen at once. Ornamental brick walls covered with creepers serve well, but better still is the high, double-faced rockery wall. You may have such a wall from 2 ft. in height upwards.

Start with a wide enough base, for both sides must slope inwards quite markedly, and yet this tapering should not bring the top of the wall to a lesser width than about 9 in. Build on the same principle of the sloping stones, to carry water to the centre,

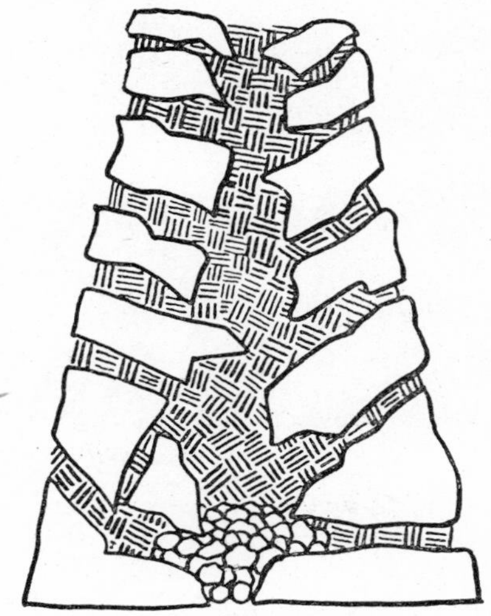

Fig. 6.—Double-face Wall

as for the single-face wall; and get in drainage rubble at the base.

Take care as you build that the soil is well packed—you do not want air cavities into which roots may later find their way. It may help to water thoroughly as you go along, if the soil be very dry. Large clumps of bulbs may be put in as you build, smaller bulbs and roots can be planted more conveniently afterwards.

When your wall is finished you may have a few flat stones on the top, on which to stand flower pots or ornaments.

The Edging or Flat Rockery.—These are often useful in lining a path,

Fig. 7.—A Children's Cubby-hole

surrounding a pond or giving variety to a large flower-bed, where a more elaborate structure would be unsuitable. You need no more than rough lumps of stone set down over the desired area. Have them large enough and frequent enough to show up well, and then put rockery and alpine plants in the surrounding soil, so that they grow over.

Sunken Gardens are useful in giving interest and variety to an otherwise flat garden surface; and also are the most satisfactory method of dealing with a garden that slopes steeply or is very uneven.

A suitable depth for a sunken garden is 1 to 3 ft., and if it is sunk from a flat surface, so that it has a bank on each side, you will have to cut a path through into it, or make suitable steps. Drainage will also have to be considered—it may be necessary to have gullies running to a soakaway.

The bottom of your sunken garden may have flower-beds with paths, or be entirely covered by crazy paving or turf. A pool, fountain or ornament, makes a good centre-piece. The sides of your garden can be dry stone walls or rockery walls, or merely banked earth. In a formal little garden, flat walls of uncemented stones look well if their front edges are straight and the stones fairly dark.

An appearance of breadth can be given to a sunken garden by banking the ground well round it. Your aim should always be to get such a level that when you are inside the rest of the garden cannot easily be seen.

Try to get as much contrast as possible between the sunken part and the neighbouring portions of your garden—in layout, style, colour scheme, perfumes, and so on.

In digging a sunken garden it is good to begin with your boundaries. Sink a trench all round to the required depth, and then level through. Remember that every bit of ground removed has to be replaced somewhere, and so plan to deal with it by working out simultaneous schemes for banks, rockeries, mounds, levelled lawn. If you get assistance for the work, a builder's labourer will be much more useful than an ordinary gardener, for the actual excavating.

Ornaments.—A suitable selection can add much to the interest and beauty of a garden, but see that colour, style, size are all in keeping.

Sundials are perhaps the commonest, and most often inappropriate, for they need to be set in old-time gardens. Bird baths and fountains can be found to harmonize with almost anything—but do not forget that they need water, which may involve at least a little daily attention. A dry bird bath is an absurdity, so is a fountain which never plays. Human figures can err most easily in size, especially if stood on pedestals—there is a grotesque effect if the figure is either too small or too large. The same applies, almost equally, to animals, reptiles or birds. With all live creatures, particularly when several are used together, you must have a sense of proportion.

The wilder the garden the rougher the material of your ornaments should be. The little painted gnomes, or mountain men, however, suit almost any secluded spot.

If you have already a fair amount of stone work in a new garden, in crazy paving and rockeries, it will not be advisable to buy too many bare ornaments until plants and flowers are beginning to cover the first stages. Even then you may first have flower vases and bowls which can introduce such splashes of colour as geraniums and fuchsias.

In setting up any heavy ornament, for instance in a flower-bed, do not place it directly on the soil. Excavate first, and put in two or three layers of bricks, getting them dead level, then place your ornament on top. There is no need to cement the bricks, the replaced soil will keep them in position and cover them adequately. In setting a sundial it will be easiest to place it in position just at noon, allowing, if necessary, for summer time.

Rustic Work looks well providing it is in good condition; when wood is rotted and nails are rusted it can give an air of dilapidation and neglect to an otherwise well-kept garden. So be sure in the first place that you have sound spars that will be hard wearing. Do not use scraps of dead branches picked up from beneath trees, but approach some wood-cutter or hedge-cutter, and get his advice about local timbers.

Have sturdy uprights, for wood rots more easily in the ground than out of it. All ends of supports must be tarred to 3 in. above ground. With trellis work, arches, and similar fitments of sawn wood you should always use some preservative—give them a good dose, for once they are overgrown it is unlikely that you will be able to treat them again.

If you buy galvanized wire arches, over which to trail ramblers, see that they are strong enough. A heavy rambler can cause a flimsy structure to collapse. To keep such an arch rigid and upright, you may drive a piece of iron or piping into the ground, and secure the side of the arch to it.

Summer Houses and arbours are less popular than they used to be. Perhaps it would be more accurate to say that the old types of structures are less popular. They seem to be so often gloomy little places cut off both from air and light, and often swarming with insects. The up-to-date summer house has for its chief purpose the providing of shade, without the loss of that "fresh air feeling."

In a small garden the position and size of a summer house matters a good deal. You do not want to take up valuable space, but you do want to have the most pleasant view available, which generally means that the greater part of the garden must be visible from the front of your little building. Since corners are always something of a problem it is an excellent plan to build your summer house into the corner. This will give you the necessary diagonal view, if your garden is square or rectangular, and at the same time will utilize a bit of space that would probably be otherwise wasted. Besides, since your structure will be so much out of the way it will appear to take up less room.

Of course you may buy a summer house ready made, of any shape or size, but it is much more interesting to build it yourself.

Get level framework and joists first, and rest it on small brick piers rather than on the earth itself, for this will give air space underneath and prevent the joists and floor rotting. Treat all wood with preservative. Then build up your framework according to taste, taking care to keep all square. For the roof you may have boards, felt, slates, tiles, iron, asbestos, thatch. Have plenty of seating inside, and a lot of open window space. Fig. 8 suggests methods of dealing with corner summer houses. This is a simple triangular structure, open at the front, and with a plain roof sloping from front to back. Fig. 9 shows a slightly more elaborate design with window and door entrances.

One of the most attractive types of summer house, which needs, however, to stand more in the middle of a garden, is that which rests on pivot or runners, and so can be turned round to face in any direction as sun or wind vary.

If you have young children, and wish to encourage them to stay in the open air, build them a cubby-hole. This can take almost any form, but one of the best and most convenient types is a large, open-fronted box-like structure, raised 3 ft. or 4 ft. above the ground. It should be large enough for at least a couple of children to sit in comfortably. It may have two methods of entry—a ladder, and a smooth sloping plank down which a youngster can slide or crawl (Fig. 7).

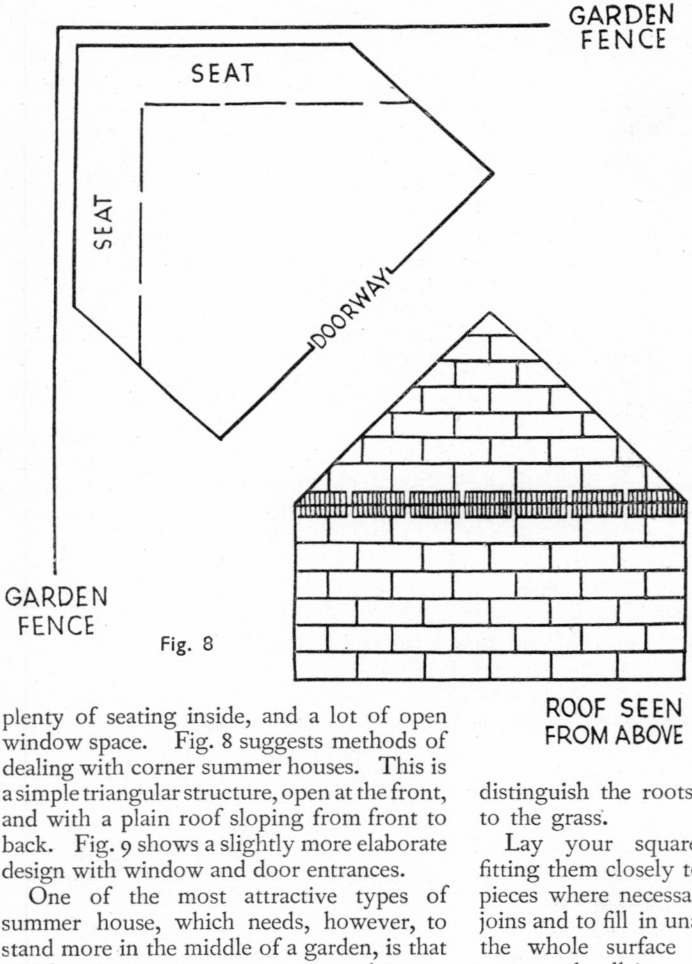

GARDEN FENCE
SEAT
SEAT
DOORWAY
GARDEN FENCE
ROOF SEEN FROM ABOVE

Fig. 8

Lawns.—A lawn, however small, is an essential part of the modern garden. You may make a lawn in three ways: turfing, working it up from rough grass, by seed.

Turf.—See that the turf is of good quality before you get it, and have it well cut. The ground should be levelled and prepared, and you should be quite sure that your lawn site is adequately drained, especially if it is clay soil.

Before laying each piece of turf unroll and examine it; from the underside you may pull out weeds by the roots—a much more effective way than trying to pull them up by the leaves the following year. It is an easy matter to distinguish the roots which do not belong to the grass.

Lay your squares of turf carefully, fitting them closely together, and slicing off pieces where necessary so as to have clean joins and to fill in unavoidable gaps. When the whole surface is finished you may water and roll it.

Providing that you get good turf, this method of making a lawn gives least trouble and best results. One big advantage is the short time in which the lawn is ready for use.

Fig. 9.—An Open Summer House at the end of a small garden

From the Rough.—If it is fairly level the making of a rough piece of ground into an attractive lawn is not too difficult a business. Patience is the chief requisite. You must keep on clearing the ground of weeds and coarse grass, and continue cutting and rolling, until you get the desired fine, level surface. Suitable fertilizers will help, and you may put in grass seeds. If any levelling has to be done it is better to leave this until the turf is in good condition—though naturally conspicuous mounds or hollows may have to be dealt with early.

Seed.—Autumn is the best time for making a lawn from seed, and the seed should be put in some time after the middle of August, for at this time of the year the soil is warm and there is a likelihood of sufficient rain to assist growth. Additionally, weeds are less prevalent than in the spring, so that your grass will have a chance of developing some sturdiness before the weeds come to life in the early part of the year. Do not delay sowing seed beyond the middle of October.

If spring, however, is warm and showery, you may make your lawn then, sowing from March to May. But cold winds and bad weather may be a serious disadvantage. Often spring-sown grass does not show before three weeks or a month, while autumn seeds may be sprouting in five to ten days.

Level your ground, removing as many stones and weeds as possible. If the soil is too heavy it is advisable to dig in sand, fine cinders, or something similar; if it is too light a few inches of loamy soil should be added. Some manure or fertilizer should be spread before putting in the seed, and the surface of the ground should finally be raked and trodden until it is firm and level, and free from any clods. Then sow your seed, using the best quality seed you can—for if you get cheap stuff you will probably be buying weeds as well as grass.

Sow on a calm, dry day, and immediately afterwards rake and cross-rake the surface, so that the seeds may be covered. You can then go over lightly with a roller.

Fix up some kind of bird-scarer—rags, tinkling pieces of glass, or something of the sort.

Watch for weeds, and remove them carefully. When the young grass is up sufficiently cut it with a mower in good condition—blunt blades may tear out the tiny plants. You may begin cutting when the grass is $1\frac{1}{2}$ in. high, and it is important that you go on cutting and rolling with regularity. Should bare patches appear, sprinkle a little seed mixed with fine soil, and pat it lightly into position with a spade.

Upkeep.—Wage constant war on weeds. You may dig out or pull most of them, but with such things as dandelions and plantains the chances are you will leave bits of the root in the ground, to come up as strongly as ever later on. But there are plenty of preparations available for killing weeds and by far the best plan is to use these.

The other principal aspects of garden planning—flowers, fruit, vegetables—are each dealt with in separate sections.

GARDEN PONDS

THE artificial pond is becoming increasingly popular, for it is adaptable to any type of garden. In size it can vary from a sunken bucket or tub to the small lake. But all ponds can have similar interest and fascination; there is so much variety—water lilies, aquatic plants, fish, and so on—and the interest remains through almost the entire year.

In constructing a pond for yourself you will naturally be influenced, as to its size, by the available space and the proportions of your garden. Take into consideration also, however, the type of objects you intend to breed or grow. The potentialities of the large shallow pool and the small deep one are quite different, even though the volume of water may be the same in each.

Water Plants. — There are roughly two kinds of water plants, the ornamental and the useful. By far the most popular of the former are water lilies. These, with the exception of a few dwarf varieties, usually need 2 ft. to 3 ft. of water if they are to grow happily. Other ornamental plants are the flowering aquatics—there are a great many of these which grow in even 6 in. of water, providing there is suitable soil at the bottom for their roots. There are also grasses, bog plants, and others which can do with even less depth, and are generally used round a pond with shallow edges to make an ornamental fringe. A number of attractive and ornamental plants are known as floating aquatics. They get their nourishment from the water; no soil is required for their trailing roots, and quite a trifling depth is sufficient.

The second variety of water plants, those which are primarily useful, are mostly submerged, and grow in almost any depth. Some of these are essential in a pond where fish or reptiles are kept, for they give a constant supply of oxygen to the water, and help to keep it clean, besides providing shelter for fishes.

Fish.—You may have fish and other live things in a pond. Clearly large fish need a large pond. Not only size but number of fish must be determined by your volume of water. A rough method of calculation is to allow 1 in. of fish to a cubic foot of water, i.e. in 9 cubic feet you could have two $4\frac{1}{2}$ in. fish or a shoal of nine "tiddlers," snails, frogs, newts, and such-like, which are very useful as scavengers. (*See* AQUARIA.)

The pond containing livestock naturally requires more attention than the one having only plants, but it is correspondingly more interesting. When you have settled on the type of pond you desire your first business will be to find a site for it.

The Site.—You should imitate nature as far as possible. Should there be some part of your garden towards which the rest of the ground slopes down, then that should be your choice. It must not, however, be in the shade; aquatic plants, like many others that bear flowers, need a great deal of sunshine.

It is possible to make your pond of clay, but the necessary quantity and quality are rarely obtainable; concrete is better.

Excavating the Pond. — Mark your outline with pegs, and give it careful consideration in respect to the character of the rest of the garden. Ponds of irregular shape are becoming increasingly popular, though if your garden is of formal character the round, rectangular, or octagonal pool may be more in keeping. Whatever shape you prefer, do not fail to allow six inches all round when you begin to dig, though a little less may do for a very small pond. If the pool is to be really large it will be advisable to dig a trench round the outline first, a foot or two wide and down to the required depth. The edges of this on the outer side can then be boarded or shored up and you can set about removing the island of soil in the middle. Remember that freshly dug soil takes up much more space than it did when packed in the ground, so have sufficient disposal room for it. In levelling your bottom through allow the same extra inches as for the sides.

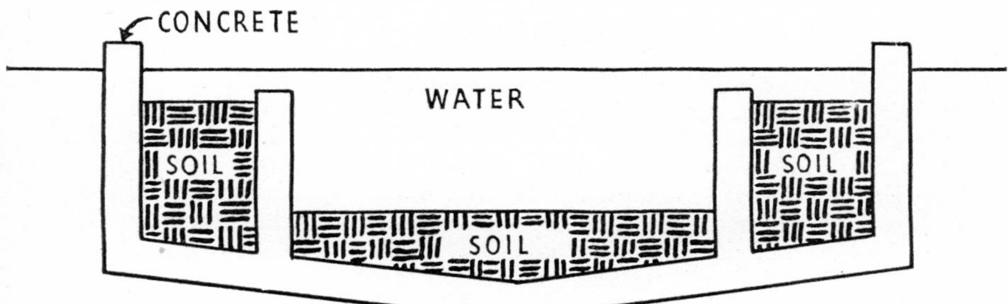

Fig. 1.—Diagram showing different depths of pond

The next thing is to ram down the soil of the finished hole until it is level and firm. At this stage you must settle whether or not you intend to have a drainage pipe by which you can empty the pond. The fixing of it involves some trouble, but since any pond must be emptied once or twice a year you must consider whether you are prepared to tackle the job with a bucket —which would probably be the alternative. And it is a small pond which does not hold a hundred buckets of water! If you are to have the pipe this must rise to the bottom of the pond where it is fitted with a plug. From the pond it runs down either to a drain, or to a soakaway—a deep hole filled with rubble and covered by soil. Whether or not you have the drainage pipe you certainly must allow for one part of the bottom to be lower than the rest, so that the water will naturally flow down into it when you are emptying by pipe or baling out.

Mixing the Cement.—Having put in your soakaway and pipe, if required, you will be ready for the concrete mixing. For the small pond three parts of sand with one of cement is the best proportion; for the larger pool you may have one part sand, one part stone chippings, one part cement. Mix this dry on a large, clean board, and gradually add water to the middle until the whole is of a fairly moist consistency. Then, with this mixture, line the walls and sides of your pond to a depth of three or four inches, pressing it down firmly but gently so that no air remains in it. Should the sides of your pond be steep and high it may be necessary to have boards along to keep the cement in place until it has dried. For a very large pond a carefully constructed boarding, preferably of matchboard, will be required. However, if your walls are no more than 6 in. in height this will be unnecessary providing your concrete mixture is reasonably stiff.

For the pond of average size you will find the most convenient method of working is to stand in the middle, and gradually to work towards your own feet, until at last you step out and put the finishing touches from a plank laid across. Be sure that the thickness of the concrete does not lessen anywhere.

A pond is much improved if, round its edge, it has a shallow ledge, indicated in the diagram, 4 in. to 6 in. below the water surface, and varying in width according to the pond measurements. On this ledge grow grasses, shallow bog plants, and such like. This ledge may be either excavated like the original hole and lined over with concrete, or it may be left with only the open soil for its bottom.

Stocking the Pond.—On several successive days you should put some water in the pool and thoroughly scrub the concrete. Then fill the pool to the brim with water in which you have dissolved enough permanganate of potash to make it a deep pink. Let this stand for ten days or a fortnight, and by this time it will have effectually neutralized the poisonous elements in the concrete. Empty once more and scrub and rinse afresh to remove any stains.

Now the pond will be ready for use.

If you fill from a tap, do not put plants or fish in until the water has stood for a few days to get aerated and warmed.

Water Lilies.—It is advisable to get catalogues from one or two leading aquatic dealers in order that you may study the plants best suited for your particular pond. There is such a wide variety that you may have almost any size or colour. Here are some particularly lovely kinds:

Odorata maxima—snow white, beautiful cup-shaped flowers with bold golden-yellow centre; *Marliacea albida*—white flowers, large and upright, frequently stained pink near the base, dark green foliage, delicious perfume, very early flowering; *Candidissima rosea*—soft rose shade, nicely scented, large globular flowers; *Fabiola*—clear pink flaked with white towards the tips of the petals, pale green foliage, big flowers, prolific from May till October; *Lucida*—pale pink deepening to vermilion, olive-green foliage marbled with bronze maroon, very large star-shaped flowers; *Venusta*—bright rose-pink flowers with saffron-yellow stamens, very fragrant; *Andreyana*—red shaded ochre, leaves spotted maroon, flowers stand high out of water; *Phoenix*—deep rose changing to brilliant crimson, large bell-shaped flowers; *Chrysantha*—soft yellow passing to vermilion, small flowers in profusion, pretty mottled foliage, suitable for shallow water; *Moorei*—canary-yellow, pale green foliage spotted purple, large open flowers; *Paul Heriot*—soft copper-rose, medium-size flowers.

For shallow pool or tub culture:

Laydeckeri purpurata—deep rosy-crimson orange-red stamens; *Odorata alba*—snow-white flowers, very fragrant, pale green foliage; *Pygmaea helvola*—soft sulphur-yellow, olive-green foliage mottled maroon, profuse with tiny flowers.

Soil is needed for planting lilies, and it must be the right sort of soil. The best mixture is good loam clay, heavy and fibrous, together with well-rotted cow manure. Do not use sand, leaf mould, or fresh manure, or sour soil from ponds or rivers—which will almost certainly contain troublesome water weeds. Coarse bone meal may be added instead of cow manure.

The whole bed of your pond may be covered with this soil to a depth of six inches or more, or you may have sufficient soil for each separate plant: the best way to arrange this latter is to set your lily in a rush or wire basket—any fishmonger can supply a rush basket (he gets large fish packed in them). Put in about three inches of soil, then the roots of your plant, and finally fill the basket. Have the soil firm and tight. If you have no basket a box will do. Whether or not you cover the bottom of the pond with soil you should allow each lily about one cubic foot of soil.

Have a variety of plants if possible, but do not crowd your pool. Lilies should have at least three feet between them; once they have settled they will grow so much that you may later have to divide up their roots because of their increasing size.

Water lilies require comparatively little attention once they are rooted. You should occasionally wash the foliage with a syringe or hose, particularly in the early part of the warm weather when the black fly is likely to make its appearance. This fly is a great pest, but if it is washed off the leaves into the pool the fish will soon make an end of it.

Water lilies should be planted not earlier than the middle of April, for about this time the plants are beginning to grow vigorously.

Tub Culture.—Small portions of root-stock with buds or young individual plants may be grown in tubs placed in a sunny corner of the garden (Fig. 2). The diagram shows method of growing. Clean water must be added from time to time.

Edging Plants.—On the shallow edges of your pond it is sufficient to have just a couple of inches of heavy loam. The smaller plants flourish here, their purpose being to add attractiveness to the pool edge. Here are some suitable for this purpose:

Acorus calamus—fragrant, more graceful and slender than the ordinary iris, long blade-like foliage; *Carex pendula*—good for small clumps, tall, with tassel-like flowers; *Eulalia gracillima*—a striking ornamental grass; *Myriophillum*—submerged hair-like foliage which sometimes turns red; *Ranunculus flammula*—spear-like foliage, useful and adaptable; *Veronica beccabunga*—oval, glossy leaves and tiny flowers of bright blue.

Aerating Plants.—You will have also to consider the submerged oxygenating plants, which are necessary to keep the water pure and clean, by absorbing the impurities and giving out oxygen—which is so essential if you are to have fish in your pond. Here are a few useful aquatic plants of this type:

Cabomba aquatica—this has attractive yellow flowers; *Cabomba Caroliniana*—an

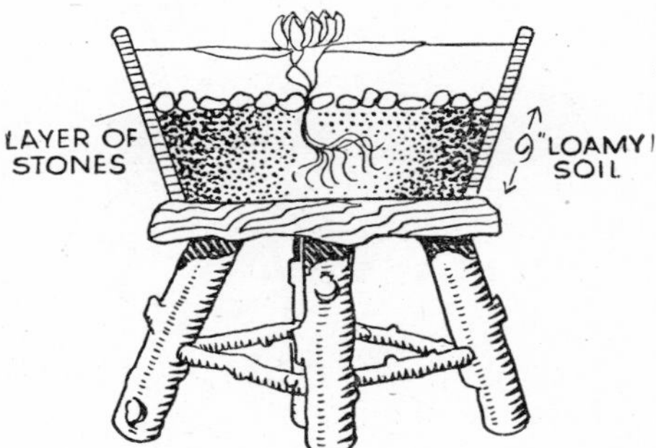

Fig. 2.—Growing Water Lilies in Tubs

excellent oxygenator, fern-like greenery beneath the water and dainty white flowers which rise just above the surface; *Chara foetida*—bristly whorls of bronze foliage, said to keep away mosquitoes; *Elodea callitrichioides*—pea-green foliage, gives useful protection for your fish; *Elodea densa*—dark green foliage, stout stems, splendid oxygenator; *Mentha aquatica*—scent like that of garden mint, most useful for keeping water clear, whorls of lilac flowers; *Myriophyllum spicatum*—tangled masses of slender, many-branched stems, leaves consisting of hair-like segments, slender spikes of greenish flowers; *Sagittaria grimineus*—grass-like leaves, excellent oxygenator; *Sagittaria sinensis*—splendid oxygenator, spikes of white flowers standing high out of the water.

Fish.—Having got your plants thoroughly settled you may think about fish. Of course, you may put fish in earlier, but without suitable plants to give shade, shelter, and purity to the water it is much more difficult to keep them in good condition.

The most popular fish are: *gold fish*—

well known because of its attractive colour, but not so hardy as the next mentioned; *golden orfe*—hardy, active, graceful, of rich salmon-pink, very pretty in shoals, stands the winter well; *primrose fish*—yellow-gold colour, vigorous, showy, keeps healthy in winter; *silver orfe*—less striking than the golden orfe, but pretty and graceful.

Fig. 3.—Water Buttercup—an oxygenator

Besides fish you should consider for your pond the introduction of various other creatures as scavengers and food for your fish. There are many possibilities—water fleas, fresh-water shrimps, aquatic snails, newts, water tortoises, fly larvæ, and so on.

The ramshorn snail, *planorbis corneus*, is one of the best scavengers, and a number of them in your pond will get rid of any food left by the fishes.

It is best to get advice on the complete stocking of your pond from some aquatic dealer. In this manner you may get a well-balanced selection at a moderate inclusive price.

Care of Fish.—If fish are to stay healthy they need some care. Their food, for instance, must be twice as plentiful in summer as in winter, for with the rising temperature of the water activity and appetite increase. Meals should be regular. If proper fish food is supplied as much as can be heaped upon a threepenny-piece is ample for two 3-in. gold fish for one day in summer. Such a meal would suffice every other day in winter. If food is placed on a small platform some inches below the surface it can be seen if the fish are leaving any ; food left uneaten is bad for the purity of the pond. By always feeding at the same spot also one can readily attract the fish, if you desire to see them or to show them to a friend. Golden orfe and gold fish are very fond of nibbling at floating pieces of bread.

When the dorsal fin of a gold fish droops it is a sign of sickness—probably some Epsom salt crystals dropped into the water instead of food will prove a remedy; if you find fish gasping at the surface it may be that you have too many in the pond, or the water is not being sufficiently oxygenated; fish attacked by fungus should be instantly removed—they may already have infected others; be sure in hot weather that you have enough shade, the shallower the water the warmer it will become under the hot sun—if the plant life of your pond is inadequate to give your fish the protection they need then several slabs of wood may be floated on the surface, temporarily, and the fish will be able to shelter under these.

Fig. 4.—Freshwater Mussel

Fig. 5.—Great Water Beetles

Scavengers for the Pond

Do not be surprised if everything does not go well with your pond at first. There is so much to learn about conditions of life in the water, and it will be surprising if you do not have some casualties among the plants and inhabitants of your pond. But profit by experience and you will find your hobby one of increasing fascination.

Other information bearing on similar topics is in the section AQUARIA of this book.

GREENHOUSES

The ideal type of house is the span roof. If this is placed in a sunny position with gables facing north and south and sides east and west the plants will have the best conditions possible. A lean-to house is good for growing fruit against a wall but is less suitable for flowers. It is, however, cheaper. Not so usual is the three-quarter span. This has a span roof with one side longer than the other, the short side dipping down to a wall which is shorter than in the other type of lean-to.

Any of those houses is better and more durable if built on a one-brick or two-brick foundation, with a bottom of cement and rubble, to the depth of about 18 in. These, however, are not regarded as tenant's fixtures, and where the house is rented, wooden structures with wooden posts fixed in the ground with rubber ring joints in the piping and boiler connections are preferable. Bolts and rubber-rings for erecting are usually supplied by firms who sell sectional buildings ready to erect and easily transported if necessary.

Heating Apparatus. — The heating apparatus should be bought from a reliable firm and built in by a capable engineer. There are many good makes of boiler on the market, supplied in sizes suitable for the amateur's greenhouse. These small upright boilers are built into the wall of the house, usually at the left-hand side of the door in houses of about 12 ft. by 7 ft., or 10 ft. by 7 ft., both convenient sizes for the small garden. A water jacket surrounds the boiler on three sides and top and connected with it are the pipes, the feed from the water supply cistern and the inflow and return pipes which go round the house at floor level. Three-inch piping is used for going round the house, about 40 ft. of piping being sufficient for a cool house about 12 ft. by 7 ft.; this giving a temperature of 45 degs. F. Ten to 20 feet more are required for a warm house, the hotter the house the larger the boiler and the greater the length of piping required. It is safer to allow more piping and a larger boiler than is actually required for the house, whatever the temperature desired, as it is better to ventilate than to overtax the boiler; the extra piping also gives one some latitude in regulating the temperature. These precautions also obviate the risk of accidents as an overworked boiler can be very dangerous as well as a lot of trouble in stoking. The return pipe should be set lower than the outflow and it is necessary to set both pipes so that there is a gradual rise from the boiler of about 1 in. in every 6 ft. An air pipe is set at the end of the inflow pipe. The piping of a span-roof house usually runs all round, but in a lean-to of small size it is usually placed along the front. The position of the piping has a good deal to do with the distribution of the heat, but for general purposes these rules are correct. Where, however, there is a cold side to a house, more piping will be necessary. If you wish to have a warmer section which can be used for raising seedlings, this should be supplied with enough piping to give at least 10 degs. extra heat and, in this case, the pipes should be fitted with valves so that the heat can be shut off or regulated as required, according to the season or the plants occupying that part of the greenhouse.

The Water Cistern may be situated near the boiler but must always be placed so that it is higher than any of the pipes. This cistern must be kept full. In small systems this is often done with a watering-can but a ball-cock is safer ; that works automatically and is connected with water pipes which supply the water tank, situated under the staging for watering. This is, of course, only possible when water is led into the house from the mains or from the house.

Fuel.—Coal, coke or dross, i.e. small pieces of coal, are suitable for using in the boiler fire, but smokeless anthracite broken into very small pieces is best. Oil heaters and gas are also procurable, but

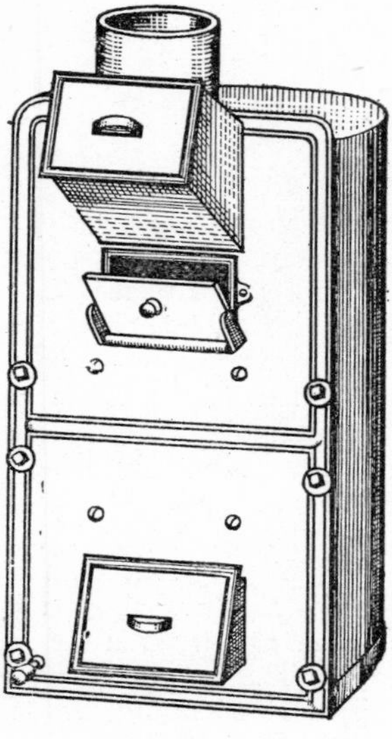

Small Boiler for Heating Greenhouse

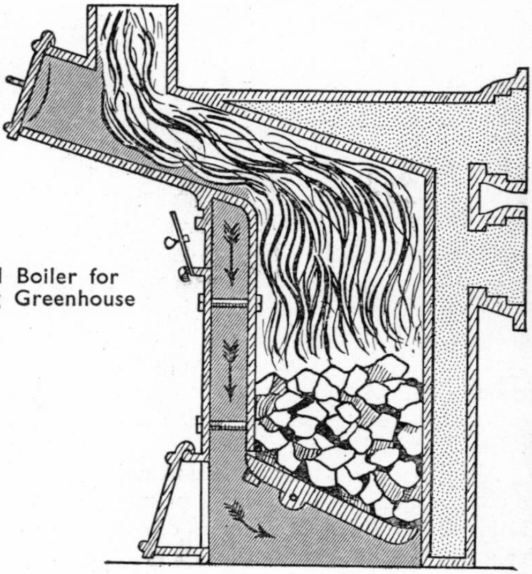

Fig. 1.—Front View

Fig. 2.—Section

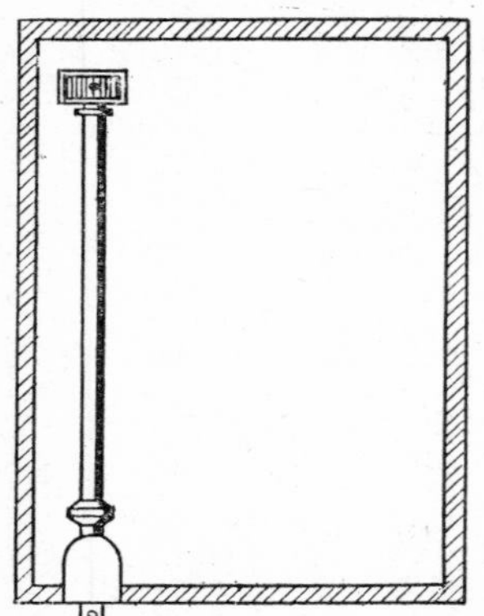
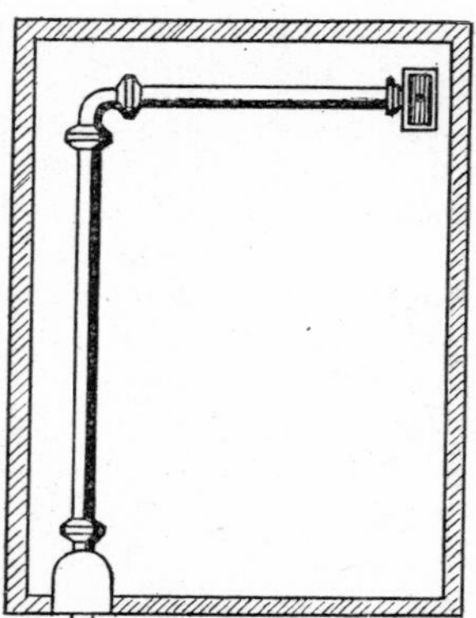
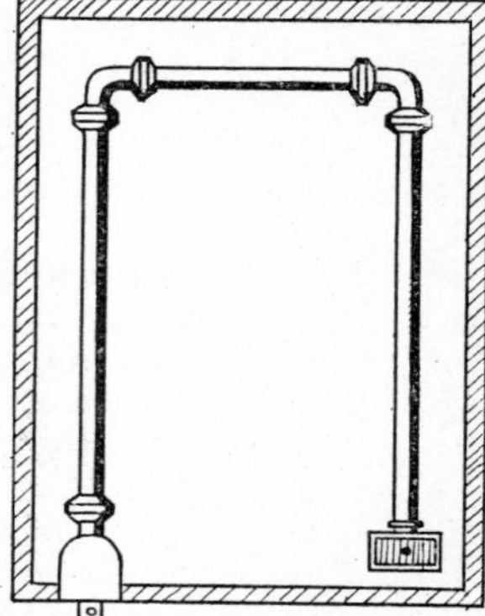

Fig. 3.—Arrangement of Boiler and Pipes

neither so economical or so suitable as coal, anthracite or coke. The hot-water system is best, as there are no harmful fumes such as might be from oil or gas.

Electricity is being introduced for heating greenhouses, but it cannot yet surpass the hot-water system. It is, however, eminently suitable for a cold house, which is used to shelter chrysanthemums just before being put into a warmer house for winter display. In one very simple system wiring is put round the house in tubing. This tubing enters the pipes which radiate the heat. The heat is governed by a thermostat which switches on automatically at 40 degrees and cuts itself off at 50. The advantage of this is very great on frosty nights. The cost depends on the local price of electricity unless you live in the country and make your own. As dry air is more suitable in winter than in summer this type of heating can be recommended for

Fig. 4.—A large Greenhouse with Central Staging

plants only needing protection against frost. Choice Alpines can be protected over winter in this way.

The Warm House which ranges from 50 degs. F. to 75 degs. F. is the best for general use. In it seedlings and tender cuttings can be raised. A very wide choice of plants is also possible and if a range of frames runs alongside it with pipes, or even just open boles through which the heat from the house can pass to them, a great quantity of material can be grown both for house and garden. These boles must be supplied with swivel wooden shutters so that they can be opened or closed.

Arrangement and Management.—The staging in a span roof should run round the house and down the centre, the side tables being about 2½ ft. wide, the central staging being as wide as space allows. This, of course, applies only to a large house. A small house has usually staging all round and only a path of about 2½ ft. down the centre. The height of staging depends on the height of plants that are to be grown, but do not have the staging too low: this is very trying on the back. The base of the staging should be of wood covered with galvanized sheeting, to hold a bed of moist sand covered with pea gravel. This is the best way of maintaining the moist atmosphere which plants revel in. A visit to a public botanic garden is very instructive. Notice the type of house, the temperature, and the method of staging the respective plants, for each amateur grower has his preferences. Orchids, some of which are not beyond the reach of the amateur, need quite a different kind of staging and treatment from ferns or pelargoniums. A friendly talk with one of the gardeners is also very enlightening.

Maintenance.—Frequent painting will be necessary inside and outside. Avoid using tar for the pipes as this is injurious to plants. A paint made from vegetable black, a little linseed oil and some dryers is harmless. Cleaning is best done in summer when the plants can safely be transferred to frames for a short time. Scrub with soap and water, and fumigate with a nicotine fumigator, sold for the purpose, to eliminate pests such as greenfly, thrips and other

Fig. 5.—Greenhouse Primulas. 1, Primula obconica. 2, 3, and 5, Sinensis Varieties. 4, Primula malacoides

troublesome insects which damage plants. These fumigators are, of course, used when the plants are in the house, but the extra precaution when the annual cleaning takes place is worth while.

Sulphur fumes are used as a disinfectant only when the house has no plants in it. The fumes are dangerous and you must not attempt to go into the house while the sulphur is being burned.

The lighting and the management of the fire are things which can be learned only by experience and the manipulation of the dampers must be understood if proper temperatures are to be maintained. Correct ventilation is also largely a matter of experience, but it is a safe general rule not to ventilate on the side from which the wind is blowing. This is a matter which depends greatly on the plants occupying the house and on the season.

Watering should be done with rain water, collected and led into a tank under the staging of the house. If possible, use rain water in the boiler as well, especially near London where a heavy deposit of lime is apt to accumulate inside the pipes. When the heating is off do not empty the pipes; they are less liable to rust if left filled with water than if kept standing empty.

A thermometer, registering maximum and minimum temperatures, will be essential. Houses are usually kept cooler in winter than in summer, plants being more active in summer and needing greater heat. A cool house ranges from 45 degs. F. to 50 degs. F. in winter to 60 to 65 in summer in the daytime. Five degs. lower are allowed for night temperatures. The warm house ranges from 55 to 65 degs. F. in winter and 65 to 75 degs. F. in summer; 5 degrees lower at night. The hot house is kept at 60 to 70 degs. F. in winter and 70 to 85 degs. F. in summer with a drop of 5 degrees at night. These are average temperatures for all-round work; special plants require special conditions and are usually grown in separate houses by experts.

Fig. 6.—A useful Span-roof Type of House

Fig. 7.—Section of Pot showing Arrangement of soil, etc.

The Potting Shed.—Beside the greenhouse or attached to one end of it a potting shed should be erected. This should be light and airy and if the hot pipes do not run through it the door of the greenhouse, if adjoining it, should be left open so that it may be more comfortable both for the gardener working there and for the plants which do not stand chilly conditions. In this shed keep a stock of pots ranging from thimbles (2 in.) and thumbs (2½ in.) right up to one large one of 20 in. in diameter and 16 in. deep. For composts, suitable for potting up, a stack of turf, some loam, leaf-mould, sharp sand and manure will be required. These with the fuel should be stored in a courtyard, however small, and it should be secluded from the flower garden, being like some other things in a garden, absolutely necessary though somewhat unsightly. A fence may surround it or a nice hedge.

A Bench is required in the potting shed, preferably with a cement top, which is very useful for mixing composts. A slab of marble from an old washstand will do admirably. A supply of compost should be kept in the shed so that it will be dry enough for potting. If it is mixed and stored outside there will be times when potting will be held up through its being in a wet, sodden condition, quite unsuitable for potting any plant.

A Propagating Frame with pipes running through it and with coconut fibre over the pipes is used for raising seedlings. One of the frames running alongside the house can be adapted for this purpose. Seeds need a temperature of from 65 to 75 degs. F., and a cold-frame is used to harden off those for bedding out in the garden. The greenhouse ones are merely transplanted into pots suitable in size for the plants or transferred to the greenhouse itself if there is room.

A Propagating Box is useful in a cool house. This should be bought as it must be well made and efficient. Home-made ones are not always successful. These boxes when well managed can be used for raising numerous seedlings and take up very little room inside the house. Their success depends on moist, close heat for the propagation of seeds. The propagating box or frame is used for raising the seeds. When they are large enough to handle they should be pricked off into pots: the larger growing kinds a single plant to a pot, the smaller ones may have three plants or more to make good clumps. Keep pots near glass when plants are small to prevent drawing them up and weakening them.

Seed pans are better than wooden boxes as they keep the soil moist and do not dry out so quickly—a fatal thing when raising seeds. Very fine compost is necessary for seed pans, the mixture being usually made up of two parts loam and one part leaf-mould with a good proportion of sand. This mixture

Fig. 8.—Greenhouse Favourites. 1 and 2, Cineraria. 3, Calceolaria. 4, Geranium

should be sieved and the pans or boxes filled to about the depth of 1 in. with crocks (i.e. broken pots or bricks or small stones for drainage), then with the soil. Seed should be sown evenly and thinly. After sowing, dip the pans up to the rims in water. Do not water overhead as this would cause hard caking of the soil. The water gradually rises from the bottom and this is usually sufficient watering till seeds appear. Cover pans with glass, from which moisture should be removed every morning, and cover with brown paper till seedlings appear.

Greenhouse Flowers.—The cheapest and quickest way to get a show the first year is by growing annuals. The half-hardy annuals do well in the cold house. A dozen or two of pots of one kind of annual can make a fine show early in the year if sown in the autumn, in August or September. Schizanthus, the Butterfly Flower or Poor Man's Orchid, is one of the most beautiful for this purpose. Its light airy foliage and dainty flowers make it a delightful flower for massing or for cutting for the table. Others which may be grown in the same way are:

Fig. 9.—Gloxinias, a showy pot-plant

Alonsoa Warscewiczii, Love Lies Bleeding, Clarkia, Dwarf Nasturtiums, Heliotrope, Impatiens Balsamina, Kochia, Lobelia, Matthiola Annual (Ten-week Stock), Petunia, Rodanthe, a beautiful everlasting, Verbena and Zinnia. For perfume, Mignonette should not be omitted.

Pelargoniums or Zonal Geraniums are the great stand-by in the greenhouse. They are of all shades of pink, crimson, scarlet and red. But if you can only have a few, choose good rose shades, some whites, and perhaps best of all, Kavolesky, a beautiful orangy or peach shade, and, by striking batches of cuttings at different times you will be able to keep the greenhouse gay practically all the year round. March, July or August and September are suitable times to take cuttings. These are cut from the old plants in the same way as cuttings for bleeding plants and are struck in pots in cold frames. The stock plant should be dry when cuttings are taken and it is usual to allow the cuttings to lie on the bench for some time before inserting in the pots. This is to prevent the fungus, Phythium Barium, the cause of "damping off," attacking them. Five cuttings are inserted round the edge of each pot and kept in the frame. In sunny districts cuttings may be struck in August and September in the open, the pots being kept moist by plunging them up to the rims in ashes. Cuttings may be struck under glass in March, the pots being kept near the glass to prevent drawing them up. A batch of well-rooted cuttings brought into the greenhouse in September, and given a temperature of 55 degs. F., should soon come into blossom, just when things are drab out of doors.

Cinerarias if sown in May or July will give a splendid show of rose, red, blue, mauve and white flowers in winter and spring. They are very easy to grow if greenfly is kept in check.

Begonias if grown in their different sorts will provide bloom all the year round. They are of various kinds, some having fibrous roots and others tuberous roots; there are summer and winter flowering kinds and they can be raised from seed or increased by cuttings or division. Some enthusiasts fill a whole house with them. Gloire de Lorraine is a fine winter-flowering one with rose flowers.

Primulas are beautiful and popular. If there is a corner of the greenhouse devoted to Alpines grown in a natural manner nothing will brighten it like the

Himalayan Primula, known as Rosea. Others are *P. Malacoides*, a dainty fairy-like blossom of different shades of pink, mauve and white, *P. Denticulata,* lilac, and *P. Cashmiriana, P. Floribunda,* yellow, *P. Kewensis,* yellow, *P. Beesiana,* magenta, *P. Bulleyana,* orange and scarlet, and *P. Cockburniana,* orange-scarlet.

Campanula isophylla, the drooping blue and white Harebells, make delightful plants for the edge of staging. Impatiens (Balsam) of a rosy shade are also suitable for this purpose. Helzine Solieroli is another with neat green creeping foliage. It is perennial.

Perpetual flowering Carnations bloom all the year round and if some of the Allwoodi's are grown, beautiful and lasting cut flowers can be gathered any time. Propagate by cuttings or layers.

Chrysanthemums brought on from cuttings or offsets and potted up in autumn for the greenhouse can fill a whole house in autumn and winter. When in the pots out of doors liquid manure should be given and disbudding will be necessary, so prolific are they. Decorative and incurved ones should be included in the collection.

Climbing plants do much to beautify the house and one of the prettiest is the Indian Mallow or Abutilion. The variegated foliage of Vexillarium and its dainty drooping red and yellow flowers make it much prized for table decoration. Plumbago capensis is a charming blue-flowered climber and, of course, some of the finer mauve and white Clematises. The Fuchsias can also be trained to climb or they may be used in hanging baskets.

Useful Shrubs for the greenhouse are: Acacia, Azaleas, Camellias, Cytisus fragrans, Deutzia gracilis, Erica, Hydrangea hortensis, and Lilac or Syringa which, when small, may be forced in the greenhouse.

Foliage Plants and ferns are indispensable as backgrounds and as a rest from the glare of too much colour. They are also worth growing for the grace and beauty of their leaves and stems. Of palms two favourites are: Cocos Weddelliana and Kentia Belmoreana. Asparagus Plumosus Tenuissimus and A. Sprengari are both excellent for decorative purposes and hardy. The very varied Coleuses are well-known and attractive plants, giving distinction to any greenhouse scheme, their rich velvety foliage being unsurpassed in the plant world. Grevillea Robusta Compacta is a very fine foliage plant with fern-like leaves. The low-growing ferns can be disposed among the brighter flowers, provided shade and sufficient moisture is ensured.

Fig. 10.—Grevillea Robusta

Watering.—It is a rule to give a good soaking rather than a mere sprinkling and in hot weather to shade either with blinds or greenhouse shading paint, sold for the purpose, and to spray the plants overhead, watering the paths in the height of summer. This gives the moist warm atmosphere necessary to the plants at this season. Dryer conditions are necessary in winter. Ventilation is also important. Open the ventilators when the temperature is too great.

GYMNASTICS and HOME GYMNASIUMS

THE principal and most interesting branches of gymnastics are—exercises on the vaulting horse, on the parallel bars and on the horizontal bar. They are here dealt with briefly in this order.

The Vaulting Horse bears some resemblance in shape and size to a real horse, minus its head, and can be used "with pommels" or "without pommels." The pommels are two upright, rigid handgrips standing about seventeen inches apart on the padded leather back. The easiest exercises for the novice are those in which the pommels are used.

The names of the various parts are as follows—*neck*, the left-hand end already referred to; *saddle*, the section between the pommels; *croup*, the right-hand end, or end opposite to the neck. The pommel names explain themselves—*neck pommel*, *croup pommel*.

When the vaulting horse is used lengthways you have the croup nearest to you, when it is used sideways, the neck should be to the left.

A Springboard may be used, to allow a performer to get extra height and vigour into his spring. This board is placed on the floor on the *near side* of the horse, the farther side being the *off side*.

Exercises customarily begin with a short run. In landing from the horse knees and ankles should yield so that the landing is springy and without shock. The height of a horse can be adapted to personal needs.

For the following exercises have the horse crossways. — Grip the pommel firmly and spring upwards, bringing one knee upwards and forward so that it comes right on to the saddle, between the arms. The other leg remains straight down, the front of the thigh touching the side of the horse. After a momentary pause the free leg should be flung back and a spring made from the knee in the saddle so that both legs come together again in the air behind and you alight on the balls of the feet, releasing your handgrips, of course.

The original spring for this exercise should have been made from both feet, and the hands should have taken their grips a little beyond the highest part of the pommels, and facing inwards towards each other.

Continue, with the reverse leg, until the exercise can be done neatly with either knee forward. Remember to spring from and land on the balls of the feet. Keep the head up and the chest forward.

Then try bringing both knees on the saddle together, side by side, making the same backward spring afterwards and landing on the point from which the leap was made.

Make the same square leap, but this time bring the knees right up against the chest so that the feet can be placed on the saddle between the arms. Be careful to retain the upright position during this momentary pause. Then spring forward, pushing clear with the hands as the legs straighten, and so landing evenly on both feet on the off side of the horse, facing forwards still.

The Through or Squat Vault.—When this can be done smoothly try jumping clean through the arms. Make the same preliminary leap, gripping the pommels firmly and rather forward. But this time do not allow the feet to touch the saddle, instead carry them cleanly through, and so straighten out on the far side. As the feet go forward clear of the horse the hands make a slight push, and release their holds, thus assisting the body to come upright for the landing. A still more spectacular form of this exercise is to spring in such a fashion that the legs rise backwards until the whole body is horizontal, with head up and back hollowed. Then the hands give a tug at the pommels and the knees come forward against the chest, so that the feet pass over the saddle and the landing is made as in the simpler form of the vault.

Other Preparatory Exercises.—There are other ways of vaulting clean over the horse, but some little introductory exercises are needed first.

Grip the pommels in the ordinary way as you make your leap, but this time fling the legs up to the left. Spread the legs when they are up, and so come down astride the neck, facing the croup. Grip the neck pommel with both hands to dismount, swinging the legs forwards then backwards, to gain impetus and allow the weight to come right over the hands. As the body reaches the horizontal position close the legs and make the landing to the off side.

The Flank or Side Vault.—Then try a complete vault to the left, letting your weight come on the right arm as the straight body reaches the horizontal level passing over the horse. The right side of the body will be nearest the horse as you go over and the left hand, of course, will have released its grip.

The Rear Vault.—Grip the neck pommel with the right hand and place the left on the neck. Then leap, turning the body to the left as you do so, so that you pass over the end of the horse in a sitting position. The left hand will have been lifted and your weight will have been on the right hand. As you alight the left hand will rest on the neck in order to steady you. It will be noticed that in this vault the body is bent into a position exactly like that of sitting on the floor, while in the former vault the body was stretched out straight and horizontal and was "on its edge," facing forwards.

Next make your leap with hands gripping the pommels normally, so that you vault over the saddle instead of just the neck. On alighting after this sitting position vault the left hand will fall on the neck pommel again and the body will be on the off side of the horse by the croup pommel.

The Wolf Vault.—In leaping extend the left leg so that it passes over the neck, and double up the right leg so that it crosses over the saddle, releasing the hands quickly, and alighting on both feet.

The Straddle Vault.—Again spring up, holding both pommels until the feet arrive on the horse with legs widely astride—left foot outside the neck pommel, right outside the croup pommel. Bring the feet in to the saddle and finish with plain forward leap.

Fig. 1.—Ready Position on Vaulting Horse without pommels

Then go on to the full straddle vault, beginning as before, raising the seat high in the flight over the horse but releasing the hands with a strong upward push and so allow the feet to come clean over without touching the horse. This exercise is best done with a friend or instructor "standing by." Be careful that you do not retain your handgrips too long, or catch your feet, or you may pitch forward and crash under the horse.

Various Somersault types of movements are possible. For instance—spring upwards, placing both hands on the pommels and, tucking the head under, arrive on the saddle on the shoulders. Allow the legs to swing on over, and at the last moment push off with the hands. You will thus have turned completely over and will arrive with your back to the horse. This should also be done in the presence of an instructor.

Spring up until you are supported against the side of the horse, with arms rigid and at full stretch, body upright. Balance support position. Now swing the left leg round and over the neck, momentarily releasing the left hand to let it pass, so that it comes to rest on the off side of the horse. Then swing the right leg round similarly over the croup. This circling of the legs can also be done backwards. And, finally, you will be

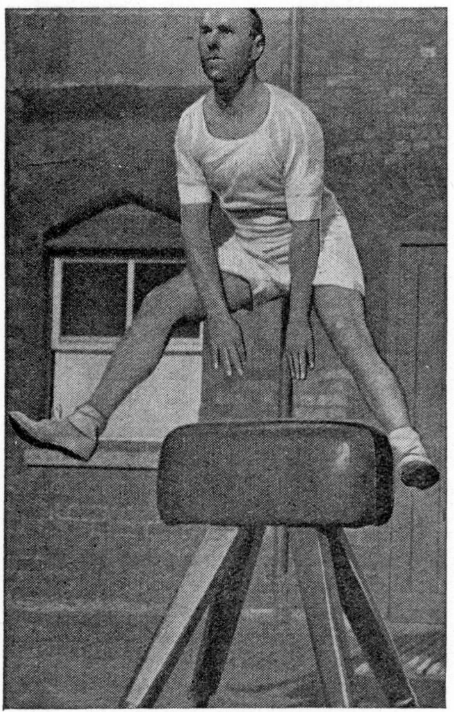

Fig. 2.—Lengthways Spring

able to swing both legs round together to one side, releasing one hand and replacing it for the clearance of the pommel.

For the following exercises the horse will be lengthways and without pommels.—Spring, by means of the hand position as before, to a seat astride the saddle, finishing with a plain vault to either side. For this latter vault hands may be placed in front or behind the body so that you make a backward or forward vault.

Place the hands on the croup and spring up so that the feet can be placed beside or between the hands. Stand up, take a step forward, and jump down over the end of the neck. After practice place the hands on the neck, following your arrival on the croup, and leap forward with legs astride, so that you "cut out" the arms and alight on the feet beyond the neck. As a variation you can bring the legs through the arms instead of outside them for the final leap to the floor.

Parallel Bar Work is unsuitable for children; for those of more mature physique it is most interesting, developing strength, quickness, poise.

Various Plain Vaults.—Stand crossways between the bars, at the middle, gripping with one hand on either side of you. This is called Cross Stand. Spring up until the arms are at full stretch, at the same time swinging the legs forward and over the right bar. Release the hands and alight on the right outer side of the bar. Do the same swing over to the left. When clearing the right bar grip this bar with the left hand in alighting, to steady the landing. In vaulting to the left the right hand finishes up holding the left bar.

Face or Front Vault.—Perform a similar swing backwards, clearing the bar in the same way—this time, at the moment of clearing, the body will be almost horizontal, and face downwards, instead of face upwards.

Rear Vault: Both Bars.—Now try a vault over both bars. Begin by standing in the middle, holding both bars. Make the same upwards swing as before, carrying the legs forward over the right bar, but instead of releasing your grips and dropping to the floor, keep hold and come to rest in an upright sitting position on the right bar, with your legs dangling down on the outside. Then lift both legs sharply, keeping them stiff, and swing them clean across to the left so that they clear both bars and you come down to the floor beyond the left bar. This same vault can be done in either direction.

Stand between the bars, near the end, facing outwards. Spring upwards to full arm stretch, and allow the legs to swing forward, then backward. As they rise behind spread the legs slightly, with feet turned out, so that the feet come down one on each bar. The arms must be rigid, and the whole body straight and stiff, with head up. Swing down to the original position, or vault to either side.

Marching or walking movements are interesting, and look well.

Get between the bars and spring up into the full-arm-stretch position. Keep arms rigid, chest forward, head up, the whole body braced. Then move each hand in turn forward a few inches, so that you travel smoothly along the bars with a sort of walking motion.

You may do the same thing backwards.

A more difficult form of the exercise, which also can be performed forwards and backwards, is that of moving both hands simultaneously. This is achieved by a series of little jumps.

All these four forms of travelling along the bars can be repeated with arms bent to right-angles at the elbows. This naturally imposes greater strain on the arms, and it is additionally hard to see that the feet remain clear of the ground.

In another form of travelling along the bars the legs play an important part.

Spring up between the bars to full arm stretch. Swing the legs forwards and upwards until they are above the bar level, then open them sideways until they come astride the bars. The legs must remain very stiff, and you will push forward from the hands, which will release their grips, until the body becomes upright supported only on the spread legs. Continue forward until the hands can grip the bars afresh, this time in front of the legs, and go over with your weight on the hands so that the legs are enabled to slide inwards over the bars and drop down into the original position—you will now be balanced at full arm stretch, vertically, but some way farther along the bars than at the outset. From this point the complete movement, beginning with the forward leg swing, will be repeated—until you have travelled right along the bars.

It is comparatively easy, when you have mastered the forward action, to travel backwards in the same fashion. This will necessitate, of course, that each time the legs are stiffly astride, the hands will be replaced behind the body instead of in front of it.

Grip the ends of the bars and raise yourself between them, facing outwards. Swing the legs forward, and then backwards, carrying them up until they can spread apart and straddle the bars. They will thus come forward astride the bars and you will be able to leap clean off the ends by releasing the hands as the legs come forward. Keep the body as upright as possible in this. If you bend you are likely to bring the head forward, and to upset your balance. Be on your guard against keeping your handgrips too long, or failing to keep the body upright, for these faults may cause you to pitch forward on your head, or at any rate to lose your balance instead of alighting properly on the balls of the feet.

This exercise is easy enough to understand as a leapfrog movement.

A good many parallel bar feats include some form of hand balance, in which the body is held vertically in the air, feet uppermost, while the weight is supported on the hands or arms. Begin such feats cautiously.

Handstand Vault.—Sit astride the bars to begin, gripping with your hands just in front of your thighs. Lean forward slowly, allowing your weight to come over on to the arms, which should be bent sharply at the elbows. Simultaneously raise the legs backwards, until they are vertical and you are firmly balanced. To continue, lower the head, curl the back, and allow yourself to go over backwards. The legs will come down over your head—and finally they will spread apart and so come astride the bars once more, as you release your grip and rise into the original position. The whole movement is almost equivalent to a forward somersault along the bars, beginning and finishing with the legs astride.

A More Difficult Handstand Vault.—Sit astride the bars, gripping their ends in front of your legs—you will thus be facing outwards. Raise yourself into a hand balance, with bent arms. But instead of holding this balance when the body is

Fig. 3.—Reversed Position on Wall Bars

vertical, allow the legs to go on over, backwards. Just as the body is past its balancing point give a push from the hands—next instant you will arrive with your feet on the floor, in a standing position.

It is possible to hold a hand balance position with arms straight and rigid, but this should not be tried until you have some facility with the bent arm work.

Another somersault movement is possible over the bars sideways, instead of down their middle. Sit on the outer side of the right bar, so that your shoulders are parallel with it. Keep the legs stiff and raise them, going backwards until your back reaches the left bar. Continue to lift the legs, and so make a sort of back somersault, reaching the floor with both feet simultaneously on the off side of the bars. Your hands will have made a slight push from the left bar at the last moment, when it became necessary for them to release their hold.

Long and Short-arm Balances are also possible on a single bar, the shoulders being parallel with the bar. Obviously, in this position, because of the more troublesome handgrips, it is more difficult to retain one's position.

Horizontal Bar.—In all horizontal bar work it is well to have a mat beneath you and an experienced companion standing by in case you take a spill; in fact, such precautions will be helpful in any gymnastics. When swinging below the bar the thumbs should be on the same sides as the fingers; when supporting yourself above the bar the thumbs will be curled round opposite to the fingers.

First learn how to alight backwards. Grip the bar above the head and draw the knees up towards the chest, forcing them on so that they pass underneath the bar, between the arms. The legs will thus hang lower and lower behind until they are almost at the ground, when you will release your handgrips and drop on to the balls of your feet.

Then acquire the knack of getting above the bar. Grip as before and bring your legs upwards, knees against chest, until you can hook the right leg over the bar, outside your right hand. At this moment you will be hanging by the hands and the right knee. Now swing the left leg down—it will previously have been stiffened and upright, lying against the front of the bar. The impetus of the downward swing, combined with a pull of the arms, will bring you right above the bar. As soon as you are here straighten and stiffen the arms, and slip the right leg back over the bar. You will now be supporting yourself at full arm stretch above the bar, with body practically vertical and straight, and legs together, with feet pointing downwards. To get down, lower yourself slowly by the arms.

In order to circle the bar from the front it is best to begin with the grip reversed, that is with the palms of the hands towards the face. Raise the legs forwards and drop them against the front of the bar, at the same time pulling upwards until the stomach comes against the bar and the weight of the legs carry you over. Afterwards try the same with an ordinary grip, palms away from the face, rising until you go over backwards with the stomach on the bar and finally come to a full arm stretch position above the bar.

Another interesting stunt is to sit up on the bar, getting up by the leg swing method already described, and slipping the left leg forward over the bar also when you are up. Your hands will thus be gripping between your legs as you sit upright. Now allow yourself to swing backwards, keeping the arms stiff and the knees hooked, and going with such impetus that you almost rise at the front into your original position. Of course, you will not quite get up, but at the highest point in this forward swing release your hands and so drop to the floor, where you will arrive right way up on your feet.

The bar can be circled on the back as well as on the stomach. Raise the legs forward, exactly as described for the first exercise (alighting backwards); but, instead of allowing the feet to drop towards the mat behind, raise them up by the bar until the body is straight, with hollowed back, and the bar rests against the backs of the thighs. Pull hard with both hands until the body is raised sufficiently for the small of the back to be on the bar. Then the weight of the legs, together with a raising forward of the head, will gradually tip you over until you come right way up above the bar, and relax into a sitting position.

It has been possible here, of course, to describe no more than a few scattered exercises, most of them quite elementary, from the various branches of gymnastics. But enough has been given to enable you to get started, and to indicate the direction of your further studies.

Home Gymnasiums.—If you are fond of making things you can get plenty of enjoyment from fitting up various gymnastic appliances in your home. Then you may have your own gymnasium.

It is not necessary to give full details here, since a fair knowledge of woodwork will enable you to plan your own constructions. Unless you have such knowledge you should hesitate to make things on which any great strain is likely to be imposed. Make your appliances strong; there must be no careless work in them and no faulty material. Get good quality ash where wood is required for bars and such like.

Punchball.—Punchball work is very fascinating. If you intend to make one of the floor-to-ceiling type you should proceed as follows:

Get a large football, and sew a strip of leather on each end of it. On each of these loops have threaded a steel ring, about the size of half a crown. Next comes the elastic. You may buy "rubbers" fairly cheaply, or strong catapult elastic will serve if doubled. Proper rubber is about ½ in. in diameter, and about 12 in. or 15 in. long. Each end of the ball has a corresponding piece fastened to the ring. A strap with buckle is fastened to the other end of each rubber—and the punchball is

Fig. 4.—Home-made Punchball

complete. Finished, it consists of five sections, approximately equal in length, 12 in. to 15 in. Thus—strap, rubber, ball, rubber, strap. The loops, rings, and joins will add to the total length, so that the completed equipment will measure about 6 ft., and the straps should be capable of extending still more.

A strong hook in floor and ceiling, or door lintel and floor, or outdoor frame and ground, and you may put your punch ball into position. It should not be necessary to stretch the elastic or rubber more than a few inches in order to get your end rings on the hooks, otherwise there will not be enough elasticity remaining. Neither should you inflate the bladder too tightly.

To use your ball wear gloves or bandages, and begin with straight, regular punches. When you can keep the ball under control you may alternate long-arm punches with short-arm jabs; and get various combinations of single and double fist work, elbow stops, right and left hooks, changes of feet, and much ordinary boxing technique.

A Heavy Punching Bag is more easily made, but much less interesting in use. Suspend your strong canvas bag from a stout hook or beam, and have it filled with leaves, paper, rags, sawdust, sand, according to materials available and the weight you require. A small bag tightly filled is better than a large one half filled.

Climbing Rope.—There is nothing to be "made" if you would add this to your home gymnasium. All you have to be careful about is that the beam, or tree branch, and the rope itself, are all of sufficient strength. Proper climbing ropes can be bought from gymnastic outfitters. Do not get second-hand ropes, especially if they have been used out of doors, for the weather may have rotted them.

Rings and Trapeze.—These also can give plenty of interesting work, even if the supporting ropes are comparatively short. It is advisable to buy rings made for the purpose, and trapeze bars need to be very strong—stout ash or steel, not too thick for a hand to grasp comfortably.

Many of the exercises described for the horizontal bars are equally suitable for these two forms of equipment.

Horizontal Bar.—It is not difficult to construct your own; on the lawn is a good place. Have your uprights of sturdy timber, and try to get a steel bar. The uprights should be strutted to ensure rigidity, and see that the ends of the bar are locked so that they cannot draw out of their sockets.

Spring Exercisers.—The component parts of such exercisers can be bought very cheaply from many popular stores. Rubber or elastic can also be made to do. The most satisfactory use of this stretching type of equipment comes from fastening it on the wall at about the shoulder level. You then stand back to the wall, holding a grip in either hand, and so proceed with your various lunging, bending, and stretching exercises.

Ladder.—An old ladder, with sound spars which have been glass-papered until they are smooth, makes an excellent piece of equipment if fixed flatly along close to a ceiling. You can then hang by the hands; swing along from one end to the other, and so on.

Stilts.—Ash poles serve best for stilts, and the foot rests should be about 3 ft. from the ground, and wide enough to stretch across the boot sole. The stilt handles should come up to the level of the shoulders.

Stilt walking is a fine exercise for developing balance and poise. You may have adjustable rests, by means of nuts and bolts —generally 3 ft. should be the maximum height, and lower levels will be very useful.

Wall Bars.—A useful makeshift is a length of ladder fixed rigidly against a wall. See that the spars are secure and smooth.

Ground Bars.—Ground bars are like abbreviated parallel bars raised just a few inches from the floor. Sturdy broom handles, shortened according to your weight, will serve quite well if notched firmly into two stout pieces of timber about 3 in. square running crossways at the ends. The bars will be parallel, about the width of the shoulders apart, and two or three inches from the floor.

Mattress.—Remember that a suitably stuffed mat or mattress is a necessary part of gymnastic equipment. An old bed mattress will do very well.

HIKING

THERE never was a time when fresh air, sunshine, and healthful exercise were more appreciated, and it is no wonder that increasing numbers of people young and old are setting out right through the year to rediscover the delights of the countryside.

Hiking can be most pleasingly adapted to individual needs and tastes, but whatever your personal preferences, the same sort of preliminary knowledge is needed if hikes are to be of maximum enjoyment.

First, dress must be considered.

Dress.—Shoes are of primary importance: boots, except in mountainous districts, are not desirable as they keep the feet unnecessarily hot. Let your shoes be well fitting and very strong; roomy shoes worn with two pairs of socks are very comfortable. They should have stout soles, nailed if any climbing is to be done. Brown are more serviceable than black, for they look well with less cleaning.

Stockings or socks should be of wool, not silk, and should be sturdy and well fitting.

Shorts are best for men in hot weather, but loose flannel trousers are useful in the colder months. Some girls like shorts—and they can look well if the rest of the dress is in harmony. But a short, loose skirt, with knickers to match, gives quite as much freedom.

For men an open-necked shirt and loose jacket; and for girls a plain blouse or jumper—with a short jacket in cold weather.

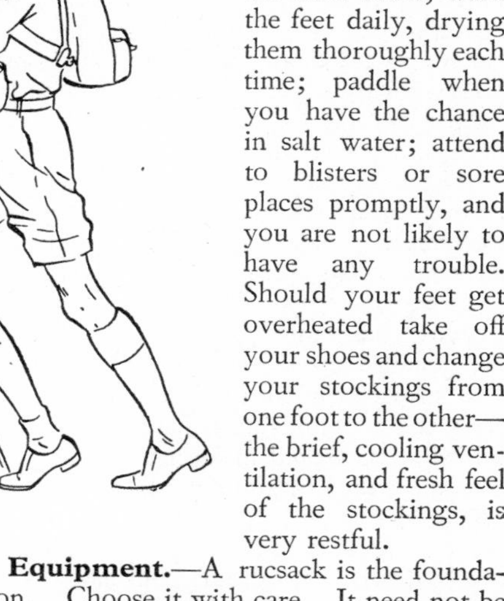

Fig. 1

Headgear should be simple—beret, cap, panama hat, or nothing at all. But have a sou'wester for wet weather, and a rainproof. A light felt hat is handy, if it can be rolled up when not wanted.

Incidentally, a simple hiking dress for girls can be made for just a few shillings. Shantung, linen, drill or similar material is best for the summer, and light woollen material for the winter. Both men and women should avoid wearing anything tight round the waist. Remember that hiking itself keeps one comfortably warm, so that not too many clothes should be worn.

Since the hiker depends so much on his feet they should be well tended. Rubbing soap inside one's stockings is quite unnecessary, though some hikers favour french chalk dusted over the feet. Keep the nails short; wash the feet daily, drying them thoroughly each time; paddle when you have the chance in salt water; attend to blisters or sore places promptly, and you are not likely to have any trouble. Should your feet get overheated take off your shoes and change your stockings from one foot to the other—the brief, cooling ventilation, and fresh feel of the stockings, is very restful.

Equipment.—A rucsack is the foundation. Choose it with care. It need not be enormous, but it should be sufficiently large. Much will depend on whether you are carrying camping equipment. You may have a limp-backed rucsack, or one attached to a frame, which distributes weight between the hips and the small of the back, and allows ventilation to the back. With this *Bergan* or *Norwegian* type the shoulders have a great deal of freedom, for the shoulder straps do little more than keep the rucsack in position. You may get a *meis*, or rigid frame, which can be affixed to almost any rucsack. Be sure to have the shoulder-straps wide enough for comfort.

Avoid old army packs, which were never meant to be carried without army equipment, and any sort of contrivance which involves straps to cross the chest.

The heavier the weight you have to carry the better it is to have a rigid frame, but a frameless rucsack is cheaper and can be very comfortable if properly packed.

A rucsack should have outside pockets in which objects are kept that may be needed frequently, a passport, for instance, if you are going abroad.

General equipment has already been dealt with in the section of this book on CAMPING, and reference should be made to that for a list of the things which should go in your rucsack, whether you intend to camp or not. It is a good plan, as you gain experience, to compile your own list of requirements, for such is obviously largely a personal matter. Then, when preparing for a hike, you can simply have your list at hand and slip the things into your rucsack as you read them.

If you do not propose to camp there will be more room for spare clothes and various oddments. It is very pleasant if you can have a complete change of clothes at the end of a hot, tiring day. But do not overburden yourself; the things you carry on your back are genuine *impedimenta*.

A strong man, with full camping kit, may carry thirty pounds quite happily, but careful selection should make it unnecessary to have more than twenty pounds, and for girls a safer maximum is fifteen pounds. If you are not camping you should get along with much less. Waterproofs add a little to weight, but it is advisable to be well prepared for rain.

Wet Weather.—The question of protection in wet weather is an important one. Opinions differ as to the best form of waterproof. Some like the ordinary storm-proof mackintosh; others prefer the light cape with chest-straps which enable the wearer to throw open the cape easily between the showers. If you favour this type of rainproof, it is a good plan to get one big enough to go right over your rucsack; see that it fastens satisfactorily round the neck, to keep out drips, and that it is of sufficient length. Some hikers follow the custom prevalent on the Continent and use a short rainproof coat, like a golfing jacket, leaving shorts or skirts unprotected. A sou'wester has already been mentioned as the best form of headgear for wet weather.

Shoes in Wet Weather.—Usually a good polish lavishly applied to your shoes will keep the leather both supple and waterproof; but if the weather is really bad, "dubbined" shoes are best. You can buy dubbin in tins from your shoemaker, or it is quite easy to make at home. A little vaseline is melted with half the quantity of paraffin; or equal proportions of tallow, neatsfoot oil and paraffin are melted together. The shoe-leather should be slightly warmed and the dubbin rubbed well in, particular attention being paid to the joins and seams. In damp weather the shoes should be stuffed with paper each night.

When wet, it is wisest to keep on walking until you can get a bath or a change of clothes. If your body keeps moving, you will rarely come to any harm from the rain.

Camping Equipment need only be very slight. Even if you intend to do much camping it is unlikely that you will stay more than one night in one place during your hike. There are plenty of tents available that need only the lightest poles, or none at all, and for the sake of your rucsack weight you may assume that you will get into some better shelter if bad weather should come on; this will allow you to have the sort of tent which will be unsuitable to withstand much rain. Aluminium utensils are useful, and can be bought in many ingenious and compact forms; but remember that they must not be washed with soda in the water.

The Youth Hostels Association has transformed things for hikers in this country. Members are now able, for the trifling cost of a shilling, to get a good bed for the night, often in the most picturesque surroundings. These hostels are scattered all over the country, at suitable distances along interesting hiking routes, so that it is possible to plan a tramp of almost any duration with the knowledge that suitable accommodation is available each night. And not merely accommodation, but congenial companionship too, for generally you will be able to meet kindred spirits. Both men and girls are catered for; cooking facilities are available, and generally meals can be secured at very moderate prices. Members use a sheet sleeping bag, the cost of which is only about 3s., the weight being 15 or 28 ounces.

The Youth Hostel movement had its origin in Germany, but it is fast becoming international and hikers of all nations frequently make happy contacts at the close of a day's journey. There is scarcely a more delightful way of spending a holiday than to go with a few friends into some neighbouring country—into Germany, for instance, where no form of holiday is more popular than hiking—through magnificent scenery with the well-equipped hostels available at night.

Other Organizations too have done a great deal for the hiker—notably the federations of Rambling Clubs which link up hikers in various parts of the country. From these you can often get valuable information as to choice of route and accommodation. Other services also are performed by these clubs, such as the safeguarding of footpaths and rights of way; and they are able to do much in the interests of hiking by encouraging the provision of National Parks and the passing of certain bills such as the Public Rights of Way and the Access to Mountains bills.

Arranging a Hike.—It is a good plan to start with a week-end. At a holiday time like Whitsun the atmosphere seems particularly suitable. If you have not been out before it is advisable to have some preparation, so that you may get hardened by degrees.

Do a few preliminary tramps of five or eight miles, with a partly laden rucsack, just to get used to the feel of the thing. You may try out your shoes in this manner, or break them in if they are new. Settle down to a steady three to four miles an hour, and keep away from main traffic-ridden roads. Have a stout walking-stick; it must be one with a crooked handle so that you can hang it on your arm when necessary.

When you have had this little practice and are confident that you can stand up to a real programme, then you may plan your hike. Allow for 10 to 15 miles a day; it is possible to do more, but no sensible hiker is out to break either speed or distance records. Have a very good idea of where you expect to stay each night. Study maps; work out distances; find out the sort of country you will pass through; note the roads and districts which are to be avoided. Requirements of the motorist and hiker, of course, are almost diametrically opposite, so that all the roads which are given precedence on a motoring map, as most useful for the motorist, are precisely the ones which the hiker will want to avoid.

The Day's Programme.—On setting out for your day's hike you should certainly have a rough idea of where you are going, particularly if you are due at a certain place by the evening. But do not have too rigid an itinerary. Always feel free to digress when you want to. There may be a church, a fine view, a curious old monument, just a mile or two off your track, which you would not like to miss, though previously you had not known of it. Your programme should always have sufficient latitude to make such a visit possible. That is an additional reason why you should not scheme to go too far each day. It is this untrammelled freedom which means so much in the pleasures of hiking.

Get going reasonably early in the morning—nine o'clock is a good hour, allowing for ample sleep and unhurried preparation. A three-hour stretch of walking will get you a good way on the day's journey, and with a brisk appetite for your midday meal. It is an advantage to get the heavier part of your hike over in the earlier hours of the day. Then take your lunch quietly, with half an hour or an hour's rest afterwards. The second stretch can be done in the afternoon, broken possibly by a halt for a cup of tea; then you should reach your destination by early evening. That will allow for a wash and change, perhaps a bathe, so that you are thoroughly ready for a substantial evening meal. This should be the heaviest meal of the day. Afterwards you may loiter round, chat, smoke, read, make acquaintances—and so to bed.

Sleep well, but rise betimes. If by any chance you have spent the night in cottage, or barn, or farm, see that you know where you may wash, and where drinking water is procurable. A town dweller often does not realize the value and importance of water to the countryman—and to put soap in a cattle trough is, to say the least, unwise.

The Hiker and the Law.—The good hiker avoids many things which are often pitfalls to the careless or inexperienced. He does not leave gates open, spread litter, break hedges, disturb cattle or trample crops. And he keeps on the right side of the law.

The hiker is apt to be somewhat afraid of the law; but in reality, if he behaves himself, he has nothing to fear. The trespassing notices and prohibitions which he sees posted up here and there are the landowners' way of protecting themselves against ignorant and destructive walkers and campers; but if he unwittingly gets himself into trespassing difficulties, he can usually extricate himself from them by politeness or by a prompt offer to pay for any damage he may have done.

Never deliberately go where you see a "trespassing" notice; but should you stray by accident on to private ground and be caught there, remember that you cannot be prosecuted unless you have done some damage. If, however, you should come to harm—be, for instance, bitten by the keeper's dog—on private land, you have no redress if you are trespassing. The tenant has the right of exerting "necessary force" to remove you from his ground; but if he orders you to go back by the way you came, you are under no obligation to do so; you will be perfectly justified in making direct for the nearest public way.

A "private road" bars cyclists as well as other wheeled traffic; but in some cases it will be found that there is a right of way for the pedestrian. These rights of way should be jealously guarded by the hiker, for they are his by right and can only cease to be so by an Act of Parliament or by an order of Quarter Sessions.

Always make enquiries before pitching your camp for the night. Many of the so-called commons and heaths which look such attractive camping-sites are governed by bye-laws which may possibly prohibit camping or, whilst permitting this, forbid the lighting of a fire.

As a matter of courtesy, of course, you will ask permission of the owner before you camp in his field; and will say "thank you" to him again in the morning.

Hikers who use country inns for the night should remember a few points of law concerning these. Generally speaking, the innkeeper cannot refuse admittance to those who ask for a bed, if there is room for them—unless they are obviously disturbers of the peace or make themselves objectionable to the other visitors. The hiker, on the other hand, does not possess the right to demand any particular bedroom, even if there seems no reason why he should not have it. The innkeeper is only responsible for the guest's property so long as the latter is not actually negligent of it. Damage or loss due to carelessness on the part of the owner cannot be compensated for.

General Hints.—Do not drink from any unknown stream or pool, unless the water is boiled. Do not pack a wet mackintosh or tent inside your rucsack; it is better, if it must be packed and carried, to roll it neatly and fasten it on the outside of your pack.

Do not throw lighted matches or cigarette ends about, or leave camp fires burning. Do not cut your name on famous buildings, or on trees or fences.

Learn to use a compass. It is a sound investment to buy a really good one. If, however, you find yourself without one, you can make your watch do just as well. Point the hour hand towards the sun; then an imaginary line dividing the angle between the hour hand and twelve noon would run north and south. You can work out which is which by remembering that the sun (not allowing for summer time) is east at 6 a.m., south at noon and west at 6 p.m. The full moon can be used for direction-finding in the same way, allowing for the moon being exactly opposite to the sun. Churches can help you to find the east; for their altars are nearly always situated at the east end of the building.

Maps and map-reading, of course, form an important part of the craft of hiking. You will add tremendously to the joy of your walking if you take a map with you. The 1-in. ordnance survey map is the best one to get. Study it at home before you set out, and make yourself familiar with the signs and contours, the meaning of which is usually indicated in the margin. When you want to find your way by the map, first find the north and adjust your map by that; then you will be able to see in what relation you stand to the places marked on the map. Or pick out some obvious landmark, or notice two objects on each side of you—say, a river to your left, and a church spire to your right, and identify these on the map; then you can find your position midway between.

Anyone with a good knowledge of the stars, of course, needs no compass on clear nights; but he will need a map all the more, since his route will be guided mainly by direction and by the number of miles covered.

Hiking Abroad.—When the hiker has walked fairly extensively in his own country, he may like to attempt a tramping holiday abroad. This is one of the best ways of exploring and enjoying a foreign country to the full. There are certain additional points, however, which should be remembered by the hiker planning a Continental holiday.

Each stage of the journey should be well thought out; passports got in readiness; and a reasonable amount of money changed beforehand, so that the hiker will not arrive on the foreign shore with only English shillings with which to tip the porters.

There should be no difficulty in getting through the Customs if the necessary items are declared frankly. Cameras, by the way, are declarable. Do not try to bring new purchases over from the Continent on your return journey, unless you are prepared for explanations to the Customs officials.

Routes from the coast are varied and numerous.

Third-class accommodation on the boat is quite adequate for the average hiker, unless he is a particularly bad sailor requiring special comforts. Third-class travelling abroad is rougher than in this country, but many a hiker enjoys it more as it affords opportunities for all kinds of interesting and often humorous contacts with the people. Many foreign railways run very good second-class sleepers for long journeys.

Cheap Fares.—Always enquire, before you book your seat on the railway, whether any cheap travelling facilities are available for the hiker; in many countries considerable discount is allowed on tickets for the English hiker, particularly if he is a member of some youth association. Often special period tickets are issued, allowing unlimited travel within a certain area, or tourist tickets which permit of certain parts of the journey being taken by train and the rest on foot.

The best months for foreign hiking are the early summer or the autumn; during holiday times there are more people abroad and hostels may be uncomfortably full and necessitate advance booking.

Keep more to the roads than you would in the normal way, especially if your knowledge of the language is scanty. Your rucsack and clothing need be very little different from those required in England—though girls should remember that in certain countries shorts are taboo. The nights are often colder abroad than they are in England, and provision should be made for this accordingly.

Make your preliminary journey as smooth as possible so that the travel will not wear you out and cause you to start your actual hiking in a state of exhaustion. It is wise to book your seat for the journey, and perhaps to book rooms for your first night at some hotel or hostel, so that you may get thoroughly rested after the crossing.

Try to plan every aspect of your hike a little more carefully than you would in England. Thus, have a clear idea of where you are going to stay the night, and do your best to get there *early* in the evening, as you never know what difficulties you may encounter through lack of knowledge of the language or of foreign customs. Continental villagers retire to bed considerably earlier than do the English, and are up betimes in the morning; often they are about in the fields before six. Attention to points such as these will make you a more welcome visitor. Be particularly careful about drinking water, and make enquiries before you bathe in lakes and pools. It is always safer, as well as more interesting, to get the services of a guide when climbing.

Hiking both abroad and at home is full of interest in itself; but when combined with some special pursuit it becomes a most fascinating hobby. Have you any particular leaning—towards photography, archæology, nature study, etc.? Then plan your hike with these objects in view.

Here are a few suggestions for hikes of various types which will link you up with your favourite pursuit.

Archæology.—For those interested in early Britain and in the Roman occupation, there is much in the way of monoliths, earthworks, early British ramparts, cromlechs and Druid circles which well repays investigation. One such route might cross Salisbury Plain, including Stonehenge; another could be planned along the length of Hadrian's Wall from the Tyne to the Solway; or round the coasts of Sussex, Kent and East Anglia along the sites of the old forts of the Saxon shore and the later mediæval Cinque Ports. The ancient way of the Chaucerian pilgrims, from Canterbury to London, or farther to Winchester, is full of romance; so are the old trackways along the Berkshire and Wessex downs; and the Roman roads traceable on the ordnance survey map of Roman Britain will well repay the hiker in archæological interest.

Architecture.—Those to whom this subject specially appeals could make the object of their hike one of the famous abbeys or cathedrals—York, Canterbury or Salisbury Cathedrals, Tintern or Buckfast or Whitby Abbey, to mention but a few—or they could visit one of the ancient cities, such as Lincoln, with its wealth of architecture, or the colleges of Oxford or Cambridge. An attractive "side-line" to these antiquarian rambles is the collecting of some special object, such as brass-rubbings from churches, quaint epitaphs, etc.

Nature Study.—This is a hobby which can lend great interest to hiking. The botanist can collect his specimens by the way, and catalogue them later during winter evenings; the naturalist can find a new pleasure in hiking at night, when wild life unknown to the daytime is about, and the habits of night creatures such as stoats and owls can be observed. An interesting nature notebook, illustrated by photographs, pressed flowers and other features, can be kept of the various nature hikes at different times of the year.

Literature.—Many an interesting pilgrimage can be made to the homes of great writers and the scenes of their books. There is the Wordsworth country; the Brontë country; Milton's cottage at Chalfont St. Giles; Gad's Hill, near Rochester, of Dickensian fame; and, to come to more recent times, the Shropshire of A. E. Housman, and the Wessex of Hardy. Have you ever taken Arnold's "Scholar Gipsy" on a walk to Bablockhythe on the "stripling Thames" near Oxford, or wandered into Hertfordshire with the "Essays of Elia," tracing Charles Lamb's old haunts?

These are but a few indications of the way in which your particular interest can be combined with that most healthful and pleasant hobby of hiking.

MAKING A HOME

CAN this be a hobby? Most decidedly. It is one that can last a lifetime. Few young couples starting life together are able to have all they want in their house at the outset, and even if money forms no barrier to the fulfilment of their wishes and they can have precisely the house they most admire it is quite certain that within a short time practical experience and developing taste will suggest all kinds of alterations. It is this aspect that makes the building of a home so fascinating a hobby.

The House.—If you are setting out on this adventurous business of building a home the house will be your first concern. It is nowadays practically as cheap to purchase as to pay rent, and new houses are becoming increasingly plentiful.

Consider fully, before settling on any particular type of house, the present tendencies of house construction. Concrete is becoming more and more popular as an alternative to bricks. Architects are beginning to throw off the ancient tradition of the sloping roof—which after all had no reason but the limitations of primitive roofing materials: it is curious how people, through long, unreasoned familiarity, believe that they can see a certain beauty in great expanses of slate and tile, and a lack of beauty in the house from which these expanses are eliminated. Actually, of course, not only is expense saved by the flat roof, but an additional area is obtained which can be utilized as playground, garden or sun parlour.

Many houses are described as "modern" merely because they have been built only a few years, yet in all essential features they may be no better than—even if as good as—their neighbours which have been standing for half a century. A house is not made modern simply by the addition of a bathroom and "space for garage." Even when it is fitted with hot and cold water throughout, that is no guarantee that it is really up to date. Modernity does not consist in the elimination of just a few of the cruder inconveniences of previous generations, but in the addition of the many items of equipment which latter-day developments have brought within our reach.

Two chief slogans apply to the modern home—"economy in upkeep" and "saving of labour." If you are building or buying a new house, you should study every detail from both points of view. For instance: a substantial item of house upkeep is painting. Windows differ enormously. Some have large amounts of exposed woodwork that will need to be painted periodically, while with others there is scarcely any wood visible. And the same remark applies to doors, porches, gables and other outside features which have to withstand the weather. A tiled bathroom is another thing to be considered. To have water splashing constantly on to walls of distemper, or paper, or paint, means that those walls, sooner or later, will need renovation. But with glazed tiling the first expense is the whole expense. If cost precludes the whole wall surface being thus treated, then let there be a high dado of tiles, and do not forget that built-in fittings, for holding soap, sponges, etc., are invaluable.

Labour-saving Devices.—Among these fitted basins with hot and cold water in bedrooms must be counted a boon. The old-fashioned washstand, with its basins and ewers, involves filling and cleaning and emptying, whereas the former needs scarcely any attention. Then, in the workaday part of the house, what an amount of strenuous cleaning has been expended by housewives on such things as kitchen tables and pastry boards! But now there are many substances available for giving durable, clean surfaces, which can be wiped over in a few seconds and made cleaner than a wood surface could ever be. No home is fully modern which has in its kitchen exposed wood surfaces that require scrubbing. Porcelain-enamelled steel and other substances have made such things unnecessary.

Fireplaces that involve almost no cleaning are another feature of the house of to-day. One can now have grates which do not contain a single particle of metal, so that cleaning consists merely in an occasional wipe over with a damp cloth.

Many rooms are fitted with grates that are much too big, throwing out an unnecessary amount of heat and burning coal wastefully. Here is a table giving approximately the width of fire generally suitable for an average living-room:

Room	11 ft. by 11 ft. . .	12 in. fire
„	14 ft. by 14 ft. . .	14 in. „
„	17 ft. by 17 ft. . .	16 in. „
„	20 ft. by 20 ft. . .	18 in. „

Gas fires, too, must not be forgotten. The modern fires are thoroughly hygienic, and involve no trouble at all in upkeep. Electric fires may be preferred—they eliminate all dust, smell, and trouble, and are available in a multitude of varieties.

"Convenience and Comfort" may be added as a third slogan, and in conformity with it the modern house can show many agreeable features.

Central heating, for instance. The days have gone when it was considered an advantage to have a house at half a dozen different temperatures, because it was more "natural." It is obviously absurd to spend an evening in a heated living-room, and then to traverse a draughty staircase and finally take off one's clothes in a bedroom with exactly the temperature of the open-air, perhaps several degrees below freezing point. Nowadays it is a simple matter to keep a whole house interior at an equable temperature and so to avoid dangerous changes and draughts.

Windows.—It may be said quite safely that sash-windows are old-fashioned and in many ways objectionable. They involve a mechanism of cords and weights that is very liable to get out of order; they necessitate a good deal of painting, both inside and out; they occupy with woodwork space that could better be filled with glass.

The modern casement window has none of these objections if it be made of metal. And windows of to-day naturally bring to mind ultra-violet-ray glass—a very important discovery. At a cost of perhaps a pound or two per window one may have this new glass fitted instead of the old. Certainly the kitchen and the nursery should be glazed with it and whichever rooms besides are much used during the daytime.

If you have a gabled roof it may help to solve the problem of storage space, for the interior of the roof itself can be used, providing a little cheap flooring is put down. It is possible to fit a patent ladder which can be brought down into position quite simply—a vast improvement on the familiar old practice of standing precariously on a step-ladder and springing up into the void. Light for this roof space can be secured by fitting a few glass slates.

Cupboards.—Be sure that you have ample cupboard room. Have one in the hall, so that unsightly clothes, umbrellas, and such like, may not litter the walls. It is generally a good plan also to have a built-in wardrobe, from floor to ceiling, on one side of a bedroom fireplace. Usually it is also possible to have a cupboard fitted in a corner of the first-floor landing. Still another cupboard should be made to enclose the hot water tank and this will serve also for airing and storing linen. In the bathroom a towel rail attached to the hot water system is a comfort.

Water.—How you get your hot water, of course, will be largely decided by the degree in which you intend to make use of it—whether from kitchen range or independent boiler; by coal, gas, or electric power; to run through the entire house or only in one section of it.

The question of filtration also arises. In a district in which the water is very hard it is an eventual economy to have the whole house supply softened, and it is certainly more healthy. Health, too, will also suggest that some sort of provision be made to keep food cool and pure—refrigerating plants are now obtainable for every type of need.

Electricity.—The electric wiring of a house deserves a good deal of thought. It is so easy to "economize" when building is in progress and to regret ever afterwards when ugly wires and cables have to be superimposed on walls and woodwork. Bear in mind at the outset possible requirements for power plugs, radio, lighting in various parts of the room. It is far better

Courtesy of the Electrical Association for Women

Fig. 1—A modern all-electric house. Above: the living-room. Below: (left) the bedroom, (right) the kitchen

to have too many points available than too few. Electric heating is coming more into vogue, and it is possible nowadays to obtain an automatic temperature control, operating through an entire house. Incidentally the same result can also be achieved by up-to-date gas, oil, or anthracite stove systems.

And as the ideal house should have no cold corners, neither should it have corners that are dark, breaks of level round the floor, necessitating dangerous steps, unnecessary passages, or steep, narrow stairs.

Having got as far as this, in actual practice, you have done no more than merely to build a sort of framework or foundation for the making of a home. You will, however, if you have been alertly concerned with all the process of construction, have the very considerable advantage of knowing all about the house in which you are to live—a most important consideration when repairs, alterations, and upkeep have to be considered.

Colour in the Home.—The next stage, and the one that will effect the greatest transformation in your home, will be the bringing in of colour—paints, distempers, papers, materials.

There are two extremes to avoid—the nervous attitude which dreads to introduce anything but pale neutral tints, and the reckless outlook which plunges into orgies of wild colour without any restraint or intelligent planning. The latter is much less in evidence than the former; the majority of people who have the least sensitiveness are so afraid of colour blunders that they take few risks.

In colouring your home you will naturally begin with the outside. There is no excuse for drabness nowadays. Concretes are available in many tones; colour washes are procurable in almost any shade; bricks and stone have almost infinite variety; glazed tiles, coloured glass, dull or glistening metal are all adaptable to building exteriors; paintwork, properly exploited, can give distinction. Yet, so customarily, outside colour is left to chance, or the whim of the builder. Properly you should consider colour at the outset, just as you do shape, bearing in mind the characteristics of the locality and the probable effects of atmosphere.

Even if you have a stereotyped house—perhaps of red brick with dark red tiles and a patch of green garden in front—it may still be given individuality by its outside paint.

Outdoor Colour Schemes.—A common procedure with such a house would be to do all painting in some characterless brown, with white window-frames, and immediately it would look like all the neighbouring houses. It could be made infinitely more attractive, however, if all doors, down-pipes, window-frames, and so on, were painted a moderately dark rich blue; especially if window sashes, beadings, and similar small sections were picked out in a warm grey. The value of these two colours for outside combination against dull red and green is widely appreciated in Continental countries, but very rarely here. Blue is admittedly a difficult colour with painters, but if surface gloss is rubbed off before the paint is very old and a fresh coat of clear varnish applied then there need be no fear of fading. No shades could be better for such a scheme than what are generally known as *bristol blue* and *parrot grey*. But get good quality paint.

An alternative, though less effective, scheme would be to have the main paintwork of the same grey, and the minor work picked out with white.

Greens often look attractive in towns where there is little natural greenery, while if you prefer to be cautious you may select quite confidently from a wide range of neutral tints—creams; stone colour; cement shades; greys; light, medium or dark browns. Among the medium browns *tan* looks particularly well; chocolates and purple browns should never be used with a red brick background. Incidentally, a full gloss finish paint best withstands normal outdoor atmospheric conditions—though whenever you think of paint you should bear in mind that there are several types of surface finish available.

Interior Colour Schemes.—You may decide to begin by linking up the interior with the exterior, and so settling first the colour scheme of the hall. For

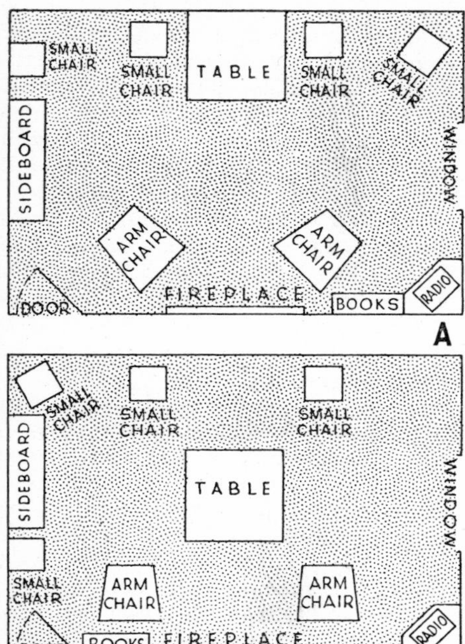

Fig. 2.—Alternative Furniture Arrangements for a Dining-room

instance, with the blue and grey, already described, at the entrance, a delightful effect would be obtained by using pale pink, with a relief of blue curtains to tone with the blue outside. The pink should be related to the grey, and this pink should cover walls, ceiling, woodwork alike, preferably with a flat rather than a glossy finish. From the hall the other rooms can be built up appropriately.

Or the hall may be linked, by means of green, with the natural colours outside instead of with the house itself. And again there would be the alternative possibility of the neutral colours. A very safe thing would be a sunny apricot tint, with woodwork and banisters in light buff. This would look particularly well if walls were dull distemper and paintwork glossy.

A great deal of thought, however, needs to be done before interior colours are decided. Individual rooms must have their own colour schemes, but they must be considered also in relation to the entire house. There should certainly be a variety of rooms, the greater the variety the more refreshing and interesting a house will be, but there must be also a unity and harmony about the whole.

Main colour outlines will naturally be determined in a large degree by the aspects of the room—north, south, west, east, light, dark, used in the evening, used in the morning, with variable lighting, with constant lighting, used for short intervals, used for long periods, needed for rest, needed for activity. When you have analysed such things as these colours will already be suggesting themselves as peculiarly appropriate, and it need not take very long to come to broad decisions.

Orange is the most joyous colour, and so suitable for northern rooms. Yellow is cheerful and gives light too. Green is good in towns, but in the country it may clash with greenery outside. Red is difficult, but very stimulating. Blues look cold, but for that reason often suit south rooms; blue too is restful. White helps much where

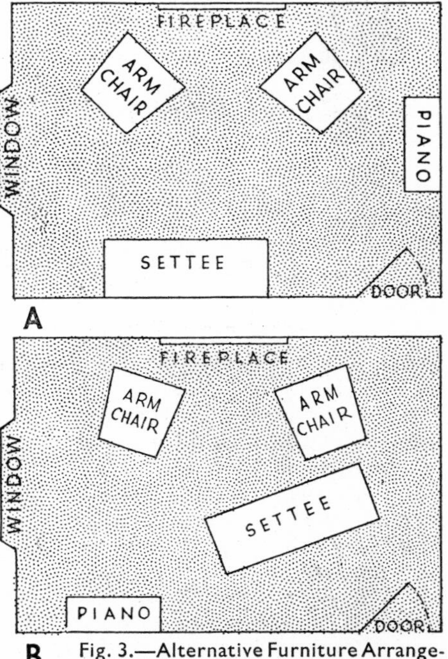

Fig. 3.—Alternative Furniture Arrangements for a Lounge

there is little light and forms an excellent background for other colours, but you must be careful to get the right surface. Cream is a safe colour and extremely useful in dark rooms. Black can be extremely effective, but it obviously needs using with discretion.

A room, however, seldom consists of a single colour, or at any rate a single shade, and when you have determined on the general effect you wish to achieve in a room you have only begun the planning.

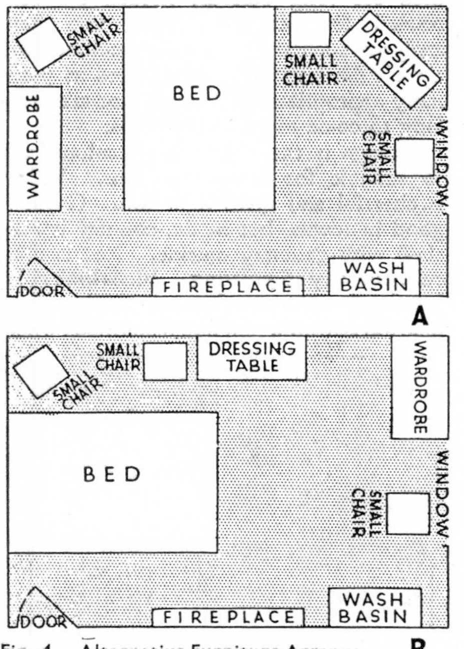

Fig. 4.—Alternative Furniture Arrangements for a Bedroom

You must now proceed to choose contrasting and harmonizing shades.

It is a sound plan to build from the floor upwards, that is to fix the colour of carpet or floor covering first and to work from that. In a large room it is all right to have walls of strongly marked colour, but in a small room walls should be less conspicuous —if they do not force themselves on the attention the room will naturally seem large, and also they will give enhanced attractiveness to furnishings and decorations. But whether bright or not the balance of values should be the same. The floor should be the darkest shade; the walls and woodwork approximately the same as each other and lighter than the floor; the ceiling lightest of all. White ceilings are seldom satisfactory; it is best to have them faintly tinted with the colour of the walls, or with some very light harmonizing shade.

Suggested Schemes.—Let us consider an actual colour scheme for a room. We will assume that it is a lounge, fairly small, which gets moderate sun. Additionally it contains piano, bookcase, and small tables in mahogany, round which the colour scheme must be built.

The floor might be covered with plain gold carpet, running right to the skirtings—this gives a much better impression of size than a square of carpet with a surround of floor. Walls and paintwork should be warm, yellowish buff, harmonizing well with the gold of the floor, the paper of good quality, rough surface, with only the least mottled pattern, so that the walls will seem to recede. The ceiling can be a pale cream. Thus the same colour tone runs from floor to ceiling, but with ascending lightness. Furniture upholstery can then be of sage green, patterned not too heavily with gold. This green provides the secondary or contrasting colour, and should be strongly marked. A third colour note may be introduced by having a lamp shade or a few other bright splashes of petunia, which itself is a link with the mahogany. Curtains, which should be patterned, seeing that floor and walls are plain, may emphasize either the green or the petunia.

Another example, this time for a dining-room of north aspect, and as an alternative to the customary orange or yellow walls:

Floor of polished parquet or oak boards; furniture in plain or polished oak; walls of canvas texture paper or ordinary distemper in apricot or light buff; woodwork of the same shade, or a little deeper, or glossy cream; ceiling a paler tone of the walls. On the floor could be used rugs in dark brown, warm golden brown, and string colour. Curtains of plain old gold, or cream patterned with golds or browns. Lamp shades could be of parchment and oak or palest peach colour glass and copper. Ornaments and fittings would be effective in brick and russet shades as well as golden browns and perhaps with touches of blue green. Copper articles would harmonize well.

The predominating colour in most rooms is naturally that of the walls and this will generally determine for you the foundation colour of the floor and the pale tint of the ceiling. The secondary colour of a room —which may be furniture, paint, curtains— should be something distinctly different. To give still more piquancy a third colour may be introduced. More than three are dangerous.

But instead of or in addition to any of these three colours it is possible to use neutral tones, which have been listed in the description of paints. A neutral colour is safe at any time, but lacks character.

Colour Combinations.—Bearing in mind the three colours possible in an ordinary room here is a list of simple combinations which will be found harmonious. Exact shades, of course, must be chosen with care:

1st Colour	*2nd Colour*	*3rd Colour*
Pale yellow	Ruby	Light blue
Yellow	Purple	Blue green
Deep yellow	Mauve	Dark green
Orange	Violet	Medium green
Pink	Dark blue	Bright green
Bright red	Bright blue	Light green
Wine	Light blue	Pale green
Ruby	Pale green	Pale yellow
Purple	Dark green	Yellow
Mauve	Medium green	Deep yellow
Violet	Bright green	Orange
Dark blue	Light green	Pink
Bright blue	Pale green	Bright red
Light blue	Pale yellow	Wine
Blue green	Yellow	Ruby
Dark green	Deep yellow	Purple
Medium green	Orange	Mauve
Bright green	Pink	Violet
Light green	Bright red	Dark blue
Pale green	Wine	Bright blue

Nature is a sure guide to the right use of colour. Study of the spectrum will yield such results as the foregoing, or one may take flower combinations and so devise other schemes equally appropriate. One simple and effective method is to examine wallpaper designs from a first-class manufacturer, and to select from colours featured there. Simpler still, any good paint or distemper maker, or experienced house furnisher or decorator, will be glad to make suggestions to you. Here are a few other schemes, with the use of neutral colours, and based on actual room parts:

Floors	*Walls*	*Ceiling*
Black & white	Pink	Cream
Dark green	Yellow	Paler yellow
Dark brown	Yellow	Cream
Beige	Pink and Blue	Pale pink
Warm buff	Pale grey	Oyster
Fawn or gold	Turquoise	Cream
Dark brown	Orange	Cream
Grey	Pink	Pale pink
Dark green	Medium green	Yellow
Medium brown	Lemon	Pale pink
Warm brown	Medium blue	Pale blue

Remember that if walls and floor are plain then curtains and furnishing materials should be patterned, or vice versa.

Choose floor coverings with care. There are so many varieties—linoleum, square or piece carpet, rubber, cork, various tiles, mosaics, parquetry, oak boards, strip oak, and so on.

Lighting.—Similarly choose your lights with care. It is possible to have frosted lamps, indirect lighting systems, shades of every colour and many different materials, various methods of eliminating unpleasant glare from direct bulb lights.

The main outlines of your rooms settled, you will come on to furniture and ornaments.

Proportion.—One important thing to keep in mind is the complete unity of any room, not only in colour, but in form and proportion. A comparatively small room, for instance, may be enhanced, as has already been suggested, by quiet toned walls. But additionally the desired impression of size may be helped by suitable flooring, perhaps narrow strip oak, which can be laid over ordinary deal boards; and also by avoiding bulky furniture. Much of the apparent size of furniture depends on its height and the degree in which it obstructs view in a room. Consequently, without sacrificing anything in quality of upholstery and comfort, you may ensure that your furniture is less conspicuous by having it low—many settees and armchairs have their backs 12 in. or even 18 in. higher than there is any need to be. As a matter of fact the nearer to the floor the seat of an easy chair is the more restful it will be.

Pictures too must have their size proportioned to that of the room. The same obstruction objection of high furniture applies to beds; in a small room you should certainly avoid the old-style high ends.

In choosing furnishing fabrics, do not buy for a lifetime. Anticipate that you will probably like a change in a few years, so there is no need to be unduly impressed by the covering that will "last for ever." But see that you get as far as possible fadeless stuffs, for the more colour you have the more dangerous the sun will be. There is a wonderful variety of furnishing materials in these days—sunproof and washproof fabrics, fadeless artificial silks, cretonnes, chintzes, printed linens.

Furniture.—When selecting furniture do not be concerned about imitating the conventional and certainly do not be completely "fitted out" by some ready-made mass-production system. Consider each room individually, the exact use to which you will put it, the personal requirements—and then buy as sparingly as possible. It is of utmost importance that quality shall stand before quantity when you are making your home. It is so easy to get a house cluttered with things which have neither beauty nor significance. Good style in furnishing, as in any of the arts, consists largely in eliminating the superfluous. A sentence loaded with adjectives is ugly, so is a room overburdened with fitments, whether intended to be useful or decorative. Besides, as you develop skill and taste in your hobby of home-making, you will discover things which you would like to add to your rooms.

Pictures.—There is particular danger of overcrowding. In so many homes pictures are quite meaningless; they are hung in profusion with some vague idea that there ought to be pictures, but they are so numerous and so lacking in character that their owners soon cease to be conscious of their existence and certainly never look at or enjoy them. It is infinitely better to have one picture in a room at which you can gaze over and over again with the same fresh pleasure. And by having just one you increase the probability that it will be noticed. Few rooms, except art galleries, can stand more than half a dozen pictures. No part of the home-making hobby is more delightful than this of searching for and securing one by one pictures that have meaning and enduring beauty for you.

Ornaments.—Even though the *whatnot* has gone, the whatnot habit of mind has not. Photographs whose only virtue is a sentimental and personal interest still lumber shelves—their worthlessness from the point of view of beauty can be judged by their complete lack of appeal to any who do not know the subjects; souvenirs, cheap vases and knick-knacks, to say nothing of odds and ends of household goods, still litter rooms. In the room that has beauty nothing out of place or worthless is allowed to obtrude. And as with pictures so with ornaments. One good vase, which can be a lasting delight, is worth twenty inferior ones. And additionally if there are only one or two ornaments you can be sure that they will be seen. It is far better to have, for instance, a lounge with no more than two or three pictures and ornaments—if they are really worth while—and wait ten years before adding another than to "fill up" with worthless things which simply obscure those that are good.

There is another side to all this, however. As taste and experience improve, and possibly financial resources also, it is very pleasant to be able to replace the less good by the better. No house should be static. The keen home-maker is always adding or increasing; his ideals are never fully achieved, nor all of his wishes obtained. You may first have to be satisfied with cheap prints of pictures you like, then with good reproductions; no one can ever get more than a few of the originals that he would like to have.

ICE SKATING

In these days there are more skaters than ever before because so many large towns have ice-rinks where this delightful sport may be practised any day; but almost every winter has one or two spells of frost when there can be outdoor skating too. Such a spell may only last a day or two, and if you would make the most of it you must be already prepared with skates in good condition, and some knowledge of skating.

Skates.—For general use you need those with curved blades—straight blades are for speed and distance work. The edges should be sharp and clean, so that they can get a firm grip of the ice, and if your own skates are not like this get them ground at once—do not wait until the frost is on you. The old wood-stock pattern skates are now quite out of date, and the best makes consist entirely of steel, either being fixed permanently to a pair of boots or having screws and nuts which allow them to be clamped on and taken off at will.

Preliminaries.—It is quite possible that you may learn to move about on skates with fair confidence in the course of a single day; but it is a common thing for a learner to take up the whole of his first visit to the ice with preliminaries which might have been overcome at home, while the ice was thickening. For instance, the chief trouble at the start is nearly always ankle weakness. It feels very odd to be balanced on two thin steel blades, which bring into play muscles that ordinarily get little use. So the beginner is held up every few minutes by the aching of his ankles, and spends a lot of his time resting. This difficulty can quite well be dealt with in your home. Put on your skates, and try walking about on a suitable floor, until you can do it with comfort. The necessary strengthening of your ankles is achieved in surprisingly quick time.

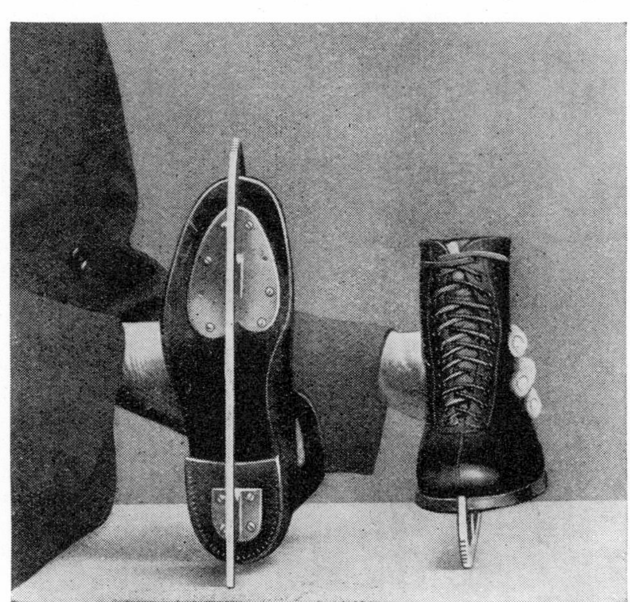

Fig. 1.—How the Skates should be fixed

You may also prepare, when the frost is starting, by getting a clear idea of the principles of skating, so that you understand exactly what to aim at when you get on the ice. It would be of no use trying to walk along in ordinary fashion, for as fast as you put one foot forward its fellow would slip back. The method must be quite different.

Stand with your feet together. Now turn the right toe outward until its skate is at right-angles with the left, and slightly to the rear. If you press against the right blade it will remain firm, so that you are sent gliding forward on the left foot. Immediately afterwards the right skate is lifted, and at the end of the glide it is put down on the ice; the left foot is turned outward and, in turn, makes its own thrust. Thus skating is simply a matter of thrust and glide on one foot then the other.

Having got so far you will be ready to begin real skating as soon as the chance comes.

Ice must be at least 2 in. thick before it is fit. Even at 3 in. it may not be safe, if it is of the white, flaky variety. The best skating ice is black and smooth. You may try its strength by thumping it with the point of a stick—if only a many-rayed scar appears then probably it is fairly safe.

But one part of an ice surface may be stronger than another. Beware of sheltered spots, where overhanging trees or banks have screened the water from the cold. A current or a spring in the water may also be a cause of danger. A word or two of warning may be appropriate here. Always be prepared for emergencies. If you chance to go through the ice, in deep water, you may hang on to the broken edge of the hole until help arrives; or you may break the edge away in front of you and so make your way to the bank. If someone else is in like danger, remember that the secret of approaching a hole in the ice safely is to spread your weight over as big a surface of the ice as possible—thus you will move along, spread-eagled; or slide any flat object—ladder, hurdle, or pole across towards the one in danger.

First Attempts.—It is best to make your earliest attempts without a stick or any other support. A few falls are inevitable, but you will soon get the knack of keeping your balance. Besides, falls need not hurt if you take care to go forward and relax all your limbs so that you just flop limply. Generally if you are leaning forward, you will do no more than drop on the hands and knees.

In the earliest stage of skating the beginner does not dare to keep his thrusting foot clear of the ice for more than the shortest time, but brings it forward and puts it down alongside its fellow as quickly as possible. Gradually, however, you should aim at lengthening the single foot glide, with the other leg stretched well behind. (Fig. 3.) Continue to develop this ability until you glide several yards from each stroke. And now correct position will matter a good deal. Your skating knee must always be well bent; the thrusting foot will be kept behind, pointing outward and downward; the body from the waist will be straight, and you will look to the front and not down at the ice.

Stopping and Turning.—To turn you must lean the body over, just as a cyclist does, and the skates will then follow round of themselves. To come to a standstill simply make a very sharp turn, until your blades are at right-angles to their former line of progress.

The Edges.—Though much time is needed to gain any wide mastery of figure skating, some of the beginnings may be learned quite quickly by anyone with fair ability at plain, straightforward skating.

Get to understand the "edges." It is rarely that a skater glides on the flat bottom of a blade, usually he is on one of the sharp edges. It is thus easy to understand an "inside" and an "outside" edge.

If you think about the matter a little more you will see that it is possible to glide on a left foot inside forward edge; a right foot outside forward—and so on. Altogether there are four such edges—two on each foot. Also, it is possible to skate backwards, on the same four edges. That makes eight in all.

You must first practise, then, taking forward glides on the various edges. Some you will master fairly easily; some will be troublesome. Aim at gliding as far as possible from a single thrust "holding your edge."

The names of the edges are usually abbreviated in print, "right forward outside" appearing as RFO. The full list of abbreviations is therefore—RFO, RFI, RBO, RBI, LFO, LFI, LBO, LBI.

Your most important edge, though not the easiest, is the "forward outside," and the best way of practising is to go round in small "cross-over" circles. For instance, for the RFO you will go round to the right, constantly crossing your left foot over the front of its fellow, and so moving forward in a series of short steps. If the circle is only 2 or 3 yds. across you will find that each time you glide on the right foot you will be leaning well on to its outside edge. Gradually lengthen your glide on the edge.

Figure Eights.—Concentrate at first on the outside forward edges, for they are most important, and difficult. Suppose you start on the right foot—as you should in commencing a figure—you will make your stroke with the left foot, keeping the right shoulder forward and the left pressed back. Your head will be turned over the right shoulder and you will lean to the right. Do not bend at the waist, but keep the whole body straight and leaning boldly across into the curve, just as a cyclist leans when taking a corner. You will probably be nervous about this leaning, and this will prevent you getting well on to the edge, but perseverance will enable you to go farther and farther over and so to hold your glide for a longer period.

When at last you can make a sufficiently strong thrust, and hold the edge long enough, you will find yourself completing a circle with a diameter of several yards. This makes you ready for a figure eight, which simply consists of two circles, one on each foot. You take one stroke, gliding on the RFO, and then when you come again to the starting point, or *centre*, the left blade is put down, a thrust made with the right foot, and the second circle of LFO completed.

Much depends on the position of your shoulders. In taking an outside edge on the left foot the left arm and shoulder will be leading; but for an inside edge the shoulder and arm over the *unemployed* foot are pressed to the front.

Backwards Skating.—Your next interest will be in backwards skating, for you should not be satisfied until you have the ability to go backwards as readily as forwards. At first keep both feet on the ice and experiment with body swaying and outward sweeps of each foot until you begin to move in the desired direction. Your knees must be sharply bent, as usual. Soon you will find yourself travelling backwards in serpentine fashion and at quite a fair pace, and then you may think about proper

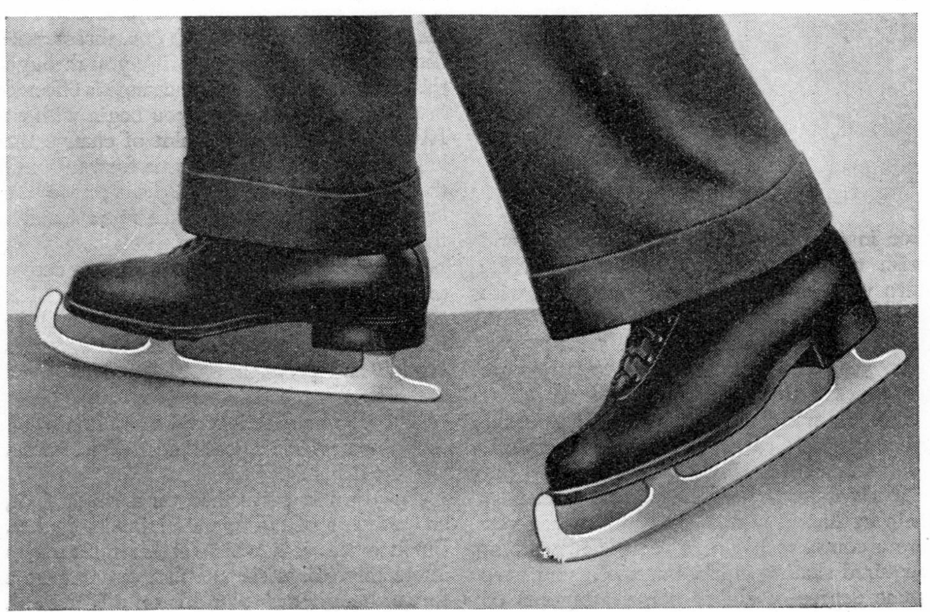

Fig. 2.—The first attempts at movement: a correct thrust

glides—just as you proceeded with your forward skating. You will thrust from each foot in turn, the toe turning inwards, and glide on the other blade in exactly normal fashion. Turn your head over your shoulder so as to look where you are going.

After this it will not need very much practice to enable you to change from forwards to backwards, or vice versa, as you are skating along. The easiest method is to change from a forward inside edge on one foot to a backward inside on the other.

Fig. 3

For instance, you are going forward, and wish to reverse. Drop on to the RFI; turn your left foot strongly outwards, with its heel following closely behind that of the right, and at the same moment as you turn your body to the left drop across on to the left foot, lifting the right clear. Thus you will find yourself travelling in the same general direction, but now backwards on an LBI.

Pair Skating.—There is no particular help in skating with a companion when you are a complete beginner; confidence is best acquired skating alone, but when you have some degree of ability pair skating can be as beneficial as it is enjoyable.

It is best to grasp hands in front, right with right and left with left; later on the two left hands can be held in front and the two rights behind your back, thus allowing complete freedom to turn. Go along in straightforward fashion, aiming to work in perfect harmony and rhythm, making your strokes exactly fit, though without glancing down at the ice. Think about style rather than speed.

You can also travel pleasantly facing each other, gripping each other's arms, or with hands on each other's shoulders. One then travels backwards and the other forwards.

More Figures.—And now may come something quite new—the *change of edge* on a single foot. This is very much like an eight, but there is not the same change of feet at the middle. You begin, for instance, with an FO curve on which you cover just half a circle; then, still on the same foot, you swing over or "change" on to the inside edge and go round in a complete circle in the opposite direction. Your thrust will need to be very strong to bring you through this circle and a half. The change is effected in this manner—suppose you begin with an RFO, as you near the point of change the left shoulder and left leg come forward until the leg is stretched to the front; then the leg is carried backward once more leaving the shoulder at the front. This change of body position will cause you to swing across on to the RFI, in which, of course, the left shoulder must lead. Be very careful to keep the body upright while making this change, and swing the whole leg freely from the hip.

The *turn* or *three* is a still more important figure, on which a great deal of advanced skating depends.

The turn is performed on a single foot, and consists of two curves joined together. But it is this join which makes the turn so interesting, for while the first curve is on a forward edge, the second is on a backward, yet there is no break nor new thrust between.

Start off on the right foot—an RFO, and cover a fair curve. Gradually twist the shoulders as you go, without bringing forward the unemployed leg, and push the left shoulder so far forward that you have a feeling that the body is being wound up. Just at the moment of maximum tautness flick your right foot round—it will go almost of itself, and at the same time carry the left shoulder back to check yourself from spinning too far. Thus you will find yourself travelling backwards on your inside edge.

In reading this it may be difficult to understand how you can continue with the backward edge. But just think of a boy going down an ice slide. Often when he is halfway along it he twists right round and finishes up with his face to the starting point, although he has been travelling smoothly all the way. It is very much like that with the *turn*, except that you do not go straight but in two equal curves. The chief difficulty is in having enough strength left in your glide to make a good second curve. In every sort of *turn* or *three* keep your skating knee well bent, but straighten slightly for the actual turn, sinking again for the succeeding glide.

Threes to a centre are the most interesting figures for practising the *turn*. Start from some definite mark on the ice and set off on an RFO; make your turn after covering a semi-circle; return to the centre by a second semi-circle of RBI; continue with a second circle of LFO; *turn*, LBI, finishing at the centre. This, of course, is a figure eight form with a turn at each extreme end. A straight line marked down the long axis should run through the centre and through the two cusps of the turns. On clean ice you will be able to see the tracings made by your blades, so make sure that the cusps point accurately to the centre, and fall exactly on this imaginary line of the long axis.

Having mastered *forward eights* of outside and inside edge you should go on to the same figure on the backward outside. These backward eights are difficult, but worth much practice. Set off on a strong RBO, holding the left foot in front, and keeping the left shoulder pressed forward. You will be looking over your right shoulder towards the centre of the circle, and almost sitting on your right heel. Gradually turn the body, carrying left leg and shoulder outward and backward and pivoting the head with them. Thus the second half of the circle is completed with the left leg leading and the head looking along the left shoulder. At the centre the left blade

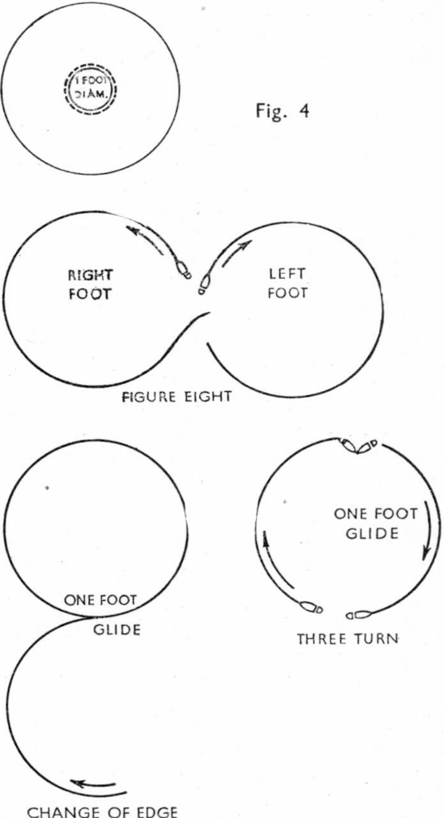

goes down and the second circle is completed in similar fashion.

General Figure Skating Hints.—Don't look down at the ice more often than necessary.

Don't let your arms flap about wildly. Use them just as much as you need, but keep them under control. The palms of the hands should face downward, or towards the sides of your body.

See that the unemployed foot points always outward and downward.

Get used to making strokes of equal strength on each foot. You are nearly certain to find one side stronger than the other at first, so aim to strengthen the latter. You do not want to be a one-legged skater.

Fig. 5

Every figure must be started from a single stroke. You should not get up speed for it. You see then how important strong strokes are. Such strong strokes are quite impossible unless the ice is gripped with the full length of your blade.

Dancing on Ice.—It is necessary to have fair ability before trying ice dances, but that ability need consist of little more than backward and forward edges and turns. The most popular dances are: waltz, fourteen- or ten-step, tango, waltz fourteen-step, fox trot.

In starting to dance on the ice you must have guidance from a competent partner; learning without systematic tuition is almost an impossibility. The best dance to begin with is the fourteen-step, then follow with the waltz.

Speed Skating.—Speed skating is for the athlete. For speed work long straight blades are used. The body crouches forward, and generally the arms are swung strongly from side to side with each stroke. Your aim must be to glide straight forward, rather than in the easy, outward curves used in ordinary skating. Particularly practise the quick cross-over steps used in taking a bend or the corners of a rink. The body must lean strongly for these and the whole action closely resembles that of running. Immediately you settle into the "straight" again return to the long glide.

KEEPING FIT

SENSIBLE moderation is the secret of good health, and it is because the great mass of people live fairly intelligently and happily, avoiding the extremes of the faddist, that general health in these days is so remarkably good. But it is not nearly what it might be, and that largely because comparatively few people make a "hobby" in any degree of keeping fit. What is needed are a few systematized, personal rules which can be worked into the daily time-table of living and become as much a matter of habit as the cleaning of teeth.

Plenty of systems have, of course, been devised; but when they involve the apportioning of even fifteen minutes daily to exercises before breakfast then they definitely do not appeal to the average person. It may be regrettable, but it is certainly true, that most of us recoil from the idea of getting out of bed a quarter of an hour earlier each morning and going through various exertions before dressing, even though we know how beneficial they would be. Fortunately, the busy man or woman can keep fit on a smaller programme, provided a reasonably balanced life is being followed. The sedentary worker, for instance, needs muscular exercise and varied interest, and he should get these by cultivating some of the open-air hobbies elsewhere described. If he swims, hikes, or cycles whenever opportunity allows, then he will be provided with much of the exercise he needs, and he will be kept fit indirectly, without concentrating attention on the matter at all.

All the same one must give a little direct attention to keeping fit, though no more than a few minutes daily may be needed.

If the body is properly fed, through lungs and stomach, and can get rid of all waste matter promptly and easily, then there will be little wrong with it. The basic principle of keeping fit is as simple as that. Add the need for recuperative rest, and for regular exercise, and there are five main headings worthy of special attention—lungs, stomach, waste products, exercise, rest.

The Lungs.—On the proper functioning of these depends the condition of the blood, on which all health rests, since the blood nourishes the tissues. Blood must get enough oxygen. The person whose work involves little physical labour, or physical labour in a vitiated atmosphere, rarely supplies his blood with the amount of oxygen it is able and ready to take. The lungs may never even be used to anything like their full capacity. There are two things, therefore, of pre-eminent importance to good health—they are, pure air and proper breathing.

Try to get as much pure, clean air as possible both day and night. If you live in a city where smoke vitiates the air, get out as often as you can into the country for week-ends and holidays and breathe deeply and regularly. Walking in the early morning or at night, when the atmosphere is clear and free from dust and grit, will help to provide the town-dweller with the oxygen he needs.

Houses should be kept freely ventilated. Windows should be open, especially at night, so that the lungs may be taking in oxygen during sleep.

Proper breathing is as essential to health as is fresh air; for unless we know how to develop our lungs, we shall be working our body machinery at only half-pressure. Not only must the air be taken in filtered and warmed through the nose, not gulped down by the mouth, but the lungs must be used as they are intended to be.

Breathing may seem the most natural thing in the world; but in actual practice most of us have to *learn* how to breathe; in the ordinary routine of modern life, which is to a large extent sedentary, our lungs do not get the chance to expand to the full. Breathing exercises are therefore essential if we want to use our lungs properly. It takes about a minute to do a dozen or so deep breathing exercises each morning on rising, but nothing else repays us so well.

Breathing should be deep, not shallow; regular in rhythm; and should bring into

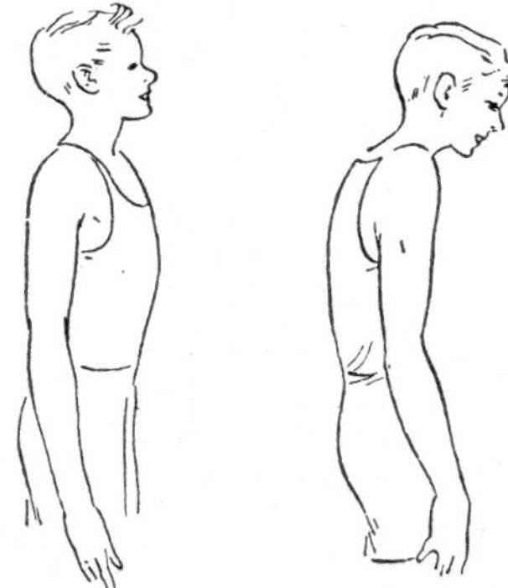

Fig. 1.—Breathing Exercise. Right and Wrong Way of Standing

play not only the upper part of the chest but the muscles of the diaphragm as well. The breathing apparatus extends right from the nose down to the diaphragm; and in the process of taking a deep breath you should start by depressing the diaphragm as you gradually expand the ribs. This greatly increases the capacity of the chest. Some breathe only by raising the ribs and puffing out the chest, and thus do not get in nearly the quantity of air they might.

Stand in the open air or at a wide-flung window when you do your daily breathing exercises; and begin by relaxing thoroughly both in body and in mind. Clear the brain as far as possible of all thoughts and concentrate on restful, recuperative breathing. Relax the muscles, and empty the chest of every particle of air. This can be done by breathing out the air already contained in the lungs, so that the shoulders fall forward and the whole of the upper body is dropping.

Then, as you inhale, fling the body back, raising the arms sideways until they are at full stretch slightly above shoulder level; rise also on the toes so that the whole body is taut by the time the lungs are full; then drop to "attention" and breathe out

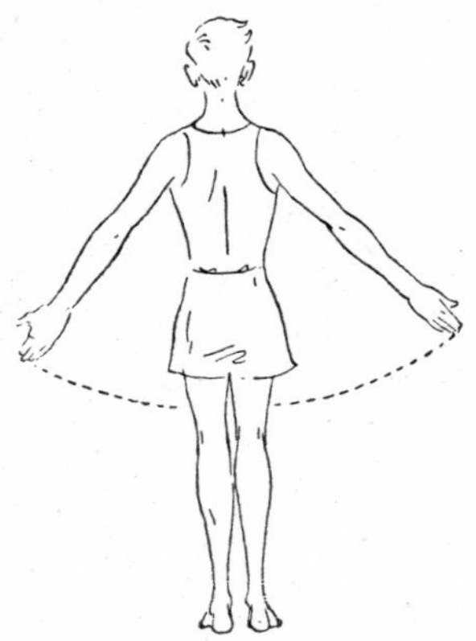

Fig. 2.—Breathing Exercise (1)

forcibly and fully. In taking a deep breath see that you are inhaling through the nose and not through the mouth, and that your shoulders are steady; the work should be done by the muscles of diaphragm and chest, the rest of the body being kept under control. Breathing out on an "ah" sound will tell you whether or not your breathing is steady and controlled. There should be no tremor in the voice as the sound is made, and it should continue with perfect steadiness till the last particle of air is expelled from the lungs.

Make a habit of taking a few deep breaths whenever during the day there is a suitable opportunity. Besides encouraging the development of the lungs and supplying the blood with oxygen, it soothes the nerves and prevents that jaded feeling at the end of the day's work.

The Stomach.—The food requirements of the body are rather like the needs of an internal combustion engine: it must be kept in running repair and it must also be provided with suitable fuel for driving power.

Six different types of food are required by the body for these two purposes. Proteins, mainly contained in meat, are needed for tissue-building and the repair of the body. Carbohydrates and fats, found in starchy and sugary foods, are necessary more particularly as a source of energy. Water is equally essential; and so are certain mineral salts and vitamins.

Your food must contain these substances in the right proportion. It is not the quantity, but the quality, of your diet that counts. A certain minimum bulk is required for the digestive processes to have full action. Part of this bulk is provided by digestible food, and part by the indigestible "roughage"—fruits and vegetables and "rough" grains, which stimulate the intestines and prevent constipation. But once the necessary bulk of food has been attained, we must consider not how much food we are to take, but what kind it is to be.

Meat is eaten because it is a concentrated form of protein; but it is not really vital to the diet. We can get on quite well without it if we take plenty of milk, cheese, eggs, potatoes and flour. Few of us, however, care to dispense with meat altogether. The

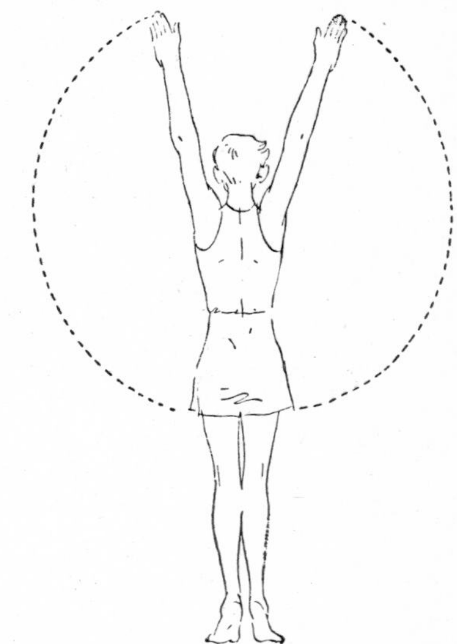

Fig. 3.—Breathing Exercise (2)

war-time ration of meat per person has been found to provide quite sufficient protein for the ordinary processes of body repair; and there is no need to exceed this if we want to keep fit.

Plenty of starchy foods, fats and sugar should also be taken to ensure the necessary quantity of carbohydrates and fats. Milk is an excellent food, and at least one quart per person should be drunk every day. Most of us drink far too little water. Two and a third pints a day should be taken, for water is very necessary for the digestion and carrying away of our food, as well as for the making of blood. Take your drinks between, rather than with, your meals; have a glass of water—preferably warm—first thing on rising, and drink at intervals throughout the day. Alcohol is harmful in whatever form it is taken. Besides water and milk, cocoa and fresh fruit drinks are very beneficial; tea—especially China—in moderate quantities does no harm if it is drunk fairly weak and not allowed to stand for more than three minutes before pouring; good coffee is also an excellent beverage.

Vitamins.—It is absolutely essential that your food should contain the necessary vitamins in addition to proteins, fats, etc. Scientists have not yet thoroughly investigated this interesting subject but though they are still unable to tell us the exact nature of the vitamins and the way they react upon our bodies, they have proved that we cannot live without vitamins. Most of them are already contained in some degree in the ordinary foods we eat; but many a minor ailment, such as poor appetite, lack of energy and resistance to colds, "nerviness," bad teeth and brittle nails, are directly traceable to vitamin deficiency.

Vitamin A, the vitamin of growth and resistance, can be obtained mainly by eating meat, fish, eggs and cheese. Liver and kidney are especially rich in this; so are the "yellow" vegetables—carrots, spinach and peas; also milk and all its products.

Vitamin B, the nerve-building vitamin, is found largely in milk; and in wholemeal bread, cabbage, carrots and nuts. Vitamin C, which tones up your body and gives you energy and vitality, is contained principally in fresh fruits and salads, especially in lemons, grape-fruit, oranges and tomatoes, and in raw vegetables or those steamed or otherwise cooked so that their essential juices are not poured down the sink.

Is vegetarianism good for those who want to keep fit? That is a question often asked by people who do not very much care for a heavy diet. Some appear to flourish on a régime devoid of meat; but for the average person it is true to say that any violent departure from the normal diet will cause the health to suffer. Eat what you like, with discretion. If you do not require much meat, concentrate on the vegetable part of your diet; but on the whole, vegetable foods are not so rich in protein as animal foods, and you will, especially while you are young and require much protein for purposes of growth, be ill advised to omit meat entirely from your diet.

Fig. 4.—Body Twist

The condition of the stomach and the other internal organs has infinitely more bearing on health than the bulk of one's muscles. Whether or not one does daily exercises to develop these latter and similar muscles does not greatly matter; but it certainly is immensely worth while that these vital internal regions should be toned up. The best way to achieve it is to follow your deep breathing with a dozen "body twists." Stand upright with hands on hips, and then, from the waist, circle the top part of the body, making as wide a sweep as you can with the shoulders. The whole figure may be understood if you think of the shape of a funnel, with legs as the spout, and the trunk sweeping round the broadening top. To avoid giddiness, make half a dozen turns in one direction and then reverse for the others. This results in a stimulating massage of the abdominal parts.

To avoid daily monotony here are two alternative exercises.

First.—Stand upright, with feet together and arms stretched out at shoulder level in front of you, parallel with each other and the floor. If you can grip a short stick with both hands it will help to keep the position. Then swing the arms and the trunk round to the right, until you face the side, and go on to swing right back again to the other side. Hold the body upright and do not move the hips more than necessary as you continue with this backward and forward twist or swing from side to side. Do it a dozen times. (Fig. 5.)

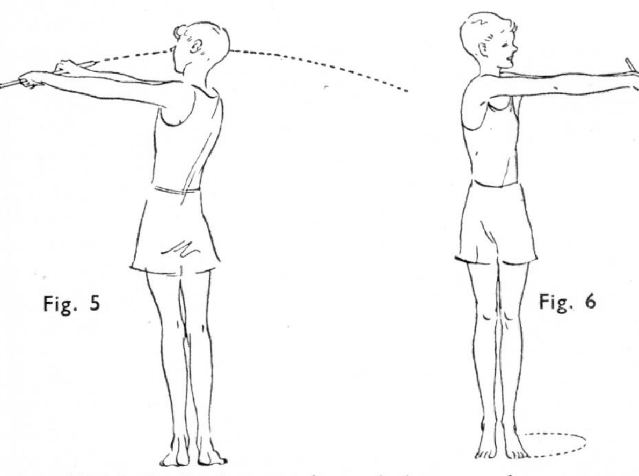

Fig. 5

Fig. 6

Second.—This is practically the same, except that now the top part of your body remains still while the lower part does the twisting. Hold the arms and shoulders steady, as in the last exercise, and then jump round, so that the feet point first to the right and then to the left. Twist from the waist. Repeat a dozen times. (Fig. 6.)

Waste Products.—Constipation is the root of much evil. The way to avoid it is not by doses of medicine which gradually become less efficacious, but by sensible diet and plenty of fluid. The long drink on rising is particularly helpful.

Remember to cultivate regular habits.

Remember, too, that the pores are excretory organs and must be kept unclogged if they are to do their work. There is no better, and more generally convenient, method than by the morning "sponge down." Cold or at any rate tepid water should be used, for this has an invigorating effect. Do this on getting out of bed, and follow, when you have put on clothes—if necessary—by the breathing and twisting exercises. In all, you need be no more than five minutes. Towel yourself vigorously, and during the pleasant glow that follows you will have the satisfaction of knowing that there is no poisonous waste left on your body to be reabsorbed during the day, and also that the pores are clear for continuing their work of exudation.

Do not depend altogether on cold water for cleansing purposes; have a warm bath at least sometimes. Very hot baths are extremely bad for the health as they tend to produce lassitude, and there is considerable risk of exposure to chill afterwards; the shock to the heart, too, on entering very hot water may have ill effects. But a brisk bath in warm water, followed by a cold sponge or shower, is refreshing and invigorating. When you first enter the bath, sponge your face at once with the warm water, so that the flow of blood to the head may keep pace with that over the rest of the body. An occasional Turkish bath is beneficial to those who can stand it; it gives a thorough "spring-clean" to the skin and encourages the excretion of waste products through the pores.

Exercise.—How much and what kind of exercise should be taken daily? This is a question frequently asked by those who want to keep fit. Especially does the answer to it affect the sedentary worker, whose only chance to get exercise is by deliberately adopting some form of sport, or some open-air pursuit.

A daily walk part of the way to work is one way of getting the air and exercise the body needs. Most people, however, feel the need of getting more exercise than this during their free evenings and at week-ends and holidays. The best possible scheme of exercise for a man was said by a well-known sportsman to consist of football in winter, and cricket in summer, both games played regularly and strenuously. Failing this, tennis, swimming and good hard walking provide the best physical exercise from the health point of view. An hour's hard "singles" is considered by physiologists to represent the minimum amount of daily exercise for the average man. Riding is also an excellent health sport. The modern week-end habit, of getting away from towns and walking, cycling or camping under the simplest conditions in the fresh air of the country, is one of the most encouraging signs of health-consciousness to-day.

Sunlight.—The vital part played by sunlight in our health has only recently been recognized by the general public. Pioneers of sun-bathing and sun-healing, like Dr. Rollier with his "sunlight centre" at Leysin, Switzerland, have proved by physiological tests the beneficial action of the sun's rays on the body. Sunlight enriches the blood, thus laying a firm foundation for good health. Samples of blood taken from sun-bathing patients show week by week a steady increase in hæmoglobin, the vital iron constituent of the blood. Sunlight moreover develops and tones up the muscles, and improves the texture of the skin in much the same way as does regular massage of the limbs.

Get out into the sunlight as much as you can, and whenever possible on holidays or at week-ends map out for yourself a daily scheme of sun-bathing. Remember that benefit is derived not from sudden and prolonged exposure to the sun, but from gradual acclimatization to it. Too much sun-bathing can do serious injury, producing lassitude, blistering and sun-stroke. Begin by exposing the body for fifteen minutes or so, and increase this time by five minutes each day for a fortnight, at the end of which you should be able to stand two or three hours' exposure without running any risk of sunburn.

Direct sunshine is not at all necessary for sun-bathing; the ultra-violet rays are contained just as much in clear, strong light as in the fierce glare of the midday sun.

Certain precautions should always be observed by the sun-bather, neglect of which may lead to serious illness. Avoid the very hot midday sunshine from eleven to two in summer; wear a hat and dark glasses when the heat is extreme; and on colder days, when there is a wind, choose a sheltered spot for your sun-bathe. Do not pass suddenly from the heat of the sun into a cool shade, thus risking a chill; and take a drink before you go into the direct sunlight, so that your body may be the better prepared to stand the heat.

Rest.—The amount of sleep needed by adults varies considerably with the individual. Some people can get along with the very minimum of sleep; others who expend much mental or physical energy during the day may require a great deal of rest to allow their bodies time to repair and recruit strength. A great many people spoil their chances of good health by sleeping too little, and just a few people by sleeping too much. The amount of sleep which you personally require can readily be discovered; if you do not feel fresh and rested when you rise, then it is likely that you have not slept enough. A rough estimate for the normal individual is from seven to eight hours.

There is, of course, not only quantity but quality of sleep. The best sleep is undoubtedly obtained before midnight, so allow yourself as much time before twelve o'clock as you can; during this period the body relaxes more thoroughly than it does throughout the rest of the night, and the brain is not so apt to be worried by dreams.

The bed should be a hard one. Feather mattresses are most injurious to health; so is too high a pillow. Avoid too many thick coverings, and never have a fire in the bedroom. Allow as much fresh air as possible to flow through the bedroom during the day; windows should be kept open, the bed stripped early and the mattress left to air; and at night, of course, as much ventilation is necessary as during the day.

Quiet rest is essential to health; and we can as a matter of fact do much more to promote real, healthful sleep than many of us imagine. Sleeping soundly is very largely a matter of habit, and can be induced by following certain rules. Worry kills sleep, as a preliminary to killing men; so let your last waking hours be tranquil, and certainly free from business cares; the pursuit of some favourite hobby is an ideal way of finishing a day, for it induces just the mood most propitious to sleep. Clear your mind of all disturbing thoughts and emotions; fix your attention on some quiet subject; try to think of a blank wall, or the colour black. When your brain is at rest, begin to relax one by one the muscles of your body, relieving all tension. Imagine that you have been dropped from a great height, or have just come to earth after a parachute flight, and that your body is altogether loose and crumpled up, offering no resistance to anything. When this stage of relaxation has been reached, deep, quiet breathing will soon bring sleep.

Practise this relaxing exercise whenever you have a spare minute during the day, especially after lunch and at the end of the day's work. Most of us keep our bodies in a perpetual state of tension, and complete relaxation is the best possible way of straightening out jangled nerves and soothing both the digestive and the respiratory system.

The question of the last meal at night largely affects the quality of sleep. Some prefer the chief meal at midday, and sleep best after a very light supper. Others find that in the evening the body is more at leisure to enjoy the main meal of the day. In this case, at least two and a half hours should elapse between the time of the meal and bedtime, so that the digestive function may be allowed its full time.

When you get up in the morning, do not spring suddenly out of bed—it is not good suddenly to race a motor engine, or a heart, that has been lying still for some time.

GENERAL HINTS

Smoking and Stimulants.—Alcohol as a stimulant is definitely bad for the health, in any form. Its action is slowly toxic to the body. Tobacco has a similar, but very much slighter, effect, and in moderation is not injurious. A certain amount of mild smoking soothes the nerves; especially the smoking of a pipe, which is much better for the health than are cigarettes. Inhaling is a dangerous practice and should be avoided as much as possible. Those with a weak stomach would do well to give up smoking altogether, as it may have upsetting effects upon the digestive system.

Though smoking may do no great harm, most physiologists agree that the body is better without it. It is a noticeable fact that all athletes in training, when they want their physical powers to be at their most vigorous, "knock off" tobacco and alcohol.

Clothing.—The simpler and looser the clothing, the better for health. The body is provided with sweat-glands regulating the temperature by excreting superfluous moisture; and these can function best when the clothing, instead of fitting tightly to the skin, leaves room for a layer of air around the body. Underwear should be as porous as possible, and should fit loosely so as to allow for this layer of air and give free flow to the circulation. The modern trend towards open-necked shirts and shorts, when circumstances make these possible, is definitely in the interests of health.

Shoes, too, should be given careful consideration by those who want to keep fit. The effect of footwear on the general health is not sufficiently recognized; but research workers in this field have found that even such ailments as headaches and insomnia are often directly traceable to badly fitting shoes, which by throwing the spine out of alignment upset the nervous balance of the body and make proper rest and poise impossible.

The line of the body should be perfectly straight from head to heel. The same height of heel should be worn all the year round, and the instep should be given proper support.

Teeth.—The care of the teeth is an important factor in this business of keeping fit. No one can enjoy really good health if the teeth are even slightly neglected. They should be brushed night and morning, of course, but even greater attention should be paid them at night, so that no traces of food are left in the mouth to decay and poison the system during the night. Eating an apple the last thing before retiring is a good way of making sure of sound teeth and preventing decay. Most of us eat far too much soft food, and we should do well to take more fresh unpeeled fruit and more crisp salads. Masticate the food well, and do not be tempted to take your meals in a hurry. "Bolted" food sets the stomach an impossible task, and leads to all kinds of digestive troubles.

Bath or sponge-down, deep breathing, body-twisting—that means just a minute or two each morning, and yet, together with plentiful water and sensible diet, it is enough to keep you fit. If, however, you care to give a few more minutes to definite exercising you may correct personal weaknesses or build up strength in particular directions.

For example, the sedentary worker has little opportunity of strengthening his arms, and he may like to do "arm pressing" exercises, lying face downward on the floor. The manual worker, so as not to be without suppleness, may prefer a few minutes of skipping. The girl anxious to develop her bust may do arm and shoulder swinging and stretching. The person who desires better ankle or calf can sit with leg outstretched and do foot-circling movements and knee-bending exercises.

So you can go on adding exercise to exercise. For instance, there is no doubt about the value of rubbing and massaging after your sponge-down—not merely the skin but the whole body can be set in a tingling glow by means of it. Similarly one can find things to benefit neck, wrists, or any part of the human frame. If you become a keen physical culturist, you will naturally follow on with many things outside the scope of this article. If you do not, then you should still adhere at least to the minimum daily routine set down here, for anything less will certainly jeopardize your chances of keeping fit!

KNITTING

KNITTING is one of the most popular hobbies for women, and it is a craft too for all ages, but, as with all crafts and in particular those related to garments, there is a constant change in fashion and new sets of designs, books, etc., dealing with the whim of the moment. To give, therefore, detailed directions for garments which are being worn at the time when this book is printed would be useless. The important point is that there are certain fundamental technical details which remain unchanged, but which are not often to be found in the knitting leaflets so easily obtainable. Beginners in the craft will find that a knowledge of these is very helpful when working from printed directions.

Wools.—These are usually sold according to the ply; that is the number of strands twisted together to form the thread actually used for knitting. It is very important to realize, however, that all four-plys are not the same thickness. This depends not on the number of strands, but on their individual thickness and the way in which they are twisted together. Some strands are very soft and thin and lightly twisted, while others are coarser and firmer and quickly twisted. The worker must therefore select the wool carefully. For underwear and baby's clothes the wool should be soft and fine; for stockings and any article to be subjected to hard wear the wool needs to be correspondingly firm.

It is most important to remember that if the knitter is following printed directions she should be quite sure to get the exact wool mentioned, or, failing that, some very similar in thickness and twist.

Needles.—These are sold in a big range of sizes. Number 9 is a very popular size. Numbers 10, 11, 12 and so on are finer, numbers 8, 7, 6, etc., become thicker. Some are pointed both ends and are useful for work on four needles, but it is usually a comfort to have a knob on one end to prevent the stitches falling off.

A good pair of knitting pins is a wise purchase. The cheaper ones may be a nuisance because of their poor surface or very sharp points or tendency to bend or break, or they may stain the wool.

A knitting pin gauge is an essential item. It costs only a few pence.

Equipment.—All work should be carefully kept in a bag or wrapper. The ends of the needles should be protected with cork or proper protectors when the work is not in use. The ball of wool should be kept in a definite place when being knitted or it will roll about and get soiled and unwound.

Following Printed Directions.—There are two main types of knitting directions. One gives the worker a diagram of the size and shape of the article planned out on a squared ground, each square representing one square inch. The directions also give the tension, i.e. the worker is told how many stitches go to the inch both across and up the knitting. The other type gives the worker the number of stitches to the inch each way but no diagram and only rough measurements.

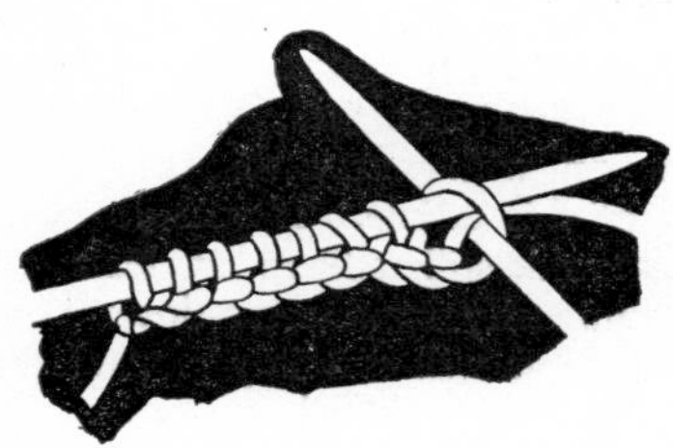

Fig. 1.—**Casting On**. Make a slip-loop and place it on a left-hand needle. Insert the right-hand needle into the loop from left to right. Pass the wool round this needle's point with the index finger of the right hand, and draw it through to form a new loop. Pass this loop from the right-hand to the left-hand needle, taking care not to allow the first loop to slip off. Insert your needle into the second stitch on the left-hand needle; and then continue the process until sufficient stitches have been cast on

It will be seen that a diagram on a squared ground is very helpful, especially if the worker has to alter the size of needle or wool or even the size of the pattern. The important thing in any case is the tension and the worker should *always*, even if needles and wool are correct, test her tension of knitting to see if it agrees with the directions. If she finds she is working on a larger or smaller scale she must either adapt her knitting or her number of stitches.

Many disappointments occur because the worker has ignored the tension.

Casting On.—It is assumed that all readers know how to cast on and off in the usual way. Space is too limited to go into details which almost everyone knows. If not, Fig. 1 will prove helpful.

When casting on, however, the worker may have found that the edge becomes very loose and not very pretty. If this happens when knitting the first row, knit in the back of the stitch instead of the front. The result is a tightening of the cast-on stitch and a much firmer edge.

Edges.—Many knitters will have noticed the tendency of knitting that is worked in stocking web fabric, i.e. one row plain and one row purl, to curl up from the bottom and in at the sides. When the stocking web pattern extends to the edges this will always happen and nothing that can be done afterwards will prevent it. It is for this reason that all wise workers plan their knitting to avoid any curling and the following hints should be carefully studied and applied.

Fig. 2.—Increasing

To prevent the bottom edge curling knit several rows of all plain knitting, or ribbing 1 plain, 1 purl, or 2 plain, 2 purl for several rows (*see* Fig. 6), or a band of moss stitch (*see* Fig. 9). The depth of the knitting in any one of these needs to be at least 1 in.

Sides.—There are two kinds of sides in most knitting. There is the edge that will be joined to another, i.e. a seam edge and the edge that will be free as down the front of a coat.

To prevent a garment in stocking web

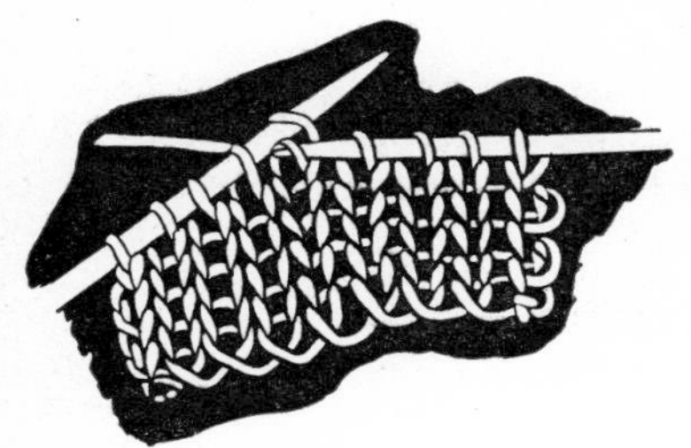

Fig. 3.—**Plain Knitting.** Insert the right-hand needle into the top stitch on the left-hand one, pass the main wool round its point and pull it through, forming a new loop as in casting on. Keep this new loop on the right-hand needle, and cast the one which is caught up with the knitting off the right-hand needle. Insert the needle into the next stitch on the left-hand needle and repeat to the end of the row. When beginning a row, the first stitch may be slipped on to the right-hand needle without knitting

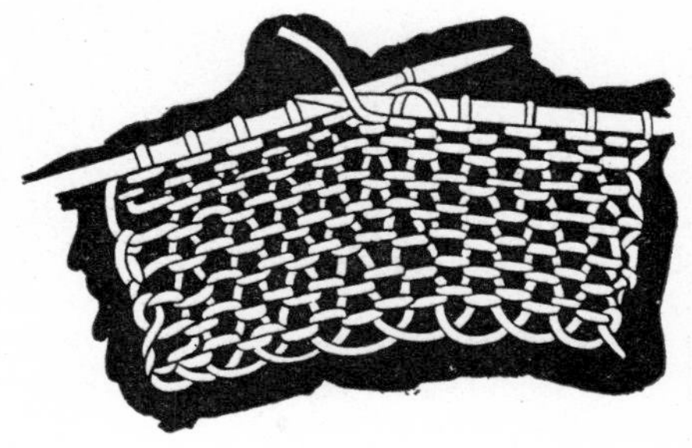

Fig. 4.—**Purling.** Purling is used when a smooth result is required. It is the opposite of plain knitting; the reverse side of a purled row is plain. Hold the wool to the front of the work. Insert the right-hand needle, from right to left, towards the front of the first stitch on the other needle. Catch the needle, draw it through, and slip the old stitch off the left-hand needle, as in plain knitting

pattern curling in down the front it is usual to knit the last 1 in. or more of stitches either in all plain knitting or moss stitch up the front. With seam edges it is advisable always to knit the two end stitches as plain. This makes a tiny notched edge which will be used when seaming the garment together.

A little experiment will also show the worker that if the first stitch is knitted the work has a tendency to tighten along the edge. If, however, the first stitch is slipped off the needle plain-wise on a plain row a chain edge will form which will be slacker than the other way.

Increasing and Decreasing.—When knitting it will be found nearly always better to make any increasing or decreasing occur two or more stitches from the edge. The most usual way of decreasing is to knit two together. Another way is to slip one, knit one and slip the slipped one over the knitted one. As it is often desirable to balance the effect of the decreasing the worker may need to use one type of decreasing at one end and the other at the opposite end.

Increasing.—Here again there are several correct ways. It is really a matter of choice. The most popular method is to knit a stitch and then take up the loop immediately below it at the back and knit it also. When increasing has to be balanced the lower loop may have to be knitted first. Another good way is to knit twice into the same stitch, first into the front and then into the back (or vice versa), without taking it off the needle.

Casting Off.—The usual method is to knit two and slip the first one over the second one knitted. Then knit one more and slip the other over it and so on. When ribbing is being cast off it is better to knit the stitches to continue the ribbing, i.e. a purl stitch is knitted as a purl even on the casting-off row.

Casting off should always be done loosely and to correspond in tightness with the rest of the work.

Patterns.—In Figs. 5 to 17 are a number of attractive and very simple patterns.

Stocking Web Fabric, Fig. 5.—This is worked one row all plain and one row all purl. It can be made interesting by knitting in bands of two or more colours.

Ribbing, Fig. 6.—Cast on any number of stitches divisible by 4.

1st Row.—* Knit 2, purl 2, repeat from * to end.

2nd Row.—** Knit 2, purl 2, repeat from ** to end.

Repeat the first and second rows.

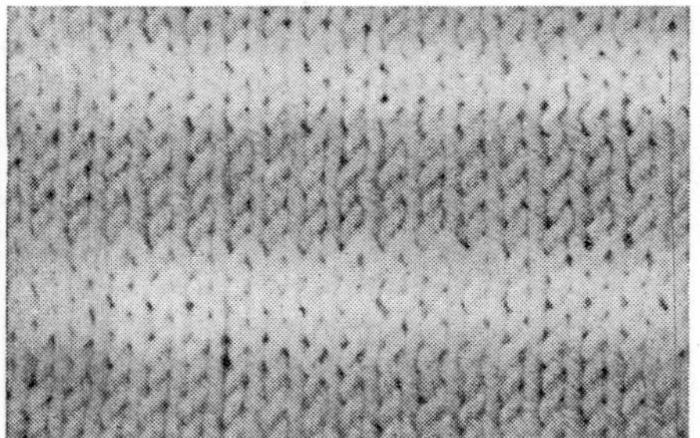
Fig. 5.—Stocking Web

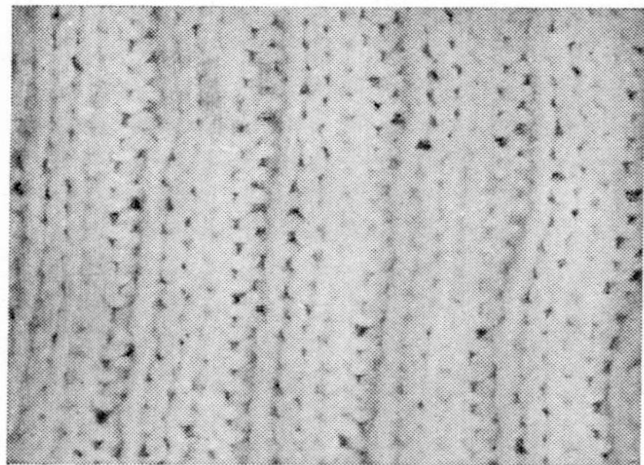
Fig. 6.—Ribbing

Ribbing, Fig. 7.—This stitch gives rather a flat rib and does not pull up so tightly as the more usual ribbings.

Cast on any number of stitches divisible by four *and one more.*

1st Row.—Knit 2, purl 2 to end and knit the last stitch.

Repeat this row all the time.

Fancy Ribbing, Fig. 8.—This is another open, flat rib.

Cast on any number of stitches divisible by four.

1st Row.—* Knit 2, purl 2. Repeat from * to end.

2nd Row.—Knit plain.

Repeat first and second rows all the time.

Moss Stitch, Fig. 9.—Cast on an even number of stitches.

1st Row.—* Knit 1, purl 1. Repeat from * to end.

2nd Row.—** Purl 1, knit 1. Repeat from ** to end.

Eyelet-hole Pattern, Fig. 10.—Cast on any number of stitches divisible by five. Knit one row plain. Now begin pattern.

1st Row (right side of work).—* Knit 3, wool forward, knit 2 together, repeat from * to end.

2nd Row.—Purl.

3rd Row.—Plain.

4th Row.—Purl.

5th Row.—* Knit 1, thread forward, knit 2 together, knit 3. Repeat from * to last four stitches; thread forward, knit 2 together, knit 2.

6th Row.—Purl.

7th Row.—Plain.

8th Row.—Purl.

Repeat these eight rows of pattern for whatever length of knitting is required.

Dice Pattern, Fig. 11.—Cast on stitches divisible by ten. Knit ribbing of 5 plain, 5 purl for six rows. On the next row reverse the ribbing by commencing with 5 purl.

The Weave Stitch, Fig. 12.—Cast on an odd number of stitches rather loosely. Work one row in plain knitting before starting the pattern as follows:

1st Row.—* Pass the right-hand needle behind the first stitch (behind *both* strands

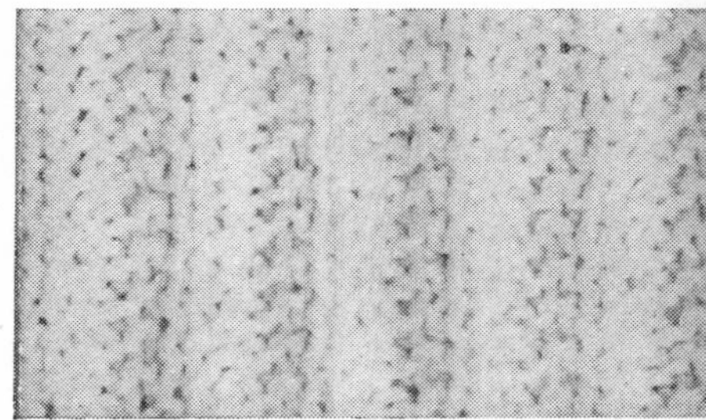
Fig. 7.—Ribbing

Fig. 8.—Fancy Ribbing

Fig. 9.—Moss Stitch Pattern

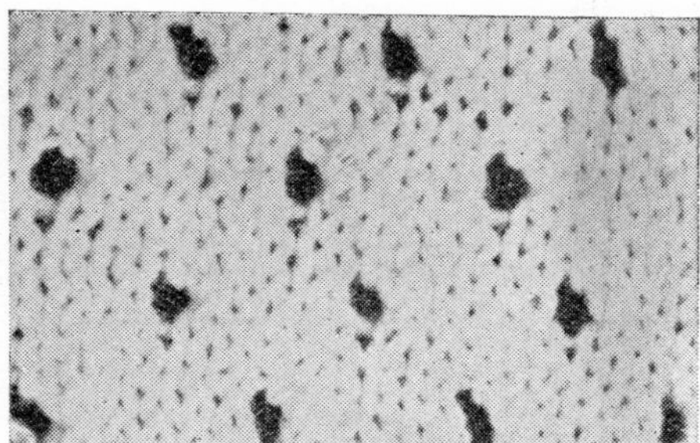

Fig. 10.—Eyelet-hole Pattern

Fig. 11.—Dice or Basketwork Pattern

Fig. 12.—Weave Stitch

of the loop), and then through the second stitch as for ordinary knitting, i.e. take it up by passing the needle from left to right through the front part of the loop. Knit the stitch but leave it on the needle. Then knit the first stitch and slip both off the needle. Repeat from * to end and knit last stitch.

2nd Row.—Pass the needle in front of the first stitch and purl the second stitch and then purl the first and lift both off together. Repeat to end and purl last stitch.

Repeat these two rows.

Openwork Pattern, Fig. 13.—Knit 8 rows of plain knitting.

9th Row.—Knit 1 * wool 3 times round needle, knit 1, repeat from *.

10th Row.—Knit 1 * drop the 3 made stitches, knit 1, repeat from *.

Knit four rows of plain knitting or as many as desired. (A small tip—the first row of knitting will seem a little loose and loopy. When you have completed it, pull the long threads of the openwork gently but firmly downwards between your finger and thumb—the stitches will then tighten.)

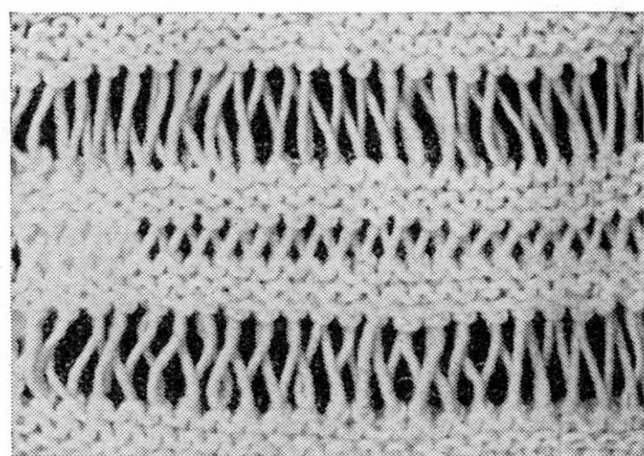

Fig. 13.—Openwork Pattern

15th Row.—Knit 1, * wool once round the needle, knit 1, repeat from *.

16th Row.—Knit 1 * drop the made stitch, knit 1, repeat from *. Knit four rows of plain knitting.

Repeat 9th and 10th Row and then knit eight rows in plain knitting.

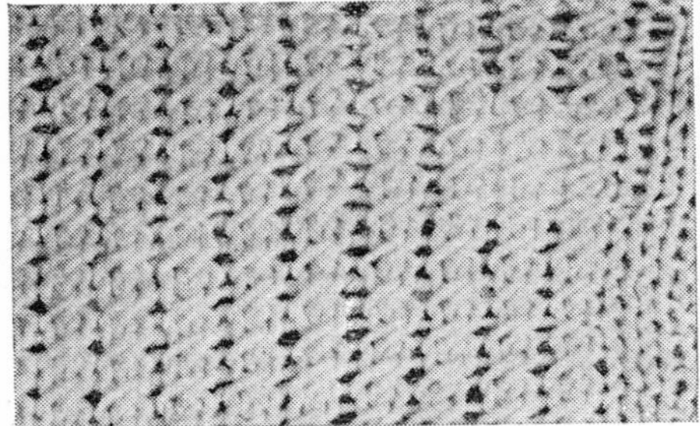

Fig. 14.—Lace Stitch

Fig. 15.—Herringbone Lace Stitch

Lace Stitch, Fig. 14.—A most effective and easy pattern for jumpers.

Cast on an even number of stitches, and knit one row plain. Now begin pattern:

1st Row (worked on right side).—Knit 2 for edge * make one by wool forward, knit 2. Repeat from * to end.

2nd Row (wrong side).—Purl 2 for edge. * Then drop the made stitch of the row below. Purl the *second* stitch on the left needle without slipping it off. Then purl the first stitch and slip both off. Repeat from * to the last two stitches and knit these without crossing. Repeat the 1st and 2nd Row.

Herringbone Lace Pattern, Fig. 15.—Cast on any odd number of stitches, and work one row plain. Now for the pattern:

1st Row.—Knit 1 * make 1 by putting wool over needle. Knit 2 together. Repeat from * to end.

2nd Row.—Purl 1 * make 1, purl 2 together. Repeat from * to end. Repeat these two rows, which make the pattern.

Feather Patterns, Fig. 16.—These make very attractive edgings for shawls, dressing jackets, the skirt parts of dresses and coats for little children and the body part of jumpers.

Cast on any number of stitches divisible by twelve. Knit four rows in all plain knitting.

1st Row of Pattern.—Knit 2 together, knit 2 together, * make 1 and knit 1, four times alternately, knit 2 together four times.

Repeat from * to within last four stitches; knit 2 together, knit 2 together.

2nd Row.—Purl.

3rd Row.—Plain.

4th Row.—Purl.

Repeat these four rows of pattern.

Fig. 17.—Cast on any number of stitches divisible by twelve. Knit four rows in all plain knitting.

1st Row of Pattern.—Purl 2 together,

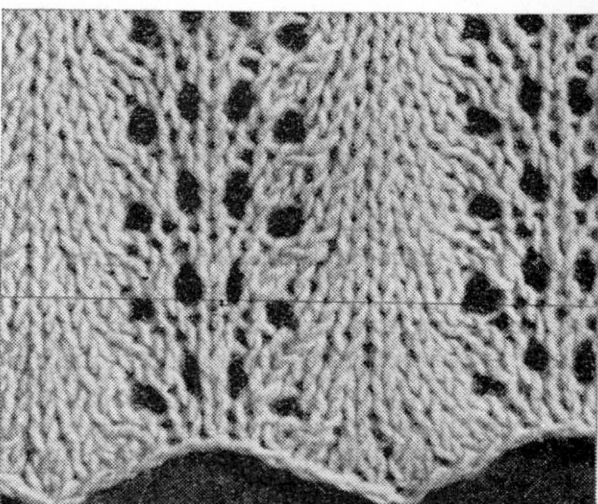

Fig. 16.—Feather Pattern

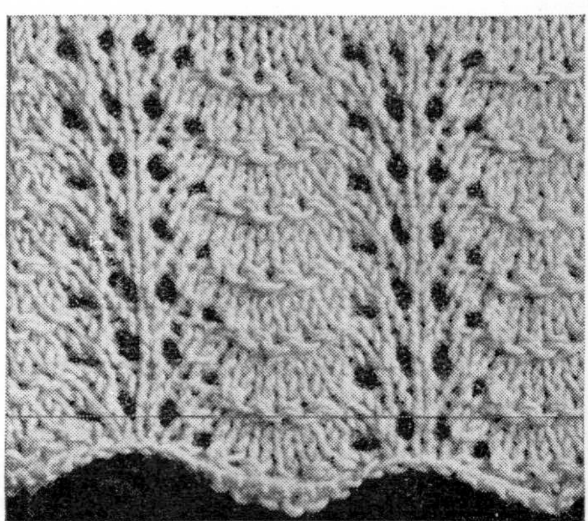

Fig. 17.—Feather Pattern

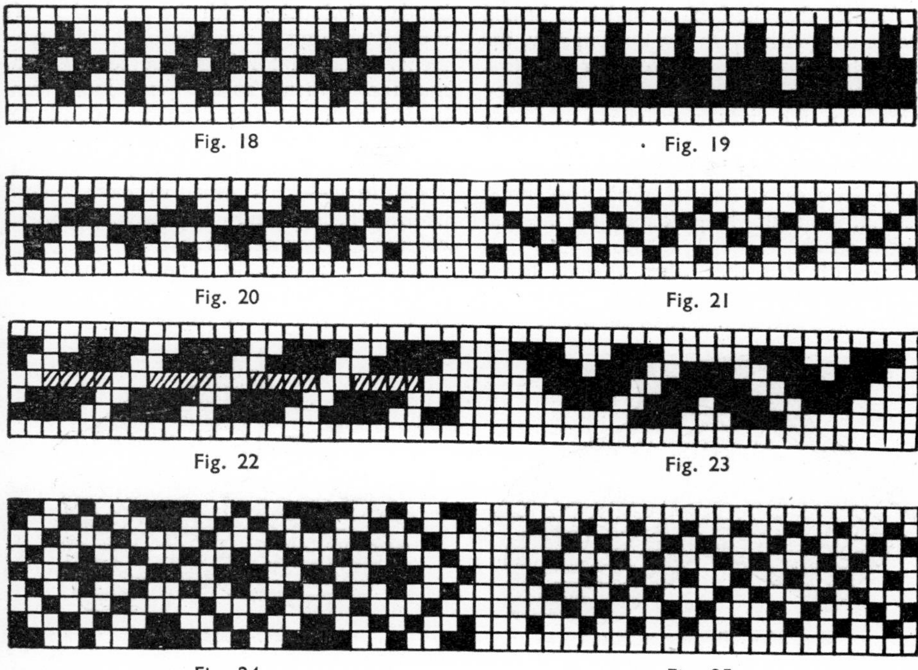

Fig. 18 · Fig. 19

Fig. 20 Fig. 21

Fig. 22 Fig. 23

Fig. 24 Fig. 25

purl 2 together, * make 1 and knit 1, four times alternately, purl 2 together four times.

Repeat from * to within the last four stitches; purl 2 together, purl 2 together.

2nd Row.—Purl.

3rd Row.—Plain.

4th Row.—Purl.

Repeat these four rows of pattern.

FAIR ISLE KNITTING

The reader who is at all interested in knitting will soon discover that there are three main ways of getting variation and interest into the knitting. There is the knitting of fancy patterns such as illustrated in Figs. 5 to 17; the use of two or more colours to give striped effects is another very usual method, while the third method of working in a number of colours in geometric shapes to form borders is known as Fair Isle Knitting.

It originated in the Hebrides where it is still practised in its traditional form often with rather a limited number of units with which to form patterns. The name is now applied to all patterns knitted in this way, an example of which is given in Fig. 31.

One of the fascinating things about this type of knitting is that the worker can very easily make up her own patterns and so make something quite original. It is far easier to make up new Fair Isle designs than new fancy patterns in knitting. A sheet of squared paper and two or more coloured pencils are the only tools needed.

Figs. 18 to 25 show designs worked out for Fair Isle Knitting.

Methods of Working.—It is usual to have only two colours in use on one row of knitting and this fact governs the design considerably. Also as one colour can only be used at a time, it is desirable that the other should not have to travel along the back too far before it is brought into use, or it may tend to strain on the work. This is another important point which influences the design.

Method 1.—For working pattern 18.

Assume that the background is light and the pattern dark. On the bottom row, the light thread would be used for the first three stitches. Then the dark would be joined in, the light put behind and one stitch only knitted in dark. The light thread would then be brought into use for three stitches while the dark one hung behind, waiting to be picked up for the next single stitch.

It is obvious that when threads travel along the back they must be kept loose; any strain is bad and puckers the work.

Fig. 26.—Slipping a Stitch

In the second row, the pattern reads * 2 light, 3 dark, 2 light, 1 dark. Repeat from *. The spot in the centre of the diamond is put there to prevent the light thread having to travel along the back of five stitches before being used again.

Second Method.—This is designed to overcome the obvious disadvantage of Method 1, i.e. the mass of strands at the back. In this second way the threads are twisted in at the back as the knitting proceeds and it is a decided advantage.

The thread not being used is held over the first and second fingers and under (or round the third finger) of the left hand. As the work proceeds the thread is lifted above the point of the right needle for one stitch and under it for the next, and so on.

The Uses of Fair Isle Knitting.—This fascinating form of knitting is frequently used on tops of gloves and stockings, for berets, jumpers, sweaters and children's clothes. It is particularly suitable for sports wear. The important thing, however, that the worker should remember is that the pattern can only be worked in horizontal bands of colouring with the result that this type of knitting is quite unsuitable for garments intended for large people. Often, too, the garments so decorated look overloaded with pattern; a border round the bottom of a jumper as in Fig. 31 is often the most effective way of using the pattern.

Colours.—It is usual to have a light neutral background and several bright colours to glow against it.

Some considerable thought should be given to the choice of colours as one unwise selection may ruin an article.

Fig. 27.—Casting Off

It is usual to choose bright strong colours that will show up at a distance and to avoid pale ones at all times. Pinks, pale blues and mauves should be avoided as they are very difficult to use with others.

One very well-known manufacturer of wools supplies a fine wool specially for Fair Isle Knitting and offers a delightful range of suitable colours.

The worker is strongly advised to endeavour to get both the best colours and the right wool, since this type of work takes longer than ordinary knitting and because of its charm deserves the very best materials.

SIMPLE ARTICLES FOR THE BEGINNER TO KNIT

As many readers will be young or inexperienced knitters or perhaps both, directions are given below for the making of three very useful and small articles. Only the foundation shapes are given because the reader can then select a pattern she likes from Figs. 5 to 17, or the Fair Isle designs, and knit the article in that.

When experience has been gained in this

way, the knitter will be able to turn with confidence to the knitting of more ambitious garments, directions for the making of which could not possibly be given here.

Foundation Shape for a Child's Beret.—Fig. 29.

The directions given are for a beret about 13 in. round the brim without stretching. Reduce the size by leaving off ten stitches; add to the size by putting on ten, or a multiple of ten stitches, i.e. one or more sections of decreasing for the crown.

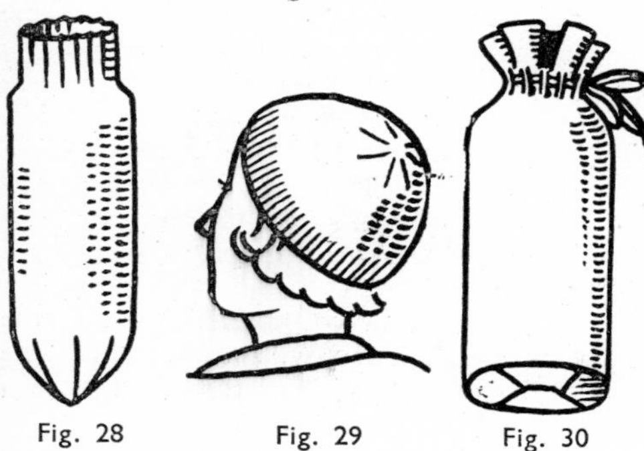

Fig. 28 Fig. 29 Fig. 30

Materials.—One or more ounces of four-ply wool, two No. 9 pins.

Tension.—About 6½ stitches to 1 in.

Cast on 80 stitches and knit for 4½ in.; longer if a turn-up brim is wanted. This part may be in any pattern desired.

Decreasing for the Crown.—* Knit 8, knit 2 together. Repeat from * to end.

Next Row.—Knit.

Next Row.—* Knit 7, knit 2 together. Repeat from * to end.

Next Row.—Knit.

Continue leaving one stitch less between the decreasings on each row until there are 24 stitches left. Then knit 2 together twelve times and draw a thread through the remaining twelve. Pull tightly and sew up down the side.

Heelless Bed Socks.—Fig. 28.

A foundation shape which can be varied with ribbing or any pattern desired.

Materials.—Two No. 9 pins and about 2 oz. of four-ply wool. Cast on 48 stitches and knit in ribbing for about 2 in. and then continue in the pattern desired for required length. This is ascertained by measuring down the back of the leg, under the heel and along the foot to within about 1 in. of the end of the toes.

Decreasing for toe.—* Knit 6, knit 2 together. Repeat from * to end.

Next Row.—Knit.

Next Row.—** Knit 5, knit 2 together. Repeat from ** to end.

Next Row.—Knit.

Continue in this way until 18 stitches are left. Cast off. Sew up the toe and side.

Note.—To reduce the width leave off 8 or a multiple of 8 stitches.

A Hot-water Bottle Cover for a cylindrical shape, approximately 12 in. round and 10 in. long. (Fig. 30.)

Materials.—About 2 oz. of four-ply wool and two No. 8 pins.

To Knit.—The directions given are for a foundation shape which can be varied by using different colours and patterns. Cast on 72 stitches for the top and knit for 1½ in.

Holes for draw-string.—Knit 1, wool forward, knit 2 together. * Knit 4, wool forward, knit 2 together. Repeat from * until 3 remain. Knit 3.

Next Row.—Knit plain.

Continue knitting until the length from the holes is sufficient to cover the bottle with its stopper, to the base.

Shaping for the bottom.—First Point.—On the first 18 stitches proceed as follows: * Knit 1, knit 2 together. Knit to last 3

Fig. 31

stitches, knit 2 together, knit 1. Repeat from * until the point is complete. Fasten off.

For the second point join on new wool and knit as for the first point. Form the 3rd and 4th points in the same way.

Press and seam up the points and the side. Make a cord and insert in the holes.

LAWN GAMES

EVEN if your lawn is very small there are plenty of games which you can play on it, many of them quite as good as tennis. To make full use of a small stretch of turf you should have a strong net—one made for ring tennis is ideal—which can be adjusted to various heights, and also a set of tapes for marking out your courts. Tapes are so much better than chalk lines, because they can be altered for varying games, or taken up altogether. If your lawn is narrow, and separated from the gardens of your neighbours only by a low fence it will be an advantage to put up nets to a height of 8 or 10 ft.

Fig. 1.—Ring Tennis

Old fishing nets serve excellently, and can be procured very cheaply at many large stores.

As several of the most important lawn games are played over a net it is an advantage to have a set of standard rules applying equally to all.

NET GAME RULES

The *singles* game has one player on each side of the net; a *doubles* game has two players on each side.

In any game like *ring tennis*, where each doubles court is divided down the middle by a line making right and left halves, the singles court may or may not have this same line—this will depend on the width available and on personal preference. In any case the size of the court can be varied to suit particular lawns. If the recommended length is not available, additional compensating width may be given to the courts, but generally it is best to preserve the standard proportions.

The choice of courts is decided at the commencement of play, by toss; and the side which wins the toss also takes first service.

The service is delivered alternately from behind the right and left halves of the court, beginning always from the right for the first service. At the end of a game the player who received now takes the first service, and the former server receives.

The server's foot must not pass in front of the rear line of the court when a service is being made—a foot is not deemed to be in front if any part of it is touching the line.

Service is made over the net to the opponent in the diagonally opposite court. Should the net be touched the service does not count. Two services are allowed, a second being taken if the first is at fault: touching the net does not constitute a fault. A game is won by the side which first scores 11 points.

When the side that is serving makes a

fault—for instance, by failing to get over the net, or getting outside the court, that should not be counted as a point by the opposing side, but instead they should take over the service and begin afresh. Thus only the side that is serving can actually score points, the service simply changing over whenever they are at fault. To make this still clearer here is an illustration of actual play: from *ring tennis :*

A wins the toss, and serves from the right-hand court. After a minute's play *B* returns a throw which *A* fails to catch, *B* does not count a point, but instead takes the service, beginning from his right-hand court. His services follow on right and left alternately—and then he beats *A* once more with a fast ring. This time *B* counts one point, and continues to serve. If the next score is also his, counting will be two-love. But if after that *B* fails to catch the ring, letting it fall inside his court, the service goes back to *A*. Thus only the serving side can count points.

It will be seen that if the score is 10-all, and *A* is serving, then *B* must score two points in order to reach eleven while *A* needs only one. This method eliminates the unfair advantage which one side would have if it retained the service all through the game.

The same player, in doubles, takes all the services until the opposite side secures them; but when it comes back to the first side the other player will serve.

After each game the players should change ends. The best of three games wins the "set."

A run may be made before the service is delivered, if desired, and after the service players may take up any position they like within their court.

Feinting or baulking in any form are forbidden in all play. Stepping over the rear line when serving constitutes a fault, and is counted as one service. Except when serving the skimming of the net is of no account.

Ring Tennis is undoubtedly the finest of all games for the small lawn. It can be very strenuous, and is always full of interest. It gives unlimited opportunity for developing fine technique.

The court for the doubles game should be 40 ft. by 18 ft. For singles a court 40 ft. by 9 ft. is satisfactory. The net should be 5 ft. high.

Fig. 2.—Tether Shuttle

On board ship, where the game originated, a rope quoit ring was often used —and this serves reasonably well. It is far better, however, to have a modern *tenikoit* ring of sponge rubber. This cannot hurt the hand, and is more satisfactory in every way. The proper dimensions of the ring are 7 in. across, $1\frac{1}{4}$ in. thick.

Throw and catch the ring by a single hand, keeping it always upright—flat rings and "wobblers" are not allowed.

There is, of course, no bouncing as in tennis, so that the players rarely need to go outside the court.

Play consists of tossing the ring backwards and forwards and a point is scored whenever a player fails to catch it or to get it into the proper court of an opponent.

Padder Tennis is real tennis, with modifications which allow it to be played on a court only a quarter of normal size.

The net is 2 ft. high, and the court should measure 18 ft. by 39 ft. Balls should be of sponge rubber, rackets made of solid wood. The racket is called a *padder*. It can be bought readily from any sports shop, or made from heavy plywood. In shape it is like an ordinary racket, but make it like a table tennis bat, measuring $16\frac{1}{2}$ in. long and $8\frac{1}{2}$ in. across at the widest part.

Play padder just as ordinary tennis—forehand and backhand play, volleying, net work and base-line driving; and so on. Scoring is also the same.

Tether Shuttle.—If you have no net around your lawn, and other games are likely to inconvenience neighbours through rings or balls going over, then try this game. In it you knock a shuttlecock backwards and forwards, but it cannot escape as it is tethered to the net. Even if it should go over a fence it can be hauled back.

Buy an ordinary outdoor shuttle, which is heavier and stronger than the shuttle used indoors, and tether it to the middle of your net by a piece of light, strong string or cord, This cord must be just long enough to allow the shuttle to reach the corners of the court.

Badminton rackets should be used, and the court can be of any size up to the official measurement of 20 ft. by 44 ft.

It is a good plan to fasten the cord to the top of the net by means of an ordinary key ring. If you have one ring permanently attached to the net the two rings can be clipped together and unclipped quite easily and there is no need to make any knots which may cause trouble when you wish to change to another game.

Naturally the string acts as a drag to the shuttle, but it is surprising how slight a hindrance it proves. Providing you hit hard you will find that the cord rarely gets entangled and you can have an excellent game exactly on the lines of ordinary badminton.

Toss Ball.—Two to eight players can take part in this, divided of course on either side of the net; 6 ft. is the best net height, and the court should be as large as you can have it, though 40 ft. by 18 ft. is ideal.

You do not require rackets. A large rubber bladder, netball, or football is used. This is tossed backwards and forwards over the net.

Fig. 3.—Toss Ball

The ball must always be thrown in an upward direction, and must not be punched or hit. It is best to use both hands in catching and tossing.

It is not permitted to run with the ball, or even to carry it a couple of steps; always it must be thrown immediately from the point where it was caught. Any player can pass to any other player on his own side—and this often allows surprising returns to be made.

When the ball falls outside the court that person or side which threw it loses a point; when it falls to the ground inside the court a point is lost by the side which failed to catch it.

Hoop Tennis gives scope for two or four players, in singles or doubles. Ordinary tennis rackets and balls are used, but the special feature of the game is a wooden hoop, measuring about 3 ft. across, which is fastened above the middle of the net — a cord running across the court, about 8 ft. from the ground, will keep the hoop upright.

Fig. 4.—Hoop Tennis

The scoring can be the same as for tennis, but an extra point is counted every time a player gets the ball through the hoop. Thus strenuous hitting is of less importance than careful aim. It needs a good deal of practice to "ring the hoop" from any angle, and as you grow more expert you may increase the difficulty of the game by reducing the size of the hoop.

Do not allow volleying from close up at the net. It is best to have a mark at least 6 ft. from the middle of the court from behind which all strokes through the hoop must be made.

Golf Croquet.—This game can be played either with golf or croquet equipment. The latter is preferable, and in either case croquet hoops must be used.

Place the hoops round your lawn as for an ordinary croquet game, and let your two or four players take their strokes in turn as usual; but, instead of continuing right round the lawn as in plain *croquet*, a fresh start must be made after each hoop, as in golf.

Hoops are therefore won or lost in turn, just like holes, and the final winner is the player who takes most hoops in the complete round.

If you have no croquet hoops available, or if you decide that they are too big, you may use sticks or stones instead, adjusting them to the desired width, and driving your balls between them. An alternative plan is to use small flower pots, laid down on their sides; of course, you cannot go "through" them, but each is considered "won" when a ball is driven into it.

Tyre Quoits.—Old motor tyres are very useful for a great many lawn games. It is worth while keeping a few on hand—any garage will be glad to give you some. Choose tyres of small or moderate size, and give them a good wash before using them for the game. For *tyre quoits* put a strong post in the ground so that it stands up about 18 ins. above ground. Then, from a distance which can be determined by the weight of the "quoit," you will roll the tyre towards it, endeavouring to encircle the post.

One point is counted if the tyre merely touches the post and drops to the ground away from it; two points if the tyre comes to rest touching the post but without "ringing" it; three points when the post is properly encircled.

It is a good plan to have two posts, one at each end of your lawn. Opponents can then play from opposite ends, so that each receives the other's tyres, thus saving a great deal of walking and carrying.

Tyre Target.—Two teams are needed, each consisting of four or five players. There must also be a referee. Bean bags, bits of stick, balls, pebbles or anything similar will do for throwing. The side which will throw first can be decided by spinning a coin—odds or evens.

The teams stand down opposite sides of the lawn, with a referee half way between them, at one end. He then rolls a motor tyre down the middle of the lawn, by giving it a single, vigorous thrust. If the *odds* are taking first throw, each one of them throws his ball, or whatever it may be, as the tyre rolls by—scoring a point if it goes through the tyre.

The *evens* then take up the balls which will have come across to them, and take their own turn as the referee rolls the tyre from the other end of the lawn.

Game should consist of 20 points.

Do not let players move from their places; they must be spread equidistant down their respective sides, and if they lose their chance as the tyre goes by they must not run along to obtain another opportunity. It is an advantage to have a line marked down the middle of the lawn, to guide the referee in bowling the tyre.

Fig. 5.—Pole Tennis

Pole Tennis.—A pole about 10 ft. high is fixed in the ground, and a strong cord tied to the top of it. This cord has its lower end attached to a tennis ball and the ball, when at rest, is suspended a couple of feet above the ground. At a height of 6 ft. above the ground a mark is painted round the pole.

Two players take part, using tennis rackets, and standing well out on opposite sides of the post. One plays in a clockwise direction, the other counter-clockwise. The aim of each is to drive the ball round so that the cord is wound on the pole above the 6 ft. mark. When this is accomplished and the ball finally comes to rest, also above the mark, then the game is won.

The start is made by one player holding the ball out so that the cord is taut and hitting it round in the desired direction. All "free hits" are taken in similar fashion. A player gives a free hit to his opponent if he causes the ball or cord to touch the post below the 6 ft. mark, or by getting his racket entangled in the cord.

It is important that players remain on opposite sides of the post; if they get near each other there is the danger that their rackets may collide.

One of the most effective ways of playing this game, which requires considerable skill however, is always to tip the ball upwards so that it just goes above the reach of your opponent, but drops again in time for your own stroke. Tremendous speed in hitting is required, because your racket is always having to overtake the ball in order to make an effective stroke and keep the ball travelling in the same direction. In ordinary tennis, of course, the racket always meets the ball when it is travelling in the opposite direction.

Clock Golf becomes the more enjoyable the larger and better conditioned is the lawn. To play it on a small, rough patch of grass where drives of no more than two or three yards are needed is a very dull business. But with really long "putts" over good turf it can be most interesting.

Press in the numbers of your clock face in regular circle formation, but do not have the hole at the centre of the circle for that will make the play all alike. By having the hole some distance from the centre you vary the length of the stroke from each figure.

There are two methods of playing. Each player can keep count of the total number of strokes required in getting right round—and the lowest score can decide the winner. Or each hole can be played separately, and a point be awarded to the one who holes with fewest strokes from each figure. Thus, in the first method the winner might have a score of *twenty-seven strokes*, and in the second *seven holes*.

In either method players follow on in turn. A single ball can be used by everybody, in which case each person must "hole out" before the next can take his turn; or each player may have his own ball, and then each can follow his neighbour with but a single stroke in turn.

Croquet.—The actual size of a standard court (35 yds. by 28 yds.) is rather large, but an excellent game can be had on quite a small lawn if the correct general principles of play are observed.

Two or four players take part—when the former, each has two balls. When there are four players they use one ball each but compete in pairs.

The balls make a complete round at least twice—round the outside and up the middle, then round once more the opposite way and down the middle—thus every hoop has to be played in both directions.

Some players prefer to stand with feet astride, so that the mallet can swing freely between the legs; this ensures good balance and ready aiming. Others like to keep the mallet at their side, standing with feet together.

When a ball has passed a hoop an extra stroke is earned. It is reckoned to be through a hoop when no part of it protrudes on the side from which it was struck. When one ball strikes another the first is placed alongside the second and a free hit is taken, which may, at the will of the player, drive the second ball in any direction. Following this still another free hit is allowed. Thus it is an advantage to hit another ball—or "make a *roquet*," for two strokes are gained.

LEATHERWORK

Many beautiful and useful articles can be made from the various kinds of leather which are nowadays available from leather manufacturers and merchants.

Materials.—The largest supply of leather for work of the kind described in this article comes from the sheep, goat and calf. It is well to understand at once that the skin of the former is stamped and coloured to represent the skin of many animals, just as the fur of the rabbit is treated to represent in both colour and "feel" the fur of many rare animals. The terms "Morocco," "Snake," "Armadillo," "Crocodile," "Python," and so on, may mean nothing more than that the surface of sheep skin has been stamped to a pattern and dyed to a colour which may make it more or less resemble the skin of these reptiles or animals.

"Suede leather" is the skin of the sheep or goat with the surface ground on an emery wheel so as to give it a smooth soft finish. It is used for many purposes in soft leather work. It is usual to begin leatherwork on this material as it is fairly cheap and easily worked. It is obtained in many colours.

"Chamois" is a split sheep skin, used mainly for gloves and window leathers.

"Skiver" is also a split sheep skin used mainly for lining bags, wallets and all kinds of fancy articles. This is the hair or grain side of the skin.

"Velvet Persian" is the name given to a skin with a fine, soft, velvety finish. "Lacing Persians" is the name given to a skin somewhat thinner than the Velvet Persian, and these are generally cut into thongs for lacing, for linings and gussets. The size of these skins varies from 4 to 10 sq. ft. and the price varies from 6d. per sq. ft. for Skivers to about 1s. 3d. per sq. ft. for Velvet Persians.

"Morocco" is the skin of the goat and in this kind of work is used in its plain colour no other decoration being necessary, unless it is improved by a contrasting or harmonizing colour in the thongs and for fittings.

Modelling is usually done on calf skin. "Natural Calf" is the most suitable for modelling and staining. It possesses a beautiful surface and for that reason it is best to avoid breaking it up with modelling and patchy colouring. Leather is not a suitable material in which to represent flowers and other naturalistic designs. It will be observed that in this section the design is restricted to that type of design which most people can with a little careful thought arrange for themselves.

Natural calf is obtainable in skins from 10 ft. to 14 ft. in area. The price varies from 1s. 3d. to 3s. od. per sq. ft. The cheapest kind is only fit for work with beginners. Natural sheep skin does not model or stain at all well as compared with calf and its use is not advisable.

When purchasing leather it must be understood that the rough edges on the legs and sides are reckoned in the area measured and charged for. The number of square feet in any skin is generally to be found in one corner on the underside of the skin—43 means $4\frac{3}{4}$ sq. ft., $52 = 5\frac{1}{2}$ sq. ft., $61 = 6\frac{1}{4}$ sq. ft.

All reputable firms can be relied on to deal fairly and helpfully with their customers and many of them will give aid with technical problems.

Thongs.—Thongs may be cut from lacing skins or may be purchased ready cut. The latter is generally the better method. If you wish to cut your own thongs it is not difficult to make a thong cutter by fixing a razor blade to a wooden stand, or an efficient pattern may be purchased.

Press Studs.—Press studs or buttons are necessary for use as fixings to purses, etc. Do not be tempted to buy cheap ones; the springs may be weak, the celluloid caps thin and easily broken and the metal cap thin and easily crushed. A great variety of fancy shapes and finishes in studs and clasps are now on the market; coloured studs can be obtained to tone with almost any colour of leather.

Frames for bags and purses can be purchased from the dealers. These are necessary for many types of work. Frames of plywood and solid thin wood are much in vogue. These can be made or purchased ready made quite cheaply.

Stones for setting into a surface can be purchased and quite often used with distinctive effect on the surface of a bag, in a belt, a book-end, etc.

Eyelets.—Eyelets are often necessary and should be stocked.

Adhesives.—Distinction should be made between pastes and glues. The former have some kind of flour as a base, the latter may be a fish glue, carpenter's glue, or any of the glues for wood. The former are useful for sticking together linings and outside leather, the latter are generally used when the ends of thongs are to be joined together or a stone fixed in its mounting. Any good paste powder to be mixed with hot water is more economical than the proprietary brands of paste.

Stains.—Stains are obtainable in powder form; it is very expensive to buy them ready mixed. Spirit stains are advised in preference to those soluble in water. The former, mixed with methylated spirit, are more convenient to use as they dry more quickly than water stains. Moreover, they are more certain and definite in their effect. The method of preparation is generally given with the stains. Mix up the whole quantity of stain at once with the spirit and keep well corked so that there is no loss by evaporation.

Polishes.—Calf skin is polished by the application of a wax polish. The best polish is obtained on a surface by rubbing well with a dry clean cloth before applying a wax polish to the surface. Wax polishes for furniture, boots, etc., are all quite suitable for work in calf.

Tools.—A six-way punch, an edge tool for paring the edges of leather, a sharp-pointed knife, pair of scissors, eyelet punch, set of tools for fixing press studs, a stitching or lacing punch, a tracer and a Dresden modelling tool form a good equipment at a very moderate cost. Other tools for punching patterns into the surface of the leather can be fairly easily made from brass screws or from pieces of bar brass of small diameter or length of side. Illustrations of

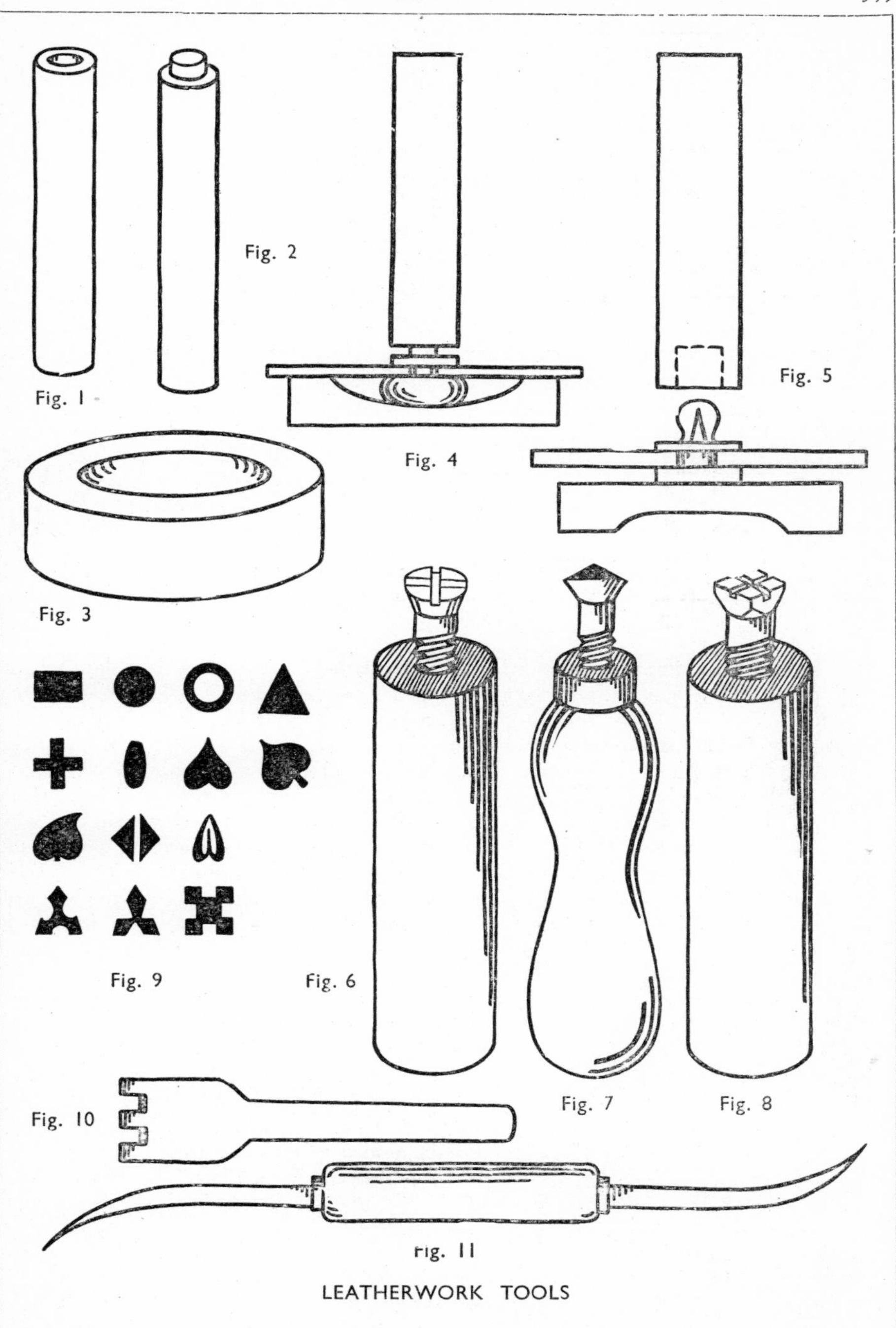

LEATHERWORK TOOLS

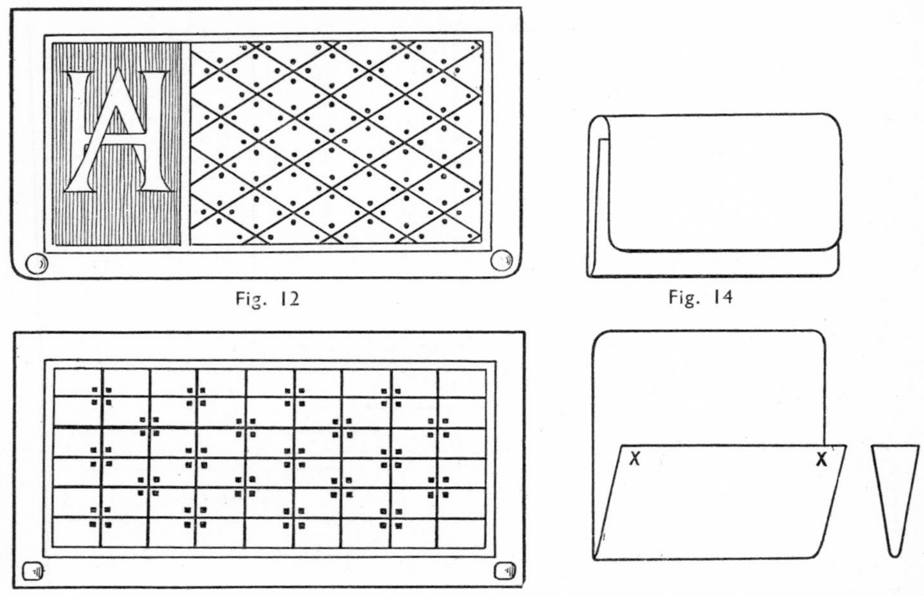

Fig. 12

Fig. 14

Fig. 13

Fig. 15

these, together with simple patterns which may be produced with them, are given on page 365.

Stamping Tools for patterns in calf. Fig. 6 shows a stamping tool which can easily be made from a brass flat-head screw turned into a handle of dowel rod, or a twig will serve. The pattern on the end of the screw is made with a small file. A 4-in. triangular file, a half-round and a knife-edge file will do most of the work on these screw heads. The cross pattern on the end of Fig. 6 is made by leaving the slot in the screw and cutting another one at right angles to it with the edge of a triangular file.

Fig. 8 shows the head of the screw filed to a square and the second slot cut. Fig. 7 shows the screw slot filed away so that the surface is clean and flat, and then filed to a triangular shape. Other suggestions for patterns are given in Fig. 9. Screws or round bars of brass are used because steel will stain the surface of natural coloured leather. Fig. 11 shows a bent tracing tool and Fig. 10 is a tool for punching slit holes for thonging.

Patterns made up from the few tool units given are shown in Figs. 12 and 13.

Staining.—Decide on the colour scheme to be used. Suppose that tones of one colour are to be used. Mix a small quantity of stain, say, a tablespoonful in a saucer and add two or three tablespoonfuls of methylated spirit to obtain a weak solution. Take a small sponge, dip it in the stain and wipe it all over the face of the leather, quickly and with even pressure, taking care not to leave any definite lines of stain. This colour will be the background. Now mix in a little more concentrated stain and obtain a darker shade. Apply this with a brush to, say, the panels of the design. Now mix a still stronger stain and apply with a small brush to the finer spots, or initial letters, or the bandings in the design. In this way a three-tone monochrome is produced.

Any mixture of colours in a scheme should be used with great restraint. Not only does this style of work require a delicate colour sense, but the pattern generally needs some considerable skill in drawing if you are to do any original designs. The geometric approach to design using a few units is much the easiest for the beginner and is to be strongly recommended.

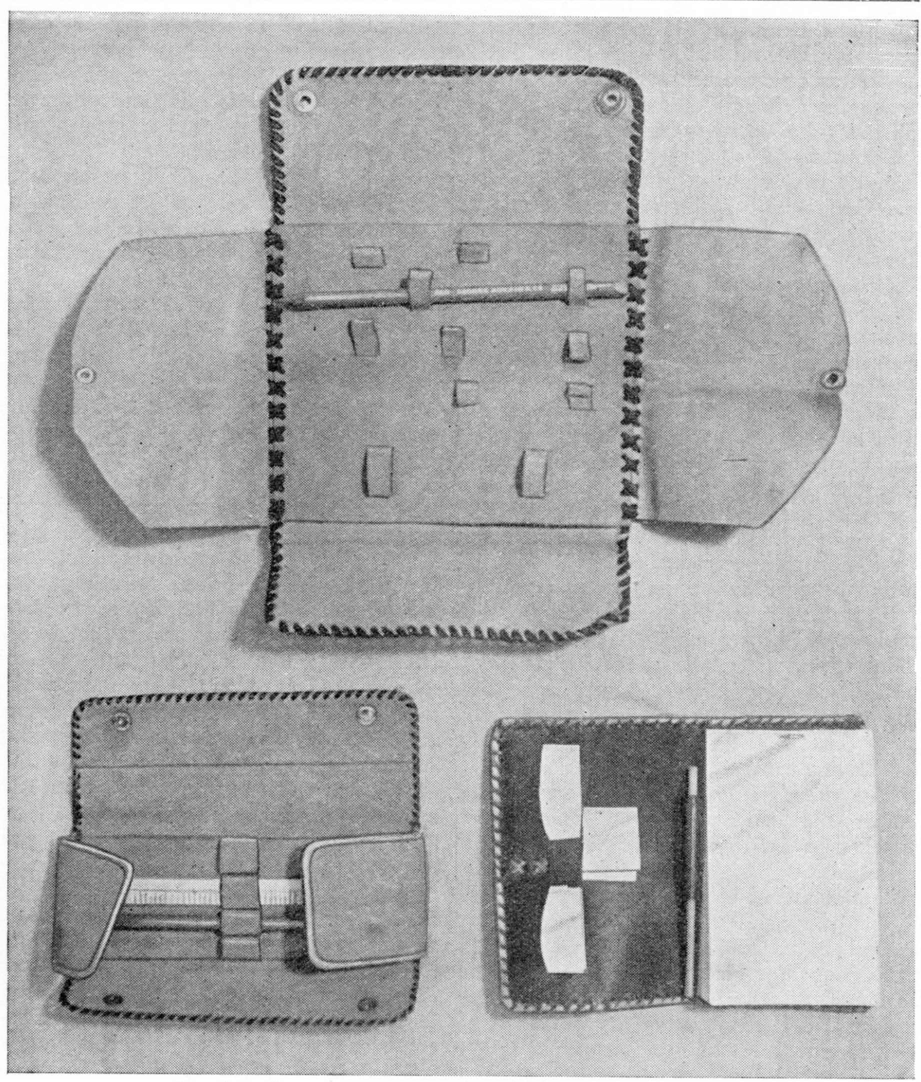

Fig. 16.—Some simple examples of Thonged Leatherwork

Lining.—After stamping and staining the calf is generally lined with skiver. This should be of a colour which tones with the outside. Cut the skiver to the size of the calf, paste the back of the latter, lay on the skiver, rub well to remove all air bubbles and lumpiness in the paste, place under pressure and leave to dry and set. If the edges of the skiver now project beyond those of the edges of the calf, they must be trimmed off with the scissors.

Making up.—If you are making a purse or a pochette, without gussets, fold up into shape as in Fig. 14; fix clips at x and x in Fig. 15 and mark out the points for the holes of the thonging, according to the dimensions given in the details on thonging. Complete the marking out on the flap and punch the holes. Begin thonging at the bottom on the outside and work round to the bottom on the other side. To calculate the length of thong required take two and a half times the length to be thonged.

Gussets.—If gussets are to be inserted (Fig. 16), cut them to the shape given in Fig. 15. Clip them in position and punch them very carefully with the sides of the pocket. The thonging would then commence at x on either side, work down the front edge, up the back and round to the other side to finish at x again. Fix the press studs and finish by polishing thoroughly with a dry cloth and then with a wax polish.

Work in Suede.—It is advisable to begin your work in the cheaper leather. Master the details of operations and gain experience in cutting and fitting and simple decoration before going on to work in calf. Begin work on single pieces of leather and make book-markers, calendars, napkin-rings, purses, belts and ties of the simplest pattern.

Figs. 17, 18, 20 and 21 give ideas for book-markers. Fig. 17 is a plain piece of leather about $1\frac{1}{4}$ in. wide, blue or red, fringed by cutting with the scissors. A small panel of grey or green leather with a pattern punched or cut out with the scissors is stuck on at the top, leaving a margin of about $\frac{1}{8}$ in. Fig. 18 is fringed and pattern punched out with the leather punch. The pattern should be punched in different sizes of holes to give more interest. Fig. 20 has one end turned over and fastened by thonging, the other end is cut away and wooden beads, of any desired shape, fixed on the two ends. Fig. 21 is fringed at both ends and a thong of harmonizing colour laced into a pattern at each end. A great variety of patterns can be arranged for thonging in this way. Fig. 19 is a tie or it may be a loose belt, cut to shape and a pattern of round holes punched in. Figs. 22, 23 and 24 show designs for calendars. The decorations are arranged from the punchings of leather which are taken from the punch. These are arranged in pattern on stems of coloured leather. Leaf shapes may be cut from scraps. Seccotine or similar adhesive is the best for this appliqué work, as it is an advantage to use a quick-setting adhesive.

Figs. 27 and 28 show simple napkin-bands, the former with a laced thong decoration threaded in as a running stitch and the latter having the ends thonged together and the decoration made by a pattern of punched holes.

Figs. 25 and 26 show small one-compartment purse with the press studs fixed as fasteners. Fig. 28 is a comb case of suede.

A few of the methods of sewing a thong are shown in Figs. 30, 31, 32 and 33.

Fig. 30 is the ordinary over-sewing stitch, or whip stitch. The holes should be spaced about twice the width of the thong apart and about one and a half times the width of the thong from the edge. The running stitch in Fig. 31 can be spaced as required and almost any width of thong can be used, according to the size of the article being put together or decorated. Fig. 32 is known as the double over-sewing or double whip. It is made by using two thongs at the same time, threading them through alternate holes. If the holes are spaced a little closer together than in the single whip stitch and thongs of different colours used, a very effective border is produced. Fig. 33 is the blanket stitch made in the same way as the needlewoman makes it, i.e. working from left to right.

Fixing Press Studs.—Figs. 25, 26 and 29 require press studs fixing in them. Figs. 1, 2 and 3 show the apparatus required for this purpose. The two former are made from $\frac{1}{2}$ in. brass bar, about 4 in. long. Fig. 1 has a $\frac{1}{4}$-in. hole drilled in one end to a depth of about $\frac{1}{4}$ in. and Fig. 2 has a projection of $\frac{3}{16}$ in. diameter and about $\frac{1}{8}$ in. deep left on the end. The former is used for fixing together the spring and the spring eyelet as shown in Fig. 5 where the anvil (Fig. 3), is shown flat side up. The positive punch in Fig. 2 is used for fixing the cap and the cap eyelet together as shown in Fig. 4 where the cap is resting upside down in the depression in the anvil.

A Pochette.—Figs. 12 and 13 give designs suitable for use on a pochette. Plan all designs full size on paper.

Use good quality calf for this work. Cut out the pattern of the purse pochette or bag in paper, apply it to the back of the large

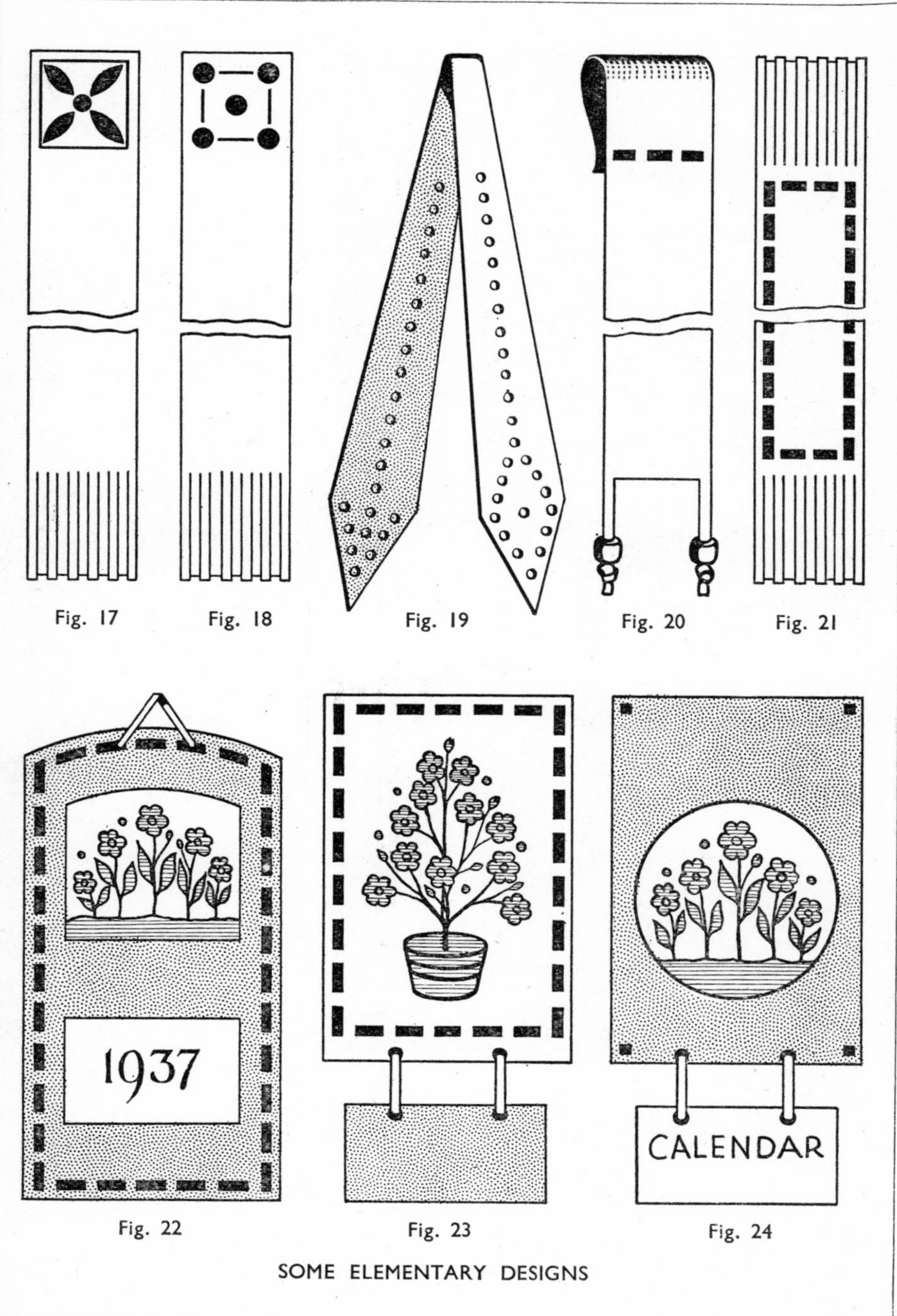

Fig. 17 Fig. 18 Fig. 19 Fig. 20 Fig. 21

Fig. 22 Fig. 23 Fig. 24

SOME ELEMENTARY DESIGNS

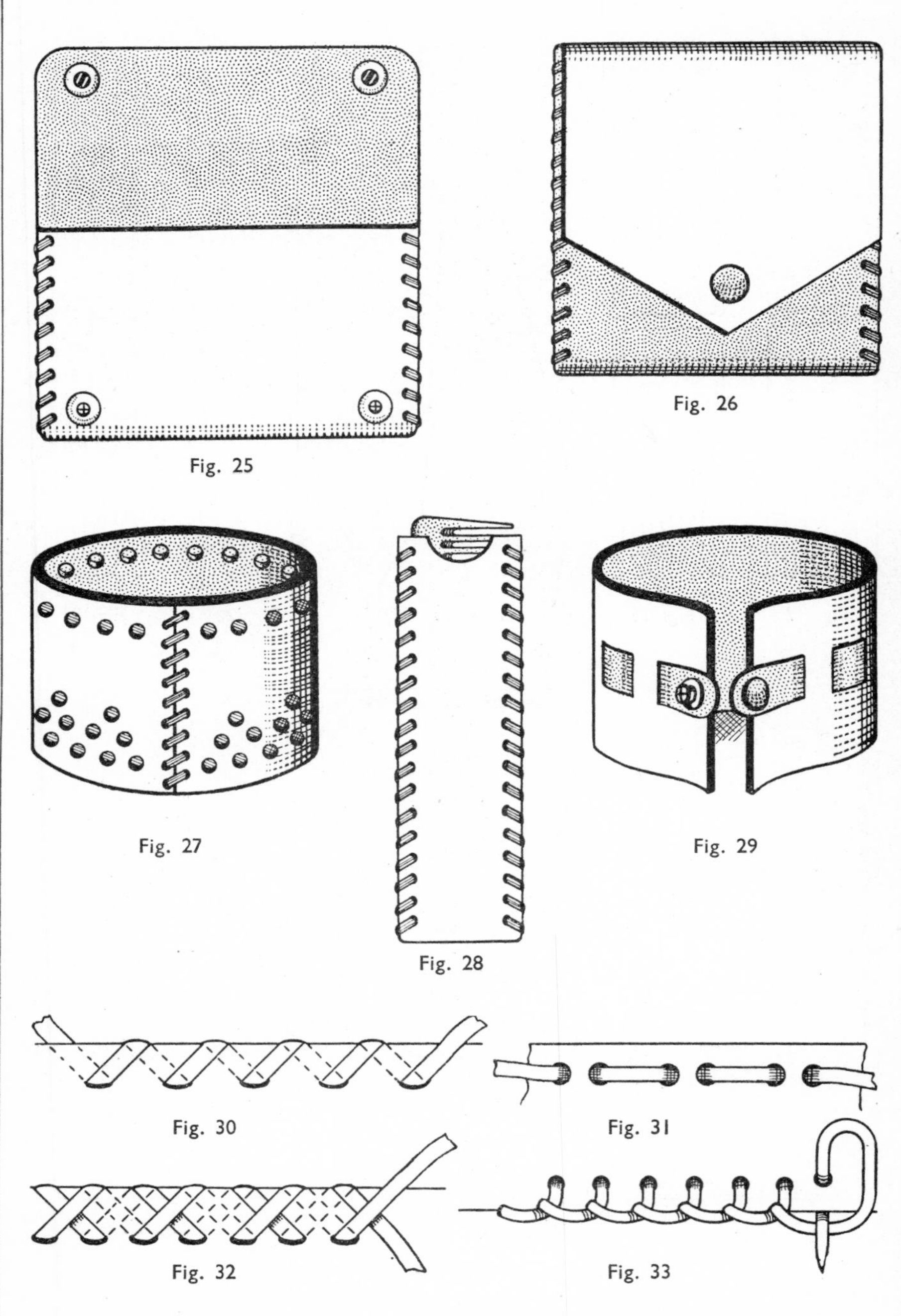

Fig. 25

Fig. 26

Fig. 27

Fig. 28

Fig. 29

Fig. 30

Fig. 31

Fig. 32

Fig. 33

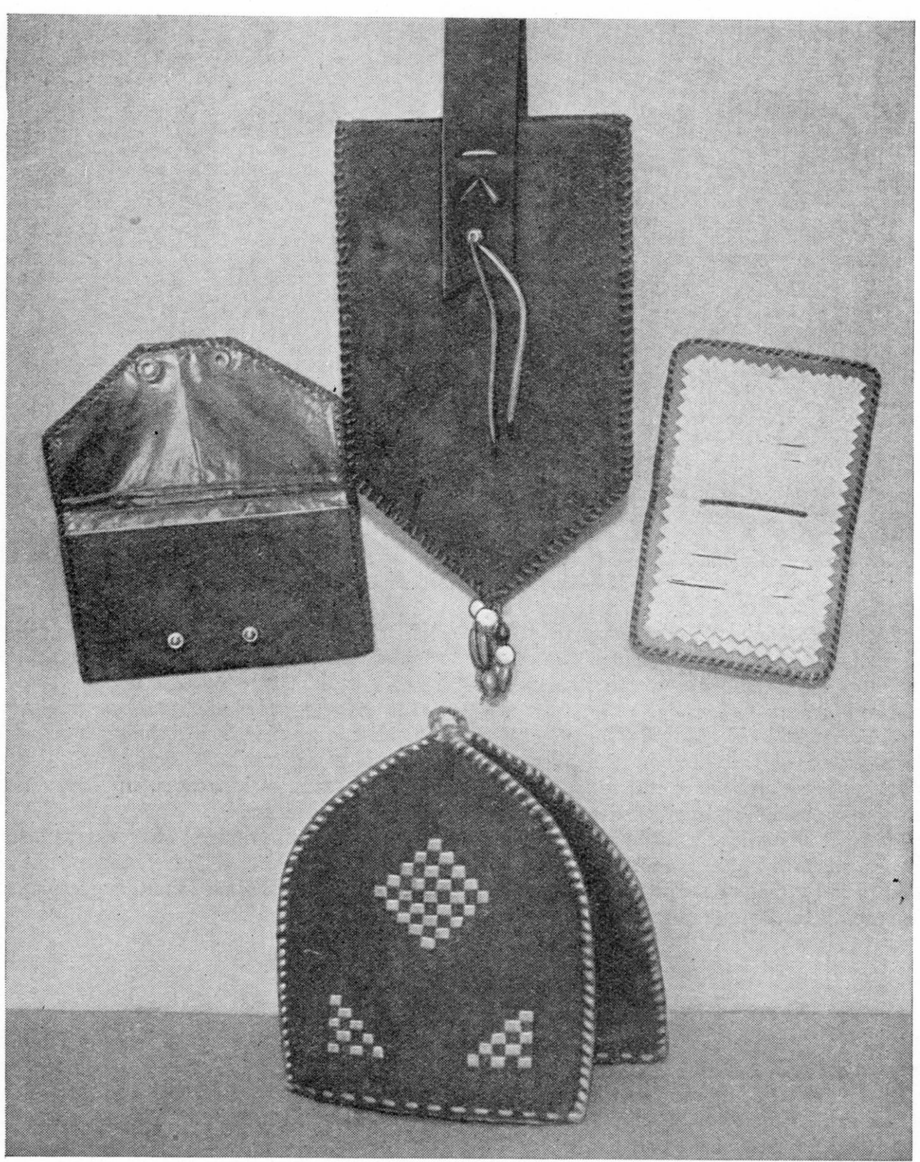

Fig. 34.—Examples showing the Decorative Use of Thonging

piece of calf and mark it out and cut out the pieces as economically as possible. Use a damp sponge and wet the surface of the piece of leather in which the pattern is to be tooled. Clip the paper on which the design is drawn accurately to the leather. Go over the design with a tracing tool. Lift the paper carefully and see whether all the pattern has been traced. If correct, remove the paper and tool in all the lines and

Fig. 35.—Examples of Tooled Leatherwork

stamps once again. If necessary to obtain clean impression, warm the tools in a gas flame and impress once more. Be careful not to burn the leather.

A Gusseted Bag.—If a purse, pochette or bag is to have a gusset all round, a long piece of leather is cut equal in length to the two sides and across the bottom of the bag. The width will depend upon the size of the article, but it should not be more than 2 in. owing to the tendency to sag in the middle of the length on the bottom edge.

Further Ideas.—There is a great scope in things which can be made in leather besides those already mentioned.

In suede—small bunches of flowers, shopping list covers, small darning hold-alls, vanity bags, spectacle cleaners, shoes, ticket and card cases, stamp cases, scissors cases, cushion covers, etc.

In calf—album covers, blotters, cases for brushes, cameras, cards, etc., seats of chairs and stools, boxes of all kinds, finger plates, chair backs and so on.

MAKING A LIBRARY

The collecting of books should be everyone's hobby. If you are fond of books it is inevitable that you shall want to possess them for yourself. A good book becomes a treasured possession—and the keen reader finds so many good ones that his shelves are constantly overflowing.

Shelves.—The first thing to decide is whether you prefer to keep your books in bookcases with glass fronts, or on open shelves round the walls. The first will keep your books clean and free from dust, but each time you want to read a book the glass front will have to be lifted up, or opened. The second method is much less expensive and gives a less formal air to the room. The books appear friendlier and are more convenient of access, but it has the disadvantage that they require more frequent dusting. A good compromise is to begin with the plain wooden shelves and to keep the majority of your books on these, but later on when you

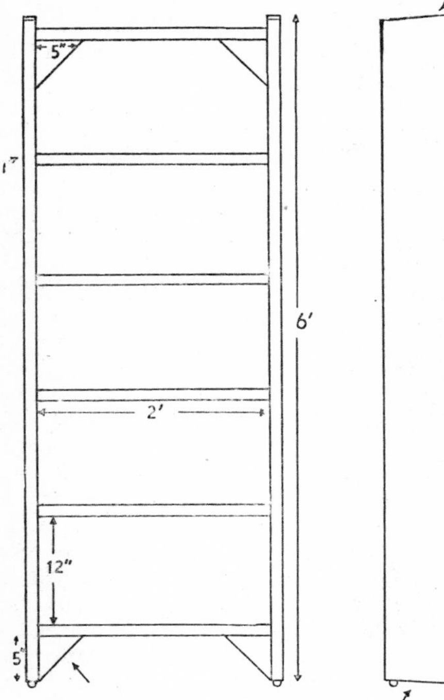

Fig. 1.—A Simple Bookcase

begin to collect a few treasures such as rare editions, or books with particularly fine illustrations, or those that for one reason or another are precious to you, then have a few shelves with glass fronts.

Be chary of purchasing an ornate bookcase of restricted dimensions. It is better to have fittings so unobtrusive that they do not detract from the volumes housed, and, more important still, fittings that are capable of easy extension. It is possible to buy shelves of this nature, suitable for any wall surface, and so made that enlargements involve no more than the fastening of a few screws. If you want cheapness, and would like to make your own book-shelves, then ordinary planed floorboard is particularly suitable. A simple, sturdy form of shelf is shown in Figs. 1 and 2, made from such floorboard. It can be finished in any stain or varnish, and will stand against a wall if tilted back slightly to clear the skirting. In making any shelves it is important that you shall allow enough depth for large books, even though you may not have any of unusual size at the moment; tall volumes have a habit of coming into your possession if your shelf space is no deeper than, say, 8 in. Be generous, allow 12 in., or even a little more, and you will never be embarrassed. The advantages of the set of shelves shown are obvious. A single set will look well against the wall and will give space for rather more than a hundred books. Then, as your library grows, you may put a second set along the same wall. Eventually you may have a thousand volumes, on ten sets of shelves, standing closely round your room even though it be small. Shelves which have to be fastened to the wall cannot be adjusted in this convenient way.

There are many forms of "adjustable" shelves available to-day, at comparatively low cost. The third illustration shows such a set, made in compact "box" sections. These sections can be built up in any formation, like a pile of child's bricks, and you can, of course, buy new sections as need arises.

Second-hand Books.—What books shall make up your library? You must try to get a lot of books for they will help to

Fig. 2.—The Bookcase in Use

make the indispensable bookish atmosphere in which your library will most readily develop. Second-hand bookshops will be particularly useful to you at this stage. Do not be afraid to go into a bookshop and browse round the shelves. If you don't see what you want, there will be no harm done in leaving your name with the bookseller and asking him to report to you when he has the sort of books you want. Most booksellers are only too anxious to help a beginner, and will take almost as much interest in your "finds" as you do. And don't forget your hobby when you visit other towns—get into the habit of taking a look at the windows and outside trays of the second-hand booksellers.

Do not despise even the "penny box." Jumble sales, auctions, street markets—from all such sources you may accumulate volumes. Only when you have a bulk on your wall of several hundreds need you begin to discriminate a little more in your purchases. But all the time, of course, you will have some general aims, some notion of the eventual contents of your full-grown library, and purchases of new books should be made as means permit. You will certainly aim to have a fine foundation of classics—books that the world knows and values—and not because they ought to be there, but because they mean a good deal to you. Thus even the classics will represent your personal taste.

When once you have acquired your mass of volumes you may gradually jettison those whose only merit is bulk until you come to have just those that are really significant to you. And when you reach limits of convenient house room, and begin to find your shelves overflowing, then you will be all the time throwing out volumes which have ceased to possess meaning and so keeping your shelves fresh and fascinating, and in addition you may replace poor copies of favourites with better and better editions.

And in choosing editions of your books do not forget the pocket editions so popular to-day. Several publishers issue these slim volumes which are very suitable for the small house or flat. They cover a wide range of subjects, are most attractive little books in good bindings, printed on good paper, and range in price from 1/- to 3/6.

Reference Books.—There are a few books which should be in everyone's library, however small. A good modern dictionary and an up-to-date atlas are two books which every reader requires to have close at hand. There are also those useful books which give information on a great variety of subjects, such as *Whitaker's Almanack*.

There are many other reference books and annuals which you can add to your reference shelf as your library grows and your interests become more specialized, but there is one "book" which everyone should try to have, and that is an encyclopædia. It is probable that the big encyclopædias such as *The Encyclopædia Britannica*, and *Chambers's Encyclopædia* are beyond the means of most people who are beginning a library of their own, and in any case these can be consulted at your public library. There are, however, small encyclopædias which can be bought a volume at a time, and which contain excellent articles written by experts in the different subjects. Everyone should try to have one of these in his library. These books are the tools which will help you to get the best out of your other books.

Building Your Library.—Possible schemes for a small library are legion, but do not have some ready-made selection all in the same binding. Let every volume on your shelves be your personal choice. One interesting way of beginning is to collect the representative books of other peoples as well as those by English writers. Here is a brief list, easily procurable in English translations:

Begin with a few books written by the ancient Greeks and Romans, because these have influenced human thought and action ever since.

GREECE.—Homer—wove stories of the Greek gods and heroes into the *Iliad* and the *Odyssey*.

Plato—the great philosopher, can be studied through his *Republic*. His idea of a perfect state is of much interest in relation to world planning of to-day.

Aristophanes, Æschylus, Euripides—dramatists.

Rome.—Virgil—in his *Ænid* has imitated Homer, and almost equalled him.

The Meditation of Marcus Aurelius—is a kindly book by a Roman Emperor, a pagan, whose ideas are strangely Christian.

India.—*The Mahabharata*—a long epic of ancient India.

Rabindranath Tagore, the modern poet, has made an almost unparalleled appeal to Europeans, particularly to English people.

France.—Balzac—was something like the *Dickens* of France.

Maupassant—has rarely been equalled, and probably never excelled, as a short-story writer.

Molière—a playwright, with much caustic humour.

Spain.—*Don Quixote*—by Cervantes, the greatest of all picaresque romances.

Vincent Blasco Ibañez—a modern author very popular in England. His finest novel is *Blood and Sand.*

U.S.A.—Nathaniel Hawthorne—in his *Scarlet Letter,* and *Twice Told Tales*, gives a picture of early Puritan America.

Longfellow—in *Hiawatha*, shows the Redskins in their own land.

O. Henry, that superb short-story writer, draws life in modern New York, and in the ranches.

Palestine.—*The Bible*—was produced in this country which stands unrivalled as the birthplace of religious literature.

Italy.—Dante—perhaps the world's greatest poet, wrote *The Divine Comedy*, which has as its three parts, *The Inferno*, *Purgatory*, and *Paradise.*

Boccaccio—writer of wonderful little short romances, which, one hundred in number, comprise the *Decameron.*

Germany.—Goethe—Germany's greatest poet, is best known here by his drama *Faust.*

Russia.—Tolstoy—can be first enjoyed in his parables and short tales, such as the volume *Master and Man.* His greatest novel is *Anna Karenina.*

Dostoieffsky—is known here chiefly for his novel *Crime and Punishment.*

Belgium.—*The Blue Bird*—a very charming symbolic play by Maeterlinck.

Persia.—*The Rubaiyat of Omar Khayyam*—a sweet but philosophically despairing poem by Omar Khayyam, achieved popularity in this country through its English translation by FitzGerald.

Norway.—Ibsen—one of the most important modern dramatists. *The Doll's House* is perhaps his best-known play.

Arabia.—*The Koran*—the Bible of the Mohammedans.

The Arabian Nights, or the *Thousand and One Nights*, is one of the most colourful and fascinating collections of stories in the world. From it come such popular tales as *Sinbad the Sailor* and *Ali Baba.*

Fig. 3.—Modern Unit Bookcases suit every size of Volume

That is, of course, a very sparse list, but space will allow no more here, for a foundation of English books is also to be suggested.

English Books.—The development of English literature may be roughly expressed thus:

From the beginning of the 17th century—Legends, poetry, drama.

18th century—Poetry, drama, prose.

19th century—Poetry, drama, prose, novels.
20th century—Poetry, drama, prose, novels, short stories.

The following list is only a skeleton outline for a collection of books which represents each stage in the history of our literature.

From the beginning to the end of the Seventeenth Century

MALLORY: *Morte d'Arthur*—a collection of the legends about King Arthur and his Knights of the Round Table.

CHAUCER: *Canterbury Pilgrims.* A picture of the life of England in the 14th century.

MORE: *Utopia*—the first English scheme for a "planned" State.

BUNYAN: *Pilgrim's Progress*—by far the most widely read of all writings produced by an Englishman. His language was derived from the Bible, simple and forceful, and he had a penetrating understanding of the human mind.

SPENSER: *Faerie Queene.*—A richly imaginative poem. Its characters are impersonal, representing abstract qualities—as glory, truth, error, justice.

SHAKESPEARE: *Plays.*—Begin with a single-volume edition.

BACON: *Essays.*—You will recognize many familiar quotations in these.

MILTON: *Poems.*—There is a good one-volume edition of these.

Unless you are very interested in the poetry of this period, an excellent plan would be to buy one or two anthologies such as the *Oxford Book of Verse*, or other similar volume, which will give you selections from all the great poets.

PEPYS: *Diary.*—The most famous diary in the world, gives a day-to-day record of what was happening in London at the end of the 17th century, besides an intimate revelation of one man's thoughts and actions.

Eighteenth Century.

JONATHAN SWIFT: *Gulliver's Travels.*—Not only a satire, but a fascinating story as well.

DEFOE: *Robinson Crusoe.*—You probably read this as a boy, without realizing that it was the "father" of the English novel.

ADDISON: *Essays.*—These were originally printed in *The Spectator*, one of the earliest English daily papers.

RICHARDSON: *Clarissa.*—The first real English novel.

FIELDING: *Tom Jones.*—A rollicking novel full of incident.

GOLDSMITH: *Vicar of Wakefield.*—The earliest English novel still widely enjoyed to-day.

JANE AUSTEN: *Pride and Prejudice*, *Sense and Sensibility*, novels, which of their kind have never been surpassed.

SAMUEL JOHNSON was a great man as well as a great writer. He is celebrated because of his dictionary. Chiefly we know him, however, because of the *Life* written by his admirer Boswell.

GIBBON was a great historian who wrote *The Decline and Fall of the Roman Empire.*

HUME was another historian, but his was a *History of England.*

For the poetry of the period choose *The Oxford Book of Eighteenth Century Verse*, it will give you all you require unless you are specially interested in one particular poet.

The Nineteenth Century is so rich in the number of authors of the first class, that it is only possible to indicate a framework which can be filled in as your library grows, and your reading tastes mature.

This period saw the great development of the English novel; the outstanding giants with one each of their representative books are:

SIR WALTER SCOTT: *Heart of Midlothian.*
CHARLES DICKENS: *David Copperfield.*
WILLIAM THACKERAY: *Vanity Fair.*
CHARLOTTE BRONTË: *Jane Eyre.*
EMILY BRONTË: *Wuthering Heights.*
GEORGE ELIOT: *Mill on the Floss.*
ANTHONY TROLLOPE: *Barchester Towers.*
R. L. STEVENSON: *Master of Ballantrae.*
THOMAS HARDY: *Tess of the D'Urbervilles.*

Short stories had existed earlier in the *Bible*, *Arabian Nights*, Boccaccio and Chaucer, but the first to treat them as serious art forms were the Americans, Poe, Hawthorne, Irving and Bret Harte.

The great poets of the century were Keats, Shelley, Wordsworth, Browning and Tennyson, for each of whom there is a good one-volume edition in the Oxford poets, or a good anthology such as the

Oxford Book of Victorian Verse will give you selections from these and many more as well.

Of the essayists the most universally popular is undoubtedly the gentle and humorous Charles Lamb in *Essays of Elia*. Two others who, because of their great influence on their contemporaries should find a place on your shelves are Ruskin and Carlyle. Begin with *Sesame and Lilies* of the former and *Heroes and Hero-worship* of the latter.

Perhaps the most widely discussed book in the whole of this period was Darwin's *Origin of Species* in which he explained his new theories of evolution.

Lord Macaulay wrote essays but is more famous for his *History of England;* another very readable *Short History of the English People* was written by J. R. Green.

Biography and memoirs have been left out—only because they are so many and so diverse that it is impossible in a short list to give a selection which would be of any use. It is sufficient to say that there is hardly a single person of any eminence in the Victorian Age whose life has not been written, often by several different people.

This is only a very meagre outline, but it will do for a beginning. When you have acquired these, the next thing is to decide where your chief interests lie. Is it in a particular form of literature such as the novel or poetry, or in a particular subject such as history or biography? Alternatively your interests may lie in the study of a special period such as the Victorian Age.

Whatever it is let that interest guide you in filling in the gaps in your outline, so that in a few years' time your library will be an index to your personal tastes—a collection of books that could only have been built up by you, and in which each book is an individual entity, chosen for some particular reason and associated in your mind with happy hours of reading.

LINO CUTTING AND PRINTING

Lino cutting and printing is one of the very fascinating crafts which can be carried on, without offence to the rest of the family, on the table of the living-room. Very little room is required for this craft and the equipment at first need be neither expensive nor elaborate.

The Material.—Any plain lino will generally be satisfactory if the surface is quite smooth and the substance hard, not spongy or coarse. Do not choose a cheap gritty lino as this will quickly blunt the edge of the cutting tool. The thickness should be about $\frac{1}{8}$ in. and scrap cuttings from the furniture dealer will be obtainable at a very cheap rate. Avoid printed or painted lino, and inlaid lino which may give trouble by breaking up. Very good lino may be purchased by the yard or foot from the contractors and pieces of special sizes may be bought mounted on plywood backs.

The Printing Inks.—Almost any ink, water, poster or oil colour can be used for making prints from lino blocks. Ordinary printer's ink in all colours, indian ink, water or oil colours in tubes, with treatment where necessary, and poster colours in pots or tubes, are all suitable. Indian ink may be used with or without the addition of a little starch paste or gloy. Water colour may be used direct from the tube or mixed with a little paste, while oil colour may be thinned down if necessary by mixing with a little paraffin, turpentine or linseed oil.

Applying the Ink.—Water colours are painted on to the block by means of a fine soft hair brush. A sponge can also be used to apply colour by dabbing. This gives a decided texture to the paint and is a method much favoured by artists. A dabber (Fig. 1), which can be made by covering an old stocking darner with a padding of cotton or wool, this being covered with a piece of thin skiver leather, also serves well. Oil colours and printer's ink can also be applied by means of a rubber roller which flattens out the colour on a glass slab and then transfers it to the block.

The Rubber.—When the printing paper is put on to the inked block it is rubbed in order to transfer the ink from the block to the paper. This rubbing can be done with the hand when the block is small, but some harder surface is generally required. The back of a dessertspoon can be quite successfully used, the smooth curved lid of a small tobacco tin, celluloid soap box, comb-back or anything similar may be used, or a baren may be purchased or made. One of these rubbers, or barens as they are sometimes called, consists of a circular disc of wood with a groove on its edge, and a handle. A circular piece of corrugated cardboard is cut to the same size as the disc and attached to the under side. A piece of hard rice-paper is then put on to cover the corrugated cardboard on the bottom surface of the disc, brought up the sides and tied into the groove with string. (*See* Fig. 2.) A rubber roller may also be used for printing.

The Tools.—As in many similar crafts a good deal can be done with simple adaptations. The ribs of umbrellas, pen nibs, etc., have been used quite successfully in conjunction with a penknife. There are, however, some simple cutters made by pen manufacturers and fitted into a well-designed handle which are admirable tools for this material. They can be purchased for a penny or two each, with handles at about fourpence each, and are well worth while. (*See* Figs. 3, 4 and 5.) Two sizes of gouges (Figs. 4 and 5), and two vee tools, one large and one small, as in Fig. 3, will be sufficient. An ordinary penknife will serve for the rest. These tools can be kept sharp either by oilstone slips or by fine emery cloth carefully applied.

Paper.—It is possible to purchase Japanese mulberry paper for this work and it is the best for fine work. Any smooth-surfaced, absorbent paper will, however,

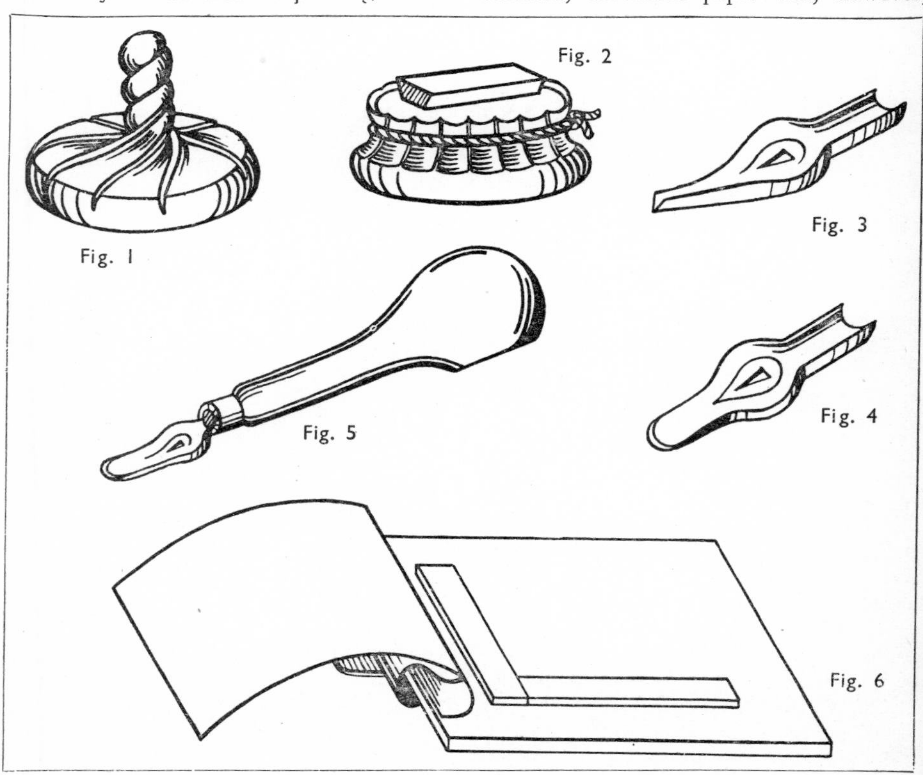

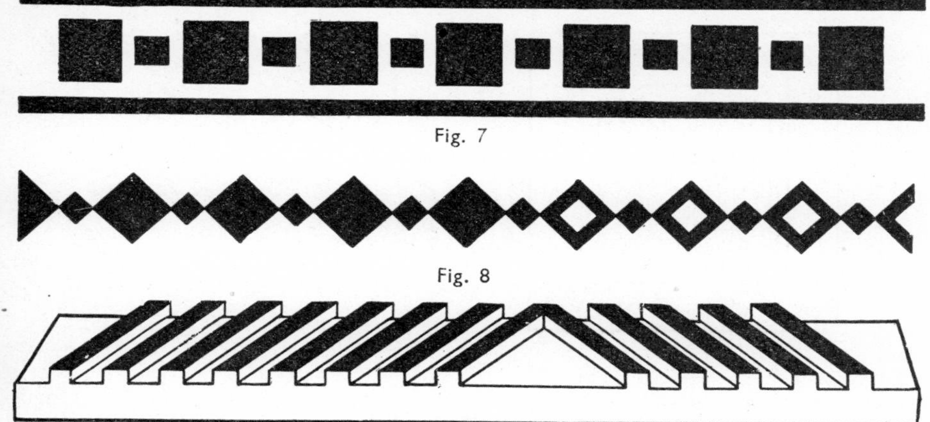

Fig. 7

Fig. 8

Fig. 9

serve the purpose. Ordinary office duplicating paper will do quite well for your early efforts. Experiments should be made in printing with damped paper, as this receives the ink more readily than dry paper. The sheets are damped by placing three sheets at a time between wet blotting paper, in series of printing paper and blotting paper to the number of sheets required. These are all placed under a flat weight and left overnight.

The Press.—An ordinary screw-down letter-press can be used for this type of work but it is rarely necessary unless it is desired that a uniform colour and texture shall appear in all the prints. A very simple press for hand printing can be made as shown in Fig. 6. It consists of a plywood board on which is fixed a right-angled frame of cardboard or wood of less thickness than the lino block which is to be fitted into it. The printing paper is held in position over the block by means of strong spring paper-clips.

The Beginning.—Quite a lot of pattern printing can be done by the use of small blocks made from cut potato, rubber, corks, cotton reels, match-sticks and so on. It is advisable to try some of this work before launching out on large pieces of work in picture making.

A few designs for all-over patterns which can be applied to articles of silk, cotton, hessian, curtain materials and linen are given in Figs. 7, 8 and 9. This kind of pattern is for use on clothing, table linen, furniture coverings, cushion covers, curtains and so on. In all this work it is essential that the material which is to be printed shall be absorbent and it is advisable to test a small piece of any material on which you wish to print before beginning on the article itself.

Water colours should not be used in this work if the material is to be washed. Oil colours are essential and these should be applied fairly thinly and pressed well into the material. Material which has been printed in this way is allowed to dry for several hours and then pressed face down on an ironing sheet with a sheet of paper between the hot iron and the printed material. Then turn the material-printed surface upwards, cover it with a damp cloth and press again with a hot iron. Thorough steaming in this way will fix the colours and the material may safely be washed.

The Operations.—Cut out a piece of linoleum to the size required. This is done by cutting a fine line on the right side alongside the ruler with the point of a knife, then bend the sheet backwards and it will crack along the line so that the canvas back can be cut with the knife or scissors.

To describe the operations and their sequence we will take a simple pattern (Fig 10) and illustrate the stages.

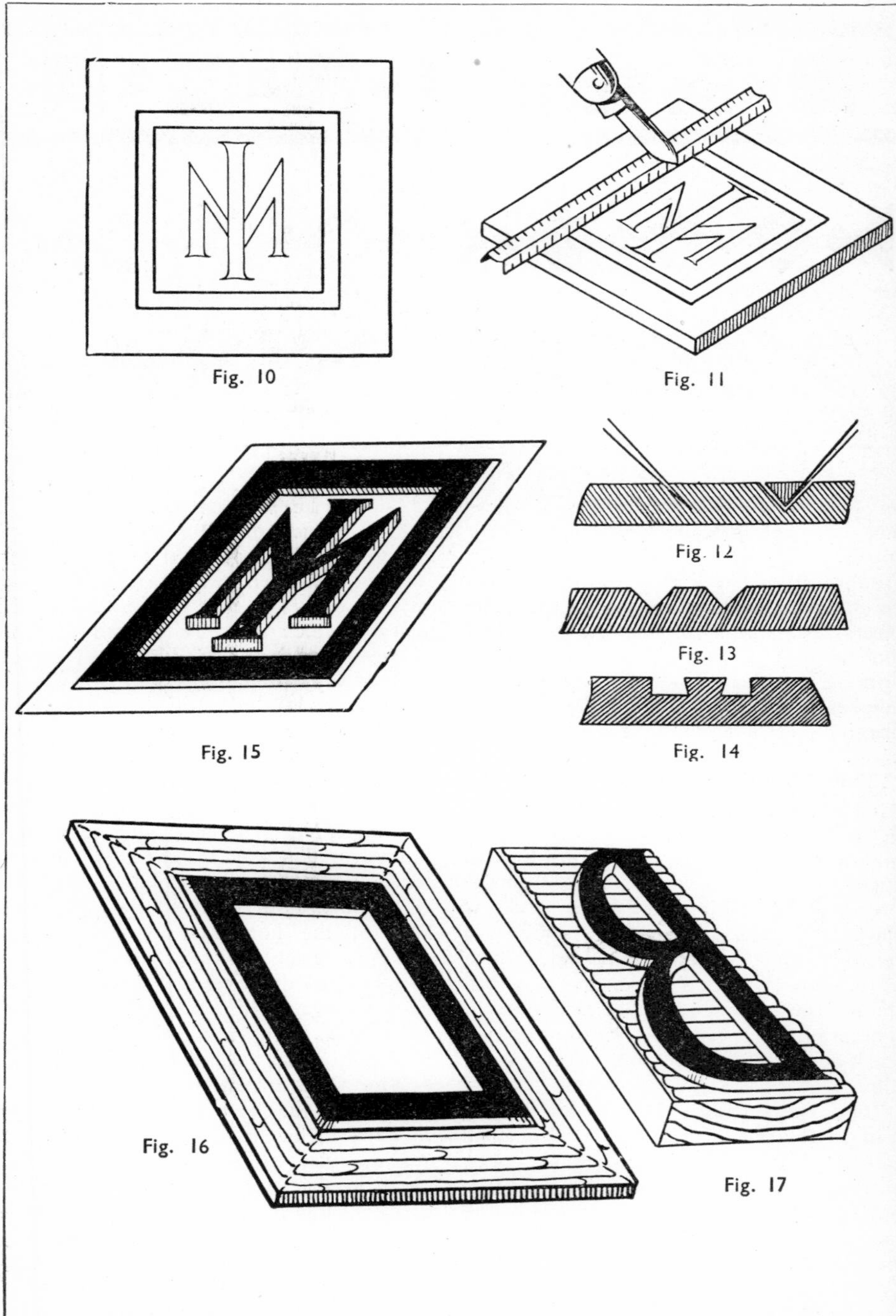
Fig. 10
Fig. 11
Fig. 12
Fig. 13
Fig. 14
Fig. 15
Fig. 16
Fig. 17

Sketch out the design full size on thin paper, place the paper on the lino, insert a piece of carbon paper between the latter and the paper and trace over the design to transfer it to the surface of the lino. If the design is not balanced it is necessary to transfer it to tracing paper and place the latter face downwards on the lino and then transfer the design through the carbon paper. Take a penknife and ruler, lay the latter alongside the inside of the margin line and, holding

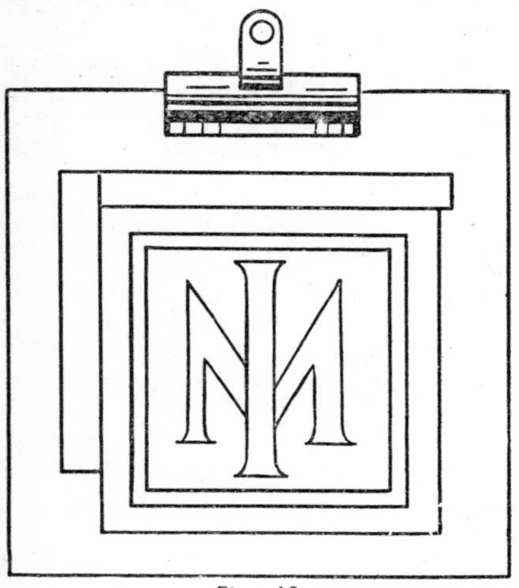

Fig. 18

the knife at an angle so as to give a cut sloping away from the line, draw it along to give a cut about $\frac{1}{16}$ in. deep. For this purpose a non-slip rule which has bevelled sides is most useful. (*See* Fig. 11.)

In this way cut round the border and then place the ruler further on the inside and cut a line about $\frac{1}{8}$ in. away from the first one and sloping towards it. Cut so as to leave a vee-shaped groove as shown in Figs. 12–14. Fig. 12 shows on the left a section of the first cut and on the right the effect of the second cut which removes the piece of lino. Now cut round the outside of the border line in the same way to give a section on the latter as shown in Fig. 13. The outward slope on all cuts is most important. If the cut is made to slope inwards as in Fig. 14 there is a possibility that the edge will soon break down when printing. (*See* Fig. 15, which shows the vee channel cut round the border.)

The outer surface around the border line can now be gouged out to give practice in the use of the gouge. This operation must be done carefully and methodically so that the gouge cuts are of regular depth, straight in line and smooth. The background of every block should be cut so neatly that it shows that a craftsman has been at work. Do not go down so far in this cutting that the canvas is reached.

Cut round the outline of the monogram

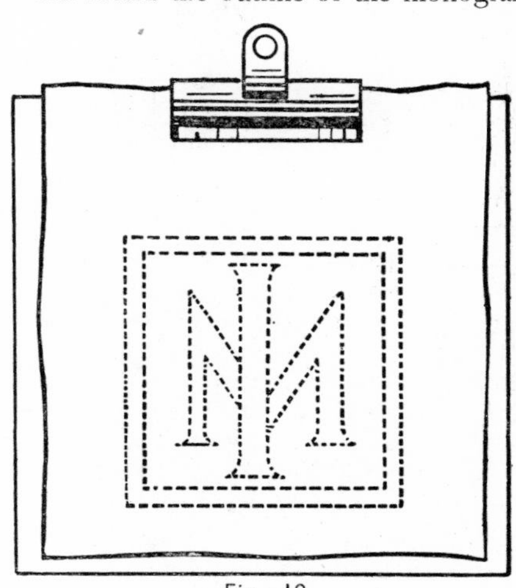

Fig. 19

with the knife in the same way as for the first cut on the border. Then take the fine vee tool and, keeping a side of the tool up to the cut, take out a vee-shaped length of lino all round the monogram. Cut out the background with the larger gouge as in Fig. 16. Take care not to push the edge of the gouge into the edge of the outline. Square up the edges of the block to fit into the right angle on the printing board.

Place the block on to the latter as shown in Fig. 18 and lay on the colour. If using the dabber, place a small quantity of printer's ink on to a sheet of glass, spread it out flat and work it up by dabbing it. Then work a little of the ink off the dabber by dabbing it on to a cleaner part of the glass. Do not overload the dabber with ink. Now dab the ink on to the block, spreading it evenly and thoroughly over the whole of the surface standing up above the background. The

Fig. 20

Fig. 21

colour may also be put on by means of a sponge, paint brushes or rollers.

Take a sheet of paper, and, if not already damped, damp it with a sponge. Push it right into the jaws of the spring clip as far as it will go. (*See* Fig. 19.) This is a simple method of registering for length position. Small pieces of paper may be glued down to the back board to act as checks for position, for correct registering. The size of the printing paper depends upon the use to which the print is to be put. If for pictorial use, without mounts, the margins must be arranged on the printing paper.

Now pull the paper over on to the block as in Fig. 19. Place a sheet or two of paper on the top and begin to rub with any one of the rubbers previously mentioned. Rub thoroughly, raise the paper—do not move it from the clip—and examine the print. Note any weak places in the print, place more colour on any part which is not clearly printed, lower the paper again and rub to take up more colour. Examine again and when satisfied with the quality of the print remove it and repeat the operations with another sheet of paper.

A good deal of variety is possible in the treatment of the prints. Quite pleasing results can be obtained by painting the background to the picture with varied water

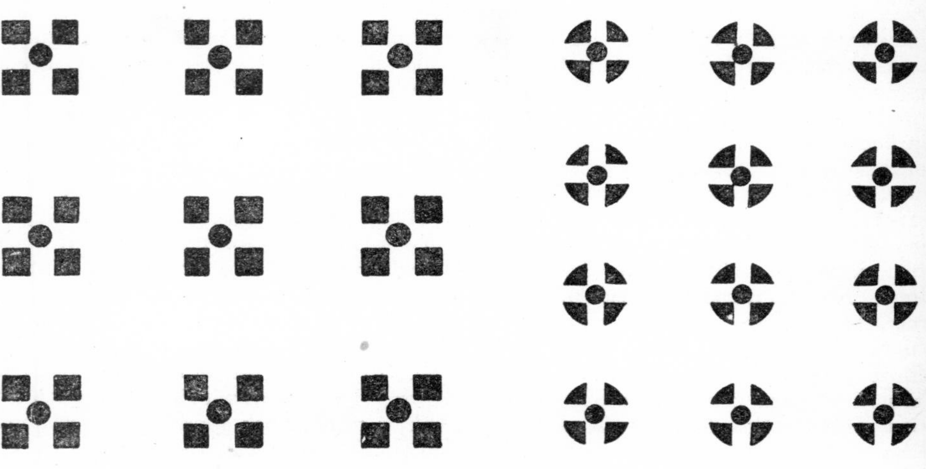

Fig. 22

Fig. 23

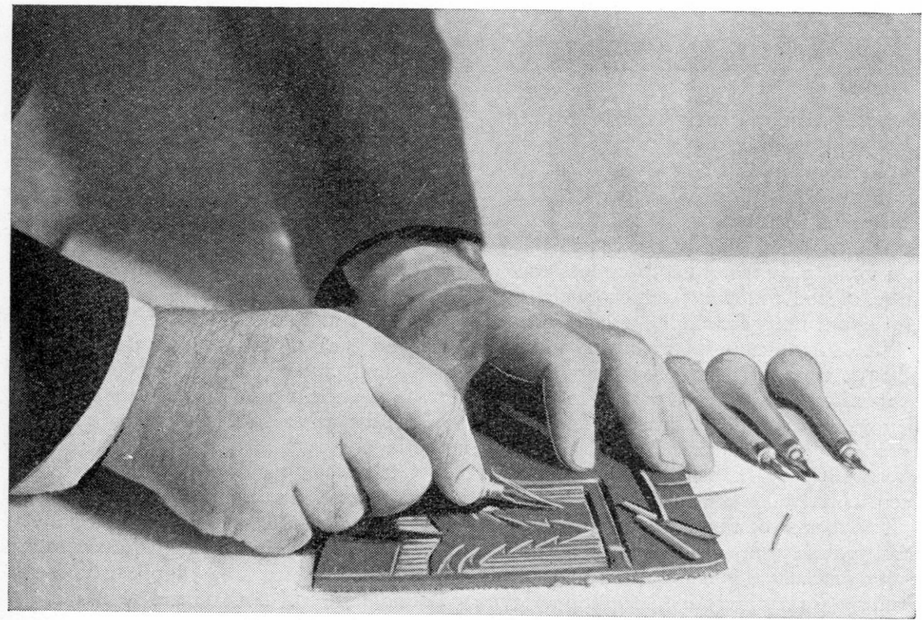

Fig. 24.—Showing how the Cutter is held

colours as a backing to the black print. This is very effective when book-plates or monograms are being printed. This colour can also be applied after the print has been made by painting it all over the printed surface. The effect is to modify the density of the blackness of the print and to give it an unusual quality. When painting the block with a brush various colours can be applied giving the effect of a multi-block printing from only one block.

Small blocks, or large blocks, to be used in a screw press can be mounted on blocks of wood. Thick plywood is best for this work as it does not lose its shape. Fig. 17 shows an initial letter so mounted. This illustration also shows that the block is a negative from which a positive is printed. It is therefore essential that all pictures which can appear in only one position should be cut negative as in this case. Figs. 20 and 21 are positives which must also be cut negative. The book-plate in Fig. 20 is a suggestion as to what may be done in this work. This kind of thing can be carried out in a large variety of treatment. For example, it may be left in the black and white, or when printed in black and dry it may be painted over with some coloured ink or very thin oil colour which will modify the contrast. The background may be painted with colour before the print is taken off. Instead of the monogram the whole name may be cut out either in solid letters as in "Ex libris," or by engraving the line as in "Greetings," in Fig. 21. Coloured paper may be used with ink of harmonizing or contrasting colour.

The picture in Fig. 21 is typical of a good deal that can be done for use as greeting cards. The pictures may be treated as suggested for the book-plate. It may be used by mounting on a large piece of good quality coloured paper or thin card. Do not forget that the designs shown in Figs. 20 and 21 must be cut in reverse.

The all-over patterns in Figs. 22 and 23 are cut and mounted on blocks about 3 in. square and are used by pressing them on to the material. From this preliminary work it is possible to go on to the production of coloured pictures, using two or more blocks.

MAGAZINES AND DIARIES

THE person with any flair for putting things down on paper has a hobby which can be exploited in many ways. Facility in writing comes largely through practice. The more writing you do, providing you do it intelligently, the better it will be. It is a good plan therefore to choose one or more of the following outlets which will give opportunity for ample, regular practice.

The Magazine.—Many business houses, schools, churches, and other organizations nowadays have their own printed magazines. If you are connected with any fairly large group of people, united by a common interest, it may be possible for you to get such a magazine launched.

The matter of filling the available pages will probably not be very difficult; the major problem is generally that of expense. Printing, or rather the setting up of type which precedes printing, is a costly business, and your first move will be to get a quotation from your local printer—perhaps for a magazine of sixteen pages. Talk it over with the printer, so that you both have a fairly good idea of what the proposed magazine will be like, and have your price based on the number of copies likely to be required. Unsold copies are of no use to you.

Then set about discovering how many regular purchasers of the magazine you will get. Unless you can depend on at least a couple of hundred purchasers a printed magazine is likely to be impracticable—assuming, of course, that it is necessary for income to balance outgoings.

Your magazine should preferably be issued once a month, and certainly not less than once a quarter, or there will be little writing for you to do, and little interest among your subscribers.

Supposing you can be sure of selling, say, 250 copies, at a few coppers each, then you can go ahead. Advertisements may possibly bring in a little money, but do not be too optimistic about this.

You will presumably be editor. In addition there should be a sub-editor to help you; a treasurer who will deal with all money affairs; a general manager who will settle publicity and distribute copies.

Get contributions from as many people as possible, for that will broaden interest. You and your assistant will write regular features; revise contributions; select matter; plan the general policy. When matter has been sent to the printer he will print it off on *galley slips*. These will come back to you, and you will correct any errors, and paste these slip proofs into a dummy copy of the magazine, so that the printer may see the layout desired.

Get freshness and variety in your pages; have competitions and aim at improving circulation by the quality of contents.

If the expense of printing is too high you may have typed and duplicated copies, bound into stiff covers, and lent round to your subscribers.

For a church magazine the simplest plan is to buy an *inset* and then to have two or three local pages and a cover attached to the outside. These are printed pages of general interest to which you may add your own pages of local news, etc. Any church headquarters will supply particulars of suitable insets.

The Club Diary.—This is particularly suitable for a young people's club. All you need is the editor and a fat exercise book.

Every time anything of special interest happens—camp, supper, holiday outing, arrival of new member, departure of old member—the editor writes an account in the "diary," and afterwards the pages can be read out to club assemblies, or borrowed.

Make all diary accounts as cheerful and frolicsome as possible. Humorous drawings may of course be inserted, and there is plenty of scope for leg-pulling. Let all writings be dated and signed, for that will make them of much more interest in later years. Whenever anything is said or done which is "fit to go in the diary" then see that it is written up straight away.

The Annual Magazine.—This is also specially suited for clubs and similar organizations. The best time to prepare it is in the winter, so that it can be "published" about Christmas time. The magazine of course is written or typed, and the editor should try to get contributions from all members. They should be written or drawn, and should be as varied as possible. Insist on original stuff—articles, stories, verse, jokes, and so on. Club announcements and news may also be inserted, and an editorial. The whole material will be bound between stiff covers.

The News Letter. — A group of friends, or members of any organization, will find this an excellent means of keeping in touch. Suppose there are eight such people, living in widely scattered places. Make a postal list with their names and addresses, putting "Editor's headquarters" at the end. Then get a large envelope or suitable portfolio and start off with your introductory letter. Post this on to the first name on the list. The recipient will read it; write a "news letter" himself, about his own affairs and whatever else he likes, and post the envelope with the two contributions on to number three. This happens until the whole list has been circulated.

Then you are really ready to begin. There are now nine contributions in your portfolio, and it is again in your hands. You will scrap the old one written by yourself, which now has been read by everyone, and replace it by a fresh letter, posting on as before to the next member. He similarly takes out his old contribution, putting in a new one and reading all the other eight letters—which of course he has not seen—before posting on to number two. Thus each member, and the editor, reads the news letter of each circle member whenever the batch comes round.

Have a strict rule that no member should keep the portfolio too long. A week is a good time.

The Quotation Book.—Every careful reader is frequently coming across passages in books that particularly impress him. It is an excellent plan to form the habit of copying these out—and perhaps to annotate or write down your own feelings regarding them. The practice is particularly useful as an exercise for the development of your own writing ability, if the passages you copy are selected primarily for their literary value.

Good writing consists largely of fresh, but lucid, expression. What you will look for is the happily appropriate phrase, the forceful compression, the striking *mot juste*. The simple act of copying such excerpts will most likely cause you to remember them, and to analyse their structure. Thus, contact with fine writing will go far towards improving your own style.

Letters.—The person who enjoys letter writing has a potential literary gift which should not be neglected. If you are such a person you should certainly exploit your talent, for good letter writers are few, and keen ones are fewer.

Most people like to receive letters, and the farther away recipients are from senders the more are letters usually appreciated. If you can correspond regularly with friends in another country, then you will be doing them a service, and you will have plenty of scope.

In writing such letters remember that it is generally the ordinary small things which are of most interest, the intimate personal touches, the recounting of familiar yet half-forgotten details.

Do not aim at "literary style"; be natural and simple. Prefer the short word to the long; the compact brief sentence to the one that rambles over many lines. Write also as you would speak, in easy colloquial fashion. Never, of course, waste ink on such hackneyed absurdities as "just a few lines to let you know."

The Personal Diary.—The regular writing of a diary is an excellent discipline. It compels that systematic practice, referred to at the beginning of this article, which is a prime factor in the developing of writing ability. So much of the great art of literature depends on seeing the drama and interest of ordinary life, life which by many might be called dull. The world's masterpieces have been written by those with a genius for looking beneath the surface and probing the deeps of the human heart. One of the great virtues of the diary is that it makes possible honest self-revelation. You may put down your inmost thoughts; you may disclose motives of which none but you are aware; you may be completely frank. The result is that you may get on to your pages the genuine stuff of human nature—which will form fascinating reading when you look back in later years.

But a diary need not be just self-centred. It can describe too the life of the times, as you see it, and the many incidents which will be a source of delight to reflect on when they have become almost forgotten—the reading of your diary pages will bring them back to vivid life.

Have a diary book of good quality and size, one that will wear well and which gives plenty of space for the daily exercise of your pen. Observe a definite plan with regard to it—let the entries be of a consistent type, so that the whole volume will have unity. And, above all, do not falter—keep on when once you have started.

Literary Criticism Group.—If you and a group of friends are equally interested in writing you will find enjoyment and benefit in a literary criticism circle. In principle it will be conducted on the lines of the *news letter* already described, a postal packet being sent round from member to member, each person inserting his own contribution and removing an old one.

The purpose now, however, will be not to hand on news from one to the other, but to criticize the literary efforts of the members. Thus the portfolio will contain stories, articles, essays, poems, and so on. If they can all be typewritten so much the better.

At the back of each "manuscript" several blank sheets of paper should be attached on which criticisms can be written. Each member will criticize every manuscript but his own. Encourage your circle to give worth-while constructive criticism. Flattering is useless, and if it is not checked the circle will deteriorate into a "mutual admiration society"—like so many literary cliques. But mere destructive criticism is almost equally valueless. You will find that competent criticism on a piece of writing is not at all easy to obtain, and your members will benefit as much from their own activities as critics as from the comments passed by others on their manuscripts.

In addition to the ordinary contributions the portfolio can contain a large exercise book in which general discussion and personal matters relating to the circle can have space.

General Hints.—In all your writing you must aim at saying just what you want to say. That may sound simple; in reality it is difficult. Few amateur writers can put down the things they intend without writing a great many more words than are necessary. There is no more important and valuable exercise than condensing what you have written. Supposing you have a page of 250 words, a first draft. Go through with the blue pencil cutting out sentences and phrases which are superfluous and you will perhaps reduce the number to 200. Persevere, cutting more phrases and words, and you may eventually have left 150. Read through when you are convinced that not any further single word can be eliminated, and you will find this new version to be altogether stronger and better than the original. Avoidance of repetition; choice of right words; a nice balance of sentences; vividness of imagery—these are the sort of things which add to your literary ability.

MECHANICAL MODELS

In dealing with mechanical models, we must divide the subject into several classes—mechanical models that are constructed by the amateur from basic prepared parts, those which are purchased ready to assemble and those ready for immediate use, such as working models of trains, etc. There is practically no limit to the number or type of model the handy-man with a mechanical bent can make. This article is only intended to indicate briefly the scope and variety of this hobby. Practical direc-

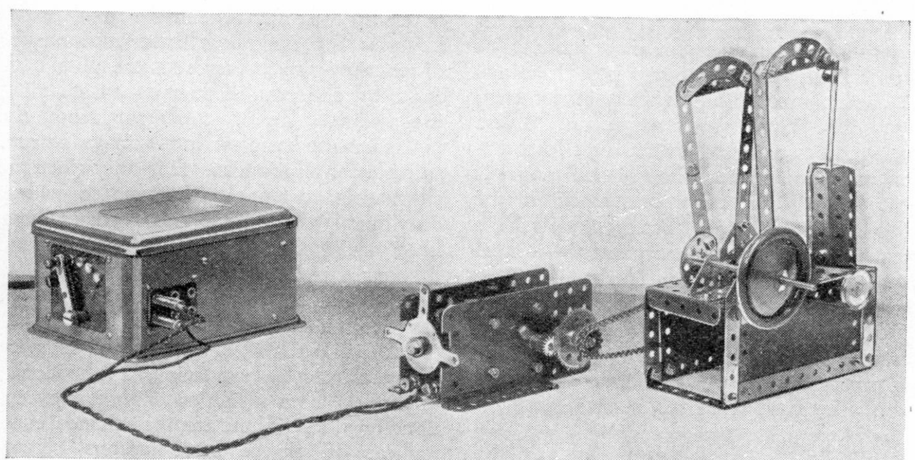

Fig. 1.—A Low-voltage Electric Motor attached to a Model *Courtesy: Meccano*

tions would occupy too large a space. As a rule every mechanically minded boy goes through several stages before he finally decides upon his life-time hobby. The simple toys—made of wood or tin—are the first stage, and it is safe to say the constructive element is so strong that no boy can resist the temptation to pull the toys to pieces in order to see how they work. It is then that he becomes interested in reconstruction and the making of things. To-day he has every opportunity, for highly ingenious outfits for model construction may be purchased for so low a price as sixpence.

Naturally these diminutive outfits have their limitations, although it must be admitted that some boys turn out some very remarkable models with them. As time goes on, however, there is a yearning to make bigger and better things, and so "part 2" of the outfit is obtained. Before going further, a word is necessary to parents concerning these construction sets. They are a real source of education to boys. They teach them to reason, to solve problems, to be practical. These qualities will stand them in good stead in later life, so any desire to construct should always be fostered.

Construction Outfits.—The cheapest outfits provide sufficient material for the construction of such things as ships, steam engines, cranes, trolleys, motor cars, and so on; and of course, as further equipment is added, so the range increases, and larger and better and more intricate models can be built. With every outfit is a booklet giving the constructional details of scores of models, and the boy who has a home construction outfit will have hours and hours of really useful enjoyment before him. A really surprising variety of models can be constructed from two sixpenny outfits. Additional parts, which can be bought at equally reasonable prices, naturally extend the scope and cater for some really elaborate constructions.

There will, of course, come a time when he wants his models to work, and it is here that greater care must be exercised in details. Stresses and strains must, to some extent come into it, so that his ingenuity is still further taxed to fit the power unit into a given space or, alternatively, to construct the appliance around the power unit.

There is no doubt that an actual steam-operated engine provides the most realism, but for domestic reasons it is not always advisable to provide either the complete unit, or the parts from which it can be made up. The modern practice is to purchase either a strong but compact clockwork motor or, as an alternative, a low-voltage electrically operated unit.

Clockwork Motors are a miracle of simplicity and power, for even the 2s. 6d. size is strong enough to work such things as cranes, mechanical navvies, motor cars, windmills, ships' coalers and so on. These little motors are fitted with a lever for starting purposes, so that the finished model is able actually to carry out work in the most approved style. Better models have reversing mechanism incorporated—a most useful device for the more intricate models. A brake is fitted to nearly all types.

One of the great advantages of the constructor sets now marketed is that all sorts of parts may be purchased as and when required. For instance, such things as

Courtesy: Meccano

Fig. 2.—Clockwork Motor

universal couplings, girders, brackets, angle pieces for bracing purposes, U channel sections, cranks and the like are all useful and enable the constructor to make many more types of models. Then there are various plates all drilled ready for assembly, axles, hooks and wheels of all descriptions.

Those who are fond of motor-car model-making will find complete outfits designed for the purpose. One can build two-seaters, chassis, four-seater tourers and saloon cars which will steer and run along quite smoothly on their rubber-tyred wheels. Those who have a desire to construct aeroplanes will find sets which will enable them to make realistic models, which, incidentally, will do anything but fly. (For Model Aeroplanes, *see* separate article.)

Undoubtedly the best type of power unit for all the models is the electric motor. This is obtainable to operate on 4, 6, 8 or 20 volts —a perfectly harmless current and one with which any boy may be entrusted with safety. Contrary to expectation it is not necessary to buy expensive and heavy batteries for operating these motors, for diminutive transformer sets are obtainable for a few shillings, these units transforming the ordinary lighting current from the mains into a harmless low-voltage current suitable for all models. It is only since the alternating current has become so widely distributed that these transformers have been marketed at a reasonable price, and they can be obtained for 100/110 volts, 50 cycles; 200/225 volts, 50 cycles; or for 225/250 volts, 50 cycles.

Model Railways.—Nearly all men are as interested as boys in trains, and the variety of models from which to choose is exceptionally wide. There are, for instance, exact replicas of all the most famous railway engines and carriages—L.N.E.R., G.W.R., L.M.S. and Southern. These models are so accurate that when compared with a photograph of the original it is sometimes difficult to tell which is which. The greatest fascination, however, lies in building a railway track—and the bigger this is, the more absorbing the hobby. It is wonderful how interesting it is to plan a whole railway, trying to overcome the obstacles imposed by the limitations as to space, planning to fit in a station or two, a tunnel, a viaduct, bridge or level crossing. When the whole plan has been thought out, a start must be made by preparing the "bed," which may be of sand, gravel, etc. Then the rails are laid and the station built and so on. Next, signals that really work are erected, the current laid on, and then comes the never-ending fun of running trains backwards and forwards, switching over from one set of lines to another, hauling diminutive goods wagons, milk trains, newspaper and mail trains, etc., at all speeds.

Not everyone can afford to purchase all the equipment necessary—or desirable—and in any case, there is much fun to be had from making one's own "scenery" and so forth. A good method of making such things as tunnels, etc., is to construct them from paper. Tear up some old newspapers and soak them in water until they become pulpy. Then squeeze them fairly dry and mix them in a paste solution made out of

Fig. 3.—A Railway System in a Back Garden

flour and water. When well mixed this provides an excellent material.

A Tunnel is constructed as follows: On a 2-ft. square of wood insert a number of small tacks the width of the tunnel (inside measurement). Then take a piece of thin cardboard, cut it to the required length and bend it over as shown in the illustration. The natural spring in the cardboard will hold it against the tacks. This forms a foundation upon which to work. If the paper pulp is inclined to be too wet, and likely to soften the cardboard, give the latter a coat of varnish or size and allow it to dry.

Now take up some of the pulp and spread it over the cardboard until the whole is covered. A thin layer will be sufficient for the first time, and this should be allowed to dry in a warm room before proceeding. When the first layer is dry add more pulp until the whole is about $\frac{1}{2}$ in. or so thick. Allow this to dry thoroughly. It will then be found to have set and formed a really strong arch. The next step is to give it one or two coats of size or thin glue, allowing this to dry also. The tunnel is now ready for decoration. Any paint will do, but

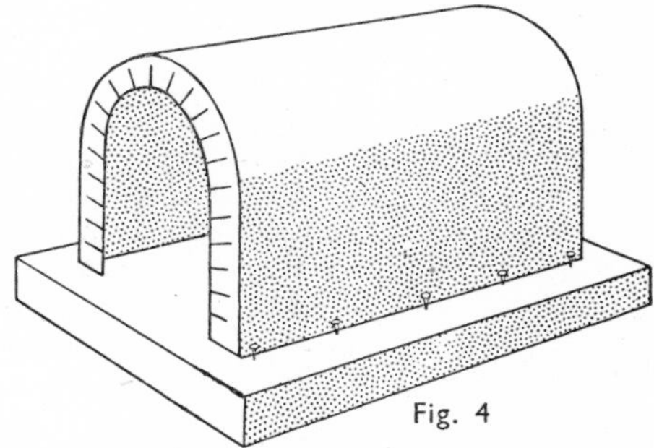

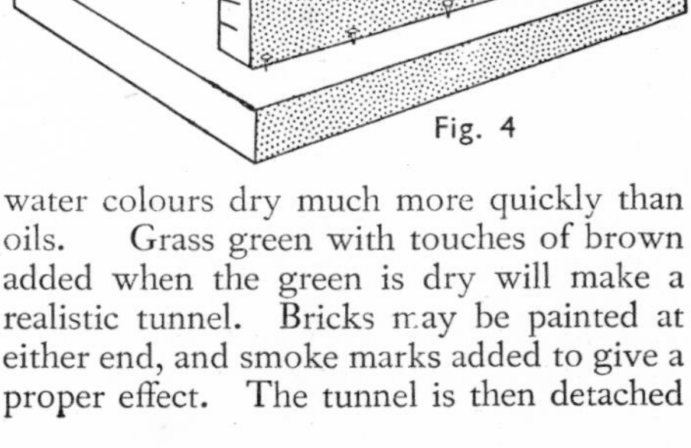

Fig. 4

water colours dry much more quickly than oils. Grass green with touches of brown added when the green is dry will make a realistic tunnel. Bricks may be painted at either end, and smoke marks added to give a proper effect. The tunnel is then detached

Fig. 5.—A Terrible Accident—in miniature!

from the board and may be placed where desired along the railway line. It is not a difficult matter to construct signals that work and stations and goods yards out of cardboard and wood. The planning alone will mean many happy hours.

Casting a Wheel.—It frequently happens that models—particularly trains—become broken. The wheels seem to suffer a great deal, and many an otherwise good engine or truck is discarded on that account. It is quite simple, however, to make another wheel, the only requisites being a small quantity of plaster of Paris, some lead, and another sound wheel. The method is as follows:

Take a couple of tablespoonfuls of plaster of Paris and mix it well with a little water so as to form a thickish paste. Then dip the sound wheel in oil and press it, flange side uppermost, into the plaster. This should be done very soon after the plaster is mixed as the mixture sets quickly. When set, remove the wheel carefully and allow the plaster to dry thoroughly. It may be placed in a warm room for this purpose, but not too near the fire. The next step is to melt a piece of sheet lead or a portion of an old lead pipe, etc., in an iron ladle. There is no need to make it red hot—just above melting point is the right temperature—and when all is ready pour quickly into the mould and let it set. When cool, break away the plaster mould and the wheel is ready. If the hub is solid, it may be drilled out to the correct size, but it is possible to insert an oiled nail into the mould when making it, thus saving the trouble of drilling.

Other Repairs may be carried out with sheets of tin and a pair of shears or strong scissors. The best plan when inserting a new panel, etc., is to remove the old one, flatten it out with a hammer and then cut the new panel using the old one as a template. Soldered repairs are by far the stronger, and provided the parts are clean and the iron is hot and well tinned, this should present no difficulty. It is wise to purchase two grades of solder, one hard, for tinning the iron, and the other soft, for the actual soldering. With a little practice one is able to turn out very neat repairs, while a small pot or two of enamel and a fine camel-haired brush will complete the jobs in such a manner that the new parts scarcely differ from the rest of the model.

METALWORK

METALWORK, like Woodwork, offers a very large field of activity for anyone interested in crafts. It has its rough heavy side as in some parts of forge work, or it can provide for the artist in precious metals. The artist is also catered for in the forging of hand-wrought gates, railings, fireside furniture and so on. The metalworker can enjoy the making of a large number of his own tools, and quite a number of household utensils can be made in tin-plate.

Equipment.—The equipment varies with the kind of work in view. If an outhouse is available, it may be possible either to build a forge in brick or to buy a portable one costing three or four pounds. A lathe may be built in a spare room, an attic, a garage or an outhouse. Vice work demands a strong bench or table and a side-bench against a wall is the best arrangement. The latter will be found to be best for most of the work as the back can be arranged as a tool-rack.

Tools.—Many of the tools are the same for all kinds of metalwork. The following selection is arranged to give a fairly representative equipment.

The file is one of the principal tools and it is known by its length, type of cut, shape and cross section. One or two bastard cuts, one smooth-cut safe edge, one half-round second-cut, all 8 in. or 10 in. long, one 6-in. three square, one rat-tail and one half-round smooth-cut will give a good start. One try-square, a scriber, centre punch, callipers (inside and outside, all home-made), cold chisel, dividers, engineers' hammer, about 1½ lb. with ball pene, tin snips, hacksaw and frame, pliers, flat and round nose, breast drill and drills, set of stocks, dies and taps, a 4-in. parallel-jaw vice, soldering stove and soldering iron, a steel rule, groover, rivet set, creasing iron, bick iron and mallet will include a large proportion of the equipment required for vice work of all kinds and tinsmith's work.

Equipment for Repoussé Work will be fairly covered by a repoussé hammer, doming block, blow-pipe and bellows, pitch block, sand-bag and various punches of tool steel which can be made at a small cost. The equipment for this branch of work is perhaps the least expensive when the high value of some of the work produced is taken into consideration.

Tools for Raising Metal consist mainly of hammers and stakes of various shapes. If equipment for forging is available, many of those can be home-made. Otherwise, it is advisable to buy a few only and extend the stock when some experience of the peculiar requirements of this work has been gained.

Where a lathe is installed it will be necessary to provide, besides the lathe equipment, a surface gauge, vee blocks, centring square and punch as well as an assortment of turning tools, either hand or machine, according to the type of lathe.

Brazing can be carried on with the blowpipe already mentioned. A small brazing hearth, which may consist of a small open sheet-iron tray filled with coke or bits of firebrick or asbestos, is necessary.

Metals.—Many of the metals available are largely confined in use to the particular branch of work to which they belong, e.g. wrought iron for forging, cast steel for tool-making, tinned iron sheet, or tinplate as it is called, for tinman's work and so on. Wrought iron, mild steel and tool steel, or carbon steel are obtainable in square, round or rectangular bars. Iron, steel, tin-plate, copper, brass, zinc, lead can be purchased in the sheet or by the pound. Solder is bought by the pound.

Operations.—As with other crafts, successful work in metals depends upon a thorough knowledge of the tools involved and their manipulation.

Filing.—Work on a level with the elbow. Grip the file with the ball of the handle in the hollow of one hand and hold the end of the file firmly in the other hand with the pressure applied on the top. Do not rock the file when pushing it. Apply pressure on the forward stroke only. Keep the file teeth clear of filings by brushing across the file with a wire brush. Do not file cast iron without first chipping off with a chisel the hard skin on the surface.

Sawing.—Purchase a saw-blade with a flexible back and so avoid a good deal of loss on breakages. Hold the handle of the frame as for the file with one hand. Grip the other end with the other hand, passing the thumb round the inside of the frame to meet the fingers outside. Apply pressure on the forward stroke only. Keep the frame upright.

Drilling.—Fix the work on the bench or in the vice so that it cannot revolve with the drill. Use carbon steel twist drills, though for a special job it may be quicker to make a flat diamond point drill. See that the point of the drill is ground at about 60 degrees to each side of the centre line; that it is central; and that the line of the small point on the end bisects the angle of the curves of the flutes on each side on the point. The cutting edge should have a clearance, i.e. the back edge should not also be in contact with the metal when the drill is revolving; the two cutting edges must be equal in length and equally inclined. Do not apply undue pressure when drilling; you might overheat the drill, reduce its temper and ruin it.

Riveting.—See that the head of the rivet inserted in the hole is properly supported under the blows of the hammer. Use the round end of the hammer, give light taps rather than heavy blows and strike a glancing blow rather than a direct one so that the metal is spread, not crushed. Do not drill the holes too large for the shank of the rivet; everything depends on its being a close sliding fit in the hole. Use a rivet set to finish off the head formed by the hammer. Do not overlook the possibilities of the rivets as an ornamental feature on a job.

Chiselling.—This operation is one which saves time and labour and other tools from damage. The narrow cross-cut chisel is used for cutting grooves and for chipping off the hard surface of a casting before using a file or a saw upon it. The flat chisel is useful for cutting out sheet metal or for cutting away superfluous metal from a job held in the vice.

Forging.—The first and most important point is a "clean" fire, i.e. a fire clear of clinker, burnt metal and fine ash. Raise the metal to its right working heat, i.e. the best heat for the particular metal before beginning to work on it. Do not continue to hammer when cool and so run the risk of splitting the metal. Keep the anvil clear of scale. Do not cut the fibres of the metal when making a bend. When forging tool steel take great care not to raise it to too high a temperature or it will be spoiled.

Soldering.—The soldering iron must be heated until a green flame is seen, filed clean, dipped in flux, then the end applied to a stick of solder to take up a coating on the point. Do not overheat the iron when reheating it; remove it from the stove at the first suspicion of white smoke coming off. Paint the joint with flux, either paste or soldering fluid. Raise the metal of the joint to a sufficient heat to melt the solder applied to it. Do not hurry the process of applying the iron to the joint as the heat is not thus transferred to the metal in sufficient quantity. Do not continue to apply the iron when the surface of the solder is crystalline in appearance and therefore cold.

Screw Cutting.—The misuse of taps for making internal threads and of stocks and dies for making external threads on metal may be expensive. Do not attempt to cut the full depth of the thread on the first cut with the dies; regulate the distance between the two halves so that you take about three cuts before the full depth of the thread is reached. Use a lubricant and do not force the die, ease it back now and again. Take care to start the cut with the die stock held horizontally or the thread will not be

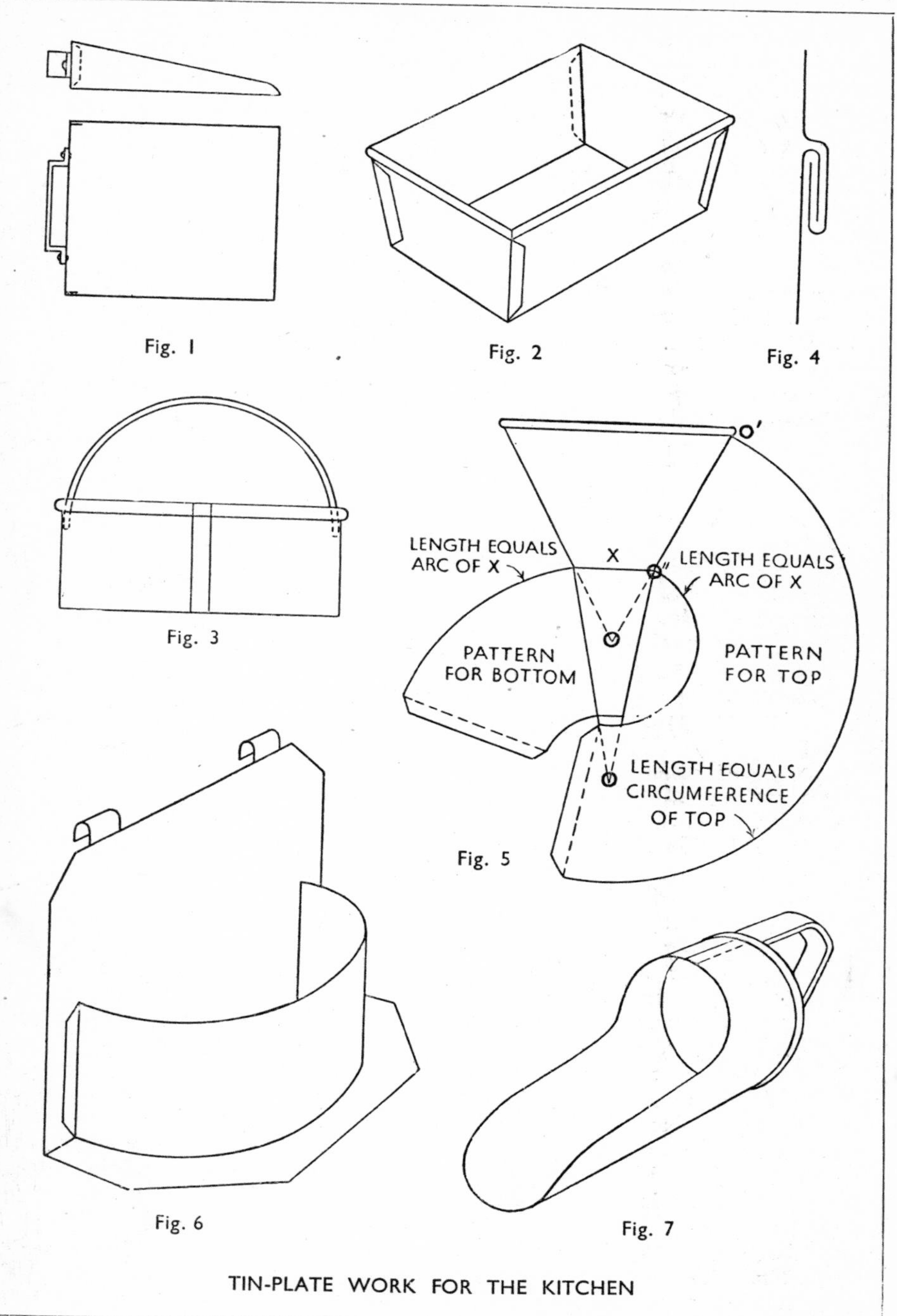

TIN-PLATE WORK FOR THE KITCHEN

true. Allow the right amount for the depth of the thread when drilling the hole to be tapped; use a tapping gauge to obtain the right drilling size for each thread. Use the taper top before the intermediate and/or plug tap so that the internal thread may be cut gradually.

Turning.—Correct setting of a piece of work in a lathe is of first importance. The holes on the ends of the piece of metal to be turned which are to fit on to the dead and live centres of the lathe must be accurately drilled and countersunk. See that the lathe centres are exactly opposite each other unless you are turning a taper. Set the cutting edge of the tool exactly on the centre line by setting to the lathe centre, or if anything slightly above, never on any account below. Use the right tool for each operation, e.g. the roughing tool for roughing off, side tool for squaring the end, parting tool for cutting in two, etc. Make quite sure that the lathe tool is ground to the correct angles for top and bottom and side rake or clearance. When using hand turning tools keep the heel of the tool as close as possible to the work. Do not use a file on the lathe any more than you can possibly help; filing is not turning.

Brazing.—Brazing or hard soldering requires a heat from a blow-pipe. For fine and small work in silver a mouth blow-pipe might be sufficient; for larger work a foot bellows is generally necessary; the larger the work, the larger the flame and the higher the heat and consequently the size of bellows required. The spelter or solder consists of brass in granular form. The more copper there is in the brass the higher the melting point, the more zinc the lower the melting point and the weaker the joint. The melting point of the spelter must be lower than that of the metals being joined or the latter will be burnt. Do not make the joint between the two pieces of metal to be united a very good fit. Allow space for the spelter to run into the joint. See that the joint is clear of foreign matter. Borax is the flux used and is better if it is first heated to drive out the moisture and then reground to a fine powder. Apply the flux and spelter together along the line of the joint after raising the work to a red heat. Where possible make vee sides on the joint so that the spelter runs towards the joint and through it. Bind parts together when necessary with thin iron wire to prevent them from moving apart under the heat. Do not quench the work in water, allow it to cool slowly.

Silver Soldering. — Silver has a lower melting point than copper and can be safely used on brass, copper and silver. Clean the work in a pickle of 1 part of sulphuric acid and 12 parts of water before applying the solder and flux. Use very small pieces of solder. Apply a small flame on a fine small job. The operations of silver soldering are the same as brazing. Immerse the work in pickle when soldered and then wash in cold water before cleaning.

Raising.—When raising a bowl by knocking it into a depression in a block of wood do not attempt to obtain great depth, 1 in. may be quite sufficient for a good finish to be secured. Do not neglect the annealing of the metal; hard metal may split under the hammer. Even placing of rows of blows from the hammer is essential. Uneven and irregular hammering simply spoils metal. Most deep shapes are best raised by coursing, i.e. hammering in rings of blows. When coursing hold the metal in contact with the stake inside the bowl at about 1 in. below the spot where the hammer is striking. Complete each course or row of blows before going on to the next course. The courses are about ½ in. apart. Pencil lines drawn concentrically on the outside of the bowl will assist in keeping the correct line of each course.

Work in Tin-plate requires very direct manipulation if the results are to be good. The surface of the metal is not improved by repeated hammering. A wood mallet should be used wherever possible.

Fig. 1 shows the details of a crumb tray made from one piece of metal. A paper pattern should be cut out to give the developed shape, i.e. a "ground plan" of the work. (*See* illustrations of pattern for funnel, Fig. 5.) The flaps on the corners are about ⅜ in. wide. They are soldered. The shape is worked up on a stake with an

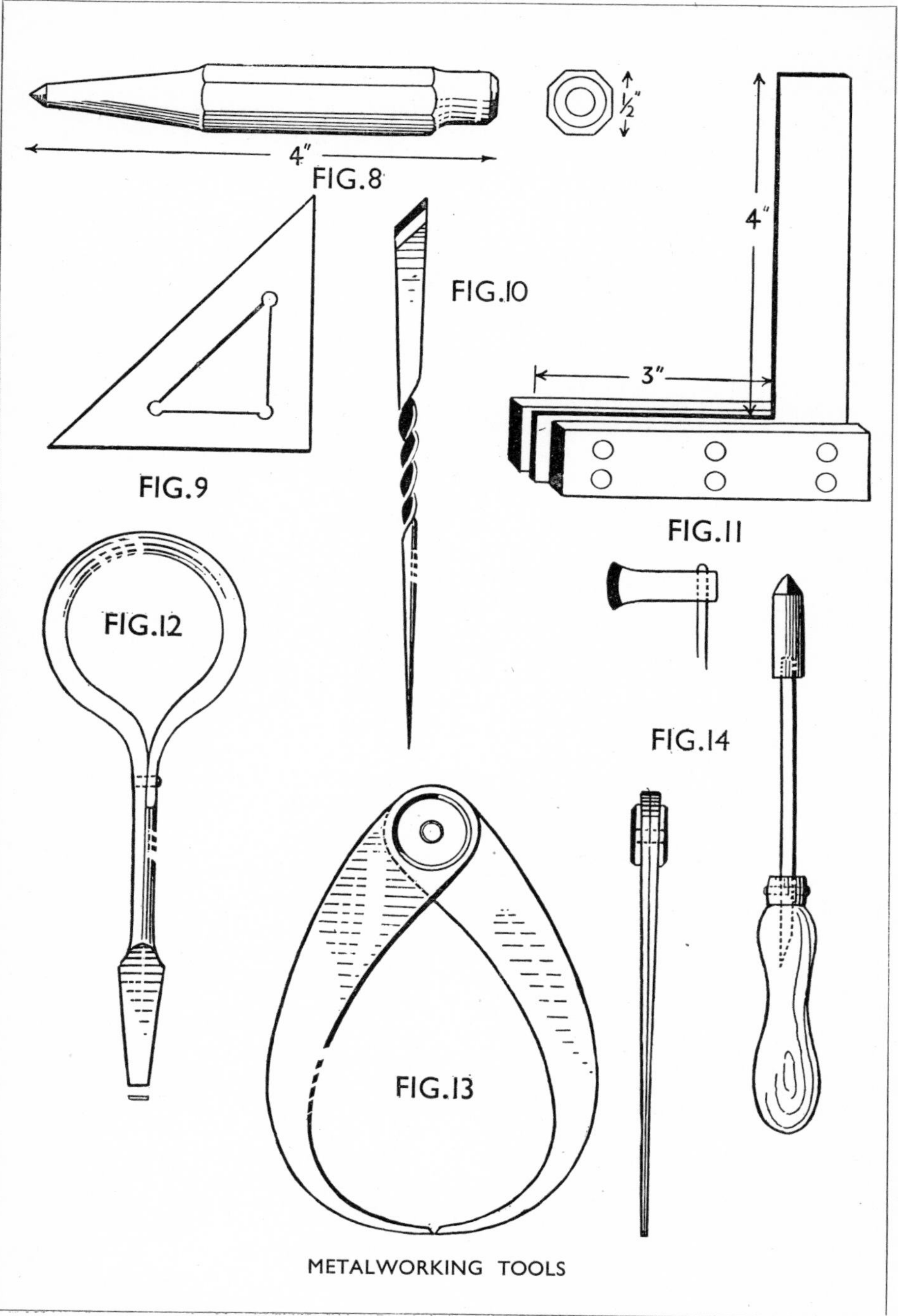

METALWORKING TOOLS

edge, either a right-angle or a sharper angle. The handle has the edges turned in and it may be soldered or riveted. The finished tray will not be very attractive if left untouched and it may be painted with enamel.

The loaf tin in Fig. 2 is a typical tray construction, made out of one piece of metal with soldered corners. Where water-tightness is not to be considered this type of tray might be made from sheet steel and riveted together. The edge in Fig. 2 is wired, by bending the edges of the sides over a sharp-edged stake, then inserting a piece of wire and tapping the edge over this to enclose it neatly.

Fig. 3 is a circular pastry cutter. These can be made of any shape, the edge wired or left plain and the joint either soldered or folded as in Fig. 4. The handle is about $\frac{3}{4}$ in. wide, the edges are folded and the ends soldered inside the body.

The Funnel.—The size of this type of article depends upon use. If it is for pouring oil into a car engine it should be about 5 in. diameter at the top. If to be used for distilled water, then a piece of very fine gauze must be fitted inside. For household purposes a diameter of about 3 in. at the top will be ample. The edge may be wired, folded or left plain. The development of the correct shape of the paper pattern from which to cut out the metal is obtained by striking curves from the centres oo with radii at o′ and o″ for the larger and the smaller cones respectively. These centres are obtained by extending the sides of the two cones in the funnel. Any size of cone can be developed in this way. The joints are soldered or folded.

The bird trough in Fig. 6 explains itself. Fig. 7 shows a scoop which can be made on the given plan to any size. The body is cut out of a rectangular piece a little longer than the circumference of the cylinder to allow for the joint. The end is made by raising the edge of a circle and fitting it on the end of the cylindrical body. The handle is soldered on last of all.

Making Your Own Tools.—Figs. 8 to 14 show several tools which you will need for most of your work in metal. The centre punch in Fig. 8 is made from a piece of $\frac{1}{2}$-in. octagonal tool steel. This steel must be softened by heating to redness and allowing to cool slowly before it can be turned in a lathe or a file will cut it easily. For a punch this length allow an extra 2 in. so that it may be fixed in the lathe for turning. If you have no lathe the shaping may be done by hand with a file. In that case you would probably not attempt to file a circular shape, but would file to a taper end with a point. After shaping, the tool must be hardened and tempered. This is a very important process with all cutting tools. Raise the metal to a bright red heat, and quench it quickly in water. That will make the steel dead hard. Now clean about 2 in. of the end and apply the heat of a Bunsen gas jet, or the gas ring, very slowly to the centre of the body of the punch. Watch the point end carefully and you will see a band of colours creeping along towards it. These are the temper colours. They indicate various degrees of temperature ranging from about 220° C. (or 428° F.) to about 300° C. (or 572° F.), and different tools are quenched off at different colours. For example, screw-drivers should be quenched off when the purplish blue colour, the high temperature, has arrived at the top; cold chisels when the purple has arrived at the cutting edge; centre punches when the orange colour is there; scribers a lighter colour and so on. When the right temper colour appears at the business end of the tool it must be picked up in the pliers at once and quenched off in water as quickly as possible. Then try the tool to see whether it will do the work it is designed to do. If it is a cold chisel try it on cast iron; if the edge turns up something is wrong. It may be you did not harden the tool properly. Try re-hardening and re-tempering. If it is still not right it may be that you have got hold of a piece of mild and not tool steel.

A Set-square, Fig. 9, is made from mild sheet steel about $\frac{1}{16}$ in. thick. Test it carefully, not with another square which might be out of truth, but by setting on edge along a line and drawing the line along the adjacent edge. Now reverse the set-square, i.e. turn it over, set the same edge

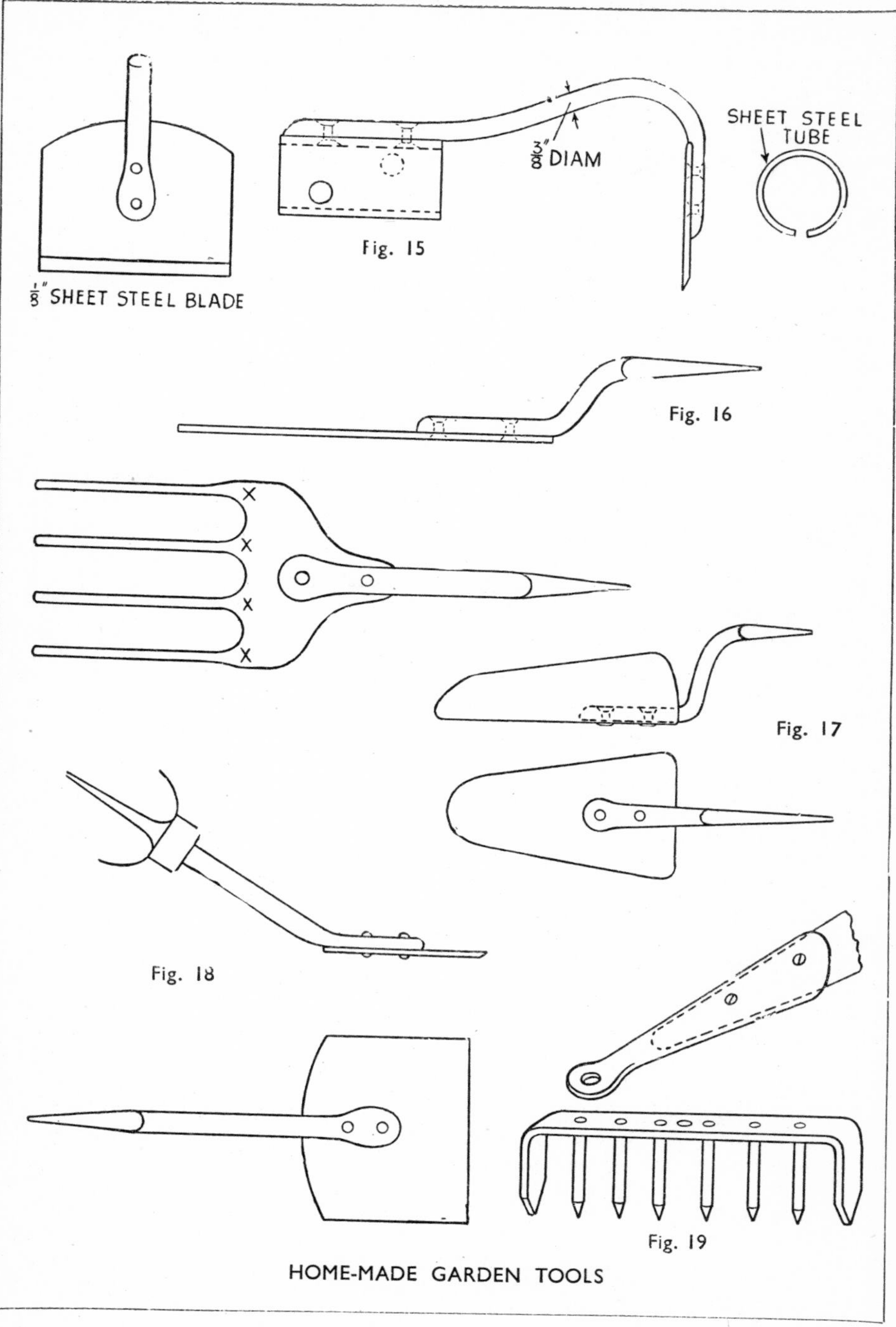

Fig. 15

Fig. 16

Fig. 17

Fig. 18

Fig. 19

HOME-MADE GARDEN TOOLS

to the same straight line and see if the upright edge coincides exactly with the first line drawn. If it does not, file the edge where necessary to make it fit perfectly.

The Scriber.—This marking-out tool is made from $\frac{3}{16}$-in. or $\frac{1}{4}$-in. square tool steel, forged down to a fine point at one end and flattened out to a blade at the other end. The metal is then heated to redness in the middle, placed in a vice, about 3 in. being held in the latter, a $\frac{1}{4}$-in. spanner put on about 2 in. above the vice jaw and a full-turn twist given to the metal to obtain the result shown in the illustration (Fig. 10). Care must be taken to keep the metal upright when pulling the spanner round. Grind the ends to shape on the grindstone or emery wheel, harden, polish and temper to straw colour.

The screw-driver in Fig. 12 must be made from $\frac{1}{4}$-in. round bar tool steel, so that the end may be hardened and tempered to a blue colour.

Fig. 13 shows a pair of callipers made from mild sheet steel about $\frac{1}{16}$ in. thick. The leg is cut out to a straight pattern and heated and shaped as shown. The rivet is of $\frac{3}{16}$-in. mild steel wire and should be a tight fit. The heads are countersunk.

The surfaces of tools like this and the square should be finished by neatly draw-filing them. That is, a "smooth cut" file is held in both hands across the work, which is generally nailed down to a piece of wood held in the vice, and drawn carefully backwards and forwards to make a series of very fine straight lines. There is always the danger that the results of this operation may be spoiled by a small piece of metal sticking in the teeth of the file. This will make an ugly scratch in the surface. It can be prevented by filling the teeth of the file with chalk.

The Soldering Iron.—Fig. 14 shows a straight soldering iron or bit and on the left a hatchet bit. Both should be made from a piece of 1-in. or $\frac{3}{4}$-in. square copper. The iron rod fitting into the handle is screwed on one end, a hole is drilled and tapped in the copper and the bar screwed into it. These two parts may be fixed without screwing by drilling a $\frac{3}{8}$-in. hole in the copper, inserting the $\frac{3}{8}$-in. iron rod and then drilling a $\frac{1}{8}$-in. hole across and through the two, this holc to receive a $\frac{1}{8}$-in. rivet which is knocked up on both ends.

Garden Tools.—Many tools for the garden can be made quite effectively. The hoe in Fig. 15 is made from a piece of sheet steel about $\frac{1}{8}$ in. thick sharpened on one edge. It is fixed to the handle by means of a piece of $\frac{3}{8}$-in. round bar iron flattened at one end and riveted to the blade, flattened at the other end and riveted to a socket of sheet steel made from No. 16 gauge. The holes in the socket are to take the screws which fix it to the wooden handle. The end view of the socket shows it not completely closed so as to allow for fitting.

The hand fork in Fig. 16 is made from No. 16 or No. 14 sheet steel cut out and riveted to a piece of $\frac{3}{8}$-in. round bar as shown. When the prongs are cut they are heated and twisted at a right angle at XXXX. This adds strength and makes the tool more effective.

The trowel in Fig. 17 is made from the same size sheet steel as the fork. The hoe in Fig. 18 is made similarly to that in Fig. 15. The rake in Fig. 19 is made from 1-in. by $\frac{1}{8}$-in. bar for the main part shaped and bent as shown and drilled to receive pieces of steel $\frac{1}{4}$ in. diameter. The rivets are shouldered to give a better grip. The socket for the handle is made from No. 16 sheet metal, shaped and hammered solid at the end so that it may be riveted and brazed to the head of the rake.

Work in Mild Steel.—There is a great deal of scope in the making of metal furniture for doors, cupboards, drawers. The door-knockers in Figs. 20 and 21 are made from sheet steel for the background, about 14 gauge is good and solid, and from bar iron of any size or section to give the required result according to position. On the outer gate of a large building a knocker about 1 ft. long and from metal about 1 in. square might not be out of place, but most people would probably be satisfied with something less and $\frac{3}{8}$-in. by $\frac{1}{2}$-in. round or square bar iron might give the result required. In the design of a knocker it should be remembered that the movable

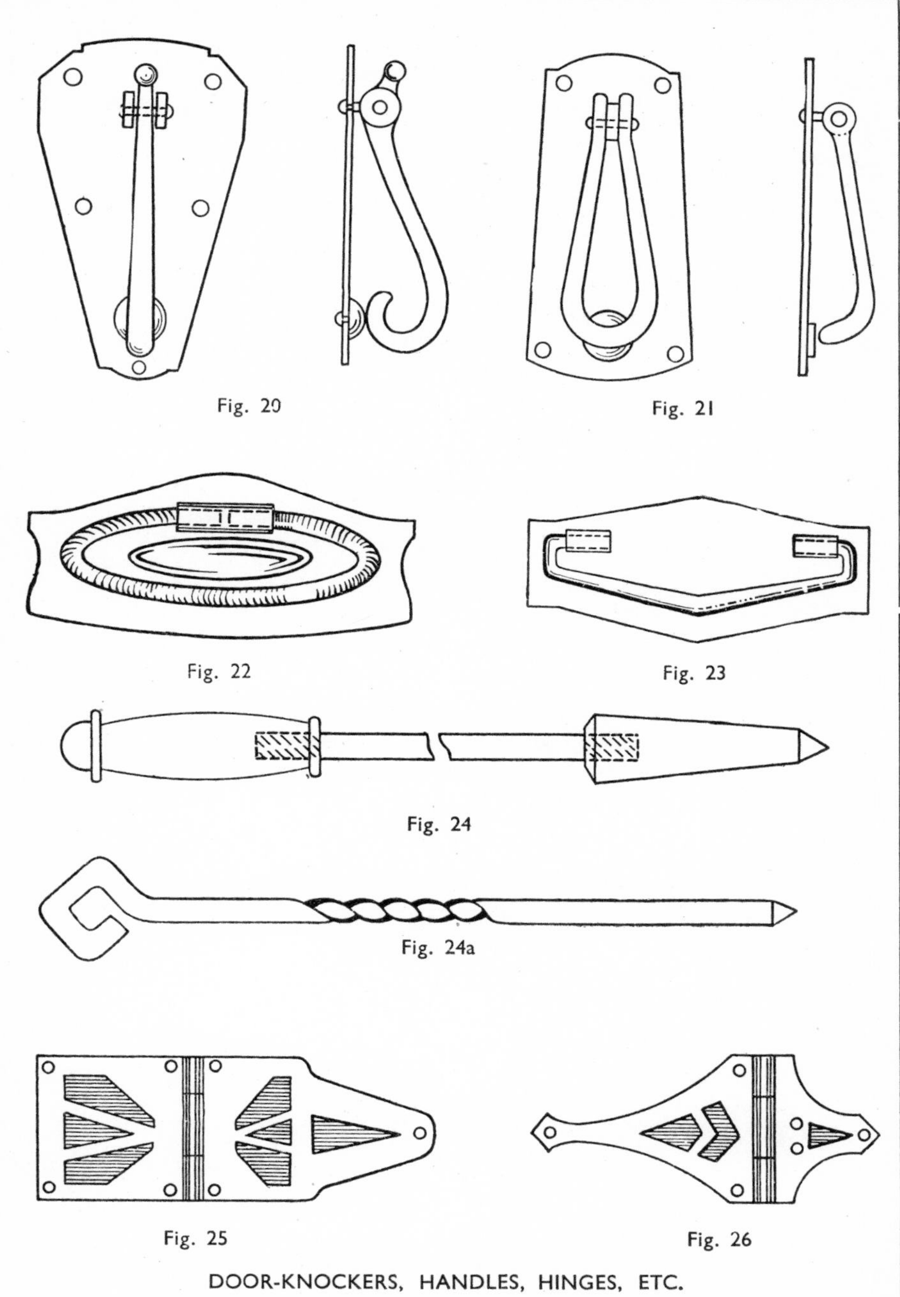

Fig. 20

Fig. 21

Fig. 22

Fig. 23

Fig. 24

Fig. 24a

Fig. 25

Fig. 26

DOOR-KNOCKERS, HANDLES, HINGES, ETC.

part must be easily gripped, lift easily and come down with an effective noise. The knockers designed like the drawer handles in Figs. 22 and 23 do not fulfil one of the above conditions.

Figs. 22 and 23 are made from sheet steel or copper or brass and the handles are made from $\frac{1}{4}$-in. round or square bar of the same metals. The hinges are made from the same gauge metal as the back, say, No. 16 or 18, and are riveted through a slotted hole in the back, the ends being turned back.

Fig. 24 is a poker which combines lathe work, tapping and screwing, forge work and fitting. It can be made into a useful part of a good set consisting of the shovel, poker, brush and a stand to hold them all. The handle and rod may be of brass or copper and the "poking" end of iron, which lasts better.

The poker shown in Fig. 24a is made from $\frac{3}{8}$-in. or $\frac{1}{2}$-in. square bar iron, the handle is forged to the pattern given or to a round shape or any shape that will be comfortable in the hand. The twist is added in the same manner as described for the scriber.

Hinge plates, escutcheon plates and drawer pulls can be made into sets of very good appearance. If made from steel and well polished, they harmonize with oak furniture very well. The making of the hinge is an operation requiring careful workmanship. When the slots have been cut out to give the shape required to form the hinge, it will be found easier to work them to the cylindrical shape if the metal is softened and turned on the same size of bar iron as is to be used for the hinge pin. Great care should be taken to fit the hinge neatly so that it works freely but not too loosely. The perforations are made by drilling holes and inserting a fine piercing saw. Cut as accurately as possible to the lines and so save yourself more filing than is necessary.

The surfaces of steel should be drawfiled, or they may be hammered with a round-nosed hammer to obtain a pitted effect. Copper and brass can be treated in the same way.

Metal Raising.—The simple raising of a small bowl from a flat piece of metal is shown in various stages in Figs. 27 to 30. A wood block is hollowed out on its end grain as in Fig. 27 and held firmly in a vice. The round thin sheet of metal from which the small bowl is to be made must first of all be softened before beginning to work it.

This is done by heating it to redness and cooling it off—unlike steel, it will be observed. Place the sheet of metal on top of the depression in the block of wood and apply the round-nosed hammer as shown. Between the blows the metal must be turned a little and kept revolving so that no place receives two successive blows from the hammer. After one revolution it will be found that the edge of the circular disc of metal is turning up.

A second row of blows about $\frac{1}{4}$ in. away from the first will give a little more lift to the edge. Notice the change in the position of the metal and of the hammer as each successive row of blows is struck. Figs. 27a, 28a, and 29a show the change in form as the hammering goes on. When the desired shape has been obtained, the edge is filed off level and the tray is put on to a stake of the shape shown in Fig. 30 and hammered carefully with the flat end of the hammer. This hardens the surface and makes it dense and results in a series of small hammer marks which give a finish to the bowl. The process is known as "planishing." The bowl may then be dipped in the acid bath previously mentioned, polished and either waxed or lacquered to preserve the surface.

Colouring Metals.—A good deal of interesting effect can be obtained by artificially colouring the metal. Copper can be coloured by applying a Bunsen flame or any other clean heat, also by immersing or painting it with a solution of sulphide of ammonia or potash.

Brass may be coloured green by painting it with a solution consisting of salt 4 oz., sal ammoniac (·880) 4 oz., ammonia 3 oz., and 1 quart of vinegar. Allow this to dry slowly on the metal; then apply a wax polish.

Armour-plate colour may be applied to steel by rubbing the surface of the metal with a piece of copper sulphate and then immersing it in a bath of ammonium

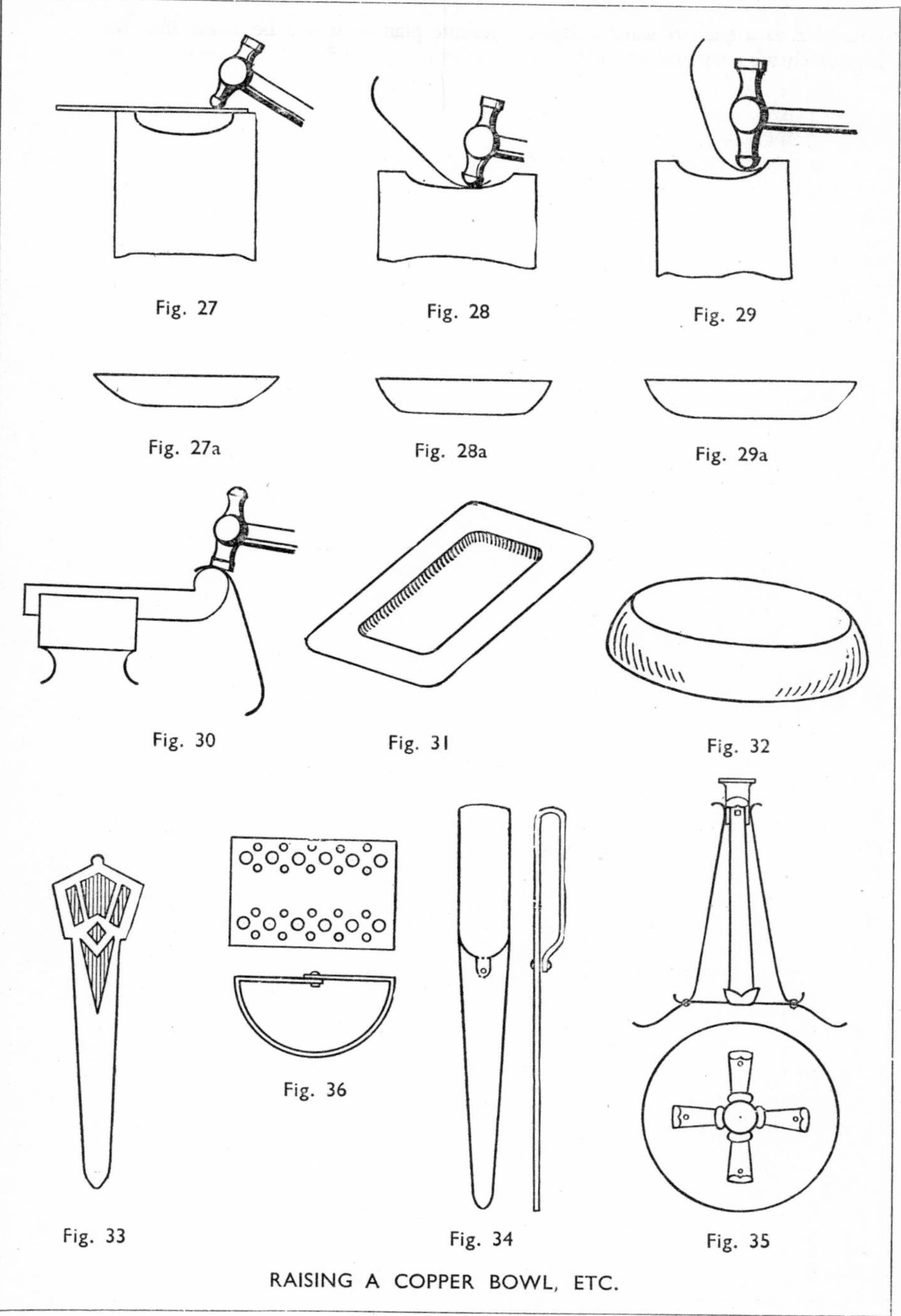

RAISING A COPPER BOWL, ETC.

sulphide, 6 oz. to a quart of water. Rinse and dry quickly when the desired colour has been obtained.

Protection of Colour.—The colour put on to metals by the above methods may be protected by lacquering. This is best put on when the article is warm. Apply the lacquer with a camel-hair brush; maintain the heat or a cloudy effect may be the result.

The very shallow desk or pin tray shown in Fig. 31 is worked by placing a sharp-edged stake under the line of the edge of the depression and tapping with a small round-nosed hammer on the upper side just outside the line of the support underneath.

The bowl in Fig. 32 is the basis of a good deal of work. It can be made into a candlestick if a centre-piece and handle are put on. It may have a flange worked on all round it of any width and so be extended into a large dish or a salver. The surface is planished (*see* page 394) to obtain a fine finish.

The paper knives in Figs. 33 and 34 are typical of a great variety of work on these lines. The ornament in the handle can be pierced, raised, etched, set with a semi-precious stone, etc. They may be made from about 20's gauge copper or brass. The whole surface may be finished by tapping all over with a round-nosed hammer.

When this finish is produced the series of hammer blows must be done on a very definite plan or it will be found that the surface is covered with a series of long parallel lines of blows, a pattern which is not interesting. The best effect can be obtained by taking one spot, striking a blow and then making a ring of blows, about six or seven, around it. Then take another spot and repeat a ring of blows around it, allowing this ring to run into the previous one.

The candlestick in Fig. 35 is an example of built-up work as contrasted with raised work from one piece.

Fig. 37.—Examples of Square Riveted and Circular Metalwork

Fig. 36 shows a napkin ring which is typical of much work that can be done from one piece of copper, etc.

Quite a lot of beautiful work may be done by combining forged steel, finished armour-bright, and hammered with copper to make electric light stands, hand or bracket, lanterns of all kinds to hold electric bulbs or candles, fruit bowls, picture frames and so on. Where there are facilities for forging —and there are many good smiths at work who began as amateurs—there is wide scope for freshness of design in gates, hearth furniture, stands for brushes, etc., outdoor electric light stands, and fitting large outer door-handles, screens, hinges and knockers, etc.

For the finer decorative work in repoussé you will find that you can forge practically all your own tools and stakes, punches, hammers. The pitch block for this work can be made by nailing a rim around a piece of wood about 3 in. thick to make a tray about 2 in. deep. Fill this with a pitch made from 7 lb. of plaster of Paris, 7 lb. of pitch and ½ lb. of tallow. Melt the pitch, add the tallow and then add the plaster a little at a time. This can be used for raising bowls instead of the block of wood, as well as for all repoussé and similar work on the surface of metal.

MINIATURE GARDENS

"MINIATURE" the dictionary tells us is "something done on a small scale," and a miniature garden must keep strictly to that definition. Whatever the size of the garden, whether it is composed of growing flowers and plants or is purely artificial, it must, to be successful, be planned on a properly thought out scale.

There are several varieties of the growing garden, but for most of them a shallow receptacle is required which will hold water. If it is to be outdoors a stone sink will serve the purpose very well (Fig. 1).

The Soil.—First put a layer of small stones for drainage, then fill with a light soil containing a certain amount of sand. For a rock garden the surface should be covered with flint chips which can be bought for the purpose. Small attractive stones, fragments of marble, or anything else of the kind available may be employed to be arranged in irregular and picturesque positions among the flints, and the plants will in time grow over these.

Some plants require shade, some more moisture than others; some like strong sunlight, and it is interesting to note that the same species of plant grown indoors will often show considerable variation from that

Fig. 1.—A Landscape Garden grown in an old stone sink

Fig. 2.—A flat "arrangement" of pebbles and stonecrop

grown outdoors, as for example the houseleek (sempervivum).

Among the easiest plants to grow in a rock garden are all varieties of sedum, stonecrop, aubretias, forget-me-not, veronicas, houseleek, dwarf trailing campanulas, or Virginia stock.

A Water Garden.—Another variety of outdoor garden is the water garden. For this prepare as before, but omit the chips. To represent a pond a flat bowl should be sunk in the soil and filled with water. For the grass, a very fine moss found by stones in moist places, makes a beautiful lawn. Small seedlings serve as trees. Such plants as aubretia, small-growing forget-me-not, Virginia stock, Swiss moss (sometimes known as "Granny's curls" or "Mind your own business"), which must be kept really wet, are suitable.

A little bridge, a cottage or a summer-house adds to the reality of the garden, with some tiny figures to make it more convincing, but it must never be forgotten that everything must be strictly in proportion if the garden is to be attractive. The figure of a man, for example, standing on the ground while his head appears above the roof of the house, quite spoils the effect.

Oak trees grow quite happily in small pots, as do the beech and sycamore maple. The earth should be changed every second year, and the roots washed and trimmed.

A very successful indoor growing garden can be grown with the many tiny varieties of cactus which can be bought from any good florist. Or if you are going on a cruise and landing on the shores of the Mediterranean,

Fig. 3.—A Cactus Garden in a tub

there are cactus hedges growing along many of the roads, from which a small seedling would be an interesting memento of your visit.

Japanese Gardens.—The cactus is also a help in the growing of a Japanese garden, which is a very popular one. This garden is really a model of something already on a very small scale. The Japanese, having very little room at their disposal, like to plan a pleasure ground with a little mount crowned with a temple or pagoda from which to view the landscape, a pond for goldfish and lotuses, and winding walks to give an impression of distance. The best effect will be obtained by including these features, and by remembering to keep the Japanese character of the landscape.

A shallow china or pottery bowl is the best for this garden, and the colour and shape of this should be carefully considered. If the colours on the outside clash with the flowers and green trees the whole effect will be spoiled.

The other requirements are fibre and charcoal (or earth if the bowl is pierced for drainage), cement, small flat stones or pieces of bath brick, dwarf trees, cactus or small ferns. A pagoda or temple, a bridge, a stone lantern and one or two figures or a little stork, can be obtained cheaply from gardening stores or an "oriental emporium." A small mirror makes a realistic pool.

Dwarf Trees as well as the cactus can be bought from most good florists, but a seedling larch dwarfs easily and produces pretty miniature flowers and cones. The stem should be tied into position with string until it has set in the quaint curves beloved of the Japanese gardener. This will take a year or two, but it is worth it since dwarf pines and cypresses are rather expensive.

The mirror should first be cemented to the bottom of the bowl. This is for the lily pond, and if possible it should be of an irregular shape. There are no straight lines in a Japanese garden.

A barrier of cement should now be built on which to lay the garden walks, thus dividing the garden into separate beds which can be filled with fibre or earth. If earth is to be used it is necessary to be careful that the cement does not interfere with the drainage or the plants will suffer. It is wiser simply to lay the stones flat on the top, pressing them firmly into the soil while it is damp.

When the cement is set the garden can be filled in with the fibre or soil, and the trees and cacti planted. The garden should not be overloaded. The keynote of everything Japanese is simplicity and a sparing use of effect. An interesting garden can be made with one tree, a couple of cacti, a tiny red bridge, and a green and gold pagoda. (Fig. 4.) The gaps should be filled with close-growing moss, pressed firmly down on to the soil and in the spaces between the stones. A piece of rock may be tilted up on end here and there to give the effect of a boulder pushing up through the grass, but these should be used sparingly so as not to distract attention from the pagoda and the tree.

Fig. 4.—A Japanese Garden

Watering.—Nothing looks worse than a dusty and neglected bowl of shrivelling plants, and it is difficult to bring back the first look of freshness if the garden has been allowed to become too dry. It should be watered overhead with a fine rose, taking care not to sprinkle the pagoda too generously, and to wipe it down gently afterwards. These little articles are made of composition, and the colour flakes easily.

There are several types of garden which,

while not being able to be kept indefinitely, may yet last for some considerable time, and take the place of flower decoration in the dark days of winter or early spring when garden flowers are scarce.

An Italian Garden will last for some weeks in the winter, and is worth the comparatively short time necessary to prepare it.

For this a shallow bowl or small metal tray is required. An oblong tray is better, as the lines in this garden should be straight.

Materials.—A few sprays of box, cypress or arbor vitæ and yew. A small round mirror. A few toy stone building blocks. If obtainable, a very small white statue will add to the reality of the garden. Sand. (Fig. 5.)

The paths should be planned on formal lines on the tray of damp sand, using the building blocks as paving stones with a little terrace at one end. Behind this terrace plant the cypress and yews clipped into shape with scissors. A long path is bordered with a yew hedge, and the twigs of box cut into small decorative trees. In the middle of the garden the mirror is placed to act as a pool, and on this stand the little white statue, masking the edge with tiny sprigs of box. The lawns should be made of fine moss, well pressed down.

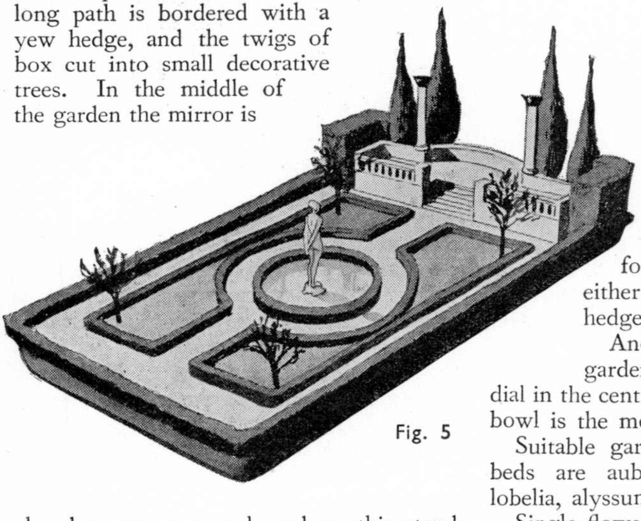

Fig. 5

There should be no flowers. An Italian garden depends for its beauty on the shape and position of trees, steps, fountains, etc. If there are enough blocks, a loggia may be built on the terrace. This is simply an open framework of four or six stone pillars with wooden bars running across the top. A little "greenhouse moss" with the end of the stem pressed into damp sand will resemble a creeper climbing up the loggia.

The details of this garden must be worked out carefully with a keen eye to the neatness of corners, and the exactness of building. The result should be a little garden in which Romeo and Juliet might have met by moonlight.

An English Garden.—For those who prefer the home-grown article, an English flower garden has a fascination of its own. The following will make a charming table garden, and last a week or more if it is kept moist.

A shallow metal tray, some sand, moss and small bright-coloured flowers are all that is required.

Fill the tray just short of the top with clean damp sand. Choose close-growing bright moss, and trim the pieces that are to go on the outside with scissors so as to get a straight edge. Lay out a lawn on the sand, leaving spaces for flower beds. A rather formal Victorian garden is the most effective, with the beds arranged in patterns like a Victorian posy. Leave the sand bare for paths, and finish off with either an outer border or a little hedge of small twigs of box or yew.

Another variety of English flower garden is a circular one with a sundial in the centre. For this a shallow black bowl is the most effective.

Suitable garden flowers for the flower beds are aubrietia, saxifrage, stonecrop, lobelia, alyssum, Virginia stock.

Single flowers should be used, and their stalks pressed into the sand one at a time. Little tufts of gypsophila can be placed here and there to soften the effect. The spikes of the rock veronica look like delphiniums, and a small twig of flowering shrub gives the impression of a whole bush.

A whole range of varieties is available

from the fields and wayside for the English garden. Among these are all the white composite flowers, cow parsley and similar plants, bed straw, sorrel, wild pansies, small heads of clover, forget-me-nots, speedwell, borage.

Wild flowers have a particularly pleasing effect as their colours are soft and delicate, and a little time spent in searching along the edge of a cornfield will yield a variety of lovely small plants, especially in the early autumn when garden flowers tend to become scarce.

A Water-lily Pond.—For a show or table decoration required for a special occasion a water-lily pond can be very successful. This can be made on a thin linoleum mat such as is obtainable in the cheap stores, or on a tray. Enough fine green moss to cover either of these should be rolled out with a rolling-pin to represent grass, first removing carefully any earth that remains on the back, so that the moss will lie perfectly flat when it is rolled.

Next a low, wide bowl, preferably black, should be pressed down where the pond is to be, the moss cut out round it, the circle under the bowl removed, and replaced by the bowl. The outside of the bowl should be concealed by coarse spikes of grass to resemble the green rush edges of a pond.

Some leaves of liverwort placed on the bottom of the bowl will give an impression of sunlight after the water has been poured in. A small flower holder is placed in the centre of the bowl, and covered with granite chips. Through the chips any water weed such as small rushes is inserted, and some tiny flowers, to give an appearance of growing from the centre rockery. Small nasturtium leaves represent the leaves of water lilies, with a little flower such as a buttercup or Japanese anemone in the centre of each leaf for the lily. A couple of tiny ducks if they can be had small enough would provide a picture of realism. One might be swimming in the water, and the other at the edge of the mound.

Miniature gardens can also be made from Barbola or sealing wax, the flowers being represented by different coloured beads. Leaves can be made from sealing wax or modelled in Barbola, painted in water colour and varnished. One of these will brighten up the most dismal room in the middle of winter.

There is plenty of scope for originality in the making of miniature gardens, and their manufacture can provide occupation for all members of the family from the youngest child of school age to the eldest. The following "Tea Garden" was designed and made by a child of nine (Fig. 6).

Fig. 6

A large black tray was covered with green paper to represent grass. At one end was an open shed made of cardboard covered with coloured paper, with a background representing a winter scene with snow-capped hills. This idea was borrowed from a skating rink where the child had been skating. The other three edges of the tray were banked with wet sand covered with moss, and hidden by every species of small flower that was obtainable, some of which took root and flourished, the others being replaced when they faded.

Lupin leaves made quite passable palm trees, and pampas grass was represented by waving seeded grass from the wayside.

In the shed was a long narrow counter for the serving of the tea, and above a placard announcing "Tea Garden." A few red tables and chairs and a red table umbrella modelled in plasticine, scattered here and there over the "lawn" added gaiety to the scene, and some tiny figures gave it life. On a dull spring day this was enough to brighten up the landscape, and the making of it kept a child happily employed.

A few general hints may be useful.

Unless they are meant to be the centre of interest houses should rarely be used in miniature gardens. It is difficult to get flowers small enough to scale.

Artificial or dried flowers should never be used in miniature gardens. They take away from the effect, very quickly losing their appearance and becoming shabby and soiled. The use of dyed shells, silver sand and pieces of coloured glass is also undesirable. They look out of place among the natural-coloured moss and flowers, and give the garden a tawdry appearance.

The colour of the bowl should be considered with care. When buying it have in mind the colour of the garden which is to be inside the bowl.

Do not buy glazed composition as the colour very quickly chips and flakes. Earthenware is best, or in the more expensive makes, Japanese pottery.

MODEL AEROPLANES

Not many hobbies have the distinction of being as new as Model Aviation, and few can equal the thrills and pleasure obtained from it.

Model aviation is a progressive hobby. One may begin by purchasing a small frail-looking craft which will behave in a most erratic manner in the novice's hands, only to find that skill must be allied with knowledge to get the best results, and before long the enthusiast finds himself master of the theory of flight and eager to design, build and pit his skill against the skill of other enthusiasts. Given a wide open space with not too much wind, model aeroplane flying offers a thrill of which young and old never seem to tire.

Initiation to the pastime frequently begins with a small son's or nephew's requests for assistance in winding up a rubber motor. Thereafter, the excitement of seeing the model aeroplane manœuvring around in the sky is sufficient to deprive the small boy of his toy for the rest of the afternoon.

Neither the building nor the flying of a model aeroplane is quite so simple as it at first appears. It requires a degree of skill equal in its way to that required of a pilot in a full-sized machine, and it also demands a knowledge of the theory of flight, if the best results in duration, climb, evolution and landing are to be obtained.

The forces by means of which an aeroplane flies are very similar to those which maintain a kite in the air. A kite is pulled against the wind by a string to get air pressure, the wind tending to blow the kite away and the string to hold it back. The result is that as long as the wind and the pull remain, the kite will tend to rise. If one of them is lost, gravity, that force which dominates the world, will drag the kite to the ground. In an aeroplane the engine and the airscrew take the place of the kite string, and these eliminate the necessity for a wind. If, therefore, a plane surface, as in an aeroplane wing, is secured at an angle and moved in relation to the air, there is a downward pressure on the air and consequently an upward pressure on the plane which tends to rise. This is illustrated in the accompanying sketch.

It will be realized that it does not matter if the inclined plane is moved through the air or if the air flows past the plane. Provided there is sufficient speed of flow there will be a pressure on the underside of the plane and a lift on the top side of the plane. Usually a cambered surface is employed as being more efficient. (*See* Fig. 1.) By increasing the angle of the plane—angle of incidence, is the technical term employed—the air both over and above the plane is deflected more violently. The same effect is provided if the speed is increased, with the result that the plane tends to rise. In exactly the same manner, if the angle of incidence or the speed decrease, the plane will descend. Below a certain speed, however, he supporting pressure becomes so small hat the plane will fall. When this occurs t is said to have stalled. Provided there is ufficient height this is not a serious matter, s the fall increases the speed of the plane nd control can be regained when speed s sufficient. A stall near the ground, owever, generally results in a crash.

The power necessary to draw forward he wing which deflects the air and thus upports the wing is furnished by the engine nd airscrew. The airscrew works in the ir in exactly the same manner as a pro- eller of a ship works in water, the only ifference being that of the density of the luids in which they operate. Power from he engine is converted into thrust by the eaction of the screw-blades on the propeller.

An Airscrew may be regarded as a air of revolving wings attached to a shaft. Owing to the angle of the wings (angle of ncidence mentioned above) and their peed when rotated, the blades have a lift which pulls the aeroplane along. Another way to consider the propeller is to regard it s a screw which bites into the air and carries he aeroplane with it in its forward movement.

Model aircraft may roughly be divided nto three classes:

(*a*) Scale models of actual machines *not* intended to fly.

(*b*) Scale models of actual machines intended to fly.

(*c*) Freak machines.

In the first group considerable attention s paid to detail with the object of achieving n actual reproduction of the full-sized nachine. The models in the second group esemble their prototypes, but have been implified. Generally speaking, the more losely a model resembles full-size form and onstruction, the less likely it is to fly.

The third class is the one most likely to nterest the flying enthusiast for, though hey may bear little resemblance to actual ircraft and consequently are called freak nachines, they can put up some wonderful erformances.

In the first section there is plenty of scope or everyone, from the youngster who, eserting his trains, puts in many happy nd hopeful hours with miniature planes to the more knowledgeable expert who, from blue prints or a kit of rough parts, builds a 42-seater Hengist or a large flying boat.

Work of this kind demands both patience and skill, but there is ample repayment for those who delight in paying meticulous attention to detail and finish. Nor is it necessary that the work should stop short at the construction of aircraft alone. There is plenty of additional scope for the enthusiast in modelling of hangars, airport buildings and accessories, though these also may be purchased complete or in kit form.

Many people, however, are not content to build models for ornamental purposes only but desire to see their handicraft in action, to see their knowledge of practical aeronautics put to the test and for these there are the two other classes mentioned. Of the two, the scale flying models are generally more difficult to construct and to fly than

LOWERING OF PRESSURE ABOVE WING

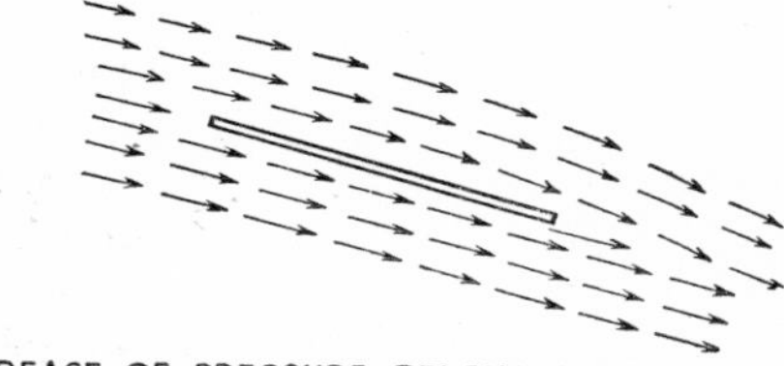

INCREASE OF PRESSURE BELOW WING

Fig. 1

the so-called "freak" machines, and their flight is much more like that of a full-sized aeroplane. The choice depends largely upon one's point of view. The flying model has the best appearance and the "freak" the best performance.

Before embarking upon the construction of any flying type or even before flying a ready-made model, the reader would do well to read the aeronautical papers and become thoroughly versed in the theories of flying. Such knowledge will be invaluable when the construction and design of models is contemplated. It is true that the information given in such technical papers relates to full-sized machines and a model built from such designs may, probably will, fail to fly; the general principles may be quite adaptable.

Having acquired a fair knowledge of

theory, the model aeroplane enthusiast should begin by building a machine from some well-known and practical design. No doubt many beginners would prefer to be unconventional, but it is better to start in the manner suggested. When the machine has been flown a good deal, experiments can be carried out with it. Rubber motors of different powers can be tried. Airscrews of differing pitch fitted. From these experiments new ideas will develop which can be embodied into a new design.

The main classes of models have been indicated, but in these classes there are subdivisions. Thus the modeller has the choice between pusher and tractor types, monoplane or biplane (with the former either high wing or low wing), as well as between fuselage and non-fuselage models.

Types of Plane.—Before discussing the design and general constructional principles, the technical terms used in connection with aeroplanes, both model and full-sized, should be mastered. Some of these are illustrated diagrammatically elsewhere in the article.

A *monoplane* is a machine with one main plane or surface.

A *low-winged monoplane* is one with the main surface beneath the fuselage.

A *high-winged monoplane* is one with its main surface above the fuselage.

A *biplane* is a machine with two wings.

The *gap* is the distance between the two surfaces (wings) or aerofoils, one above the other.

The *fuselage* is the body of the aeroplane.

Stagger is the amount that the top wing of a biplane is placed forward of the bottom wing.

Airscrew—propeller. When this is placed in front the machine is called a tractor; if behind the main plane, a pusher.

Aerofoil is a supporting surface, the term usually applied to the wing. It is more accurate than "plane," which is a flat surface. Wings are usually curved or cambered.

Camber is the curving or arching of the wing or aerofoil.

Dihedral angle is the angle which each plane makes with the horizontal. (*See* Fig. 2.)

Angle of incidence. The angle an aerofoil makes with the horizontal. (*See* Fig. 3.)

Leading edge. Front edge of wing.

Trailing edge. Rear edge of wing.

Loading is the weight carried per unit o wing area. For example, a model weighin 10 oz. and having a wing area of 288 in. would have a loading of 5 oz. per sq. ft.

Pitch of airscrew. The distance an air screw would advance per revolution if ther were no slip.

Elevator. An auxiliary plane to alte angle of machine.

Tailplane. A horizontal subsidiary plan fixed some distance behind the main plan

Construction.—When constructing model aeroplane the first thing is to kno what you want to build. The beginne would be well advised to build from som well-known design, blue prints of which ca be obtained from various suppliers. If yo decide to make your own design, it is advis able to prepare a rough drawing givin dimensions of main parts together with thei shape and area. It is unwise to copy a full sized design, as what may be quite satis factory in the original will be unreliable an extremely complicated when "scaled down."

The object is to make a plane perform certain task, and superfluous constructio should be avoided. Details should be a simple and light as possible and the utmos care should be taken to make them as neatl and accurately as possible. What is don should be well done, so pay attention t finish as well as to method.

When details have been worked out o the rough drawing, a full-sized or half sized drawing can be prepared which shoul contain all details. Such a drawing no only facilitates construction, but serves a a record for the future. The next thing t decide is what is wanted in the way of too and materials to do the job. Many goo model aeroplanes have, in the past, bee built from odd scraps of metal, wood an fabric, with the aid of perhaps a knife or fi and a pair of scissors. Admirable though may be to construct in this way with th minimum of assistance, much more efficie models can be constructed in far less tim with thought, tools and materials. The to kit need not be an extensive one, but shoul contain several light hammers, including tack hammer; several wood saws, fine set; fret-saw and hack-saw; keyhole saw and set of blades; square bevel gauge, compasses, calipers (inside and outside); foot-rule; folding rule; screwdrivers; twist drills (all the small sizes up to $\frac{1}{4}$ in.); bradawls; braces with ratchets; several small chisels and gouges; jack plane and small iron plane; files and rasps—various sizes; pliers of assorted types and sizes; a pair of wire cutters; several clamps, a glue pot and a soldering iron.

With the tools enumerated here it should be possible to make almost any type of model aeroplane. The materials used depend largely upon the design, but the following list includes all that is generally necessary.

Woods.—Spruce, birch, balsa, cane, walnut—three-ply, deal.

Fabric and other Materials.—Silk, tissue paper, glue—seccotine, etc.; rope, varnish, etc., cotton, thread, fine wire; sheet brass, iron, aluminium, tinned iron; piano wire; and elastic (for motors)—size varies with weight of models.

Wing Construction.—Wings or planes can be classified under three main headings according as the frames are made of wood, wire or cane. Each produces equally good results, and the choice is largely a matter of personal preference. The wire plane is much stronger, offers less resistance to the air and is much neater in appearance than the others, but is somewhat heavier. A wooden plane is light and has a good appearance, but it is inclined to be weak. Woods which can be used are birch, spruce and balsa, the latter being extremely light in weight. Spruce is heavier than balsa but lighter than birch. When cane is used for the wing plane it must be bound and glued as it is not possible to pin it. This results in a very strong and flexible frame that will stand a good deal of knocking about, but naturally has not the pleasing appearance of the others.

There are various fabrics which may be used for covering wings. One is the special material used by model aeroplane manufacturers and which may be obtained from various suppliers. Another material which is very suitable is Jap silk, which can be obtained at most drapers. It is quite light and requires only a small quantity of "dope" and may be obtained in various shades.

When wire wings are used the fabric is sewn on to the wing frame with an over and over stitch. The overlap can then be glued down. With wooden wings the material is stretched tightly over the frame and glued down to it, drawing-pins being used to maintain it in position until the glue is set. After the wings have been completed they must be "doped." This applies also to rudder, elevators, tailplane and fuselage also, if this is a fabric-covered type.

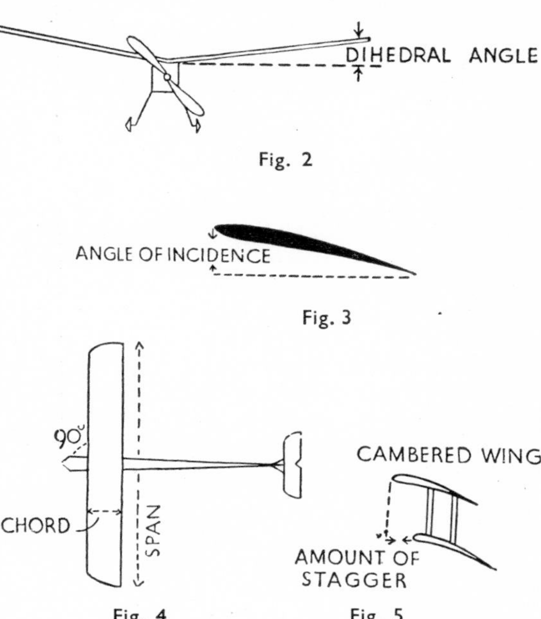

Fig. 2

Fig. 3

Fig. 4

Fig. 5

A good dope or proofing material can be made by diluting varnish with linseed oil in the ratio of about 3 : 1.

Frames.—Most so-called freak machines with a single airscrew have a single spar frame which may be either solid or hollow. The former is heavier but easier to construct, since it is merely a piece of wood of the right section cut to suitable length to which undercarriage, wings and tail assembly are fitted. The hollow spar, which is lighter, can be made by cutting a deep groove in the spar and covering the open side with a thin strip glued on. If it will be necessary to drill holes through a hollow spar, small pieces of wood should be inserted and glued in position in the groove where necessary before covering the groove.

If the model is to have two propellers, either a "T" type frame or an "A" type frame should be employed. Fuselage models can be made in a variety of ways, and drawings should be obtained from which to work.

Undercarriages.—The purpose of the undercarriage is to assist (*a*) in "taking off" and (*b*) in landing. For the latter purpose it should be located well forward in order to prevent the model "nosing over" when the wheels touch. For the former it must be farther back. One must therefore compromise by bearing it as far backward as possible without affecting landings. As the undercarriage is of no use whatever in flight, merely adding to the weight and causing considerable "drag," it should be as light as possible. The wheels may be of wood with rubber tyres, metal disks or of three-ply covered with silk. The metal disks are usually of aluminium and are to be recommended to those who would rather purchase than make their own.

Propellers or Airscrews.—The propeller of an aeroplane is the means by which the power of the engine is converted into work. It follows, therefore, that the airscrew should be of the most efficient design possible.

The operation of an airscrew may be likened to a bolt turning in a nut. If the nut is held and the bolt rotated the bolt must move forward. If it has ten threads to the inch a complete revolution of the bolt will move it forward $\frac{1}{10}$ of an inch. This is called the pitch and the pitch of an airscrew is the distance it should move forward during one revolution. In actual practice it will seldom move forward more than 75 per cent. of its theoretical pitch and this loss of efficiency is referred to as slip and is a percentage of theoretical pitch. Thus a screw with a theoretical pitch of 4 ft. with 75 per cent. efficiency has an effective pitch of 3 ft. The better the design of screw the lower the percentage of slip.

Propellers for model aircraft are of various types. Some are of bent birchwood. The propeller blades are cut out then held in a steam jet and slowly twisted until the correct angle has been obtained. Another type is carved from a solid block of mahogany, spruce, whitewood or walnut. Still a third type is made from layers of wood glued together and is called a laminated airscrew. This type of construction, which incidentally is employed for full-sized wooden airscrews, is much stronger than the other types mentioned and if made of alternate layers of whitewood and mahogany, gives a pleasing finish. In addition to those mentioned, metal airscrews may be obtained, the efficiency of which is very high.

When making an airscrew the points which have to be considered are the loading per square foot of wing area, the speed of the model, the theoretical and effective pitch of the airscrew, and finally its balance. Aeromodellists who are interested in making their own airscrews are advised to obtain tables which give pitches, loading and speeds of various sized airscrews. Such tables can be found in books devoted to this subject.

For single-screw models the diameter of the airscrew should be about $\frac{1}{3}$ of the wing span. The width of the blade should be $\frac{1}{8}$ of the diameter. Airscrews of comparatively large diameter and small pitch, rotating at slow speeds, give much better results than those of small diameter, long pitch and high speed.

Elastic Motors.—The most widely used method of providing power for the model aeroplane is the elastic motor, though compressed-air containers and motors are sometimes used, and for the really large models diminutive petrol engines have been constructed. Even superheated steam has been employed for this purpose. Elastic motors have the merit of being easily operated, are of light weight, and generally adaptable to all types of model aeroplanes.

There is no hard and fast rule as to the amount of elastic to be employed in driving

Fig. 6.—Flying Model Aeroplanes

ι model, but generally it should weigh ıbout $\frac{1}{6}$ of the total weight of the model. Γhe best quality elastic should be used and ectangular section is better than square ·ection. If too much elastic is used the nodel will tend to climb and stall. If nsufficient elastic is used, the model, being ınderpowered, will fly sluggishly. The ıctual number of strands required can only ɔe discovered by trial and error or by past :xperience. The energy stored in an elastic notor is not given out at a steady rate, the ›utput being large at first, falling to zero. Γhis is quite satisfactory from the modellist's /iewpoint as most power is required at the ›eginning of the flight to lift the model from he ground or to climb steeply. As it eaches its maximum height the motor which s running down permits the model to lescend in a long glide.

Lubrication.—Elastic should not be ısed dry, but should be lubricated with pure oft soap. The strands should be smeared o that they slide smoothly over one another. Care should be taken not to overwind new elastic. The motor should be used a number of times with an increase of turn each time until the maximum has been reached.

How to Fly a Model Aeroplane.—Flying a model aeroplane, successfully that is, is not so easy as many people imagine. Unlike many mechanical models which merely require winding up in order to function perfectly, the model aeroplane has to be carefully adjusted, properly wound and correctly launched if the flight is to be successful. Perhaps this is why the flying of models is so intriguing. It certainly calls for a good deal of skill and air sense if the best results are to be obtained. Furthermore, as with full-sized machines, each type has its own characteristics, an understanding of which will tend to improve performance.

If the model which is to be flown has been purchased complete, first read the instructions carefully and assemble the model to the directions given. These will tell you how the wings should be fixed and the precise spot, how the rudder and tailplane should be attached and how many turns have to be given to the airscrew. It is assumed that the motor is of the elastic type which is most common at the moment. The wings are curved and must therefore be fitted the right way round. The wings, rudder and tail assembly and frame should all be perfectly true, viewed from every angle. Standing on the floor the model should stand quite true, each wing tip the same distance from it.

Before winding up the airscrew it is well to see that the rubber motor is lubricated. This has the effect of increasing the life of the rubber and since it allows a greater number of turns being given to the airscrew, it also makes for longer flights.

Tubes of lubricant can be purchased, but green soft soap boiled in water will be found quite suitable. The rubber is dipped in the solution and the surplus drained off. The use of this adds surprisingly to the resiliency of the rubber. The motor should be lubricated after each dozen flights.

Winding the Airscrew.—When the elastic is lubricated place it on the hooks provided on the propeller and frame, taking care to see that the propeller bearing is lubricated also. A little vaseline will do this. Give the airscrew a few turns and then release to see if it is running true. If it is out of alignment carefully bend the shaft until the airscrew is quite free from wobble. Note the way in which the airscrew should be wound. The directions given will probably tell you, but a glance will show the way it must run in order to screw itself forward into the air. Whether the model is a tractor, i.e. with the airscrew in front, or a pusher, i.e. with the propeller behind, the air must be driven to the rear.

It is a good plan to test the adjustment of the plane before actually commencing the flight. This is done by launching it forward, without the motor wound up, in a glide. If properly assembled, the plane will gracefully glide forward and land on its wheels. If it tends to dive forward suddenly, the centre of gravity is wrong and the main plane should be moved forward a short distance until the correct position is found. If the plane tends to nose up or glide in a series of swoops, the main plane is too far forward and should be shifted back slightly.

Contrary to the practice with a full-size machine, a model aeroplane, unless of great power, should be launched with the wind and not against it. Hold the model at arm's length above the head with the left hand holding the airscrew and the right gripping the fuselage. Tilt the nose of the machine slightly downward and launch the model firmly but gently forward. Do not throw it; and keep the nose down. Launching slightly nose down enables the model to gather speed rapidly and then climb rapidly, but if too steep an angle is given it will zoom and then probably stall. An explanation of these terms will be found at the end of this section.

Launching nose upward will nearly always result in a stall followed by a spin—and a crash. Watch the performance carefully on each flight, making minor adjustments as required and very quickly a knowledge of the art of flying models may be acquired.

Below will be found a list of faults and their remedies.

Model Rises Sharply then Nose dives to Earth.—Move main plane back.

Model Dives to Earth.—Move main plane forward.

Model Rises, Loops and then Nose-dives.—Model over-elevated, adjust elevators to give flatter diving angle.

Model Climbs, Dives, then Repeats the Process.—Model slightly over-elevated.

Model Goes Backward.—Motor wound in wrong direction.

If Model Turns Sharply to Left or Right.—Adjust rudder.

If Model Rocks from Side to Side, it has insufficient dihedral angle. (*See* list of terms on earlier page.)

Avoid windy days for flying models. Choose a calm day and let your "aerodrome" be as large as possible.

Model Gliders.—Quite a lot about the behaviour of aircraft in the air can be learned from model gliders. These can very easily and quickly be made from a sheet of stout paper. They obtain their flying power from the force of gravity. A well-designed glider is one that has the flattest gliding angle, i.e. will travel the greatest distance for a given loss of height. A gliding angle of one in seven is quite possible, which means that if launched from a height of 6 ft. it should touch earth about 42 ft. away.

A glider can be made to perform many stunts and evolutions in the air, such as looping-the-loop, and rolling.

Societies and Clubs.—Every aero-modellist and flier should, if possible, become a member of a club where he will meet with people of similar interests and will be able to exchange experiences, opinions and ideas.

The sport of model flying is controlled by the "Society of Model Aeronautical Engineers," to whom enquiries should be addressed regarding clubs, etc. The address of the Secretary is E. S. H. Cosh, 35 Maple Crescent, Sidcup, Kent.

MODEL YACHTING

Few hobbies can claim so ancient and so honourable a lineage and few have been so assiduously practised, partly as an example of craftsmanship on the part of the model maker and partly as a healthy outdoor pastime.

Young and old alike respond to the fascination of the miniature ship, and are intrigued by the lifelike motion of the sailing model, responsive to every passing change of wind and water.

Wide as the ocean itself, model yachting has something to offer to all. The tiny toddler pulling his toy boat along with a string—the competitive schoolboy with a boat of his own building, the serious student of naval architecture, keen club men with "class racers" competing in organized club and inter-club racing—all feel something of the lure and romance of the sea and ships.

Despite their diminutive size, all model yachts are essentially scientific in conception and are fashioned with due regard to the same laws that govern the design of full-size craft; the results obtainable being largely governed by the correctness of the original design and the skill with which the model is sailed.

Model yachting can be enjoyed by the individual sailing alone on any piece of water deep enough to float the boat or he can join a club and fraternize with kindred spirits.

Organized Model Yachting.—There are numerous clubs in Great Britain, many of them with their own club house and other amenities; most of them appeal to the adult who is keen on the active pursuit of the hobby, but several of them have in addition a juvenile section where youngsters are initiated into the correct methods of sailing. Clubs organize their own races, generally held once a week for prizes and in some cases for handsome trophies and awards.

Inter-club and international racing is organized under the control of the Model Yachting Association, which body issues the recognized standard sailing and other rules for the well-being of model yachting in general.

International model yacht races are held, and those organized by the M.Y.A. are a well-known and highly appreciated feature of the model yacht world.

The model equivalent of "Cowes Week" is the annual contest for the "Yachting Monthly" 100-guinea cup—competed for by entrants from most of the European nations and from America. This event is preceded by a series of elimination contests to decide the boat to sail on the great day to defend the prestige of Great Britain against the selected boats of all other nations. Naturally enough every keen model yachtsman aspires to this honour, but to be successful demands the possession of the best boat of the year allied with a very great skill and ability for sailing. In its way it is the equivalent of winning the Derby or the championship of Great Britain at lawn tennis.

Those who have not tried a really good "class" racing model yacht may be inclined to scoff at the foregoing statement, but a brief trial will soon convince that while it is possible for anyone to have plenty of fun and amusement with a model yacht, the highest possibilities can only be realized after lengthy experience and the acquisition of ability to handle the model successfully under all conditions of wind and weather.

It is just because of this personal element that model yachting has such a definite and persistent appeal; the model yacht is merely the instrument, it is the personality of the skipper, his sportsmanship and sailing abilities that really count in the long run. Organized model yachting therefore becomes a contest of skill between individuals, and it is the aim of all to win only by superior skill and seamanship; the hobby thus becomes a monitor of good qualities and is a definitely beneficial stimulus to the development of such desirable human attributes as patience, observation, sound judgment, courtesy and mutual helpfulness.

Principal Parts of a Model Yacht.—The technology of model yachting is based on ancient nautical phraseology. For example, the body of the boat—or that part that floats in the water is called the "hull"—the front end is named the "bow"

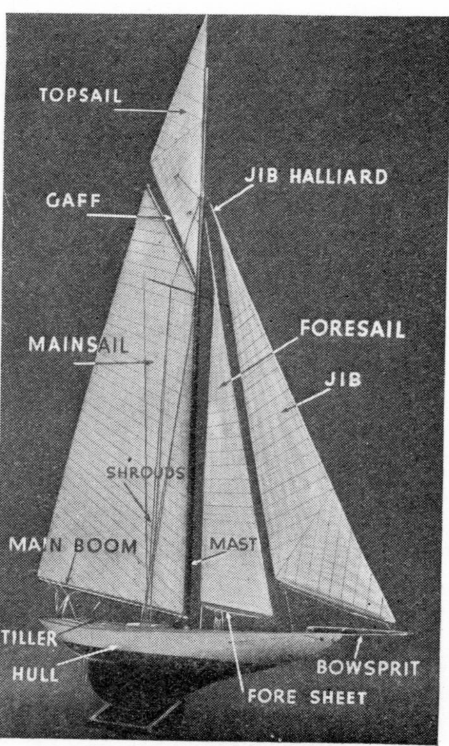

Fig. I.—The Principal Parts of a Yacht

the back end is called the "stern," th bottom part of the hull is called the "keel, the movable piece near the stern is calle the "rudder." The rudder can be move by means of a bar called the "tiller" whic may take various forms.

The upper covering of the hull is calle the "deck"—the removable cover thereo is called the "hatch" and is provided t enable access to the interior or "hold."

An upright stick fixed in the hull is calle the "mast" and is used to hoist the sail The mast is kept upright by means of cord called "shrouds" when they are fixed to th side of the boat and "stays" when they ar fixed lengthways—or "fore and aft" to th hull.

The linen or silk material hoisted on th mast is called the sail and is extended o "spread" at the bottom by a stick called "boom" and sometimes by another stick a the top called the "gaff."

The various sails have distinguishin names, that in front of or "before" the mas is called the "foresail" when there is onl one, or in cases where there are two th outer sail is called a "jib," while if a third i hoisted above the other two it is called "jib topsail." The sail behind the mast i called the "mainsail" and another if hoiste above it is called the "main topsail."

Strings or thin specially made cords ar attached to the sails to enable them to b raised and adjusted—a process called "setting" the sail; the string used to raise th sail is called a "halliard," that used t control the amount the sail can swing outwards at the bottom is called a "sheet," whil to distinguish one from another the nam of the sail is prefixed to that of the string For example, "jib halliard" means the string used to hoist the jib; similarly "mainsheet" means the string used to control the bottom of the mainsail and so on.

The controlling strings are attached a one end to the sail and at the other end to the deck and some means of adjusting the effective length of the string is provided. On very simple boats a metal pin is fixed a one end of the string and is plugged into any one of a series of holes either in the boom or in the deck as may be required.

Fig. 2.—Competing in the International Model Yacht Races at Fleetwood

On all better class models the string is passed through two screw eyes on the boom, the end of the string is doubled back on itself and fastened to a little piece of wood or ivory called a "bowsie." This is like a tent runner and has two holes in it—one slides on the long part of the string, the other is fixed to the end of the string—consequently any pull on the opposite end of the string is transmitted to the outer end of the bowsie which then acts as a lever and locks itself, thus preventing endways movement.

This simple device enables a very delicate adjustment of the length of the string and thereby permits the position of the sail relative to the centre line of the ship to be set to any desired angle. Such adjustment constitutes one of the elementary methods of controlling the "course" or direction in which the ship will sail.

Sizes and Classes of Model Yachts.—Toy boats are made in lengths from a few inches upwards, the smallest practical model measures 18 in. long, the length being that of the hull and exclusive of any projecting booms or other parts.

The two best classes or sizes for juvenile and general use by those who do not wish to go in for the more elaborate boats are the 24-in. and the 36-in. "L.O.A." classes. The letters L.O.A. mean "length over all," and this is the only governing or limiting factor in the class—boats to be eligible must not exceed the stated total length.

The 30-in. L.O.A. restricted class is another good size for general use, but in this case the hull length must not exceed 30 in.; the "beam" or maximum width of hull must not exceed 8 in.; the depth must not exceed 9 in., nor may the weight exceed 9 lb.

The 36-in. L.O.A. restricted class is one of the very best for general sailing, the limits of the hull are 36 in. long, 9-in. beam, 11-in. draught and 12 lb. in weight.

The stated weights must include the mast, sails and gear, and when racing, the model must exhibit on the mainsail her class mark and registered number.

Models used extensively for club and inter-club racing include the popular "Length and Sail Area" 10 raters, an average size of boat under this rule measures 60 in. long and weighs about 18 lb.

Other popular classes rather larger and considerably heavier are known as the "10 metre" and the 12 metre, but these are becoming displaced by the largest sized boats generally known as "Class A." These boats are built under a rather complicated formula and rating rules; but can be regarded as real racing yachts in miniature and are used in the annual international races.

The novice will be well advised to commence with a 36-in. boat and after gaining some practical experience of model yacht sailing going in for a larger boat.

In each class there are various characteristic forms of hull, some are relatively shallow, others are deep and more or less rounded in shape. Each has some distinguishing quality, for example, a very shallow hull with a deep "fin" or plate keel will sail very well in light winds; a more rounded or "full bodied" hull is more suitable for use on exposed ponds where the normal wind is stronger than it would be on a sheltered inland pond.

Consequently, when buying a model yacht have in mind the normal conditions under which the boat will be sailed. For use on sheltered inland ponds select a moderately shallow hull with a deep keel—a hull that when viewed from the bows is more or less like the letter T.

The sails on such a boat should be as tall and narrow as possible because the wind is always stronger above the water than it is near the surface, consequently the tall sails catch the wind better.

When the sailing water is a pond on an exposed common or near the sea, a lower sail spread is preferable associated with a medium-bodied hull, more like a V in cross section.

For use on the sea coast or in very exposed conditions choose a boat with a fuller bodied hull—more like the letter U in cross section, and preferably of the "cutter" rig with jib, foresail, mainsail and a topsail.

With this arrangement the jib and the topsail can be removed when the wind is very strong, whereas with the more generally used "Bermuda" rig consisting of a tall triangular mainsail and a single foresail, it is necessary to have two or more "suits" of sails—a normal set for use in light winds, a smaller suit for use in heavy winds and a very small suit for use in quite stormy weather.

Practical Sailing.—The art of model yacht sailing can only be acquired by actual experience—but a few fundamentals can be set forth to aid the novice and pave the way to greater exploits.

For example, suppose this page represents a pond, and that the model is at the bottom centre and the wind blowing from the right hand top corner towards the boat. The easiest course for the boat to take would be towards about the centre of the left-hand side—a course in respect of the wind that is called "reaching."

Before releasing the boat it is necessary to realize that the direction the boat will take is governed entirely by the wind and the angle of the sails. When "reaching" the sails should be set so that the jib is about 30 degs. to the centre line and the mainsail about 45 degs. For a first attempt, adjust the sails in this way, put the boat in the water, let the wind "fill" or extend the sails so that they "draw" or pull the boat, then gently release it and watch the action of the boat while in motion. Assuming that the wind remains steady all the time, then if the sails flap about and the boat tends to travel towards the bottom left-hand corner it indicates that the foresail is too slack and it should be drawn in a trifle.

This will cause the boat to travel faster because the sails will now draw properly and not flap about, but the course may still not be correct and the boat come ashore too near the bottom of the pond. This indicates that both sails are slacked out too much and they should be drawn in somewhat, but in the same proportions as before. With this alteration the course should be correct and the boat can be sailed backwards and forwards, but will make little or no progress towards the top of the pond.

To do this requires that the boat shall sail

much more towards the wind—a course known as "beating to windward"—which is one of the most difficult to accomplish and is the greatest test of model and sailor.

To induce the boat to "beat to windward" both sails must be drawn in towards the centre of the ship as closely as they will go without "spilling" wind or going "into stays," that is causing the sails to turn from one side to the other without materially driving the boat forwards. When this phenomenon is experienced very slightly slacken either the foresail or the mainsail—or both if necessary. Note the position for future use as once the best sailing position is found it can always be repeated on some future occasion under similar conditions of wind.

Having succeeded in sailing direct to the top of the pond, the only remaining problem is to sail back again—a course known as "running" or, "before the wind." To do this attach a swing rudder, if one is provided with the model. It should, however, never be used when reaching or beating, or if a rudder with tiller is fitted, adjust it so that the rudder swings over a little on the same side as the main boom; then slacken out the main boom as far as it will go and slacken the jib or foresail to an angle of about 45 degs. and all being well the boat should sail straight down the pond and reach its original starting point, thus showing that the sailor has passed his novitiate and is well on his way to becoming a real skipper.

MOTOR-CARAVANING

Caravaning is one of the most pleasant and at the same time healthiest of recreations and although its joys increase with experience, the beginner will find it full of charm and fascination. The motorist who tows his mobile home is free to wander where he likes and stay where he pleases for as long a time as holidays permit. The caravan holiday has a wider appeal to ladies than has camping, for besides ensuring perfect protection in all weathers, the caravan gives almost as much comfort as the modern bungalow or flat. It is indeed a luxury vehicle with its well sprung mattresses, carpeted floors, built-in cupboards, sink, cooking range, electric light, leaded windows and so on.

Choosing a Caravan.—There is a

Fig. 1.—A Serviceable Type of Motor-trailer Caravan

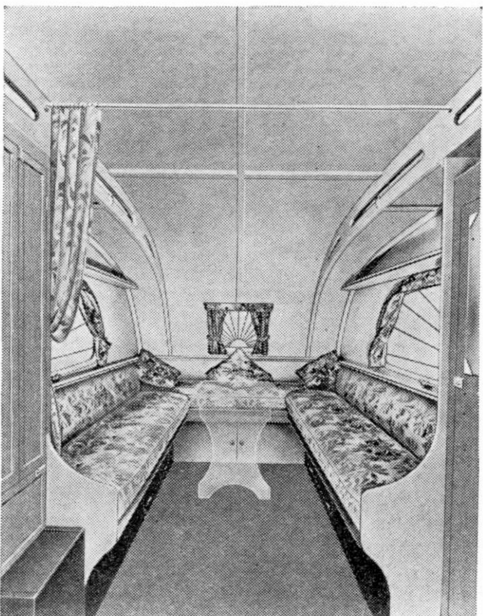
Fig. 2.—Interior, showing Position of Table

wide variety from which to make a choice, prices ranging from £50 or so upwards. Before choosing a caravan, however, it is necessary to know what weight one's car will haul with comfort, and a good rule is to base the weight on the horse-power rating, allowing one hundredweight per horse power; thus a 12 h.p. car will be able to pull a 12 cwt. caravan without difficulty, even in hilly districts, while an 8 h.p. car should be given an 8 cwt. van and so on.

Many have queried the advisability of using so low a horse-powered car as an "8" for such towing, but experience proves that these little cars are quite capable of pulling caravans, even in hilly country. The weight to be towed should naturally be kept down to the minimum, but the modern light car is quite capable of towing a four-berth caravan with ease.

Fig. 1 shows a popular van for light cars. It is 11 ft. long, 7 ft. 6 in. high, and 6 ft. 4 in. wide in the centre, tapering to 6 ft. at the ends. The interior is well appointed and has sliding doors for dividing the van into two separate compartments. One of these contains a double bed-settee and the other two bunk-type beds which also form a settee for day use.

A full-length wardrobe, large lockers and cupboards are provided and there is a neat stove and oven fitted into an aluminium lined recess. A feature of this van is that there are windows at each end (in addition to the sides), so that the driver of the car is able to see right through when on the road.

There is also a two-berth caravan made especially for seven horse-power cars. Its weight is only 5½ cwt. and it can be towed anywhere by an Austin Seven or even a motor-cycle combination.

Towing a vehicle does not impose any strain on the car itself, although obviously the clutch has to do more work. Once the maximum weight has been ascertained the choice of a caravan will depend generally upon the depth of one's pocket.

The question of storage when the caravan is not in use is one that must not be overlooked, and it is here that the folding caravan deserves mention. There is one type marketed which "collapses" to a height of about 4 ft., but when open provides a rigid roof and stout canvas sides for the upper half of the walls and doors. This, of course, is not as comfortable as the rigid vans, but it is considerably cheaper.

Towing.—It is necessary for the car to be fitted with a towing bracket and usually this is supplied by the maker of the caravan, and in cases where the van itself is hired for a short period an allowance is made for the return of the bracket. Automatic brakes are essential to comply with the requirements of the law and these generally operate through the tendency of the caravan to over-run when the brakes of the car are applied. Provision should be made for illuminating the rear number on the caravan; the number should, of course, be the same as that of the car. Most caravans are fitted with a domestic-sized 5 amp. 2-pin plug socket so that it is a simple matter to fit up a length of flex to make connection with the car battery.

Towing presents no difficulty after the first few miles, but until one has become used to the additional length it is wise to keep the speed down. Reversing requires a certain amount of practice, but usually before the holiday is over the motorist is able to reverse in an expert manner. Climbing hills should be accompanied by an early change of gear, for with most modern cars the power output depends upon a high rate of r.p.m. Make sure, when travelling, that the windows of the caravan are securely closed, as otherwise they may become damaged in transit.

Up to the present there is no extra tax for towing a caravan, and a speed of 30 miles per hour is permissible except in the case of a four-wheeled caravan, when the limit is 20 miles per hour. It should be noted that the full length of the trailer, excluding the draw-bar, should not exceed 22 ft., whilst the width should not be greater than 7 ft. 6 in.

Insurance.—It is as well to inform one's insurance company that a caravan is to be towed, and to obtain their sanction in writing. Many companies will give this without additional charge. The caravan itself should, of course, be insured. Where the outfit is hired, insurance is covered by the hiring fee. The rates are about 25*s.* for three months for vans up to £100 in value with an additional 12*s.* 6*d.* per £50 above this figure. Proportionate rates are quoted for shorter periods than the three months.

General Equipment of the caravan. Hired outfits usually contain cooking utensils and a stove; the hirer provides his own bedding and in some cases crockery and cutlery. Stocking the caravan prior to a holiday should be undertaken carefully, for it is quite easy to take far more than is really necessary, and so to reduce the amount of space in which to live.

Camping.—Upon arrival at the camping ground be careful not to take the car or caravan down a steep grass slope, because a heavy dew or rain will render the grass so slippery that it may be impossible to climb out without the aid of horses. It goes without saying that as level a pitch as possible should be chosen in order to keep the caravan "on an even keel."

Camping sites are not, as a rule, difficult to find but speaking generally it is wise not to get too far from a farmhouse from which food supplies may be obtained. Water, of course, should be available within easy distance. Some caravans are fitted with a water tank, and in such a case it is not so essential for the camp to be pitched close to a running stream or other supply. The usual charge for camping is one shilling per night, although some farmers make an additional charge for the car. Lists of camping sites are published from time to time in motoring and other papers, whilst A.A. patrols will give every assistance. Railway companies issue lists of camp sites. A.A. and R.A.C. will supply lists to members.

The Camping Trailer.—Those who cannot afford to purchase or hire a caravan will find the camping trailer, which costs from £15, a very useful substitute; not that the trailer itself is sufficiently large to live in, but it will accommodate everything that is necessary for a good holiday under canvas. Of course, where room is available in the car it is cheaper and frequently better to carry everything inside, but if four people are spending their holiday together, the trailer should most certainly be considered. This usually consists of a flat truck body mounted on pneumatic tyres and towed in the same way as a caravan. A stout canvas top supported on a wooden frame

Fig. 3.—The "Kitchen"

Fig. 4.—The Morning Toilet in Camp

gives the necessary protection. The trailer itself may be used as a bedroom if required.

Camping has been dealt with in a separate section of this book, but there is a big difference between ordinary camping and camping by car. In the former case lightness is of paramount importance, but with a car a larger and stronger tent may be taken, whilst such luxuries as a collapsible bath, washing bowl, camp chairs and so on all add to the comfort of the holiday. Many people use the trailer as a kitchen, and it is certainly an advantage to keep the smell of cooking away from the living or sleeping tent. It is unwise to cook with the heating apparatus under canvas owing to the condensation that forms on the walls. The modern wickless paraffin stove may be obtained in a model designed for outdoor use, although it is usually wise to use some sort of a screen to keep off the wind.

Camp and Caravan Cooking can be fun or it can be sheer misery—it depends largely upon the equipment. Open fires are nice when the weather is fine and fuel dry and plentiful, but many farmers will not permit open fires on their land. Petrol stoves do not give out as much heat as the paraffin variety and although one has fuel always at hand, not every car is fitted with a tap which will enable replenishments to be made easily. One or more water buckets should be included in the equipment, the canvas rectangular type being the best. This costs about 2*s.* for the 12-pint and 2*s.* 6*d.* for the 24-pint size. Of the smaller items to be taken much depends upon the requirements of the campers, to say nothing of the capacity of the car. Unbreakable crockery can now be purchased very cheaply as also can stainless cutlery.

The tent, like the caravan, may be either purchased or hired, but when purchasing a tent the motorist should get the best possible.

As a guide to size, one that is 8 ft. long over all, 6 ft. high, and 5 ft. 6 in. wide will accommodate three people without crowding. This tent may be obtained in light-weight proofed Egyptian cotton, and with or without a fly sheet; fly sheets, however, are always worth the little additional cost for they give extra protection from sun and rain. A tent that has a round end is particularly useful, for a fair amount of kit may be stored in this recess. The average price, complete with ground sheet and fly sheet is £5 in tan and about 15*s.* cheaper in white.

Those few hardy individuals who can sleep anywhere usually scorn anything softer than mother earth for a bed, but the average camper likes to be as comfortable as possible. Camp beds have been developed to a wonderful degree of lightness during the last year or two, and really excellent ones can be purchased for 13*s.* 6*d.* The selection of the beds should always follow that of the tent, as the question of wall height has to be taken into consideration. Some of the modern beds are only 6 in. high, and fold into surprisingly small space, while air beds are becoming very popular, chiefly on account of their compactness when deflated. They can be inflated from a tyre pump in a few minutes, and they provide a most comfortable couch.

MOTOR CYCLING

MOTOR cycling is a hobby which is not only healthy but of absorbing interest to the mechanically minded. To many, however, it is far more than a hobby, because it provides the cheapest form of mechanical transport whilst at the same time it is one of the most reliable. There are dozens of makes of machines from which to choose, ranging from the diminutive "baby" or light-weight of 150 c.c. to the big twins and four-cylinder machines of 7 and 8 or more horse-power.

The Two-stroke Engine. — The principle of the motor-cycle engine (the Otto four-stroke, that is) is exactly the same as that described under MOTORING (q.v.). There is one type of engine, however, that is seldom to be encountered in cars, and this is the two-stroke. The Otto cycle is complete in every two revolutions of the crankshaft, giving thereby the induction, compression, ignition and exhaust strokes. With the two-stroke machine, the operation is completed in one revolution of the crankshaft, and reference to Fig. 1 will show the principle in which the two-stroke engine works. It should be noted that there are no valves in the ordinary sense of the term, the two-stroke being the simplest type to manufacture. Part way down the cylinder wall is an opening or port, communicating with the crankcase and also with the carburettor, while on the other side of the cylinder is an exhaust port. As the crankcase is air-tight, it follows that when the piston rises it forms a vacuum, and the vaporized fuel is sucked into the crankcase. As the piston descends it uncovers the transfer port and allows the partially compressed fuel vapour to pass into the cylinder. It will be noted that the piston is not of the usual type, for it has what is called a deflector top, and it will be seen from the illustration that the fuel is deflected up one side of the cylinder and round the top, the idea of this being to expel the burned gas which passes out the other side into the silencer. The piston rising closes both ports and finishes compressing the fuel. At top dead centre, or thereabouts, ignition takes place, and the cycle of operations is continued. Thus it will be seen that every time the piston reaches top dead centre firing takes place, whereas with the ordinary four-stroke type of engine firing takes place at every alternate top dead centre.

Lubrication.—Two-stroke engines are extremely reliable and, as we have said before, very simple. One outstanding feature of a large number of them is that they are lubricated by what is known as the Petroil system. Lubricating oil is mixed with the fuel, the proportion by bulk being about one of oil to about eight of petrol. When, therefore, the mixture is drawn into the crankcase a definite amount of oil is also present, and this serves to keep the engine lubricated. The method is extremely satisfactory, although should the two-stroke machine be left standing for a considerable time it is likely that the oil that is mixed with the fuel in the carburettor will sink to the bottom of the float chamber and so make starting a little difficult. Some manufacturers, of course, keep to the usual force feed type of lubrication on the grounds that it is simpler and less messy.

The majority of motor cyclists prefer to carry out their own repairs, although, of course, such jobs as cylinder reconditioning and so on are best left to the expert. Nearly every motor cyclist of experience can tell by the way an engine stops exactly what is wrong with it, whilst the old hand will almost invariably be able to pick out immediately the faults of any machine which he handles for a few minutes. The diagnosis list which appears under the motoring section covers most of the faults likely to be experienced with a motor-cycle engine, so we can now turn to general hints on maintenance.

Decarbonizing a motor-cycle engine is quite a simple job, despite the fact that there are four main types, namely (*a*) Side-valve engine, (*b*) Overhead-valve engine, (*c*) Overhead cam-shaft engine, and (*d*) Two-stroke engine. The first three types are illustrated.

When tackling an engine overhaul it is wise to make preparations for handling the parts and for cleaning them thoroughly. A small pail with about half a gallon of paraffin together with a stiff paint-brush and a number of clean rags will make all the difference when working.

The Side-valve Engine, particularly if it is of modern design, is the simplest of the four kinds mentioned. All that it is necessary to do is to unscrew half a dozen or so cylinder-head bolts which will expose the piston valves and of course the cylinder head itself. In most cases the sparking plug must be removed before attempting to remove the head. If the cylinder head itself is not detachable the usual plan is to take out the sparking plug and unship the carburettor, after which the four holding-down nuts at the base of the cylinder are removed and the cylinder itself gradually lifted off. For this perhaps it may be found advantageous to turn the fly-wheel so that the piston is at the bottom of its stroke. It is sometimes possible to do this without disturbing the carburettor, while the throttle and air slides, petrol feed and exhaust pipes, of course, have to be undone. The actual decarbonizing job is the same as with cars and has been described in that section.

The Overhead-valve Engine is also extremely easy to dismantle, although in many cases it is necessary to remove the fuel tank. All overhead-valve engines, of course, have detachable heads and before these can be removed the overhead-valve mechanism and push rods must be taken off.

The Overhead Cam-shaft Engine is increasing in popularity. This does not present any great difficulty in dismantling, although care should be used in case the valve timing is altered.

The Two-stroke Engine requires practically no skill or knowledge to dismantle, for after the carburettor, petrol pipe, exhaust pipe and pressure release valve have been removed the cylinder can be lifted straight off when the holding-down nuts have been unfastened.

As a rule when decarbonizing a motor-cycle engine the piston itself is taken off so that the piston rings and their grooves can be cleaned thoroughly. The method of removing the gudgeon pin naturally depends upon the type used. With most modern engines the gudgeon pins may be pushed out with the fingers after removing piston (Fig. 2). Make a mark on the front inside of the piston, in order that the piston may be replaced the same way as it came out. It is not always easy to slip the piston rings off without breakage. Rings are of cast iron and are exceptionally brittle and as a rule they cannot be sprung out wider than the diameter of the piston. The best method is to use three strips of tin about three-eighths or so of an inch wide. The slot in the ring is prised up and a strip of tin inserted so as to hold the ring clear of the groove. The tin is

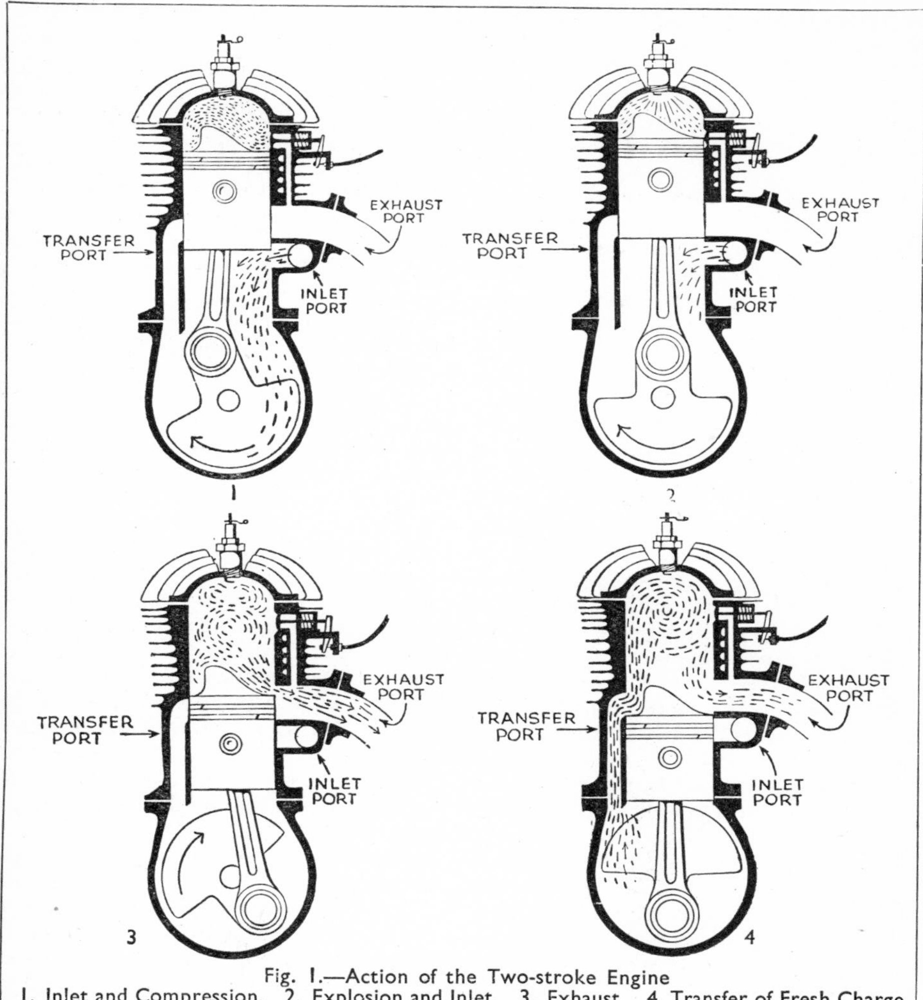

Fig. 1.—Action of the Two-stroke Engine
1. Inlet and Compression. 2. Explosion and Inlet. 3. Exhaust. 4. Transfer of Fresh Charge

then moved round slightly and another piece inserted. The first piece is then moved round still more and eventually a third piece inserted. They are then evenly spaced around the piston when the ring may be gently drawn off. There are, of course, special tools designed for piston-ring removal and fitting, but as the average motor cyclist would not want to use such an appliance more than once a year, or twice at the most, he may not feel it worth while buying.

Loosening Parts.—It sometimes happens that piston rings are so badly stuck that it is scarcely worth while spending time in removing them whole, although there is a special tool designed for the purpose. If the piston is soaked in paraffin for a few hours it will loosen and soften the carbon and will possibly allow the ring to be withdrawn fairly easily. Valve caps, which are of course found on side-valve engines, very often become exceedingly stiff to remove. Paraffin spread on and allowed to stand may sometimes loosen them, but a very good loosener is a mixture of creosote, engine oil (thin) and a little flaked graphite. The creosote and engine oil will do the loosening, whilst the graphite will tend to prevent further sticking.

Motor-cycle Carburettors operate on exactly the same principle as those designed for car use, but frequently there are two separate controls. One is the main control and is usually termed the petrol lever, whilst the other enables extra air to be given to meet conditions. There are, of course, a large number of single-lever carburettors in use, but the majority of motor cyclists prefer the two-lever control as it gives finer adjustment and enables better fuel consumption to be obtained.

Magnetos are also similar in design to those fitted to cars, but of course there is no need for the elaborate distributor, as the contact breaker carries out this function. In single-cylinder engines there is one cam on the contact breaker ring, whilst on twins there are two set opposite each other. There are, of course, in this case two high-tension leads taken from opposite points on the slip ring.

Motor-cycle Transmission has gone through various phases during the past twenty years or so, and in the early models the power was transmitted by means of a V-belt which ran direct from the engine pulley to the rear wheel. This had many disadvantages, apart from the fact that the machine was nearly always of the single-gear type. Canvas and rubber belts stretch, and slip badly in wet weather. A decided improvement was made with the system known as the chain-cum-belt. In this method the engine pulley was replaced by a sprocket and a chain took the drive to the gear-box. Although this was undoubtedly a great improvement on the all-belt drive, the disadvantages mentioned were not entirely overcome. The modern drive is of the all-chain type, one chain driving to the gear-box and the others from thence to the rear wheel. Usually the first chain is guarded against wet either by means of a metal cover or by its total enclosure in an oil bath. Chains when properly looked after have a very long life and transmit about 99 per cent. of the power. They should, however, be kept well lubricated and correctly adjusted. The method of testing is to insert a finger underneath the chain between the two sprockets. On the front chain, play should not be more than $\frac{3}{16}$ in. in an up and down direction, whilst on the rear chain, $\frac{1}{2}$ in. is the limit. Adjustment is carried out in the first instance by slackening off the gear-box bolts and moving this unit back the required amount, whilst the rear chain is adjusted by undoing the rear wheel nuts and moving the wheel itself bodily back. This will alter the brake adjustment in most cases.

Brakes are in modern motor cycles of the internal expanding type, both on front and on rear wheels. Great care should be given to brake adjustment for it is vital to safety. The greatest efficiency is reached just before the wheel ceases to revolve, although, according to law, riders must be able to lock the wheel if required. It should always be borne in mind that the effective brake power depends entirely upon the grip between the road and the tyre, the surface giving the best grip being that of rough concrete. Tests should therefore be carried out on this type of surface in order that the maximum efficiency be obtained. Motor cyclists are desired by law to have two independent brakes, one on each wheel.

Motor-cycle Gear-boxes are very similar in construction to those on cars, and details of these will be seen under the motoring section. The majority of motor cycles to-day have three-speed gears. Clutches are usually of the single-plate type, and these also are illustrated in the motoring section.

Lighting.—Most lamps to-day are electric and are either run off an accumulator or receive their current direct from the magdyno. There are really three systems, however, for on some machines current is taken from the primary winding of the magneto, which, of course, is a low-tension current, and taken direct to the lamp bulb. This method is quite satisfactory and has been extensively employed in recent years. It is necessary, however, for either a dry battery or an accumulator to be used, because naturally the lights will otherwise go out when the engine is not running. The simplest and incidentally the cheapest form of electric lighting is that provided by the battery system. Batteries can be used with or without a dynamo for recharging; in the latter case, of course, the batteries must be charged at a proper charging station. Larger motor-cycle outfits are provided with a dynamo which charges the necessary battery. The magdyno is a combination of magneto and dynamo. This instrument provides a six-volt current at five amperes or thereabouts. With this method also an accumulator is used. Well-made lamps are necessary, and readers are advised not to purchase cheap foreign productions. A spare bulb or two should be included in the tool kit.

The Controls of motor cycles are now practically standard. The handlebars are provided with two grips, one at each extremity, the left one being the exhaust valve lifter, and the right the front brake. On the left-hand side the clutch lever comes next, followed by the ignition control, whilst on the right bar the two carburettor control levers are clamped. The gear levers may either be fixed to the right-hand side of the petrol tank or they may be operated by a foot lever. In front of the two foot-rests are foot-operated pedals, the left being the clutch and the right the rear brake pedal. Some manufacturers fit a twist grip control for ignition and carburettor, and the standard practice is for an inward turn to advance the spark or to open the throttle. Usually an extra air lever is incorporated on the handlebar.

When Choosing a New Motor Cycle consideration must be given to two points: first the purpose for which the machine is to be used, and second, the price one is prepared to pay. There are motor cycles on the market with a cubic capacity of 100, whilst there are others which employ engines with the same cubic capacity as the well-known Austin Seven. The rider who is content with low speeds and who has no intention of taking a passenger will find that anything up to 200 c.c. will be ample for his requirements. These machines can be obtained very cheaply indeed, and almost without exception they are very reliable and cost little to run. In the 250 c.c. class are machines capable of sufficient power to satisfy the majority of riders—that is, of course, for solo work. They have considerable reserve of power in comparison with 100 or 150 c.c. models and enable one to maintain quite a good average speed.

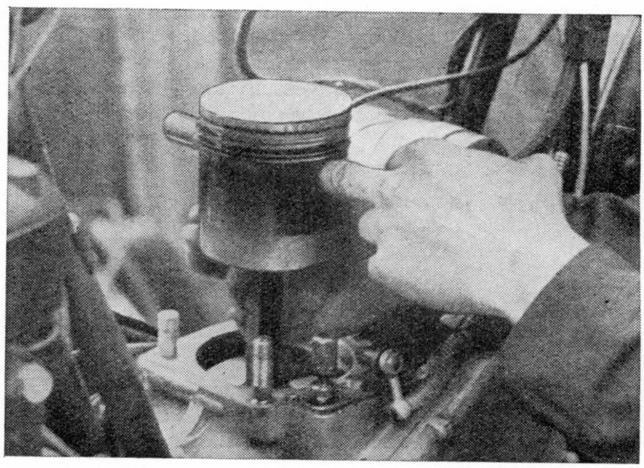

Fig. 2.—The Gudgeon Pin should be pushed out with the finger

When Choosing a Second-hand Machine the following points should be observed: First of all make sure that the engine is cold and then stand on the kick-starter pedal against compression. This should bear one's weight for about a minute on a four-stroke machine of about $3\frac{1}{2}$-horse power. If possible take hold of the engine pulley and rock it to and fro, listening for big end play, and up and down for looseness in the crankshaft bearings. Then start the engine and note the noise in the valve tappets, etc. An engine that is in good condition will tick over very slowly. Place the machine on the stand and shake each wheel for bearing slackness. Inspect the front spring shackles for play, then test all controls, looking particularly for frayed Bowden cables. If possible the condition of the brake linings should be ascertained, and in any case the brakes should be thoroughly tested. The lamps should be switched on to see if the ammeter is working. The condition of the tyres and the contents of the tool kit should also be noted.

Sidecars.—Modern sidecars are built on extremely pleasing lines, and give great comfort to the occupant. Supplied in a variety of types they may be either open or closed, or even of the saloon type with winding windows. Driving a sidecar outfit is, of course, vastly different from riding a machine solo. The controls are exactly the same but the steering is absolutely different. To mount the sidecar machine for the first time, after having ridden solo, provides a number of thrills, and the novice is advised to practise sidecar work in a quiet road. The solo rider to a great extent steers his machine by balancing, but of course the sidecar will not respond to this treatment. The front wheel must definitely be pointed in the direction in which it is intended that the machine shall travel, and this gives an utterly different feel to that of solo work. It is in turning a corner, however, that the greatest difficulty is encountered, for the centrifugal force tries to turn the machine over when it is rounding a corner. It is the wheel that is inside that tends to lift. On a right-hand corner, of course, the weight of the machine and rider prevents such a thing from happening, but on a left-hand corner, and particularly if no passenger is in the sidecar, the inside wheel will very easily come off the ground. The driver, and the passenger if carried, should lean to the left when turning a left-handed corner. It requires very little practice, however, to take corners at fair speeds.

Fig. 3.—Cylinder-head Nuts should be tightened diagonally

It is not considered advisable to fit a sidecar to a machine of less than 250 c.c. Some of the smaller machines will pull a light sidecar but for general all round work a 250 c.c. machine is the minimum. The most common sidecar machine is the 500 c.c. outfit. This will take two or more passengers up any ordinary hill at a good speed, whilst it has even been known to tow a light caravan or trailer.

Insurances.—Motor cyclists, whether of solo machines or of combinations, are subject to the same highway law as motorists, and care should be exercised at all times. A copy of the Highway Code can be obtained from any licensing authority. All machines must be insured against third party claims, under the Road Traffic Act, and machines must, of course, be licensed. At the time of writing the rates are as follows:

Solo motor cycle not exceeding 150 c.c. engine capacity 12/– per annum.

Solo machine 150–250 c.c. £1 2s. 6d. per annum.

Solo machine exceeding 250 c.c. £2 5s. 0d. per annum.

Extra charge for sidecar 15/– per annum.

Licensing.—Every driver of a mechanically propelled vehicle must possess a driving licence and an insurance policy. The minimum age at which this licence may be obtained is 16 years if a motor cycle is driven, and 17 years in the case of a car. The licence costs 5/– and lasts twelve months from the date of issue. Temporary licences are issued to learners who must pass an official test within six months from the date of issue.

Learners must attach a letter "L" in red on a white background, the letter itself measuring 4 in. deep, 3½ in. wide and 1¼ in. thick. The card must be 7 in. square.

If the motor cycle is used to carry a pillion passenger the machine must be fitted with a proper pillion seat, and the passenger must ride behind the driver and astride the machine. These regulations do not apply to sidecar outfits. If it is intended to carry

Fig. 4.—When working on a machine have it at a convenient height

a pillion passenger, make sure that the insurance company is aware of this fact and has given the necessary permission. In most cases an additional premium will be required. Only one passenger may be taken on a solo machine. (*See* insurance regulations in article on MOTORING.)

Motor-cycle Touring provides one of the most interesting and at the same time cheapest forms of holidaying. Packing all one's necessaries on to a solo mount, is, however, quite a job to the uninitiated. Suit-cases are apt to become much the worse for wear if they are strapped on to carriers without the interposition of a sheet of felt, whilst if more than two cases are carried, some difficulty may be experienced when mounting and dismounting.

Undoubtedly the best way to carry loads is to make use of the pannier type of holder. The bags are slung over the rear carrier, being fastened at several points with straps to prevent movement. With a couple of these pannier bags and a waterproof canvas bag strapped on to the carrier itself, one is able to carry everything one needs with the greatest ease and safety—even to the extent of camping equipment. When camping by motor cycle a middle course must be chosen between walking and motoring equipment. If both of these sections are read, the motor cyclist will be able to find out all that is required as regards equipment. There are several extremely light vans now obtainable that have been designed for towing behind light-weight vehicles, and a powerful motor cycle and sidecar is quite capable of hauling one of these.

Before starting out on a tour, always make sure that the machine is in thoroughly sound mechanical condition, as trouble on the road is likely to prove costly. The engine should be decarbonized, valves ground in, tyres removed and the covers rendered free from stones and flints. The wheel bearings should be thoroughly lubricated, and all spring shackles given their quota of grease. The engine should be warmed up, and then drained of oil and replenished with the proper grade and quantity. The carburettor should be dismantled and cleaned, and the contact breaker, lights, dynamo, etc., looked to. All control wires should be examined and replaced if at all frayed.

Sidecar connections must be tightened, and the springs supporting the body lubricated. Make sure that the hood and side-screens are sound and waterproof, and that the luggage grid is sufficiently strong to carry its load. It is only by giving careful attention to such details that a trouble-free run is assured. Always use the best petrol, for although the machine may appear to run just as well on an inferior fuel, more miles per gallon and easier starting are obtained from first-class fuel. The latter point will be appreciated if a camping holiday is undertaken, for during the cold nights the oil in the sump will thicken. Cheap oils should be definitely avoided at all times: they will almost certainly cause trouble sooner or later.

MOTORING

A GOOD motorist understands his car, and as a knowledge of the working principles of the motor vehicle greatly enhances the pleasure of motoring and also enables the owner-driver to reduce his running costs, we begin by stating how a car works.

The Engine.—Modern engines are of several kinds and operate on what is called the four-stroke principle. However many cylinders the engine may have, the principle is the same throughout, so, for the sake of simplicity, we will consider the single-cylinder model. This is not unlike a gun in its operation, the cylinder taking the place of the barrel, the piston the bullet, and petrol in vapour form, mixed with air, the explosive mixture. Instead, however, of the "bullet" being ejected entirely from the barrel, it is harnessed in such a way that its momentum is directed to the rotation of wheels, the bullet itself returning to secure more power. In the petrol engine the piston is connected to what is called a crankshaft (i.e. a shaft that is cranked) by means of a rod which is suitably named the connecting rod. At each end of this is a bearing, the one fitted inside the piston being called the gudgeon - pin bearing, whilst that embracing the crankshaft is usually termed the big end. Attached to the crankshaft is the flywheel and this is connected through a clutch, via gears, to the rear axle and thence to the road wheels.

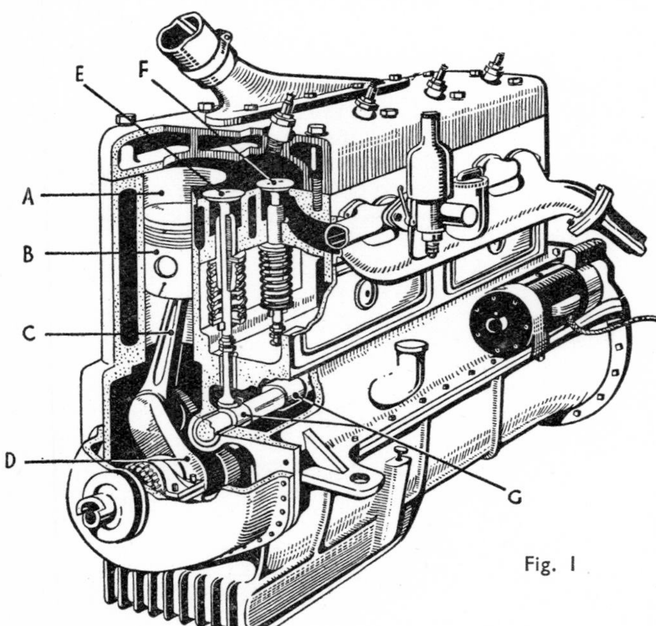

Fig. 1

Leaving out for the moment, however, the connection between the engine and the road wheels, let us see how the engine itself develops power. As the piston is made a close sliding fit in the cylinder it is practically gas tight, so that when descending, or leaving the closed end of the cylinder, suction is set up. By mechanical means described later a valve is opened and a supply of vaporized petrol and air is drawn into the cylinder. As the crankshaft rotates the piston rises, at the same time the inlet valve, that is the valve through which the petrol vapour entered, is closed and the mixture is compressed. At the top of the piston stroke the compressed mixture is ignited by means of electricity and the resultant expansion of the gas forces the piston down to the bottom once more. Another valve opens and the upward sweep of the piston forces the spent gas through this exhaust valve and thence by the exhaust pipe and silencer to the open air. This is the completion of the cycle. We therefore have the four operations which are known as Induction, Compression, Ignition, and Exhaustion.

The features of an engine, then, are the cylinder, piston, connecting rod, crankshaft, valves, petrol supply and means for igniting the vapour. The accompanying diagram (Fig. 1) will make the foregoing clear: (*a*) is the cylinder, (*b*) the piston, (*c*) the connecting rod, (*d*) the end of the crankshaft, (*e*) and (*f*) are the inlet and exhaust valves respectively, (*g*) being the cams which raise the valves at the desired time. Valves are, of course, closed or returned to their seatings by means of springs, and in some engines the valves are side by side, that is, they are set actually in the cylinder block itself, as in the diagram, or they are of the overhead type, which means that they are set in a detachable cylinder head and operate over the top of the piston.

The Carburettor.—Fig. 2 will show the general principles of a modern carburettor. The petrol enters the carburettor float chamber through the pipe and strainer (*a*). It then passes through a needle valve operated by the float (*b*). As the float sinks, so the valve opens and more petrol enters, whilst as the float rises it reduces the aperture and so cuts off the supply. From the float chamber the petrol flows to the bottom of the main jet (*c*) whilst a small tube allows the supply to run to the starting jet (*d*). Then, when the engine is started, the main jet supply is cut off by means of a shutter (*e*) but a small hole in this shutter permits a pure supply of petrol to run past and into the cylinders. As soon as the engine is started the throttle is opened, thus causing air to enter at (*f*) and pass over the main jet.

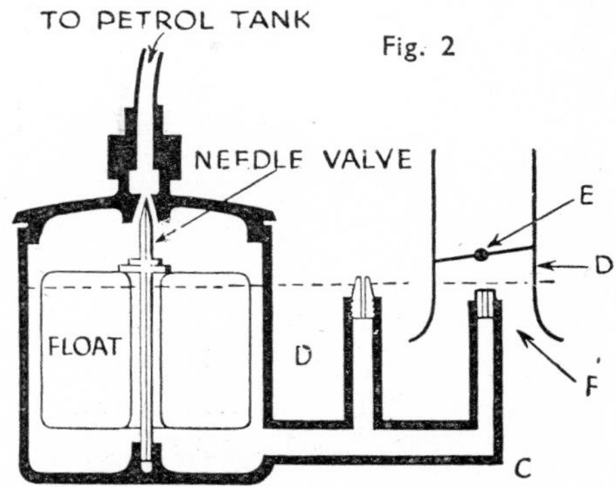

This rush of air sucks up the petrol through the main jet, atomizes it and carries it into the engine.

It will be realized that as both the main and starter jets are so small, proper filtration of the petrol is necessary. If no filter is incorporated either in the tank or in the carburettor itself, frequent jet clogging may result.

Carburettors are usually set for a good grade petrol, and should a lower-quality fuel be used the setting of the carburettor may need some adjustment to compensate for the difference in specific gravity. It is wise for the owner to have his carburettor tuned by a competent man. Should a carburettor need cleaning, the jets must first of all be removed. The method of doing this naturally depends upon the design of the instrument. Jets should then be blown through in the reverse direction to that in which the petrol flows. They should on no account be cleansed with a pin, although sometimes a primus stove cleaner will remove the obstruction. The float should be taken out by removing the covering from the float chamber (usually held on by a spring), and the float chamber itself carefully wiped. Shake the float to see if there is any petrol inside it. This will affect consumption considerably. Do not attempt to solder a leak in a float, but take it to a garage man.

The Ignition.—The next part to be considered is that which provides the electric spark. In the majority of modern cars electricity is drawn from the car battery. The battery consists of an acid-proof box containing a number of positive and negative plates covered with a solution of diluted sulphuric acid. The battery stores electricity in a chemical form; it is kept charged by the dynamo driven by the engine. Current is drawn from the accumulator and passes round a coil of fine copper wire. Outside this coil is a second coil composed of a very large number of turns of fine stranded copper wire. These two windings are known as primary and secondary respectively. By mechanical means the current through the primary winding is switched on and off at intervals corresponding to the speed of the engine, and it is the cessation of current, or collapse of field as it is termed, in the primary winding that induces a current in the secondary coil. This induced current is of very high-voltage, and is of sufficient power to jump across the spark gap provided by the sparking plug. The distributor directs the high-tension current to each plug in turn, the spark occurring at the top of the compression stroke. Failure of the ignition system can therefore be traced back to its source if the principle of operation is known. Thus, in the event of a car's failing to start, if the ignition is suspected, the sparking plugs are first of all tested by shorting with a wood-handled tool (to avoid shock), then the faulty one can be removed. If the plugs are all right a test is made of the leads themselves and so on, right back to the battery.

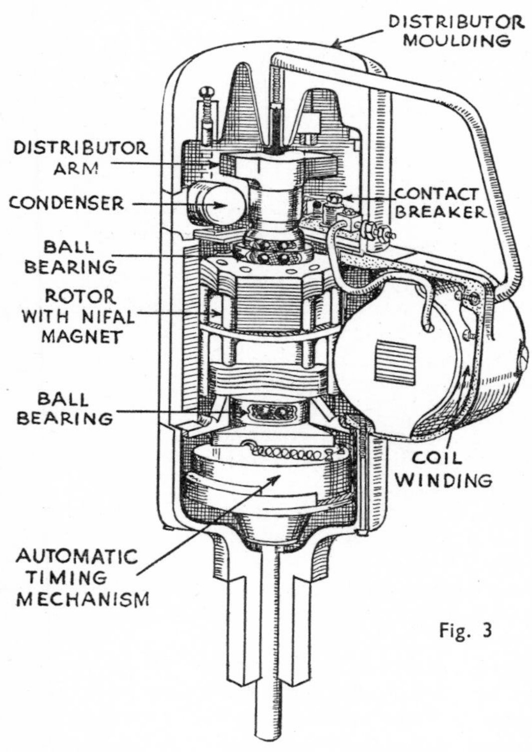

Fig. 3

The Magneto.—The magneto is a self-contained instrument which makes its own electricity. Rotating between the poles of a permanent magnet is the armature, which, like the coil, is composed of two windings —primary and secondary. Lines of magnetic force flow through the primary winding but cease at intervals. This cessation induces a high-tension current into the secondary winding, and the contact breaker and distributor, which are all combined in the one instrument, direct the current to the plugs. The accompanying sketch (Fig. 3) will show the general construction of a magneto. These instruments are exceedingly reliable, and, speaking generally, if they fail to function first thing in the morning, it is because the rocker arm of the contact breaker is stuck. The little cap for excluding dust is removed and the contact breaker rendered free either by moving with the fingers or by taking it out and cleaning the bearing. The central screw holds the contact breaker in position, thus rendering a small magneto spanner necessary in the tool kit.

The Transmission.—The means of breaking connection between the engine and the road wheels and also of connecting them up gradually are the gear-box and the clutch. These lie between the rear axle and the engine, the latter-named component being next behind the engine. Clutches are of several types, the simplest form being what is known as the cone clutch. Inside the flywheel is a cone-shaped recess whilst the clutch itself is constructed to fit closely inside this recess so that when pressed home by springs, under the driver's control through the clutch pedal, it transmits the power from the engine to the gear-box. Cone clutches are usually faced with some material such as leather or bonded asbestos. The more common type of clutch is known as the disc or plate. The operation of this can be seen by reference to Fig. 4. Modern cars are being fitted with a fluid flywheel, which functions as a clutch, comprising a number of vanes rotating in a casing full of oil. One set of vanes is fastened to the side of the flywheel nearest the engine, whilst the other is connected to the gear-box. As the engine rotates, so it passes oil through channels to the second set of vanes, and the force with which the oil is thrown outwards transmits the power to the gear-box.

The Gear-box.—Fig. 5 shows the general principle of them all. The driving shaft, which is connected to the engine via the clutch, rotates the lay shaft through pinions which are in constant mesh. On this lay shaft are other pinions of different sizes. In alignment with the driving shaft is the driven shaft, and at the driver's will this may either be connected direct to the driving shaft, or the sliding pinions on the driven shaft may be engaged with those on the lay shaft, thus transmitting power in a roundabout direction. It is these pinions which provide the changes of speed. When a small pinion on the lay shaft is driving a large one on the driven shaft, the gear is low, which means that the engine revolutions are high in proportion to those of the rear wheels. When, however, a large wheel on the lay shaft is driving one of equal size or one slightly smaller on the driven shaft, a correspondingly higher gear is obtained, so that although the engine may revolve at the same speed as before the vehicle moves much more quickly. As far

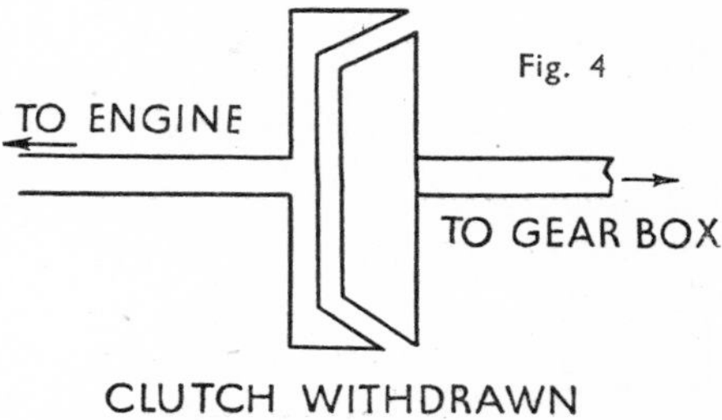

Fig. 4

CLUTCH WITHDRAWN

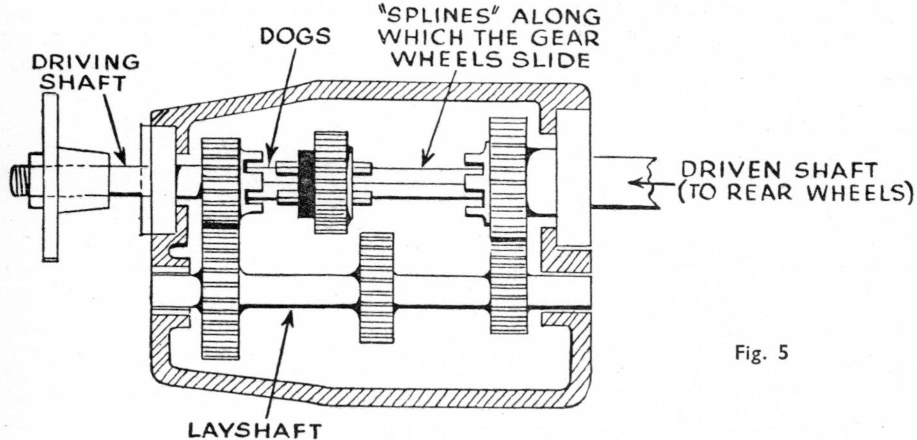

Fig. 5

as top gear is concerned, the two dogs (*see* illustration) are engaged, providing a direct drive from the crankshaft to the driven shaft, the necessary reduction in gear being obtained through the back axle.

To allow for the rise and fall of the rear axle as the car bumps over the road, it is necessary to have some means of flexible transmission, and the apparatus which carries out this job is known as the universal joint. Usually there are two universal joints, depending upon the design of the car, and reference to Fig. 6 will show how these joints operate.

Lastly we come to the rear axle and universal joint. The drive is taken from the

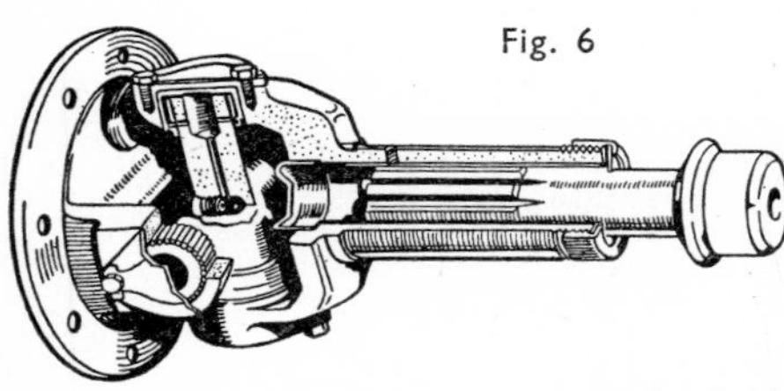
Fig. 6

gear-box via a shaft to a small bevel wheel situated in the rear axle housing. This bevel wheel (which may be spiral bevel, herringbone or hypoid bevel) rotates the crown wheel which is connected to the rear axle via the differential gear. The job of the differential gear is to provide for the faster rotation of the outside rear wheel when turning a corner.

Decarbonizing.—The modern car engine is almost a miracle of reliability, but owing to the nature of the fuel used a deposit gradually forms on the top of the piston and round the cylinder head. This deposit has the effect of lowering the efficiency of the engine, and periodically the carbon should be removed. It is quite a simple—if messy—job to do this, and whilst the manufacturers' service books give every detail of this operation, the following general principle should be adopted. Remove the bonnet, drain the radiator and loosen the water-pipe connections. Then take off the sparking plug leads, and if the engine is of the side-valve type, loosen the cylinder nuts with a box spanner. The best method of doing this is to start with the centre nuts or studs and loosen them a quarter to half a turn, then work outwards either side and loosen the others a like amount, returning to the first and taking off altogether. By turning the starting handle once or twice sharply with the ignition switch off, the compression will very often loosen the head, which may then be lifted off and placed on a bench. Between the cylinder head and the cylinder itself will be found a gasket or washer, which must be carefully removed and put in a place of safety. With a blunt chisel scrape the deposit from the piston heads, making sure that the piston itself is not damaged by the use of too sharp a tool. Attention should then be given to the cylinder head itself, the sparking plugs removed, and the head scraped clean and finally washed with petrol.

The Valves.—As a rule when the engine needs decarbonizing the valves also need attention. Valves, as we see by referring to the first illustration, are usually of the mushroom type, the seating being a bevel. After much use this bevelled surface becomes pitted, and is no longer gas-tight. To restore its efficiency the valve is taken out by compressing the spring, removing the cotter pin or locking ring and lifting the valve out. To grind in, procure a tin of carborundum paste or powder. Powder should be mixed with oil to the consistency of paste before using. After the seatings of both valve and cylinder have been wiped clean, a small quantity of paste is applied evenly around the edge, and the valve dropped back into position. With a screwdriver grind the valve backwards and forwards on its seating, lifting occasionally to enable the abrasive to get into a different position. It is not necessary that the seating be the entire width of the bevel, for as long as there is contact all the way round the valve will be gas-tight. Proceed with each valve in turn until all have been properly ground in, then wash both valves and seatings with paraffin oil and replace. It may be necessary after grinding in valves to alter the valve tappets, which are the short rods operating the valves. The amount of clearance to be given varies with the different makes of cars, and the manufacturer will supply the necessary data. The cylinder-head gasket should now be wiped over and given a slight coating of gold-size on both sides before being placed in position. The cylinder-head facing is also coated with gold-size and then carefully replaced on the studs, making sure that the gasket is not damaged. The holding-down nuts are then tightened up carefully, starting at the centre and working outwards as before. The water pipes are connected, the radiator filled up and the engine started. When warm it should be switched off and the cylinder nuts tightened up again. The average owner-driver should be able to decarbonize his car in five or six hours.

The reader who has followed the explanation above concerning the operation of a car and its main components will now be in a position to understand fully the following trouble-finding data.

Failure to Start.—Failure to start may be due to one of three main causes: mechanical faults, lack of fuel, no spark. Under mechanical faults will come such things as valve-timing out of gear, breakages, and so on, but if the engine is known to be in good mechanical condition attention should be given to the ignition and carburettor. (Modern plug testers can be obtained very cheaply.) If a second person is present he should depress the starter switch so as to turn the engine over whilst the plugs are tested to see if a spark takes place. If there is no spark, disconnect leads in turn and hold metal end ¼ in. from cylinder head and turn engine again. If there is still no spark, remove the cover of the contact breaker to see if this is working. If the contact breaker is operating, remove distributor brush and see if it is glazed. Test the gap between platinum points. Watch for sparking in the contact breaker. If no sparking occurs at any of points tested it is probable that either the magneto condenser is burned or its armature windings are burnt out. If spark appears at end of leads but not the plugs, the latter are at fault and should be removed, dismantled and cleaned, the point gap being checked.

With coil ignition the trouble may be due to a run-down battery, loose connections, damaged coil, contact-breaker points being dirty or needing adjustment, punctured condenser and so on. It is understood, of course, that the main switch of the engine was put on in the first instance. If the ignition is sound, the carburettor should be attended to next.

Fig. 7.—A hammer can be used for testing faulty plugs

See that petrol is turned on and that carburettor floods when needle is lifted or depressed. If no flooding, make sure that there is sufficient fuel in the tank. Remove jets and clean. Watch for presence of water in float chamber, also see that throttle is not too wide open. This will be denoted by the absence of suction sound.

Misfires and Stops.—As with the previous section the faults are traceable to mechanical troubles, ignition failure and carburettor faults. Speaking generally, if a car has been running fairly well the mechanical trouble will not be anything

Fig. 8.—Cleaning Distributor Contacts with petrol-rag

serious, but will be confined, most likely, to the valves and their operation. Remove the valve cover and check the valve items: valve springs—one or more of these may be broken, which will result in the valves being stuck, with a consequent loss of compression. The valve cotter may have sheared through, giving the same effect. The valve may be burned and no longer gas-tight. The stem may be bent and stuck so that there is no gas-tight seating; or the valve itself may be broken. If the engine is mechanically sound, spluttering may be due to a faulty plug. Perhaps the insulator is cracked, the gap between the points is too wide, or there is oil on the electrodes, causing a short. A broken carbon brush in the magneto slip-ring will also cause misfiring, as will a badly worn distributor, a dirty slip-ring, which, of course, prevents proper contact, faulty connections or a loose magneto coupling. The most frequent cause of misfiring and refusal to run is, however, traceable to the carburettor. With many cars, if the throttle is not set correctly the engine will not run. If an engine starts well and gradually dies out, it is quite likely that the jet is partially choked. An over-rich mixture may also prevent the engine from running properly, and this may be due to a punctured float. If a vacuum feed is fitted, this should be checked over to see that it is working properly. Water in the carburettor will also cause intermittent firing. Make sure, too, that the air vent in the petrol tank cap is not stopped up.

Lubrication. — It is essential that all parts of the car receive their proper amount of lubricant which should be of the right kind and quality. Cheap oils and greases are bad for cars and should be avoided. It is true that the motorist may not notice any difference in the running of the engine when cheap oil is used, but sooner or later trouble will occur, particularly at high speeds. Lubrication should be carried out at frequent intervals, and charts giving the grades of oil, etc., may be obtained from any oil manufacturer.

The chassis of most modern cars are now fitted with grease nipples instead of cups, the application of a grease gun being all that is required to lubricate the various parts efficiently. Regular lubrication of the chassis is strongly recommended, for not only does it increase the life of the car but it renders the vehicle safer to run and also enables a higher price to be obtained for it when it is sold. The majority of car tool kits include a small pressure grease gun, and with this it is possible to secure a pressure of several hundred pounds to the square inch. If a gun of this nature is unable to force the lubricant through a nipple, the car should be taken along to a proper service station which will have a high-power grease gun capable of giving pressures up to five or more thousand pounds per square inch. The advantage of this high-pressure lubrication is that old and spent grease is forced out of the bearing, the new charge taking its place.

Tyres.—Under-inflation is the cause of most tyre trouble and pressures should be checked regularly with the proper gauge. It is impossible to tell the pressure in a tyre merely by looking at it. The front tyres especially should be watched to see if there is any feather edge on the tread projections. If these are noticed, the alignment should be checked by a mechanic. Misaligned wheels may cause a tyre to wear completely through in a few hundred miles. Good tyres are advised and the reader warned from purchasing those of cheap quality or those labelled "seconds." The price is usually low because of interior weaknesses. A good set of tyres will last from ten to fifteen thousand miles. They should, however, be inspected at intervals, and stones removed from the tread or they will work through and penetrate the tube.

As far as puncture repairing is concerned patching is quite simple and most reliable if carried out properly. The tube should be thoroughly roughened and cleaned before the rubber solution is applied. The self-vulcanizing patch strip may be relied upon implicitly.

The Law.—Every private motor vehicle must be registered and a licence fee paid. This is based upon the R.A.C. horse-power rating. The rates are obtainable from the local council. Third party insurance is also compulsory by law, and the reader is advised to deal only with reputable companies. This point cannot be overstressed, for should the insurance company fail, or refuse to meet the claim, the private motorist is himself liable even though a premium has been paid.

All insurance contracts are based on the facts contained in the proposal form, and should these, whether intentionally or unintentionally, be untrue, the contract itself is voidable and the company can refuse to meet the claim. Note any conditions regarding fire-extinguishers in car or garage.

All drivers are required to take out a driving licence, which may be obtained for 5/- from the local authorities.

For Learners' Licences *see* Motor Cycle section.

Choosing a Car.—There are many points to be considered when choosing a new car, the first usually being the question of price. Once the maximum figure has been decided upon, the cost of tax, insurance, fuel and general running costs should be considered, as also should such features as ease of driving, comfort, appearance and so on. The choice of a second-hand car, however, demands greater consideration, and the reader is advised either to take along with him some friend who is competent to examine the car, or to seek some garage proprietor in whom implicit trust may be placed. One or two of the motoring journals should be studied in order to get an idea of the prices now obtaining for vehicles of a given age and type, and the intending purchaser should bear in mind not only the year of manufacture, but the condition of the body-work, paint, upholstery, tyres and equipment. If these are

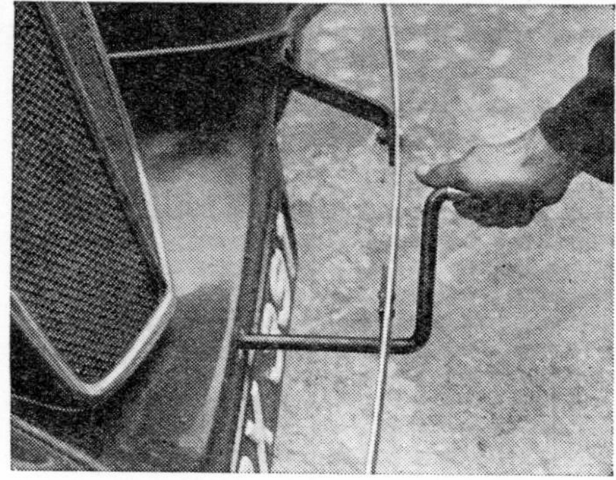

Fig. 9.—Keep the thumb on the same side as the fingers for safety when starting

satisfactory, attention should be given to the engine. The prospective buyer should have an opportunity of examining the car before the engine has been started up in order both to discover whether it starts easily and to find out the state of its compression. This is best ascertained by taking hold of the starting handle and turning the engine over slowly to note whether the compression on each cylinder appears equal. Whilst the engine is being thus turned, listen for leakage past pistons and valves. Remove the valve cover and see if the valves themselves can be moved from side to side. Movement indicates worn valve guides. Then see if the engine starts readily. Throttle it well down to see how slowly it runs. It is possible to learn far more from a slowly running engine than from one that is turning over at several thousand revolutions per minute. Whilst the engine is ticking over, listen carefully for knocks, and when the engine is warm remove the oil-filler cap of the crank-case and watch for the presence of fumes. Puffs of faintly blue smoke will show that there is leakage past pistons and that a rebore is necessary. Then jack up the front axle by its centre and test the wheels for play. Note, too, whether there is excessive play in the steering wheel. The outer edge of this should not move more than 1½ in. before taking up the strain. Then take the car on to the road and note the noise in all gears. Remove the foot occasionally from the accelerator so that the car overruns the engine. Excessive noise or rattle will denote looseness of the transmission gear. Listen also for rear-axle noises. The differential gear condition can be ascertained by cornering. The reader is advised to let someone else drive, and to sit in the back seat in order to hear these noises. A car with a noisy rear axle should definitely be rejected as trouble in that quarter is most expensive to remedy. Back in the garage, jack up one rear wheel and turn it backwards and forwards whilst the car is in gear. This will show back lash in the transmission. The brakes should receive careful attention and if possible the brake drums be removed and the condition of the linings ascertained. If the brakes of a car will not stop the vehicle in 50 ft. when driving at 30 m.p.h., adjustment is necessary. Finally the electrical equipment of the car should be tested; lights switched on, the horn used, windscreen wiper operated and the ammeter watched to see whether the dynamo is charging or not.

Be sure that spare parts are still procurable.

Touring.—The pleasures of touring by car are greatly enhanced if careful preparation is made beforehand. Not only should the car itself be thoroughly greased and tightened up and necessary adjustments and repairs carried out, but the entire route should be planned and a good map obtained.

Always make sure that the tool kit is complete and that the spare wheel is in good condition and fully inflated.

MUSHROOM GROWING

THE person who wishes to grow mushrooms will require some kind of shed or a cellar, a garden with an entrance other than through the house so that manure can be brought into the shed or cellar without damage to furniture and carpets, a small amount of capital, and, last but not least, patience to wait about three months for results.

The Bed.—The first step is to prepare the medium on which the mushrooms are to be grown. Get some absolutely fresh horse manure—20 bushels or one load will be enough for 50 square feet of bed area—from a stable where the horses are fed on dry food, are healthy, and not being physicked.

The manure will most likely contain a proportion of straw litter; if this litter is deficient add fresh wheat straw, and if there is too much of it fork out the longer pieces. Mix the manure thoroughly and moisten any parts that seem dry. Then stack it into a neat square pile and sift about 3 in. of good garden soil on to the top.

Leave it thus for a week and then examine it to see if there are any signs of heating-up. You really need a thermometer to keep an accurate check on this heating-up process; the mercury tube from an ordinary wall thermometer will serve quite well, or you can buy a special mushroom-bed thermometer with higher readings for about 5/–.

At this first examination the temperature under the surface of the manure will probably be about 90 degrees Fahrenheit.

When heating-up has started give the heap a thorough re-mixing, turning the inside out and the outside in. Make sure that the manure is uniformly moist by sprinkling any dry parts with water, and shake out every forkful, so as to avoid lumps. Care must be taken not to over-water as this can ruin the compost. On top of the second pile sift a 1-in. layer of soil.

This re-mixing process must be repeated at intervals of six days or more till the manure is sufficiently "composted," which may be in about three weeks—more or less according to weather conditions. If the pile is backward in heating-up give it a higher, more conical shape.

You can easily judge when the final condition is reached because the following changes will have taken place: the unpleasant odour of the manure will have been replaced by a sweet smell; the colour will be dark brown but it should not be black; the straw will have lost its toughness and should break easily; the manure will be soft and will cling together, yet will not contain so much water as to drip when squeezed; the temperature will have dropped from the peak point (round about 140 degrees Fahrenheit) to approximately 120 degrees Fahrenheit. At this stage the manure is called "compost," which "sounds better."

Where to Grow Mushrooms.—While it is reaching this condition you may prepare the growing premises. If you are building a special mushroom-house, make the walls of double planking with straw or shavings stuffed between them. Ventilation should be arranged so that a current of fresh air passes continually through the house without any draughts playing on the beds.

An old shed can easily be adapted, however. Adequate ventilation and some means of excluding direct sunshine are the only essentials. Heaping earth against the walls, covering the roof with straw or turf, installing a slow-combustion stove (with a pan of water on top to keep the atmosphere moist), are some methods which are commonly used to keep the temperature high; other ideas especially suitable for your circumstances may occur to you.

To get the biggest possible bed area you should build plank bunks in tiers to hold the compost. The accompanying sketch suggests dimensions and lay-out for a small house. You will notice that the beds are far enough apart to allow the use of a watering-can, and not so large that some mushrooms cannot be reached. These are points that many beginners forget.

Constructing the Beds.—When both the premises and the compost are ready

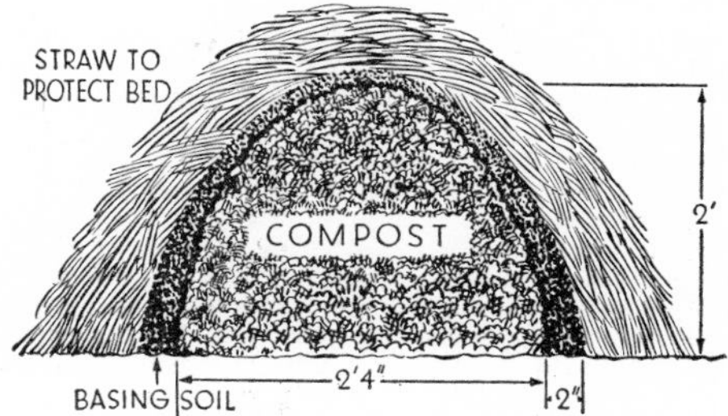

Fig. 1.—Section of a small ridge bed

Fig. 2.—Protect your compost from the rain

you may make up the beds. Carry the compost in buckets and pack it firmly and evenly into the "bunks" to a depth of from 6 to 8 in. Then leave it for a day or so with the ventilators closed. In all probability the compost will go through another heating-up, perhaps reaching the temperature of 140 degrees Fahrenheit. Open the ventilators and let the beds cool down to about 70 degrees before planting the spawn.

If the compost refuses to heat-up in the beds, it may be too moist. In this case you should loosen it so that the air can get into it and dry it. Afterwards press it down firmly again. On the other hand, the reason for not heating may be that it is too dry; by handling a little of the compost you will soon detect this. The remedy is to water the beds with a fine spray. Even if all your efforts fail to secure a rise in temperature, you will have just as good a crop if other conditions are right, but it will be longer coming.

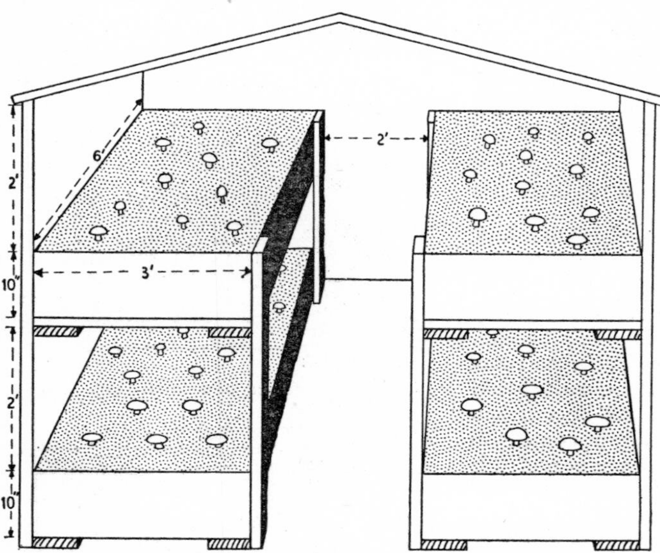

Fig. 3.—Diagram showing dimensions of Mushroom Shed

Planting the Spawn.—You can obtain it from almost any seedsman for about 7/6 a quart. Planting is quite a simple job. A quart will be enough to plant from 30 to 40 square feet. Break it up into about 40 pieces, each about half the size of a golf ball. Plant these $1\frac{1}{2}$ in. below the surface and 8 to 10 in. apart, making a small hole in the compost, inserting the spawn and pressing the compost back into place. Spawn is expensive, so be careful to plant every scrap—even the dust—it is all productive.

The beds will not need any more attention for a week or two except for a light watering with a rose spray if they seem dry, and you can meanwhile prepare the "casing" or "surfacing" soil. To do this get some good quality garden soil, entirely free from decayed vegetable matter, and sift it thoroughly. Mix into it enough lime to lighten the colour, moisten it if necessary, and stack it ready for use when the spawn has begun to "run" in the beds.

This should be between a week and a fortnight after it has been planted—if the surrounding temperature has been about 50 degrees Fahrenheit. You can tell when the time has come by lifting the compost gently from one of the spawn lumps. If there is a kind of cobwebby mildew spreading from it you may proceed with casing. If it is very dry you may give the compost a last watering, then spread the casing soil evenly over it to a depth of $1\frac{1}{2}$ in.

For a month or more you have nothing to do now but watch the beds, only watering them if they seem very dry and taking prompt measures against any pests that may appear. Then will come the glorious day when the beds show the first signs of life. At first there will be little more than a dab of white over the places where spawn was planted, but in a day or so tiny, pin-head mushrooms will be visible in large numbers. Though these pin-heads will develop to the size of the top of a match-stick, all of them will probably turn brown and die, when you can pick them off carefully and throw them away.

Bogus mushrooms with long stems and tiny heads may also appear at this stage, and these too must be picked and destroyed, lest, decaying in the beds, they encourage the deadly mushroom "molds."

There can be no mistaking the first-fruits of the real crop; they usually break the surface with round heads like peas, and five to six weeks from the time of spawning. A light watering every other day will bring them on till they are just larger than shillings, and then they can be left alone altogether.

During the cropping period the sun must be kept off the beds. High temperature will cause the mushrooms to grow lanky and small headed. Plenty of ventilation and the comparatively low temperature of 55 degrees will ensure healthy growth.

The best time to pick the mushrooms is just before the heads begin to flatten. Flat heads may look larger but they are not as heavy nor as succulent as round ones. Twist the whole stem from the soil and fill the hole which is left with soil prepared in the same way as the casing.

The Crop may last anything from six weeks to six months, according to the temperature, the quality of the beds and spawn and the way you tend them. When the crop is finished remove the old compost, which you should be able to sell for a good price to a local market-gardener or to a sports ground. Before you re-fill the beds wash them out thoroughly with water tinged with disinfectant, also sweep the floor and sprinkle it with lime-wash.

It is possible to grow mushrooms out of doors, the best time to make up the beds being from September to May. Choose a sheltered spot and spread out a thin layer of damp stable litter. On this the compost, prepared as already described, should be made into a long, ridge-shaped bed about 2½ ft. high in the middle. Plant the spawn while the bed still has a fairly high temperature, case the bed, and then cover it with a thick coat of straw. Sacking should also be laid on the straw to give protection from rain.

Pests.—The most common insect pest attacking the mushroom is the mushroom fly, a small, gnat-like insect which lays its eggs round the mushroom stems. From these eggs maggots hatch which burrow into the stems and so into the caps. Ordinary insect powder—but *not* a liquid insecticide—should be used promptly, but if the flies are once allowed to increase, it becomes almost impossible to exterminate them. The insect powder will be cheaper and more effective if mixed with lime, the mixture being shaken into the air between the beds.

Springtails are another unwelcome visitor. They are tiny, grey, long-bodied insects, and can easily be distinguished because they hop like fleas. They eat the mushroom caps and gills, disfiguring and even destroying them. Insect powder and lime and a little lime in the water with which the beds are watered will keep them down.

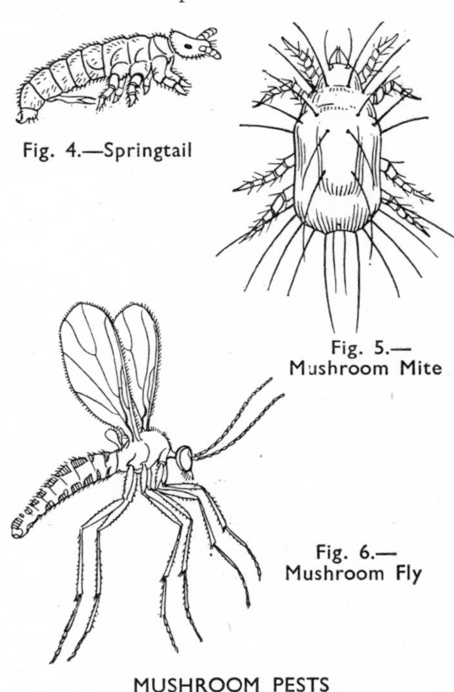

Fig. 4.—Springtail

Fig. 5.—Mushroom Mite

Fig. 6.—Mushroom Fly

MUSHROOM PESTS

If your mushrooms are weakly and dark coloured, you may suspect the mushroom mite. This very small, egg-shaped insect digs down into the compost and even reaches the spawn. It is a very light colour, and only the most careful examination will detect it. In identifying this and other pests a cheap microscope will prove very useful. The mites are most evident when the beds are heating-up as then they come to the surface. At this stage paradichlorbenzine, or moth crystals, spread over the beds will prove extremely effective. Half a pound of crystals is enough for 50 square feet of bed area.

Tiny red spiders will do no harm to the mushrooms; they are even beneficial for they feed on other insects which are more harmful.

There are many other kinds of insects harmful to mushroom growth, but they are by no means common and, if you keep the premises perfectly clean with no litter on the floor, you should not have trouble from them. Still, it is always as well to take precautionary measures by fumigating the house just before spawning the beds.

Seal all cracks and raise the temperature as high as possible, then burn a sulphur candle or flowers of sulphur in a pan floating in a bucket of water. An alternative method is to place a tablespoonful of insect powder on a red-hot shovel; this will produce very powerful fumes. Keep the house sealed for 36 hours at least.

So much for the prevention of insects. The attacks of disease are also deadly, though fortunately not as common as those of living pests. "Molds" are green or white patches which appear on the beds, usually when a crop has been gathered. When they appear the entire patch must be removed to the depth of a ¼ in., and the surface made up with clean soil.

"Bubbles" is the most dreaded of all mushroom diseases, and results from using casing soil in which the disease exists. Infected mushrooms become pulpy and round like puff-balls. They should be picked immediately and destroyed, and the bed round them should be soaked with fairly strong Lysol solution. If the disease once gets a hold of the beds nothing can save them, and the wisest course is to sell the compost as manure. Do not use it on your own garden or the next crop will probably be infected also if that soil is used for casing new beds.

Mushroom growing is not a long and tedious business, fraught with big chances of failure. It sounds more difficult than it really is, and all your labours will be well repaid when you see your beds thick with white caps. You will not grumble if your arm aches with picking them.

PRACTICAL MUSIC

It is not easy for the amateur to get advice on those points which so clearly distinguish him from the professional musician. This is largely because of the difficulty of deciding just where the distinction lies. It may perhaps be best expressed by stating that the professional is generally much more "practical" than the amateur. This short outline has to do with the things that go to make up "practical ability."

Solidness.—Most musicians are familiar with "solid" playing but not all understand it. It is not violence or loudness, but a quality suggesting mastery of expression and power. Notice, for instance, how an experienced solo pianist contrives to make his playing sound full and sufficient.

A common fault of the amateur pianist is the playing of chords *arpeggiando* or in a broken, straggling manner. The best cure for this is plenty of chord-playing, care being taken that the notes are driven down with great vigour and absolute unanimity. Much benefit can also be obtained from slow scale-playing in double thirds. For the string player, double stopping, slow, *fortissimo* scales, and chord-playing are best for forming a good solid style—providing the bow arm aims at accuracy of movement rather than pressure.

Whatever the instrument, it is always quality of tone that really gives quantity: the rough, forced note never carries well.

"Attack" has much to do with solidness. Any ordinary note should begin firmly and remain even throughout. Players of wind and string instruments in particular are apt to begin a note uncertainly and feebly and only to reach the proper loudness towards the middle of the note. Decisive, firm attack applies to all playing, and to singing.

Notes are often cut short—and in this way power is lost. Still another fault is to let an ordinary note fade away towards its end, instead of maintaining its power until the succeeding beat.

Accent and rhythm also make for solidness. There must be a decided accent after each bar line. Should the number of beats in a bar be divisible by two, another accent will occur at the second half of the bar—in six-eight time, for example, the first and fourth beats are strong. A group of two, three, or four notes must always be accented at its beginning.

Sight Reading.—The method of practising sight reading is neither specially pleasant nor artistic, but it is essentially practical.

Get a big pile of music in front of you—all sorts from comic songs to concerti—and play straight through, without slackening over difficult phrases or pausing over mistakes, but "keeping the time going" at all costs. For this sort of practice do not touch anything familiar. Simply open the music, glance rapidly at key, time signature, tempo, repeats, and so on, and plunge straight in. Do not hesitate or lose the vital rhythm, despite wrong notes and blurs, until you emerge grimly and triumphantly at the final chord.

Even the complete beginner should sight read. Hymns do very well in early stages, but get plenty of varied music so that you can always fall back on things which are almost or quite unknown. And be strict with yourself—do not slacken when you come to a patch of semiquavers or when difficulties crop up.

Memorizing.—You cannot always have a roll of music in your pocket. In the twilight, at an impromptu singsong, for an emergency solo, to try out an instrument—there are so many occasions when the ability to do something from memory is of great value. And you can develop the ability with perseverance.

It will help to consider an actual illustration, to show a method of memorizing. Many would-be musicians simply try to fix a long composition in their minds without any clear method; actually analysis and intelligent understanding are necessary before the memory is called for.

Chanson Triste, by Tschaikovsky, is so well known that any musician should perform it without music. On analysis it will be found an easy task, because of its regular structure.

A complete little phrase is contained in the first two bars, and a second phrase in bars three and four. You can well imagine that bars one and two ask a question, and bars three and four answer them. A rather similar question is asked in bars five and six, and the seventh and eighth answer in the same way. If these eight bars are played over a few times, the two-bar sections being kept in mind, you will find it quite easy to repeat them without looking at your music.

In the ninth and tenth bars the original question is asked again, but the reply is different, for this time the notes ascend one by one. Then come four two-bar questions each at a lower pitch than the preceding one.

That completes the first movement.

Try over each question and answer separately; then join them together; then add the next section—and you will very soon memorize the whole movement. The rest of the piece can be divided up just as readily. There is the second or middle movement, and then the beginning is recapitulated, and, to make a proper ending, a *tail* or *coda* is added.

There is the method—you may deal with any piece of music similarly.

Do not trouble about necessary expression until you have the mere notes safe. Often you will find it helpful to visualize the actual music page, particularly places where rests come. And remember that crescendos occur most frequently in ascending passages and decrescendos in descending.

Italian.—Italian words are inseparable from music, and it is essential that one should be able to pronounce them boldly and accurately. Mispronunciations like—an-dan-tee, ca-preesio con-shir-to—are terribly common. Here are a few simple rules. First the vowel sounds:

A is *ah;* E is *ay;* I is *ee;* O is *oh;* U is *oo.*

Practically all consonants are pronounced as in English, though H is never sounded.

The last syllable but one of a word is usually accented.

When two vowels come together each is pronounced.

In the following all the vowels occur:

Vivace (lively) pronounced—vee-*vah*-chay.

Giusto (just, exact)—*joost*-oh.

Notice the C and G. These letters are always hard, as in "catgut," except when they are followed by I or E—thus the I in *giusto* and the E in *vivace* soften the two letters.

Con grazia (with grace) pronounced—con *grat*-zea.

A single Z is sounded like TZ, but ZZ, as in *mezzo*, is like DZ—thus "medzo."

S is as in English, though more like a Z when coming between two vowels.

GN, coming before a vowel, is like the "ni" of "bunion." Thus *segno* (sign) is pronounced *say*-nyo, the accent falling on the usual penultimate syllable.

CH, is pronounced like "ch" in "chord."

SC, is like "sh" in "shake" if it is followed by I or E, otherwise it is sounded like "sc" in "scale."

Master these few rules; practise them thoroughly; get to understand the meanings of Italian musical phrases so that you can speak them with assurance and recognize them readily.

Time Keeping.—Keeping time is, of course, developed by sight reading, but it is of such prime importance that it needs study for itself too.

One of the difficulties in the way of mastering the time in any troublesome piece of music is that the attention is naturally distracted by the actual mechanism of playing. But there is one most valuable way of practice in which the whole attention can be given to the time study. In this you do not play at all, but simply tap out the time with your fingers.

Spread the music on your knee, with right hand lying on the page, fingers in readiness for tapping.

Count aloud. For every note tap a finger down, preferably under the printed note, and keep the finger down for the exact duration of the note. Mark accents by emphasis in the taps. For a group of rapid notes use several fingers, as if you were a pianist. Tests should be marked by the raising of the finger tip.

It is helpful with tied notes or syncopated bars to give a sharp pressure to the finger to keep in your mind where the unmarked beats fall. If, for instance, in waltz time the third crotchet is tied to the first crotchet of the succeeding bar, make a sharp pressure of the finger on this first beat so that you are reminded of the rhythm, although the finger does not lift and drive down afresh.

Another thing that bothers many learners is the fitting in of groups of notes on single beats. You will be greatly helped in judging the subdivision, so that the speed of your small notes is right, if you tap them out with a group of fingers. Do plenty of practice—with twos, threes, fours, and then with larger numbers and uneven or compound groups. Consider a five as a slightly slow three with a slightly fast two; a six as two triplets; a seven as a four and a three—and so on.

Repeats.—*Repeats* often cause much trouble to the amateur. They need not.

First make yourself familiar with the common terms associated with musical repetitions.

Da—from.

Al, alla—to the.

Dal—from the.

Capo—head, beginning of piece.

Fine—end.

Segno—sign, usually written **$**.

Poi—then.

Coda, ⊕—tail, concluding movement, and sign which marks it.

E—and.

Ripetizione—repetition.

Senza—without.

1st. 1—bar to be played with first performance of movement.

2nd. 2—bar to be played with second performance of movement.

In very simple solos few repeat signs occur, except perhaps a few double dots between the lines as indicated on p. 439. In sonatas, selections, overtures, and compositions of regular classic form, the repeats are a little more varied but generally straightforward. It is especially in orchestral music that the full complications are met with—the sort of music in which economy of space is important and so printing is reduced to a minimum. It is when the novice begins to meet phrases like "*dal segno senza ripetizione e poi alla coda*" (from the sign, without repeat, and then to the coda) that some real understanding is needed.

An ordinary sort of waltz, in an orchestral edition, is very commonly arranged in the following manner:

An introduction opens, leading up to a double-bar, over which a **$**, and after which come two or four dots, placed vertically in the spaces of the stave. At the end of, probably, thirty-two bars occurs another double-bar preceded by a similar two or four

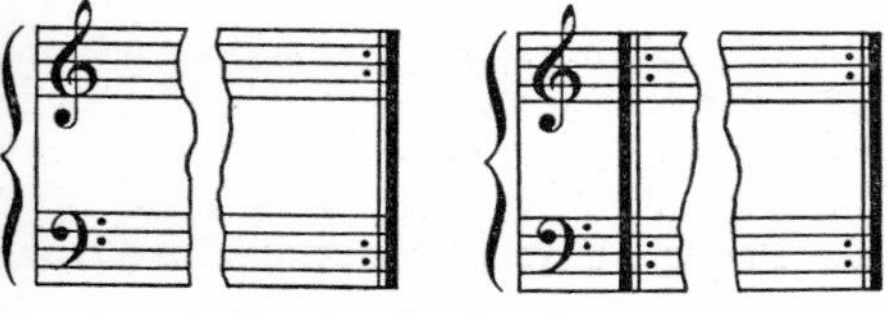

Fig. 1.—Repeat Signs

dots. These signify that the movement is to be repeated from the previous dots. But over the thirty-first and thirty-second bars is a straight line with 1 or 1st marked. The measures under this line are called the "first-time bars." At the repetition of the movement the "first-time bars" are omitted, and the player jumps to the "second-time bars," which follow the double-bar. Now comes a straight stretch, unrepeated, in which a certain sign is passed, marked "to ⊕," but this should be ignored as yet; and then the Trio is reached.

The Trio probably has one or two movements which may or may not be repeated, but at the end of it is D.S. or *Dal Segno* or just **$**.

You must now recommence, without loss of time, at **$**, which was near the beginning; this repeating of the whole composition is often called the *Da Capo*. In a *Da Capo* no repeats are taken, so that all first-time bars will be omitted, and you will play through until *Coda* ⊕ is reached. From here you jump directly to the *Coda*, usually marked ⊕. This is the final movement of the composition, and leads directly to *Fine*, or "the end"—often indicated by a pause written over a double-bar.

When there is no introduction to a piece *Da Capo al Fine* may take the place of *Dal Segno e poi alla Coda*. This means that you will go right back to the beginning and play through without repeats until *Fine* is reached.

Occasionally a "last-time" bar follows the "second-time" bars—this will be understood as *Fine*, and will be played only in the final repetition.

Practice.—It is a mistake to practise too long without a break. If you are playing for four hours, it is advisable to take five minutes off each hour. But one hour is not too long for concentrated work—many dabblers at music get tired after much less. If you have only sixty minutes available pack every second with effort.

As a rule it is good to get through the least attractive part of your work first. Few people, for instance, are much in love with diminished sevenths—very well, get through those first. Similarly, you may be none too fond of chromatic progressions. But vary the order of your practice, so that it seems always fresh—and vary the type of work you are doing too. Variety is tremendously important in maintaining interest, and without interest practice may be so much waste of time. You can freshen things by changing the hours of your playing, from evening to morning, or from one long spell into several shorter ones.

Do not make the mistake of thinking that you are studying a piece when you are merely playing it through. You may go straight through it a dozen times and be little the better—especially at those one or two bars where you always stumble. You should work harder at the more difficult places, giving them much more time than the passages which run smoothly. Obviously, if one section is bristling with difficulties the effect you make when you play the whole piece will depend almost entirely on that passage.

In the case of a study the germ of the whole thing is often contained in just a few bars, and it is helpful to concentrate on these until the particular bit of technique embodied in the study is in some degree mastered by the constant repetition. After that the full composition may be tackled.

If you are having lessons make a note of all problems that crop up during home practice, so that they can be brought up when next you see your teacher.

Be regular. A half-hour every day is much more beneficial than two or three hours sometimes. And even a half-hour can achieve a great deal if it is used honestly and strenuously day after day.

During your practice period, when you are supposed to be playing, see that you really do play. Do not be side-tracked by any alluring little excursions into matters of theory, or musical history, or anything of that sort. Keep your fingers working every minute.

Do not despise scales and arpeggi; on the other hand, do not worship them. Remember that they have no value in themselves, but are the means to an end. They are a gymnasium for the fingers or voice.

But do not imagine that when you have done a few major scales that you have made full use of the gymnasium. Remember there are chromatic scales, harmonic and melodic minors, scales in thirds, sixths, octaves, tenths, and in double thirds, most of them to be played, by the pianist, in similar and contrary motion. Then there is the twin world of the arpeggio with its major and minor triads, its dominant and diminished sevenths, and its almost numberless inversions. All have their special uses.

One great value of the scale and arpeggio is that it allows full attention to be given to special points of technique—like playing *staccato*, *saltato*, *martellato*, *legato*, *spiccato*. In addition, they give familiarity with keys, and help to make the fingers work smoothly through long, swift runs. (*See also* PIANO PLAYING, SINGING AND OTHER MUSICAL ARTICLES.)

NATURE STUDY

THE study of British Wild Animals is one which, in these days of cheap transport, must commend itself as a hobby to those who need something inexpensive, interesting, and inexhaustible. It is cheap, because the beginner needs nothing but his eyes, and a note-book and pencil for jottings and rough sketches, field glasses and a camera can be added later: it is vitally interesting because it is a study of individuals in whose lives so many human parallels may be seen, and it is inexhaustible because each day brings new facts to light. Anybody can add to the sum total of our knowledge of the wild.

The first thing to do is to learn something of the appearance, homes, and habits of our wild animals; then you can apply that knowledge to interpret the signs of their existence in the countryside: you may then build up your own histories of the wild folk, for, although the main habits of individuals are characteristic of the race, localities make a difference to individual behaviour.

It will be easier for the beginner, and more helpful to the older naturalist to divide the countryside into: *Woods and their Outskirts*, *Fields*, *Forests*, *Moors and Dry Highlands*, *The River Bank*, and consider the types of wild life found in each.

Apart from the little apparatus necessary, there are several general rules to be observed. Go alone to study Nature, the quieter you are the more you will see. If you have a companion don't talk more than necessary. A walk through a wood or along a field's edge is enough to start a train of investigation—a trail of feathers or a rabbit runway followed up usually leads to some place where an observation stand may be taken, and the rest of the story found out. Some of the most interesting glimpses into the life of the wild are obtained by chance, when the naturalist is keeping his eyes and ears open.

Taking Cover.—The secret of taking cover when studying wild animals is to do so in such a way that the outlines of trees, bushes, etc., with which they are familiar remain unchanged. Do not therefore stand behind rocks or trees and peer round them at the spot you wish to watch; stand flat against them facing the place you are observing. Again, however, you will spoil your chances if you dress in blue or black, or any bright colour, as you will show up against the background. Greeny-grey tweeds or grey flannels are by far the best wear as they fit in with most backgrounds.

If there is a convenient bush use that as your cover, but if not, lying flat on the ground is quite satisfactory, and discomfort may be minimized by digging out a shallow depression to take your hip bone. It is quite useful to cover yourself with bracken, branches, hay or heather when lying thus.

When watching in the open and you have to move a limb do so smoothly and slowly. There must be no smoking, and you must bear insect bites. Anti-sting lotions usually smell so strongly that they will keep the animals as well as the insects away. A high-necked jersey, or a muffler, gauntlet gloves, a cycling helmet and very thick stockings will protect you from them.

Travel towards your observation point and take cover with the wind coming towards you, so that the animals have no warning of your intentions.

In the winter when further observation is possible in woods bare of leafy undergrowth, guard against cold, wet feet. Well dubbined boots and leather gaiters, or shooting stockings over woollen socks are the greatest help.

The Various "Seasons"—hunting, shooting, etc.—offer opportunities to the naturalist for unexpected sights of the wild. Cub-hunting begins in August, and grouse shooting on the twelfth; partridge shooting on the first of September; pheasant shooting on the first of October, and beagling the same month; fox-hunting begins in November; the last two continuing till April. In February, when the shooting seasons are over, the keeper goes ferreting.

A good time for observation is at sunrise and sunset, as animals are either going out, or returning from feeding. But often the best view of an animal comes by chance during the day and signs which, rightly interpreted, will add much to your knowledge, must be looked for at any hour of the day or night.

Make friends with a keeper, both for what he can tell and show you, and because so many of the best woods are private. Though the law of trespass says that damage must be proved for a successful prosecution, flattening down grass blades can technically be called damage. Leave all gates as you find them, unless this is obviously wrong, i.e. in the case of pastures where animals are grazing.

WOODS AND THEIR OUTSKIRTS

Foxes. — The fox earth is chiefly found in a mixed oak or pine wood. It often opens in a tangled thicket, and one with a patch of level ground before it is chosen by the vixen for her earth. The cubs are born in April and can be seen at the den mouth at sunrise and sunset soon after their eyes are open, i.e. in 15–20 days. The vixen and the dog-fox hunt for them, bringing frogs, mice, birds and rabbits as soon as they can eat. The dried remains of these found at the den mouth in early summer tell of an occupied earth. Take cover nearly an hour before sunset and you will see the cubs come out and play like kittens with these remains. The mother will be hiding near them.

In summer the fox often lies out in the undergrowth and then you may start him. Foxes often have a regular hunting plan, searching definite bushes, ditches and spinneys in turn. They hate getting their feet wet, so a fallen log or a shooters' bridge is used for crossing wide streams. On February nights you may hear the dog-fox uttering a series of dog-like yaps, and the vixen's blood curdling screams in reply.

Squirrels.—The American grey squirrel has almost exterminated the English red squirrel in the woods in and around the Home Counties. The habits of both are similar, but the former is the greater egg stealer.

Look for squirrels in mixed woods and particularly pine plantations. Cones stripped of their scales, empty hazel nut, acorn and beechmast shells tell of squirrels nearby. They only come to the ground in search of food, and do all their travelling from place to place through the tree-tops.

Look for their nests or dreys in winter, when the large structures of dried, leafed branches, built in the crotch of an oak, tell of winter nests. Squirrels sleep in these or in hollow trees during the cold weather, coming to ground to visit one of their stores of nuts and seeds on mild days. These are often in tree stumps. They also bury acorns and nuts where they find them, scratching there weeks later, when food is scarce. The four young are born in June on a nest of leaves and moss in a hollow tree.

Dormice.—Strong claws, bulging eyes and a furry tail, show that the dormouse is not of the mouse family: he comes between the mice and the squirrels. You must watch for him at sunset when he comes out in search of nuts, acorns and seeds. He sleeps by day in a round nest of twigs and moss hung in rose or honeysuckle bushes.

The blond, naked young are born in a larger but similar nest in May. The dormouse hibernates in winter and fattens in autumn. His chief food is hazel nuts. All winter he sleeps in a hole in a bank or tree.

Stoats and Weasels. — The long, thin-bodied weasel is often confused with the stoat, for they are both sandy-coloured, with light underparts and flat heads; but the stoat is the larger and has a black-tipped tail. They both hunt by scent, searching the woodside and wayside ditches, and often cross the road when on the prowl. Owing to their difference in size, the stoat tracks rabbits, even in the burrows, and also game birds; but the weasel chiefly uses the mice runs which intercross the fields and woods' edge, killing the inhabitants in hundreds; and haunts the hedges after small birds.

The stoat steals game birds' eggs, and often has a hidden store of food. Frogs, worms, and eggs hidden in a hollow tree belong to him. Where the rabbits feed at dawn you may see a stoat steal out of the bushes and attract their attention by jumping and frisking. The fascinated rabbits do not move until the stoat has pounced on one of them, and sunk its teeth behind the ears. This neck bite may be seen on the bodies of rabbits otherwise whole, for the stoat often kills for fun, and leaves his prey uneaten.

The stoat, with the dead rabbit in his teeth, will make for cover in a series of short rushes. Follow it if you can for it is probably on its way to its nest of grass and leaves in a wall or tree stump, where the April-born young await it. The young, of which there is one litter a year, soon hunt with the old ones.

Weasels choose sunny banks in which to build their grass nests. They have litters during the summer, and the mother plays with the young like a cat with its kittens.

Hedgehogs. — Hedgehogs are insect eaters, and are to be found searching for worms, slugs and snails in ditches along woods and copses but, according to the part of the country where they are found, they also eat birds and their eggs, rabbits, and rats. They take young rabbits out of the nests, and grown ones out of snares, though if you find the remains in the latter is a skin turned inside out, it is the work of a badger.

Go with a torch at night to the wood's edge, or stream, to look for hedgehogs. Usually they will continue their insect hunt unconcerned if the light is not too bright. Four to eight young are born in spring and in autumn. The nest is in the undergrowth, and though you can hear the family moving among the leaves, you can rarely see the young before they are three weeks' old. Their spines are first white and soft, then barred with grey, and finally, dry and brittle.

Bank Voles.—This chestnut-coloured vole is about 3 in. long with a bristly tail, and large ears. His runs are found in woodside and wayside banks in certain districts. The mother often uses an old bird's nest instead of making one of grass and feathers, for her litters. About six young are born, both blind and naked.

Snakes.—The only snake found in the woods is the harmless grass snake. It is greeny brown, about a yard long, and sometimes has a yellow ring round its neck. It can swim, and feeds on frogs and newts. It hibernates, and in spring lays numerous parchment-covered eggs, which take nine weeks to hatch, in manure and rubbish.

FIELDS

Hares and Rabbits.—Though hares and rabbits may be classed as field dwellers, there are many rabbit warrens found in woods where the soil is sandy. Keepers of young plantations wire against rabbits because they bark the young trees and so destroy them. Hares do not frequent woods; they prefer fields of tussocky grass, root-crops, or scrubland.

The habits of hares and rabbits differ far more than their appearance, though at near view the larger sandy body, powerful hind legs and black ear-tips of the hare are evident. A hare lives a solitary life, the rabbit a communal one; the former's home is above ground, the latter's below. A hare depends upon its speed to save it from its enemies, a rabbit depends on bolting to a hole. Both are rodents, feeding on grass, clover, root crops, garden vegetables and the bark of trees. Pine and larch branches, blown or cut down in winter, are stripped of their bark in a night by hungry rabbits.

Fig. 1.—Harvest Mouse

Fig. 2.—House Mouse

Fig. 3.—Field Mouse

Warrens, long established, or just begun, are easily found on sandy soil. From them hundreds of tracks lead to the feeding grounds. You may watch them going out at dusk or dawn, led by an old doe, nibbling their way along these runways towards the turnip and clover fields. When rain is coming at night the rabbits will feed during the day.

From March to September the mother rabbits dig shafts away from the warren, ending in a round nursery for each litter. The naked, blind babies lie on a nest of grass, and fur pulled from the doe. When she leaves them she stamps down the earth at the end of the shaft, making a "stop" against stoats. Hedgehogs will dig out the shaft, but a badger, smelling the young from above, digs straight down from the surface.

Leverets are born in an open "form." Any slightly hollow spot in the bracken or coarse grass, such as the hare sleeps in, serves. No track leads direct to it as the hare leaps the last few yards when reaching and leaving it. The leverets are born with fur and open eyes. In a few days each is moved to its own form, and directly they can feed on grass the mother ceases to visit them. You can put up a hare in autumn in fields of kale or root crops; and on March nights when the moon is full, jack hares may be seen boxing and wrestling together on high ground.

Moles.—The mole is an insect eater and spends a great deal of time underground. Certain pastures are honeycombed with mole runs and the "hills" which he heaves up as he tunnels after grubs, worms and snails.

A mole emerges from a hill and hunts for a while above ground, and if you watch a mole-ridden pasture in autumn, when they are more than usually active, you may catch sight of him. You can watch his progress across the field by the succession of hills which arise. A mole eats about every two hours, and he tunnels to eat. One tunnel always leads to water. He uses his snout and pink forepaws to dig, pushing up the accumulated earth every so often with his back. The actual home is under a large heap, protected by a bush or thicket; and in a smaller chamber the mother makes a grass nest for the three to seven blind babies in spring.

Mice.—The house mouse, the harvest mouse and the long-tailed field mouse are to be found in the fields. The house mouse is easily seen round corn ricks and farm

Fig. 4.—Shrew

buildings, the harvest mouse in cornfields' and the field mouse in hedges. In the country the house mouse feeds chiefly on grain, the kernels of fruit stones, and seeds. If you find gnawed remains of rose or hawthorn seeds beneath a bush, it is the work of these mice. The harvest mouse climbs the corn stalks after the ears of wheat and barley, but the field mouse climbs trees after nuts and berries as the sun sets; he digs for the bulbs of spring flowers, too.

The house mouse makes a straw nest in the country, in any odd corner, and as many as twelve young are born at a time. Although the adult harvest mice live and hibernate in burrows under the fields, the half-dozen young are born in a round grass nest woven round the corn stalks. The field mouse hibernates too, but in a burrow under roots of trees, where the young are born in grass nests.

Shrews.—Shrews are often mistaken for mice, but the long, thin snout, dark coat, pinky tail, and musky scent mark them out from the mice. Though cats and dogs will kill shrews, this scent stops the animals from eating their catch.

Unlike mice, shrews are insect eaters; they like caterpillars which they climb plants to catch; and insects which hide under burdocks and other broad-leaved plants. It is possible to watch them feeding, as they are short-sighted; but at the least movement on your part, they will rapidly dig themselves in. The young are born in round nests of grass set in hedges, but the side entrance marks these out from the entirely closed nests of dormice. In September many dead shrews may be seen on paths and in the grass, but there is no explanation as yet of this yearly happening.

Voles.—The animal with the short muzzle, stumpy body and tiny ears which gnaws the grass roots in the pastures, and eats off the young shoots and leaves, is not a mouse, but the field vole. His habit of biting through any root in his way as he tunnels is destructive to pasture; and as there are numerous families each year, born in moss nests set on the ground, this vole is a pest to the farmer. Small runways found in the long grass belong to him too, though they are probably used by the mice as well.

Bats.—You can see bats flittering over the fields at dusk, or hanging down from the rafters in outbuildings during the day, suspended by their hind legs. There are twelve kinds of British bats, and they are all insect eaters. They catch insects while on the wing, their sharply toothed mouths making an effective trap. Like the swallows they do not eat each insect immediately, but instead of keeping it in their mouths, they tuck it into a kind of pocket between their legs. When you see bats pausing in flight this is what they are doing.

The hearing and sight of bats are good, but they are helped in flight by sensitive hairs on their wing tips and muzzles which, when touching any object, warn the bat to steer clear of it. Bats hibernate during the winter in barns and church towers.

FORESTS

Deer.—There are three kinds of British deer, the red deer, which is the largest, the fallow deer, and the roe deer, which is the smallest of the three. The red deer roams the Scottish Highlands and the open lands of Devon and Somerset; fallow deer may be seen in Richmond Park and Epping Forest; while Scotch woods or the New Forest

Fig. 5.—A typical Badger's Sett

must be visited for a sight of the roe deer, which, unlike the two others, roam in families and not in herds. Besides the difference in size, the main difference between the deer is their antlers.

In each case it is the males only which are antlered. The red stag's horns are large with many branches, those of the fallow deer are flattened and widely curved, and the roe deer has straight three-pointed ones. The red and the fallow male deer show the beginning of antlers in the form of knobs at the age of one year; during their second year they both grow one branched antler, the red male being called a *brocket*, and the fallow male a *pricket*. At this age the roe deer grows knobs. Up to the fifth year the antlers of each type grow more branched, the red deer becoming a *stag royal* when he has three points on the top of his antlers. The roe deer's antlers never have more than three branches. Each year the antlers are shed in some solitary place in March, growing to their characteristic lengths during the summer.

The does all have their young in the deepest thickets hidden away from the males, though when the fawns are about a month old they may be seen with their mothers in the usual feeding grounds. Besides grass, deer like horse-chestnuts, acorns and tree shoots.

The Badger.—Though badger setts are found in woods, they are more numerous in the forests. The badger, with its yellowish grey coat and striped face, is definitely a creature of the night, sleeping by day underground in one of the many passages of the sett. It has been seen abroad by day and does sleep in the sun at the sett mouth on a bed of grass, but he disappears instantly at any strange sound.

The best way to see him is to find and watch an occupied sett. Its large opening in a thicket or in a tree's roots is marked by the presence of some of its grey hairs sticking to the walls, and by the nearby heaps of bracken and grasses, its discarded bedding. These heaps are large in spring and autumn, at which seasons he gives a thorough cleaning to the home. Take up your position behind convenient cover in the early evening. You must wait till dark, and even then you may only hear them go out, so well do their striped faces and dark bodies blend with the background.

Fig. 6.—Red Deer

Fig. 7.—Roe Deer

Fig. 8.—Fallow Deer

The cubs are born in early April, and come to the sett mouth several times before they are taken out by their mother to hunt woodlice under the bark of rotten logs, and to dig bluebell roots in the glades. Robbing rabbit stops and vole burrows comes later.

HEATHS, MOORS AND DRY HIGHLANDS

Reptiles.—Although foxes, hares, etc., may be seen in these districts, bird and reptile life is more prolific. Here are found the adder (our only poisonous snake), the smooth snake, the slow worm, and the common and sand lizard.

The adder's two-foot body is thick, brownish-black with a wavy line down its spine, and its small flat head has a V-shaped black mark on it. Adders feed on mice, shrews, voles, newts, frogs and slugs. In winter it hibernates under the heath, or in an old bird's nest. Unlike the grass snake, the mother lays her eggs in August and they hatch immediately. The young are 6 in. long.

The smooth snake, rather like a grass snake, only smaller, is reddish brown and darkly spotted, with a dark head. Underneath it is reddish, grey, or orange. It is very fond of mice and sand lizards, and pounces almost like an animal on its prey. This mother also lays eggs on the point of hatching, in August; the young are light brown above and blue beneath. The bite of this snake is not poisonous.

The slow worm is really a lizard without legs, and he leaves his tail in his captor's hands, as a lizard does. It is perfectly harmless. Numbers may be found together under stones on dry, sandy heaths. They are about 15 in. long, and have small eyes and hooked teeth. The young, born late in summer, are about 2 in. long. Slow worms often hibernate under stones in companies.

The female common lizard is about 7 in. long and is bigger than the male. They are both reddish brown above, but the male is orange underneath and the female yellowish green. Unlike snakes, lizards have eyelids and sleep with them closed; but they do lay eggs on the point of hatching. The black, 2 in. young can look after themselves from birth. Lizards can climb heather stems in search of insects, but move in a glide when on the ground.

The sand lizard is larger, sandy in colour, with striped back and sides, and pale green under-parts. They are found chiefly in Dorset, Surrey and Hampshire.

THE RIVER BANK

Otters.—Otters frequent certain rivers, ponds and lakes. Otters travel ceaselessly from one stretch of water to another, except when bringing up their young. Although they hunt chiefly by night, you may see them in the daytime on lonely river banks. A trout or salmon with one bite out of the shoulder lying on the grass tells of the passage of an otter. He seizes moorhens from under water by the legs, and eels he loves. In periods of drought otters often travel miles overland in search of well-stocked pools.

Some otters are born in sea caves, travelling up the rivers when they can swim well; and it is a saying that otters always return to the sea to die. Inland, the mother breeds in a riverside holt, i.e. an old drain or a hollow in the tree roots, with an under-water entrance. The young have to be taught to swim and dive and fish by their parents; you may see them on summer nights, guessing their exact whereabouts by their soft whistle.

Rats and Water Voles.—Each spring the brown rats leave the farm buildings where they have wintered and travel down to the river banks. They drive away countless water voles from their riverside tunnels and live there themselves, the voles retreating chiefly inland. Hence we get the mistaken term "water rat." The rat you see swimming in the streams in

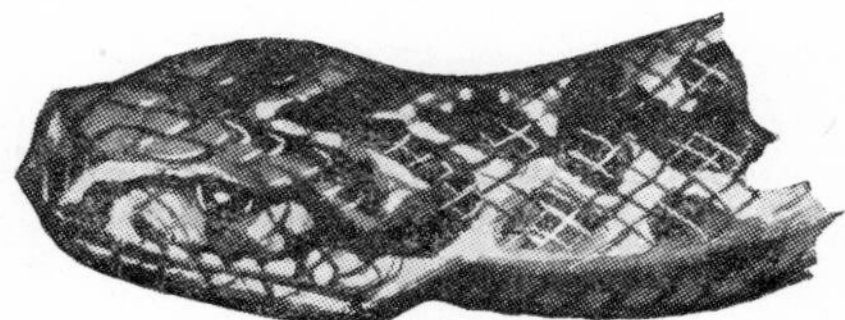

Fig. 9.—Adder

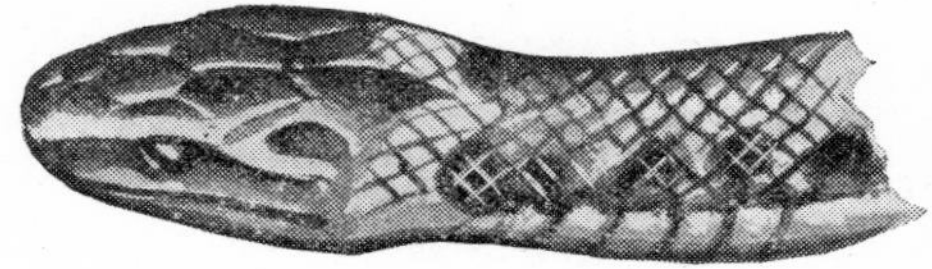

Fig. 10.—Smooth Snake

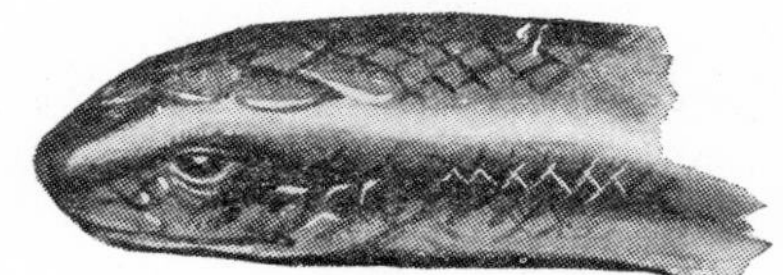

Fig. 11.—Slow Worm

summer is the brown land rat. The young birds, eggs, young mice and voles and rabbits have brought him and his kind out of their winter quarters in pursuit of different diet.

Very little observation is necessary to determine whether it is a brown rat or a water vole you see on the bank's edge. A rat has a pointed snout and ears, and a long scaly tail; a water vole is plumper, with round head, ears and snout, and he has a hairy tail. Their habits too are different. The water vole is a vegetarian, living on leaves, bark, and the succulent stems of rushes and flags; the rat is omnivorous. The vole journeys always by water when possible, the rat runs along the bank.

OUTDOOR GAMES

WHAT shall we play? The question is always arising, not only with children during their holidays, but with grown-ups too—in camp, garden, or party on the sea-shore, or at a picnic.

In the following pages are described all sorts of less formal games, which can be enjoyed by mixed groups of almost any age, and with no preliminary experience. They are such that adaptations of numbers and methods can be used whenever necessary—and if equipment is needed it can be readily improvised.

Human Croquet is a placid sort of game but it can give scope for a good deal of skill; and a large number of players can take part. It is played after the manner of ordinary croquet—though mallets, balls, and hoops, of wood and iron, are not required.

Pairs of players form the *hoops*, by standing face to face with hands clasped high in the air. Then there are the *players*, who are active in the game, not passive like the hoops. Finally there are the *balls*—blindfolded people, one allotted to each player.

To begin, the first *player* puts his *ball* facing the desired *hoop*, and says "Go!" The *ball* then trots forward until "Stop!" is called. If he succeeds in going through the *hoop* another "stroke" is allowed to his *player*; if not the second *player* takes his turn. If one *ball* collides with another it is awarded an extra stroke.

The winner, of course, is the *player* who first gets his *ball* round through all the *hoops* in proper order. A hoop must be passed from the proper side; if a *ball* runs by it must naturally be brought back to negotiate the *hoop*.

It is not necessary for *hoops* to remain with hands clasped high in the air throughout the game—they need only take up the position when the *ball* is actually playing to them.

Pebble Chase.—If a pebble is not available then a button, marble, or any similar small object may be used.

The players form a large ring, each standing with his hands in front of him, palms pressed flatly together—the forearms are thus jutting out horizontally from the body.

One player stands at the middle, his hands stretched similarly to the front, but between his palms he holds the pebble—it is, of course, so small that it makes no perceptible difference to the hands.

This middle player goes round to each other person in turn, and places his hands momentarily between the flat palms of the others—these palms open at the top to allow the entry, and close again immediately the visiting hands are lifted.

Nothing happens in nearly every instance. But in one pair of hands, however, the pebble is dropped. The player receiving it tries to give no clue either by expression or movement of hands. His aim is, when the first player has completed the full round and returned to the middle, to dash in and to give back the pebble before being touched by any other player.

Of course, everyone standing round is looking suspiciously at everyone else. It is even permitted to run and touch a suspected player at any time, and if the suspected one has the pebble he may flee and still try to get back to the centre man. This latter must never go to meet an incoming player, when one is dashing towards him he must always stand still with waiting palms.

When the centre man has completed his round and returned to the middle the one who has the pebble is not allowed to pause, but must dash at once to the centre. If he is wise he will take the shortest route—for the whole ring of players will be in pursuit of him. If he fails to move promptly the centre man may count three and disqualify him—either compelling him to drop out of the game, or to become centre man himself.

Bottle Ball is planned on the same general lines as football and can be equally strenuous. Have a moderate sized "field."

Fig. 1.—Leg Cricket

Instead of a goal at each end stand up a bottle, and round it mark a circle with a radius of 3 yards—if you have no bottle an Indian club, a stick lightly pressed into the ground, or anything that can be knocked over easily will serve.

Teams of six to twelve players take part. The object of each is to knock over the bottle of the opponent—this counts as a goal, and after it the ball is centred afresh.

Use a large ball, and allow handling only, no kicking. The ball must always be thrown from the point where it was caught, the player must not run along carrying it.

No player is allowed within the circles. You may permit tackling, in rugger fashion, if you think it desirable. There is no reason why the bottle should be broken, but remember not to leave the bottle or any broken glass where it may be a source of inconvenience to anyone else.

Punch Ball.—Use a football, not too tightly inflated, or one of those large, reinforced rubber bladders for this. A "net" is needed, but it can be improvised by a length of string, or even a row of deck chairs. If you use string, thread a few pieces of paper on to make it more conspicuous, or hang one or two jackets over it. Have the net 5 or 6 ft. high. Mark out court boundaries, something like tennis size—just a stone or stick at each corner will serve.

About four players should be each side of the net. Play goes on in the same general manner as tennis, except that the ball must be punched or hit with the fist.

Serve by a punch from the back corners. Handling or catching of the ball is not allowed.

Tyre Toss.—Lay an old motor tyre flat in the middle of the "field." The half-dozen or so players who take part stand round at equal distances, about 20 ft. from the tyre.

The game consists in tossing bean bags, pebbles, balls, into the tyre—even stones or bits of stick will serve.

Each player tries in turn, and every successful throw gains 2 points. *Game* is 11 points. If a bean bag drops and stays on the tyre itself, without touching the ground, it scores one point. And if such a bag is knocked into the tyre by a succeeding throw then the player who knocks the bag in gains the extra point. By having partners in the game players may often help each other.

Leg Cricket.—This very popular and strenuous game, which has different names in various parts of the country, requires a fair amount of space. It yields most fun when about a dozen players are taking part.

One person is the *batsman*. He stands at the centre, with feet together, holding a stick with which to protect his legs. A tennis racket will serve if it is gripped by the sides and held upside down so that the handle can be used as a stick. The rest of the players stand round in a fairly large ring. It is their object to hit the legs of the batsman with a tennis ball.

All the players must retain their positions while the throwing is on. Anyone getting the ball can throw it, and the person at the centre makes a stroke whenever he gets the chance, in this manner warding off the ball from his legs. He must not move otherwise than to turn about with his feet together so that he can always face the opponent—indeed, if the odds seem too much in his favour, he may be forbidden even to move at all.

When his legs are touched he drops the stick, and the one who hit him must dash to the middle and take his place. The new batsman is open to be thrown at the instant that he snatches up the stick.

A small cricket bat can be used in another form of this game. Instead of being compelled to stay in one spot, he may run and dodge wherever he likes, and so protect himself as much by his agility in getting clear as by striking at the ball.

Peanut Hunt—Some preliminary preparation is needed for this. You will scatter a large number of peanuts about the ground hiding them in spots that are not too hard to find.

All the players will be divided into two teams, the *dogs* and the *cats*. Each team has a leader.

When the signal to start is given all set off to find the nuts. When a *dog* discovers one he sits up and barks until his leader comes and takes it from him. A *cat* miaows. Only the leaders are allowed to pick up the nuts.

The winning team is the one which discovers the larger number. It is generally advisable to let the leaders bring their nuts, as each is found, to some central point—perhaps to a *referee*.

Sackball.—As many sacks as there are players are needed for this, and a football or something similar.

A "goal" is fixed at each end of the "field"—it may be formed of two sticks, or a bucket or tub into which the ball must be dropped.

The general planning of the game is as in football, with teams, centring, and so on, but every player stands in a sack which is tied about his waist.

Kicking, handling, throwing—anything should be allowed that is fair play. The fewer rules you have the better.

There are few games which give more delight to spectators than sackball.

Three-legged Football is a rather similar game which can often be improvised more conveniently than sackball. Everyone has tried three-legged racing, but this football is less familiar.

Couples stand side by side with inside ankles tied in the usual way. The "field" should not be too large. About half a dozen couples in each team is quite suitable.

To get still more thrills handling may be allowed as well as kicking. The three-legged goalkeepers in particular are likely to have an exciting time.

Tree Ball.—A small tree, or post, which has clear flat ground around it is needed. To the base of it fasten a 10 or 15 yard length of cord or rope, to the other end of which you have secured a football.

Four players can take part, or just two at a time. One "side" tries to wind the cord round the tree in a clockwise direction and the other counter clockwise.

The players kick the ball whenever they have the chance, but must not handle it. A free kick is given to the opponent whenever a player becomes entangled with the cord.

The game continues until the cord is wound completely round and the ball thus comes to rest against the tree. Opposing players must stay on opposite sides of the tree so as not to interfere with each other

Triangular Tug of War is played by three people.

Three motor tyres are required. These are laid flat on the ground, so that they touch each other. The three players sit on them, with their feet towards the centre, and clasp hands so that they form a triangle. In this position they begin a tug of war. Anyone touching the ground with foot or body drops out. When the first has gone the two remaining players continue their struggle until a win is scored.

Tyre Quoit Race.—Motor tyres are needed for this game also, one for each competitor.

A number of posts are fixed in the ground at intervals around the "course."

The players start off in turn, tossing their tyres and endeavouring to encircle the first post, as in a game of quoits. Only one throw is allowed to each, then when all have gone each tosses again, and so on.

A player cannot go on to the second post until he has ringed the first.

In order to avoid confusion in taking turns, do not have too many players together.

Toeball.—This game is most suitable for the seaside, when you are sun-bathing after a swim. The equipment needed is a large ball—perhaps a football—to which is attached a 2 ft. length of cord. At the end of the cord make a loop.

Plan the game in competitive fashion. Each person lies flat on his back with his heel against a "starting mark." The cord loop is slipped over his toes, and the ball lies at full stretch beyond his foot. Now, the leg is kicked upwards and the ball is flung upwards and backwards over his head, the loop slipping freely from the toes as it goes. The person who sends the ball farthest is the winner.

To become an expert at this you must not only kick hard, but must be able to make the ball go straight. Point your toes as you kick so that they do not unintentionally catch the loop.

Pie Slicing is a game which children will enjoy at the sea. Two at a time should take part.

Turn up a bucket of damp sand so as to make a *pie*. Then two youngsters in turn begin to cut slices from it, with their spades. When the pie finally collapses the player who took the last slice loses the game. The best way of determining a collapse is by noting when the top itself breaks.

Both players should have the same sort of spade—an iron one is better than a wooden.

Spearing the Ring.—This is an ideal camp game.

The "ring" should be a small iron or wooden hoop, a tenikoit ring, or an old motor tyre. The "spear" is a stick or pole 5 or 6 ft. long.

Four or six players take part at a time.

Mark two lines down the course—the bowling line and the running line. They are about 20 ft. apart, and parallel.

Play starts from the head of the lines. The ring is rolled down the bowling line, hard and straight, by one player. At the same time the remaining players run one behind the other down the other line, carrying their spears.

The front player throws his spear first, endeavouring to get it through the ring. If he is unsuccessful he drops to the side and the second player takes a throw. If the second fails the third tries, and so on. Those who have not thrown keep running, of course, at the speed of the "ring."

The one who *spears* the ring bowls it for the next round, the person whom he replaces going to the rear of the running line. Each player who fails to score drops in turn also to the rear of the line.

A ring is considered to be *speared* if only the point of the stick goes through it.

Horseshoe Ringing is an interesting form of outdoor quoits.

Two or four players can take part, each being provided with a horsehoe. Use fairly light shoes. They can be purchased from a blacksmith for a few pence. Get him to knock the points down when you buy them.

A standard pitch is 40 ft. long, though you may do with less. At the end of it fix a strong stick or piece of iron pipe so that it stands 8 in. out of the ground. Around this mark two circles, one with a radius of 8 in. and another of 3 ft.

A throw is made by each player in turn. The object is to ring the peg. No horse-

Fig. 2.—Horseshoe Tossing

shoe may be picked up until all four have been sent down—with a pair of players there are two shoes for each.

Three points are won when the shoe encircles the peg—the test is whether the two ends of the horseshoe are far enough across to allow a straight stick to touch them both whilst being clear of the peg which is encircled. Two points are scored if the shoe falls within the 8 in. circle, without ringing the peg; and 1 point is for a shoe between the 8 in. and the 3 ft. circle.

Much skill is needed to play this game well. Grip the end of the horseshoe, and throw with a smooth sweep, rather like the underarm bowling of cricket. Of course, to score a *ringer* a horseshoe must reach the peg with its open ends forward. This means that the shoe has to revolve just the required amount. It is usual to make 1½ or 2½ spins in the air—the number depends on the length of the rink and the speed of the throw.

Should a horseshoe be knocked by a succeeding throw its score will be determined by the position it finally occupies.

Hole Ball.—You may dig a hole for this, about 9 in. square by 6 in. deep. Better still, sink a box of about this size, so that the bottom and sides are firm.

The game consists of rolling or bouncing tennis balls, from a distance of about 30 ft. so that they come to rest in the hole. One point is counted for each successful throw, and 11 points is "game." Additional interest is given if a post is fixed in the ground to one side of the box, and a yard or so from it. Balls can then "cannon," from the post. In this form of the game you may count 1 point when the post is hit, 2 for an ordinary throw into the box, and 3 when the ball arrives in the box "off" the post.

Tyre Tag.—Everyone knows the ordinary game of tag, in which *it* pursues the rest of the players until he touches or "tags" one. But now a number of motor tyres are needed. These are strewed about the ground, and any player is safe from being tagged while he stands inside a tyre. He must not stay in the tyre,

Fig. 3.—Human Croquet

however, but is allowed to jump inside only to escape being tagged. *It*, from a distance of 2 yards, may count any player out—if, by the time ten is counted, the one inside the tyre does not jump clear, he becomes *it*.

Balloon Tennis.—This can often be improvised, and can give plenty of fun. For the *net* you can use a fallen tree, a fence, a length of string, even a mark on the ground. Perhaps the best way of all, in suitable weather and dress, is to play it across a small stream.

Any number of players can take part, and the balloon is batted backwards and forwards, by hand, a point being scored each time that it goes outside the agreed boundaries, or falls to the ground. You should have a few spare balloons by in reserve.

Deck Chair Race.—You may arrange this as a contest for individuals, if you have enough chairs; or as a relay team race, when two chairs will suffice.

Lay the chairs flat on the ground, and start off the competitors from a suitable distance. Each runner must go down the course; lift and put up the chair in proper fashion; sit in it; fold it flat and replace it on the ground; and return to the starting point.

It is surprising how many people find deck chairs to be quite unmanageable things.

Shadow Tag is possible only when the sun is bright. It is on the lines of the familiar *tag*—but now *it* does not seek to touch another person — only the other's shadow. The game may even be complicated by insisting that *it's* shadow must touch the other shadow.

Players should spread apart well, so that their shadows do not become confused with each other. This game can be relied on to give plenty of fun, for it is extremely difficult to anticipate where your shadow is going to fall.

Pitch Pebble belongs naturally to the seaside. Dig a hole, or better still bury a bucket so that its mouth is flush with the surface of the ground. Then the leader must get a good handful of small pebbles and take up his place with the other players, about ten paces from the hole.

The complete handful of pebbles are tossed together to the hole. Those which go in the leader takes out and retains,

Fig. 4.—Pebble Chase

counting them as his score. The second player collects and tosses all that remain, and in turn picks up those that stay in the hole. The third does the same, and so on.

When all the pebbles are used the next round is started, the player who was second leading off with the original big handful, and the one who previously started now coming last. Continue until all have taken their turn to start a round, and then discover who has thrown most into the hole—it will be necessary to keep careful count if players are to remember their scores.

Shoe Race.—The ground must be dry and smooth for this, and your players must be in the right sort of rollicking mood.

All who are to compete take off their shoes and pile them into a jumbled heap at the end of the course. Then a straightforward race is started. Each person runs down to the pile and back again. But, arriving at the pile, the player's own shoes must be sorted out and put on.

Make sure that the winner has on his own footwear, and that laces or straps are properly fastened.

Hand Tennis.—This is a game that can be improvised on any fairly level piece of ground—a makeshift net and court have already been described. In addition you need only a ball. A tennis ball is unsuitable; something softer is required. A toy football, tightly inflated, suits most sorts of ground.

The game is played exactly like ordinary tennis, but the ball must be batted with the flat hand instead of with a racket. Remember that you can speed up the game by reducing the size of the court; your court measurements, in fact, should be determined by the character of the ground and the type of ball available. If desired, three or four players may take part on each side.

Outdoor Draughts necessitate some preparation, but when you have your equipment the game can be most interesting —to spectators as well as to players.

The "board" can be 6 ft. or 8 ft. square. It can be marked out with whiting on turf, or scratched on a hard stretch of sand. For draughts you can have tin lids, or pebbles. A fishing net or a long cane can be used for lifting or pushing the draughts from square to square; or you may have a magnet on a fishing line. There is endless scope for ingenuity in preparation of your equipment.

Players, of course, stand at their respective sides of the board, and the game proceeds in ordinary fashion.

Tyre Quoits.—A stout stick or peg must be driven into the ground, standing about 18 in. high. A motor tyre is bowled from a distance of about 10 yards in an endeavour to make it drop over this peg.

Three points are counted when the peg is encircled; two if the tyre comes to rest touching the peg but without encircling it; one if the tyre touches the peg but falls to the ground away from it.

Two or more players may take part, and you may have 11 or 21 points for a game.

Diabolo is a game which seems to have enduring popularity. It is centuries old, and yet enjoys a new vogue at fairly frequent intervals. Undoubtedly it is fascinating, and gives scope for much ability. One advantage of the game is that it can be played alone, and the equipment, which can be bought for even less than a shilling, is so small that it can be packed by any holiday-maker. There is scarcely a better place to practice than on a seashore where there are not too many people.

The main difficulty in diabolo is in starting. The knack of the thing lies in keeping your left hand still and whipping the right up and down, fairly close to the other. Increase the speed and vigour of your movements until the cone is humming strongly. If it is liable to tilt you may save it by pushing out or drawing in your stick.

Continue until you can toss and catch your spool; remember to keep your string taut when making a catch.

With a companion of equal ability you may have most interesting play by hurling your spool backwards and forwards, gradually increasing the distance between you.

Sprint Tug of War.—For this both rope and teams are exactly the same as in an ordinary tug-of-war bout. The rope, however, is not held at the beginning but is stretched out straight on the ground.

Each team then takes up its place about 20 yards from its respective end. When the

Fig. 5.—Rhubarb Race

word is given all sprint for the rope, and that team wins which first succeeds in getting the rope back to its own starting point. It is not allowed for any person to touch the half of the rope belonging to the opponents.

A good plan is to have your fastest runner at the front of the team so that he can get to the rope first. Generally the bout ends with quite an exciting tussle, for there is little opportunity for either team to get "set" in the ordinary way.

Tyre Wrestling. — Again two old motor tyres are needed. Put them flat on the ground and have one person standing in each of them. These two then come to grips, and wrestle in any fashion they like. The one who first compels his opponent to place his foot down outside the tyre becomes the winner.

With three tyres three wrestlers may take part similarly—all standing up to begin, with arms gripped together. The first to step outside his tyre is, of course, eliminated, and the two remaining wrestle to a final decision.

Rhubarb Race.—With the same two tyres a strenuous and comic race can be run. Three or four boys stand inside each tyre, holding it up about their waists. They are thus kept together in a tight bundle, like rhubarb sticks, and in this position they run the race. This game must be played on turf, for obvious reasons.

Duck Stone is a fine old game. It can be played almost anywhere, providing there is reasonable space, and the necessary stones or pebbles are available.

Each player must have a stone about the size of an orange. A much larger, flat stone is at the centre of the "field." This is called the *duck*. By it stands *it*, whose own stone rests on the *duck*.

The other players stand at the *home* line, which is marked across about 10 yards from the *duck*. From here they take turns to throw, trying to knock *its* stone from the *duck*. Having thrown, their aim is to fetch their own stones back *home* without being touched by *it*.

Anyone is liable to be tagged, or touched, once he has gone forward over the *home* line, unless he is standing with his foot touching his own stone.

Should *its* stone be knocked from the *duck* he must immediately replace it, and this gives players the chance to recover their own stones and to dash *home*. They have a chance also when *it* is pursuing any other player.

If *it* succeeds in catching a person the two change places.

When a player has picked up his stone he remains liable to capture until he gets across the home line. *It* can continue to pursue so long as his own stone does not fall from the *duck*; if it does he must return and replace it.

PAINTING

In painting, both in water-colours and in oils, as in sketching, the artist must be careful to let his eyes, rather than his brain, control his work. He knows, for instance, that all elm leaves are the same colour, that a flower pot is red, that the face of his model is creamy with pink cheeks, but, if he painted them in flat washes of colour, they would look wrong. Light plays a tremendously important part in painting, it gives gradations of colour which are not actualities, but which must be observed and reproduced by the artist whose picture is going to be any good. Shadows also vary greatly in tone and colour.

Side by side with the question of light is the question of contrast, of the ability of one colour to kill or enrich another. Yellows against blues, pinks against reds, blues against blacks or reds, greens against blues and browns, are contrasts to be experimented with. Brightness of a colour is not therefore always achieved by depth of colour, but by placing it against a colour which throws it up. Life and warmth exist in a picture to the extent of the colour contrasts, and pictures which look utterly lifeless can often be brought to a successful completion by judicious touches of colour.

Into these questions of light and contrasts comes again the question of shadows. Shadows are light and dark by comparison. When you are blocking in your shadows at the beginning do not be trapped into making dark shadows too dark, or the result will be heavy. Compare them with the darkest colour in the group, background, or landscape, and get their relative strength from that.

Water Colours.—Water-colour painting has much to recommend it as a hobby, for though water colours are not an easier medium to work with than oils, as is often supposed, they require little attention when not in use and are easier to mix, and to carry, when outdoor work is meditated.

Just as experiment in mediums was advisable in sketching, so experiment in mixing and the laying on of washes, can teach much which cannot be learned in any other way. There are, however, several main points which must be observed by all.

Buy the best artist's water colours you can afford. Cheap paints give a gritty and spotty surface when dry, and in two-colour mixtures this is very evident, for cheap colours do not combine, and give a dirty tint spotted with the two plain colours. It is better to get an empty japanned box and start with a few pans of colour, adding to it as time goes on, than to buy a ready fitted box of many inferior paints.

The following colours will be excellent for a start: Prussian Blue, Cobalt Blue, French Ultramarine, Burnt Sienna, Raw Umber, Light Red, Yellow Ochre, Aureolin, Gamboge, Alizarin Crimson, Viridian Green, Vermilion, Ivory Black.

Sable hair brushes are the best, but are expensive, and for the larger brushes camel hair will do very well. Nos. 5 and 7, in camel hair, and 3 and 4 in sable hair, are sufficient for a start.

The best paper is Whatmans', with a "not" surface, bought either in sheets which can be stretched on a drawing board, or on a block ready stretched. This last is the more convenient.

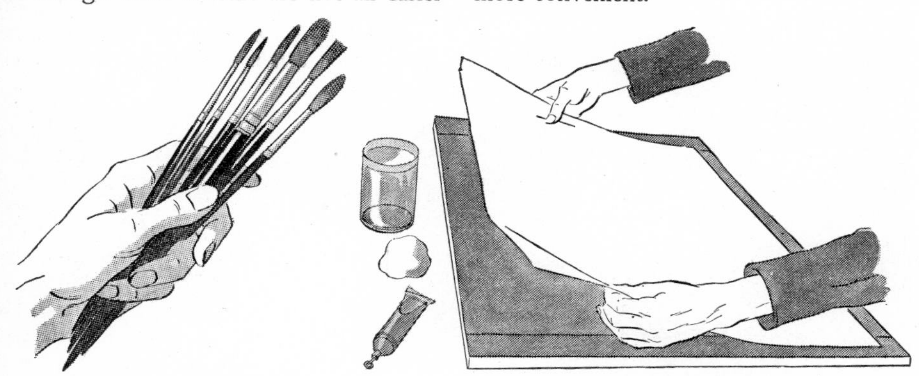

Fig. 1.—Water-colour Brushes

Fig. 2.—Stretch Paper

Before actually beginning to paint a picture, experiments must be made in laying flat and mixed washes. To do this successfully take the largest brush and wash the surface to be painted over with water. If you work with your block tilted or on an easel, the superfluous water will run to the bottom of the page, where it can be absorbed with clean blotting-paper. Having mixed enough of the required colour, start with a full brush while the paper is still moist, and draw it across the top of the area to be covered; then paint in horizontal lines, letting each stripe overlap the previous one a little. Use plenty of water, absorbing the residue of colour at the bottom with a clean and almost dry brush. Generally, water should be used plentifully while making a water-colour picture.

The mixing of two colours to obtain a

third can either be done on the picture or on the palette; the former often gives better results. In such cases the paper must be well washed with water, and the second colour laid on before the first has started to dry. Light Red or Brown Madder over Cobalt or Ultramarine, for skies or shadows; Yellows and Siennas over Blues for the production of Greens may be treated this way, always remembering to use the colder colour for the first wash, or the richness will be lost.

Care must be taken not to mix those colours which have an injurious effect on each other, one killing the other in time. Among such mixtures are Aureolin and Crimson Lake, and Emerald Green with Vermilion, also Alizarin Crimson with Ultramarine.

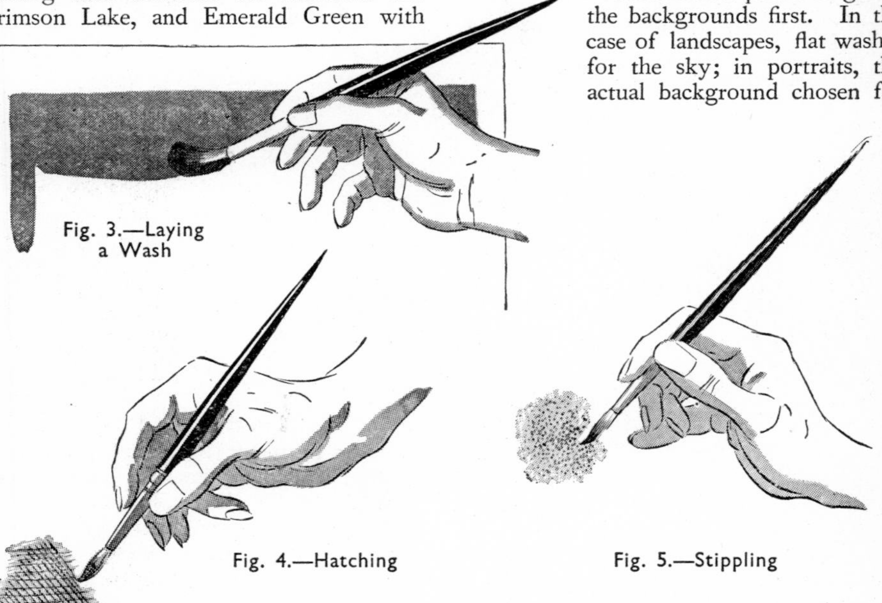

Fig. 3.—Laying a Wash

Fig. 4.—Hatching

Fig. 5.—Stippling

Two colours mix satisfactorily, and three sometimes. Often three, and always more than three, result in a mud colour, which is quite hopeless, so the artist must again experiment.

Another thing to be careful about is the use of fugitive colours, i.e. those which fade when subjected to ordinary exposure. For example, Prussian Blue is inclined to fade in the light, but seems to deepen again when kept in the dark; and Alizarin Crimson fades when used in light washes. Lists have been made of permanent, durable, and fugitive colours, and these may be consulted when doubt arises.

When you start painting a picture, sketch in lightly in pencil the group, figure, or landscape you have chosen. If you can work very lightly, the amount of lead on the paper will not smudge when washed over with water. Some sketches are strengthened by the pencil outline remaining visible, but should you wish otherwise, rub the paper with fine breadcrumbs, which will leave the lines just distinct enough to be seen.

Some artists prefer to get in the backgrounds first. In the case of landscapes, flat washes for the sky; in portraits, the actual background chosen for the model. In the latter case, it must be borne in mind that the arranged background must enrich and not detract from the colouring of your model. Try pinning sprays of flowers against various coloured cloths, and study the resultant colour schemes.

Treatment.—After the background is finished the shadows may be put in, flat washes of main colour laid on and, lastly, detail built up. Various effects may be obtained by stroking, i.e. short parallel lines of colour; hatching, i.e. long lines of different colours crossed at an angle;

spotting, i.e. spots of plain colour near together; or by stippling, which is done by tapping the surface with a fairly dry brush with a little dry colour on it. High lights are best obtained by washing out. Wash with water the dry, painted surface in which you require light; let it stay a moment, then blot with clean blotting-paper, repeating if necessary. Soften the edges by painting out the hard outlines with a moderately dry, clean brush. This softening of outline is necessary the whole time the picture is being built up. Finally, touches of colour are added to heighten contrasts, tiny washings out are done to lighten heavy blocks of colour, and any blurred outlines are tightened up.

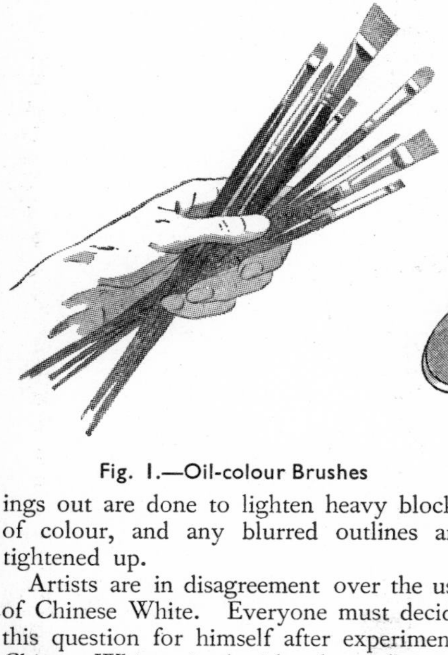

Fig. 1.—Oil-colour Brushes

Artists are in disagreement over the use of Chinese White. Everyone must decide this question for himself after experiment. Chinese White mixed with other colours is useful for getting misty distances, etc. Unlike other pigments, white is stronger when dry than when wet, so less should be used than seems necessary at the outset. White tends to kill the life in colours and makes them look cold, so that it is better left alone by the beginner.

Oil Painting.—Oil paint is not a very easy medium and much experiment is necessary to find the results that can be obtained by different ways of painting. Yet, because nearly all forms of pictorial beauty can be expressed successfully in this medium, and because the result is permanent, oil painting is a hobby to be considered seriously, although hard work is involved.

When one is first experimenting with methods of laying on paint, the less expensive colours are quite satisfactory. Later, when painting something whose permanence is of importance, best-quality paints must be used. White is used more than any other pigment, being frequently mixed with other colours. It is also used plain as an "undercoat" and therefore the best paint must be used. Both Flake and Zinc Whites are employed, the former drying more quickly than the latter, but needing to be varnished.

The Palette.—It must be realized that the fewer colours you have on your palette the cleaner and clearer will be your effects. It is better to start with just a few tubes of colour, and to obtain variety by mixing.

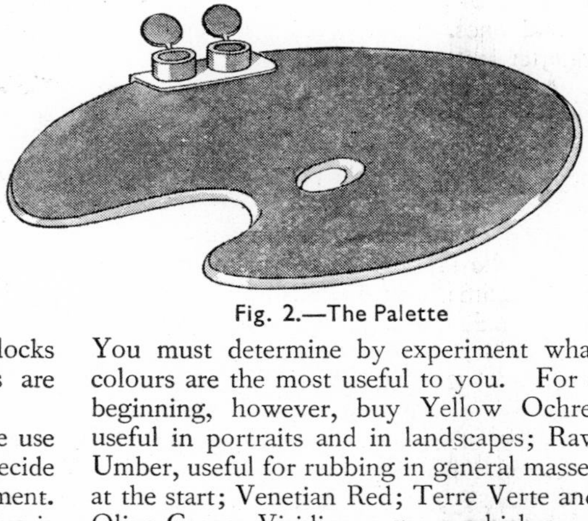

Fig. 2.—The Palette

You must determine by experiment what colours are the most useful to you. For a beginning, however, buy Yellow Ochre, useful in portraits and in landscapes; Raw Umber, useful for rubbing in general masses at the start; Venetian Red; Terre Verte and Olive Green; Viridian, a green which must be used with care; Lemon Chrome; Vermilion; Light Red; Burnt Sienna; Cobalt Blue; French Ultramarine; and Ivory Black.

Media.—Paints may be mixed with pure linseed oil, or a mixture of poppy oil and linseed. Some artists prefer to use only turpentine oil or medium-drying petroleum spirit; but here again experiment will decide for you. Both Copal and Amber oil varnishes are often used as mediums for thinning one's colours, but do not use them when intending to paint over that surface again as they dry hard, and painting on a slippery surface is most unsatisfactory. Mastic varnish is used to coat a finished picture in order to preserve it, but the final varnishing is a matter of taste.

When buying a palette on which to squeeze your paints, get one you can hold comfortably, and keep it clean. Each time after use the paint that is left should be taken off with a palette knife and put aside; then the whole palette can be cleaned with the knife and rag before the colour is returned to it. Always squeeze your colours on to your palette in the same order, not putting similar ones side by side, for fear of mistakes.

Buy the very best brushes, and keep them thoroughly clean with soap and water, though this takes longer than with turpentine. As it is best to paint with the largest brush possible for your subject, get long-haired flat brushes with rounded corners, as they are easier to handle than round ones. Half, five-eights, and three-quarter inch wide are the most useful sizes.

A medium-grained white canvas is best.

Treatment.—For backgrounds and for blocking-in the general masses of your picture, brush strokes should be in every direction and not straight up and down. Later, horizontal and vertical strokes can be used with the same effect as shading in a drawing. Do not hold the brush near the tip, and only dip the tip of it in the paint.

The easiest method of putting on paint is to rub in a thin tone with the flat of the brush. This is for backgrounds, and is one of many different methods. Colours may be mixed with white in varying quantities, according to the depth of tone required; or if preferred a thin coating of white may be put over the surface, allowed to dry a little, and then the main colour painted over it. Colours may also be glazed over a dry white coat, using a mixture of oil and turpentine with the paint. When painting out an unsatisfactory passage, always give it a thin white coat, and repaint over this dry. Outlines may be sharpened by a thin edging of the same colour in a deeper tone, or an edging of a different colour.

PAINTING ON WOOD AND GLASS

WOOD and glassware are much used in the home. The painted articles which come from other countries are often greatly admired and there is no reason why English craft-workers should not be equally successful in their efforts. A keen appreciation of colour and ornament help towards the finished results. A visit to one of the handicraft exhibitions, held annually all over the country, will give the amateur many fruitful suggestions.

Choosing and Preparing White Wood.—Wood should be preferably smooth and free from knots, grease, and dirt marks. Grease is not always traceable until water-colour paint or transparent stain is applied to the wood. Light spots are noticeable where the colour refuses to go over the grease marks. All such marks should be attacked with a piece of clean rag dipped in benzine or by rubbing with pumice powder on a piece of cotton-wool. Grain-marks are also to be avoided when buying wood, as they often spoil the effect of a design. The large stock of white-wood articles now on the market range from napkin-rings to hair-brushes and are specially suitable for the craft-worker.

The woods used are sycamore, chestnut, limewood and maple. Limewood, being softer, is more suitable for chip-carving than for painting.

Experiment first on a flat-surfaced article. The wood supplied for painting is apparently smooth until painted on. To prevent roughness treat the surface before starting work. If this is left until later, damage will be caused to the design. First smooth the parts to be decorated with very fine glass-paper. Following this, pumice-stone or pumice-powder is sometimes used, after which the surface is cleaned and dusted. To ensure adequate preparation, a thin coat of size can be applied with a camel-hair brush. Use packet size, which is easier to dissolve than the loose kind. Two teaspoonfuls dissolved in a cup of warm water will be sufficient. Allow the size to soak thoroughly in and dry. Any further roughness which appears should be sand-papered down and the treatment repeated before beginning to paint.

Another way of bringing out roughness is by damping the surface with a clean wet rag. When dry, rough patches can be removed with glass-paper. This should be done until the wood remains smooth after being redamped, proving that it is ready to take colour. Preliminary preparations may be rather tedious, but it should be remembered that the smoother and cleaner the surface the crisper will be the decoration applied to it. The grain will rise when not treated before being painted on.

Drawing and Design.—A study of styles of ornament is of great value to the designer. Many useful books are available, though much of the best work is to be seen in some of the London museums. The Persians and the Indians in particular understand how to cover an entire surface with pattern. Varied form and exquisite drawing make the richness of their design a pleasure to the eye. Unless the student has considerable skill and patience in drawing, the pattern should be kept simple, however.

First decide on the parts of the article to be decorated. If design is a difficult problem, take an interesting unit and trace it at intervals to make a border or a happy arrangement. Only the practised craftsman should draw direct on to the wood. If a faulty pencil line is rubbed out it will frequently make the surface greasy. When a suitable design has been planned it should be spaced out on tracing paper for tracing. Figs. 1-5 are simple geometric borders based on squares. Figs. 6 and 7 are two suggestions for book-ends; while Figs. 8-12 are simple motifs for use separately or together.

Geometric patterns can be used with good effect. Naturalistic flower and fruit clusters are not so successful in repetition. Too many set rules in design tend to confusion. It is better to use any form, floral or animal, abstract or naturalistic, which appeals to the designer. Designs are sometimes evolved out of varying articles. By arranging pennies, halfpennies and farthings in relation to each other and drawing round the edges, flower designs can be made. The addition of a contrasting colour to the flower centres and wavy lines round the edges will make the pattern more interesting. Before tracing, any cracks or holes should be filled up with plastic wood and afterwards rubbed down to the surface-level with sand-paper.

The Ground Colour.—This is the first point to be decided in painting on wood. When transparent colour is used, the ground and the pattern are often painted separately. This means that either the pattern is painted first and the ground, including the areas between the pattern, is filled in after, or the pattern carried out in opaque colours over the stained surface.

The pattern should be traced after the ground has been stained. A method sometimes used when oil colour or enamel is combined with a water-stained ground is to cover the entire article with a coat of fine size. This is obtainable from any oil and colour man. Allow the coat to dry and paint the pattern over it. When the colours have dried and hardened the size can be washed off with warm water and the wood is ready for the water stain. This may be taken over the whole surface. Being transparent it does not injure the opaque colour, though it is advisable to remove any slight marks with a damp wash-leather when the stain is dry. In using lacquer paint, give two coats of the background colour. The first coat should be thinnish and worked with the grain and not across it. If this is not done, the paint will work up and be uneven. The backs and sides of articles should be done before the tops. Allow the first coat to dry and rub over lightly with fine glass-paper to make a tacking for the second one. Only two coats should be needed. Enamel takes well on a lacquered surface. When the background is left uncoloured, do not remove the coating of size. Polish over this. Size prevents the colour running at the edges.

Transferring the Design to the Wood.—A single design can be drawn on to the wood without previous preparation, but to ensure correct placing, it is often better to trace from a drawing that has been planned out on paper. Having made your design, trace it, and then go over the back of the tracing with a soft pencil, carefully following the outlines of the pattern. Another method of transferring is to use a piece of smooth tissue paper that has been lightly rubbed all over with a soft pencil (Grade 3B). This is laid under the tracing with the pencilled surface next to the wood and the impression is made by going round the outlines of the design with a well-sharpened H pencil. Except in special cases, do not use carbon paper as it is greasy and therefore unsuitable for transparent colour.

Stencilling.—Owing to the limitations of stencilled design, it should only be used for highly decorative work. (*See* separate article.)

Pouncing.—A third method of tracing is the pricked outline known as pouncing. The outlines of the design are pricked at intervals of a quarter of an inch either with a wheel tracer or a darning needle. (If the eye of the needle is fixed into a cork it is easier to hold.) A pounce can be made from a wad of cotton-wool or by tightly rolling a strip of felt. When the design is in position, dip the pounce in powder colour and smear over the pricked holes, leaving the pattern in dotted outline on the article. The colour can either be fixed by spraying with a weak solution of permanganate of potash, or the outline drawn in with indigo or sepia.

Colour.—When your article is ready to be painted, decide if the colour is to be transparent, as with water-colour or a specially prepared stain or ink, or whether opaque colours, oils, tempera, enamels or lacquer paints are to be used.

Colour always gives an added interest to work, especially when it is in harmony with its surroundings. When vivid colour is required, enamels and lacquer paints are more forceful than the softer and more harmonious appearance of stains. In using stains, several applications of one colour may be needed before the right depth of tone is achieved. Prepared stains and waterproof inks may be diluted with water as required. Choice of colour is largely governed by personal taste. It is a good plan to decide whether a colour scheme is to be delicate or rich before starting to paint. Avoid the use of delicate shades with deep rich colour. This does not mean that contrasting colours should not be used together so long as they are of the same strength in tone.

Black is valuable as a forcing colour when not used in large quantities. Gold greatly enriches a design and is most satisfactory for outlining and details. Sable brushes are better to work with than camel-hair ones. Paint the pattern in the same way that flat washes would be painted on paper, working in one direction only.

Polishing.—Polish is easily and inexpensively made at home. Wax polish gives a mellow surface that is very suitable for stained work. Shred a small lump of bees'-wax and allow it to absorb enough turpentine thoroughly to soften it. Whenever possible this should be done overnight so that the polish will be ready the next day. Paraffin wax can be prepared in the same way. A polish should not be put on too lavishly. Even distribution and vigorous rubbing with a silk rag or a piece of felt are more important. Friction is the main factor in giving a good surface to wax polish. It is absolutely essential for the wood to be thoroughly dry before polishing is commenced. Better results are obtained with three polishers, one for applying the wax, a second for rubbing, and a third for finishing off finally. The insides and undersides of articles, which are more out of sight, must not be neglected. When these are left unpolished and unstained there is a sense of incompleteness. A better finish is given by colouring the unstained parts to match the dominant colours in the design. Another neat finish is to leave the wood unstained, and to polish it, first removing all roughness.

Painting on Glass.—Glass is used as much as wood among household accessories. Painted glassware has largely supplanted cut glass, and a revolution in this craft has come about with the increased supplies of paints and enamels which are permanent without firing. As in painting on wood and modelling in barbola, first designs should be made on an article that is small and flat surfaced. To get used to the limitations of

Fig. 1
Fig. 8
Fig. 2
Fig. 9
Fig. 3
Fig. 10
Fig. 4
Fig. 11
Fig. 5
Fig. 6
Fig. 12
Fig. 7

the craft, try out the colour to be used on a spare piece of glass.

The Design is best planned as a stencil plate. Each of the parts which go to make up the whole will then be separate pieces in themselves. In this way contrasting colours can be used without waiting for one colour to dry before the next is applied. Shading and stippling are quite unsuitable for glass. A brown or black outline will always give a delicate forcefulness to the pattern, and an even distribution of spotting in the background spaces gives an additional richness. Spotting and outlining are most useful in giving variety when the design is in one colour.

Untarnishable gold paint looks equally well on wood and glass. Grounding with an uneven network of gold lines can be used with patterns which are sufficiently bold in themselves.

Transferring Designs to Glass.—See that the glass is quite clean. All smears can be removed by wiping over the surface with a clean rag soaked in methylated spirit, and afterwards finishing with a chamois leather and a polisher. In preparing a design many of the same rules apply as in painting on wood. Take the exact measurements of the article to be decorated and space out the design accordingly. The rim of a glass or the lid of a powder bowl can easily be measured by laying the article on paper and running a pencil line round the circumference. If the design is a repeating one, draw each section of it within the space indicated. Mark off uniform widths round the circumference and the correct spacing is obtained by extending the lines to the point where they meet in the centre of the circle. The tracing is fitted to the underside of the glass with strips of stamp paper to secure the edges, so that the design will show through and can be painted in the same way. A pattern can be cut up and re-arranged to suit articles of different shapes.

It is not always possible to fix a tracing on the underside or inside of an article. Glass bottles require another method. Trace the design and use blue or red carbon paper for transferring it. Trace only small portions at a time as carbon is greasy and inclined to smear. Paint in the parts as soon as they are traced so that there is no opportunity for smudging.

Colour.—The colour can be transparent or opaque. Quick-drying colours facilitate work. Enamels give a glossy, opaque finish. Twopenny tins of these colours are useful where small quantities are needed. Ordinary students' oil colour is quite effective when mixed with a quick-drying medium. For transparent painting there are coloured varnishes. Some of these can be used for painting the pattern and for staining the whole surface of the glass. They should be applied in flat washes with a soft camel-hair brush. Transparent oil colours may be used if mixed with a suitable medium. Use sable brushes for oil paint and camel-hair brushes for varnishing.

Entire designs can often be carried out in gold which looks its best on glass that has been tinted all over. Untarnishable gold, or a gold bronze used with a quick-drying medium, are the simplest and most effective methods. In using gold with a quick-drying medium, first treat the part to be decorated with the medium, and dip a camel-hair brush or a piece of chamois leather into the bronze powder and dust over it. The enamelled or varnished parts of the design should be quite dry before this is done; if not, flecks of bronzing powder will adhere and give a smudged appearance.

Painting.—Unless a space is left between each colour, as described above, the one colour must be allowed to dry before the next is painted on. Some students use pointed wooden sticks in preference to brushes. By this method, painting is commenced in the centre of the design and the colour spread with a circular movement until it reaches the outer edges. Even distribution is essential. When using a brush it is better to lay the colours on rather than to paint them. The shiny surface of the glass will show through in streaks if there is any attempt to work the colour in. Quick application is important when coloured varnish is being used. When possible, avoid going over the colour twice.

Spotting and Outlining—Spotting can be done by dipping the end of a stick

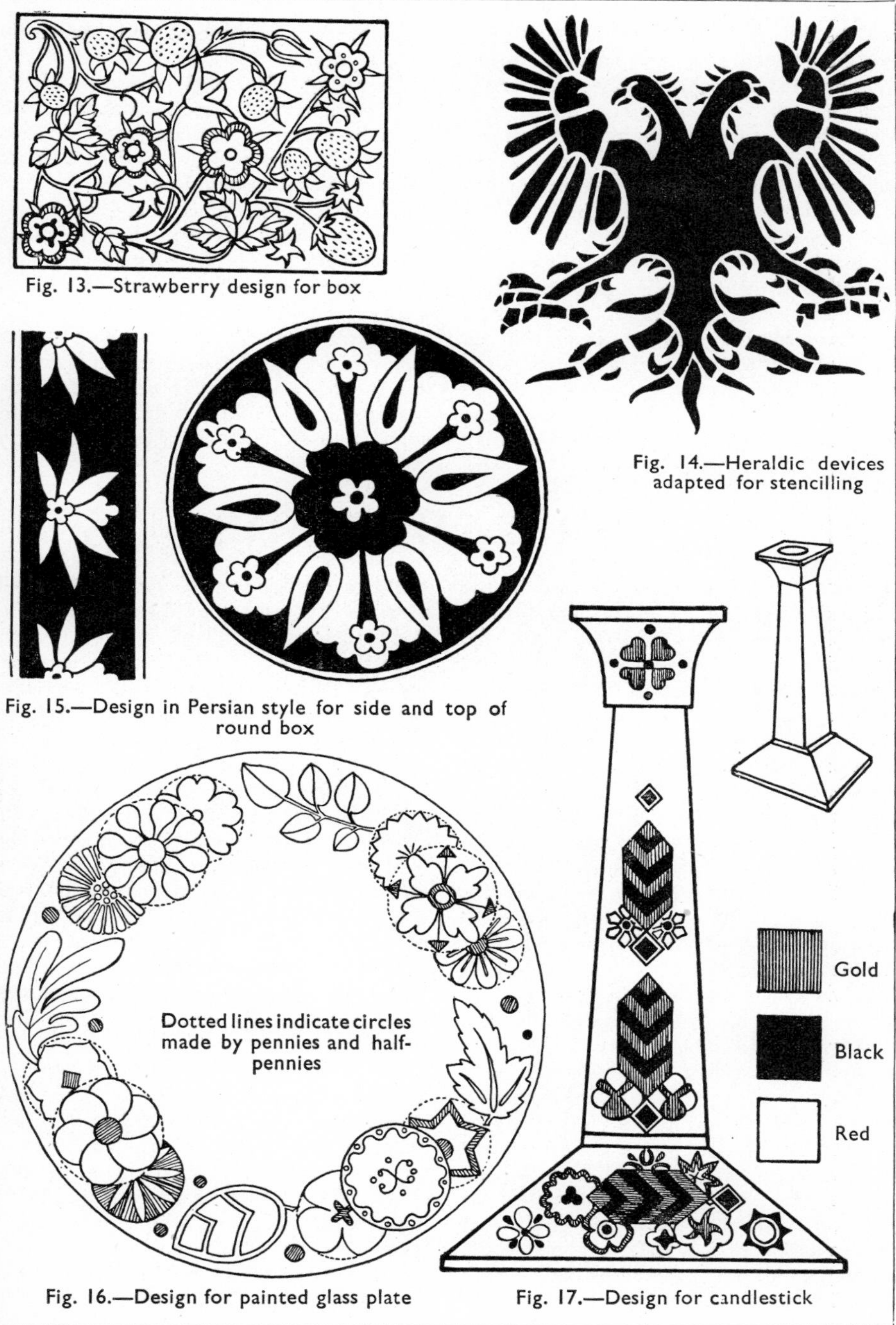

Fig. 13.—Strawberry design for box

Fig. 14.—Heraldic devices adapted for stencilling

Fig. 15.—Design in Persian style for side and top of round box

Fig. 16.—Design for painted glass plate

Fig. 17.—Design for candlestick

into the colour and holding it upright to drip the enamel or varnish on to the glass. Spots vary in size according to the stick used.

Before outlining a design the student should be sure that he has the steady hand so essential to the neat drawing which outlining requires. When colouring is to be done with varnish, a mapping pen and outlining ink No. 2 are needed. *Encre grasse* (oil-colour ink) is another good medium. If the outline is to be washed off after the painting is done, use an ink which is not waterproof. When the pen is charged draw it lightly over the glass so that the ink will flow evenly. The pen should glide over the surface leaving a fine black line varying in width. Keep the outline thin for delicate patterns and heavier for bolder ones.

Cleaning Painted Glass.—Methylated spirit used as described above is one of the best ways of cleaning glass. The side of the glass on which the design is not painted can be carefully polished.

When washing, it is necessary to use warm water without soda. Brushes should always be cleaned immediately after use. A cleaner is sometimes provided with the enamel. Failing this, the worst of the paint should be cleaned away with turpentine, and the brushes finished off by washing in the usual way. Keep all bottles tightly corked and lids on tins. Colours exposed to air quickly harden.

PAPER LAMPSHADES

LAMPSHADES are a definite feature in the decoration of the house. Concentrated spots of strong colour are often used in the decoration of a room. These may be in the form of cushions, ornaments, candle or lampshades. Whatever colour is used it should harmonize with the surroundings. If a room is decorated in a dainty, pale colour scheme, then the lampshade should be in the same tone, not in strong colour which would be likely to attract too much attention to itself.

Special thought must be given to the choice of colours used in the shade. It should not be forgotten that a good effect obtained by daylight may be quite unsuitable when a light is shining through at night. Blue, green and mauve shades may be very pretty during the day, but with an artificial light shining through they give a very cold appearance, and are unflattering to the faces around them. This can be modified to some extent by lining the shade with white paper or silk. The warmer colours are usually quite successful in shades, either in the paper or silk itself or in the decoration of the shade. Such colours as orange, red, pink and yellow add warmth and brightness to a colour scheme both in daylight and artificial light.

When considering the size of the shade to be used you must consider the size of its stand, the position of the light, its distance from the floor and the direction in which the light is generally required. A reading lamp is generally used on a table, therefore the shade must not be too large. Most of its light is required on or near the table, so that a fairly strongly coloured or more opaque shade must be used. A floor-stand about 5 ft. high would require a larger shade.

Most of the light is required to illuminate the room so that a good portion of the shade would be undecorated or the whole thing must be made of fairly translucent material.

Before deciding upon a colour-scheme experiment use odd scraps of parchment paper and judge the effect by holding them to the light.

When working out shapes it is a good plan to make them first in any kind of clean paper, fit them in position, make any adjustments required and then use this as a pattern on the parchment paper to give the final shape. This is very necessary when mounting panels on home-made wire frames as they often vary slightly in size.

To Make and Decorate Shades.—Parchment paper for making lampshades may be purchased from the stationer for a

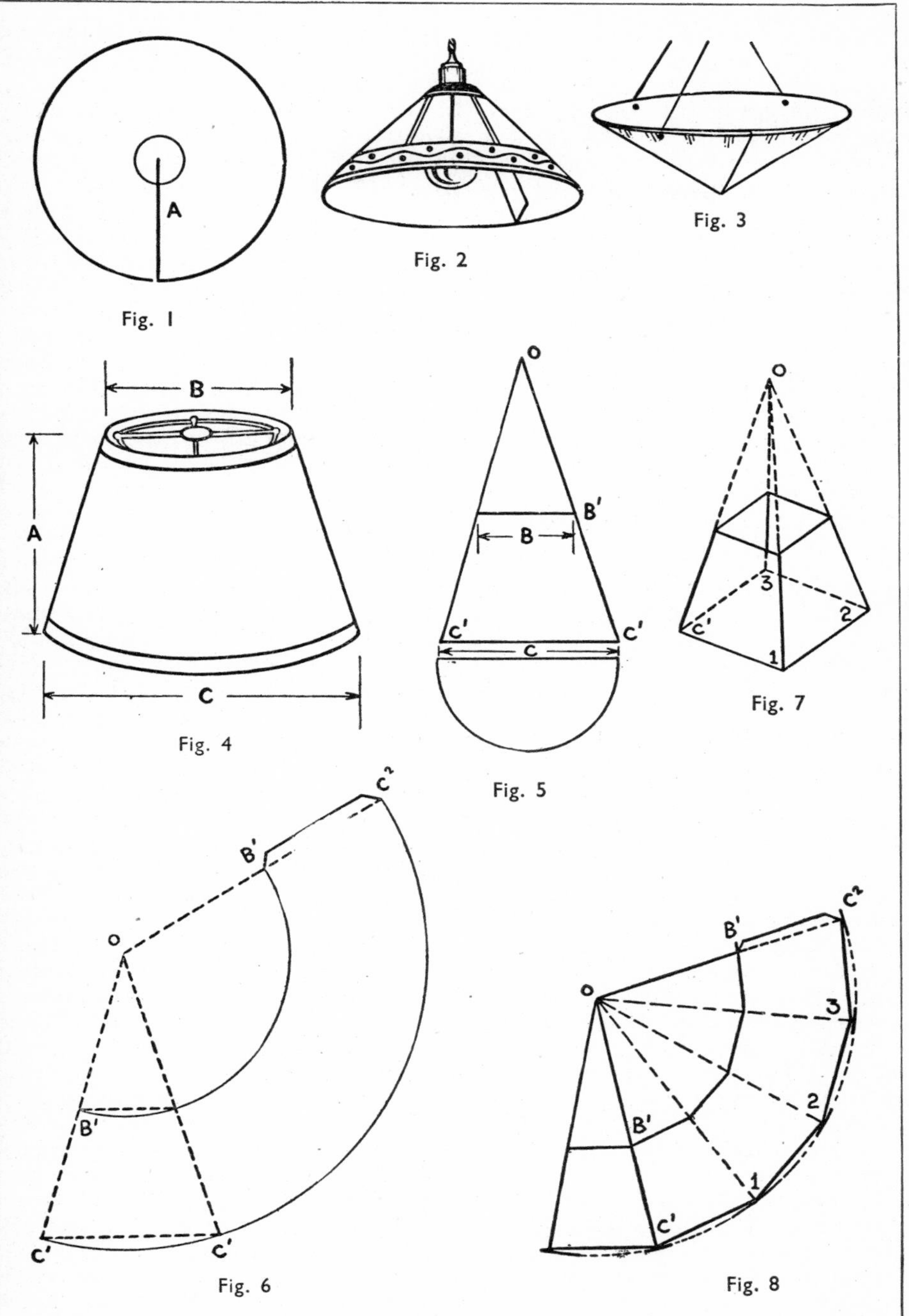

Fig. 1

Fig. 2

Fig. 3

Fig. 4

Fig. 5

Fig. 6

Fig. 7

Fig. 8

few pence per sheet or it may be prepared from cartridge paper or manilla paper by painting the whole surface with a mixture of turpentine, raw linseed oil and methylated spirits, equal quantities of each.

The liquid will soak through the paper and make it fairly transparent. Leave it to dry before beginning to cut it to shape. If manilla paper is used it will be found that it possesses a beautiful mottled surface which is intensified by the oiling. If any decoration in water colour is to be applied to the surface of the lampshade it should be applied previously. It is then necessary to paint the oil on the undecorated side of the shade so that the colour is not softened or

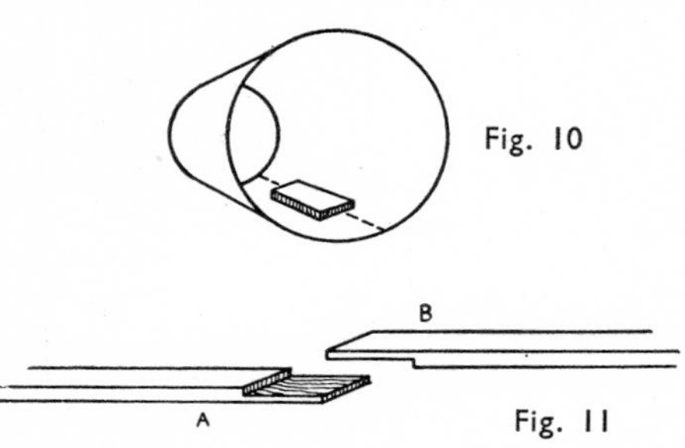

Fig. 10

Fig. 11

brushed off. If oil colour is used it may be possible, though not always desirable, to apply it after the oiling process. But as a general rule oil colour is too opaque for general use. Water colours can usually be applied fairly easily to parchment purchased from a stationer if the surface to be decorated is first rubbed with a little pumice powder; or the damp brush is first lightly rubbed on a piece of yellow soap before loading it with colour. Waterproof lampshade inks can be obtained in a variety of colours.

Old parchment documents can be used with delightful effects for lampshades if the ink is washed off as much as possible, and the parchment pinned out flat and left to dry.

Lampshades can be easily and very effectively decorated by marbling as described in the section for CARDBOARD WORK. This is done after the shape has been cut and before the surface has been oiled. There are a few definite standard shapes upon which the forms of most lampshades are based. The wire frames can be purchased, or made at home if you have the soldering apparatus. It is a good plan to paint or enamel the frames before covering.

Wire Frames.—Having decided on the shape you require, or purchased the wire frame, it will probably be found in one of the classes shown in Figs. 1 to 8.

Fig. 2 is the simplest form. It is made from a circle of paper or parchment with a radius equal to *a* (Fig. 1). Draw the circle with a pair of compasses, cut it out and then cut along *a*, fold to the shape and diameter required as in Fig. 2, cut out all excepting ½ in. of the overlap and fix with seccotine or any other liquid glue, leaving it flat on a table with a heavy weight over the join as in Fig. 10. Or it may be fixed by punching holes with a ticket or leather punch and lacing with a leather thong. To make an invisible join, pare ½ in. off top of used thong [(*a*) in Fig. 11], and ½ in. off new thong (*b*), glue together as indicated and leave till dry. Thick embroiding silk or wool, silk cord, raffia or even thick new white string are also useful for lacing. The inverted shape (in Fig. 3) is obtained by the same method excepting that the centre is not cut away.

The shape of Fig. 4 is obtained by measuring the height *a*, the top and bottom diameters *b* and *c* and setting them out and joining their ends as shown in Fig. 5. Now extend the sloping sides *d* and *e* to meet in *o* (Fig. 5). With the radius o—c^1 draw the shape given in Fig. 6, marking on it also o—b^1. The distance c^1, c^2 in Fig. 6 is obtained by measuring the circumference of the circle, half of which is shown in Fig. 5 and setting it along the curve c^1, c^2. This can be done by stepping it off in short distances with the compasses. Draw a line from c^2 to *o* on the right-hand side, add ½ in. for a flap and cut out the shape. After decorating the surface fold into the form in Fig. 4 and fasten the ends together.

For a very large shade you may need the whole of a table-top when setting out, and a pin with a piece of thread attached to one end and a pencil at the other for use instead of a compass when drawing the circular lines.

The pyramidal type of shade shown in Fig. 7 is set out somewhat similarly to the conical one just described.

As before, take the measurements of the bottom and top of the cut-off pyramid and set them out as in Fig. 5. Extend the sloping lines to meet in *o*. Draw the part of a circle with *o*—*b* as radius and also draw the curve o^1—c^2, as in Fig. 8. Now take the length of each side of the square, or it might be a rectangle, and set it off along the curve in Fig. 8 as c^1 1, 2, 3, c^2. Draw lines from these points to *o* and join c^1 1, 2, 3, c^2 in straight lines on both circles. Add a flap of ½ in. Cut out the shape, crease it sharply along the lines, open out flat, decorate it and make up to its final shape.

PARTIES AND ENTERTAINING

One great secret of successful entertaining is for the host and hostess not to attempt more than they can comfortably manage. In households where there are two or three servants, entertaining can be done on a grand scale; but in the smaller home, where there is no domestic help, or, at most, one maid, it is important that the pressure of domestic duties should not reduce the hostess to that frenzied condition in which it is impossible for her to perform her social duties.

The informal dinner party is an excellent method of entertaining a comparatively small number of friends. Where domestic help is lacking an easily managed menu would be soup, joint or poultry and a sweet followed by coffee. The table should be simply decorated—a few flowers are all that is necessary, though ornamental candles add to the effect. The knives and forks, etc., should be arranged with military precision if the table is to look at its best. Folded table-napkins add a festive touch and provide a receptacle for a roll, or, in the case of a children's party, for bon-bons, paper caps or some little novelty gift.

A leisurely meal followed by conversation over coffee in the drawing room, with perhaps a game of bridge or a little music later, is a sufficient entertainment in itself if the guests are well chosen.

A Buffet Supper.—If, however, younger folk are to be entertained the games will need to be a little more hilarious, and it is better to invite the guests to an early buffet supper, rather than to a formal dinner. This is a very easy way of entertaining people to a meal, because such excellent cold sweets can be obtained from popular caterers in an easily negotiable form.

Sandwiches should figure prominently on the menu. Excellent "sandwich spread" can be bought in bottles, or chicken, sardine, cress, tomato, cheese, and olive, scrambled egg, foie gras or "gentleman's relish" sandwiches can be prepared at home. The considerable labour of cutting up is dispensed with if small bridge rolls are used instead of bread. These can be ordered from the baker or confectioner.

Lobster or meat patties can be bought, or small sausage rolls made at home.

Most "home-made" tea shops will make these things to order, though the cost will probably be higher than if they were procured from a branch of the multiple caterers.

The sweets should include jellies, trifles, charlottes, fruit salad, crêmes, etc., which can be purchased already prepared, or made at home. Individual sweets in small fancy cardboard containers, free glasses or crockery for other things. Ices or iced soufflés are of course ideal, but unless you have a refrigerator it is hardly worth the trouble of making them at home.

Coffee, tea and lemonade are indispensable, but to these may be added a variety of drinks to suit the means of the host.

A little lively gramophone music can be played while the guests are assembling and introductions are being effected.

The host and hostess must be ready to organize parlour games, but in practice it usually happens that a few bright spirits among the guests will make suggestions, and there will be more spontaneity about the entertainment. The host and hostess must fill in any awkward pauses, or prevent the games becoming of such a nature that all cannot join in.

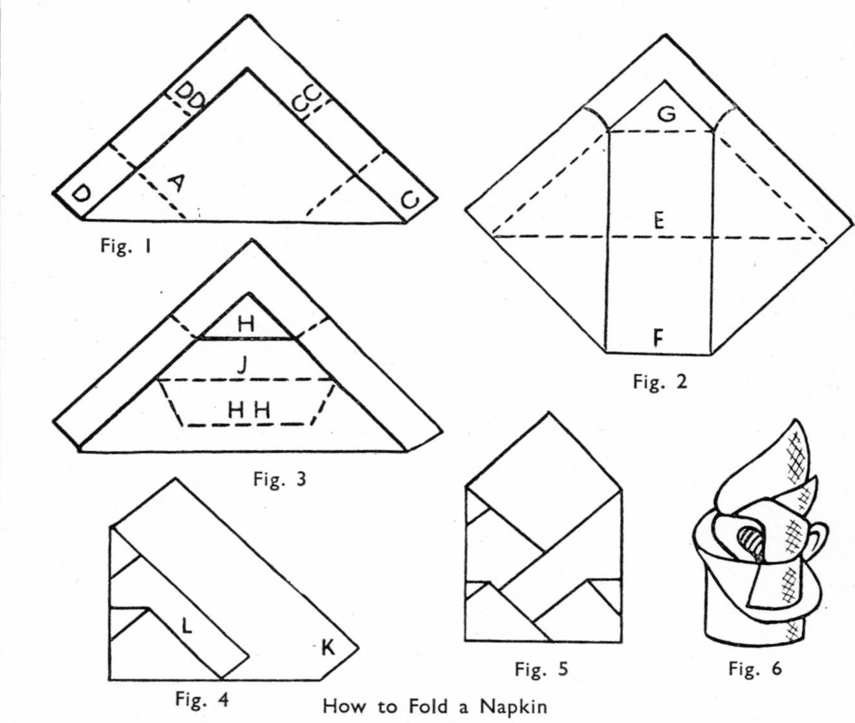

How to Fold a Napkin

Place the table napkin cornerwise before you, and fold the bottom point over as in Fig. 1. Then fold at lines A and B until D rests on DD and C on CC as in Fig. 2. Next fold at line E until F rests on G. The result should be as in Fig. 3. Then fold H on to line HH, folding at J. Reverse the napkin and fold back one side, as shown in Fig. 4, about a third the length of the base, and then tuck point K into pleat L. The result will be as in Fig. 5. The centre can be hollowed out and the points standing up can be turned down into the pleats. The final effect should be something like Fig. 6

Supper should be served about half way through the evening. The buffet supper should be set out in the dining-room, and if space is limited the hall could be utilized for drinks. Plenty of seating accommodation should be provided—cushions on the stairs or garden chairs in the conservatory appeal to the young people.

After supper the company will drift back to the drawing-room, and it will be found that at this point the livelier and more boisterous games are appreciated.

Children's Parties.—These can follow much the same procedure. In place of the buffet supper a "sit-down" tea should be provided. The food should be simple, but decorative, with such delicacies as sponge cake with a little icing (not too much cream), junket decorated with "hundreds and thousands," jellies, blanc mange, etc.

At Christmas time the party usually centres round the Christmas tree, and some method of distributing the presents has to be devised. To ensure that each child receives the present intended for it, the articles on the tree can be numbered and the little guests each given an appropriately numbered ticket in a sealed envelope. If the envelopes are not opened until the last minute the element of surprise is maintained. Another method is to have presents approximately suitable for all children, and let the children draw numbered tickets from two hats, one containing odd numbers for boys and the other containing even numbers for girls.

Games should be chosen from such old favourites as Blind Man's Buff, Musical Chairs, Oranges and Lemons, etc.

A more ambitious party would include an entertainment by a ventriloquist or conjurer, or a Punch and Judy show. Sometimes a home cinema entertainment can be arranged. If the children are all of a suitable age a story told by one who really understands the art will provide a restful interlude.

Birthday Parties.—For children these can generally follow the plan suggested above, with a birthday cake decorated with an appropriate number of small candles. For the more auspicious twenty-first birthday party a more ambitious programme might be arranged. The meal should be a little more formal, perhaps the health of the person whose birthday it is being proposed

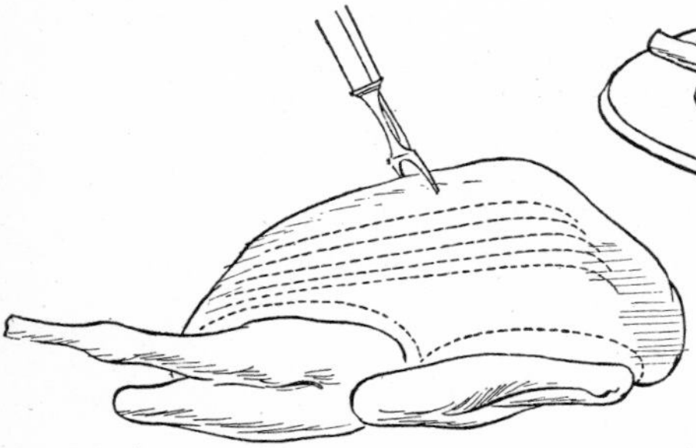

Fig. 7.—How to Carve a Chicken.

in a short speech. Whether the main meal be tea, dinner or supper, the menu should within reason, be as elaborate as the domestic arrangements permit.

Decorations should be definitely festive. Remarkable effects can be obtained with crêpe paper, and the dining-room transformed into a veritable fairyland at very little cost. Walls, light fittings, as well as tables can be decorated with this material in many charming shades. Spend a little time deciding upon a colour scheme, keeping in mind the normal colours in the room. In decorating tables avoid decorations which interfere with the flow of conversation across the tables.

Dances.—If there is a fair-sized room available an evening's dancing is always enjoyed. All unnecessary furniture should be removed and the seating accommodation should be arranged round the walls. The ideal floor is a polished wooden one, and if the room is usually covered by a carpet it is worth while taking it up and staining and polishing the boards. Polished linoleum also makes a good dancing floor, but for a dance with a more or less informal and family

Fig. 8.—How to Carve a Leg of Mutton

atmosphere almost any type of floor can be used.

Music is best provided by a gramophone. The duties of gramophone attendant might be undertaken by a member of the family who does not wish to dance, or the duties shared in rotation. The record should be selected with care. Fox-trots, one-steps and waltzes are likely to prove most popular, but there should be a sprinkling of tangoes, rumbas and less familiar dances. The possibility of introducing some of the old dances should also be kept in mind.

It is better to draw up a well-balanced programme at the beginning of the evening and work steadily through it, than to leave it to the fancy of the moment.

Breaks in the programme should be made at the end of every few dances, and, again, these should be carefully planned. These short intervals should be filled in various ways, such as—a few stories told by a good raconteur; a musical item; a few conjuring tricks; a game of the restful type; a humorous gramophone record. A couple of specially good dancers could demonstrate

Fig. 4.—How to Set a Place at Table

one of the latest dances. If a wireless set is available one of the breaks might coincide with the News.

Refreshments should be provided by means of a buffet supper, with drinks, sweets and cigarettes handed round during the shorter breaks.

For Book-lovers.—Serious minded people are still interested in good plays and books, and the hostess who enables a group of friends to meet together to discuss matters in which they are mutually interested will be doing something more than providing a pleasant evening's entertainment. In a family in which there are several young people in their 'teens this type of evening has the advantage of keeping the young people at home and at the same time providing them with an opportunity of meeting their friends. The guests, who would have to be really interested in books, could meet and discuss a particular book which they had all been reading, one or two being asked to be ready to open the discussion.

The reading of plays—both ancient and modern—could also be the main object of the evening, the guests each taking different parts.

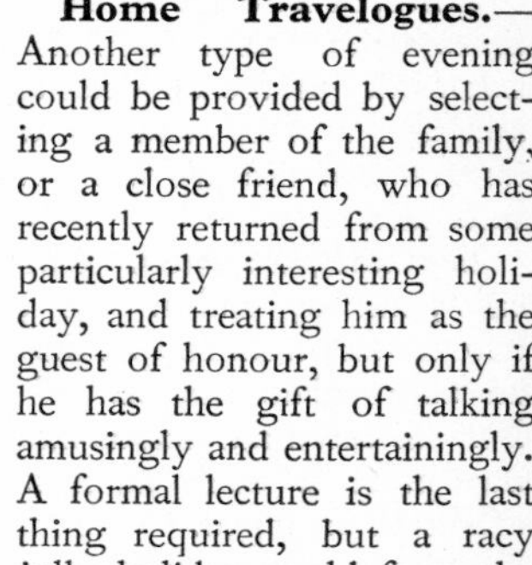

Home Travelogues.—Another type of evening could be provided by selecting a member of the family, or a close friend, who has recently returned from some particularly interesting holiday, and treating him as the guest of honour, but only if he has the gift of talking amusingly and entertainingly. A formal lecture is the last thing required, but a racy account of a jolly holiday could form the chief interest of the evening, especially if photographs or lantern slides or a miniature cinematograph film could be shown. Refreshments and a little music and general conversation ought to complete a quiet but pleasant evening.

A Large Scale Party, if it is to be organized for some club or society, should be departmentalized, and individuals, or small committees, made responsible for various tasks—decorating the hall, arranging the refreshments, organizing the games and music, etc. There should be an M.C. to co-ordinate the efforts of the committees and see that nothing is overlooked, and also someone to look after publicity or issue invitations and inform all concerned as to the number likely to be present.

INDOOR PARTY GAMES

INDOOR parties are always enjoyable if they are properly planned. Whether you are catering for four people or forty, whether young or old, almost everything depends on having plenty of varied games. Draw up a programme beforehand, bearing in mind the people who are to take part. Then you can go straight ahead without any of those dull moments when interest has flagged and no one knows quite what to do next. Remember to drop a game at once if it is not going well—and it is never possible to predict with certainty just how a game will go, so much depends on the individual players, and on the mood of the moment.

As a general rule it is advisable to start off with some game in which all can join, so that everyone gets moving and the proper "play atmosphere" is produced.

Musical March.—Have a large ring of chairs or seats facing outwards, and seat your players so that every place is taken.

As the pianist begins, or the music is switched on, all begin to march round, in single file, but when the music stops each must try to get back to his own place as quickly as possible. It is not permitted to run backwards; every player must just dash on round in the same direction until the proper seat is reached. The one who is last to take his seat is "out"—and so remains in his place when the music restarts and the others get up and renew their march. So the game goes on until only the winner is left.

It is advisable to have a judge to determine which player is last each time.

Forty Ways of Getting There.—The middle of the room is left clear, all the players sitting down the sides to watch the fun. Then each in turn goes down the room and back again—walking, running, or by some other method. No "way of getting there" must be used twice.

The game, of course, is a test of inventiveness, as well as of other qualities. There are endless ways of "getting there."

Here are some suggestions: walking—forwards, backwards, sideways, with long steps, with short steps, with feet crossing over each other; moving on hands and knees; running—in similarly varying manners; hopping; jumping; corkscrewing; gliding along; with waltz step; hobbling like a lame man; bowling an imaginary hoop; pretending to bounce a ball; making the motions of swimming; walking on the toes—and so on.

Stop the Stick.—A ring of players is formed. All are numbered round. One person in the middle has a walking-stick, which he supports in an upright position on the floor by holding his finger against the top of it. He suddenly calls out any number—and takes away his finger from the stick. The player called tries to catch the stick before it crashes to the floor. If he succeeds he returns to his place; if not he stays in the middle and calls out a new number himself.

The Bellman.—Any number can take part. Everyone is blindfolded except one player who carries a bell, which he must ring constantly. The rest, guided by the sound, pursue him—all of them, of course, are blindfolded. If he is captured the successful player in turn becomes *bellman.*

Feeding the Zoo.—Get all your people in a ring, giving them no inkling of the trick you propose to play on them. Put down on the floor, in the middle of the room,

Fig. 1.—Stick Stepping

a bun, or anything similar that is eatable. Say that you are going to give each person the name of some animal, but all are to keep their names secret. Then go round and whisper to everyone the same word—"bear."

You will now explain that when any player has his name called he must at once rush forward and seize the bun. Begin to call out various names—lion, elephant, deer, panther. It may be well to pause here, as if surprised, and remind each to keep his name in mind. Then—"bear!"

Next moment there will be a confused heap over the bun.

Live Target.—All the players stand scattered about, only one being allowed to move. He is the *target.* It is his business to avoid being hit by the ball which is thrown by the others, and he is allowed to dodge about as he likes. The rest can only get the ball when it comes near, and must throw it at once. When someone hits the *target* the two change places.

Jumping the Stick.—The agile ones of the party will enjoy this most, but there will be plenty of fun for those who merely watch.

A walking-stick is laid on the floor. Then you bend forward and grip it with both hands, a comfortable distance apart. Bring the stick against your toes and try to jump over it without releasing your hold. It is not so easy as it may sound, and you will be well advised to practise it a good many times before showing others "how simple it is."

Tight-rope Walking.—Put a mark or tape along the floor to serve for a tight-rope. You can have either team contests or individual exhibitions. After some straightforward walking make your players do something more difficult—walking backwards. Disqualification follows, of course, overbalancing from the "rope."

A B C Race.—This is like an ordinary relay contest, but instead of letting each player simply touch off the next runner, make him recite the whole alphabet through—the letter Z will be the signal for the next team member to set off. As a variation, make all competitors say the alphabet backwards, and run backwards too.

Juggler's Race.—Each person carries a walking-stick the end of which is balanced vertically on the flat palm of his hand.

Crab Race.—Everyone taking part goes along on hands and feet—but goes sideways.

Kangaroo Race.—Each competitor travels along the course by jumping, keeping his feet together and holding a ball between them. A tennis ball serves very well. If it is dropped it must be replaced before the player goes on.

Spotted.—Select a small object to be hidden, such as a thimble, and choose one player to hide it. All the others taking part go out of the room while the object is concealed. Then the player seats himself somewhere and calls "Come in." The rest enter and begin to search for the object. As each player catches sight of it he returns to the middle of the room and calls out "Spotted." Those who have been successful take their seats, until there are no others left searching.

Then the one who first found the object lets the rest go out of the room again, and so takes his turn to hide the object.

Thief! Thief!—All players sit in a large ring, one being in the middle. This latter has a bean-bag (a calico bag about 6 in. by 2 in. filled with beans or counters), and hands it to any person, "to hold for a moment," but it is immediately tossed to any other player, and the game begins. The bag is passed round from hand to hand as quickly as possible, and the one in the middle dashes after it, trying to touch a person who is actually holding it. A player tagged while the bag is in his hands changes places with the one in the middle. Throwing the bag across the ring is allowed, but should not be encouraged. The bag need not always travel round the same way.

The Ghost Hand.—Invite any person who would "like to feel the touch of a ghost hand" to come out from the others and stand against the wall by himself. Fold his hands flatly across his chest. Then you will stand facing him, pointing straight at his eyeballs with the middle finger of each of your hands. Your other fingers will be doubled up on to your palms. Tell him that you are merely going to put a finger on each eyelid, so that he shall know where your hands are; and that a second later he will feel the ghost hand touch his own wrist.

Your fingers will slowly advance, until, when they are almost touching his eyes, the lids will instinctively close to protect the eyeballs. At this instant the first finger of your left hand will stretch across and touch the left eye while its fellow finger touches the right. Thus your right hand will be free to give the ghostly pressure, and will return up to its former place without, of course, touching the left eye. The first finger will then double up, and by the time the eyes open, both hands, with their second fingers still outstretched, will be seen drawing away.

Whirligig Race.—This is a team game. It is pretty strenuous, and a fair amount of space is needed. Each team should consist of six players. They stand in straight lines, one team member behind another, with a yard or two between each pair. When the starting signal is given each leader turns outward; runs down the length of his team; round the bottom, and up to the front again. Here he turns outward once more, but his coat-tail or hand is clutched by the second player, who follows on for the second round. For the third round the third runner joins on behind. So it goes on, the string of runners increasing, and whirling in a smaller circuit each time, until the last one joins on. To finish, the whole team makes a straight run to a fixed point.

Hen and Eggs.—When you have a lot of players who do not know each other's names, this game will give all the opportunity of becoming mutually acquainted.

Arrange the seats in horseshoe formation, and make all sit down—you, as leader, sit at one end, and a selected player, who has been prepared beforehand, has the last seat but one at the other end of the horseshoe. Begin by asking every person to discover the name of his right-hand neighbour. Supposing the first five people are: Leader, Mr. A., Mr. B., Miss C., Miss D. You will turn to your neighbour, Mr. A., and remark:

"They say Farmer Simpson has a hen. Does she cackle?"

Then your neighbour, like all of those who follow, refers you on to his neighbour, thus:

"*Mr. A.*—Mr. B. says . . . "

"*Mr. B.*—Miss C. says . . . "

"*Miss C.*—Miss D. says . . . "

Thus it goes on until the last but one has been reached—his neighbour may be Mrs. Z., and so he gives the final answer to your query in this fashion:

"Mrs. Z. says it does cackle."

After that make a new start, turning to your right-hand neighbour and saying:

"What colour eggs does it lay?"

The replies follow as before—Mr. A. says; Mr. B. says; Miss C. says; and so on—until the last but one ends up—"Mrs. Z. says they are brown."

At the next and final round you ask: "How many are there?"—then the reply is given:

"Mrs. Z. says there are plenty for breakfast."

Head Slap.—Only two can take part at a time. They stand face to face, one with

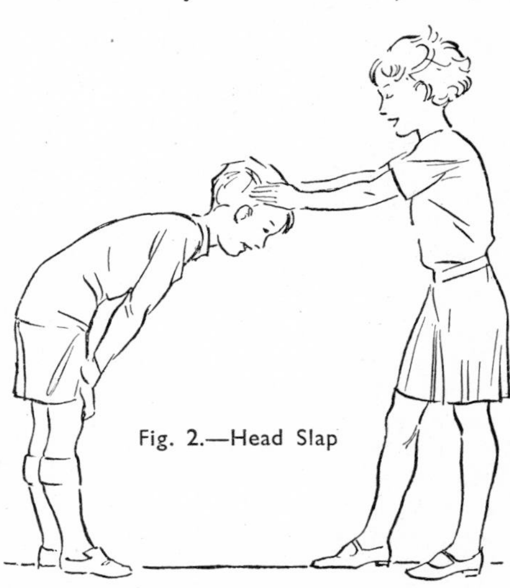

Fig. 2.—Head Slap

his arms stretched straight out in front of him, parallel with the ground and with each other, and with palms facing inward. The other bends forward at the waist, so that his head is between his companion's hands, but just below them. Then this second player, without any warning, jerks his head upward, and the pair of waiting hands try to slap the ears as they rise. Each player should have three slaps. It is not often the head gets touched—although the person who is to bob up cannot help anticipating a fearful whack!

Astride Ball.—A fair-size ring of players is formed, all facing inward. Each should have his legs widely astride, and should be bending forward with hands on knees. One player stands in the centre, with a ball, and tries to get it between the legs of anyone in the ring, by throwing it. Any person who moves his hands from his knees, except for actually stopping the ball, has to change places with the one in the middle, so also does anyone who lets the ball through.

One-foot Tug.—A pair of opponents compete, clasping hands. Each stands on one foot—right hand should hold right. Each grips his own raised ankle with his free hand. Then they have a tug-of-war, that one winning who first compels his opponent to put his raised foot down. Of course, hopping about is permitted.

Adders' Nest.—Mark a ring about a yard across on the floor or spread a newspaper. This is the *adders' nest*. The players, any number, clasp hands and form a large ring around it. The object of each one, in the struggle that ensues, is to drag his neighbours on to the nest, while keeping clear himself. Anyone whose foot touches the fatal area is "bitten" and drops out of the game. The one who remains in last is, of course, the winner.

Sound the Gong.—From the ceiling suspend a hoop, measuring about 3 ft. across, so that it hangs 5 or 6 ft. from the floor. A hoop can easily be improvised if necessary from a fresh-cut stick or some wire. In the middle of the hoop hang the *gong*—a tin lid. The game consists of throwing balls at the *gong*. Each time it is hit count two points; if the ball goes through the hoop without touching the *gong* count one.

If the room is large enough it is a good plan to have opposing players at equal distances on opposite sides of the hoop so that each can then catch and return the balls of the opponent.

Hog Tie.—Do not try this except in suitable clothes, which will not suffer from rough usage.

Two take part. Each is given a yard length of strong cord—then they hurl themselves on each other. Each, of course, is both *hog* and *farmer* at the same time. That one wins who first succeeds in tying his opponent's ankles together.

Take the Toss.—If you are leading you will stand in the middle of the room with a football. All those taking part stand round in a large ring: the circle consists of two teams, and each team is numbered. Thus each two players with the same number will be on opposite sides of the circle. The ball is thrown into the air and at the same time you call out any number. Instantly—assuming that they are alert—the two corresponding players dash to the middle; and the one who first touches the ball scores a point for his team. No one is allowed to push or impede another player.

Game is 11 points.

Knock the Hat.—This is a boxing contest though there is no real need for gloves, since each boxer tries, not to hit his opponent, but merely to knock off the hat he is wearing. If bouts seem likely to last too long you may confine the boxers within a circle, marked on the floor, and measuring 2 or 3 yards across.

Fishing.—This is a most fascinating and laughable game. Some equipment is needed, but it can easily be prepared.

First, half a dozen *fishing-rods*—each consisting of a light stick or cane with a 5-ft. length of string fastened to the end, and a metal or wire hook tied to the end of the string. For the *fish* you need twenty or thirty cotton spools; to the top of each you will fasten a small loop of string into which the fishers can get their hooks. An alternative plan is to drive a small wire or brass staple into the top of the reel.

A small carpet in the middle of the room will serve for the *fish pond*, or you may mark it out—it should be about 6 ft. across. Inside this stand all the cotton spools, loops upward.

The half-dozen players start fishing together, and land as many fish as they can, until there are no more in the pond.

But the chief fun of the game lies in the fact that inside each spool a small cut-out paper fish is coiled, and on this is written some weight, from 1 oz. to 5 lb. Thus no one can tell, when catching a fish, what weight it will be—and the final winner is the one who secures the heaviest total catch.

Be careful to get the weights of your fish fairly varied. If you have two dozen they might run as follows: three 5 lb., three 4 lb., three 3 lb., two 2 lb., two 1 lb., two 8 oz., three 4 oz., three 2 oz., three 1 oz.

Hello Circle.—At any sort of party or social in which a fair number are attending it is a good plan to start with this.

Suppose you are leader. Get all the players to stand in a circle, facing inwards, you taking your place with them. Then turn to your right, shake hands with your neighbour, and say "Hello." Continue on round the inside of the circle, doing the same to each person in turn. Your neighbour meanwhile will also have turned to the right and will be following on in just the same fashion. His right-hand neighbour comes behind him, and so on. Thus the circle will presently be turning in on itself, and everyone will shake hands with everyone else. The only person who does not move at all will be the last one in the ring, who was your left-hand neighbour at the outset.

Crosswires.—It is great fun to have a room full of people all trying to do this together; it is still greater fun to have one at a time performing so that the others can look on and laugh.

It seems so simple. All you have to do is to hold your nose with your right hand and your right ear with your left hand; then loose your grips; clap your hands once, and reverse the holds—left hand to nose, right hand to left ear. Continue—clapping and reversing over and over again. It is curious how many people cannot even find their nose for the first change. Of course, the thing must be done briskly.

That Reminds Me.—The players sit round for this quiet game, and each speaks in turn.

The one who starts off says:

"I was thinking of"—here he may say anything, perhaps it may be—"oak."

His neighbour, like all who follow, then says what springs into his mind suggested by this word "oak"—though each following player will refer to the last-spoken word —and not to the first one.

Thus the second may say:

"That reminds me of—furniture."

And the third:

"That reminds me of—sideboard."

The list may run on:—oak, furniture, sideboard, oranges, Italy, Romans, chariot, wheels, bicycle, cycle tour, camping, earwigs, and so on.

Hidden Treasures.—This is a game on the same lines as the familiar *Musical Chairs*, but some little preparation is needed.

Get a packet of chocolate and tie it up with paper and string. Wrap it up again, and again, until it has at least a dozen separate coverings. This is your "hidden treasure."

Let the players sit round in a ring. While the music is playing the package must be passed round from hand to hand. But whenever the music stops whoever chances to have the package may begin to unwrap it, and to tear off string and paper just as long as the music is silent—the instant that it restarts the package must be passed on.

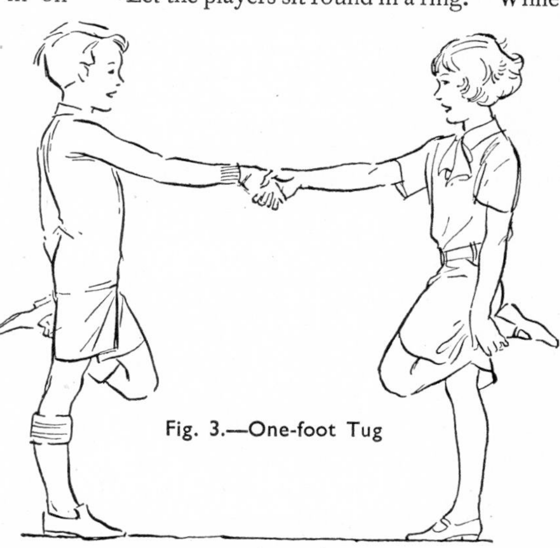

Fig. 3.—One-foot Tug

Thus the coverings are gradually removed during the short pauses, until at last someone strips off the last paper, and is allowed to keep the chocolate as a reward.

Relay Bangs.—If you have a sufficiently large room, and a jolly group of people, relay races can always be depended on to go well. Probably the most amusing type of race is the *Relay Bang*.

Have your two teams, perhaps each containing a dozen people, sitting in two parallel straight lines down the middle of the room, facing each other. Each player is seated on a paper bag.

When the starting word is given the two end players, *number one* in each team, spring to their feet; dash down the middle, round the ends, and back behind their respective teams and so again to their places. On arrival each snatches up his paper bag; inflates it, and bursts it with his free hand. The explosion is the signal for the next team number to set off down the middle. Each bang thus starts off a new runner until the whole team have competed.

Sugar Hat.—This is a little trick which can only be worked off once on the same people.

Place three hats on a table in front of you and do some suitable talking to impress the onlookers with the surprising performance which you are about to give.

Produce a lump of sugar, and tell them that you propose first to eat it, then to make it come under any one of the hats they may choose. Raise the hats in turn to show that no sugar is beneath them now. Then pop the lump into your mouth and let them hear you crunch it up.

Invite your audience to select the hat under which they would like the sugar to come—then lift it and put it on your head. You will have fulfilled your promise.

Passing the Basket.—Music is required for this, either a piano or a radio set will serve.

The players sit round in a large ring, passing a small basket from hand to hand, so that each in turn holds it for an instant. The music breaks off at unexpected intervals, and each time it stops whoever happens to be holding the basket drops out of the game. Eventually only the winner is left.

If the basket falls on the floor that player who last touched it must recover it. As the numbers are reduced players should spread out so that the passing distances for the basket remain roughly equal.

Winking.—A ring of chairs is needed. Girls sit down in these, facing inwards. One chair is left empty. Behind every chair, including the vacant one, stands a man.

It is this man who has no partner who begins the game. He winks at any girl he chooses, and she tries to spring up from her place and run across to the vacant chair. But the man behind her, if he can, seizes her shoulders and prevents her escape. If, however, she does get away the one who is left without a partner now winks at any other girl, including his former companion, and so tries to fill his chair again.

A man can wink at one girl after another till at last someone manages to escape across to him.

No man must keep his hands on his partner's shoulders. No girl must refuse to go when she catches a wink.

After a time, of course, the men may go into the ring and the girls stand behind the chairs.

Two Dogs and a Bone.—Two teams of eight take part in this, lined up across opposite ends of the room. In the middle of the room stands an Indian club, or anything suitable, for the "bone." Each team is numbered, from one to eight.

The leader calls out any number he chooses, and the players of that number dash to the centre, each trying to get back to his end carrying the "bone," without being touched. There will, naturally, very often be a good deal of feinting. Should any player be touched whilst actually carrying the object he loses a point, but by getting back safely with it he gains one.

The leader must keep a record of scores and must call numbers in irregular fashion so that none of the players know what to expect. Nine points make *game*.

Back and Front.—This also is a team game. It is exciting, but not strenuous.

The teams stand facing each other in two straight lines. At the top ends are two plates or saucers each holding a dozen dried peas.

When the starting word is given each end player begins passing down the peas, one at a time. They go down in front of the players, round the end team member, and up again behind the backs of the team.

It is most confusing to be trying to pass things in front of you and behind you at the same time, especially in opposite directions.

That team wins which safely gets all its peas on to the plate.

Stick Stepping.—Hold the walking-stick in front of you in both hands, so that it is stretched across at the level of your knees. Then step over it, first with one foot then the other, and immediately afterwards step back again.

See how many times you can step forward and backwards without your feet touching the stick.

Crossed Scissors.—Get your players in a ring, seated, and then go ahead to puzzle them. Take a seat yourself and hold a large pair of scissors conspicuously in front of you. Shut or open these scissors, whichever you like, and pass them to your neighbour, saying either: "I pass them crossed," or, "I pass them uncrossed."

Then let him pass on to the next, and so on round the ring. Each time a player passes on the scissors you may declare whether or not he has done the thing correctly. Probably they will usually be wrong, until they tumble to the secret.

Actually the scissors are merely a bluff, and correctness depends not on them at all, but in crossing or uncrossing your legs to suit the words you speak.

Let those who get the solution stay in, of course. It is still more puzzling to those who have not yet guessed the secret when their neighbours are getting your "right" each time—no matter what they do with the scissors.

Blindfold Supper.—Two take part in this—they should be good-humoured people, for most of the fun is for the onlookers.

They sit facing each other. Both are blindfolded. Each has a saucer or basin of crumbled biscuit, dry cereal, or something similar, on his knee, and a wooden spoon in his right hand.

With the spoon each tries to feed the other—and you can imagine that the contents of the basins are as likely to go down the players' necks or over their heads as in their mouths!

Witch Doctors.—The players are divided into two parties, about a third of them being *witch doctors*. It is helpful if they can be distinguished by badges, or paper hats, or something else.

It is the business of the witch doctors to pursue the others, putting on *spells* by touching them. Anyone touched must remain still, and is under the spell until released by the touch of any free person.

Thus the game is a race between the witch doctors putting the spells on and the others taking them off.

Alphabet Jaunts.—Players sit in a ring, each in turn describing some "jaunt" which he intends to take—but in each a particular letter of the alphabet must appear three times—as a destination, as a verb, as a noun. No letter must be missed, and every player must take his turn promptly—or else drop out. Thus the first half-dozen might begin like this:

"I am going to Assam to animate the ant eaters."

"I am going to Birmingham to buy a bicycle."

"I am going to Canada to catch a cheetah."

"I am going to Dundee to delve into Doric."

"I am going to Ecuador to earn my expenses."

"I am going to Florence to find some fabrics."

Jogging the Lemon.—This is an amusing race game, for which a fairly large room is needed with a clear floor. Any number can take part.

Each competitor holds a walking-stick, and with the point of this he must jog a lemon up the room and back again. No hitting is allowed.

Until you have tried to poke a lemon along in this fashion you can have no idea how unruly a thing it may be.

Nose Race.—Pairs compete in this. Each couple stands face to face, supporting between them a matchbox cover which is held on their two noses.

Cigarette Blowing.—Three or four people sit down either side of a table, facing each other. The cigarette is placed in the middle of the table, and they set to blowing their hardest. That side wins which first makes the cigarette roll over the opponents' edge of the table.

Hands on Knees.—All taking part sit in a ring, their hands flat on their knees. One player is in the middle, and is compelled to stay on his feet until he succeeds in slapping the hand of some person. For this purpose he dashes and dodges about, slapping here and there as unexpectedly as he can. Any person is allowed to slide his hands down the sides of his legs to avoid an actual slap, but all the rest of the time he must keep them flat on the top of his knees, and even when he has slid them down he must bring them up again immediately the one in the middle has slapped at them.

A person who has his hands slapped must change places with the one in the middle.

PETS

CATS.—The easiest pet to keep is a cat. In good health, no animal could be less trouble, and, despite many reports to the contrary, a well-treated cat is a very faithful and affectionate pet.

Most people acquire a cat either because a stray has come to them, or because someone gives them a kitten. Persian and Siamese kittens, however, usually have to be bought, and the price given for them varies according to the prize value of the strain. Persian and Siamese cats are perhaps more delicate than others, and the latter sometimes become fierce unexpectedly, but the rules of feeding, breeding, and nursing are the same for all.

Many people who only intend to keep one cat, find that a neuter, i.e. a castrated male, is the most satisfactory; they do not stray for days as toms are apt to do, and they are cleaner. Four months is a good age at which to take a male kitten to the vet., but castration can, of course, be done any time after that age, though it is cruel to leave it too long. This operation should be done by a vet. and not by just anyone who says he can do it, for an unskilled person may cause much needless suffering.

On the morning you have arranged to take your kitten to the vet., do not give it any breakfast, except perhaps just a drink of milk. You will be able to have him back in a few hours, when he may seem a little sleepy, but otherwise all right, and can be given a light meal of milk and boiled fish.

If you are given a female kitten it is possible to have an operation to prevent her from having kittens, but, besides being cruel, it is unsatisfactory. She will come "on heat" just the same and the nuisance of neighbouring toms hanging about the garden is not avoided. It is better not to allow a female to have kittens before she is a year old. She will come "on heat" before that age, but by careful watching and a judicious shutting up—providing her with a box of sand and plenty of food and drink—it can be prevented.

When a cat is carrying her kittens she must be given plenty of milk and nourishing food. A word here about general diet, then, will not be out of place. Although many people feed cats on the floor or on paper, it is unwise, as germs are often picked up that way and tiresome illnesses result. Each cat should have its own tin plate and tin saucer, which must be washed at least once a day, or gastric trouble and diarrhœa are likely to result. Two good meals a day with a saucer or so of milk between are what a cat needs. Fish, boiled or fried, but not salted; any meat, cooked or raw; liver and lights; green vegetables and potatoes are liked by cats. All food should be "good" and not just "going bad."

Diet.—Too much fish means a type of phosphorous poisoning which, being cumulative, takes a long time to manifest itself definitely. Then increasing listlessness, shedding of the coat, and, in acute stages, the cornea covering half the eye, shows what is the matter. It takes a long time to get the phosphorus out of the system, but it can be done by first giving a teaspoonful of castor oil, followed by a dessertspoonful of liquid paraffin every morning; and by keeping fish out of the diet for a while, giving instead mixed meat and vegetables.

Too much meat means a poor coat, so let the cat's evening meal at least be a real "dog's dinner" of meat, cut small, vegetables, and potatoes, all mashed with gravy. For breakfast, fish—occasionally given raw, which acts as an aperient—or boiled lights;

Fig. 1.—Long-haired Cats should be combed daily

or raw liver, or minced meat, may be given alone if liked. A varied diet is what is necessary.

Despite belief to the contrary, it is better to cut cats' food up small, as if it is given in chunks, they bolt it whole and their hunger is not so easily appeased, while digestive troubles result. Bones which splinter should not be given but hard bones are good for the teeth.

Water must be accessible, for all cats like it, however much milk they drink.

A cat carrying her kittens needs the same type of meals, but more milk should be included in the diet. Occasionally it is a good idea to give lactol, a richer mixture than cow's milk. This may be given to kittens, too, because it more resembles their mother's milk, which is three times stronger than that of the cow.

Kittens.—A cat carries her kittens about sixty-three days, and, during the last fortnight, she will be looking for a bed in boxes, cupboards, drawers, and wardrobes. This is the time to make ready a bed and put her in it once or twice so that she becomes accustomed to it.

Because she prefers a dark place out of a draught, an ideal bed is a large, square, cardboard hat box, with a hinged lid. Strip the edging from the lid and cut a quarter of it away so that the cat can get in and out and have air. Crumpled tissue paper makes a soft bed, and can easily be removed, and a piece of soft blanket substituted after the event. Place the bed somewhere quiet, and the cat will retire to it quite happily when ready.

Usually the kittens are born easily, but if there is any difficulty, you must call in the vet., who, with the aid of whelping forceps, will help their birth.

A healthy cat can bring up four kittens, but unless you are deliberately breeding cats, you will only want to keep one or two. It is cruel to take away all the kittens, for it endangers the mother's health; but if you must do it, do so immediately, before they have begun feeding. Decide which kittens you are keeping, and then take the others away the first time the mother leaves the bed. You can either drown them at once in a bucket of cold water, fitting a tin plate in the water over them so that they are submerged; or you can have them chloroformed.

As kittens' eyes are not open till ten days after birth, the cat should stay in the box, but after the eyes are open it is a good plan to remove the mother and kittens to a round cat basket which can be purchased cheaply. Many kittens have a discharge from the eyes when first open, and this can be cured by frequent bathing with warm boracic lint.

Examine the mother's teats from time to time, as sometimes one goes "blind" and the milk will not flow. Inattention results in swelling, and eventually an abscess forms. Bathe with hot boracic lotion and wool, and try, by gently squeezing, to get the milk through. If, after many attempts, you are unsuccessful, call the vet.

Encourage the kittens to lap at 24 days, and begin giving them bits of boiled fish and scraps of meat at seven weeks. Kittens can be house-trained by providing them with a box of sand, or sand and earth, for their needs. Where cats have no ready access to a garden, such a box, changed frequently, is a necessity.

A cat's natural medicine is grass, so if you live in a flat you must grow a regular supply in pots for it, either oats or cocksfoot grass (*Dactylis glomerata*), both of which can be bought in packets.

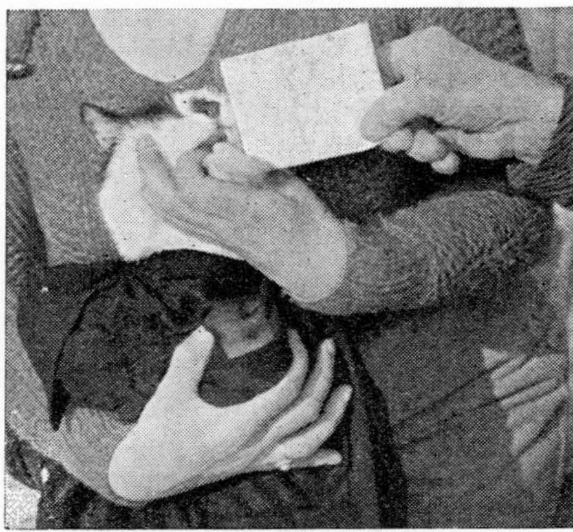

Fig. 2.—When giving a cat a powder or oil be sure to wrap it in a shawl first

When a cat is ill it is advisable to call the vet. at once, but there are several common illnesses which you can recognize and treat quite successfully yourself, and, incidentally, learn to avoid.

Long-haired cats often get a ball of fur in the stomach, particularly during the spring moult. The signs are listlessness, and a disinclination to eat; the cat becomes thin and its coat staring. Give a large teaspoonful of castor oil first thing in the morning and see that the cat can get out of doors as it acts quickly. Then for the three following mornings give a dessertspoonful of liquid paraffin. See that the cat has plenty of grass.

If you give a dessertspoonful of olive oil regularly, once a week, and comb the cat daily, this trouble can be avoided (Fig. 1).

To give cats various oils successfully, warm both the spoon and the oil, letting a little warm water remain in the former so that the oil runs off. Wrap the cat in a shawl, leaving only the head out (Fig. 2). Be quiet and gentle, and talk to it, for, once frightened the cat will resist all efforts. Get someone to hold the cat. Take its head in your left hand, and hold its nose up; place the spoon between the teeth and the left or right cheek, letting the oil slowly pour in. The oil will trickle through the teeth on to the tongue, when the cat will swallow it. Special medicine spoons for cats can be bought cheaply and are a great help in giving medicines (Fig. 4).

Pills are given by opening the mouth and placing the pill far back on the tongue; then the mouth is closed and held shut, while the throat should be stroked as this induces the cat to swallow.

Colds are common among cats and are characterized by frequent sneezing, running at the eyes, and sometimes dribbling. Don't let the cat out of doors at all; provide it with a box for its needs, and give it raw meat to eat. If, however, it is off its food, a tonic powder can be given. A neglected cold can be serious.

Bronchitis is marked by persistent dribbling, coughing, and wheezing, and a disinclination for food. Give a dose of

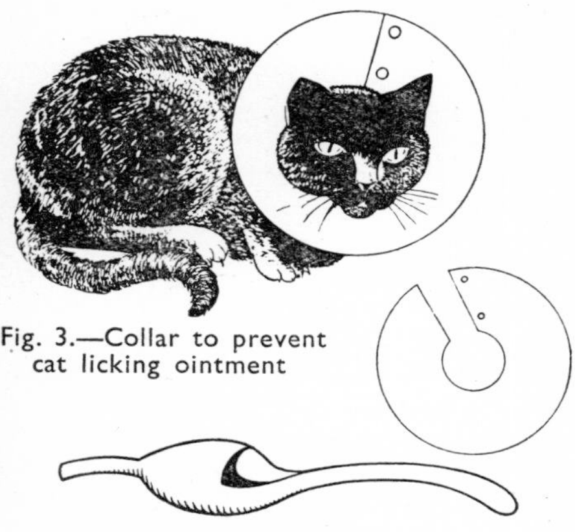

Fig. 3.—Collar to prevent cat licking ointment

Fig. 4.—Medicine Spoon

liquid paraffin, and fever or cough powders. Much relief is afforded by giving a camphorated oil inhalation. When the cat is dozing, place some boiling water in a jar and pour some oil on it; place the jar on the ground so that the cat gets the rising steam. A tent made of newspaper over the chair-top helps.

Pneumonia is more serious. Very quick breathing, no desire for food, occasionally a cough, and tenderness of the chest when pressed, a staring coat, and a very hot nose are signs of this. The temperature, taken with an ordinary half-minute thermometer left three minutes between the hind leg and the body, is 104°–105°. Start by giving a teaspoonful of castor oil, but be very careful how you give it as any excitement or struggling is most dangerous at this time. Make a pneumonia jacket from a piece of flannel about 18 in. wide and 12 in. long, according to the size of your cat. The photograph shows how to put it on. Line the chest part with double lint or wadding, not thermogene. Keep the patient in a warm place, and inhalations may be given as for bronchitis. Give lactol, juice from raw meat, meat jellies from a spoon or, if very ill, ten drops of brandy in milk every four hours. When the cat shows interest in food give a little raw meat, a raw egg beaten up in milk, a little boiled fish, and so on. Guard against constipation by giving liquid paraffin in the morning.

Fleas are often present in long-haired cats and nearly always on kittens. Anti-insect powder of a reliable make (specially prepared for cats) should be sprinkled on the coat, and the cat combed in the garden. Do not do this in a room as the fleas drop off and will live in warmth, and may be picked up again.

Mange is another disease from which even the best-cared-for cats suffer, as they pick it up from walls and posts visited by mangy toms. The commonest kind attacks the head and ears. The cat is always scratching and the hair comes off and leaves a grey, scaly surface and tiny red pimples. Treat with sulphur ointment or a reliable skin cure for four days, then wash with formalin soap and warm water, taking care to dry the places well. Repeat the treatment if necessary.

Fig. 5.—Pneumonia Jacket. Note draw-string at neck

Wounds must be bathed with boracic or permanganate of potash solution, and sores treated with sulphur ointment. But in cases of canker in the ear, jaundice, distemper, etc., it is better to consult a vet,

The main thing to remember when dealing with illness is to avoid excitement. Be gently persistent, talk to the cat, avoid getting scratched—if you do, paint the wound with iodine at once—and remember the value of castor oil and liquid paraffin.

GUINEA-PIGS, or cavies as they are known among fanciers, make most satisfactory pets as they are not difficult to rear, or expensive to buy. There are three chief kinds of cavies—the English, or smooth-coated, which may be purchased in any colouring; the Abyssinian, with its fur growing in a series of rosettes, which can be had in red, tortoiseshell, or tortoiseshell and white; and the long-haired Peruvian.

For the beginner either of the first two is preferable as Peruvians need a tremendous amount of attention in order to keep their coat from matting, daily brushing being a necessity, while at the same time they are not so hardy.

English and Abyssinians can both be housed successfully in out-of-door hutches, but the Peruvian needs an indoor house. There is no doubt, however, that the Peruvian, with its long, silky coat in fawn and white, or agouti and white, is the most attractive in appearance, and for those of you who are taking up the breeding of cavies seriously and wish to exhibit, it is a breed which offers tremendous possibilities.

Whatever kind of guinea-pigs you intend to have, however, the chief rule is to buy good stock. Do not be tempted by those exhibited in the streets or by itinerant vendors in open-air markets. Go to a reliable breeder and take his advice. It may cost a little more, but it is well worth it.

Guinea-pigs make successful pets for children, though it is rather cruel to keep a single sow or boar in solitary confinement as people often do. If you are going to keep guinea-pigs for pleasure only, you will need to buy only a boar and a sow, and it is a good plan to get the fancier to point out to you any weak point in the sow you choose and ask him to let you have a boar who is perfect in these points. Then, when they mate, you may have some perfect specimens in the litter. It is just as easy to remove some of the young cavies soon after birth and drown them as you do kittens if you want to reduce the number of the litter. If, on the other hand, you want to breed a good number of youngsters, a boar will serve up to three sows quite satisfactorily.

When you begin breeding from your own stock you will find it very much wiser not to breed from sows until they are about a year old.

Hutches.—You can keep your guinea-pigs out of doors all the year round as long as you do not place your hutch in a draughty spot, or facing north where they get no sun. Many people have the hutches in sheds, however, and others just build a lean-to of tarpaulin with no sides under which the hutches can be placed in winter. Hutches should be built of thick wood, and be divided by a wooden partition, rather more than half having a ½-in. wire-mesh front, and the other a wooden front. The latter, as in the photograph, can be a complete door, or there can be two small doors, one in each half. The roof should slope down towards the back and be covered with tarpaulin, tarred and sanded to make it waterproof.

Single hutches may well be made from sugar boxes, but if you are keeping any number of cavies, batches of six hutches, arranged in two tiers of three are often used. On the outside of each hutch there should be a holder for a card on which must be written details of mating, diet, etc., of the inmate. It is worth while to fit small padlocks on the doors.

Whether hutches are housed in a shed or out of doors they should be raised from the ground, preferably on trestles. It is a good idea to have a waterproof sheet which can be hooked across the fronts of outdoor hutches in bad weather.

For Abyssinian and English cavies excellent bedding can be made from a layer of sawdust or cedar litter covered with hay. The sawdust and litter are absorbent and deodorant. For Peruvians it is unwise to give either sawdust or hay as both tend to matt their coats; straw cut up fairly small makes ideal bedding for them.

Cleaning out the hutches is not a pleasant task, but the longer you leave it the worse it will be, besides being very bad for the

Fig. 6.—Group of Cages for Cavies or Rabbits. Note dark compartments

animals. You should have set days on which to do it, and periodically scrub them out with warm water in which some permanganate of potash crystals have been dissolved.

Cavies are all the better for exercise although many people provide no run for them. It is easy to construct a wire run in the form of a long, rectangular box of wire mesh, about 1 ft. in height, with wooden supports at the corners and a door at one end. The animals can either be transferred by hand to it, or sloping wired boards leading from the hutches, down which they can walk into the "run," can be made. If the run can be placed on the grass, the cavies will be able to nibble the grass through the wire bottom.

Diet.—Cavies are easy to feed, but, as with cats, variety in their food is necessary if you wish to keep them healthy. Feeding troughs can be bought very cheaply and are much the best way of giving them mashes and bran. These should be scrubbed once a week with warm water containing permanganate of potash, or digestive troubles and diarrhœa may result. Two good meals a day are ideal for ordinary stock, though young ones and sows carrying their young need a midday meal. Avoid, at all costs, the indiscriminate giving of tit-bits by visitors as cavies are very liable to indigestion, which sets up constipation and brings a train of other ills in its wake.

Garden produce in the form of lettuce, carrot roots and tops, and hedge food in the form of dandelions, hedge parsley, and sow thistle is good. With the morning meal of green stuff give some dry bran. About five o'clock in the afternoon give either oats or a barley meal mash. Swedes, turnips and cabbage stumps should be given now and then as the nibbling of them is good for the teeth. Water, milk and water, and sometimes pure milk should be given them to drink, and it is a good plan in hot weather to mix a little flowers of sulphur in the milk to act as a cooling medicine.

Breeding.—It is very important to note the exact date of service of each of your sows so that you can put the boar into a hutch by himself at the right time, and can prepare a nursery for the sow. Seventy days is the time which sows carry their young, and it is much better to take the boar away after 40 days. After that time take great care not to fuss or disturb the sow in any way, or the results will be bad. If you can possibly make her a new nursery in a different hutch it is well worth while. See that the interior of the hutch is scrubbed with disinfectant—not a strong-smelling one, or she will be upset: permanganate of potash crystals in solution are most satisfactory as they are odourless.

If you cannot have another hutch, let the sow spend a morning in the wire run a few days before the litter is expected, and scrub out her hutch, giving her plenty of bedding, particularly in the dark part of the hutch. You must clip any long-haired sow from motives of cleanliness.

During the whole 70 days and for 28 days afterwards it is advisable to give your sow green stuff in the middle of the day, with a bread-and-milk breakfast instead of the usual food, and boiled oats or mash for supper. The ordinary drinking water should be supplemented with milk, for the young will drink this and begin to take some of the bread and milk when a week old.

Give the sow plenty of milk to drink as long as the young are with her. In a month's time begin taking the young away from her and putting the young sows in one hutch and the young boars into another. If you take all the young away at once the mother's supply of milk cannot regulate itself to the sudden change, and the effect on her health will be bad.

Cavies well repay attention to their toilet, even though you may not want to exhibit them. The English ones should be well brushed towards the tail with a soft brush and then smoothed with the hands. The Abyssinians, on the other hand, need brushing with a stiff brush, for they are wiry coated, and towards the head. Each rosette needs teasing out with a small brush. The Peruvians respond to an oil dressing before brushing.

Coughs and Colds beset guinea-pigs just as they do cats. In either case give plenty of warm milk and a warm mash at night. For a cough give a teaspoonful of glycerine twice a day, the same method of dosing as for cats being successful. A persistent cold yields to three drops of sweet spirits of nitre in milk twice a day.

Diarrhœa calls for castor oil, an egg-spoonful being enough. While the animal is suffering from this give dry bran and dry oats.

Skin Diseases in cavies usually mean that the blood is out of order. Give milk of magnesia in their drinking milk for a few days.

PARROTS.—Most people choose to keep a parrot as a pet for the joy of teaching it to talk. If this is your chief consideration you will do well to buy a grey parrot or a blue-fronted Amazon, as they are definitely the most teachable. Naturally, as with humans, individuals differ, and some parrots can be taught to talk more readily than others of the same species. Some people maintain that a cock bird is better than a hen for teaching purposes, others the opposite, but no hard and fast rule can be laid down about this.

Cockatoos can also be taught to talk with care, but not so fluently as the others; and there is no doubt that they scream horribly. Their appearance is attractive, however, and the crest which can be raised and lowered at will, gives them a fascinating appearance. If you do choose to buy one, the greater sulphur crested, or the rose breasted are the most attractive, and, with patience, some of these make most successful pets.

The Grey Parrot.—The approximate age of this steel-grey bird with its crimson tail and black beak can be told by the iris of the eye, which is grey when the bird is young and pale yellow when it is older. Like a good many of the parrots there is no difference in the colour of the plumage of the hen and cock birds; but possibly, on comparison, the cocks are slightly larger and their heads more rounded.

Though the ordinary screeching voice of the parrot is far from musical, it is so easy to teach them to imitate the human voice and the birds themselves so delight in indulging in their repertoire that one is seldom bothered by the screeching. Grey parrots can mimic animals, can carry on almost a conversation, and can be taught popular songs. They are, however, shy of performing in front of strangers.

The Amazons.—Although there are at least nine types of Amazon parrots, the ones usually found in bird fanciers' shops are the mealy, the blue-fronted, and the yellow-shouldered. The mealy Amazon, as its name suggests, is characterized by its mealy appearance. Its back is brighter green than its underparts, while its under-tail coverts, forehead and cheeks are yellow. The centre of its head is yellow too, but often spotted with red, and its nape feathers are edged with black. The red edging, its black and bluish wings, its grey beak, orange-marked mandibles, and orange-rimmed brown eyes make it an attractive-looking bird.

One point in its favour is that it is not spiteful as many other parrots are, but certain of this type are frightful shriekers.

The Blue-fronted Amazon is a hardier bird than the mealy and much more talkative. It is a large, bright green bird with a blue forehead. Its face and throat are yellow, and it has two red and two blue primaries (i.e. large quill feathers in the wing). Its beak is dark and it has orange-centred eyes. The amount it can be taught is enormous, and a parrot of this kind will abundantly repay the care and attention bestowed upon its education.

The yellow-shouldered Amazon is another green parrot, but all its feathers have black edges. The forehead and beak are white, and the top of the head and ear coverts, throat and cheeks, as well as the top of the wings, are yellow. There are red feathers in its wings and the red and blue tail feathers are banded with yellow.

The female of the species is marked by a difference in plumage, for it is duller in colour, and the lower underparts are bright blue. This, however, is a parrot which you must take on chance, for some are easy to teach and some are quite hopeless.

Parrots are comparatively expensive birds to buy. The main thing again when purchasing your pet is to get it from a reliable dealer. The itinerant vendors of parrots who occasionally haunt the streets may be able to offer you a healthy bird, but it is wise not to buy from them. If your parrot is alive two months after you have bought him, you can be sure it is a healthy bird.

Fig. 7.—Best Type of Parrot Cage

Cages for parrots should be large, and preferably square, as in Fig. 7. The bottom tray should be of metal as it is easier to keep clean. The seed box and drinking bowl should be porcelain lined, and if a swinging perch is included, it should not get in the parrot's way when it is sitting on the perch.

Sand for the tray should be sea sand and not shell sand as the salt in the former is beneficial to the bird, while the fragments of shell in the latter, when swallowed, are liable to injure the intestines. If, however, your parrot manifests that appalling habit of eating the excreta, a wire rack must be fitted over the bottom of the cage through which it cannot get its claws, and grit given for eating in a box.

Possibly the reason for the early loss of many parrots is incorrect diet. Parrots are not used to animal or sloppy food—the former, and an excess of the latter, lead to digestive troubles. Boiled maize can be given twice a week—young birds should be given it until they are weaned on to dry seeds. Boiled potatoes may be given occasionally, but you should avoid feeding parrots with scraps from the table. Besides giving it a mixture of hemp, wheat, and canary seed, or sunflower sometimes instead of hemp, give it a little fruit. Pieces of ripe orange, apple and pear, or grapes, and bananas especially, are very much liked by greys and Amazons. A leaf of lettuce, a fresh green pea-pod, or a shelled walnut stuck through the bars are also appreciated. You *must* provide a piece of cuttle-fish bone which the bird can chew.

Sick Birds, unlike sick animals, can not so readily be cured, although there are many advertised cures for all ills on the market, and success with them is not unknown. However, there are one or two mild ailments to which they are prone, and which can be cured with a little trouble.

Just as cat lovers keep castor oil and liquid paraffin handy, parrot keepers must keep glycerine. Colds so often caught by leaving the cage uncovered at night—do not forget to leave an opening for air, by the way—can be cured by putting six drops of glycerine in the drinking water, which should never be given stone cold, but with the chill taken off it. Some chillies should be mixed in with the seed. Some people also put a rusty nail in the drinking water in order to supply the bird with a little tincture of iron. Asthma, too, calls for glycerine in the drinking water but you must be careful not to give too large a dose.

Diarrhœa can be alleviated by giving Epsom salts in the drinking water in the proportion of half a teaspoonful to a large breakfast cup, followed, the next day, by a few drops of whisky in the drinking water. Drinking water must be changed at least twice a day.

Feather Eating is one of the vices that may be indulged in by all parrots, and can be of two kinds: the bird either pulls a feather out deliberately and chews the end; or, when appearing to be preening itself, pecks at the soft base of the quill, causing the feather to droop. Then the bird finally bites it off. Some people say that giving it bones is the cause of this, but it is often caused by skin irritation or by boredom. It is rather difficult to cure.

Try clipping the wings and letting the parrot loose in a room where there are some non-poisonous tree branches on which it can perch and peck. Give it some Epsom salts in its drinking water or one of the reliable feather-eating cures advertised. When recaged, give it a piece of wood to chew, and occasionally some liquid magnesia in the drinking water.

RABBITS.—Many of the illnesses to which rabbits are subject are due to bad housing conditions, so, before you purchase your stock, be sure that you have the right type of home ready for them. The essentials are: warmth, dryness, fresh air, and avoidance of draughts. As with guinea-pigs, rabbits may be housed in single hutches, or in tiers of hutches; and these may be entirely out of doors, or placed in a shelter. In either case they should face south and be sheltered from the east winds.

An excellent shelter may be made by erecting a sloping roof of corrugated iron with the angle of two walls making two sides, the others being left open. Hutches placed in this on trestles—never on the ground or flat against the wall—will ensure that your rabbits are unlikely to get colds, chills, inflamed eyes, or cramp.

Hutches similar to those made for guinea-pigs, but larger, can be made from boxes obtained from the grocer, or specially constructed from thick wood. An ideal hutch is 5 ft. long, 3 ft. wide, and 2 ft. high, with small mesh wire two-thirds of the way along its front. This can be used to house several bucks, or does, or by putting in a partition, as a breeding hutch.

If the hutch is partitioned for breeding purposes, it must have a door in the wire run too, to avoid disturbing the nesting doe. Nesting boxes may be purchased from dealers, or copied from illustrations. A type often used is rectangular, with a hinged lid covering part of the top, and a hinged flap in front, which comes half-way up the box and is let down when the young rabbits can open their eyes.

Troughs with weighted bases should be used for mashes and as drinking vessels, and a wire hammock rack, which can easily be made at home, fitted at the side to hold greenstuff and hay. Throwing food on the floor, as many people do, contaminates it and results in digestive troubles. Although rabbits obtain much moisture from their green food, water should be given, especially to does in kindle, as then they are very thirsty. Hutches must be cleaned at least twice a week and food receptacles kept clean, or diarrhœa and parasitical infections will result.

Sawdust is the best litter for the run, and hay and straw cut in short lengths for the nesting box. Sawdust should not be used, however, for long-haired rabbits. A few holes bored in the bottom of the hutches keep the floors dry.

Whatever your reason for keeping rabbits, go to a reliable breeder. Some people think it unwise for a beginner to buy a buck and a doe, but advise the purchase of one well-bred doe about eight months old, housing her for a month and then sending her to the breeder for "service."

Breeds.—*Dutch* rabbits as pets, with their rounded bodies and short ears, and their amusing half white, half brown, grey, fawn or black coats, are very satisfactory. *English* rabbits are attractive too, with their dark-striped spines, cheek spots, and moth-shaped markings on their mouths, showing up well against their white pelts. *Blue Beverans*, as their name suggests, are beautifully coloured, and vie with the *Silvers* in appearance and all-round utility, being successfully bred for pelt and table.

Among rabbits whose worth lies in their fur, the *Angora* comes first to the mind; but *Belgian Hares*, *Flemish Giants*, *Chinchillas* and *Havanas* are also very profitable.

The whole secret of Angora keeping lies in roomy hutches and daily care of the coat. Nothing looks and is more miserable than a neglected specimen. In health the Angora's fur is silky and the eyes wine red. The fur obtained from daily grooming with a stiff brush is kept, and three crops of fur a year from each rabbit is usual. These are obtained by clipping with scissors. Straw cut in short lengths must be used on the floor of the hutches and very little mash is required for feeding.

The golden tan pelt of the Belgian hare is ticked with dark hair except on its chest. This animal must be given roomy quarters, as must the grey Flemish Giant. Chinchillas and brown Havanas are expensive to buy but well worth considering by the serious breeder.

Having chosen your variety—and you should have only one breed to start with—matters of feeding will now occupy your attention. Remember that rabbits are greedy and will eat more food than they need when in confinement. Two meals a day,

Fig. 8.—Angoras are best kept in wire-bottomed cages to prevent their fur matting

one of solid food and one of greenstuff are necessary. Green food must be increased during the summer and solid food cut down, but not altogether omitted.

Feed at a regular hour each day, and make the morning meal a crumby mash of about two ounces of bran and of barley meal, with sometimes half an ounce of fish meal per rabbit. Or a mash of boiled wheat and oats, or household scraps such as chopped cheese rind, fruit parings, and dry bread may be added to a mash of bran. In the evening half a pound of greenstuff per rabbit is enough; but these amounts must be balanced according to the season. Broccoli and cauliflower are preferable to cabbage; parsley, dandelions, sow-thistles, lettuce, pea-pods, apple and hawthorn leaves, carrots, swedes, and turnips, may all be given; but change of greenstuff must be gradual, or digestive troubles will result. Does with young may be given bread and milk at midday, and milk also to drink, but the milk must be boiled first.

Breeding.—A doe indicates she is "in season" by behaving oddly. The young are carried for 30 days and just before they are born the doe makes a nest of fur plucked from her own body in the hay. Cover the hutch while she is having her young and keep her very quiet. Disturbance sometimes results in her killing the young. The litter can be examined for weaklings when she has gone into the run to feed. Leave the young rabbits with the doe for at least six weeks, and separate the bucks from the does at three months. Does can be hutched together until they are eight months old, but bucks must be separated sooner, as they fight.

Colds can be cured by a bread-and-milk diet, with a few drops only of glycerine added at night. Diarrhœa needs dry mashes and no green food, while constipation can be cured by giving more green food and a little liquid paraffin. Bathe inflamed eyes in warm boric lotion. Other more serious diseases are better treated by a vet.

PIGEONS.—At first sight pigeons may not appeal to the town dweller as pets. Certainly the word "pigeons" conjures up a picture of a farmyard with Fantails or Pouters strutting among the hens at feeding time. But though both these breeds can be kept in town, as also can Tumblers and Magpies, the Homer, or Messenger, pigeons are the ones which have a universal appeal. There is more fun to be had out of keeping them, for, what could be more exciting than the training of Homers?

Their natural instinct is, of course, to return home the moment they are released, or "tossed" as it is usually called. If you begin with a half-mile toss, and gradually increase the distance you can train your birds to return home from miles away. The only thing to remember is to start training in the summer at the age of three and a half months, and to take them out about twice a week. Later, you may enter them in contests, and in meeting various other owners you will learn more of pigeon management than in any other way.

Whatever kind of pigeons you choose, buy good stock from a reliable fancier. It is a good idea to start with one or two pairs only.

As with most pets, illness among pigeons is usually due to bad housing and improper feeding, so care must be taken to house and feed them correctly.

The Loft or Cote.—If you are definitely going to breed pigeons, you should have a loft. If you intend only to keep a few, a pigeon cote made from an old barrel and thatched as in the illustration is quite satisfactory. It is supplied inside with perches and its construction makes it unnecessary to wire the windows as must, however, be done in an ordinary loft as a protection against cats.

Pigeon lofts can be purchased at a reasonable price, but if you are building one, a wooden shed, 15 ft. by 9 ft. and about 8 ft. high, divided in half horizontally, so that the pigeons can use the top half, i.e. the loft, and the ground floor can be used to store food, etc., is very satisfactory. The loft should have wire-netted windows along the top front, opening upwards, and held by a chain, for pigeons must have light and

Fig. 9.—A Novel Dove-cote made from an old barrel

air. Tiers of perches, made of boards about 6 in. wide and divided off every foot by vertical boards like an enormous egg box, placed well out of any draught, is an arrangement which gives every bird a perch to itself and avoids squabbling in the loft.

Sand the floor of your loft, and also provide extra grit in a pan. Suitable grit is specially sold for the purpose. Plenty of water both inside and outside the loft should be available. All the drinking bowls must be emptied twice a day and properly refilled—do not just add a little more water to them. Perches should be scraped every day, and the loft tidied daily also, and thoroughly cleaned at least once a week with an occasional dusting with one of the standard disinfectant powders.

Pigeons love baths and will attempt to use their drinking bowls for the purpose if none are provided. This means contaminated water and resultant illness. Buy a galvanized bath about 24 in. square and be sure always to have at least 3 in. of water in it.

Nesting Boxes can be purchased cheaply, but do not fit them into the loft as they will be hard to clean and are also a temptation to the birds to go broody at the wrong time. Early in March divide off one end of the loft temporarily and put in the nesting boxes together with lengths of straw and hay to aid them in building.

Diet.—Feed your pigeons morning and evening, and do it at the same hour each day. Ready-mixed pigeon food is quite cheap. It is largely composed of dried peas, tick beans, wheat, barley and maize. Feed the birds out of doors if possible. If you feed in the loft in pans, clear up as soon as possible any remains on the floor, or the birds will eat the dirty grain later, and be ill.

The hen will make a nest soon after pairing and will lay two eggs. Above all, do not fuss her when she is sitting. A fortnight later, after the eggs are hatched, the two young should be feeding themselves, and a new nesting box must be given to the hen, as she will lay two more eggs.

When the birds are moulting after the summer, put a rusty nail in their drinking water, as this adds the necessary percentage of iron to it. Give them a handful of linseed to every dozen birds each day, and hang a cauliflower or a cabbage in reach over the floor, but remove daily any leaves thrown on the floor. Clean the loft floor every day so that the loose feathers are removed and parasitical infection avoided. Incidentally, it is a good plan to sprinkle nesting boxes with insecticide.

It is advisable to divide your loft into two parts, with perches in each during the winter months, i.e. October–February, and keep the hens and cocks separate during this time.

When a bird looks seedy, try giving it half a teaspoonful of olive oil. Unless it is really ill, it will recover quickly. A bird, which is undoubtedly ill, however, should be killed.

Study the pigeon fanciers' papers, join a pigeon racing club, and get to know other fanciers if you want to get the most fun out of your pigeon pets.

General Hints—(*a*) Give clean wholesome food in clean utensils.

(*b*) Keep liquid paraffin, flowers of sulphur, milk of magnesia and olive oil handy.

(*c*) Scrub houses with permanganate of potash solution, and see that they are dry and draught-proof.

(*d*) Feed all pets regularly and avoid giving tit-bits.

(*e*) Be consistent in your treatment of them; do not speak harshly, but be firm.

(*f*) Take the advice of Fanciers—they know from experience.

PHOTOGRAPHY

SOME people regard photography as a matter of pressing a button and letting the chemist do the rest. It *can* be as easy as that, but even if you do not wish to trouble about the developing and printing of your pictures there are certain things it is necessary for you to know about the principles of photography if you are to get satisfactory results and the greatest pleasure out of your hobby.

Types of Camera.—The beginner has first to decide on the type of camera. The simplest to handle are the box-form, roll-film cameras, and although these cost only a few shillings each the standard makes are remarkably efficient. The details of the working of these cameras differ slightly, but with each one a booklet of instructions is given, and the beginner will be well advised to spend half an hour or so reading the booklet and examining the inner workings of the camera—in so far as they are visible without taking the camera to pieces.

The shutter, which permits the light to enter the camera, is normally set for snapshot work, and if you take away the back of the camera and hold the body up to the light and press the shutter release, you can see how the shutter opens for a fraction of a second—generally about one twenty-fifth of a second in the cheapest cameras. Now set the shutter for a time exposure. Press the shutter release once and the shutter will open and remain open until the release is pressed the second time. While it is open examine the stops, or different-sized openings, by means of which the amount of light entering the camera can be regulated.

A great deal depends upon getting the exposure correct, and as this type of camera has only one snapshot, or instantaneous speed, the exposure can only be regulated by means of the stops. On a bright day in the open country the smallest stop can be used, but if the sky is overcast, and the light poor, the largest stop will be necessary in order to get the maximum amount of light through to the film.

Most people know that the photograph is taken by the light rays striking upon the sensitive emulsion on the film or plate at the back of the camera after they have passed through the lens. The film or plate must not be exposed unless in a dark room illuminated only by a safe light, which is generally a deep ruby light. This is because the red light has no effect upon ordinary and orthochromatic films and plates.

Charging the Box Camera.—The user of the box camera, however, does not

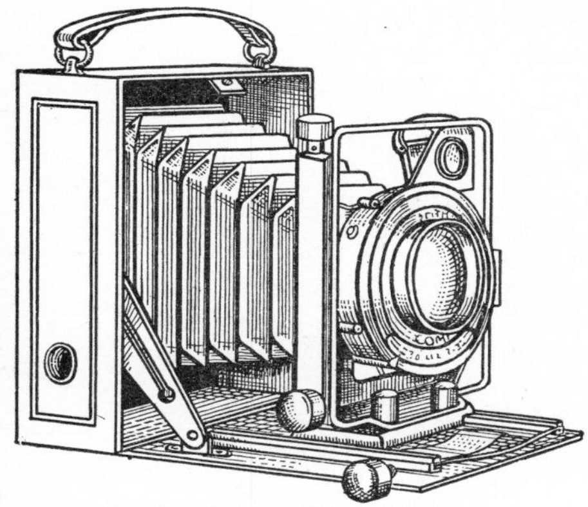

Fig. 1.—Folding Plate Camera

need a dark room for loading and changing films, because the films are supplied wrapped round with light-proof paper which is not unrolled until the spool on which the film and paper is wound is actually in the camera. The dealer from whom the film is purchased will show how it should be inserted in the camera. When the spool is in position the film is unwound on to an empty spool so that after the preliminary protecting paper has been unrolled the film is brought into position at the back of the camera. As this operation is being performed keep your eye on the little red peep-hole at the back of the camera, and stop winding when the figure "1" comes into view.

You are now ready to take your first photograph. In selecting your subject remember that although the cheap camera will take satisfactory pictures of many things, it will not take all subjects in all circumstances. Good light is necessary. Choose first a few landscape scenes, or views in which any near objects are well lighted. The view-finder will enable you to aim the camera accurately. If the view-finder is of the direct-vision type (that is, the type through which you look with the camera held at eye level) so much the better, though you have to be more careful in its use. Generally you get better results with the camera held at eye level—you do not normally view from breast or hip level.

Lighting.—A useful rule for beginners is to have the light behind them so that it falls directly on to the object photographed, but often more effective pictures can be taken "against the light," or with a good side light. It is important never to permit the rays of the sun to shine directly into the lens.

Choosing the Picture.—If your snapshot album is to be an interesting one great care must be taken in the selection of scenes photographed. If you are lucky enough to take a photograph of the Taj Mahal, do not let there be a huge figure of Mary or Tommy standing self-consciously in the foreground. It certainly adds to the personal interest of a photograph for a member of the party to be included, but let the personal figure be incidental to the picture.

Panoramic scenes and wide landscape views are all very well once in a while, but often the wide expanse that looks impressive to the eye is disappointing as recorded by the camera. Snaps of more restricted scenes generally provide better pictures—the old water mill, the thatched cottage, the fisherman mending his nets, the picturesque corner of the village street, etc. Some old churches and inns provide pretty snaps, but care should be taken to find the most

Fig. 2.—Folding Roll-film Camera

artistic viewpoint. Pictures are often improved if they have a natural "frame." Many a view can be photographed through an archway or doorway. The branches of an overhanging tree may also help to provide a good "frame."

Snaps of animals and children at play provide some of the best pictures, but they should be as natural as possible. If you wish to take a snap at fairly close quarters you may find it difficult to get the focusing correct unless you are good at judging distances. The beginner is advised to decide on which spot he wishes the subject to stand, and then to take up an appropriate position, and wait patiently until the subject, either naturally or by tactful persuasion, achieves the desired pose. Figures should be taken against a suitable background, wherever possible, and not against the sky. Avoid taking portrait snaps of people with their legs closer to you than their bodies—distortion follows and the feet look much too big.

As a rule the camera should be held straight and upright, but do not be afraid to experiment and take shots from unusual angles.

Immediately you have taken one picture, wind the film into the second position. Get into the habit of doing this immediately—it will save many double exposures.

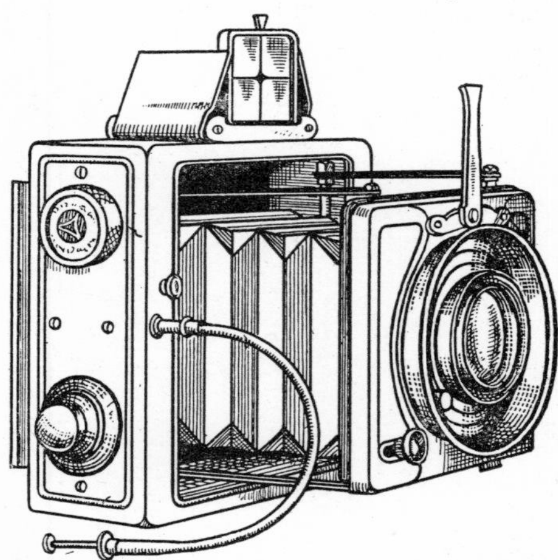

Fig. 3.—Folding Camera (press type) with Focal-plane Shutter

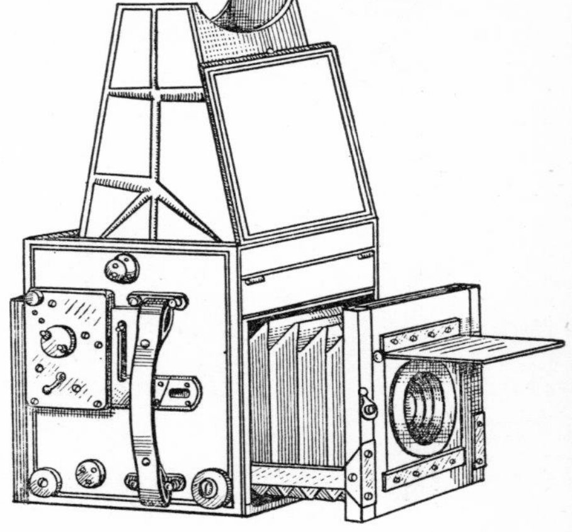

Fig. 4.—Reflex Camera

When the spool is finished continue winding until the protecting paper is off the original spool, seal the used film and hand it to the chemist for developing and printing. You can develop your own films but before dealing with that we will consider other types of cameras.

The Folding Roll-film Camera is very compact and easily handled. Apart from its compactness it has generally a better lens than the box form, and has a focusing adjustment that enables near objects to be photographed. With box cameras you cannot as a rule get nearer than a dozen feet, though some are fitted with focusing attachments, and even for the simplest box camera a portrait lens can be purchased that will fit on the front, enabling photographs to be taken at short distances.

Folding Plate Cameras are popular with amateurs who wish to do their own developing, partly because plates are cheaper than films, and partly because there is no need to wait until six or more exposures have been made before starting to develop. Plates are much heavier and more bulky to carry, but by means of a film pack adapter it is possible to overcome this difficulty and use flat films. These are supplied in a film pack, which is an ingenious device whereby twelve flat films are packed in a kind of box and placed in the adapter at the back of the camera. As each exposure is made a new film is brought to the front of the pack by pulling a paper tab bearing the number of the film exposed.

A plate camera is almost invariably fitted with a focusing screen, a piece of ground glass which is placed in the plate position, and upon which the picture about to be photographed is thrown. This enables the picture to be focused accurately and also more easily composed. An additional refinement with which this type of camera is usually fitted is a double extension which enables photographs to be taken of objects quite close to the camera, and copying work to be done.

The Reflex Camera is rather bulky and heavy, but it has a number of advantages. It is fitted with an additional focusing screen on the top, the picture being reflected upwards by means of a mirror which automatically slips out of the way just as the exposure is about to be made. This top focusing screen is viewed through a hood, and the photographer is able to view and focus his picture up to the moment of exposure.

Having decided which type of camera to use, the next point to settle is the size. The smallest vest-pocket cameras are extremely convenient to carry, are inexpensive to run, and satisfactory enlargements can be made from the negatives. On the other hand people who wish to do their own developing and printing generally prefer something a little larger. The $3\frac{1}{2}$ in. by $2\frac{1}{2}$ in. size is large enough for pleasing contact prints (prints made direct from the negative without enlargement) though perhaps the ideal size for the serious-minded amateur is the quarter-plate ($3\frac{1}{4}$ in. by $4\frac{1}{4}$ in.).

The cost of cameras varies enormously—from three or four shillings to £50 to £100—and it is safe to say that generally the more spent the better proportionately the value obtained.

The Lens is the most important part of the camera. The cheapest cameras are

Fig. 5.—Scenic effects should not be obscured by "human interest" even though it is improved by some living object

fitted with single achromatic lens. Next comes what is known as Rapid Rectilinear lens (commonly known as R.R. lens). These give a picture that does not show curvature of straight lines, and are more efficient. A great improvement on these two types is the Anastigmatic lens. The speed of a lens depends upon the largest size of aperture or stop with which it can be satisfactorily used. The apertures or stops are numbered according to the "F." system, and the number is arrived at by calculations involving the focal length of the lens, and the size of the stop opening. The smaller the opening, the higher the "F." number. A cheap lens has to be used with an aperture of a comparatively high "F." number, because with a larger aperture the picture would not be sharp and clear all over. Thus the lens that works satisfactorily with the largest aperture (that is, a small "F." number) is the fastest because the greatest amount of light passes through the lens and the plate receives a satisfactory impression in the shortest space of time. There is another system of marking stops known as the Uniform Standard. These numbers are described as U.S. numbers and as this system is used in many cameras a table is printed on this page giving the comparative exposure required for a given subject.

U.S. No. . . .	1	2	4	8	16	32
F. No. . . .	F.4	F.5·6	F.8	F.11	F.16	F.22
Comparative Exposures	1 sec.	2 secs.	4 secs.	8 secs.	16 secs.	32 secs.

From this it will be seen that with an F.11 stop twice the exposure is required as would be the case with an F.8 stop.

Although it is an advantage to have a fast lens, you do not always want to use the largest aperture, for with a large aperture there is a decrease in the depth of focus. For instance, with an aperture of F.4 or larger, it is necessary to focus accurately on the main object, and it will be found that objects a little nearer or further away are out of focus or fuzzy. By using a smaller stop, say, F.8, the range at which everything is in focus is increased. Incidentally, this depth of focus is greater in small cameras than in larger ones. The beginner who is using a hand camera has to judge his distances more accurately with the larger camera because generally speaking the larger the camera the greater the focal length of the lens, and the greater the focal length of the lens the smaller the depth of focus.

Shutters.—Most hand cameras are fitted with between lens shutters, giving instantaneous exposures ranging from 1/250 sec. to 1 sec., and also enabling time and bulb exposures to be taken. Reflex cameras and some folding cameras of the type used by press photographers have focal-plane shutters which operate immediately in front of the plate or film. When these shutters are released a blind with a slit in it flashes across the plate, the exposure being regulated by altering the width of the slit, and by adjusting the tension of the spring which works the shutter.

A tripod or stand is useful for all types of cameras and is really indispensable for the serious worker.

The Choice of Plates.—Plates differ considerably in sensitiveness or speed, and the speeds are indicated by an H. and D. number on the box. For ordinary purposes these numbers range from H. and D. 200 to H. and D. 1 400. The beginner should avoid an ultra fast plate—H. and D. 300 is a good speed to begin with. He should keep to one make until he is familiar with it, as different makes of plates vary slightly in their reactions to the developer.

Ordinary plates do not reproduce colour values accurately. For instance, reds and yellows appear darker in the finished print than they should, and blues appear nearly white. This fault can be corrected by using orthochromatic or panchromatic plates or films as described later. A simpler method is to use plates which include a filter in the emulsion. These are sold by most makers under such names as anti-filter, non-screen, etc. These give excellent results and are fast enough for ordinary purposes.

Exposure.—The best way of calculating the exposure is by means of an exposure meter which can be bought at varying prices. The best are those that measure the light by means of a piece of sensitized paper. The following factors have to be taken into account : Light, speed of plate or film; aperture, subject, distance. Photographic periodicals usually print monthly exposure tables, and these are very useful, for the light varies considerably from month to month. The exposure table given here can be taken as a rough guide when using plates of about 300–400 H. and D. between the hours of 11 a.m. and 3 p.m. in the months of May, June and July, with a stop of F.8. who has not an ultra rapid shutter should use the fastest speed he has and the largest aperture and note the result. Street scenes can be registered at exposures from 1/25 sec. to 1/100 sec. It will be understood that in many cases moving objects have to be under-exposed.

Open Landscape beach scenes.	Landscape with moderate foreground.	Street scenes and views with heavy foreground.	Portraits out of doors in shade	Portraits in ordinary rooms.
1/100	1/50	1/25	1/10	½ to 3 secs.

These exposures are for a fine sunny day. Reference to the table of stops will enable exposures with stops other than F.8 to be calculated. Multiply by 2 for diffused light and by 3 for dull light. Further multiplication must be made according to the month (April and August, 1¼ times; March and September 1½ times, etc.). Earlier and later in the day the exposure must be further prolonged, and as the days shorten the period when the light is considered brightest should be lessened to two hours, in the middle of the day.

Moving Objects are hardly suitable subjects for the beginner, but most amateurs like to have a shot at them. Snap them as they move obliquely towards the camera, rather than as they move directly across the field of view. This lessens the apparent motion. For foot sports an exposure of 1/250 sec. to 1/500 sec. should be given; for fast moving motor-cars or trains from 1/500 sec. to 1/1000 sec. The amateur

Dark Room.—Although roll films can be developed in daylight tanks, and it is thus possible to do without a dark room, the amateur who is really going to enjoy developing and printing his pictures needs one. If he has a small room or cupboard or shed that can be exclusively devoted to his photographic work he is fortunate. If not, then he must adapt the bathroom or scullery or some other part of the house temporarily. Light must be excluded, and if this cannot easily be done by heavy curtains it is well worth while making a light wooden frame covered with opaque material that will fit tightly into the window space. A curtain over the door may also be necessary. Guard against a makeshift arrangement. To have to pin a piece of blanket here and a piece of brown paper there, and to have to roll some rag to stop a light leak elsewhere, is very irritating and wastes time. A dark room lamp is needed. Electric light is best, but oil is quite satisfactory. The best type of lamp is fitted with a clear glass, a ruby glass and an orange glass. When developing bromide prints the orange glass is sufficient, but for plates the red glass should also be brought into use. A very dark green safe-light is necessary for panchromatic plates and films. If water is not laid on in the room, a supply of water in jugs or pails will be necessary as well as a pail for waste water.

Get into the habit of loading plates into the dark-slides, or containers, in the dark. It is quite easy to tell by touch which is the emulsion side of the plate, and an additional check is afforded by the fact that plates are invariably packed film to film in pairs. A changing bag in which this operation can be performed even in daylight is a useful little extravagance. Plates can also be changed under the bedclothes if the authorities of the household do not object, and this method is to be commended when on holiday. A dark raincoat is a useful help. The coat should be buttoned up and placed breast downwards on the bed with plate holders and box of plates inside in the middle. The top and bottom of the coat should be turned under and the photographer's arms pushed down the sleeves of the coat. A companion's help is useful in pulling the bedclothes over the whole and another precaution is to draw the curtains or blinds. With a little practice plates can be changed quite quickly.

Dark Room Equipment.—For developing plates of quarter-plate size the following will be required. One quarter-plate dish for developing, one whole plate dish for fixing, and a plate-washer, which can be the article specially designed for this purpose or any suitable dish or basin. A 4-oz. graduated glass measure and a 10-oz. measure and a drying rack are also required. It is a great convenience, of course, if the number of dishes can be at least duplicated.

For printing a printing frame is also required.

Developers.—If developers are to be made up scales are wanted. There are several excellent single solution developers sold ready made up in packets for dissolving in water or ready in solution form. A popular single solution developer is metol-hydroquinone. This gives clear negatives and is quick working: a useful formula is as follows:

Metol . . .	20 grains
Sodium sulphite .	1 oz.
Hydroquinone . .	25 grains
Sodium carbonate .	$\frac{3}{4}$ oz.
Distilled water to .	10 oz.

For use mix with an equal quantity of water.

Greater control in development is secured by using a two-solution developer. A pyro soda developer is favoured by many professional workers, and all plate makers give a formula on each box. For amateurs' work where under-exposure is at all likely a pyro metol developer is very good. This can be made up as follows:

No. 1 solution:

Metol . . .	20 grains
Potassium meta bisulphite . .	65 grains
Pyrogallic acid . .	30 grains
Potassium bromide .	10 grains
Water up to . .	10 oz.

No. 2 solution:

Sodium carbonate (cryst.) . .	2 oz.
Water up to . .	10 oz.

Dissolve in the order given. For use take equal quantities of Nos. 1 and 2.

An acid fixing bath should be made by dissolving 4 oz. of hyposulphite of soda in one pint of water, and adding $\frac{1}{2}$ oz. of potassium meta bisulphite.

Developing Plates or Films.—In developing a plate you may work according to the Time-Temperature method adopted by professional photographers who develop films by the thousand. The plates or films are developed for a period which depends upon the strength of the developer and the temperature of the solution. For this purpose it is better to buy packets of developer specially made up giving the appropriate times at different temperatures.

It is more interesting to give each plate individual treatment. Before taking the exposed plate out of the slide see that everything in the dark room is ready. Assuming the exposure was about correct, prepare enough developer (2 oz. for a quarter-plate). Turn out the white light, and with the ruby light only showing place the plate, emulsion upwards, in the developing dish, and flood the plate with developer, taking care that it is quickly and completely covered. Rock gently. After about half a minute the image will begin to appear, first the high lights, or light portions of the picture which will appear on the plate as black, and then the medium tones, until all the detail of the picture can be faintly traced. The beginner will find it difficult to decide when the developing has gone far enough. Only experience can tell, for different makes

Fig. 6.—A view is often improved when framed as if by chance

of plates differ slightly in appearance as they develop. As a rough guide, the negative is ready to come out of the developer when a fair amount of the detail can be seen through the glass side.

The plate should be given a slight rinse in clean water and placed in the fixing bath. The white light can be turned on soon after the negative is in the fixer, but it is better not to expose it much until fixing is practically complete. This is from ten to twenty minutes after the creamy appearance has gone from the negative. It should then be washed for an hour in running water, or in continual changes of water for a similar period, and then stood up to dry.

When over-exposure is suspected, increase the proportion of the No. 1 solution, and add a few drops of a ten per cent. solution of potassium bromide. This will retard development and prevent the negative becoming too dense. With a single solution developer all that can be done is to add a little ten per cent. potassium bromide. For under-exposure, increase the proportion of the No. 2 solution and double the amount of water. Warming the developer slightly helps matters, but tends to cause fog. With a single solution developer dilute with water. Another tip for under-exposure is to take the plate out of the developer immediately the image appears and place it in a dish of clean water for half an hour. At the end of this time a great deal of detail will probably have developed, but the negative will have no density. Place it back in the developer again for density to develop. The great thing to guard against in under-exposure is excessive contrast, and diluted developer tends to soften contrasts.

The Factorial Method.—This is another method of developing. The time elapsing between the immersion of the plate in the developer and the first appearance of the image is carefully noted. This period of time is multiplied by a given factor which varies according to the developer used, and the result of this calculation gives the total time for developing. The factor for pyro-soda developer varies according to the formula used, but a general factor that suits a number of the formulas suggested by plate-makers is 5. The factor for M.Q. developer is 14, and that for pyro-metol, 9. If the first trace of the image appears in 60 seconds, and the factor of the developer is 5, the plate should be developed for five minutes. The above-mentioned factors should be modified if necessary after trial. If the negatives are too soft, increase the factor; if too harsh, decrease it.

The development of roll films and film packs should be done in the same way. Special dishes with a roller in can be bought for the roll films, but the films can be developed quite easily in an ordinary dish by holding one end in each hand and see-sawing up and down so that the film is constantly moved through the developer.

Do not let plates or films lie on top of each other in the developer or fixer, but see that the solution is kept moving from time to time.

Intensification.—Negatives which lack printing density and therefore produce flat prints may be improved by intensification. There are several methods of doing this, and a number of firms sell intensifiers of different types ready mixed in packet or tablet form. An easy intensifier to handle is chromium. Two solutions are required because the working mixture does not keep well.

Solution A:

Potassium bichromate .	1 oz.
Water	25 oz.

Solution B:

Hydrochloric acid .	½ oz.
Water	25 oz.

The negative should be bleached in a mixture of equal parts of A and B and then washed until the yellow stain is removed. It is then re-developed in a strong developer. This operation can be performed in the ordinary white light of the dark room.

Reduction.—A negative that is too dense to print satisfactorily can be improved by the process known as reduction. A ten per cent. solution of potassium ferricyanide, is required. Make up a solution of hypo (1 oz. in 5 oz.) and add enough of the ferri-cyanide solution to turn it a pale yellow. The negative should be placed in this and left until the desired degree of reduction is nearly reached.

Printing.—The photographic dealer generally uses gas-light paper for printing, and this is most popular with the amateur because it can be handled in ordinary artificial light without the need for a special dark-room lamp. The paper must, of course, be handled carefully and exposed as little as possible, and then only to a weak light. If care is taken to get negatives of uniform density and contrast, one stock of gas-light paper will be sufficient. The best type of negative is one with plenty of detail, rather thin, and not too contrasty. For this a vigorous paper is best. For negatives that tend to be harsh and very contrasty, a soft paper is required. The packet of paper should be opened in the darkest corner of the room or behind a screen, and placed in contact with the negatives in the printing frame. The exposure is made by holding the printing frame about six inches from the artificial light. Judging the correct exposure is a matter of experience. Experiment by covering three-quarters of the negative with a piece of cardboard and exposing the one end for ten seconds. Then shift the card so that another quarter of the negative is uncovered, and expose for another ten seconds. Repeat again and then again, so that the four quarters of the negative have been exposed respectively for ten, twenty, thirty and forty seconds. When this trial piece has been developed, it will be easy to see which section was most correctly exposed.

It is best to develop the prints in the developer recommended by the makers of the paper. In most cases it can be purchased in packets ready for dissolving in water.

Development should be complete in about thirty seconds. After development the print should be rinsed quickly and plunged into an acid fixing bath for ten minutes and then washed thoroughly.

Yellow stains may be due to over-development, weak or exhausted developer, contamination of the developer or print with hypo, or undue exposure to the light at any stage before fixing is complete. Dishes, measures, etc., should be kept scrupulously clean, and while developing it is better not to permit the fingers to come into contact with the hypo but to keep the prints in the fixing bath on the move by means of a rod.

Printing Papers are made with various surfaces—glossy, matt, satin, etc. For small prints, glossy paper brings out the fine detail better, especially if glazed. This can be done by squeegeeing the wet prints on to prepared glass or ferrotype plates. The plates need careful polishing or treatment with glazing solution which can be bought fairly cheaply. The prints should be placed face down on the treated plates, covered with a sheet of blotting paper and then squeezed until the moisture is all pressed out. They should then be left to dry in a warm airy place until the prints practically drop off. A cheap polish for applying to ferrotype plates is made by dissolving 20 grains of bees-wax in 1 oz. of turpentine. This should be applied very lightly with cotton wool—a mere touch is enough—and the plates thoroughly polished with another pad of wool.

An old-fashioned printing method is that known as P.O.P. (printing out paper). It is much less sensitive to light and can be placed in the printing frame in weak daylight. Developing is not required as the printing is done as the printing frame is exposed to the bright daylight, though not to the direct rays of the sun. The paper has to be examined from time to time by carefully turning back a corner, and the printing is carried a little farther than is desired because the fixing bath has the effect of reducing it slightly. A self-toning paper is best as it requires to be fixed only. This is done by immersing in a solution of hypo (2 to 3 oz. to the pint of water according to the makers' instructions). An acid fixing bath must *not* be used.

Enlarging.—This is perhaps the most fascinating part of photography, for an enlarged print not only brings out many good points not readily observed in a small contact print, but by enlarging only a portion of the negative it is often possible to get a much more artistic result. The best work is done with an enlarger using artificial light. The diagram will illustrate the principle on which the enlarger works. The greater the distance between the lens and the easel the greater the degree of enlargement, though focusing adjustments have to be made altering the distance between the lens and the negative. Focusing is best done with a spare sheet of paper on the easel. Some enlargers are automatic in focusing, the adjustment between negative and lens and easel being made with one movement so that the image is always in focus. Then a yellow cap is fitted over the lens (because bromide paper is not sensitive to yellow light), a piece of bromide paper of appropriate size fixed to the easel and the exposure made by removing the yellow cap.

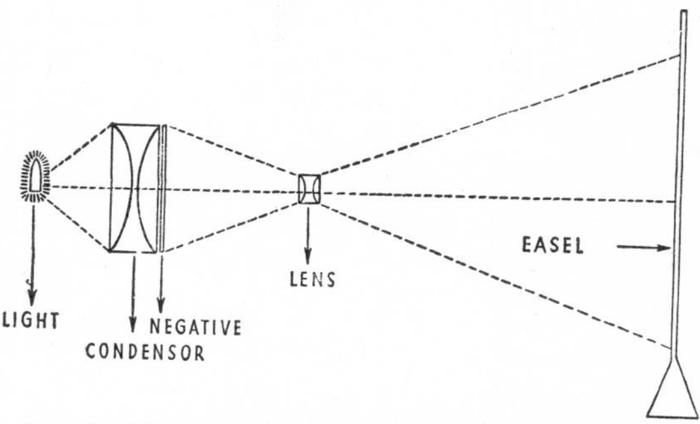

Fig. 7.—Diagram showing principle of enlargement

Bromide paper must not be exposed to white light. A trial exposure on a narrow strip of paper should be made first. The exposure will vary considerably according to the strength of the light, the aperture of the lens, the density of the negative, and the

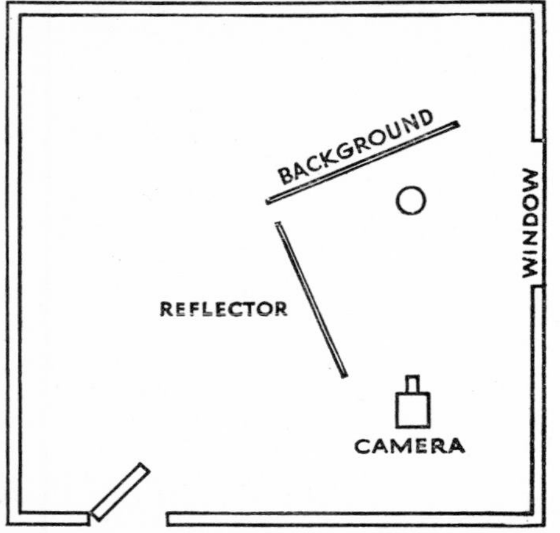

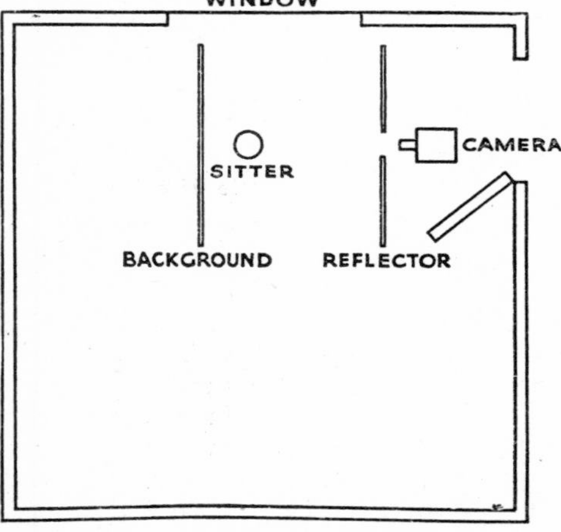

Fig. 8.—Two arrangements for portraiture. Note position of camera pointed through reflector in lower diagram

speed of the paper. Commence the experiment with exposures from thirty seconds to five minutes. The development of bromide prints is much the same as with gaslight paper, except that it takes about two minutes. If the enlargement is a big one, it is best to soak the paper in water for a minute before pouring the developer over it. An MQ developer is suitable for bromide paper. Many photographers consider amidol the ideal developer for bromide prints, and it certainly gives beautiful black tones. Unfortunately it does not keep well in solution so has to be frequently made up. Another disadvantage is that it stains the fingers very badly and rubber gloves or finger stalls are necessary. A good formula is as follows:

Amidol . . .	25 grains
Sodium sulphite .	300 grains
Water . . .	10 oz.

A good deal of local control can be exercised in enlarging. Dense parts of the negative can be given additional exposure by shading the thin parts of the negative during exposure. Pieces of paper with various sized and shaped holes can be used.

Bromide paper is also supplied in various grades—contrasty, medium and soft. If the negatives are kept fairly thin and soft, contrasty or medium paper will be found most useful.

Toning.—Bromide and gaslight prints may be toned to a variety of artistic shades and colours, the most popular being sepia. For this two solutions should be made up.

Stock sulphide solution

Pure sodium sulphide .	4 oz.
Water to . .	20 oz.

Bleaching Bath

Potassium ferricyanide	1 oz.
Potassium bromide .	1 oz.
Water to . . .	20 oz.

The prints, after thorough washing and fixing, should be placed in the bleaching bath. In a few minutes only a faint yellow image will be left. The prints should then be quickly rinsed for half a minute and re-developed in a solution made up of 3 oz. of the stock solution and 17 oz. of water. This re-development, or toning, only takes a few seconds, after which the prints should be washed for half an hour. The bleacher can be used until exhausted, but the re-developer should not be kept longer than a day after use. The stock solution will not keep in diluted form. The bleaching solution should be kept in the dark.

Home Portraiture.—This is an interesting side of photography, and successful work depends very largely on the arrangement of the lighting. The subject should be posed so that the light from the window falls from one side and slightly above, with a reflector placed so as to illuminate the other side of the figure, and prevent harsh contrasts (*see* diagram). If a background is necessary this can be made of some plain material either light or dark. A reflector can be provided by some light material thrown over a screen or balanced on a music stand. Other lighting effects can be obtained by pointing the camera through a hole in the reflector so that light is reflected on to the front of the subject. Get a sympathetic friend to pose while you experiment in rearranging the lighting, and get familiar with the possibilities. Use the largest stop possible, not only to shorten exposure, but to prevent more than the actual subject being in focus. A background that is sharply in focus detracts from the portrait.

Flashlight provides interesting work for dark evenings. Flash powder is bought ready mixed, and although a patent flash lamp is an advantage one can improvise one from a piece of tin (say the lid of a biscuit tin), bent to an L shape and fixed to a wooden handle. This provides a pan for the powder and a reflector for the flash. Patent lamps ignite the flash powder by means of a spark from a flint or electric current, but for the home-made lamp the touch-paper provided with the powder should be used. A diluted developer will help to prevent harsh contrasts. Flashlight is very useful sometimes when photographing dark interiors where the light is uneven, and where there are large patches of dark shadow. Give a daylight exposure calculated to be sufficient for the middle lights and finish off with a small flash to lighten the shadows.

The latest flashlight apparatus is an electric lamp which fires a flash inside a glass bulb thus avoiding any smoke or danger. For the amateur this works out rather expensive.

Panchromatic Work.—Reference has already been made to panchromatic plates

Fig. 9.—Intensifying effect of steepness by lowering camera

Fig. 10.—Night lighting transforms the simplest objects

and films. Although orthochromatic plates and films certainly give truer rendering of colour values than ordinary plates the fastidious will not be satisfied. Better results are obtained if the orthochromatic plates or films are used in conjunction with a light filter or colour screen. This is placed so that the light reaching the emulsion passes through it and has the effect of increasing the exposure necessary by two, three, five or more times the normal. These filters can be bought at various strengths. Graduated filters are also obtainable. In these the depth of colour diminishes from top to bottom, and enables the sky portion of a landscape to be shown with the clouds rendered in their appropriate tones when in the ordinary way the sky would probably be dead white if the foreground were correctly exposed. Some workers, however, look with suspicion on graduated filters.

The ideal method of rendering colour values is to use

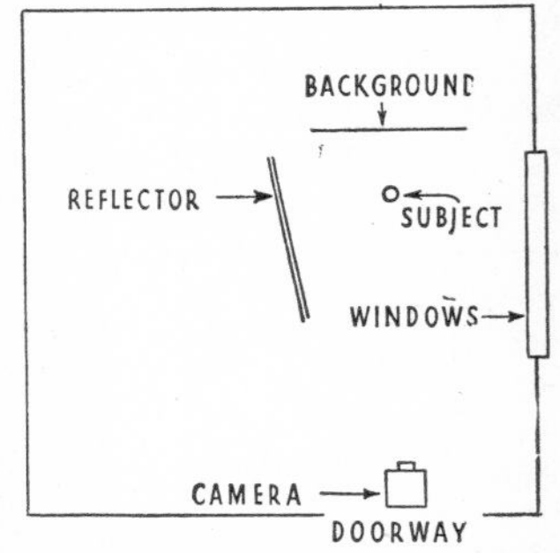

Fig. 11.—Further portraiture arrangement

panchromatic plates or films. These are sensitive to all the colours of the spectrum, and require the use of the special deep green safe light already referred to. The use of desensitising preparations, several of which are on the market, enable panchromatic plates to be developed in ruby light after they have first been placed in the desensitising preparation for a period in accordance with the makers' directions. This desensitising preparation, by the way, is useful with all plates and films where the dark room is not very light tight. If the time and temperature method is used panchromatic plates and films can be developed in complete darkness.

Miniature Precision Cameras.—Quite a modern development in photography has been the popularizing of the miniature precision camera.

These modern miniature cameras are

exquisitely made with lens, shutters and focusing arrangements of remarkable strength and precision. The most popular form uses films of the standard cinematograph kind, giving 36 exposures to the roll, each about $1\frac{1}{2}$ in. by 1 in. Ultra fast lens are fitted about 2 in. focal length and of apertures from F 3·5 to F 1·5. Using the fast films now on the market they enable photographs to be taken under conditions undreamed of only a few years ago, and the resulting negatives enable enlargements to be made up to ten or fifteen times linear, or even more.

The successful worker with these cameras has to avoid the "blaze away and let the chemist do the rest" technique. The exposure must be just right. How important this is may be gauged by the fact the electric exposure meters costing about £5 each are on the market for use with these cameras, and at least one model has a photo - electric cell meter incorporated. Very efficient meters are also sold costing much less, but in every case the human element comes in and to that extent they are less reliable than the electric meters which are entirely automatic. The aiming or sighting of these small cameras is also important and quite a range of additional gadgets are sold to make this operation more or less foolproof.

Developing.—To get the best results from a perfect exposure, perfect development is essential, and special developers are sold which are designed to minimize grain in the negative.

Absence of grain, which is vital if good enlargements are to be made, is impossible if development is prolonged or forced. In developing films care should be taken to have all solutions and rinsing and washing water of the same temperature. The time and temperature method is best, and development should be stopped a little earlier than normal to keep the negatives fairly thin and soft, so that they will yield the best enlargements. Washing should be done in half a dozen changes of water that has been standing for some time in the dark room, rather than in running water from the tap.

The wet negatives should be handled with great care and hung to dry where there

Fig. 12.—A composition based on right angles

will be no risk of their being marked by dust.

The enlarging process should follow the normal routine, but again every operation must be undertaken with special care. Fresh developer and fixing bath, equal temperature for all solutions, perfect exposure and development are again essential.

Of course, all this emphasis upon precision can be applied with equal validity to any photographic operation, but for the miniature worker it is absolutely essential.

PIANO PLAYING

Only the virtuoso can fill great concert halls with audiences and thrill them by brilliant performances; but it is within the power of most ordinary people to become useful pianists and obtain pleasure and satisfaction from their efforts.

Of the great number who start to learn to play the piano, only a very small proportion intend to, or ever do, become professionals. The rest can be divided into those who learn because they are fond of music and those who try to learn because someone else wishes them to.

It is to those of all ages who want to be able to play for the love of it that this article is mainly addressed.

When to Begin.—The best age for the average child to begin to learn is about eight years, though some naturally gifted children can safely start at five or six. Within reason, it is never too late to start to learn, although difficulties are naturally increased with age.

The Instrument.—There is nothing like a bad instrument to kill a beginner's interest. Many non-musical parents think that any instrument will do for a child to learn on. This is a great mistake, for if a child, or any beginner, cannot make their first efforts sound pleasing, they are readily discouraged. It is wise to buy the very best instrument that can be afforded.

A good second-hand piano is better than a very cheap new one. The case is of little importance compared with the inside. When buying a piano it is best to have the advice of someone who understands piano construction, and who can judge whether the tone will last, etc.

Care of the Instrument.—Having got a good instrument it pays to look after it. It should be tuned regularly two or three times a year.

Never let the piano get so badly out of tune that it is noticeable to the listener. If possible, keep it in an even temperature. It is very bad for the instrument to be kept in a room where there is a fire one day a week and on the other days the room is cold and damp. Neither should the piano be always closed or always open. A good arrangement is to open it during the day, even if it is not used, and to close it at night.

The dusting tools of an electric vacuum cleaner are excellent to clean the action—that is, the springs and hammers—both by suction and by reversing the operation and blowing. The keys should be cleaned with a damp cloth and polished with a soft dry duster. Very bad finger marks may be removed with a rag dipped in methylated spirit.

The Teacher.—When selecting a teacher do not be guided entirely by the possession of a number of diplomas: they may or may not be the sign of a good teacher. Careful inquiries should be made as to the methods of the teacher and as to the class of players produced. The teacher who slavishly follows a college syllabus is not to be recommended, nor is the "crammer" who rushes students through examinations to a degree without any real knowledge to support it. The right teacher is one who can adapt his methods to the individual ability and requirements of each pupil.

Ideal teaching comprises theoretical knowledge, technical training, solo playing, accompanying, sight-reading, memorizing and musical history.

The first illustration shows the correct position of the player's hands.

Music and Fingering.—The student should familiarize himself with the meaning of the various expression marks, pedalling, fingering, tempo, etc. It is sometimes a good plan to play the same piece from music printed by a different publisher. The appearance of the notes differs sufficiently to make a useful check on accuracy.

There are two types of fingering. The continental system, which is more general, indicates the thumb by the figure 1 and the other four fingers by 2, 3, 4, and 5 respectively. The English system uses a cross (+) to indicate the thumb, the index finger as 1, the middle finger as 2 and so on.

Practice.—A lesson is not of much use unless followed up by regular daily practice. Several brief spells during the day are better, as a rule, than one long one. If the student can manage half an hour before school or office, so much the better.

All piano playing, if done in the right spirit, should be practice and all practice should be enjoyed as playing.

Scale and Arpeggio Practice is essential, though it need not be overdone.

Fig. 1.—Position of Hands for turning over thumb

To be able to play scales in all keys and not to be able to read a simple piece at sight is absurd. Scales and arpeggi provide excellent technical work, especially if they are played fast and slow, legato and staccato, and with graduated tone. To gain confidence at the keyboard, it is a splendid thing to close the

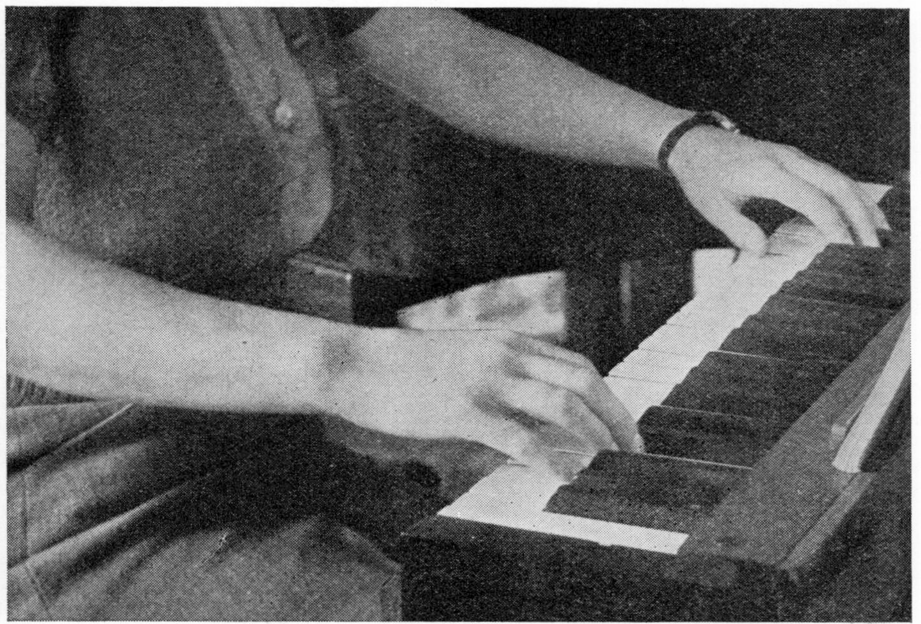

Fig. 2.—Keep Elbows away from Sides so that they may move freely

eyes while playing scales and arpeggi. If played intelligently, they also produce a sound and ready knowledge of all the keys, which is invaluable.

Studies should also form an important part of the practice. There are a number of good graded schools of studies and one such set should be worked through conscientiously, but they should be supplemented by other complete single volumes of studies by various other composers.

Each study deals with a special technical or time difficulty and, before attempting the study, its purpose should be clear to the performer, and kept in mind all through.

The value of studies is that each difficulty is introduced over and over again so that it has to be conquered if the whole piece is to be played; whereas in an ordinary composition that particular difficulty may only occur once or twice and might be skipped by the performer without noticeably spoiling the whole.

Hand Development.—Another part of the practice time should be devoted to hand development. It is a very valuable thing to be able to strike a large chord quickly and cleanly. A useful exercise for this purpose is to place the first finger (continental fingering) on any white key and place the other four fingers—one at a time —on alternate white keys.

If this cannot be done at first, do it as nearly as possible and then allow the hand to remain in the position for a few moments and then relax. Repeat this with both hands at intervals during the practice and gradually increase the compass until some pairs of fingers can stretch two keys.

The five-finger position—i.e. with the thumb and fingers on consecutive white notes of key C or G—is the basis of all playing and books can be obtained with many exercises of this kind. A few moments given regularly to the strengthening of the five-finger position will develop and maintain the ability to use all the fingers with equal control. With a little imagination the student can invent exercises on the five-finger position, working the fingers in pairs as well as individually, to correct any special personal weakness.

All scales, arpeggi, studies and exercises should be taken slowly at first and the speed gradually increased, without sacrificing accuracy. Effort should always be made to understand the principles of the fingering employed so that they can be applied naturally to music in which the fingering is not indicated.

It is also a good thing to spend part of the practice time working at one composition until it is mastered. There are some compositions which cannot be read at sight and there is great value and also some sense of satisfaction in having conquered one such piece.

Sight-reading.—Every player should aim at being able to read at sight and there is only one way to be able to do this—to be always trying fresh music.

A part of each day's practice should be devoted to this most fascinating and useful accomplishment. Any sort of music will serve the purpose—the greater the variety, the better.

It is not difficult to obtain a good supply of fresh music as it can be bought very cheaply, second-hand; and friends will also lend or exchange. Of course, to be able to read at sight correctly, one must understand the principles of time-keeping. (*See also* the section on Sight-reading under PRACTICAL MUSIC.)

The Importance of Tempo.—Children more easily appreciate the relative values of the different notes if they are compared to something they know, such as, a semibreve is worth a penny; a minim, a halfpenny; a crotchet, a farthing; a quaver, a half-farthing.

If everything relating to the relative value of notes and rests has been properly taught from the beginning, there is no difficulty, but if this important part has been neglected every effort should be made to remedy the defect. Music played in wrong time is like a drawing out of perspective.

It is a great help to time-keeping to take a piece of music and tap the melody out on a table.

Playing With Others.—The pianoforte has been called "the instrument of the solitary," but this need not be so.

Pianoforte duet-playing is a much neglected art, but it can be very interesting and capable of giving great pleasure to the performers. There are many fine original compositions, by great composers, for four hands as well as arrangements of standard works.

Duet arrangements of symphonies, overtures and other orchestral works are most helpful towards a better understanding of the orchestral score. Piano concertos with orchestral part arranged for another player are also interesting to try, but these are best for two pianos and are rarely possible for amateurs.

Duets can also be obtained for players of unequal abilities, where one part is elementary and the other more advanced. These are very suitable for pupil and teacher.

Accompanying. — Among amateurs the good accompanist is rare and in great demand. The art of accompanying on the piano is full of interest and well worth studying.

The duty of an accompanist is to support the soloist and to remember that the soloist must always be prominent. However good the solo, a bad accompaniment will spoil it.

A soloist may be very erratic, but wherever he goes, the pianist must keep up with him—and support his melody with his own, subdued but never weak.

As in sight-reading the only way to be proficient in this branch of the pianist's art is to work at it. Take every opportunity of playing accompaniments of all sorts and, if done with interest and intelligence, the ability will come.

Solo Playing.—The purpose of a solo is to give pleasure to others. The performer should always remember this and select pieces which, if played well, will achieve that end.

An ideal solo for ordinary purposes should be reasonably brief, good without being highbrow, and well within the ability of the performer. A simple thing played well is better than a difficult one performed badly.

If possible, a solo should be played from memory. Some find it a simple matter to memorize, to others it is almost an impossibility. The average player will find it best to play the required piece through many times from music before attempting it without. It is helpful to sit away from the instrument and "think" the piece right through.

When playing your solo keep calm, and if a mistake is made do not embarrass the audience by murmured apologies or shrugs. It can only pass unnoticed or the mistake is obvious to them, in which case apologies or fuss cannot help.

Fig. 3.—Right Foot Forward helps Balance

Improvising.—There are occasions when a pianist is required to improvise—if he can. Comparatively few can.

Some players have a natural ability which

makes it easy for them to improvise in an elementary fashion, but to do so on a given theme, as was once popular, requires much careful study and practice. However, almost everyone can improvise, given some knowledge of the major and minor keys, and the rules of harmony.

You should be quite familiar with the major and minor chords and the dominant and diminished seventh chords, and their inversions, in all keys. These should be practised also as broken chords. A good test is to play each of those four chords, beginning on every note in turn of the chromatic scale. Even without theoretical knowledge a person with a good ear for music can arrange pleasing progressions from these chords alone.

The Aim.—The aim of every piano student should be "all-round achievement." The person who can play decent solos, read at sight, memorize, improvise, accompany a solo, or lead community singing, not only gets the most out of his ability himself, but is able to give fine service to his fellow men. (*See also* PRACTICAL MUSIC.)

PIANO ACCORDION AND HARMONICA PLAYING

ALMOST the first question asked by most prospective players of the piano accordion is, "How long will it take me to learn?"

The best attempt at a reply would be that, while anyone should be able to play a number of simple tunes after a few weeks' acquaintance with the instrument, the serious student will find sufficient material for many years of increasingly interesting study.

Holding the Instrument.—As is the case with every musical instrument, there is a right and a wrong way of holding the piano accordion. The correct method is as follows:

First of all, make sure that the "piano" keyboard, with its black and white keys, is on the right-hand side, and the "button" keyboard on the left. Place the right arm through one of the straps and get the strap well on to the shoulder. Do the same with the other arm, so that the weight of the instrument is evenly distributed on the shoulders. The top of the accordion should be two or three inches below the chin (12-bass and 24-bass models may be carried three inches or so lower).

In this position, as long as the player does not stoop, the accordion will feel surprisingly light in weight. At first, it is better to sit down for practice. The music stand should be kept high enough for easy reading when the player is sitting upright. As soon as the shoulders are fully accustomed to the feel of the instrument, the player should do part of his practice while standing.

The left hand is inserted under the strap which runs from top to bottom of the instrument. Not only the hand but part of the wrist as well, goes under the strap. When the *tips* of the fingers can be placed vertically on the buttons, the correct position will have been found.

Many people, on first examining the buttons of the left-hand keyboard of the piano accordion, are immediately convinced that they present an almost insuperable difficulty. This is not the case.

These buttons, whether they number 8, 12, 24, 48, 80 or 120, are arranged in a very convenient manner. The musical theory upon which their position is based is one of extreme simplicity.

This is of great importance when it is borne in mind that the accordion is the only type of portable musical instrument enabling the player to accompany a tune with appropriate full harmony. The violin, 'cello, cornet and other easily-carried instruments give melody only. The nearest approach to the accordion, in this respect, is the small folding type of reed organ, which can hardly be called "portable" to the same extent!

It is not necessary to enter into a theoretical discussion on harmony in order to demonstrate the simplicity of the accordion

Accordion Times

Fig. 1.—The Instrument

instrument. Then, shorter oblique lines will be seen, consisting of two, three, four, five or six buttons (according to the size of the instrument) running diagonally *across* the keyboard.

Keeping to the idea of a harmonic family, the vertical lines may be said to represent the surnames (technically, the keynotes). Each *oblique* row of buttons contains the "family" bearing that surname. Every one of these buttons. It is sufficient to say that very many tunes may be accompanied by the use of six (and in some instances, only four) of these buttons. Moreover, those required for the purpose will always be found in a compact group, no matter what may be the keynote of the tune.

Should the reader be a musician, he will realize that this is brought about by the Tonic, Dominant and Subdominant harmonies in every key always being found on adjacent rows of buttons.

Even those with no knowledge whatever of music will have noticed that a pianist, when playing the ordinary type of "vamping" accompaniment, first plays one single low note following it with a group of three or four notes higher up the keyboard, and so on. This group of notes (which is known as a "chord") always "blends" with the previous single note. To the ear, it is apparently the *only* group of notes that could be played in conjunction with the single "bass" note. The theoretical explanation of this is that the bass note and the chord belong to the same "harmonic family," as it were.

The Left-hand Keyboard.—When the left-hand keyboard of an accordion is examined, it will be seen that the buttons are arranged in rows which follow two distinct geometrical patterns. First, there is a vertical line, from top to bottom of the

Brit. Coll. Accordionists

Fig. 2.—How to Hold it

families is closely related to those immediately above it and below it.

This explanation will show that there is really nothing bewildering about the left-hand keyboard. However many buttons it may contain, each group of three oblique rows contains in itself the harmonic accompaniment to a simple melody, no matter what may be the "family name" or keynote of the tune.

It may, however, be remarked that on the larger instruments each oblique row contains five or even six buttons, and that it is difficult to know which to begin with. That is even more easily explained.

One particular button will be found to differ from all the rest. On some makes of accordion it is indented; on others, scored with shallow grooves. This is known as the "C" button, because it produces the single note "C". All the buttons in that *vertical* row are known as "fundamental basses." They produce single notes only —the low played by the pianist before he plays his chord.

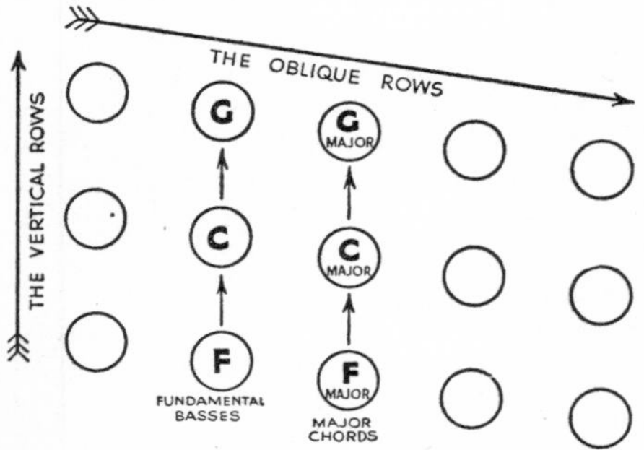

Fig. 3.—The Left-hand Keyboard

Fingering.—If the tip of the middle finger is placed on the "C" button, it will be found that the index finger lies over the next one in the same *oblique* row. This button will produce *three* notes which are those of the chord most commonly used in accompaniment, known as the "major" chord.

Opening the bellows with a steady movement, press these buttons alternately. As in the case of the pianist's "vamping," a bass note will be heard, followed by a chord, and the chord will blend with it.

The middle finger may be used for "experimental" purposes but, in actual practice, it will be better to use the ring finger.

Then move the fingers upward until they rest on the corresponding buttons of the next oblique row above, and repeat the action. Immediately, the note and chord produced will strike the ear as the most appropriate to follow the first. The ear is a true judge in this matter, for the harmony being played ("G") is that most closely related to that of the keynote ("C").

When a few minutes have been spent in moving between the "C" and "G" buttons, a further experiment may be tried. From the "C" row, move the fingers to the corresponding two buttons of the next row *below*, which produce the bass note and chord of "F". Here again, a very familiar movement of sound will be heard.

A pleasing accompaniment is to be derived from the use of these three pairs of buttons. The diagram below will assist in committing to memory their relative positions. This shows a section of the left-hand keyboard of an 80-bass piano accordion. Only those buttons referred to in this article are named. The others need not be considered at present. The outer vertical rows of buttons will not be found on 12-bass and 24-bass instruments.

The Right-hand or " Melody " Keyboard of the piano accordion is very similar to that of the pianoforte, except that it is shorter and the action or "touch" of the keys is different. The actual range of notes varies according to the size and make of the instrument. For any practical purpose, however, a compass of two octaves (25 notes) is the minimum.

Those with a knowledge of the piano will experience no difficulty whatever in using this keyboard. They will, in fact, find it very interesting. Not only can it be used in the same manner as that of the piano, with a "detached" or "staccato" touch, but the organ-style of sustained playing can also be adopted.

When a pianoforte key is struck, the sound produced begins to die away at once. With the accordion, the sound continues just as long as the key (or button) is held down and the bellows are operated.

As to the actual "learning" of the instrument, it must not be imagined that this entails drudgery in any form. During recent years great advances have been made in methods of tuition and self-tuition. Music, once popularly supposed to be a mysterious science understandable only by professors, has proved to be a fascinating hobby. If it were more simple, it would not be worth the trouble of learning. As it is, very few interests will be found more absorbing than the study of simple music.

A system of "symbols" has been introduced in order to simplify the playing of the left-hand keyboard of the accordion. These symbols are supplementary to the musical notation. No such system is possible, or really necessary, for the right-hand keyboard.

In this connection it is strongly urged that players should *not* be content to rely entirely upon the symbols or upon playing melodies "by ear." A little concentration on the study of musical signs and notation will prove how interesting the subject can be.

As an experiment, a simple but pleasing effect may be produced from the piano accordion by the use of only *two* buttons. To demonstrate this, here is the first part of a tune that everyone knows, "Home, Sweet Home." (Fig. 4.)

As we are merely "experimenting" it will be permissible to first "pick out" the melody with the right hand. The first note of the tune ("C") can be easily identified by the non-musician. When the instrument is in the playing position, this note is on the white key immediately above a *pair* of black keys (not a group of three). Having discovered this note, it should be a fairly simple matter to play the rest of this familiar tune.

Fig. 4

After a few attempts, it will be found possible to accompany the tune by the use of the "C" and "G" *fundamental bass buttons only* as indicated by the letter-symbols under the musical example.

It must be borne in mind that this simple "vamping" style of accompaniment is by no means the sole use for which the left-hand keyboard may be employed. In spite of its simplicity (perhaps it would be more true to say *because* of the rational lay-out of the buttons) an immense range of harmonic effects can be produced.

Bass solos, played on this keyboard and accompanied by the right hand, give an excellent effect and are not difficult.

To ensure a correct action of the left arm when using the bellows, the left hand should describe an elongated "figure eight." The bellows should commence opening at the top, the hand moving outwards and slightly downwards. At the end of the movement, the hand should be gently turned palm downwards as it begins to return, so that the closing movement of the bellows also begins at the top of the instrument.

The piano accordion is unique in that it affords pleasure to the casual player who is content with an elementary knowledge, while giving full scope to serious and ambitious musical students. Many who take up the instrument as a hobby eventually enter the ranks of thorough-going enthusiasts.

As to the instrument itself, its uses are manifold. Accordion solos are always received with acclamation. There is no better accompanying instrument for vocal music.

The growing popularity of harmonica

bands has opened yet another sphere of activity for the accordion. It has been found invaluable, adding a depth of tone and fullness of volume that improve even the most skilful efforts of harmonica players.

Fig. 5.—How to Hold the Harmonica

types in general use are the 10-, 12- and 16-hole Chromatic Harmonicas. On these instruments any piece of music can be played in any key. Like the ordinary type harmonicas, they are simple in construction and easy to learn.

In choosing your harmonica, you will no doubt be guided by the type of music you wish to play. As you read on, you will be guided in your choice also by reading about the uses of the three groups of instruments.

An infallible guide for learning to play these instruments is, that each of them, by blowing, produces only the doh, me, soh, doh chord; the other notes of the tonic sol-fa scale are produced by drawing, as shown below in Fig. 6.

To play the harmonica, hold it in the left hand between the thumb and forefinger, with the low notes to the left. Place the right hand in the position you see in the illustration, so that it forms a cup over the left hand.

You can obtain various effects on the harmonica by manipulating the cupped hand as follows:

1. Opening and closing the right hand

BLOW NOTES.—	DOH		ME		SOH		DOH
DRAW NOTES.—		RAY		FAH		LAH TE	

Fig. 6

THE HARMONICA

There are a number of types of harmonicas. They fall into three main groups:

Group 1. The 10-, 12-, 14-, 16-, 20-, 24- and 28-hole harmonicas. These instruments are of different designs, shapes, and sizes. The most popular keys are G and C.

Group 2. Specially-designed Harmonica Band instruments: Tremolo, Organ, and Alto Tuned Harmonicas, with a Vineta Accompanying Harmonica, for playing bass and accompaniment. These Tremolo, Organ, and Alto Tuned instruments can also be used as solo instruments. They are 20-hole harmonicas.

Group 3. The Chromatic Harmonicas. As there are different types of ordinary harmonicas, so there are different types of these advanced instruments. The three main

while playing; this at different speeds, according to the speed of the piece you are playing.

2. In playing marches, a good effect is the movement of the right hand a few inches from the left, and bringing it down lightly upon the left hand back to the cupped position while playing.

Always cup the hands over the part of the instrument you are playing.

To Form a Harmonica Band, discuss the matter with your friends. If you agree to form the band, decide upon the type of harmonica the players are to use. You may select any of the types in Groups 1, 2 and 3, provided they are the same type and key.

Instruments in key G will give you quite a large range of music; if you add key C harmonicas, you will add variety to your band playing, be able to play most popular songs and increase the band's repertoire.

Part Playing.—Get your instruments, appoint a band leader, choose your programme of music, and go ahead. This will be only melody playing. Now no band is likely to exist for long that plays only the melody. When you think about a band, you think about part-playing. The most useful instruments for the early stages of this part-playing are the Tremolo, Organ, and Alto Tuned Harmonicas, with the Vineta Accompanying Harmonica, described in Group 2. Later your band will be able to advance to the instruments described in Group 3.

Below are a few bars of a piece of music to illustrate this part-playing.

A band may have any number of players. For a band of 6, there should be 3 Tremolo, 1 Organ, 1 Alto, and 1 Vineta. Keep this proportion, whatever the size of the band. This, for best balance of instruments.

The Tremolo, Organ, and Alto Tuning instruments have holes or notes numbered 1–20. All the odd numbers are blow notes; all the even numbers draw notes. The figures above the music are the harmonica notation, the even numbers being bracketed to distinguish blow from draw notes. As the harmonica notation is the same for Tremolo, Organ, and Alto instruments, all the players can play each of the parts.

As the harmonica notation is the same for key G and key C instruments, the piece of music may be played with instruments in either of these keys.

Take up your harmonicas. See that the numbers are on the far side from you, with No. 1 to the left. Place the instrument well into the mouth, and cover holes 2, 3 and 4 with the surface of the tongue, leaving hole 5 exposed to the breath. The following illustration will show you how this is done.

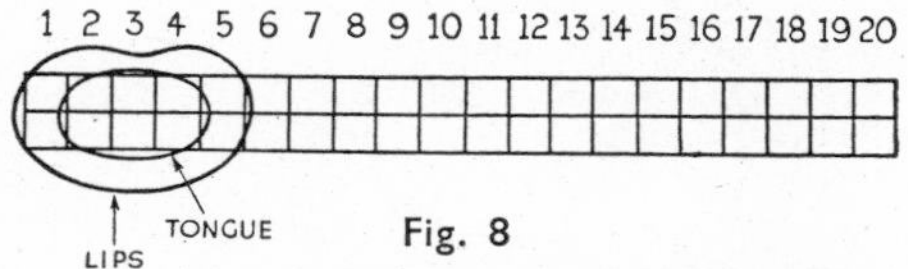

Fig. 8

Blow into the exposed 5th hole, and you will produce the 1st note of the Tremolo (T) part of the piece of music. Now play to the end of the Tremolo part, blowing or drawing the notes according to the harmonica notation. While doing so, see that the tongue is properly placed on the instrument, as instructed.

In the same way all the players play through the Organ and Alto parts.

Fig. 7.—T—1st or Tremolo Part for the Tremolo Tuning Harmonicas. O—2nd or Organ Part for the Organ Tuning Harmonicas. A—3rd or Alto Part for the Alto Tuning Harmonicas. V—the Vineta Accompanying Harmonica part

Fig. 9.—A "Uniformed" Harmonica Band in Action

Playing the Vineta.—The capital letters are played in the small holes; small letters are played in the large holes. As shown, the letters above the Vineta dividing line are blown and the letters below that line are drawn. The letters opposite V are the Vineta notation.

Now separate the players into their respective parts—T, O and A—and, with the Vineta player accompanying, play the piece of music. You are now a band playing in parts!

The piano, piano-accordion, guitar, banjo, drums, and other musical instruments form useful additions to a harmonica band.

Care should be exercised in adding other instruments to a harmonica band. It is well to bear in mind the band is primarily a harmonica band, and that the added instruments must not overshadow the harmonica playing. The adding of these instruments lends variety to the band playing, improves the tonal quality, and adds volume. If the players of the added instruments play softly, the harmonicas will be heard to the greatest advantage.

Lastly we come to the Chromatic Harmonicas (Group 3). These instruments are the very latest development in harmonica construction. They provide the half-tones or semi-tones not found in the instruments described in Groups 1 and 2. These half-tones are obtained by pressing a lever or slide while playing. Let us proceed to see how easy it is to learn to play this instrument. Take a 12-hole Chromatic Harmonica in key C. Holding the instrument in the left hand, between thumb and first finger, as directed, the low or bass notes to the left, place the instrument well into the mouth, and cover holes 2, 3 and 4 with the surface of the tongue, leaving hole 5 exposed to the breath. Now blow into the exposed 5th hole, and the note C (or Doh) will respond. Blow this note several times, until you are sure you can produce a clear single note. Now draw the breath through the same hole, and you will produce the note D (or Ray). Blow and draw these two notes until you can play them clearly and distinctly.

Playing the Scale.—Playing the scale is just like going up a ladder step by step. Following the instructions below, play the scale, remembering to keep the tongue properly placed upon the playing surface of the instrument while doing so.

Blow in hole 5—1st note of scale—C (Doh).
Draw in hole 5—2nd note of scale—D (Ray).
Blow in hole 6—3rd note of scale—E (Me).
Draw in hole 6—4th note of scale—F (Fah).
Blow in hole 7—5th note of scale—G (Soh).
Draw in hole 7—6th note of scale—A (Lah).
Draw in hole 8—7th note of scale—B (Te).
Blow in hole 8—8th note of scale—C (Doh).

(NOTE that the sequence of blow and draw notes changes at hole 8, to draw and blow.)

In playing a 12-hole Chromatic Harmonica in key G, follow the same procedure as in the case of the key C instrument. Only remember that in a 12-hole Chromatic Harmonica in key G, the first note Doh will be G, and not C. The sequence of draw and blow notes is the same as for the key C instrument, when playing the scale. You can now proceed to play the scale in this key.

Having proceeded thus far, you should now be able to play simple pieces of music. This done, you can proceed to part-playing.

PICKLES AND SAUCES

PICKLING is not really difficult. It is, in fact, one of the branches of cookery where it is easy to do well. At the same time, it offers scope for originality; for the addition or omission of a spice or a flavouring is going to turn your effort into something a little bit different and that is the sign of a good cook. Experiment with confidence.

Besides providing pickles for home consumption, the housewife can turn this branch of cooking into a very profitable hobby, for this age of machine-made goods has paradoxically created a demand for home-made ones. If you want to make money out of your pickles, first of all make them look attractive. Screw-cap jars can be bought and decorated with a border depicting the vegetable contents painted in sealing wax round the base. Thus, in the case of Pickled Cabbage, a border of red cabbages done in magenta wax—or of Tomato Chutney, tomatoes and apples, or tomatoes alone. It will be necessary to charge a small deposit on such jars, refundable on return, unless you include the price of it in the price of the pickles. Such attractively packed pickles would have an enormous sale at the local tea rooms, so make friends with someone who runs one in order to work up a connection. You can decorate old jam jars the same way and use cellophane or any of the other covers now on the market for pickles which do not require keeping long. The kind of cover does not really matter as long as the jar is perfectly airtight—that is the important point.

Do not make too many pickles of a standard kind; people get used to a particular brand and it will not be easy to break into that market. But a certain amount of experimenting will enable you to produce some special pickle, a sweet one will probably sell best, where you can create your own market.

General Rules.—There are a few hard and fast rules which must be followed in every kind of pickling. Always use an enamelled or aluminium pan for cooking, never an iron or tin one because of its effect on the vinegar. Use a wooden spoon for stirring, and, if possible, do not use the pan or the spoon for anything else. The vinegar used should be the very best obtainable, and although there are ready-spiced pickling vinegars on the market, most pickle makers will like to spice their own to their taste. Malt vinegar is most frequently used, with white wine vinegar for light-coloured vegetables. The spices for flavouring are sometimes bottled with the pickle, but otherwise tie them in a muslin bag with one long end of string, by means of which they can easily be removed.

Jars and bottles must be perfectly dry before being filled, otherwise the pickles will not keep. To make certain of this, place them in a cool oven to dry off. A circle of waxed paper should be folded over corks and if the pickle needs keeping a long time, seal over these with sealing wax.

Pickled Red Cabbage.—This is one of the easiest pickles to make, and it has the advantage of being ready for use less than a month after sealing and also of keeping a reasonably long time. Red cabbages are at their best after a touch of frost. November is a good month in which to make this pickle. Take off the outer leaves of the cabbage, wash, quarter, cut out the stump, then drain. Shread the quartered cabbage finely and place it either on wire racks or in an old clothes-basket, not on a dish; sprinkle well with salt. If the cabbage is allowed to stand flat in the brine which will run from it, it is apt to go flabby, a frequent fault with this pickle. Let this stand from twenty-four to thirty-six hours, according to the amount of cabbage, then tip it into an old cloth and shake to remove surplus moisture. Pack the cabbage into jars to within about 1 in. of the top and completely cover them with malt vinegar in which mixed pickling spice has been boiled in the proportion of half an ounce to a quart. The vinegar is poured over cold and the spice is left in it. Seal in three days' time.

Pickled Onions. — This is another easy pickle to make and very popular with men. Make a brine of salt and water in the proportion of two tablespoonfuls of salt to one quart of water. The onions should be small and when they are peeled, leave them to soak in the brine for thirty-six hours. Drain and wipe dry. Pack the onions into jars, trying to put those of the same size together. Cover them with white wine vinegar in which mixed pickling spice and white sugar have been added in the proportion of one ounce of spice and two tablespoonfuls of sugar to the quart of vinegar. The vinegar can be poured over hot or cold, and the jars sealed the next day.

Mustard Pickle.—Almost any diced vegetables can be used for this pickle; onions are added whole, and chopped apple, prunes, and sultanas may be added later. Break up cauliflower into small pieces, dice cucumber, gherkins, etc., sprinkle with salt and leave for eighteen hours. Drain them and shake in a cloth. Put them into the pan and add any chopped fruit except the sultanas. Make this mash up to three quarts with vinegar and bring slowly to the boil. Take dry mustard in the proportion of seven ounces to the gallon of vinegar, add one tablespoonful of curry powder, one cupful of brown sugar, and four tablespoonfuls of flour. Mix to a paste with a little cold vinegar, and add vinegar from the vegetables till thoroughly thinned. Return to the pan, add the sultanas and bring to the boil. Boil for fifteen minutes. Pour into jars and seal when cold.

Marrow Pickle.—Cut a large ripe marrow into inch cubes. Chop up half a pound to a pound of onions according to the size of the marrow and mix with a pound of chopped apples. Place alternate layers of marrow and mixed apple and onion well sprinkled with brown sugar in the preserving pan. Just cover with malt vinegar and cook until the marrow can be pierced easily with a fork. Put half an ounce of mixed spice into a bag and throw into the pan, together with pepper and salt to taste, and some sultanas. Boil till thick, remove spice and bottle before it is cold. Seal the next day.

Lemon Pickle.—This is a very old recipe. Lemon pickle made in this way is a rarity, though it is excellent. The only drawback is that it cannot be eaten earlier than three years after it is made, and it reaches perfection at five. However, if you begin now, and make it regularly every year when the new lemons come in at the beginning of November, a regular supply will be assured later. Eaten with cold chicken or veal there is nothing to surpass it.

Cut six almost green lemons across in four parts at the pointed end, making the cuts half-way through the lemon. Mix a quarter of an ounce of cayenne pepper with an ounce of white pepper and as much salt as you wish. With the aid of a spoon fill the cuts in the lemons with this mixture and place them in a bowl. Leave for ten days, turning them every day, then pack them in a large earthenware jar. Boil sufficient vinegar to cover them and let it get quite cold before pouring over the lemons. Seal the jar, but open it every six months to see if it is necessary to add more boiled vinegar, as the lemons absorb it considerably.

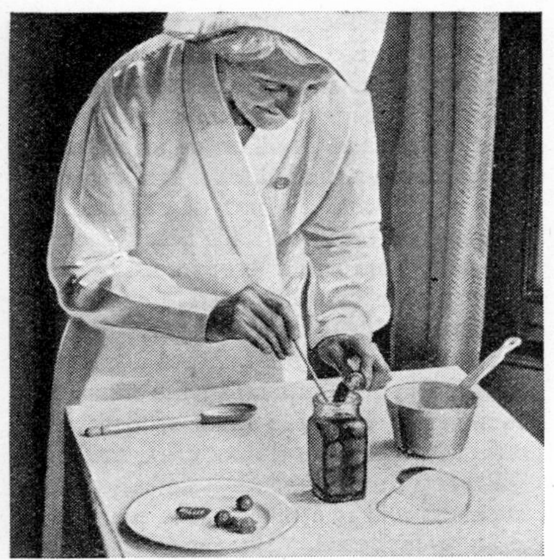

Fig. 1.—Bottles should be packed with a stick

Damson Pickle.—Damsons, small black plums, or prunes make an excellent pickle. To every three pounds of fruit take two pounds of lump sugar, one ounce of mace, a little cinnamon and a few cloves if liked. Prick each fruit with a steel knitting needle (but on no account stone them, or the flavour will be spoiled), and place in an earthenware bowl. Tie the spices in a bag and boil in the vinegar with the sugar till the liquid is nicely flavoured. Then pour it over the damsons and let it stand for twenty-four hours. Now boil all in a preserving pan very gently for five minutes, except prunes which take longer before the skin breaks. Pour into jars and when cold, seal. Keep for five months before using.

Chutneys.—Chutney may have for its chief ingredient apples, tomatoes, both green and ripe, green gooseberries, marrow, and rhubarb; all these being added to a good chutney foundation. One good way of making this is to chop a pound of onions, and a pound of apples, add a pound of sultanas and a quarter of a pound of chopped orange peel (candied), or to two pounds of brown sugar, according to the sourness of the main ingredient, three-quarters of an ounce of ground ginger, half a teaspoonful of cayenne, one teaspoonful of salt, and one and a half to two pints of vinegar to cover. To this foundation add either two pounds of green gooseberries topped and tailed, or four pounds of diced marrow, or two pounds of sliced green tomatoes, or two pounds of ripe tomatoes, sliced and sprinkled with salt, which have stood for a night, or two pounds of apples. Boil this till it is the consistence of jam; put in jars and seal when cold.

When experimenting with this and other pickles write down each time the quantities you are using, so that when you achieve something extra good you have a permanent record of it. A handful of this, and a little of that, is not wise. Do not forget also to taste what you are making frequently, for ingredients must vary in their quality.

SAUCES

Mayonnaise.—Here is a mayonnaise which is a half-way house between sauces made for immediate consumption and those which will keep, for if kept in a covered jar it will be good for two weeks.

Take the yolks of two new-laid eggs and beat them with a fork. Add an eggspoonful of dry mustard and mix; then add salad oil slowly until the mixture thickens, about a breakfastcupful altogether will give a good consistency. Add either a tablespoonful of vinegar, or a dessertspoonful of vinegar and a tablespoonful of lemon juice, salt and pepper to taste. If a sweet mayonnaise is preferred, a dessertspoonful upwards of

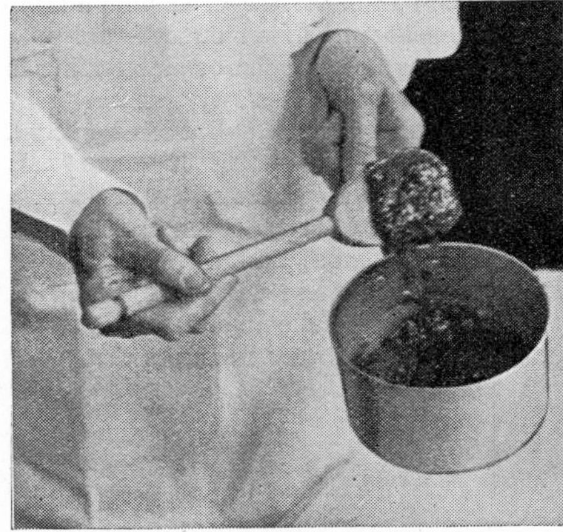

Fig. 2.—Chutney should not be too liquid

Fig. 3.—Clipping the edge of the cover to ensure a better fit

white sugar can be added now. Parsley or sorrel boiled and rubbed through a sieve may be added to this on serving to produce a green mayonnaise, or the vinegar in which beetroots have been steeping—together with a little cochineal, to serve as a red mayonnaise. Both these are excellent with fish.

Salad Dressing. — There are many bottled salad dressings on the market, but here is one with an individual flavour that will keep well. Beat three eggs thoroughly with a gill of milk, add a saltspoonful of salt and of pepper, a tablespoonful of white sugar also. Mix a teaspoonful of Worcester sauce into a tablespoonful of salad oil and add slowly to the egg mixture. Now put in a gill of vinegar slowly, a lump of butter—about half an ounce—and pour all into a double saucepan or jar standing in a saucepan, and cook slowly, stirring persistently until it is thick. Bottle when cool.

Tomato Sauce.—This is a very old family recipe, and produces a sauce with a subtle flavour. Take seven pounds of large firm tomatoes and three pounds of large cooking apples; wipe them and core the apples, then bake in tins in the oven until tender. Rub the tomatoes through a sieve, then free the apples from the skins and sieve. Boil the tomato and apple pulp for an hour, then add one and a half ounces of salt, eight ounces of brown sugar, half an ounce of garlic and half an ounce of shallot chopped and pounded, half an ounce of white pepper and a pinch of cayenne, and half a nutmeg, grated. Tie a tablespoonful of mustard seed and a teaspoonful of mixed pickling spice in a bag, and pour over all a pint of the best malt vinegar. Boil for several hours until the mixture is perfectly smooth, stirring frequently; the number of hours varies with the kind of fruit used. Bottle while hot, but do not cork until cold.

Harvey Sauce.—This is added to many hot sauces and is a most useful member of the store-cupboard. Put into the pan five pints of malt vinegar, two pounds of black treacle, the juice of four lemons, a dessertspoonful of cayenne, half an ounce of garlic cut in small pieces, and half an ounce of mixed pickling spice. Boil this mixture for an hour, and then strain it. Bottle when cold.

Mint Sauce.—Everyone can make mint sauce when fresh mint is in season, but bottled mint sauce is not often satisfactory. Here, however, is a recipe for a really good one. Take one and a half pints of vinegar and a pound of brown sugar and boil them for six minutes; let this go cold. Fill jars three-quarters full with mint chopped with a little granulated sugar; pour over this the cold vinegar, and seal carefully.

Mushroom Ketchup.—Take any quantity of large mushrooms picked on a dry morning; those picked in the rain will give a musty flavour. Peel and break up small, then put layers in a pan, sprinkling salt on each layer. Let them stand for thirty-six hours, stirring occasionally. Strain off the liquor, and to every pint add half an ounce of allspice, ten cloves, grated nutmeg to taste, and boil gently for half an hour. Let it stand for a day, then strain into bottles.

PICTURE FRAMING

The vogue of many styles of picture frame belongs to the past. The age of frames covered with plush, corks, shells, beads, elaborately carved moulding, and so on, has gone, and the amateur can, with present-day styles, turn out more work and at much less cost of money and labour than was the case not very many years ago.

The equipment required is neither large, nor expensive. A few simple cramps, mitre block, saws, hammers, bradawls, Archimedean drill, rebate plane, cutting gauge, bevel, mount cutter's knife, bevelled-edge rule, Jack and smoothing planes, bench and vice, try-square, together with the necessary panel pins, glue-pot, screws and hanging plates will enable you to do a large amount of work. Figs. 1 to 4 illustrate a few of the above, many of which can be made at home.

The extended use of three-ply and laminated wood has found its way into picture framing and many beautiful examples of neat simple frames can be made from this material. We give a few designs in Figs. 5 to 8. You are advised to begin on something orthodox and safe if you wish to win fairly general approval for your frames.

Ordinary picture moulding can be purchased quite cheaply at a price per foot which depends upon its size and the shape of its section.

You can make practically all your frames direct from plain material and use other joints besides the mitred joint in its various forms.

Making Narrow Black Picture Framing.—A good deal of narrow black framing is used nowadays for framing all kinds of prints, etchings and photographs. This framing can be purchased in lengths fairly cheaply ready for cutting, but if you cannot obtain it this way or prefer to make your own the following will enable you to do so.

Prepare lengths of fine-grained wood, such as bass-wood or bay-wood, say $\frac{1}{2}$ in. by $\frac{5}{8}$ in, or $\frac{5}{8}$ in. by $\frac{5}{8}$ in., and take out a rebate $\frac{1}{4}$ in. wide by $\frac{3}{8}$ in. deep as in Figs. 11, 12 and 13. Obtain half a pint of shoemaker's ink and give the lengths one or two coats. Allow to dry and then paint with one or two coats of spirit-black stain. You can make this stain by dissolving half an ounce of aniline black in one pint of methylated spirits, adding to it a little french polish to make it bind and act somewhat as a filler. Now fill the grain with a black paste filler. Leave each coat to dry before applying the next. Now finish according to the degree of brightness required on the surface. That is, apply wax for a dull polish, white french polish or a brushing cellulose lacquer for a high polish. Leave to set and then cut up as previously described.

Plywood Frames.—A great deal of work can be done in framing small pictures by the use of plywood. This can be obtained either in birch or alder, with a plain surface to be finished in one of many ways, or in oak- or mahogany-faced plywood. The details of construction are very simple. (*See* Figs. 9 and 10.) The back rebate is formed after the hole is cut. A good deal of the effect is obtained by the right placing of the hole cut out to receive the photograph or picture; Figs. 5 to 8 give a few suggestions. Notice that the hole is never placed exactly in the centre of the slab of wood. As shown, it is more interesting when it is placed either to the right or the left or above the centre with a larger space of wood underneath than at either side or above the picture.

As previously stated, there are several ways in which these frames may be finished. For example, as the surface of birch or alder plywood is not very interesting it is better to size it and paint with cellulose or other enamel in a colour to harmonize with the picture and the surroundings. If oak-faced plywood is used, it may be fumed, stained, painted with a solution of common soda, or limed and polished with wax or french polish. If the plywood is faced with

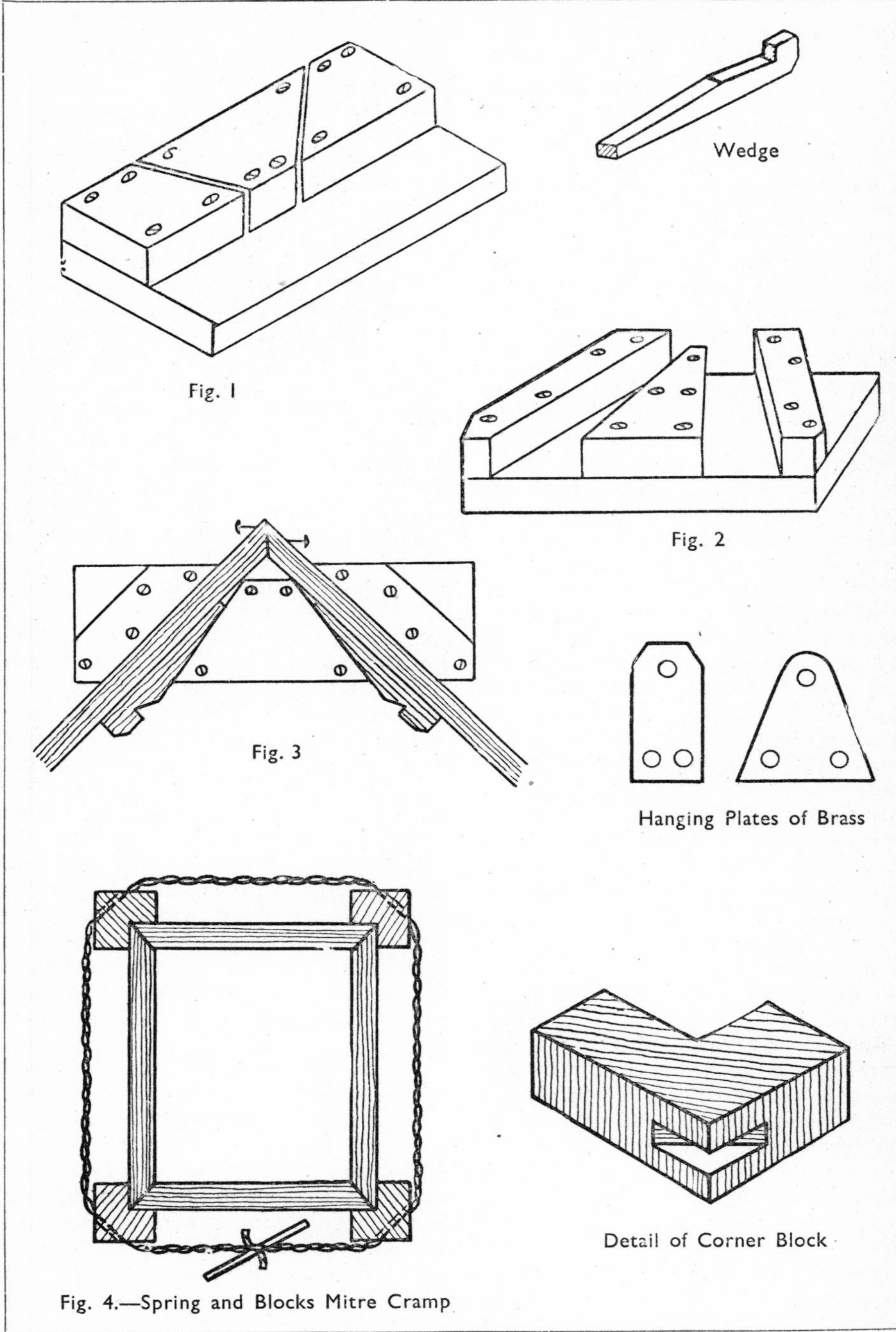

Fig. 4.—Spring and Blocks Mitre Cramp

mahogany it may be waxed or polished without staining, or stained with bi-chromate of potash and waxed or french polished.

Again, if birch or alder plywood is used it may be veneered all over with any veneer, edged with a stringing of ebony or box and french polished. The back should be veneered as well as the front so as to counteract the pull of the veneer.

Another variation would be the inlaying of a band either into the surface of the oak or mahogany plywood or into the veneer itself.

Really first-class work can be produced by any of the above methods. Still another method is to cover the whole of the frame with textile material. Coarse linen or fine hessian, or even coarse hessian, in various colours can be used and very attractive results obtained. It is understood, of course, that this method may be considered not quite so satisfactory because of the tendency for the material to catch dust.

Making Mounts and Mounting Pictures.—A few hints on mounting pictures will probably save a good deal of spoiled work. You can buy mounts ready made, but they are rather expensive and the method of making them is practically the same as that for the actual picture mounting itself. It must be remembered that great care should be taken to prevent dirt or paste being picked up by the picture. The use of plenty of waste paper, clean dusters, clean water, paste without alum or other chemicals likely to attack the photograph or the colour in the picture, is essential.

A perfectly laid picture should be without a trace of a wrinkle. Take the mounting paper, lay it face down on the piece of thick cardboard it is to cover, damp it all over with a sponge and water. It will probably curl up, so it must be held down carefully to prevent the wet surface from getting into contact with the front of the paper and marking it. After a few minutes damp it again and it will stay flat.

Now paste it all over with a coat of ordinary flour or starch paste. Pick it up carefully and lay it in position on the cardboard. Cover it with a piece of clean paper and, working from the centre with a duster, rub it carefully down until all air bubbles and wrinkles disappear. Place the mount on a flat surface, cover it with a clean sheet of cardboard and put a number of books on the surface to keep it quite flat until dry.

In choosing the colour of the mount for a picture consider the dominant colour in the picture and either make it tone or contrast with it. If mounting a picture in a light tone of colour, choose a mount of a slightly darker shade or tint. This generally adds richness to the quality of the picture. Remember also that when a picture without a margin or border has been mounted, it may appear a little unconvincing as it lies on the mount. If the mount is light, a fairly thick dark line, drawn round the picture and at a short distance away from it will make all the difference. If the mount is a dark, coloured one use a light line. Do not try any "fancy work" on the line; just allow it to speak for itself. You will find it much more satisfying than an elaborately decorative line which will take the eye away from the picture.

Joints in Framing.—The principal joint in the construction of picture frames is the mitre-joint. It is cut with a saw on the mitre-block, shown in Fig. 1. The method of obtaining the length of the pieces of framing is shown in Fig. 14. To fix the joints, glue, then fold in a cramp, and nail together, or make saw kerfs as shown in Fig. 15 and insert thin glued strips of plywood and leave to set.

Dowelled, butt, half-lap, mitred half-lap, mortice and tenon joints are also used. Sketches of these joints are shown in the section on WOODWORK.

PASSE-PARTOUT FRAMING

There are many photographs, pen-lettered quotations, small pictures, etc., which you may like to preserve in some kind of frame but do not wish to put into wooden frames. A simple, inexpensive and effective method is to bind together the picture, using a backing of cardboard and a covering of glass with an edge-binding of paper.

Tools and Materials.—The tools and materials required are quite few.

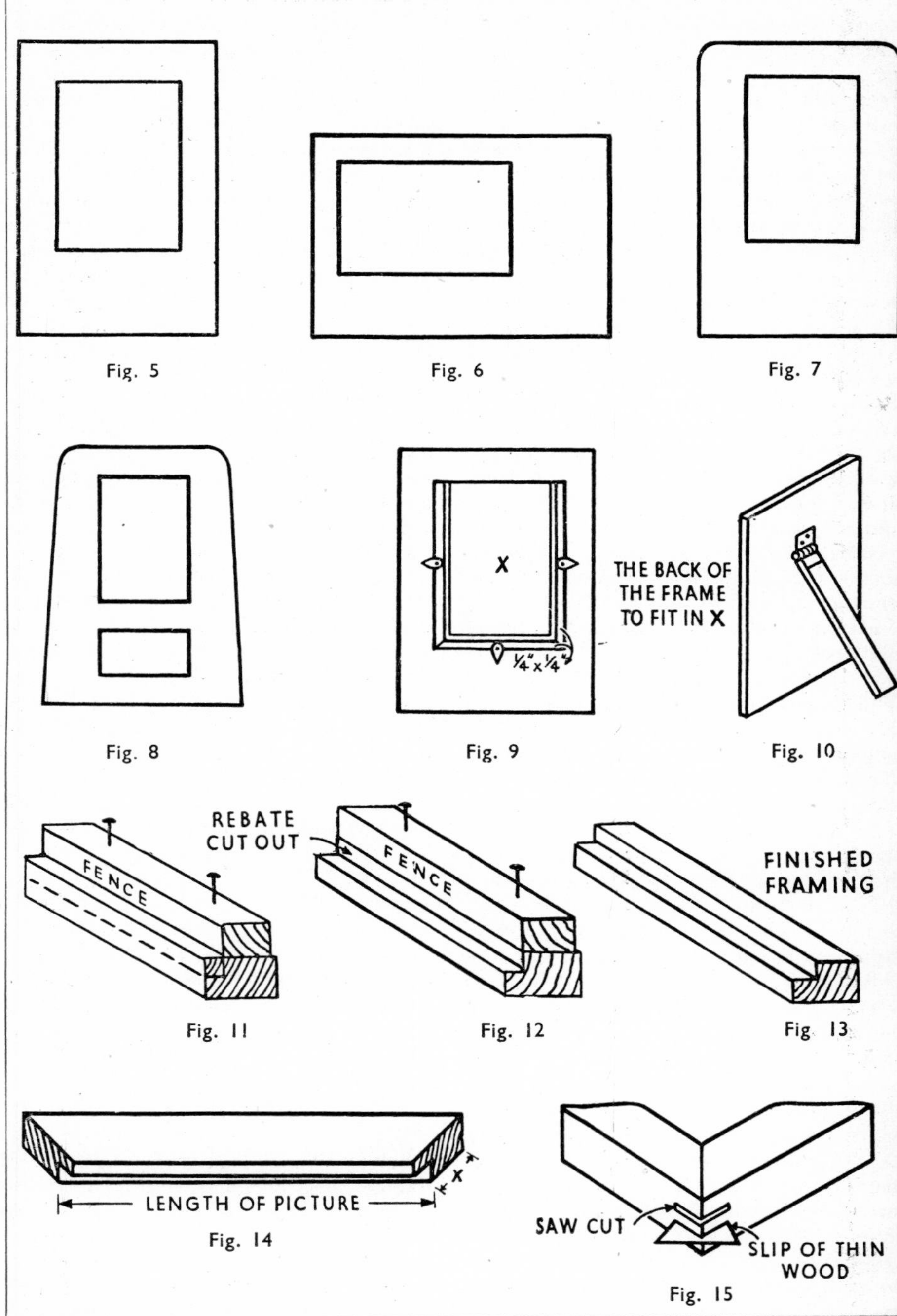

Fig. 5

Fig. 6

Fig. 7

Fig. 8

Fig. 9

Fig. 10

Fig. 11

Fig. 12

Fig. 13

Fig. 14

Fig. 15

Strawboard or cardboard for backing, lightweight picture glass, brass hangers, passe-partout binding, a Dennison creaser for creasing the latter accurately to the required width before placing it in position on the picture, a pair of scissors, a ruler, a sharp-pointed knife and a glass-cutter. Old photograph negatives are quite useful and cheap for this work.

Any cardboard from boxes will generally cut up into useful material for backing boards.

Many kinds of binding can be purchased in various colours and plain or patterned surfaces. Fancy bindings are not advised as they may take attention from the picture. Rather the binding should form an unobtrusive part of the whole picture. Plain black binding is most generally used, but there is no reason why you should not use a coloured binding which will harmonize with the main colour in the picture and the mount used as a background. For sepia prints a brown binding might be best. A dark blue binding would do for a small seascape; a red binding would do well on some highly coloured landscape pictures.

The small brass ring hangers (Fig. 19) can be purchased quite cheaply and, if unobtainable, rings or loops may be made of string or plain rings used and a strip of tape fixed to take the place of the small metal strip.

Mounting.—The picture or photograph may require mounting. This is very necessary as it is important that the picture should be thick enough to prevent the raised ends of the brass hangers showing through on the front of the picture. The mounting is therefore best done on thick paper or thin cardboard. Again, you should consider the colour of the picture in deciding upon that of the mount. The mount should always be plain so that it sets off the details of the picture rather than detracting from the latter.

It is important that the proportions of the mount should be carefully thought out. Do not place a picture exactly in the geometric centre of the mount, with an equal margin all round. The margins may be equal on the two sides and the top with a larger margin below or the side margins may be a little wider than the top with the still greater bottom margin. (*See* Figs. 16, 17, 18.)

If you can arrange your own size of mount a very fine proportion can be obtained by using an oblong, eight units long by five units wide. These units may be in half-inches, inches, inches and a half, or anything else, according to the size of the picture required.

Preparing the Work.—First of all see that your working surface, i.e. the table or bench top, is quite clean and protected with a clean piece of paper. Mount the picture on a mount of the size required and leave to set under flat pressure till dry. Cut a backing board of cardboard to the same size as the picture. When deciding on the thickness of the backing board remember that it is not desirable to have a very thick edge to the picture. Cut a piece of glass to the same size. When cutting glass take care that it is resting on a perfectly flat surface or you might break it when holding the ruler in position.

Clean the glass thoroughly on both sides. Decide on the position for the brass hangers, pierce holes with a bradawl, a knife point, the point of the scissors or a bodkin, insert the metal strips with the prongs horizontal and press back the ends, as in Fig. 20. The position of these hangers is important as they affect the angle at which the picture will hang. The distance from the top will vary from 1 in. to 2 in., according to the size of the picture, and about 1½ in. from the sides. When the ends of the hanger are turned back tap them with a hammer so as to knock them level with the surface of the cardboard. Pieces of narrow tape can be used instead of these rings. With a knife make slits in the backing boards wide enough to take the tape. Push the ends of the tape through with the point of a knife, turn them back one each way and paste them down. (*See* Fig. 21.)

Binding the Edges.—Now stick together the picture and the backing board at the top corners only. Seccotine or similar tube glue is probably most convenient to use for this work as there is less difficulty in obtaining the necessary tackiness to enable the work to be carried on quickly than there is when a flour paste is being used.

Begin binding with the two long sides

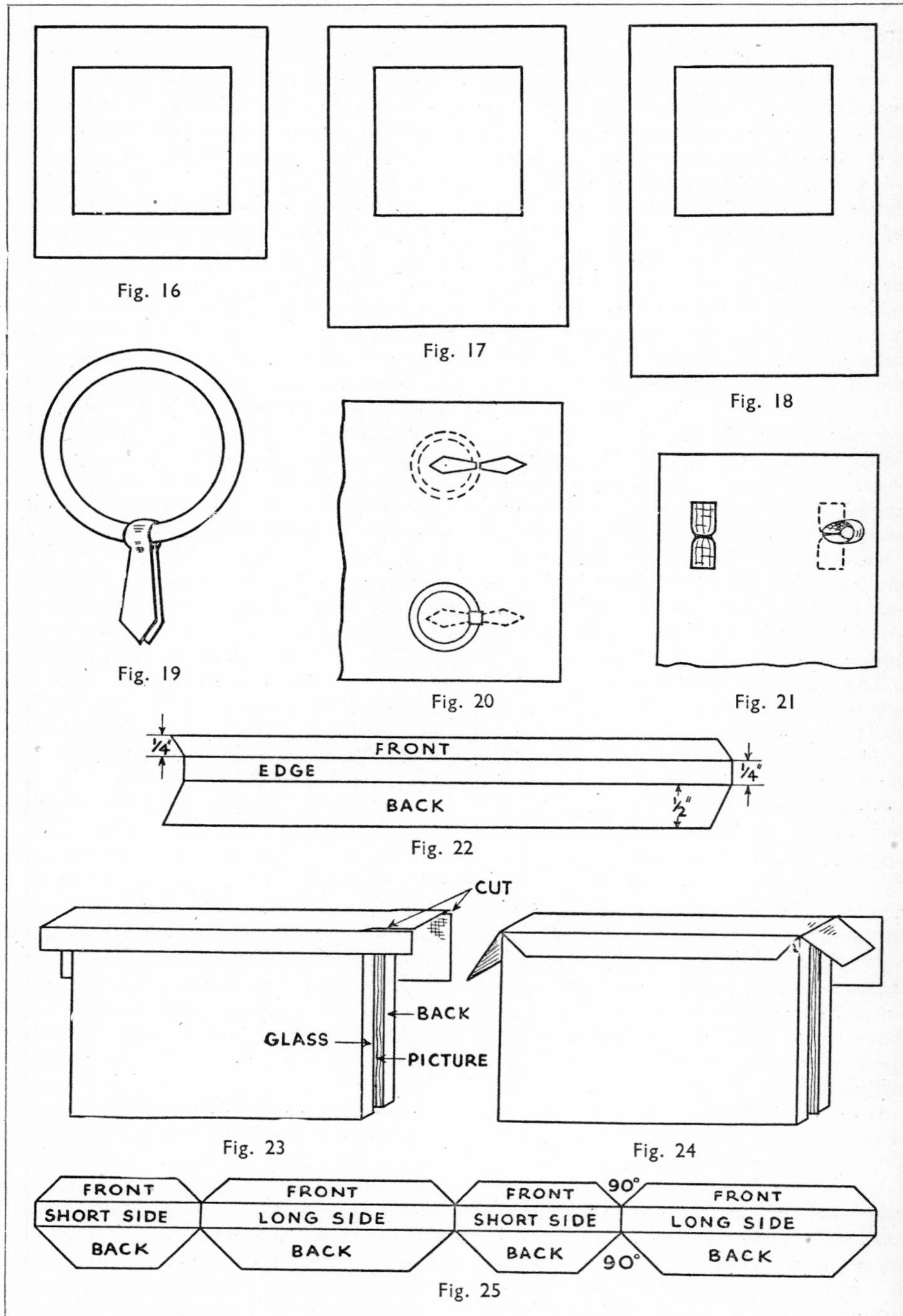

Fig. 16

Fig. 17

Fig. 18

Fig. 19

Fig. 20

Fig. 21

Fig. 22

Fig. 23

Fig. 24

Fig. 25

of the glass. Measure and cut off binding, allowing about ½ in. longer than required. Always start with the long side directly in front of you. Moisten binding well and apply quickly to glass, making sure that the edge of the binding is parallel with the edge of the glass. (A light pencil line made on the mount beforehand will be helpful.) Pressure should be used until the binding is well set.

Turn glass and picture over, being careful to keep them exactly level, remoistening binding if necessary, and fastening down quickly, pressing from the middle outwards to exclude all creases and air bubbles. Cover the other long side in the same manner.

Before putting the binding on the two short ends, the surplus binding on the long edges should be trimmed off about ⅛ in. from the edge of the glass, and the ends neatly folded over the corners. The corners are now ready for mitring.

Mitring the Corners.—Cut the binding for the two short ends leaving an extension of about 1 in. for mitring corners, as illustration No. 23. Moisten binding and apply as before. Cut the extensions of the binding through the middle of the fold. Cut off surplus binding and fasten to the picture, trimming the corners carefully.

Picture Hanging.—If, when you have framed your pictures, they are not hung to the best advantage, a good deal of the enjoyment of your work is lost. First of all, a few "don'ts."

Don't hang the pictures on a damp wall; don't hang the pictures with a tilt outwards, or hang a glazed picture opposite a window, the strong light from which falling directly upon it will cause objects in front to be reflected in the glass and render the picture itself invisible; don't hang an oil painting where it is likely to be exposed to the glare of the hot sun or it may be cracked and blistered; don't hang very large pictures in very small rooms.

Try the effect of two single hanging wires hanging straight down instead of the usual wire going to one point and forming a triangle above the frame. Also arrange the hanging wire so that it is concealed behind the picture and see how you like that instead of the usual arrangement.

If you have a number of small pictures to hang on a wall try the effect of grouping them and treating each group as a unit and arranging for the eye level to pass through the frames with a greater amount of picture above the line than below it. If you are hanging one picture only, place it just above the eye level. If you are hanging a large picture and a small one, one above the other, place the larger one on top.

POSTER DESIGNING

Socials, parties, dances, meetings, sports, whist drives, bazaars, rummage sales, concerts and hundreds of other similar events are organized everywhere, every day. Many of them are small affairs and the organizers cannot afford to pay heavy printers' bills. How then can they be advertised? It usually falls to the lot of one member of the organization to do the posters.

Now the writing of a reasonably good poster is not difficult; it can be a very fascinating hobby and one that is sure to be useful and quite possibly remunerative. The following introduction to this interesting craft is intended rather for the beginner than for the expert who has already acquired skill in lettering and design.

Essentials of a Good Poster.—It must be read quite easily at a distance.

It must attract the attention of the passer-by.

The essential facts must be so stated and written that the reader instantly grasps them.

They must be the right size for the place where they will be put up.

Each of these points is vitally important and no amount of colour, fancy designs, pictures, etc., will help if attention has not been paid in the first place to these points.

Easy to Read at a Distance.—Many notices fail in this respect and yet it is the first thing at which the designer should aim. The following points will help:

Size of Paper.—It must be remembered that a sheet of paper pinned on the board in front of the artist looks quite large, but if he or she walks to the other side of even a small room and looks at it, it seems very much smaller. This is partly due to perspective and partly to its size in comparison with other objects around it. Choose therefore a good size for the paper and before setting to work test it at a distance to see if it looks large enough and will carry all the words that must be written on it.

The letters must be large enough to be read easily at the required distance. They must also be simple in shape and heavy enough in line to be easily distinguished.

The beginner frequently attempts very fancy shapes and adds "twiddly bits" in all sorts of unexpected and wrong places. These confuse the eye of the reader who cannot, as a result, recognize the letters. Fig. 1 gives the simplest possible shapes of all the letters. They are the foundation shapes and can, of course, be thickened as illustrated in order to make them show up. Look at a number of big posters on the hoardings and you will be surprised to see how many designers have used only this type of letter—just because it is quite the clearest and most easily read.

Letters in Good Proportion.—This is very important as the eye has been trained from infancy to look for certain proportions, and we read far more quickly if the letters are made as we have always learned to expect them to be. In Fig. 1 the letters of the alphabet are set out in their usual proportion taking a square as the unit. It will be seen that some fit into a square, some are not quite as wide as they are high and some are surprisingly slender, being only half as wide as they are high. These last ones are often very maltreated. We see B's and P's in particular looking clumsy and stout, while S, the "dainty lady" of the alphabet is very often made to look very much too rotund.

The amateur will be very wise if she or he spends a number of hours sketching these letters and trying to form them well and in their correct proportion, until it becomes second nature to do them correctly.

Spacing.—This is the pitfall of many and it can so easily be avoided if the following points are realized:

Letters which are spread out too much are difficult to read, e.g. L E T T E R I N G F O R P O S T E R S is not nearly so easily read as LETTERING FOR POSTERS. Therefore place the letters together so that each word stands out as a mass—but test it at a distance to see that the letters do not run together and become illegible. Leave good spaces between the words. There can be no definite rule for the placing of the letters, e.g. one cannot decide that all letters shall be $\frac{1}{8}$ in. apart. As an example, take the word ENTERTAINMENT in Fig. 4. In the upper of the two words each letter is placed the same distance from its neighbours. This results in two big ugly spaces as indicated caused by a T and an A, and a bad massing of a number of vertical lines which would be difficult to read at a distance. In the lower word these points have been corrected by a closer spacing of NTE and RTA and a wider spacing of INMEN. The result is a saving of space and a more-easily-read word.

This overlapping of letters is important and while it cannot always be done when one would like, opportunities often occur and examples are given in the words "Party," "July," "You," "Lost," "WANTED" at the bottom of Fig. 4. It will be seen that A, P, T, V, L, Y, J are the letters which give rise to awkward spaces in words.

The spacings of A S O C I A L E V E N I N G illustrate the danger of too wide spacing between letters and how much more pleasant and legible the words are when the letters are closer. Also notice that in the lower example the space between the lines is lessened to advantage.

The Poster Must Attract Attention.—This is the second essential and after all it is the primary object of any poster. How then can this be done? Any or all the following suggestions will help:

The whole poster must be large enough;
Bold, clear and easily read lettering;
Bright colours;

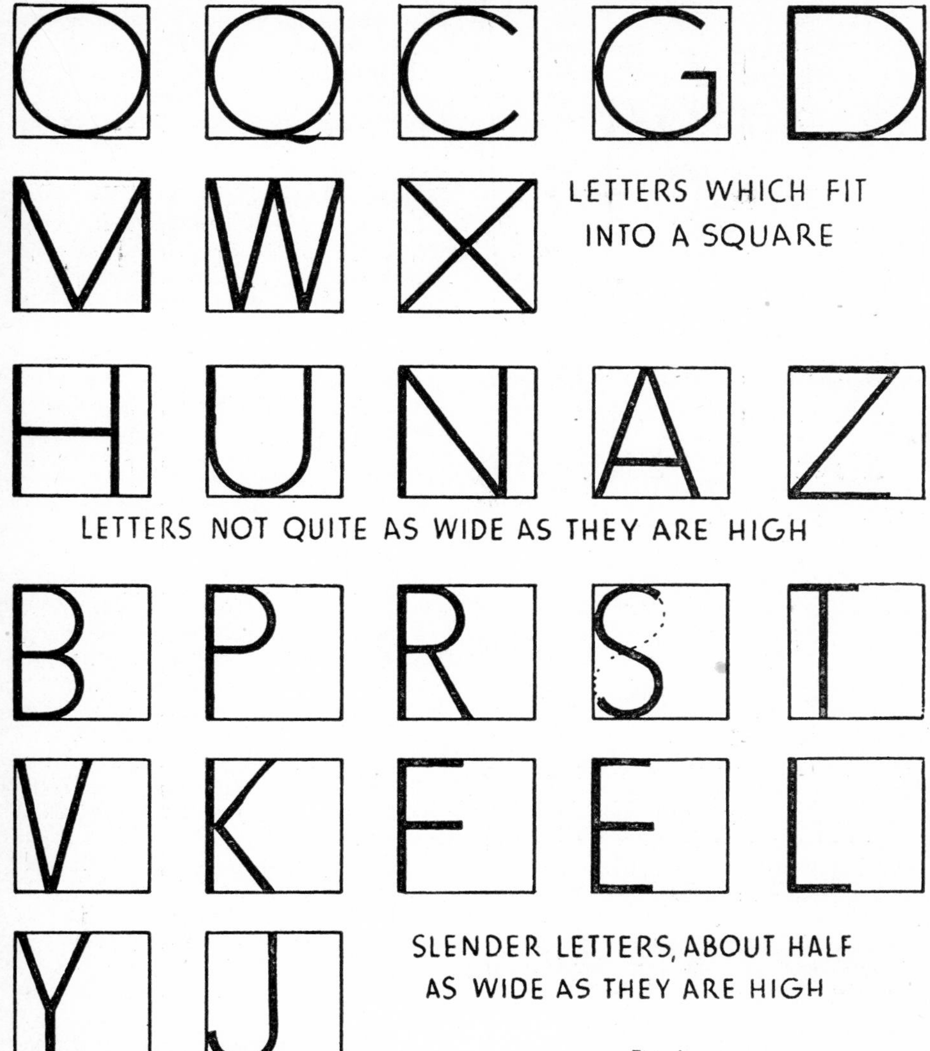

Fig. 1

BNGSAT

SHOWING HOW THE FOUNDATION SHAPES CAN BE TREATED TO MAKE THEM SHOW AT A DISTANCE

Fig. 2

Some word written much larger than the rest to catch the eye;

Some discordant "note," e.g. of colour or a word written at a slant;

A picture or sketch such as a Father Christmas for a party, or several playing cards for a Whist Drive.

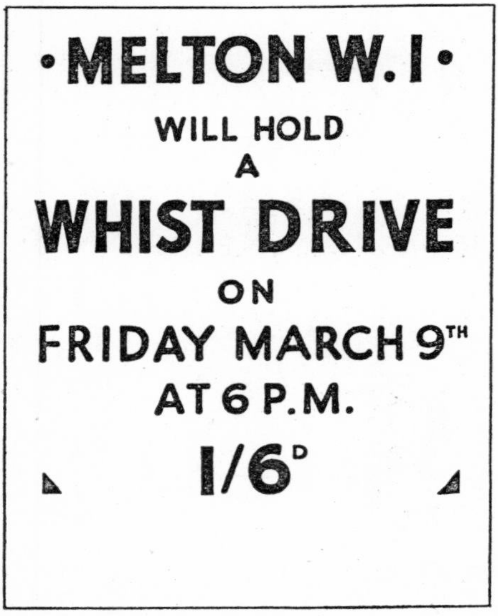

•MELTON W.I•
WILL HOLD
A
WHIST DRIVE
ON
FRIDAY MARCH 9TH
AT 6 P.M.
1/6D

Fig. 3

An extremely well-written poster with well-formed letters, etc. This, because of its restraint and dignity, commands immediate attention.

Important Facts Must Stand Out.—This is important as the reader must see instantly what the poster advertises. This can be done in several ways:

One or two words written much larger than the rest, e.g. JUMBLE SALE, the place and date being in much smaller letters.

The important words painted in a bright colour.

Arrows or lines leading the eye to the word.

Arranging the wording to form a triangle pointing downwards to the main word.

Leaving a large area of plain space round the word.

It is not always easy to decide on the most important word. Usually it is the type of meeting, e.g. SALE OF WORK, CONCERT, DANCE, etc. Sometimes if it is a lecture, the subject is the important word, while it may be that the person coming to perform or talk is so well-known that their name written large will attract attention.

The name of the organization running the affair should usually be fairly large and at the top. The date should be, of course, of a size that stands out clearly and if it is FREE it is as well to advertise the fact! Other facts should be written large enough for readers to see easily after they have been arrested by the larger words.

Avoid wherever possible putting in too much. Brevity and simplicity are very important.

Large and Small Posters and Notices.—The actual size of posters is an important consideration and while no definite ruling can be given as circumstances are different in every case, those planning the advertising should realize one or two points. The first is that very large posters are not welcomed by shops. The writer knows of one instance where a large number of rather large posters were ordered and when efforts were made to distribute them not a single shop would display them. The next year much smaller ones were printed and no difficulty was found in placing them

ENTERTAINMENT

AWKWARD SPACES

TOO CLOSE

ENTERTAINMENT

THE ABOVE MISTAKES CORRECTED

A SOCIAL EVENING

TOO SPREAD OUT TO BE EASILY READ

A SOCIAL EVENING

MORE EASILY READ BECAUSE MORE COMPACT

PARTY JULY YOU

LOST WANTED

EXAMPLES OF CLOSE SPACING OF LETTERS WHERE OTHERWISE THERE WOULD BE AN UGLY SPACE

Fig. 4

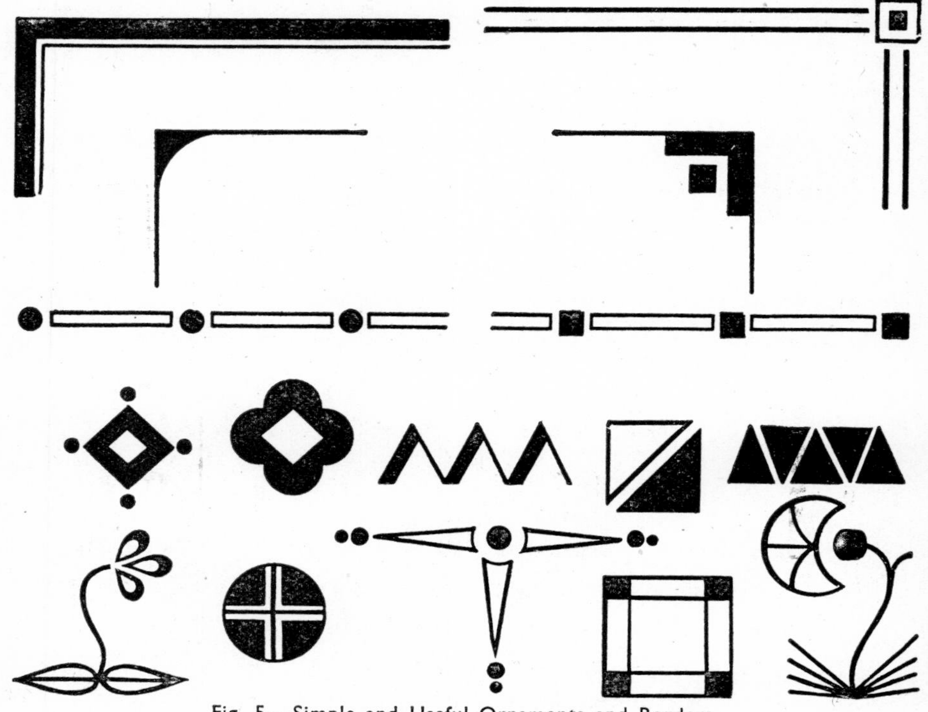

Fig. 5.—Simple and Useful Ornaments and Borders

in shops. A number of small posters is better than one or two large posters that only a limited number of people will see.

Tools and Materials.—A drawing board about 22 in. by 16 in. is essential and can be obtained for a very small outlay; soft pencils and a soft rubber; ruler, T square; drawing-pins; one or two good medium thick brushes, indian ink (water proof), black ink, poster paints, including white. All kinds of pens will be useful, e.g. mapping, ball pointed and later very wide-ended pens with which a special type of writing called script can be done which is not dealt with here. Compasses with pen attachments and ruling-pens that carry a good deal of ink are useful.

For paper, a visit should be paid to the local art-shops to find out what different kinds of inexpensive paper is easily obtainable. Ordinary cartridge and tinted papers will probably be easily found. Good kitchen paper is also useful at times.

Planning a Poster.—First decide on the size and shape of the poster. The proportion 5 units wide by 8 units long is good. Then write down the minimum of words and underline the most important ones. Then sketch very roughly various possible arrangements of the words commencing with the important word or words and deciding on their position in the panel. This is best well above the middle, see Figs. 2 and 3, never right across the middle. Suggestions for lay-outs are given in Figs. 2 and 3, and notice that in each case there is a good plain area at the bottom which is always effective.

When a pleasant plan has been evolved, it must then be carefully planned *faintly* in pencil on the full-size poster. All measurements should be accurately taken. The T square is a valuable tool for planning lines, etc. Mark the centre, plan for a generous border and then adapt the general sizes of the letters to the poster and the space at your disposal.

When everything is sketched in, rule all straight lines and then carry it out in the selected medium, ink, coloured inks or poster paint. Do not be too disheartened if mistakes occur. Remember that if you are working on white paper, Chinese white covers a multitude of sins, and if the background is coloured a patch of stuck-on paper will not show a little way off.

Finishing Touches.—Borders and line fillings are often useful for finishing posters. They should always be simple and inconspicuous as they are not the important part of the notice. When selecting them choose simple and quickly done bands or spots and practise doing the latter free hand. The additional units of decoration can often be done in colour repeating the colour of the important words.

One final word of advice. If colours are chosen be careful to use those which can be seen at a distance, and certainly do not use together a weak one and a brilliant one. A little experiment will soon prove if one colour fades out at a distance before the others.

Contrasting colours always give a brilliant and startling effect, e.g. black and white, black and yellow, red and green, blue and orange, yellow and violet.

Possibilities of this Craft.—Only the very elementary side of poster work has been dealt with here, and the need for simplicity has been emphasised. This is one of the essentials of all good posters. Often the design or picture may be very advanced but you will always find that it has been executed in a very bold and simple way.

Once the beginner has acquired a good technique and the idea of planning before actually doing the final poster, all kinds of possibilities will be visualized. In the hands of someone with originality and some skill in doing quick sketches, there is no limit to what can be done in this fascinating craft.

POULTRY KEEPING

POULTRY keeping is a hobby which makes considerable demands on the enthusiast. You must take these into consideration before you start. Are you prepared, summer and winter, to devote a minimum of half an hour daily to your fowls? Can you make arrangements for them to be attended to while you are away on holiday? Can you afford to lay out about 5/- per head on the birds for their upkeep till they start laying?

Of course, poultry keeping has its attractions, and these should be considered. It has all the fascination of other pet-keeping hobbies, and in addition produces a concrete return, in the form of fresh eggs and fattened fowls, for the work it entails.

If you feel the pros outweigh the cons, your next step is to decide on what system you are going to keep your fowls. There are three systems possible: the extensive, the semi-intensive, and the intensive. The first of these is only possible if you have a field, an orchard, or, at least, a large garden, because it means allowing your birds to range freely, only returning to their small houses to lay and at night. Its advantages are that the fowls get a large proportion of their food without cost to their owner; they are kept in the pink of condition by the free life, and they benefit the land over which they run.

Under the semi-intensive system the birds are given the freedom of a small enclosed run and have a moderate-size laying house and perhaps a scratching shed. In the average garden this plan is the best.

But in back-yards and small city gardens the intensive system is often the only one practicable, for intensively reared birds are kept constantly in a house, and have not even the liberty of a small run. Properly carried out, this method brings quite good results, and is no more cruel to the fowls than the confinement of rabbits to hutches or of canaries to cages. Your own judgment based on your circumstances must decide which system will suit you best.

The next question is the breed of fowl you are going to keep. For general purposes the Rhode Island Red is most popular. The Wyandotte also is a good favourite.

Buff or White Orpingtons (old type), and Buff Plymouth Rocks are also good if a real laying strain is chosen.

For laying only, without regard to table qualities, the white, black, brown or buff Leghorn is unbeatable; while, solely for edible purposes, the Sussex or Orpington (old type) is best.

If you intend to breed your own replacement pullets by hatching eggs under a hen, you will find that all the breeds mentioned above are sitters except the Leghorn.

Before you can actually get your stock, however, you will have to prepare suitable accommodation for them. Coops, small runs, and the other things necessary for bringing up chicks will be described later. First of all you must know the requirements of laying hens.

Poultry Houses.—There are many excellent firms which specialize in building poultry houses. These firms advertise in the "Feathered World," and from any one of them you should be able to get a ready-made laying house quite cheaply. You should, if possible, see the house before buying. Make sure that it is strongly constructed, with the framework well braced and the wall-boards not less than $\frac{3}{4}$ in. thick (nominal, which is actually $\frac{5}{8}$ in.). If it is for use in an enclosed garden, a sectional building should be chosen.

Of course, you can cut down expenses considerably by building the house yourself. This will present no difficulty if you have a working knowledge of carpentry, and use a fairly simple design. The Ministry of Agriculture supplies these very cheaply. With a little ingenuity such second-hand materials as the wood from old boxes, old linoleum, odd pieces of glass, and empty oil-drums flattened out can be utilized.

For use with the extensive system "slatted-floor" houses are ideal. These have a floor of slats placed a little less than 1 in. apart, beneath which is a boarded tray to catch the droppings which fall between the slats. This tray is made to slide out for cleaning purposes.

There must be at least two large windows, and the upper part of one wall should consist of wire netting. This can be covered during the cold nights by a wooden shutter, but ventilators set high in the ends of the house should always be left open.

The row of nest boxes should be, as far as possible, in shadow, and the boards in the wall at the back of them should be hinged so that eggs can be collected from outside the house. Each nest should measure about 14 in. square, and about one nest for every five fowls should be enough, for, during the heavy laying period, you can temporarily increase the number of nests by putting in one of those sectional orange-boxes.

No perches are necessary in the slatted house, as the fowls sleep on the floor, but some arrangement should be made to stop them from spending the night on the nests—a wire netting frame to fit in front of the nest boxes is the best thing.

The roof of the house can be made most cheaply of boards covered with felt. Battens must be nailed over the felt about 2 ft. apart to prevent the wind lifting it off the boards. Be careful to nail them down the slope, and not across it, or they will stop the rain from running off.

Corrugated iron is more durable, but unless there is an inner lining of matchboard with an air space of 2 in. between it and the corrugated iron, the house will be too hot in summer and too cold in winter. It will also help to keep the house at a healthy temperature if, during the summer, the roof is coated with whitewash in which is a little size or starch.

A Slatted-floor House such as I have described is quite suitable for semi-intensive poultry keeping, too, and can carry twice as many fowls, though a house similar in other details but with a plain boarded floor is generally used. In the latter, perches must be supplied. These should consist of strips of wood 2 in. by 2 in., with the top edges rounded. Immediately under them, "droppings boards" must be fitted; they must be easily removable for cleaning. By collecting the droppings from the birds on the perches during the night, they will greatly simplify the task of keeping the house clean.

If the laying house is lifted about 2 ft. from the ground on wooden posts, there

A badly designed type of poultry house

Fig. 1.—Right and wrong types of poultry houses. The top specimen is clumsy to move, has insufficient light and ventilation and little facility for cleaning. The specimen in the lower picture has these faults remedied

will be no possibility of it harbouring rats, and, in addition, a lower story will be formed which will make a fine scratching shed. A board with strips of wood across it to give foothold will have to be sloped up to the entry trap-door, however, to form a ladder for the birds.

For intensive purposes the lower scratching shed must be wired round with netting, and a "staircase" will need to be made from within it to the upper laying house.

An enclosed run for the semi-intensive system can easily be laid out with wire-netting nailed to wooden posts. A height of five feet should be sufficient as, if you find the birds flying over, you can clip their long wing feathers and so stop them.

Having made ready the pens and houses, you can now proceed to get your stock. The cheapest way to do this is to buy sitting eggs in January or February and hatch them under a broody hen. By the time these birds lay, their total cost will have been about 5/- each.

Day-old Chicks.—By purchasing these for about 1/- each, you may save yourself the small trouble of hatching, but the cost of these chicks will work out at about 5/6 each by the time they lay. In any case, you should avoid buying "cheap" chicks.

An even simpler but still more expensive method is to buy three-months-old pullets at the beginning of July, for about 3/6 each, or laying pullets in September. If you decide to avoid the trouble of rearing chicks, and to buy laying pullets, your best plan will be to buy half first-season birds and the other half second-season birds. Then, each year following, you need replace only the older half of your stock.

In order to take the business of rearing poultry from the very beginning, let us suppose that you have decided to hatch a sitting of eggs under a hen to get your first chicks.

Buy the eggs from a reputable breeder, making certain that they are from a really good laying strain. They will cost 7/6 a dozen at least if any good. They should be as fresh as possible—certainly not more than a week old. If you have to keep them, lay them in a tray of bran and turn them every day to prevent displacement of the germ due to the yolk rising.

Sit three to four times as many eggs as the number of pullets you require; this will allow for infertile eggs and cockerels. Thirteen eggs may be placed under one hen.

The nest should be in a darkened, secluded spot. It can be made from a wooden box, measuring about 14 in. in each direction, tipped on its side.

The lid should be sawn across into three equal parts. The lower piece should be nailed across the front of the box to keep the nest in place. One of the other pieces must be made to fit loosely to the box, so that it can be removed to allow the fowl to be taken out. The remaining section of the lid need not be used at all; the gap it leaves will serve for ventilation.

The Nest itself should consist of first a foundation of moist, sifted earth, moulded into a hollow; then a layer of hay also shaped into a hollow.

Before putting the hen on the real eggs try her on some dummy eggs for a day or two. You will then get some idea whether she is going to settle down. If she seems to sit tightly you can give her feathers a dusting with insect powder, let her have a meal, and then set her to work on the real eggs. She should commence sitting on the real eggs in the evening, for she will settle down better during the night.

Regularly each day the hen must be taken off and given a good feed of wheat and maize. When you lift her off the nest be careful that she does not bring out any eggs tucked under her wings, or they will drop and be smashed. Provide her with clean water, flint grit, and a dust bath. But prevent her from reaching any green stuff unless she is constipated, as it is a laxative.

The nest and eggs should be cleansed if necessary—the former by adding clean hay, and the latter by washing in warm water.

The amount of time the hen is away from the eggs can be lengthened from ten minutes during the first week to twenty minutes during the final week. She should, while off the nest, pass large, moist fæces. In very cold weather the eggs should be covered with flannel while the hen is off.

Testing for Fertility.—At the end of the first week the eggs can be tested. Cut an egg-shaped hole slightly smaller than an egg in a thick piece of cardboard. Fit the eggs into this hole large end uppermost, and hold them up to a light in a dark room. You will be able to see right into them. If they are infertile they will be quite clear, but, on turning a fertile egg round you will see a dark spot with streaks radiating from it, looking very like a spider. A second test should be made a week later, and then the developing germ should be so plainly visible that all doubt will be removed and the infertile eggs may be taken away.

On the morning of the twenty-first day some of the chicks should be hatched. Do not worry the hen by looking under her too often. On the other hand, contrary to general practice, you may safely remove the chicks more or less as they come off, taking away also the broken shells lest they cup over the unhatched eggs and make it impossible for the chickens in them to break through. As you take the chicks away, put them into an enclosed basket lined with warm flannel, and place the basket itself somewhere in the warm.

When all the chickens are off, let the hen have food and exercise, then give her the chicks. Unless they show signs of hunger, no food should be given the little things till thirty-six hours after they have been hatched. Then feed them on one of the better-known proprietary chick foods. These are graded to suit chickens of different ages, and should be fed according to the directions which are usually given.

Meals.—Generally speaking, six meals a day should be given during the first three weeks ; for the fourth and fifth weeks four meals will be sufficient; while at the sixth week the number can be reduced to three. Of these one can consist of scalded biscuit meal dried off with middlings, and the other two of small wheat.

The Coop into which you put the chicks with their mother during the first few weeks can be quite a simple affair. A packing case measuring about 2 ft. high, 2 ft. wide and 3 ft. long can be used. The lid should be covered with felt and hinged to the box to form the roof. One of the long sides must be knocked out and vertical spars about 3 in. apart nailed in its place. In order to admit the hen, the middle spar must be removable. The spars should be covered at night by a wooden shutter in which are ventilation holes.

Fig. 2.—A serviceable Chicken Coop. Note triangular white patch which is of a translucent waterproof cloth

A small enclosed pen to fit against the sparred front of the coop must be made. The best type is of wire netting on a light wooden framework, with a hinged roof. It need not be higher than about 18 in.

Do not let the mother into the pen with her chicks till they are strong enough to scramble out of her way when she scratches or dust-bathes. When they are about six weeks old, the chickens will be able to do without their mother. But before you take her from them, put her with them into their new laying house so that she can teach them to use the perch at night.

Separate the Cockerels from the Pullets as soon as you can distinguish them. If you do not wish to keep them for stock purposes, put them into a small run for fattening. Feed them on a mixture of equal parts of Sussex ground oats, middlings, and barley meal mixed with water or, better still, with skim milk. Gradually increase their rations and when, in a few weeks, they show signs of going off the food, they should be ready for the market, or the table.

At about six months your pullets will begin to lay. Earlier laying should be discouraged for it results in small, valueless eggs, and weakens the birds. Pullets which show signs of laying too soon may be held back if you feed them solely on grain and a little greenstuff.

You have now reached the stage where your pullets are laying and your cockerels are either ready for sale as stock birds or have been disposed of for the table. But if you had preferred to hatch and rear your chicks by artificial methods, it would simply be a matter of getting to understand the machines used.

The Incubator.—Although you may only need a small model, you would do well to get a good one. There are two types: hot-air, and hot-water incubators. The former is usually the cheaper to buy, but the latter is slightly the more reliable.

Place your incubator in a well-ventilated room where the temperature is as constant as possible. Do not put it anywhere where the sun will shine on it. See that it is dead level and quite steady. Also make sure that the moving parts of the automatic temperature controller are working freely.

Try the incubator for a few days before putting any eggs into it. Use a good quality paraffin, and be careful not to get any spilt on the incubator, or the eggs may be tainted.

Full directions are supplied with every incubator; read yours carefully and you should soon get used to controlling the machine. As the procedure varies with the different makers it would be useless to give any general instructions; but here are three important "don'ts." Don't try to squeeze in more eggs than the tray is supposed to hold, thinking that when the infertile eggs are removed there will be more room. Don't add more eggs at a later date; and don't forget to replenish the moisture device if it should need it.

If all goes well the eggs will be seen to be chipped on the twentieth day. The chicks which hatch out can be put into the drying chamber. They can be given to a broody hen which has been sitting on dummy eggs for a week or two. If the eggs are taken from under her at night and the chicks substituted, she will take to them readily.

The Brooder.—The alternative is to rear the chicks in a brooder. Here again you should buy a good model, even if it costs a little more, and follow the directions supplied. You can soon check the temperature of the brooder by watching the behaviour of the chicks. When they are cold they will huddle closely together, and when the heat is too much for them they will try to get as far away from each other as possible, and they will show signs of weakness.

The best litter for the brooding compartments is crumbled peat moss, which has fine deodorizing properties, or fine chips and sawdust or chopped straw. Peat moss, however, you should be warned, tends to get very dirty in a brooder.

At about seven weeks the chicks can be taken from the brooder and put into the laying house, where they will progress in exactly the same way as naturally hatched birds, so we can now pass on to their management when they start to lay.

Diet.—The most important factor in securing good egg production is correct feeding. A laying fowl can hardly eat too much; but *what* it eats is all important. To be successful, a diet must combine all the elements a bird's body needs in, as nearly as possible, the proper proportions.

There are three kinds of food in the ordinary poultry diet: grain, greenstuff and mash. Grain can be bought in ready-made mixtures, but these are not recommended as the quality of the grain they contain is often poor. Wheat alone, or a simple mixture of wheat and kibbled (i.e. coarsely ground) maize in equal parts is best for laying fowls. Oats are too dear and often too husky. Kibbled maize is excellent, plus *short clipped* oats if you like. The myth that maize is "heating" in the summer has been exploded.

Greenstuff may take the form of cabbage, tender grass, sanfoin, lucerne, or practically anything green and juicy. Lawn clippings are excellent, though if you have only a small garden, you may find the provision of sufficient greenstuff difficult. If so, you should try germinating grain. Wheat and oats are suitable for this treatment.

Half fill a bucket with grain and then fill it up with lukewarm water. Let the grain soak for twelve hours. Spread it evenly on trays which should, if possible, be kept in a warm atmosphere.

Keep them for about a week, sprinkling the grain with warm water occasionally, and by then it should have sprouted an abundance of green shoots.

The Mash is the stimulating part of the fowls' diet. You *can* make your own mash if you wish to, but whether you are to use wet or dry mash must be decided by your circumstances. For the small-scale poultry-keeper wet mash is cheaper to make than dry as it can be made chiefly from kitchen scraps which would in the ordinary way be wasted. But feeding dry mash means less work, because a whole week's supply can be mixed at one time and can be left in the hopper from which the birds will help themselves when they feel hungry. As regards results there is nothing to choose between the two methods, though the small man would probably find it cheaper still to buy a good proprietary mash.

To make a wet mash, keep an old saucepan into which all your kitchen scraps, except very rich ones or excessive quantities of meat, can be thrown. Let them simmer in a little water for a few hours then chop them up fairly fine. It only remains to stir in just enough of the following drying-off mixture to make up a moist, crumbly mash: middlings seven parts, Sussex ground oats (or maize meal which is equally good and much cheaper) two parts, and meat meal one part. The meat meal must be omitted if the scraps include any meat.

In winter the drying-off mixture may be changed to: middlings six parts, Sussex ground oats one part, maize meal two parts, and meat meal one part.

A good dry mash can be made by a mixture of the following meals: maize meal three parts, bean meal one part, barley meal three parts, bran two parts, clover meal one part, meat meal one-third of a part. In summer, leave out the maize meal.

Feeding Time-tables.—We must next see how to give it them.

Working on the wet mash system, give them a good ration of grain, say one handful to four birds, first thing in the morning. Bury it well under the litter, so that the fowls will have to scratch for it. This will keep them occupied for some time—and busy fowls make the best layers. The disadvantage of giving a mash meal in the morning is that the birds fill their crops without any trouble and are content to mope about for the rest of the morning.

At midday, give them a helping of greenstuff with a little grain. The greenstuff must be fresh—not decayed or sour or it will bring on looseness of the bowels.

Finally, at night, about an hour before sunset, a meal of wet mash should be given followed by a few handfuls of grain. Thus the birds will be sent to their perches with full crops, which is an important point.

The method of feeding dry mash is a little different. Having mixed the mash, put it into a hopper and leave it always in the pen. A simple hopper may consist of a box about 18 in. long, 12 in. wide, and 9 in. deep at the back and 4 in. deep at the front. A sloping lid is hinged at the back and reaches to within 4 in. of the front, leaving a space through which the fowls peck. The morning ration of grain should be smaller than under the wet mash system, and a meal of grain should be given at night.

Besides the foods mentioned above you should give your fowls plenty of grit. Birds which range freely do not need this so much because they can get grit from the ground; but for those confined to a small run a box containing oyster-shell grit or limestone grit should be hung on the wall of the laying house within easy reach. The oyster-shell will keep the birds supplied with eggshell-forming materials.

Powdered vegetable charcoal is an excellent thing for keeping the birds healthy and a little should be mixed with the mash occasionally.

Water.—Plenty of clean water is essential. Self-replenishing fountains, especially home-made ones, are usually difficult to keep clean. All that is necessary is a jam jar or two. Swill them out and fill them afresh when you give the meals.

A feeding experiment worth trying is that of "night lighting" the laying houses. This means putting a lamp into the house for about an hour after the fowls have gone to roost, through the winter nights. By this artificial light you can give the birds an extra feed of grain. A distinct rise in egg production should result.

In order to check the effects of such experiments on the egg yield and to help you keep your layers up to scratch, you should keep a record of the number of eggs collected each day. Also jot down your expenses, and, at the end of the year, total these up; balance them against the income of eggs and table birds. You will probably be surprised to find how profitable your hobby is proving.

Cleaning.—You cannot expect to get the best out of your fowls unless you keep them in conditions of perfect cleanliness. To give them a good start in life the incubator in which they are hatched must be thoroughly cleaned out and sprayed with any mild disinfectant except creosote before the eggs are put in. Fumigation with a sulphur candle is an added safeguard.

Laying houses must be cleaned out at least once a week and sprinkled with lime. If sand or dry earth is shaken on to the droppings boards dirt will not stick to them and can be shaken off more easily.

Even the ground in semi-intensive runs should be kept sweet and clean, either by shifting the pen to a fresh patch frequently, or by digging lime into the soil.

By taking these precautions you will not only keep the birds in better general health, but also you will make them much more immune from the attacks of such pests as fleas, lice, and red mite. But with all your care, these insects may gain a footing in the hot weather so you should know how to deal with them.

Pests.—Lice infest the birds' feathers and should be driven off by dusting the feathers with insect powder. Fleas are to be found most in the nest boxes; clean these out and treat them with creosote. However, you must remember that eggs taint easily; several days must elapse after creosoting before using the nest boxes again. As a preventive, sprinkle the nests with insect powder occasionally. Red mite are the most serious of the common insect pests. They are to be found in nooks and crannies—round the sockets of the perches is a favourite spot—where patches that look rather like greyish dust will be found (actually these are the cast skins of the mites). At night they leave their hiding-places and attack the birds, giving them no rest and so indirectly lowering the egg yield. The only cure is to paint or spray the house thoroughly with creosote thinned out with paraffin, or to paint the cracks and ends of perches with paraffin. Do not let the hens into the house till it is quite dry.

A Dust Bath helps to keep the fowls insect-free. A fairly large, shallow, wooden box half-filled with dry earth, ashes, and a little flowers of sulphur will serve admirably.

Other "troubles" that usually visit every pen at some time or another are egg-eating and feather-eating.

Egg-eating is usually the result of wrong diet or insufficient lime. Weak-shelled eggs (these are more often the result) are laid, which get broken in the nest and the fowls peck at them out of curiosity. So the habit is formed. Give a fresh supply of oyster-shell, and catch those birds which have the habit. Isolate them lest they lead the others into bad ways also. Give them the two halves of an eggshell filled with mustard and stuck together to resemble an egg, and take away whatever eggs they lay as soon as possible. If this treatment does not bring about a cure, the bird should be killed, for an egg-eater is quite useless.

Feather-eating is only too common among confined fowls. It may be the consequence of wrong diet, i.e. lack of animal food, overheated blood, or of lack of other amusement. Sprinkle flowers of sulphur on the mash, and hang up cooked meaty bones for the fowls to peck at. Also bury the grain food under the litter so that the birds may find distraction in scratching for it. As a final measure smear the birds' backs with Stockholm tar. If only one bird has the habit, isolate her.

Moulting.—Loss of feathers does not necessarily indicate feather-eating. It may be that the birds are beginning their annual moult. This occurs at the end of the summer, the old feathers being cast off and a new set grown. For from eight to fifteen weeks your birds will be short of feathers—and there will be no eggs. Obviously it is to your benefit to get the moult over as quickly as possible, and at a time when eggs are cheap as they always are at the beginning of August. At about this time, then, cut down the birds' food rations, leaving out mash altogether, and confine the fowls to their houses. A little linseed meal and bone meal forming, say, a sixth part of the mash will also work wonders.

Just before the moult at the end of the second season is generally reckoned to be the best time to dispose of fowls. They are then deemed to have finished their profitable laying life. But, for the amateur, it is often worth while to keep really good birds for a third season.

When one of your birds shows signs of illness—drooping attitude, colourless comb and wattles, or loss of appetite—isolate it at once, and, by careful observation, make a diagnosis. If the ailment is infectious, or if it is likely to affect the bird's powers even should a cure be made, you had best kill it at once. Burn its body or else bury it deeply in order to avoid further infection.

Bronchitis is often the consequence of a neglected cold. A rattling in the throat and difficulty in breathing are present in addition to the ordinary cold symptoms. Keep the bird in a warm but well-ventilated place and make it inhale the steam from boiling water to which has been added a little friar's balsam.

Colds are usually the result of damp, draughts, or of being turned straight out of hot, badly-ventilated houses into the chilly morning air. The symptoms are sneezing, coughing, and discharge from the eyes and nose. Wash away this discharge and cleanse the face and head with warm boracic lotion or permanganate of potash or mild Condy's fluid. Give a two-grain quinine pill just before the hen goes to roost. The drinking water should be coloured with permanganate of potash.

If the face swells and the nose and mouth become choked with foul-smelling discharge, instead of permanganate of potash put a dessertspoonful of the following mixture into 1½ pints of water: Copper sulphate 2 oz., iron sulphate 1 oz., water 1½ pints. Alum lotion tinged with permanganate of potash should be used for washing out the fowl's mouth and nostrils.

This disease is very infectious and, unless you value the affected bird highly, you would be advised to kill and burn it.

Comb Troubles.—In frosty weather Leghorn fowls' combs are sometimes frozen, becoming hard and blue. Soften them by rubbing gently, and then paint them with camphorated oil. Ulcers forming on the comb should be first treated with paraffin and then dressed with sweet oil. Tincture of myrrh is an excellent dressing for wounds on the comb.

Constipation, the symptom of which is vain attempts to pass motions. Increase the ration of greenstuff and encourage the bird to take more exercise.

Cramp.—This is a trouble which affects young chicks rather than adult fowls. The legs bend up and lose their power. Bathe them in warm water and work the joints gently, then dry them thoroughly and rub on embrocation. Keep the chicken in a cosy nest of flannel.

Crop Binding.—The crop swells and refuses to function. This may be the result of over-eating or of swallowing something which has caused a blockage, such as long, coarse grass or a fragment of bone. First try kneading the crop. If this is useless, liquefy the contents of the crop by giving the bird two teaspoonfuls of glycerine and then kneading it again. Turn the bird head downwards and try to press out the contents of the crop through the bird's mouth. If this does not effect a cure probably the best thing for an amateur to do is to kill the bird. There are other remedies but they are hardly ever successful except in the hands of a real expert.

Diarrhœa may be caused by wrong feeding, by some poison in the system, or by cold and damp. The bird's health will usually improve if the bird is given correct feeding or put on to a grain diet only.

Egg Defects. — Double-yolked eggs are sometimes due to an overstimulating diet. Spots of blood in the eggs show that the hen has ruptured a blood vessel. Isolate her and give her a rest by feeding a less stimulating diet.

Foot Troubles.—A hard corn sometimes appears on the under part of a fowl's foot. This is sometimes caused by the bird continually jumping down from a high perch on to a hard floor. Paint the corn with lunar caustic and confine the hen to a soft-floored coop. Sometimes, while scratching, a bird's foot is cut by glass or wire. From this a soft swelling may develop. The swelling should be fomented, then lanced. Squeeze out all the matter and bathe in weak permanganate of potash solution. Finally, the foot should be bandaged.

Gapes.—The chickens or fowls will open their mouths as if yawning, cough, and even run backwards. This is due to small, red, gape worms in the birds' throats. It is a difficult complaint to deal with as the ground over which the chickens run is often infested with these worms and the trouble is renewed even after a cure has been effected. Try putting the birds into a box in which is a mixture of one part powdered camphor and two parts powdered chalk. Shake the box and the birds will inhale the powder. This should make them cough up the worms.

Scaly Leg is caused by a parasite which burrows under the scales on the legs, making them thick and rough. Soak the legs up to the hock joint in warm water, then brush them with an old toothbrush dipped in paraffin or, better still, in carbolized vaseline. Next dip them into linseed oil and repeat the dressing. Give this treatment every day till the thick scales are loosened and drop out.

PRESERVE MAKING

There are still those who take a pride in having well-stocked shelves of neatly labelled jams and jellies, and there is a satisfaction in having such a reward for the hot busy days spent in picking and cooking the fruit.

The equipment required is not an elaborate one. A preserving pan, a long wooden spoon, scales for weighing, a pint or quart measure, a silver knife, a jelly bag or linen cloth are almost all the extras required. No iron or tin should be allowed to come in contact with the fruit. Our grandmothers would have looked askance at anything but a copper or brass preserving pan, but nowadays aluminium is very popular as it retains the heat well and is easily cleaned.

General Advice.—All the utensils must be perfectly clean, but metal polish should not be used on brass or copper pans immediately before cooking with them. The pan must not be greased, or placed over a smoky fire.

If the jam or jelly is being made with a gas or electric stove it is best to use an asbestos mat under the preserving pan.

Jars for potting will also be required, preferably of glass. The 2 lb. or the 1 lb. size are the most universally used. The jars must be perfectly clean, dry and warm.

As soon as the jam has been put into the jars it should be covered with circles of waxed paper, such as are supplied with ordinary parchment or cellophane covers. These should fit exactly, and be put in wax side down so that the heat will melt the wax and make the jam airtight.

Some people prefer to tie the jam down immediately it has been poured, and declare that it keeps better if this is done. Others prefer to see the set and wait until it is cold. Much, however, depends on the keeping place, which all are agreed must be perfectly dry and airy.

Each jar should be labelled clearly and the date added, so that it can be used in the right order.

Only sound fresh fruit should be used, and it must be free from dust, grit or stain. If it is firm and only just ripe it is not damaged by rinsing. It is best picked on a dry day.

Very soft fruits such as strawberries and raspberries will not bear handling beyond picking over. Gooseberries, cherries and currants can all be washed, a few at a time, and drained. Plums can be wiped or washed. Remove all bruises and stains.

It is very important that the fruit should not be over-ripe, as the pectin, which causes the jam or jelly to set or firm, is at its best in fruit slightly under-ripe, and scarcely exists in that which is over-ripe. There are substitutes for the natural pectin on the market, but if the fruit has only just reached maturity these need seldom be used. Some fruits are more rich in pectin than others and set more easily. Such are gooseberries, plums, currants, damsons and raspberries. Strawberries, cherries, rhubarb and marrow contain very little pectin, and require the necessary equivalents to be added. The juice of one lemon to each pound of fruit, or half a level teaspoonful of tartaric acid added as soon as the fruit is in the pan, helps to break down the pectin cells and frees it more rapidly during evaporation.

Only pure granulated or preserving sugar should be used. An inferior quality of sugar not only spoils the colour and flavour, but it throws up scum which is wasteful. The sugar, particularly for jelly, is better heated in the oven before adding to the fruit or fruit juice.

There are several different ways of making jam. A syrup of the sugar and water can be made and the fruit put into it; the fruit and sugar can be put on together, or the fruit can be boiled first and the sugar, warmed and crushed, added after. The general rule of a pound of sugar to a pound of fruit or a pint of fruit juice is a good one to follow, but some fruits require slightly more or less.

Fig. 1.—Have a saucer handy to prevent drips

To judge if the jam or jelly is set a simple test is to cool a teaspoonful on a plate. If it crinkles when pushed back with the finger it is ready.

An easy way of pouring the jam into the jars is by means of a cup and saucer. The saucer is held in the left hand, and receives the drips from the cup. Jars should always be wiped with a damp cloth when they are hot as a splash is then easier to remove.

The jam should cool down slightly in the pan before filling into the jars. This prevents the fruit floating to the top.

GOOSEBERRY JAM

4 *lb. gooseberries*, 4 *lb. sugar*

Pick the stalks and stems from the gooseberries, and wash them well. Put them on in a preserving pan with the sugar, half a pint of currant juice or water, and stir frequently till boiling. Boil for quarter of an hour.

RASPBERRY JAM

Allow 1 lb. of sugar to each pound of fruit

Place the raspberries in a preserving pan without water, and simmer over a gentle heat until cooked. Heat the sugar before adding to the fruit. Boil quickly and take up when set.

STRAWBERRY JAM (1)

To 2 pints gooseberry pulp allow 4 lb. strawberries and 6 lb. sugar

Top and tail gooseberries, wash them well and drain. Put them wet, but without any additional water, into a large jar and steam them until they are reduced to a pulp. When ready rub them through a hair sieve, measure the pulp thus obtained, and allow sugar and strawberries in the above proportion. Put sugar and pulp into a preserving pan and stir constantly until the mixture has come to the boil and has boiled for ten minutes. Then add the strawberries which must be dry and carefully picked. Cook rapidly from ten to fifteen minutes longer, or until the jam will set. Cool slightly and pot.

STRAWBERRY JAM (2)

To 3 lb. strawberries allow the juice of one lemon and 2½ lb. sugar

Small or medium-sized strawberries are the best for jam. Pick the fruit and carefully reject any that is unsound. Put into the preserving pan and bring to the boil, stirring all the time. Have the sugar weighed out, and made very hot in the oven. Add it gradually to the fruit without letting it go off the boil. Pour in the strained lemon juice, and boil until set.

CHERRY JAM

To 4 lb. cherries weighed after stoning allow 1 pint gooseberry or red-currant juice and 3½ lb. sugar

Stalk and wash the cherries and cook them slowly without any water until they are tender enough to stone. Do not use the juice which has been drawn from the cherries as it will not stiffen. (It will make a summer drink or a sauce.) Put the fruit juice and sugar into the preserving pan, bring to the boil, and boil quickly for ten minutes. Then add the cherries and cook a few minutes longer, or until the jam will set. Stir occasionally while cooling to keep the fruit mixed. Kentish or Morella cherries are best.

PLUM JAM

To 6 lb. fruit, unstoned, allow 5 lb. sugar

Pick, wash and stone the plums and put them while still wet into a preserving pan. Do not use a steel knife. No additional water is required. Allow them to cook for a few minutes. Then add the sugar and cook until the jam will set. This jam sets very easily and over-cooking will make it dark and stiff, and quite spoil the colour.

RHUBARB JAM

7 lb. rhubarb, ½ lb. preserved ginger, sugar

Wipe the rhubarb, trim and cut in half-inch lengths. Let it lie in a basin for forty-eight hours to dry. Weigh it now and allow an equal amount of sugar. Return to the basin with a layer of sugar over each one of rhubarb and stand for twenty-four hours. Cut up the ginger in small pieces and put all into the preserving pan together, bring to the boil and boil for twenty-five minutes, stirring frequently. Turn into heated pots and cover.

DRIED APRICOT JAM

1 lb. dried apricots, 3 pints cold water, sugar, juice of 3 lemons

Soak the apricots in 3 pints of cold water and lemon juice for twenty-four hours. Simmer until tender. Weigh the pulp and allow ¾ lb. sugar to each pound of pulp. Stir constantly, and do not over-boil. An ounce of sweet almonds blanched and halved added just before the jam is cooked is an improvement.

ORANGE MARMALADE

5 Seville oranges, 1 sweet orange, 2 lemons, sugar

Weigh fruit. Cut into halves, take out pips, and strain juice. Put the skins through a mincer (or slice them if preferred), place in a deep basin, and allow 2½ pints of water to a pound of fruit. Let it stand overnight. Next day boil until tender (about two hours), take off and leave for twenty-four hours. Weigh again, and allow 1½ lb. of sugar to each pound of pulp. Boil quickly for three-quarters of an hour, or until it jellies.

JELLIES

The same general directions as for jam apply, with a few additions, to the making of jelly.

Small amounts set better, and only small jars should be used. 1 lb. or even the ½ lb. size are the most suitable.

It is not considered necessary nowadays to make a special jelly bag, as a clean white linen cloth is all that is required. To strain the jelly, turn a kitchen chair or stool seat down on a table, and place a basin on the upturned seat. Tie strong linen tapes to the corners of the cloth and to the legs of the chair. Be sure that the tapes are strong and well secured or the weight of the jelly will bring down the bag. Scald the cloth with boiling water before using.

Do not hurry the process of straining, but leave the jelly throughout the night if necessary. If you squeeze the bag you will get cloudy jelly.

STRAWBERRY JELLY

Put fruit in preserving pan with juice of 1 lemon to each 3 lb. of strawberries. Allow fruit very gradually to get hot enough for the juice to be pressed out. Do not boil the fruit. Strain. To each pint of juice allow 1 lb. of sugar. Boil twenty minutes without the sugar, then add sugar hot. Bring to boil, skim well, and boil fifteen minutes.

GOOSEBERRY JELLY

4 lb. gooseberries, ½ lb. red currants, sugar

Wash the gooseberries and currants, and put them in a preserving pan with four breakfastcupfuls of water. Boil gently for five minutes and strain. To each pint of juice allow 1 lb. of sugar. Stir frequently till this boils, and boil for ten minutes.

Some housewives, although successful with other kinds of jams and jellies, find red-currant jelly a difficulty. The recipe below has been in use for generations, and if the instructions are carefully followed a beautiful firm jelly will result. The secret

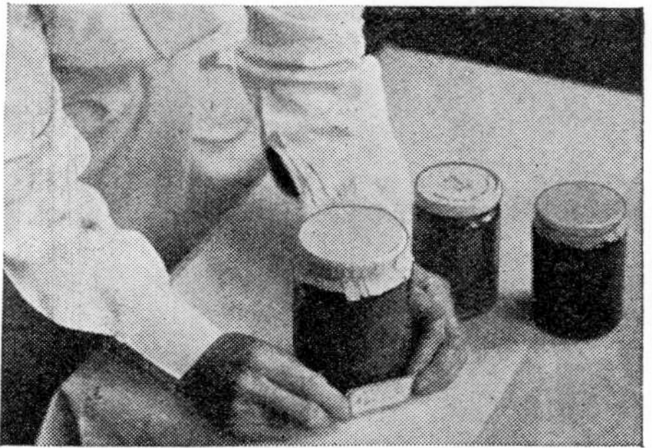

Fig. 2.—Labels look neatest at the base of the jars

of success is in slow heating to release the juice, fairly fast boiling during the few minutes required, and the prompt removal of the preserving pan when the time has expired.

RED-CURRANT JELLY

4 lb. currants, 1 lb. raspberries, sugar

Pick the larger stalks and leaves from the currants and raspberries, and wash the currants in cold water. Put in preserving pan with four breakfastcupfuls of water, and allow to heat gradually to boiling point, stirring frequently, then let them boil gently for about ten minutes. Strain. To each pint of juice allow 1 lb. of sugar, and add ½ lb. more. Stir this frequently until it boils, allow it to boil for five minutes, then lift pan away from the heat, skim and pot.

APPLE JELLY

To 1 pint apple juice allow 1 lb. sugar and 1 lemon

Wash the apples—crab apples may be used—and cut them in pieces without peeling or coring. Remove any damaged parts, and put the apples into a preserving pan with sufficient cold water to cover them, or 4 quarts of water for 8 lb. of apples. Bring to the boil and cook slowly until the apples are reduced to a pulp. Strain and let the juice drip all night. Measure the juice into a clean preserving pan, add sugar in the above proportions, also the strained juice and thinly peeled rind of the required number of lemons. Stir carefully until the sugar is melted, and then boil until the jelly will set when tested on a plate. Remove any scum, pour into small pots, and cover when cold.

RASPBERRY JELLY

This is prepared in the same way as red-currant jelly, with the same amount of sugar and the same time for cooking. It is considered an improvement if some red-currant juice is added and a $\frac{1}{4}$ pint to each pint of raspberry juice. The sugar need not be increased if this is done.

RHUBARB JELLY

This is best made in September. Choose red rhubarb, cut it into short lengths and put them in a large jar. To each 6 lb. of rhubarb add the peel of three lemons. Put the jar into the oven, let the rhubarb get quite soft, and the juice will flow freely, then strain, and squeeze through flannel.

Put the juice into the preserving pan, or into an enamelled saucepan, with the juice of the three lemons. Add $1\frac{1}{2}$ lb. of sugar to each pint of rhubarb juice, and, when dissolved, bring all to the boil and simmer for about $\frac{3}{4}$ hour, stirring well and skimming. Test by putting a little on a cold plate, and if it jellies it is done. Pour into jars and cover when cold.

BLACKBERRY JELLY

Gather the blackberries in dry weather if possible. Pick them and put in preserving pan. To about 4 lb. of blackberries allow 1 lb. of apples, washed and cut up without paring. Cover with cold water. Boil this gently for fifteen or twenty minutes until the fruit is quite a pulp. Strain and let it drip perhaps all night. To each pint of juice add 1 lb. sugar. Bring to the boil slowly, then boil rather quickly from ten to fifteen minutes.

GRAPE FRUIT AND ORANGE JELLY

To 2 lb. grape fruit allow 2 lb. sweet oranges, 2 lemons, 4 pints of water, sugar

Wash and dry all the fruit and then grate off the yellow rind only. Remove the white skin which is not to be used, and cut the remainder into small pieces. Put the fruit into a preserving pan with the water and boil one hour, stirring frequently. Strain and leave to drip. Next day measure the juice into a clean pan, add the grated rind with 1 lb. of sugar to each pint of liquid, and boil until it will jelly. Skim, pour into pots, and cover when cold.

PRINTING FOR AMATEURS

THERE is something most fascinating about producing "real print" and there are hundreds of things for which print is better than duplicating or typing—tickets for social evenings, menu cards, concerts and amateur theatrical programmes, trade announcements, labels, letter headings, visiting cards and so on. The man who makes a hobby of printing will find that he has ample scope for his work, and incidentally he may, at the same time, make it a paying proposition.

If outside work is to be done, the possession of a really efficient outfit however small is an absolute necessity. There is always the temptation to purchase a cheap machine and a lot of type in preference to a better machine and just one or two type faces, but the latter is the better way to start. The first thing to decide is the size of work one will undertake. To buy a press that will print a width and depth of, say, 5 × 8 in. and then to discover at no too distant date that a larger press is needed means great disappointment on the one hand, and additional expense on the other.

Types of Press.—There are two main types of press suitable for amateur work: the vertical platen and the horizontal platen. The platen is the flat metal surface which presses the paper on to the type. Both kinds can be purchased for operation either by hand or treadle. Naturally treadle operation is better, especially if much work is carried out, but the hand press is not to be despised. The horizontal platen press is shown in Fig. 1. It may be purchased quite cheaply, and if used intelligently will turn out really excellent work.

The Type.—The printing machine, however, is not the only appliance necessary, for there are many other little pieces of apparatus which save both time and labour. These will be dealt with as we proceed. The next step is to select the type. Type is now known by the name system, in which certain "faces" are called by certain names. Some of the most commonly used are "Cheltenham," "Garamond," "Gill Sans" and "Plantin," whilst for every one of these types companion faces are available in italic, bold and bold italic, and figures. The beginner may at first see little difference in type faces, and so, in order to avoid trouble, he should study the following specimens:

9-point PLANTIN
9-point PLANTIN Bold
10-point OLD FACE
10-*point OLD FACE Italic*
12-point CHELTENHAM
12-point CHELTENHAM Bold
14-point GILL SANS
14-point GILL SANS Bold

It will be noted in the above examples that figures appear such as "9 point," "10 point," "12 point," etc. These figures relate to the size of the type body.

Readers who are buying type for the first time should purchase only those faces which are in common use. Caslon is a good face, so is Garamond, with Gill Sans Bold for display work.

Type Founts. — Types are usually bought in founts and comprise both small and capital letters, known respectively as lower and upper case, a few of the most common diphthongs, and such signs as full stops, commas, colons, semi-colons, exclamation marks, brackets, numbers and so on. Each fount has a complete series of any one special size face, and it includes a larger number of the more common letters. For instance, one particular fount may have as many as 50 letter a's, 8 q's, 12 k's, 50 i's and 60 e's. Included in every fount is a number of pieces of type-metal which are used for spacing. The largest is called an "em" and is always the square of the body of the type. Then we have the "en" which is half that size, and there are sometimes three other spaces known as thick, mid and thin, respectively. In addition to these are "quads" which are similar to the spacing material but are much longer. It should be noted, of course, that each size of type requires its own size quads and spaces. Still larger are the pieces known as metal furniture, which are very similar to quads but are larger and wider. These pieces are used for filling in vacant spaces in the frame. Reglet is the name given to wooden spacing material, this being cut to the desired length by the type-setter. Then there are quoins, which are small wooden wedges to hold the type securely in the frame or chase as it is called. Lastly there are the various kinds of rules, usually made of brass strips, and designed for printing either plain, dotted or fancy lines. As far as rules and borders are concerned, however, the amateur printer should be careful in his choice, for flowery designs are not looked upon with so much favour as they were, a few plain rules being more in demand.

Composition comprises the operations of picking up single letters and arranging them into words, inserting punctuation marks, and spacing and justifying the type into lines.

A composing stick is "made up" by adjusting and fixing the slide at the same distance from the head as the length of the line to be composed.

A setting-rule of the length of the line is put inside the stick next to the flange, with its ear towards the end of the stick. The compositor stands in front of the type case, holding the stick loosely in the palm of his left hand with the fingers grasping the flange, and the thumb extended over the front of the plate till it touches the flange. He then reads a few words of his copy, glances at the box containing the first letter to be set, and having located a particular type and carefully noted the position of its nick, he picks it out of the box with the forefinger and thumb of his right hand, and places it, face upwards and nick outwards, against the rule and next the slide.

The second letter is taken from its box and placed against the side of the one already in the stick, the thumb of the left hand being lightly pressed against each letter as it is deposited to keep it in position, and so on with other letters and the spaces separating the words until the line is completed. A slight inclination of the stick upwards also tends to keep the letters close together and prevent their falling down.

There will probably be a space left at the end of the line into which an entire word cannot be placed, and as all lines except display lines and last lines of paragraphs should be of a uniform length, the compositor cannot insert spaces after the last letter to "justify" the line, or fill it out exactly to the measure of the stick. There are, however, three courses open to him: if one or two letters are required to complete the last word, he may bring all the words in the line closer together by taking out the thick spaces placed between them as they were set and substituting thinner spaces to "get in" the remaining letters; he may "drive out" by increasing the spaces between the words to fill out the line; or he may divide the word according to recognized rules (inserting a hyphen to show that the word is divided) and place the remainder of the word in the next line. After the line has been justified to fit the measure of the stick, the setting-rule is removed to the bottom, or nicked side, of the composed line to form a smooth resting-place for the letters of the next line. Succeeding lines are composed and justified in the same way until the setting has been completed.

Fig. 2 shows a general view of a high-speed press of popular design. In this outfit there is a metal box-like tray in which the type is actually set. In the larger machines the type is set in a rectangular metal frame called a chase. The chase has no bottom so it must be placed upon a flat surface while the type is being set. We will, however, turn to this type of machine presently.

Assuming that the reader has a high-speed type of press as illustrated in Fig. 1, he should set about the work of type-setting in the following manner. The frame or box will be found to have four small set screws running through the sides, two at one side and two at the end. The box should be tilted at an angle so that the long plain side is nearest the type set up. A strip of metal is then inserted on the left to take the pressure from the set screws.

Storing Type.—The type itself should be stored in a box with many compartments so that each letter may be selected quickly. Suppose you are setting the words "Daily Herald," you search in the D box and take out a capital D. It will be found that on one side of this piece of type are two grooves or nicks, and the metal must be placed in the tray so that these nicks are away from the setter. Next the a, i, l, y must be set in lower case, or small letters. After these must be a space, and a thick space is inserted. A capital H followed by the other letters and concluding with a full stop would complete the setting. Make sure that the first letter always starts nearest to you on your left and with the nicks away from you. (*See* Fig. 3.)

If more than two lines are to be set, the requisite spacing should be inserted above each line and the process carried on until the complete setting is finished. Next comes the job of locking it securely in the frame, and this is carried out by packing with wood and finally screwing down the set screws. Always remember that type is made with mathematical precision. It consists of a number of squares, and in order to hold the type securely every line must be accurately spaced to the same width in the frame.

In Fig. 2 the type is set in a metal frame called a chase. The chase is removed from the machine and placed on a flat surface. This may be supplied with the machine or the amateur printer may use a wooden bench, a slab of marble fixed to a table or other suitable surface. A slightly different method of type-setting is used with the larger chase, for a kind of inner framework is constructed of wood, a rectangle being left the size and depth of the type area. In this rectangle the type is set. Remember that the first letter is set to your left hand with the nicks in the type body away from you. As each line

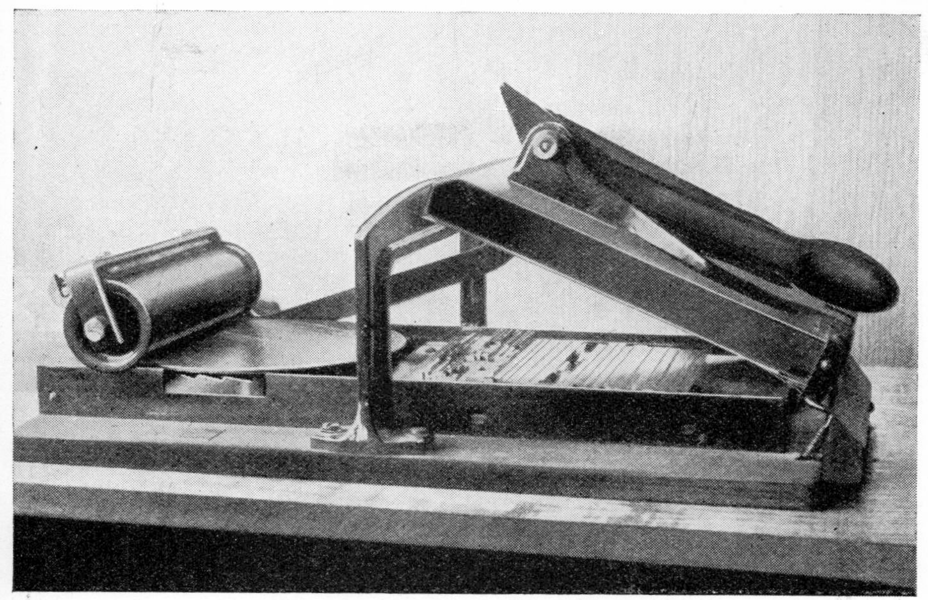

Fig. 1.—A Horizontal Platen Press

is composed, leads (pronounced "leds") are inserted to space them out. These leads are simply strips of metal or wood, made in various thicknesses, but always of the standard width. The type-setter should cut these to length as required.

When all the matter has been set up and checked over, the space between the wooden frame and the chase is packed with furniture and finally wedged with wooden wedges to hold it rigid. Great care must be exercised in seeing that the whole of the type matter is locked up solid, otherwise when the chase is lifted from the metal plate the type will collapse and all the work will have to be done again. One should make a point of having plenty of wedges and, of course, plenty of strips of wood to fill up the blank spaces.

Occasionally one may find it desirable to keep the type standing, which means that the particular chase or forme, as it is now called, is merely lifted out of the machine and stored until required again. This necessitates the purchase of additional chases, but these are quite inexpensive.

With a machine such as that we are discussing, it is possible to print a small poster measuring 16 × 10 in., for this is done in two operations. The actual inside measurements of the chase are $7\frac{1}{4}$ in. × $9\frac{3}{4}$ in., so that all sorts of bill heads, letter headings, circular letters, etc., can be printed in the one operation. After the type has been set in the bed of the machine, the next thing is to take off a proof.

Inking.—Take a small piece of printers' ink and place it on a flat piece of glass or other level surface, and with the soft hand-roller, roll it many times, until an even surface is obtained. Then run the hand-roller over the ink disk or plate on the machine. Never apply the ink actually to the machine itself in lump form or blotchy printing will result. The biggest difficulty with most beginners is with regard to the ink, but it is far easier to add a little more than to take some away. The roller of the machine is then passed over the ink disk several times and then over the newly set type. A piece of paper is next laid on the tympan card, which, as the machine is operated, carries it over and presses it on to the type. The proof itself should then be very carefully checked for errors and also for inequalities

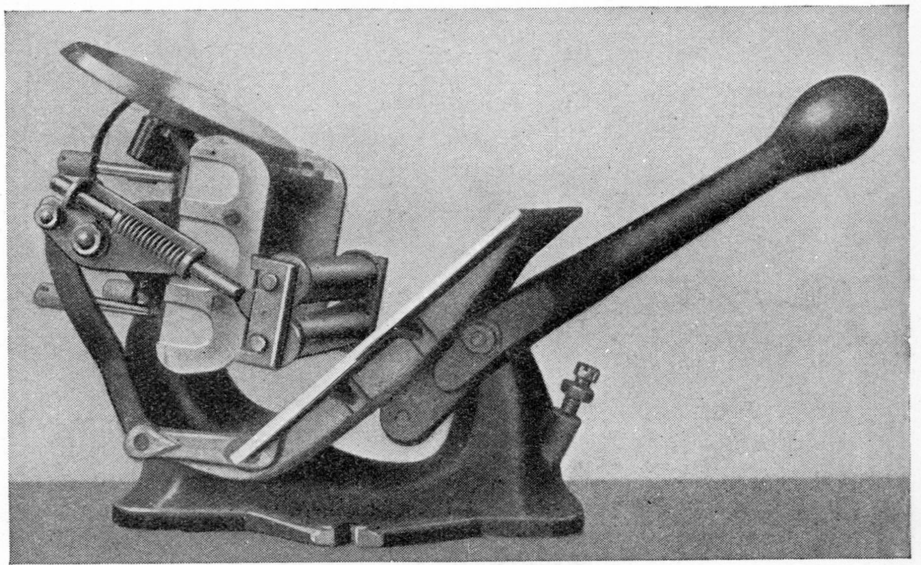

Fig. 2.—Another useful type of Press

of impression. There are standard signs used in the printing trade for proof correction, and it is well for the reader to learn these as quickly as possible. Below is a list of the most common of the signs.

Proof-correcting Signs

caps/	Change to capitals.
l.c./	Change to lower case. (Not capitals.)
ital/	Change to italic.
b.f./	Change to bold face.
——	Under word means "Put this in italic."
stet/	Retain crossed-out word or letters.
. . . .	"Let it stand" (used in conjunction with stet in the margin).
see copy	Omission. See the copy.
run on	Make no break in the reading.
run over	Run this word over to the next line.
run back	Run word back to the preceding line.
N.P./	Start a paragraph here.
run on	No paragraph.
wf./	Wrong fount.
₰	Take out the crossed-out type, word or sentence.
ʼ/	Insert apostrophe.
" "/	Insert quotation marks.
∧	Make correction indicated in margin.
||	Line up—that is, make the lines even with other matter.
///	Straighten lines or type out of line.
⊙	Insert period.
⊙	Insert colon.
,/	Insert comma.
;/	Insert semi-colon.
-/	Insert hyphen.
9	Upside down. Reverse.
#	Insert space here.
⁀	Close up. No space.
←	Move this to the left.
→	Move this to the right.
⊼	Raise to proper position.
⊥	Lower to proper position.
⊥	Push down this lead or space.
×	Battered type. Change.

When the proofs have been passed, attention must be given to inequalities of impression. It is likely that with new type the resultant impression will be excellent, but wear gradually takes place, and some of the letters as they are used more frequently than others will give a very faint impression. Should this happen, they must be lifted slightly in order to bring the printing surface on a level with the rest of the type. The usual method is to paste a very thin piece of tissue paper beneath each letter or portion of the whole. This part of the process is called the "make ready." The actual work of printing can now be undertaken, bearing in mind that ink should be sparingly used.

It may be that your first results will be rather disappointing, not from the actual printing point of view so much as from that of lay-out. The art of designing printed matter can only come with practice, and the best plan is to use every opportunity of composing neat yet effective typographical arrangements. They can, of course, be designed on paper, it being unnecessary to set them up in type. It is a good plan to study examples of lay-outs, for from these good ideas may frequently be obtained and adapted to suit special requirements.

Paper.—It is necessary for the amateur printer to obtain samples of papers from the various suppliers, and a postcard will ensure that samples of the latest products are sent regularly. There are five chief sizes in which paper is bought, these being:

Crown	20 × 15 in.
Demy	$22\frac{1}{2}$ × $17\frac{1}{2}$,,
Medium	23 × 18 ,,
Royal	25 × 20 ,,
Double Crown	30 × 20 ,,

From these sizes it is a simple matter to calculate the particular sheets required, but be sure to leave a margin of $\frac{1}{2}$ in. or so for trimming. For instance, a double crown sheet cut into eight will give sheets $7\frac{1}{2}$ × 10, but the finished job will be nearer 7 × $9\frac{1}{2}$. Always use great care when choosing paper sizes to avoid cutting to waste. There are various stock sizes for cards and boards, the chief ones for visiting and business cards being "Thirds"—3 × $1\frac{1}{2}$ in., and "Extra Thirds"—3 × $1\frac{7}{8}$ in.

Illustrations.—Those you will use are of two kinds—line and half-tone. A line block is cut from a zinc plate, and records outlines and solid masses. Shading can be introduced by means of mechanical tints and consists of various combinations of lines and dots, or each separately. The photographs reproduced throughout this book are in half-tone, and the sketches are in line—study them well and note the differences. Both types of block may be "stereoed" which means that from the originals duplicates can be cast in a softer kind of type-metal. Some firms supply stock blocks to meet all requirements, but care should be taken to see that the blocks chosen are neither out of date as regards design, nor worn, for a worn block will print badly. The blocks you will purchase thus will be already mounted, usually on wood to the correct type height, so that they need to be merely set into position when the typescript is set, and locked.

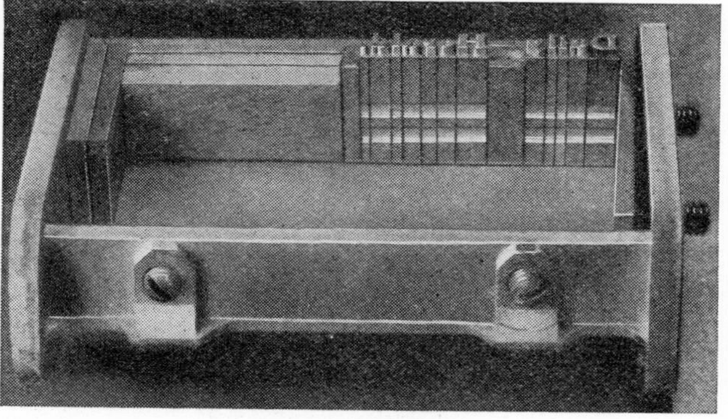

Fig. 3.—The Chase

Finally, remember to keep your machine clean. Rub it over with a soft cloth that has been moistened with paraffin, and do not forget to clean the rollers as well, or extra work will be necessary when starting on the next job. Keep the machine well oiled and dry, and you will be assured of low costs as well as good printing.

READING

Reading can scarcely be termed a hobby, rather it should be classed with such normal activities as talking, without which man cannot be said fully to live. Yet the habit of reading does not come by chance, certainly not the habit of worth-while reading: that must be cultivated. When once a person has gained the "freedom of literature" illimitable enjoyment awaits him; he can meet the great spirits of every age and have within his reach all the wisdom and learning of mankind.

To have a proper appreciation of books one must understand something of their great complexity. There are so many types—novels, books of reference, collections of short stories, technical handbooks, essays, biographies, books of travel, histories, memoirs, plays, and so on. Obviously such a diversity of books are not to be read all in the same manner; and, as Bacon says in his essay on *Studies*—"Some books are to be tasted, others are to be swallowed, and some few are to be chewed and digested."

Fig. 1.—It is better to use a magnifying glass than strain the eyes over small print

But books form only one section of the great quantity of reading matter. There are more than three thousand newspapers and periodicals published in this country, and it is almost as essential that one should distinguish between these as that one should have an appreciative knowledge of books. The simplest type, appealing to the most undeveloped intelligence is the *comic.* Many of these are intended for children, but some cater for the adult of elementary taste. A step higher comes the *popular weekly*. These do not profess to be erudite; their purpose is to amuse. Then there are *popular monthlies*, costing rather more. Of somewhat higher standard are a few weeklies which aim to be educative in a popular way, and there are quite a number of important, serious, weekly reviews which do not aim at simply reporting news like newspapers but in giving considered judgments on the facts. Lastly, there are the better monthly and quarterly magazines and reviews, catering for readers of considerable knowledge and discernment.

One should take regularly such journals as one can afford, striving to educate one's taste so that eventually the best things are enjoyed.

The great mass of special interest periodicals, like women's papers, trade and technical journals, form a special realm outside that of general reading and naturally make individual appeals.

How to Read.—Even after good reading matter can be chosen it is necessary that one shall know how to read. Ruskin has said—"If you read ten pages of a good book, letter by letter—that is to say, with real accuracy—you are for evermore in some measure an educated person."

This does not mean skimming over the pages to get the "gist" of the author's meaning; it means using your mind actively all the time that your eye travels down the page. Ask yourself if you have really understood the page you have finished; if there were any unfamiliar words look them up in a good dictionary. It will soon become a pleasure to watch out for any words which are peculiar to a certain author. Read with a pencil always beside you—if the book is your own you can mark passages which you especially want to remember. In any case it is a good plan to use the blank page at the end of the book for making a very brief note on each chapter, and months after you have finished the book a glance at this will bring it back vividly to your mind.

The Commonplace Book. — Even better than this is the keeping of a Commonplace Book. An ordinary large well-bound exercise book will do admirably for this purpose. When you come upon a saying or paragraph in a book which appeals particularly to you, copy it into your Commonplace Book, with the author's name, the title of the book and the number of the page. The very act of copying the passage out will impress it more firmly in your mind, and gradually you will acquire a book of quotations made by yourself which will be a pleasure to read over and which will also show the development of your taste and critical ability.

It will be even more useful if you use a few pages at the end of the book for an index, divided into two parts, the first under the subject, the second under the author. For instance suppose you had been reading Emerson's essay on *Friendship* and you wished to remember these fine words with which he ends it, "The essence of friendship is entireness, a total magnanimity and trust. It must not surmise or provide for infirmity. It treats its object as a god that it may deify both." In your subject index this would appear thus:

Friendship page . . .

and in the author index

Emerson, R.W. page . . .

Happily there are so many "good books" that no reader need ever read anything that he does not enjoy. This test of a book is quite adequate, especially in early stages of acquiring the "reading habit"—read only what you enjoy. Samuel Johnson himself has given this welcome dictum.

Acquiring Books.—In the section of these pages on MAKING A LIBRARY the purchasing and collecting of books is dealt with. There are other channels, but very few people can hope to buy all the books they wish to read. There are some books which are quite interesting at the time, but which are not worth shelf room in the small library; others which are too expensive, and yet others which for one reason or another you do not want to have for your own. How are you to borrow these books? First, there are the multiple branch lending libraries, with their well-stocked shelves in almost every town; books may be borrowed from these at varying charges according to the type of book required and the promptitude with which you want to read the newest books.

Public Libraries.—But for many people, and certainly the student, there is a better way. Join your Public Library. There is hardly a town or village in England to-day which has not a library which is free to the residents of that place. It is quite a simple matter to become a member; usually a form has to be filled in and the signature of a householder obtained; when this is completed, one or more tickets will be given to you.

How to Use the Library.—If your library is in a fair-sized town, you may be a little put off by its size and apparent complexity. The easiest and best thing to do as soon as you have your tickets is to ask an assistant to explain simply how to find a book and any special things you ought to know.

The first thing is to realize that the books are shelved according to their subject and that allied subjects are grouped together and the key to their position is in the catalogue. In the illustration you will see a borrower consulting the catalogue to see if the library has the book he wants. Having found that it is in the stock of the library, it is then a simple matter to ask an assistant to help you to find it. But perhaps the

Fig. 2.—Library users can make recommendations in the Suggestions Book

book is not in the stock of the library, and you think it is a worth-while book which others would like to read besides yourself. Then ask if there is a Suggestions Book, and write down the particulars in that, as you see someone doing in the illustration. It will probably be considered by the Library Committee and you will be notified as to their decision.

But the book you require may have been in the stock of the library, but not on the shelves at the moment. Most libraries will allow you to reserve it at a charge of 1d., and a card will be sent to you as soon as it is available.

These are only two ways in which you can make a fuller use of your public library —there are probably many others and the only way to find them out is to ask a member of the staff. You will find that they are only too anxious to help you to make the fullest possible use of what after all is your own library, paid for out of the rates.

All the public libraries are linked together by the National Central Library and if your particular library has not the book you want, then it is possible for them to try and borrow it for you from some other library. In this way even if you live in a small village you can borrow the books you require.

There is another department of a public library which you will find useful, that is the Reference Library. Here you can consult those books of reference such as the big encyclopædias and dictionaries, or the quick reference books such as *Who's Who* or *Whitaker's Almanack*. If your problem is not one that can be solved quickly, then ask the assistant on duty to help you. He has access to a wide range of information and from one source or another can probably give you the answer you require.

The British Museum.—But it may be that, good and far-reaching as this service is, you require something more. Then for you are the great national collections, chief of which is the British Museum. This is one of the large libraries of the world and is intended only for the serious student who, having tried all the resources his local public library can offer, needs something else. Ticket-holders only, who must be over twenty-one years of age, are admitted to the British Museum Reading Room. Applications for a ticket must be made in writing to the Director, The British Museum Library, Bloomsbury, W.C.1. You must state your profession or business and also your reason for wishing to use the library, and the application must be accompanied by the recommendation of a householder who can personally vouch for you. It is obvious that the use of the Reading Room must be kept for those who are engaged in some serious work of research, and cannot obtain the book they require in any other way. Of course no books can be borrowed from the British Museum, but must be read in the Reading Room. But if you do wish to consult some old books for your study, then the best plan is to ask the librarian of your public library to help you with your request to read at the British Museum. His object is to assist you to read the books you want, and he will do all in his power to help you.

What to Read.—Do not read the new books merely to be in the fashion. There is no more ridiculous snobbery than that of reading in order that one may talk the current jargon of "literary" cliques. Whether you know the latest best-seller is of no real importance; whether you are finding new books that mean something to you personally is something that matters very much more.

But in order to be able to appreciate the best in modern books, you must have some standards by which to judge them, and the only way to train this critical faculty is to read those books which have lived because the "passionate few" in every age have rediscovered their value and beauty. Those books are the classics; but do not be put off them by that label. A classic is merely a book that people have refused to allow to die, one which has endured, when all the ruck of mediocre stuff written in the same age has sunk out of sight. It is essentially a book which others before you have enjoyed and which has in some measure enriched their lives. If after reading such a book you get nothing out of it, the fault lies with your taste, rather than with the book.

Taste.—But, you ask, how am I to arrive at this stage of caring for the classics? There is no short cut to this. Just as you only get out of life in proportion to what you bring to it, so in reading. If you have never done any serious reading before, you may find the book you have chosen dry and dull. Do not give it up in disgust and go back to your thrillers and say that that kind of book is all right for some people, but not for you. Think about what you have read, try to understand it, always remembering that other readers have enjoyed it immensely and it is probable that you will too. Then try again. If you have a friend who is also taking up this hobby, then you can discuss the book with each other. If it is a novel that you have been reading, the descriptions of the places and events should make you able to see them for yourself. The characters should behave in such a way that you know without any doubt that that is how they really would behave in real life. For the great touchstone of every great book is that it must be true.

Truth in Fiction.—Truthfulness should be the prime requirement in our reading. It may be understood in many ways. For instance, here is a paragraph from a novel concerning a girl who picked up a violin for the first time:

"She laid it on her breast, dropping her chin on it and drew the bow softly across the strings. One after another she tested the open notes. They reminded her of things. Gradually her stroke ceased to tremble and she drew the bow firmly. Then her fingers began to fall and softly, slowly, she searched up and down those strings for sounds she knew. From the first day the instrument became hers she spent half her practice time in imitating the sounds of all outdoors, and improvising the songs her happy heart sang."

Now, to write about a girl, untutored, making anything but very unpleasant noises when first she picks up a fiddle is absolute nonsense, as any violin teacher will tell you, and a writer guilty of such sentimental rubbish does not lead one to expect *truth* in his or her writings.

But against this example let us compare an extract from *The Professor at the Breakfast Table*, by Oliver Wendell Holmes. He is describing the slow processes by which a violin comes to maturity:

"—played on by ancient maestros until the bow-hand lost its power and the flying fingers stiffened. Bequeathed to the passionate young enthusiast, who made it whisper his hidden love, and cry his inarticulate longings, and scream his untold agonies, and wail his monotonous despair. Passed from his dying hand to the cold virtuoso, who let it slumber in its case for a generation, till, when his hoard was broken up, it came forth once more and rode the stormy symphonies of royal orchestras, beneath the rushing bow of their lord and leader. Into lonely prisons with improvident artists; into convents from which arose day and night holy hymns with which its tones were blended; and back again to orgies in which it learned to howl and laugh as if a legion of devils were shut up in it; then again to the gentle dilettante who calmed it down with easy melodies until it answered him softly as in the days of the old maestros. And so into our hands, its pores all full of music; stained, like a meerschaum, through and through, with all the concentrated hue and sweetness of all the harmonies which have kindled and faded on its strings."

That paragraph is sheer beautiful truth —one cannot help trusting an author who writes like that.

There is another sort of truth—truth of character. If we look at Oliver Twist we find that he is consistent; his experiences fall naturally. We get to know and believe in him. But supposing we read in some novelette of a boy who, walking along a road, sees a man attacked by six robbers. The boy puts them to flight, and finds that the man he has saved is a millionaire. The boy, who is ambitious to fly, is promptly put in charge of an aeroplane by the millionaire, who chances to have one ready for a world flight. Now that is all absurd; it does not carry conviction at any point; it is not *true*.

Every reader must be his own judge of the value of the books he reads. Opinions taken from others, second-hand judgments, are worthless. It is far better to hold a view contrary to others, if it is held honestly, than to coincide with the crowd merely because they are the majority. The most famous picture in the Louvre is Da Vinci's *Mona Lisa*. No matter when one visits it there is sure to be a little, worshipping cluster of people standing round, for the reputation of *Mona Lisa* is world-wide. In the course of a few hours, in the *Salon Carré* where it hangs, one can hear ecstatic admiration of its beauty in many languages. Yet one candid visitor has said that he could not understand why people admired the picture, he could never see in it anything more than a fat, ugly woman with an unpleasant leer on her face. It is to be feared that some of the other people who look can see no more, despite what they say. And as with pictures so with books—have your own opinions.

Poetry.—There is one section of reading more worth cultivating than any other; it is poetry. It will be illuminating, though rather depressing, to ask all your acquaintances one day which of them has read any poetry during the previous week or month. You will be fortunate in your friends if some can say they have, assuming that they are normal, non-literary people.

The whole trouble lies in the fact that

Fig. 3.—Standard Reference Books are a valuable feature of the Public Library

Fig. 4.—Encourage your Children to use the Public Library

comparatively delicate taste is needed to appreciate this highest form of literary art, and such taste is not acquired easily, nor by accident. But it is worth all the pains involved, for once this genuine love of poetry is obtained it remains a source of pleasure throughout a lifetime, deep satisfying pleasure of a kind that few other experiences can give.

How to Read Poetry.—One of the simplest methods of beginning to enjoy poetry, and one of the surest, is to start with comparatively modern writers who use familiar language and live in the sort of world we know. Short poems are best, and there are any number of modern anthologies from which you may choose. Read and explore until you find just a few which give you pleasure. Read those again and again, pondering on the sources of your enjoyment. It will be simple to widen your reading when once you have a sincere delight in even a single poem. Everything depends on the start, and in following up assiduously. If possible get a companion for your readings—there are few happier ways of spending an evening than in having a pile of anthologies on a table from which you and your friend read favourites. Remember that narrative poems are generally the easiest to appreciate, and there are plenty of really great works which simply "tell a story" beautifully.

Your Illimitable Choice.—But apart from poetry what will you read? You have decided to read a book that has stood the test of time rather than a new book; your object is not to become a student of literary history, but to gain enjoyment and to enrich your life, so begin with a book that you expect to be interested in, either because the idea in the story appeals to you, or because you are interested in the author, or perhaps because you know the district in which the scene is laid. Try and have some object in view. Arnold Bennett has said, "Your paramount aim in poring over literature is to enjoy, but you will not fully achieve that aim unless you have also a subsidiary aim which necessitates the measurement of your energy. Your subsidiary aim may be æsthetic, moral, political, religious, scientific, erudite; you may devote yourself to a man, a topic, an epoch, a nation, a branch of literature, an idea—you have the widest latitude in the choice of an objective; but a definite object you must have."

Make a plan then, but do not adhere too rigidly to it, or your reading will become a task and not an enjoyment. Sometimes one book will suggest another and having rambled down this byway for a little you will return refreshed to the main road. Do not be afraid to try new authors—it is as easy to become hidebound in your choice of reading as in any other activity. If your natural taste inclines you to books of travel, sandwich in a volume of essays sometimes for a change.

Biography.—You may see a film based on the life of a great man, such as "Disraeli," and when you come out of the cinema you wonder how far the film was true to the facts. For it must always be borne in mind when seeing a film based on a well-known novel, or a great historical personage, that the scenario writer may for his own purposes have completely altered the story, or emphasized only one aspect in the character of the great man. So that having seen this film on the life of Benjamin Disraeli, Earl of Beaconsfield, you decide to read a short biography for yourself; and a very good one for your purpose would be a book called "Disraeli," by André Maurois. Although this is written by a Frenchman, it gives an excellent picture of the statesman. From this it is an easy transition to the novels which Lord Beaconsfield wrote as a young man; they were best sellers in their day and some of them are supposed to be largely autobiographical. Begin with "Coningsby" and then "Sybil." If your interest has been sustained thus far, and there is no reason why it should not be, because "Disraeli" is a most fascinating character to study, then you will probably want to read something about that other great statesman, who was equally worshipped by his followers and detested by his opponents—William Ewart Gladstone. Having read about the two great statesmen, what about Queen Victoria herself? A most interesting study of her is "Queen Victoria," by E. F. Benson. And

Fig. 6.—The Card Index of a Public Library is arranged in two sections

so you go on, one book leading to another, the memoirs of one man suggesting that of another, the biography which eulogizes is matched by that which attempts to "debunk" and from them all you can gradually build up your own picture of an epoch, which is just what Arnold Bennett recommended to you as one of the main objects of your reading.

Very few people want to read only the one book at a time. Moods change and with a different mood comes the desire for another kind of book. Most people find it advisable to have a lighter book of some kind, novel or play, or essays, to alternate with their main reading.

It may be for that delicious half-hour in bed before you put the light out, that you want something less stimulating to the mind than what you have been reading. Keep one or two books on your bedside table—preferably old friends that will not require too much effort.

Suggestions.—Here are a few suggestions for different types of books round which you can build up your reading plans.

A Novel.—"David Copperfield," by Charles Dickens. This is one of the most popular novels that Dickens wrote, and you may have seen the film of the story. It will therefore make a good starting-off point for you. It is largely autobiographical in the description of David as a boy at school and in London—this will naturally lead you to a short study of the author himself and of the times he lived in. Life in those days was very hard for the poor—people could be imprisoned for debt and schools were places of misery. Dickens saw all these wrongs and determined to do what he could to right them. After you have finished "David Copperfield," read some of the other novels and these in their turn will lead you to other books about London at that time. One of his novels, "A Tale of Two Cities," deals with the French Revolution and the reign of terror; you may wonder as you read it, if it is a true picture. Read a history of it and form your own opinion. If you are fascinated by the period, as many people are, there are countless memoirs and studies of the chief actors in the drama.

An alternative suggestion would be to read the novels of Thackeray, George Eliot and Charlotte Brontë, all of whom were writing about this time, and between them all you will get a vivid picture of what different parts of England were like, and how people behaved in those years.

Diaries and Memoirs.—If you are one of those people who prefer real life to even the best novel, then your taste will lead you to diaries and memoirs, and you cannot do better than begin with "Pepys' Diary." It is one of the most fascinating diaries that has ever been written, largely because Pepys wrote it in a private shorthand, entirely for his own pleasure, and put down quite frankly all he did, or saw or thought. He began it in 1660 and had to leave off in 1669 when his eyes began to trouble him. It describes minutely all his doings of every day—what he ate, how he bought a fine new coat, how he quarrelled with his wife and made it up again, how he went to the theatre, constantly against his private vows, how he never could resist kissing a pretty woman. It is all put down simply and without excuse and as Professor Cordon has said, "The first thing we note about the 'Diary' is that it puts every reader in a good humour. For in the first place Pepys himself enjoys everything so much."

There are endless ramifications from this book—Pepys was devoted to the theatre; perhaps you would like to read some of the plays he saw. He lived through the Plague, being one of the few officials brave enough to remain in London, and saw the Great Fire.

Essays.—The most lovable and human of essayists is Charles Lamb and to really appreciate his "Essays of Elia" you should know something about the man himself. He was an accounting clerk in the East India House for thirty-three years and wrote his essays to please himself. When he was only twenty-one his sister developed insanity and Lamb undertook to look after her and for the rest of his life they lived together under this shadow. But no sense of this calamity appears in his essays which are full of a tender humour and a very fine philosophy of life. When you have read the Essays, read the Letters which he wrote, find out something about his friends, and who else was writing at the same time. No one can read much of Lamb without becoming aware how much he loved London, so that you will want to know something about the London of his day.

These are only a few suggestions. There are countless others and if you come to a time in your reading, when you cannot think what book to begin on next, see if your Library cannot help you in suggesting a few books which will link up together to form a definite little group.

RUG MAKING

HOME-MADE rugs, providing they are well done and well planned, are most decidedly worth doing. If care is taken to ensure that the materials are good and durable, the rug will last a lifetime and added to this the worker will have the pleasure of seeing a very definite result for his or her efforts. It is possible, of course, to plan delightful rugs in just the colours one desires, and to arrange for the pattern to be in keeping with the rest of the room for which it is destined.

Cost.—Compared with the cost of a small piece of embroidery or knitting, hand-made rugs are not cheap, though they may cost less than the same quality rug in a shop. There are two main kinds of rugs, and the price of the materials vary accordingly. First there is the pile rug with which most people are acquainted. These are definitely expensive owing to the amount of wool needed for the pile. The average size of a rug is two yards long and three-quarters of a yard wide, and this, in a long pile of a good quality Turkey rug wool on a good canvas would cost not less than £2 0s. 0d., as one rug uses about ten to twelve pounds of wool. A shorter pile on the same size rug would cost perhaps 10s. 0d. less.

The rugs which are worked with a needle, such as cross-stitched ones, are the cheapest and for a rug of the average size about four or five pounds of wool is needed. The cost, if carried out in suitable wool, is from 15s. od. to 17s. 6d.

It is, of course, possible to make rugs of "thrums," i.e. lengths of wool left over by the manufacturer, but often these require a great deal of sorting and it is most annoying to find that the very colour of which one will need the largest amount is in the smallest quantity. It is the cheapest way of buying the wool but it involves much waste of time and much planning.

Thrift rugs can cost very little. In these, instead of wool, the worker uses old pieces of material or stockings which must of course be washed first. The material is then cut up into small lengths to be used in the same way as wool. The great disadvantage of thrift rugs is their excessive weight which makes them impracticable.

A Craft for all.—Quite apart from the fact that rug making is a craft well worth doing, it is also one which can be worked on a communal basis, providing the method of working and the pattern are both simple. It is possible to talk and listen to the wireless when rug making and many men find in it a very pleasant fireside occupation. Children, too, can make remarkably good rugs.

A fairly large rug of simple pattern is an excellent piece of work to plan for the long winter evenings to occupy the hands of any member of the family who may be at home with little to do.

Storage Room.—A rug is of course bulky, and it is necessary to have a definite corner in which to keep it when it is being made. It should be wrapped round in a cloth and the wool kept preferably in a large box where it is easy to see the colours at a glance. Wool should be wound into balls and the smallest quantity desired can be cut off.

Every worker should wear some sort of apron as the fluff from the wool easily gets on to the clothes. A table on which to keep the rug while working is a help but not a necessity.

Fig. 1.—A Cross-stitch Rug

Type of Work.—Most people enjoy making rugs because it is rather a bold technique. The tools and threads are large and there is no strain on the eyes. Many who are not happy with fine needlework thoroughly enjoy rug making. Those readers who contemplate starting on a rug will be well advised to give some time and thought to the planning of it so that they will choose the materials and method of work which they are most likely to appreciate best and the following facts may be helpful.

Choice of Wool.—For pile rugs a Turkey wool or thrums gives the best result, but for rugs to be worked with a needle, e.g. in cross stitch, Sirdar or Persian or Herdwick wool is recommended. The last mentioned is made from the fleece of the sheep of the Lake District and is very hard-wearing and reasonably priced.

Canvas.—The worker is strongly advised to buy the best quality; it lasts longer and does not cut the wool. This is especially important for needleworked rugs and, moreover, in those cases the amount of

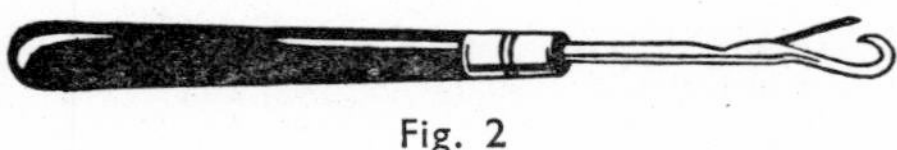

Fig. 2

wool used is relatively small and a heavier canvas is necessary. An excellent background for needleworked rugs is Helvellyn canvas made of jute and sold by all firms who deal in rug materials.

Needles.—For pile rugs, the patent latch-hook (Fig. 2) is recommended and for needleworked rugs select a coarse Persian rug needle. A strong steel crochet hook is necessary for finishing the edges. For thrift rugs special hooks are sold.

Choice of Design.—There are a number of good designs to be purchased which are worked out on squared paper and are easy to follow. It is possible also to buy canvas with the design already stamped on it, but this is a very expensive way of beginning. Any reader who has a little idea of pattern, and likes his or her work to be her own entirely, is strongly urged to make a simple pattern. The rug in Fig. 1 is an excellent example of a simple but well-designed rug. The rug is worked in cross stitch but can be carried out equally well as a pile rug.

Fig. 5 shows an original design for a pile rug adapted from a Persian carpet.

Very effective rugs usually have a good area of plain colour as the one in Fig. 1. It makes the pattern more important and is restful to the eye.

Type of Design.—No matter how the worker obtains the pattern she is strongly advised to avoid any which include realistic birds, beasts, fishes, landscapes,

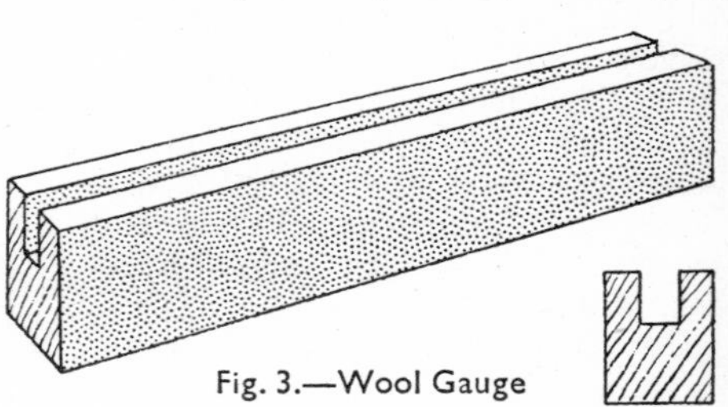

Fig. 3.—Wool Gauge

figures or large floral patterns. None of these is suitable for a floor and the eye quickly tires of them.

Choose a design that can be looked at with comfort from all angles. And remember that a small pattern is better for a small room but that too niggling a pattern defeats its own ends.

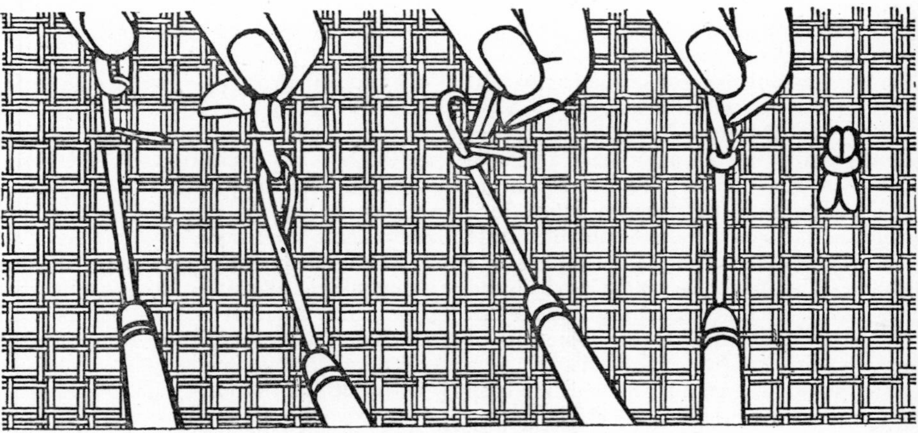

Fig. 4.—How the wool of a pile rug is knotted

Fig. 5.—A Pile Rug design adapted from a Persian Carpet

The beginner is advised to make a small slip mat as a first exercise. A narrow border as in Fig. 13, with a plain centre, is easy to do and exceedingly effective.

Colours.—The colours of rugs soon get drabbed with use; therefore the wise worker chooses strong colours, mixed of course with a judicious selection of neutral shades.

Pastel tints such as pink, blue and mauve fade and soil quickly, so it is well to avoid them unless your rug is for a bedroom or drawing-room.

Any good Persian carpet will inspire effective colour scheme for living rooms, as for example, dark blue, Indian red and sage green, with camel or nigger brown as a background.

A rug is always an important item of furniture and the colour scheme should be selected so that it harmonizes with its surroundings. If the room is in browns, fawns and oranges, it will be wise to make these predominate in the rug too. Similarly if the room is in a colour scheme of blues or greens or reds, the rug should echo the colours so that it will be an additional attraction to the room.

METHODS

Pile Rugs.—The wool is first wound round a wooden gauge and cut into equal lengths (*see* Fig. 3.) Each little length is then knotted into place with a patent latch-hook or a crochet hook. The effect is as in Fig. 4. The canvas should have 9 holes to the square inch.

A Short Pile Rug can be made with a needle. A narrow strip of wood is used for working over and a special stitch is worked to fasten each loop that passes over the wood. The loops are cut before the gauge is removed. This is one of the most satisfactory ways of making a pile rug and almost every firm which supplies rug wool

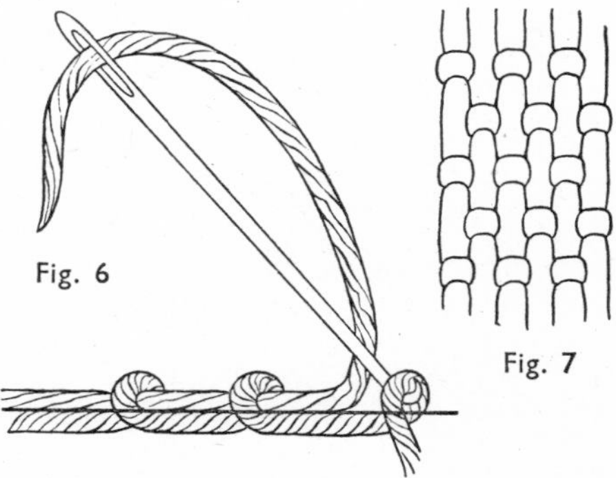

and canvas has leaflets giving directions for working. (*See* Fig. 10.)

Locker Rugs.—These are worked

with a combined needle and hook. Wool is threaded though the eye of the needle. The hook end is then inserted through a hole in the canvas and picks up another length of wool which is under the canvas. The loop is brought up through to the right side of the canvas and kept on the needle, while the hook is passed through the next hole and picks up another loop. This continues until the needle has on it sufficient loops. The needle is then pulled through all the loops and pulls with it the wool inserted in the eye. This wool locks all the loops. This is an economical and quick method but intricate designs cannot be worked in it. (*See* Fig. 6.) Fig. 7 shows the appearance of the surface.

Embroidered Rugs.—These include all the ways of making rugs with tapestry stitches. Rug wool is used on heavy jute canvas which is preferable for this type of work to the ordinary rug canvas. They are usually very economical and clean wearing. About $\frac{1}{4}$ lb. wool is required for a square foot.

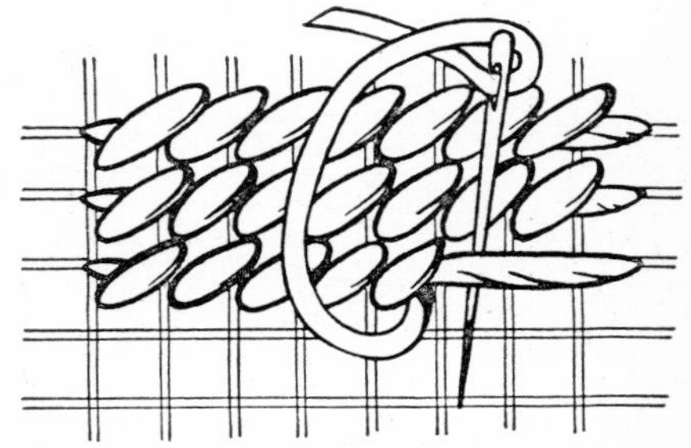

Fig. 8.—Sloped Gobelin Stitch with padding

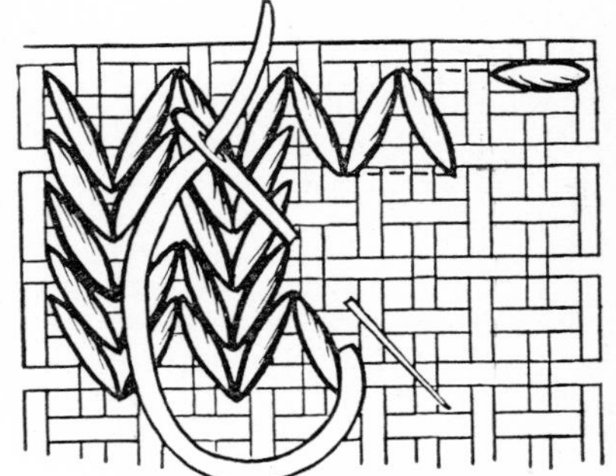

Fig. 9.—Knitting Stitch

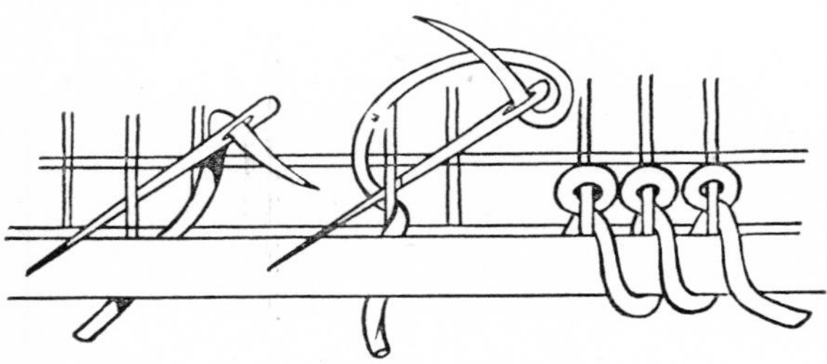

Fig. 10.—Short Pile Stitch using wooden gauge

The best stitches are:—Cross stitch, Gobelin stitch, either straight or sloped, various Hungarian stitches, the Kelm or knitting stitch, knotted stitch and chain stitch. Several of these are given in Figs. 8, 9, 11 and reference should also be made to the section on EMBROIDERY in this book. Any stitch described there is equally applicable to rugs.

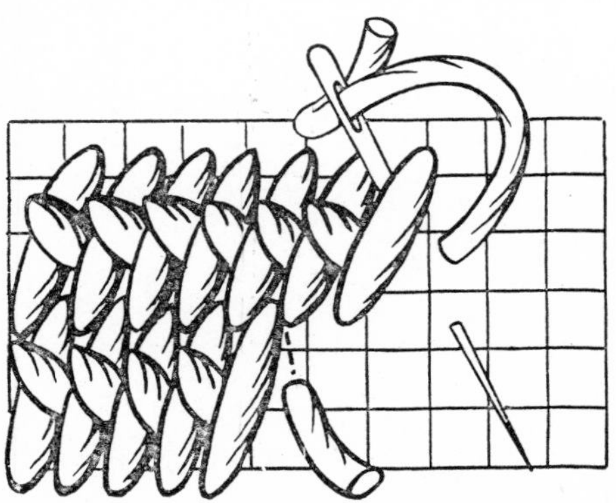

Fig. 11.—Knotted Stitch

Needlewoven Rugs.—These are quite different from any of the above types. The worker must first purchase a length of heavy woollen or jute material. Threads of the fabric are then withdrawn and rug wool or jute thread inserted in their place. The type of embroidery known as needle-weaving is often employed here most effectively and really handsome borders can be built up. The jute material is not expensive and can be obtained in several excellent ground colours. Also it is exceedingly durable. It is, however, not quite the right material for a sitting room, yet in passages, bedrooms, country cottages, on stone floors, etc., it is particularly satisfactory.

Woven Rugs.—These are made on a simple loom with a warp of twine or yarn which ultimately makes a fringe. This is the least usual type of rug but any reader with a little knowledge of weaving could construct a loom on a big packing case. These woven rugs are exceedingly pleasant; inevitably simple in design, they depend a great deal on colour and texture for their effect and the result is very satisfying.

Fig. 12.—An Effective Modern Design

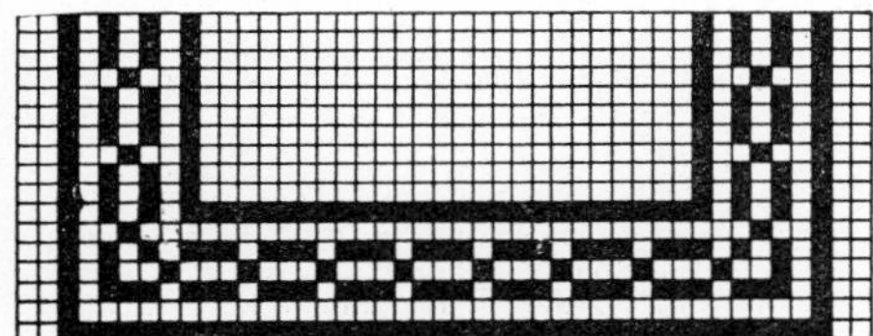

Fig. 13.—A Simple Border

THE PREPARATION AND FINISH OF A RUG

It is in the finishing of a rug that many amateurs go astray. A successful finish depends on the careful preparation of the rug before work is commenced. Firstly, the cut ends should be hemmed down before beginning the work and one or two rows of holes left unworked. When the pile or embroidery is complete, work in double crochet all round the rug over the selvedge and cut ends (which have been turned back), using the same coloured wool as in the border. (*See* the edge of the rug in Fig. 1.)

If preferred, blanket stitch may be used and if the wool does not quite cover the canvas one or two strands may be laid on the hem and worked over. In this case the blanket-stitching should be fairly close to hold the laid wool firmly in place.

The Back of the Rug.—Lining is *inadvisable* as dust collects between it and the canvas. If, however, a lining is desired, leave one end loosely tacked so that it may be opened at intervals and the dust can be shaken out.

Enough has now been written to give the reader a general idea of this most fascinating craft which offers so many possibilities to those who enjoy work of this kind.

SELF-DEFENCE

SELF-DEFENCE may seem a queer sort of hobby, but it is closely allied with jiu-jitsu, wrestling, boxing and tumbling, and many people practise it merely as a form of athletic recreation. It does happen sometimes, even in this country, that one needs to know what to do against an unprovoked attack, and it is then that the methods of self-defence have real practical value. But even if you seldom or never have occasion to use them you will find that the study and practice of them will keep you congenially occupied for a long time, and will give you not only interest and health but self-confidence too. Incidentally, self-defence is as worth while a hobby for girls and women as for men.

Very often a threatened attack can be prevented by a sufficient show of courage on the part of the intended victim. Just as

Fig. 1.—Blow with elbow to remove assailant on running-board

a snarling dog is most dangerous if it senses that you are nervous and will probably not attack you if you are not afraid, so if you chance to meet a rough-looking character on a country road and are suspicious of his intentions your safest plan will be to walk boldly towards him. Seeing your self-reliant air he will probably think twice about interfering with you. The same applies if you are cycling.

Should you be walking in the dark and have reason to suspect that you are being followed you will find that your hearing is more sensitive if you open your mouth. And if you are sitting by a camp fire when an unwanted intruder suddenly arrives, spring aside into the shadows, leaving him in the firelight while you are concealed. What to do if you actually come to grips in the foregoing emergencies will be dealt with later.

Attacking Animals.—The safest way to deal with a charging bull, if you cannot get to a fence or gate in time, is to leap to one side and throw your coat or jacket over his horns so that he is momentarily blinded. An attacking dog can be dealt with by a kick under the jaw if you have previously held a hat or something similar in front of you in which he can first fix his teeth.

A Hold-up.—Should an attacker leap on to the running-board of your car, on the driving side, you can get rid of him, if windows allow, by a strong upward and outward jab of elbow or wrist which will take him in the throat or under the chin. Even in a hold-up by a revolver you are not necessarily at the mercy of the other man. Suppose you are standing facing him and have obeyed his order to put up your hands. Fix his eyes with yours, talking perhaps as you do so in order to distract him. Your arms will be above your head, but do not keep them together; let them sag and spread sideways as widely as possible. By doing so you will prevent your attacker from keeping his eye on both simultaneously—and that may give you the opportunity to swing down the hand of which he has for the moment lost sight and so to knock aside or seize the weapon. Fortunately criminals in this country do not often risk shooting or even carrying weapons, if they can possibly avoid doing so. But you must be extremely careful when firearms are concerned.

One useful way of temporarily disabling an attacker is to seize the lapels of his jacket and jerk them outwards and backwards so that the jacket is snatched clear of his shoulders and half down his back and remains hamperingly around his elbows. (Fig. 2.)

There are many more vigorous ways of dealing with an attacker. For example, suppose one is coming towards you with upraised bludgeon or weapon, so that he is upright. A very effective counter is to duck sharply in front of him, going down on one knee so that your head goes between his legs and your shoulders are pressed against his shins. If you now clutch his ankles from behind and tug them sharply, jerking them upwards, at the same time pushing with your shoulders, you will fling him over backwards—probably his head will strike the ground with such force as to stun him. In practising this and similar throws with a friend you must use a mattress and proceed cautiously, as you would for jiu-jitsu work.

An alternative way of getting control is to grab the right wrist of your opponent with your own right hand and to get behind his right arm. If you now thrust your left arm under his right arm-pit and clutch his jacket somewhere near the left lapel, keeping your arm rigid you will find that you can strain his right wrist back and get an arm-breaking pressure on his right elbow which will be running across your own left arm. The front of his wrist should be held to the front, so that the pressure you exert strains his arm in the way in which his elbow cannot possibly bend—without breaking. The least pressure you give will be very painful so be very, very careful if you practise this with a friend.

An Ordinary Umbrella, properly wielded, can be a most effective weapon against an attacker. Do not try to hit with it, for the ribs and cover will muffle the blow, and the stick will most likely break. The point is the effective part. Hold the umbrella, point forward, as if it were a foil. A straight hard jab in face, throat, or stomach will be pretty certain to put any attacker out of action. Fencing, by the way, apart from its own interest and value, is a most excellent exercise from the point of view of self-defence, for it teaches you how to make forceful, well-aimed thrusts with any available weapon.

A walking-stick is infinitely better than an umbrella, in fact walking-stick defence is quite a study in itself, and if you customarily carry a stick when out walking, you will

Fig. 2.—A Temporary Disablement

Fig. 3.—Defending oneself with a walking-stick

find the proper handling of your stick a most fascinating study. The same stabs with your ferrule can be depended on to ward off an attack, and if you have an opponent on the ground you can place the point of your stick in the pit of his stomach and hold him helpless. The slightest vertical pressure will convince him of the serious danger of trying to escape, as effectively as if you had a rapier point at his throat.

Blows With a Stick.—It is not merely the point of the stick which is of value. You may hit with the whole length of it too. Be careful where you hit—some portions of the anatomy are much more susceptible than others, and to put your opponent out of action promptly you should aim at such points as the collar-bone near the neck, the tip of a shoulder, inside of a knee, outside of forearm, back of hand, elbow or shin.

Do not make a straight, square stroke. Not only is this less efficacious but it gives your opponent a chance to grab the stick while it lies dead against his body. Cultivate a stinging, slicing stroke. This is far more painful, and also ensures that the stick comes immediately out of reach, ready for further use.

In making any blows at the head or shoulders of your companion keep your own hand as high as possible, for this will enable you to strike downward over his guard, and will also ensure that at least one of your arms is raised as a protecting guard for yourself should you need it.

When you go for a walk with your stick cultivate the ability to swing it freely, whilst keeping it under firm control. When you can make it whistle through the air in great sweeping circles you will have a defence which the boldest antagonist would hesitate to break into.

Single-sticks.—It is well when practising with a friend that you shall also occasionally let him use a stick against yours—you may follow this up by equipping yourself with proper head guards and weapons and so taking up the old hobby of single-sticks.

If your opponent has a stick and you have none your safest plan will be to get in promptly to close quarters where his stick cannot be used.

Boxing is naturally another excellent method of self-defence, and, even if you do not make a proper study of it, it is worth while at least to acquire the ability to make a few strong punches correctly.

Punches with the fist are not always, however, the best way of persuading an assailant to leave you alone. A clenched fist, arriving flatly and solidly, may have little effect—like the stick which is driven straight and square at the body. Often, a blow given sharply by a smaller edge is much more potent. Clench your right fist for instance, and with the back knuckles give a sharp blow on the back of your left hand. It will be very painful! Now imagine that you are clutched round the body from behind. Your attacker is not likely to retain his hold long if a similar knuckle blow is delivered really hard on the back of his hands.

You may also make very painful blows with the edge of the hand between the little finger and the wrist. If you hold your hand stiff and flat and deliver the hit in some vulnerable spot, such as the outer side of the arm between shoulder and elbow, your attacker will not want more.

When at close quarters with an assailant there are a number of methods of dealing with him. A knee jab in the stomach may put him *hors de combat.* You may stamp on his feet. If you are held from behind, you may give some terribly effective blows in his face with the back of your head. If you have a walking-stick which cannot be used in any other fashion, its crook handle may trip him up or, snatched around his neck, may jerk him to the ground.

When you are actually gripped it is important that you should know how to get free. A grip round the body or throat may be dealt with in one of the various ways already described, or you may seize the little finger of one of your attacker's hands and tug it backwards. The little finger will have no strength to resist, and unless the rest of the hand yields with it the finger is liable to be broken.

Should you be seized round the neck from in front, hook your left hand round behind the small of the other's back; bringing your right hand up so that its palm rests under his chin while your fingers spread over his face. Now pull with the left hand and push vigorously with the right, and his grip will be broken. Probably he will tumble on his back. A rather similar method can be used if you are gripped round the body from in front. Get your left hand behind him, your right under his chin, and your right knee high up against his stomach or chest. Then thrust him away with knee and right hand. As his head goes back, of course, he cannot save himself. If the left hand is not needed behind in order to pull at your opponent, then the left too may be able to come up and push against the chin. In either methods of breaking front holds you may the better ensure that your assailant crashes on to his back by getting one foot behind his to trip him.

A Nose Grip.—At the moment when an attacker is about to encircle you with his arms you may be able to prevent him by seizing his nose and grimly hanging on to it. His disconcerting difficulty in breathing will almost certainly make him abandon his intended clutch in order to tear your hold away.

Sometimes a body hold may be countered by bending forward or backward and pulling the other's feet from beneath him. If you are seized round the body from behind—assuming that your arms are free—simply spread your legs, and stoop forward till you can seize his ankles and so drag his legs forward between your own. (Fig. 4.) As he falls on his back, you will probably knock the wind out of him if you allow yourself to go down also. You may sometimes use this same method when you are seized from in front—reaching round the backs of your legs in order to seize his ankles, and pushing

Fig. 4.—Countering a Body Hold

forward with your head against his body as you do so.

The arms may not be free, however, and when you are seized from behind this will completely change your problem, and the method of solving it. You will now aim to throw your attacker completely over your head, by bending forward sharply at the waist, so that his head comes down and forward whilst your legs and his are hurled upwards and over. It will help you considerably if you are able to clutch his coat near the neck or shoulders. Remember when you fall that it will ease things if all your muscles are relaxed—never fall with any part of the body stiff, except the neck, which may be necessary to prevent the head from bumping, or the limbs which are being used in a jiu-jitsu breakfall movement.

The Value of Tripping an Opponent is considerable, for the trip seeks to catch him off his balance and bring about a violent fall. This type of defence naturally leads into jiu-jitsu—a most fascinating hobby—but without going into that thoroughly you may acquire a few particularly useful tips that will be useful in self-defence.

There is no easier and more effective trip than the ankle throw. As your opponent comes forward at you, you give way, clutching the left lapel of his coat with your right hand and the back of his sleeve just behind his right elbow with your left. Then, just as he is about to put his right foot down in a normal step forward, you push your left foot inwards against the outer side of his right ankle. His right leg will slip across from under him just as his weight is coming over on to it, and if you give a sharp tug he will crash to the ground by the side of you.

An even easier back trip can be used very often in similar circumstances, when an attacker has approached you with one arm and one leg forward—an almost inevitable position.

Supposing his right foot and right arm are nearer. You will seize his arm somewhat near the elbow with your left hand, and get your right hand up by his left shoulder. At the same time you must move slightly to the left. From this position you will now be able to pass your own right leg outside and round behind his right leg. If you then do a sharp backward kick with your right foot, you will knock *his* right foot forward clean off the ground. Simultaneously you must jerk him sideways by an outward tug of his right elbow with your left hand and a push on his left shoulder with your right hand—and he will inevitably crash on to his right side or his back.

The same trip can, of course, be performed from the other side—your left leg hooking behind the left. Throws of this sort need a great deal of practice if they are to be performed with the requisite assurance and speed. So much depends on catching your opponent just at the right instant. Try all these methods over very frequently therefore, with a companion, until you are proficient. See that he has something soft to fall on!

Different tactics can sometimes be used against an assailant who has one arm upraised to strike or stab. If you are able to seize his wrist with one or both hands, you may twist round so that your back is to him and so bring the arm down across your near shoulder. Providing the front of his wrist is turned upwards you may get a most painful pressure on his elbow which, supported by your shoulder, cannot bend against the direction of the joint. A violent jerk could quite easily break an arm held in this position, and it is certain that your attacker will not long hold his weapon when he discovers how much he is in your power.

Kicks.—Sometimes an attack may come from the feet instead of the hands; a ruffianly assailant may try to kick his victim.

If you see the kick coming, and are far enough away, stretch out your nearest foot and try to receive it on the sole, aiming to catch his shin rather than his foot. With a stiff knee and the hard edge of a shoe sole you may make him regret that kick, for it may almost break his shin. Should his leg come high enough for you to clutch it will be easy to upset his balance by a strong body punch in almost any direction, but preferably hit or push him from the right side if you have seized his left leg or vice versa. Should it chance that you have seized his foot with both hands you may exert a very painful and effective pressure by twisting it violently—this will certainly bring him to the ground heavily, unless he is holding on to something with his hands.

When you have overcome an attacker and wish to take him along with you, how shall you do it? The most effective "come along with me" method is that in which you walk by his side with his near arm locked in such a position that you might even break his elbow if he compelled you to such extremes. Suppose you are on his right side, you will grip his right wrist with your right hand, so that his palm is facing forward. Your left arm will be passed over the front of his right arm so that your forearm is able to bend back underneath his elbow. Your left hand will then clutch your right wrist. In this position you are able to exert strain on his right elbow by pressing his wrist down with your right hand—you can adjust the painfulness of the pressure to the amount of trouble he gives you.

Frog-marching is familiar to most people, from school-days. By holding both arms of a person, and bending one or both up behind his back, you may cause him to bend forward and walk along helplessly at your direction.

It may be necessary to secure a criminal while you go for help. A chair is convenient if you have enough cord, for arms and legs may be fastened separately to

Fig. 5.—A Temporary Tie-up. This is painful and must not be continued too long

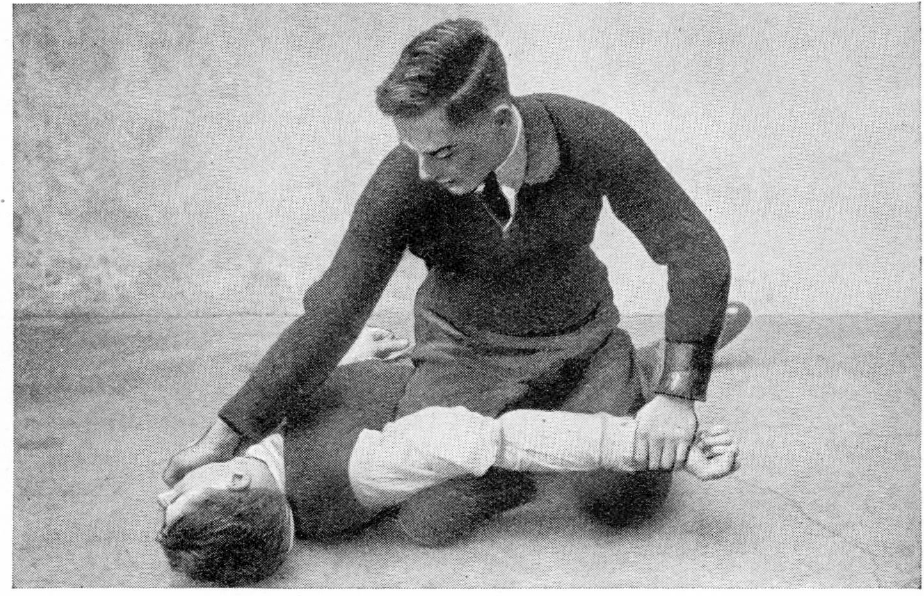

Fig. 6.—The Arm and Head Hold

strong spars. A quick, but effective method of service for a very short time—as for instance, whilst telephoning for police—is to tie his thumbs together behind his back—a shoe-lace will serve. Lay him face downward on the floor as you do it, and then drag one of his feet backward and hook it through under the tied thumbs. This method can be very painful to the prisoner if he struggles or is left too long, so use it with discretion. (*See* Fig. 5.)

Handcuffs. — If you wish to fasten a man's hands behind his back see that they are in such a position that the fingers cannot get at the cord. The best plan is to fold the arms across the small of the back so that the forearms are lying against each other. The wrists can then be knotted together, and the hands will be spread in opposite directions, unable to reach each other or the cords. (Fig. 7.)

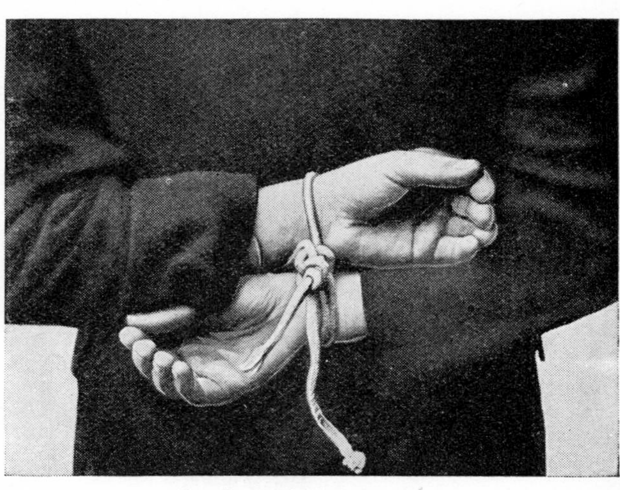

Fig. 7.—Makeshift Handcuffs

Jiu-jitsu Holds.—There are a number of important jiu-jitsu holds. One of the most effective is the arm lock with foot on chest. Be cautious how you apply this, as you may quite easily injure your opponent.

When your opponent is on his back grip his right arm, holding it upwards, with the palm of your hand passing over the front of his wrist. Stand at his side, by his shoulder, and place your right foot on his chest just at the right armpit. You will thus hold his right arm extended across your shin, and will be able to exert very severe and painful pressure on his elbow. For extra control you may grip his wrist with both hands; the important thing is to have his arm so turned that the back of the elbow is against your leg.

The Arm and Head Hold.—A similar method is used, but with the complication of a special head position. (Fig. 7.) Your opponent must be on his back as before, and you will kneel or crouch at his right side. Your right foot must be near his right hip, and your right knee passed up behind his armpit. You will thus be able to grip his right wrist with your left hand and hold his right arm fully extended over your right knee. Your right hand will be stretched across so that you are able to grip his chin, and by pushing on this you may force his head down so that it lies with the left cheek on the floor and cannot move. Your opponent will be exceedingly uncomfortable, so do not be too harsh, either with his head or his right arm.

SINGING

So many people would like to sing, but are so thoroughly shy that they are afraid to open their mouths unless they are in a crowd of would-be singers. These few pages are to encourage and to help them, and those who know nothing of nerves, to

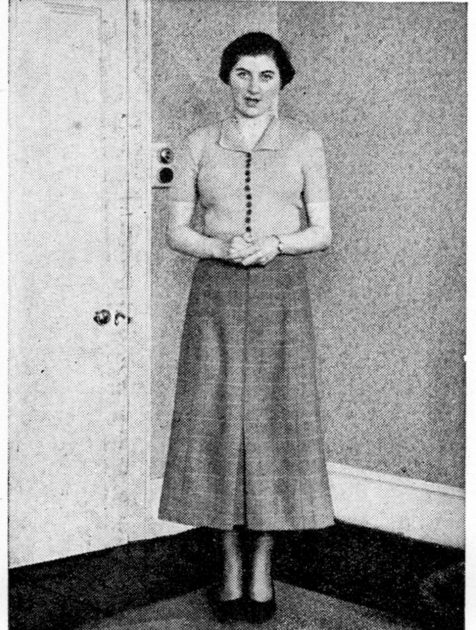

Fig. 1.—A Bad Position

Fig. 2.—A Good Position

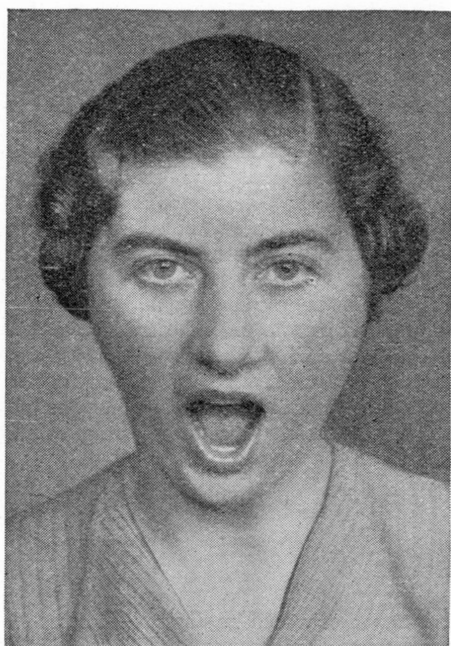

Fig. 3.—Bad Mouth Opening

Fig. 4.—Good Mouth Opening

progress towards clearly defined standards of ability.

Breathing.—The source of easy singing is correct breathing. If you have only a little breath your sounds will be weak, but plenty of breath means plenty of strength for singing. It is not easy to harness this great power, but you can soon learn the way. Thinking is the first and last part. You can do a great deal by sitting still and planning the procedure.

Stand up, put equal weight on both feet, the right foot slightly in front of the left. Feel the whole world belongs to you. Your shoulders will not be stiff, but just well set: your back will be straight, and your ribs well out to allow for the expansion of your lungs. Now experiment. Breathe as *deeply* as you can, imagining you are utterly excited at the prospect of the greatest moment of your life, then relax again, breathe in as deeply as before, this time feeling as exasperated as you can imagine with someone or something. Did you not, this second time, have the sensation of being filled with breath, as before, but of the breath being quite out of control?

Right breathing is at the foundation of things; and right feeling. When you "feel things deeply" the nerve centre is affected. That is where one gets the feeling of having been "knocked out" when troubles have been overwhelming. But only when you breathe down deeply do you reach this centre of deep feeling, which will so affect your singing.

When you have taken your breath, do not let it go at once. "Poise" it, or "weigh" it, as you might take a package in your hand and try to judge the cost of the postage. Do not "hold" your breath. That suggests tension, which must be avoided. It is essential to get balance or control before attempting to use the motive power behind the voice. A helpful aid to getting this "poise" is to stand, holding the hands at waist level loosely. Do not clasp each individual finger, but just let one hand rest in the other, and you will feel they are "weighing" your breath for you. Then begin to sing out gently, and you will notice how it all feels within your power. Practice breathing as you walk along the street, though at first not too strenuously, and not too often. Three times in succession is enough for a day or two, as you will be using muscles that have been neglected previously, and common sense advises that moderation is wise whenever you start something new.

Do not worry too much about exercises, as exercises. A few will be suggested later, but the most practical thing to get in mind is "Take care of the words, and the tone will take care of itself." So use songs with words very often. All vowel-sound practice is inadvisable. You may see the wisdom of that later, and will prove it in your experience.

Never be insincere in your singing. Sing what your inner self tells you is the right thing. If you have no one else to advise you, saturate yourself in the folk melodies of your own country, for they have come down from the ages and have stood the test of time.

Phrasing.—Supposing, then, you have chosen a song for your studies—perhaps you heard it on the radio or at a recital and thought you would like to know it better. Read it through; study the words, the mood, phrases, and find the climax, to which you must work. The phrases will tell you the obvious breathing places, but, occasionally, they are too long to be managed with ease, especially in these early stages of your venture. So re-read, and let the words take first place, and you will find the music will give way for the moment—as long as you do not break the rhythm. You must never be late for a new phrase. To be in time, plan to take a little of the value from the note preceding. Here is an illustration:

‖ 𝅗𝅥 𝅗𝅥 | 𝅗𝅥 ♩x ♩ | 𝅗𝅥 𝅗𝅥 | 𝅝 ‖

Let us presume the above phrase is too long to be sung at one stretch. A breath should therefore be taken after the first crotchet in bar 2, at x, and that crotchet will be slightly shortened, say to a quaver, and the balance of the value of the note, that is a quaver rest, should be spent in taking and poising the breath in readiness for the timing of the second crotchet at the 4th beat of that second bar—not a fraction too soon or late, but *on* the 4th beat. So now you would see the phrase as this:

‖ 𝅗𝅥 𝅗𝅥 | 𝅗𝅥 ♪ 𝄾 ✓ ♩ | 𝅗𝅥 𝅗𝅥 | 𝅝 ‖

A good general rule is—take a big breath before a song begins and between each verse, and only "*replace*" the breath used at each phrase or other breathing places. It is perhaps simpler to say—take a large breath at the long stopping places and a small breath at the short stopping places. Keep reminding yourself to stand well, and make sure that you can turn your head easily without hindering the singing. Shoulders will never want to "heave" if you are standing correctly.

Tone.—For some time indulge only in quiet singing, remembering that just as much breath is required as for very loud production. Any one can "yell," but few can sing with lovely, clear, open quality of tone on quiet notes, a sort of miniature of the larger tone. Listen for what you are planning and make sure that you get that result. If you want a crescendo, plan one, and begin quietly enough for the increase of tone to be really gradual and steady. The reverse applies for a decrescendo, which must begin loudly enough to allow the desired result. Never force yourself to take a note too high or too low. Work over "safe" ground for a time, and soon the voice will show it has expanded considerably without actual practising on those outer notes.

Your Mouth.—Have you ever realized that you cannot lift the top part of your face unless you tilt your head backwards? Therefore you will have to let your lower jaw drop a good deal if your mouth is to open widely. A very little practice will get this little difficulty out of the way, and your mind will be able to concentrate on more urgent matters. Meanwhile, if you drop the lower jaw, and say "Ah," you will get the wide-shaped mouth which is correct, and which gives a more pleasing expression than the long-shaped mouth. It is the more natural, but you need not exaggerate it—like a toothpaste advertisement. In order to get your highest note you must have this wide mouth. As long as you can get the tips of your little fingers in between your side teeth—from *outside* your face—you will have a good open throat, and the secret for the easy singing you are hoping to get. In former days it was thought the mouth should be open in front sufficiently to allow two fingers to be fitted in between the teeth. That encourages the long shaped mouth with the consequent malformed vowel sounds.

Use your tongue, teeth and lips well.

Vowels and Consonants.—Many people insist on vowel practice entirely, forgetting the importance of consonants, which represent the "clothing" of vowels. Consonants help to send the voice away from the singer to the audience. You will find you can seldom practise with no hearers about, whether willing or unwilling, so do your best that they shall have "music" to listen to all the time, as far as is possible! Take great care of the whole of each word you sing. So often words start off well, but get lost, and are hardly recognizable by their end. *Concentrate on listening to everything you do.* Your ears will soon warn you if there is anything wrong with what you are working at, and will show you exactly where are the weak spots.

Sing "through" your eyes. Let them do the expressing for you, while your face is busy with the producing of the voice in general. Eyes let an audience know at once whether your mind is on what you are doing. Set your gaze on a steady point a little above eye-level, not much higher, or you will show only the whites of your eyes. Singing "through" the eyes will help to bring the voice to the front of the face, where so many little resounding spots and cavities exist, and you will begin to hear the "ring" of your notes for yourself.

Practising.—Test your voice from the A above Middle C downwards, and take notice where the sound is less pleasing or comfortable to produce. Do the same from the same A upwards. Then hum from the note below your top "easy" one down an octave and up again, about 3 times. Do this from the next note lower, and work that octave down and up, and so on, until you have reached the note *above* your most "easy" lowest note. For example, suppose you found the B below Middle C was the lowest "easy" note, and the 2nd E flat above Middle C was your highest. That is not a very wide compass of course, but it will serve for illustration. You will now hum from D, the note below your highest at present, then from D flat, and so on until you have arrived at Middle C, as your *lowest* note. You must play for safety for a few weeks, getting good breath control over the easy range of notes. Hum to a quiet "m," "n," or "ng"; for you can do no harm with those sounds. When your limit is reached you will know it at once, for the humming sound will just stop. Such humming will also prove invaluable in giving you the forward and lovely "taut" quality which every singer desires, and without which a voice will not carry.

For increasing breath control, sing on a monotone, very slowly, May, Me, My, Mo, Mōo, on the middle notes of your compass; or count from 1 to 5 in one breath. Later to 8, 10, 12, or, in time 20, without feeling any strain. Think always of words and not just figures. When they occur in a song, they are used as words, and so are more "sympathetic" to the voice. For example—"One morning," or "Two lovers," or "Three fishers," or "Four jolly sailormen."

Vowel Sounds.—These must be clear, and so must be mentally correct at the first approach.

"a" is really "e-î" (as in "egg-it").

"ee" as in "easy."

"i" (not "ah-î," but "û-î" as in "up-it.") The old form "ah-î" tends to produce the Cockney "oi," and is extremely difficult to eradicate once it has taken root.

"O" is almost "aw-oo" (as in "saw-you"). The usual fault in this is generally caused by laziness! The completion of the word is neglected. The "oo" *is* necessary —it *can* be achieved by itself, "o," plus the

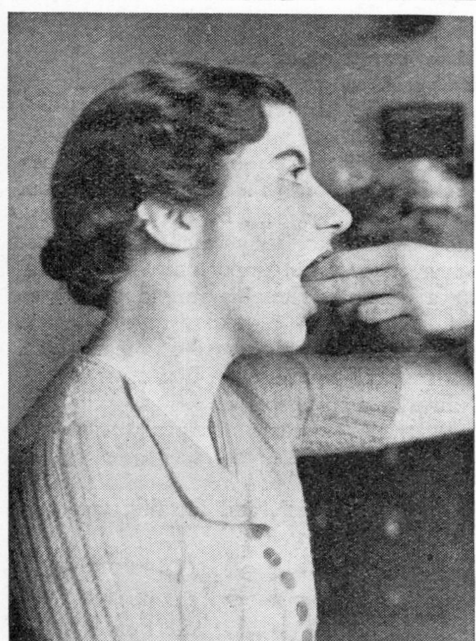

Fig. 5.—Old Style of Teaching Mouth Opening

"oo" ending, viz.: "o-oo," but do not forget the ending.

Try many ways; experiment is the finest teacher you can have for home study. The ears will get so acute that they will warn you directly you are off the track, and will prompt you how to put the matter right.

"U" is "ĭ-oo" as "in-June." Spend very little time on the first part of the sound.

Beware of some of those individual sounds. Each separate part of each word needs great care, if there is to be no slovenly result.

"ĭ" as in "pin" or "pick" not "peak."

"oo" as in "coon" not "cook."

"ee" as in "peat" not "pin."

The sounds so easily get slipshod.

Difficult Words.—Let us now examine a few words that often present difficulties:

"Mouth." Think of this as "mah-ooth" and link the divisions neatly.

"Think, these, things." Notice the first and last of the 3 words. They have the same light sound. The middle word is deeper in quality. The "th" in 1 and 3 is light as in "pith" and the vowels are light also, as in the word "pith" again. In 2, we have "th" as in "leather," and "ee" as in "peat" once more.

When words begin with "wh," visualize the "wh" as "hoo," e.g. whether = "hoo-ether." When "w" is the first letter, then translate it to "oo," and make "weather" sound like "oo-eather." Read the following slowly, and speak it first as an exercise: "When we went where witches were, we watched while we wished what we were wishing we would win." Write it out with the "hoo" or "oo" as explained above. Tongue, teeth and lips are to be well worked in this sort of thing. Monotone the above on one note, or move up a semitone for each word, or down a semitone.

Another important thing to guard against, is "er" appearing between words or even syllables of words. It is a common fault in churches, where there has been no speech training. Try this: "Give me your smile, the sunshine in your eyes." Add "er" wherever you can, and you will get: "Give (er) me (er) your (er) smile (er),

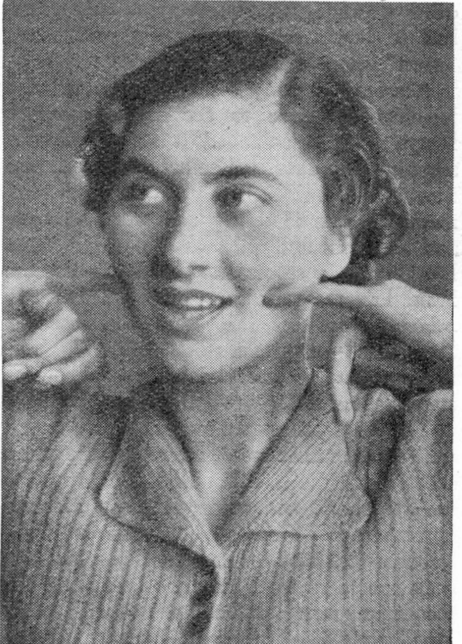

Fig. 6.—Modern Style of Teaching Mouth Opening

the (er) sun (er) shine (er) in (er) your (er) eyes (er)." To ensure a correct enunciation of this continue the same vowel sounds that each word contains, but *only mentally*. The above would then read something like this: "Give (î) me (ee) your (aw) smile (i), the (er) sun (û) shine (i) in (î) your (aw) eyes (i)." The letters in brackets should not be heard, though there might be a "hint" of the sound where the word ended with a consonant, as in "Give," "smile," "sunshine," "in," "eyes." Go over everything really slowly, and you will find it all quite manageable. Then practise the following in that same way:

"Church" (er), "laugh" (ah), "joke" (o), "boot" (oo), "fight" (i), "morn" (aw). Many other words you can discover for yourself.

Another error, often heard, is the heavy ending given to such words as "slowly," "country," "happy." They should never be "slowlee," "countree," "happee," but the "i" should be as in "lift." "Slowly" would be sung as "slow-lî(ft)" and the other words in the same way. Think how bad it would be to talk of "sin" when "seen" was intended.

Accompanying.—It is something of a handicap to have to accompany oneself. But, if it can be achieved, it is a tremendous asset in these days. The handicap is caused through—*a*, having to sit down; *b*, because, mentally, one is doing two very separate and concentrated jobs at the same time. Reading as a soloist *and* as a pianist, the brain has a tremendous piece of work to achieve. Soloists lead, and accompanists "go with"—they do not "follow." The hands; feet, at the pedals; tongue, teeth and lips, are all at work at once.

To play your own accompaniment, sit well on the music stool, the right foot at the right pedal, the left foot back, but opposite the left pedal, and ready to move forward if required. This should give a well-balanced feeling. The song should have been learnt, away from the piano, and the accompaniment studied separately, too. Much practice of the voice part should be done standing away from the piano, in order to get that sensation of singing "away from one's self." The left-hand part of the accompaniment is too often neglected, and yet it has so often the most important notes of the harmony. If there are ornaments in both piano and vocal parts, make them exactly match one another. They should "flow" into the whole composition, not be "bumped" in, by sheer fright and knowledge that they are weak spots! Never neglect the opportunity of playing for a friend. There is untold advantage in playing with a violinist, or 'cellist. "Strings" are so akin to the human voice, and musical phrasing is often most clearly shown by a string player.

When there are two or more notes to one word or syllable, remember this rule—Look after the second note (or those notes following the first), and the first will take care of itself, e.g.

All day. All . . . . day. All . . . . day. And another pitfall—never anticipate a consonant, e.g. me . . . elt, *not* me . . ool . . . t. The "lt" should come at the right spot, and there *is* only one spot for it—the last fraction of the sound. Actually every word which begins and ends with a consonant is made up of the first fraction of the sound sung to the first consonant, followed by the vowel immediately, which must be continued unto the final fraction of the sound, when the last consonant is promptly and neatly sung. Take the word "Nought." It is sung in this way "Naw . . . awt." As nearly as can be expressed on paper. "Fall" is very difficult to manage easily. Think "Faw . . . awl" or it will arrive as "Faw . . . ool," or "Faw . . . ler."

Do not roll an "r," unless it is followed by a vowel. For instance, in "far away," it would not do to sing, "Fah away," yet only a "tinge" of the "r" is required to send that little bit of "a" on to the "way." On the other hand, "Far back" needs none of the "r" at all. "Charming" should never be "Charrrrming." Singing is only

Fig. 7.—Correct Position for Accompanying

Fig. 8.—Bad Position for Accompanying Oneself

"coloured speech," and who would speak this word with the rolled "r"?

Where the same two letters follow one another, they should both be sung, unless intended to be silent. Consider the second of the two as a capital letter, and this difficulty is such no longer. For instance —"was set." Make that, "was Set" in your mind. And so with—"it Teemed," "did Dance," "come My," and so on. You will be amply repaid for the care you take over your diction.

Sight Reading.—A very important part of any musician's equipment is the ability to read well at sight. One may be called upon to fill a gap at a moment's notice. A singer may have failed at the "eleventh hour," and it is no use having the required voice for the "part." One must be able to learn that part very quickly indeed. And only good reading will enable that to be done. The eye will help the ear, when, if learning by ear alone, one or two points may be missed. No up-to-date conductor will admit a person to his choral society if he, or she, cannot read with a certain amount of reliability. On the lowest level, surely, one should feel it a disgrace to stumble over every other note, in a new work. How many novels would be read, nowadays, if the prose reading was as poor as the music reading? How dull it would be to read so unintelligently, even to oneself. Do not neglect this vital matter. You will find it most enjoyable and stimulating, as a few bars studied daily soon give the necessary confidence to plunge into longer works. Confidence is of first importance. Begin with something really simple. The best way is to get a "sight reader" from a music shop. If you have other friends who are interested in this subject, each could purchase a separate edition and exchange from time to time.

Always get the time pattern settled in your mind first of all. It is the most important part of sight reading, though not always the most difficult; but you will clear the way for the melody, which may be a little harder. Tap out the rhythm on a table, or on the woodwork of the piano, but do not play the tune on the piano until you have attempted to sing it through once, at least. Try to keep the rhythm going, and so pass through where possible, without halting. Stumbling, and going back to the first bar again cause "stammering," and that very soon becomes a habit.

"Portamento" is important. It is the gliding of the voice from one note to another. Very careful study is necessary if it is not to become a permanent "scoop." It should be avoided like the plague, except for special effects. Just as a little vinegar enhances the flavour of some dishes, so a hint of this portamento enriches certain phrases. It is almost a caress round one word in a sentence, and must be most beautifully done. In a word like "lullaby." especially if the phrase of notes descends, it can be sheer beauty. No one should detect the way it is done, it should just "happen" the only "court of appeal" is the ear.

Exercises.—Sing plenty of scales, but most often from the top note and down, first. This gets the voice well-placed. Hum to "n" for two beats, then change to a vowel. The "n" lifts the voice to where it should be, and the vowel following should just flow from that. "Aw" and "oo" are excellent for forward tone. Be sure that the "oo" is as to the fore as was the "aw." There is a tendency to let the "oo" fade out, or to be "drawn in." For "ee" the lower jaw must be well-relaxed, and so the side teeth will be well apart. Try singing this "ee" with teeth closed and then again with them open. The latter will give the richer tone.

The tongue has not been mentioned. We are told it is an unruly member, and so long as we ignore it, it has no chance to be a nuisance. The more notice that is taken of it, the more troublesome it seems to become.

Think about the sound you wish to secure, and the mouth will fall into the right shape, and the tongue, teeth and lips will act as part of the mouth only. Just let it all be a natural process. Find exercises in the songs you are studying. The consonants and vowels will be heard in their right perspective. When the voice feels tired, just hum gently to "m," "n," "ng." One excellent thing is to hum those sounds in succession. It should sound as if an apostrophe was placed between each of the sounds, but as if "M-un-ung" was intended. The result should be almost as if there was a twang from a banjo. Energy of tongue, teeth and lips will certainly be necessary here. Work up and down in semitones for each sound or for the group of the 3 sounds.

Diet.—Do not be fussy about your food. After a good practice one is inclined to feel ravenous. It is as well to eat a little slowly at first if this is the case. Singing should help one to keep well. One cannot sing when ailing, so the best thing is to take an entire rest from even an attempt to sing. A day or two's rest is good for the voice at all times, during a period of intensive study. It is a wise plan to rest for an hour after a meal, as one foregoes a hot bath for that time. The control of breath is weakened, also the digestive organs have begun their work, and should not be upset. But, on the other hand, if one is needing a meal, it is foolish to begin any concentrated practising. A little warm milk, and well-buttered bread will do no harm. Do not eat biscuits, if you intend to sing. They are dry and rough. Just a little refreshment to guard against strain is all that is needed, and really will not interfere with the breathing apparatus.

Meals.—The mind cannot work if the body is faint for food. After long hours in an office, with "just a cup of tea" at 4 o'clock, home at 6, or even later; realizing there will have to be a wait of an hour if the proper meal is taken, one is too weary to make the sudden plunge into a solid practice. Such "driving" of oneself would be harmful. If the blood-stream does not function properly, the breathing department will also not be up to pitch, and then the vocal cords will be strained. It is wiser to cut out the actual work until a more appropriate time. There is no harm in having a good square meal, and then getting the song, and studying it mentally. Or, one might hum a few sight-singing exercises. "Flat" singing is often caused by singing when physically tired, or when in a stuffy atmosphere. The lungs are unable to take in sufficient oxygen to keep the muscles in sound working order. There is the opposite kind of faulty intonation, that of singing "sharp," and usually caused by too much effort being expended, and no poising of the breath before using it. The over-zealous fall into this trap very easily. A cure can be effected by pitching a song higher for "flat singing" and lower for "sharp singing", and more conscious care of the breathing will help enormously. Many people imagine they would never hear these faults, but constant listening will train the ear to be very critical, and the student will certainly realize something is wrong and will soon be able to adjust matters without prompting from a listener.

Tobacco and Alcohol.—Beware of smoking, and alcohol. Moderate smoking need be no hindrance. Some, realizing the delicacy of the coating of the vocal organs, will wish to cut out anything which is likely to irritate or harden; others will consider saving money to spend on increasing repertoire—quite an expensive item. It really depends a great deal on the person's own judgment. Have a will of your own, and that, in itself, will strengthen the singing. Forget yourself, for that is one of the surest ways of finding yourself, if you are utterly sincere in this search for art and beauty.

Whenever moving from a different atmosphere, heat to cold or cold to heat, be sure to breathe through the nose, with lips closed. The air is filtered, and warmed when necessary, before it enters the lungs, and so a good deal of trouble is avoided. After having a cold, a singer is well-advised to begin work very gently; and, in order to set the vocal cords vibrating normally once more, use a light "coo" (as in "cook") for several days. Also, he should cut down the length of practice for a day or two.

General Hints.—Aim at "ease" in everything you do. That does not mean laziness! It involves constant hard work, not odd spurts from time to time.

At the outset, be warned about "frog-in-the-throat." Often it is a nervous complaint. Listen to the experienced broadcaster, or soloist in church or concert hall, or speaker. Watch them take up a position on any platform. They walk on quietly and stand easily, obviously quite calm—and all goes well. So when you feel a "frog," take a big breath and forget there is such a thing. If it won't be ignored, try and sing *through* it, and you will find that this will do the trick completely. Any violent clearance of the throat is likely to cause irritation, and more harm than good.

As a final suggestion, try and hear all the great singers and string players you possibly can. A violin will demonstrate the good "singing phrases" each singer should aim to secure.

William Byrd wrote, in the sixteenth century

"Reasons set down . . . to perswade every one to learne to sing.

First it is a knowledge easely taught, and quickly learned where there is a good Master and an apt Scoller.

2. The exercise of singing is delightful to Nature & good to preserve the health of Man.

3. It doth strengthen all the parts of the brest, and doth open the pipes.

4. It is a singular good remedie for a stutting & stammering in the speech.

5. It is the best meanes to procure a perfect pronunciation & to make a good Orator.

6. It is the onely way to know where Nature hath bestowed the benefit of a good voice, which guift is so rare, as there is not one among a thousand, that hath it: and in many, that excellent guift is lost, because they want Art to express Nature.

7. There is not any Musicke of Instruments whatsoever, comparable to that which is made of the voyces of Men, where the voyces are good, and the same well sorted and ordered.

8. The better the voyce is, the meeter it is to honour and serve God therewith: and the voyce of Man is chiefely to be imployed to that ende.

. . . .

Since singing is so good a thing,
I wish all men would learne to sing."

SKETCHING

Sketching as a hobby may well be regarded under five headings: Still-life and Interiors; Figures; Architecture; Landscapes; and Seascapes; the last three probably appealing to the layman most. Apart from water colours and oils, which are dealt with in another section under the title of Painting, the commonest mediums for sketching any of these five are: Pencil—easily first and of all-round value; Charcoal; Pen and Ink; Coloured Chalks; and Pastels.

Pencil.—The beginner would do well to concentrate on the use of pencil at first; an HB of good quality is excellent to start with; B's and BB's, and so on, being of increasing softness and tone. Sharpen your pencil to a point or wedge; and for paper use a moderately heavy Cartridge or Bank paper in block form.

Charcoal, by reason of the depth of tone it offers, is a favourite medium for quick sketches, such as figures, or a landscape where the dominant note is dark masses. A variety of tones can be obtained when charcoal is employed; rubbing with blotting-paper stubs or finger-tips should be avoided as they destroy the freshness of a sketch. Charcoal can be procured in various sizes in both vine and willow; when the sketch is finished spray with "Fixitif" and a diffuser to prevent smudging. Both can be obtained from a dealer in artists' materials. It is sprayed from about a foot and a half distant in a slanting direction. Cartridge paper can be recommended when using charcoal.

Pen and Ink.—A beginner will wisely draw his proposed pen and ink sketch in pencil first. The pencil can be rubbed out when drawing is completed. Quill or reed pens may be used, but a variety of nibs should be tried in order to find what type of line can be achieved with each. In a pen-and-ink drawing every line must be a working unit, and must be considered well before drawing, because it is often the omitted line which tells the story.

Indian ink bought ready mixed in bottles is the best medium, an unspillable bottle wedged in a box is useful for outdoor work.

Fig. 1.—Illustrating principles of perspective. Parallel lines meet at horizon, horizontal lines above eye-level slope down to horizon, below eye-level they slope up

Fig. 2.—Comparatively low horizon line with dominant interest in sky masses

For thin line sketches Bristol board may be used, but for a bolder and more expressive drawing a rough cartridge or board is advisable. The type of board or paper used is entirely a matter of taste and depends on the kind of drawing intended.

Coloured Chalks, coated with wood, like a pencil, are useful for rapid colour-notes which present themselves unexpectedly. Cartridge paper is the best to use in conjunction with these.

Pastels may be used to advantage when broad colour masses are required rather than a delicate, tinted drawing. Most landscapes and seascapes are best attempted in pastel. They break easily, but can be carried in a box in rows of corrugated cardboard, with the ends wedged with wadding.

Pastel sketches tend to rub, and as they are best unsprayed, they should be protected by tissue covers. Buy special pastel paper for this type of sketching, and rely on the advice of the artists' colourman.

Choosing the Subject.—To assist the amateur to select his composition, a set of cards with various-sized rectangles cut out of them can be made at home. These should be used as view-finders.

The great thing to remember when sketching is, not to attempt to use yourself as a camera. If you want some scene faithfully reproduced down to the smallest detail, take a snapshot of it. But if the grouping of some trees, a gated corner leading into a pasture, some city by-way where the eaves of old houses lean to one another across the road, take your fancy, then get out your sketching block.

When you meet a person for the first time there is always some feature of the person or clothes which dominates your impression of that person. If you compare your impression with that of someone else's, you will find that they will differ. In a similar way sketches of the same scene by different people will differ, because a sketch is a personal interpretation of the impression you get of the scene before you.

If you are sketching a town or country scene you must decide upon what particular aspect of that scene is the dominant point to you, and make that the main feature of your sketch. Quite interesting effects can be obtained by treating the adjacent portions less emphatically, also by the employment of a vignette. It is for this reason that directly you begin to search for "bits" that will make a good sketch when you are on a country walk, you may come to the conclusion that there are not such things. Whenever a bridge, or perhaps a woodland scene, appeals to you, there will be too many trees, or bushes around. But you must not be discouraged; choose the dominant note of the scene, be it the shadows thrown on the water under the bridge, or the bole of a beech, and draw in just as much of the accompanying scenery as balances your object.

Balance of Composition.—This question of balance is a very important one. It allows you in sketching from nature to shift a bush a little to the right, to engineer cloud effects, and so on, so that the balance of light and shade in the picture shall be good. The most strict rule is that the main object of your sketch should not be in the middle of your drawing; that is very bad craftsmanship. See always that the other objects included in the composition lead the eye to the dominant point, or climax, of your sketch.

Fig. 3.—High view-point sketch. The Sky is left clear

Landscapes.—When you have settled the composition satisfactorily, making sure that your paths look as if they lead somewhere, and that your trees are growing in a possible way, you must balance your shading too. A dark object needs light relief to balance it, but the balance of light and dark must not be distributed so that the sketch will divide into two distinct halves, one light, one dark.

One of the best ways of avoiding this is to experiment with the horizon line, lowering it or lifting it. This will show you just where it should be fixed to give the sketch the most vitality. Sketches of rolling pastures and low hills, for instance, can be treated from a high or low view-point. In the former, where there is more earth than sky, details of light and shade must be concentrated on in it, and the sky left clear. In the latter, the sky must not be left bare, or the picture will be dull and uninteresting; cloud effects must be introduced to complete the balance. (*See* Figs. 2 and 3.)

When you are choosing the dominant note of your sketch, remember that a series of horizontal lines convey immobility, vertical lines convey strength, and curved lines give life and movement.

Seascapes.—This needs to be remembered very carefully when doing seascapes—the most difficult type of outdoor sketching. In the seascape proper, instead of the static earth, you have a large expanse of water which is not motionless. Boats on the water move, too; the sails of fishing boats belly in the breeze; there is movement of people on the sands. It is only in seascapes where colour and tranquillity are the dominant note, and where the space allotted to the actual sea is small, that the artist can disregard the necessity of curved lines of movement.

Figures.—It is difficult to sketch figures well without constant practice, preferably practice in sketching from the nude. But the introduction of figures into landscapes should not be omitted because of that, for figures add life to the dullest of sketches.

When introducing a figure as an integral part of a landscape, great care should be taken that the figure or figures do not become the dominant feature, unless so required; but always be conversant with the structure of the figure; this also applies to the drawing of trees which need close study before their various characteristics can be successfully interpreted. Very important is the fact that the artist should appreciate the depth or third dimension of a tree, figure or any other object occurring in his composition, which brings us to the problem of perspective.

Perspective.—This subject should be

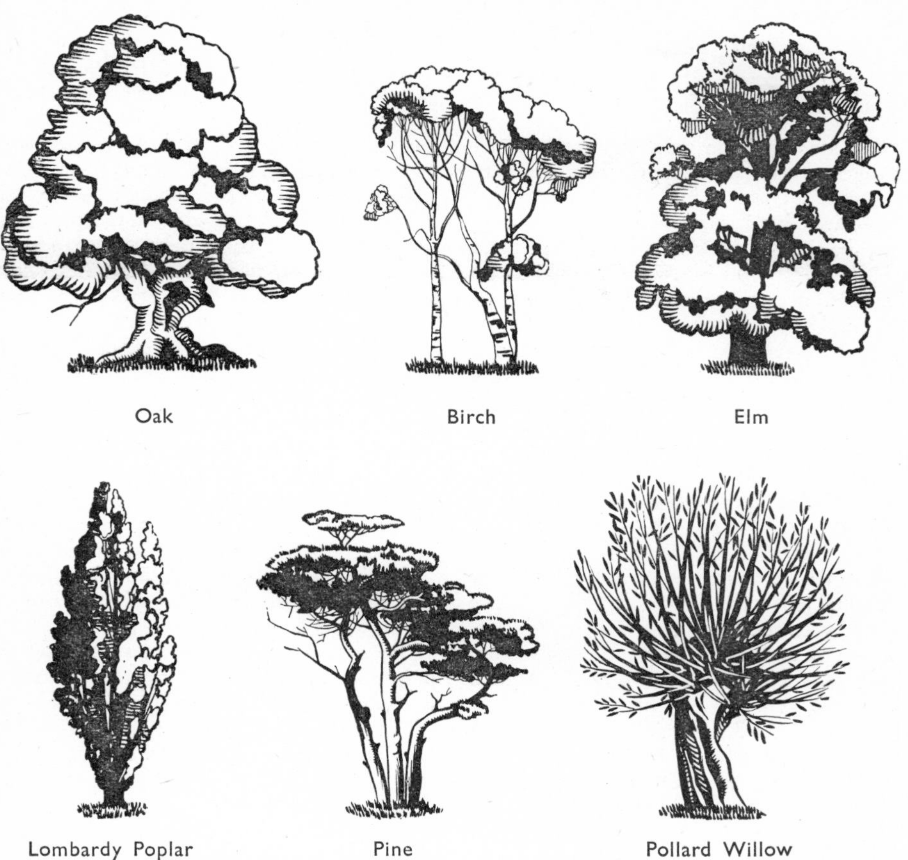

Fig. 4.—The Significant Forms of Trees

carefully studied. Distances though are as equally important as length and breath, and the juxtaposition of the individual elements can be controlled by a knowledge of perspective; it is well to remember that parallel lines travelling away from you converge to a given point on the horizon. Thus the horizontal lines of a building going away from you below the eye-level, i.e. your horizon line, slope up from you to it; and if the lines are above your eye-level, they slope down from you towards it. (*See* Fig. 1.)

Experimenting with media is the surest way of finding just which of them will give you the effect you need. Experiment, too, in types of sketching until you find the one you like best. Sketching is one of the few arts wherein the beginner should not begin by copying the work of others. Study the sketches of the masters with a dissecting eye to see how they get their effects. But do not make repeated copies of their sketches. You can only gain real satisfaction and a measure of success by putting on paper your interpretation of any scene that pleases you.

SOFT TOYS

Toy making is an art that appeals to all ages. With children their efforts may be crude but the results are none the less appreciated by the makers. When, however, the skill of the fingers is developed and is backed by good ideas and the ability to plan and design, there is no limit to the delightful articles that can be made, many of which are really beautiful.

There are a large number of branches of toy making, many of which could not be dealt with in this book. There is, however, one branch, that of soft toys or "Cuddle Toys," which is easy to do at home and which takes up no more room than an ordinary piece of needlework.

"Soft Toys" has now come to be applied only to toys that are really soft and cuddly and suitable for the very little folk. There are many stuffed toys that must have wire, glass eyes and hard parts to make them complete. These are an obvious source of danger.

Materials.—All materials for this type of toy making must be suitable to the style of toy. Fine felt is always effective and there are all kinds of materials specially made to look like fur. They are ideal if one can afford them. The beginner, however, will be wise to use oddments of cloth from the piece bag and only invest in the rather expensive fabrics when she is quite sure she is going to enjoy the craft.

Oddments of wool and thread are useful, while stout cotton and strong needles are essential.

Kapok, a vegetable down, is used for stuffing and is obtainable at most soft furnishers. It is extremely light and a little goes a long way. Blanket combings from a blanket factory are also good and cheap.

Tools.—A wooden skewer for stuffing the toy, fairly long needles, stout cotton, tailor's chalk, good scissors, pins, etc.

Stitching.—All stitching should be done by hand. Back-stitching is far more secure than machine-stitching. In the latter one thread may be tighter than the other that will break when a strain occurs.

Raw Edges.—These should be snipped frequently and in the case of sharp points, as at the tips of ears, the material should be cut off as near as possible to the stitching.

Felt or Cloth Balls.—(*See* Fig. 13.) This is a very simple and effective toy to make. It consists of six pieces of the same shape as in Fig. 1, sewn together. The pieces may be of felt or from soft cloth and as many colours as desired may be used. Felt, of course, is easier as the edges do not fray and the pieces can be over-sewn together, but be careful not to pull the sewing too tightly or a ridge will form.

If cloth is used turnings must be allowed and the sections back-stitched together on the wrong side.

To obtain the pattern mark a piece of paper out in ½-in. or ¾-in. or 1-in. squares as shown. The size will depend on the size of ball required. The dimensions given in Fig. 1 make a felt ball 12 in. round. Then study the diagram carefully and draw the shape on the squares to correspond with the one in the plan. Turnings are not allowed for. Cut out the pattern, pin it carefully on the material on the wrong side and draw round it with a soft dark pencil. There is no right side to felt, but the pencilled side should count as the wrong side. In the case of a material with a warp and weft try to get all the "selvedge" threads travelling the same way on all the pieces. Sew up all the seams with the exception of the middle half of the last one. Stuff through this aperture. Avoid making the ball too hard. Close the opening with top-sewing.

Woolly Ball.—This is ideal for a baby and for indoor play and as it can be made out of all kinds of oddments of wool it can cost nothing. These balls, however, take much more wool than is generally thought, so only little ones should be made at first. Wool used from un-

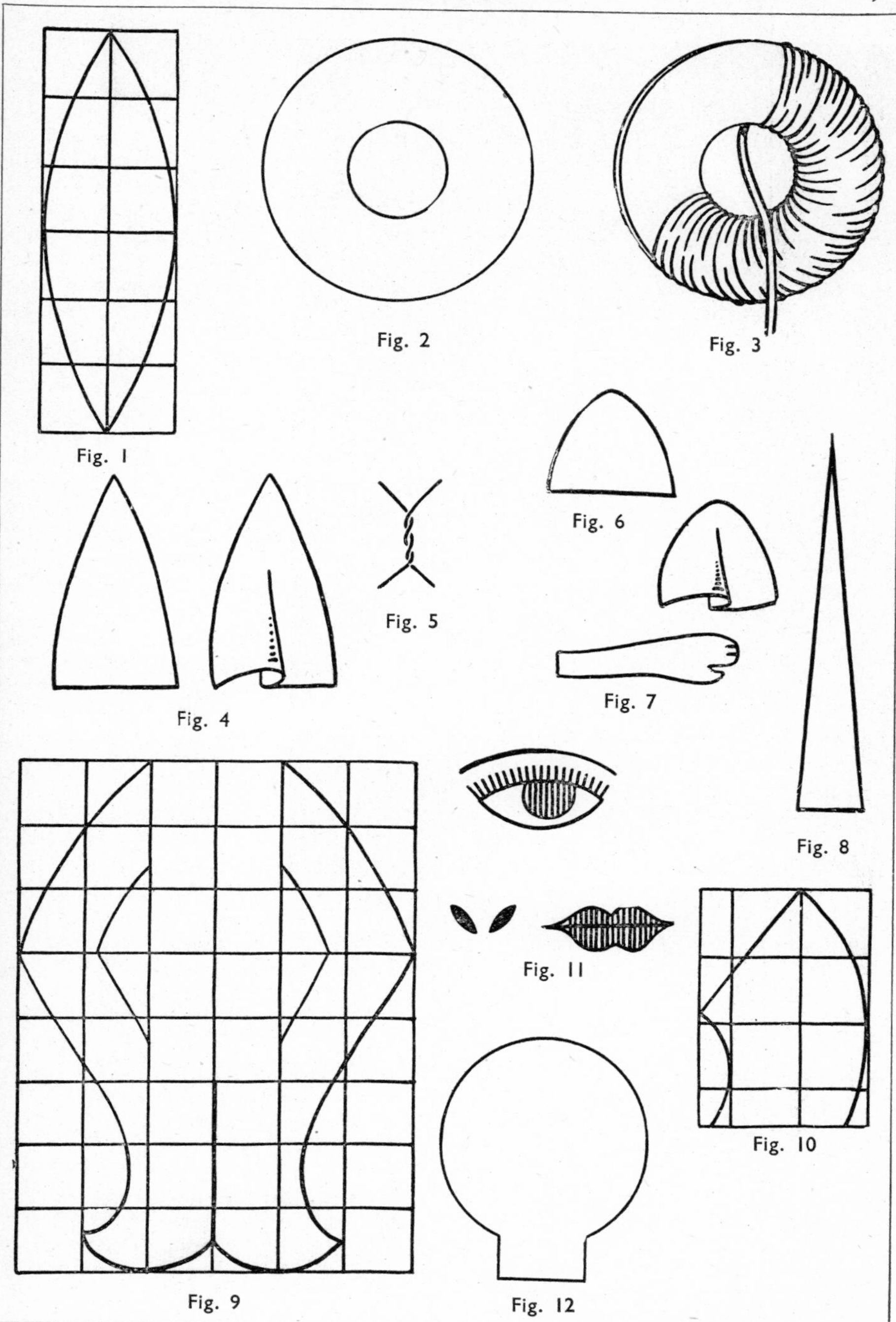
Fig. 1
Fig. 2
Fig. 3
Fig. 4
Fig. 5
Fig. 6
Fig. 7
Fig. 8
Fig. 9
Fig. 10
Fig. 11
Fig. 12

Fig. 13.—The Finished Toys

fine string and insert it through the outer edge of the wool and feel the way between the two thicknesses of cardboard. Work the needle all the way round in between and bring it out where it started. Tie tightly, then begin to cut the wool parallel with the outer edges of the cardboard until all the loops have been cut. Tighten the string round the centre of the ball as soon as possible and later make it extremely secure and firm. Tear away the cardboard as soon as all the cutting has been done.

Shape the ball with scissors by cutting away all loose ends and if necessary cutting away an even depth all over to make a firmer surface.

Billy Bunny and Baby Owl (*see* Fig. 13) are made with the woolly balls described above. One ball is smaller and should be securely tied to the other so that it is close up to the body. Circles of black felt or boot buttons can be used for eyes. Billy Bunny has two large flabby ears cut from an old felt hat, and the shape of his nose and mouth can be marked with black wool (*see* Fig. 5). The eyes are inserted to the side of the face.

Baby Owl is made of brown marled wool such as is used for stockings and men's pullovers and is rather more loosely wound to give a fluffy undershaped effect.

When the ball for the head is being cut do not cut the outer edge of the loops for about $\frac{1}{16}$ in. of the circumference. These threads being tightly stretched on the cardboard give a shiny effect for the beak and if a piece of black cotton is sewn over them

ravelled knitting is useful as it is curly and makes a very close ball.

Cut out two circles of stiff card as in Fig. 2. If compasses are not to hand, draw round a tumbler turned upside down, for the outside ring and a smaller circular object for the inside. It should be realized that the outside circumference of the cardboard ring is a little larger than that of the finished ball.

Place the two rings of cardboard together and wind the wool over and over the card as in Fig. 3. It should be firmly, evenly and systematically wound in order to get an even distribution of the wool. When it is quite impossible to wind any more, thread a darning needle with really stout thread or parallel to the edge of the cardboard they are fixed in position. Do not remove the cardboard from just behind this place. Two little brown or fawn felt or cloth ears can be inserted well to the side, pointing a little forward and two flat buttons facing straight forward do for the eyes.

Mother Mouse and Baby Mouse (*see* Fig. 13) are a real delight. Both are made with two woolly balls as above, but a good deal of the outside wool is cut away to give a firm surface. At one place when the winding is in progress white wool can be added to form a patch on the underside of the body. The shape of the ears is shown in Fig. 6. The tails are made of soft leather from an old glove stuck round a piece of string. Mother mouse's paws are little strips of leather widening at the end. In both cases the face is cut rather pointed and the chest flattened by cutting away wool.

The Elf is a very nice cuddly toy for a child. It can be made of any odd pieces of material. Fig. 9 shows the pattern drawn out on squared paper. The squares can be any size desired and according to the amount of material to spare. Cut out a back and a front in material and allow turnings.

Stitch all round except at the neck. Turn right side out and stitch seam between legs and inside bend of arms. Fill with Kapok until the body is about 1 in. thick. Commence with the toes and fill all the corners first, pushing the stuffing into place with skewer and being careful that all corners are filled.

The face is a moulded cardboard one, obtainable from toy shops for a few pence. The head is made of two pieces of material shaped as in Fig. 12, sewn together and stuffed. Take in a dart or two so that it is a nice, rounded shape. Sew the face on to one side and sew into position at the opening for the neck.

If a face cannot be obtained sew a piece of flesh-coloured material on to the pad and embroider or paint in the eyes, nose and mouth as in Fig. 11.

Make a hood from the pattern shown in Fig. 10. It has a seam up the front and down the back. Turn in the edge round the face and fix back with stitchery. Place the hood over the head and ease in round the neck and secure.

Make the neck frill and cuffs of fur, marabout, wool, ruched silk, etc.

All these toys are very easy to make because the patterns are so simple. The moment, however, the worker commences to make animal or bird shapes it is necessary to have a reliable pattern. For this reason it is quite impossible to deal with these here.

STAINING AND POLISHING

STAINING and polishing the pieces of furniture you have made may either improve or entirely spoil the appearance of your work.

There are various kinds of stain, viz. water, oil, varnish, spirit, wax, and chemical. Any of these may be purchased already made up, may be made up by a painter, or you may make them up yourself. The worker should consider the character of the wood of which a piece of furniture is made when deciding on the kind of stain to use and the general finish to apply.

Stains in powder form, requiring only the addition of water or spirit, are very useful and generally easy to apply with hope of success. Water stains are easier to apply than spirit stains as they do not dry so quickly. They are therefore not so patchy in effect. The disadvantage of water stain as compared with spirit stain is that it raises the grain of the wood. Furthermore, water stain cannot be successfully applied to a surface previously polished or varnished. Water stains include vandyke brown, raw umber, burnt umber, raw sienna, burnt sienna, aniline dyes and various prepared stains, such as Johnsons and Stephens. They may be bought as vandyke crystals (brown), walnut crystals (warm brown), mahogany crystals (dark red), black, bichromate of potash (red on mahogany, warm brown on oak). These can be mixed together to obtain various shades of mahogany and walnut colour.

Oil stains consist of the above-mentioned stains ground in oil. Japan black thinned with turpentine is a very useful stain which gives a good range of colour according to the amount of turpentine used. Various forms of creosote can also be mixed with turpentine and effectively used.

Varnish stains, so easily obtained at the cheap stores, are oil stains to which varnish has been added. They are the least satisfactory of all stains and you are advised to avoid them as they do not penetrate the wood, but lie on the surface and hide the grain of the wood.

Spirit stains are most easily made from spirit-soluble aniline dyes, such as bismarck and vandyke brown. Most druggists sell these dyes at about 1s. 6d. per ounce. Green, yellow and black stains are also obtainable. When purchasing stains it is useful to mention the purpose for which they are required.

Wax stains are made from beeswax dissolved in turpentine and stained with oil colours. Chemical stains are most commonly used in the form of permanganate of potash, ammonia, soda, carbonate of soda, bichromate of potash, salt, etc.

Preparing the Wood.—The preparation of a piece of work for staining begins as soon as the work is being put together. You must remember when putting your job together that if glue overflows from the joints on to the surface of any part it must be wiped off at once. If it is left to dry, it fills the grain of the wood and no stain can enter. Consequently the surface will be patchy in colour.

All surfaces must be glass-papered until they are quite smooth, rubbing finally with No. 0 glass-paper with the grain. Awkward corners, the angles between shelves and sides, rails and stiles and all junctions must have special attention. Wrap the glass-paper round a block of wood or cork.

Remove all oil or grease spots with a rag dipped in turpentine or benzine. If the wood is of poor quality, or not well finished, or coarse in grain, as oak, ash, etc., it will be advisable to fill the grain with a mixture which will help to make a smooth, even surface, and at the same time save a considerable amount of polish. There are many fillers which can be used for this purpose. Whiting and turpentine is a very simple filler for amateurs to use. Glue size may also be used—a quarter of a pound of size to a half gallon of water gives a useful strength. This is painted on, allowed to dry and then papered down. If the filler is too thin it will run, if too thick it cannot be rubbed into the pores, so the proportions of the mixture are easily determined.

If the filler is to be coloured, the usual pigments may be used, e.g. venetian red for mahogany, burnt umber or vandyke brown for walnut, dark oak, etc., and lamp black for very dark work.

Varnish may also be used as a grain filler. It should be papered down when set.

Polishing.—The easiest, and the oldest, method of polishing is by means of beeswax and turpentine. It is an old-fashioned method, but like many old-fashioned things, it is very good and has never been entirely displaced by the newer french polishing. You should try this method and so obtain experience of the ease with which fine results can be obtained before you attempt other methods.

Although it is customary nowadays to confine the use of wax polish to oak, there is no reason why it should not be used on almost any other wood. Time and "elbow grease" are the main factors in the production of a finely polished surface with an egg-shell gloss.

Where white woods are being polished white wax should be used, but for most jobs yellow beeswax is mixed with turpentine to be dissolved into a mixture of a consistency which may vary from a liquid state to that of soft butter. Whatever consistency is required can be obtained by adding either more wax or more turpentine. To dissolve the wax either shred it or warm it and add the turpentine. Be careful not to pour the turpentine on to the molten wax while it is near a flame or both wax and turpentine may catch fire.

When the mixture is cold it is ready for use. The wax is applied either with a brush or a rag. It should not be applied too thickly and should be rubbed well into the wood with a pad of coarse rag such as

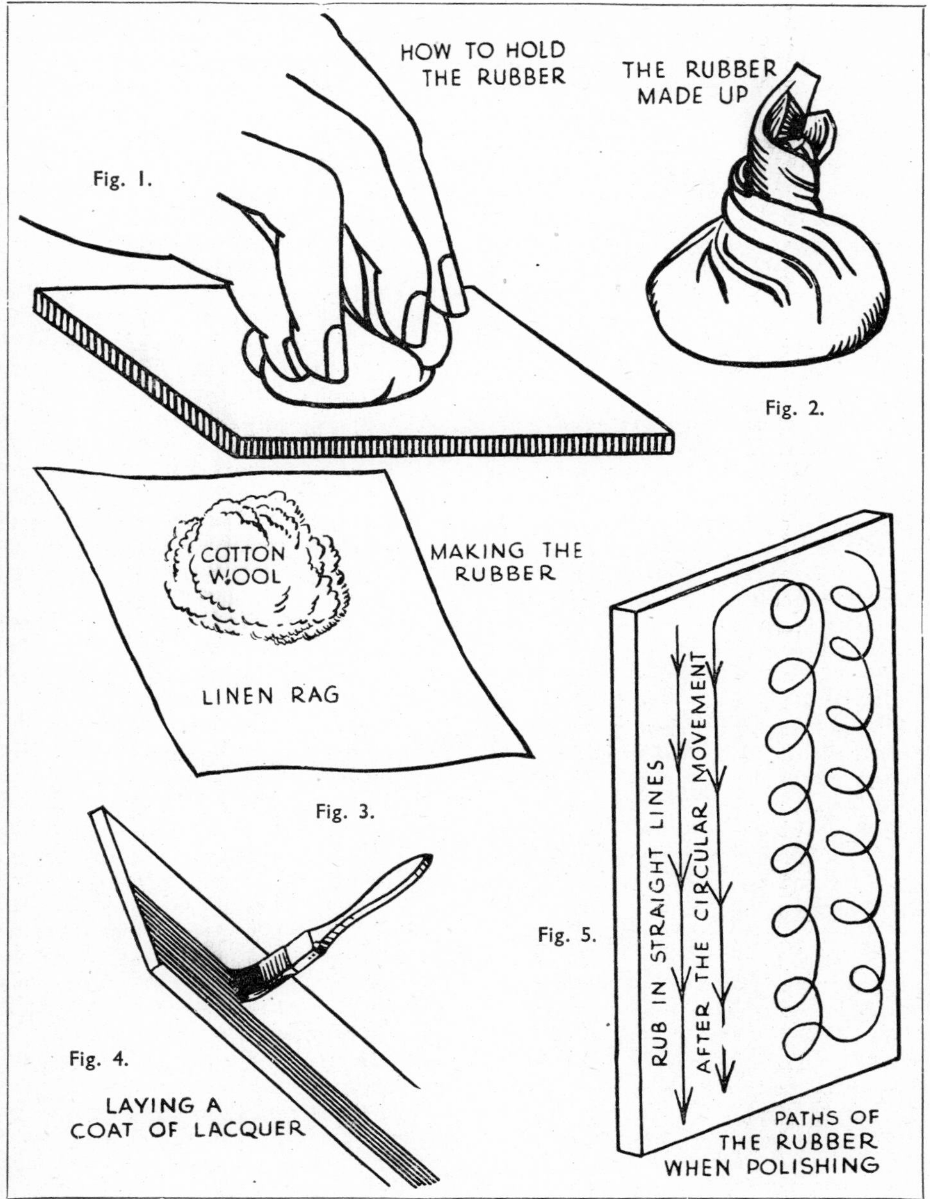

hessian. Next rub well with a softer rag of flannel or felt. If a smeared result is obtained, too much wax has been put on. Further vigorous rubbing will remedy this. If a sufficiently good smooth polish is not produced by the first rubbing, leave the wax to set for a day or two, apply another coat and rub thoroughly again. It is impossible to rub too much or too hard. If the wax is to be applied to a piece of carving or to an elaborate ornament or moulding, it should be soft and applied with a brush, rubbing with a stiff brush to obtain a polish.

Wax polishing is very suitably applied to oak which has been fumed, a process of colouring which will be described later.

French Polishing.—This is one of the commonest forms of finish. The preparation of the wood is carried out as previously described, the aim being to obtain a smooth hard surface on which to build up the polish.

French polish is made from shellac and methylated spirit. If a white polish is required which will not affect the colour of the wood, white shellac is used. If brown or orange shellac is used, the polish will slightly darken any wood on which it is used.

The polish can be bought ready made, and some of the proprietary brands are very easy to use, or it may be made by yourself. The latter method is strongly advised as by it you will learn more about the effects of slight differences in composition and be able to account for and correct any faulty work.

To make the polish put about 6 oz. of shellac in a pint of spirit, or put a quantity of shellac in a bottle and add spirit to about twice the height and leave it to dissolve. The bottle should be kept well corked when not in use or the spirit will evaporate and leave a thicker polish.

The Rubber.—A rubber with which to apply the polish is made from a piece of old linen rag and a pad of cotton-wool. The cotton-wool is placed in the centre of the piece of rag. A small amount of polish is poured on to it. The rag is folded carefully over the wool so as to leave the ends as a handle to the pad. The polish is squeezed through the wool and rag to the surface of the pad. The latter must be quite smooth, without creases. (*See* Figs. 1, 2, and 3.)

Bodying-in.—The surface to be polished having been "filled" and glass-papered perfectly smooth it is now ready for "bodying-in." The pad should be fairly wet for this initial operation. Rub lightly across the grain all over the surface and when well covered leave to set for a few hours. If rubbing is continued too long, the polish already laid will be lifted. When putting on the next and subsequent layers rub with a circular as well as a transverse motion. Do not work with a dry rubber and do not let the latter harden. Before putting on the second layer rub lightly with old fine glass-paper. Put a few drops of raw linseed oil on the paper and so prevent scratching of the surface. All lumpiness in the polish on the surface must be removed. Add another coat or two until a smooth body of polish is laid. Leave to set for a few days.

Working Up.—Glass-paper the surface until quite flat and dead, without shine. Wipe off the dust and rub over the surface lightly with a rag dipped in linseed oil. Charge the rubber with polish. Put a few spots of raw linseed oil on the surface of the rag which will be in contact with the wood—this will prevent the pad sticking and dragging the polish. The method of handling the rubber at this stage will make or mar the surface. Do not dab the rubber on the surface; do not rub heavily, or begin and end abruptly; do not use too much oil on the pad; keep the latter in motion while it is in contact; move with a circular motion.

If you wish to do a really good piece of work, keep the job in hand for several days, giving it a coat of polish and a light rubbing, then leaving it for a day to set. If the polish seems to have gone off a bit after standing for a day, you can conclude that it has sunk into the wood. The bodying process must therefore be continued until the surface remains good.

About four separate applications should be sufficient to work up a good polish on a close-grained wood. One or two more may be necessary on oak or ash.

As soon as any irregularity is noticed in the surface during the rubbing stop at once and leave to set and paper down to a smooth surface. If the surface of the polish is rough it may be due to using too little oil on the rubber. If the polish comes away in pieces or seems to break away, too much oil is being used.

Spiriting Off.—The durability and general excellence of polishing depends upon the thoroughness of the "bodying-in," the brightness depends upon the final process known as "spiriting off." This finishing process is similar to bodying excepting that, instead of polish in the rubber, towards the end methylated spirit alone is used. By it all the smears and rubber marks previously made must be removed till a glossy hard film of shellac, quite free from oil, remains. The amount of methylated spirit put into the rubber is increased as the amount of polish is reduced until all the polish is worked out of the rubber and the operation of spiriting off really begins. It must not be forgotten that an excess in the quantity of the spirit will be apt to wash the body of the polish away. Rub very lightly at first, increasing the pressure as the rubber dries. Towards the finish rub rather more in the direction of the grain than with a circular motion. The complete absence of oil may be detected by breathing on the work. If the moisture from the breath takes some time to evaporate, oil is still there; if oil is absent, the moisture disappears at once.

Fuming Oak.—As a means of colouring oak without raising the grain, fuming with ammonia is easily the best method. The effect on the wood is to colour it a greyish-brown and when this is wax-polished a delightful permanent finish is obtained. Very strong ammonia is used, i.e. with a strength known as ·880. Care must be taken not to release the fumes carelessly or unnecessarily as they are very pungent, and if the cork is removed from the bottle and the latter applied to the nose a nasty shock may result. There is no danger if ordinary care is taken.

The fuming takes place in a box which is fairly air-tight, and large enough to contain the piece of furniture to be fumed. The joints can be made air-tight by sticking strips of paper over them. A three-ply tea-box is very useful for this purpose.

The article is placed in the box and one, two or three saucers of ammonia placed in with it (the quantity depending upon the size of the article and the depth of colour required), and the lid put on; or the saucers containing ammonia are placed on or around the article and the box put on over the top of all.

The time of exposure depends upon the darkness of the colour required, the longer the exposure given the darker the resultant colour. If the article is left in for one night, a fairly dark colour is obtained.

The progress of fuming can be observed by boring a hole in the side of the box, inserting a stick of the same oak as that being fumed, and withdrawing it periodically for inspection.

It is of interest to know that this system is the modern substitute for leaving furniture in a stable to be acted upon by the ammonia fumes which are naturally present, a method which is still effective for those who have the use of a stable occupied by horses.

The box may be filled with articles to be fumed, so saving space. It must not be overlooked that some varieties of American oak are not susceptible to ammonia vapour, but remain unchanged in colour. Any wood can be tested by holding it for a few moments over the mouth of the ammonia bottle. Sapwood will not take fume and comes from the box almost white. If this has happened the light portions must be stained to match.

Walnut is always richer in colour if it is oiled before polishing. It is not necessary to stain this wood, indeed you spoil good wood if you do so before polishing.

If you oil oak before polishing, do not forget that a yellow tinge will result which may not be the colour you require before finishing with white wax. Wax and oil-polishing table tops do not suffer from the application of hot tea-pots, etc.

Staining and Polishing the Floor Margins.—The floor should be cleaned and a coating of glue size painted on. Leave this to dry. Rub down with fine glass-paper. Mix the powder stain thoroughly with equal quantities of varnish, linseed oil and turpentine. Brush on carefully and leave to set for a day or two. Rub down again with fine glass-paper, stop up all nail holes and open joints with stained putty. The latter is made by mixing some of the powder stain with a little oil and working into the putty. Wipe over with a damp rag or leather and varnish. A second coat of varnish of good hard-drying quality will give a very durable finish. Another cheap and effective floor stain is made by mixing paraffin with ordinary creosote, thinning it down to the colour required. This may be equally well applied to the ceiling joists and beams in an open ceiling.

A good polisher for use when wax-polishing the floors can be made by covering a brick with layers of old blanket and fixing it to the head of an old sweeping broom.

Varnishing.—There are various kinds of varnish. Do not use cheap varnish. Clear varnish is used in all cases where it is desired to show up the grain beneath to the best advantage. A very good effect can often be obtained when it is applied to the bare unstained wood, or the work may first be stained and then varnished.

When there are no special reasons why the grain should be shown up, e.g. when a piece of inferior wood has been used, a varnish stain may be used, that is a varnish with which a dye has been mixed. This is especially useful for renovations or where a piece of new wood has been put into an old piece of furniture and it is desired to match up with the old work. Also, where it is necessary to recolour a part of a piece of work that has already been varnished, it is advisable to wash the whole of the work with weak soda water, wash off with clean water, leave to dry and then give a coat of varnish stain. In such a case the latter should be at least as dark in colour as the old varnish. Do not mix varnishes of different makes. Varnish will not dry on an oily surface.

Brush Lacquering.—Cellulose lacquer may be obtained in a wide range of colours. Cellulose has the advantage over enamel and paint in that it dries fairly quickly and flows out well, leaving no brush marks.

When using lacquer on wood it is advisable to consider the character of the wood to be lacquered. Close-grained woods such as birch and beech take lacquer much more effectively than open-grained woods like oak. The grain must, in any case, be carefully filled. Paint the surface with a glue size, that is, ordinary glue thinned down with water. Apply it with a brush; do not brush vigorously to froth up the size and take care not to allow the corners to be filled up. Allow the size to dry out thoroughly. Rub down with fine glass-paper. Rub well with a rag to remove all dust.

As cellulose lacquer hardens rapidly it cannot be worked with a brush in the same way as varnish is worked. Once laid on evenly it should be left. It is best to have the work lying in a horizontal position. A flowing coat is applied with a flat brush, the surface being covered as quickly as possible. This is allowed to dry thoroughly hard. If a second coat is necessary or another colour is being applied on top of the first it is best to leave the work overnight. Any of the colours can be mixed together to produce a special shade or tint.

An "egg-shell" finish, slightly duller and smoother than the straight lacquer finish is obtained by sprinkling fine pumice powder over the surface and rubbing briskly in one direction with a soft pad. This kind of finish can be applied to furniture of all kinds, large and small. It can also be used to add a line or a spot of colour to a stained and polished piece of work. The edge of the base or side of a tray, a box or a bookstand, handles and knobs of drawers and doors, etc., can be so treated with pleasing effect.

Other Finishes.—Enamels in a great variety of colours can be used to put a finish on much of the work done by the amateur. Gold lacquer and aluminium paint are suitable for picture frames and similar pieces of work. Such finishes are very useful when a frame requires freshening up a little.

Wood dyes can be obtained in a wide range of colour. Polish which can be easily applied with a flat brush is now available. Special wood fillers, coloured to fit specified woods, are also obtainable, as are coloured wax polishes and french polishes. All these make the work easier to do and a good finish less difficult to obtain.

Various Hints.—Before re-polishing furniture it should be thoroughly washed, but not soaked. Use very soapy soft water and a piece of cheese cloth and wash all parts. Then wring out another piece of cheese cloth in hot water and put on it a little furniture polish or reviver, and rub well on to the furniture.

Mahogany is easily darkened by fuming. It can also be darkened and made richer in colour by rubbing with raw linseed oil. Do not use too much oil as all this must dry out before polish can be applied. This wood can also be darkened by means of a solution of bichromate of potash. Obtain a few pennyworth of bichromate of potash crystals from the chemist, place a tablespoonful in an 8-oz. medicine bottle and leave to dissolve. It is not necessary to wait until all the crystals are dissolved before painting the liquid into the wood. This stain will raise the grain of the wood. It will therefore be necessary to rub down with fine old glass-paper.

If it is desired to stain oak to a very dark colour to match "antique" furniture, add a little Brunswick black to the brown stain being used.

Various coloured stains can be made from the spirit dyes usually sold for leather work. Ordinary inks are also useful for producing special effects.

A good deal of oak work is now finished without staining. If this work is accidentally stained with ink, etc., the marks can generally be removed by bleaching with a weak solution of oxalic acid. The strength of the solution is about one pennyworth of acid to a pint of hot water. This is painted on to the stain.

A still weaker solution is most useful for removing stain and polish from any oak job it is desired to put into modern finish, i.e. a natural colour with a wax polish.

Oak can be slightly stained by painting with a solution of washing soda and water.

Limed oak finish can be easily produced by painting the work with ordinary limewash and leaving it for two or three days. Then rub off the limewash and polish with a rubber of coarse hessian. A brownish colour is also given by this process. There are patent mixtures now on sale which give the same results.

During the process of polishing bruises may be seen on the surface of the wood which have previously been overlooked. If the fibres are not cut but simply crushed, they may be raised by wetting well with water. Cover the place with a piece of paper and apply a hot flat iron. When the fibres are swollen back to the surface rub with fine glass-paper and proceed with the polishing.

Do not use too much stain as this may cause the wood to swell; it will also weaken the glue joints. If too much stain is used on veneer, the stain may go right through to the glue beneath and loosen it.

Do not try to mix spirit and oil stains with water stains.

Do not brush on the stain near to other work. The brush may splash and spoil it.

To finish basswood and other white woods, stain with a solution of vandyke crystals as a base; leave to dry and observe the colour; if too cold and dull add a further coat of mahogany (red) stain. Experiments should be made on a spare piece of wood to obtain the desired shade. Wax polish with one of the commercial polishes or a mixture of beeswax and turpentine.

Another method is as follows. After staining apply a coat of french polish with a camel-hair mop. This coat of polish may be tinted, to improve the colour, with any of the spirit stains previously mentioned. Allow this coat to dry and carefully rub down the surface with a fine glass-paper. Apply another coat of polish, glass-paper down again when dry and then polish with wax.

Another method is to stain, rub down with fine glass-paper, restain if necessary, and paint with varnish. Leave to set, rub down with fine glass-paper, varnish again, leave to set, rub down again, varnish a third time and leave to set. If the surface is not absolutely smoothly varnished repeat the operations. A quicker result will be obtained if, after staining and glass-papering and staining again, a coat of glue size is applied. Leave this to set and then rub down with glass-paper. Now apply the varnish. One coat may be sufficient, but if the surface is not perfect, glass-paper it down and apply a second coat.

A smooth finish, slightly less shiny, may be obtained by working on the first hard coat of varnish with a wax polish.

TO FINISH OAK

Natural Colour.—Apply wax polish, rubbing it in with hessian or shavings, finishing with a soft cloth. Do not expect a high polish from this method, nor a quick one. If the operations are repeated in a few days' time, a higher polish will be obtained. A good result is obtained with less labour if, after applying the wax, it is rubbed in with the hessian and left to set for a day. It should then be rubbed with a soft cloth.

Yellowish-brown.—Rub in raw linseed oil, leave to dry and finish with wax polish.

Dark Brown or Antique Shade.—Stain with vandyke crystals to the desired colour. Leave to set. Rub down with fine glass-paper. Apply a small amount of raw linseed oil and leave to dry. Apply one or two coats of french polish with a camel-hair mop. Leave to set, then glass-paper, and finish with wax polish.

Another method is to paint the work with liquid ammonia, then apply a coat of soda water. Leave to set, glass-paper down, give two coats of polish and finish with wax polish.

Another method still is to thin down creosote with paraffin; brush on until the desired shade is obtained, leaving the work to dry after each application. Glass-paper down, apply french polish and wax polish as above.

To match up antique work it may be necessary to add a little black stain to the brown.

Light Oak.—Stain with a weak solution of vandyke crystals or a weak solution of bichromate of potash, glass-paper down when dry and then finish as above. If the colour is too warm in tone add a little green stain or tint the polish with a green spirit stain.

Black Oak.—Stain with black water stain; when dry rub down with fine glass-paper and apply two coats of black polish made up by adding spirit black to the polish. Finish as above.

Weathered Oak.—Stain with a weak solution of black and vandyke water stain, to a greyish shade. Finish as for brown oak.

To Finish Walnut.—The beautiful colour of walnut is best finished by simple wax polish. It may be darkened, and still preserve its beauty, by applying a coat of raw linseed oil. This must be left to dry and a wax polish then applied. Any sap-wood should be stained to match before oiling or polishing.

To Finish Mahogany.—A good colour is obtained by staining with bichromate of potash; when dry the grain is filled with a paste made of fine plaster of Paris. This is well rubbed into the pores of the wood and the surplus removed by rubbing vigorously with hessian before the paste sets. Clean out all angles and corners with a pointed stick. The paste may be tinted with any reddish powder to avoid it showing white in the grain. There are many patent wood fillers on the market which can be used instead of the one mentioned above. When the filler has hardened, rub the surface with a small amount of raw linseed oil to bring up the colour. Rub carefully with fine glass-paper and then with a soft cloth. Leave the work for several hours and then apply a coat of polish with the mop. Leave to set; rub down, apply another coat of polish and repeat the setting and rubbing processes and then finish with wax polish. If it is desired to apply a finish of french polish proceed as previously described instead of wax polishing.

STAMP COLLECTING

To few of us is given the opportunity to travel, and whilst books which tell of the adventures of others are of great interest, there is no volume which will give its owner so much joy as that containing a personally collected series of postage stamps of all nations.

The keen philatelist, or stamp collector, learns a great deal of world history, is able to visualize foreign lands, and is able, by studying his collection, to trace events, both political and industrial, of all the countries in the world.

There are several ways of commencing a stamp collection. One can, of course, obtain many from friends who work in offices, or one can buy and exchange. The first method is not always satisfactory for unless one's friends work in the offices of firms with world-wide business, the stamps of only a few countries will be secured, and as a rule these will only be of the usual letter-post face value.

Packets of stamps can be purchased at almost any stationers, and whilst this method of collecting is satisfactory for the beginner, the stage is soon reached when any one packet will yeild perhaps no more than one fresh specimen. This naturally adds to the cost but not to the value of those selected for the album. We are speaking, of course, of the cheap packets which are sold from 2d. to a shilling or so each.

As the collection progresses, more expensive packets are bought, and later, stamps will be purchased singly from the regular dealers in stamps.

Before going further into the ways of acquiring stamps foı the collection, however, let us see how the collection should be kept. Possibly after a few weeks' work you have gathered a thousand or so stamps, many of which may be duplicated. Most keen collectors know immediately whether or not they have any given stamp in their collection, but the novice has not yet arrived at this stage.

Undoubtedly the only method of classifying the stamps satisfactorily is first of all to sort them into countries and then into age and face value. It is here that one of the several stamp catalogues published will prove of value. We will return to these catalogues later, however. We must first know how to keep the stamps so that they are not only classified, but are available for instant inspection.

Albums.—The variety of albums on the market is legion, and the prices range from two shillings up to several pounds. The cheaper type of album will do very well for a start, but as the collection increases in value as well as in numbers, the collector is advised to invest in a loose-leaf album, the stamps being fixed on one side of the page only. This is necessary because some foreign stamps are not printed with permanent inks, and if these come into contact with the faces of other stamps, both the appearance and the value is likely to be damaged.

A further advantage of the loose-leaf system of cataloguing is that, as political events move so rapidly to-day, new stamps are more frequently issued than they were a few years ago, and any system that enables these new issues to be added without upsetting the existing arrangements is of real value.

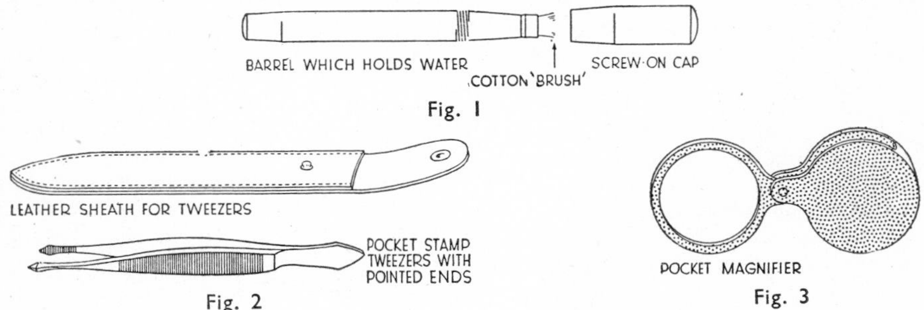

Fig. 1

Fig. 2

Fig. 3

Many albums are so printed that a space is left for certain stamps, small facsimile diagrams sometimes being printed in the space to indicate the places.

The Identification of Stamps is a matter of concern to the beginner, for in a good many cases, no indication as to the country of origin is printed on the stamp. Where the postmark is decipherable, of course, this simplifies matters considerably, but the percentage of readable postmarks or franks is none too high. British stamps do not have the country of origin printed thereon, but of course, they are easily identified by the portrait of the ruling sovereign of the time of issue. Most colonial stamps give the name. The names of foreign stamps are not, of course, printed in English or even always in Roman characters. Bavaria appears as "Bayern." France appears as "Republique Francaise," and so on.

Russian and Chinese stamps are printed in their own particular characters.

In order to assist readers to identify stamps, a short list is given below showing the marks on the stamps and the country of origin.

A & T—Annam and Tonquin.
Açores—Azores.
A Payer te Betalen—Belgium.
B.C.A.—British Central Africa.
Bengasi—Tripoli.
British South Africa Company—Rhodesia.
Buchanan—Liberia.
C Ch.—Cochin China.
Ceskych Skautu }
Cesko Slovenska } Czecho-Slovakia.
Chine—French China.
Colonies Poste—French Colonies.
Correio—Portugal.
Correo Oficial—Spain.
Cote d'Ivoire—Ivory Coast (Fr.)
CTOT—Bulgaria.
Deficit—Peru.
Deutsche Reich—German Empire
España—Spain.
Filipinas—Philippine Islands.
Franco Bollo di Stati—Italy.
Franco Bollo Postale Toscano—Tuscany.
Frimarke—Norway.
Helvetia—Switzerland.
Impuesto de Guerra—Spain (war tax).
Kais Kon. Zeitungs Stampel—Austria.
Kongeligt Post—Denmark.
Lima—Peru.
Maroc—French Morocco.
Mejico—Mexico.
Napoletana—Naples.
Nederland—Holland.
Norge—Norway.
Orts Post—Switzerland.
Polska—Poland.
Post Zegel—Holland.
Rayon—Switzerland.
Republica Portuguesa—Portugal.
Rn or Rin—Japan.
Romana—Rumania.
Sen.—Japan.
Tical—Siam.
U.G.—Uganda.
Van Diemen's Land—Tasmania.
Zeitungs—Austria.

This is by no means comprehensive but it will be useful to the beginner.

Having classified the stamps according to countries, the next step is to affix them in the album in their correct places. As has been said, many albums are real guides in this respect, but as one may frequently have to move stamps to another position, it is obviously necessary that they be stuck in quite lightly.

The best method of affixing stamps to pages is by means of the small gummed transparent mounts especially supplied for the purpose. These mounts are quite cheap, costing about a penny a hundred (if bought in small quantities). First of all, however, we must remove the collected stamps from the portions of envelopes to which most of them adhere. This is best done by putting the stamps face down on a piece of blotting paper, and then damping the backs with water applied with a small camel-hair brush. The envelope paper can then be peeled off quite easily. The stamps should next be placed on another sheet of blotting paper until they are quite dry.

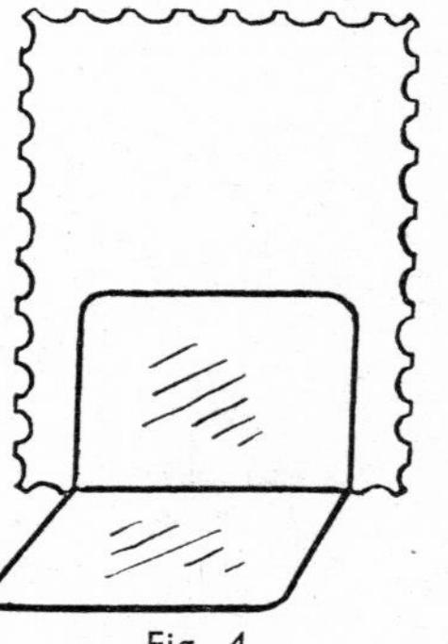

Fig. 4

The accompanying illustration shows how to affix the mounts to stamps. It is better to fix them sideways than at the top, for they are then less likely to be damaged when closing the album. Stamps should be set in the album in chronological order, each set, of course, being placed in order as regards face value.

Those who take stamp collecting seriously will never mount in their albums a stamp that is in any way damaged—for instance, one having a torn corner, perforations and so on. The beginner may like to put them in until he obtains better specimens, but apart from personal gratification, there is no point to be served by doing so.

Sooner or later the collector will find that he needs to know more about stamps than how to discover their country of origin, and

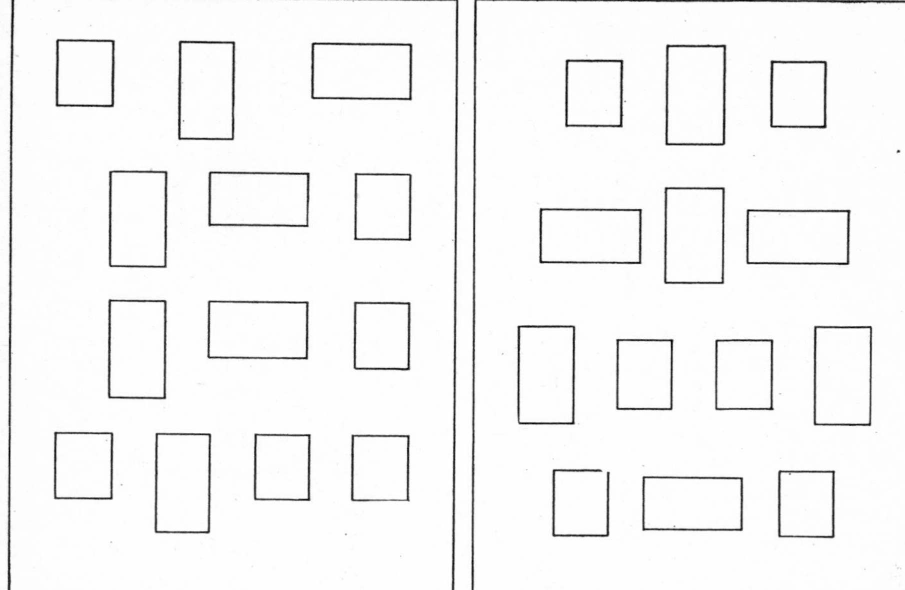

Fig. 5.—Bad Page Arrangement

Fig. 6.—Same Stamps, but Better Arrangement

it is here that the stamp catalogues previously referred to will be of the greatest value. There are several such catalogues on the market, and the best plan when buying is to go to a reputable dealer and obtain his advice. The same thing applies to information concerning fakes, watermarks, overprintings, reprints and so on. As far as faked stamps are concerned, these were — and still are — produced for the express purpose of deceiving collectors. Naturally those stamps that are rare are the chief object of attention. Apart from the printing of faked stamps, there are such things as faked watermarks, imperforate stamps, overprints and so on. The detection of fakes is no easy matter and many an expert has been deceived.

Much may be done, however, if the collector tackles the job in the right way, without hurry, giving to his task every care and attention. The design of the stamp should first of all be considered. Where possible the suspected stamp should be compared with the genuine one. In the days when stamp faking was first begun, the fakes were rather crude, and a comparison between the fake and the genuine stamp quickly brought to light the differences. To-day, however, the process of reproduction has so much improved that it is not so much in the general design as in the smaller features that mistakes are discovered.

Watermarks.—Only much study will give the collector the requisite knowledge of watermarks and so on, and here again, the faker has been busy. A watermark is "moulded in" the paper, usually at the time of manufacture, although a very few countries adopt the principle of adding an imitation "watermark" afterwards. When held up to the light, a design or other form is readily visible. The new issue (begun in August, 1934), of British stamps shows up the watermark better if the stamp is placed, face down, on the table.

A good method of detecting any watermark is to place the stamp face down in a black dish, such as is used by photographers for developing negatives, and to drop a small amount of benzine on the back of the stamp. The watermark will then show up very distinctly. The benzine evaporates quickly and will not damage the stamp in any way.

One London dealer has invented a special watermark detector consisting of a card in which are punched a number of holes covered by coloured transparent material. The stamp is placed on one of the "holes" and held up to the light and the watermark is then visible. Most stamp catalogues reproduce specimen watermarks of the different countries, and these should be studied.

No outline of the subject of stamp collecting, however brief, would be complete without reference to the various societies and periodicals devoted to the study of stamps. There are not many journals on the subject, but the reader is advised to subscribe regularly to one or other of them if he wishes to learn much about his hobby. Every ardent collector, however, will wish to join a philatelic society. The Royal Philatelic Society is the goal at which to aim. There is, however, the Junior Philatelic Society, membership of which costs very little, whilst the benefits it confers on its members are large. By mixing with other enthusiasts, the collector will not only add to his store of knowledge, but will be given advice as to the purchase of stamps of all kinds.

There are, of course, local clubs which it is well worth joining, and for the beginner these provide excellent opportunities for the sale and exchange of good specimens.

STENCIL CRAFT

A LARGE amount of decorative work of all kinds is done nowadays by means of stencils. These are made from pieces of stiff paper or thin metal with holes cut in them to form a pattern. Colour is applied to the surface to be decorated by dabbing with a stiff bristled brush through the holes. The method offers good opportunities to those people who have good taste in decoration but cannot handle a paint brush or pencil in the ordinary way.

A very great variety of use can be found for stencilling. Stencilled patterns can be applied to almost any material that will take colour. Curtains, bed-spreads, clothing, tea-cosies, cushions, door- and wall-panels, articles of painted furniture, book-covers, table-cloths and runners, leather goods and many other articles can be effectively decorated in this medium.

Tools and Materials are few and quite inexpensive. A sharp pointed knife is necessary. Any kind will do provided the blade is of good steel that can be brought to a fine point and maintained. Small blades called carton nibs which can be fitted to a pen holder can be purchased quite cheaply. (*See* Fig. 2.) The point of the cutter is kept sharp by constant rubbing on a piece of fine emery cloth glued to a piece of wood as in Fig. 1. Special stencil paper can be prepared by painting thick paper, such as manila paper, with a mixture of boiled linseed oil and turpentine and leaving it to dry. The surface upon which the paper is cut should be firm but not hard. If wood is used, the point of the knife will be dragged with the grain, if a zinc slab is used the point of the knife will be quickly blunted. Cardboard is the best material for use as a cutting board provided it is frequently renewed.

The object of coating the paper with oil is to make it resist the action of any paint that will be deposited upon it. Another method of waterproofing is by the application of "knotting" varnish. This is painted all over one side of the paper, which is hung up to dry before the other side is covered. Waterproofing can be applied either before or after the pattern has been cut.

If oil colours are used in stencilling, the plates are cleaned with a cloth soaked with turpentine. If water colour or distemper is used, the plate should be washed with water as the paint becomes dry and renders it brittle and liable to break, besides filling up the small holes and spoiling the outlines.

Brushes.—Any short stiff bristle brush will do for dabbing on the paint. Gloy brushes can be used for small work, old shaving brushes can be cut down to a

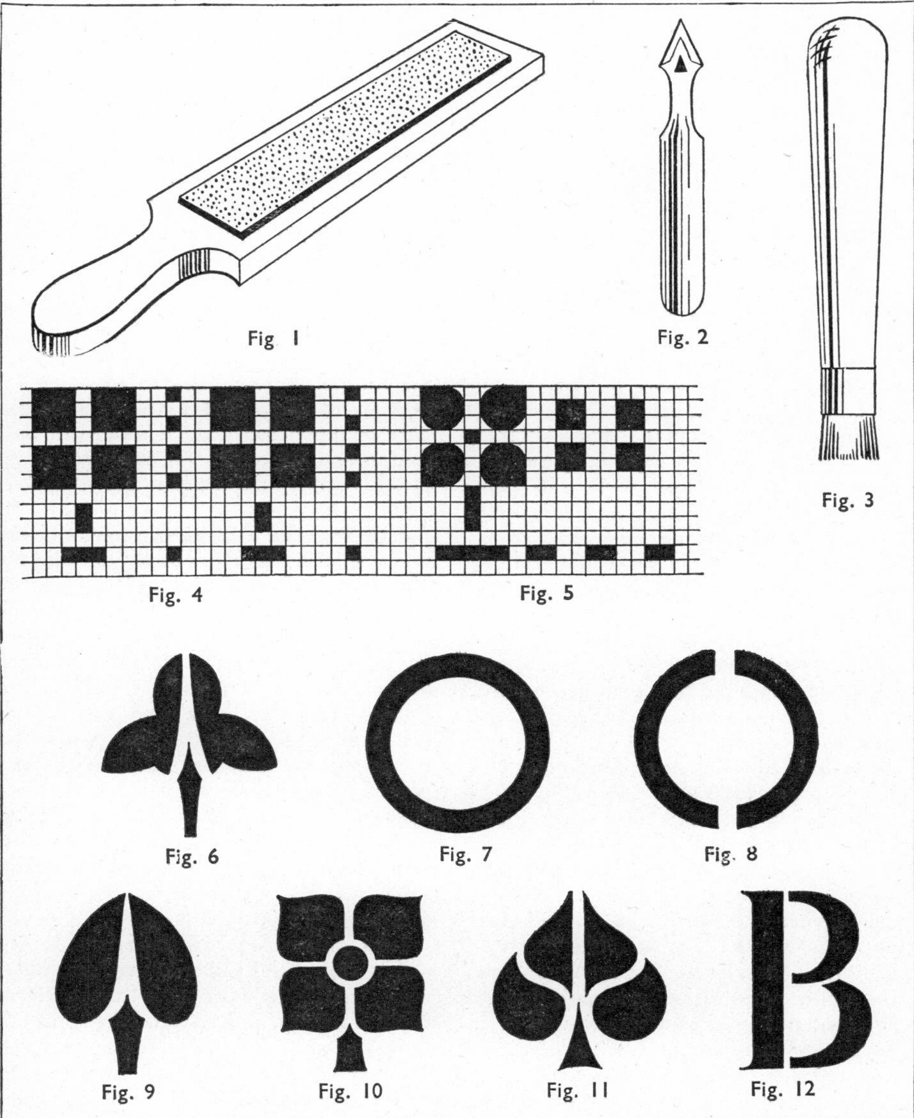
Fig. 1 Fig. 2 Fig. 3 Fig. 4 Fig. 5 Fig. 6 Fig. 7 Fig. 8 Fig. 9 Fig. 10 Fig. 11 Fig. 12

square-ended short bunch of bristles for larger work, or special stencil brushes may be purchased for a few coppers each. (*See* Fig. 3.)

The Colours.—You are advised against using artists' oil-colours unless they are mixed with a copal varnishing medium to speed up the drying.

Stencil oil colours already mixed with medium can be purchased in tubes or bottles and, provided the instructions given with them are followed, they are the best to use on all articles which are to be handled or exposed to the weather. Ordinary water colours, poster colours, stains, dyes and coloured inks are all useful on various materials or in certain circumstances, dark patterns, for instance, on a light ground.

Designing Stencil Plates.—You should begin on a simple design. Not only will you learn a good deal about the possibilities but you will also discover some of the difficulties which might just as well be met on a simple job involving only a small waste of time in the event of failure.

Patterns can be either positive or negative. If you want a pattern in the positive cut it out and leave the background. You will then apply the paint through the holes and obtain a positive. result. If you want a negative pattern cut away the background and apply the paint to it.

The very best way to begin designing stencil plates is to use squared paper as a background. For small work this paper can be cut and prepared and give quite satisfactory service.

Fig. 4 shows a simple pattern cut in squared paper which could be used on a wall, on a door or almost anything and which will vary in size according to the use. Fig. 5 shows the same idea made a little more interesting by taking off the corners of the squares, and adding one or two other lines.

Use of Ties.—This preliminary use of squared paper will make it easy for you to realize that the pattern in stencil plates must be tied together with narrow bands which prevent pieces of the pattern dropping out. Fig. 7 shows what happens to the letter O if no ties are left and Fig. 8. shows where they may be placed to hold the centre in position. The ties prevent the completion of the letter when the paint is applied to the plate, but this is a legitimate feature in all stencilling In order that the ties shall not upset a design they are used as lines in the construction of any pattern. As, for example, veins in a leaf shown in Figs. 6, 9, 10 and 11 and in the letter B in Fig. 12.

Figs. 13 and 14 show more suggestions for simple designs based on squared paper.

Transferring the Pattern.—Having sketched out the design it can be transferred if necessary, to the specially prepared paper, that is if it has not already been drawn direct on to the latter. The transfer can be made by placing the original underneath the prepared paper and tracing over the lines which are seen underneath. If the pattern cannot be seen through the prepared paper the following method can be adopted. Rub with soft lead pencil the back of the paper on which the design is drawn, covering the whole of the area of the design. Now place this paper on top of the prepared paper and draw over the lines of the pattern with a hard pencil. This will transfer the pattern in black line on to the prepared paper. You will find this hint invaluable when you cannot use a piece of carbon paper for transferring a pattern of any kind. If you want to transfer lines on to a black or dark coloured background instead of black lead pencil use chalk on the back of the paper bearing the design and transfer a white line.

Cutting the Plate.—Cutting a stencil plate is just another form of drawing. Use your knife as you would a pencil, but keep it a little more upright. Do not allow the knife to lean over sideways either to the right or the left so as to cut under the line or to make a bevelled cut sloping inwards. If the paper is torn when the knife is being used any broken tie can be repaired by means of strips of gummed paper. Any patches put on in this way must be waterproofed. See that the cut is made clean through the paper at the very commencement of the stroke. Start at the centre of a pattern and so avoid dragging the plate.

It is difficult to cut small round holes with a knife. A punch, as used for leather work, will do the work more easily and give a better result. The punch cutter must be kept sharp or a rough edge will be produced. This can be done by rubbing the outside of the cutter carefully on a piece of fine emery cloth, revolving it in the fingers as it moves backwards and forwards. Remove the slight burr from the inside of the cutter by putting the end of a pencil into it and working it round firmly. This will turn the burr back again and it is removed by a light rub on the emery cloth.

If you hold up the cut plate against the light or against a piece of paper you will

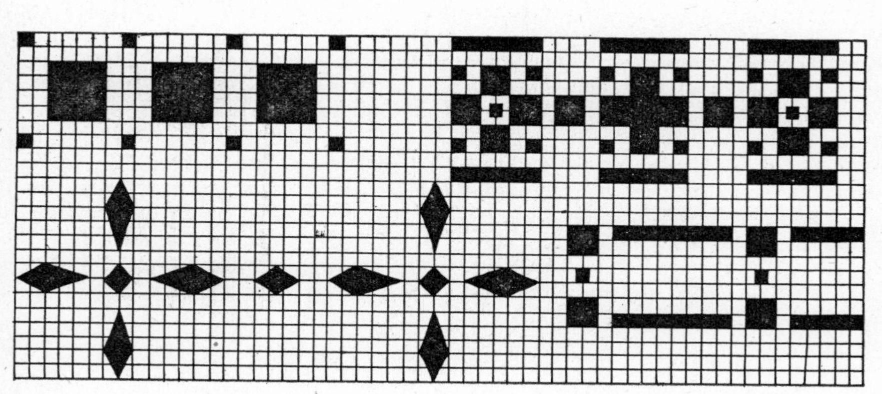

Fig. 13

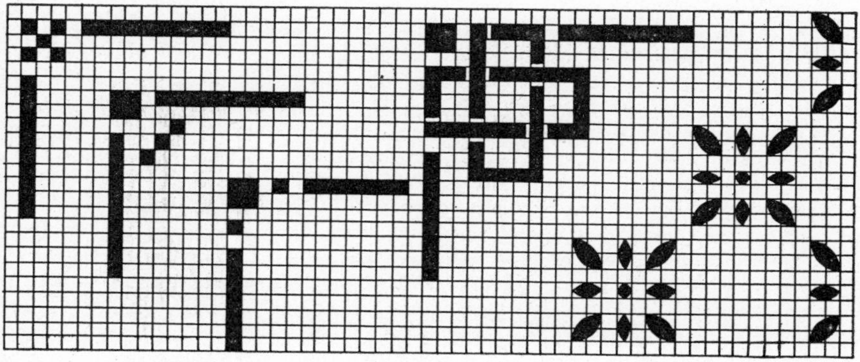

Fig. 14

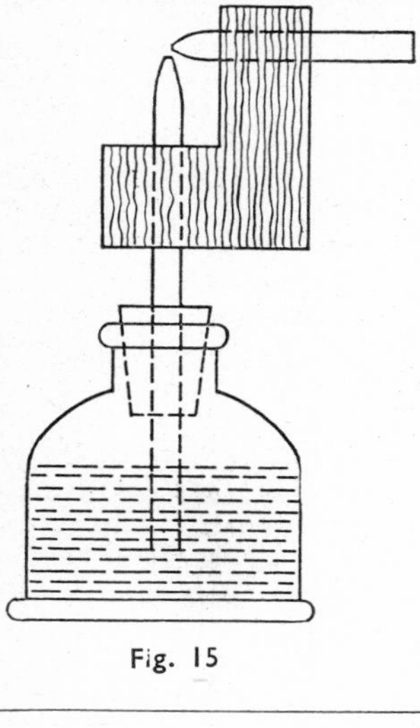

Fig. 15

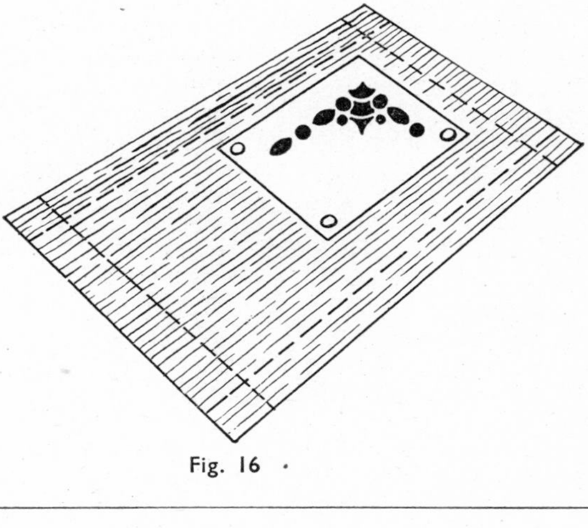

Fig. 16

get a fair idea how it will look when colour is stencilled through it.

Applying the Colour.—It is advisable to begin stencilling with a thick or opaque water colour. A little practice on paper will be useful because there are several little things to be guarded against and you might as well learn them at the outset. Lay the paper to be stencilled on a smooth surface such as a pad of blotting paper. It is best to get into the habit of using the latter as textile materials must have an absorbent material underneath to take up an excess of paint. Pin the stencil down over the paper. Put out a small quantity of paint. Do not dip the brush into this little heap of paint or you will ruin your work as soon as you begin to dab it on the stencil. Flatten out the heap of paint with the blade of a knife so as to reduce it to a thin layer. Take the brush in the hand as you would a pencil, but hold it quite vertical and dab, dab, dab it lightly in the paint so as to pick up on the ends of the bristles only. This dabbing action works from the wrist only. *Do not* keep a stiff wrist; work from the elbow or you will put on so much weight that you will ruin the brush in five minutes. Do not use the stencil brush for mixing the colours.

Now apply the paint through the stencil with the same light dabbing action. This is the only good method of applying paint through a stencil as the paint is less likely to be deposited in lumps or in the corners of the holes. Never use a painting stroke with a stencil brush. Moreover, when applying paint to textile materials it is essential that it should be driven well into the texture of the material and not allowed to stand on top of it and spoil its appearance as a textile. If the brush is overcharged with colour or the colour is too thin, it might work its way underneath the plate and spoil the outline. If the colour is too thick it will be difficult to drive it into the small holes and fine corners.

Fig. 16 shows a stencil plate pinned down to a table cloth or centre ready for the paint to be applied.

Where more than one colour is to be used, use a separate brush for each. Mix a sufficient quantity of colour to finish the work in hand as it is difficult to match colours at times, especially when working in artificial light, and while the fresh mixture is being made an unfinished detail may be drying; the result is an ugly patch or line where the fresh colour is applied.

General Hints.—If you are applying water colour or stain to wood, first size the surface so that the colour does not spread. If you wish to decorate the walls of a room use distemper. Many delightful dadoes, friezes and effective spots of colour and pattern can be put on at practically no cost whatever. On textile materials use stencil oil colours only. Waterproof inks of various colours can be well used on wood. Shading and tinting can be obtained by the addition of white or black paint on top of the background colour; also by varying the pressure on the brush. Colours can be blended by varying the pressure on the brush.

Always stretch textile material to remove all creases by pinning down over the pad of blotting paper or over a pad of calico sheeting or similar material. When applying colour to light or delicate fabrics such as silk, satin, georgette, ninon, etc., apply only a small amount of colour. On thick or coarse materials more colour is necessary and it should be mixed a little thinner; also it should be driven well into the texture.

When designing for small articles such as dress details, tea-cosies, scarves, lampshades, make the size of the pattern conform to the size of the article; do not overload the article with the size and apparent weight of the decoration. Curtains, theatrical costumes, table-cloths and runners, cushion covers, bed spreads, window drapery and so on will generally take bolder pattern with larger masses.

Spraying.—Colour can be applied to all materials by spraying it through the plate from a diffuser. An ordinary scent spray will do quite well for this work or a simple form shown in Fig. 15 can be made or purchased for a few pence. The latter is more easily cleaned than the former when it is required to change the colour. Clean water is blown through either of them to clean out all colour. When using the scent spray fill the bottle with coloured ink

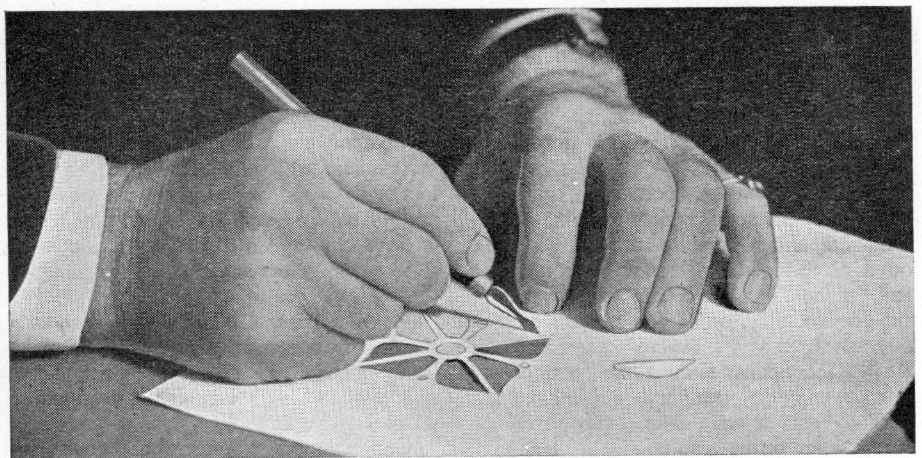

Fig. 17.—How to Cut the Stencil

or stain or water colour and spray it in the usual way on to the stencil plate pinned in a *vertical* position. Stand two or three feet away from the plate when spraying and observe the strength of the deposit. Regulate the colour by moving towards or away from the plate. To use the diffuser shown in Fig. 15 place the long tube in the liquid and the end of the shorter one in the mouth and blow. A fine spray issues from the top of the long tube and is blown away in the line of the direction of the short one. Watch carefully to see that the spots of colour are not so heavy that they run.

Washing Stencilled Materials.—It must be remembered that articles stencilled in water colours cannot be washed and retain the colour. Articles stencilled in oil colours can be quite safely washed. It should be remembered that if you wish to remove a smear of paint from a piece of fabric you generally use turpentine or benzine and, or, a solution of strong soap and water together with a good deal of vigorous rubbing. Therefore you must avoid strong soap and vigorous rubbing in the wash. Use pure soap flakes to make a strong solution with the soap and boiling water, add cold water to give lukewarmness. Rub the article quite gently, do not rub the stencilled parts and do not allow the article to stay in the water longer than is necessary to clean it. Rinse it in lukewarm and then in cold water to remove all traces of soap; roll it in a towel and while still damp iron it, using only a moderately hot iron.

SWEET MAKING

Sweet making is a hobby which must appeal to every intelligent woman because it is one which allows scope for individuality. Even some of the simplest of sweets which need no cooking and no apparatus in their preparation, can, with a little experiment, become your speciality.

It will be easier to regard sweet making under four headings—Unboiled sweets, Candied Fruits and Fudges, Toffees, and Chocolates. There are certain general rules which apply to the making of all of them, and the first of these is—do buy the best ingredients. It is far better to make half a pound of sweets from the best materials than to buy cheaper sugar, etc., in order to get more and then find that the whole thing is a failure. Special sweet-makers' icing sugar can be purchased, but ordinary best quality icing sugar from the grocers will do perfectly well provided that you rub it through the finest of sieves to remove the lumps which are usually in it. Where recipes need white of egg in them, be sure that the egg is really new laid, the white of pickled eggs, for instance, is most unsatisfactory.

Implements.—A porcelain or china bowl is the best in which to mix the ingredients, and if possible roll out the pastes on a marble slab with a glass bottle as a rolling pin. You can obtain a slab of marble quite reasonably, or, if you possess a spare marble topped washstand, why not try that? Saucepans should be copper or aluminium; do not try boiling sugar, toffees, etc., in enamel ones: you will be sure to get burnt results.

One thing you must have is a palette knife, an ordinary knife is useless for getting round the corners of a saucepan. Accuracy of measurement is important, so purchase a gill measure; for although a pint measure with gills marked looks accurate, it is easier to be accurate with something smaller.

If you are going to make a business proposition of your hobby you will need to buy special packing materials. Corrugated waxed paper squares, tinfoil, and boxes with frilled edges are not expensive and add just that touch which makes all the difference.

Unboiled Sweets.—By unboiled sweets we mean creams of all kinds, and also marzipan. The foundation of creams is made from one pound of icing sugar, a pinch of cream of tartar, the white of an egg, and perhaps a few drops of water if the egg white is not very large. Ready-made foundation, "fondant," can be purchased, and by adding various flavourings to this fondant—made workable by being heated in a jar standing in hot water—cream sweets can even more easily be made. But making your own is better.

The whole secret of making a successful foundation is to make haste slowly. Begin by whisking the egg, but not unduly. Add a pinch of cream of tartar, and then begin to add the sieved icing sugar slowly, beating the mixture as hard as you can so that a constant smooth paste is the result. When you have used up about half the sugar, add whatever flavouring and colouring you have chosen, and a very few drops of water. Add as much of the rest of the sugar as will make a very stiff paste. Dust your slab and rolling pin with icing sugar and roll out your paste to about a quarter of an inch in thickness. Cut out in rounds or squares and place them on sheets of waxed paper or on china plates to dry for a few hours.

Here are a few suggestions for using the foundation.

Peppermint Creams.—Add enough oil of peppermint and stamp in rings. A small pastry cutter, a wine glass, or the special round cutters used by professionals will achieve this.

Confectioners' colourings and flavourings will be needed for the production of other "creams"—or you can buy a flavoured colouring also.

Violet Creams.—Add violet colouring and flavouring to taste; roll out half an inch thick and stamp in ovals. Put a crystallized violet on each.

Rose Creams.—Add raspberry colour and flavouring, roll out a quarter of an inch thick, stamp in circles and put a crystallized rose petal on each.

Lemon, Orange and Crême de Menthe Creams.—Add lemon, or orange, or crême de menthe, colour and flavouring, roll out half an inch thick, stamp in ovals and make a pattern on the top with a fork.

Coffee Almonds.—Flavour with coffee essence, cut out as for lemon creams and press an almond on top of each.

Walnut Creams.—Colour the foundation green and put half a walnut on top of each.

Brazil Bon-bons.—Flavour the foundation with vanilla, roll into a thin sheet, stamp into circles the size of a crown, and wrap round each brazil nut.

Cherry Delight.—Use half orange juice and half white of egg to make your foundation. Roll out to a quarter of an inch in thickness, cut out in rounds with a fluted cutter and press half a glacé cherry on the top of each.

Ginger Creams.—Add half ginger syrup to half an egg white and enough

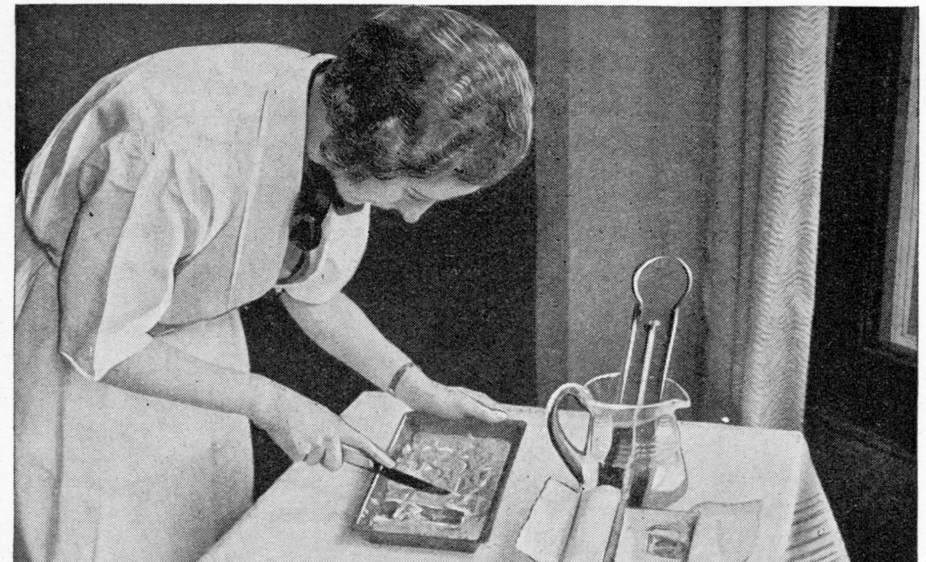

Fig. 1.—Cut Fudge into convenient pieces with a sharp knife

grated chocolate to colour lightly. Cut in circles and decorate with crystallized ginger.

If the sweetmeats used in decoration will not stay on the sweets, dip each in a little white of egg before pressing in place.

Marzipan.—Confectioners' marzipan can be bought ready made. It is mixed with about its own weight in icing sugar. You may, however, prefer to make your own foundation. A very good one can be made from half a pound of ground almonds mixed with about three-quarters of a pound of icing sugar. Begin by mixing half a pound of sieved icing sugar with the ground almonds dry, then add this slowly to the lightly beaten white of an egg, add as much extra icing sugar as is necessary to make it workable but not sticky.

Neapolitan Marzipan.—This marzipan can be used in many ways. To make delicious marzipan sweets, separate into three different portions, and colour and flavour two of them to choice, leaving one portion plain. Roll out each separately, fairly thinly, keeping them as square in shape as possible. Place one layer in a tin on greaseproof paper, brush it over with white of egg and lay the second layer on it. Treat this in a similar way and when the third is added press together, dust a piece of greaseproof paper with icing sugar, place on top of the marzipan—and a tin lid with a moderately heavy book on it as a weight. Leave for twenty-four hours and then cut in cubes.

Stuffed Cherries.—Flavour the marzipan with orange essence. Roll some glacé cherries in icing sugar till they are no longer sticky. Put a small ball of marzipan in each cherry and a thin strip of angelica sticking out of the top of each.

Stuffed Dates.—The best box dates should be used for this: dates which are pressed together in slabs are rather messy to work with and do not look so well. You will need also some shelled walnuts broken into quarters. Stone the dates by making one slit down the side with a silver knife. Roll a quarter walnut in enough marzipan to fill the cavity left. Stuff the date and roll in icing sugar. Each should have its own paper case for packing.

Hedgehogs.—Roll oval balls of marzipan flavoured with vanilla or lemon, in powdered chocolate. Shred some almonds coarsely, and stick all over the back to form the prickles.

Coconut Ice.—Many people make this pleasant sweetmeat by the boiling method, but it can be made very successfully as an unboiled sweet. Mix two tablespoonfuls of condensed milk with the white of an egg; add half a pound of sieved icing sugar gradually. Then mix in six ounces of desiccated coconut. Halve this mixture, add to one part enough cochineal and raspberry flavouring to suit and then add further icing sugar until the whole mixtures are really stiff. Roll out three-quarters of an inch thick, keeping each the same shape. Brush over the white layer with white of egg, place the pink one on it, and when fairly dry cut into bars.

Boiled Sweets.—Directly you contemplate boiled sweets of any kind you will find it ever so much more satisfactory to buy a sugar thermometer. The secret of producing candies, fudges, toffees, etc., which come out exactly as you expect them to do, lies in the heating of the mixture to the same temperature always. You can make quite good fudges and toffees by testing for the critical point by dropping bits from the spoon into a cupful of cold water. But the chances are against you getting the same result twice—sometimes you will get a sugary mass, at others it will be complete stick-jaw.

A Sugar Thermometer is not unduly expensive, and treated with care will last a long time. Do be careful, however, to dip it into hot water before putting it into your boiling mixture, and wash it in hot water afterwards. (Fig. 2.)

Fudges and candied fruits require boiling to 245° F. and toffees from 275°–300° F. according to whether they are to be soft toffees or hard toffees. When melting sugar, which in the case of toffees and fudges can either be loaf or granulated, but preferably not beet sugar, put a gill of water to each pound of sugar and add a pinch of cream of tartar when the sugar is melted. Use a large saucepan, for sugar mixtures are like boiling milk, and blow up over the top of the saucepan in no time. It is a good plan too, to grease the bottom of the saucepan very slightly before putting in the sugar and water. Tins, must of course be greased. It is easy to do this with a brush and some melted butter; do not use margarine for the purpose.

Candied Fruits.—Tangerine, lemon, and orange quarters, and dates can be candied in this way. Melt a pound of sugar in a gill of water very slowly so that the liquid does not boil before the sugar is melted, add a pinch of cream of tartar and boil to 240° F. Put in your fruit and boil for two minutes, then take the saucepan off the fire and beat till it thickens and fluffs. Pour out on to a sieve set over a plate so that the surplus syrup runs through.

Fudge.—This sweetmeat is definitely easy to make. There are several recipes for fudge, but a standard foundation, to which various flavourings and colourings can be added, is perhaps the most useful. Here is a good one. Melt an ounce and a half of unsalted butter in your saucepan and then add two gills of condensed milk and a pound of granulated sugar. Do not forget a pinch of cream of tartar. Boil the mixture, stirring the while, until it reaches 240° F. Then take the saucepan off the fire and add whatever flavouring you have chosen, except in the case of chocolate, finally beating with a wooden spoon till it goes thick. Pour on to a buttered plate or tin, press it flat, and leave for a hour.

To this foundation you may add vanilla essence, orange essence, pineapple essence (decorated with crystallized pineapple), cochineal and raspberry flavouring for Raspberry Fudge; or use half honey and half condensed milk and add hazel nuts for Maple Fudge; or a half a gill of strong coffee to one gill of condensed milk for Coffee Fudge; or two ounces of grated chocolate to the milk and sugar before boiling for Chocolate Fudge.

Toffees and Fudges can be cut with a palette knife, but dip the knife in warm water first; or else you can buy special toffee cutters quite cheaply, these being easier and quicker to use.

Fruit Drops.—Dissolve a pound of loaf sugar in 2 gills of water add a pinch of cream of tartar and boil to 300° F., or when it will set hard enough to snap in water, if you have no thermometer. You may find that scum rises to the top of the liquid, in which case you must skim it. Add any flavouring you like; pineapple, pear, raspberry etc., and then pour into your tins to cool. Cut in strips and then into squares.

Toffee.—Nowadays when glucose is considered such an addition to diet, you may like to follow the example of many toffee makers and add it to your recipes. A good proportion in which to add it is to use a quarter as much glucose as sugar; and it is preferable to add it when your mixture has begun to boil. For dark toffees such as Treacle or Russian Toffee, you may use brown sugar.

Nursery Toffee.—Melt a pound of brown sugar in a gill of water and then add four ounces of butter in small pieces. When boiling add the glucose if liked, and boil to 300° F., or when it cracks easily in water. You can add lemon flavouring if you like. Pour into tins and break with a toffee hammer when cold.

Milk Toffee.—Dissolve a pound of loaf sugar in three gills of condensed milk, stirring all the time. When this is thoroughly liquid add six ounces of butter in pieces, stirring slowly all the time. Boil till this reaches 275° F. or when a piece dropped in water will bend easily. Pour into tins and cut when half cold. This toffee may be flavoured with oil of peppermint.

Treacle Toffee is made by adding half a pound of black treacle to the nursery toffee recipe, or if you use Golden Syrup, which is not so sweet, use about three-quarters of a pound. Nuts may be added to the Nursery Toffee recipe, and different flavourings used. By experiment, and by writing down what you have done each time you may evolve some delightful toffees.

Barley Sugar.—You can either make it by dissolving a pound of loaf sugar and three ounces of glucose in a gill and a half of water, boiling till 310° F. is reached, and then colouring and flavouring it with lemon; or you can use, instead of water, the liquid left when two ounces of barley and the rind of a lemon have been boiled in a pint and a half of water for two hours, allowed to settle, and the top water poured off. In both cases pour into a buttered tin, and when half cold, cut into strips and twist.

Chocolates.—The making of chocolates is regarded by many people as too difficult, but provided that you take care, are patient, and are prepared to experiment in the matter of centres, you will find it quite possible, and certainly it is the most fascinating branch of sweet making.

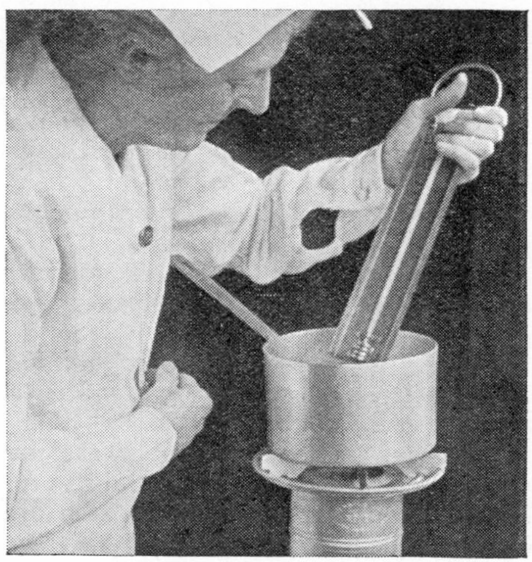

Fig. 2.—A Sugar Thermometer

You will probably find it easiest to start with something solid for centres. Such as almonds, hazel nuts, brazils, or raisins. The only thing to remember is that your chocolates will set better if your centres are warmed. You can easily warm nuts on sheets of greaseproof paper in the oven.

You can use ordinary three-pronged forks for dipping, and you will find it helpful to buy an oval and a round dipping fork too.

Chocolate Nuts.—Have your centres ready near you before you begin dipping. While the nuts are warming you can make the coating chocolate. Melt three-quarters of an ounce of coco butter in a jar standing in hot water if you have not got a double saucepan, and then grate into it half a pound or more of confectioners' chocolate. Stir this with a wooden spoon until it has

Fig. 3.—Making Marzipan Walnuts

really melted and then take the jar or the top saucepan away from the hot water container and beat the mixture till it is quite smooth and thick. Put the mixture back to heat again and bring it up to a temperature of about 85° F., but you can test by seeing if a dipped chocolate takes about five minutes to set, which is a reasonable time. Do not get it too hot, or your coating will just run off the centres and make a puddle at the bottom of them.

Now you are ready to dip. Take the whole thing off the fire, but leave the water in the surrounding receptable to keep the chocolate liquid; you can aid this by stirring after dipping each centre. Take a centre on your dipping fork and drop into the chocolate; leave it there for a minute, then lift it out, holding it above the mixture for a minute to let any superfluous chocolate drain off; then pop it on to a sheet of corrugated wax paper at your side. Pat the top with your fork, or make a scroll or twist on it unless you wish to decorate the top otherwise. If the chocolate gets too stiff, add more hot water to the surround.

Chocolate Marzipans are just squares of marzipan flavoured and coloured but not pressed. If you make your marzipan in a bowl standing in a basin of hot water, they should be warm enough for dipping when you have shaped the centres. The same procedure is followed as for the dipping of nuts. A good marzipan centre can be made if a little marmalade is added to vanilla marzipan.

Peppermint Creams made the unboiled way and dipped soon after they are made are most successful. It is usual to decorate these with an *M* made with the dipping fork.

Other cream centres may be made from unboiled creams, or from ready prepared fondant, bought by the pound. This is warmed in a basin surrounded by hot water to make the foundation creamy enough. Or you can make your own boiled fondant from the following recipe: take a pound of lump sugar and dissolve it in a gill of water, then add a dessertspoonful of glucose and boil until it will make a soft ball in water, 240° F. Pour into a china bowl and leave it till you can bear to touch it with your fingers. Beat it till it turns white, then turn it out on to your slab and knead it till you get a paste the consistency of the inside of chocolates. This paste can now be flavoured and coloured to suit your requirements, and shaped into balls, cakes, or rolls for dipping. But if you do not want to use it till the next day, do not shape, but store in bulk in a basin. This can be stood in a bowl of hot water and worked again until soft enough to flavour and shape.

Squares of milk toffee, preserved ginger and pineapple too, can be coated quite successfully. Later, when more experienced, you can deal with nougatines, pralines and truffles.

Do not forget to decorate your creams with crystallized rose petals, violets, and nuts, according to their centres; and make use of orange, lemon, vanilla, and coffee essences.

TABLE MATS

MATS are a necessary part of the equipment for a meal whether you prefer the cloth-covered table or the more austere plain, uncovered oak. If you live in a district where lamps are still in use a further need is felt to prevent damage to other articles of furniture. The following are a few of the methods which can be adopted for making mats. The style you choose will depend upon your age, special requirements and your taste.

Cardboard Mats.—Figs. 1 and 2 show a mat made from cardboard and covered with cretonne, casement cloth, plain linen, etc. Cut out two pieces of cardboard, any kind will do, about 6 in. diameter, and two pieces of the material which you are going to use as a covering, to a radius of ¾ in. or 1 in. more. Use a fairly thick paste and paste one side of the cardboard, rubbing it well with a stiff brush or the edge of a piece of stiff cardboard or piece of wood to flatten out the paste and so prevent ugly lumps showing in the surface of the covering material. Allow this paste to dry a little until the cardboard can be lifted by adhesion to the ends of the fingers. This will prevent the paste working through the texture of the covering material and spoiling it. Now place the cardboard in the centre of the material as in Fig. 1. Paste the surface of the cardboard for about ¾ in. from the edge and all round. Turn over the projecting material on to this ring of paste and flatten it down carefully. A wider margin than ¾ in. on the material will cause lumpiness and make folds.

Make two of these for each mat. Stick them together by pasting the uncovered sides and leave under flat pressure to dry and set. Now over-sew the edges carefully together and the mat is complete.

If you wish to make a washable mat there is now available quite good material with a waterproofed surface which can be dealt with in the same way. If it is a heat-resisting mat that you require, purchase the circular asbestos mats now obtainable and use them as the foundation instead of cardboard.

Should you not desire to use the two thicknesses of covered cardboard use one piece only and cover the under side with a piece of material carefully sewn to the edge of the piece first put on.

Rush Mats.—Many people who use an oak dining-table find mats made from rushes either in natural or dyed colour give a very agreeable touch of colour to the table, at the same time as being thoroughly useful. Moreover, these mats can be increased in size for use on the floor of the bedroom, kitchen, bathroom, or indeed almost any place. They are very cheap to make and wear quite a considerable time.

The materials required are plaited rushes, coloured or natural coloured twine and a packing needle. You can dye the rushes by soaking them in ordinary dyes of any colour, though the dye will probably fade out after a time.

You can either buy the rushes ready plaited or make the plait yourself. In the latter case soak the rush in water for a few minutes and leave it to mellow for 24 hours. Pin or tie the ends of three rushes to any immovable piece of wood, say a deal table-top, and make an ordinary plait. The thickness of the plait should be as regular as possible, so you must work the thick end of a rush into the thin end of the preceding one. Work a long length of plait and then cut off it for use on small articles. For a dinner mat about 9 in. diameter cut off about 7 ft. Bind both ends with string to prevent the plait coming undone and begin to coil it to form a solid centre about 2 in. diameter. Pass the needle and string right through this, two or three times to tie up the end and fix it solidly. Then coil on another piece, sew through the centre of its depth into the previous coil with stitches about 1 in. apart. Continue to the required diameter. (*See* Fig. 3.) It will be found easier and more effective if the plait is coiled on its edge, not the flat way,

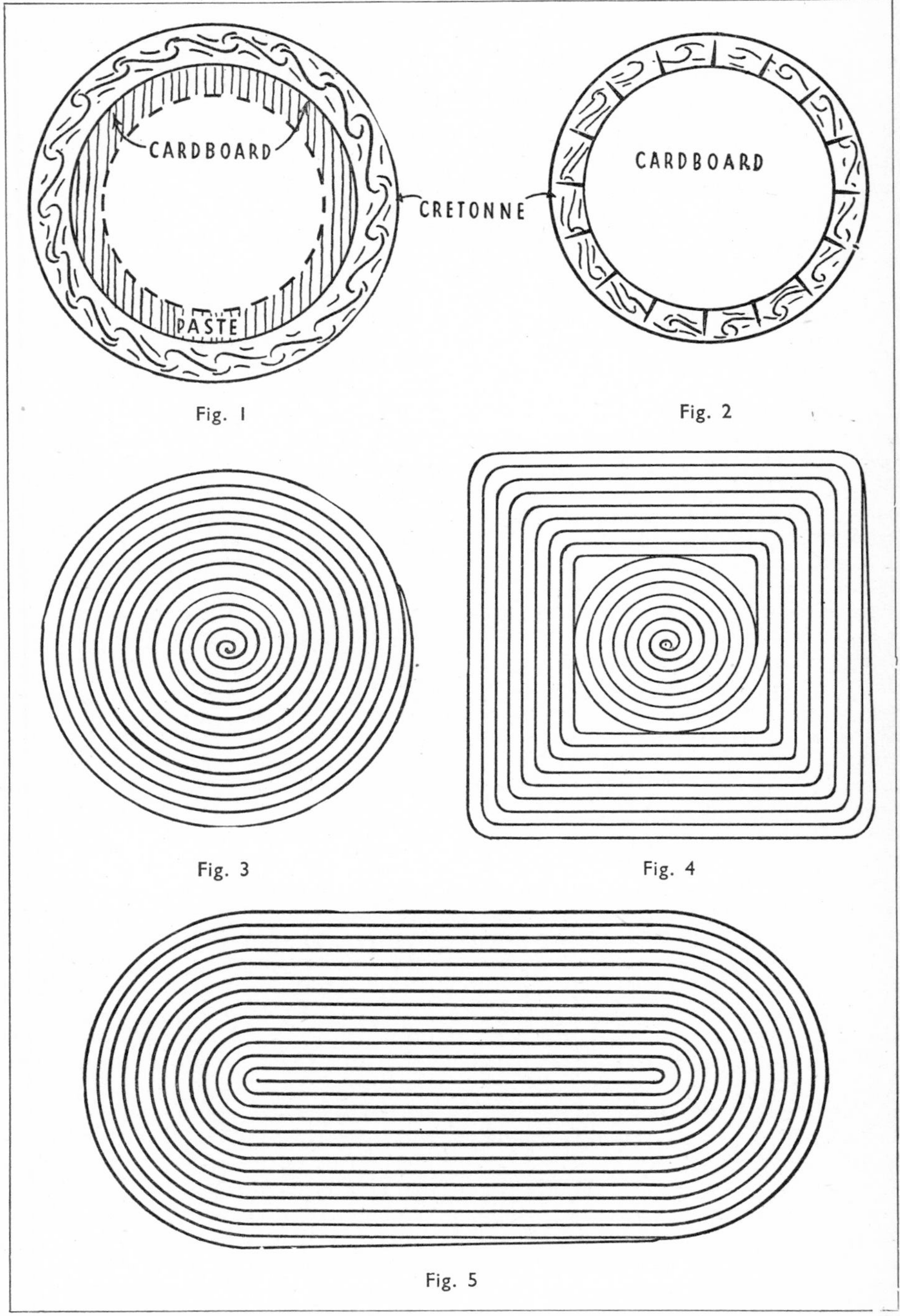

Fig. 1

Fig. 2

Fig. 3

Fig. 4

Fig. 5

which will be more difficult and give a thinner mat.

These mats can be made in many simple shapes. Fig. 5 shows a rectangular mat which instead of the plain centre might have a centre of scrolls or coils. A square one could be started on the basis of a circle and then turned sharply at right angles to work out to the square. The space between the square and the circle is left empty or may be filled in with a pattern sewn in string. (*See* Fig. 4.)

Mats with finer detail in them can be made in the above way from plaited natural or coloured raffia.

Raffia Mats.—Very nice mats can be made from raffia and cardboard of circular shape as shown in Fig. 7. Cut a circular disc of cardboard of the diameter required with a hole of one or two inches diameter in the middle as in Fig. 6. Decide on the colour scheme in raffia and plan its lines in pencil on the cardboard as in Fig. 6. Begin winding with one of the colours of the raffia fixing the end by laying it sideways on the surface of the cardboard and wrapping over and over it, through the hole, out and over the edge, round the other side and through the hole again. Repeat the operation until one section is complete. Then take the coloured raffia for the next section and proceed as before. When finished, as in Fig. 7, fix the strands of raffia on the edge by a blanket stitch running round the edge and catching up almost every strand. The middle hole may be filled with a pattern of stitched raffia caught on to the strands covering the edge of this circle, stitching a set of threads across the hole and then weaving a darning thread in and out of these threads. If the hole is a large one it may also be filled by making a small circle on the same plan as the large one with a small hole in the centre. This can be fixed into the large hole by stitching together the strands covering the inner edge of the latter and those covering the outer edge of the smaller one.

Cork Mats can now be bought quite cheaply. These can be made much more attractive by making a stencil pattern with which to decorate the surface in oil colour.

Very good results can also be obtained by fixing square or round wooden beads round the edge. Obtain a few gross of square beads of different colours about $\frac{1}{4}$ in. size. They cost about 2s. 6d. per thousand and are perforated for threading as shown in Fig. 9.

To fix the beads first draw a pencil line parallel to the edge of the mat about $\frac{1}{4}$ in. away and set out on it divisions $\frac{1}{4}$ in. apart as in Fig. 8. Use a strong needle or a fine bodkin and pierce a hole at each point. Thread your needle with button-hole twist or mercerized cotton of the colour desired, pass the needle through a hole, leave a long end, thread a bead on to the needle and thread and place it against the side of the mat. Pass the needle through the next hole in the mat, thread another bead, then form a connection with the previous bead by passing the needle and thread through the loop between it and the edge of the mat to form a blanket stitch. Then thread again through the third hole in the mat and so on to the end as in Fig. 9.

Woven Mats.—The beginning of a simple woven mat which can be made by the children is shown in Fig. 10. Take a piece of cardboard, pierce an uneven number of holes in it about $\frac{1}{4}$ in. from the edge and about $\frac{1}{2}$ in. to $\frac{5}{8}$ in. apart. Cut out the centre to about 1 in. diameter. Begin to thread up a warp of thin twine (macramé twine is very good) by passing the thread through a hole near the circumference, then through the centre hole to the other side, up through the next hole, across to the centre hole, through it back to the next hole, and so on until every hole is filled and there is a series of warp threads covering both sides of the cardboard as in Fig. 10. Begin to weave on this warp with raffia, string, wool or coloured macramé string. Start in the centre and weave one under and one over for about 1 in. Then begin to work pattern by taking up, say, two strands or any such combination you may desire. Do not forget that the colour scheme should be planned beforehand. Beat up the weft threads tightly towards the centre as the weaving proceeds. When the weaving has been worked in as far as it will go at the edge the finishing can be done in one of two ways. You may break away the cardboard on the

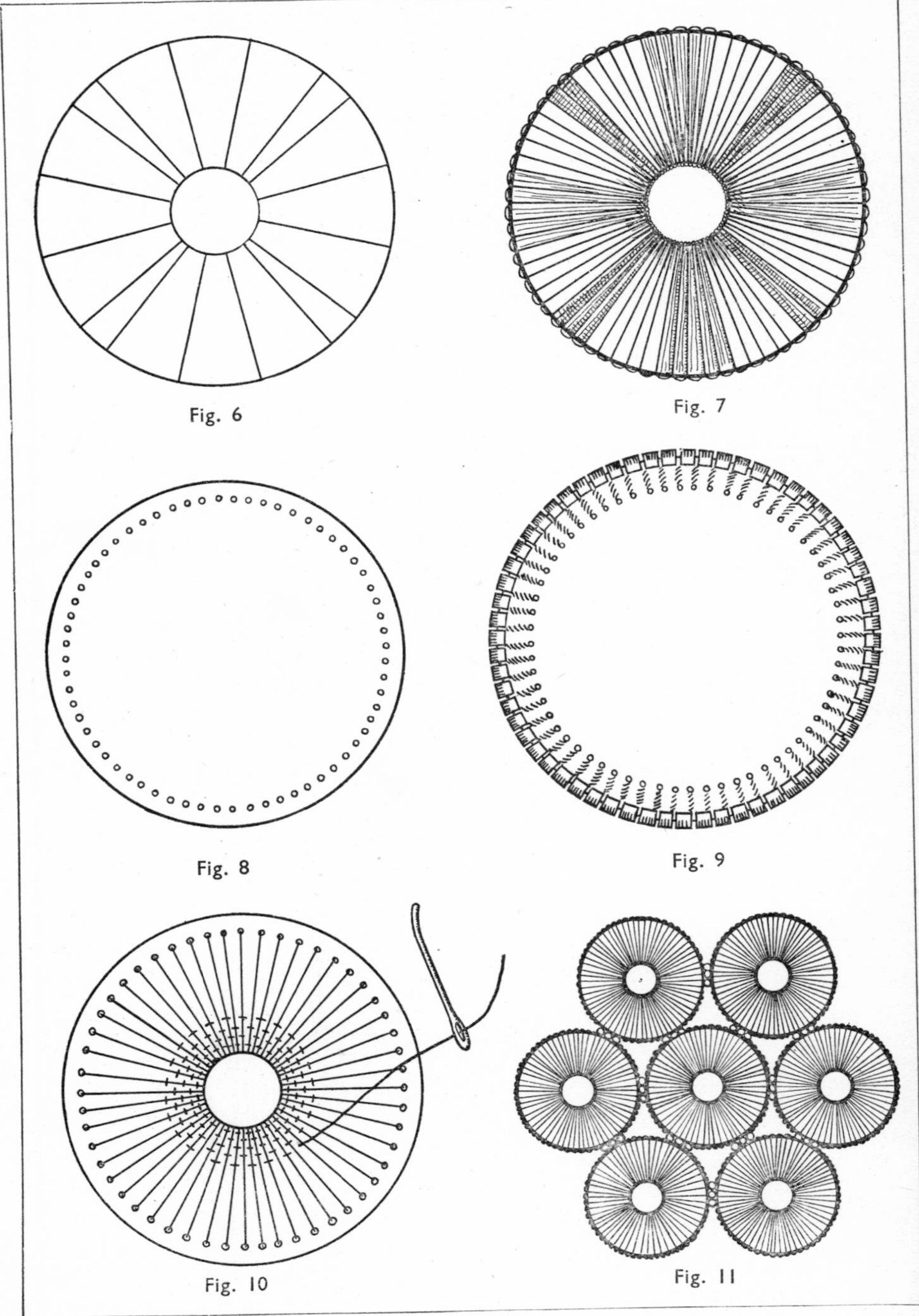

Fig. 6

Fig. 7

Fig. 8

Fig. 9

Fig. 10

Fig. 11

side of the holes, and not covered, and take a number of strands of the weaving material and lay them on the edge to cover the cardboard which is still visible. Now over-sew this into position by a thread of the same material in a contrasting colour, which passes through each hole in turn.

In the other method you do not break away the cardboard but take a larger bundle of threads, lay it along the flat surface of cardboard exposed on both sides and over the edge to cover it completely. Then over-sew as before. In this method instead of a bundle of threads make two plaits of them, one for each side. Lay these plaits on the uncovered parts of the cardboard on each side so that they are completely covered.

Fig. 11 shows a mat made from small circles of cardboard covered with raffia. These are sewn together to make any size.

TABLE TENNIS

TABLE TENNIS has become a deservedly popular game, of international importance, a strenuous game calling for skill, speed, physical fitness. Not all who play are even yet familiar with the rules. Here is a brief summary of them:

The Rules.—The ball must be perfectly round and not less than $4\frac{1}{2}$ in. or more than $4\frac{3}{4}$ in. in circumference. It must weigh not less than 2·40 grammes and not more than 2·53 grammes. The net, running across the middle of the table, must be $6\frac{3}{4}$ in. high, and 6 ft. long, projecting 6 in. over each side of the table. The table must measure 9 ft. by 5 ft., and its surface must be $2\frac{1}{2}$ ft. from the floor. A game consists of 21 points; each player is allowed five serves, after which the service goes to his opponent. Should the score reach 20–20 two successive points must be taken to win, and service is changed for every point. Singles or doubles can be played. For service the ball must first be played into the server's half of the table so that it bounces over the net into the opponent's half. In doubles the serve is made to the diagonally opposite opponent. Should a server miss the ball in serving he loses a point. A *let* is allowed when a service ball touches the top of the net in going over, and the receiver may claim another service. At other times it is permissible for the ball to touch the net. A ball can be returned round the net posts. If a player has hit a ball off the table the opponent may forfeit a point if he touches the ball with his racket and so "plays" it. A player moving the table in making a stroke forfeits the point, so he does if he puts a hand on the table for support; his body may touch the table subject to the first condition. Volleying is not allowed. In doubles, partners must hit the ball alternately—a point is lost by going out of turn. Service is always taken by the right-hand player. After five serves the partners change places, and the opponent who was previously receiving becomes the server.

Rackets and Balls.—Since rackets are so cheap—the best quality costs only a few shillings—it is advisable to start off with a good one. The light cork-faced bats have now been superseded by sturdy rackets having a roughened surface of rubber on each side. You may need to change rackets a few times before you find the weight and grip which best suit you, but having made up your mind stick to your choice. Buy good balls too. To test the quality of a ball bounce it. If dropped from a height of 12 in. on to a proper table it should bounce up again 8 in. It is best to have half-a-dozen balls on hand, for when one gets split or dented it should be scrapped—the old method of forcing out dents by heating in front of a fire so that the air inside expands and pushes out the celluloid may be economical but it does not improve the shape of the ball. You may prove the roundness of a ball by spinning it on a table with your fingers, just as you would a top—if it spins smoothly it is all right.

Gripping the Racket.—The handle of the racket must be gripped very firmly. The handle passes naturally across the palm,

Fig. 1.—Back View of Grip

Fig. 2.—Front View of Grip

with the little finger and its two neighbours curling round it, close up to the flat part of the racket. The thumb lies flatly across rather on its edge, on the rubber, and of course, on the front of the racket. The forefinger lies outstretched, slanting similarly across the flat rubber of the racket back—as shown in the illustrations. Though this is the standard grip there are some players who find some variation of it suits them better. You are not bound to adopt it if some other method proves more comfortable and effective.

When making any stroke you should not let the ball get too close to you otherwise the movement of the playing arm will be hampered. Neither should you stand close to the table end. The position naturally depends on the actual needs of play, and varies according to the strokes a player is using and whether he is attacking or defending. A good player may remain much of the time about 5 ft. from his end of the table, and may sometimes retreat to double that distance in order to receive fast shots.

Serving.—The ball must be made to bounce first in your court, after you have struck it, before it crosses and bounces in the court of your opponent, and it must be tossed up before you hit it. Later, when you have gained confidence, you may acquire the knack of spinning the ball with your fingers as you toss it to your racket—but do not bother about finger spin yet.

Plain forehand and backhand strokes can be used equally for services. Later you will learn to impart various sorts of "spin" to the ball, by "stroking" the racket in a certain direction at the moment of impact instead of making a square, plain hit. Back spin can be imparted by a sharp, downward, chopping stroke.

In the main your first service aim should be to develop fast low shots. If you serve a few balls in this fashion, compelling your opponent to keep well back, then change abruptly to a short ball you may get him by surprise and so upset his return stroke.

In receiving service your methods must be determined by the balls that are being sent across. If the service is a plain one it can be met, if desired, by a plain return. But if your opponent has put spin on the ball it is no use attempting a plain stroke. Spin in one stroke must be countered by spin in the return hit. Noting the "slice" or "chop" which the other player puts into his stroke you will seek to counteract the effect by slicing or chopping so that the ball is struck in the opposite direction. Thus the spin is nullified and you are able to keep control of the ball. In receiving service keep well back, but always on your toes in case there is need to dash to the net.

In all play you will keep your eye on the ball, never in any circumstances lose sight of it. But, almost in a subconscious way, you may watch your opponent too.

The Strokes.—Most net game strokes are practicable in table tennis, and can be played either from the forehand or the backhand. And, as in lawn tennis, it is the backhand that usually needs most attention. In a table tennis backhand stroke the forefinger is on the side of the racket nearest to your opponent.

The commonest and most useful stroke is the *drive*. This is a long, straight shot, generally taken well out from the net, or away from the table. The ball is driven very hard, and reaches the selected spot on the opponent's court by the shortest route. The drive should be low so that the ball bounces swiftly from the table at a flat angle. Let your racket "follow through." This following through applies to practically all strokes, as it does in most ball games. The racket must continue in the same direction without any check after the impact with the ball, as if it were trying to keep pressed against the ball for as long as possible. This not only ensures a smoother action and fuller power but prevents the muscular strain involved in suddenly stopping the arm.

The Forehand Drive should begin with the racket back behind the hip and finish with the racket just above shoulder height. Lean slightly forward so that you are over the ball, or rather your arm has that sort of feeling, as you make the drive. As you make the forehand drive with the right arm back, the right foot should be back too, and your weight should be on the left foot at the moment of impact.

The Backhand Drive.—The position of the feet is reversed, the right being forward, and the left foot and hip being back because the right hand is stretched across to the left-hand side of the body. As for the forehand stroke, slope the racket surface forward over the ball so that you impart top spin as you make the stroke. Get a good swing of the arm, and plenty of vigour. These two strokes, the forehand and backhand drives, are the most important of the game.

The lawn tennis *lob*, or its table tennis equivalent, is used much less frequently than the drive, but it is appropriate when you want to tempt an opponent or to deceive him as to your intentions. The ball is sent fairly high, and right on to the back edge of the table.

S. & G.

Fig. 3.—Demonstration of the Forehand Drive at the World Table Tennis Championships

The Smash.—Get well over the ball, and drive down with full vigour. A ball that is being returned too high, or has only just been returned with an effort, rising above the net with scarcely energy to get over it—these are the sort of replies that give you your chance for the smash, and perhaps for the kill which will be quite unplayable by your opponent. But even when smashing do not play wildly; know just where you intend the ball to go, and then put it there with all your force. A carelessly placed smash may send the ball so high that your opponent may in turn be given a chance to kill on your side of the net.

The Drop-shot is also adaptable to table tennis. It is the gentle stroke in which the ball is made simply to trickle over. There are roughly two types of drop-shots. You may play them right from the back of the table, with such care that the ball stops when it has crossed the middle and falls so closely to the net that it cannot be returned. Or you may play it from near the middle of the table, just lifting the ball over the net, so that it seems to crawl over with tantalizing slowness and lack of force. The drop-shot is used chiefly for taking an opponent off his guard.

Remember to develop backhand as well as forehand play, so that you can make any stroke from either side of the table. A backhand defence is always best against fast attacking shots. Some players shirk their backhand, and endeavour to run across so as to take everything with the forehand. Such a player, having got round to the left-hand side of the table, is right out of position and will probably fall easy prey to the opponent's next return. If your backhand is weak that is all the more reason why you should work it hard. In backhand strokes the arm is slanted across the front of the body, and it is the thumb instead of the forefinger which gives pressure on the racket. In forehand play the forefinger presses consciously.

Don't be afraid of using the full length of the arm and the full weight of the body in your big strokes. But, equally, don't forget the use of the wrist.

It is a great asset if you can make your strokes to look alike, for then your opponent will never know what to expect. The wrist is of great importance in making this sort of feinting possible; it also gives the additional bit of power which augments the force of an arm stroke; and, besides, it imparts unexpected spin to a ball by a quick slice or chop.

It is the wrist flick which deals with most balls which come just over the net, and the same smart flick which puts the final sting into all smash strokes.

Footwork is of the greatest importance. Your poise should be relaxed, not rigid, but must always have tense preparedness. The effect of your general bearing on an opponent can be considerable. As a general rule you should be at the middle of your table end, though of course not close against it. Do not move from your position unless the requirements of a stroke compel you to. If you are forced out of position get back again as quickly as you can. After a drive, in which the feet have been one behind the other to allow the sideways position of the body, you should bring the rear foot forward again, so as to be in readiness to play the next stroke from the opposite side if necessary.

The Doubles Game.—Footwork is particularly important in doubles play. In the doubles game partners take strokes alternately, and each must therefore step in for his hit then step quickly back to make way for his partner. Take care to step always to that side of the table which is away from your partner, so that you do not obstruct him as you move or force him to lose sight of the ball. Keep your eye on the ball all the time, not on your partner. To make a good pair for doubles the same partners should play always together, so that they get to understand each other and to combine in the most effective fashion.

Strategy.—Though the offensive is almost always the best game it is sometimes necessary to be on the defensive. In attacking you will play close up to the table, giving the opponent no rest. Mislead him as much as possible, by putting spin on your balls. In playing a defensive game get well back from the table—a fierce drive, for

S. & G.

Fig. 4.—Demonstration of a Backhand Stroke at the World Table Tennis Championships

instance, has lost most of its force and sting if you receive it several yards back. But in getting right back be on your guard against short drop-shots. Remember to counteract spin when you receive the ball—killing top spin, for instance, by getting your racket face upwards and slicing under the ball.

A defensive player can be very irritating, but you must concentrate on varying your strokes so that he has no chance of really settling down. In most play it is subtlety that wins quite as much, or even more, than hard hitting. You should be able to drop the ball always on that part of the table which is most inconvenient for your opponent.

In meeting a strange opponent do your best to explore his play by trying him with a variety of strokes until you discover his weak points. If his backhand drives are bad—then compel him to play them at every opportunity. You may find that when he has scored well from a particular stroke he will be tempted to repeat the same stroke frequently, so that if you give him chances, unobtrusively, you will know what to expect—and such knowledge will enable you to cope effectively with his returns.

Be on your guard against a left-handed player. It is difficult to get used to his returns, and what would be weak points for another person will be strong ones for him. If you chance to be left-handed don't try to change; your peculiarity may be an advantage rather than otherwise.

Practice.—Get in as much practice as you can. You can rehearse footwork and stroke movements without table or ball, just as a boxer does shadow boxing. By pushing the opponent's end of a table up against a wall you can play by yourself. Drive the ball on to the farther court, in the usual manner, but with top spin, and it will then bounce against the wall and come back on to your own end of the table.

In practising with a friend give all your attention to technique. Let him feed you with regular returns so that you may play a particular stroke over and over again in the same fashion. Concentrate on each stroke in turn, and on planned pieces of footwork and strategy.

TELEVISION

TELEVISION like most scientific "marvels" is, when shorn of its technical phrases and the many details added to secure perfection, quite simple in principle. Any amateur with access to a supply of wireless parts and some mechanical skill can make a simple "televisor" which will give moderately good reception. That, however, is by the way. Before dealing with "how it is done," it is as well to follow the efforts of the pioneers faced with a jungle of ignorance on the subject. To know what they had to face and cut a way through to make seeing by electricity possible, helps not only to understanding the problems solved, but also to doing it for oneself.

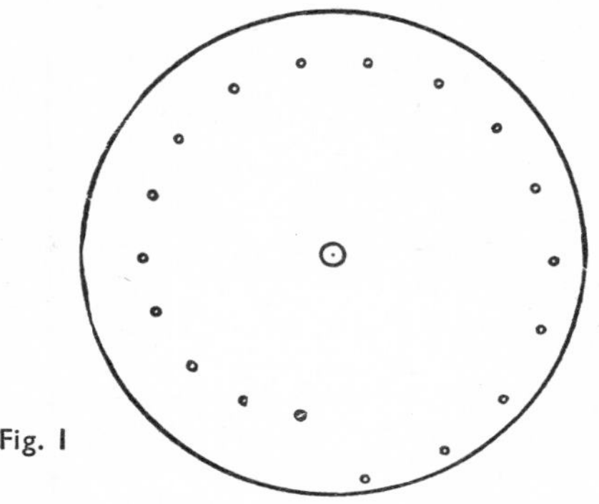
Fig. 1

Early Experiments.—As soon as the telephone was invented the possibility of seeing by electricity was thought of, but it was not until 1873 when it was found that Selenium allowed more or less current to pass according to the light falling on it that the first hesitant steps were taken. Of the many complicated and ingenious methods evolved one only need be mentioned. It employed a disc perforated with a series of holes on its edge arranged in a spiral form to both break up the image for transmission and to reform it at the receiving station. (Fig. 1.)

All the early efforts, however, came to grief through a few definite causes. Selenium as a means of converting light variations into electrical current variations was slow in operation—it had a time-lag as it is called—there was no convenient and easy way of turning a varying electric current into a varying source of light and in any case there was no means of turning the very feeble currents the Selenium cell passed into currents powerful enough to work the crude apparatus available.

The whole thing had to wait until electrical engineers had learned how to employ free electrons to control electric currents, to produce light and to follow and trace rapid current fluctuations. The current-controlling device when invented was called a "thermionic valve," we call them "wireless valves" now; the second device was the "gas discharge lamp," of which the neon lamp is a popular example; and the third is the "cathode ray tube," a not-so-well-known piece of apparatus but invaluable in the laboratory for following and recording exceedingly rapid current fluctuations.

Those three made television really possible and their development and improvement have largely conditioned the improvement in television systems. There is another device known as a "photo-electric cell" which operates much more quickly than a Selenium cell, but it was more in the nature of a refinement than an essential in early television work, for ways were discovered of overcoming the Selenium time-lag.

The first step in any television system is to convert the picture or image to be sent into electric currents varying in intensity strictly with the light and shade in the original. How was it to be done?

One inventor suggested a large screen made up of a number of Selenium cells, before which the object to be televised would be placed. Each cell would be connected through its own current supply to an electric lamp forming part of a large screen at the receiving end. According to the light falling on the cells the lamps would light, partly light, or not light at all. The arrangement would have worked if the Selenium cells could have passed enough current to light the lamps (such an arrangement of lamps in a screen was used later to give public demonstrations), but the arrangement was insufferably clumsy and complicated.

Another suggested arrangement was that *one* cell should be caused to inspect the whole of the scene so rapidly that the eye could not follow its movement. Impossible as this may seem it was really very simple and was done by means of the disc already mentioned.

The required scene was picked up by a lens and focused on to the surface of the rapidly rotating disc. (Fig. 2.) As the spirally arranged holes passed they allowed the light from a definite portion of the picture to fall on the cell and so operate it. The current fluctuations so caused were used to operate a light source placed behind an identical disc rotating at the same speed at the receiving end. When both discs were rotating at a speed of 750 revolutions a minute the eye, unable to follow the individual holes, merely saw a more or less stable picture.

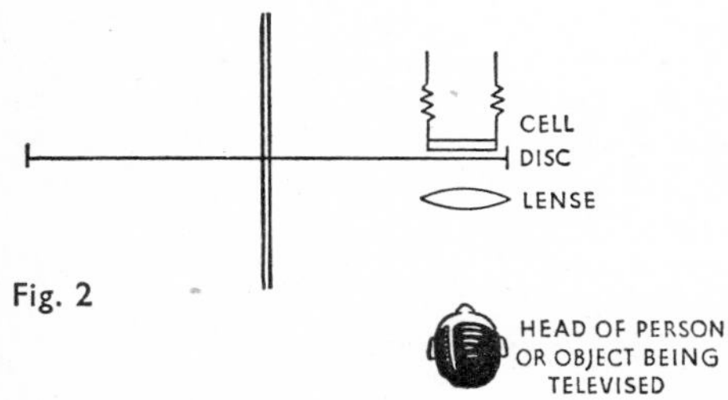

Fig. 2

It may be helpful before going further if one makes a simple disc as in A Fig. 3 with only four holes in it. Pin it down before a picture and trace out the area and shape of the portion of the picture before which the holes pass. It will be seen that approximately an area as at B is seen through the holes. The diameter of the wheel and the number of the holes in it fix definitely the size of the picture as to height and width.

Such a very simple arrangement, however, would give a very crude picture, so crude in fact as to be almost unrecognizable. If we want more detail we must have more holes and about the least number we can tolerate for reasonable detail is 30, and on this number much of the early television research was done. Thirty holes, by the way, demand a disc 20 in. in diameter if the picture is to measure 3 in. by 1 in.

When experimenting with the simple four-holed disc a number of defects inherent in any disc used for television purposes will be noticed. As it is impossible for one light source to be both bright and dull at the same time, it is obvious one hole of the disc must have left the picture before another starts to pass over it. This accounts for the wedge form given the picture in Fig. 4 B. Although as the disc is made larger and the holes more numerous the perfect rectangle is more nearly approached, but the distortion of shape is always present. It will be noticed, too, that if the holes are not correctly placed on their respective radii there will be some portions of the picture which are uncovered twice while other portions are not uncovered at all. Fig. 4 illustrates this diagrammatically with three adjacent holes. Much the same defect is caused also if the holes are incorrect as to size. The path traced out by one hole should lie beside and just touching but not intruding upon the path traced by the preceding or succeeding holes.

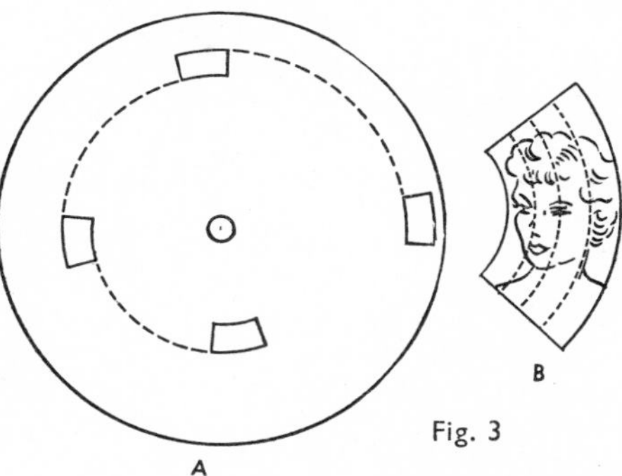

Fig. 3

With a pair of such discs, a Selenium cell behind the transmitting disc and a neon lamp behind the receiver all the early work on television was done. It was even used to demonstrate stereoscopic television and television in natural colour.

Apparatus Required.—To return to

simple television, however, the only additional apparatus required is a couple of electric motors to drive the discs and two wireless amplifiers, one to amplify the tiny currents passed by the Selenium cell and the other to make the received signal strong enough to work the neon lamp. The means of linkage between the two stations may be either wire or wireless.

Any amateur mechanic can make the discs, the chief skill needed being accuracy and patience in marking out and cutting the holes. If the disc is 20 in. in diameter and there are 30 holes each hole will have to be $\frac{1}{30}$ in. in diameter (that is if the picture is to be 1 in. wide by 3 in. high which is the standard shape in this country). The best material to use, because clean holes can be readily cut in it, is very thin aluminium or steel sheet not more than five to ten thousandths of an inch thick and perfectly flat. It can be purchased of any metal dealer.

To drive such a disc at least $\frac{1}{8}$ of a horse-power motor will be necessary, for the motor must run steadily and be well up to its work.

If such apparatus is constructed, and an attempt made to use it, one of the early difficulties of television will be met. However well made the motors and however reliable the current supply it is almost impossible to get two identical motors to run at the same speed, or even within ten revolutions of one another. For television

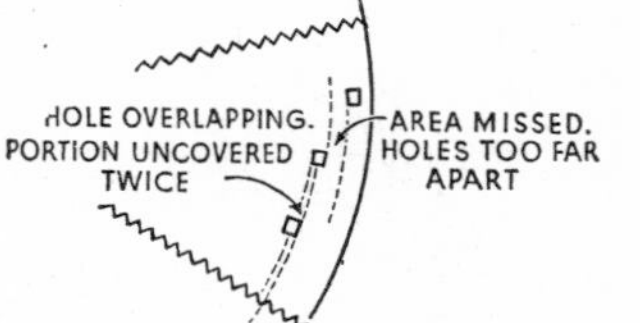

Fig. 4

not only must they run at the same speed precisely, even $\frac{1}{30}$ of a revolution fast or slow if there is a 30-hole disc is enough to put the image out, but they must be in step in relation to the holes in their respective discs. When the first hole in the transmitting disc begins its journey across the cell the first hole in the receiving disc must be beginning its journey across the neon lamp.

If the two motors are out of step some of the queer results shown in Fig. 5 will be seen, while if their speeds are different one may see merely a rapid succession of black dots travelling in a diagonal direction, or the picture one should see is travelling down or up like a cinematograph film being slowly passed before one.

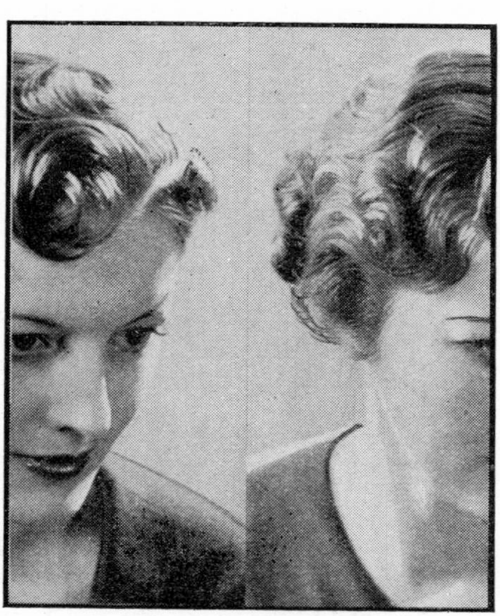

Fig. 5.—Effects when Transmitter and Receiver are out of step

The Television Signal.—To keep the two motors in step the television signal is used. If one considers the matter it will be realized that the transmitting station is sending out a succession of current impulses corresponding to the passage of the holes in the disc before the Selenium cell, each one separated from the next by a brief pause. This interrupted current is used to control the speed of the receiving motor. The received signal after being amplified is tapped. The main portion of it goes to the neon lamp to form the image. The other portion is fed to a piece of apparatus shown diagrammatically at Fig. 7.

Fig. 6.—Effect when Transmitter and Receiver speeds are at variance

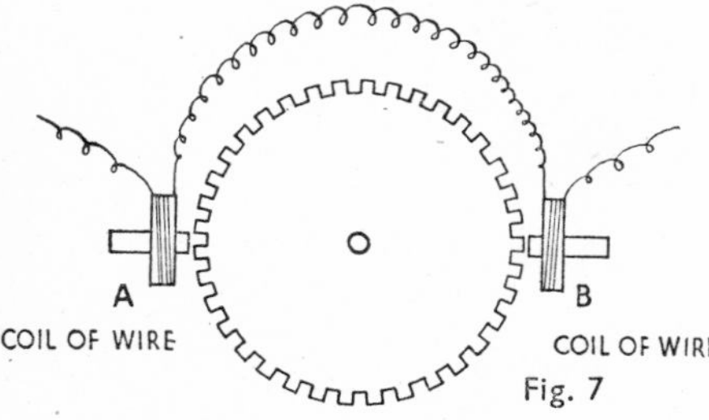

Fig. 7

The toothed wheel has a tooth for each hole in the disc. It is made of cast iron and mounted rigidly on the receiving motor shaft. The current running through the coils of wire A and B has no effect if both motors are running at the same speed, i.e. receiving and transmitting motors, but if the receiving motor goes slow the teeth on the wheel will be approaching the electric magnets formed by the coils A and B and they will tend to pull the wheel round or hurry it up. If, on the other hand, the motor is fast the pull will have the effect of slowing it. The receiving motor is initially adjusted to approximately the correct speed by means of a resistance.

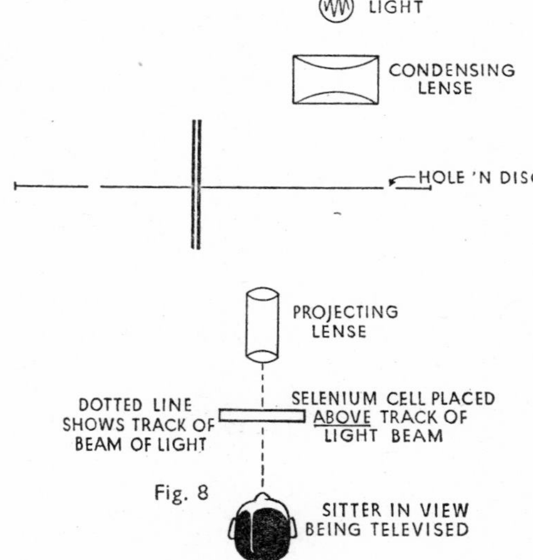

Fig. 8

With this simple apparatus television was proved and such outstanding events as transmission to America and to the *Berengaria* in mid-Atlantic in 1928 were carried out.

It was soon found, however, that it was not only costly to flood with intense light whatever was to be televised but it was in addition very unpleasant for any person in that light.

To get over the difficulty the transmitter was rearranged as in Fig. 8 so that a tiny beam of intense light swept step by step over the subject. The Selenium cell instead of being behind the disc was placed in front and immediately before the scene to be looked at and received the full light reflected back from it. This meant of course that there must be no light present other than that from the flickering beam—a much more pleasant state of affairs for whoever happened to be televised. It also made possible an extension of the area being transmitted. With the previous

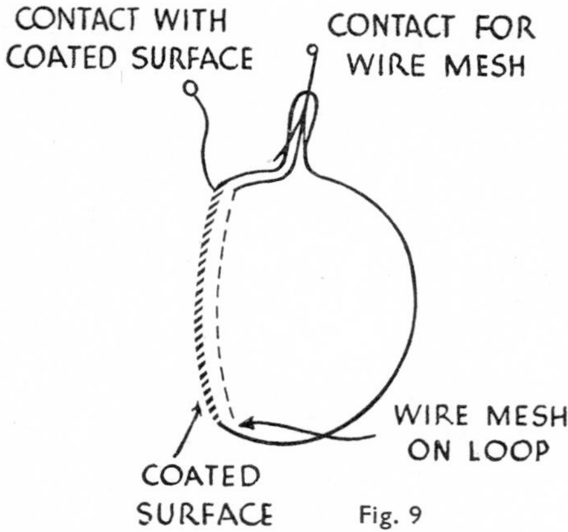

Fig. 9

arrangement it was not possible to do much more than the head and shoulders of a person—the light obtainable from any larger view being far too weak to have any appreciable effect. Now two or three full-length figures became possible and at the same time quite tiny objects within the definition imposed by the 30 lines per picture were recognizable.

About this time (somewhere about 1928) electrical engineers had developed to a useful degree a property of some of the rarer metals, notably Caesium and Potassium. These when sprayed thinly over a glass surface emit, when in a complete vacuum, a feeble stream of electrons strictly proportional to the amount of light falling on them, and with far less time-lag than Selenium.

The illustration Fig. 9 shows the general arrangement of one of these "photo-electric" cells as they are called. A is the coated surface and B a fine wire mesh or a wire loop placed before and fairly close to it to catch the electron stream and so conduct it to an ordinary wireless amplifier to be brought up to usable strength. The whole, of course, is placed in a highly exhausted glass bulb. The better the vacuum the better the cell works. Furthermore, a whole group of such cells can be used together, thus making possible a useful result from faint gleams of light which before were undetectable.

The Mirror Drum.—Together with the development of the photo-electric cell the neon lamp was developed. The "beehive" type in which a spiral coil of wire was made to glow speedily disappeared and in its place was produced a lamp having a large flat metal plate which glowed. The voltage necessary to work it, also, was reduced to a manageable figure. At the same time a fresh type called a "crater neon" was produced. In this the glow

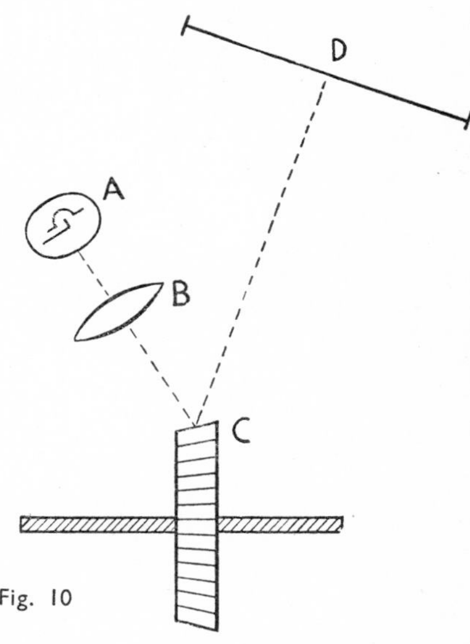

Fig. 10

took place in a small cup and was intensely bright. This led to a further improvement in television receivers. The perforated disc was discarded at the receiving end and in its place a wheel was used, around its rim being arranged 30 small mirrors each set at a slightly different angle to the spindle of the wheel in such a way that a beam of light would be reflected successively over 30 adjacent paths on a screen, giving a similar effect to the disc. Fig. 10 shows this diagrammatically—A is the crater neon, B a lens to focus it on to, C the mirror drum as it is called, and D is the screen where the image is seen.

The mirror drum made possible a very much larger, brighter and more satisfactory image.

Speed of Transmission.—While television was struggling forward, and by television is meant the transmission of living images by wire or wireless *without* photographic aid in any form, other methods of picture transmission also were going ahead. Some workers, in Germany principally, used cinema film with television systems as a useful aid to experiment and telegraph engineers generally brought the telegraphing of ordinary photographs to such a stage of perfection that the original could only be told from the transmitted photo with the aid of a microscope. All systems worked on the line of varying light to build up their pictures, but where television was tied to 30 lines *per picture*, irrespective of size, the transmission of photographs telegraphically used something like 100 *lines per inch* and if necessary took as much as an hour or longer to send a single picture. Television on the other hand had to send something like $12\frac{1}{2}$ pictures per second to present movement with reasonable fidelity.

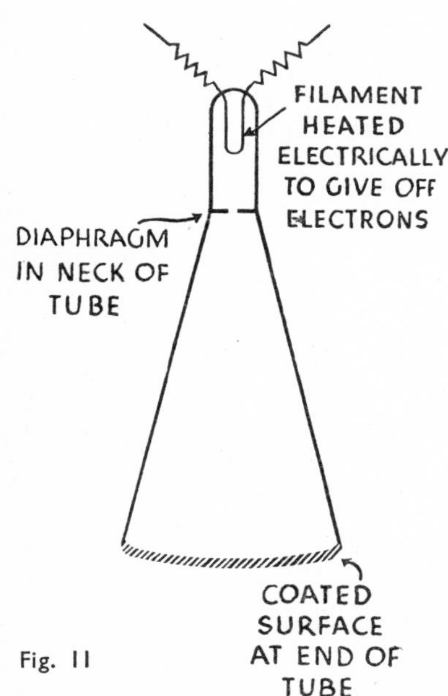

Fig. 11

If anything better was to be done some new method had to be tried, and again it was an electron-operated device which offered a solution. It is known as a cathode-ray tube.

In this a heated filament gives off a stream of electrons which are passed through a diaphragm having a small aperture, and allowed to fall on a screen composed of a mixture of Calcium, Tungsten and Zinc silicate. This glows or fluoresces brilliantly when the electrons fall on it.

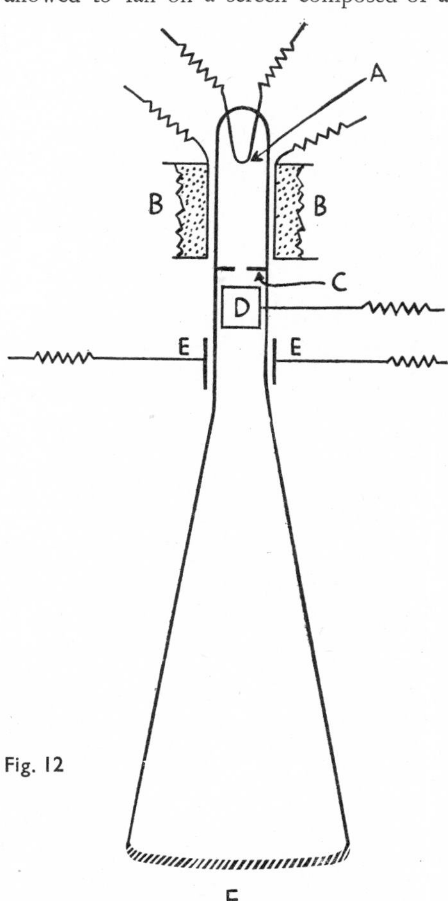

Fig. 12

The tube, shown diagrammatically in Fig.

12, has to have, as in the case of the photo-electric cell, as nearly perfect a vacuum as is physically possible.

The electron stream (the cathode rays) can be deflected from their normal straight ahead course either by a magnetic field or by passing it between parallel plates to which a high voltage is applied. In Fig. 12 is shown a cathode-ray tube set up for television. A is the heated filament emitting the electrons, B is a large coil arranged round the narrow portion of the tube to concentrate the rays, C the diaphragm through which they pass, D and E are either coils of wire forming electric magnets or plates to which a high voltage is applied and which divert the beam, F is the fluorescent screen on which the image appears.

The cathode-ray tube has no limit of operation as regards speed for the ray is without weight or inertia and responds instantly to any current variation on D and E. With it any number of lines per picture or even per inch can be secured and any number of complete pictures per second. A re-arrangement of it combined with the photo-electric cell is available for the transmitting end to convert any image or scene into current impulses. Its only limitations are the size in which it can be made and the fact that glass at times is porous and allows air to leak in and spoil the vacuum. The strength of the glass also imposes a limitation.

As there are no motors, synchronization difficulties are simplified. Two alternating current signals at widely separated frequencies being all that is required to keep both transmitter and receiver in step. These two signals are sent out with the main television signal and filtered out at the receiving end, a piece of wireless wizardry that development in that art has made a commonplace for many purposes.

Television, like wireless, has gained much from amateurs—it is still open to those who can afford the rather costly cathode-ray tube—and it must not be forgotten that John L. Baird, the man who has done more for television in England than anyone else and whose early work started other countries taking a serious interest in it, was himself an "amateur" in the beginning and had to find out everything for himself with the simplest of apparatus and next to no cash for experiments.

THEATRICALS

To see a play is a good thing but to take part in one is infinitely better. Apart from the pleasure which can be derived from acting or reading plays many people are realizing that a new world is before them, a world of culture, of literature and art, and a place where they can find opportunities for self-expression so often lacking in their ordinary life.

There is a wealth of fresh knowledge to be derived from the study of plays and when this study is combined with the development of voice, manner, gesture, poise and self-confidence, in an atmosphere of delightful comradeship, the advantages of such a study are very attractive.

Play Reading.—To the many who shun the glare of a public performance or to the small society which has yet to feel its feet, a play-reading circle is suggested as the best way in which to begin. It must be remembered that royalties have to be paid for the performing rights of most modern plays and the cost of this should be ascertained before a play is decided upon. Such royalties are not necessary if the play is done privately. There are, however, many good plays on which there are no fees, and works by Shakespeare, Sheridan, etc., can be done without payment. Members of the circle should meet at regular intervals to read and discuss plays. One person should be chosen to direct the proceedings, allot the parts, etc. His leadership must be followed and his orders accepted as final, otherwise there is a tendency to bicker and argue even among friends.

The members should sit at ease, preferably

in a semi-circle. It is sometimes a good thing—especially when reading plays by modern authors such as Shaw or Barrie—to appoint someone to read the stage-directions.

No attempt is made to act the plays though the readers will naturally interpret the characters to the best of their ability. By this means, at comparatively little cost, a preliminary knowledge of stage technique is acquired, and there is a further advantage that plays which are, for many reasons unsuitable for production by a small society, can be interpreted and enjoyed in this manner. From this it is but a short step to the production of a play.

Choosing a Play.—Considerable care will have to be taken. Many types of plays are available for performance by amateurs, but for a first production the play should be of the simplest nature, and well within the capacity of those taking part.

Contrary to general belief a farce is difficult to produce and still more difficult to act. It must be carried through at high speed, cues must be picked up rapidly and the utmost use made of the improbable situations which arise. When an audience is very hilarious, great restraint on the part of the actors is necessary, the desire to join in their laughter being sometimes almost overwhelming. Drama, too, of the more serious type, should be avoided in the early stages, though after a little experience, there is no reason why this type of play should not be essayed.

Costume plays, too, must be considered carefully, since they generally necessitate, in addition to costumes, extensive sets and period furniture. This does not mean, of course, that costume plays should not be undertaken by dramatic societies—they are extremely interesting and also popular with the general public—but the ultimate cost must be calculated before such a play is attempted. If the costumes can be made by the members so much the better, but remember that any suggestion of "home-madeness" in either scenery or costumes will ruin the effect. A straight comedy offers the best vehicle for an inexperienced cast, though any straight play should also be suitable.

It is a good idea for all who contemplate either reading or acting plays to get into touch with the English Drama League, which will be found most helpful.

Stage and Cast.—When choosing a play one should bear in mind, first of all, the limitations of the stage upon which it is to be performed. The production of many good plays has been spoiled by the unsuitability of the stage. Next comes the question of the number of players. It is better to avoid plays with a large cast, though if the membership of the society is large and the size of the stage permits it, there is no objection to numbers, and a large cast usually means a good sale for tickets. Too small a cast imposes a great deal of work on the principals and may also result in the society having a number of disgruntled members whose abilities have been overlooked. A cast of about eight or twelve is generally satisfactory, though, of course, if some of the parts are minor ones, this number can be exceeded; but "doubling," or the playing of two parts by one person, may have to be resorted to in this case.

Scenery.—Some plays are unsuitable for amateur production on account of the changes of scenery. Small halls are badly designed from this point of view, and although audiences usually expect long waits between scenes at amateur productions, they have never become accustomed to them. Many good plays have been written in which the same scene is used throughout, and this is a very desirable type of play to choose. The "set," as it is called, can be carefully prepared beforehand, and being of a semi-permanent nature can be much more effective than one which has to be "struck" after a few minutes. When changes have to be made, the scenery used should be as light and simple as possible, and rehearsals should be held of the changing of the set so that this can be done in the minimum of time.

Scenery is always a problem to small societies. It may, of course, be hired and if the setting required is an elaborate one or back cloths are necessary, this is to be recommended. The cost of hiring is not great, but in remote districts the cost of carriage may be so high as to make hiring

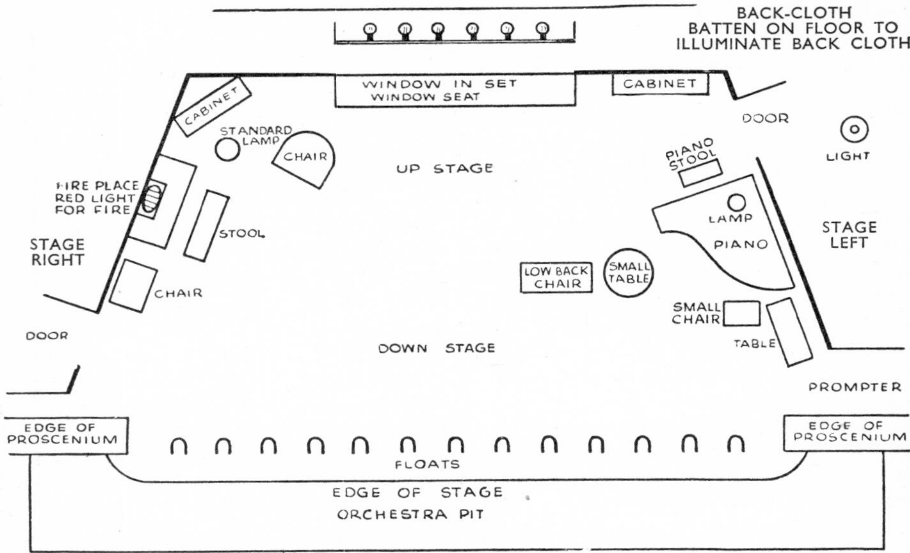

Fig. I.—Typical arrangement for a Living Room Set on small Stage

impossible. After all, there is nothing like making one's own, and every society is bound to have a handy man who can knock up some screens. They should be about 3 ft. by 8 ft., depending, of course, on the size of the hall. The framework is of battens, properly cross braced and covered on the one side with canvas. This can be painted, papered or distempered. If hooks are attached to each screen, as in the illustration (Fig. 2) or a cord tied to one of the top hooks, a number of screens can be quickly attached to form a setting and as quickly released when a change is necessary. It cannot be too strongly emphasized that plain background-curtains of a neutral colour, aided, of course, by suitable furniture on the stage would, in many cases, make a much more effective setting than elaborately painted scenery. "The greatest art is to conceal art," but a good deal of stage scenery falls short in this respect. Simplicity, as far as possible, should be sought in every production, for, after all, "the play's the thing."

Lighting.—This important subject is unfortunately one that depends too much upon individual circumstances for any detailed advice to be given. Theatres, of course, have their own lighting staff who will be able to meet the requirements of most amateur producers; but when the performance is to take place in a hall or assembly room, the amateur is usually confronted by difficulties that are best overcome by consulting a local electrician. He will be able to state whether it is possible to have foot-

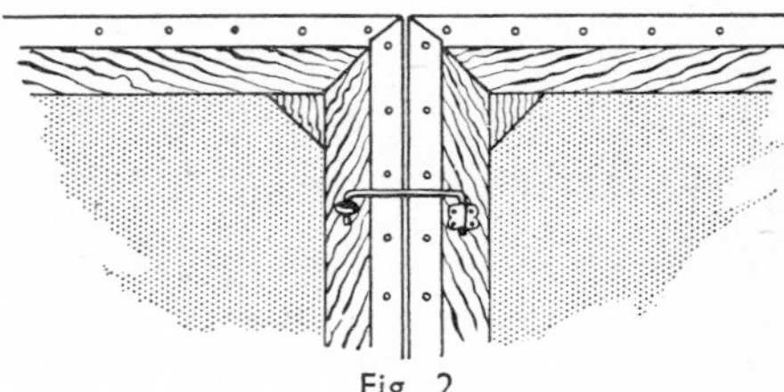

Fig. 2

lights or "floats," overhead lights (arranged in rows called battens), and incidental lights for flooding a back-cloth, illuminating a fire or window or "spotting" a particular person or place on the stage, and whether the installation will permit the use of "dimmers," etc.

The Producer.—In the production of any play the producer is the most important person, for upon him the success of the play largely depends. A producer should have a thorough understanding of stage technique, a complete knowledge of the play, an unfailing sense of humour and infinite patience. If the society does not number such within its boundaries, it would be better to have an outsider. In many cases this is advisable since he is less likely to be accused of favouritism. The producer in conjunction with the committee will then proceed to the casting of the play. Characters should each be carefully considered and the name or names of the persons most suited to the parts in question noted. This should be followed by a reading, when the persons selected for the parts should be asked to go through certain passages of the play, after which the final selection should be made. It is advisable to have understudies, particularly for the principal parts, though with many societies this is impossible. Such understudies could, of course, take minor characters in the play if their services are required. Rehearsal dates must then be arranged and strictly adhered to. In many societies it is a practice for the players to give written undertakings to the producer to appear at all rehearsals unless he has given them permission to be absent.

Rehearsals.—The first rehearsal or two should be devoted to going through the whole play with books or script, so that the players will become accustomed to the sound of their own voices and also to the movements that are required of them. Necessity for making the correct movement at the right time should be insisted upon from the beginning so that proper habits may be formed. The synchronizing of the movement with a particular word or line will also assist in memorizing the part. A definite start should be made on the first part of the play and only when this is well in hand and its purpose thoroughly understood should movement be made to the next. Some people can memorize much more quickly than others, so the use of books may be permitted for some time, though naturally real acting cannot be attempted until the players are word perfect.

Memorizing.—At this point it would perhaps be as well to indicate how parts can best be studied and memorized. The play should first of all be read through very carefully and visualized as far as possible. Then the speeches of the player should be marked in the book and read through a number of times until the sense, if not the actual words, is memorized. This is of considerable importance. To memorize in parrot fashion is extremely difficult, but provided the sense has been grasped the correct words may be acquired at a little later date. Cue words—those immediately before the player's speech—must also be memorized so that the player can pick up his cues immediately.

Movement and Timing.—Considerable attention should be given to these. Incorrect timing may mean an actor completing his lines before arriving at the right spot, and wrong movements will frequently result in interference and bad grouping of the players. Gestures should be made deliberately and without any jerkiness. Players who are not speaking should be careful about their movements, as any sudden action on their part, even the raising of a hand, will distract attention from the speaker. Exits also have to be very carefully timed and the player would do well to mark his book in such a manner that he knows exactly when to make the proper move.

Many players seem to be at a loss to know what to do with their hands, but these should not normally be moved unless required to emphasize some part of the speech or to carry out some definite action. At other times they should hang by the side, not however, in any rigid manner.

Turns on the stage should always be made towards the audience; in other words the player should never, unless the play definitely calls for it, turn his back to the audience. Nor should he look out into the audience, except perhaps at a critical moment of the play when his gaze, attention and voice should all be directed to the gallery or the back of the hall.

Make-up.—Half the enjoyment in taking part in a play is derived from making up in the character it is desired to portray. Clothes must, of course, be in keeping, attention being paid to all details. There is not sufficient space here to indicate more than a few features of the art of make-up and the player would do well to obtain one of the many handbooks published on this subject.

As a general rule, however, make-up for amateur productions is of the lightest description, the stage lighting of small halls being seldom as brilliant as that found on the professional stage. Whatever the character it is desired to portray, the groundwork of suitable colouring should first of all be worked into the skin, to be followed by linings and rouge as required.

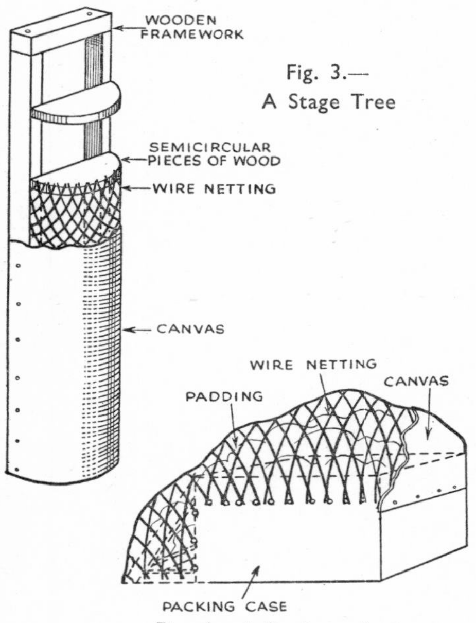

Fig. 3.—A Stage Tree

Fig. 4.—A Rock or Bank

For juvenile parts no lines are necessary, but for older characters lines may be drawn as lightly as possible with a lake pencil backed by a white liner, thus giving the effect of furrows. High spots on the cheek bones can be emphasized by the use of white merged into darker colouring below. The appearance of the face at a very short distance can be altered in this way. Nose paste can be used for any considerable changes in features, but is not recommended to the amateur. Make-up should never be too heavy. Lines should be suggested rather than definitely drawn. The whole make-up should be finished off with powder applied with a hare's foot or large woollen puff. Care should be taken to see that the make-up does not stop short behind the ears or under the chin, and the hands too must be made up in accordance with the character required. Wigs should be avoided when possible, but if used, the actor's head must be carefully measured in order to make sure of a good fit. These wigs can be hired from any reputable agency. The front part of the wig is carefully "joined up," i.e. merged with grease paint, in such a way as to make the joint indistinguishable. All wigs should be carefully brushed before fitting.

The Dress Rehearsal should be carried out in exactly the same manner as the real performance. The curtain should go up on time, all properties should be at hand, all effects used, and the Prompter should be in attendance on the correct side of the stage. (*See* Fig. 1 for stage directions.) Timing of the play should be taken in order to see whether any speeding up is necessary so that the play may finish at the proper hour. It should not be necessary for the producer to interrupt the play during the dress rehearsal, he should leave any criticisms he may have to make to the end of the act. The orchestra should, of course, be in attendance, particularly if musical effects are required during the play.

Now comes the night! The advertising manager has done his part and the players theirs by selling tickets as well as by rehearsing, and the hall should be comfortably filled. The producer hands over his responsibility to the stage manager, who thereafter takes control and the curtain goes up on a performance that will not only give pleasure to the spectator, but also make the players and supernumeraries feel that their labours have been really worth while.

TRAVEL

THE best hobbies are those which are never exhausted—and among these *travel* ranks high. Once the fascination has taken hold of you it is almost certain that you are a devotee for life. Even when age or circumstances prevent your further wanderings, a memory richly stored with experiences will give you delight, and the still-stirring *wanderlust* will find fresh outlets in reading, lectures, and varied studies. Life is never long enough for anyone who loves to travel to see and do all for which he yearns. If you know one country well—and who ever does?—then there are other countries around; and beyond one's continent are other continents.

Seeing things is not the whole of travel, and no one who really travels would care to be mistaken for one who merely tours. There are peoples in every land, curiously alike the world over, yet curiously different even in neighbouring districts. To appreciate the qualities of different peoples, to recognize their peculiar virtues, and become absorbed in their atmosphere so that ever afterwards you know something of their point of view and have perhaps given them to understand a little of your own—that is not only a most fascinating sort of hobby, but an immensely worth-while bit of work in the world to-day, when perhaps the greatest need is a friendly unity of all peoples.

How shall your travels begin?

Well, travel definitely does not consist in buying "comprehensive tickets" at London; journeying with a party who carry their national atmosphere round with them; being met at every stage of the journey, and staying at cosmopolitan hotels crowded with other tourists. That way one may become an experienced tourist, but never a traveller.

You must begin to travel by going alone, or with just one or two well-chosen companions. You will make your own arrangements—and the fewer you make in England the better, from the point of view of experience. If you have never been abroad before you cannot do better than begin with France or Belgium. A brief trip across the Channel need cost little more than a visit to an English coastal resort, yet it can be the beginning of this thrilling new hobby of yours. A couple of days, well used, can teach a great deal. If economy is of first importance some port like Dieppe, Boulogne, or Ostend, will suit. But take pains to avoid, so far as you can, English-speaking places and people.

Passports.—You will need a passport, not necessarily for the little trip just mentioned, but with your eye on future jaunts. Send for necessary forms to the Passport Office, Westminster, S.W.1.

If you have wife and children, get them included, even if they are not travelling with you immediately—it may be useful later on.

Travelling Sickness.—Do not be deterred because you are a "bad traveller." Train, sea, air sickness can often be completely overcome by persistent effort—frequently they are no more than the result of lack of practice in journeying. Eat a normal meal before setting out, with plenty of sugars and starches, but little fat, and that in itself will safeguard you. In the train sit facing the engine and have the compartment ventilated, but not draughty; shut the window in tunnels; eat an occasional piece of barley sugar—this is useful in other than train travel. In a ship, stay on deck, if you feel like sitting up, or lie flat on your back in a bunk—providing below deck is not too stuffy; do a little light reading to divert your thoughts; do not walk about; have a hot drink when you come ashore. In an aeroplane keep your thoughts occupied cheerfully; have some chewing-gum, but not too much of it; do not be afraid to look down.

Luggage.—The less luggage you have with you the better; the ideal way to travel is with no more than a rucsack or a single suitcase. The rucsack's marked advantage over the suitcase is that it allows both hands to be free. Additionally, of course, a load on one's back seems much lighter than in one's hand; and you will appreciate not having a clumsy bag dangling at your side when you get in the crowd by the gangway as you leave your ship at your Continental port, and go through the Customs. By the way, never attempt to conceal anything from the Custom's officers, it is neither honest nor does it pay!

Language.—It is possible to visit a country without knowing the language, but no sensible traveller does it if he can help it. A great deal of enjoyment comes from trying to understand and making yourself understood in the national tongue. For practical purposes it is surprising how little is essential. Here is a list of words and phrases which, translated and memorized will get you through in ordinary circumtances:

Yes;
No;
Please;
Thank you;
Good day;
Good night;
Sir;
Madam;
Miss;
I want to go to ——;
Is this the way to ——?;
Is it near?;
One third-class ticket for ——;
Return ticket;
Where is the luggage office?;
Which is the train for ——?;
Is this a through carriage to ——?;
Can I change money here?;
I want a room for one night;
What is the price?;
That is too dear;
I will take that;
Breakfast;
Lunch;
Dinner;
Water;
Coffee;
Bread and butter;
What stamp does this letter require?;
Have you any ——?;
Is there a bus to ——?

You will find, generally, that you will be able to make yourself understood in another language much more easily than you can understand when it is spoken to you—that will be chiefly because the few words which are familiar will be lost in a flood of words you do not know. Listen hard therefore for the familiar, and cling to them. For instance, a Parisian may, while giving you directions, speak a long sentence, in which you may recognize only *deuxième* and *gauche*, but they will be the key words, and that second turn on the left may be exactly what you needed to know, helpful as the other particulars may have been.

If you are very unsure of pronunciation it is good to point to your word or sentence in your phrase-book, when some friendly person is available, and then, when he repeats it, to write down the sound as well as you can for your own guidance.

Incidentally, Esperanto is a language which already can be of considerable service in almost any country, not merely because there are to be found many people with some knowledge of it, but also because it simplifies the matter of learning almost any national language because it is based on so many of the basic roots of human speech.

Money.—Get used to the currency of the country in which you travel as quickly as possible, and also learn the numbers up to a hundred—usually a fairly easy task.

Letters.—If you want letters posted to you you can leave your address in England as "Poste Restante, *Paris*," or wherever you propose to be. When you call to enquire for letters, have your passport with you.

Food.—You will do well to get familiar with the terms of the menu quite early. In most Continental countries "fixed price" meals are obtainable very reasonably, sometimes extraordinarily cheaply. If economy is important you should get all your meals at outside restaurants of suitable type rather than in the hotel dining-room. Your breakfast, for instance, in France, will invariably cost you more at your hotel than if you take a *café complet* round the corner. Do not look for English food when abroad, any more than you would look for English customs. Find the best in the new country—and in most Continental countries it is a rather wonderful best—and experiment and learn until you can order an agreeable meal with confidence. Remember that restaurant waiters often pay the proprietor for the privilege of holding their posts, and so depend for their earnings entirely on tips. Ten per cent. of the bill is the accepted standard; do not go below it. If, to your account, *service* is added, the matter will be settled without further trouble to you, and you need not tip.

Finding Your Way.—On arriving at a new city, buy a plan of it at or near the railway station, and set about studying the layout of the place. First find the station where you are, and then discover the relative position of the heart of the city. If there is an important river or waterside you will almost certainly find that the principal street runs parallel with it, with other main streets at right angles. It will be unlikely that the city on either side of a river will be of similar importance or character—all London's best-known streets are north of the Thames.

Accommodation.—Assuming that you have booked nothing in advance you will need to look for lodgings. Policemen may direct you to a suitable district, and then enquiries and comparisons may at last bring you to a decision. If you would travel cheaply much will depend on your willingness to find out prices. Possibly, however, you will have had recommendations or information before leaving England. It should certainly be your habit, before going abroad, to find out everything possible about the places you propose to visit. Books, maps, talks with people of experience, all such things will smooth out later difficulties and make your trip more enjoyable. Much of the pleasure of travel lies in anticipation, and to collect and pore over the literature so readily available from the London offices of other countries, around the Haymarket, lengthens the joy of one's proposed journey.

Forming the Travel Habit.—It is good to form the habit of regular travel. When once the determination to go out of England, say once a year, has been formed, it is surprising how somehow one finds the opportunity to do it. Gradually one's journeys lengthen, increasing experience giving more confidence, and more longings. The trip to the French coast will inevitably be followed by a visit to Paris. Paris is the stepping-off place for so much of Europe. It will be helpful to suggest a few journeys which may follow a visit to Paris, beginning with those which can be done most easily and cheaply.

Suggested Journeys.—Dover, Ostend, Bruges, Ghent, Brussels, London. This need cost no more than a trip to Paris, and it has the advantage that from Ostend one may just slip across the frontier into Holland and so have a glimpse of an additional country. Before starting this or any other trip time-tables and booklets can be obtained from the principal London termini to help in making your plans.

Paris, Lyons, Geneva, London. This allows also for Dijon—Rouen can be taken on the way to Paris. And at Geneva, the "world's centre," one can get a unique taste of the new internationalism which is breaking down old isolations and prejudices. On the return one may go through Lille or Amiens, or by way of Belgium. It is good to become familiar as soon as possible with the various cross-Channel routes—Southampton–Cherbourg, this can be done by Atlantic liner; Southampton–Havre; Newhaven – Dieppe; Folkestone – Boulogne; Dover–Calais; Dover–Ostend; Tilbury–Dunkirk; Tilbury–Flushing; Harwich–Rotterdam, and so on. Use one route for the outward journey and another for the return.

Paris, Lucerne, Cologne, London. This will allow you to get in France, Switzerland, Germany, Belgium or Holland. And if you care to visit Geneva too you may make a trip from there to Chamonix at the foot of Mont Blanc.

Amsterdam, Hague, Rotterdam, Brussels. This short journey brings you right down Holland and gives an opportunity of returning to Croydon by air—a comparatively short and inexpensive, but satisfying flight.

Paris, Bale, Milan, Venice, Bologna, Genoa, London. The Italian lakes can be seen in this lovely north Italian trip.

Genoa, Pisa, Rome, Naples, Sicily, Florence, Milan, London. This may be varied by going from Naples, via Syracuse, to the lovely little island of Malta, thence to Tunis—to set foot in Africa with its sun and sand and teaming bazaars; then back to London via Marseilles.

Paris, Bordeaux, Madrid, Seville, Lisbon, London. Spain and Portugal are countries to loiter in, and, for new experience, one may slip across to Tangiers.

Marseilles, Athens, Belgrade, Trieste, London. There is almost infinite variety of route when one begins to go so far afield as this. It is tempting to go the little farther into Asia, and to see Istanbul, Sofia, Bucharest, Budapest, Vienna, Prague.

Berlin, Warsaw, Moscow, Leningrad, London. Here again there is so much in the intervening distances.

And so one might go on. Once you are started on this hobby of travel, imagination knows no limits. And, since shipping companies cater so well in these days for those who must consider costs, one easily continues to think of voyages to the east and the west, the north and the south. One other complication, however, comes in at this point—time is required for longer journeys, and that for many keen travellers, makes impracticable, at any rate for a great part of their lives, the more distant wanderings. But if you are bound in all your journeyings to just a few weeks there is practically the whole of Europe still available and the exploration of this medley of little countries can well take a lifetime—for even if the United States of Europe should arrive before you have done it is quite certain that all the fascinating differences of the component peoples will not be obliterated.

Cruising.—For those who love the sea a new form of travel has come—*cruising*. This, while not giving many contacts with other countries, is attractive because of the ease of travel, the healthfulness of the life aboard, and the comparative luxury and freedom from care which the organizers of cruises make possible.

The minimum cost of a pleasure cruise can be reckoned as a pound per day, and it is possible to take such cruises from about three pounds upwards.

Cruising Kit.—Though you may set off on a Continental ramble happily enough with a rucsack, the requirements for a cruise are rather different. Dress, for instance, has much to do with proper enjoyment. A man, to be well equipped, should have one or two lounge suits, sports clothes, dinner jacket, light mackintosh, warm coat, two swim suits and a wrap. For women, of course, there is more varied scope—a warm coat is essential, evenings aboard are chilly. Then tweeds, which always are popular; mackintosh; several washing frocks, and frocks for the evening; swim suits and wrap; berets or small felt hats; a broader hat for the sun; sandals, tennis shoes; and possibly a fancy dress. High-heeled shoes are not worn on deck—sports clothes are the rule right through the daytime.

The Daily Routine.—When you have found your cabin and unpacked make the acquaintance of the appropriate stewards and arrange times for your morning bath and so on, also discovering when and where you are to have meals.

In the daytime, games like ring tennis, bullboard, deck quoits, shuffle board, deck golf, will probably be available. So will bathing. Take full advantage of the open-air swimming pool, but do not overdo sun bathing, or you will regret it the rest of the cruise.

The "utility services" on a ship are surprisingly thorough. If you are ill there is, naturally, the surgeon available. But in addition you can probably have any photographic work done; buy such things as cigarettes, chocolates, stationery, stamps; have hair dressing and manicuring; get full information about shore trips or anything else; have clothes pressed and laundered; buy souvenirs, and the many odds and ends whose need you do not realize until you begin the cruise.

At the office of the purser you may mail letters, change money, send telegrams and wireless messages, and get assistance in such predicaments as the losing of anything.

Deck chairs are obtainable free from the deck steward, and boots are cleaned without cost by the Boots.

Take care what souvenirs you buy at ports of call—there is usually so much rubbish awaiting you, often at exorbitant prices. Get information aboard first as to what things will be liable to duty—if you have to pay heavily at the Customs it may make the cost out of proportion to value.

Tipping.—It is best to allot ten per cent. of the total passage money to tips—three pounds if your ticket has cost thirty.

Divide this into three equal parts—one-third to bed-room service, one-third to dining-saloon service; one-third to other and personal services.

VEGETABLE GROWING

GIVEN a good sized rectangle with sheltering walls, fences or hedges, with a good exposure to the sun, any amateur ought to get good results. A level stretch is the easiest to work, provided it is not in a hollow; an elevated spot is best, to avoid frost which always falls.

Plan the Vegetable Garden.—Plans, as usual come before practice. Reserve space for a tool shed, for frames and manure and have, if possible, a wide enough path to allow for carting manure; if this is not possible have it wide enough for wheeling a barrow along. Fruit may be grown on the walls and there may be espalier fruit trees along the margins of paths. Herbs may be grown on small beds under the lee of the walls but the main cropping ground should be well out in the sun and with as few paths as possible. And these should only be soft paths in the soil about a foot wide; for they will vary with every different crop and are therefore only temporary, at any time. The wide path should, however, be well made and drained. Edgings may be of brick, wood or tiles. Tiles, if a little expensive at first, are very satisfactory and lasting. This preserves a neat appearance and is better than a live edge of plants; these are apt to harbour slugs and pests.

Tools.—Buy the best tools you can afford. A good Skelton spade, a digging fork, a wide pronged fork for lifting manure, hoes and rakes, a good line and a measuring rod. A wooden dibber and a trowel will also be necessary. A hand fork for weeding is useful. Gradually you will acquire other tools but buy as few as possible to begin with until you have a knowledge of good and bad ones.

Soil.—A good turfy loam is best, but as in the flower garden, one has to make the best of the soil one has and to improve it as one goes along as knowledge increases. Much depends on the crops to be grown at any given time. In an old garden the soil, having been much used, is sometimes sour. Lime is beneficial—6 oz. to the square yard. This should, however, be applied only if no stable manure is being dug in at the same time.

The chief thing is the deep working of the soil, trenching and proper cultivation are absolutely essential if good vegetables are to be grown. Trenching is carried out as for the flower garden and manure applied in the same way; except where carrots or beetroot are to be grown. No manure should be used for these crops.

All plants have certain chemical constituents and some of these they draw from the soil, namely, nitrates, potash, phosphates and lime. Nitrates make good green foliage and increased growth; phosphates feed the flowers and seeds, potash supplies starch and lime sweetens. Constant cropping of the ground exhausts the soil of these and for this reason manures are used to return them to it, and to improve deficient soils. Horse manure or mixed horse, cow and pig manure are the best. Horse manure should be dug in at the rate of one ton to ten square rods or four large barrow-loads to every 20 square ft.

The Cropping Plan.—In planning the crop rotation you must plan for three years ahead. First mark off enough ground to contain permanent crops such as rhubarb, asparagus, artichokes, and herbs. Annual crops are grown in the remaining ground. The main thing is not to grow the same things in the same ground two years running. Green crops are followed by roots and roots by fibrous rooted plants. After making a list of the plants desired, each kind must be assigned to its proper place in the plan. For instance: Cabbages, brussels sprouts, leeks, cauliflower, peas, beans, carrots and turnips, onions and beet, celery and potatoes, lettuce and parsnip might all be included in the list.

The First Year.—Divide the ground into three portions. In the first grow cabbages, cauliflower, sprouts and leeks. In the second grow peas and beans. In the third, grow potatoes and parsnip. In the third grow also carrots and beetroot with no manure or on a bed manured the previous year.

The Second Year crop the plots thus:

1. Peas, beans, lettuce, parsnips or potatoes;
2. Beet, carrots, leeks, cabbages, cauliflower or sprouts, lettuces or turnips;
3. Onions, turnips and lettuces.

The Third Year.

1. Beet, carrot, leeks;
2. Turnips, parsnips or potatoes;
3. Cabbages, cauliflower, sprouts and leeks.

Early Spring Work.—For the production of early vegetables a hotbed is necessary. This can be made at any season of the year for forwarding seeds and plants. It is perhaps most valued at the beginning of the year. As the harvest can only be gathered three months after the beginning of the work, if crops are desired in January the hotbed will require to be made in October. January is, however, a popular month for starting to make one.

Fresh hot manure and leaves are the best materials for building a hotbed, though in these days gardeners are resorting to other materials such as wool shoddy or coco-nut fibre. Manure, however, is always necessary whatever other material may be added to the heap unless a pit heated with water pipes is used. Early carrots, cauliflower, lettuces, peas and beans and leeks being only a few of the things that can be grown thus.

The Hotbed.—Procure a load of fresh manure and some litter of leaves. Mix these and leave for a week, taking care to see that the heap is kept moist. Turn occasionally and at the end of a week enough heat should have been generated. As a frame has to be fitted over the bed, measure the frame and then proceed to build the materials into a packed heap, making it a few feet wider than the frame. Tread well to make firm. The deeper the bed the greater the heat. A piece of wood is sometimes stuck into the heap and when this is warm the bed is ready for use. If a thermometer is used make it as high as possible or of a temperature suited to the seeds. When the bed has reached its greatest heat, soil to the depth of a few inches should be added to the top of the bed and seed sown. Frame lights should be adjusted and protecting mats used for frost. As plants should not be grown on the same bed from which they were raised from seed, two hotbeds will be necessary. If, however, the seedlings have commenced their life in a glass-house one bed will be sufficient. Sometimes the heat goes out of a bed before the crop is ready. This is a disaster and the only remedy is to remove some of the material from the outside of the bed and add fresh hot manure to keep it going for the required length of time.

Outside Work in the early part of the year consists of reducing the soil to a fine tilth or crumbly condition, suitable for sowing seed. Hoe well and where necessary single digging should be done. If the plan is ready and seeds ordered the next thing is to wait on the weather. Seed should never be sown in wet weather or when the soil is pasty. If the instructions given for the raising of annuals out-of-doors are faithfully followed for vegetables, fine seedlings will result. When March dust is flying sow your seed. A warm sunny day is the best to choose. It is a mistake to sow thickly; it is wasteful and as the tiny seedlings have no room to develop at a delicate state of their existence, healthy plants cannot result. Small seeds should be covered with about an inch of soil.

As soon as seedlings are large enough to handle, begin thinning. Move along the drills and as you pull out the surplus plants with one hand, hold down the plant to be left, and see that it is firmed; otherwise it will die. Some thinnings can only be thrown away. Cabbages, cauliflower, lettuce and even turnip can be transplanted. This work should be done in showery weather and if there is no rain, water should be given. A good soaking will be necessary, mere sprinkling will do more harm than good.

Hoeing.—Once the plants are thinned and transplanted hoeing must go on all season or until the crops are harvested, for two reasons, to keep the soil friable and do away with the necessity for watering and to keep weeds in check. If hoeing is neglected, many hours of weary weeding will have to be put in, and poorer crops gathered when done.

Planting should always be firm; a loosely planted plant might as well be thrown away; it will either die or be sickly. Use the measuring rod or line to ensure straight lines. A dibber is chiefly used for thinned plants, but for those transplanted from boxes it is important to use a trowel to ensure that the ball of earth be kept intact.

Rhubarb.—January and February are the months when rhubarb can be forced. When the leaves have withered lift roots and throw out into the open so that they can be frosted for a night or two. Then plant the crowns either under the staging of a heated greenhouse or in the hotbed. Keep the roots moist. A temperature of about 50° is sufficient. Sacking may be hung round the staging of the greenhouse to ensure darkness for forcing. Mats on the hotbeds will be needed. If the plants are to be forced outside, cover each root with an earthenware pot with lid, or an old apple barrel or box with lids. Before covering the roots outside, surround with stable manure, though in rich soil this is unnecessary. Do not force the same roots two years in succession; indeed forced roots are so exhausted that they take a few seasons to recover and should not even have stalks pulled during the year following forcing. It is well therefore to force only part of your stock in one year and a different part the following and so on. The best kinds for forcing are Victoria and Champagne Red.

Ordinary garden rhubarb needs deep working of the soil, much stable manure and, during the growing months, much liquid manure.

Green Crops.—Green vegetables such as cabbage, cauliflower, broccoli, brussels sprouts and kale or borecole are usually grown in such a way that there are several crops in a year. Cauliflower, being perhaps the choicest of them all, is grown succulent and tender in frames or hotbeds prepared as early as January or even in November or December. They should only be risked out-of-doors at these times in very mild districts such as Cornwall. And even in mild districts it is not the true cauliflower but broccoli that is produced from autumn to April, but, on the market, they are cauliflower.

Cauliflower.—In the open two crops of cauliflower are possible, autumn and summer. Rich soil is best. For the summer crop sow in February or March; for an autumn crop sow in April. Where a winter crop is possible sow also in August. Consult seedsmen's catalogues for early and late varieties. For forcing, Feltham Forcing is good; for summer, Sutton's First Crop and Snowball; for autumn, Autumn Giant or Dwarf Mammoth; for winter, plant Broccoli Roscoff because in doubtful districts cauliflower has to be wintered in frames and planted out in spring. Seedlings should be transplanted in the open, 4 in. apart; later they should be planted in their permanent quarters, 2½ ft. apart.

Broccoli, or hardy cauliflowers, are of two kinds, the ball and the sprouting. They may be raised in frames but are finished out of doors in rich soil. Sow in the open in April or May. Sow seeds about an inch deep in drills a foot apart, then transplant 2½ ft. apart. In autumn sow Leamington and Purple Sprouting. For autumn use, sow A1, Walchern or Veitch's Self Protecting; for Christmas, Early Penzance.

Cabbage needs rich, deeply dug soil prepared a few months ahead. Early spring is the time when they are appreciated so sow in July or August for cutting in April. Four sowings may be made in the year; in February or March—if in February under glass in heat, out of doors in March; for later crops sow in April and May. Seedlings should be transplanted in moist weather and final planting in rows 18 in. apart and plants 2½ or 2 ft., according to the variety being grown. Cabbages respond well to top dressings of Nitrate of Soda, Nitrate of Lime or Peruvian Guano, if for show purposes. Horn and hoof manures and superphosphates are also good. Conical shapes are the earlies, flat drumheads are usually late. Spring cabbage: First and Best or Flower of Spring. Dwarf kinds for spring: Ellam's Early Dwarf and Harbinger. Summer and autumn, Enfield Market and Leeds Market, Nonpareil and Winningstadt, the latter a very popular one for exhibition. Drumheads and Christmas Drumhead are both hardy for autumn and winter. For pickling: Dutch Blood Red and Dwarf Blood Red. Coleworts are loosely hearting cabbages used for spring. Savoys are a rough leaved type of cabbage

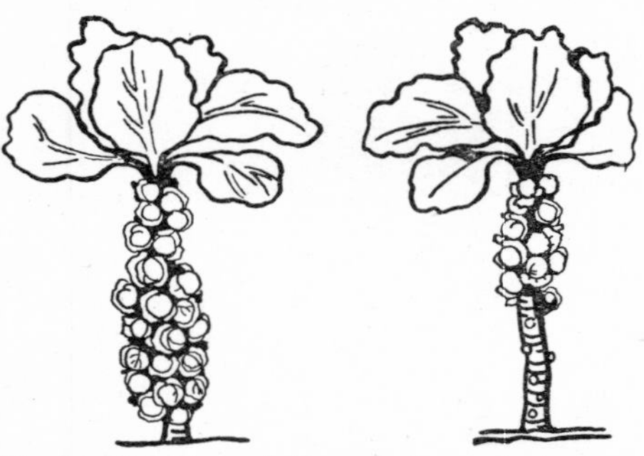

Fig. 1.—Pick Brussels Sprouts from the bottom of the stem

introduced from Savoy. They are invaluable in the north. For winter use Ormskirk is good; Tom Thumb is a small type. Earlies are Earliest of All and Favourite. They need the same conditions as for cabbages; if grown after potatoes, do not add any manure to the soil before planting.

Brussels Sprouts.—Three sowings may be made; the first in heat in March, the second out-of-doors in April, the third in July or August. Rich soil is essential but do not over feed either with horse manure or artificials or the sprouts will come loose and coarse. When cropping begins do not cut off tops as this arrests the development of sprouts. When planting it is important to make soil very firm; this means more sprouts and earlier; loose soil results in more leaves than sprouts. Good kinds to grow are, The Wroxton, dwarf; Dwarf Gem, Aigburth, a good one for either early or late sowing and sturdy.

Borecole, or Scotch Kale, is invaluable as a winter vegetable and is easy to grow. Sow in March or April and transplant when quite small to permament quarters. Spring greens may be obtained if the variety Asparagus Kale is sown in autumn. Webb's Hardy Sprouting or Cottager's Kale are also good for spring cropping. For autumn and winter use Tall Curled Scotch or Christmas Curled Scotch.

" Catch Crops."—A gardener who knows his business and has a small piece of ground to use, economizes in space by growing catch crops. In this way he increases the yield of his garden and is making the maximum use of it. Radishes, lettuce, spinach, coleworts, and even the larger growing things like kale, sprouts, borecole and broccoli can be used as catch crops. These crops are grown between other crops and are gathered before the main crop has reached full size. This is a very good way of making the most of space, provided it is not indulged in to the injury of the more important crop.

For instance coleworts, or spring cabbage, can be grown between the summer cropping cabbages. Lettuce may be grown between cauliflower, while cauliflower itself may be grown between rows of potatoes.

Spinach is easy to cultivate and is useful for sowing between cauliflowers. It should get plenty of moisture while growing and needs a deep soil in a shady position for the summer crop. Sow a pinch of seed where the plants are to grow, between the cauliflower plants, and thin when large enough to handle. Victoria Imperial Round is a good one to grow either for summer or winter use. For summer sow in March: for winter, in August, September or October.

New Zealand Spinach or Prickly are good types. Others are Long Standing and Carter. The Prickly ones are said to stand the winter better than the others and there is a kind known as Perpetual Spinach, good roots of which may be forced.

Root Crops.—The root vegetables are carrots, turnips, beetroot, leeks, onions, parsnips, potatoes, shallots and artichokes. Carrots present difficulties to the amateur which need not be. The first secret of successful carrot growing is to grow them on land which has not been specially manured for them but on good soil which has been manured in the previous year for a different crop, such as leeks. Freshly manured soil gives forked diseased roots. The tap root of the carrot needs a sandy soil so that it can pierce down easily and form long straight roots. If the soil be heavy or clayey pierce holes deep enough to hold the root and fill up with sand. Then sow the seed thinly, a pinch at each place. Cover with an inch of soil. Sow in dry sunny weather and not too early in the spring. Thin out all surplus plants, leaving only one plant to develop at each place. Carrots, like all tap roots, will not stand transplanting. Keep plot free from weeds, and water if necessary. Use as required and store surplus crop in dry sand clamps or in dry shed. Carrots and turnips are ideal vegetables for forcing in frames or hotbeds early in the year when they are appreciated. Early Nantes are good forcing carrots. Outdoors early croppers are Shorthorns; for general crop, New Red Intermediate, Altrincham or Sutton's Favourite.

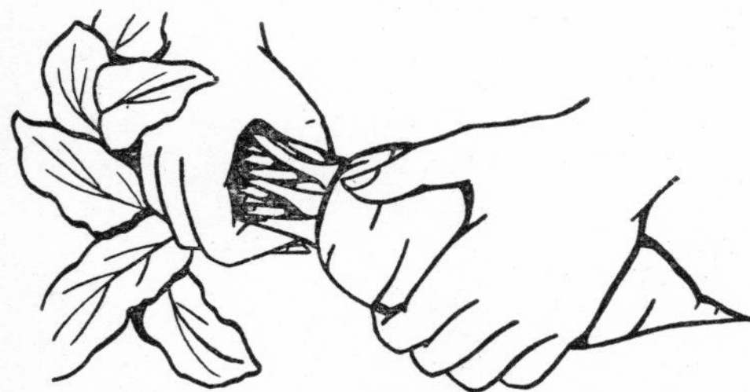

Fig. 2.—Remove Beetroot leaves by twisting

Beetroot should also be grown on ground manured for a previous crop. Sow in sunny weather in spring in rich, not too heavy, soil and thin out from 4–6 in. apart according to the size of kind being grown. The long beets are best for flavour and for storing but most housewives prefer the short and ball type as being more suitable for the pot. Purple Galloway and Bell's Nonbleeding do not bleed. Improved Globe is early. Crimson Ball and Sutton's Market Favourite are both good.

Turnips may be forced or grown in one or two crops in the open. Sow not too early in drills in rich well-manured soil and thin to single plants, the distance apart being governed by the size grown. Although turnips may be sown in March, April and May, growers in cold districts, troubled by late frosts, make nothing but work for themselves if they sow too early as often crops are nipped by frosts and new sowings have to be made. Use Early Paris Market for forcing or Red or White Milan. Golden Ball is a good general cropper and Swede cannot be beaten for standing frost.

Fig. 3.—Top: Sprouts emerging wrongly. Bottom: A properly sprouted Potato

Potatoes do best in sandy loam. The best seed potatoes come from Scotland. There are numerous varieties but only seed potatoes passed by the Board of Agriculture are permitted to be grown in private gardens. So the best types are better to be ascertained from a reliable firm of nurserymen. Sets sprouted in a dark place give the best crop. Planting should be wide apart; earlies being set 24 in. between drills and 12 in. apart; maincrop and late kinds having more haulm should be set 30 in. between drills and 16 in. apart. At least three sprouts should be left on each set and it is better, if no increase of stock is needed, not to cut the potatoes into pieces. Kidneys should never be cut. As the plants grow earthing up should be proceeded with. When haulms turn yellow lift and store in clamps. Earlies are lifted as required for the table.

A Clamp.—To make a clamp dig a trench in a dry part of the ground 2 ft. wide and 1 ft. deep. This should be a square

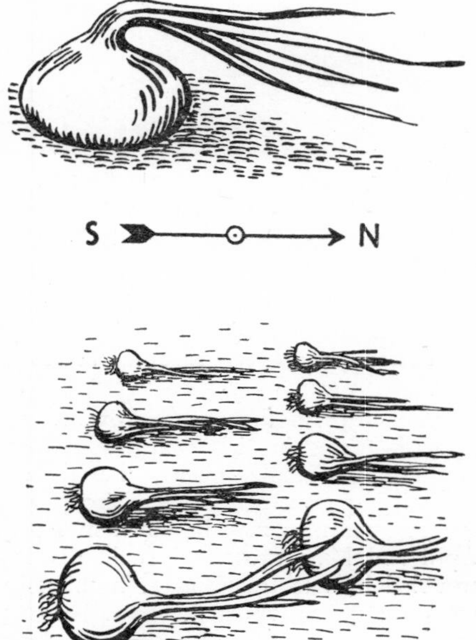

Fig. 4.—Lift Onions to dry and lay towards the North

surrounding the place where the clamp is to be. Raise the bed of clamp with the displaced soil of the trench and then pile the potatoes in a rounded heap and cover them with clean straw. Insert a long piece of wood in the centre for ventilation. Then cover the whole with a foot of soil and clamp down firmly. In severe frosts further protect with a layer of litter and open clamps occasionally for the purpose of removing any diseased potatoes.

Jerusalem Artichoke tubers should be planted in March or April in soil which has not been too much enriched. These tubers being hardy they may be left in the plot all winter.

Onions should be sown for summer use in March or April; for autumn in July, August or September. Sow in drills on land which has been made firm; this ensures good sets. Onions need sun, manure—buried deeply—and a friable soil. Thin out to 9 in. apart keeping rows 12 in. apart. Bending over of the tops is a method whereby ripening is hastened; it is usually done in September. The Onion Fly is a troublesome pest and it is well to know how to cope with it. It attacks the roots and whenever these turn yellow it is a bad sign. Lift the bulbs and destroy them. Apply paraffin to the soil where these plants have been to prevent further damage to crop. Autumn sown crops are not so liable to attack nor are earlies as the maggot is most active in June and July. Shallots are also subject to this trouble; otherwise they are easily grown. Plant the sets half way in the soil in a sunny place and no further work is required except weeding.

Leeks are heavy feeders and much manure must be dug into the deeply worked plot which should be prepared in the autumn or winter. The best leeks are obtained if seedlings are forwarded in frames or under glass in heat. When the plants are large enough, and the weather genial, transplant either on flat ground or drop each leek into a deep hole made with a dibber. Earth up as they grow, to blanch them, if grown in trenches; if on the flat paper bands are used but these must be attended to and not kept too tight to allow of good development. During growth feeding with liquid manure is good. Make this by using 2 gallons of horse or cow manure to a large barrel of water and add some soot. After standing for a week this will be ready for use. Improved Lyon Leek is a favourite for blanching for exhibition. Prizetaker is another. For household purposes the best is the Musselburgh. Leeks remain in the soil throughout the winter and are used as needed.

Parsnips should be sown in March or April in soil which has been trenched and having the manure placed deep down. Thin to single plants and keep clean; the roots being hardy can be lifted as required all through the winter; no storing being needed. Grow the Student or Hollow Crown.

Broad Beans are easy to grow; an early crop being obtained if they are sown in November or December. All the beans, broad, kidney or French, and runner like a deeply trenched soil, plenty of manure and sun. Light soils are benefited by the addition of $1\frac{1}{2}$ oz. Superphosphate and 1 oz. Kainit to the square yard, dug in at the end of the year. Sow in drills 18 in. apart with about 8 in. between each seed. When plants are up about 6 in. earth up, and when well in flower pinch off tops to encourage formation of pods. Successional sowings may be made right on to May but not later. Mazagan is the best earlier cropper or use Early Green Long Pods. Giant Windsor is a good one for the main crop or The Cropper, a long pod bean.

Kidney or French Beans.—Sow in May or June, first soaking seeds in warm water. Sow seed 3 in. apart and 2 in. deep in drills 18 in. apart. Thin to 8 in. apart. The best dwarfs are Canadian Wonder, The Wonder, and for late sowing, Newington. The tall varieties need the same conditions but need to be staked.

Runner Beans.—Sow in May in drills; seeds being put 3 in. deep with about 6 in. between each seed and 12 in. between the rows. A later sowing may be made in June. As soon as they begin to run strong stakes about 8 or 9 ft. should be put in.

Peas.—Grow in soil in which cabbage has previously been grown; this will prevent over development of the peas and yet give them sufficient nourishment; failing that dig in well-rotted manure, keeping it in the second spit, for the roots descend very deep and this food will be available when most required. Some growers make a shallow ditch at each side of the drill for watering in dry weather, but some prefer to surround the rows with green mulch of vegetable refuse or grass cuttings. Sow in flat drills about 6 in. wide and 2 or 3 in. deep. The distance between rows depends on the height and habit of growth; enough room must be allowed for development of the haulm. A good rule is to allow a foot more than the height of the pea; if it grows 4 ft. allow 5 ft. between rows. Use soot water for warding off slugs and run lines of black thread across beds if birds are troublesome. When plants are 6 in. or even 4 in. high put in branches as stakes making them firm, or use wire pea trainers. Dwarf kinds are good for small gardens and give heavy crops if properly grown. Early sowing may begin in March or April according to the district and condition of the soil. The early crops should be ready in about three months. Successive sowings may be made every fortnight up to May or June. Earlies are Gradus, Bedford Champion and Duke of Albany. For later crops use Duke of York, Veitch's Perfection. Dwarfs are Little Marvel and Lincoln.

Salads have become prominent in our diet. Lettuces, being the most popular salad plants, should receive special attention. There are two kinds of lettuce, the round Cabbage, and the long Cos. All lettuces need a deep rich soil but manure should be placed at about a spade's depth down; otherwise the plants will bolt. This is one vegetable that is worth forcing, the tender plants being so much more acceptable than the tough leathery ones so often grown out-of-doors. Seed may be sown in heat in December but this is a precarious proceeding even for market growers and costly. It is safer to sow in February or March under glass. After that sowings may go on at regular intervals right up to the autumn in the open garden. Sow in drills a foot apart and thin to about 6 in. apart.

Lettuces are often transplanted but the best plants are those grown where sown. Much water is necessary. But no plant should be watered overhead after it has begun to heart. This causes rot. The soil round the plants should be watered and any adjoining path should be a soft soil one, kept covered with straw to prevent being trodden hard. This ensures watering to the roots by percolation and no damage is done to the tissue of the plants.

Tie in Cos lettuce when almost ready for cutting; this blanches the hearts. This is not required for Cabbage lettuces. Keep any transplanted plants moist and free from weeds.

Under glass grow Tom Thumb (cabbage). For out-of-doors good cabbage types are Giant White Cos, All The Year Round and Favourite. Cos types are, Paris White, and Winter White or Dwarf Perfecta.

Mustard and Cress come next to lettuce. They are both cultivated in the same way but mustard takes longer to be ready for use so should be sown about four or five days before the cress. For indoor growing, either in a room or in the greenhouse or frames prepare boxes or shallow seed pans and fill with a layer of very fine soil. Scatter the seed thickly over this and cover for a few days. Keep moist and when seedlings are 1 in. high gradually give them light. Cut and use before the second or true leaves develop. Sow broadcast in the open in moist sunny place. Some gardeners do not cover the seeds at all with soil others just cover slightly. To keep up the supply seed must be sown frequently. Triple Curled Cress is good and there is the common one. Use either Brown or White mustard.

Celery is best raised under glass. Sow in March for early crop, in April for later. When plants are large enough transplant into boxes and harden off in cold frame. Trenches about 3 ft. deep with plenty of manure should be prepared in the garden and the plants put into these about 4 in. deep; the plants are not to be put in deeply although the trench was deeply worked. Keep plants about 10 in. apart. As they grow they should be earthed up at intervals, the leaves being tied together so that no soil shall fall into the heart of the plant. Paper collars are not good; they cause rot. It is better to tie and undo the ties when earthing up has been done. Liquid manure is beneficial for this crop. For early use sow Sandringham White or White Gem; for later crop use Sultham Prize Pink or Matchless Red. Lettuces may be grown along the edges of celery trenches as a catch crop.

Fig. 5.—Double Crop Beds

WEAVING

The weaver, the potter and the gardener will probably never agree as to the justice of the claim of each to be recognized as the oldest of all crafts. The craft of weaving is now very largely carried on by means of power-driven looms and the complexity of the modern Jacquard loom is probably beyond the understanding of most people. It should nevertheless be remembered that the basic principle of weaving is that of common darning and that every contrivance for weaving only performs three major operations, viz., it separates one set of threads from another set, making what is known as a "shed" through which a shuttle containing thread is passed to perform the second operation; the third operation is that of "beating up" this thread to take its place alongside a thread laid in by the previous "throw" of the shuttle. All these operations were first of all, and still are, performed quite efficiently by hand and the machine simply makes possible many elaborations of the patterns it is possible to weave.

Nomenclature.—The frame upon which the weaving is done, no matter how simple or how complex, is called a loom, the threads which run lengthways are called the warp and the cross threads thrown by and from the shuttle are called the weft, or more poetically, the woof. The frame generally used to lift the threads to form the shed is

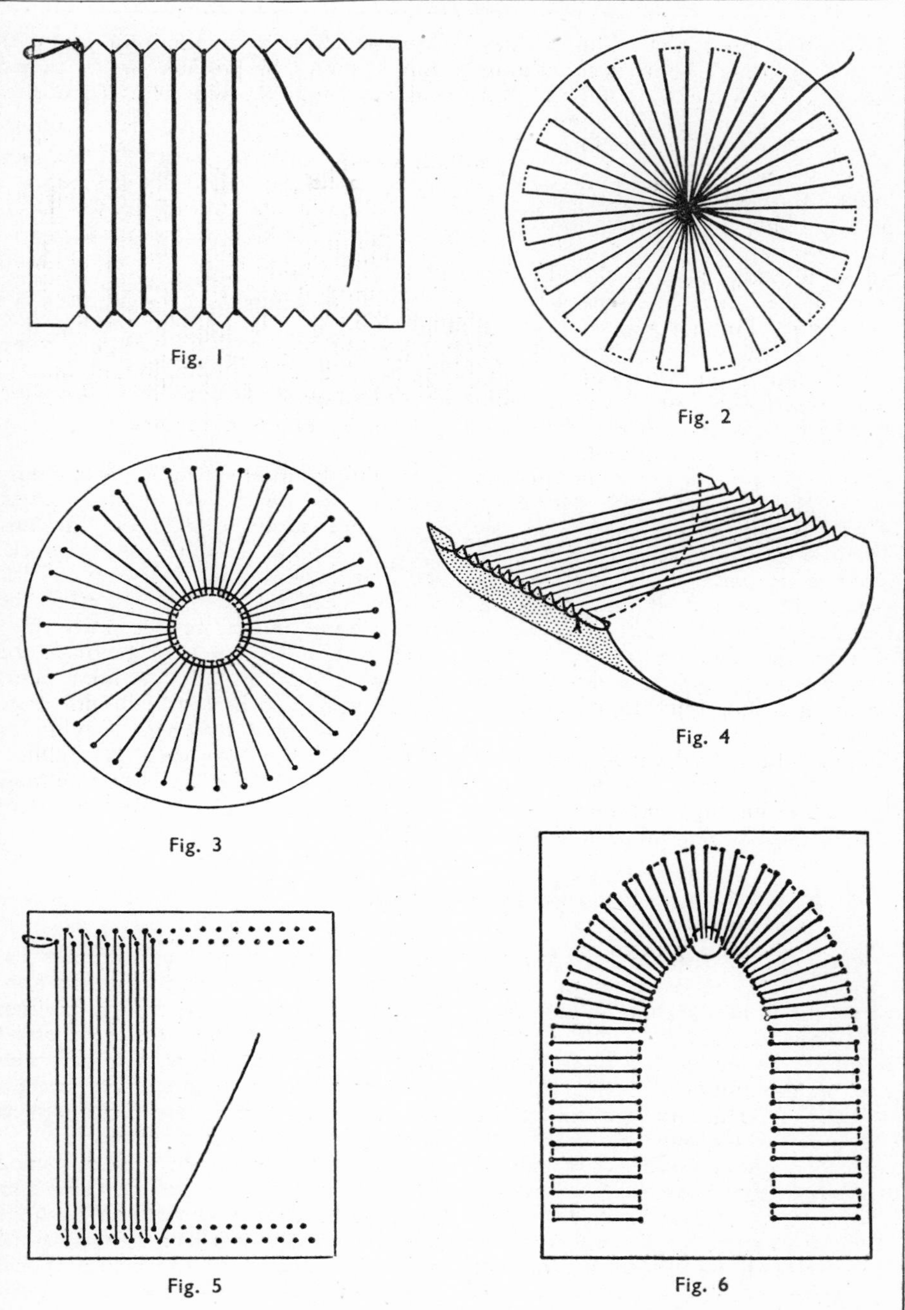

Fig. 1

Fig. 2

Fig. 3

Fig. 4

Fig. 5

Fig. 6

called the heddle, and the weft threads are knocked up by a reed or beater, referred to later on in this section.

The Materials.—The materials for this craft are many and varied as there is such a large variety and style of work which can be done. Rug weaving requires rug wool, articles of clothing can be woven in two-, three- or four-ply wool, cotton, mercerized cotton or linen. Bags, tea-cosies, curtains, hats, pochettes, belts, ties, scarves, etc., can all be woven out of these materials. Strips of felt, raffia, string, strips of old cloth, straws can be made into mats for various purposes.

Looms.—A good deal of work can be done with home-made looms of quite simple types. Indeed it is advisable to practise pattern-making on small looms made from pieces of strong cardboard as shown in Figs. 1–6. Fig. 1 has teeth cut on opposite edges, about $\frac{1}{6}$ in. apart. Fig. 4 is so shaped because it is easy to hold between the knees and to weave the weft threads. In Fig. 5 the holes are spaced $\frac{1}{4}$ in. apart on each of the rows which are also $\frac{1}{4}$ in. apart. Fig. 2 shows a circular loom in which the holes are about $\frac{1}{2}$ in. apart, and odd in number. This loom is useful for tam o' shanters, mats, and circular gabs. Fig. 3 is similar but with a larger central hole and the warp is the same on each side. Fig. 6 is a loom on which slippers can be woven. The holes are about $\frac{1}{4}$ in. apart and the warp is threaded up as shown. This type of work is most suitable for people who must work under exceptional circumstances.

Flat boards can also be used effectively for a large variety of work. Fig. 7 shows a $\frac{1}{2}$ in. board which can be made up to about 18 in. by 12 in. with raised ends about 1 in. high. The latter are made from hard wood such as birch or beech and saw cuts through which the warp threads are passed from end to end are made about $\frac{1}{6}$ in. apart and $\frac{3}{16}$ in. deep. Fig. 8 shows how this board loom can be raised to allow the warp threads to pass round it and so give a longer warp, suitable for a scarf.

Frame Looms.—Fig. 9 shows a small frame loom which is easily made. The warp threads on this are threaded through the holes in a piece of canvas with about $\frac{1}{10}$ in. mesh which is doubled and fixed with drawing pins or tacks so that the folded edge is towards the centre of the loom. The warp threads are passed through every alternate hole in a straight line, using a needle for threading the wool.

A larger size of the same type of loom is well adapted for rug weaving. This is made from 2 in. by $\frac{3}{4}$ in. wood put together as shown in the photograph (Fig. 12B) i.e., with pairs of end pieces fixed to the long sides and together by means of $\frac{1}{4}$ in. bolts.

A photograph (Fig. 12A) of a loom "set up" with a warp is shown on page 646. The use of canvas is clearly seen.

Box Looms.—Boxes can be made into very efficient looms. Figs. 10 and 11 illustrate this type. In this type the warp is wrapped round the box as in Fig. 8.

Roller Looms.—Fig. 13 shows a small loom and Fig. 14 a large one fitted with rollers. The rollers carry the warp threads which are wrapped round them at each end thus allowing several feet of length to be woven for one setting up of the loom. This is a considerable advantage as the "setting up" of a loom, i.e. the arranging of the threads of the warp, fixing and winding them on to one roller, known as the warp beam, threading them through the heddle and winding them on to the other roller, known as the cloth beam, takes a considerable amount of time. It may indeed take longer than is required to weave the piece of material after the setting up is finished. Larger roller looms which will weave material over 12 in. wide are shown in Figs. 12C, 12D and 12E. These frames can be enlarged to give a greater width. A large amount of weaving can be done on the looms mentioned so far and you are advised to learn the work from the simpler looms rather than attempting at once to work with a loom having more than one heddle. In this way you will learn all the simple processes and patterns and will find that the mastery of a four-heddle loom does not present so many problems as it does without a background of personal experience in handling a simple type of machine.

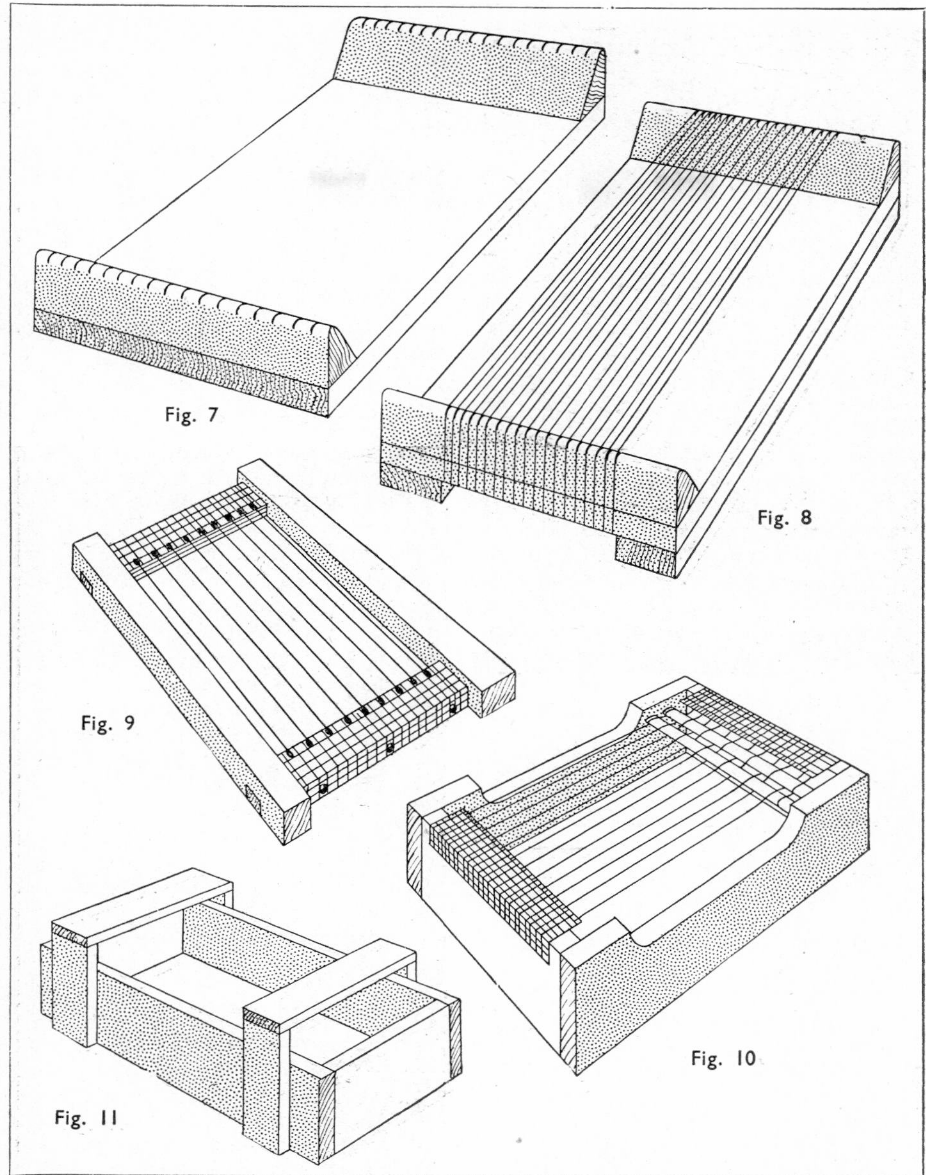
Fig. 7
Fig. 8
Fig. 9
Fig. 10
Fig. 11

The Shuttle.—A good deal of simple weaving can be done with a large needle, passing it in and out among the warp threads as in darning. Simple forms of shuttle are shown in Figs. 15 and 16. These should be made from a smooth close-grained wood like box-wood. An ordinary wooden ruler can be cut to shape.

Heddles.—Lifting the warp threads one by one by means of a needle is very slow work and a variety of means of speeding up the work by lifting a group of threads

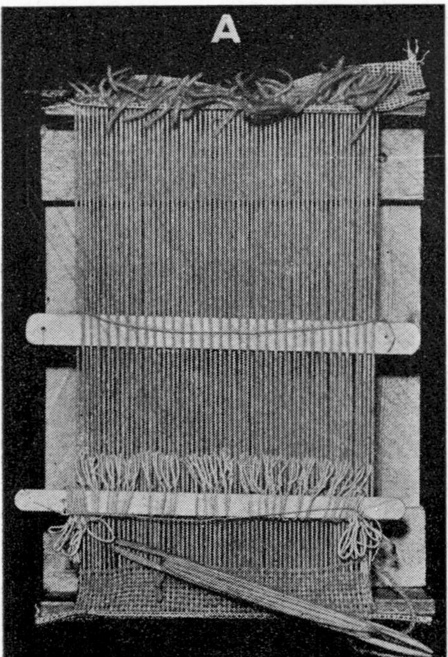

Fig. 12.—Showing String Leashes

together have been evolved in the leash rods and heddles shown in Figs. 12A, 12B, 12D and 12E. The warp threads are threaded through these when they are being put on the loom. The photograph 12A shows how the leashes can be made from thin white string knotted into loops at intervals of about 3 in. The loops so formed are passed on to a flat stick about $\frac{3}{4}$ in. wide. This can be made from $\frac{3}{16}$ in. plywood. The spaces between these loops are formed into loops passing under every alternate warp thread so that threading of loops on to the leash rod is done at the same time as the looping of the warp threads, i.e., one loop on to the leash rod, loop up the end warp thread, the next loop on to the rod, loop up the next warp thread but one and so on until all the loops are on the rod and all the alternative threads are looped up. A few spare loops are shown at each end of the rod in 12A. When the leash rod is lifted, half the warp threads are lifted and the shuttle carrying the weft thread can be passed quickly across. The alternate shed is made by a shed stick which is a wide flat stick about an inch or more wide by $\frac{1}{4}$ in. thick which is threaded through the warp threads alternately in and out, i.e. one thread on top and one underneath the stick in such a way that when the latter is turned on its edge it pushes down the set of threads in the leashes and raises the alternate half to form a shed through which the shuttle can now be passed in the opposite direction. This can be seen in 12A and in 12B where it is on its edge in the frame sides and making a "shed."

Metal heddles as in 12D and 12E are obtainable as also are heddles made from celluloid, string, string and metal eyes, wood.

Fig. 12 (*cont.*).—Formation of a "Shed"

The work of the heddle is shown in 12E where a shed is formed by depressing the threads in the holes of the heddle.

The Beginnings.—Figs. 1–6 show cardboard looms which can be used for making small things such as purses, mats, pochettes. These are also useful for trying out patterns. The latter is an important part of this craft as it is only by experimenting that originality can be developed. Pattern may be quickly tried out by weaving in straws such as are used with ices and drinks. The looms in Figs. 12A and 12D have a piece of open-meshed canvas, about $\frac{1}{10}$ in. mesh fixed on each end as previously mentioned. This canvas is also used on the roller looms to give a grip for the warp threads.

The photograph 12A shows the warp set up and tabby weaving begun. In Figs. 12D and 12E the heddle is of twisted wire. Notice the two pieces of wood passed through the warp threads near the end of Figs. 12B, 12C and 12D, are fixed together at the ends. These are the laze rods and are used to keep the warp threads at equidistant spaces to prevent them overlapping each other

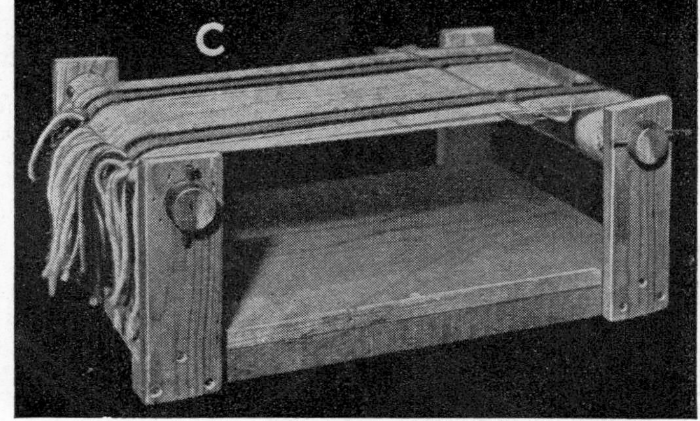

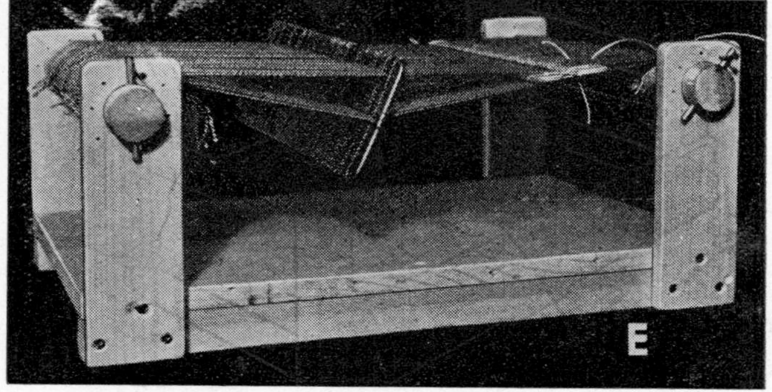

Fig. 12 (*cont.*).—Photographs showing heddles and formation cf sl.eds

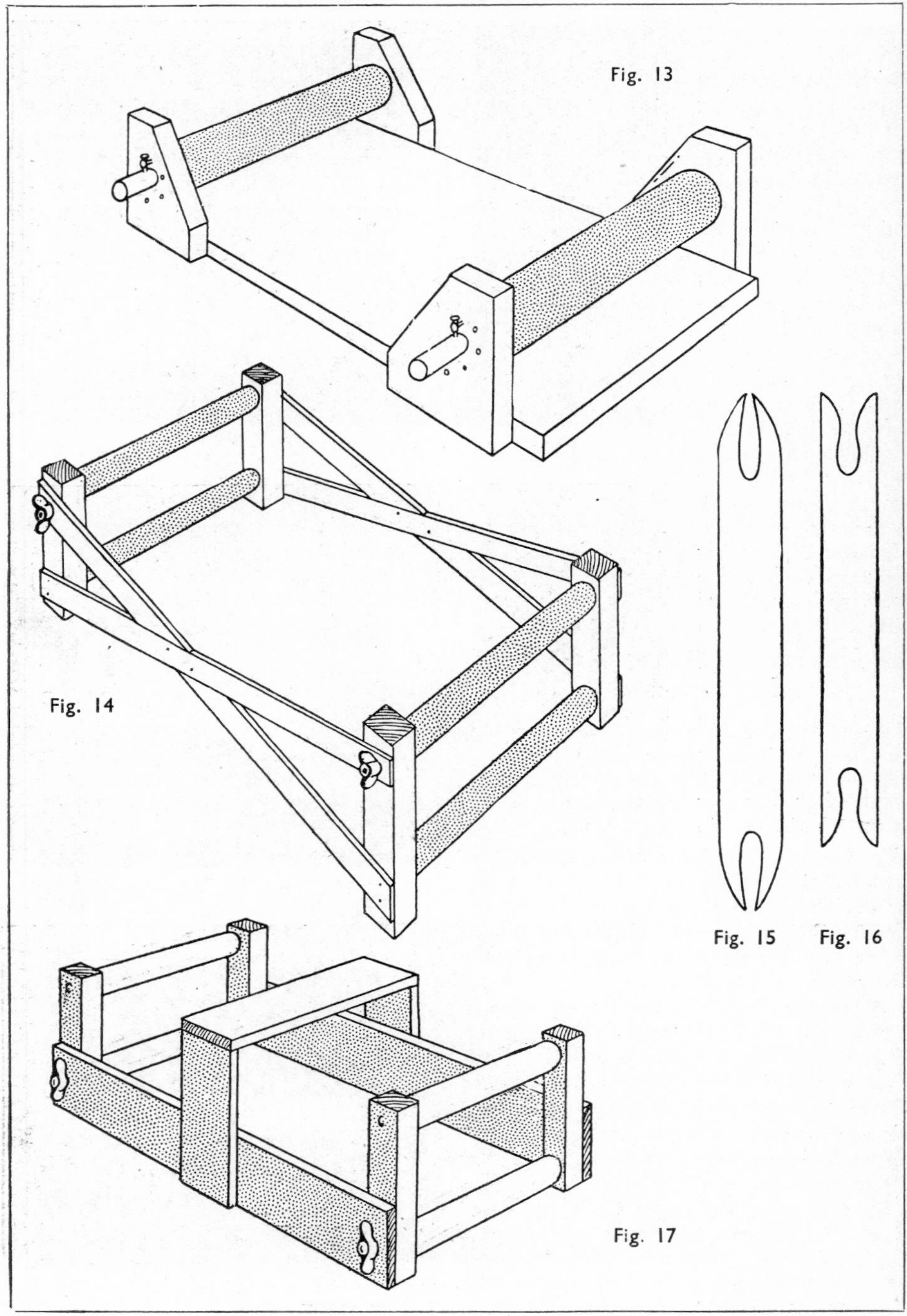
Fig. 13
Fig. 14
Fig. 15
Fig. 16
Fig. 17

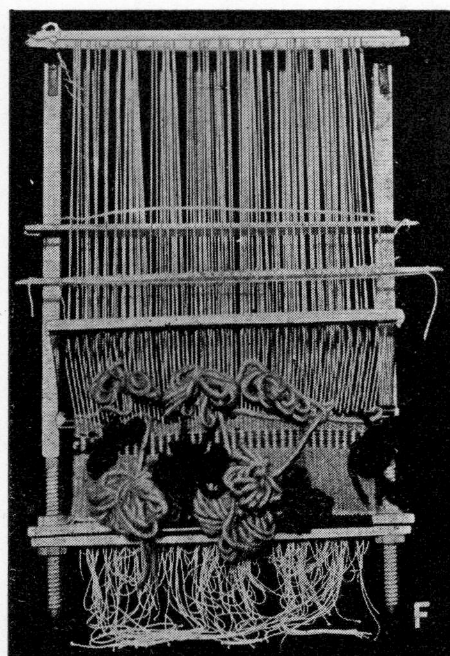

Fig. 12 (*cont.*).—A Tapestry Loom

and spoiling the weaving. These rods are threaded through alternate threads in such a way that one half of the warp threads cross underneath the next rod in the middle of the space between them. (*See* Fig. 10.) This is known as the cross and in large work it is generally formed on the frame of pegs on which the warp is wound in order to arrange the threads easily on the beams and of the required length for the material to be woven.

Pattern.—Having set up the warp in the colours required, the pattern to be woven is now worked out, if indeed it has not already been worked out, before setting up the loom. That of course is the general procedure when you are expert. Patterns are worked out on squared paper, $\frac{1}{8}$ in. squares as in the illustrations given.

The plainest and most straightforward weave, as patterns are called, is the "one under one over," known as "tabby." (Fig. 18.) A good deal of variety can be put into this by means of coloured threads in the

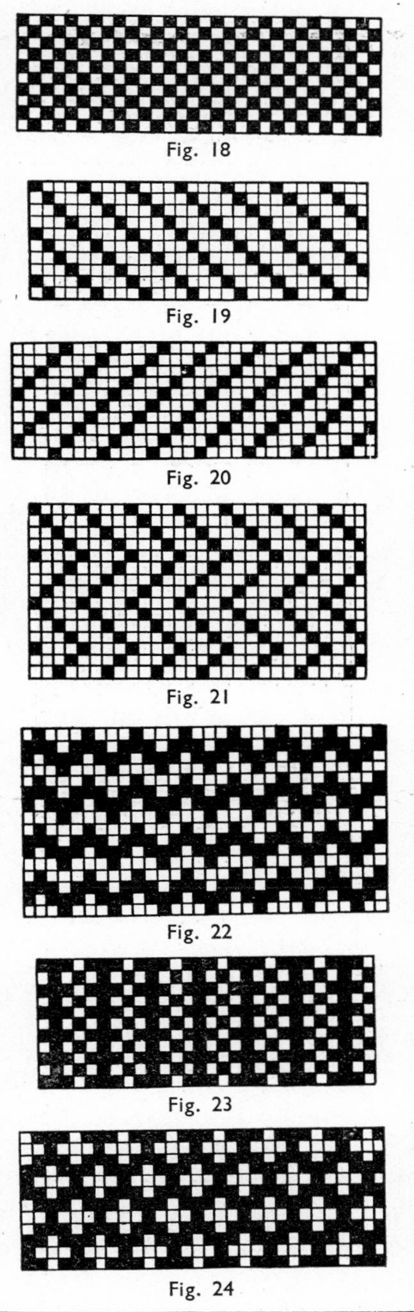

Fig. 18

Fig. 19

Fig. 20

Fig. 21

Fig. 22

Fig. 23

Fig. 24

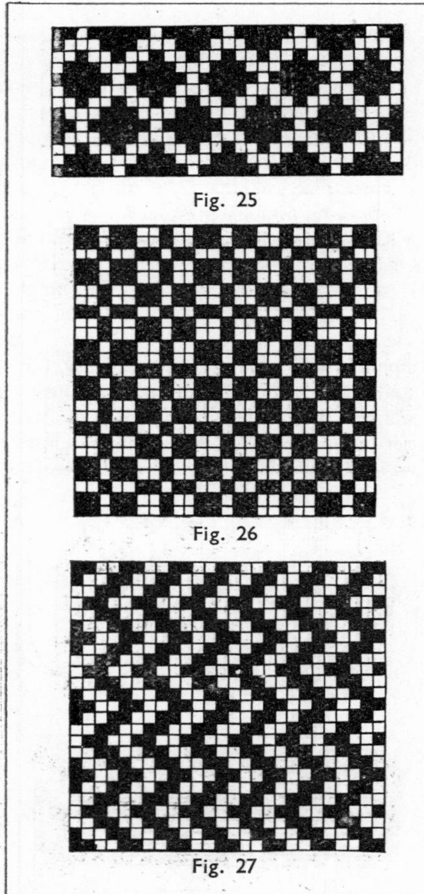
Fig. 25

Fig. 26

Fig. 27

warp and in the weft. The latter would precede the former. Then a combination of the two will give a tartan. Next the twills right and left hand, and zig-zag as in Figs. 19, 20 and 21. It will be observed that in weaving patterns such as are shown here, the lifting of warp threads to give the pattern will be done either by threading in and out, lifting and leaving the required number of threads or, excepting in the case of the tabby weave, with the aid of more than one heddle. Such work immediately leads on to the more elaborate table loom which can be purchased with up to four heddles and on which there is not much limit in the way of pattern designing.

Fig. 22 shows a horizontal zig-zag pattern made by lifting threads as shown by each line of weaving. Fig. 23 shows an interesting check pattern. Notice that one row of warp threads are lifted in the order three up, one down, while the next row every alternate thread is lifted for the shuttle to pass through. The patterns in Figs. 24, 25, 26 and 27 can be easily followed.

Rug Looms.—The rug loom in photograph 12B shows an oriental rug in the making with the short ends of rug wool knotted on to the warp threads. After each row of knotting a row or two of string weft is woven in to hold the knots firmly in position.

The photograph 12F shows a tapestry loom with pattern in different colours just beginning. The groups of warp threads, which are of string, to be raised to give the necessary design are lifted by the fingers being passed behind them and dragging them forward while the appropriate bunch, spool or shuttle of wool, is passed through the shed so formed.

Very fine and valuable work can be done on this type of loom and this is probably the section of weaving which yields the best profit.

COLLECTING WILD FLOWERS

Collecting wild flowers is a hobby which most people have indulged in some time during their youth; but it is definitely a hobby which is worth consideration by the adult.

Those who have not much space at their disposal and are not keen on doing things with their hands will most profitably join a botanical society. One of the aims of members is to find as many different kinds of wild flowers during the year from March 1st as possible, marks being allotted accordingly, and extra marks for those actually found on the first of March.

Collecting is done with the aid of some standard Flora. The one used by botanists

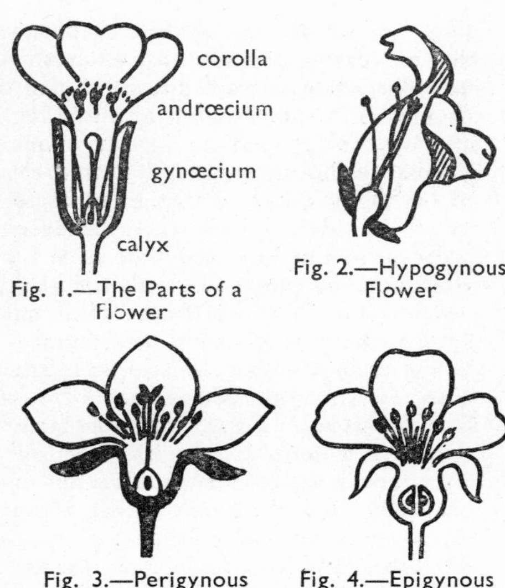

Fig. 1.—The Parts of a Flower

Fig. 2.—Hypogynous Flower

Fig. 3.—Perigynous Flower

Fig. 4.—Epigynous Flower

until they are far advanced is "British Flora," by Bentham and Hooker, and "Illustrations of the British Flora."

People who collect flowers in this way pick one or two good specimens, except in the case of rare flowers (when looking at the growing plant only, is permitted), and bring them home, after noting height, surrounding herbage, etc., for identification. *It is never necessary to uproot a plant for purposes of identification.* Then the corresponding illustrations in the illustrated "Bentham" are painted in, in correct colours, the date and locality being added beneath. A member of a botanical—or wild flower—society will then enter in the book supplied for the purpose, the date and exact places where the specimens were found.

Forming a Herbarium.—If, on the other hand, you are good with your fingers, the actual collecting of wild flowers to form a herbarium, will interest you most. The principal requirement is some really good drying paper, blotting paper is not substantial enough. Botanical drying paper is bought by the ream. Besides this some small squares of glass are useful for keeping down petals which will curl up; 3 in. square is a good size for them. Presses can be bought but you can make them quite easily out of three-ply wood. Cut out two pieces the size of your drying paper, and cut some pieces of cardboard this size too. The specimens, placed between layers of drying paper, are put between these boards, and a weight is placed on top, or the frame may be bound with webbing or string and hung in a warm place to dry. An old brush, a pair of scissors, and a penknife, are also needed.

Obtaining Specimens.—Go out armed with a notebook in which to write date, locality, type of soil, and also height of plant, colour of flower and leaves, which may alter as the specimen dries. Take a small trowel for digging up plants, but you must not do this in case of rare ones, or if notices are posted forbidding it, without permission. It is this indiscriminate uprooting of wild flowers which is forcing

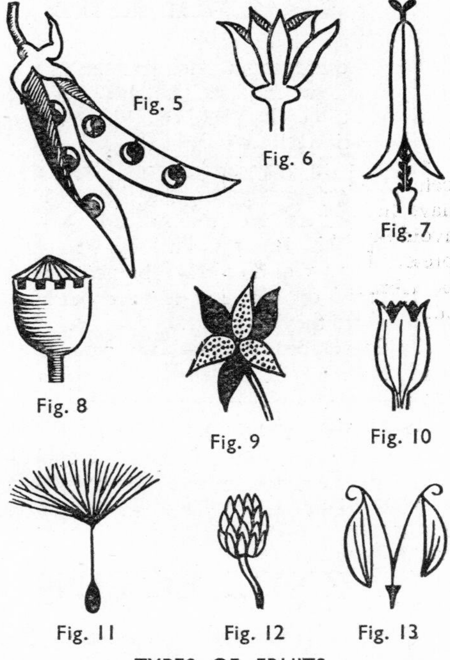

TYPES OF FRUITS

Fig. 5.—Legume of Pea. Fig. 6.—Follicle of Marsh Marigold. Fig. 7.—Siliqua of Wallflower. Fig. 8.—Poppy Capsule. Fig. 9.—Pansy Capsule splitting down midriff. Fig. 10.—Primrose Capsule. Fig. 11.—Dandelion Seed with Pappus. Fig. 12.—Achenes of Buttercup. Fig. 13.—Schizocarp of Fennel.

into the ranks of rarities those plants which a few years ago were locally profuse.

Besides these, you will need something in which to take your plants home. Some botanists use a japanned box, known as a vasculum, but a portable press is often handier. Make it out of two pieces of cardboard with a strip of linen, which will form the hinge, joining them at the back. Place sheets of drying paper inside, and slip a rubber band or two over it to keep it closed.

A specimen should consist of root, stem, leaves, buds, flowers, and fruit. Some specimens will of course be too big to deal with in their entirety, so cut them into sections with scissors. In the "Illustrated Bentham" all plants showing sections are tall ones.

Any plants with bulbous roots, and any heathers should be plunged into boiling water (not the flowers), in order to kill them. This stops them from going brown when drying, and prevents the leaves from falling off heathers when dry. A label must be attached to each plant marking name, family, variety, locality and date.

Plants with very thick roots, like bluebells or big flower heads like thistles, may have the underside of them sliced away to avoid squashing them when they are in the press. Leaves or flowering branches may be trimmed off too, but leave enough to show where they do grow.

Drying Specimens.—Many people get much better results if their drying paper is hot first before placing several sheets of it on one of the boards of the press. When you have your first specimen arranged naturally, clip some drying sheets to the top of your board, and then fold over your plant, removing any glass squares you have used as you go. If you have a stout plant to deal with, be sure to put several sheets of drying paper between it and the next one, and after ten specimens, put in one of the cardboards. When you have got all your plants in, put on the top board, and add a light weight.

After a few hours change your drying sheets and put on a heavier weight. Do this from time to time for about four weeks, after which the plants should be really dry. Then they can be mounted on separate sheets of cartridge paper or Bristol board. Most botanists prefer fish glue or a flour paste, with some preservative, as a sticking medium. Brush it sparingly on the underside of the specimen, and smooth it on to its mount with a very clean rag. Put these mounted ones back in the press between sheets of drying paper for two days.

Write on each mount all details concerning the specimen. The finished articles can be kept in a cupboard fitted with sliding racks. Flake naphthalene should be left in the cupboard to ward off insects.

Classification.—Flowering plants are classified into *families*. Each family is distinguished from another by differences in stems, leaves, flowers and fruit. According to details of these, sub-divisions: *Genera*, are made; and these again are divided according to smaller differences, into *Species*. The number of genera and species which belong to a family varies considerably.

Each plant then, has two Latin names; its genus and its species. The common groundsel, for instance, is a member of the family *Compositæ*, but its botanical name is *Senecio Vulgaris*, it is of the genus *Senecio* and the species is *Vulgaris*.

It is necessary first to find to what family your specimen belongs; but a good deal of preliminary searchings in *Bentham* will be saved if you learn what are the common variations in the parts of a plant, and also what are the characteristics of the largest flower families.

Annuals are plants which flower and die the same year they are planted, biennials, those which flower the year after they are sown, and then die; and herbaceous perennials are plants which flower and make seed each year, but which die down above the ground each winter. Shrubs and trees are woody perennials which usually shed their leaves in winter.

Roots are *fibrous* when their branches are thin and numerous, e.g. grass; they are *tuberous* when any branch thickens into a tuber, e.g. Celandine: they are *tap roots*, when the main root is thickest and throws off small branches only, e.g. Wallflower. This is the commonest root form.

The Stem.—The part where it leaves the root is called the *rootstock*; and this sometimes grows horizontally just under the surface, in which case it is called a *rhizome*, e.g. Iris; or it may be in the form of a *bulb*, e.g. Daffodil; or form a rounded tuberous rootstock called a *corm*, e.g. Crocus.

The way the stem grows is important when determining species. It is called *erect* when it grows straight up from the ground, *prostrate* when lying flat, and *creeping* when it grows fresh roots downwards at the joints.

Branches as well as leaves can be *alternate* when they grow singly up the stem, *opposite* when in pairs, and *whorled* when a circle round the stem.

A Leaf has two parts, the blade, or *lamina*, and the stalk, or *petiole*. When leaves have no petiole, they are *sessile*, and if they encircle the stem, they are *perfoliate*. Leaves which grow from the root-stock are *radical*, those from the stem, *cauline*. Some plants, such as the Field Buttercup, have both types. Leaves may also be *simple* or *compound*, the latter when they are composed of leaflets joined to a mid-rib, e.g. Rose. Their edges may be toothed, i.e. *dentate* or *serrate*, like a saw.

A Perfect Flower consists of a *calyx*, a *corolla*, an *andrœcium*, and a *gynœcium* arranged in whorls round one another. The calyx is composed of sepals, free or joined, and numerous, according to the family. The corolla is composed of petals which may be of any number, free, or joined into a tube, in which case the corolla is said to be *tubular*. If the petals are of different shapes the corolla is called *irregular*.

The andrœcium is composed of stamens. The anthers, or pollen bags are generally attached to stalks, i.e. filaments, but sometimes sessile on the corolla. The number and arrangement of stamens is a very great help in determining the genus and species. The gynœcium, or pistil, consists of stigma, style and ovary; the style is often absent or rather so short that the stigma appears to join directly to the ovary. This is divided into a number of carpels.

The Receptacle is that part on which the actual flower grows. If the pistil grows on top of the receptacle, with the calyx, corolla, and stamens growing beneath it, the flower is *hypogynous*, when the receptacle is cup-shaped, the pistil growing on it, and the calyx, corolla and stamens from the edge of it, the flower is *perigynous*: and when the receptacle grows over and encloses the ovary, and only the stigma protrudes, the flower is *epigynous*. These positions are important when verifying specimens.

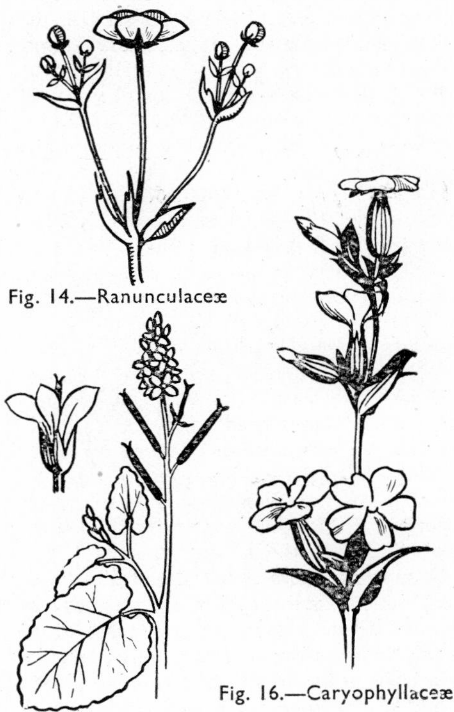

Fig. 14.—Ranunculaceæ

Fig. 15.—Cruciferæ

Fig. 16.—Caryophyllaceæ

THE FLOWER FAMILIES

Seeds and Fruits.—The differences in fruits often determine species, so try always to get a specimen with fruits attached. The three chief pod-like fruits are: the *legume*, splitting down the margin and mid-rib, e.g. Pea; the *follicle*, splitting down the margin only, e.g. Marsh Marigold; and the *siliqua*, splitting from the base upwards, with seeds attached to a replum, e.g. Wallflower.

Capsules are seed boxes which open in various ways. Those from which the seed escapes through pores or valves include the Snapdragons and Poppies. Violets and Pansies grow capsules which split down the mid-rib, and Primroses have capsules opening by teeth.

Many plants have dry, indehiscent, i.e. non-splitting fruits; these are *nuts* and *achenes*, and are of many shapes. Others enclose their seeds in succulent covers, berries, drupes and pomes; of such are gooseberries, cherries and apples.

Among the two hundred and fifty flower families perhaps the biggest are: *Ranunculaceæ*, the buttercup family; *Cruciferæ*, the wallflower family; *Caryophyllaceæ*, the pink family; *Geraniaceæ*, the geranium family; *Papilionaceæ*, the pea family; *Rosaceæ*, the rose family; *Umbelliferæ*, the parsley family; *Compositæ*, the daisy family; *Scrophulariaceæ*, the snapdragon family; and *Labiateæ*, the dead-nettle family.

Ranunculaceæ.—With the exception of the clematis, these plants are herbs with radical and cauling leaves, often much cut. The flowers have five free sepals and petals, sometimes modified; but all the flowers have numerous free stamens with separate carpels, and the flowers are hypogynous. The fruits are achenes or follicles. To this family belong all the buttercups, the meadow-rues, the anemones, the hellebores, the columbines, and the larkspurs.

Cruciferæ.—Members of this family are easy to distinguish by the four petals and sepals arranged in the form of a cross. They also have six stamens, four long and two short, and a siliqua fruit. The leaves are alternate. To this family belong the stocks, wallflowers, all the cresses, the mustards, the cabbages, and the shepherd's purse.

Caryophyllaceæ. — The outstanding characteristic of this family is the way the stalks are swollen where the opposite pairs of entire leaves join them. No wild flower belonging to this family is yellow. The sepals vary from four to five, and are often united to form a tube, while the petals are twisted when in bud. There are eight or ten free stamens but it is the difference in numbers in the floral whorls which determine the genera of this family. To it belong the pinks, the campions, the sandworts, the chickweeds, and the stitchworts.

Geraniaceæ.—Although the five petals of these flowers are also twisted in the bud as in the pink family, plants belonging to this order have opposite, divided or compound toothed leaves, with stipules; and the fruit is a capsule separating into five parts, in the form of a stork's bill. There are five sepals and petals, and five or ten stamens, sometimes united. To this family belong the crane's bills, the stork's bills and herb robert.

Fig. 17.—Geraniaceæ

Fig. 18.—Rosaceæ (Great Burnet)

Fig. 19.—Another type of Rosaceæ (Field Rose)

Papilionaceæ.—Herbs, shrubs, and trees can all be found belonging to this family, but members of it are easily recognized by reason of the flower which is always like a pea. The leaves are alternate, simple or compound, with stipules. In the flower itself, the five sepals join to form a single calyx; and the irregular five-petalled corolla is composed of one large petal, the standard, two smaller, called wings, and two central ones united to form a keel. There are ten stamens, either all united or nine united and one free. The fruit is a pod. Among members of this family are the furzes, brooms, medicks, clovers, trefoils, vetches, and peas.

Rosaceæ.—This is another large family including in its members herbs, shrubs and trees. The leaves are alternate, toothed, and both simple and compound. The outstanding characteristic of this family is the numerous stamens growing round the top of the receptacle, and all the flowers, except the apple, are perigynous. The genera belonging to this order do differ from one another a good deal owing to the form of the receptacle; and although the number of sepals and petals is usually five, the latter are sometimes absent. The fruits may be follicles, drupes, pomes, berries or achenes. Among this family are found sloe, cherry, apple, blackberry, roses, meadow sweet, the avens, cinquefoils, tormentils, silverweed and agrimony. Those lacking petals are salad and great burnet, and lady's mantle.

Umbelliferæ.—This family takes its name from the way the flowers are arranged in little bunches radiating from a central point, i.e. umbels. These plants are herbs and have alternate leaves cut and divided. Most of the umbels have bracts at their base. The calyx is five-toothed, and the petals, sometimes notched and irregular in size, grow round a disk on top of the ovary, the five stamens alternating with them. The fruit is separating, but it is differences in shape of the fruit, besides the arrangements of bracts and the size of the petals, which mark out the various species. So when you are collecting specimens of this order, take one with ripe fruits attached. In this family you will find parsleys, hemlocks, celery, carraway, dropworts, fennels, sweet cicely, chervils and carrot.

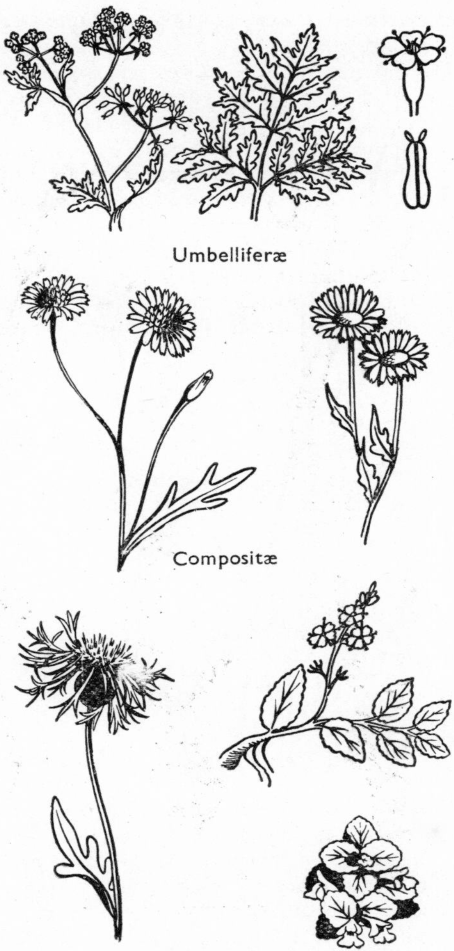

Umbelliferæ

Compositæ

Another type of Composital Scrophulariaceæ

Compositæ.—This is the largest flower family. The flowers belonging to it are really flower heads. Masses of tiny flowers or florets grow on a receptacle surrounded by bracts which serve as a calyx. There are numerous genera belonging to this family, but it is easier to regard them in three main divisions: those which have florets all of the same type, i.e. strap-shaped, like the

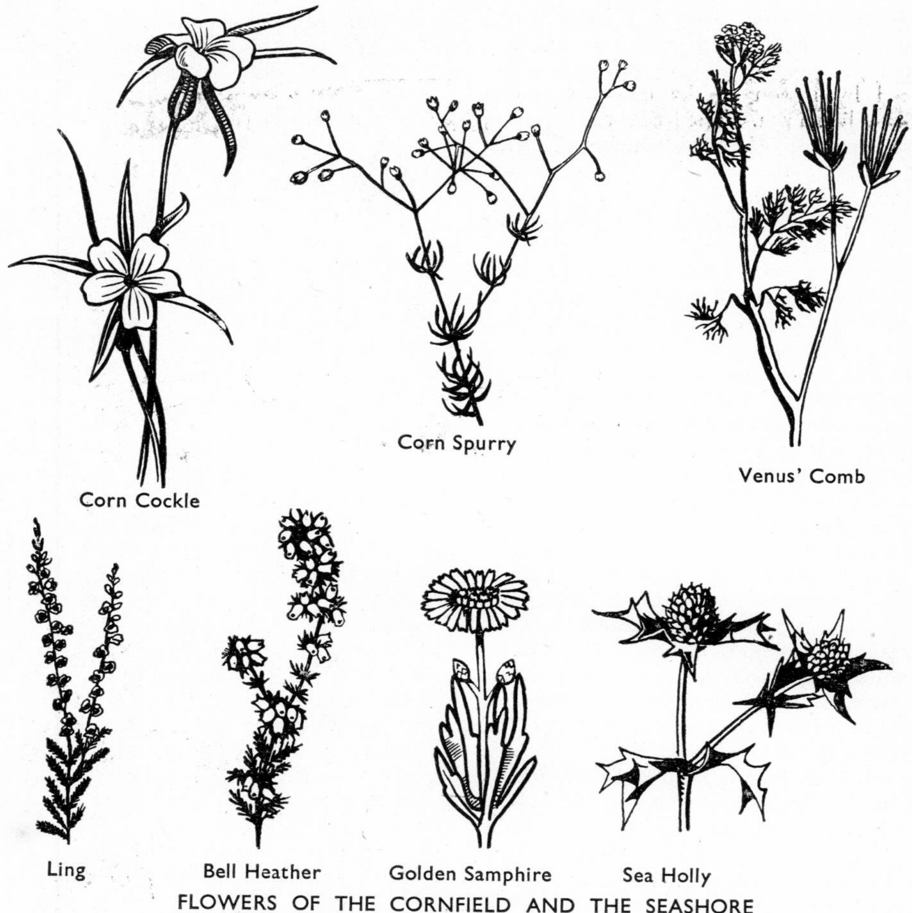

FLOWERS OF THE CORNFIELD AND THE SEASHORE

dandelion, those which have disk florets surrounded by strap-shaped ray florets like the daisy; and those which have tubular florets, like the cornflower, or only disk florets, like the groundsel.

The leaves of the compositæ are alternate or opposite, and the fruits achenes attached to a pappus. Here again the different species depend upon the form of the achene and of the pappus.

Among those with strap-shaped corollas are hawkbits, hawksbeards, hawkweeds and sow thistles. The commonest flowers with both ray and disk florets are daisies, corn marigolds, chamomiles and the yarrow. Thistles, hardheads, knapweeds and groundsels all have tubular florets.

Scrophulariaceæ.—The main characteristics of this family are the two-lipped corolla, the pairs of stamens, either two or four; and the two-celled capsule, each cell of which contains several seeds. The corolla have three different forms, five lobed in the mullein, four lobed in the speedwells, and mouth-like as in the snapdragon. All the English members of this family are herbs, the leaves are simple and usually opposite. Toadflaxes belong to the snapdragon group; and there are 16 different speedwells, besides bartsias, rattles, and cow wheats.

Labiatæ.—Though at first sight this family can be confused with the last because of its two-lipped tubular corollas, yet there are marked differences. The stalks are always square, the leaves and branches are always opposite, while the flowers grow in the axils of the leaves, mostly in a whorl. Most members of this family have a strong scent, for to it belong the sages, thymes, mints, horehound, betony, and also the dead-nettles, woundworts, and the bugles.

WIRELESS

When anyone says "Wireless," we instinctively think of Broadcasting, and this is the kind of wireless that this article is chiefly about. Everyone nowadays either has a wireless set, or often listens to the programmes, either B.B.C. or from foreign countries. It is so easy to take this tremendous achievement for granted, that it is difficult to realize that it is almost a mushroom growth. For most of the progress that has taken place has been the result of intensive work during the last ten years or so. Of course, the growth of high-powered broadcasting stations all over Europe has immensely stimulated the expansion of listening, so much so that when some great political leader, or man of science addresses the microphone, he may be fairly certain of a national hearing, not to say an international one.

It would, therefore, be quite true to say that wireless is *the* national hobby, both for the technically minded, and also for those who switch on to hear music, news, and the immense variety that the broadcast programmes have to offer.

The wireless set of the present day, with its continental range, differs as much from the crystal set of the early broadcast days as the programmes of to-day surpass the first broadcasts in variety, richness and quality. However, the crystal set is by no means to be despised, even nowadays, and when near to a high-powered station, it can give very satisfactory reception indeed. It is quite a simple matter to design a crystal set to separate the programmes from a twin wave Regional station at close range—it costs nothing to run (with the exception of the annual 10*s*. licence), and it is a very useful standby should the valve receiver "pack up" for any reason, or the batteries give out. Even if the electric light goes out, the crystal set will still continue working, and one has the comforting assurance that news, time signals, etc., are always available.

However, nearly everyone wants loud-speaker reception, and here the valve set comes into its own. Two valves will give satisfactory reception from the "local station," while three will give good results from the B.B.C. stations, and a good selection of foreign programmes into the bargain.

How a Wireless Set picks up Programmes.—The microphone at the transmitting studio or elsewhere picks up the sounds and, like a telephone mouth-piece, converts the sound vibrations into variations of an electric current. These variations are transferred to an amplifier, having generally three stages of amplification, and the output of this amplifier is transferred to another and similar amplifier, and the resultant current, after having been suitably controlled and modified by the control engineers, passes to the transmitting station. They are there once more magnified and "mixed" with the carrier wave of the station, which consists of high-frequency oscillations. This mixture is then fed into the aerial of the transmitter, and any listener's aerial within range of the transmitting station will pick up the combined signals, if the set is tuned to a similar frequency to that of the sending station.

The receiving aerial is very simply brought into "tune" with the "frequency" of the transmitting station, as it is connected to a coil of wire in the receiving set. This coil of wire can be made to respond to any desired frequency by connecting a variable condenser across it. This has the effect of making the aerial and coil "vibrate"—electrically, of course—in sympathy with the vibrations sent out by the transmitting station.

The Detector.—Having secured the particular "vibrations" we wish, the next thing we have to do is to rectify them, or "detect" them. This we do by passing them through a "detector," which may be either a crystal in a simple crystal set, or a detector valve. Broadly speaking, this "detector" is like a "one way" street, and has the result of passing through the electrical impulses in one direction only, and stopping the others. The resulting one-way current is then magnified by being passed through other valves until, finally, it is powerful enough to operate our loud speakers.

The Valves.—Let us examine in greater detail just how a wireless valve works. The ordinary triode valve consists of a filament heated by a battery, a grid and a plate or anode. When the filament is heated by passing a current through it, it proceeds, so to speak, to "evaporate" electrons, which fly towards the plate. The positive pole of a high tension supply of electricity is connected to the plate, and the negative end of the supply to the filament. The positively charged plate has a strong attraction for the negative electrons thrown off by the filament, but, in the meantime, these have to pass through the meshes of the "grid," which is in the way. The grid is connected to our tuning coil, so that variations in signals received by the aerial have the effect of controlling the flow of electrons from the filament to the plate. In this way we get great magnification of any signals applied to the grid of a valve.

Sets.—You often hear the question asked, "Which is the best set to use?" The answer is, there is no best set—it depends entirely on what is required. If you want the B.B.C. programmes only, and are fairly close to a broadcasting station, then quite a simple set will serve your requirements. If, on the other hand, you want a good supply of foreign stations, then a much more complex set is necessary, because, not only must it be more sensitive, but it has also to be more selective in order to pick out the programmes you wish from the others of, perhaps, higher power.

Then, again, there is the question of quality. If you are near a B.B.C. station and only wish to hear the local programmes, it is quite easy to design a set which will give good quality, but to combine high quality with the ability to reproduce programmes from a variety of different stations, is neither easy nor inexpensive. We have already mentioned the crystal set for satisfactory head-phone reception of programmes from the local station. The one valve set will also give very satisfactory and reliable reception of the local station on head-phones—it has also a greater range, due to the incorporation of "reaction"—and will, in favourable conditions, bring in programmes from quite a number of foreign stations as well. For loud-speaker reception, however, we need power, and the smallest number of valves for practical purposes is two, although a pentode one-valve set can be designed for loud-speaker reception of a nearby transmitting station.

Wireless receiving sets can be roughly divided into two classes, "straight" sets, and superheterodynes. The straight set consists, basically, of a detector valve, followed by a low frequency magnifying stage or stages; although in most modern designs there is only one stage; the output valve feeding the loud-speaker being either a power, pentode, or super-power type. The detector valve may or may not be preceded by one or more stages of high frequency amplification, for which a screened grid valve or high frequency pentode valve is used.

The Superheterodyne works on a very interesting principle—it is a receiver and miniature transmitter combined. First of all it receives the signal to which it is tuned—then it generates a high frequency oscillation on a different wave length. The two waves, the incoming one from the station desired, and the wave generated by the oscillator portion of the superhet are mixed together, the result being a third and different wave length. This is amplified by suitable valves, and then "detected" and amplified again before passing to the loud speaker. The chief virtue of this superheterodyne type of set is very high selectivity, and for the consistent reception of numbers of different stations it is probable that the superheterodyne is the best all-round design, although at the same time it must be said that the straight set, properly designed, is a powerful rival.

We may sum up by saying that for loudspeaker reception of the local station a "straight" set of two or three valves is all that is generally needed. In a two-valve set the first valve will be a detector, coupled by means of a transformer to a power valve. But the transformer must be a good one, or the quality of the output will suffer, and so will the amplification, for the cheap transformer, although of the same nominal ratio as the expensive one, will not give the same amount of amplification. Or a three-valve set, consisting of a detector valve, followed by two stage of resistance capacity coupling, may be used. In many ways this is preferable to using two valves and a transformer—the quality is generally better, and the amplification decidedly greater than can be obtained from the two valve set, unless a very expensive transformer indeed be used. If situated at some distance from a Regional station, the best set would probably be a three valve set, consisting of one stage of high frequency amplification, for which a screened grid or high frequency pentode valve is used, followed by a detector valve, and then a power valve, pentode or super-power valve.

Home-built Sets.—There have been few movements of recent years which have had such widespread and rapid growth as the hobby of building wireless sets, both for the technical interest of the thing, and for the entertainment afforded by the finished article. By building your own set, you will acquire a valuable insight into the basic principles of electrical and wireless engineering—should your set fail to work properly at any time, you will be able to rectify the fault without delay. Should you wish to experiment with the short waves, you can proceed to adapt your set, or build a separate one, and at a considerable saving of money as compared with the commercially produced article. In passing, may we venture to drop a hint to the budding or, it may be, advanced home constructor? It will be found better in every way if, first, one set is constructed for the reception of the local station. If this is done, and the set is permanently left in good working order, the household will never drop heavily on the unfortunate wireless fan, because, perchance, the set is being rebuilt just when everyone else wants to use it. The experimental set will, you will find, never be completed; there is always some new circuit to be tried, some elusive station to be logged. In the end you will find that this will even prove an actual economy in £ s. d., and the comfort and convenience of this arrangement has to be tried to be believed.

Fig. 1.—A home-built Set

The Moving Coil Loudspeaker.—A big step forward in really good reproduction of broadcast programmes was made with the invention of the moving coil loudspeaker. But, if you have, or are thinking of making a battery operated receiver, do not just buy any moving coil speaker just because you may have heard it is a big advance on the older fashioned cone or moving iron-balanced armature speaker. It is really a question of the amount of power available—if you have only a small set, powered by the standard-sized high-tension battery, then you will do better to get a balanced armature unit, or an inductor speaker. Both these types are much more sensitive than the average moving coil, and are capable of giving very satisfying reproduction indeed. But, you may say, what about Class B amplification or Quiescent Push Pull? You can certainly, with either of these systems, work a moving coil speaker at fine volume, but you cannot do so with a small high-tension battery. It should be at least double capacity, or preferably triple, capacity. Even then, you must take steps, either to add a booster battery, or replace with a new one when the battery begins to run down, as these systems of amplification are more sensitive to variations in high-tension voltage than the ordinary, or Class A system. When Class B amplification was first announced, people thought that it was going to be the salvation of the battery user, in the sense that it was going to reduce his replacement costs radically. But it is truer to say that, although it does not do this, it certainly makes moving coil quality and volume available to the man without electric mains. However, it may be said that anyone who wishes to effect a real economy in high-tension costs would do well to instal a battery economizer, which can either be obtained commercially, or can be made up for a few shillings. Briefly, this is an arrangement whereby, on no signal intervals, or during soft passages of music, etc., the output valve is heavily overbiassed, with considerable economy in high-tension current. The idea is quite sound, and there are no snags. As much as fifty per cent. saving may be expected.

Selectivity.—Earlier in this article, we stated that it was a comparatively easy matter to design a set to give good quality on the local station. Now, quality and selectivity are two things which simply do not mix, unless you care to go to some expense to make them do so, and it is very interesting to see why this is so. When a broadcasting station radiates a programme on its carrier wave, it takes up a certain amount of space in the ether to do so. The carrier wave may be imagined as having a certain width, and the broadcasting stations next in order of wave length, both below and above, occupy the next bands, which should not overlap. Now, if we are near to a station, we can design our receiving set so as to receive the complete width transmitted by the station without any danger of interference from another station, as we need not worry much about the sensitivity of our set, in view of the power of the "local." On the other hand, if we happen to be near a Regional station and wish to receive some distant station, we have to arrange matters so that our set is sensitive enough to "hear" the distant signal, and selective enough only to receive it well within the band width of the desired station. Generally, this means cutting off a certain amount of the high notes, so that really good quality is difficult to get. Since, however, most people want to listen to the local station as distinct from experimenting with distant reception, this turns out to be fairly satisfactory to everyone. Some modern commercial mains driven receivers are designed with this difficulty in mind, so that, when really good reception is required of the local, one can increase the band width being received, with a gain in the upper register, or top notes, or, alternatively, when interference is being experienced, due to the adjacent station, we can then adjust the receiver so that it receives a narrower band of frequencies.

Reproduction.—We may say that the ratio between the softest and the loudest note of the orchestra is 1–100 in degrees of loudness, as heard in the concert hall. But, for technical reasons, we cannot broadcast such a wide variation in sound, so that the transmitting stations have to compress this ratio so that it becomes only 1–10 approximately. But it is surprising how accommodating is the human ear, and in spite of this perhaps only technical difficulty, we find that we can quite well appreciate a fine concert, and can almost imagine ourselves on the spot during a running commentary or a play.

Good quality reproduction in a wireless

set is very largely dependent upon the use of the correct valves for the several positions in the set. Take the case of the ordinary two or three valve set. If it is a two valve set, the first valve should be of the L. F., or special detector type, as it is generally transformer coupled to the power valve. These detector valves have what is called an "impedance" of about 10,000 ohms or so, and if the best quality is required, this is the kind to use. If the set is a three valve one of the detector, two L. F. type, then the first valve can well be one of 20,000 ohms impedance, as this is generally resistance capacity coupled to the next stage. The next valve in this case should be of the L. F. type, of 10,000 ohms impedance, as it is really a power stage in miniature. The impedance should be low, because this valve is generally coupled by a transformer to the last valve, which drives the speaker.

Resistance.—Earlier in this article we mentioned the case of a three valve set designed for local station reception in which all the valves are coupled together by means of resistances and condensers, or R. C. C., as it is usually termed. Many old sets of this general type are still in use, but the resistances used in the plate or anode circuits of the valves are too high in the light of modern practice. In general one may say that a resistance value of 50,000 ohms should not be exceeded in the anode circuit of the detector valve, and 25,000 ohms is quite sufficient in the plate circuit of the L. F. valve. It is better to avoid the use of the so-called R. C. type of valve, which has an impedance of about 50,000 ohms or so, because, although slightly higher amplification may be gained by its use, the quality will not be quite so good as with the H. L. type of valve, and reaction will not be so easy to control, so that on balance, the lower impedance valve will give better all-round results.

Screened Grid Valves are available in two general classes, viz. high and low impedance. Where the set has only one stage of high frequency amplification, it may safely be taken that the high impedance type should be chosen, as greater amplification is obtainable from it. If there are two stages, however, the other type should be chosen, as two high efficiency valves will be found very difficult to stabilize, and the resulting amplification will not be greater, as it will not be possible to work the valves "all out."

Power Valves fall into two general classes, small power valves and super-power types. Here the problem of choice is really conditioned by the nature of the power

Fig. 2.—A Main's Unit

supply—we may here say that we have the battery user in mind. The super-power valve is to be preferred generally, even for the two valve set; owing to its grid swing and low impedance it will give better quality than the small power valve. But the price to be paid is rather high from the point of view of the high tension supply, and a double or triple capacity battery will be needed. The best solution is the use of H. T. accumulators, which can be purchased, or hired at very reasonable rates, and it is quite safe to say that no one who has enjoyed the uniformly high quality which can be obtained from a constant and unvaryingly high tension supply will ever go back to the small high tension dry battery.

The super-power valve is often, and wrongly, considered to be the best because it is more powerful than the small powered type. It is not more powerful, in fact it is less so than the smaller valve, which has a much higher amplification factor, but it will not over-load so easily, and given an adequate signal from the preceding valve it will deliver a large volume with ease, where the smaller valve would not do so. There is another type of output valve, the pentode, which we have not considered as yet. This is like a combination of the small power and the super power types, because it will give quite a large output from a small signal input. In the more simple types of sets, however, such as those we are considering, the pentode is best avoided. To get the best out of the valve, the circuits have to be more carefully designed, and the valve has to be matched to the loud speaker very much more critically than in the case of the power valve, so that in the end it often pays, in simple sets, to add another stage of L. F. amplification and use a big triode output valve where good quality is the primary consideration, and this should always be the case, apart from the experimental set of the keen amateur.

We have already considered another type of output valve, viz., the Class B valve, and there is also a double pentode valve, which is really two pentode valves in one bulb. This also works on the quiescent push pull principle, and is capable of giving sufficient power satisfactorily to work a moving coil speaker.

The Mains Operated Electrically Heated Valve.—There is another sort of valve, basically the same, which can be run from the electric mains, either A. C. or, less usually, D. C. mains. These have a grid and plate, or anode, as in the battery operated valve, but the arrangements for heating the filament are different. In the mains operated indirectly heated valve, as it is called, there is a heater connected with a supply of low tension current, either A. C. or D. C., and this is surrounded by a tube called the cathode. This, when heated, gives off electrons in the same way as the filament of a battery valve. For several reasons the mains valve is very much more efficient than its battery counterpart, and if electric mains are available it is always better to build a set which uses mains valves, so that one can make the fullest use of the greater power and better quality which will be available. It may not always be convenient, however, to get rid of an old set as soon as the mains become available, and in this case a good compromise may be made by getting a mains unit, which takes the place of the high tension battery. A good mains unit will not only give an unfailing high tension supply, but will also provide a low tension supply in the form of a trickle charger, so that your accumulator may be kept up to the mark.

Car Radio.—A very interesting development of modern wireless broadcasting has been the introduction of car radio. This has been brought to a high pitch of perfection, mainly in the United States, but the British manufacturer has, as usual, risen to the occasion, and can now supply installations which are quite as good, if not better than anything hitherto available. Many technical problems have had to be solved before the difficulty of programme "fading" under bridges, etc., could be met, and there was also the question of interference to be dealt with. When the engine of a car is working, the electrical side, viz., the ignition coil, sparking plugs, etc., act as miniature transmitters, and give rise to all kinds of trouble. These all had to be tracked to their sources and cured without affecting the performance of the engine, so that now it is possible to drive about the country and receive literally dozens of transmissions at good quality. The type of set used for this work is usually a superheterodyne, and the power supply comes from the car battery.

It is perhaps out of the scope of this article to make any comments on the safety or otherwise of listening to the wireless whilst the car is on the move, but on the whole there seems to be no real reason why this new development should add to the present difficulties of driving, while the set will be found invaluable for entertainment during picnics, etc.

Short Wave Transmission.—Everyone has heard of the B.B.C. Empire transmitter, which transmits the programmes on several different wave lengths to our Colonies. These operate on what are known as the short waves, and this remains probably the most fascinating field for experiment and research that the most ardent wireless fan could wish for. It is

Fig. 3.—Car Radio unobtrusively installed between the accumulators

possible with a well designed and constructed one valve set to tour the world, and it is indeed amazing what enormous distances these short waves cover. It is possible to build what is called an adaptor which can be attached to any ordinary broadcast receiving set, by means of which the programmes from short wave stations all over the world can be tuned in. It is much better, however, for the experimenter to build an entirely separate set for the short waves. The frequencies on which the programmes are transmitted are so exceedingly high that quite different values of components are necessary for good reception. The conditions under which the short waves are received are continually changing—one has to put up with fading, atmospherics, heterodynes, and often the required station is not there at all! A really good slow motion condenser is a prime necessity and it should be about ·00015 mfd. in value. The grid condenser should be ·0001 mfd., and the grid leak should have a much higher value than is usual for the broadcast set, anything up to, say, 5 megohms or so. A potentiometer across the low tension supply is also a help to get really smooth reaction, without which nothing can be done; the end of the grid leak being taken to the slider, so that the best position can be found by trial. It is possible to obtain a special short wave coil so that the whole of the short wave band from, say, 12 to 80 metres, can be covered without changing coils. This is, of course, a great convenience, and there are no ill effects, apparently, from the switching system which has to be used.

An interesting feature of short wave reception is that quite often one cannot hear a comparatively nearby station when it is transmitting, but other stations two or three thousand or more miles away, come in at full strength when tuned in. The reason is this. When we listen to our local broadcasting station on the medium or long waves, we are listening to what is called the ground ray. The transmitting aerial sends out wireless waves in all directions, and a proportion are radiated shywards. These travel until they meet the Heaviside Layer, when they are reflected back to the surface of the earth again. Should our receiving station happen to be located near the point at which this reflected ray meets the earth, we can naturally hear it when we tune in. Now the short waves have only a limited range as regards the ground or direct ray—consequently it soon dies out, and we have to be situated at some distance from the station before we can pick up the indirect or reflected ray.

Ultra Short Waves.—You may have heard something about the experiment which the B.B.C., amongst others, have been conducting with what are called the ultra short waves, i.e. those of seven metres and even less. These waves have interesting properties, one of which is that they behave like rays of light. That is, they will only operate a receiving set provided that set can be "seen" by the waves in the same way that we could see, say, a distant building from the top of a tower. If the building were out of sight, say, beyond the level of the horizon, we naturally could not see it, and similarly, these ultra short waves have only what is called optical range. It is thought that, because of this property, they may provide for really high quality broadcasting from local stations at some time in the future. Quality, as we have pointed out earlier, is really a question of the width of the frequency band which can be transmitted without interference from adjacent stations, and in this case there could not be any adjacent stations, as they would be quite out of range. It may, however, be pointed out that experiments are still being actively conducted about these waves, and it is possible that fresh discoveries may yet be made about their properties, both in regard to range and ease of reception.

Hints for the Home Constructor.—The tools required are simple and few. Get a small pair of round-nosed pliers, an electrician's screw-driver, and some emery cloth. You will find the pliers essential for making loops at the ends of pieces of wire for connecting up the various component parts. A small pair of long-nosed pliers will be useful for tightening nuts, etc. Use No. 22 tinned copper wire (bare) for the wiring up, and get some lengths of insulated sleeving to slip over the bare wire so as to avoid any chance of short circuits. Several yards of 14/36 rubber-covered flex will be needed for the battery connections, and it is well also to use flex for wiring up the low tension circuits to the valve-holders.

In general it always pays, even with a powerful set, to put up an efficient aerial. This need not, however, be of the outdoor variety, as our experience has been that indoor aerials can be extraordinarily efficient. They can often be erected in the loft, and one of the best conductors to use is ordinary single rubber covered flex, 14/36, or the slightly smaller variety of flex which is used for electric bells. We have found that an extraordinarily efficient indoor aerial can be made, using what is called Litz wire. This is a flexible wire, consisting of some nine, eighteen, or more, wires, but each strand is insulated from the others, either by enamel or by a covering of silk.

Before attaching the end of this Litz wire aerial to the set's aerial terminal, you must remove the insulation from each strand for a distance of, say, an inch or so, and then twist the bared strands together. Indoor aerials should be suspended clear of walls, to avoid high frequency leakages to earth.

The best wire to use for outdoor aerials is 7/22 copper wire, bare or enamelled. The enamel insulation will not, of course, offer any barrier to the passage of the wireless waves, but will prevent or defer corrosion, especially at the seaside. Use as short a length of wire as possible for the earth connection. Rubber covered flex is good, and 23/36, as used for domestic electrical appliances, cannot be improved upon. A water pipe makes an excellent earth, but clean off the paint first, then wind the wire round it, and finish off with a binding of insulating tape.

WOOD CARVING

Carving in wood implies something to carve. You will find therefore that this craft is best taken up when you have made a piece of furniture, and so designed it that carving is an essential part of the whole, and not an afterthought.

Restraint in decoration is a most important principle. Up to within recent times a great deal of time was put into the carving applied to furniture and buildings and some magnificent work has been left to us. It is, however, a mistake to copy much of what was done and apply it to furniture of modern design. That carving was done in a period when the rush of life did not make such demands as at the present time and men had more time to express themselves. Modern furniture is much more restrained and simple in form and decoration and the beginner in carving can now do plenty of satisfying work without the necessity of first taking a course of instruction in modelling.

Much simple ornament can be done in the form of simple chisel and gouge cuts and low relief carving is not difficult to accomplish.

What to Carve.—The days are gone, we hope, when enthusiastic would-be carvers would remove the door of the perfectly plain and well-designed grand-father clock and "ornament it" by carving on it a pattern which was neither necessary nor fitting. You should resist the temptation to carve on anything that presents a plain surface. The chair backs are probably quite well designed and plain and will not be made either more comfortable or more interesting nor will they be easier to keep clean if they are cut about. A carved chair seat or table top are not very practicable from the user's or the housewife's point of view.

There is, however, a fairly wide scope of work to which carving can safely be applied and the articles should be made with a view to completion in this way. Tea-caddies, book stands, pipe racks, fire screens, cigarette boxes, stands of all kinds, candlesticks, ash trays, fruit bowls, brackets, picture and mirror frames, clock cases, stools, tables, log boxes, plant stands, and so on are among the small articles which lend themselves to the work. Larger pieces of furniture include tables, hall stands, folding screens, sideboards, book tables, chairs, etc.

The Equipment.—A strong table or bench is essential. To be comfortable the work-table should be at least 6 in. higher than the normal height of a table. If it is necessary to work on the kitchen table, an extra top at least 1 in. thick, well battened and strong, can be clamped to the ordinary table top. If the driving of screws and boring of holes in the kitchen table top does not matter, the extra top can be dispensed with.

Tools.—The cutting tools are chisels and gouges, the former straight and flat at the end and in the blade, the latter hollow. These chisels and gouges, unlike the carpenter's or joiner's tools are always ground on both sides as in Figs. 1 and 2. Figs. 3 and 4 show a chisel and a gouge. The cutting tools are also made bent or curved in the shank. This enables hollow cuts and deep ones to be made with better results than are possible with a straight chisel or gouge. Vee tools, which end in the form of the letter V are largely used in carving. Figs. 5, 6 and 7 show curved and vee tools. There is a large variety of sizes and curves in cutting tools, but the beginner is advised to avoid purchasing "a set of tools" and to confine himself to a few of each kind such as a $\frac{3}{4}$ in., $\frac{1}{4}$ in. (A, B), $\frac{3}{4}$ in., $\frac{1}{2}$in. and $\frac{1}{4}$ in. flat gouge (C, D and E), $\frac{3}{4}$ in., $\frac{5}{8}$ in., $\frac{3}{8}$ in., $\frac{1}{4}$ in. quick gouge (F, G, H, J), a $\frac{1}{4}$ in. bent quick gouge, $\frac{1}{4}$ in. bent chisel, one right-hand skew and one left-hand skew $\frac{1}{4}$ in. chisel (K, L) in Fig. 8 and one $\frac{5}{16}$ in. vee or parting tool. You may, of course, require smaller tools for more delicate work. They are made as small as $\frac{1}{16}$ in.

Holdfasts, Clamps and Screws.—Carving is two-handed work, the tools requiring considerable effort of control in both hands so that good, accurate and clean cuts can be made. It is therefore essential

or in a rack where each tool is separated from its neighbours. To store in a box without a set of trays with a compartment for each tool is asking for trouble and work in sharpening.

Grinding.—A grindstone, oilstone and leather strop are necessary. The chisels and gouges should have grinding bevels from $\frac{3}{8}$ in. to $\frac{1}{2}$ in. long, so as to reduce the amount of rubbing necessary on the oilstone.

2 in. by $\frac{3}{4}$ in., two slips about 4 in. by 2 in. by $\frac{1}{2}$ in. and a slip for use on parting tools will be necessary. A slip is a piece of oilstone shaped as in Fig. 12. The parting or vee tool slip is shown in Fig. 13 and is made to fit various curves. Washita stones are very good for this work. Use neat's-foot oil as the lubricant on the stones and slips.

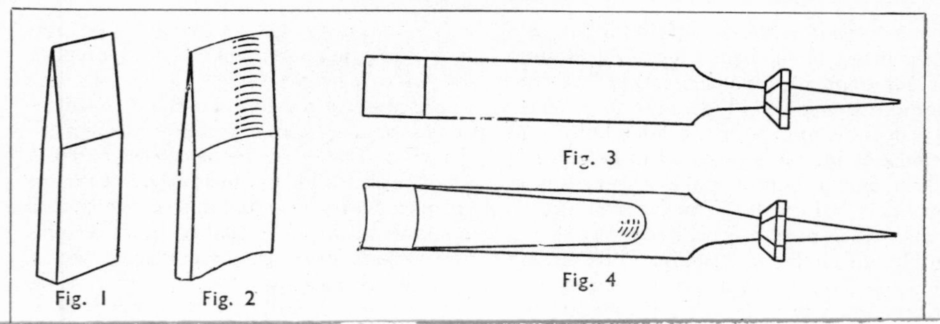

Fig. 1 Fig. 2

Fig. 3

Fig. 4

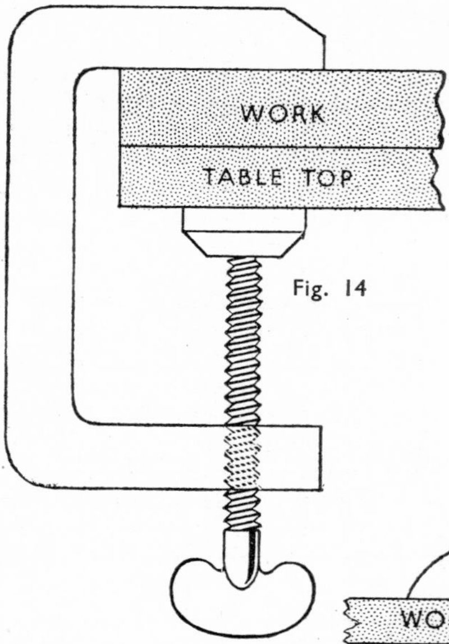

WORK
TABLE TOP

Fig. 14

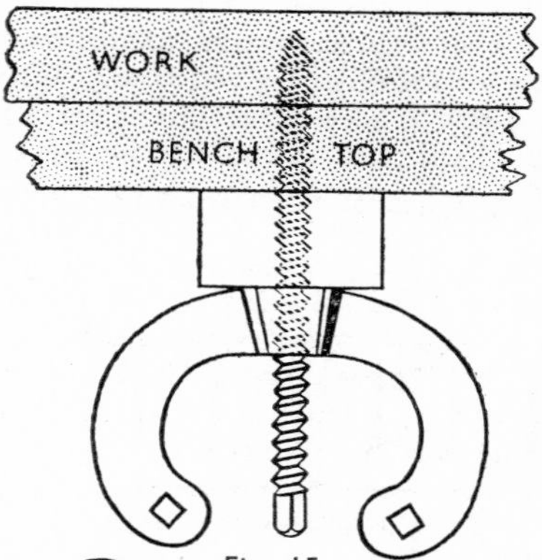

WORK
BENCH TOP

Fig. 15

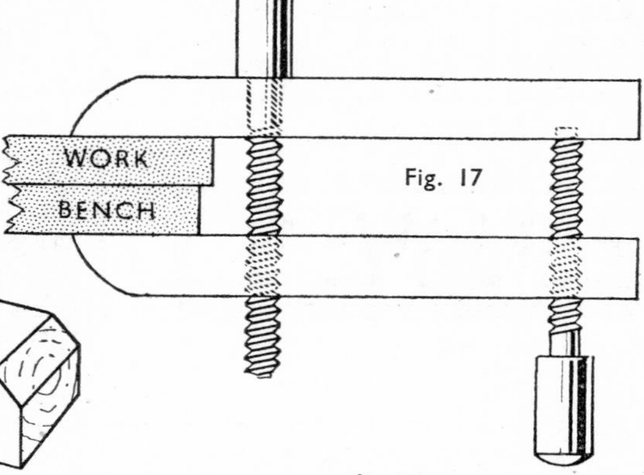

WORK
BENCH

Fig. 17

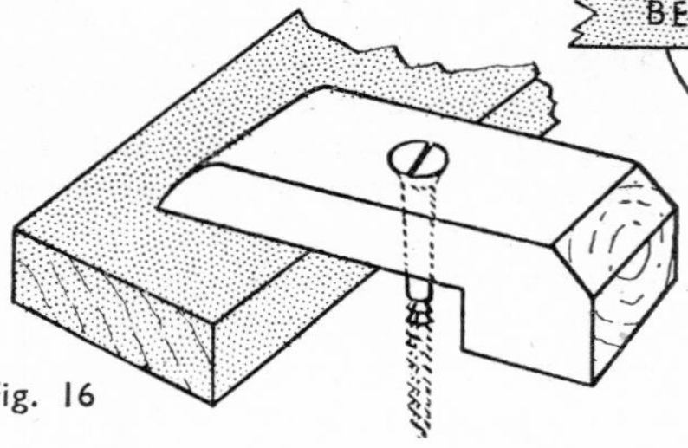

Fig. 16

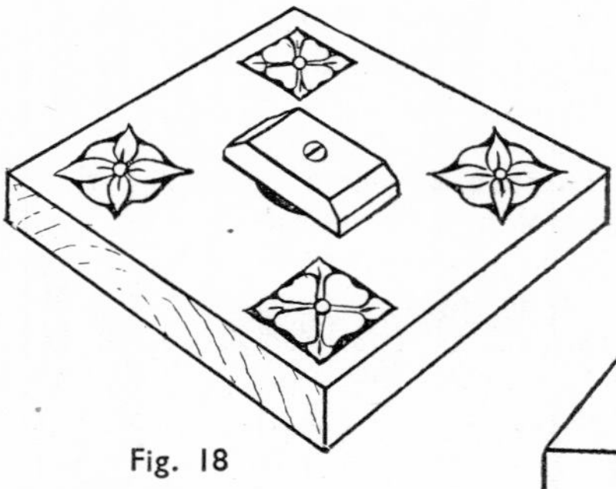

Fig. 18

WOOD TO BE CARVED

Fig. 19

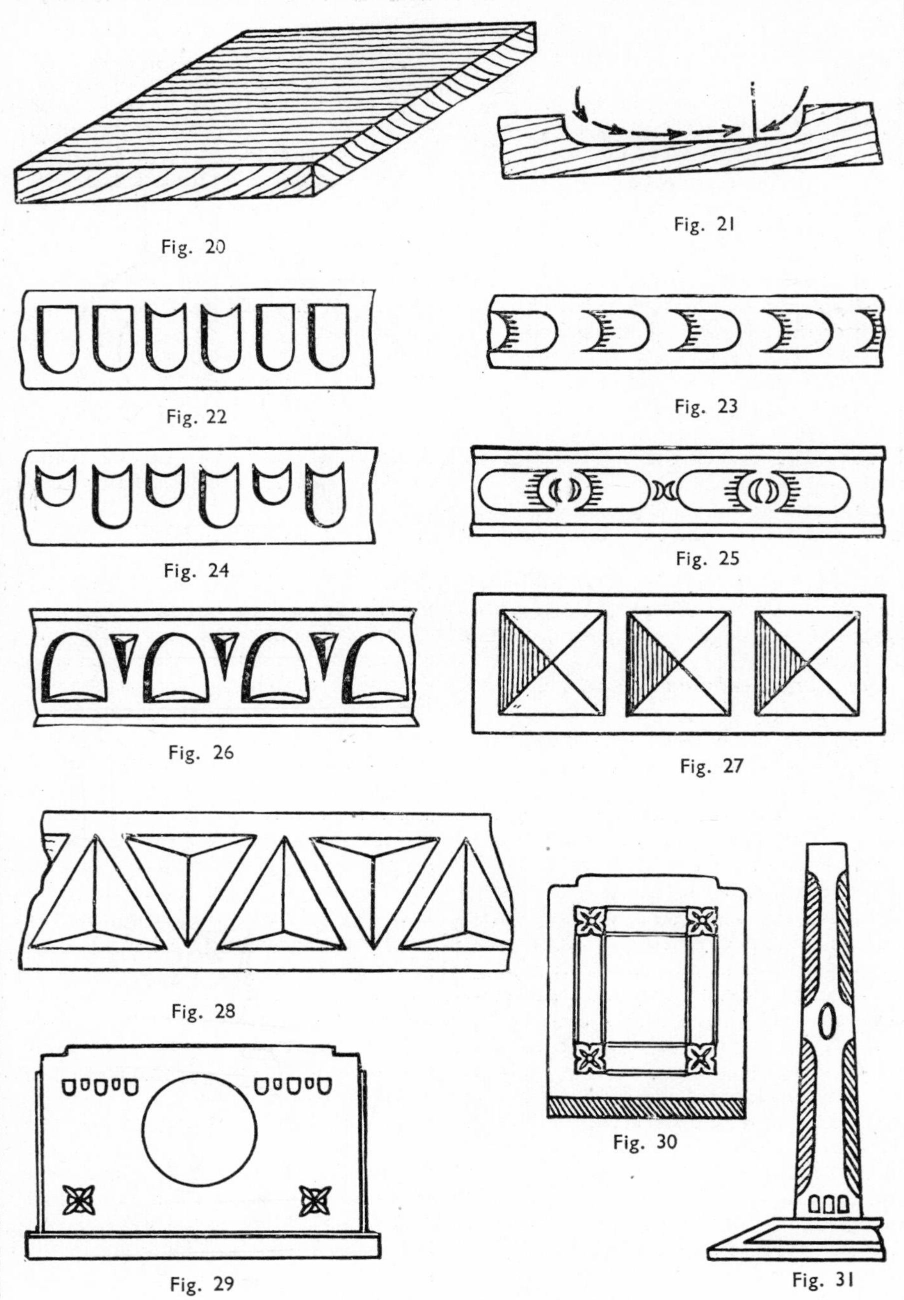

Fig. 20

Fig. 21

Fig. 22

Fig. 23

Fig. 24

Fig. 25

Fig. 26

Fig. 27

Fig. 28

Fig. 29

Fig. 30

Fig. 31

Great care must be taken in rubbing the edge of the gouge on the oilstone. For the beginner it is easiest to place the tool on its back at right angles across the stone. Raise it to an angle of about 25 degs. and rub it up and down the length of the stone, at the same time rolling it a little in the hand so that the whole of the edge is brought into contact with the stone on each journey up and down the stone. When the old edge has been removed take the oilstone slip of the size and shape that will fit roughly the curve of the gouge, hold the latter by the handle in the left hand, rest it against the edge of the bench and rub the inside bevel with the slip. This should bring up a keen edge, but if it is still not perfect then a rub on the outside and another light one on the inside may put it right.

The vee tool must be handled very carefully so as to keep the end quite square to the side of the blade.

Keep the stone lubricated with oil or the particles of steel rubbed off the blades will choke its surface and prevent it cutting efficiently.

Stropping.—Make a strop by gluing a piece of hard smooth leather, such as leather belting, at least 2 in. wide, on to a flat piece of wood. Prepare the surface with oil and emery powder.

Remove wire edge from the tool and bring it to a razor keenness by drawing first one side and then the other of the edge sharply down on to the surface of the strop. The inside edge of gouges or vee tools can be done on the edge of the strop, or, if the latter is not glued to a board, you can bend it to fit the gouge and then stroke the latter on it.

Wood.—The best wood for the beginner to use is yellow pine. It is a soft wood of fine, even and straight grain. It is not much use in the making of the articles we have enumerated but it is excellent for the practice which is necessary for the worker to master a few manipulations and to learn something about the direction of grain and the possibilities of a few tools. When this skill has been gained, the worker should learn to carve oak and mahogany, as these are probably the timber she will generally use for the construction of the articles mentioned.

Operations.—It is best to begin with a few simple cuts so that you may become accustomed to the tools and the grain of the wood. A few designs which are suitable for beginners are shown in Figs. 22 to 31.

The following are a few hints about the grain of wood. A little experience and observation will show you that there is generally a right way and a wrong way both to plane and to cut a piece of wood with chisels and gouges. It is essential for success in carving that this should be clearly understood.

Fig. 20 shows a piece of wood with the annual rings which make the grain. If this piece of wood is planed from A to B the surface will be smooth. If it is planed from B to A it will be plucked up and rough. If a bevel is planed or chiselled from C to D it will not give so clean an edge as will be produced if it is cut in the direction from D to C. If you wish to cut the surface of the board in the direction C to A it will not be so easy as cutting from A to C. It will always be found more difficult to cut against the grain than with it, and keener control of the cutting tool is necessary if clean results are to be obtained in the former case.

When gouging out hollows in wood the arrows in Fig. 21 show the direction in which the best results will be obtained.

The Designs.—A few suggestions for simple cuts and grouping of cuts are given in Figs. 22 to 31. Figs. 22, 24 and 25 show lines of gouge cuts which might be used as bands running round a box, along a rail of a table, dinner-wagon, the rail of a fairly large frame, etc. Figs. 23 and 25 are suitable for narrow bands or wide edges. Figs. 27 and 28 would fit a wider rail. Fig. 29 shows the grouping of simple gouge cuts as in Figs. 22 or 23 applied to a clock case. Conventional foliage form is shown applied to the end of a book stand in Fig. 30 and the candlestick in Fig. 31 has the edge worked quarter-circle with a scratch tool and then a vee tool used to cut up the bead thus formed into cable ornament. These simple beginnings should lead you on to an appreciation of the more advanced forms of carvings and give you skill to work them.